ROME I AND ROME II IN PRACTICE

ROME I AND ROME II IN PRACTICE

Edited by
Emmanuel Guinchard

INTERSENTIA
Cambridge – Antwerp – Chicago

Intersentia Ltd
8 Wellington Mews
Wellington Street | Cambridge
CB1 1HW | United Kingdom
Tel: +44 1223 736 170
Email: mail@intersentia.co.uk
www.intersentia.com | www.intersentia.co.uk

Distribution for the UK and
Rest of the World (incl. Eastern Europe)
NBN International
1 Deltic Avenue, Rooksley
Milton Keynes MK13 8LD
United Kingdom
Tel: +44 1752 202 301 | Fax: +44 1752 202 331
Email: orders@nbninternational.com

Distribution for Europe
Lefebvre Sarrut Belgium NV
Hoogstraat 139/6
1000 Brussels
Belgium
Tel: +32 (0)800 39 067
Email: mail@intersentia.be

Distribution for the USA and Canada
Independent Publishers Group
Order Department
814 North Franklin Street
Chicago, IL 60610
USA
Tel: +1 800 888 4741 (toll free) | Fax: +1 312 337 5985
Email: orders@ipgbook.com

ISBN 978-1-78068-671-4
D/2020/7849/101
NUR 822

British Library Cataloguing in Publication Data. A catalogue record for this book is available from the British Library.

CONTENTS

LIST OF CASES

COURT OF JUSTICE OF THE EUROPEAN UNION

AUSTRIA

BELGIUM

BULGARIA

CROATIA

CYPRUS

CZECH REPUBLIC

FRANCE

GERMANY

GREECE

HUNGARY

IRELAND

ITALY

LATVIA

LITHUANIA

LUXEMBOURG

THE NETHERLANDS

POLAND

PORTUGAL

SLOVAKIA

SLOVENIA

SPAIN

UNITED KINGDOM

LIST OF CONTRIBUTORS

Marie-Elodie Ancel
Professor at Université Paris II Panthéon-Assas, France

Apostolos Anthimos
Attorney-at-Law, Thessaloniki, Greece

Davor Babić
Professor at the University of Zagreb, Croatia

Laura Maria van Bochove
Assistant Professor at Leiden University, the Netherlands

Petr Bříza
Senior Lecturer at the Commercial Law Department of Charles University, Czech Republic; Partner at Bříza & Trubač law firm, Prague, Czech Republic

Geert Van Calster
Professor at KU Leuven, Belgium; Member of the Belgian Bar

Marcin Czepelak
Assistant Professor at Jagiellonian University, Kraków, Poland

Aleksandrs Fillers
Researcher at the University of Antwerp, Belgium

Pietro Franzina
Professor at the Catholic University of the Sacred Heart, Milan, Italy

Emilia Fronczak
Avocat à la Cour, Loyens & Loeff, Luxembourg

Aleš Galič
Professor at the University of Ljubljana, Slovenia

Uglješa Grušić
Associate Professor at University College London, United Kingdom

Emmanuel Guinchard
Senior Lecturer at Northumbria University, United Kingdom

Tomáš Hokr
Partner at Bříza & Trubač law firm, Prague, Czech Republic

Csongor István Nagy
Head of the Department of Private International Law at the University of Szeged, Hungary

Elena Judova
Lecturer at Matej Bel University, Banská Bystrica, Slovakia

Inga Kačevska
Attorney at Law and Associate Professor at the University of Latvia, Latvia

Thomas Kadner Graziano
Professor at the University of Geneva, Switzerland

Jerca Kramberger Škerl
Associate Professor at the University of Ljubljana, Slovenia

Miloš Levrinc
Lecturer at Matej Bel University, Banská Bystrica, Slovakia

Christiana Markou
Attorney-at-Law at Markou-Christodoulou & Polycarpou LLC, Cyprus

Valentinas Mikelėnas
Professor at the University of Vilnius, Lithuania

Nikolay Natov
Professor at Sofia University St Kliment Ohridski, Sofia, Bulgaria

Máire Ní Shúilleabháin
Assistant Professor at University College Dublin, Ireland

Vassil Pandov
Assistant Professor at Sofia University St Kliment Ohridski, Sofia, Bulgaria

Afonso Patrão
Professor at University of Coimbra, Portugal

Michel José Reymond
Attorney-at-Law at Byrne-Sutton Bollen Kern, Switzerland

Diana Sancho-Villa
Senior Lecturer at Westminster University, United Kingdom

Stephan Walter
Research Fellow at the Institute for German and International Civil Procedure at the University of Bonn, Germany

Matthias Weller
Director of the Institute for German and International Civil Procedure at the University of Bonn, Germany

Dora Zgrabljić Rotar
Assistant Professor at the University of Zagreb, Croatia

INTRODUCTION

Emmanuel GUINCHARD

Resolving disputes which arise under contracts or out of torts may be complicated enough in the domestic context. The task becomes even more complex in the presence of a foreign element, in particular if the parties are based in different states or the contract should be enforced abroad or the tort was committed in a foreign country. In those circumstances, it is essential to establish what law will apply to such a contract or tort, possibly before the parties enter into any binding agreement or the tort arises. In the European Union (save Denmark), the Regulation (EC) No. 593/2008 of the European Parliament and of the Council of 17 June 2008 on the law applicable to contractual obligations (Rome I)[1] and Regulation (EC) No. 864/2007 of the European Parliament and of the Council of 11 July 2007 on the law applicable to non-contractual obligations (Rome II)[2] are the key Regulations on the law applicable to obligations. They derived from the initiatives of the European Commission following the Treaty of Amsterdam, which, according to Article 65(b) of the EC Treaty, gave the Community competence to take measures to promote the compatibility of conflict-of-laws rules applicable in the Member States insofar as was necessary for the proper functioning of the internal market. The idea was that substantive contract and tort law differed considerably across Europe (they still do). In the absence of a unified European contract or tort law, rules on conflict of laws were therefore crucial (they still are). However, those rules themselves differed. This, it was argued, hindered the proper functioning of the internal market, hence the need to harmonise these rules in order to increase legal certainty.

With slightly confusing numbering to the outsider, Rome II was enacted before Rome I. It was a ground-breaking instrument: the first European Regulation ever on the applicable law. Of course, several EC instruments already contained choice-of-law rules covering a particular area, but the main focus of these instruments had never been the choice of laws itself. Rome II lays down the conflict-of-law rules applicable to a wide range of non-contractual obligations in civil and commercial matters. For its part, Rome I draws heavily on an earlier instrument – the 1980 Rome Convention on the Law Applicable to Contractual

[1] OJEU, L 177, 4 July 2008, p. 6.
[2] OJEU, L 199, 31 July 2007, p. 40.

Obligations – albeit with some notable differences in terms of both substance and institutional context (jurisdiction of the Court of Justice as of right). Both Rome I and Rome II follow the traditional choice-of-law methodology, that is the enactment of conflict-of-laws rules that may be overshadowed by *lois d'application immédiate* (overriding mandatory rules) and lead to a law which may be set aside by *ordre public*. The conflict-of-laws rules themselves may be, at times, characterised by some innovation, the degree of which differs according to the national background.

Rome I and Rome II are Regulations of paramount importance, for reasons including their topic (obligations law), which notably covers most of business life, their historical role in the creation of a genuine European private international law, and their universal application (any law may be specified as the law applicable to the contract or tort/delict, whether or not it is the law of an EU Member State). Their significance is highlighted by the choice made by the United Kingdom to apply Rome I and Rome II to settle conflicts between the laws of its different parts – for example, between England and Scotland – as well as its agreement to apply them long after the end of the transition period (currently scheduled on 31 December 2020) as Rome I will apply to contracts concluded before the end of the transition period and Rome II to events giving rise to damage which occurred before the end of the transition period.[3] Moreover, the United Kingdom intends to unilaterally apply Rome I and Rome II even afterwards. Their high status (if not stature) in private international law worldwide is demonstrated by their influence on several recent codifications of private international law in non-EU Member States (including draft codifications),[4] prompting questions about the rise of a global private international law.

Rome I and Rome II provide uniform conflict-of-laws rules in order to avoid undue forum-shopping before the courts of EU Member States (save Denmark): no matter where in the EU an action is brought, the rules determining the applicable law will always be the same. So goes the theory at least. It is clearly of value to see, after ten years of application of Rome I and Rome II, whether this theory has been put into practice and to what extent, as well as to assess any difficulty that may have arisen in the interpretation and application of these Regulations. Such information is essential for a variety of stakeholders: judges looking at their colleagues' judgments for inspiration or confirmation in order to reach a better-informed decision; practitioners dealing with a complex multi-jurisdictional dispute and reflecting on their international litigation strategy as counsel; policy-makers pondering a reform of, or complement to, these

---

3 Article 66 of the Agreement on the withdrawal of the United Kingdom of Great Britain and Northern Ireland from the European Union and the European Atomic Energy Community, OJEU L 29, 31.1.2020, p. 7.

4 Notwithstanding the previous influence of the 1980 Rome Convention on the Law Applicable to Contractual Obligations.

instruments and actively involved in the ongoing construction of a true and far-reaching European private international law and considering whether some of the essential features of Rome I and Rome II should create a 'precedent' for future negotiations and instruments; and academics and students assessing the functioning of the existing Regulations and researching ways to improve them.

To this end, a team of authors from the widest range of Member States possible was assembled and a questionnaire drafted.[5] The authors were selected on the basis of their high-level expertise on the law applicable to obligations at national as well as at European level. Many have both academic and practical experience. All are multilingual. They devoted a great deal of time and effort to the collection and the critical analysis of case law on the Rome I and Rome II Regulations before the Court of Justice of the EU and in their respective jurisdictions, thus producing a fine-grained picture of the judicial practice on these Regulations before the CJEU and in the vast majority of the EU Member States, often offering unprecedented access in English to national case law. These authors, to whom we can only express our deepest gratitude and thanks, are (in the alphabetical order of the countries they reported on,[6] save for the CJEU, which has pre-eminence as the supreme authority on the interpretation of the Rome I and Rome II Regulations): Thomas Kadner Graziano and Michel José Reymond (CJEU), Matthias Weller and Stephan Walter (Austria and Germany), Geert Van Calster (Belgium), Nikolay Natov and Vassil Pandov (Bulgaria), Davor Babić and Dora Zgrabljić Rotar (Croatia), Christiana Markou (Cyprus), Petr Bříza and Tomáš Hokr (Czech Republic), Marie-Elodie Ancel (France), Apostolos Anthimos (Greece), Csongor István Nagy (Hungary), Máire Ní Shúilleabháin (Ireland), Pietro Franzina (Italy), Inga Kačevska and Aleksandrs Fillers (Latvia), Valentinas Mikelėnas (Lithuania), Emilia Fronczak (Luxembourg), Laura Maria van Bochove (The Netherlands), Marcin Czepelak (Poland), Afonso Patrão (Portugal), Elena Judova and Miloš Levrinc (Slovakia), Jerca Kramberger Škerl and Aleš Galič (Slovenia), Diana Sancho-Villa (Spain) and Uglješa Grušić (United Kingdom). We would like to pay particular tribute to Professor Nikolay Natov, who sadly passed away during the course of this project.

We hope that this book – the first Europe-wide study exclusively devoted to the judicial application of the Rome I and Rome II Regulations – will be of assistance to legislators, judges, practitioners and academics of the EU and beyond, as well as contribute, even modestly, to the construction of a true European private international law.

---

5 It was sent to the authors of the national reports, with the proviso that the list of questions was not exhaustive and that authors were invited to bring to the readers' attention other issues emerging from practice specific to the jurisdiction. The questionnaire can be found after this introduction.

6 Austria and Germany are the object of a single report.

QUESTIONNAIRE FOR THE NATIONAL REPORTS

Please note that the list of questions below is not exhaustive. Authors of the national reports are invited to bring to the readers' attention other issues emerging from practice specific to their jurisdiction.

THE NATIONAL LANDSCAPE

Are there any national measures facilitating the application of Rome I / Rome II?

Have the rules of Rome I / Rome II been extended beyond their normal scope of application, for example to defamation, either by a piece of legislation or by case-law?

How many decisions from national courts applying Rome I / Rome II in your country?

How many arbitration awards applying Rome I / Rome II (if this datum is made publically available, even redacted, for ex. some ICC awards)?

What are the five most applied provisions of Rome I / Rome II?

How many decisions in your country which should have applied Rome I or / and Rome II but ultimately, and wrongly, applied a different set of rules (such as former national rules on the law applicable to obligations)?

How many arbitration awards which should have applied Rome I or / and Rome II but ultimately, and wrongly, applied a different set of rules (if this datum is made publically available, even redacted, for ex. some ICC awards)?

THE OPERATION OF THE ROME I AND ROME II REGULATIONS IN PRACTICE

LOIS D'APPLICATION IMMÉDIATE (OVERRIDING MANDATORY PROVISIONS)

Is the identification of *lois d'application immédiate*, so called overriding mandatory provisions, an issue?

Do the Courts tend to unduly extend the definition of, or overapply, the *lois d'application immédiate* instead of Rome I / Rome II conflict of laws rules stricto sensu, for example by going beyond their famous definition by Ph. Franceskakis (endorsed by the Court of Justice in Arblade, case C-369/96)?

What are considered as *lois d'application immédiate* in your country? Please give examples of *lois d'application immédiate* in both contractual and non-contractual obligations.

Should the treatment of third States' *lois d'application immédiate* be reconsidered, taking into account the differences between Articles 9 Rome I and 16 Rome II and their practice?

PARTY AUTONOMY

Should Article 3 Rome I be amended, for example because of an excessive use of *dépeçage* or the need to choose the *lex mercatoria*?

Has the introduction of party autonomy in Rome II (Article 14) given rise to difficulties of application or negative consequences for the parties involved? How have the concept of commercial activity and the guarantee of an agreement freely negotiated been understood?

ABSENCE OF CHOICE OF LAW

Has the move towards fixed rules in Article 4 Rome I been adhered to or resisted?

Is Article 4(1) Rome II as easy to apply as it is to understand, notably in terms of localisation of the place of direct damage, for ex. in case of delayed poisoning, data theft, or res in transitu?

Have the Courts apply Article 4(2) Rome II in case of a multitude of tortfeasors or victims and how?

ESCAPE CLAUSES

Are the escape clauses of Rome I and Rome II (e.g. Articles 4(3), 5(3), 8(4) Rome I / Articles 4(3), 5(2) Rome II) truly the exception in practice or are they overused by the Courts? In this respect, does Article 4(3) Rome I have any impact in practice (from a more close connection in Article 4(5) of the Rome Convention to a manifestly more close connection)?

Could you attempt to categorise the typical situations in which the escape clauses were applied?

Have the Courts apply Article 4(3) Rome II in case of collision of ship in international waters and how?

SPECIFIC RULES

Have the specific rules to certain contracts in Rome I (contracts for the carriage of goods (Articles 5(1) and 5(3)), contracts for the carriage of passengers (Articles 5(2) and 5(3)), consumer contracts (Article 6), insurance contracts (Article 7) and individual employment contracts (Article 8)) worked well in practice?

Have the rules for specific torts and delicts in Rome II (namely product liability (Article 5), unfair competition and acts restricting free competition (Article 6), environmental damage (Article 7), infringement of intellectual property rights (Article 8), and industrial damage (Article 9)) worked well in practice? For example, how have key concepts of Article 5 Rome II such as the marketing requirement or the foreseeability defence been understood?

RULES APPLICABLE TO NON-CONTRACTUAL OBLIGATIONS OTHER THAN TORTS / DELICTS

How have the concepts of unjust enrichment (Article 10 Rome II), *negotiorum gestio* (Article 11 Rome II) and *culpa in contrahendo* (Article 12 Rome II) been understood in your country?

RULES OF SAFETY AND CONDUCT

What is the position of Courts on rules of safety and conduct of Article 17 Rome II, notably in relation to foreign administrative permits?

SCOPE OF APPLICABLE LAW

Is there any question not expressly listed in Article 12 Rome I / Article 15 Rome II (scope of the law applicable) but which Courts have included, as this article draws a list which is non-limitative ('in particular')?

Is there any characterisation issue in relation to Article 12 Rome I / Article 15 Rome II?

RENVOI

Are there cases where *renvoi* would have been helpful in order to reach international harmony of decisions?

FOREIGN LAW

Is access to foreign law for the purposes of Rome I / Rome II adequate?

What is the treatment of foreign law, for example in terms of burden of proof and rank with national law?

What support is available to Courts in respect of foreign law?

Are you aware of any case in which the *lex fori* was applied, despite Rome I / Rome II, because of a difficulty to establish with sufficient certainty the foreign law applicable? Is the universal application of Rome I (Article 2) / Rome II (Article 3) compromised?

ORDRE PUBLIC

Are you aware of any case in which the *lex fori* was applied because of the inconsistency of the foreign applicable law with international *ordre public* of the forum (Articles 21 Rome I and 26 Rome II)?

COMPENSATION

Is the level of compensation awarded to cross-border victims of delicts / torts, for example of road traffic accidents, satisfactory?

RELATIONS WITH INTERNATIONAL CONVENTIONS

For those countries which apply a Hague Convention (which supersedes Rome I / II: Article 25 / Article 28) do you think that in many cases the solutions are truly different (in practice and not just in theory) from what an application of Rome I / II would have resulted in? How many cases are we talking about in terms of percentage of the total number of cases (applying a specific Hague Convention)? For those cases where the application of the Hague Convention clearly led to a different result (not in theory but in practice), do you think the application of Rome I / Rome II would have been more appropriate? Whose party's interests are favoured by the application of the Hague Convention? Which party would benefit from the application instead of Rome I / Rome II?

GENERAL EVALUATION

Have the innovations brought in by the Rome I and Rome II Regulations proved wise / satisfactory/ successful?

Is there more uniformity now in comparison with the pre-Rome I and Rome II regimes?

Was the previous PIL Regime (whether national for non-contractual obligations or para-EU for contractual obligations – the 1980 Rome Convention) a better one?

Has the taxonomy used by both Regulations proved practical, that is: is it easy to identify a specific contract or tort / delict and its corresponding rule, or are there characterisation issues such as overlaps?

Do you see any gaps, for example in relation to quasi-delicts?

Have the courts applied the relevant Regulation in the light of its spirit and not only its letter?

Do you see negative consequences arising from the application of the Regulations in particular situations arising from case law?

CONCLUSION

SUMMARY OF FINDINGS

What lessons may we learn from the practical application of the Rome I and Rome II Regulations?

Which provisions are the most unclear / impractical / out of line with recent policies?

MAIN RECOMMENDATIONS, ESPECIALLY IN PREPARATION FOR THE REFORM OF ROME I / ROME II

What could be improved either from a judicial or legislative perspective at the national level?

What could be improved either from a judicial or legislative perspective at the EU level?

What are the new challenges ahead such as those raised by the rise of collective actions or the private enforcement of competition law in Europe?

THE APPLICATION OF THE ROME I AND ROME II REGULATIONS BEFORE THE COURT OF JUSTICE OF THE EUROPEAN UNION

Thomas KADNER GRAZIANO and Michel José REYMOND

1. INTRODUCTION

The Rome I and Rome II Regulations[1] entered into force in the EU Member States in 2009 and 2007 respectively. They introduced common rules determining

[1] Regulation (EC) No. 593/2008 of the European Parliament and of the Council of 17 June 2008 on the law applicable to contractual obligations [2008] OJ L 177/6 (Rome I) and

the applicable law in contractual (Rome I) and non-contractual (Rome II) matters in all EU Member States except Denmark. They designate the same applicable law, regardless of the country in which the case is brought. Rome I and Rome II establish foreseeability of outcome in individual cases, create legal certainty as to the applicable law, and eliminate forum shopping within Europe. Since the entry into force of both Regulations, discussions in the field of the private international law of obligations have taken place at a considerably higher, more sophisticated level, leading to greater justice and fairness in cross-border cases.

The clarity of the rules in both Regulations has had the further effect that, up until now, the Court of Justice of the European Union (CJEU) has rarely been called on to answer questions of their interpretation. Indeed, a cursory look at the existing case law reveals a relative scarcity of decisions. The CJEU has cited the Rome I Regulation in around 28 cases, with less than half of these actually examining one or several of its provisions as a subject of enquiry.[2] Meanwhile

---

Regulation (EC) No. 864/2007 of the European Parliament and of the Council of 11 July 2007 on the law applicable to non-contractual obligations [2007] OJ L 199/40 (Rome II).

2 Cases mentioning the Rome I Regulation that are not dealt with in the present survey fall into four categories. First are cases focusing on the interpretation of the Rome I Convention in which the Regulation is brought up either to be excluded or as used a means of comparison; see Case C-483/14, *KA Finanz AG v. Sparkassen Versicherung AG Vienna Insurance Group*, ECLI:EU:C:2016:205, para. 43; Case 305/13, *Haeger & Schmidt GmbH v. Mutuelles du Mans assurances IARD (MMA IARD) and Others*, ECLI:EU:C:2014:2320, paras. 39 and 50; Case C-64/12, *Anton Schlecker v. Melitta Josefa Boedeker*, ECLI:EU:C:2013:551, para. 38; Case C-29/10, *Heiko Koelzsch v. État du Grand Duchy de Luxembourg*, ECLI:EU:C:2011:151, para. 46; also included in this category – though unrelated to the Rome I Convention – is a decision issued on 9 October 2019 in which the CJEU excluded, for lack of a relevant rule, the application of the Rome I Regulation when determining the law applicable to the third-party effects of assignment claims when multiple assignments are performed by the same creditor to different assignees, see Case C-547/18, *BGL BNP Paribas SA v. TeamBank AG Nürnberg*, ECLI:EU:C:2019:848. Second are cases in which the Regulation is mentioned as a source of inspiration or as an illustration for the interpretation of other community regulations, in particular in the field of consumer contracts; see Case C-249/16, *Saale Kareda v. Stefan Benkö*, ECLI:EU:C:2017:472, para. 32; Case C-149/18, *Agostinho da Silva Martins v. Dekra Claims Services Portugal SA*, ECLI:EU:C:2019:84 (otherwise focusing on the Rome II Regulation, as described in the present contribution), Case C-508/12, *Walter Vapenik v. Josef Thurner*, ECLI:EU:C:2013:790, para. 29; Case C-208/18, *Jana Petruchová v. FIBO Group Holdings Limited*, ECLI:EU:C:2019:825; paras. 60–66; Case C-190/11, *Daniela Mühlleitner v. Ahmad Yusufi and Wadat Yusufi*, ECLI:EU:C:2012:542, para. 33; Joined Cases C-585/08 and C-144/09, *Peter Pammer v. Reederei Karl Schlüter GmbH & Co. KG and Hotel Alpenhof GesmbH v. Oliver Heller*, ECLI:EU:C:2010:740; Case C-34/18, *Ottília Lovasné Tóth v. ERSTE Bank Hungary Zrt.*, ECLI:EU:C:2019:764, para. 63. The third category comprises a single case in which the Rome I Regulation was applied to determine the law applicable to a contract but was otherwise not central to the questions referred to the CJEU, see Case 198/18, *CeDe Group AB v. KAN Sp. z o.o. in bankruptcy*, ECLI:EU:C:2019:1001, para. 15. Finally, a couple of cases were either left unreported or outright dismissed by the CJEU; see Case C-169/16, *Moreno Oscar*; Case C-397/15, *Raiffeisen Privatbank Liechtenstein AG v. Gerhild Lukath*, ECLI:EU:C:2016:16; Case C-475/14 *Gjensidige Baltic*; see finally Case C-396/13, *Sähköalojen*

the Rome II Regulation only features prominently in around seven cases, out of a total of 18 cases in which it is referenced at all.[3] Furthermore, it may also be noted that a large part of this body of case law addresses issues relating to the procedural framework of the two regulations, such as their scope of application or their relationship with each other or with other instruments of EU law. From 2015 onwards, however, there has been an increase in decisions addressing applicable law, culminating in four major rulings in the cases *Republik Griechenland v. Grigorios Nikiforidis*, *Florin Lazar v. Allianz SpA*, *Nintendo v. BigBen Interactive*, and *Agostinho da Silva Martins v. Dekra Claims*, rendered in December 2015, October 2016, September 2017, and January 2019 respectively.

2. DECISIONS ON THE TEMPORAL SCOPE OF APPLICATION

In two decisions, the CJEU was required to clarify the scope *ratione temporis* of the Rome I and Rome II Regulations respectively.

2.1. ROME I

In accordance with Article 28, the Rome I Regulation applies to 'contracts concluded after 17 December 2009'. In the case of *Republik Griechenland v. Grigorios Nikiforidis*,[4] one of the issues before the CJEU (for further issues

ammattiliitto ry v. Elektrobudowa Spolka Akcyjna, ECLI:EU:C:2015:86, in which the CJEU applied Directive 96/71 on the posting of workers in the framework of the provision of services in order to determine the law applicable to the question of the assignability of a claim in payment made by a labour organisation; while both the referring court and the Advocate General relied on the Rome I Regulation, and in particular its Art. 14(2), the CJEU did not address or mention the Regulation at all in its final decision.

3 In addition to the unreported *Gjensidige Baltic* case mentioned in n. 2 above, several cases mention the Rome II Regulation in passing; see Case C-535/17, *NK v. BNP Paribas Fortis NV*, ECLI:EU:C:2019:96, para. 22; Case C-272/18, *Verein für Konsumenteninformation v. TVP Treuhand- und Verwaltungsgesellschaft für Publikumsfonds mbH & Co KG*, ECLI:EU:C:2019:827, para. 5 (otherwise focusing on the Rome I Regulation, as detailed in the present contribution); Case C-451/18, *Tibor-Trans Fuvarozó és Kereskedelmi Kft. v. DAF TRUCKS N.V.*, ECLI:EU:C:2019:635, para 35; Case C-173/11, *Football Dataco Ltd and Others v. Sportradar GmbH and Sportradar AG*, ECLI:EU:C:2012:642, para. 7; Case C-172/18, *AMS Neve Ltd and Others v. Heritage Audio SL and Pedro Rodríguez Arribas*, ECLI:EU:C:2019:674, para. 31; Case C-45/13, *Andreas Kainz v. Pantherwerke AG*, ECLI:EU:C:2014:7, para. 20; Case C-27/17, *AB 'flyLAL-Lithuanian Airlines' v. Starptautiskā lidosta 'Rīga' VAS and 'Air Baltic Corporation' AS*, ECLI:EU:C:2018:533, para. 41; Case C-25/18, *Brian Andrew Kerr v. Pavlo Postnov and Natalia Postnova*, ECLI:EU:C:2019:376, para. 7 (also otherwise focusing on the Rome I Regulation); Case C-22/12, *Katarína Haasová v. Rastislav Petrík and Blanka Holingová*, ECLI:EU:C:2013:692, para. 36.

discussed in this case, see below section 3.1) was the application of this rule to long-term employment contracts. In this case, an employment contract between Mr Nikiforidis and the Hellenic Republic had been concluded in 1998, well before the entry into force of the Rome I Regulation. Later, the Greek state reduced the employee's gross salary for the period from October 2010 to December 2012, that is, for a period commencing after the entry into force of the Rome I Regulation. This led the referring court to consider whether this modification to the contractual terms created an independent date of conclusion which would then allow the contractual relationship between the parties to fall under the temporal scope of application of the Rome I Regulation, or whether the date of the conclusion of the initial contract was relevant for the whole contractual relationship between the parties.

For two reasons, the CJEU preferred the second solution. First, the legislative history of the Rome I Regulation showed that the EU legislator purposefully avoided the application of the Rome I Regulation to obligations arising after 17 December 2009 but based upon contracts concluded before that date. Indeed, as the Court noted, an earlier draft of the Regulation had stated that it would apply to 'contractual obligations' arising after that moment, whereas the final and current wording of Article 28 states that '[the] Regulation shall apply to contracts concluded after 17 December 2009'. Second, the Court argued that applying the Rome II Regulation to a long-term contractual relationship concluded before its entry into force following the modification of the contractual terms would be detrimental to the principles of legal certainty and foreseeability of the applicable law. These principles are not, however, absolute, and the CJEU went on to add that a modification of the contractual terms which is 'of such magnitude that it gives rise not to the mere updating or amendment of the contract but to the creation of a new legal relationship between the contractual parties' could create an independent starting date relevant for the purposes of Article 28.[5] Whether this was the case in the proceedings at hand was then left for the referring court to determine.

2.2. ROME II

The very first decision of the CJEU with respect to the Rome II Regulation also concerned its scope *ratione temporis*. In the case of *Deo Antoine Homawoo v. GMF Assurances SA*,[6] which was decided by the CJEU in November 2011, the facts

---

4 Case C-135/15, *Republik Griechenland v. Grigorios Nikiforidis*, ECLI:EU:C:2016:774.

5 *Ibid.*, para. 37.

were quite simple: Mr Homawoo, an English national domiciled in that country, was injured in a road traffic accident while in France. He brought a claim before the English courts in order to claim damages from GMF Assurances SA, a French insurance company. Before the High Court, he argued that the assessment of damages for his claim was governed by English law, as designated by internal English conflict-of-law rules. As the accident had occurred on 29 August 2007, the Rome II Regulation was, at first sight, inapplicable *ratione temporis*, due to the interplay between Articles 31 and 32, which state that '[the] Regulation shall apply to events giving rise to damage which occur after its entry into force' and that '[it] shall apply from 11 January 2009'. The defendant, however, contended that the Rome II Regulation did apply because, since neither Article 31 nor Article 32 address the question of the Regulation's date of entry into force *stricto sensu*, that date should be determined according to the default rule laid down in Article 297 of the Treaty of the Functioning of the European Union, according to which legislative acts 'enter into force on the twentieth day following that of their publication'. Under that reading, the Rome II Regulation, which was published in the Official Journal on 31 July 2007, would have entered into force on 20 August 2007. The accident would then, according to a textual interpretation of Article 31, have occurred 'after its entry into force' and would thus have fallen within the temporal scope of application of the Regulation. The CJEU thus had to decide whether the language of Article 31 referred to the application date set out in Article 32, that is, 11 January 2009, or to the date of the Regulation's actual entry into force, that is, 31 July 2007.

The CJEU began by recognising that the Rome II Regulation did not address the date of its own entry into force and that, according to Article 297 TFEU, it did indeed enter into force on 20 August 2007. Nevertheless, the Court induced that the only effect of this would be that, from this date onwards, the Commission and the Member States could begin to fulfil their obligations under the Regulation, such as establishing a list of related international conventions as required under Article 29 of the Rome II Regulation. By contrast, the actual date on which the Regulation became applicable to non-contractual obligations was that stated in Article 32, i.e. 11 January 2009. This solution was justified by the need to safeguard legal certainty for tortious events that had occurred between those two dates, such as in the case at hand. Finally, the Court underlined that the date of the commencement of proceedings had no effect upon this determination at all.

---

6 Case C-412/10, *Deo Antoine Homawoo v. GMF Assurances SA*, ECLI:EU:C:2011:747.

3. ROME I: KEY DECISIONS ON APPLICABLE LAW

3.1. OVERRIDING MANDATORY PROVISIONS (*LOIS DE POLICE*)

In what is arguably the most important CJEU case on the Rome I Regulation so far, *Republik Griechenland v. Grigorios Nikiforidis*, decided on 18 October 2016 (and briefly introduced above),[7] the Court provided guidelines on overriding mandatory provisions (*lois de police*) under the Rome I Regulation. The facts were as follows: Mr Nikiforidis, a Greek national, had been employed by the Hellenic Republic since 1996 and held a teaching position at a primary school located in Nuremberg, Germany. In 2010, the Greek legislature adopted two laws, Law 3833/2010 and Law 3845/2010, both implementing budget measures negotiated between the Hellenic Republic and the European Commission, European Central Bank and International Monetary Fund during its economic crisis. These laws had the cumulative effect of reducing the remuneration of public officials by around 15 per cent, regardless of the place of their employment. Thus, Mr Nikiforidis's salary was reduced for the period covering October 2010 to December 2012. Arguing that German rather than Greek law applied to his employment contract, thus excluding the application of the two budget laws to his salary, Mr Nikiforidis brought proceedings against his employer before the German courts seeking payment of the unpaid amounts. The German *Bundesarbeitsgericht* (Federal Supreme Labour Court) arrived at the conclusion that German law was applicable to the employment contract and considered whether the austerity measures should nevertheless apply as overriding mandatory provisions (*lois de police*) of a foreign (in this case Greek) law. The *Bundesarbeitsgericht* referred two principal questions to the CJEU. Given that the employment contract had been concluded before the entry into force of the Rome I Regulation, the first question concerned the issue of whether the Rome I Regulation applied at all to determine the law applicable to the contract (see section 2 above). The second question concerned the interpretation of the Rome I Regulation in relation to mandatory provisions (*lois de police*).

The provisions of the Rome I Regulation regarding overriding mandatory provisions (*lois de police*) take a more restrictive approach than those of its predecessor, the Rome I Convention. Whereas the Rome I Convention did not specify which mandatory rules should be taken into account by the judge of the forum, and to what extent they had to be followed,[8] the Rome I Regulation

---

[7] See n. 4 above.

[8] Convention 80/934/EEC on the Law Applicable to Contractual Obligations, opened for signature in Rome on 19 June 1980 [1980] OJ L 266/1, Art. 7(1) and (2). Even under the

states that effect may be given to the application of the mandatory provisions of either the law of the forum, as foreseen by its Article 9(2), or the law(s) of the place of performance of the contract, 'in so far as those overriding mandatory provisions render the performance of the contract unlawful', as provided for by its Article 9(3). In the case at hand, since both the forum and the place of performance of the contract were located in Germany, neither of these rules designated Greek law. The *Bundesarbeitsgericht* submitted the question to the CJEU as to whether the designation of relevant mandatory provisions in Article 9 of the Rome I Regulation should be regarded as a *numerus clausus*, or whether effect could still be given to mandatory provisions of the law of another state. Only the latter interpretation would have allowed the Greek austerity measures to apply to the employment contract. The referring court also considered whether the duty of sincere cooperation between Member States pointed towards this solution,[9] given the financial situation of the Hellenic Republic.

In its decision, the Court started by noting that the Rome I Regulation rests upon the principles of both freedom of contract and of legal certainty. Article 9 on *lois de police*, being an exception to the principle that parties be able to choose the law applicable to their contractual relationship, has to be interpreted in a restrictive manner so as not to frustrate the parties' legitimate expectations with respect to the applicable law. In particular, courts should not be allowed to apply mandatory provisions (*lois de police*) of states other than those expressly designated by the provision. In the specific case of employment contracts, the Court added that any other decision would unduly weaken the right for workers to rely on the protective provisions of the law of the place of their habitual work. The Court also noted that the nature of the current provision, which was more restrictive than the one found in the Rome I Convention, was a clear legislative signal that had to be respected. Thus, the Court concluded that the two Greek laws, being neither part of the law of the forum nor of the law of the place of habitual work, could not be applied as *lois de police*.

However, the CJEU added a caveat: while Article 9 of the Rome I Regulation operates to restrict the range of *lois de police* that may be applied in a given case, it does not restrict the range of mandatory provisions that may be taken into account within the context of the applicable law. This further distinction somewhat limits the impact of the restrictive interpretation of Article 9(1) and (2). While the mandatory provisions of only a limited range of states may indeed be *directly* applied under this provision, the *lois de police* of

previous Convention, *lois de police* were however applied in a rather restrictive matter; see Case C-184/12, *United Antwerp Maritime Agencies (Unamar) NV v. Navigation Maritime Bulgare*, ECLI:EU:C:2013:663.

9 Treaty on the Functioning of the European Union [2007] OJ C 326/1, Art. 4(3).

any other state may be considered when applying the law designated by the Rome I Regulation and may thus still influence the outcome of a given case. In the case at hand, this meant that while the *Bundesarbeitsgericht* could not apply the austerity measures to the employment contract between the Hellenic Republic and Mr Nikiforidis as part of Greek law, it could still take them into account within the boundaries of the applicable substantive law, which was German law.[10]

3.2. LAW APPLICABLE TO PAYMENT OBLIGATIONS ARISING FROM DECISIONS TAKEN BY PROPERTY OWNERS IN THEIR GENERAL ASSEMBLY

In *Kerr v. Postnov and Postnova*, the CJEU had to characterise the nature of payment obligations arising from decisions taken by an association of property owners.[11]

The case involved Mr Postnov and Ms Postnova, two Irish residents, who in May 2008 had acquired an apartment situated in an apartment block in Bansko, Bulgaria. The apartment block was managed by the association of its owners. The association took its decisions in its annual general assembly. At the assemblies for years 2013 to 2017, they adopted yearly budgets for the maintenance of the common areas. Mr Postnov and Ms Postnova did not pay their yearly contributions and the building manager lodged an application for payment before the *Rayonen sad Razlog* (District Court of Razlog, Bulgaria).

On appeal, the *Okrazhen sad Blagoevgrad* (Regional Court of Blagoevgrad, Bulgaria) referred several questions to the CJEU.

The main question was whether the courts in Bulgaria had jurisdiction under the Brussels I Regulation, and, if so, under which provision. Drawing upon its previous case law according to which payment obligations arising from the relationship between an association and its members are to be regarded as 'matters related to a contract', the CJEU concluded that the obligation at hand also fell within that characterisation. Neither the fact that the owner's association

10 See on this case also Estelle Fohrer-Dedeurwaeder, note on *Republik Griechenland v. Grigorios Nikiforidis Journal du Droit International*, Vol. 1, 2017, 202. The author argues that since consideration of a foreign *loi de police*, rather than outright application of it, is the preferred methodology in practice, the decision has the effect of severely curtailing the actual usability of Art. 9(3) of the Rome I Regulation.

11 Case C-25/18, *Brian Andrew Kerr v. Pavlo Postnov and Natalia Postnova*, ECLI:EU:C:2019:376; see also case note by P. Mankowski, 'Zahlungsklagen gegen Wohnungseigentümer im europäischen Internationalen Zivilprozessrecht', *ZMR* 2019, 565–569; A. Schwartze, 'Konzentration der Verfahren in Wohnungseigentumssachen am Ort der Liegenschaft auch bei Zahlungsklagen gegen Wohnungseigentümer im Ausland', *ZWE* 2019, 480–483.

was constituted by law – rather than through agreement – nor the fact that the defendants did not participate in the budget decisions were sufficient to find otherwise. Consequently, the Court concluded that the payment obligation due by Mr Postnov and Ms Postnova fell under the scope of Article 7(1)(a) of the Brussels I Regulation (recast), granting jurisdiction over disputes related to a contract at the place of performance of the contractual obligation in dispute.

As for the issue of applicable law, the Regional Court of Blagoevgrad requested the CJEU's guidance on (i) whether the Rome I Regulation applied at all to determine the law applicable to the payment obligation due by Mr Postnov and Ms Postnova and, if so, (ii) whether the underlying contract giving rise to said payment obligation was to be characterised as either a contract for the provision of services or a contract relating to a right *in rem* or a tenancy contract as the latter two types of contracts fall under a specific provision of the Regulation, i.e. Article 4(1)(c).

With regard to the first issue, the CJEU, having already held that the payment obligation in the case at issue was contractual in nature, considered the scope of application of the Rome I Regulation. Noting that Article 1(2)(f) of the Regulation, which excludes from the Regulation's scope all questions 'governed by the law of companies and other bodies, corporate or unincorporated', the Court found that such exclusion only applied to the structural aspects of companies, that the obligation to pay in the case at hand did not fall under that exclusion, and that the Rome I Regulation thus applied to determine the applicable law.[12]

As to the second issue, the CJEU considered whether the contracts at hand fell under the scope of Article 4(1)(c) of the Rome I Regulation, which provides that the law applicable to contracts related to a right *in rem* and to tenancy contracts is the law of the country where the property is situated. To answer this question, the Court referred to its case law developed in the context of Article 24(1) of the Brussels I Regulation (recast), which also provides a specific regime for the same categories of contracts by allocating exclusive jurisdiction at the place where the related property is located. According to that case law, which the Court found to also be applicable to the Rome I Regulation, the notion of actions *in rem* and actions over tenancy contracts do not encompass all actions concerning rights vested in immovable property but only those 'which both come within the scope of that regulation and are actions which seek to determine the extent, content, ownership or possession of immovable property or the existence of other rights in rem therein and to provide the holders of those rights with protection for the powers which attach to their interest'.[13] This was not the case of the obligation

---

12 *Ibid.*, paras. 32–36.

13 *Ibid.*, para. 37, citing Case C-605/14, *Virpi Komu and Others v. Pekka Komu and Jelena Komu*, ECLI:EU:C:2015:833, para. 26; Case C-417/15, *Wolfgang Schmidt v. Christiane Schmidt*, ECLI:EU:C:2016:881, para. 30.

to pay in the case at hand, which consequently did not fall under the specific rule in Article 4(1)(c) of the Regulation for *in rem* contracts.

Ultimately, the CJEU found that, since the contribution owed by Mr and Ms Postnova was to cover charges for the maintenance of the common areas of the apartment they owned, it stemmed from a contract for the provision of services and consequently fell under Article 4(1)(b) of the Rome I Regulation, which designates the law of the country where the service provider has its habitual residence.

3.3 APPLICATION OF THE RULES ON CONSUMER CONTRACTS TO INVESTMENT FUND TRUST AGREEMENTS

In the decision *Verein für Konsumenteninformation v. TVP Treuhand- und Verwaltungsgesellschaft für Publikumsfonds mbH & Co KG*, issued on 3 October 2019,[14] the CJEU addressed the question of whether investors may benefit from the protections granted to consumers under the European regime of Private International Law. The issue is highly relevant given the consequences that such client protection entails for the activities deployed by investment firms.

TVP, a company incorporated in Germany, managed investment funds and offered shares in these funds on the basis of subscription-based trust agreements. TVP operated out of Germany, while its investment products were marketed and sold in Austria by one of TVP's sister companies. The individual trust agreements, which TVP issued to its prospective clients for their signature, contained a choice-of-law clause in favour of German law. The *Verein für Konsumenteninformation*, an Austrian consumer protection association, lodged an injunction before the *Handelsgericht Wien* (Commercial Court Vienna) seeking to prohibit TVP from invoking its choice-of-law clause, on the basis that such clause contravened EU law and Austrian consumer law.

The main issue referred to the CJEU centred on whether Article 6 of the Rome I Regulation governing consumer contracts applied to TVP's investment products. However, since the lower courts had already determined that TVP's offerings were consumer contracts, the CJEU did not have to address this issue.[15] The Court focused on a narrower question submitted by the *Oberster Gerichtshof*. According to Article 6(4)(a) of the Rome I Regulation,

---

14 Case C-272/18, *Verein für Konsumenteninformation v. TVP Treuhand- und Verwaltungsgesellschaft für Publikumsfonds mbH & Co KG*, ECLI:EU:C:2019:827.

15 In a subsequent decision issued on 2 April 2020, the CJEU clarified the notion of consumer in financial and banking contracts. According to the Court, the protective regime applies 'if the conclusion of that contract does not fall within the scope of [the] person's

the protective rules on consumer contracts 'do not apply to a contract for the supply of services where the services are to be supplied to the consumer exclusively in a country other than that in which he has his habitual residence'. Given that TVP's management of its funds was performed from its offices in Germany, and that the company notably did not perform its fund management from Austria where the customers were domiciled, it was unclear whether the exception of Article 6(4)(a) operated to preclude the application of the Regulation's protective regime for consumers to TVP's products.

To answer this question, the Court was first led to determine whether TVP's offerings were 'contracts for the supply of services' under Article 6(4)(a) of the Regulation. Considering that, under TVP's agreements, 'the trustee carries out the activity of administering the trust property in return for remuneration', the Court found that this was the case.[16]

Second, the Court had to determine whether the place where 'the services are to be supplied' under Article 6(4)(a) was to be determined by reference to the terms of the contract as interpreted by the *lex contractus*, or by reference to the place where the services were actually supplied by the service provider. The Court considered that the first option would essentially allow professionals to manipulate the analysis of Article 6(4)(a) to their benefit by unilaterally defining the place of performance of their services in their contracts. As such a result was undesirable from the point of view of consumer protection, the CJEU concluded that the second option was preferable and that the place of the supply of services had to be determined by locating the place of their actual supply by the professional.[17]

The CJEU then applied the above standard to the case at hand, noting in particular that TVP's Austrian customers (i) paid their subscriptions fees to an Austrian bank account; (ii) received dividends and activity reports in Austria; and (iii) exercised their voting rights from Austria through a website portal. Though TVP's fund management was entirely conducted from the company's offices in Germany, these points of contact with Austria led the Court to nonetheless find that TVP's services were supplied at least partly in Austria, i.e. the habitual residence of its clients. Therefore, since TVP did not supply its services '*exclusively in a country other than that in which [the consumer] has*

professional activity [...]'. Other factors, such as the volume and amounts of the said client's transactions, or even whether he or she would be deemed as a 'retail client' under Directive 2004/39/EC on markets in financial instruments, are irrelevant to that determination, see Case C-500/18, *AU v. Reliantco Investments LTD and Reliantco Investments LTD Limassol Sucursala București*, ECLI:EU:C:2020:264, para. 57. Though the decision concerned the Brussels I Regulation (recast), these considerations are applicable by analogy to the definition of consumer found in Article 6 of the Rome I Regulation.

16 *Ibid.*, para. 47.

17 *Ibid.*, paras. 48–52.

his habitual residence', the exception in Article 6(4)(a) did not apply and TVP's Austrian customers benefitted from the consumer protection offered under Article 6 of the Rome I Regulation.

Ultimately, the Court did not determine the law applicable to TVP's contract, nor did it decide on the issue of the validity of TVP's choice-of-law clause contained therein. It instead considered that under Article 6(1) of the Rome I Regulation, Austrian law, as the law of the country of the consumers' habitual residence, should in principle be the law that applies to the investment contracts concluded by TVP. On the other hand, Article 2 of the Regulation gave TVP the possibility to insert a choice-of-law clause into its contracts if such insertion was validly made under TVP's designated law, i.e. German law and in particular Directive 93/13 on Unfair Terms in Consumer Contracts. The CJEU thus referred the case back to the lower courts for their determination on this issue.[18]

With this decision, the CJEU has confirmed that the protective regime established as an exception by the Rome I Regulation for consumers will readily apply to international investment and financial contracts regardless of whether the professional concentrates its fund management activity in its home jurisdiction. In this regard, the Court has emphasised that the exception under Article 6(4)(a) should be interpreted restrictively. As to the issue of the validity of the choice-of-law clause, the CJEU, by referring to Directive 93/13, seems to have adopted a 'transparency control' approach by reference to material consumer law to protect unsuspecting consumers against such clauses.[19]

4. ROME II: KEY DECISIONS ON APPLICABLE LAW

Motor vehicle accidents are the most common cause of personal injury and extra-contractual liability claims brought before European courts. Regarding liability for traffic accidents, the domestic laws in the EU vary considerably between countries and the question of which liability law applies may consequently have a decisive impact on the success of a claim. As a result, it is not surprising that two of the CJEU's decisions on Rome II deal with road traffic accidents, while a third one deals with a helicopter crash.

4.1. DAMAGE CLAIMS BROUGHT BY SECONDARY VICTIMS

On 10 December 2015, in *Florin Lazar v. Allianz SpA*, the CJEU decided for the first time which law should apply under the Rome II Regulation to a claim

---

18 *Ibid.*, paras. 55–60.

19 In this sense, see Case note by P. Mankowski, 'EuGH: Internationale Zuständigkeit bei Treuhandvertrag über die Verwaltung einer Kommanditbeteiligung', *LMK* 2019, 422737.

in damages brought by a family member of a victim who had lost his or her life in an accident.[20] A young woman of Romanian nationality and residing in Italy (the *primary victim*) had died in a road traffic accident in Italy. The vehicle that had caused the accident could not be identified. The father of the young woman, Mr Florin Lazar, a Romanian national residing in Romania (the *secondary victim*), requested compensation for the pecuniary and non-pecuniary harm which he had suffered following the death of his daughter. Under Italian law, in cases where the identity of the driver that caused the accident remains unknown, compensation is provided by a guarantee fund that is required to designate an insurer, which in the present case was Allianz SpA. Mr Lazar thus brought a claim in damages against Allianz SpA before the *Tribunale di Trieste* (district court in Trieste, Italy).

In the majority of European jurisdictions, in cases such as these, close family members are entitled to recover certain pecuniary losses (in particular loss of financial support or maintenance) and damages relating to non-pecuniary harm that they suffer following the death or, as we are witnessing now in more and more jurisdictions, severe injury of a loved one (in the case of death, referred to as *bereavement damages*). Nevertheless, the conditions and amounts of these damages vary widely. In the past, divergences between national laws regarding liability for bereavement damages often led secondary victims to bring their case to the highest courts to seek application of their desired liability law.

In the *Florin Lazar v. Allianz SpA* case, the first possible approach was that claims brought by secondary victims ought to be assessed under Italian law, since the accident had occurred in Italy and the primary victim lost her life there. A second, alternative approach was to apply Romanian law instead, given that the secondary victim had his domicile (or habitual residence) there and had to live with the consequences of the accident in Romania. Both jurisdictions provide damages for bereavement. Those granted in Italy are, however, the most generous in Europe.[21]

---

20 Case C-350/14, *Florin Lazar v. Allianz SpA*, ECLI:EU:C:2015:802. Case note e.g. by T. Kadner Graziano, 'The Law Applicable to Tort Claims Brought by Secondary Victims, The *Florin Lazar v. Allianz SpA* and *Germanwings* Cases', *Yearbook of Private International Law*, Vol. XVII, 2015/2016, 477.

21 See E. Gallmetzer, 'Hinterbliebenengeld als Grundrecht? – Einführung und neueste Entwicklungen in Italien', in: C. Huber, T. Kadner Graziano and J. Luckey (eds.), *Hinterbliebenengeld*, Baden-Baden: Nomos, 2018, pp. 212–235; M. Wenter, 'Die Ansprüche naher Angehöriger von Unfallopfern im italienischen Schadensrecht', *zfs* 2012, 1; G. Christandl and D. Hinghofer-Szalkay, 'Ersatzansprüche für immaterielle Schäden aus Tötung naher Angehöriger – eine rechtsvergleichende Untersuchung', *ZfRV* 2007, 44, 58 ff. See for Romanian law: Art. 1391(1) and (2) of the Romanian Civil Code (*Codul civil*) providing (in English translation): 'Non-pecuniary loss. (1) In cases of the violation of physical integrity or health, compensation may also be granted for diminished opportunities for a family life or social life. (2) The court may also grant compensation to ascendants, descendants, brothers, sisters or a spouse for pain and suffering caused by the death of the victim, and to any person who can prove the existence of such pain or suffering.'

The CJEU opted for the first approach, submitting all damage (i.e. initial damage and damage suffered by secondary victims) to the law of the place where the event of their common cause of action had taken place (which in this case was Italy). The Court thus refused to localise the injury suffered by the secondary victim separately, that is, detached from the analysis of the law applicable to the primary victim which could have led to treatment of primary and secondary victims under different laws. In its reasoning, the CJEU relied upon three central arguments.

Firstly, the CJEU referred to the wording of Article 4(1) of the Rome II Regulation. It states that the applicable law is generally that of the country in which the damage occurred, provided that this place can be determined; in the case of traffic accidents, the place of the damage is usually identified without any major difficulties. This law then applies 'irrespective of the country or countries in which the indirect consequences of that event occur', including – according to the CJEU – damage suffered by a secondary victim. The Court held that '[t]he damage sustained by the close relatives of the deceased, must be regarded as indirect consequences of the accident […] within the meaning of Art. 4(1) of the Rome II Regulation.'

Second, the CJEU referred to Article 15(f) of the Rome II Regulation stating that '[t]he law applicable to non-contractual obligations under this Regulation shall govern in particular […] persons entitled to compensation for damage sustained personally.' The Court deduced from this provision that the law applicable to claims of primary victims needs to first be determined, and that once this determination is made, this same law subsequently applies in order to determine who, and in particular which secondary victims may be deemed to be 'entitled to compensation'.

Third, the CJEU referred to Recital 16 of the Rome II Regulation, according to which the applicable law must be foreseeable to both parties. The Court stressed that it should avoid a situation in which 'the tort or delict is broken up into several elements, each subject to a different law according to the places or the persons other than the direct victim who sustain damage'.

It is indeed true that, were the place of injury suffered by secondary victims to be determined autonomously and depending on their domicile, the law applicable to their claims would hardly be foreseeable, either before or shortly after the accident. The solution chosen by the CJEU leads, on the contrary, to the application of the same law to damage claims brought by both primary victims (should they have survived the accident) and secondary victims, hereby avoiding such uncertainties. Arguments relating to foreseeability of the applicable law, simplicity and consistency thus all favour the solution found by the CJEU.

4.2. LIMITATION PERIODS AS MANDATORY PROVISIONS?

Limitation periods for claims in extra-contractual liability vary considerably in Europe, ranging from one year to ten years (or more) depending on the country. Consequently, the question of the applicable law might well be crucial for the outcome of a case. A short limitation period under a foreign applicable liability law may cause a very unpleasant surprise for the victim of an accident and may make the difference between winning a deserving case and a total dismissal of the action.

On 31 January 2019, in *Agostinho da Silva Martins v. Dekra Claims*, the CJEU issued its first decision on the question of whether the Rome II Regulation allowed the victim of a road traffic accident to avoid the application of a particularly short limitation period contained within a foreign applicable law through the mechanism of overriding mandatory provisions of law (*lois de police*).[22]

In August 2015, in Spain a passenger car registered and insured in Spain crashed into the back of a vehicle registered in Portugal, causing serious damage. The damaged car was towed back to Portugal and repaired there. The Portuguese accident insurer of the damaged car, AXA Portugal, covered the property damage. Since the driver of the Spanish car was solely responsible for the accident, AXA Portugal was subsequently reimbursed by Dekra Claims, the Portuguese partner of the Spanish car's motor vehicle insurer Segur Caixa. So far, it was a standard case.

In addition to the repair cost, the driver of the Portuguese car requested compensation for certain indirect damages, but without success. On 11 November 2016, approximately 15 months after the accident, he filed a claim for these indirect damages against the insurer before the courts at his Portuguese domicile.

The defendant insurance company invoked the statute of limitations under Article 1968 of the Spanish *Código civil* which provided for a short limitation period of one year. According to Article 498 of the Portuguese *Código civil*, the limitation period for extracontractual claims is three years and the action would not have been time-barred.

According to Article 11(1) of the Portuguese Decree-Law No 291/2007, compulsory motor vehicle liability insurance covers civil liability in case of accidents occurring in Portugal and abroad. In the latter case, if Portuguese law

22 Case C-149/18, *Agostinho da Silva Martins v. Dekra Claims Services Portugal SA*, ECLI:EU:C:2019:84. For more on the mechanism of mandatory provisions of law, see the above report of the *Republik Griechenland v. Grigorios Nikiforidis* case in which the CJEU dealt with it from the perspective of the Rome I Regulation.

provides for a higher level of cover than the foreign applicable law, Portuguese shall apply instead of the otherwise applicable foreign law. Article 11(1) of the Portuguese Act may thus lead to the application of a law different from that designated by the Rome II Regulation. The claimant invoked this provision and requested the application of the longer Portuguese limitation period to his claim.

The claim against the insurance company was brought before a Portuguese court. Portugal is not among the Contracting States of the Hague Convention of 1971 on the law applicable to traffic accidents, leading to a determination of applicable law according to the Rome II Regulation. Since the accident happened in Spain, the claim was in principle governed by Spanish law, according to Article 4(1) of the Rome II Regulation.

The question submitted to the CJEU was whether Article 11(1)(b) of the Portuguese Decree-Law, together with the longer limitation period of the Portuguese *Código civil* were to be regarded as 'overriding mandatory provisions' pursuant to Article 16 of the Rome II Regulation. Article 16 states that '[n]othing in this Regulation shall restrict the application of the provisions of the law of the forum in a situation where they are mandatory irrespective of the law otherwise applicable to the non-contractual obligation.'

In its decision, the CJEU first emphasised that the Rome II Regulation declares as applicable the law of the country in which the damage occurred, i.e. in which the accident happened. According to Article 15(h) of the Rome II Regulation, this same law also explicitly applies to the question of limitation periods.[23] With respect to the exceptional application of mandatory rules under Article 16 of the Rome II Regulation, the Court recalled its previous case law according to which 'it must be borne in mind that [...] the plea relating to the existence of a "mandatory rule" within the meaning of the legislation of the Member State concerned must be interpreted strictly'. This applied not only to the Rome I Regulation but also to Article 16 of the Rome II Regulation.[24]

Regarding the definition of the concept of 'mandatory provision', the Court referred to Article 9(1) of the Rome I Regulation which 'defines mandatory provisions as provisions the respect for which is regarded as crucial by a State for safeguarding its public interests, such as its political, social or economic organisation, to such an extent that they are applicable to any situation falling within their scope, irrespective of the law otherwise applicable to the contract under that regulation'.[25] When analysing whether a provision of national law is mandatory in the sense of Article 16 of the Rome II Regulation, a national court 'must find, on the basis of a detailed analysis of the wording, general scheme, objectives and the context in which that provision was adopted, that it is of

23 *Ibid.*, paras. 24–25.
24 *Ibid.*, paras. 26, 28–29.
25 *Ibid.*, para. 27.

such importance in the national legal order that it justifies a departure from the applicable law, designated pursuant to Article 4 [of the Rome II Regulation]'.[26]

While it is the national court that is expected to carry out this analysis with respect to its own national law, the Court pointed to the fact that the European legislator was well aware of the variety of limitation periods in the national domestic laws when it enacted Article 15(h) of the Rome II Regulation and yet explicitly submitted limitation periods to the law which is applicable according to Article 4 of the Regulation.[27] The Court concluded that '[i]n those circumstances [...] the application to an action seeking compensation for damage resulting from an accident of a limitation period other than that laid down in the law designated as applicable would require the identification of particularly important reasons, such as a manifest infringement of the right to an effective remedy and to effective judicial protection arising from the application of the law designated as applicable pursuant to Article 4 of the Rome II Regulation.'

Therefore, the Court went on: 'Article 16 of the Rome II Regulation must be interpreted as meaning that a national provision [...] which provides that the limitation period for actions seeking compensation for damage resulting from an accident is three years, cannot be considered to be an overriding mandatory provision [...] unless the court hearing the case finds, on the basis of a detailed analysis of the wording, general scheme, objectives and the context in which that provision was adopted, that it is of such importance in the national legal order that it justifies a departure from the law applicable, designated pursuant to Article 4 of that regulation'.[28]

In light of this reasoning, the conditions for an exception under Article 16 will hardly ever be met with respect to foreign limitation periods. The Court's reasoning is straightforward and the arguments are convincing. The drafters of the Rome II Regulation in the Commission were indeed well aware of the problem that short limitation periods may cause in cross-border cases, and the decision to extend applicable law under Article 4 Rome II to issues of limitation in Article 15(h) was made in full awareness of this issue.[29]

And yet, the application of short foreign limitation periods may lead to extremely harsh results. Short one-year limitation periods are made, and may be fit, for domestic situations, and for such situations only.[30] Cross-border

---

26 *Ibid.*, paras. 30, 31.

27 *Ibid.*, para. 33.

28 Paras. 34, 35.

29 On this issue T. Kadner Graziano, 'Die kumulative Anknüpfung der Verjährung „in favorem actionis" – Ein Vorschlag zum Opferschutz in grenzüberschreitenden Fällen', *Recht der internationalen Wirtschaft (RIW)* 2007, 336–340.

30 And even there they may lead to harsh results. In response to an asbestos case, the Swiss legislator recently abandoned its short one-year limitation period in torts, for further information see <https://www.admin.ch/opc/fr/federal-gazette/2018/3655.pdf>.

scenarios are, by the simple fact that they are cross-border, too complex to be fit for short limitation periods. In cross-border cases parties are faced with additional layers of complexity which are absent in purely domestic scenarios. The present case illustrates this well: determining the applicable law; finding out whether, under the standards of the applicable liability law, the victim was expected to have the car repaired close by or whether towing costs back to Portugal would be admitted and covered; identifying the relevant insurer and its representative in Portugal; organising the repair; calculating the amount of additional damage; negotiating recovery under the applicable foreign law with an insurer; estimating the chances of success of a potential claim, again under the applicable foreign law; consulting a lawyer and finding a corresponding foreign lawyer able to give advice on the content of the applicable foreign law; finally, preparing and bringing the claim … All this took the victim in the present case approximately 15 months. Under Portuguese law and its three-year limitation period, this would have been amply sufficient, but not under Spanish law with its short one-year limitation period.

De lege ferenda, harsh results due to particularly short limitation periods of an applicable foreign law could be easily avoided if, for limitation periods, an alternative connecting mechanism were adopted. The relevant rule in amendment of the Rome II Regulation could read:

> **Limitation periods.** The claim for extra-contractual liability is time-barred only if the limitation period of the applicable law and the limitation period of the law of the country of the victim's habitual residence at the time of the accident have expired.

If this rule were adopted, the claim of Mr da Silva Martins would only have been time-barred if both the (one-year) limitation period of Spanish law and the (three-year) limitation period of Portuguese law had been expired. The victim of the accident would have had the time to prepare his case and he would have avoided the unwelcome surprise that a claim brought 15 months after the occurrence of the accident was already time-barred under the applicable foreign law. The *Agostinho da Silva Martins v. Dekra Claims* case, and many more similar cases in Europe, may give cause for concern about whether such an amendment of the Rome II Regulation would be worth considering.

4.3. DIRECT ACTIONS AGAINST LIABILITY INSURERS

The case *Eleonore Prüller-Frey v. Norbert Brodnig and Axa Versicherung AG*, decided on 9 September 2015, brought clarifications with respect to the victim's direct right of action against the insurer of a vehicle.[31]

---

[31] Case C-240/14, *Eleonore Prüller-Frey v. Norbert Brodnig and Axa Versicherung AG*, ECLI:EU:C:2015:567.

Ms Prüller-Frey, an Austrian national domiciled in Austria, was interested in purchasing an aloe vera plantation located in Spain. In order to survey the plantation, she boarded an autogiro (a vehicle resembling a small helicopter), which was piloted by its owner, Mr Preiss. The vehicle was insured against civil liability with the insurance company AXA Versicherung AG, established in Germany. The policy, however, had not been contracted under the name of Mr Preiss, but under the name of an associate, Mr Brodnig, who was at the time resident in both Spain and Austria and who had managed to obtain favourable conditions due to his experience in air transport. The insurance contract contained a choice-of-law clause in favour of German law.

During the trip, the vehicle crashed near Jerez de la Frontera, in Andalusia (Spain). Ms Prüller-Frey, who was injured in that event, sued both Mr Brodnig and AXA Versicherung in Austria before the *Landesgericht Korneuburg* (Regional Court of Korneuburg, Austria), seeking approximately €143,000 in damages, along with a declaration of joint liability for any future damage stemming from the accident. The claim was thus brought by a claimant domiciled in Austria before Austrian courts against, among others, a defendant insurance company established in Germany for damage suffered in Spain.

The defendants argued that, since the insurance contract was subject to German law, the action could not be brought directly against the second defendant (the insurance company), because in such scenarios (an aircraft crash), German law does not allow the victim to bring a direct action against the liability insurer. The question before the CJEU was thus whether the Rome II Regulation, applicable to the case at hand,[32] allowed for a direct action against the insurer in such circumstances.

According to Article 18 of the Rome II Regulation, victims can bring a direct action against an insurer if either the law applicable to the insurance contract or the law applicable to the non-contractual obligation allows a direct claim. In its decision, the Court held that, even if Ms Prüller-Frey was not able to make a direct claim against AXA Versicherung AG under German law as the law applicable to the insurance contract, she could nevertheless invoke this law if the law applicable to the accident, as determined pursuant to Article 4 of the Rome II Regulation, allowed a direct claim against the liability insurer. The CJEU concluded that it was for the *Landesgericht Korneuburg* to examine whether this was the case.

---

32 A preliminary issue, which will not be related in detail in this contribution, was whether the Rome II Regulation applied to the case at hand as it was possibly pre-empted by the Montreal Convention for the Unification of Certain Rules for International Carriage by Air of 28 May 1999. The CJEU answered that the Convention did not apply, and thus continued its examination on the basis of the Rome II Regulation.

4.4. ROME II: LAW APPLICABLE TO MULTI-JURISDICTIONAL INFRINGEMENTS OF COMMUNITY DESIGN RIGHTS

Most elements pertaining to unitary Community design rights are directly governed by the Regulation on Community Designs.[33] For matters, actions or remedies not covered by that Regulation, Article 8(2) of the Rome II Regulation contains a choice-of-law rule designating 'the law of the country in which the act of infringement was committed.'

On 27 September 2017, the CJEU rendered the *Nintendo v. BigBen* decision, in which it interpreted the application of Article 8(2) pertaining to infringements committed across several Member States, in particular through websites offering infringing goods for sale to potential buyers in multiple countries at once.[34]

The facts concerned the Japanese video game manufacturer Nintendo and the marketing of its Wii video game console in Europe, along with several official accessories such as the Wii remote control, the 'Nunchuck' controller add-on, the 'Wii Motion Plus' remote add-on and the fitness oriented 'Wii Balance Board' connectable mat. In relation to these accessories, Nintendo held several registered Community designs.

BigBen France manufactured remote controls and several accessories compatible with Nintendo's Wii console. It sold these goods directly to consumers located in France, Belgium, Luxembourg and others. It also sold them to BigBen Germany, a subsidiary which then resold them to consumers located in Germany and Austria through its own dedicated website. BigBen Germany, however, had no stock of accessories of its own and directly forwarded the orders it received from consumers to its parent company.

Nintendo alleged that the two companies infringed its registered designs through both the sale of their compatible accessories and through the use of advertisements depicting the use of Nintendo accessories. The company brought several actions before the *Landgericht Düsseldorf* (Regional Court of Düsseldorf, Germany). It sought, firstly, a declaration from the court that its registered designs had been infringed and, secondly, the imposition of several orders against the defendants with the objectives of the disclosure of several documents; the payment of Nintendo's legal fees along with further compensation; and the destruction or, subsidiarily, the recall of the infringing products.

---

33 Council Regulation (EC) No. 6/2002 of 12 December 2001 on Community Designs [2002] OJ L 3/1.

34 Joined Cases C-24/16 and C-25/16, *Nintendo Co. Ltd v. BigBen Interactive GmbH, BigBen Interactive SA*, ECLI:EU:C:2017:724; see also case notes by L. Idot, Europe, n. 12, December 2019, comm. 524; J. Schulte, 'Gemeinsam verzockt: Zuständigkeit und Anknüpfung bei Verletzung eines Gemeinschaftsgeschmacksmusters durch mehrere Schädiger', *IPRax* 2019, 202–208.

The *Landgericht Düsseldorf*, applying the Regulation on Community Designs, held that BigBen France and BigBen Germany had indeed infringed upon Nintendo's registered Community designs, yet only insofar as the sale of accessories was concerned. With regard to the measures that Nintendo had sought to impose upon the defendants, the Court considered that the imposition of such measures fell outside the scope of the Regulation on Community Designs and that, as such, they had to be examined under the law(s) designated by Article 8(2) of the Rome II Regulation. Finding that this led to the distributive application of German, Austrian and French law, given the nature of the sales of goods operated by the defendants through their respective websites, the Court granted the orders sought by Nintendo. Regarding BigBen France, however, it limited the scope of the orders to the sale of its goods to BigBen Germany and not to the rest of its activities.

Upon appeal to the *Oberlandesgericht Düsseldorf* (Higher Regional Court of Düsseldorf, Germany), Nintendo argued inter alia that German law should have applied to its claims against BigBen Germany and that, correspondingly, French law should have applied to its claims against BigBen France. Unsure of which law was applicable to the infringements at hand, especially given the geographically distributed nature of the sales operated by the defendants through their respective websites, the *Oberlandesgericht Düsseldorf* decided to refer the matter to the CJEU to clarify the application of Article 8(2) in this context.[35]

The CJEU began by confirming that Article 8(2) of the Rome II Regulation applied to the determination of the law applicable to the measures sought by Nintendo. According to Article 89(1)(d) of the Regulation on Community Designs, a court may impose any measures not foreseen by the Regulation itself but which are 'provided by the law of the Member State in which the acts of infringement or threatened infringement are committed, including its private international law.' The latter reference to rules of private international law, the CJEU reasoned, was to be understood as designating the Rome II Regulation as the generally applicable regulation in conflict-of-law matters for non-contractual obligations in the EU.[36] Therefore, one had to look at the rules of Rome II and, in particular, Article 8(2), in order to identify the law governing such measures.

Referring to the *Homawoo* decision presented above, the Court then recalled that the Rome II Regulation was aimed at ensuring the predictability of outcomes, the legal certainty of the law applicable to non-contractual obligations and its uniform application throughout EU Member States. The Court argued that these principles came under particular strain when applied to disputes over intellectual property infringements committed across several countries,

35 *Ibid.*, paras. 33–36.

36 *Ibid.*, para. 93.

as they potentially lead to the cumulative application of the law of several Member States simultaneously.[37]

The CJEU interpreted Article 8(2) as designating the law of the country in which the event giving rise to the damage occurred, i.e. the country in which the infringing act was committed. In cases where a number of infringements are distributed across multiple Member States, this place was to be localised through 'an overall assessment of that defendant's conduct in order to determine the place where the initial act of infringement at the origin of that conduct was committed or threatened,' rather than through a consideration of each separate act of infringement. As such, the Court deduced from Article 8(2) a single connecting factor, identifying a single law applicable to the whole range of infringing activities.[38]

Regarding the situation of BigBen France, which had offered infringing goods for sale in multiple countries through its commercial website, the Court designated the applicable law as the one of 'the place where the process of putting the offer for sale online by that operator on its website was activated.'[39] Regarding BigBen Germany, which did not actually ship the infringing goods itself and merely forwarded orders to its parent company, the Court still declined to provide a clear answer and only repeated that an overall assessment of its conduct was to be performed.[40]

The CJEU's approach in *Nintendo v. BigBen* seeks to avoid fragmentation of the law applicable to a multi-jurisdictional infringement of unitary Community designs. However, it does not actually solve the issue of the uncertainty of the applicable law that the Court had rightfully identified in such cases. On the contrary, the standard seems to simply kick the can of uncertainty further down the road and maintains the question of the 'global assessment' of the infringing party's conduct.

The CJEU's designation of the place of activation of the infringing party's website as the place of the commission of the infringement in cases of direct sales is particularly ill-defined as activation is a purely technical operation bearing no relation to the marketing or sale of infringing goods. Furthermore, the activation and operation of e-commerce websites and platforms are routinely delegated by commercial operators to specialised subcontractors who may or may not be localised in jurisdictions relevant to the main operator's business activities. The CJEU's solution thus muddles, rather than clarifies, the choice-of-law inquiry in such situations. The fact that the Court did not provide an answer regarding

37 *Ibid.*, para. 99.
38 *Ibid.*, para. 103.
39 *Ibid.*, para. 108.
40 *Ibid.*, para. 109.

the more complex situation of BigBen Germany is telling of the fragility of its approach.

We must keep our fingers crossed that the CJEU will not extend its judgment in *Nintendo v. BigBen* to Article 8(1) of the Rome II Regulation covering infringements of general intellectual property rights. Such an extension would, in our view, be in stark contrast to the wording and rationale of Article 8(1). In fact, Article 8(1) designates the 'law of the country for which protection is claimed' without specific reference to the commission of an act of infringement, as is the case for Article 8(2) on Community designs.

5. RELATIONSHIP BETWEEN ROME I AND ROME II

Two decisions of the CJEU have addressed the relationship between the Rome I and Rome II Regulations in complex cases, along with the delimitation between contractual relations falling under the ambit of the Rome I Regulation, and non-contractual relations governed by the Rome II Regulation.

The first decision, *Ergo Insurance v. If P&C Insurance*,[41] raised this issue in relation to contribution claims made between several insurers involved in the same incident. It concerned two joined cases: in the first case, a tractor unit coupled with a trailer overturned during a manoeuvre on a road near Mannheim, Germany. As the driver of the tractor unit was found to be responsible for the accident by the local authorities, the insurer of that vehicle, a company based in Lithuania, subsequently paid about 7,760 Lithuanian *Litas* in compensation to the victims. It then brought an action against the insurer of the trailer – which was insured by a different insurance company – requesting reimbursement of half of the amount paid for compensation.

The second, joined case concerned a nearly identical fact pattern, with an accident that had occurred in Germany, and with the Lithuanian insurer of a tractor unit taking action against the insurer of its affixed trailer following compensation for damage done to third parties. Both referring courts, the *Vilniaus miesto apylinkės teismas* (District Court of the City of Vilnius) in the first case and the *Lietuvos Aukščiausiasis Teismas* (Supreme Court of Lithuania) in the second, asked the CJEU to clarify how the law applicable to these actions should be determined. In particular, it was unclear whether such analysis had to be performed with reference to the law applicable to the insurance contracts under the Rome I Regulation, or whether the law of the place of the accident as designated by Article 4(1) of the Rome II Regulation applied instead. In short, the question was

41 Joined Cases C-359/14 and C-475/14, *ERGO Insurance SE v. If P&C Insurance AS and Gjensidige Baltic AAS v. PZU Lietuva UAB DK*, ECLI:EU:C:2016:40.

whether this was an action in contract, subject to the Rome I Regulation, or in tort, subject to the Rome II Regulation.

Drawing a parallel between the material scope of each Regulation and the definition of 'matters relating to contract' and 'matters relating to tort, delict or quasi-delict' under Article 7(2) of the Brussels I Regulation (recast), the CJEU reasoned that the scope of the Rome I Regulation, as set out by Article 1, covers legal obligations 'freely consented to by one person towards another', while the scope of the Rome II Regulation covers 'all actions which seek to establish the liability of a defendant and [which] are not related to a contract'. Following its Article 2, the Rome II Regulation includes unjust enrichment, *negotiorum gestio* and *culpa in contrahendo* in that definition.

Applying this to the cases at hand, the CJEU began by remarking that there was no contractual relationship between the insurers. As the claims in compensation did not arise out of any particular contract, but rather from the concomitant liability of the insurers, the Court concluded that Article 4 of the Rome II Regulation, designating German law as the *lex loci delicti* in both scenarios, should be applied in order to measure each insurer's contribution to the compensation for the damage. With that being said, the Court also considered that there remained a contractual element to that determination, since each insurer's coverage obligations stemmed from their contractual relationship with their respective insured party. Thus, it also concluded that Article 7 of the Rome I Regulation, governing insurance contracts, applied to determine the law applicable to that particular aspect of the two disputes.

Before moving on to the second decision, it should be mentioned that in the *Kareda v. Benkö* decision rendered in 2017, the CJEU, citing *Ergo*, confirmed that the delimitation between contract and tort matters should be consistent between both jurisdictional and choice-of-law matters.[42] In that case, the Court concluded inter alia that a recourse claim made between joint debtors to a loan contract was a contractual matter falling under the ambit of Article 7(1) of the Brussels I Regulation (recast). The Court noted that such solution was consistent with Article 16 of the Rome I Regulation which links the relationship between joint debtors to the contractual relationship with the creditor.[43]

The second decision, *Verein für Konsumenteninformation v. Amazon EU Sàrl*,[44] concerned the topic of consumer contracts and unfair terms. A consumer protection association located in Austria requested an injunction against the European branch of the online retailer Amazon.com, established in Luxembourg, before its home courts. The order, which was based upon Directive 2009/22/EC

42 Case C-249/16, *Saale Kareda v. Stefan Benkö*, ECLI:EU:C:2017:472.
43 *Ibid.*, para. 32.
44 Case C-191/15, *Verein für Konsumenteninformation v. Amazon EU Sàrl*, ECLI:EU:C:2016:612.

on injunctions for the protection of consumers,[45] sought to stop Amazon from including certain contractual clauses in its standard terms, as these were deemed unfair by the association.

At the heart of this case was the question of which law was applicable to determine the unfair nature of the standard terms. On the one hand, the courts of first and second instance, noting that one of the clauses at issue was a *choice-of-law clause* in favour of the law of Luxembourg, applied Article 6(2) of the Rome I Regulation (the provision determining the law governing consumer contracts), which states that such provisions are permitted in consumer contracts under certain conditions. However, they reached opposite results: the first instance court eventually considered that the choice-of-law clause was invalid and applied Austrian law to the standard terms as the law of the place where consumer protection was sought. The appellate court, by contrast, retained the validity of the choice-of-law clause and applied the law of Luxembourg instead. The Austrian *Oberster Gerichtshof* (Supreme Court) had doubts as to the applicable instrument: since the injunction was made *in abstracto*, independent of any particular contract, there were also grounds to consider that it fell outside the realm of the Rome I Regulation. The applicable law in that case would have to be determined according to the Rome II Regulation. In order to obtain clarity on this point, the *Oberster Gerichtshof* submitted the question to the CJEU.

In its decision, the CJEU reasoned in two steps. In the first step, it characterised injunctions brought by consumer protection associations as non-contractual in nature. Indeed, in the 2002 *Henkel* decision, it had already decided in this manner in the context of the Brussels I Regulation, reasoning that such actions, since they are preventive and stem from the professional's liability for unfair commercial practices, do not qualify as contractual.[46] Applying this reasoning to the contractual clauses in the present case, the Court held that such actions fall under Article 6(1) of the Rome II Regulation, addressing unfair competition and designating the law of the place of the affected market, here understood as the place where competitive relations and the interests of consumers are affected. The Court also made it clear that the mere presence of a choice-of-law clause made in favour of a specific law was not sufficient to lead to the application of that law as the one most closely connected to the case under Article 4(3) of the Regulation, as such a solution would allow the professional to choose the applicable law and thus bear the risk of circumventing the aim of protecting the interest of consumers against unfair contract terms.

In a second step, however, the Court distinguished two aspects of the case: the injunction itself, which, as mentioned above, was subject to the Rome II

[45] Directive 2009/22/EC of the European Parliament and of the Council of 23 April 2009 on injunctions for the protection of consumers' interests [2009] OJ L 110/30.

[46] Case C-167/00, *Verein für Konsumenteninformation v. Karl Heinz Henkel*, ECLI:EU:C:2002:555.

Regulation, and the 'examination of the unfairness of terms … which are the subject of the action for an injunction [and which] must be determined independently in accordance with the nature of those terms'.[47] Regarding the latter analysis, the Court reasoned that the Rome I Regulation, and in particular Article 4(1) or alternatively Article 6(2) on choice of law in consumer contracts, was applicable. The Court argued that applying the law of the place of the affected market pursuant to Article 6(1) of the Rome II Regulation to the examination of the clauses would create 'a risk that the criteria of [that] examination would be different from those applied in an individual action brought by a consumer'.[48] This would 'have the effect in particular of abolishing the consistency of assessment between collective actions and individual actions'.[49] Thus, the Court concluded that while Article 6(1) of the Rome II Regulation applies to an injunction brought by a consumer protection association 'where what is alleged is a breach of a law aimed at protecting consumers' interests with respect to the use of unfair terms in general terms and conditions', the Rome I Regulation applies to determine 'the law applicable to the assessment of a particular contractual term … whether this is in an individual action or in a collective action.'

6. RELATIONSHIP WITH OTHER INSTRUMENTS OF EU LAW

In a number of cases situated outside of the scope of application of the Rome I Regulation, the CJEU incidentally addressed the question of its relationship with other instruments of European law.

In *Hermann Lutz v. Elke Bäuerle*,[50] which was decided in April 2015, a question was raised by the German *Bundesgerichtshof* (Federal Court of Justice) regarding the application of the Rome I Regulation to a contract falling under Regulation 1346/2000 on insolvency proceedings.[51] The facts were as follows: Mr Lutz, an Austrian resident, had bought a car from the Austrian subsidiary of ECZ GmbH, a German company registered in Tettnang. As the company failed to deliver the good, the buyer filed a claim for recovery of the purchase price before the *Bezirksgericht Bregenz* (Distinct Court of Bregenz) in Austria. On 17 March 2008, he succeeded in obtaining an enforceable payment order of around €10,000 plus interest. Shortly thereafter, on 20 May 2008, assets in the amount

47 *Ibid.*, para. 49.
48 *Ibid.*, para. 55.
49 *Ibid.*, para. 56.
50 Case C-557/13, *Hermann Lutz v. Elke Bäuerle*, ECLI:EU:C:2015:227.
51 Council Regulation (EC) No. 1346/2000 of 29 May 2000 on insolvency proceedings [2000] OJ L 160/1.

of that sum were frozen in three bank accounts owned by the company until the order was executed, much later, on 17 March 2009. During that period, starting from August 2008, insolvency proceedings had however been opened against the same debtor company. At the moment of the payment, the liquidator in charge of the insolvency proceedings filed a claim before the *Landgericht Ravensburg* (Regional Court of Ravensburg) in Germany, seeking to set aside the order and asking for the recovery of the payment sum. The case then went on appeal to the *Bundesgerichtshof*, which then referred a series of questions to the CJEU.

Stated in broad terms, the main issue tackled by the CJEU in that case was whether the law applicable to the claim of the liquidator was the *lex loci concursus*, applicable according to the general principle laid down by Article 4(2)(m) of Regulation 1346/2000, or if the *lex causae* was applicable instead following an exception laid down by Article 13 on acts detrimental to all creditors. In the course of its analysis, the Court clarified that the choice-of-law system contained in the insolvency regulation was a *lex specialis* to the Rome I Regulation. Thus, the CJEU restricted the scope of its arguments to the four corners of the insolvency regulation,[52] ultimately arriving at the conclusion that the *lex causae* was applicable.[53]

The CJEU's conclusions in *Lutz* were confirmed, obiter dictum, in the decision *Vinyls Italia SpA v. Mediterranea di Navigazione SpA*, rendered in June 2017.[54] In that case, the Court found that Article 3(3) of the Rome I Regulation, which affirms, in the context of a choice-of-law clause, the application of the mandatory laws of the Member State in which all of the elements related to the contract are located, was inapplicable to the setting aside of a contract payment in the context of insolvency proceedings, as such matters fall exclusively under the insolvency regulation.[55] As the Rome I Regulation was inapplicable in the case at hand, the Court merely mentioned it as source of inspiration when interpreting Article 13 of the insolvency regulation.[56]

A similar result was reached by the CJEU in *Höszig Kft. v. Alstom Power Thermal Services*,[57] which was decided in July 2016, and in which it had to delineate the respective scopes of application of the Brussels I Regulation[58] and the Rome I Regulation in assessing the validity of a forum-selection clause.

---

52 In particular, it declined to take inspiration from Art. 12(1)(d) of the Rome I Regulation regarding the question of whether the law applicable to the contract at whole also applied to limitation periods and time bars, see *ibid.*, paras. 45–46.

53 See *ibid.*, paras. 53–55.

54 Case C-54/16, *Vinyls Italia SpA v. Mediterranea di Navigazione SpA*, ECLI:EU:C:2017:433.

55 *Ibid.*, paras. 48–49.

56 *Ibid.*, paras. 42–43.

57 Case C-222/15, *Hőszig Kft. v. Alstom Power Thermal Services*, ECLI:EU:C:2016:525.

58 Regulation (EU) No. 1215/2012 of the European Parliament and of the Council of 12 December 2012 on jurisdiction and the recognition and enforcement of judgments in civil and commercial matters (recast) [2012] OJ L 351/1.

The case concerned a series of work contracts entered into by Technos Cie., a French company, and Höszig Kft., a Hungarian company, under which the Hungarian company was to manufacture metallic structures that had to be integrated by the French company into various power plants located in France. The first contract made reference to the general conditions of the supplier and that document contained a choice-of-forum clause in favour of 'the courts of Paris' and a choice-of-law clause in favour of French law. As a dispute arose between the parties regarding performance of the contract, Höszig brought action before the *Pécsi Törvényszék* (Court of Pécs) in Hungary, a move that Alstom, which had succeeded to the rights of Technos Cie. in the meantime, opposed due to the existence of the choice-of-forum clause.

During the proceedings, the main object of contention between the two parties was whether the general conditions, and in particular the choice-of-forum and choice-of-law clauses, were validly integrated into the contract. Both parties based their arguments upon the text of Article 10 of the Rome I Regulation, which states that the existence and/or validity of a contract or a contractual term is to be examined by the law applicable to the contract, or, exceptionally, by the law of the habitual residence of a party arguing lack of consent if the application of the general rule was found to be unreasonable given the circumstances of the case. This led the referring court to request an interpretation of this provision from the CJEU. The Court replied that the issue of the validity of a choice of jurisdiction clause was to be examined exclusively under Article 23 of the Brussels I Regulation, and that the Rome I Regulation was inapplicable by virtue of its Article 1(2)(e) ('The following shall be excluded from the scope of this Regulation: … arbitration agreements and agreements on the choice of court.'). Finding that the choice-of-forum clause was validly integrated into the contract under the standards of the relevant provision, the CJEU concluded that the *Court of Pécs* did not have jurisdiction. There was thus no need to examine the integration of the choice-of-law clause pursuant to Article 10 of the Rome I Regulation.

Finally, a short mention may be made of *Calberson GE v. European Commission*,[59] a case decided in February 2016, in which the Court examined a very specific issue, namely the role of the Rome I Regulation as a choice-of-law instrument when dealing with transport contracts concluded in the context of the adjudication procedure envisaged by the European Union's programme for the supply of agricultural goods to the Federation of Russia. The Court concluded that all of the contractual elements not already covered

59 Case T-164/14, *Calberson GE v. European Commission*, ECLI:EU:T:2016:85.

by the existing legal framework of that programme, which was set out in several Regulations,[60] had to be resolved according to the law otherwise applicable to the contract as determined by the rules of the Rome I Regulation.

7. CONCLUSIONS AND PROSPECTS

The limited number of cases for preliminary rulings on issues regarding the interpretation of the Rome I and II Regulations that have been submitted to the CJEU so far seems to confirm the high degree of legal certainty that both Regulations have achieved. There have been almost as many cases on the *relationship between* the different private international law instruments and on the relationship between these Regulations and other EU instruments as there have been cases on the *interpretation of the connecting factors* used in Rome I and Rome II. This may arguably be an indication that the time has come to commence preparatory work for a comprehensive EU Private International Law Regulation bringing together the current Regulations on jurisdiction, applicable law and the recognition and enforcement of judgments in one single instrument. Such an instrument could help to avoid uncertainties and frictions between the scopes of application of different EU instruments in cross-border cases and hereby contribute to even more legal certainty in cross-border cases in Europe.[61]

---

60 Commission Regulation (EC) No. 111/1999 of 18 January 1999 laying down general rules for the application of Council Regulation (EC) No. 2802/98 on a programme to supply agricultural products to the Russian Federation [1999] OJ L 14/3, amended by Commission Regulation (EC) No. 1125/1999 [1999] OJ L 135/41.

61 See the proposal by T. Kadner Graziano, 'Codifying European Private International Law: The Swiss Private International Law Act – A Model for a Comprehensive European Private International Law Regulation?', *Journal of Private International Law* 2015, 585.

THE APPLICATION OF THE ROME I AND ROME II REGULATIONS IN AUSTRIA AND GERMANY

Matthias WELLER and Stephan WALTER

1. GENERAL OVERVIEW

Unlike all the other contributions in this book, this contribution features the court practice of two distinct Member States, namely Austria and Germany. The reasons for this approach are manifold. Not only do Austria and Germany share a common language, but they also belong to the same legal family (the German or Germanic legal family)[1] which they represent within the European Union. Moreover, Austrian courts often refer to German decisions and German legal literature (and sometimes vice versa).[2] Against this background, a joint analysis of the case law of these two Member States is instrumental to bring to light both commonalities and differences in their application of the Rome I and Rome II Regulation. In order to identify such trends and tendencies in the practice of Austrian and German courts, more than 500 decisions that were publicly available on 1 January 2020 were taken into account.

In general, the case law shows that the application of the Rome I and Rome II Regulations has been correct to a large extent. In particular, it seems that the courts are usually aware of the Regulations' existence and functioning,[3]

1 See Konrad Zweigert/Hein Kötz, Einführung in die Rechtsvergleichung (1996), p. 130 et seq.

2 See e.g. Austrian Supreme Court of Justice (OGH), docket no. 2 Ob 204/14k; Austrian Supreme Court of Justice (OGH), docket no. 2 Ob 18/16k; Austrian Supreme Court of Justice (OGH), docket no. 3 Ob 8/14v; Regional Court of Munich, docket no. 12 O 730/17, para. 229.

3 See Florian Heindler/Bea Verschraegen, in Paul Beaumont et al. (eds.), Cross-Border Litigation in Europe (2017), Austria, p. 243, 245.

although it is technically impossible to comprehensively collect from the databases all the decisions that overlooked the applicability of the Regulations. Some decisions, however, have suffered from fundamental misunderstandings. For example, the universal scope of the Regulations has sometimes been ignored and it has wrongly been required that the defendant or both parties had their habitual residence in a Member State.[4] Furthermore, some courts have ignored the exclusion of the *renvoi* in Article 20 Rome I Regulation and Article 24 Rome II Regulation,[5] or relied on the Regulations to determine the international jurisdiction.[6] Yet such blatantly wrong decisions are very rare and do not appear to be representative. On the contrary, the vast majority of the decisions dealt with a variety of micro-level issues. Given the large number of decisions, only a selection of the most telling cases can be discussed here in detail.

2. ROME I

2.1. OVERVIEW

After 10 years of application, there is already a huge body of case law on the Rome I Regulation. More than 260 decisions rendered by German courts and about 30 decisions by Austrian courts are publicly available. The most frequently applied provisions are (in descending order) Articles 3, 4, 5, 6, and 8 Rome I Regulation (Germany) and Articles 4, 3, 8, 15, and 6 Rome I Regulation (Austria).

By contrast, both the Rome I Regulation and the Rome II Regulation do not play any noticeable role in arbitral proceedings. Although it is argued that arbitral tribunals are obliged to apply the Regulations,[7] there are no arbitration

---

4 E.g. Higher Regional Court of Koblenz, docket no. 2 U 1050/11, para. 31; Higher Regional Court of Cologne, docket no. I-6 U 87/10, 6 U 87/10, para. 10; Regional Court of Frankenthal, docket no. 4 O 155/09, para. 24; Local Court of Frankenthal, docket no. 3a C 158/13; Administrative Court of Minden, docket no. 11 K 2675/11, para. 46; Local Court of Würzburg, docket no. 16 C 207/13, para. 18; however, only in one case did a court apply the former German autonomous rules on non-contractual obligations instead of the Rome II Regulation even though the Regulation had entered into force several years before: Higher Regional Court of Cologne, docket no. I-6 U 87/10, 6 U 87/10, para. 10.

5 Regional Court of Cologne, docket no. 20 O 195/13, para. 8; Local Court of Geldern, docket no. 4 C 356/10, para. 10.

6 Regional Court of Frankfurt, docket no. 2-24 O 142/10, para. 24; Regional Court of Düsseldorf, docket no. 14c O 292/11, para. 90; Regional Court of Stuttgart, docket no. 30 O 26/17, para. 48.

7 E.g. Béatrice Blümel, ÖJZ 2015, 343 et seq.; Dietmar Czernich, Wirtschaftsrechtliche Blätter 2013, 554 et seq.; Mary-Rose McGuire, SchiedsVZ 2011, 257, 266 et seq.

awards publicly available where the Regulations were actually applied. Of course, it cannot be ruled out that some arbitral tribunals may have applied the Regulations in unpublished awards. However, it is a clear indication that arbitral tribunals do not feel bound by the Regulations. This is in line with the prevailing view in the literature.[8]

2.2. SCOPE

2.2.1. Temporal Scope: Article 28 Rome I

According to Article 28 Rome I Regulation, the Regulation shall only apply to contracts concluded as of 17 December 2009. Nonetheless, some German courts have applied the Rome I Regulation to long-term contracts concluded before this date,[9] even though Article 28 Rome I Regulation also applies to such long-term contracts.[10] If, however, a long-term contract concluded before the relevant date is subject to an alteration or amendment afterwards, the question arises as to whether this may lead to the application of the Regulation on the contract as a whole.[11]

The German Federal Labour Court (*Bundesarbeitsgericht*, BAG) referred this question to the CJEU for a preliminary ruling,[12] and it was held that a contract concluded before 17 December 2009 could fall within the scope of the Rome I Regulation only in so far as the contractual relationship 'has undergone, as a result of mutual agreement of the contracting parties which has manifested itself

8 Dieter Martiny, in Jan v. Hein (ed.), Münchener Kommentar zum Bürgerlichen Gesetzbuch Vol. 12 (7th ed. 2018), Vorbemerkung zu Art. 1 Rom I-VO, para. 102; Alexander Grimm, SchiedsVZ 2012, 189, 200; Michael Nueber, SchiedsVZ 2014, 186, 188 et seq.; Thomas Pfeiffer, NJW 2012, 1169, 1170 et seq.

9 Higher Regional Court of Hamm, docket no. I-4 U 36/15, para. 40; Higher Regional Court of Hamm, docket no. I-4 U 138/15, para. 39 (ultimately, the German Federal Court of Justice (BGH) has rectified both decisions, see German Federal Court of Justice (BGH), docket no. I ZR 113/16, para. 17 and German Federal Court of Justice (BGH), docket no. 114/16, para. 17); Higher Regional Court of Hamm, docket no. I-27 127/10, 27 U 127/10, para. 62; Labour Court of Stuttgart, docket no. 23 Ca 8738/11, para. 94; by contrast, see Higher Regional Court of Stuttgart, docket no. 2 U 156/12, para. 66 (application of the former German autonomous rules on contractual obligations, even though the court correctly assumed that the Rome I Regulation was applicable).

10 See e.g. German Federal Labour Court (BAG), docket no. 6 AZR 430/15, para. 35; Peter Mankowski, in Ulrich Magnus/Peter Mankowski (eds.), European Commentaries on Private International Law Vol. II – Rome I Regulation (2017), Article 28, para. 4; Sebastian Omlor, in Franco Ferrari (ed.), Rome I Regulation: Pocket Commentary (2015), Article 28 Rome I, para. 1.

11 See Peter Mankowski, in Ulrich Magnus/Peter Mankowski (eds.), European Commentaries on Private International Law Vol. II – Rome I Regulation (2017), Article 28, para. 6.

12 German Federal Labour Court (BAG), docket no. 5 AZR 962/13 (A).

on or after that date, a variation of such magnitude that a new [...] contract must be regarded as having been concluded on or after that date'.[13] Although the underlying policy decision appears to be convincing, it is of course a challenge to decide in the particular case at hand whether the alteration amounts to such an intensity that the entire contract must be regarded as having been concluded on or after that date.[14] Thus far, there have been no decisions on this issue. The German Federal Labour Court (BAG) has not found any alteration of the contract in the case that gave rise to the reference to the CJEU.[15] In another case, the Higher Regional Court (*Oberlandesgericht*) of Oldenburg has not discussed the intensity of an alteration of the contract in question because both the Rome I Regulation and the German autonomous conflict-of-laws rules have referred to the law of the same country.[16]

2.2.2. *Material Scope: Article 1 Rome I*

The German legislator produced a lacuna for contracts falling outside the scope of the Rome I Regulation because the autonomous private international law provisions dealing generally with the law applicable to contractual obligations (Articles 27 et seq. German Introductory Act to the Civil Code) were repealed when the Rome I Regulation entered into force. As a consequence, German courts have applied the Rome I Regulation by analogy to the material validity of choice-of-court agreements, notwithstanding their exclusion from the Regulation's scope in Article 1(2)(e) Rome I Regulation.[17] In contrast, German courts have thus far not applied the Rome I Regulation to arbitration agreements.[18] This problem does not arise under Austrian law since section 35

---

13 CJEU, decision of 18 October 2016, Case C-135/15, *Hellenic Republic v. Grigorios Nikiforidis*, ECLI:EU:C:2016:774, para. 39.

14 Konrad Duden, EuZW 2016, 940, 943; Daniel Valdini, GWR 2016, 488; also see Felix Maultzsch, EuZA 2017, 241, 248.

15 German Federal Labour Court (BAG), docket no. 5 AZR 962/13, para. 32.

16 Higher Regional Court of Oldenburg, docket no. 11 U 7/17, para. 41.

17 Regional Court of Munich, docket no. 33 O 8184/16, para. 45; affirmative: Rainer Hüßtege, in Heinz Thomas/Hans Putzo (founders), Zivilprozessordnung (39th ed. 2018), Vorb §38, para. 6; Karsten Thorn, in Otto Palandt (founder), Bürgerliches Gesetzbuch (78th ed. 2019), Art. 1 Rom I-VO, para. 11 with further references; for a different view (application of the repealed Articles 27 et seq. German Introductory Act to the Civil Code) see Christian Heinrich, in Hans-Joachim Musielak/Wolfgang Voit (eds.), Zivilprozessordnung (16th ed. 2019), §38, para. 18; Stefan Smid/Sabine Hartmann, in Bernhard Wieczorek/Rolf A. Schütze (eds.), Zivilprozessordnung Vol. 1/2 (4th ed. 2015), §38 ZPO, para. 104.

18 See e.g. Higher Regional Court of Saarbrücken, docket no. 4 U 44/16, para. 48; Higher Regional Court of Hamm, docket no. I-21 U 16/13, para. 61; nonetheless, some authors argue in favour of an application of the Rome I Regulation to arbitration agreements: see Karsten Thorn, in Otto Palandt (founder), Bürgerliches Gesetzbuch (78th ed. 2019), Art. 1 Rom I-VO, para. 11; Rolf A. Schütze, SchiedsVZ 2014, 274, 275; the prevailing view in the literature, however, applies Article V(1)(a) of the 1958 New York Convention on the Recognition and Enforcement of Foreign Arbitral Awards by analogy: see e.g. Rainer Hausmann,

Austrian Act on Private International Law covers all contractual obligations falling outside the scope of the Rome I Regulation.[19]

When confronted with a question of the material scope of the Rome I Regulation (and of the Rome II Regulation as well) the Austrian Supreme Court of Justice (*Oberster Gerichtshof*, OGH) rightly deduced from Recital 7 that the terms used in Article 1(2) Rome I Regulation (and Rome II Regulation) should be interpreted consistently with the Brussels I Regulation (now the Brussels I *bis* Regulation) and its predecessor.[20] Therefore, in line with case law by the CJEU on the Brussels Convention and with reference thereto,[21] the Austrian Supreme Court of Justice (OGH) held that the exclusion of obligations arising out of matrimonial property regimes pursuant to Article 1(2)(c) Rome I Regulation does not encompass legal relationships between the spouses which have no connection with the marriage.

The Austrian Supreme Court of Justice (OGH) referred the question to the CJEU whether the exclusion of Article 1(2)(f) Rome I Regulation applies to agreements between a beneficiary and a fiduciary who holds an interest in a limited partnership on behalf of the beneficiary, particularly where the partnership agreements and the fiduciary agreements are interwoven.[22] The CJEU answered in the negative.[23] Hence, the Rome I Regulation applies in such a scenario.

Moreover, the Higher Regional Court of Saarbrücken asked the CJEU if the Rome I Regulation – and in particular Article 14 Rome I Regulation – determines the law applicable to third-party effects of assignments of claims.[24] The CJEU held that Article 14 Rome I Regulation is not designating, directly or by analogy, the applicable law concerning the third-party effects of the assignment of a claim.[25] Consequently, autonomous private international law provisions have to be applied on this issue – at least for the time being.[26]

---

in Christoph Reithmann/Dieter Martiny (eds.), Internationales Vertragsrecht (8th ed. 2015), para. 8.239; Dennis Solomon, in Stephan Balthasar (ed.), International Commercial Arbitration (2016), §2, para. 120; Stefan Kröll, IPRax 2016, 43, 46.

19 Brigitta Lurger/Martina Melcher, Handbuch Internationales Privatrecht (2017), para. 4/61; Dietmar Czernich, SchiedsVZ 2015, 181, 183.

20 Austrian Supreme Court of Justice (OGH), docket no. 6 Ob 29/15f, para. 1; affirmative: Marianne Andrae, IPRax 2017, 526. See also Matthias Weller, in Gralf-Peter Calliess (ed.), Rome Regulations (2nd ed. 2015), Rome I Article 1, para. 1.

21 CJEU, decision of 27 March 1979, Case 143/78, *Jacques de Cavel v. Louise de Cavel*, ECLI:EU:C:1979:83, para. 7.

22 Austrian Supreme Court of Justice (OGH), docket no. 6 Ob 5/17d.

23 CJEU, decision of 3 October 2019, Case C-272/18, *Verein für Konsumenteninformation v. TVP*, ECLI:EU:C:2019:827, para. 41.

24 Higher Regional Court of Saarbrücken, docket no. 4 U 109/17.

25 CJEU, decision of 9 October 2019, Case C-548/18, *BGL BNP Paribas SA v. TeamBank AG Nürnberg*, ECLI:EU:C:2019:848, para. 38.

26 See the Proposal for a Regulation of the European Parliament and of the Council on the law applicable to the third-party effects of assignments of claims of 12 March 2018, COM(2018) 96 final.

Lastly, the Higher Regional Court of Frankfurt held that in the case of a litigation in one's own name on another's behalf (*Prozessstandschaft*) the Rome I Regulation applies to the granting and scope of standing while the *lex fori* determines if representative standing is permitted in the proceedings in the first place.[27]

2.3. *LOIS DE POLICE*

The identification of overriding mandatory provisions (*lois de police*) has played a major role in German and Austrian case law, mostly in labour law disputes. Even though there is general agreement among the courts that Article 9 Rome I Regulation has to be interpreted narrowly,[28] this has not prevented some of them from dealing with overriding mandatory provisions in a rather superficial way.[29] In most cases, however, the courts have denied the existence of an overriding mandatory provision.[30] The following provisions have been characterised as overriding in the sense of Article 9 Rome I Regulation: section 1 of the Kuwaiti Ordinance no. 21/1964,[31] section 24 of the Austrian Commercial Agents Act (*Handelsvertretergesetz*[32]),[33] section 20 of the German Minimum Wage Act (*Mindestlohngesetz*[34]),[35]

---

27 Higher Regional Court of Frankfurt, docket no. 19 U 67/18, para. 56 et seq.

28 German Federal Labour Court (BAG), docket no. 10 AZR 200/11, para. 14; German Federal Labour Court (BAG), docket no. 10 ABR 33/15, para. 106; Regional Court of Kleve, docket no. 4 O 272/12, para. 21.

29 Regional Court of Kleve, docket no. 4 O 272/12, para. 43; Administrative Court of Schleswig-Holstein, docket no. 8 B 60/12, para. 12; Administrative Court of Schleswig-Holstein, docket no. 8 B 61/12, para. 12.

30 German Federal Labour Court (BAG), docket no. 10 AZR 200/11, para. 13 et seq.; German Federal Labour Court (BAG), docket no. 10 AZR 191/14, para. 19; Regional Labour Court of Lower Saxony, docket no. 15Sa 14/14, para. 71 (section 2 of the German Continued Remuneration Law); Regional Court of Kleve, docket no. 4 O 272/12, para. 21 (sections 305 and 305a of the German Civil Code); German Federal Court of Justice (BAG), docket no. 10 AZR 191/14, para. 19 (section 615 of the German Civil Code); Austrian Supreme Court of Justice (OGH), docket no. 9 ObA 65/11s, para. VI (section 102 of the German Works Constitution Act); also see Austrian Supreme Court of Justice (OGH), docket no. 9 Ob 53/16h, para. 4 (section 1(2) and section 20 German Minimum Wage Act) and Austrian Supreme Court of Justice (OGH), docket no. 2 Ob 204/14k, para. III (section 13a(2) and section 6(3) Austrian Consumer Protection Law).

31 Ordinance no. 21/1964 concerning the consolidated boycott of Israel law as published in the Official Publication no. 479 of 31 May 1964; Higher Regional Court of Frankfurt, docket no. 16 U 209/17, para. 40.

32 *Handelsvertretergesetz* of 11 February 1993, BGBl. 88/1993, p. 1151, most recently amended by BGBl. I 29/2016.

33 Austrian Supreme Court of Justice (OGH), docket no. 5 Ob 72/16y, para. IV.6.

34 *Mindestlohngesetz* of 11 August 2014, BGBl. I p. 1348, most recently amended by Art. 14 of the Law of 11 July 2019, BGBl. I p. 1066.

35 Fiscal Court of Berlin-Brandenburg, docket no. 1 K 1174/17, para. 79.

section 22a(1) number 4 of the German Law Concerning Arms Control (*Waffengesetz*[36]),[37] the data protection regimes of the German Federal Data Protection Act (*Bundesdatenschutzgesetz*[38]) and of the German Telemedia Act (*Telemediengesetz*[39]),[40] section 9 number 2 and section 10(4) of the German Law on Temporary Work (*Arbeitnehmerüberlassungsgesetz*[41]),[42] section 2 of the German Posted Workers Act (*Arbeitnehmer-Entsendegesetz*[43]),[44] and section 3 of the German Continued Remuneration Law (*Entgeltfortzahlungsgesetz*[45]).[46] In the latter decision, the German Federal Labour Court (BAG) held that a sufficient connection with the enacting state is necessary to apply an overriding mandatory provision.[47] This view corresponds with the prevailing view on the former German autonomous rule regarding overriding mandatory provisions of the *lex fori* (Article 34 German Introductory Act to the Civil Code).[48] Although the wording of Article 9(2) Rome I Regulation makes no reference to such a requirement, there is widespread consensus in the legal literature that a close connection with the enacting state is implicitly required because there would be neither need nor justification to apply the overriding mandatory provision otherwise.[49] Of course, this poses the follow-up question

---

36 *Waffengesetz* (WaffG) of 11 October 2002, BGBl. I p. 3970, 4592; 2003 I p. 1957, amended most recently by Art. 7 of the Law of 20 November 2019, BGBl. I p. 1626.

37 Regional Court of Kleve, docket no. 4 O 272/12, para. 43.

38 *Bundesdatenschutzgesetz* of 30 June 2017, BGBl. I p. 2097, amended most recently by Art. 12 of the Law of 20 November 2019, BGBl. I p. 1626.

39 *Telemediengesetz* of 26 February 2007, BGBl. I p. 179, most recently amended by Art. 11 of the Law of 11 July 2019, BGBl. I p. 1066.

40 Administrative Court of Schleswig-Holstein, docket no. 8 B 60/12, para. 12; Administrative Court of Schleswig-Holstein, docket no. 8 B 61/12, para. 12; this is, however, disputed: see Regional Court of Berlin, docket no. 16 O 551/10, para. 80.

41 *Arbeitnehmerüberlassungsgesetz* as updated in the Official Publication of 3 February 1995, BGBl. I p. 158, most recently amended by Art. 48 of the Law of 15 August 2019, BGBl. I p. 1307.

42 Regional Labour Court of Rhineland-Palatinate, docket no. 2 Sa 65/15, para. 53.

43 *Arbeitnehmer-Entsendegesetz* of 1 March 1996, BGBl. I p. 227, most recently amended by Art. 1 of the Law of 22 November 2019, BGBl. I p. 1756.

44 Fiscal Court of Baden-Württemberg, docket no. 11 K 2644/16, para. 43 et seq.; Fiscal Court of Baden-Württemberg, docket no. 11 K 544/16, para. 38 et seq.

45 *Entgeltfortzahlungsgesetz* of 26 May 1994, BGBl. I S. 1014, 1065, most recently amended by Art. 9 of the Law of 22 November 2019, BGBl. I p. 1746.

46 German Federal Labour Court (BAG), docket no. 10 AZR 200/11, para. 18; German Federal Labour Court (BAG), docket no. 10 AZR 191/14, para. 19.

47 German Federal Labour Court (BAG), docket no. 10 AZR 200/11, para. 18.

48 German Federal Labour Court (BAG), docket no. 5 AZR 255/00, para. 41; Jan Kropholler, Internationales Privatrecht (6th ed. 2006), §52 IX 1, p. 498.

49 Andrea Bonomi, in Ulrich Magnus/Peter Mankowski (eds.), European Commentaries on Private International Law Vol. II – Rome I Regulation (2017), Article 9, para. 96; Rupert Doehner, in Rainer Hüßtege/Heinz-Peter Mansel (eds.), NomosKommentar Vol. 6 – Rom-Verordnungen (3rd ed. 2019), Artikel 9 ROM I, para. 24; Dieter Martiny, in Jan v. Hein (ed.), Münchener Kommentar zum Bürgerlichen Gesetzbuch Vol. 12 (7th ed. 2018),

of the connection's necessary intensity.[50] A preliminary ruling by the CJEU would be desirable to clarify these uncertainties.

Three decisions concerned the treatment of third states' overriding mandatory provisions pursuant to Article 9(3) Rome I Regulation. The Austrian Supreme Court of Justice (OGH) denied the application of the rules of the German Minimum Wage Act after a thorough balancing of interests between the nature and purpose of the provision and the consequences of its application or non-application because, in the court's view, it would have led to predominantly negative consequences for the employer.[51] In another case, the German Federal Labour Court (BAG) referred the question to the CJEU for a preliminary ruling on whether Article 9(3) of the Rome I Regulation solely excludes the direct application of overriding mandatory provisions of another country in which the obligations arising out of that contract are not to be performed, or have not been performed, or whether that provision also excludes indirect regard to those mandatory provisions in the law of the Member State the law of which governs the contract.[52] The CJEU held that Article 9(3) Rome I Regulation precludes

> 'overriding mandatory provisions other than those of the State of the forum or of the State where the obligations arising out of the contract have to be or have been performed from being applied, as legal rules, by the court of the forum, but as not precluding it from taking such other overriding mandatory provisions into account as matters of fact in so far as this is provided for by the national law that is applicable to the contract pursuant to the regulation. This interpretation is not affected by the principle of sincere cooperation laid down in Article 4(3) TEU'.[53]

Unfortunately, but unsurprisingly, the decision left a number of questions unanswered. For example, it remains unclear where to draw the line between taking account of an overriding mandatory provision and its application as legal rule.[54]

Finally, the Higher Regional Court of Frankfurt refused to take section 1 of the Kuwaiti Ordinance no. 21/1964 into account, although the requirements of Article 9(3) Rome I Regulation were met. The rule, which prohibits the

---

Artikel 9 Rom I-VO, paras. 109 and 124 et seq.; for a different view see Martin Schmidt-Kessel, in Franco Ferrari (ed.), Rome I Regulation: Pocket Commentary (2015), Article 9 Rome I, para. 38.

50 See e.g. Rupert Doehner, in Rainer Hüßtege/Heinz-Peter Mansel (eds.), NomosKommentar Vol. 6 – Rom-Verordnungen (3rd ed. 2019), Artikel 9 ROM I, para. 24.

51 Austrian Supreme Court of Justice (OGH), docket no. 9 ObA 53/16h, para. 5.4. et seq.; also see Fiscal Court of Baden-Württemberg, docket no. 11 K 2644/16, para. 44 et seq.

52 German Federal Labour Court (BAG), docket no. 5 AZR 962/13 (A), question 2.

53 CJEU, decision of 18 October 2016, Case C-135/15, *Hellenic Republic v. Grigorios Nikiforidis*, ECLI:EU:C:2016:774, para. 55.

54 Konrad Duden, EuZW 2016, 940, 943; Thomas Pfeiffer, LMK 2016, 382315; Doris-Maria Schuster, ArbRAktuell 2016, 550.

transportation of citizens of Israel by Kuwaiti air carriers, was considered to be irreconcilable with European and German values.[55] In the same decision, the court argued that the 'country where the obligations arising out of the contract have to be or have been performed' in the sense that Article 9(3) Rome I Regulation should not be equated with the 'place of performance of the obligation' in the sense of Article 7(1) Brussels I *bis* Regulation.[56] It held, in line with the prevailing view in the German literature,[57] that Article 9(3) Rome I Regulation should envisage all places where the performance is *de facto* carried out.[58]

2.4. PARTY AUTONOMY

The German and Austrian courts have rendered numerous decisions based on Article 3 Rome I Regulation. Yet neither *dépeçage* nor a choice of the *lex mercatoria* were a particular issue. With regard to the latter, it should, of course, be noted that such a possibility may be seen as desirable.[59] However, *de lege lata*, this has only theoretical significance. Of practical significance were the following issues.

2.4.1. Choice-of-Law Clauses in Consumer and Employment Contracts

Whereas the validity of choice-of-law clauses has not been called into question in labour law disputes,[60] a number of (lower) courts have declared choice-of-law clauses in consumer contracts invalid.[61] This is due to a misunderstanding of

---

55 Higher Regional Court of Frankfurt, docket no. 16 U 209/17, para. 44 et seq.

56 Higher Regional Court of Frankfurt, docket no. 16 U 209/17, para. 42; also see Dieter Martiny, in Jan v. Hein (ed.), Münchener Kommentar zum BGB Vol. 12 (7th ed. 2018), Art. 9 Rom I-VO, para. 117.

57 See Felix Maultzsch, in Christine Budzikiewicz/Marc-Philippe Weller/Wolfgang Wurmnest (eds.), BeckOGK – Rom I-VO (01.12.2018), Artikel 9, para. 114 et seq. with further references.

58 Higher Regional Court of Frankfurt, docket no. 16 U 209/17, para. 42.

59 Boris Schinkels, GPR 2007, 106, 111 (arguing that the exclusion of the choice of non-state law amounts to a violation of constitutional rights).

60 German Federal Labour Court (BAG), docket no. 2 AZR 223/19, para. 12; German Federal Labour Court (BAG), docket no. 2 AZR 54/18, para. 27; German Federal Labour Court (BAG), docket no. 6 AZR 430/15, para. 40; Regional Labour Court of Hesse, docket no. 6 Sa 567/18, para. 24; Regional Labour Court of Baden-Württemberg, docket no. 19 Sa 65/14, para. 110; Regional Labour Court of Mecklenburg–West Pomerania, docket no. 2 Sa 172/13, para. 57; Regional Labour Court of Rhineland-Palatinate, docket no. 4 Sa 709/14, para. 51; Labour Court of Düsseldorf, docket no. 2 Ca 5395/10, para. 46.

61 Regional Court of Karlsruhe, docket no. 14 O 27/11 KfH III, para. 62; Local Court of Bremen, docket no. 9 C 0270/12, 9 C 270/12, para. 22; Local Court of Brunswick, docket no. 118 C 3557/13, para. 13.

Article 6(2) sentence 2 Rome I Regulation: these courts wrongly assumed that the law of the country where the consumer has his habitual residence shall govern the contract in every single case and that only a choice of this country's law is permissible.[62] In sum, however, these decisions have remained exceptional.[63]

2.4.2. Implied Choice of Law in a Contract

A number of factors were considered as evidence of a choice of law in a contract. First and foremost, the reference to specific rules of national law in the contract was often deemed to be sufficient.[64] By contrast, and while there is consensus that these aspects have to be taken into account, there is inconsistent case law on the weight to be given to the language of the contract,[65] the place where the contract was concluded,[66] and the contractually agreed currency.[67] The Higher Regional Court of Stuttgart argued that an exclusive choice of court agreement has to be considered as well.[68] On the other hand, the mere place of performance

---

62 See Regional Court of Karlsruhe, docket no. 14 O 27/11 KfH III, para. 62; Local Court of Brunswick, docket no. 118 C 3557/13, para. 13.

63 Article 6(2) Rome I Regulation is generally applied correctly; see Austrian Supreme Court of Justice (OGH), docket no. 5 Ob 194/18t, para. 1.2; German Federal Court of Justice (BGH), docket no. III ZR 183/17, para. 20; German Federal Court of Justice (BGH), docket no. I ZR 47/16, para. 27; German Federal Court of Justice (BGH), docket no. I ZR 40/11, para. 33; Higher Regional Court of Munich, docket no. 18 W 1873/18, para. 12; Higher Regional Court of Cologne, docket no. I-6 U 90/15, 6 U 90/15, para. 70; Regional Court of Frankfurt, docket no. 2-04 O 214/18, para. 51; Regional Court of Dortmund, docket no. 3 O 610/15, para. 17; Regional Court of Hamburg, docket no. 327 O 779/10, para. 66; Local Court of Bremen, docket no. 9 C 337/13, para. 24; Local Court of Würzburg, docket no. 16 C 207/13, para. 16.

64 German Federal Labour Court (BAG), docket no. 6 AZR 430/15, para. 45; Higher Regional Court of Stuttgart, docket no. 10 U 152/18, para. 58; Higher Regional Court of Brandenburg, docket no. 3 U 22/18, para. 82; Higher Regional Court of Munich, docket no. 23 U 1848/16, para. 37; Higher Regional Court of Saarbrücken, docket no. 4 U 109/14, paras. 26 and 31; Higher Regional Court of Stuttgart, docket no. 10 U 102/14, para. 23; Regional Labour Court of Hesse, docket no. 6 Sa 567/18, para. 24; Regional Labour Court of Baden-Württemberg, docket no. 19 Sa 65/14, para. 110; Local Court of Cologne, docket no. 142 C 232/13, para. 16.

65 German Federal Labour Court (BAG), docket no. 5 AZR 767/14, para. 25; German Federal Labour Court (BAG), docket no. 6 AZR 430/15, para. 43; Higher Regional Court of Brandenburg, docket no. 3 U 22/18, para. 82; Higher Regional Court of Cologne, docket no. 19 Sch 17/13, para. 38; Higher Regional Court of Saarbrücken, docket no. 4 U 109/14, paras. 26 and 32; Higher Regional Court of Hamm, docket no. I-32 SA 90/11, 32 SA 90/11, para. 26; Labour Court of Stuttgart, docket no. 23 Ca 8738/11, para. 94.

66 German Federal Labour Court (BAG), docket no. 5 AZR 767/14, para. 26; German Federal Labour Court (BAG), docket no. 6 AZR 430/15, para. 44; Regional Labour Court of Baden-Württemberg, docket no. 19 Sa 65/14, para. 110; Higher Regional Court of Saarbrücken, docket no. 4 U 109/14, para. 30; Higher Regional Court of Hamm, docket no. I-32 SA 90/11, 32 SA 90/11, para. 26.

67 German Federal Labour Court (BAG), docket no. 5 AZR 767/14, para. 25 et seq., esp. para. 27; but compare German Federal Labour Court (BAG), docket no. 6 AZR 430/15, para. 45.

68 Higher Regional Court of Stuttgart, docket no. 10 U 152/18, para. 58.

and the habitual residence of only one party are factors that did not establish an implied choice of this country's law.[69] Lastly, the context of the contract may be relevant.[70]

These decisions show that an implied choice of law in a contract is very difficult to ascertain in practice. The courts have to identify the real intention of the parties, since an imputed intention does not suffice.[71] Therefore, a careful review of the contractual terms in light of the particular circumstances of the individual case is essential.[72] In the majority of the cases, the courts took adequate account of these demands. However, it would be worth discussing why a reference to statutes or specific rules of national law in the contract should per se be enough to assume an implied choice of law to the entire contract. For example, such a reference may only aim at incorporating a provision into the terms of the contract without the intention to make the entire contract subject to the law of this country.[73] Therefore, a reference to particular rules of national law should only be regarded as further (strong) evidence of a choice of law.[74]

2.4.3. Subsequent Choice of Law

While many decisions have concerned a subsequent choice of law, only a few of them have involved an express one.[75] In the absence of an express choice of law, both the German and the Austrian courts have inferred an implied choice of law if both parties plead on the basis of the same law, usually the law

---

69 Higher Regional Court of Saarbrücken, docket no. 4 U 109/14, para. 32; Local Court of Cologne, docket no. 142 C 232/13, para. 16.

70 Higher Regional Court of Saarbrücken, docket no. 4 U 109/14, para. 32; Local Court of Cologne, docket no. 142 C 232/13, para. 16.

71 Stefan Leible, in Rainer Hüßtege/Heinz-Peter Mansel (eds.), NomosKommentar Vol. 6 – Rom-Verordnungen (3rd ed. 2019), Artikel 3 ROM I, para. 49; Matthias Wendland, in Christine Budzikiewicz/Marc-Philippe Weller/Wolfgang Wurmnest (eds.), BeckOGK – Rom I-VO (01.12.2018), Artikel 3, para. 132.4; Francesca Ragno, in Franco Ferrari (ed.), Rome I Regulation: Pocket Commentary (2015), Article 3 Rome I, para. 34.

72 See Stefan Leible, in Rainer Hüßtege/Heinz-Peter Mansel (eds.), NomosKommentar Vol. 6 – Rom-Verordnungen (3rd ed. 2019), Artikel 3 ROM I, para. 50.

73 Francesca Ragno, in Franco Ferrari (ed.), Rome I Regulation: Pocket Commentary (2015), Article 3 Rome I, para. 40.

74 See comprehensively Matthias Wendland, in Christine Budzikiewicz/Marc-Philippe Weller/Wolfgang Wurmnest (eds.), BeckOGK – Rom I-VO (01.12.2018), Artikel 3, para. 161 et seq.; Stefan Leible, in Rainer Hüßtege/Heinz-Peter Mansel (eds.), NomosKommentar Vol. 6 – Rom-Verordnungen (3rd ed. 2019), Artikel 3 ROM I, para. 56; also see Dennis Solomon, ZVglRWiss 115 (2016), 586, 589 et seq.

75 Higher Regional Court of Hamm, docket no. I-27 U 127/10, 27 U 127/10, para. 62; Regional Court of Kiel, docket no. 14 O 63/11, para. 51; Local Court of Frankfurt, docket no. 385 C 2455/10 (70), para. 15.

of the forum.[76] However, the German Federal Labour Court (BAG) held in a case on a contract for the benefit of third parties that this does not suffice if the parties in the court proceedings are not the parties to the contract.[77] This holding mirrors the German doctrine on contracts in favour of third parties, according to which only the parties, and not the beneficiary, may alter the contract, but may also be considered part of the foundations of Article 3 Rome I Regulation ('law chosen by the *parties*').

In a decision of the Higher Regional Court of Stuttgart, it was held to be sufficient that the parties argued on the basis of German law in pre-trial correspondence and imposed the burden of proof on the respondent that this did not constitute a choice of law.[78] In addition, the Higher Regional Court of Cologne concluded that an implied choice of law existed because the court of first instance applied the substantive law of the *lex fori* without any objections by both parties.[79] Both of the latter two decisions appear to go too far in inferring a choice of law by the parties.[80] Moreover, the German courts tend to resort to a subsequent choice of law even when the 'chosen' law is applicable by virtue of an objective connecting factor or a manifestly closer connection.[81] Again, this appears hardly convincing.[82]

---

76 Austrian Supreme Court of Justice (OGH), docket no. 3 Ob 116/18g, para. 1.3; Austrian Supreme Court of Justice (OGH), docket no. 1 Ob 67/15g, para. 1; Austrian Supreme Court of Justice (OGH), docket no. 1 Ob 222/15a, para. 1; Higher Regional Court of Vienna, docket no. 133R7/19f, para. 2.11; German Federal Labour Court (BAG), docket no. 5 AZR 767/14, para. 28; German Federal Labour Court (BAG), docket no. 6 AZR 430/15, para. 47; Higher Regional Court of Frankfurt, docket no. 16 U 209/17, para. 28; Higher Regional Court of Cologne, docket no. I-3 U 108/14, 3 U 108/14, para. 28; Higher Regional Court of Munich, docket no. 23 U 2854/13, para. 15; Higher Regional Court of Saarbrücken, docket no. 4 U 130/13, para. 89; Regional Court of Munich, docket no. 37 O 28331/12, para. 164; see also Austrian Supreme Court of Justice (OGH), docket no. 4 Ob 225/14p, para. 3, leaving this question open.

77 German Federal Labour Court (BAG), docket no. 5 AZR 767/14, para. 28.

78 Higher Regional Court of Stuttgart, docket no. 3 U 184/12, para. 50.

79 Higher Regional Court of Cologne, docket no. I-3 U 108/14, 3 U 108/14, para. 28.

80 See also Peter Mankowski, in Ulrich Magnus/Peter Mankowski (eds.), European Commentaries on Private International Law Vol. II – Rome I Regulation (2017), Article 3, para. 114; Brigitta Lurger/Martina Melcher, Handbuch Internationales Privatrecht (2017), para. 4/63.

81 See Higher Regional Court of Frankfurt, docket no. 16 U 209/17, para. 28 et seq.; Higher Regional Court of Munich, docket no. 23 U 1928/16, para. 43; Higher Regional Court of Hamm, docket no. I-32 SA 90/11, 32 SA 90/11, para. 26; also see Labour Court of Stuttgart, docket no. 23 Ca 8738/11, para. 95; this assessment is contested by some commentators, see e.g. Jan v. Hein/Hannah Dittmers, in Paul Beaumont et al. (eds.), Cross-Border Litigation in Europe (2017), Germany, p. 145, 152.

82 Gralf-Peter Calliess, in Gralf-Peter Calliess (ed.), Rome Regulations (2nd ed. 2015), Rome I Article 3, para. 38.

Finally, the Higher Regional Court of Berlin rightly held that a subsequent implied choice of law agreement can even supersede an earlier express choice of law agreement.[83]

2.4.4. Choice-of-Law Clauses in General Terms and Conditions

Because of Article 3(5) in conjunction with Article 10(1) Rome I Regulation, a choice of German law contained in general terms and conditions entails a review of the clause by virtue of the German law on general terms and conditions (sections 305 et seq. German Civil Code).[84] In the case of a contract concluded with a consumer with habitual residence in Germany, these rules also apply, on the basis of Article 6(2) sentence 2 Rome I Regulation, irrespective of the chosen law, since they are provisions that cannot be derogated from by agreement by virtue of German law.[85] These provisions prohibit, in particular, so-called 'surprise' and 'non-transparent' clauses (section 305c German Civil Code). Whether the clause should be regarded as surprising or non-transparent depends on the perspective of an average consumer.[86] The exact scope of the transparency control is, however, a matter of dispute.[87] For example, the choice of the law of the professional's seat was not deemed to be surprising.[88] By contrast, in the case of a contract concluded with a consumer with habitual residence in Germany, the German Federal Court of Justice (BGH) held that a choice-of-law clause stating that the law of the Netherlands should exclusively apply for all legal disputes arising out of the business relationship violates the principle of transparency pursuant to section 307(1) and (2) German Civil Code because the clause presented an incorrect picture of the existing legal remedies.[89] In particular, the clause did not indicate that Article 6(2) sentence 2 Rome I Regulation ensures the protection afforded to the consumer by

---

83 Higher Regional Court of Berlin, docket no. 26 U 108/17, para. 23.

84 Higher Regional Court of Hamm, docket no. I-7 U 26/15, 7 U 26/15, para. 31; Higher Regional Court of Düsseldorf, docket no. I-18 U 124/13, 18 U 124/13, para. 19; Regional Court of Nuremberg-Fürth, docket no. 16 O 8856/12, para. 87; Regional Court of Kleve, docket no. 4 O 272/12, para. 20.

85 German Federal Court of Justice (BGH), docket no. I ZR 40/11, para. 33; Regional Court of Ulm, docket no. 4 O 66/13, para. 120; Regional Court of Dortmund, docket no. 3 O 610/15, para. 17.

86 German Federal Court of Justice (BGH), docket no. V ZR 184/94, para. 9; Regional Court of Munich, docket no. 12 O 7134/11, para. 51; Jürgen Basedow, in Wolfgang Krüger (ed.), Münchener Kommentar zum Bürgerlichen Gesetzbuch Vol. 2 (8th ed. 2019), §305c BGB, para. 7; Astrid Stadler, in Rolf Stürner (ed.), Jauernig – Bürgerliches Gesetzbuch (17th ed. 2018), §305c BGB, para. 2.

87 See e.g. Wulf-Henning Roth, IPRax 2013, 515, 524.

88 Regional Court of Dortmund, docket no. 3 O 610/15, para. 17.

89 German Federal Court of Justice (BGH), docket no. I ZR 40/11, para. 38.

provisions that cannot be derogated from by agreement by virtue of the law of his habitual residence. For the same reason, the Regional Court (*Landgericht*) of Ulm declared another choice-of-law clause invalid.[90] Moreover, the Regional Court of Frankfurt invalidated a choice-of-law clause included in a contract for the transportation of a passenger (Article 5(2) Rome I Regulation).[91] While Article 6(2) Rome I Regulation does not apply to a contract of carriage (Article 6(4)(b) Rome I Regulation), the court held the clause to be non-transparent because it did not indicate that only certain laws may be chosen pursuant to Article 5(2) subparagraph 2 Rome I Regulation (in the given case, the chosen law was one of these laws). This decision was later overturned by the Higher Regional Court of Frankfurt.[92] In the court's view, Article 5(2) subparagraph 2 Rome I Regulation cannot be equated with Article 6(2) Rome I Regulation. Therefore, it is not necessary to make references to the eligible laws. While the reasoning appears to be convincing, the court missed the opportunity to refer this question to the CJEU. A subsequent reference for a preliminary ruling by the Local Court (*Amtsgericht*) of Nuremberg[93] was later withdrawn.

2.5. ABSENCE OF CHOICE OF LAW

2.5.1. Article 4 Rome I

The application of Article 4(1) Rome I Regulation, in particular the determination of the scope of the specified types of contract, has not caused any particular problems for German and Austrian courts. For example, it was held that internet auctions of movables do not fall within the scope of Article 4(1)(g) Rome I Regulation because a place of the auction cannot be determined, and that, instead, Article 4(1)(a) Rome I Regulation applies.[94] Contracts for medical treatment and contracts between a lawyer and his client are usually considered as a contract for the provision of services and are thus governed by Article 4(1)(b) Rome I Regulation.[95] Furthermore, the donation of land has been characterised

---

90 Regional Court of Ulm, docket no. 4 O 66/13, para. 143.

91 Regional Court of Frankfurt, docket no. 2-24 O 8/17, para. 32 et seq.

92 Higher Regional Court of Frankfurt, docket no. 16 U 15/18, para. 25 et seq.

93 Local Court of Nuremberg, docket no. 19 C 1084/18.

94 Higher Regional Court of Brandenburg, docket no. 11 U 44/14, para. 18; it is submitted, however, that Article 4(1)(g) Rome I Regulation is applicable if there is a real auction place and the bidders just place their bid via the Internet: see Ulrich Magnus, in Ulrich Magnus/Peter Mankowski (eds.), European Commentaries on Private International Law Vol. II – Rome I Regulation (2017), Article 4, para. 653.

95 Regional Court of Detmold, docket no. 10 S 229/11, para. 15; Regional Court of Mönchengladbach, docket no. 6 O 175/11 (contract for medical treatment); Higher Administrative Court of Berlin-Brandenburg, docket no. OVG 2 M 30.11, para. 2

as a contract relating to a right *in rem* in immovable property (Article 4(1)(c) Rome I Regulation).[96] By contrast, a suretyship,[97] a sale of rights,[98] an acknowledgment of debt,[99] a donation of objects other than immovables,[100] and a licence contract[101] cannot be categorised as a contract specified in Article 4(1) Rome I Regulation. Hence, the courts have had to determine who effects the characteristic performance of these contracts in the sense of Article 4(2) Rome I Regulation. Again, this has not posed major difficulties.[102] Nonetheless, some uncertainties exist with respect to licence contracts. In simple licence contracts, the licensor usually carries out the characteristic performance.[103] However, the

---

(contract between a lawyer and his client); Gerhard Hohloch, in Barbara Grunewald/Georg Maier-Reimer/Harm Peter Westermann (eds.), Erman – BGB (15th ed. 2017), Art. 4 Rom I, para. 14; Dieter Martiny, in Jan v. Hein (ed.), Münchener Kommentar zum BGB Vol. 12 (7th ed. 2018), Art. 4 Rom I-VO, paras. 71 and 76.

96 Higher Regional Court of Brandenburg, docket no. 5 U 60/14, para. 33.

97 Regional Court of Kiel, docket no. 16 O 37/12, para. 31; Ulrich Magnus, in Ulrich Magnus/Peter Mankowski (eds.), European Commentaries on Private International Law Vol. II – Rome I Regulation (2017), Article 4, para. 464; but compare Dieter Martiny, in: Christoph Reithmann/Dieter Martiny (eds.), Internationales Vertragsrecht (8th ed. 2015), para. 6.475.

98 Higher Regional Court of Munich, docket no. 23 U 1250/15, para. 38; Gerhard Hohloch, in Barbara Grunewald/Georg Maier-Reimer/Harm Peter Westermann (eds.), Erman – BGB (15th ed. 2017), Art. 4 Rom I, para. 14; Ulrich Magnus, in Ulrich Magnus/Peter Mankowski (eds.), European Commentaries on Private International Law Vol. II – Rome I Regulation (2017), Article 4, para. 282 with further references.

99 Regional Court of Mönchengladbach, docket no. 6 O 175/11; Stefan Leible, in Rainer Hüßtege/Heinz-Peter Mansel (eds.), NomosKommentar Vol. 6 – Rom-Verordnungen (3rd ed. 2019), Artikel 4 ROM I, para. 154; Dieter Martiny, in Jan v. Hein (ed.), Münchener Kommentar zum BGB Vol. 12 (7th ed. 2018), Art. 4 Rom I-VO, para. 240.

100 Higher Regional Court of Düsseldorf, docket no. I-16 U 108/14, 16 U 108/14, para. 39; Stefan Leible, in Rainer Hüßtege/Heinz-Peter Mansel (eds.), NomosKommentar Vol. 6 – Rom-Verordnungen (3rd ed. 2019), Artikel 4 ROM I, para. 100; Ulrich Magnus, in Ulrich Magnus/Peter Mankowski (eds.), European Commentaries on Private International Law Vol. II – Rome I Regulation (2017), Article 4, para. 294.

101 Higher Regional Court of Cologne, docket no. I-6 U 60/14, para. 67; Regional Court of Mannheim, docket no. 2 O 147/14, para. 85; Ulrich Magnus, in Ulrich Magnus/Peter Mankowski (eds.), European Commentaries on Private International Law Vol. II – Rome I Regulation (2017), Article 4, para. 597 (with reference to case law by the CJEU on the Brussels I Regulation: CJEU, decision of 23 April 2009, Case C-533/07, *Falco Privatstiftung and Thomas Rabitsch v. Gisela Weller-Lindhorst*, ECLI:EU:C:2009:257, para. 44).

102 Regional Court of Kiel, docket no. 16 O 37/12, para. 31 (suretyship: surety); Higher Regional Court of Düsseldorf, docket no. I-16 U 108/14, 16 U 108/14, para. 39 (donation: donor); Higher Regional Court of Munich, docket no. 23 U 1250/15, para. 38 (sale of rights: seller); Regional Court of Mönchengladbach, docket no. 6 O 175/11 (acknowledgment of debt: acknowledging party).

103 See Higher Regional Court of Cologne, docket no. I-6 U 60/14, para. 67; Regional Court of Mannheim, docket no. 2 O 147/14, para. 85; Stefan Leible, in Rainer Hüßtege/Heinz-Peter Mansel (eds.), NomosKommentar Vol. 6 – Rom-Verordnungen (3rd ed. 2019), Artikel 4 ROM I, para. 167; but compare for a different view Dieter Martiny, in Jan v. Hein (ed.), Münchener Kommentar zum BGB Vol. 12 (7th ed. 2018), Art. 4 Rom I-VO, para. 265 et seq. with further references.

particular circumstances of the case have to be taken into account. If, for example, both parties grant each other a licence (cross-licence contract), the question arises as to whether Article 4(2) Rome I Regulation is still applicable.[104] When confronted with this problem, the Regional Court of Mannheim left this question open because it found that both countries' substantive laws were identical.[105] From the viewpoint of methodology, this solution is not convincing.[106] A reference to the CJEU for a preliminary ruling would have been preferable.

2.5.2. *Specific Rules*

2.5.2.1. Overview

An evaluation of the case law on the specific rules for certain contracts indicates mixed results. On a quantitative level, the introduction of these rules has proven to be justified, as can be seen by the very large number of decisions on Articles 5–8 Rome I Regulation. Moreover, the application of Articles 5 and 7 has not caused any major problems.[107] In the only noteworthy decision, the German Federal Court of Justice (BGH) decided that in the context of Article 5(2) Rome I Regulation the place of departure of the first route segment is decisive if a flight connection consists of more than one route segment and there is no considerable layover.[108] Of course, this decision raises the question of what constitutes a 'considerable' layover. Nonetheless, this rather minor problem sharply contrasts with a number of critical issues concerning the application of Articles 6 and 8.

---

104 Against the application of Article 4(2) Rome I Regulation e.g. Ulrich Magnus, in Ulrich Magnus/Peter Mankowski (eds.), European Commentaries on Private International Law Vol. II - Rome I Regulation (2017), Article 4, para. 600.

105 Regional Court of Mannheim, docket no. 2 O 147/14, para. 86.

106 Dennis Solomon, ZVglRWiss 115 (2016), 586, 599; this approach raises additional concerns in cases when one of the laws is the *lex fori* and the other one a foreign law because of the differing treatment of domestic and foreign law by the courts; on the application of foreign law in general see below at section 4.

107 For Article 5 Rome I Regulation, see e.g. Austrian Supreme Court of Justice (OGH), docket no. 7 Ob 5/13f, para. 2; Austrian Supreme Court of Justice (OGH), docket no. 7 Ob 105/14p, para. 3; German Federal Court of Justice (BGH), docket no. I ZR 64/18, para. 47; German Federal Court of Justice (BGH), docket no. I ZR 216/14, para. 12; German Federal Court of Justice (BGH), docket no. I ZR 212/13, para. 19; Higher Regional Court of Düsseldorf, docket no. 18 U 149/17, para. 24; Higher Regional Court of Brandenburg, docket no. 7 U 142/13, para. 30; Regional Court of Bremen, docket no. 3 S 315/14, para. 31; for Article 7 Rome I Regulation, see e.g. Austrian Supreme Court of Justice (OGH), docket no. 7 Ob 144/16a, para. I; Higher Regional Court of Frankfurt, docket no. 5 U 17/13, para. 25; Local Court of Cologne, docket no. 268 C 89/11, para. 28.

108 German Federal Court of Justice (BGH), docket no. X ZR 128/11, para. 30.

2.5.2.2. Article 6 Rome I

Firstly, the German Federal Court of Justice (BGH) held in 2009 that the law applicable to injunction actions brought against the use of unfair contractual terms towards consumers must be determined by the Rome II Regulation, whereas the law applicable to the assessment of a particular contractual term has to be determined pursuant to Article 6 Rome I Regulation.[109] This was far from an *acte clair* and thus would have required a reference to the CJEU.[110] The Austrian Supreme Court of Justice (OGH) showed more sensitivity in this issue and referred the question to the CJEU.[111] The CJEU eventually affirmed the position taken by the German Federal Court of Justice (BGH), in that it decided that the Rome II Regulation applies with regard to the action for an injunction, whereas the particular contractual term must be determined pursuant to the Rome I Regulation, irrespective of whether that assessment is made in an individual or a collective action.[112] However, the case once again demonstrated that the German courts can be quite reluctant to refer questions to the CJEU.

Secondly, German courts rightly held that the application of Article 6 Rome I Regulation is neither subject to a maximum monetary threshold,[113] nor limited to specific types of contracts.[114]

Thirdly, numerous decisions involved the issue of whether or not the professional directed his activities to the country of the consumer's habitual residence in the sense of Article 6(1)(b) Rome I Regulation. There is consensus that it has to be the professional's intention to target consumers in the country in question.[115] The Regional Court of Bonn even found that a Turkish seller who worked together with a German travel agency with the intention to lure tourists from Germany into his business premises in Turkey – but without making a profit-sharing arrangement – targeted German consumers.[116] It is disputed if

---

109 German Federal Court of Justice (BGH), docket no. Xa ZR 19/08, para. 18 et seq.; affirmative evaluations of this decision e.g. by Wolfgang Hau, LMK 2009, 293079; Astrid Stadler, VuR 2010, 83, 87.

110 Astrid Stadler, VuR 2010, 83, 87; Ansgar Staudinger/Paul Czaplinski, NJW 2009, 3371 et seq.

111 Austrian Supreme Court of Justice (OGH), docket no. 2 Ob 204/14k.

112 CJEU, decision of 28 July 2016, Case C-191/15, *Verein für Konsumenteninformation v. Amazon EU*, ECLI:EU:C:2016:612, para. 60; see Peter Mankowski, NJW 2016, 2705 et seq.; Peter Rott, EuZW 2016, 733 et seq.; Felix M. Wilke, GPR 2017, 21 et seq.

113 Regional Court of Ulm, docket no. 4 O 66/13, para. 124; also see Higher Regional Court of Stuttgart, docket no. 5 U 98/17, para. 126.

114 See (implicitly) German Federal Court of Justice, docket no. III ZR 183/17, para. 20.

115 Higher Regional Court of Cologne, docket no. I-6 U 90/15, 6 U 90/15, para. 69; Higher Regional Court of Hamm, docket no. I-4 U 36/15, 4 U 36/15, para. 40; Higher Regional Court of Hamm I-4 U 138/15, 4 U 138/15, para. 39; Regional Court of Frankfurt, docket no. 2-04 O 214/18, para. 46; also see Local Court of Würzburg, docket no. 16 C 207/13, para. 20; a very superficial analysis on this issue was conducted by the Local Court of Charlottenburg, docket no. 203 C 47/16, para. 22.

116 Regional Court of Bonn, docket no. 1 O 101/18, para. 39 et seq.

this finding is convincing.[117] Moreover, the case law existing so far does not give much guidance on websites. The Higher Regional Court of Cologne put an emphasis on the website's top-level domain,[118] whereas the Local Court of Brunswick held that a website is directed to every state, at least if the website's language is the same as the consumer's local language.[119] In light of Recital 7 and the CJEU's decision in *Pammer* and *Alpenhof*, which listed a number of criteria to be considered when assessing whether the professional targeted a certain Member State in the context of Article 15(1)(c) Brussels I Regulation (now Article 17(1)(c) Brussels I *bis* Regulation),[120] the courts' considerations remained too superficial. Lastly, and perhaps even more importantly, the Local Court of Brunswick held that no specific nexus between the activity and the contract is required.[121] This seems to conflict with the requirement that the contract shall fall 'within the scope of such activities' and with Recital 25, which specifies that the 'consumer contract has [to be] concluded as a result of the professional['s]' activities.[122] However, this time the court took account of Recital 7 and rightly referred to the CJEU's decision in *Emrek*, where it was decided that Article 15(1)(c) Brussels I Regulation (now Article 17(1)(c) Brussels I *bis* Regulation) does not require the existence of a causal link between the activities of the professional and the conclusion of the contract with the consumer.[123]

2.5.2.3. Article 8 Rome I

Consistent interpretation of all instruments of EU private international law, as well as primary law touching upon the issue in question (*rechtsaktübergreifende Auslegung*), as required (partly) in Recital 7 of the

---

[117] See on this issue Gerhard Hohloch, in Barbara Grunewald/Georg Maier-Reimer/Harm Peter Westermann (eds.), Erman – BGB (15th ed. 2017), Art. 6 Rom I, para. 25; Stefan Arnold, IPRax 2016, 567 et seq.

[118] Higher Regional Court of Cologne, docket no. I-6 U 90/15, 6 U 90/15, para. 69.

[119] Local Court of Brunswick, docket no. 118 C 3557/13, para. 12.

[120] CJEU, decision of 7 December 2010, Joined Cases C-585/08 and C-144/09, *Peter Pammer v. Reederei Karl Schlüter GmbH & Co. KG (C-585/08) and Hotel Alpenhof GesmbH v. Oliver Heller (C-144/09)*, ECLI:EU:C:2010:740, para. 93; also see Gottfried Musger, in Helmut Koziol/Peter Bydlinski/Raimund Bollenberger (eds.), ABGB – Kurzkommentar (5th ed. 2017), Art. 6 Rom I-VO, para. 3.

[121] Local Court of Brunswick, docket no. 118 C 3557/13, para. 12; affirmative e.g. Dieter Martiny, in Jan v. Hein (ed.), Münchener Kommentar zum BGB Vol. 12 (7th ed. 2018), Art. 6 Rom I-VO, para. 47; Bettina Heiderhoff, in Thomas Rauscher (ed.), Europäisches Zivilprozess- und Kollisionsrecht Vol. 3 (4th ed. 2016), Artikel 6 Rom II-VO, para. 37; cautious Gottfried Musger, in Helmut Koziol/Peter Bydlinski/Raimund Bollenberger (eds.), ABGB – Kurzkommentar (5th ed. 2017), Art. 6 Rom I-VO, para. 3.

[122] Gralf-Peter Calliess, in Gralf-Peter Calliess (ed.), Rome Regulations (2nd ed. 2015), Rome I Article 6, para. 53; Giesela Rühl, in Christine Budzikiewicz/Marc-Philippe Weller/Wolfgang Wurmnest (eds.), BeckOGK – Rom I-VO (01.12.2018), Artikel 6, para. 196; Matthias Klöpfer/Christoph Wendelstein, JZ 2014, 298, 300.

[123] CJEU, decision of 17 October 2013, Case C-218/12, *Lokman Emrek v. Vlado Sabranovic*, ECLI:EU:C:2013:666, para. 32.

Rome I and Rome II Regulations, has again played a major role in the context of Article 8 Rome I Regulation. The German Federal Labour Court (BAG) rightly held that the term 'employee' in the sense of Article 8 Rome I Regulation has to be interpreted autonomously and with respect to the jurisprudence of the CJEU on Article 45 TFEU.[124] Hence, 'the essential feature of an employment relationship is that for a certain period of time one person performs services for and under the direction of another in return for which he receives remuneration'.[125] Whether such a relationship exists must be assessed 'on the basis of all the factors and circumstances characterising the relationship between the parties'.[126]

Furthermore, the German Federal Labour Court (BAG) held that the term 'country where the work is habitually carried out' in the sense of Article 8(2) sentence 1 Rome I Regulation is interpreted extensively and consistently with Article 6(2)(a) Rome Convention.[127] Referring to the decisions of the CJEU in *Koelzsch*[128] and *Voogsgeerd*,[129] the court decided that this term must be understood as referring to the place where or from where the employee actually carries out his working activities and, if there is no centre of activities, to the place where he carries out the majority of his activities.[130] Only if no such place can be identified does Article 8(3) Rome I Regulation apply.[131] With regard to the place where a temporary worker habitually carries out his work, both the Austrian Supreme Court of Justice (OGH) and the German Federal Labour Court (BAG) make the following distinction: if the temporary worker carries out his work in only one country, that country is the place where he habitually carries out his work, irrespective of the employer's place of business;[132] if, on the other hand, the temporary worker works in various, ever-changing countries, Article 8(3) Rome I Regulation applies, leading to the application of the law of the country where the place of business through which the employee was engaged is situated.[133] Of course, the escape clause could still lead to the application of the

124 German Federal Labour Court (BAG), docket no. 6 AZR 430/15, para. 54.

125 CJEU, decision of 10 September 2015, Case C-47/14, *Holterman Ferho Exploitatie BV et al. v. Friedrich Leopold Freiherr Spies von Büllesheim*, ECLI:EU:C:2015:574, para. 41.

126 CJEU, decision of 10 September 2015, Case C-47/14, *Holterman Ferho Exploitatie BV et al. v. Friedrich Leopold Freiherr Spies von Büllesheim*, ECLI:EU:C:2015:574, para. 46; CJEU, decision of 9 July 2015, Case C-229/14, *Ender Balkaya v. Kiesel Abbruch- und Recycling Technik GmbH*, ECLI:EU:C:2015:455, para. 37.

127 German Federal Labour Court (BAG), docket no. 6 AZR 430/15, para. 56.

128 CJEU, decision of 15 March 2011, Case C-29/10, *Heiko Koelzsch v. État du Grand Duchy of Luxembourg*, ECLI:EU:C:2011:151, para. 45.

129 CJEU, decision of 15 December 2011, Case C-384/10, *Jan Voogsgeerd v. Navimer SA*, ECLI:EU:C:2011:842, para. 37.

130 German Federal Labour Court (BAG), docket no. 6 AZR 430/15, para. 57.

131 German Federal Labour Court (BAG), docket no. 6 AZR 430/15, para. 57.

132 Austrian Supreme Court of Justice (OGH), docket no. 8 ObA 86/10w, para. 2; German Federal Labour Court (BAG), docket no. 10 ABR 33/15, para. 105; German Federal Labour Court (BAG), docket no. 10 ABR 48/15, para. 88.

133 German Federal Labour Court (BAG), docket no. 10 ABR 33/15, para. 105; German Federal Labour Court (BAG), docket no. 10 ABR 48/15, para. 88.

law of a different country.[134] This approach takes due account of the particular circumstances of the individual case at issue without disregarding the structure of Article 8 Rome I Regulation. The courts correctly held that temporary workers can also have a place where they habitually carry out their work.[135] Although there is a risk that some courts could resort to the escape clause too hastily, this solution is convincing.[136]

Lastly, the Regional Labour Court of Mecklenburg–West Pomerania decided in regard to a choice of law and its limitations on the basis of Article 8(1) sentence 2 Rome I Regulation that the employee has to state which law would govern the contract in the absence of a choice of law agreement[137] – a decision that must be rejected since the provision in question has to be applied *ex officio*.[138] In addition, the approach taken by the court would improperly burden the employee.

2.6. ESCAPE CLAUSES

The German and Austrian courts resort to escape clauses rather restrictively. For example, there are only two decisions in which Article 4(3) Rome I Regulation has been applied,[139] and the courts have not resorted to this escape clause even in cases virtually predestined for the escape clause to apply, for instance in the case of a cross-licence contract or an acknowledgment of debt.[140]

---

134 On this issue in general see the next section on escape clauses.

135 Dieter Martiny, in Jan v. Hein (ed.), Münchener Kommentar zum BGB Vol. 12 (7th ed. 2018), Art. 8 Rom I-VO, para. 68; Frank Bayreuther, DB 2011, 706, 708; Martin Franzen, EuZA 2011, 451, 456.

136 See Dieter Martiny, in Jan v. Hein (ed.), Münchener Kommentar zum BGB Vol. 12 (7th ed. 2018), Art. 8 Rom I-VO, para. 68 with further references.

137 Regional Labour Court of Mecklenburg–West Pomerania, docket no. 2 Sa 172/13, para. 57.

138 Oliver L. Knöfel, in Christine Budzikiewicz/Marc-Philippe Weller/Wolfgang Wurmnest (eds.), BeckOGK – Rom I-VO (01.12.2018), Artikel 8, para. 44; Oliver L. Knöfel, IPRax 2014, 130, 131 et seq.

139 Higher Regional Court of Karlsruhe, docket no. 13 U 130/16, para. 39 (the court applied German law instead of Swiss law to a suretyship because it found that all 'substantial' circumstances were connected with 'German law'; the nationality of the parties, their place of residence and the place where the contract was signed were deemed to be insignificant); Higher Regional Court of Munich, docket no. 7 U 4830/11, para. 16 (the court applied German law to a promissory note, even though its issuer as well as the payee had their seat in Spain – which would have led to the application of Spanish law pursuant to Article 4(2) Rome I Regulation – because the promissory note was drafted in German and issued in Germany, the place of fulfilment was Germany, and the issuer was founded by German investors and still had a German management).

140 Regional Court of Mönchengladbach, docket no. 6 O 175/11; Regional Court of Mannheim, docket no. 2 O 147/14; see e.g. Ulrich Magnus, in Ulrich Magnus/Peter Mankowski (eds.), European Commentaries on Private International Law Vol. II – Rome I Regulation (2017), Article 4, para. 491 (arguing that the close connection between the acknowledgment and the acknowledged debt may lead to the application of the law governing the debt by virtue of Article 4(3) Rome I Regulation); doubting Austrian Supreme Court of Justice (OGH), docket no. 2 Ob 71/18g, para. 2; with regard to a cross-licence contract one could

Furthermore, the escape clauses of Article 5(3) Rome I Regulation and Article 7(2) subparagraph 2 sentence 2 Rome I Regulation have not been applied at all.

With respect to labour contracts, the courts tend to be more liberal. This is in line with the wording of Article 8(4) Rome I Regulation, which does not – in contrast to Article 4(3) Rome I Regulation – require a 'manifestly' closer connection. For example, a secondment contract was deemed to be more closely connected to Germany than to the place where the employee habitually carried out his work. The contract was drafted in German, it contained a call-back right for the employer, and in case of a conflict of interest with the German parent company the loyalty to the parent company should prevail.[141] In another decision, the German Federal Labour Court (BAG) suggested the application of Article 8(4) Rome I Regulation regarding the employment contract of a temporary worker if both parties' citizenships or places of residence or business coincide.[142] The Austrian Supreme Court of Justice (OGH) seems to be more restrictive, since it did not even consider the application of the escape clause in a similar case.[143]

2.7. SCOPE OF APPLICATION

The German Federal Court of Justice (BGH) clarified that Article 12(1)(e) Rome I Regulation ('the consequences of nullity of the contract') encompasses certain claims based on unjust enrichment as well.[144] In these cases, the Rome I Regulation takes precedence over Article 10 Rome II Regulation. While this finding was undisputed in the literature,[145] the court of previous instance had applied Article 10 Rome II Regulation.[146]

2.8. PUBLIC POLICY

There has not been a single case in which Austrian or German courts have affirmed a violation of public policy. In fact, only two courts have considered an infringement of public policy at all. Firstly, the Regional Court of Kleve decided

also consider an application of Article 4(4) Rome I Regulation: see Dennis Solomon, ZVglRWiss 115 (2016), 586, 599.

141 Labour Court of Stuttgart, docket no. 23 Ca 8738/11, para. 94.

142 German Federal Labour Court (BAG), docket no. 10 ABR 33/15, para. 105; German Federal Labour Court (BAG), docket no. 10 ABR 48/15, para. 88.

143 See Austrian Supreme Court of Justice (OGH), docket no. 8 ObA 86/10w, para. 2.

144 German Federal Court of Justice (BGH), docket no. IX ZR 92/17, para. 27.

145 Ulrich Spellenberg, in Jan v. Hein (ed.), Münchener Kommentar zum BGB Vol. 12 (7th ed. 2018), Art. 12 Rom I-VO, para. 164 with further references.

146 Higher Regional Court of Berlin, docket no. 14 U 20/16.

that Article 22(1) of the Dutch Forwarding Conditions (FENEX Conditions), a simple choice-of-law clause,[147] clearly did not constitute a violation of public policy.[148] Secondly, the Regional Court of Frankfurt did not find a violation of public policy in a case where foreign law (the law of Kuwait) was decisive to determining whether a claim for performance was excluded because the performance was impossible for the obligor or for any other person (section 275(1) German Civil Code).[149] These cases show that the courts handle the frequent party submissions to consider a violation of public policy quite well.

3. ROME II

3.1. OVERVIEW

The body of case law on the Rome II Regulation has evolved significantly since the Regulation entered into force. Nearly 200 decisions by German courts and about 50 decisions by Austrian courts are publicly available. The most frequently applied provisions are (in descending order) Articles 4, 6, 8, 32, and 31 Rome II Regulation (Germany) and Articles 1, 4, 6, 8, and 28 Rome II Regulation (Austria).

3.2. SCOPE

The scope of the exclusion of non-contractual obligations arising out of violations of privacy and rights relating to personality, including defamation, (Article 1(2)(g) Rome II Regulation) has given rise to a number of uncertainties. This applies, in particular, to its personal scope: while it is undisputed that the exclusion covers claims by natural persons,[150] it is far more controversial whether this is also the case for claims by bodies corporate or incorporate.[151] The Higher Regional Court of Koblenz applied Article 4 Rome II Regulation in a case of defamation to an Internet

147 Article 22(1) FENEX Conditions reads: 'All contracts to which the present conditions apply shall be governed by Dutch law'.

148 Regional Court of Kleve, docket no. 4 O 272/12, para. 21.

149 Regional Court of Frankfurt, docket no. 2-24 O 37/17, para. 47 et seq.

150 German Federal Court of Justice (BGH), docket no. VI ZR 93/10, para. 14; German Federal Court of Justice (BGH), docket no. VI ZR 217/08, para. 22; Austrian Supreme Court of Justice (OGH), docket no. 6 Ob 26/16s, para. 2; Austrian Supreme Court of Justice (OGH), docket no. 6 Ob 106/14b, para. 1; Higher Regional Court of Stuttgart, docket no. 4 U 78/13, para. 102; Regional Court of Frankfurt, docket no. 2-03 O 315/17, para. 74; Regional Court of Schweinfurt, docket no. 22 O 934/10, para. 54; Regional Court of Tübingen, docket no. 7 O 525/10, para. 19; the exclusion in Article 1(2)(g) Rome II Regulation has been overlooked by the Higher Regional Court of Vienna, docket no. 5 R 5/17t, para. 11.

151 See Robert Magnus, RabelsZ 84 (2020), 1, 7 et seq.; Axel Halfmeier, in Gralf-Peter Calliess (ed.), Rome Regulations (2nd ed. 2015), Rome II Article 1, para. 58; Andrew Dickinson, The Rome II Regulation (2008), p. 239 et seq., para. 3.227.

provider, without considering a possible exclusion by virtue of Article 1(2)(g) Rome II Regulation.[152] On the other hand, the German Federal Court of Justice (BGH) seems to hold that claims of legal entities are generally excluded from the Regulation's scope by virtue of this provision.[153] According to the prevailing view in the literature, at least acts falling within the scope of Article 6 Rome II Regulation do not fall within the exclusion in Article 1(2)(g) Rome II Regulation.[154] It is unfortunate that the courts did not refer this question to the CJEU for a preliminary ruling.

Moreover, it is a matter of dispute whether the right to a name falls within the exclusion in Article 1(2)(g) Rome II Regulation.[155] The German Federal Court of Justice (BGH) expressly left this issue open,[156] whereas the Austrian Supreme Court of Justice (OGH) answered the question in the negative without even considering a possible exclusion.[157] Again, only a preliminary ruling by the CJEU could give a definitive answer.

3.3. *LOIS DE POLICE*

In contrast to the Rome I Regulation, overriding mandatory provisions have merely played a minor role in the context of the Rome II Regulation. The Austrian Supreme Court of Justice (OGH) relied expressly on the CJEU's decision in *Arblade*[158] when it held that Article 16 Rome II Regulation shall only apply to national provisions compliance with which has been deemed so crucial

---

152 Higher Regional Court of Koblenz, docket no. 10 U 108/11.

153 See German Federal Court of Justice (BGH), docket no. VI ZR 269/12, para. 11.

154 Axel Halfmeier, in Gralf-Peter Calliess (ed.), Rome Regulations (2nd ed. 2015), Rome II Article 1, para. 58; Andrew Dickinson, The Rome II Regulation (2008), p. 240, para. 3.227.

155 See Matthias Lehmann, in Rainer Hüßtege/Heinz-Peter Mansel (eds.), NomosKommentar Vol. 6 – Rom-Verordnungen (3rd ed. 2019), Artikel 4 ROM II, para. 66; Peter Mankowski, in Peter W. Heermann/Jochen Schlingloff (eds.), Münchener Kommentar zum Lauterkeitsrecht Vol. 1 (2nd ed. 2014), Teil II. Internationales Wettbewerbs- und Wettbewerbsverfahrensrecht, para. 266 et seq.; Matthias Neumayr, in Helmut Koziol/Peter Bydlinski/Raimund Bollenberger (eds.), ABGB – Kurzkommentar (5th ed. 2017), Art. 1 Rom II-VO, para. 7; Marc-Philippe Weller, LMK 2013, 344766.

156 German Federal Court of Justice (BGH), docket no. I ZR 82/14, para. 35.

157 Austrian Supreme Court of Justice (OGH), docket no. 17 Ob 6/11y, para. 3.1.; if one agrees with the opinion that the right to a name falls within the scope of the Rome II Regulation, the follow-up question is raised as to which provision governs these claims. With regard to the legal name of a business, the Austrian Supreme Court of Justice (OGH) held that Article 8 Rome II Regulation applies. The court based this finding on an autonomous interpretation of the term 'intellectual property' and referred to Article 1(2) of the Paris Convention for the Protection of Industrial Property, where 'trade names' are expressly mentioned as being within the scope of 'industrial property'.

158 CJEU, decision of 23 November 1999, Joined Cases C-369/96 and C-376/96, *Criminal proceedings against Jean-Claude Arblade and Arblade & Fils SARL (C-369/96) and Bernard Leloup, Serge Leloup and Sofrage SARL*, ECLI:EU:C:1999:575, para. 30.

for the protection of the political, social or economic order in the Member State concerned as to require compliance therewith by all persons present on the national territory of that Member State and all legal relationships within that state.[159] The court concluded that rules on liability insurance fulfil these prerequisites because they also serve public interest.[160] The Regional Court of Neuruppin held that the German rules on damages cannot be regarded as overriding mandatory provisions.[161]

3.4. PARTY AUTONOMY

The practical impact of Article 14 Rome II Regulation has also remained rather limited so far. Only seven decisions have been rendered and all of them concerned a possible implied *ex post* choice of law by virtue of the parties' conduct in court proceedings.[162] The courts have taken a very liberal approach: in five cases, they inferred a choice of law solely on the ground that both parties pleaded on the basis of the substantive law of the *lex fori*.[163] Furthermore, the Higher Regional Court of Düsseldorf based a tacit choice of law on the fact that both parties made no objection to the application of the substantive law of the Netherlands.[164] These decisions resemble the requirements imposed on a subsequent implied choice of law in the context of the Rome I Regulation.[165] Again, and in particular in light of Article 14(1) subparagraph 2 Rome II Regulation and Recital 31 sentence 3 – according to which an implied choice of law shall be demonstrated with reasonable certainty by the circumstances of the case and with respect to the parties' intentions – the courts tend to assume a choice of law too easily. In particular, active consent cannot be established in a situation where there is simply no objection against the application of a certain

159 Austrian Supreme Court of Justice (OGH), docket no. 2 Ob 40/15v, para. 4.2.4.

160 Austrian Supreme Court of Justice (OGH), docket no. 2 Ob 40/15v, para. 4.2.5.

161 Regional Court of Neuruppin, docket no. 1 O 120/14, para. 34.

162 Austria: Austrian Supreme Court of Justice (OGH), docket no. 1 Ob 33/19p; Austrian Supreme Court of Justice (OGH), docket no. 1 Ob 67/15g; Austrian Supreme Court of Justice (OGH), docket no. 1 Ob 222/15a; Germany: Higher Regional Court of Stuttgart, docket no. 1 U 205/18; Higher Regional Court of Düsseldorf, docket no. I-18 U 27/12, 18 U 27/12; Higher Regional Court of Hamm, docket no. I-28 U 59/10, 28 U 59/10.

163 Austrian Supreme Court of Justice (OGH), docket no. 1 Ob 67/15g, para. 1; Austrian Supreme Court of Justice (OGH), docket no. 1 Ob 222/15a, para. 1; Higher Regional Court of Stuttgart, docket no. 1 U 205/18, para. 47; Higher Regional Court of Frankfurt, docket no. 6 U 3/18, para. 57; Higher Regional Court of Hamm, docket no. I-28 U 59/10, 28 U 59/10, para. 85; in one case, on the other hand, the parties pleaded on the basis of a foreign law, Austrian Supreme Court of Justice (OGH), docket no. 1 Ob 33/19p, para. 3.

164 Higher Regional Court of Düsseldorf, docket no. I-18 U 27/12, 18 U 27/12, para. 65.

165 On the similar issue under the Rome I Regulation, see above at section 2.4.3.

substantive law.[166] Furthermore, proceeding on the basis of a certain substantive law because it is believed to be applicable anyway is insufficient for building consent because in this case the parties do not have the intention of choosing the applicable law.[167] Finally, under Austrian domestic law an implied choice of law by the parties' conduct in court proceedings is not possible at all (section 11(2) Austrian Act on Private International Law),[168] and it is far from certain that the parties are aware of the new legal landscape. Therefore, the courts should ensure that the parties are cognisant of their power to choose the applicable law before they hastily presume a choice of law.[169]

3.5. TORTS

3.5.1. Article 4 Rome II

Article 4(1) is one of the Rome II Regulation's provisions that is applied most often by the courts in Germany and Austria.[170] Although its application usually does not cause any problems in practice, a number of decisions regarding injunction actions against the use of unfair contractual terms (especially in general terms and conditions) towards consumers merit closer examination.

---

166 Helmut Ofner, ZfRV 1995, 149; Helmut Ofner, ZfRV 2016, 80; Peter Mankowski, in Ulrich Magnus/Peter Mankowski (eds.), European Commentaries on Private International Law Vol. II – Rome I Regulation (2017), Article 3, para. 143.

167 Helmut Ofner, ZfRV 1995, 149; also see (with regard to Article 3 Rome I Regulation) Peter Mankowski, in Ulrich Magnus/Peter Mankowski (eds.), European Commentaries on Private International Law Vol. II – Rome I Regulation (2017), Article 3, para. 143; Brigitta Lurger/Martina Melcher, Handbuch Internationales Privatrecht (2017), para. 4/63.

168 See Brigitta Lurger/Martina Melcher, Handbuch Internationales Privatrecht (2017), para. 4/63.

169 Abbo Junker, in Jan v. Hein (ed.), Münchener Kommentar zum BGB Vol. 12 (7th ed. 2018), Art. 14 Rom II-VO, para. 33; Martin Gebauer, in Rainer Hüßtege/Heinz-Peter Mansel (eds.), NomosKommentar Vol. 6 – Rom-Verordnungen (3rd ed. 2019), Artikel 14 ROM II, para. 21 et seq.; Matthias Neumayr, in Helmut Koziol/Peter Bydlinski/Raimund Bollenberger (eds.), ABGB – Kurzkommentar (5th ed. 2017), Art. 14 Rom II-VO, para. 3.

170 Most German cases concerned road traffic accidents; see e.g. Higher Regional Court of Saarbrücken, docket no. 4 U 18/17, para. 48; Higher Regional Court of Munich, docket no. 10 U 2408/16, para. 8; Higher Regional Court of Hamm, docket no. I-9 U 30/15, 9 U 30/15, para. 3; Regional Court of Neuruppin, docket no. 1 O 120/14, para. 20; Regional Court of Saarbrücken, docket no. 13 S 21/15, para. 13; Regional Court of Kleve, docket no. 5 S 128/11, para. 12; Regional Court of Frankenthal, docket no. 4 O 155/09; Local Court of Heinsberg, docket no. 18 C 27/17, para. 13; Local Court of Landsberg, docket no. 2 C 141/18, para. 3; Local Court of Frankenthal, docket no. 3a C 158/13; this is different in Austria, since it is a contracting state to the Hague Convention of 4 May 1971 on the Law Applicable to Traffic Accidents.

As discussed above,[171] the German Federal Court of Justice (BGH) held that said actions are governed by the Rome II Regulation.[172] However, the court left open the question whether Article 4(1) or Article 6(1) Rome II Regulation is applicable.[173] Again,[174] the court deemed a preliminary ruling by the CJEU on this question to be unnecessary. Subsequently, the German courts have applied either Article 6(1) Rome II Regulation or (predominantly) Article 4(1) Rome II Regulation to these actions.[175] With regard to the latter, the courts have located the place where the damage occurred at the place where the allegedly unfair contractual terms were presumably used, because this was the place where the protected collective interests of the consumers were affected.[176] At first sight, such an approach makes a distinction between Articles 4(1) and 6(1) Rome II Regulation superfluous. Yet, only the law applicable by virtue of Article 4(1) Rome II Regulation is subject to a manifestly closer connection to another country (Article 4(3) Rome II Regulation). Therefore, it makes a difference which provision applies.

The matter was settled when the Austrian Supreme Court of Justice (OGH) referred the question to the CJEU of whether Article 4 Rome II Regulation is applicable to injunction actions.[177] The CJEU answered in the negative and held that Article 6(1) Rome II Regulation applies.[178] This decision is in line with the prevailing view in the literature.[179] Further, the Austrian Supreme Court of Justice (OGH) discussed how to determine the place where the damage occurred pursuant to Article 4(1) Rome II Regulation in the context of Article 6(2) Rome II

171 See above at section 2.5.2.2.

172 German Federal Court of Justice (BGH), docket no. Xa ZR 19/08, para. 18.

173 German Federal Court of Justice (BGH), docket no. Xa ZR 19/08, para. 19.

174 See above at section 2.5.2.2.

175 See e.g. German Federal Court of Justice (BGH), docket no. Xa ZR 5/09, para. 12; German Federal Court of Justice (BGH), docket no. Xa ZR 68/09, para. 17; Higher Regional Court of Cologne, docket no. I-6 U 90/15, 6 U 90/15, para. 49; Higher Regional Court of Frankfurt, docket no. 16 U 86/12, para. 20; Regional Court of Berlin, docket no. 15 O 601/12, para. 82; Regional Court of Frankfurt, docket no. 2-24 O 1420/10, 2/24 O 142/10, para. 27.

176 German Federal Court of Justice (BGH), docket no. Xa ZR 19/08, para. 19; German Federal Court of Justice (BGH), docket no. Xa ZR 5/09, para. 12; German Federal Court of Justice (BGH), docket no. Xa ZR 68/09, para. 17; Higher Regional Court of Cologne, docket no. I-6 U 90/15, 6 U 90/15, para. 49; Higher Regional Court of Frankfurt, docket no. 16 U 86/12, para. 20; Regional Court of Berlin, docket no. 15 O 601/12, para. 82; this was highly controversial: see e.g. Dietmar Baetge, ZEuP 2011, 930, 937 et seq.; Astrid Stadler, VuR 2010, 83 et seq.

177 Austrian Supreme Court of Justice (OGH), docket no. 2 Ob 204/14k.

178 CJEU, decision of 28 July 2016, Case C-191/15, *Verein für Konsumenteninformation v. Amazon EU*, ECLI:EU:C:2016:612, para. 60.

179 Dörte Poelzig/Matthias Windorfer, in Christine Budzikiewicz/Marc-Philippe Weller/Wolfgang Wurmnest (eds.), BeckOGK – Rom II-VO (01.12.2018), Artikel 6, para. 87; Josef Drexl, in Franz Jürgen Säcker/Roland Rixecker/Hartmut Oetker (eds.), Münchener Kommentar zum BGB Vol. 12 (7th ed. 2018), Internationales Lauterkeitsrecht, para. 137 et seq.; Dietmar Baetge, ZEuP 2011, 930, 937 et seq.; Björn Steinrötter, NJW 2013, 2605, 2608.

Regulation. In the court's view, neither the place of the affected market nor the place where either the central administration or the branch affected is located is decisive.[180] Instead, the court favoured the place of the first interference in the competitor's legal sphere.[181] The Austrian Supreme Court of Justice (OGH) based its reasoning on the CJEU's decisions in *Marinari*[182] and *Kronhofer*.[183]

3.5.2. *Specific Rules*

3.5.2.1. Overview

From a quantitative point of view, the specific rules on product liability, environmental damage and industrial damage do not have any substantial relevance. So far there is no German or Austrian case law on Articles 7 and 9 Rome II Regulation and only two decisions on Article 5 Rome II Regulation, and the substance of the latter were minimal: the Austrian Supreme Court of Justice (OGH) held that the burden of proof in regard to the foreseeability defence pursuant to Article 5(1) sentence 2 Rome II Regulation lies with the person claimed to be liable[184] – a position undisputed in the literature.[185] Furthermore, the Higher Regional Court of Koblenz rightly pointed out that Article 4(2) Rome II Regulation takes precedence over Article 5 Rome II Regulation ('without prejudice to Article 4(2)').[186] Hence, the heated debate that surrounded the introduction of these provisions and their proper application has no correlation with their importance in court practice. This is in sharp contrast with the practical impact of Articles 6 and 8 Rome II Regulation, two of the most often applied and most controversial provisions.

---

180 Austrian Supreme Court of Justice (OGH), docket no. 4 Ob 12/11k, para. 5.1.1.; Austrian Supreme Court of Justice (OGH), docket no. 17 Ob 6/11y, para. 4.1.(b); affirmative Josef Drexl, in Franz Jürgen Säcker/Roland Rixecker/Hartmut Oetker (eds.), Münchener Kommentar zum BGB Vol. 12 (7th ed. 2018), Internationales Lauterkeitsrecht, para. 179; Peter Mankowski, in Peter W. Heermann/Jochen Schlingloff (eds.), Münchener Kommentar zum Lauterkeitsrecht Vol. 1 (2nd ed. 2014), Teil II. Internationales Wettbewerbs- und Wettbewerbsverfahrensrecht, para. 253; but see Dörte Poelzig/Matthias Windorfer, in Christine Budzikiewicz/Marc-Philippe Weller/Wolfgang Wurmnest (eds.), BeckOGK – Rom II-VO (01.12.2018), Artikel 6, para. 105 with further references.

181 Austrian Supreme Court of Justice (OGH), docket no. 4 Ob 12/11k, para. 5.1.3.

182 CJEU, decision of 19 September 1995, Case C-364/93, *Antonio Marinari v. Lloyds Bank plc and Zubaidi Trading Company*, ECLI:EU:C:1995:289, para. 21.

183 CJEU, decision of 10 June 2004, Case C-168/02, *Rudolf Kronhofer v. Marianne Maier et al.*, ECLI:EU:C:2004:364, para. 21.

184 Austrian Supreme Court of Justice (OGH), docket no. 3 Ob 8/14v, para. 1.2.

185 Martin Illmer, in Peter Huber (ed.), Rome II Regulation: Pocket Commentary (2011), Article 5, para. 46; Abbo Junker, in Jan v. Hein (ed.), Münchener Kommentar zum BGB Vol. 12 (7th ed. 2018), Art. 5 Rom II-VO, para. 55; Andreas Spickhoff, in Dietmar Baetge/Jan v. Hein/ Michael v. Hinden (eds.), Die richtige Ordnung: Festschrift für Jan Kropholler zum 70. Geburtstag (2008), p. 671, 682.

186 Higher Regional Court of Koblenz, docket no. 5 U 926/18, para. 14.

3.5.2.2. Article 6 Rome II

First and foremost, the courts have rendered numerous decisions on the determination of the country where competitive relations or the collective interests of consumers are, or are likely to be, affected in unfair competition cases pursuant to Article 6(1) Rome II Regulation. As a continuation of the case law established under autonomous law, German courts have applied the market effects principle and thus the law of the country where the competitive interests collide.[187] Even though there is consensus that a country's market has to be consciously targeted,[188] it is unclear whether the conduct complained of must have a sufficient economic impact in this country.[189] The Commission's proposals expressly required that the competitive relations or the collective interests of consumers were, or were likely to be, directly and substantially affected. By contrast, the wording of Article 6(1) Rome II Regulation makes no reference to such a 'substantiality requirement'. This suggests that there is no threshold requirement of economic impact.[190] In any case, a reference to the CJEU for a preliminary ruling would be necessary. In relation to advertising and marketing measures, the target market has to be determined.[191] This becomes particularly problematic when conduct via the Internet is at issue, because websites can be

---

187 German Federal Court of Justice (BGH), docket no. I ZR 253/14, para. 42; German Federal Court of Justice (BGH), docket no. I ZR 225/13, para. 16; German Federal Court of Justice (BGH), docket no. I ZR 253/14, para. 40; Higher Regional Court of Frankfurt, docket no. 6 U 3/18, para. 56; Higher Regional Court of Düsseldorf, docket no. I-15 U 48/19, para. 49; Higher Regional Court of Düsseldorf, docket no. I-2 U 34/19, para. 6; Higher Regional Court of Düsseldorf, docket no. I-2 W 58/10, 2 W 58/10, para. 8; Higher Regional Court of Thuringia, docket no. 2 U 524/17, para. 26; Regional Court of Düsseldorf, docket no. 37 O 133/18, para. 34; also see German Federal Court of Justice (BGH), docket no. I ZR 131/12, para. 38.

188 German Federal Court of Justice (BGH), docket no. I ZR 131/12, para. 38; Higher Regional Court of Berlin, docket no. 5 U 20/14, para. 47; also see Regional Court of Karlsruhe, docket no. 14 O 27/11 KfH III, para. 52.

189 Affirmative: Higher Regional Court of Berlin, docket no. 5 U 20/14, para. 47; Josef Drexl, in Franz Jürgen Säcker/Roland Rixecker/Hartmut Oetker (eds.), Münchener Kommentar zum BGB Vol. 12 (7th ed. 2018), Internationales Lauterkeitsrecht, para. 199; also see Christian Handig, GRUR Int 2008, 24, 28.

190 Matthias Weller, in Rainer Hüßtege/Heinz-Peter Mansel (eds.), NomosKommentar Vol. 6 – Rom-Verordnungen (3rd ed. 2019), Artikel 6 ROM II, para. 20; Steffen Pabst, in Thomas Rauscher (ed.), Europäisches Zivilprozess- und Kollisionsrecht Vol. 3 (4th ed. 2016), Artikel 6 Rom II-VO, para. 38 et seq.; Rolf Sack, WRP 2008, 845, 854.

191 German Federal Court of Justice (BGH), docket no. I ZR 225/13, para. 16; Austrian Supreme Court of Justice (OGH), docket no. 4 Ob 12/11k, para. 6.1.; Austrian Supreme Court of Justice (OGH), docket no. 17 Ob 6/11y, para. 4.1.(a); Austrian Supreme Court of Justice (OGH), docket no. 4 Ob 29/13p, para. 1.1.; Austrian Supreme Court of Justice (OGH), docket no. 4 Ob 202/12b, para. 1.2.; also see Regional Court of Karlsruhe, docket no. 14 O 27/11 KfH III, para. 52; Dörte Poelzig/Matthias Windorfer, in Christine Budzikiewicz/Marc-Philippe Weller/Wolfgang Wurmnest (eds.), BeckOGK – Rom II-VO (01.12.2018), Artikel 6, para. 76.

viewed in almost any country. Some courts have held that online advertising measures should, where there is doubt, be considered to be targeted globally, unless their content clearly suggests that only certain markets are targeted.[192] In contrast, a number of other courts have required the website in question to meet certain positive criteria.[193] For example, emphasis should be placed on the language of the website and whether the website can be accessed within the country.[194] Furthermore, the Higher Regional Court of Berlin decided that the use of a disclaimer may indicate that certain markets are not targeted if the disclaimer is clear and unambiguous and can be regarded as genuine.[195] For this reason, a disclaimer included in general terms and conditions may be insufficient.[196] Moreover, a disclaimer is held to be invalid if the advertising company does not comply with it in practice.[197] This is convincing.[198]

In four decisions, the Austrian Supreme Court of Justice (OGH) dealt with multi-state acts of unfair competition. In the case of a non-contractual obligation arising out of a restriction of competition, Article 6(3)(b) Rome II Regulation provides that a person seeking compensation for damage who sues in the court of the domicile of the defendant may choose to base his or her claim on the law of the court seised. By contrast, there is no such rule in Article 6(1) Rome II Regulation. Recital 22 sentence 3 – which states that in cases where the market is, or is likely to be, affected in more than one country, the claimant should be able in certain circumstances to choose to base his or her claim on the law of the court seised – only refers to Article 6(3)(b) Rome II Regulation. Furthermore, there is no escape clause that could lead to the application of the law of only one country. Hence, if conduct affects various countries, the market effects principle leads to the cumulative application of the laws of all of these countries (the mosaic approach).[199] This can lead to unsatisfactory results and has given

---

192 Higher Regional Court of Hamm, docket no. I-4 U 196/10, 4 U 196/10, para. 82; Regional Court of Karlsruhe, docket no. 14 O 27/11 KfH III, para. 52.

193 Joint Senate of the Highest Courts of Justice, docket no. GmS-OGB 1/10, para. 15; Higher Regional Court of Hamm, docket no. I-4 U 100/13, 4 U 100/13, para. 37; Regional Court of Berlin, docket no. 91 O 102/12, para. 15.

194 Higher Regional Court of Hamm, docket no. I-4 U 100/13, 4 U 100/13, para. 37; Higher Regional Court of Berlin, docket no. 5 W 221/17, para. 3; Regional Court of Berlin, docket no. 91 O 102/12, para. 15; see also Joint Senate of the Highest Courts of Justice, docket no. GmS-OGB 1/10, para. 15.

195 Higher Regional Court of Berlin, docket no. 5 U 16/14, para. 31.

196 Higher Regional Court of Berlin, docket no. 5 U 16/14, para. 32.

197 Higher Regional Court of Berlin, docket no. 5 U 16/14, para. 31.

198 See Dörte Poelzig/Matthias Windorfer, in Christine Budzikiewicz/Marc-Philippe Weller/Wolfgang Wurmnest (eds.), BeckOGK – Rom II-VO (01.12.2018), Artikel 6, para. 143 with further references.

199 Matthias Weller, in Rainer Hüßtege/Heinz-Peter Mansel (eds.), NomosKommentar Vol. 6 – Rom-Verordnungen (3rd ed. 2019), Artikel 6 ROM II, para. 19; Josef Drexl, in Franz Jürgen Säcker/Roland Rixecker/Hartmut Oetker (eds.), Münchener Kommentar zum BGB Vol. 12 (7th ed. 2018), Internationales Lauterkeitsrecht, para. 187; Martin Illmer, in Peter Huber (ed.),

rise to a heated debate about the proper approach towards multi-state acts of unfair competition under Article 6(1) Rome II Regulation.[200] For example, some argue that Article 6(3)(b) Rome II Regulation may be applied by analogy,[201] a view rejected by most commentators.[202] Unfortunately, the Austrian Supreme Court of Justice (OGH) did not pick up this issue. Instead, the court followed the mosaic approach without any further discussion.[203]

A number of decisions have dealt with the relationship between Article 6(1) Rome II Regulation and the country-of-origin principle in Article 3(1) Electronic Commerce Directive. Whether the latter provision (and its transposition into national law) constitutes a conflict-of-laws rule, taking precedence over Article 6(1) Rome II Regulation, or whether the country-of-origin principle is a corrective at the substantive law level, is a matter of dispute.[204] The German Federal Court of Justice (BGH) referred the question to the CJEU for a preliminary ruling on whether Article 3(1) and (2) Electronic Commerce Directive should be attributed a conflict-of-laws character in the sense that in the field of private law they also require the exclusive application of the law applicable in the country of origin, to the exclusion of national conflict-of-laws rules, or whether they operate as a corrective at a substantive law level, by means of which the substantive law outcome under the law declared to be applicable pursuant to the national conflict-of-laws rules is altered and reduced to the requirements of the country of origin.

Rome II Regulation: Pocket Commentary (2011), Article 6, para. 55; Matthias Neumayr, in Helmut Koziol/Peter Bydlinski/Raimund Bollenberger (eds.), ABGB – Kurzkommentar (5th ed. 2017), Art. 6 Rom II-VO, para. 2.

200 See Josef Drexl, in Franz Jürgen Säcker/Roland Rixecker/Hartmut Oetker (eds.), Münchener Kommentar zum BGB Vol. 12 (7th ed. 2018), Internationales Lauterkeitsrecht, para. 198 ('maybe the most important conflict-of-laws problem').

201 Gerhard Wagner, IPRax 2008, 1, 8; also see Helmut Heiss/Leander Loacker, JBl. 2007, 613, 630 (extension of Article 6(3)(b) Rome II Regulation to Article 6 Rome II Regulation *de lege ferenda*).

202 Steffen Pabst, in Thomas Rauscher (ed.), Europäisches Zivilprozess- und Kollisionsrecht Vol. 3 (4th ed. 2016), Artikel 6 Rom II-VO, para. 71; Martin Illmer, in Peter Huber (ed.), Rome II Regulation: Pocket Commentary (2011), Article 6, para. 55 with further references.

203 Austrian Supreme Court of Justice (OGH), docket no. 4 Ob 29/13p, para. 1.1.; Austrian Supreme Court of Justice (OGH), docket no. 4 Ob 202/12b, para. 1.2.; Austrian Supreme Court of Justice (OGH), docket no. 4 Ob 12/11k, para. 6.1.; Austrian Supreme Court of Justice (OGH), docket no. 17 Ob 6/11y, para. 4.1.(a).

204 See Matthias Weller, in Rainer Hüßtege/Heinz-Peter Mansel (eds.), NomosKommentar Vol. 6 – Rom-Verordnungen (3rd ed. 2019), Artikel 6 ROM II, para. 21 et seq.; Dörte Poelzig/Matthias Windorfer, in Christine Budzikiewicz/Marc-Philippe Weller/Wolfgang Wurmnest (eds.), BeckOGK – Rom II-VO (01.12.2018), Artikel 6, para. 112 et seq.; Josef Drexl, in Franz Jürgen Säcker/Roland Rixecker/Hartmut Oetker (eds.), Münchener Kommentar zum BGB Vol. 12 (7th ed. 2018), Internationales Lauterkeitsrecht, para. 62 et seq.; Martin Illmer, in Peter Huber (ed.), Rome II Regulation: Pocket Commentary (2011), Article 6, para. 25 et seq.

The CJEU held that Article 3 Electronic Commerce Directive:

> 'must be interpreted as not requiring transposition in the form of a specific conflict-of-laws rule. Nevertheless, in relation to the coordinated field, Member States must ensure that, subject to the derogations authorised in accordance with the conditions set out in Article 3(4) [Electronic Commerce Directive], the provider of an electronic commerce service is not made subject to stricter requirements than those provided for by the substantive law applicable in the Member State in which that service provider is established'.[205]

This decision did not, however, settle all disputes and there are still uncertainties in practice. For example, in its final judgment in the case that gave rise to the reference to the CJEU, the German Federal Court of Justice (BGH) decided that section 3 German Telemedia Act does not constitute a conflict-of-laws rule but a prohibition of restrictions on the substantive law level.[206] The Higher Regional Court of Hamburg held the opposite.[207] The German Federal Court of Justice (BGH) reversed this decision and emphasised once more that section 3 German Telemedia Act does not constitute a conflict-of-laws rule.[208]

By contrast, the Austrian Supreme Court of Justice (OGH) held in 2012 that section 20 Austrian E-Commerce Act, the Austrian legislation implementing the Electronic Commerce Directive, constitutes a conflict-of-laws rule that takes precedence over Article 6(1) Rome II Regulation.[209] In 2013, however, the Austrian Supreme Court of Justice (OGH) made the following distinction: Within the scope of the Rome II Regulation, section 20 Austrian E-Commerce Act does not constitute a conflict-of-laws rule and does not take precedence over Article 6(1) Rome II Regulation by virtue of Article 27 Rome II Regulation, because this rule only encompasses conflict-of-laws rules based in EU law and not cases within the scope of autonomous national law merely making use of the implementation legislation (*überschießende Umsetzung*).[210] On the contrary, Article 6(1) Rome II Regulation would supersede such a conflict-of-laws rule.[211] Outside the scope of the Rome II Regulation, especially in cases of non-contractual obligations arising out of violations of privacy and rights relating to personality, including defamation (Article 1(2)(g) Rome II Regulation), section 20 Austrian E-Commerce Act should be regarded as a conflict-of-laws rule.[212]

---

205 CJEU, decision of 25 October 2011, Joined Cases C-509/09 and C-161/10, *eDate Advertising GmbH et al. v. X and Société MGN LIMITED*, ECLI:EU:C:2011:685, para. 68; also see Rolf Sack, EWS 2011, 513 et seq.

206 German Federal Court of Justice (BGH), docket no. VI ZR 217/08, para. 34.

207 Higher Regional Court of Hamburg, docket no. 3 U 86/13, para. 151.

208 German Federal Court of Justice (BGH), docket no. I ZR 253/14, para. 34 et seq.; also see Higher Regional Court of Munich, docket no. 18 W 1383/18, para. 15.

209 Austrian Supreme Court of Justice (OGH), docket no. 7 Ob 189/11m, para. 1.2.

210 Austrian Supreme Court of Justice (OGH), docket no. 4 Ob 29/13p, para. 1.2.(c) et seq.

211 Austrian Supreme Court of Justice (OGH), docket no. 4 Ob 29/13p, para. 1.2.(c) et seq.

212 Austrian Supreme Court of Justice (OGH), docket no. 4 Ob 29/13p, para. 1.2.(e).

This distinction is not conclusive. For example, it is already doubtful whether a national transposition of Article 3 Electronic Commerce Directive as a conflict-of-laws rule is really a case of going beyond the requirements of the Directive.[213] Notwithstanding the above, from a conceptual point of view a solution at the substantive law level is preferable.[214]

In a number of cases, German and Austrian courts have had to decide whether an act of unfair competition exclusively affects the interests of a specific competitor, leading to the application of Article 4 Rome II Regulation by virtue of Article 6(2) Rome II Regulation. There is consensus that Article 6(2) Rome II Regulation is rather narrow in scope[215] and that Article 6(1) Rome II Regulation applies if the conduct also impacts the interests of the public[216] or likely misleads the opposite side of the market.[217] The Austrian Supreme Court of Justice (OGH) has rightly applied Article 6(2) Rome II Regulation in domain-grabbing cases, at least if the person claimed to be liable only tries to lock up domain names and does not use the domain for his own business activities.[218] If there is the latter kind of (ab)use, Article 6(1) Rome II Regulation applies, because this use likely misleads the opposite side of the market.[219]

3.5.2.3. Article 8 Rome II

There are considerable uncertainties as to the scope of the *lex loci protectionis* determined by Article 8(1) Rome II Regulation.[220] This is due to the rather

---

213 Matthias Weller, in Rainer Hüßtege/Heinz-Peter Mansel (eds.), NomosKommentar Vol. 6 – Rom-Verordnungen (3rd ed. 2019), Artikel 6 ROM II, para. 25b.

214 Matthias Weller, in Rainer Hüßtege/Heinz-Peter Mansel (eds.), NomosKommentar Vol. 6 – Rom-Verordnungen (3rd ed. 2019), Artikel 6 ROM II, para. 25 et seq.; Josef Drexl, in Franz Jürgen Säcker/Roland Rixecker/Hartmut Oetker (eds.), Münchener Kommentar zum BGB Vol. 12 (7th ed. 2018), Internationales Lauterkeitsrecht, para. 78; Dörte Poelzig/Matthias Windorfer, in Christine Budzikiewicz/Marc-Philippe Weller/Wolfgang Wurmnest (eds.), BeckOGK – Rom II-VO (01.12.2018), Artikel 6, para. 117.

215 Too superficially and hastily: Regional Court of Düsseldorf, docket no. 14d O 3/15, para. 57.

216 German Federal Court of Justice (BGH), docket no. I ZR 201/16, para. 23; German Federal Court of Justice (BGH), docket no. I ZR 131/12, para. 37; Higher Regional Court of Brandenburg, docket no. 6 W 9/19, para. 33; also see German Federal Court of Justice (BGH), docket no. I ZR 253/14, para. 43.

217 Austrian Supreme Court of Justice (OGH), docket no. 4 Ob 106/13m, para. 2.

218 Austrian Supreme Court of Justice (OGH), docket no. 17 Ob 6/11y, para. 4.2.(b).

219 Josef Drexl, in Franz Jürgen Säcker/Roland Rixecker/Hartmut Oetker (eds.), Münchener Kommentar zum BGB Vol. 12 (7th ed. 2018), Internationales Lauterkeitsrecht, para. 175; also see Austrian Supreme Court of Justice (OGH), docket no. 17 Ob 6/11y, para. 4.2.(b) (leaving this question open).

220 E.g. Michael Grünberger, in Rainer Hüßtege/Heinz-Peter Mansel (eds.), NomosKommentar Vol. 6 – Rom-Verordnungen (3rd ed. 2019), Artikel 8 ROM II, para. 38 et seq.; Josef Drexl, in Franz Jürgen Säcker/Roland Rixecker/Hartmut Oetker (eds.), Münchener Kommentar zum BGB Vol. 12 (7th ed. 2018), Internationales Lauterkeitsrecht, para. 175 et seq.; Mary-Rose McGuire, in Christine Budzikiewicz/Marc-Philippe Weller/Wolfgang Wurmnest (eds.), BeckOGK – Rom II-VO (01.12.2018), Artikel 8, para. 207 et seq.; Matthias Neumayr, in Helmut

complex interplay between Article 8(1) Rome II Regulation and Article 15 Rome II Regulation. For example, it is disputed whether the existence of an intellectual property right, its initial holder and its transferability are governed by Article 8(1) Rome II Regulation or by the national rules on private international law.[221]

The differing views on these questions are also reflected in the case law. Tending to a narrow scope, the Regional Court of Munich suggested that the protectability of an intellectual property right is determined by the national rules on private international law of the *lex fori*.[222] Furthermore, the Austrian Supreme Court of Justice (OGH) was uncertain whether Article 8 Rome II Regulation applies to the ownership of the intellectual property right.[223] By contrast, the German Federal Court of Justice (BGH) seems to favour the view that Article 8 Rome II Regulation governs not only the content of protection of the intellectual property right but also its existence and ownership.[224] This problem is not of purely theoretical significance. Firstly, the national rules on private international law are quite diverse in the Member States (especially in Greece, Portugal and Romania) and do not per se lead to the application of the *lex loci protectionis*.[225] Secondly, there is no exclusion of *renvoi* in the autonomous rules on private international law. Therefore, a decision by the CJEU would be essential.

Moreover, the Austrian Supreme Court of Justice (OGH) derived from the wording of Article 8(1) Rome II Regulation – which states that 'the law of the country for which protection is claimed' is applicable – that the applicable law depends on the pleading of the claimant.[226] Although this means that, in principle, it is in the claimant's power to 'choose' the applicable law, it does not give him an unreasonable advantage because the question whether there is in fact an infringement of an intellectual property right is decided on the level of the

---

Koziol/Peter Bydlinski/Raimund Bollenberger (eds.), ABGB – Kurzkommentar (5th ed. 2017), Art. 8 Rom II-VO, para. 1.

221 Josef Drexl, in Franz Jürgen Säcker/Roland Rixecker/Hartmut Oetker (eds.), Münchener Kommentar zum BGB Vol. 12 (7th ed. 2018), Internationales Lauterkeitsrecht, para. 176 et seq; Steffen Pabst, in Thomas Rauscher (ed.), Europäisches Zivilprozess- und Kollisionsrecht Vol. 3 (4th ed. 2016), Artikel 8 Rom II-VO, para. 8 et seq.

222 Regional Court of Munich, docket no. 21 O 14914/09, para. 43.

223 Austrian Supreme Court of Justice (OGH), docket no. 4 Ob 184/13g, para. 2.2.1.(a).

224 German Federal Court of Justice (BGH), docket no. I ZR 201/16, para. 22; German Federal Court of Justice (BGH), docket no. I ZR 11/16, para. 13; German Federal Court of Justice (BGH), docket no. I ZR 76/11, para. 18; also see Regional Court of Munich, docket no. 37 O 5140/18, para. 40; Regional Court of Munich, docket no. 37 O 22800/16, para. 109; Regional Court of Düsseldorf, docket no. 4a O 54/12, para. 168; Regional Court of Düsseldorf, docket no. 4b O 273/10, para. 184; Regional Court of Düsseldorf, docket no. 4b O 274/10, para. 183.

225 See Josef Drexl, in Franz Jürgen Säcker/Roland Rixecker/Hartmut Oetker (eds.), Münchener Kommentar zum BGB Vol. 12 (7th ed. 2018), Internationales Lauterkeitsrecht, para. 175.

226 Austrian Supreme Court of Justice (OGH), docket no. 17 Ob 6/11y, para. 3.2.

'chosen' substantive law, and the substantive law will usually require territorial links of the action purported to be infringing ('territoriality principle').[227]

Furthermore, one decision dealt with the disputed question of whether Article 8 Rome II Regulation requires a significant domestic connection. Its wording, as well as the recitals, do not provide for such a restriction. However, it is argued that this requirement can be deduced from the territoriality principle on which this article is based.[228] If one accepts this conclusion, it then has to be decided whether this problem should be discussed at the conflict-of-laws or substantive law level.[229] The Higher Regional Court of Munich followed the former view without discussing this problem at all.[230]

Like Article 6(1) Rome II Regulation,[231] Article 8(1) and (2) Rome II Regulation do not provide a solution for multi-state torts. The Austrian Supreme Court of Justice (OGH) rightly held that in the context of Article 8(1) Rome II Regulation the mosaic approach applies.[232] Since a mosaic approach is generally seen to be inefficient, some commentators have proposed a noticeable influence requirement.[233] This solution has, however, been almost unanimously rejected.[234] By contrast, in the case of a non-contractual obligation arising from an infringement of a unitary EC intellectual property right, for any question that is not governed by the relevant EC instrument, Article 8(2) Rome II

227 Josef Drexl, in Franz Jürgen Säcker/Roland Rixecker/Hartmut Oetker (eds.), Münchener Kommentar zum BGB Vol. 12 (7th ed. 2018), Internationales Immaterialgüterrecht, para. 12; Steffen Pabst, in Thomas Rauscher (ed.), Europäisches Zivilprozess- und Kollisionsrecht Vol. 3 (4th ed. 2016), Artikel 8 Rom II-VO, para. 21; for a different view see Nadine Klass, GRUR Int 2007, 373, 376; Benedikt Buchner, GRUR Int 2005, 1004, 1006.

228 Benedikt Buchner, in Gralf-Peter Calliess (ed.), Rome Regulations (2nd ed. 2015), Rome II Article 8, para. 18.

229 For the former see Benedikt Buchner, in Gralf-Peter Calliess (ed.), Rome Regulations (2nd ed. 2015), Rome II Article 8, para. 21; for the latter see Andreas Spickhoff, in Heinz Georg Bamberger/Herbert Roth/Wolfgang Hau/Roman Poseck (eds.), BeckOK BGB (52nd ed. 2019), VO (EG) 864/2007 Art. 8, para. 4.

230 Higher Regional Court of Munich, docket no. 29 U 3496/11, para. 46.

231 See above at section 3.5.2.2.

232 Austrian Supreme Court of Justice (OGH), docket no. 4 Ob 12/11k, para. 4; Austrian Supreme Court of Justice (OGH), docket no. 4 Ob 190/12p, para. 1.1.; Steffen Pabst, in Thomas Rauscher (ed.), Europäisches Zivilprozess- und Kollisionsrecht Vol. 3 (4th ed. 2016), Artikel 8 Rom II-VO, para. 22; Andreas Spickhoff, in Heinz Georg Bamberger/Herbert Roth/Wolfgang Hau/Roman Poseck (eds.), BeckOK BGB (52nd ed. 2019), VO (EG) 864/2007 Art. 8, para. 4; Matthias Neumayr, in Helmut Koziol/Peter Bydlinski/Raimund Bollenberger (eds.), ABGB – Kurzkommentar (5th ed. 2017), Art. 8 Rom II-VO, para. 4.

233 See Benedikt Buchner, GRUR Int 2005, 1004, 1007; Frank Beckstein, Einschränkungen des Schutzlandprinzips (2010), p. 199.

234 Mary-Rose McGuire, in Christine Budzikiewicz/Marc-Philippe Weller/Wolfgang Wurmnest (eds.), BeckOGK – Rom II-VO (01.12.2018), Artikel 8, para. 175; Josef Drexl, in Franz Jürgen Säcker/Roland Rixecker/Hartmut Oetker (eds.), Münchener Kommentar zum BGB Vol. 12 (7th ed. 2018), Internationales Immaterialgüterrecht, para. 12; Steffen Pabst, in Thomas Rauscher (ed.), Europäisches Zivilprozess- und Kollisionsrecht Vol. 3 (4th ed. 2016), Artikel 8 Rom II-VO, para. 22.

Regulation provides for the application of the law of the country in which the act of infringement was committed. In this context, the Higher Regional Court of Frankfurt left open the question of whether a mosaic approach has to be applied or whether the law of only one state should be applicable (for example the law of the state where the infringement was essentially committed).[235] The Higher Regional Court of Düsseldorf referred this question to the CJEU for a preliminary ruling.[236] In its decision the CJEU rejected a mosaic approach, instead affirming that a court has to make 'an overall assessment of the defendant's conduct in order to determine the place where the initial act of infringement at the origin of that conduct was committed or threatened'.[237]

In this regard, it is noteworthy that it has been a matter of debate whether the term 'committed' used in Article 8(2) Rome II Regulation refers to the place where the event which gave rise to the harm occurred or to the place where the harm arose.[238] Without discussing this problem, the German Federal Court of Justice (BGH) followed the former view because, in the court's opinion, this provision resembled the former German autonomous rule on non-contractual obligations.[239] This position has been confirmed recently by the CJEU's decision in *Nintendo*.[240]

3.6. RULES APPLICABLE TO NON-CONTRACTUAL OBLIGATIONS OTHER THAN TORT

By contrast to the provisions on torts, the impact of Articles 10–12 Rome II Regulation has remained rather limited so far. For example, the only notable issue in practice with Article 10 Rome II Regulation is its distinction from Article 11 Rome II Regulation.[241]

---

235 Higher Regional Court of Frankfurt, docket no. 6 U 4/15, para. 64.

236 Higher Regional Court of Düsseldorf, docket no. I-20 U 225/13, I-20 U 226/13, 20 U 226/13.

237 CJEU, decision of 27 September 2017, Case C-25/16, *Nintendo Co. Ltd v. BigBen Interactive GmbH, BigBen Interactive SA*, ECLI:EU:C:2017:724, para. 103.

238 E.g. Mary-Rose McGuire, in Christine Budzikiewicz/Marc-Philippe Weller/Wolfgang Wurmnest (eds.), BeckOGK – Rom II-VO (01.12.2018), Artikel 8, para. 218 et seq. with further references.

239 German Federal Court of Justice (BGH), docket no. I ZR 253/14, para. 106.

240 CJEU, decision of 27 September 2017, Case C-25/16, *Nintendo Co. Ltd v. BigBen Interactive GmbH, BigBen Interactive SA*, ECLI:EU:C:2017:724, para. 98.

241 See German Federal Court of Justice (BGH), docket no. VIII ZR 266/13, para. 28 (the court expressly left open the question of whether a voluntary payment of another's debt falls in the scope of Article 10 Rome II Regulation or Article 11 Rome II Regulation); Austrian Supreme Court of Justice (OGH), docket no. 6 Ob 29/15f, para. 2.2. (claims for reimbursement of expenses pursuant to section 1042 Austrian General Civil Code are governed by Article 10 Rome II Regulation and not by Article 11 Rome II Regulation; in a prior decision, the court had left this question open: Austrian Supreme Court of Justice (OGH), docket no. 3 Ob 42/14v, para. 2.2.); also see Matthias Neumayr, in Helmut Koziol/Peter Bydlinski/Raimund Bollenberger (eds.), ABGB – Kurzkommentar (5th ed. 2017), Art. 10 Rom II-VO, para. 3.

Article 11 Rome II Regulation has raised the most questions in practice. Apart from the aforementioned decisions, two further German cases have dealt with the scope of Article 11 Rome II Regulation. The Higher Regional Court of Düsseldorf held that Article 4 Rome II Regulation rather than Article 11 Rome II Regulation applies if the intervenor acts *mala fide* because he knows that he is not entitled to take action (*angemaßte Eigengeschäftsführung* or *Geschäftsanmaßung*).[242] Furthermore, the Regional Court of Munich decided that *negotiorum gestio* as understood in Article 11 Rome II Regulation refers to both measures of assistance and measures of interference taken in the interest of another, irrespective whether these measures corresponded with the other's actual or assumed interests.[243] This reflects the prevailing view in Germany.[244] In the latter decision, the court also ruled that the law of the place of execution applies if this place differs from the place of effect.[245] In the court's opinion, the escape clause of Article 11(4) Rome II Regulation provides sufficient protection against alleged manipulations of the connecting factors.[246] Therefore, it rejected the view of most commentators that the place of effect is decisive.[247] Finally, for reasons of legal certainty, the court agreed with the prevailing view in the literature[248] that the law of the country in which the performance started applies

242 Higher Regional Court of Düsseldorf, docket no. I-18 U 27/12, 18 U 27/12, para. 64; this view is shared by Dominique Jakob/Peter Picht, in Thomas Rauscher (ed.), Europäisches Zivilprozess- und Kollisionsrecht Vol. 3 (4th ed. 2016), Artikel 11 Rom II-VO, para. 7; Francis Limbach, in Rainer Hüßtege/Heinz-Peter Mansel (eds.), NomosKommentar Vol. 6 - Rom-Verordnungen (3rd ed. 2019), Artikel 11 ROM II, para. 6; Timo Nehne, IPRax 2012 136, 137.

243 Regional Court of Munich, docket no. 10 O 6084/12, para. 24.

244 Dominique Jakob/Peter Picht, in Thomas Rauscher (ed.), Europäisches Zivilprozess- und Kollisionsrecht Vol. 3 (4th ed. 2016), Artikel 11 Rom II-VO, para. 7; Boris Schinkels, in Gralf-Peter Calliess (ed.), Rome Regulations (2nd ed. 2015), Rome II Article 11, para. 3 et seq.; but see for a more restrictive view Francis Limbach, in Rainer Hüßtege/Heinz-Peter Mansel (eds.), NomosKommentar Vol. 6 - Rom-Verordnungen (3rd ed. 2019), Artikel 11 ROM II, para. 6.

245 Regional Court of Munich, docket no. 10 O 6084/12, para. 47; also see Abbo Junker, in Jan v. Hein (ed.), Münchener Kommentar zum BGB Vol. 12 (7th ed. 2018), Art. 11 Rom II-VO, para. 17; Francis Limbach, in Rainer Hüßtege/Heinz-Peter Mansel (eds.), NomosKommentar Vol. 6 - Rom-Verordnungen (3rd ed. 2019), Artikel 11 ROM II, para. 13; Matthias Neumayr, in Helmut Koziol/Peter Bydlinski/Raimund Bollenberger (eds.), ABGB - Kurzkommentar (5th ed. 2017), Art. 11 Rom II-VO, para. 3.

246 See Regional Court of Munich, docket no. 10 O 6084/12, para. 48.

247 Andreas Spickhoff, in Heinz Georg Bamberger/Herbert Roth/Wolfgang Hau/Roman Poseck (eds.), BeckOK BGB (52nd ed. 2019), VO (EG) 864/2007 Art. 11, para. 6 with further references.

248 Abbo Junker, in Jan v. Hein (ed.), Münchener Kommentar zum BGB Vol. 12 (7th ed. 2018), Art. 11 Rom II-VO, para. 18; Matthias Neumayr, in Helmut Koziol/Peter Bydlinski/Raimund Bollenberger (eds.), ABGB - Kurzkommentar (5th ed. 2017), Art. 11 Rom II-VO, para. 3; for a different view (application of the law of the centre of action), see Peter Huber/Ivo Bach, in Peter Huber (ed.), Rome II Regulation: Pocket Commentary (2011), Article 11 Rome II, para. 22; Francis Limbach, in Rainer Hüßtege/Heinz-Peter Mansel (eds.), NomosKommentar Vol. 6 - Rom-Verordnungen (3rd ed. 2019), Artikel 11 ROM II, para. 13.

if the act is performed in more than one country.[249] Of course, the escape clause of Article 11(4) Rome II Regulation could still lead to the application of the law of the centre of action.[250]

In one of the very few decisions on Article 12 Rome II Regulation, the Higher Regional Court of Koblenz held that a non-contractual obligation arising out of dealings prior to the conclusion of a contract shall only be governed by Article 12 Rome II Regulation if there were at least serious contractual negotiations.[251] Furthermore, the court stressed that a direct link between the non-contractual obligation and the dealings prior to the contract is required,[252] a finding in line with Recital 30 of the Rome II Regulation.[253]

3.7. ESCAPE CLAUSES

There are no typical situations in which the escape clauses have been applied. On the contrary, and in line with the case law on the Rome I Regulation, it has to be noted that the courts have favoured a restrictive approach.[254] Hence, the mere habitual residence of one party has repeatedly been held to be insufficient.[255] Furthermore, in one decision concerning a road traffic accident in Greece, the Higher Regional Court of Nuremberg dealt with the controversial question of the circumstances in which, in spite of a common habitual residence of the parties (in this case, Germany), a return to the *lex loci damni* is possible.[256] The court took a very restrictive position and denied the application of Article 4(3) Rome II Regulation even though the place where the car was registered and insured coincided with the place of the accident.[257] However, a manifestly closer connection could be conceivable if, in addition, all the parties to an accident share the nationality of the place of the accident.[258]

---

249 Regional Court of Munich, docket no. 10 O 6084/12, para. 41.

250 Regional Court of Munich, docket no. 10 O 6084/12, para. 41.

251 Higher Regional Court of Koblenz, docket no. 10 U 108/11 = IPRspr. 2011 Nr. 41.

252 Higher Regional Court of Koblenz, docket no. 10 U 108/11 = IPRspr. 2011 Nr. 41.

253 Christine Budzikiewicz, in Rainer Hüßtege/Heinz-Peter Mansel (eds.), NomosKommentar Vol. 6 – Rom-Verordnungen (3rd ed. 2019), Artikel 12 ROM II, para. 17; Abbo Junker, in Jan v. Hein (ed.), Münchener Kommentar zum BGB Vol. 12 (7th ed. 2018), Art. 12 Rom II-VO, para. 18.

254 See e.g. Austrian Supreme Court of Justice (OGH), docket no. 6 Ob 233/18k, para. 1.3; Regional Court of Munich, docket no. 10 O 6084/12, para. 52; but see for a more liberal approach for financial market torts Regional Court of Stuttgart, docket no. 22 O 101/16, para. 174 et seq.; also see Higher Regional Court of Stuttgart, docket no. 1 U 205/18, para. 47.

255 Higher Regional Court of Koblenz, docket no. 10 U 108/11 = IPRspr. 2011 Nr. 41; Regional Court of Hamburg, docket no. 329 O 343/14, para. 32.

256 See Jan v. Hein, in Gralf-Peter Calliess (ed.), Rome Regulations (2nd ed. 2015), Rome II Article 4, para. 45; Abbo Junker, JZ 2008, 169, 176.

257 Higher Regional Court of Nuremberg, docket no. 4 U 1839/14, para. 24.

258 Higher Regional Court of Nuremberg, docket no. 4 U 1839/14, para. 24.

Moreover, the Regional Court of Munich held in the case of *negotiorum gestio* that an application of the escape clause could be considered if a party manipulates the connecting factors.[259]

As a sharp contrast to these decisions, the Austrian Supreme Court of Justice (OGH) applied Article 4(3) Rome II Regulation when two claimants were affiliated group companies and the place where the tortious act was committed coincided with the place of central administration of one of the claimants.[260]

Furthermore, the Higher Regional Court of Nuremberg held that a manifestly closer connection can be deduced from a marriage between the parties if the dispute is sufficiently linked to the marriage.[261]

Finally, it is worth mentioning that a number of courts have carried out relatively superficial examinations; in particular, they did not determine the applicable law under Article 4(1) or (2) Rome II Regulation. Though it is accepted that a court may leave open the issue of exactly localising the place of damage in complex scenarios,[262] they did not in fact deal with this question at all.[263]

3.8. RULES OF SAFETY AND CONDUCT

In the German and Austrian case law, the application of Article 17 Rome II Regulation has not posed any particular problems to date. In accordance with Recital 34 sentence 2, the Austrian Supreme Court of Justice (OGH) interpreted the term 'rules of safety and conduct' as referring to all regulations having any relation to safety and conduct.[264] In the same vein, the Higher Regional Court of Munich classified the – private – FIS (*Fédération Internationale de Ski*) Rules of Conduct as 'rules of safety and conduct'.[265] Apart from this, the German courts applied Article 17 Rome II Regulation in a number of cases concerning road traffic accidents, taking into account the road safety rules of the place where

259 Regional Court of Munich, docket no. 10 O 6084/12, para. 57.

260 Austrian Supreme Court of Justice (OGH), docket no. 4 Ob 12/11k, para. 5.1.3.

261 Higher Regional Court of Nuremberg, docket no. 7 UF 617/18, para. 32.

262 Jan v. Hein, in Gralf-Peter Calliess (ed.), Rome Regulations (2nd ed. 2015), Rome II Article 4, para. 50; but see Matthias Lehmann, in Rainer Hüßtege/Heinz-Peter Mansel (eds.), NomosKommentar Vol. 6 – Rom-Verordnungen (3rd ed. 2019), Artikel 4 ROM II, para. 140.

263 Higher Regional Court of Cologne, docket no. I-13 U 41/11, 13 U 41/11, para. 16; Regional Court of Düsseldorf, docket no. 14d O 3/15, para. 58; Regional Court of Hamburg, docket no. 329 O 343/14, para. 31; also see on Article 11(4) Rome II Regulation Regional Court of Oldenburg, docket no. 5 O 860/18, para. 20.

264 Austrian Supreme Court of Justice (OGH), docket no. 6 Ob 57/14x, para. 1.

265 Higher Regional Court of Munich, docket no. 3 U 2750/16, para. 17; also see Regional Court of Cologne, docket no. 30 O 53/17, para. 47; but see the criticism by Yannick Diehl, IPRax 2018, 371, 373 et seq.

the accident occurred (as explicitly envisaged by Recital 34 sentence 2),[266] whereas the Austrian Supreme Court of Justice (OGH) also took into account the provisions of Romanian insolvency law.[267]

3.9. SCOPE OF APPLICABLE LAW

Unlike in relation to Article 12 Rome I Regulation, Austrian and German courts were confronted with several issues of characterisation in relation to Article 15 Rome II Regulation. Most notably, the Higher Regional Court of Düsseldorf referred the question to the CJEU for a preliminary ruling on whether Article 15(a) and (g) Rome II Regulation are to be interpreted as meaning that the law determined is also applicable to participatory acts of other persons.[268] However, the CJEU rejected this question as inadmissible because the referring court had not set out the reasons which prompted it to inquire about the interpretation of Article 15 Rome II Regulation.[269] Moreover, the Austrian Supreme Court of Justice (OGH) extensively discussed whether, in the light of Article 15(a) and (f) Rome II Regulation, the right to bring proceedings is characterised as being a procedural or substantive matter.[270] Ultimately, the court left this question open.[271] The same applies to the question whether the ownership of an intellectual property right is governed by Article 8 Rome II Regulation by virtue of Article 15(f) Rome II Regulation.[272] In a more recent decision, the German Federal Court of Justice (BGH) seemed to answer this question in the affirmative.[273] However, the court did not take recourse to Article 15 Rome II Regulation, let alone discuss this point in detail.

266 Higher Regional Court of Hamm, docket no. I-9 U 30/15, 9 U 30/15, para. 3; Higher Regional Court of Munich, docket no. 10 U 2408/16, para. 16; Higher Regional Court of Munich, docket no. 10 U 2443/17, para. 5; Regional Court of Saarbrücken, docket no. 13 S 21/15, para. 20; Regional Court of Kleve, docket no. 5 S 128/11, para. 12; Local Court of Frankenthal, docket no. 3a C 278/16.

267 Austrian Supreme Court of Justice (OGH), docket no. 6 Ob 57/14x.

268 Higher Regional Court of Düsseldorf, docket no. I-20 U 225/13, 20 U 225/13, para. 48; Higher Regional Court of Düsseldorf, docket no. I-20 U 226/13, 20 U 226/13, para. 45; see Annette Kur, GRUR Int 2014, 749, 756.

269 CJEU, decision of 27 September 2017, Case C-25/16, *Nintendo Co. Ltd v. BigBen Interactive GmbH, BigBen Interactive SA*, ECLI:EU:C:2017:724, para. 110.

270 Austrian Supreme Court of Justice (OGH), docket no. 4 Ob 147/14t, para. 1.3. et seq.; Dörte Poelzig/Matthias Windorfer, in Christine Budzikiewicz/Marc-Philippe Weller/Wolfgang Wurmnest (eds.), BeckOGK – Rom II-VO (01.12.2018), Artikel 6, para. 40 et seq.

271 Austrian Supreme Court of Justice (OGH), docket no. 4 Ob 147/14t, para. 1.4.; see Florian Heindler/Bea Verschraegen, in Paul Beaumont et al. (eds.), Cross-Border Litigation in Europe (2017), Austria, p. 243, 247.

272 Austrian Supreme Court of Justice (OGH), docket no. 4 Ob 184/13g, para. 2.2.1.(a).

273 German Federal Court of Justice (BGH), docket no. I ZR 76/11, para. 18.

3.10. PUBLIC POLICY

Like under the Rome I Regulation, Austrian courts have not rendered a single decision concerning an infringement of public policy within the scope of the Rome II Regulation. The German courts, on the other hand, have discussed Article 26 Rome II Regulation in five cases. In the first case, a prima facie evidence rule was unknown to the substantive law;[274] in the second case, the applicable law provided a right to remuneration for their finders on the basis of *negotiorum gestio*;[275] in the third case, the compensation awarded under the applicable law was lower than the compensation awarded under the law of the claimant's habitual residence,[276] in the fourth case, the applicable law prescribed a limitation period of one year in the case of personal injury,[277] and in the fifth case, a respondent who had to provide securities at the interlocutory proceedings stage was not granted damages under the applicable law although the claimant – as was shown in the main proceedings – did not have a claim.[278] In all five cases, the courts ultimately did not find a violation of public policy. In particular, they correctly held that legal provisions deviating from German law do not per se constitute a violation of public policy.[279] Again it becomes apparent that the courts handle quite well the frequent (and quite often obviously unfounded) submissions by parties of a violation of public policy.

3.11. COMPENSATION

The level of compensation to a cross-border victim of a tort has given rise to discussions in very few decisions. As mentioned above, the Regional Court of Neuruppin had to decide whether it is a violation of public policy that the compensation awarded under the applicable law is lower than the compensation awarded under the law of the claimant's habitual residence.[280] The court held that only in exceptional cases could there be considered to be a violation of public policy, for example if the applicable law does not grant any or only very low compensation.[281] Additionally, the court decided that the German rules on damages are not overriding mandatory provisions.[282]

---

274 Local Court of Geldern, docket no. 4 C 356/10, para. 18.
275 Regional Court of Munich, docket no. 10 O 6084/12, para. 109.
276 Regional Court of Neuruppin, docket no. 1 O 120/14, para. 31 et seq.
277 Higher Regional Court of Hamm, docket no. 9 U 44/19, para. 22 et seq.; also see Regional Court of Dortmund, docket no. 7 O 95/15, para. 39.
278 Higher Regional Court of Hamburg, docket no. 3 U 182/17, para. 88 et seq.
279 Higher Regional Court of Hamm, docket no. 9 U 44/19, para. 25; Regional Court of Munich, docket no. 10 O 6084/12, para. 109; Local Court of Geldern, docket no. 4 C 356/10, para. 18.
280 Regional Court of Neuruppin, docket no. 1 O 120/14, para. 31 et seq.
281 Regional Court of Neuruppin, docket no. 1 O 120/14, para. 35.
282 Regional Court of Neuruppin, docket no. 1 O 120/14, para. 34.

In another decision, the Local Court of Frankenthal correctly relied on Recital 33 and took into account all the relevant factual circumstances of the specific victim when it quantified damages for personal injury in the case of a road traffic accident that took place in a state other than that of the victim's habitual residence.[283]

Whereas the case law does not indicate an unsatisfactory level of compensation, some commentators have made the criticism that in the case of multiple victims, the applicable law may differ, which could ultimately lead to the level of compensation differing significantly as well.[284] Therefore, introducing a uniform 'accident statute', leading to the application of the same law to all victims of an accident, has been suggested.[285]

3.12. RULES ON THE BURDEN OF PROOF

With regard to the scope of Article 22 Rome II Regulation, the issue of how to deal with so-called prima facie evidence is highly controversial. On the one hand, the Regional Court of Saarbrücken held that it could be applied even though foreign substantive law governed the legal issue.[286] On the other hand, the Local Court of Geldern decided that rules on the burden of proof in the sense of Article 22 Rome II Regulation have to be understood as substantial rules, even if they are qualified as procedural rules according to national law and irrespective of whether they are written rules or established by case law.[287] Therefore, a prima facie evidence would not apply if it was not recognised by the *lex causae*. Regardless of whether or not one agrees with the latter view, it is unfortunate that the court did not refer this question to the CJEU for a preliminary ruling, since it is clearly not *acte clair*.[288]

---

283 Local Court of Frankenthal, docket no. 3a C 158/13.

284 For example, if one compares the very restrictive German approach to the one taken by US courts, in particular with regard to the possibility of awarding punitive damages.

285 Marc-Philippe Weller/Bettina Rentsch/Chris Thomale, NJW 2015, 1909, 1913 et seq.; but compare Frederick Rieländer, RabelsZ 81 (2017), 344 et seq.

286 Regional Court of Saarbrücken, docket no. 13 S 21/15, para. 22; also see Andreas Spickhoff, in Heinz Georg Bamberger/Herbert Roth /Wolfgang Hau/Roman Poseck (eds.), BeckOK BGB (52nd ed. 2019), VO (EG) 864/2007 Art. 22, para. 3; Jan v. Hein/Hannah Dittmers, in Paul Beaumont et al. (eds.), Cross-Border Litigation in Europe (2017), Germany, p. 145, 153; Christoph Thole, IPRax 2010, 285, 287.

287 Local Court of Geldern, docket no. 4 C 356/10, para. 17; affirmative Abbo Junker, in Jan v. Hein (ed.), Münchener Kommentar zum BGB Vol. 12 (7th ed. 2018), Art. 22 Rom II-VO, para. 8; Matthias Neumayr, in Helmut Koziol/Peter Bydlinski/Raimund Bollenberger (eds.), ABGB – Kurzkommentar (5th ed. 2017), Art. 22 Rom II-VO, para. 1; Ansgar Staudinger, NJW 2011, 650 et seq.; Wolfgang Wurmnest, ZVglRWiss 115 (2016), 624, 639.

288 See also Wolfgang Wurmnest, ZVglRWiss 115 (2016), 624, 639.

3.13. RELATIONS WITH OTHER CONVENTIONS

Germany is not a contracting state to either the Hague Convention of 2 October 1973 on the Law Applicable to Products Liability or the Hague Convention of 4 May 1971 on the Law Applicable to Traffic Accidents, while Austria is a contracting state to the latter. Correctly, Austrian courts concluded that the Convention takes precedence over the Rome II Regulation pursuant to Article 28(1) Rome II Regulation.[289] In two cases, the application of the Convention ultimately led to a different result than the application of Article 4 Rome II Regulation.[290] Even though it cannot be said that either the Hague Conventions ultimately or the Rome II Regulation favour one of the parties in general, the mere existence of different regimes determining the law applicable to certain non-contractual obligations in the Member States is seen as unsatisfactory.[291] This issue should be addressed during the revision process for the Rome II Regulation.

4. APPLICATION OF FOREIGN LAW

In Germany and Austria, foreign law is regarded as 'law' and not as 'fact'.[292] Furthermore, the content of foreign law has to be ascertained and applied *ex officio*. In Austria, this is expressly provided in sections 3 and 4(1) sentence 1 Austrian Act on Private International Law. The wording of the German counterpart – section 293 German Code of Civil Procedure – is less clear, but it is unanimously

289 Austrian Supreme Court of Justice (OGH), docket no. 2 Ob 9/19s; Austrian Supreme Court of Justice (OGH), docket no. 2 Ob 50/16s; Austrian Supreme Court of Justice (OGH), docket no. 2 Ob 35/15h; Austrian Supreme Court of Justice (OGH), docket no. 40/15v; Austrian Supreme Court of Justice (OGH), docket no. 2 Ob 65/16x; Austrian Supreme Court of Justice (OGH), docket no. 136/15m.

290 Austrian Supreme Court of Justice (OGH), docket no. 2 Ob 50/16s, para. 2 (application of the law of the state where the accident occurred instead of the law of the common habitual residence); Austrian Supreme Court of Justice (OGH), docket no. 136/15m, para. 2.4. (application of the law either of the state of registration or of the state in which the vehicles are habitually stationed instead of the law of the state where the damage occurred).

291 See e.g. Matthias Neumayr, in Helmut Koziol/Peter Bydlinski/Raimund Bollenberger (eds.), ABGB – Kurzkommentar (5th ed. 2017), Art. 28 Rom II-VO, para. 2; Martin Illmer, in Peter Huber (ed.), Rome II Regulation: Pocket Commentary (2011), Article 5, para. 7; Wolfgang Wurmnest, ZVglRWiss 115 (2016), 624, 643.

292 Austria: Matthias Neumayr, in Helmut Koziol/Peter Bydlinski/Raimund Bollenberger (eds.), ABGB – Kurzkommentar (5th ed. 2017), §3 IPRG, para. 1; Germany: Hanns Prütting, in Thomas Rauscher/Wolfgang Krüger (eds.), Münchener Kommentar zur Zivilprozessordnung Vol. 1 (5th ed. 2016), §293 ZPO, para. 1; Andreas Spickhoff, ZZP 112 (1999), 265, 286 et seq.

interpreted in this sense.[293] As a consequence, the parties do not need to plead foreign law or to prove it.[294] Additionally, the courts have to apply foreign law in the way it is applied in its originating country. While this is again expressly provided in section 3 Austrian Act on Private International Law, the same applies to German courts by virtue of standing case law.[295] In both countries, the courts have discretion on how to establish the content of foreign law.[296] According to section 293 sentence 1 German Civil Code, the court may base its decision on its actual knowledge of the foreign law. In Austria, section 4(1) Austrian Act on Private International Law is understood in the same way.[297] If the court lacks actual knowledge of the foreign law, it can rely on any auxiliary means deemed appropriate.[298] This follows from section 293 sentence 2 German Civil Code and section 4(1) sentence 2 Austrian Act on Private International Law. The latter contains a non-exhaustive list of possible auxiliary means, such as the assistance of the parties or expert opinions.[299] Due to the

---

293 German Federal Court of Justice (BGH), docket no. XII ZR 266/91, para. 7; German Federal Court of Justice (BGH), docket no. III ZR 151/79, para. 28; Higher Regional Court of Munich, docket no. 10 U 2627/17, para. 27; Michael Huber, in Hans-Joachim Musielak/Wolfgang Voit (eds.), Zivilprozessordnung (16th ed. 2019), §293 ZPO, para. 8; Hanns Prütting, in Thomas Rauscher/Wolfgang Krüger (eds.), Münchener Kommentar zur Zivilprozessordnung Vol. 1 (5th ed. 2016), §293 ZPO, para. 12; Jan v. Hein/Hannah Dittmers, in Paul Beaumont et al. (eds.), Cross-Border Litigation in Europe (2017), Germany, p. 145, 154; Michael Stürner, ZVglRWiss 117 (2018), 1, 2; Clemens Trautmann, ZEuP 2006, 283, 287.

294 Matthias Neumayr, in Helmut Koziol/Peter Bydlinski/Raimund Bollenberger (eds.), ABGB – Kurzkommentar (5th ed. 2017), §2 IPRG, para. 1; Hanns Prütting, in Thomas Rauscher/Wolfgang Krüger (eds.), Münchener Kommentar zur Zivilprozessordnung Vol. 1 (5th ed. 2016), §293 ZPO, para. 6; Ivo Bach/Urs Peter Gruber, in Carlos Esplugues/José Luis Iglesias/Guillermo Palao (eds.), Application of Foreign Law (2011), Austria and Germany, p. 101, 102.

295 German Federal Court of Justice (BGH), docket no. II ZR 192/13, para. 15; German Federal Court of Justice (BGH), docket no. IVb ZR 643/80, para. 19; German Federal Court of Justice (BGH), docket no. II ZR 28/62, para. 7; Higher Regional Court of Munich, docket no. 10 U 2627/17, para. 27.

296 Matthias Neumayr, in Helmut Koziol/Peter Bydlinski/Raimund Bollenberger (eds.), ABGB – Kurzkommentar (5th ed. 2017), §4 IPRG, para. 1; German Federal Court of Justice (BGH), docket no. II ZR 192/13, para. 15; Michael Huber, in Hans-Joachim Musielak/Wolfgang Voit (eds.), Zivilprozessordnung (16th ed. 2019), §293 ZPO, para. 4; Michael Stürner, ZVglRWiss 117 (2018), 1, 2.

297 Walter Rechberger, in Hans W. Fasching/Andreas Konecny (eds.), Kommentar zu den Zivilprozessgesetzen Vol. 2 (2nd ed. 2004), §271 ZPO, para. 1.

298 Austria: Matthias Neumayr, in Helmut Koziol/Peter Bydlinski/Raimund Bollenberger (eds.), ABGB – Kurzkommentar (5th ed. 2017), §4 IPRG, para. 1; Walter Rechberger, in Hans W. Fasching/Andreas Konecny (eds.), Kommentar zu den Zivilprozessgesetzen Vol. 2 (2nd ed. 2004), §271 ZPO, para. 4; Germany: Michael Huber, in Hans-Joachim Musielak/Wolfgang Voit (eds.), Zivilprozessordnung (16th ed. 2019), §293 ZPO, para. 5 et seq.; see in more detail Oliver Remien, in Yuko Nishitani (ed.), Treatment of Foreign Law – Dynamics towards Convergence? (2017), Germany, p. 183, 192 et seq.

299 Matthias Neumayr, in Helmut Koziol/Peter Bydlinski/Raimund Bollenberger (eds.), ABGB – Kurzkommentar (5th ed. 2017), §4 IPRG, para. 1; Walter Rechberger, in Hans W. Fasching/Andreas Konecny (eds.), Kommentar zu den Zivilprozessgesetzen Vol. 2 (2nd ed. 2004), §271 ZPO, para. 4.

good legal infrastructure in Austria and Germany, adequate access to foreign law is provided, at least generally.[300] For example, the courts' libraries are sometimes well equipped with foreign legal literature and there are a number of institutions that can give competent advice on foreign law.[301] If, nonetheless, the foreign law cannot be ascertained within a reasonable time, section 4(2) Austrian Act on Private International Law provides that Austrian law applies. Although there is no such provision in Germany, there is standing case law that German law applies if the court fails to ascertain the foreign law.[302] However, there is no Austrian or German case available in which this has been the case with regard to the law determined by the Rome I Regulation and the Rome II Regulation.[303] Having established that foreign law is treated very similarly in Austria and Germany, there is one important exception: whereas Austrian procedural law (section 502 (1) Austrian Code of Civil Procedure) in principle allows a review of foreign law by the Austrian Supreme Court of Justice (OGH), at least if it is important for legal certainty,[304] the German Federal Court of Justice (BGH) has repeatedly declined such a review,[305] although a recent (but unrelated) change of the wording of section 545(1) German Code of Civil Procedure suggests

---

300 Ivo Bach/Urs Peter Gruber, in Carlos Esplugues/José Luis Iglesias/Guillermo Palao (eds.), Application of Foreign Law (2011), Austria and Germany, p. 101, 106 and 113; Jan v. Hein/Hannah Dittmers, in Paul Beaumont et al. (eds.), Cross-Border Litigation in Europe (2017), Germany, p. 145, 154; Oliver Remien, in Yuko Nishitani (ed.), Treatment of Foreign Law – Dynamics towards Convergence? (2017), Germany, p. 183, 192 et seq.; but see Michael Stürner, ZVglRWiss 117 (2018), 1, 10.

301 See Ivo Bach/Urs Peter Gruber, in Carlos Esplugues/José Luis Iglesias/Guillermo Palao (eds.), Application of Foreign Law (2011), Austria and Germany, p. 101, 113; Jan v. Hein/Hannah Dittmers, in Paul Beaumont et al. (eds.), Cross-Border Litigation in Europe (2017), Germany, p. 145, 154.

302 German Federal Court of Justice (BGH), docket no. IVb ZR 643/80, para. 21 et seq.; German Federal Court of Justice (BGH), docket no. IV ZB 7/77, para. 18; this approach is criticised by some commentators, see Hanns Prütting, in Thomas Rauscher/Wolfgang Krüger (eds.), Münchener Kommentar zur Zivilprozessordnung Vol. 1 (5th ed. 2016), §293 ZPO, para. 61 et seq.

303 But see Higher Regional Court of Munich, docket no. 10 U 2372/16, para. 18, rightly criticising the Regional Court's conclusion that the content of the applicable Portuguese law could not be determined simply because one research institution rejected to prepare an expert opinion.

304 Austrian Supreme Court of Justice (OGH), docket no. 6 Ob 666/84; see Austrian Supreme Court of Justice (OGH), docket no. 10 Ob 147/00s; Walter Rechberger, in Hans W. Fasching/Andreas Konecny (eds.), Kommentar zu den Zivilprozessgesetzen Vol. 2 (2nd ed. 2004), §271 ZPO, para. 4.

305 German Federal Court of Justice (BGH), docket no. II ZR 192/13, para. 14; German Federal Court of Justice (BGH), docket no. V ZB 197/12, para. 18 et seq.; affirmative Wolfgang Krüger, in Thomas Rauscher/Wolfgang Krüger (eds.), Münchener Kommentar zur Zivilprozessordnung Vol. 2 (5th ed. 2016), §545 ZPO, para. 11; Raphael Koch, in Ingo Saenger (ed.), Zivilprozessordnung – Handkommentar (8th ed. 2019), §545 ZPO, para. 10.1; Herbert Roth, NJW 2014, 1224 et seq.

the opposite.[306] Furthermore, in labour law disputes it is undisputed that the German Federal Labour Court (BAG) has to review the application of foreign law by virtue of section 73(1) sentence 1 German Labour Court Act, a provision nearly identical to section 545(1) German Code of Civil Procedure.[307] Instead, the German Federal Court of Justice (BGH) reviews the proper application of section 293 German Code of Civil Procedure and is quite strict in doing so.[308] Ironically, this will sometimes result in a *de facto* review of foreign law.[309]

5. CONCLUSIONS

It will be no surprise that one of the central conclusions of this chapter must be that the courts in Germany and Austria (as probably elsewhere) are often too reluctant to refer questions to the CJEU.[310] Compared to the large number of open questions on the application and interpretation of the Rome I and II Regulations, the number of judgments by the CJEU is far too small. Of course, this is partly due to the CJEU being overloaded with work, but the answer to this problem cannot be the violation of Article 267 TFEU. Rather, options relating to the organisation and structure of the CJEU – general enlargement, special chambers for private international law and/or judicial cooperation, etc. – should be reconsidered.

Secondly, the courts of the Member States should pay more attention to a systematic interpretation as expressly required by Recitals 7 of the Rome I and Rome II Regulations in order to support coherence and predictability.

Thirdly, certain issues deserve a conceptual rethinking, such as certain aspects of Articles 6 and 8 Rome II Regulation, in particular the mosaic principle. The reality seems to go further towards multi-state torts affecting a large number of jurisdictions (e.g. antitrust, intellectual property, internet, personality rights

306 Hanns Prütting, in Thomas Rauscher/Wolfgang Krüger (eds.), Münchener Kommentar zur Zivilprozessordnung Vol. 1 (5th ed. 2016), §293 ZPO, para. 68; Burkhard Hess/ Rudolf Hübner, NJW 2009, 3132 et seq.; Thomas Riehm, JZ 2014, 73, 74; Michael Stürner, ZVglRWiss 117 (2018), 1, 9 et seq.

307 German Federal Labour Court (BAG), docket no. 2 AZR 128/74, para. 38; Oliver Klose, in Christian Rolfs/ Richard Giesen/Ralf Kreikebohm/Peter Udsching (eds.), BeckOK Arbeitsrecht (54th ed. 2019), §73 ArbGG, para. 3.

308 See e.g. German Federal Court of Justice (BGH), docket no. IX ZR 304/13, para. 15; German Federal Court of Justice (BGH), docket no. II ZR 305/01, para. 10 et seq.; also see Oliver Remien, in Yuko Nishitani (ed.), Treatment of Foreign Law – Dynamics towards Convergence? (2017), Germany, p. 183, 212; Ingo Saenger, in Ingo Saenger (ed.), Zivilprozessordnung – Handkommentar (8th ed. 2019), §293 ZPO, para. 19.

309 Thomas Riehm, JZ 2014, 73, 77; Matthias Weller/Stephan Walter, WuB 2017, 231, 235.

310 This view is shared by Florian Heindler/Bea Verschraegen, in Paul Beaumont et al. (eds.), Cross-Border Litigation in Europe (2017), Austria, p. 243, 248.

in general), and the solutions produced by any mosaic principle tend to lose plausibility or seem to require restrictions.[311]

Finally, this chapter supports the proposition that an effort should be made to unify and codify general aspects of the choice-of-law process. For example, one of the most relevant issues in practice turned out to be the requirement (and limits) of a valid choice of law by the parties, in particular where an implicit choice is concerned, by pleading on the basis of a certain substantive law (usually the *lex fori*) for instance. These recurrent issues should be addressed in more detail and more coherently for all EU instruments, or at least for the Rome I and Rome II Regulations, be it in amended recitals or in an entire general instrument ('Rome 0 Regulation'[312]) that could also address issues like the application of foreign law by domestic courts and other pervasive problems affecting the choice-of-law process. This would certainly bolster a central objective of the EU's choice-of-law instruments, which is to increase legal certainty and predictability in cross-border legal relationships.

311 On the level of jurisdiction the latest case law has been restrictive, see e.g. Case C-194/16, *Bolagsupplysningen OÜ Ingrid Ilsjan v. Svensk Handel AB*, ECLI:EU:C:2017:766: no delictual jurisdiction under Article 7(2) Brussels I *bis* Regulation for an action for rectification of defamatory information and removal from the internet before the courts of each Member State in which the information published on the internet is or was accessible.

312 See Stefan Leible/Hannes Unberath (eds.), Brauchen wir eine Rom 0-Verordnung? (2013), passim; Brigitta Lurger/Martina Melcher, Handbuch Internationales Privatrecht (2017), para. 8/12 et seq.

THE APPLICATION OF THE ROME I AND ROME II REGULATIONS IN BELGIUM

Geert VAN CALSTER

1. THE NATIONAL LANDSCAPE

As a preliminary note, it is crucial to underline that Belgium has an abysmal method of publishing – more appropriately hiding – case law. The very highest courts of the land – the Constitutional Court, the Supreme Court in Ordinary (Cour de Cassation/Hof van Cassatie, hereinafter referred to as the 'Supreme Court') and the Supreme Administrative Court (Raad van State/Conseil d'Etat) – each publish their case law on a separate dedicated website (all three of which have search functions that are severely wanting). All other courts do not. Belgium does not seriously take part in the ECLI. Further, Belgium's page on the EU's e-Justice Portal links to juridat.org, which only contains a selection of relevant case law.

The unacceptable reality in Belgium is that editorial committees of legal reviews scramble to network courts and clerks in order to get their hands on interesting case law. This results in a rather haphazard selection of published material, of which one can say with certainty that it does not provide an accurate picture of the application of EU law, or indeed any other law, in the country.[1]

Moreover, anonymity of judgments in Belgium is taken to absurd lengths. Even in commercial cases, the identity of parties is limited to the use of their initials.

Finally, the Supreme Court applies an extreme form of judicial economy, often limiting itself to an observation that the lower courts (typically a court of appeal) have correctly or incorrectly applied the law, without much explicit analysis of the legal reasoning behind it. Its judgments are often extremely short with little indication of what the court suggests the future interpretation should be.

The application of Rome I in the Belgian legal order is greatly facilitated by the insertion of Article 98 paragraph 1 of the Belgian Act on Private International Law,[2] which provides that (my translation):

> 'The law applicable to contractual obligations shall be determined in accordance with [Regulation 593/2008[3]]. Except if otherwise determined by this Act, contractual obligations excluded from the scope of application of [this Regulation] shall be subject to the law determined by [it].'

This proviso is a clear indication of the direction Belgium takes in its development of residual conflict of laws: increasingly, the residual space is filled with a copy/paste of the EU rules.

The same is not true for non-contractual obligations under Rome II. Given the general direction of EU conflict of laws just referred to, had Rome II existed at the time of writing of the Belgian Private International Law Act, it would not have been at all surprising had Belgium followed the copy/paste route (presumably then following Rome II's general *lex loci damni* rule) for the excluded areas. Since the adoption of Rome II, there has been no proposal to amend the Act so as to mirror Rome II for the excluded areas.

The overall direction of the application of Rome I and II (with the express caveat made above, that case law is only reported in piecemeal fashion) is one of fairly unspectacular application, not always entirely correct but not woefully inadequate either.

---

1 A good free source for collated case law (taken from judgments published in reviews) is the site managed by my colleague at Antwerp, Prof. Thalia Kruger: <http://www.eurprocedure.be/?language=nl&form_type=basic>.

2 Act of 16 July 2004, Official State Gazette, 27 July 2004.

3 The Act itself refers to the 1980 Rome Convention.

2. ROME I

2.1. SCOPE OF APPLICATION

2.1.1. Posted Workers

There is first of all continuing difficulty in clearly delineating the exact *scope of application* of, and the congruence between, the various relevant instruments with regard to *posted workers* (tax, social security, and labour law).

The question of the relationship between the Posted Workers Directive and Rome I was raised in *Y.F.M.M.D. v. R.E.D. bvba*, before the Supreme Court.[4] At issue was, among other things, whether the qualification as either an employee or self-employed person could be made under the laws of the forum (Belgium) or rather under the laws of the Member State from which he/she was posted. The Court of Appeal had seemingly done the latter. It was argued before the Supreme Court that this was incompatible with both the Posted Workers Directive and Article 3 (not further defined, but presumably referring to Article 3(3)) and Article 8 (the special regime for employees) of the Rome I Regulation. The Supreme Court however held the argument inadmissible as the conclusion it would lead to had already been held inapplicable as a result of social security legislation.

2.1.2. Distinguishing between Contracts and Torts

Belgian courts do not escape the difficulty of distinguishing between contractual and non-contractual liability, especially in the event of concurrent liability. This issue was highlighted by *NBI v. AG HIV et al*,[5] a case between a Belgian operator of a renewable energy facility, the German installer of a number of its technical facilities, and the latter's insurer and re-insurer. The judgment in substance concerns jurisdiction for provisional measures only, which however triggered a review of Rome I.

The commercial court at Hasselt considered whether it had jurisdiction over the substance of the case, although there was no doubt that it had jurisdiction to order provisional measures. The court entertained the issue of substantive jurisdiction to assist the plaintiff with recognition and enforcement. The Brussels I Recast only accommodates easy recognition and enforcement for measures issued by courts that have jurisdiction over the substance of the case.

---

4 Cass. (2e k.) AR P.15.0846.N, 2 February 2016, *Y.F.M.M.D. v. R.E.D. bvba*.

5 See Kh. Antwerpen (afd. Hasselt) 2 July 2015, Tijdschrift@ipr.be 2015, issue 3, 62 and <http://www.ipr.be/> (13 October 2015).

Section 4.6.2.2 of the relevant certificate annexed to the Brussels I Recast, as the court noted, contains a specific instruction to indicate whether the court that issued the decision for which recognition and enforcement is being sought has jurisdiction over the substance of the matter.

Now, in insurance matters, Article 13(2) Brussels I Recast engages Articles 10, 11 and 12 for actions brought by the injured party directly against the insurer, (only) where such direct actions 'are permitted', which should be read to mean 'are permitted by the applicable law'. Article 13 therefore requires the application of either Rome I or Rome II to then determine jurisdiction. In the case at hand, the obvious difference of opinion between parties related to such direct action existing in the circumstances of the case under Belgian law, but not under German law. The court held that the case was subject to Rome I as it concerned a contractual relationship. It made no reference to CJEU precedent. Recent precedent such as *Brogsitter*,[6] *Ergo*[7] and, even more recently, *Kareda v. Benkö*[8] had not yet been issued at the time of the judgment. However, the court conducted an analysis that would likely have been the same as that of the CJEU. It held that the issue was contractual, given the close link between the action and the contractual arrangement. The Belgian court noted in paragraph 16 of its decision that direct action is an exception to the privity of contracts, and that as such the interests of the insurer need to be taken into account. This, it suggested, would be best achieved by applying the *lex contractus* to the relationship between the insurer and the injured party too. Finally, the court referred to Article 12(1)(b) Rome I, which provides that the *lex contractus* governs in particular, inter alia, 'performance' of the contract.

The plaintiff's argument that Article 9 Rome I's overriding mandatory provisions should apply was summarily dismissed. A mere finding that the Belgian law at issue constitutes mandatory law evidently does not suffice to render it overriding mandatory law.

The eventual decision was therefore taken on the basis of German law, the *lex contractus*, which does not provide for direct action. The court held itself to have jurisdiction for provisional measures only – not over the substance of the case.[9]

---

6 Case C-548/12, *Marc Brogsitter v. Fabrication de Montres Normandes*, ECLI:EU:C:2014:148.

7 Joined Cases C-359/14 and C-475/14, *Ergo Insurance*, ECLI:EU:C:2016:40.

8 C-249/16, *Saale Kareda v. Stefan Benkö*, ECLI:EU:C:2017:472.

9 Although not relevant to the issues under discussion in this volume, it is interesting to note that Justice De Bus adopted a narrow view on the scope of provisional measures available under Article 35 Brussels I Recast. He suggested that the article must not be used to grant parties a measure that they could not obtain in the substantive procedure. Other courts undoubtedly may take a more expansionist view: as long as the measure meets the Van Uden criteria, the nature of the measure is not a limitative requirement.

2.2. RESPECT FOR PARTY AUTONOMY AND THE ESCAPE CLAUSE

Belgian courts of course safeguard party autonomy in choice of law for contracts, and are not tempted to resort to the Regulation's escape clause too readily. *C.H.N. IMPORT- EXPORT & Rafik C v. SOLAREC*[10] concerned the application of Article 5(1) Brussels I, now Article 7(1) Brussels I Recast, and subsequently the application of Article 4 Rome Convention: the 'closest connection'/proper law of the contract, and the presumptions included in same. The court held that Article 4's presumption was just that, and the closest connection in fact was with Algerian law. The case of course shows the relevance of the Rome I Regulation having tightened the presumptions, while at the same time still allowing for rebuttal of the presumptions.

BZ v. SAHK,[11] too, concerned the application of the escape clause of then Article 4(5) of the Rome Convention. The habitual residence of the party carrying out the characteristic performance (the contract concerned maritime towing services) was the Netherlands; however, the Court of Appeal at Brussels held that this was the only factor connecting the contract to the Netherlands, and held in favour of Belgian law.

Article 12 Rome I's list of issues covered by the *lex contractus* was used as an extra argument to support a finding on the privity of contracts. Deciding on direct action by subcontractors in *BB (a company) v. TT et al*,[12] Justice De Bus held that direct action is an exception to the privity of contracts, and that as such the interests of (in this case) the owner in commissioning building works need to be taken into account. Selection of a governing law by the owner enables him to foresee the possibility of direct action by potential subcontractors. Reference was also made by the Court to Article 12(1)(b) Rome I, which provides that the *lex contractus* governs in particular, inter alia, 'performance' of the contract.

On the related issue of Article 18's provisions on burden of proof being subject to the *lex contractus*, in *PE v. Juwelier de Greef*,[13] the Supreme Court succinctly sanctioned the Court of Appeal's application of what was then Article 14 Rome Convention (now Article 18 Rome I), which holds that

---

10 Liege 2011/RG/769, 22 November 2012.

11 Brussel (4e k.) 21 December 2010, Tijdschrift@ipr.be 2011, issue 2, 84.

12 Kh. Antwerpen (afd. Hasselt) (8e k.) no. A/12/3632, A/12/3692, 8 October 2014, RABG 2015, issue 12, 897, note B. Volders; TBH 2015, issue 1, 113 and <http://www.rdc-tbh.be/> (18 February 2015); Tijdschrift@ipr.be 2014, issue 4, 74. The direct action issue is discussed in particular in para. 18 ff. (p. 91 ff. of Tijdschrift@ipr.be 2014, issue 4).

13 Cass. (1e k.) AR C.12.0483.N, 12 April 2013, *P.E. v. Juwelier Degreef nv*; NJW 2013, issue 291, 848, note M. De Potter de Ten Broeck; Pas. 2013, issue 4, 863; RW 2013–14, issue 41, 1615; TBBR 2013, issue 291, 478; TBH 2013, issue 7, 675, summary K. Cox.

determination of the burden of proof is subject to the *lex contractus* (in the case at hand to show that the party was not materially able to supply the contracted goods).

2.3. APPLYING FOREIGN LAW IN ACCORDANCE WITH HOME RULES

In *BNP Paribas v. RL*,[14] on the issue of application of foreign law as *lex contractus*, the Supreme Court held that that law should be applied as it would be by the foreign 'home', reminiscent of the challenge before the Court of Appeal for England and Wales in *Wall v. Mutuelle De Poitiers Assurances*.[15] Under Belgian private international law, foreign law is to be applied in accordance with its interpretation 'at home'. The Supreme Court found that the Court of Appeal's judgment suffered from internal incoherence – conceptually the judgment is neither surprising nor extraordinary.

Gecamines v. RL and Umicore,[16] also concerned the application of foreign law in accordance with the foreign state's own interpretation. This judgment illustrates the Supreme Court's view of statutes of limitation as being covered by the *lex causae* (in the case at issue, Congolese labour law) and not *lex fori*. Neither the Rome Convention nor the Rome I Regulation are clear on how EU private international law sees this issue.

2.4. OVERRIDING MANDATORY LAW

2.4.1. Unamar

One of the most discussed parts of Rome I is of course the rules on overriding mandatory law, and no case on this issue has received more attention than *Unamar*.[17] Of preliminary importance is to note that the case concerns the Rome *Convention's* provisions on overriding mandatory law. The exact relationship

---

14 Cass. (1e k.) AR C.12.0330.F, 28 March 2013, *BNP Paribas v. R.L.*, JT 2013, issue 6525, 437; Pas. 2013, issue 3, 807.

15 [2014] EWCA Civ 138.

16 Cass. (3e k.) AR C.12.0031.F, 18 March 2013, *La générale des carrières et des mines v. R.L., Umicore*, JTT 2013, issue 1161, 271; Pas. 2013, issue 3, 682; RABG 2013, issue 18, 1263, note M. Baetens-Spetschinsky; Rev.dr.étr. 2013, issue 173, 354; RW 2014–15, issue 7, 254; Tijdschrift@ipr.be 2013, issue 2, 11.

17 Cass. (1e k.) AR C.11.0430.N, 12 September 2014, *United Antwerp Maritime Agencies (Unamar) nv v. Navigation Maritime Bulgare*, <http://www.cass.be> (5 October 2014); RABG 2015, issue 9, 661, note S. Cnudde; RW 2015–16, issue 14, 537 and <http://www.rw.be/> (11 January 2016).

between mandatory and overriding mandatory provisions of EU and national law was to some degree clarified by the CJEU in *Unamar*.[18] Belgium's stronger protection of the agent – long held by Belgian law to be of 'special' (in the Rome Convention's jargon) mandatory rules status – gold-plates the regime of the Commercial Agents Directive 86/653. In *Unamar*, the parties had agreed that Bulgarian law would be the applicable law (as well as incidentally that the case would have to go to arbitration in Bulgaria first, circumventing Belgian law, which proscribes the use of arbitration for disputes such as those at issue). The question therefore arose whether Belgian law, the *lex fori*, could justifiably trump Bulgarian law (although no suggestion was made that it did not meet the minimum standard set out in the Commercial Agents Directive). In 2005, Unamar, as the commercial agent, and NMB, as the principal, concluded a commercial agency agreement for the operation of NMB's container liner shipping service. The agreement was for a one-year term and was renewed annually until 31 December 2008. It provided that it was to be governed by Bulgarian law and that any dispute relating to the agreement was to be determined by arbitration in Bulgaria. On 19 December 2008, NMB informed its agents that it was obliged, for financial reasons, to terminate their contractual relationship. The agency contract concluded with Unamar was extended only until 31 March 2009. Unamar brought an action on 25 February 2009 before the Antwerp Commercial Court for an order that NMB pay various forms of compensation provided for under the law on commercial agency contracts. NMB in turn brought an action against Unamar for payment of outstanding freight. In the proceedings brought by Unamar, NMB raised a plea of inadmissibility, alleging that the Belgian court did not have jurisdiction to hear the dispute before it because there was an arbitration clause in the commercial agency contract. In its judgment of 12 May 2009, after joining the cases referred to it by each of the parties, the Commercial Court ruled that NMB's plea of lack of jurisdiction was unfounded. As regards the applicable law in each of the two disputes, the court ruled, inter alia, that Article 27 of the Belgian law on commercial agency contracts was a unilateral conflict-of-law rule that was directly applicable as a 'mandatory rule' and thus rendered the choice of foreign law ineffective.

---

18 Case C-184/12, *Unamar v. Navigation Maritime Bulgare*, ECLI:EU:C:2013:663. The question referred to read 'having regard, not least, to the classification under Belgian law of the provisions at issue in this case (Articles 18, 20 and 21 of the Belgian Law of 13 April 1995 relating to commercial agency contracts) as special mandatory rules of law within the terms of Article 7(2) of the Rome Convention, must Articles 3 and 7(2) of the Rome Convention, read, as appropriate, in conjunction with Council Directive 86/653/EEC of 18 December 1986 on the coordination of the laws of the Member States relating to self-employed commercial agents, be interpreted as meaning that special mandatory rules of law of the forum that offer wider protection than the minimum laid down by Directive 86/653/EEC may be applied to the contract, even if it appears that the law applicable to the contract is the law of another Member State of the European Union in which the minimum protection provided by Directive 86/653/EEC has also been implemented?'.

On appeal, the case was referred for judicial review to the CJEU. The Court did *not* rule on the issue of jurisdiction, given that the Supreme Court had not raised this in its request. This means that the debate on whether Belgian's trumping of foreign arbitration in cases such as these continues to be unresolved. According to NMB, the application of the law on commercial agency contracts to the dispute in the main proceedings could not be considered to be 'mandatory' within the meaning of Article 7(2) of the Rome Convention, given that the dispute concerned a matter covered by Directive 86/653 and the law chosen by the parties was the law of another Member State that had also transposed that Directive into its national law. Thus, according to NMB, the principles of the freedom of contract of the parties and legal certainty preclude the rejection of Bulgarian law in favour of Belgian law.

The CJEU emphasised the harmonising purpose of the Commercial Agency Contracts Directive. It also highlighted that the wording of Article 7(2) of the Rome Convention does not expressly lay down any particular condition for the application of the mandatory rules of the law of the forum. However, the CJEU then insisted (para. 46) that the possibility of pleading the existence of mandatory rules under Article 7(2) of the Rome Convention does not affect the obligation of the Member States to ensure the conformity of those rules with EU law. The CJEU will therefore test such national legislation in light of the TFEU, in particular the exceptions allowed to the EU core freedoms. It may therefore allow such restrictions on the basis that they constitute overriding reasons relating to the public interest (applying the *Arblade* case-law).[19] The classification of national provisions by a Member State as public order legislation applies to national provisions compliance with which has been deemed to be so crucial for the protection of the political, social or economic order in the Member State concerned as to require compliance therewith by all persons present on the national territory of that Member State and all legal relationships within that state.

The plea relating to the existence of a 'mandatory rule' within the meaning of the legislation of the Member State concerned, as referred to in Article 7(2) of the Rome Convention, must therefore be interpreted strictly: for otherwise it risks upsetting the core rule of that Convention, which is parties' freedom to choose the applicable law.

The Court finally held that it is for the Belgian court:

> 'in the course of its assessment of whether the national law which it proposes to substitute for that expressly chosen by the parties to the contract is a "mandatory rule", to take account not only of the exact terms of that law, but also of its general structure and of all the circumstances in which that law was adopted in order to

19 Joined Cases C-369/96 and C-376/96, *Criminal proceedings against Jean-Claude Arblade and Arblade & Fils SARL (C-369/96) and Bernard Leloup, Serge Leloup and Sofrage SARL*, ECLI:EU:C:1999:575.

> determine whether it is mandatory in nature in so far as it appears that the legislature adopted it in order to protect an interest judged to be essential by the Member State concerned. As the Commission pointed out, such a case might be one where the transposition in the Member State of the forum, by extending the scope of a directive or by choosing to make wider use of the discretion afforded by that directive, offers greater protection to commercial agents by virtue of the particular interest which the Member State pays to that category of nationals.' (paragraph 50)

The Court then distinguished *Ingmar*,[20] in which the law that was rejected was the law of a third country. In *Unamar*, on the other hand, the law that was to be rejected in favour of the law of the forum was that of another Member State which, according to all those intervening and in the opinion of the referring court, had correctly transposed Directive 86/653. The Court concluded:

> 'Articles 3 and 7(2) of the Rome Convention must be interpreted as meaning that the law of a Member State of the European Union which meets the minimum protection requirements laid down by Directive 86/653 and which has been chosen by the parties to a commercial agency contract may be rejected by the court of another Member State before which the case has been brought in favour of the law of the forum, owing to the mandatory nature, in the legal order of that Member State, of the rules governing the situation of self-employed commercial agents only if the court before which the case has been brought finds, on the basis of a detailed assessment, that, in the course of that transposition, the legislature of the State of the forum held it to be crucial, in the legal order concerned, to grant the commercial agent protection going beyond that provided for by the directive, taking account in that regard of the nature and of the objective of such mandatory provisions.'

The Court's instructions were therefore clear: there was a strong presumption against mandatory law, in light of the correct implementation by Bulgaria; and the national court had to conduct an in-depth review of the preparatory works of the relevant Belgian Act that transposed the Directive. Discussions in Belgian scholarship reveal that there is no clear view on the exact nature of the 'mandatory' character of the gold-plated provisions.

The CJEU also referred in passing to the Rome I Regulation. This Regulation, as noted, introduces two types of mandatory provisions: simple 'mandatory' ones, with reference to national as well as to EU law and with specific reference to gold-plating for the latter; and 'overriding mandatory' ones, with reference to the *Arblade* criteria but no reference to gold-plating.

It is not therefore entirely certain what the precedent value is of *Unamar* in terms of the future application of the Regulation. The Supreme Court, to which the case was referred back, did not carry out any research into the

20 Case C-381/98, *Ingmar GB Ltd v. Eaton Leonard Technologies Inc.*, ECLI:EU:C:2000:605.

travaux préparatoires of the 1995 Act. It simply annulled the judgment of the Court of Appeal (which now has to be revisited by another Court of Appeal) for 'lack of justification'. In doing so, it (only) referred to the CJEU's dictum, in full, followed by the conclusion that the Court of Appeal had not duly justified its decision. Now, as I noted in my introduction, Belgian Supreme Court judgments are not necessarily easy to read: lengthy and verbatim reference is often made in particular to applicants' legal argument, followed by a much more succinct conclusion by the court itself. Interpretation therefore hinges on being able to identify those specific arguments which may have swayed the court. There is no hint of these in the finding in *Unamar*.

In my view, the CJEU's judgment clearly implies a presumption against the mandatory nature of gold-plated provisions:

> 'only if the court before which the case has been brought finds, on the basis of a *detailed assessment*, that, *in the course of that transposition*, the legislature of the State of the forum held it to be crucial, in the legal order concerned, to grant the commercial agent protection going beyond that provided for by the directive, taking account in that regard of the nature and of the objective of such mandatory provisions.' (emphasis added)

The Court of Appeal at Antwerp had focused its analysis on the correct transposition of the minimum requirements of the Commercial Agents Directive into Bulgarian law. It had referred to discussion in the Belgian parliament, suggesting the altogether limited mandatory character of the Belgian rules from the moment a conflict-of-laws context is present.

In other words, paraphrasing the CJEU, there was no '*detailed assessment*, that, *in the course of that transposition*, [Belgium] held it to be crucial, in [its] legal order, to grant the commercial agent protection going beyond that provided for by the Directive'. Neither, though, did the applicants' arguments, at least as referred to in the Supreme Court's judgment, include such detailed assessment. Had that been present in the applicants' submission, I would have assumed the Court would have referred to it.

There is in my view *no* active requirement for the courts to scout for indications of mandatory character in the provisions of the applicable law at issue. The default position is against such character. In the absence of the presence of *detailed* assessment (not just one or two references to passing discussion in parliament) by the applicants themselves, I believe the Antwerp Court of Appeal has been wrongly rebuked for not having duly considered such assessment.

The case now has gone back to appeal (this time at the Brussels Court of Appeal). The ball must be squarely in the court of the applicants. They are seeking to establish the mandatory character: they ought to provide the 'detailed assessment' that the CJEU requires, by which the Brussels Court of Appeal in its turn may or may not be convinced.

Were the case to have been decided under the Rome I Regulation, I would argue in view of the *effet utile* argument made above, that in the absence of a reference to gold-plating in Article 9, and its presence in Article 3, that the EU's allowance for national rules of overriding mandatory nature does not cover gold-plating.

2.4.2. Orcon

The same provisions of overriding mandatory law under the Rome Convention were also the subject of a judgment by the Supreme Court in *Orcon*.[21] The Court emphasised the exceptional nature of the correction mechanism of overriding mandatory law, holding that the notorious (in the area of conflict of laws at least) Belgian Act on concession agreements only identifies the rules with respect to the ending of the contract as being of overriding mandatory order – not any of the other rules with respect to the contract.

2.5. PROTECTED CATEGORIES: EMPLOYEES

On the question of protected categories – specifically employees – in *J v. Navimer*,[22] the Supreme Court reaffirmed the CJEU's analysis in C-384/10 *Voogsgeerd* of (now) Article 8(3) Rome I's 'place of business through which the employee was engaged'. The Court of Appeal had justifiably ignored the place of actual employment once Article 8(3) is engaged. The applicant's attempt to link the *Voogsgeerd* analysis to the place of actual employment failed.

3. ROME II

3.1. DISTINGUISHING BETWEEN CONTRACTS AND TORTS

It is not always easy to precisely distinguish between contractual and non-contractual relations where the two parties do have a contract. However, that does not mean that it is not in some cases straightforward. In *Antwerp Distribution and Product Operations NV v. Gebroeders Raaphorst Transport BV*,[23] the Commercial Court at Ghent (Dendermonde) had to determine the

21 Cass. (1e k.) AR C.07.0076.N, 28 February 2008, *Orcon v. Carrier Espana S.I.*, Pas. 2008, issue 2, 571; RW 2008–09, issue 18, 751, note D. Mertens.

22 Cass. (3e k.) AR S.09.0013.N, 25 November 2013, *J. v. Navimer*.

23 Kh. Gent (afd. Dendermonde) no. A14/03283, 6 February 2015, Eur.Vervoerr. 2015, issue 2, 238.

applicable law for tort per Article 4 Rome II. The parties' contractual relations were subject to the UN convention on the Contract for the International Carriage of Goods by Road. For damage caused to goods other than the transported goods, however, the Convention provides that damage is determined in accordance with the applicable national law. The Court simply concluded that Belgian law, the *locus damni*, applied per Article 4.

3.2. THE CORE RULE AND THE ESCAPE CLAUSE

A similarly textbook application was at stake in *Oberbank v. Group C AG.*[24] The Commercial Court at Eupen applied Article 4(1) Rome II in the context of discounted bills of exchange. Payment had been effected on the Belgian accounts of the creditor, which was identified as the *locus damni*. There were no indications that any other laws had a closer connection to the case.

In *Google v. Copiepresse and Union of Journalists*,[25] the Brussels Court of Appeal nevertheless assessed the general rule of Article 4(1) Rome II, and contemplated but rejected the closer connection test of Article 4(3) (which in fact it also identified as the general rule: applicable law should be the law with the closest connection). This case involved the distribution, with the violation of copyright, of works protected under Belgian intellectual property law (with a link to the relevant Berne Convention). Google had argued that, under the Berne Convention, the applicable law was the *lex loci delicti commissi*. The Court of Appeal discussed the Berne Convention and decided it instructed that the *lex loci damni* should apply. The Court then considered Rome II for support, ignored Article 8's specific rule on infringement of intellectual property rights (citing the same lack of clarity as it has discussed in relation to the Convention) and came to the same *lex loci damni* rule as under the Berne Convention. Rome II in fact did not apply to the facts at issue *ratione temporis* – the reference to it was one in support of the Berne findings.

3.3. *CULPA IN CONTRAHENDO*

The Commercial Court at Dendermonde followed an exemplary methodological approach to Rome II's rules on pre-contractual liability *culpa in contrahendo* in *N (a Belgian company) v. NN (a Dutch company)*,[26] albeit with an awkward

---

24 Kh. Eupen (1e k.) no. 132/2011, 19 September 2013, DAOR 2013, issue 108, 431; Le droit des affaires (Revue internationale du droit des affaires).

25 Brussel (9e k.) no. 2007/AR/1730, 5 May 2011, AM 2012, issue 2–3, 202; Auteurs en media / Auteurs et média. Also RDTI 2011, issue 44, 35, note A. De Francquen.

26 Kh. Dendermonde (2e k.) 29 December 2011, RW 2013–14, issue 5, 184, note B. Ponet.

pedagogical style (the court takes the reader on an introductory course into commercial conflict of laws). Via Article 12's putative law (the law which would apply, were the contract to be valid), the Court ends up with Dutch law applying to the liability issue.

3.4. APPLYING THE RULES ON UNFAIR COMPETITION

I have often flagged that applying the choice-of-law rules on unfair competition is not straightforward. The Liege Court of Appeal's judgment in *easyJet v. Test-Achats*[27] is a classic illustration of this, and of the challenges of applying conflicts law in cyberspace. Test-Achats/Testaankoop is a consumer organisation. Although the object of its suit was easyJet's general terms and conditions, and although the legal grounds for the suggested illegality of these terms and conditions was the Belgian Act on unfair competition and the protection of the consumer, the Court of Appeal at Liege held that the action was one in tort. It then pointed to Article 6(1) Rome II's reference to the market where the collectivity of consumers' interest is affected. Recital 21, too, was quoted as emphasising that consumer protection is one of the intended aims of competition law and of the laws on unfair competition. The Court then identified some of the provisions of the relevant Belgian Act as being of overriding mandatory law character (*lois de police* or *lois d'application immédiate*), trumping the choice of law made in favour of English law by consumers resident in Belgium who had bought their easyJet tickets via the Internet. It also held that even if one were to contest the application of Belgian law as overriding mandatory law, it would apply by default per Articles 4 and 6(1) Rome II.

This seems a bit of an unnatural sequence of analysis, probably the result of the qualification of the relevant Belgian Act as overriding mandatory law having been discussed by a number of scholarly sources. The Court's view on Article 16 also seems at odds with the CJEU's finding in *Unamar*, referred to above, which points to a strict reading of the possibility of applying national law as overriding mandatory law in the event of harmonisation of the subject matter by EU law (here, consumer law).

If nothing else, both the Court of Appeal's judgment and the judgment at first instance[28] highlight the difficulty in application of Rome II's Article 6 on unfair competition (and acts restricting free competition).

27 Luik (7e k.) no. 2011/RG/1202, 23 April 2013, DCCR 2014, issue 105, 68, note T. Kruger and R. Steennot.

28 Kh. Namen (3e k.) 10 March 2010, DCCR 2011, issue 92–93, 46, note T. Kruger.

Article 6 Rome II was also at issue in *NV D v. NV M*, a 2010 decision of the Court of Appeal at Antwerp[29] concerning two Belgian companies but with the involvement of a Danish lawyer acting on behalf of one of them: this escalated the issue to a conflict-of-laws issue, triggering Rome II. The facts were qualified as constituting unfair trade practices, in that the lawyer, upon the instruction of his client, had forwarded a copy of a judgment in an earlier tussle between the parties to one of the opponent's clients. The Court held that only the interests of the competitor had been affected,[30] therefore engaging Article 6(2), which in turn makes the general rule of Article 4 applicable. The defendant's suggestion that Danish law was manifestly more closely connected was rejected: the mere physical presence of the lawyer in Denmark did not suffice to displace the overall rule of Article 4(1) or indeed, as in the case at issue, the specific exception of Article 4(2) (person claimed to be liable and person sustaining damage with domicile in the same Member State).

29 Antwerpen (5e k.) no. 2009/AR/2316, 25 March 2010, Jaarboek Marktpraktijken 2010, 386, note B. Keirsbilck. A similar decision (only impact on the competitor) was reached by the Court of First Instance in Brussels on 20 April 2018, Rb Brussel, 20 April 2018, Tijdschrift@ipr.be 2018, issue 2, 53.

30 I do always find this a tricky call. I can think of very few infringements of competition law or unfair trading practices that are so removed from the market that there is no impact on consumers.

THE APPLICATION OF THE ROME I AND ROME II REGULATIONS IN BULGARIA

Nikolay NATOV* and Vassil PANDOV

* Professor Nikolay Natov sadly passed away during the project.

1. THE NATIONAL LANDSCAPE

1.1. ROME I

Before the Rome I Regulation came into force on 17 December 2009, the Rome Convention on the Law Applicable to Contractual Obligations[1] applied in Bulgaria for a relatively short period – between 15 January 2008 and 17 December 2009. Bulgarian legislation has not been adapted in line with the Rome I Regulation and there are no national rules facilitating the application of the Regulation. However, the Bulgarian Code of Private International Law (CPIL) had been intentionally brought into line with the conflict-of-law rules of the Rome Convention prior to the accession of Bulgaria to the European Union on 1 January 2007. The ratification of the Rome Convention was an obligation carried out by Bulgaria under the rules of Annex I to Article 3(3) of the Protocol concerning the conditions and arrangements for admission of the Republic of Bulgaria and Romania to the European Union.[2] In the course of the national legislative procedure, Bulgarian lawmakers decided to incorporate into the CPIL the provisions of the Rome Convention and, furthermore, to draft a special rule regarding the application of national rules in line with the Convention. According to Article 103 CPIL, in the interpretation and application of the provisions of the CPIL, regard must be had to the fact that these provisions are aligned with the Rome Convention, and to the need to achieve uniformity in the manner in which the rules of the Rome Convention are interpreted and applied in the states for which it is in force. After the entry into force of the Rome Convention, and now of the Rome I and II Regulations, this provision (Article 103 CPIL) has lost its importance, but it has not been expressly removed from the text of the Code.

The rules of the Rome I Regulation have not been extended beyond their scope of application as defined in the Regulation. Bulgarian courts are not tempted to widen the scope of application of the Rome I Regulation and they stick to its original scope and meaning.

1 Ratified by Law of Bulgarian Parliament of 07 March 2007, published in State Gazette vol. 24 of 20 March 2007.

2 [2005] OJ L 157/29.

Using a specialised e-database of national law to search for court practice on the application of the Rome I Regulation resulted in about 70 cases found.[3] There are naturally court cases in which the foreign element in the relationships and the proceedings go unnoticed by the courts because the parties remain silent about it and, as a result, there is no reference to Rome I Regulation. Nevertheless, the body of cases is enough to convey the main trends in the application in practice of the Rome I Regulation in Bulgarian courts.

The most commonly applied provisions of the Rome I Regulation are Articles 4(1)(a) and (b), 3(1), 5 and 6. Our analysis showed that relatively few of the decisions had wrongly applied Rome I Regulation (about five per cent). The source of mistakes is the Regulation's temporal scope – *ratione temporis*. Some courts apply different sources of law that were successively applicable, but not at the same time, to the same contracts simultaneously. For a series of contracts concluded between 2008 and 2010, the court founded its reasoning on the CPIL, the Rome Convention and the Rome I Regulation, without specifying which one was relevant to the separate agreements. The applicable law was determined on the basis of Article 4 of the Rome Convention, Article 94 CPIL and Article 4 of the Rome I Regulation. The underlying and stated ratio is that all three provisions of different sources contain the one and same conflict-of-law rule:

> 'when parties have not exercised freedom of choice, the contract is governed by the law of the country with which it is most closely connected, the closest connection being presumed to be with the country where the party required to effect the characteristic performance of the contract has his habitual residence.'[4]

Even when court defines the applicability of the Rome I Regulation *ratione temporis* to the contract in the case, the provision of Article 94 CPIL is cited as analogous to Article 4(1)(a) of the Rome I Regulation, without paying special attention to the fact that Article 94 CPIL, being harmonised with Rome Convention, contains the general presumption of closest connection. Finally, the applicable law of the country where the seller of goods is habitually resident is applied on the grounds of Article 4(1)(a) of the Rome I Regulation and Article 94 CPIL. By this the court ignores the prevalence of the Regulation and the impossibility to refer to different sources of law.[5]

In conclusion, courts feel in a way more comfortable arguing the definition of applicable law based on both national and EU conflict-of-law sources. It is interesting that there is no choice of the wrong set of rules; instead there is a reference to two or three different set of rules, with no special attention being paid to their subsequent and mutually exclusive operation in time. On the other

3 As of April 2020.
4 Decision 644 of 11.04.2016 Sofia City Court, commercial case 8529/2013.
5 Decision 176 of 05.11.2014 Dobrich District Court, commercial case 76/2014.

hand, we have not identified a trend towards widening or wrongly interpreting the material scope of the Rome I Regulation.

1.2. ROME II

Bulgarian national sources of private international law were not amended before or after the entry into force of the Rome II Regulation in order for additional rules similar to the ones of the Regulation to be inserted into Bulgarian law. There are no provisions concerning or facilitating the operation of the Rome II Regulation. However, like for the Rome I Regulation, the Bulgarian CPIL was drafted in line with the Proposal for the Rome II Regulation.[6] The CPIL's provisions are pretty much the same as those in the Proposal.[7] Thus, the CPIL regulates non-contractual obligations arising out of privacy and personality rights. Although after intensive discussions these kinds of torts were dropped from the final text of the Rome II Regulation, the CPIL was enacted in 2005[8] before the publication of the final Rome II Regulation.[9] As per Article 108(1) CPIL, entitled 'Violation of Rights Relating to the Personality', the obligations arising from a violation of personality rights by mass media – and in particular print publications, radio, television or other means of proliferation of information – shall be governed, upon choice of the person suffering damage, by:

1. the law of the state in which the said person is habitually resident, or
2. the law of the state within the territory of which the damage occurred, or
3. the law of the state of the habitual residence or the place of business of the person claimed to be liable.

After the entry into force of the Rome II Regulation, its scope has not been subject to any extension or conversion. The defamation cases are governed either by Article 108 CPIL in cases of tort caused by the media, or by the general provision of Article 105 CPIL in all instances not related to the media.

There is no great variety or abundance of Bulgarian jurisprudence on the Rome II Regulation. About 30 cases were tracked down using specialised e-database of national law.[10] Almost all claims referring to the Rome II Regulation are related to damages resulting from traffic accidents and the respective responsibility of insurers or compensation bodies under different schemes of

6 COM (2003) 427 final of 22 July 2003.
7 B. Musseva in 'Party Autonomy in Private International Law', Society of SYLFF Fellows in Bulgaria (SSFB), Sofia 2008, p. 44.
8 State Gazette vol. 42 of 17 May 2005.
9 [2007] OJ L 199/40.
10 As of 15 April 2020.

coverage. The most commonly applied provisions of the Rome II Regulation are without doubt the general tort rules of Article 4. Due to the considerable difference in the number of court decisions referring to Rome I and to Rome II, this chapter deals more extensively with the practice on the Rome I Regulation. As a results, not all of the sections below refer to the Rome II Regulation because of the lack of authorities on the matter.

2. THE OPERATION OF THE ROME I AND ROME II REGULATIONS IN PRACTICE

2.1. *LOIS DE POLICE* (OVERRIDING MANDATORY PROVISIONS)

The court practice is not really representative of the position of the Bulgarian judiciary on the application of *lois de police* or overriding mandatory rules. The requirement for notification on every instance of export of wastes as per Regulation 1013/2006 on shipments of waste is treated as a public law matter and not related to the contract law regime as a *loi de police.*[11] After defining the applicable law as per Article 4(1)(a) of the Rome I Regulation, the court has been addressed by parties with objections that intra-EU shipments of waste were not duly accompanied by the documentation required under Article 18 of Regulation 1013/2006, the lack of said mandatory documentation being directly related to the performance of obligations under the contract. In fact, the provisions of Regulation 1013/2006 pertaining to shipments of waste between Member States can be treated as mandatory and enforceable irrespective of the applicable law because their purpose so requires and the situation is closely connected with the EU.[12] However, the court did not apply Article 9(1) of the Rome I Regulation and Article 18 of Regulation 1013/2006 as community *lois de police* even though the situation was intra-EU, stating that the public nature of the substantive rules is a matter of administrative law and provides for a sanction. An example of *lois de police* in court practice are the rules related to conditions for acquiring rights *in rem* by foreign citizens over real estate on the territory of Bulgaria, including when the transfer of rights stems from a contract.[13] On the contrary, the rules for the period of prescription as per foreign law (UK Limitation Act 1980) do not qualify as overriding mandatory provisions.[14]

---

11 Decision 1003 of 21.12.2015 Varna District Court, commercial case 1537/2015.

12 Opinion of AG Szpunar in Case C-507/15, *Agro Foreign Trade & Agency Ltd v. Petersime NV*, para. 41. Case C-381/98, *Ingmar* [2000] ECR I-09305.

13 Decision 646 of 03.12.2014 Rousse District Court, civil case 977/2014.

14 Decision 23 of 15.01.2020 Varna Appellate Court, commercial case 606/2019.

In Bulgarian law theory and court cases, instances of substantive rules that have characteristics of overriding mandatory rules include: public law sources regarding the regime for the import and trade of medicines and weapons; rules on the preservation of nature and ecological standards; provision of medical care; rules on the protection of competition and consumers, etc.[15] This first group of rules protect society as whole, whereas the second group of overriding mandatory rules are aimed at defending individuals– rules for the protection of consumers; rules for full or partial exemption from civil liability for breach of contractual obligation.[16]

Having in mind the too-flexible attitude of Bulgarian courts to EU mandatory rules, there are serious doubts about the practical operation of Article 9(3) of the Rome I Regulation related to mandatory provisions of the law of the country where the obligations arising out of the contract have to be or have been performed. The attitude of Bulgarian courts is to treat foreign mandatory rules more like fact or (*local data*),[17] closer to the operation of Article 17 of the Rome II Regulation.[18]

2.2. PARTY AUTONOMY

2.2.1. Rome I

The jurisprudence of Bulgarian courts is indicative of the level of will of the parties to enter into choice-of-law agreements and especially whether the choice is expressly or clearly demonstrated by the terms of the contract or the circumstances of the case, including the behaviour of parties, as per Article 3 of the Rome I Regulation. In several cases, the choice of law was contained in general terms and conditions drafted and presented by one of the parties to the contract. The established notion is that the implied choice of law could be accepted on the basis of standard form contracts and general terms and conditions to contracts that contain choice-of-law agreements.[19] If invoices for the price of goods contain a reference to a set of general terms and conditions predefined by the seller, the choice-of-law provision in such terms and conditions can be upheld only if the buyer has expressly been informed about

15 N. Natov, *Commentary on the Code of Private International Law*, Ciela Soft and Publishing, Sofia 2006, pp. 389–390.

16 Supra n. 14.

17 B. Musseva, *Tort in Private International Law*, Sibi, Sofia 2011, p. 248.

18 Supra n. 5.

19 Report on the Convention on the law applicable to contractual obligations by Mario Giuliano, Professor, University of Milan, and Paul Lagarde [1980] OJ C 282/1; D. Sarbinova, 'Some Tendencies to Contract Choice of Law and its Limits' (2012) 2 *Legal World* 80, 83.

the date and the contents of the terms and conditions. Otherwise there is no guarantee for the buyer that the terms and conditions referred to are the same as those put forward by the seller:[20]

> 'Since invoices do not specify the general terms by their date or by name, and since the defendant disputes the contents of the terms presented by the claimant, the phrase "in addition to our general terms and conditions" in the invoices issued by the seller shall not be tantamount to a reference to the specific terms and conditions.'

In the case of an offer for road transport of goods including a provision that shipment is governed by the UN Convention on the Contract for the International Carriage of Goods by Road and the national law of an EU Member State, the general acceptance of the offer by the shipper is not decisive to entering into a choice-of-law agreement if the other party has not separately and expressly given consent to the party autonomy provision.[21]

The courts clearly distinguish between choice of law for contracts and the nationality of applicable law to the court proceedings. The objection that Bulgarian laws are to be applied, since Bulgarian courts are competent to hear the case and since the parties have exchanged statements (claim and response to the claim) following the Bulgarian Code of Civil Procedure, is unfounded. The procedural law (*lex magistratus*) is not to be mixed up with applicable law to the substance matter of the dispute.[22]

Courts have expressly discussed the relationship between party autonomy and the application of the UN Convention on Contracts for the International Sale of Goods (CISG). If the application of the CISG has not been expressly excluded by the parties, a choice of the law of a contracting state to the Convention will lead to its application:[23] since the CISG is part of the legal system of the state whose law has been chosen, it follows that it will apply to the case. The presumed application of the CISG to contracts for the sale of goods in instances where the parties have chosen the laws of a contracting state to the convention under Article 3 of the Rome I Regulation is also prevalent in Bulgarian private international law theory.[24] However, a different view states that a choice of the substantive law of a CISG contracting state excludes the application of the CISG,[25] since, in the absence of an autonomous choice of laws by the parties, it is the CISG that generally governs the sale of goods. The choice of law is construed as willingness to submit the contract not to the CISG but to the chosen law.

---

20 Decision of 10.11.2014 Sofia County Court, civil case 52412/2011.

21 Decision of 29.12.2014 Belogradchik County Court, civil case 83/2013.

22 Supra n. 14.

23 Decision 1419 of 08.08.2014 Sofia City Court, commercial case 5078/2011.

24 D. Sarbinova, supra n. 19, p. 88.

25 Decision 1419 of 08.08.2013 Sofia City Court, commercial case 5078/2011.

In conclusion, the overall attitude of Bulgarian jurisprudence toward implied choice of law as per Article 3(1) of the Rome I Regulation could be defined as restrictive and based on high standards of legal certainty. In most cases, parties have to prove not only that general terms, offers, invoices and other documents exchanged between them contained a choice-of-law agreement, but also that the counterparty has either expressly received the actual draft agreement containing the choice-of-law clause or accepted it. On the other hand, in court practice there are no instances of excessive use of *dépeçage* – the application of different laws to different part or parts of the contract under Article 3(1) of the Rome I Regulation. As to the use of *lex mercatoria*, in Bulgaria it is not permissible, including in arbitration proceedings, since Article 38(1) of the International Commercial Arbitration Act limits party autonomy to the 'law', and not 'rules of law', chosen by parties. A possible change to the Rome I Regulation permitting the application of soft law and commercial usages sources to international commercial contracts would bring more flexibility and competitiveness to EU forums.

There is an established pattern of Bulgarian courts disregarding, and not considering as valid, choice of law for compensation claims against air carriers (mostly for the laws of the home state of the carrier), as per Article 5(2)(b) of the Rome I Regulation. The jurisprudence is related to the application of Regulation (EC) No. 261/2004 of the European Parliament and of the Council of 11 February 2004 establishing common rules on compensation and assistance to passengers in the event of denied boarding and of cancellation or long delay of flights, and repealing Regulation (EEC) No. 295/91. The choice-of-law clause contained in the general terms and conditions of carriers is considered to be an unfair term as per Directive 93/13/EEC of 5 April 1993 on unfair terms in consumer contracts as amended by Directive 2011/83/EU of the European Parliament and of the Council of 25 October 2011 on consumer rights. The courts are of the position that Article 5(2) together with Recitals 32 and 23 of the Rome I Regulation exclude passengers' contracts from the scope of the special rules concerning consumer contracts (Article 6 of the Rome I Regulation), but this cannot deprive natural persons from special protection. The choice-of-law provision in the general terms and conditions is considered unfair since it could not reasonably be expected that the average informed customer would choose the law of a state, with which he or she has no economic or personal connection, having in mind that the centre of the vital interests of the consumer is in another Member State. The courts make no reference to the Judgment of the CJEU of 28 July 2016 in Case C-191/15, *Amazon*, where it was observed that choice-of-law agreement in consumer cases cannot be treated as unfair per se. The choice of applicable law is unfair only in so far as it displays certain specific characteristics inherent in its wording or context which cause a significant imbalance in the rights and obligations of the parties. The unfairness of such a term may result from a formulation that does not comply with the requirement of being drafted in plain and intelligible language set out in Article 5 of Directive 93/13. Where the effects of a term are specified by mandatory statutory provisions, it is essential that the carrier informs the passenger of those provisions.

2.2.2. Rome II

In the study, no cases of party autonomy in non-contractual obligations were identified. This is related to the dominant position before the adoption of the CPIL and the Rome II Regulation that, since substantive tort rules are mandatory in nature, choice of law is not permitted. Since most claims arise from traffic accidents with parties habitually resident in different countries, the probability of reaching a choice-of-law agreement after the event is very low. In practical terms, party autonomy, as per Article 14(1)(b) of the Rome II Regulation, can be identified in complex commercial contracts that expressly make the parallel tortious relationship subject to the same substantive regime of laws as the contract, also chosen by the parties.

2.3. ABSENCE OF CHOICE OF LAW

2.3.1. Rome I

The reform of the general conflict-of-law rule of Article 4(1) of the Rome Convention in favour of fixed and special rules related to the type of contractual relationship has been adhered to by court practice and legal theory. The improved foreseeability of conflict-of-law rules brings more certainty in the process of application for the judiciary as well as for the parties.[26] Jurisprudence confirms that the rules of the CPIL, the Rome Convention and the Rome I Regulation are all based on the underlying principle of the closest connection being with the country of habitual residence of the party owing the characteristic performance.[27] Moreover, in their desire to reaffirm the application of the presumption of the closest connection to the habitual residence of the party with the characteristic performance, courts have applied the fixed criteria of Article 4(1) alongside (2) to a contract for services.[28] Both the provisions of Article 4(1) and Article 4(2) of the Rome I Regulation are cited as grounds for applying the law of the country of the provider of services. The provision of Article 4(2) of the Rome I Regulation is considered a connecting factor confirming the principle in Article 4(1) stating the presumption. This mistake

---

26 B. Musseva, 'Regulation Rome I', in N. Natov (ed.) commentary, Ciela, Sofia 2009, pp. 89–90.

27 Decision 200 of 11.07.2013 Varna Appellate Court, commercial case 332/2013.

28 Decision 83 of 21.10.2013 Vratsa District Court, commercial case 43/2013.

of simultaneous application of mutually exclusive provisions is due to the texts of Article 4(1) and (2) of the Rome Convention being similar to the default rule of Article 4(2) of the Rome I Regulation.

Otherwise, fixed rules do not pose difficulties to courts in defining their scope – Article 4(1)(f) being correctly applied to distribution agreements,[29] Article 4(1)(a) to contracts for the sale of goods,[30] Article4(1)(b) to an agency contract[31] and so on. The list of rules for different contractual relations brings added value to court practice since not all of the connecting factors are related to the habitual residence of a party (Article 4(1)(c), (g) and (h)), but the principle of habitual residence of the party with characteristic performance is not relevant for defining the applicable law. However, since not all factual cases could be defined in conflict-of-laws rules, keeping the general presumption in Article 4(2) of the Rome I Regulation strikes a fair balance, which is approved of by the Bulgarian judiciary.

2.3.2. Rome II

All the court decisions examined where the Rome II Regulation was applied were connected specifically to the operation of Article 4(1), which is the general localisation principle for the country where the damage occurs, irrespective of the country in which the event giving rise to the damage occurred and irrespective of the country or countries in which the indirect consequences of that event occur. In general, it could be said that courts do not encounter great difficulties in interpreting and following the logic of the place of direct and initial injury as per Recital 17 of the Rome II Regulation.[32] In instances of pecuniary damage to property, the courts do not take into account the country where the damage was rectified and the country where the cost of rectifying the damage was determined. For example, in instances of traffic accidents on the territory of Bulgaria, the fact that the affected vehicle was transported to and serviced in another Member State does not influence the fact that the initial damage to the property was suffered in the territory of Bulgarian courts.[33] The place where the car was repaired and where the cost of the repairs has been paid

---

29 Decision of 10.11.2014 Sofia County Court, civil case 52412/2011; Injunction 78 of 18.04.2017 Supreme Court of Cassation, Commercial Division, 2nd commercial circuit, commercial case 645/2016.

30 Decision 1341 of 24.07.2013 Sofia City Court, commercial case 3150/2011.

31 Decision 1192 of 01.07.2019 Sofia City Court, commercial case 58/2018.

32 Decision 2390 of 24.03.2016 Sofia City Court, civil case 8592/2015; Decision 110 of 10.03.2014 Kiustendil County Court, civil case 835/2013; Decision 2379 of 05.06.2013 Plovdiv County Court, civil case 1061/2012.

33 Decision 16198 of 11.08.2014 Sofia City Court, civil case 14722/2013; Decision of 13.02.2012 Sofia City Court, civil case 16068/2011.

represents an indirect consequence of the event, and taking that into account would undermine the clear and predictable determination of the substantive law. The Supreme Court of Cassation reaffirmed this practice, stating that the rule in Article 4(1) of the Rome II Regulation accepts as the principal criterion for establishing the nexus of the damage the place where initial injury occurred, whereas the place where the costs of rectifying the damage were suffered and paid is not relevant to determine which country's tort law is applicable.[34]

Bulgarian courts have taken opposing positions in relation to the place where the damage occurred in cases of personal damages. Even when the damage as a result of traffic accident occurred abroad, the court went on applying the *lex fori* without mentioning the rules of Article 4(1) of the Rome II Regulation.[35] In cases of progressive additional worsening of the health of the damaged person after returning to their country of habitual residence, the fact that the initial harm was suffered abroad is disregarded.[36] If the victim has returned to his/her country of residence very shortly (one day) after the accident, *loci damni* becomes the country of habitual residence of the victim and not the country where the initial injury occurred.[37] They have interpreted the term 'the place in which the damage occurs' within the meaning of Article 4(1) of the Rome II Regulation in the context of claims for compensation for non-material damage brought by close relatives of a person who has died as a result of a road traffic accident that occurred in a state different from the one where family members were resident and where they suffered the damage. Some courts have accepted that personal damages caused by the death of a close relative in a traffic accident are sustained in the country where the claimant has his or her habitual residence and not the country where the death occurred.[38] The place of residence of a person who undergoes psychological trauma and emotional suffering caused by the death of a relative represents, as per Article 4(1) of the Rome II Regulation, the place where the damage occurred, irrespective of where the accident took place.[39] On the other hand, some courts have accepted that the only location that is important in establishing the place where the damage occurred is of the place where the tort initially and directly arose – i.e. the country where the road accident occurred. The latter approach also prevails in cases of personal emotional and psychological suffering caused by the death of relative in a state that is different from the habitual residence of the claimant.[40]

---

34 Injunction 898 of 27.11.2015 Supreme Court of Cassation, Commercial Division, 1st commercial circuit, commercial case 3751/2014.

35 Decision 3737 of 23.05.2019 Sofia City Court, civil case 2858/2017.

36 Decision 4923 of 20.07.2018 Sofia City Court, civil case 6200/2015.

37 Decision 6173 of 21.08.2019 Sofia City Court, civil case 159/2018; Decision 4380 of 17.06.2019 Sofia City Court, civil case 9742/2017.

38 Decision 7850 of 25.11.2013 Sofia City Court, civil case 3423/2010.

39 Decision 6667 of 01.10.2015 Sofia City Court, civil case 8115/2012.

40 Decision 7830 of 16.11.2015 Sofia City Court, civil case 10390/2013.

It should be noted that this varying practice by Bulgarian courts took place prior to the official, authoritative interpretation of the place where the damage occurs in instances of personal damages arising from the death of a relative provided by the CJEU in the *Florin Lazar* case.[41] The CJEU took the view that the damage sustained by the close relatives of the deceased must be regarded as the indirect consequences of the accident and that the country where the direct damage occurs is the country where the physical injuries of the deceased were suffered, no matter where the habitual residence of the affected person happens to be. After the decision of the CJEU in the *Florin Lazar* case, the highest national instance in Bulgaria, the High Court of Cassation, strictly followed the reasoning of CJEU that the suffering of relatives amounts to indirect consequence. The place of damage for all claims regarding traffic accidents is the place where the accident and initial injury took place.[42]

An interesting approach has been found in applying the rule of Article 4(2) of the Rome II Regulation as to the law of the common habitual residence of the person claimed to be liable and the person sustaining damage. The claim was filed by a natural person with habitual residence in Bulgaria against the Bulgarian national compensation body as per the Fourth Motor Insurance Directive (Directive 2000/26/EC) called the Guarantee Fund. The place of the injury and the harm occurred in another Member State. The court, although stating that the compensation body was responsible for the third party's tort, accepted that, since the person that inflicted the damage was not found and since both parties (the compensation body and the victim) had common habitual residence in Bulgaria, Bulgarian law applied.[43] This jurisprudence has not been followed by other courts who have, in similar circumstances, applied the law of the country in which the initial injury occurred, as per Article 4(1) of Rome II Regulation, irrespective of the fact that the defendant is a compensation body with habitual residence in Bulgaria.[44]

---

41 Case C-350/14, *Florin Lazar*, decision of 10.12.2015.

42 Injunction 154 of 19.07.2017 Supreme Court of Cassation, Commercial Division, 2nd commercial circuit, commercial case 557/2017; Injunction 342 of 10.07.2017 Supreme Court of Cassation, Commercial Division, 1st commercial circuit, commercial case 1435/2017. Also – Decision 313 of 05.02.2018 Sofia Appellate Court, civil case 4039/2017; Injunction 546 of 09.08.2019 Supreme Court of Cassation, Commercial Division, 2nd commercial circuit, commercial case 2790/2018; Injunction 544 of 02.08.2018 Supreme Court of Cassation, Commercial Division, 2nd commercial circuit, commercial case 520/2018; Injunction 425 of 14.06.2019 Varna Appellate Court, commercial appeal case 302/2019; Decision 519 of 23.01.2019 Sofia City Court, civil case 10962/2015; Decision 8804 of 23.12.2019 Sofia City Court, civil case 10378/2018; Decision 2506 of 23.04.2018 Sofia City Court, civil case 3357/2015; Decision 3932 of 31.05.2019 Sofia City Court, civil case 16627/2015; Decision 1188 of 19.02.2019 Sofia City Court, civil case 5480/2014; Decision 8048 of 30.11.2017 Sofia City Court, civil appeal case 3593/2017.

43 Decision 421 of 16.01.2020 Sofia City Court, civil case 9838/2018.

44 Decision 485 of 11.12.2019 Rousse District Court, civil case 309/2018.

A possible flaw in the interpretation of the CJEU's jurisprudence and, namely, the decisions in Joined Cases C-359/14 and C-475/14, *ERGO Insurance*, which made a difference between the legal regime governing the right of a third party to substitute the damaged person and the regime of the tort responsibility, is to apply to the entitlement of compensation as well as the method of determining the amount of non-pecuniary damages in accordance with the insurance contract law (Rome I Regulation).[45]

2.4. ESCAPE CLAUSES

2.4.1. Rome I

The escape clauses of Articles 4(3), 5(3) and 8(4) of the Rome I Regulation are an exception to the general conflict-of-law rules that define the applicable law using fixed criteria. Bulgarian jurisprudence adopts a strict and conservative attitude towards the use of escape clauses, thus being in line with the reform brought in with the text of Article 4(3) of the Rome I Regulation, as compared to Article 4(5) of the Rome Convention. The new general escape clause rule of Article 4(3) of the Rome I Regulation requires the qualified conditions of being 'clearly' demonstrated and 'manifestly more closely connected' to be met. The courts are free, based on the circumstances of the case, to take into account all the possible connections of the contract, regarding the parties or regarding its contents, to a country different from that of the fixed rules. In the practice of Bulgarian courts, such additional connecting factors have been: the country where the contract was concluded; the place of business of a proxy of the seller; and the place where the offer to enter into the agreement was sent. Electronic ways of communication between parties, as well as the INCOTERMS standard clauses for transfer of risk over goods, have been used by the parties to argue for a closer connection as per Article 4(3). However, in all the established judicial sources, the application of the escape clause has been rejected. In one case, for example, the fact that the place of business of the agent or proxy of the seller was in the territory of Bulgaria, combined with the transfer of risk over the goods on the territory of Bulgaria, as per a CIP Incoterms standard clause in the contract, was not enough for the court to decide that Bulgaria was more closely connected with the case, the habitual residence of the seller being in Romania.[46] Thus, the escape clause remains truly an exception in the practice of Bulgarian courts and there are no reported cases of its use. The fact that the escape clause could lead

45 Decision 208 of 15.05.2019 Veliko Tarnovo District Court, commercial case 129/2018.

46 Decision 131 of 14.02.2013 Varna District Court, commercial case 516/2011; Decision 200 of 11.07.2013 Varna Appellate Court, commercial case 332/2013.

to the application of domestic law of the court was not a factor and has not influenced the decision of the courts. As to special escape clauses of Articles 5(3) and 8(4) of the Rome I Regulation, the underlying principle would remain the same, although there is no case law as yet.

2.4.2. *Rome II*

Bulgarian courts are not easily tempted to apply the escape clause of Article 4(3) of the Rome II Regulation in order to make the dispute subject to the *lex fori*. No instance of the application of Article 4(3) of the Rome II Regulations was identified in our search. On the contrary, courts expressly stress that there is no ground for the case to rely on the nexus with the country with which the non-contractual relationship is more closely connected,[47] the substantive tort law being that of the country where the initial and direct damage was sustained.

There have been no cases before Bulgarian courts regarding claims arising from the collision of vessels in international waters. In those cases, the courts would most probably resort, as additional connecting factors for the operation of escape clauses, to a provision of the Bulgarian Merchant Shipping Code – Article 14(2) and (3). According to Article 14(2), in cases of collision of vessels in waters or waterways over which no state exerts sovereignty, the law of the country of the court or the law of the arbitration tribunal is applicable. There is a special rule under Article 14(3) that if all affected vessels operate under the same flag, the law of the *lex banderae* is applicable. In the latter case, the common flag of vessels could fall within the scope of Article 4(2) of the Rome II Regulation – the law of the country of the common habitual residence of the parties.[48] Although said provisions of the Merchant Shipping Code are no longer applicable since the coming into force of the Rome II Regulation, they could be a source of reference for the appreciation of factors regarding close connection under Article 4(3) of the Rome II Regulation.

2.5. SPECIFIC RULES

2.5.1. *Rome I*

The specific conflict-of-law rules for different type of contractual relations in Articles 5–8 of the Rome I Regulation work well in the court practice of

---

47 Decision of 13.02.2012 Sofia City Court, civil case 16068/2011; Decision 7830 of 16.11.2015 Sofia City Court, civil case 10390/2013; Decision of 28.08.2012 Sofia City Court, commercial case 12035/2010.

48 B. Musseva, supra n. 17, pp. 205–206.

Bulgarian courts. Competent authorities point out the different scope of the general rules of Article 4 of the Rome I Regulation and that of the special rules of Articles 5–8 of the Regulation.

The *contract for the carriage of passengers* by air was governed by Article 5(2) of the Rome I Regulation in a case concerning a claim for compensation for a flight cancelled by the air carrier. Since the passenger and the carrier had different places of habitual residence, the relationship entered into the ambit of the Rome I Regulation.[49] The underlying logic of the court was that the contract had a connection with more than one country and resort to private international law sources was needed. The court went on to apply the Rome I Regulation, without giving any reason why the Montreal Convention for the Unification of Certain Rules for International Carriage by Air[50] was not relevant to the case. The court decided that the applicable law was that of the country of the habitual residence of the passenger (as per Article 5(2) of the Rome Regulation), without checking the additional requirements for either the place of departure or the place of destination to also be situated in that country. More interestingly, the court made a characterisation of the claim between tort and contract not on the basis of the autonomous meaning of the legal figures as per the Rome I and Rome II Regulations, but on the grounds of the *lex fori* being the Bulgarian law. The claim was characterised as contractual in nature as per Bulgarian laws even though the Rome I Regulation was already in force.

Consumer contracts are characterised on the basis only of the general features of Article 6(1) of the Rome I Regulation – a contract concluded by a natural person for a purpose which can be regarded as being outside his trade or profession (the consumer) with another person acting in the exercise of his trade or profession (the professional). The court did not succeed in arguing for the additional requirement for directed activities as per Article 6(1)(a) and (b) of the Rome I Regulation. The defendant professional was a Spanish financial institution with no information on how it directed activities towards Bulgaria, nor did it perform its activities on the territory of Bulgaria (the habitual residence of the consumer) or direct its activities toward Bulgaria.[51] This considerable flaw in the court's argumentation was in the course of a small claim procedures under Regulation 861/2007 setting up a European Small Claims Procedure.

The special rules for *insurance contracts* in Article 7 of the Rome I Regulation pose some characterisation issues for courts, especially as regards the meaning of the terms 'large risk', 'risks for which a Member State imposes an obligation to take out insurance' and the connection of 'the country in which the risk is situated'. The judge decided that a contract for transport insurance of cargo

49 Decision of 24.10.2013 Sofia County Court, civil case 19467/2012.
50 Ratified by the Bulgarian Parliament on 16 July 2003, in force as of 9 January 2004.
51 Decision of 19.02.2016 Sofia County Court, civil case 56422/2012.

fell within the category of large risk insurance contracts, which is in line with definition of large risk in EU law – Article 13(27)(a) of Directive 2009/138/EC on the taking-up and pursuit of the business of insurance and reinsurance. The applicable law was that of the country of habitual residence of the insurer.[52] In other cases of cargo insurance contracts, the court found that large risk insurance is most closely connected with Bulgaria (instead of the insurer's country of habitual residence), since the goods are loaded in Bulgaria and the destination of the goods is different from the insurer's place of habitual residence.[53]

Regarding contracts for insurance, Bulgarian courts make reference to CJEU decisions in Joined Cases C-359/14 and C-475/14, *ERGO Insurance*, in the sense that the obligation for an insurer to compensate the damage caused to a victim arises not from the damage caused to the latter but from the contract between it and the insured party who is liable. Such compensation is therefore based on a contractual obligation, since the law applicable to such an obligation must be determined in accordance with the provisions of the Rome I Regulation.[54] The right of subrogation of a third party in the right for a victim's compensation is governed by the applicable insurance contract law – Article 19 of the Rome II Regulation together with Article 7 of the Rome I Regulation.[55]

Special conflict-of-law rules for the determination of the law applicable to *individual employment contracts* take precedence over the general rules of Article 4 of the Rome I Regulation. The courts unmistakably establish the relationship between said provisions on the basis of the maxim *lex specialis derogat legi generali*. In a case concerning the alleged unlawful termination of an employment contract by a foreign embassy, the Bulgarian Supreme Court reaffirmed the opinion of the lower court that Article 8 of the Rome I Regulation should apply instead of Article 4 of the Rome I Regulation.[56] First, the court overturned an application for immunity from civil jurisdiction on the grounds that the foreign embassy had voluntarily entered into the private contract and was thus subject to labour law; as a result, the employee was entitled to the right to a defence as the weaker party in the legal relationship in question and that the rules of Article 9 of the Rome I Regulation are applicable. The court emphasised the universal effect of the Regulation's conflict-of-law rules when it comes to employment contracts. The court then went on to assess the choice of foreign law in the employment contract, which was judged to be valid. However, following the ratio of the lower courts,[57] the Supreme Court decided that provisions of

[52] Decision 5754 of 23.07.2014 Sofia City Court, civil case 11253/2013.

[53] Decision 2101 of 22.11.2019 Sofia City Court, commercial case 2060/2018.

[54] Decision 65 of 20.08.2019 Targovishte District Court, commercial case 19/2019.

[55] Decision 468 of 14.12.2018 Pazardjik District Court, civil appeal case 752/2018.

[56] Decision 11 of 15.05.2015 Supreme Court of Cassation, Civil Division, 3rd civil circuit, civil case 4455/2014.

[57] Decision 2134 of 28.03.2014 Sofia City Court, civil case 9355/2013.

Bulgarian law (as the law of the place where the employee habitually carried out his work) applied directly and could not be derogated from by agreement. The foreign law applied alongside the mandatory rules of Bulgarian employment law, since the latter afford employees protection in the event of the termination of their employment contract. No attention was paid to establishing the content of the chosen foreign law in order to verify whether it provided the same or a higher level of protection. An observation is made that, from a factual point of view, no analogous procedure equivalent to that in the Bulgarian Labour Law could be followed under the chosen foreign law. The court proceeded directly to applying – by their very nature mandatory – rules from the Bulgarian Labour Code on employee protection, which set out a special procedure for the selection of the individual employee among the employees as a whole whose contract is to be terminated before issuing the act for firing the claimant. Under Bulgarian law, when there is more than one employee in the same or similar jobs, a formal procedure for selecting the best qualified and skilled one or ones must be followed. The foreign employer did not do so and so the court held the termination of the contract illegal on the grounds of these rules that cannot be derogated from by agreement. A possible problem in characterising the contract as falling outside the scope of employment contracts, as opposed to a contract for services, is that the criteria for determining the type of contract are not taken from the autonomous meaning of the Rome I Regulation's provisions, but are based on national sources.[58]

The courts also applied without much discussion the rules regulating the voluntary assignment of a claim against a third party – Article 14 of the Rome I Regulation. In a case concerning the contractual assignment of claims arising out of a licence agreement, the competent authority resorted to Article 14(2) of the Rome I Regulation and as a result the foreign law chosen by the parties in the initial agreement was followed to determine the relationship between the assignee and the debtor, as well as the conditions under which the assignment could be invoked against the debtor.[59] The position of the debtor was assessed according to the law expressly chosen by the debtor and the assignor in the initial licence agreement. Thus, the interests of the debtor were duly considered, since he was not aware preliminarily of the assignment of claims. The assignability of the claim was construed as accomplishing the general conditions for the transfer of the claim between assignor and assignee, as well as aspects related to the performance of the agreement by the debtor.

---

58 Decision 143 of 20.11.2019 Supreme Court of Cassation, Commercial Division, 2nd commercial circuit, commercial case 527/2019.

59 Decision 1871 of 18.11.2015 Sofia City Court, commercial case 8148/2014.

2.5.2. *Rome II*

The study has identified relevant court practice on the application of specific rules on the law applicable to torts regarding intellectual property rights torts – Article 8(1) of the Rome II Regulation. Most cases concerned claims for damages due to unauthorised use of photographs or literature being tortious in nature. The courts have a clear tendency to apply Bulgarian substantive copyright law and, especially – the Bulgarian Copyright and Related Rights Act. In one of the cases there is an express reference to the conflict rule of Article 8(1) of the Rome II Regulation for the law of the State for which protection is claimed.[60]

With regards to unjust enrichment caused by an unauthorised bank transfer from a Canadian bank account to a Bulgarian bank account, the court applied Article 10(3) of the Rome II Regulation. The court stated that the place where the unjust enrichment took place was Bulgaria, where the enrichment materialised in the form of the deposited sum in the bank account. The court subsequently applied Bulgarian law.[61]

2.6. SCOPE OF APPLICABLE LAW AND CHARACTERISATION

2.6.1. *Rome I*

Article 12 of the Rome I Regulation seems to meet the expectations of the Bulgarian judiciary as a provision detailed enough to ascertain the scope of the applicable material law. There are no instances of the scope of the applicable law being widened in light of the fact that the list in Article 12 of the Rome I Regulation is not exhaustive, except for the rescission of the contract. Under Bulgarian contract law, if a party does not fulfil its obligation after due notice, the other party is untitled to unwind (rescind) the contract. As a consequence, the party may make a claim for contractual restitution and/or compensation since the contractual relationship is deemed to be extinguished *ex ante*. Claims regarding the consequences of rescinded contracts do not expressly fall within the ambit of Article 12(1)(e) of the Rome I Regulation; however, without providing any substantial reasoning, the courts apply the rules of the Rome I Regulation to the consequences of rescinded contracts.[62]

A sensitive issue seems to be the characterisation of legal notions in applying the Regulation. Some Bulgarian courts do not follow the established principle of the autonomous interpretation of the legal terms used in the

60 Decision 1327 of 25.06.018 Sofia City Court, commercial case 1432/2017.
61 Decision 963 of 23.05.2019 Sofia City Court, commercial case 56/2019.
62 Decision 373 of 27.12.2013 Varna Appellate Court, commercial case 592/2013.

Regulation, following its express meaning and the guidance provided by the jurisprudence of the CJEU on references for preliminary rulings. Thus, the court first establishes the characterisation of the contract under Bulgarian national sources of contract law and then, following its 'national' characterisation, submits the question to the relevant provision of the Rome I Regulation.[63] The use of this approach in several decisions points to a possible issue in the application of the Regulation. In one case, a claim for restitution following a rescinded contract was characterised under Bulgarian law. Since the type of contract (forming a contractual joint venture) was not subject to a special conflict-of-law rule in the Regulation I Rome, the court directly applied Bulgarian law, from which it derived the criteria for characterisation, even though the contracts fell within the scope of Article 4(2) of the Rome I Regulation.[64] In another case, a contract for construction was subjected to Bulgarian contract law, without characterisation of its nature as a contract for the provision of services, under Article 4(1)(b) of the Rome I Regulation.[65] However, the wrong approach to characterisation did not affect the application of the conflict-of-law rule itself, which was the right one.

2.6.2. Rome II

Bulgarian courts have not encountered characterisation difficulties in applying the Rome II Regulation. All the reported court practice is related to torts arising from physical damage to property or to persons as a result of traffic accidents. The courts have only discussed the issue of the Regulation's operation *ratione temporis*. Before the start of application of the Rome II Regulation, all non-contractual obligations were governed by the conflict-of-law rules of Part Three, Chapter 11 CPIL. The courts clearly and unmistakably distinguish between whether the CPIL should apply or the Rome II Regulation based on when the event giving rise to the damage occurred.[66] The court expressly refers to the CJEU's decision in *Homawoo*[67] and states that under Article 31, the Regulation applies to events giving rise to damage occurring after the date given in Article 32, namely 11 January 2009.[68]

Courts have refused to apply the rules for the applicable law of the Rome II Regulation regarding powers of the manager of condominiums for common areas in residential buildings. As per Bulgarian laws the owners of all residential

---

63 Supra n. 62.
64 Decision 571 of 28.03.2016 Sofia City Court, commercial case 2382/2012.
65 Supra n. 62.
66 Decision of 28.08.2012 Sofia City Court, commercial case 12035/2010.
67 Case C-412/10, *Homawoo* [2011] ECR I-11603, para. 31.
68 Decision 7850 of 25.11.2013 Sofia City Court, civil case 3423/2010.

buildings shall elect a person to take charge of the management of common areas of the building. The court rejected the allegation that the relationship between the manager and individual owners is one of *negotiorum gestio* as per Article 11 of the Rome II Regulation, giving the reason that a special management contract regulated by law has been concluded between the manager and the owners.[69]

2.7. APPLICATION OF FOREIGN LAW

In conformity with Article 43 CPIL (entitled 'Ascertaining the content of foreign law'), Bulgarian courts and other judicial bodies ascertain the content of the foreign law *ex officio*. In doing so, they have several means at their disposal: first, to use the mechanisms as provided for in the international treaties; second, to request information from the Ministry of Justice, or from another state body; third, to request foreign law expert statements; and fourth, to request statements from specialised institutions (domestic or foreign). The parties may support these efforts, for example, by submitting documents that contain foreign law, such as state gazettes or similar. Under Article 43(2) CPIL, the parties *may* assist in situations where foreign law was selected by a conflict-of-law rule; under Article 43(3), where the parties have specifically chosen the applicable foreign law, the court or other judicial body may *oblige* them to assist in determining its content. However, the duty to ascertain the content of foreign law does not shift from the court or other judicial body to the parties at any point during this process. This means that the parties may assist of their own motion or may be obliged to assist by the court or other judicial body, but if the parties fail to assist or decline to assist, their failure or refusal does not discharge the court or other judicial body from its official obligation in law to ascertain the content of foreign law. The burden of ascertaining foreign law rests with the court or other judicial body without any legal possibility to shift it to the parties. Once the content of foreign law has been determined, the court or other judicial body is obliged – in conformity with Article 44 CPIL – to interpret and apply this law as it is interpreted and applied in the state that created it. Failure to apply foreign law, or the incorrect interpretation and application of it, is grounds for appeal. The court is considered to have failed to apply foreign law if it did not follow the conflict-of-law rules of Bulgarian private international law, including the rule in the Rome I Regulation which requires the court to apply foreign law, i.e. the application of conflict-of-law rules of private international law is compulsory for courts and other judicial bodies in Bulgaria. Incorrect interpretation and application of foreign law is considered to have occurred if the court or other

[69] Injunction 500 of 28.08.2018 Dobrich District Court, civil appeal case 379/2018.

judicial body did not interpret and apply this law in the way it is interpreted and applied by the competent bodies of the state that enacted it.

2.7.1. Rome I

It seems that access to foreign law for the purposes of the Rome I Regulation is adequate. The courts and other judicial bodies may make use of the options provided by the international treaties (particularly the European Convention on Information on Foreign Law (the 1968 London Convention)), the European Judicial Network in Civil and Commercial Matters, the European Notarial Network, assistance from the Ministry of Justice and the Ministry of Foreign Affairs (which can supply foreign official documents and texts, mainly through the legal aid channels of the Ministry of Justice or the diplomatic and consular channels of the Ministry of Foreign Affairs), foreign law expert opinions, and statements from specialised institutions in Bulgaria and abroad.

Foreign law is treated as being equal to national law. The process of ascertainment of the content of foreign law is based on the co-operation between the courts or other judicial bodies and the parties, but the duty to determine the foreign law is an official one and rests with the courts and other judicial bodies alone. As mentioned above, the Ministry of Justice and the Ministry of Foreign Affairs support the courts and other judicial bodies in their work of establishing the content of foreign law. There are just a few cases where the courts applied the *lex fori* despite the Rome I Regulation being applicable because of a difficulty in establishing with sufficient certainty the applicable foreign law. In the first such case, the court applied Article 14(2) of the Rome I Regulation to the assignment of claims under a licence agreement. The court held that the foreign law had to be ascertained by the parties and, in breach of its own legal obligation to do this, the court decided that the failure of the parties to ascertain the content of foreign law meant the claim should be rejected. In other words, the lack of ascertainment of foreign law by the parties was considered by the court as a ground for rejection of the claim.[70] Another case was related to regular commercial transactions between a Bulgarian company and a company registered within another EU Member State. The court committed an error in the application of the Rome I Regulation. At the beginning of the trial, it correctly stated that the Rome I Regulation was an applicable instrument, but ultimately the court applied the CPIL instead. Further, the court referred to Article 4(1) of the Rome I Regulation, citing as grounds for the parties' obligation to ascertain the contents of foreign law.[71] This is without doubt an incorrect application and

[70] Decision 1871 of 18.11.2015 Sofia City Court, commercial case 8148/2014.

[71] Decision 151 of 04.12.2014 Pazardjik County Court, commercial case 125/2013.

understanding of the Rome I Regulation, which led the court not to fulfil its duty to ascertain *ex officio* the content of foreign law. Based on the above examples, we can infer that some Bulgarian courts tend to compromise the universal application of the Rome I Regulation by replacing it with the *lex fori.*

2.7.2. Rome II

It seems that the access to foreign law for the purposes of the Rome II Regulation is adequate too. The situation is the same as that for the Rome I Regulation, as described above in section 2.7.1. Foreign law treated as equal to national law. The process of the ascertainment of the content of foreign law is based on the co-operation between the courts or other judicial bodies and the parties, but the duty to determine the foreign law is an official one and rests with the courts and other judicial bodies alone. As mentioned, the Ministry of Justice and the Ministry of Foreign Affairs support the courts and other judicial bodies in their work of establishing the content of foreign law. We identified no cases where the courts applied the *lex fori* despite the Rome II Regulation being applicable because of a difficulty in establishing with sufficient certainty the applicable foreign law. As a consequence of the lack of case law, it is not possible to say whether the universal application of the Rome II Regulation is compromised or not.

2.8. *ORDRE PUBLIC* (PUBLIC POLICY OF THE FORUM)

2.8.1. Rome I

The public policy (*ordre public*) exception is well known to the contemporary private international law systems of the EU Member States. The autonomous terms inserted in Article 21 of the Rome I Regulation (which is identical to Article 26 of the Rome II Regulation) have been more a topic for academic discussions in Bulgaria than a challenge in the jurisprudence. The concept of public policy is generally applied at the stage of the recognition and enforcement of foreign decisions, rather than in the process of applying foreign law within the ambit of the Rome Regulations. It is used very rarely in court practice, proving its exceptional nature. Courts are not tempted to excessively use or even further abuse the recourse to public policy in order to apply Bulgarian law. The general rule of Article 45(3) CPIL is that where an incompatibility with public policy is established, another appropriate provision of the same foreign law shall be applied. In the absence of such a provision, a provision of Bulgarian law shall apply, if necessary for regulating the relationship. Since public policy is more appropriate for more sensitive areas such as family law, courts have not used it in contract law except in cases of discrepancy in the requirements of form between

Bulgarian and foreign law. In one case, the court accepted that a mandatory rule for the written form of a contract for legal services in Bulgarian law represented grounds for the application of public policy exception.[72] However, this ruling was overturned by the higher instance court, which pointed out that public policy is not to be referred to in every case of a difference between the material provisions of the *lex fori* and foreign law, as is the case with the formal validity of a contract.[73] The public policy exception can be activated only in the event of a breach of such imperative conditions of Bulgarian law that are at the basis of the Bulgarian legal order and are tantamount to basic principles of jurisprudence with a universal bearing. Moreover, the contradiction must be a qualified one – there must be an intolerable discrepancy with *lex fori* principles. Thus, fact that the conditions for the formal validity of a contract for court representation by a lawyer are different under Italian Code of Civil Procedure from Bulgarian procedural rules does not give rise to the public policy exception under Article 21 of the Rome I Regulation. The manifestly incompatible difference with domestic law should be considered only individually on a case-by-case basis and it must lead to substantially detrimental consequences for legal certainty.[74] Thus, the more liberal conditions of German law on the formal validity of a contract for the transfer of a vehicle were not relevant to engage the rules of the *ordre public*. The difference in the period of prescription in the UK Limitation Act 1980 compared to Bulgarian laws is not a ground for the refusal to apply foreign law as contradictory to public policy of the forum. The limitation period as per UK law is longer the same as the one regulated by Bulgarian civil law.[75]

In conclusion, court practice has been very cautious in its reference to public policy in contract obligations, having in mind its character as a tool of last resort. In all cases, the content of the public policy was subjected to domestic sources and no 'international' public policy was applied. Courts have not neither fundamental rights nor the basic principles of human rights under EU law.

2.8.2. Rome II

The public policy rule of Article 27 of the Rome II Regulation has not been used by Bulgarian courts to affect the application of foreign law as far as can be seen from the publicly reported case law. According to established Bulgarian academic authorities, public policy provisions of EU or national source cannot be resorted to except in cases of substantial and real inconsistency of the consequences of the operation of foreign legal rules *in concreto* with basic notions of Bulgarian

72 Decision 698 of 14.08.2014 Sliven County Court, civil case 450/2013.
73 Decision 14 of 21.01.2015 Sliven District Court, civil case 584/2014.
74 Decision 81 of 07.01.2015 Blagoevgrad County Court, civil case 1161/2014.
75 Supra n. 14; Decision 62 of 07.05.2019 Dobrich District Court, commercial case 208/2018.

law and morals.[76] The Bulgarian concept of public policy is familiar and 'accepts the assessment' of the proximity of the situation with Bulgaria and the intensity of the link. As per Article 45(2) CPIL, the application of the *ordre public* is a function of the strength of the nexus of the relationship with Bulgarian public policy and the significance of the consequences of the application of foreign law. The criteria for the application of the public policy under Bulgarian legislation are expressly stated to be in line with the French notion of *ordre public de proximité* or the German one of *Inlandbeziehung*.

2.9. RELATIONS WITH INTERNATIONAL CONVENTIONS

2.9.1. Rome I

The application of the international conventions to which Bulgaria was a party at the time the Rome I Regulation was adopted and which lay down conflict-of-law rules relating to contractual obligations has not been an issue, since Bulgaria is not a party to the Hague Convention of 15 June 1955 on the Law Applicable to International Sale of Goods (CISG).

Courts have focused their attention on the relationship between the scope of application of the CISG and that of the Rome I Regulation. However, the CISG lays down a uniform contract regime for the international sale of goods through its substantive rules and self-regulates its applicability in its Article 1. The rule in Article 25(1) of the Rome I Regulation is not relevant to the operation of the CISG because the two instruments refer to different types of the norms – those of the Regulation being conflict-of-law rules and those of the CISG being substantive ones with direct application. Surprisingly, the jurisprudence of the Bulgarian courts indicates uncertainty as to how direct application of the Convention, as per Article 1(1)(a) CISG, works, which is a flaw in the interpretation of the CISG and not of the Rome I Regulation. Most of courts first establish the law applicable to contracts for the sale of goods as per Articles 3(1) and 4(1)(a) of the Rome I Regulation, then make the observation that the CISG is an integral part of the domestic law of any country that is a contracting state to the CISG. This is a serious inconvenience for the court authorities' ratio, since the indirect application of the CISG through the rules of the Rome I Regulation is only possible in the instance of Article 1(1)(b) CISG when the state in which the parties' place of business is situated is not a contracting state to the Convention. The direct application of the CISG as per Article 1(1)(a) is independent of conflict-of-law rules, including those of the Rome I Regulation, and the Regulation does not

---

76 N. Natov, supra n. 15, pp. 366–370.

apply if the place of business of the parties is located in a contracting state to the CISG.[77] In a series of decisions, Bulgarian civil and commercial courts have referred to the Rome I Regulation as a stage in the process of operation of the CISG, even though the conditions for its direct application were fulfilled and there was no need to establish the applicable substantive law of the contract, the CISG being an integral part of it.[78] The applicable law was defined as that of the country of the habitual residence of the seller, as per Article 4(1)(a) of the Rome I Regulation, and since that country was a contracting state to the CISG, the latter was applicable.

On the other hand, in a minority of cases, courts have proceeded to the direct application of the CISG as per Article 1(1)(a) of the Convention, without any recourse to the Rome I Regulation.[79] In cases of contracts for the transport of goods by road, the 1956 Convention on the Contract for the International Carriage of Goods by Road (CMR) has been ruled to be directly applicable without any relationship to the Rome I Regulation. The CMR is directly applicable as it contains substantive rules and prevails over the Rome I Regulation in matters relating to contracts for the carriage of goods by road.[80]

For topics outside the scope of the CISG or the CMR, the conflict-of-law rules of the Rome I Regulation are subsidiarily applicable to define the set of national rules on the matter. The typical example is the provision of Article 78 CISG, which does not fix the amount of the interest in the event of late payment. If parties have not set or agreed on how to determine this issue, the applicable substantive law as defined by the Rome I Regulation will be used to do so.[81]

2.9.2. Rome II

Courts strictly follow the universal character of the rules of the Rome II Regulation. The Regulation's interplay with the Hague Convention of 4 May 1971 on the Law Applicable to Traffic Accidents is not at issue since Bulgaria is not a contracting state.[82] Since most of jurisprudence concerns claims arising from

---

77 P. Schlechtriem and I. Schwenzer, *Commentary on the UN Convention on International Sale of GOODS (CISG)*, 2nd ed., Oxford University Press, Oxford 2005, p. 33.

78 Decision 176 of 05.11.2014 Dobrich District Court, commercial case 76/2014; Decision 644 of 11.04.2016 Sofia City Court, commercial case 8529/2013; Decision 1003 of 21.12.2015 Varna District Court, commercial case 1537/2015; Decision 1693 of 24.04.2013 Plovdiv County Court, commercial case 8664/2011.

79 Decision 571 of 28.03.2016 Sofia City Court, commercial case 2382/2012; Decision 1419 of 08.08.2013 Sofia City Court, commercial case 5078/2011.

80 Decision 54 of 12.02.2015 Bourgas District Court, commercial case 81/2013.

81 Decision 644 of 11.04.2016 Sofia City Court, commercial case 8529/2013; Decision 200 of 11.07.2013 Varna Appellate Court, commercial case 332/2013; Decision 228 of 03.05.2019 Stara Zagora District Court, commercial case 137/2018.

82 Decision 7850 of 25.11.2013 Sofia City Court, civil case 3423/2010.

traffic accidents, the courts feel obliged to stress that the Hague Convention is not relevant to the case. On the other hand, special sources of EU substantive law prevail over the Rome II Regulation as per Article 27. In one case, the court applied the substantive rules of Regulation 1408/71 on the application of social security schemes to employed persons and their families moving within the Community on the grounds of Article 27 of the Rome II Regulation, which deals with the subrogation of social security in a claim against an insurer for medical treatment costs.[83] The court's assessment of the relevance of Article 27 of the Rome II Regulation is questionable since Article 93(1) of Regulation 1408/71 contains substantive and not conflict-of-law rules.

3. GENERAL EVALUATION

It seems that the innovations brought about by the Rome I and Rome II Regulations have proved wise and successful. This chapter has shown that a relatively small proportion of decisions in Bulgaria have wrongly applied the Rome I Regulation (about five per cent).

The previous regime in Bulgaria was almost the same as the regime of both Regulations. There is now more uniformity in comparison with the pre-Rome I and Rome II regimes. Although the corresponding rules of CPIL were drafted following the models of the Rome I and Rome II Regulations, the national character of the Code excluded its compulsory application by the courts and other judicial bodies of the EU Member States. While the EU origin of the Rome I and Rome II Regulations ensures that the courts of the EU Member States shall apply both instruments and by this the uniformity will be strengthened.

The taxonomy used by both Regulations has proved practical. No gaps were tracked and, especially in relation to *quasi-delicts*, no gap was seen. It is easy to identify a specific contract or tort/delict and its corresponding rule. A sensitive issue seems to be the characterisation of legal notions in applying the Rome I Regulation. Some courts do not follow the established principle on the autonomous interpretation of the legal terms used in the Regulation following its express meaning and the guidance provided by the jurisprudence of CJEU on references for preliminary rulings.

It seems the courts apply the relevant Regulation in the light of its spirit and not only its letter. The courts are not tempted to widen the scope of application of either Regulation and they stick to its original scope and meaning of the rules.

As regards the Rome I Regulation, some cases reveal that a foreign element in the relationships and the proceedings may go unnoticed by the courts if the

[83] Decision 47556 of 15.02.2016 Sofia County Court, civil case 47556/2014.

parties do not expressly mention it and, as a result, no reference to the Regulation is made. The escape clause remains truly an exception: the courts are not easily tempted to apply the escape clause of Article 4(3) of the Rome I Regulation in order to make the dispute subject to the *lex fori*. Some courts consider the failure of the parties to ascertain the content of foreign law as a ground for the rejection of the claim. Some courts wrongly refer to Article 4(1) of the Rome I Regulation as a ground for a legally non-existent obligation of parties to ascertain the content of foreign law, which has in some cases led the court to fail to fulfil its own duty to ascertain the content of foreign law *ex officio*. This is a trend that undermines the universal application of the Rome I Regulation by replacing it with the *lex fori*.

4. CONCLUSION

In general, it could be said that Bulgarian courts do not encounter great difficulties in interpreting and following the logic and the spirit of both the Rome I and Rome II Regulations. The judiciary feels comfortable with the new legal regime established by the Regulations and, with some exceptions, correctly applies the norms of these instruments.

With regard to the Rome I Regulation, the provisions on the application *ratione temporis* have proved to be most unclear. Some courts apply different sources of law to the same contracts simultaneously. In the case of a series of contracts concluded between 2008 and 2010, the court founded its reasoning on the CPIL, the Rome Convention and the Rome I Regulation without specifying which one was relevant to the separate contracts; as a consequence, the applicable law was determined on the basis of Article 4 of the Rome Convention, Article 94 CPIL and Article 4 of the Rome I Regulation. As far as the Rome II Regulation is concerned, Bulgarian courts have encountered difficulties when determining the place where the damage occurred in cases of personal injury.

The national judiciary should be more decisive when applying both Regulations and particularly should not dismiss claims if parties failed to assist in ascertaining the content of foreign law for the purposes of application of both Regulations. Courts should also improve their approach to the *ratione temporis* clauses of both Regulations.

A possible change to the Rome I Regulation permitting the functioning of soft law and commercial usage source (e.g. Incoterms) to international commercial contracts would bring more flexibility and competitiveness to EU forums.

The arbitration exception seems to be a challenge that will attract more attention in the future, taking into account the fact that an increasing number of disputes arising from international commercial contracts and non-contractual commercial disputes are being resolved by arbitration.

THE APPLICATION OF THE ROME I AND ROME II REGULATIONS IN CROATIA

Davor Babić and Dora Zgrabljić Rotar

1. THE NATIONAL LANDSCAPE

The Croatian legal system belongs to civil law systems, with elements of the Germanic and the Romanic legal families.[1] For historical reasons, Croatia does not have a civil code or a commercial code. Instead, the dominant sources of private law are statutes governing individual fields of law such as the law of obligations, property law, inheritance law, private international law, etc.[2]

Private international law has been codified in Croatia since 1982 when the Private International Law Act[3] was originally enacted as a federal statute

---

1 H. Ernst, 'General Introduction', in T. Josipović (ed.), *Introduction to the Law of Croatia*, Wolters Kluwer, Alphen aan den Rijn 2014, p. 4.

2 H. Ernst, supra n. 1.

3 *Zakon o rješavanju sukoba zakona s propisima drugih zemalja u određenim odnosima*, *Narodne novine* (Official Gazette), No. 53/91.

of the former Socialist Federative Republic of Yugoslavia.[4] The original text of the law was taken over as the law of Croatia in 1991, when the country declared independence.[5] The Private International Law Act has not been affected by the major legislative reforms carried out in 1990s, when Croatia underwent a transition from a socialist economy to a market-based economy.

With the need for reform of private international law, the bill for a new Private International Law Act was passed by the Croatian Parliament on 4 October 2017 and came into effect on 29 January 2019.[6] Until that date, the 1982 Private International Law Act was in effect in Croatia.[7]

Both the 1982 Private International Law Act and the 2017 Private International Law Act are comprehensive codifications of private international law. The 1982 Act establishes rules on the law applicable to status, family law matters, property law relationships, and other substantive legal relationships involving a foreign element. Further, the Act establishes rules concerning the jurisdiction of courts and other bodies, in cases involving a foreign element, and rules for the recognition of foreign judgments (Article 1). Although the codifications are comprehensive, some areas of private international law governing certain specific areas are codified in special laws. Thus, for example, private international rules relating to maritime law are codified in the Maritime Code.[8]

General rules on the law governing contractual obligations are contained in Articles 19–25 of the 1982 Private International Law Act. The rules on the law governing contracts in maritime and airline traffic are found in the Maritime Code (Articles 971, 973–975, 978–985) and the Act on Obligations and Property Rights in Air Traffic[9] (Articles 176–180), respectively. Certain provisions relevant to determining the law governing contractual obligations are found in the Consumer Protection Act (Article 4).[10]

---

4 Službeni list SFRJ (Official Gazette SFRY), No. 43/82 and 72/82.

5 D. Babić, 'Private International Law', in T. Josipović (ed.), *Introduction to the Law of Croatia*, Wolters Kluwer, Alphen aan den Rijn 2014, p. 439. The only major change since 1982 was that the rules on recognition and enforcement of arbitral awards were abolished and replaced by the Arbitration Act of 2001 (*Narodne novine* (Official Gazette), No. 88/01, Art. 50).

6 *Zakon o međunarodnom privatnom pravu, Narodne novine* (Official Gazette), No. 101/17.

7 The original name has been changed from 'Act concerning the resolution of conflicts of laws with the provisions of other countries in certain matters' (*Zakon o rješavanju sukoba zakona s propisima drugih zemalja u određenim odnosima*) to 'Private International Law Act' (*Zakon o međunarodnom privatnom pravu*). The old name of the statute is not only lacking in elegance, but is also misleading – the Act does not govern only conflict of laws, but also other aspects of private international law in the wider sense, such as international jurisdiction and the recognition and enforcement of foreign judgments.

8 *Pomorski zakonik* (Maritime Code), *Narodne novine* (Official Gazette), Nos. 181/04, 76/07, 146/08, 61/11, 56/13, 26/15.

9 *Zakon o obveznim i stvarnopravnim odnosima u zračnom prometu* (Act on Obligations and Property Rights in Air Traffic), *Narodne novine* (Official Gazette), Nos. 132/98, 63/08, 134/09, 94/13.

10 *Zakon o zaštiti potrošača* (Consumer Protection Act), *Narodne novine* (Official Gazette), Nos. 41/14, 110/15, 14/19.

For the most part, the Croatian codification of private international law of torts is reduced to a single provision contained in Article 28 of the 1982 Private International Law Act. That provision applies to nearly all the types of tort liability (e.g. personal injury cases, violation of privacy and personality rights, intellectual property infringements, damage arising from the violation of competition laws, etc.).[11] Specific statutory rules on the applicable law are provided only for maritime and airline traffic accidents, which appear in the Maritime Code and the Act on Obligations and Property Rights in Air Traffic. Importantly, Croatia is party to the Hague Convention of 4 May 1971 on the Law Applicable to Traffic Accidents, the Hague Convention of 2 October 1973 on the Law Applicable to Products Liability, and the Vienna Convention on Civil Liability for Nuclear Damage of 21 May 1963.[12] Given that, according to the Croatian Constitution (Article 140), treaties in effect in Croatia have precedence over statutory law, conflict-of-laws provisions found in those laws do not apply within the field of application of those conventions.[13]

Croatia joined the European Union on 1 July 2013. Since that date, the Rome I and Rome II Regulations take precedence over national conflict-of-laws rules that coincide with their scope of application. For the purpose of the Regulations' transitory provisions, the date of Croatia's accession is treated as the day of the entry into force of the Regulations.[14] Thus, in line with the principle of non-retroactivity,[15] the Rome I Regulation applies in Croatia to contracts

11 The scope of the law governing the tort has neither been defined, nor have there been published court decisions on this issue. Academic commentary suggests that this law governs all the substantive tort law issues, such as the legal basis for the liability, causality, delictual capacity, vicarious liability, grounds for limitation or exclusion of liability, joint liability, types and quantum of indemnification and prescription (limitation) of claims. I. Grbin, 'Vanugovorna odgovornost za štetu u međunarodnom privatnom pravu' (1973) 5 *Naša zakonitost* 470; V. Tomljenović, *Pomorsko međunarodno privatno pravo,* Pravni fakultet Sveučilišta u Rijeci, Rijeka 1998, p. 196.

12 Službeni list SFRJ (Official Gazette SFRY), International Treaties, No. 26 of 1976 and No. 8 of 1977. Pursuant to the notification of succession, which was submitted by Croatia on 22 January 1994, Croatia has been a party to the Convention since 8 October 1991 (*Narodne novine – Međunarodni ugovori* (Official Gazette – International Treaties), No. 4/94).

13 The courts occasionally fail to give effect to the applicable international treaties and instead apply the rules of statutory law. See e.g. High Commercial Court, Judgment No. Pž-335/92, 24 March 1992; High Commercial Court, Judgment No. Pž-1010/93, 18 May 1993 (applying Art. 28 Conflict of Laws Act and not the 1971 Hague Convention on the Law Applicable to Traffic Accidents); Supreme Court of Croatia, Gzz 28/92, 5 May 1993 (applying Art. 31 Conflict of Laws Act and not the 1961 Hague Convention on the Conflicts of Laws Relating to the Form of Testamentary Dispositions) (K. Sajko, H. Sikirić, V. Bouček, D. Babić and N. Tepeš, *Izvori hrvatskog i europskog međunarodnog privatnog prava,* Informator, Zagreb 2001, pp. 148–149).

14 Art. 2 Act Concerning the Conditions of Accession of the Republic of Croatia to the Treaty on European Union, the Treaty on the Functioning of the European Union and the Treaty Establishing the European Atomic Energy Community.

15 D. Babić, 'Opće uređenje starnačkog izbora mjerodavnog prava prema Uredbi (EZ) 593/2008 o pravu mjerodavnom za ugovorne obveze (Rim I)' (2016) 5(3) *Zagrebačka pravna revija* 273.

concluded after 1 July 2013 (Article 28 Rome I), and the Rome II Regulation to events occurring after 1 July 2013 (Article 31 Rome II).[16] The law applicable to contracts that were concluded and events that occurred prior to that date is determined according to the rules of Croatian Private International Law Act of 1982 and other rules of internal Croatian private international law.[17]

The Croatian legal system does not accept the doctrine of precedent; however, lower courts are influenced by the decisions of the appellate courts, as well as the decisions of the Supreme Court and the Constitutional Court.[18] At the time of writing, there are two reported appellate court decisions applying the Rome I Regulation and no appellate court decisions applying the Rome II regulation. Some, but not all, of the decisions on the application of the 1982 Private International Law Act provisions concerning contractual and non-contractual obligations have been published, as have some decisions on the application of the relevant Hague Conventions.

In the Croatian legal system, unlike some other legal systems, conflict-of-laws rules are mandatory in nature.[19] There is a significant number of cases where the courts have applied substantive domestic law without consulting conflict-of-laws rules at all. Similarly, courts have often ignored the international treaties that are in force in Croatia. Appellate courts increasingly quash lower court decisions for failure to apply private international law and international treaties.[20] In both reported decisions applying the Rome I Regulation, the appellate court returned the case back to the lower court based on the fact that the lower courts failed

---

16 The same principle applies to the timely application of other European regulations in Croatia. For example, the Brussels I Regulation applies to legal proceedings instituted and to documents formally drawn up or registered as authentic instruments after 1 July 2013 (Art. 66 Council Regulation (EC) No. 44/2001of 22 December 2000 on jurisdiction and the recognition and enforcement of judgments in civil and commercial matters). D. Babić, 'Vremenske granice primjene uredaba 44/2001 i 1215/2012 u Hrvatskoj', in J. Garašić (ed.), *Europsko građansko procesno pravo*, Narodne novine, Zagreb 2013, p. 140.

17 D. Babić, supra n. 15, p. 273.

18 H. Ernst, supra n. 1.

19 H. Sikirić, 'Primjena kolizijskih pravila i stranog prava u sudskom postupku' (2006) 56 *Zbornik Pravnog fakulteta u Zagrebu* 672; K. Sajko, *Međunarodno privatno pravo*, Narodne novine, Zagreb 2009, p. 229; M. Župan, *Pravo najbliže veze u hrvatskom i eurospkom međunarodnom privatnom ugovornom pravu*, Pravni fakultet u Rijeci, Rijeka 2006, p. 199.

20 Constitutional Court, Judgment No. U-III/1162/2001, 5 December 2001; High Commercial Court, Judgment No. Pž-632/03, 9 July 2005; High Commercial Court, Judgment No. Pž 4546/03-3, 13 December 2006; High Commercial Court, Judgment No. Pž 2729/06-3, 13 February 2007; High Commercial Court, Judgment No. Pž-5414/04, 4 July 2007; High Commercial Court, Judgment No. Pž 7719/04-3, 18 September 2007; High Commercial Court, Judgment No. Pž 3345/05-3, 30 October 2007; High Commercial Court, Judgment No. Pž 1115/05-4, 18 January 2008; High Commercial Court, Judgment No. Pž 4459/05-4, 26 June 2008; High Commercial Court, Judgment No. Pž 2467/02-3, 17 May 2005; High Commercial Court, Judgment No. Pž 254/03-3, 15 February 2006; High Commercial Court, Judgment No. Pž 802/03-3, 7 September 2006.

to apply the relevant provisions of the Rome I Regulation in a dispute arising out of a contract with an international element and applied Croatian substantive law instead.[21]

There are several institutions that administer arbitration in Croatia. The Permanent Arbitration Court of the Croatian Chamber of Economy (*Stalno arbitražno sudište pri Hrvatskoj gospodarskoj komori*), the leading arbitration institution in Croatia, has a long tradition. The Court administers all types of disputes. The types of cases vary from general commercial transactions, such as sale of goods, to complex infrastructural or financial disputes.

Awards and other decisions of arbitral tribunals are not publicly available. Sanitised excerpts of certain arbitral decisions are occasionally reported in connection to a specific topic. Selected excerpts from arbitral decisions have been published in the Croatian Arbitration Yearbook and other scholarly writings. There are no published arbitral decisions regarding the application of Rome I or Rome II.

According to the Croatian Arbitration Act, the application of the conflict-of-laws rules of any legal system is not mandatory in arbitral proceedings.[22] Parties are free to choose the applicable law and, where a choice has not been made, the arbitral tribunal shall apply the law most closely connected with the dispute. A 2002 study on practice in arbitrations administered by the PAC CCE[23] showed that arbitrators nevertheless tended to apply Croatian conflict-of-laws rules.[24] However, the rules were not always applied in the same manner as they are usually applied before a state court. For example, like in judicial proceedings, the choice-of-law in arbitral proceedings does not have to be explicit, but not all factors are given the same weight as before a state court. Choice of the seat of arbitration will not be as strong an indicator of the implicit choice of law, while a choice of court could be considered an indicator that the parties also opted for the application of the *lex fori*.[25] In all six reported cases, the decision on the applicable law was based on the conflict-of-laws rule set out in Article 20 of the Croatian Private International Law Act, but mindful of the purpose to apply the law that is most closely connected to the dispute, which is not otherwise

---

21 High Commercial Court, Judgment No. Pž-5942/2015-2, 18 May 2017; High Commercial Court, Judgment No. Pž-4902/2017-2, 5 September 2017.

22 D. Babić, 'Rome I Regulation: binding authority for arbitral tribunals in the European Union?' (2017) 13 *Journal of Private International Law* 71.

23 The research reported six cases: Permanent Arbitration Court of the Croatian Chamber of Economy (PAC CCE) IS-P-16/97, 15 December 1998; PAC CCE IS-P-32/94, 10 July 1995; PAC CCE IS-P-12/93, 13 April 1994; PAC CCE IS-P-5/93, 24 May 1994; PAC CCE IS-P-16/93, 2 June 1994; PAC CCE IS-P-15/96, 15 September 1997.

24 D. Babić, 'Određivanje prava mjerodavnog za ugovore u praksi Stalnog izbranog sudišta pri Hrvatskoj gospodarskoj komori' (2002) 12 *Hrvatska pravna revija* 156.

25 D. Babić, supra n. 24, p. 154.

seen in practice of the state courts.[26] The result in all six cases would have been the same if, instead of Croatian conflict-of-laws rules, the Rome Convention on the Law Applicable to Contractual Obligations had been applied.[27]

In addition to the Permanent Court, two specialised arbitration institutions have been established in Croatia. The Arbitration Court of the Croatian Olympic Committee administers sport-related arbitration disputes. The institution has created a Sports Arbitration Council that renders decisions in specific cases. The Arbitration Court established by Carnet, the domain name server of .hr (the Croatian domain name), resolves disputes over domain names. Arbitration is conducted by a sole arbitrator named by the Hr Governing Committee and chosen from a list of arbitrators. The two specialised arbitral institutions have handled a small number of cases so far that have not been publicly reported.[28]

2. THE EXTENSION OF THE APPLICATION OF THE ROME I AND ROME II REGULATIONS' RULES ACCORDING TO THE CROATIAN PILA

Rome I Regulation applies, in situations involving a conflict of laws, to contractual obligations in civil and commercial matters and does not apply, in particular, to revenue, customs or administrative matters (Article 1). Article 1 further sets forth a list of contractual obligations or other related matters that are explicitly excluded from the scope of application of the Regulation. Nothing in the Regulation, or EU law in general, precludes Member States from creating rules on excluded matters as they see fit, including by an extension of the rules of the Rome I Regulation.[29]

According to Article 25(2) of the 2017 Croatian Private International Law Act, the law applicable to contractual obligations that fall outside of the scope of application of the Rome I Regulation, and are not governed by another provision of national or international law in force in Croatia, is determined according to the provisions of the Rome I Regulation applicable to such contractual obligations.

The Rome II Regulation applies, in situations involving a conflict of laws, to non-contractual obligations in civil and commercial matters and, like

26 D. Babić, supra n. 24, p. 162.

27 D. Babić, supra n. 24, p. 162.

28 D. Zgrabljić Rotar, 'Arbitration – Country Report for Croatia', in A. Nuni et al. (eds.), *Civil Law Forum for South East Europe – Collection of studies and analyses*, Centre for SEELS, Skopje 2014, p. 226.

29 M. Weller, in G.P. Calliess (ed.), *Rome Regulations – Commentary*, Wolters Kluwer, Alphen aan den Rijn 2015, p. 58.

the Rome I Regulation, does not apply, in particular, to revenue, customs or administrative matters, or additionally to state liability for acts and omissions in the exercise of state authority (*acta iure imperii*) (Article 1). As in the Rome I Regulation, this provision of the Rome II Regulation is followed by a list of explicitly excluded non-contractual obligations. According to Article 26(2) of the 2017 Croatian Private International Law Act, the law applicable to non-contractual obligations that fall outside of the scope of application of the Rome II Regulation, and are not governed by another provision of national or international law in force in Croatia, is determined according to the provisions of the Rome II Regulation applicable to those non-contractual obligations.

This extension of the two Regulations will have to be interpreted in accordance with the other provisions of the 2017 Private International Law Act and the existing interpretations of the Rome I and Rome II Regulations respectively. Four requirements will have to be met to apply the conflict-of-laws rules found in the Rome I and Rome II Regulations to matters that are explicitly excluded from their respective scopes of application.

Firstly, per its scope of application as set forth in Article 1, the Croatian Private International Law Act can only apply to a private law matter. Private law matters include matters of general civil law (such as property law, the law of obligations and succession law), as well as family law, commercial law, labour law and other areas of private law. Private law matters are distinction from matters of public law, in which issues of the applicable law typically do not arise, since public law is generally considered according to Croatian law to have a territorial effect.[30] The term 'private law matter' is equivalent to the term 'civil and commercial matters' used in both the Rome I and Rome II Regulations. In this context, Croatian courts should rely on the meaning of 'private law matters' as understood in the Croatian national legal system (as opposed to the autonomous interpretation required when applying the Regulations), since the basis for the application of the European rules would not lie in one of the two Regulations but in the Croatian Private International Law Act.

Secondly, the legal relationship at issue must involve a foreign element. The foreign element may consist in the affiliation of a party with a foreign jurisdiction (e.g. seat, domicile or habitual residence abroad), the location of the subject matter (e.g. property located abroad), or in the fact that the substance of the legal relationship is otherwise connected with a foreign jurisdiction (e.g. contractual performance to be effected abroad).[31]

---

30 D. Babić, supra n. 5, p. 441.

31 T. Varady, *Međunarodne i unutrašnje kolizione norme – odnos i sadejstva, posebno prema ustavima u SFRJ*, Savremena administracija, Belgrade 1975, p. 28; M. Dika, G. Knežević and S. Stojanović, *Komentar Zakona o međunarodnom privatnom i procesnom pravu*, Nomos, Belgrade 1990, p. 10; D. Babić, supra n. 5, p. 441.

Thirdly, the matter has to involve a contractual obligation (in the case of the extension of the Rome I Regulation) or a non-contractual obligation (in the case of the extension of the Rome II Regulation). Whether or not the legal relationship is a 'contractual obligation' or a 'non-contractual obligation' is to be interpreted in accordance with Croatian national law. Under Croatian law, a contract is said to have been concluded when the parties have agreed on the essential parts of the contract.[32] Contractual liability arises as 'a result of non-performance or delay in performance of a contractual obligation'.[33] Extra-contractual or non-contractual liability arises as a result of a tort or delict, and the following conditions must be met: the subjects, i.e. the tortfeasor and the victim, must have a legal relationship; there must be a wrongful act; damage must result; there must be a causal link between the wrongful act and the damage; and there must be unlawfulness in an objective sense, meaning the wrongful act or omission is contrary to a legal provision.[34]

Finally, for the Rome I or Rome II Regulations to apply on the basis of the extension provided by national law, there cannot be any other provision of national or international law governing the same issue in Croatia. Where a matter is governed by a *lex specialis* or an international treaty, the extension of the rules of the Rome I or Rome II Regulations is not possible.

In practice, there are very few possible situations in which the Rome I and Rome II Regulation rules could apply based on the extension provided in Articles 25 and 26 of the 2017 Croatian Private International Law Act. Conflict-of-laws rules for the majority of the excluded matters are found either in other EU regulations, or in international or national sources of law in force in Croatia. The 2017 Private International Law Act, for example, sets forth the rules for questions involving the status or legal capacity of natural persons[35] and the rules for questions governed by the law of companies and other bodies, corporate or unincorporated, such as the creation (by registration or otherwise), legal capacity, internal organisation or winding-up of companies and other bodies, corporate or unincorporated, and the personal liability of officers and members as such for the obligations of the company or body.[36] The 1958 New York Convention on the Recognition and Enforcement of Foreign Arbitral Awards arguably provides for a conflict-of-laws rule on the validity of arbitration agreements;[37] and the Brussels I Regulation (recast) provides a

---

32 Art. 247 *Zakon o obveznim odnosima, Narodne novine* (Official Gazette) Nos. 35/05, 41/08, 125/11, 78/15.

33 M. Baretić, 'Tort Law', in T. Josipović (ed.), *Introduction to the Law of Croatia*, Wolters Kluwer, Alphen aan den Rijn 2014, p. 163.

34 M. Baretić, supra n. 33, p. 164.

35 Art. 1(2)(a) Rome I Regulation.

36 Art. 1(2)(f) Rome I Regulation.

37 Art. 1(2)(e) Rome I Regulation.

conflict-of-laws rule on the validity of choice-of-court agreements.[38] There is the possibility of extending the rules of Rome I Regulation to the constitution of trusts and the relationship between settlers, trustees and beneficiaries,[39] but only insofar as such a relationship may be characterised as either a contractual or non-contractual obligation.[40] Another possibility lies in the last exclusion listed in Article 1 of the Rome I Regulation,[41] introduced with the aim of avoiding any influence on the Member States' social security systems.[42] Since there is no *lex specialis* or international instrument governing this matter in Croatia, the general rules on insurance contracts found in Article 7 of the Rome I Regulation could apply to this specific type of insurance contract as well. As far as the extension of the Rome II Regulation rules is concerned, there are also two situations in which that would be possible. The first situation is, for similar reasons as the extension of the Rome I rules, the matter of non-contractual obligations arising out of the relationship between the settlors, trustees and beneficiaries of a trust created voluntarily.[43] The second situation is that concerning non-contractual obligations arising out of violations of privacy and rights relating to personality, including defamation.[44]

3. THE OPERATION OF ROME I AND ROME II IN PRACTICE

3.1. *LOIS DE POLICE*

The 1982 Croatian Private International Law Act does not contain a general provision on *lois de police*, or overriding mandatory provisions. The Act only specifies that certain rules of Croatian substantive law govern specific aspects of a legal relationship directly, i.e. regardless of the otherwise governing law.

---

38 Art. 1(2)(e) Rome I Regulation.

39 Art. 1(2)(h) Rome I Regulation.

40 This extension is also in line with the fact that 'legal relationships under continental civil law functionally equivalent to trusts fall within the Rome I Regulation as soon as they are of a contractual nature'. M. Weller, supra n. 29, p. 68.

41 Art. 1(2)(j) Rome I Regulation: 'insurance contracts arising out of operations carried out by organisations other than undertakings referred to in Article 2 of Directive 2002/83/EC of the European Parliament and of the Council of 5 November 2002 concerning life assurance (14) the object of which is to provide benefits for employed or self-employed persons belonging to an undertaking or group of undertakings, or to a trade or group of trades, in the event of death or survival or of discontinuance or curtailment of activity, or of sickness related to work or accidents at work'.

42 M. Weller, supra n. 29, p. 70.

43 Art. 1(2)(e) Rome II Regulation.

44 Art. 1(2)(g) Rome II Regulation.

Thus, for example, according to Article 32(2) of the 1982 Private International Law Act, even if a person may enter into a marriage according to the law of the country of their nationality, they may not enter into a marriage in Croatia if, with respect to that person, there is an impediment relating to the existence of a prior marriage, kinship or mental incapacity.

The concept of overriding mandatory provisions has however been recognised in the doctrine. Adopting the French legal terminology (*règles d'application immédiate*), academic commentary refers to these norms as the 'rules of immediate application' (*pravila neposredne primjene*).[45] It is generally accepted that foreign rules of immediate application may be applied by Croatian courts if they are a part of Croatian law or when they form part of the law governing the substance of the case.[46] It is less clear whether courts could apply, or take into account, rules of immediate application of a foreign country whose law does not govern the case. According to some commentators, this question should be answered in the negative, as this possibility was never considered during the drafting of the 1982 Private International Law Act.[47] Other authors take the position that it would be possible, even in the absence of an explicit norm, to at least take into account third-country rules of immediate application.[48]

The issue has been, to some extent, resolved in the 2017 Private International Law Act, which contains a general provision on overriding mandatory rules. Adopting almost word-for-word the language of Article 9 of the Rome I Regulation, the 2017 Private International Law Act provides in Article 13 that the courts shall always give effect to the overriding mandatory rules of Croatian law, defined as 'provisions the respect for which is regarded as crucial by a country for safeguarding its public interests, such as its political, social or economic organisation'.[49] The court may apply an overriding mandatory provision of a third country if it renders the performance of the whole contract or a part of the contract unlawful.[50]

There has been no published case law on the application of the overriding mandatory rules by Croatian courts within the meaning provided in the Rome I and Rome II Regulation. Although the courts have in the past applied Croatian overriding mandatory rules and their identification was generally not a problem, they do not expressly refer to an applied rule as a *loi de police.*

---

45 K. Sajko, supra n. 19, pp. 279–282; M. Dika, G. Knežević and S. Stojanović, supra n. 31; T. Varadi, B. Bordaš, G. Knežević and V. Pavić, *Međunarodno privatno pravo,* Pravni fakultet Univerziteta u Beogradu, Belgrade 2016, pp. 165–174; D. Babić, supra n. 5, p. 443.

46 T. Varadi, B. Bordaš, G. Knežević and V. Pavić, supra n. 45, p. 171.

47 M. Dika, G. Knežević and S. Stojanović, supra n. 31, p. 18.

48 T. Varadi, B. Bordaš, G. Knežević and V. Pavić, supra n. 45, pp. 171–173.

49 Art. 13(1) Conflict of Laws Act.

50 Art. 13(2) Conflict of Laws Act.

3.2. PARTY AUTONOMY

According to Article 19 of the 1982 Private International Law Act, a contract is governed by the law chosen by the contracting parties, unless statutory law or an international treaty provides otherwise.

Although the law does not expressly so provide, commentators agree that, under this provision, choice of law may be express (i.e. in the form of a contractual choice-of-law clause) or inferred from the terms of the contract or the circumstances of the case.[51]

The parties' choice of law under Article 19 means the selection of the actual governing law, not the mere incorporation of the chosen law into the contract. The chosen law applies to the exclusion of any other law, subject only to the public policy exception.[52] The chosen law has to be a law of a specific country; the parties cannot choose a unified set of rules or the *lex mercatoria* to govern their contract. According to commentators on the 1982 Private International Law Act, like now under Recital 13 of the Rome I Regulation, the parties can incorporate a uniform set of rules into their contract.[53]

For certain types of contracts, the freedom to choose the applicable law is excluded or restricted by the 1982 Private International Law Act. For example, contracts involving immovable property are governed exclusively by the law of the country in which the property is situated and the parties may not select a different law (Article 21). This restriction has been criticised in the literature, because the rationale for the application of the *lex rei sitae* for rights *in rem* does not apply to bilateral legal relationships, such as contracts.[54] In consumer contracts, choice of law is allowed, but it may not deprive the consumer of the protection afforded under Croatian law, if the consumer is a resident in Croatia (Article 4).

Article 19 does not mention the possibility of *dépeçage*, and although there were different opinions by different scholars, the idea that the parties are, in general, not allowed to choose different laws to govern different parts of their contract, has prevailed.[55]

---

51 Ž. Matić, 'Mjerodavno pravo za ugovore prema Zakonu o rješavanju sukoba zakona s propisima drugih zemalja iz 1982. Godine' (1985) 2–3 *Zbornik Pravnog fakulteta u Zagrebu* 214; G. Knežević, *Merodavno pravo za trgovački ugovor o međunarodnoj prodaji robe*, Belgrade 1989, p. 49; K. Sajko, supra n. 19, p. 144; M. Dika, G. Knežević and S. Stojanović, supra n. 31, p. 74.

52 M. Dika, G. Knežević and S. Stojanović, supra n. 31, p. 75; T. Varadi, 'Spoljnotrgovinska arbitraža i internacionalističko koncipiranje autonomije volje' (1970) *Zbornik Pravnog fakulteta u Novom Sadu* 149.

53 M. Dika, G. Knežević and S. Stojanović, supra n. 31, p. 74.

54 D. Babić, 'Izbor nadležnog suda i mjerodavnog prava u ugovorima o nekretninama s međunarodnim obilježjem' (2007) 7 *Pravo i porezi* 48–52.

55 M. Dika, G. Knežević and S. Stojanović, supra n. 31, p. 75.

The reported Croatian courts' judgments on the Rome I Regulation dealt, in essence, with the party autonomy in contracts with an international element. In one decision, the High Commercial Court held that, contrary to the plaintiff's claims, the plaintiff had not proven that the parties had chosen Croatian substantive law as the applicable law.[56] Thus, the lower court should establish, in accordance with Article 3 of the Rome I Regulation, whether the parties have validly chosen the applicable law. In the other decision, the High Commercial Court quashed the decision of the lower court by which the Croatian substantive law is applicable in a case between an Austrian seller and a Croatian buyer because the parties had not chosen the applicable law.[57] The High Commercial Court found that the applicable law should, based on Article 4 of the Rome I Regulation, be the law of the seller, i.e. Austrian law.

The 1982 Private International Law Act does not provide for party autonomy in tort cases. To the extent that the substantive legal rules of the *lex loci delicti* give the parties the freedom to regulate their relationship as they wish, they may incorporate the rules of another law as a part of their agreement. The ability to choose the governing law for non-contractual obligations was, for the first time, introduced through the provisions of the Rome II Regulation. Although some scholars had argued that party autonomy in non-contractual obligations should be allowed even before Croatia joined the EU,[58] because that would be in line with the Stabilisation and Association Agreement between the EC and Croatia, there is no published case law indicating that this interpretation has been accepted by the courts.

3.3. ABSENCE OF CHOICE OF LAW

The fixed rules on the law applicable to specific types of contracts found in Article 4 of the Rome I Regulation are not a major novelty for the Croatian legal system. According to Article 20 of the 1982 Private International Law Act, if the parties have not chosen the applicable law, the law provides for connecting factors for specific types of contracts, such as sale of goods, service contracts, agency, forwarding, loans, etc. Thus, connecting factors were, in Croatian law, listed in a manner resembling Article 117 of the Swiss Private International Law Act or Article 4 of the Rome I Regulation.

---

56 High Commercial Court, Judgment No. Pž-4902/2017-2, 5 September 2017.

57 High Commercial Court, Judgment No. Pž-5942/2015-2, 18 May 2017.

58 V. Bouček and M. Sente, 'Stranačka autonomija kao poveznica deliktnog statuta u Uredbi Rim II' (2009) 48 *Pravo u gospodarstvu* 1291.

For most types of contracts, the Croatian Private International Law Act indicates that the law of the characteristic performer applies.[59] Thus, for example, sales contracts are governed by the law of the seller (point 1), agency contracts by the law of the agent (point 3), loans by the law of the lender (point 8), insurance contracts by the law of the insurer (point 13), etc. For some types of contracts, the law does not follow the principle of characteristic performance. For example, contracts made in a regulated market are governed by the law of the market (point 15) and technology transfer agreements by the law of the transferee (point 18).

The most important deviation from the principle of characteristic performance is found in the general clause of item 20, which provides that contracts not listed in the preceding points are governed by the law of the offeror. Given that many types of contracts – such as a distributorship, franchise, joint venture, purchase of shares and other financial instruments, etc. – are not listed in points 1–19, the provision point 20 is wide in scope. The rule on the application of the law of the offeror has been rightly criticised on two counts. First, this connecting factor appears to be random. One cannot expect that the contract will automatically have a closer connection with the law of the offeror as opposed to the law of the offeree. Second, it may be difficult in many cases to determine which party in a chain of offers and counteroffers was the offeror and which the offeree.[60]

According to Article 28(1) of the 1982 Private International Law Act, the law governing tortious liability is the law of the place where the act was performed or the law of the place where the consequences occurred, whichever is more favourable for the victim.

This provision codifies the *lex loci delicti* as the fundamental principle of tort conflicts. It explicitly adopts the so-called principle of ubiquity of cross border torts – if a tortious act committed in one jurisdiction (*lex loci actus*) produces a harmful effect in another jurisdiction (*lex loci damni*), the tort is deemed to be located in both jurisdictions. The choice between the two laws is resolved in accordance with the *favor laesi* principle, which states that the courts shall apply the law that is more favourable to the victim. Commentators agree that it is clear from the wording of Article 28 that it is for the court to determine *ex officio* which law is more favourable to the victim. The law does not give the victim the option to choose between the two laws.[61] The disadvantage in practice

---

59 Ž. Matić, supra n. 51, p. 218; M. Dika, G. Knežević and S. Stojanović, supra n. 31, p. 79; K. Sajko, supra n. 19, pp. 163–164.

60 M. Dika, G. Knežević and S. Stojanović, supra n. 31, p. 80; D. Babić, supra n. 54, pp. 48–52.

61 K. Sajko, supra n. 19, p. 154; M. Pak, *Međunarodno privatno pravo*, Naučna knjiga, Belgrade 1986, pp. 865–866; M. Ilešič, A. Polajnar-Pavčnik and D. Wedam-Lukić, *Mednarodno zasebno pravo, zakon s komentarjem*, Uradni list SR Slovenije, Ljubljana 1983, p. 47; M. Dika, G. Knežević and S. Stojanović, supra n. 31, p. 99.

is that, rather than leaving it to the plaintiff to determine which law is most favourable to his or her interests, the court must determine the content of both laws, compare them and decide which benefits the victim most. Not only does this inquiry require time and expense, it may not always be easy to tell which law is more favourable to the plaintiff (e.g. one law may be more favourable to the plaintiff with respect to liability, another with respect to the quantum).

Courts generally see it as their duty to determine which law is most favourable to the victim,[62] and in some cases they have applied the law on which the plaintiff relied in the pleadings.[63]

The court practice has been inconsistent on the issue of whether indirect harmful effects – such as the harm the victim suffers in the place of his or her habitual residence to his or her assets, health or well-being – should be taken into account when determining the applicable law. In a case decided in 1992, the plaintiff domiciled in Germany sued for the damage he suffered as a result of an accident that happened in Croatia. The High Commercial Court held that the harmful effect occurred not only in Croatia, but also in Germany, because it was there that the plaintiff suffered indirect consequences of the accident.[64] In a landmark 2007 decision, the Supreme Court adopted a different view, albeit in the context of jurisdiction. It held that Croatian courts may not assume jurisdiction under Article 53 of the Private International Law Act on the basis of mere indirect harmful effects. The case involved a suit by the widow and daughter of a crew member on a Croatian ship who lost his life in an accident that occurred in Piraeus, Greece. The court held that in that case the harmful effect took place only in Greece, not in Croatia, where the plaintiffs suffered the consequences of the loss of life of their relative.[65] Although the case concerned jurisdiction, the reasoning of the court is equally applicable in the context of determining the governing law.

If the harmful effects occur in more than one jurisdiction, the courts seem to apply the most favourable law to the entire claim, rather than applying different laws to effects in different countries (mosaic approach). A case in point is a decision of the Supreme Court,[66] where the plaintiff domiciled in Croatia sued the Slovenian newspaper *Delo* for libel. *Delo* is primarily distributed in Slovenia and only a very small number of copies are sold in Croatia. The court held that Croatian law, as the law more favourable to the plaintiff, applied to the

62 High Commercial Court, Judgment No. Pž-1010/93 of 24 March 1992; High Commercial Court, Judgment No. Pž-1010/93 of 18 May 1993; V. Tomljenović, supra n. 11, pp. 193–194.

63 High Commercial Court, Judgment No. Pž-6257/03-3, 22 November 2006; Supreme Court of Croatia, Rev 3197/1995-2, 22 November 1995.

64 High Commercial Court, Judgment No. Pž-335/92, 24 March 1992; K. Sajko, supra n. 19, p. 148.

65 Supreme Court of Croatia, Revt 51/03-2, 27 February 2007.

66 Supreme Court of Croatia, Rev 3197/1995-2, 22 November 1995.

entire claim, including the harmful effects produced by the publication in Slovenia.

The law sets out a special rule on conflict relating to the issue of the unlawfulness of the harmful action. Article 28(3) of the Private International Law Act specifies that, for the purposes of determining tortious liability, an act shall be considered unlawful if it is unlawful under either the law of the place where the act was performed or where the consequences occurred. If the act was performed or the consequences occurred in more than one place, it is sufficient that the act is unlawful according to the law of any of those places. This provision affords additional protection to the victim. Under this provision, it is possible for one law to apply to the issue of unlawfulness, and another law, which is more favourable in any other respect, to all other substantive issues.[67]

3.4. SPECIFIC RULES

There are no decisions by Croatian courts on the specific rules on contracts of carriage, consumer contracts, insurance contracts and employment contracts in the Rome I Regulation.

The primary connecting factor for all four types of contract was party autonomy, set forth in Article 19 of the 1982 Private International Law Act. Consumers in Croatia were protected through a provision, similar to the one currently found in Article 6 of the Rome I Regulation, that was part of the Croatian Consumer Act.[68] According to Article 4 of the Croatian Consumer Act, 'the consumer shall have the right to protection on the basis of this Act, regardless of the fact that the foreign applicable law has been chosen by the contract'. Although the underlying idea is, like in the Rome I Regulation, consumer protection, the provision is essentially a unilateral norm. It does not guarantee consumers residing abroad application of the consumer protection laws of their country of residence.

If the parties do not make a choice of law, Article 20 of the 1982 Croatian Private International Law Act includes fixed rules on the applicable law: for the contracts of carriage, this is the law of the place where the carrier was domiciled or had its seat at the time of the acceptance of the offer;[69] for insurance contracts, the law of the place where the insurer was domiciled or had its seat at the time of the acceptance of the offer;[70] and for property claims arising out of employment contracts, the law of the state were the contract was to be or

[67] M. Dika, G. Knežević and S. Stojanović, supra n. 31, p. 99.

[68] *Zakon o zaštiti potrošača*, *Narodne novine* (Official Gazette), No. 96/03.

[69] Art. 20(12) 1982 Conflict of Laws Act.

[70] Art. 20(13) 1982 Conflict of Laws Act.

was performed. For all these categories, an escape clause was allowed to cover the situations where 'special circumstances of the case' refer to another law. Thus, all of the solutions found in the 1982 Conflict of Laws Act were essentially in line with the Rome I Regulation's special provisions currently in force. The only conflict-of-laws rule that stands out is that used to determine the law applicable to consumer contracts in the event that the parties have not chosen the applicable law and the contract does not fall within one of the categories listed in the fixed rules. The rule for all contracts not specifically listed is that the applicable law will be the law of the place where the offeror was domiciled or had its seat at the time of the acceptance of the offer.

Further, there is also no case law on the application of the Rome II Regulation's specific rules on product liability, unfair competition and acts restricting free competition, environmental damage, infringement of intellectual property rights and industrial damage. However, some of the concepts introduced by the Rome II Regulation were already present in Croatian legal system through other sources of law.

Croatia is party to the Hague Convention of 2 October 1973 on the Law Applicable to Products Liability. Since the rule on product liability laid down in Article 5 of the Rome II Regulation relies heavily on the solutions adopted by the Hague Convention,[71] the system for determining the applicable law for product liability under the Rome II Regulation was already known to the Croatian legislator and in practice.[72]

3.5. RULES APPLICABLE TO NON-CONTRACTUAL OBLIGATIONS OTHER THAN TORTS OR DELICTS

While other non-contractual obligations within the meaning of the Rome I and Rome II Regulations, such as unjust enrichment (Article 10 Rome II), *negotiorum gestio* (Article 11 Rome II) and *culpa in contrahendo* (Article 12 Rome II) are to be interpreted autonomously, without recourse to national law, it is perhaps worth noting that the concepts are known in Croatian national law and that their definitions under Croatian law do not significantly deviate from the prevailing understanding of the concepts in other civil law jurisdictions.

Culpa in contrahendo, or pre-contractual liability, is defined as liability for damage sustained by one party to the negotiation that occurred as a result of an act by the other party during negotiations which was contrary to the principle of good faith, especially if the party disrupted the negotiations contrary to

71 C. Schmid and T. Pinkel, in G.P. Calliess (ed.), *Rome Regulations – Commentary*, Wolters Kluwer, Alphen aan den Rijn 2015, pp. 536–537.

72 See, for example, the judgment of the Supreme Court of the Republic of Croatia, Rev 17/2007-2, 10 May 2007.

good faith or entered the negotiations without a real intention to conclude the contract (Article 251 of the Croatian Obligations Act).[73] Thus, it must be proven that one party acted in a manner contrary to the principle of good faith – since according to Article 4 of the Croatian Obligations Act, the good faith principle equally applies in the course of creating the obligations as well as in course of performing them – and proven that the act occurred during the actual negotiation process.[74] In the Croatian legal system, pre-contractual liability is not considered part of contractual or extra-contractual liability, but rather a separate type of liability.[75]

Condictio sine causa, or unjust enrichment, is understood and defined in the Croatian legal system in a similar way to that in Article 10 of the Rome II Regulation. Unjust enrichment is regulated in Articles 1111–1120 of the Croatian Obligations Act. The presumptions of *condictio sine causa* are that one party increased their assets, that the other party had a decrease in their assets, that there was a causal link between the increase on the one side and the decrease on the other, and that it was caused by an unjust factor.[76] The key concept is the definition of 'unjust'. In the Croatian legal system, the understanding of 'unjust' is almost identical to the one in the Rome II Regulation. Under both the Croatian Obligations Act and the Rome II Regulation, the concept implies 'the lack of legal cause or entitlement' that is 'neither contractual nor tortious'.[77]

The understanding in the Croatian legal system of the concept of *negotiorum gestio*, referred to in Article 11 of the Rome II Regulation, is also in line with the interpretation of the application of Article 11. The concept is governed by Articles 1121–1126 of the Croatian Obligations Act. There must be a relationship between the agent/intervener (*negotiorum gestor*) and the principal (*dominus negotii*), and this relationship must be caused by the agent's intervention without the authority of the principal so as to affect the affairs of the principal.[78] The act must be in the interest of the principal.[79]

From the above, it is likely that the courts in Croatia will not have a problem in applying Articles 10 and 11 of the Rome II Regulation.

---

73 P. Klarić and M. Vedriš, *Građansko pravo*, Narodne novine, Zagreb 2014, p. 606; M. Baretić, supra n. 33, pp. 186–187.

74 M. Baretić, supra n. 33, p. 186.

75 P. Klarić and M. Vedriš, supra n. 73, p. 607; M. Baretić, supra n. 33, p. 163.

76 P. Klarić and M. Vedriš, supra n. 73, p. 646.

77 B. Schinkels, in G.P. Calliess (ed.), *Rome Regulations – Commentary*, Wolters Kluwer, Alphen aan den Rijn 2015, pp. 660–661; P. Klarić and M. Vedriš, supra n. 73, p. 646.

78 B. Schinkels, supra n. 77, p. 676; P. Klarić and M. Vedriš, supra n. 73, pp. 652–653.

79 P. Klarić and M. Vedriš, supra n. 73, p. 652. Some scholars find that, in regard to the application of Art. 11 Rome II Regulation, there is some uncertainty as to the possibility that the agent can intervene in his own interest as well, but those kinds of cases would in practice be extremely rare (B. Schinkels, supra n. 77, p. 677).

3.6. FOREIGN LAW

The application and the position of foreign law is an issue not dealt with in the Rome I and Rome II Regulations, and is thus governed by national law. In Croatia, it is currently governed by Article 8 of the 2017 Private International Law Act. The 2017 Croatian Private International Law Act, which has replaced the 1982 Act, has a slightly different provision on the application of foreign law.

The application of conflict-of-laws rules is mandatory in Croatia.[80] Foreign law has the same position as domestic law and is not, as in some other legal systems, considered a fact. Parties are allowed all available legal remedies in the event of its wrongful application, as well as in the event (more often seen in practice) that the court does not apply a foreign law where the conflict-of-laws rule would render it applicable.[81] There is a significant number of cases where courts have applied substantive domestic law without consulting conflict-of-laws rules at all, which has usually led to a successful appeal by the parties.[82]

According to both the 1982 Private International Law Act and the 2017 Private International Law Act, the principle of *iura novit curia* applies with respect to foreign law. The court or another competent body shall determine *ex officio* the content of foreign law.[83] The 2017 Private International Law Act clarifies that foreign law shall be applied as in its country of origin.[84] The provision already existed in the 1982 Private International Law Act, but is for the first time part of the same article as the *ex officio* determination in the 2017 PILA.

Notwithstanding the *iura novit curia* rule, it is a recognised fact that judges cannot be expected to know the laws of foreign jurisdictions, and thus provisions aiming to facilitate the understanding of applicable foreign law have been introduced into the Private International Law Act. Both the 1982 and the 2017

80 H. Sikirić, supra n. 19, p. 672.

81 H. Sikirić, supra n. 19, p. 672; M. Dika, G. Knežević and S. Stojanović, supra n. 31, p. 50.

82 Constitutional Court, Judgment No. U-III/1162/2001, 5 December 2001; High Commercial Court, Judgment No. Pž-632/03, 9 July 2005; High Commercial Court, Judgment No. Pž 4546/03-3, 13 December 2006; High Commercial Court, Judgment No. Pž 2729/06-3, 13 February 2007; High Commercial Court, Judgment No. Pž-5414/04, 4 July 2007; High Commercial Court, Judgment No. Pž 7719/04-3, 18 September 2007; High Commercial Court, Judgment No. Pž 3345/05-3, 30 October 2007; High Commercial Court, Judgment No. Pž 1115/05-4, 18 January 2008; High Commercial Court, Judgment No. Pž 4459/05-4, 26 June 2008; High Commercial Court, Judgment No. Pž 2467/02-3, 17 May 2005; High Commercial Court, Judgment No. Pž 254/03-3, 15 February 2006; High Commercial Court, Judgment No. Pž 802/03-3, 7 September 2006.

83 Art. 8 2017 Croatian Conflict of Laws Act; Art. 13 1982 Conflict of Laws Act.

84 Art. 8(2) 2017 Croatian Conflict of Laws Act.

Private International Law Acts direct the courts to request, when appropriate, the information on foreign law from the Croatian Ministry of Justice. The 2017 Private International Law Act introduces the possibility of requesting the information from an expert or another body or specialised institution.

As of 2013, the European Convention on Information on Foreign Law is also in force in Croatia.[85] Under the Convention, Croatia is obligated to set up or appoint a single body to receive requests for the information from another contracting party and to take action on these requests. The appointed transmitting agency in Croatia is the Department for European Affairs, International and Judicial Cooperation, attached to the Croatian Ministry of Justice.

According to both the 1982 and 2017 Private International Law Acts, the parties to the proceedings may submit an official document on the content of the foreign law. However, such documents will have the same position as all other authentic documents,[86] making the content of such a document, as well as its authenticity, only a rebuttable presumption, allowing the court to apply the foreign law according to its own understanding of it.[87]

A new element in the 2017 Croatian Private International Law Act is the introduction of a provision according to which the court may apply Croatian law in the event that it cannot establish the content of the applicable foreign law.[88] It is generally accepted that the court cannot dismiss an action solely because it cannot determine the content of the applicable foreign law.[89] Following the suggestions made in scholarly writings,[90] the 2017 Private International Law Act provides that in such cases courts shall apply Croatian law.

3.7. *ORDRE PUBLIC*

According to Article 4 of the 1982 Private International Law Act, 'the law of a foreign state shall not apply if that would be contrary to the basic principles of state organisation laid down by the Constitution of the Republic of Croatia'. *Ordre public* does not include all mandatory law, but encompasses only the most fundamental values of Croatian law that have to be protected, even if a foreign

---

85 *Narodne novine – Međunarodni ugovori* (Official Gazette – International Treaties), No. 13/13.

86 H. Sikirić, supra n. 19, p. 673.

87 M. Dika, G. Knežević and S. Stojanović, supra n. 31, p. 50; H. Sikirić, supra n. 19, pp. 673–674.

88 Art. 8(5) 2017 Croatian Conflict of Laws Act.

89 H. Sikirić, supra n. 19, p. 675; K. Sajko, supra n. 19, p. 223, M. Dika and S. Triva, *Građansko parnično procesno pravo*, Narodne novine, Zagreb 2004, p. 183.

90 H. Sikirić, supra n. 19, p. 678; M. Dika, G. Knežević and S. Stojanović, supra n. 31, p. 50; K. Sajko, supra n. 19, p. 229.

law is otherwise applicable.[91] The prevailing view is that Article 4 of the Private International Law Act should not be interpreted as restricting the *ordre public* exception to constitutional norms.[92] The courts may refuse to apply foreign law only if the specific result reached by applying that law would violate *ordre public*. The courts should not examine whether the law of a foreign state is *in abstracto* compatible with the public policy of Croatia.[93]

In line with the scholarly interpretations of the provision on *ordre public*, the 2017 Private International Law Act sets forth a slightly changed provision, according to which 'rules of foreign law applicable according to this law shall not apply if the effect of such application is manifestly incompatible with the public policy of the Republic of Croatia.'[94] This provision now uses a similar wording to that in, for example, Article 21 of the Rome I Regulation and Article 26 of the Rome II Regulation.

According to both scholarly[95] and judicial interpretation,[96] the public policy exception should be construed narrowly. Croatian courts normally take for granted that the application of foreign law usually does not violate Croatian *ordre public*. Court decisions almost never discuss whether or not applying a particular foreign rule of law would violate the fundamental principles of Croatian law, although the parties often invoke the public policy exception during proceedings. There is almost no published case law on the public policy exception in the context of the application of foreign law.

One published court decision has dealt with this topic in a disappointing manner. In a 2007 appellate decision, the High Commercial Court held that Czech law, which the parties had chosen in their agreement, could not be applied because it would lead to a violation of Croatian public policy. The court held that the contract at issue created a severe disparity of rights and obligations, in favour of the Czech party. The court failed to explain which particular principle of Croatian law would have been violated and why that principle should be elevated to the rank of public policy.[97]

---

91 See e.g. T. Varadi, B. Bordaš, G. Knežević and V. Pavić, supra n. 45, p. 154; M. Dika, G. Knežević and S. Stojanović, supra n. 31, p. 15, 47; M. Pak, supra n. 61, p. 607; I. Grbin, *Priznanje i izvršenje odluka stranih sudova*, Informator, Zagreb 1980, p. 117.

92 M. Dika, G. Knežević and S. Stojanović, supra n. 31, p. 16. According to Polajnar-Pavčnik, Art. 4 should be interpreted as restricting the public policy exception only to constitutional principles (supra n. 61, p. 20).

93 K. Sajko, supra n. 19, p. 259; M. Dika, G. Knežević and S. Stojanović, supra n. 31, pp. 16–17; T. Varadi, B. Bordaš, G. Knežević and V. Pavić, supra n. 45, p. 194; M. Pak, supra n. 61, p. 598.

94 Art. 12 2017 Croatian Conflict of Laws Act.

95 M. Dika, G. Knežević and S. Stojanović, supra n. 31, p. 19.

96 Supreme Court of the Republic of Croatia, Revt 74/2007-2, 7 October 2009 (the decision emphasises that not all mandatory rules are a part of public policy); High Commercial Court, Judgment No. Pž-7632/11-3, 10 May 2012, Supreme Court of the Republic of Croatia, Judgment No. Gž 29/11-2, 21 September 2011.

97 High Commercial Court, Judgment No. Pž-2008/04-3, 16 May 2007.

Case law on the application of the *ordre public* exception in the context of the judicial review of arbitral awards offers hope that the above decision of the High Commercial Court will remain an isolated deviation. On several occasions, the courts have held that the public policy exception is a very narrow ground for refusal of enforcement of an arbitral award, and encompasses only the most fundamental principles of the Croatian legal order.[98] As yet, no arbitral award has been set aside or denied enforcement on public policy grounds.

98 See e.g. Supreme Court of the Republic of Croatia, Judgment No. Gž 17/06-2, 11 July 2007; High Commercial Court, Judgment No. Pž-4908/04-3, 17 October 2006; High Commercial Court, Judgment No. Pž-5712/03-3, 8 November 2006; High Commercial Court, Judgment No. Pž-1574/04-6, 12 December 2006.

THE APPLICATION OF THE ROME I AND ROME II REGULATIONS IN CYPRUS

Christiana Markou

1. INTRODUCTION

This chapter explores the application of the Rome I and Rome II Regulations in Cyprus. It starts by explaining the sources of private international law in Cyprus in an attempt to show the position of EU Regulations and hence of the Rome I and Rome II Regulations in Cypriot private international law and their relationship with the rest of its sources. It then inquires into the extent to which and how the two Regulations have been utilised by Cypriot courts, starting with the Rome I Regulation and continuing with the Rome II Regulation. As will be seen, though the two Regulations are directly applicable in Cyprus and supersede other relevant laws, their use in practice is limited and the relevant case law scarce. The Cypriot experience with the Regulations cannot therefore offer substantial lessons with regard to their practical application, though a few issues can be identified that should be of concern to the judiciary at national level and/or the legislature at EU level.

2. SOURCES OF CYPRIOT PRIVATE INTERNATIONAL LAW AND ROME I AND ROME II

Private international law in Cyprus is largely non-codified and spread across multiple sources, briefly described by Emilianides et al. as including EU law, common law, statutory law, multilateral and bilateral treaties and, to a lesser extent, doctrine.[1]

Since Cyprus is an EU Member State, EU law – i.e. Regulations, Directives, Decisions and CJEU case law – is applicable in Cyprus and takes precedence over national law, including the Constitution. This supremacy of EU law is uncontested in Cyprus and is expressly stated in Article 1A of the Constitution, which provides as follows:

> 'No provision of the Constitution shall be deemed to annul laws enacted, acts done or measures taken by the Republic which become necessary by reason of its obligations as a member state of the European Union, nor does it prevent Regulations, Directives or other acts or binding measures of a legislative character, adopted by the European Union or the European Communities or by their institutions or competent bodies thereof on the basis of the Treaties establishing the European Communities or the Treaty on European Union, from having legal effect in the Republic.'

It follows that the Rome I and Rome II Regulations governing the issue of applicable law in international disputes in contractual and non-contractual matters respectively are applicable in Cyprus; unlike Denmark, Cyprus has not sought any exemption from the application of these Regulations.

As Cyprus used to be a British colony, the Cypriot legal system has greatly been influenced by English law. Thus, common law is recognised as a key source of Cypriot law in Article 29(1)(c) of the Court of Justice Law 14/60. Though this provision makes it clear that common law is applicable only in the absence of Cypriot statute or case law on a given matter, it is nevertheless a principal source

1 A. Emilianides et al., *IEL Private International Law in Cyprus*, Kluwer Law International 2015, pp. 24–27.

of Cypriot private international law, given that Cypriot statutes governing private international law issues are extremely limited. Moreover, no statute exhaustively or extensively dictates private international law rules in relation to a particular matter or domain. As the Supreme Court of Cyprus has stated, 'the principles of Private International Law are part of the law of Cyprus, in so far as they form part of the common law in England';[2] indeed, Cypriot case law on matters pertaining to private international law is often based on references to common law, often accompanied by doctrine, in particular English textbooks, such as *Dicey's Conflict of Laws*.

International conventions, including Hague Conventions, on private international law take precedence over domestic law by virtue of Article 169 of the Cypriot Constitution. However, in relation to the law applicable to contractual and non-contractual obligations, which is governed by the Rome I and Rome II Regulations respectively, Cyprus has not ratified any of the Hague Conventions to which non-EU Member States are parties. Thus, though such Conventions, unlike those solely between EU Member States, supersede the relevant Regulations by operation of Article 25(2) Rome I Regulation and Article 28(2) Rome I Regulation, no issue of overlap between the Regulations and any of the Hague Conventions can arise in Cyprus.

Cyprus has also entered into certain bilateral agreements governing specific private international law issues with countries such as Syria, China, Russia and other non-EU countries.[3] These do not, however, include any rules on the law applicable to contractual and non-contractual disputes and do not therefore affect the application of the Rome I and Rome II Regulations.

3. ROME I

3.1. THE NATIONAL LANDSCAPE

Prior to 2006, when Cyprus implemented the 1980 Rome Convention on the Law Applicable to Contractual Obligations,[4] the rules governing the law applicable to contracts in Cyprus were the corresponding common law principles, according to which the contract was governed by the law chosen by the parties and, in the absence of such choice, by the 'proper law' of the contract (a common law concept referring to the most appropriate law with the closest connection

2 *Kochino Siddika Mehmet and Others v. Dervishe Irfan* (1976) 1 CLR 240.

3 Office of the Law Commissioner, *Part I – Bilateral Treaties and other International Agreements*, 2013 <http://www.olc.gov.cy/olc/olc.nsf/dmlparti_en/dmlparti_en?OpenDocument>.

4 The Convention on the Accession to the Rome Convention on the Law Applicable to Contractual Conventions (Ratification) Law (Law 15 (III)/2006).

to the court).[5] Approximately three years later, the Rome Convention was replaced by the Rome I Regulation, which is directly applicable in Cyprus, meaning that there was no need to introduce any national implementing measures. There are no measures intended to assist with its interpretation either. Case law on the Rome I Regulation is scarce, as is case law on the Rome Convention it has replaced. More specifically, following a quick search, only two judicial decisions have been found to contain a reference to the Rome Convention and even those do not involve an application of any of its provisions: the first simply states that the Convention is the predecessor of the Rome I Regulation[6] and the second is a decision on an interim application based, amongst other instruments, on the Rome Convention.[7]

As far as the Rome I Regulation is concerned, there are very few judicial decisions applying its provisions. Three of them concerned Article 3(1) and a resulting acknowledgement (or finding) that the contract at issue was governed by the law expressly chosen by the contracting parties.[8] All three concerned contractual clauses that involved the choice of a single law. Therefore, there is no experience in Cyprus on the (judicial) treatment of *dépeçage*, i.e. the choice of different laws for different parts of one contract, which, as Emilianides et al. observe, 'is a major novelty, as far as the Cypriot private international law of contracts is concerned'.[9] One of these cases concerned a choice of Greek law, and additionally of Cypriot law, but as auxiliary or supplementary to Greek law.[10] The applicants did not sufficiently prove the relevant provisions of the Greek law before the court[11] and suggested that the court should, based on the specific choice-of-law clause, apply Cypriot law. The court refused to do so, stating that given that the Greek law could not be applied, Cypriot law – as it was only auxiliary or supplementary to Greek law – could not be applied either. As a result, the court rejected the applicants' application, confirming that a failure to prove the applicable law can be fatal to the success of an application or legal action. Obviously, however, this does not constitute *dépeçage*, as the two chosen laws were not intended to apply to different parts of the contract.

A choice-of-law clause that in fact involved *dépeçage* appeared in *Hampton Advisory Group*,[12] which involved a dispute over a contract of services. The clause

5 See *Economides v. M/V Cometa 23* (1986) 1 CLR 443, where the relevant common law principles are adopted.

6 *Lanuria Limited v. Utterlan Limited and others*, civil action no. 2176/2016, 18.10.2016.

7 *The Best MCC Ltd v. Dulevo International SpA*, civil action no. 9832/07, 12.06.2009.

8 *Geniki Taxydromiki Ellados (Cyprus) Courier Services Ltd v. Nan Global Ltd*, civil action no. 2650/2015, 22.12.2015; *Marios Taramides v. Abercrombie Kent Ltd*, civil action no. 8328/12, 29.05.2015; *Aimiliou Stylianou v. Andreas Karasiazis and others*, civil action no. 5928/15, 19.08.2016.

9 Emilianides et al., supra n. 1, p. 58.

10 *Geniki Taxydromiki Ellados (Cyprus) Courier Services Ltd v. Nan Global Ltd*, supra n. 8.

11 For the need to prove foreign law under Cypriot law, see infra at section 3.6.

12 *Hampton Advisory Group SA v. Bost AD and others* (2012) 1 CLR 549.

read as follows: 'This Agreement shall be governed by the Bulgarian law for the Advance and for the Price, and by the laws of Cyprus for the exercise of the option and related registrations and for the maintaining of the value of the Shares'. The court, however, did not get to deal with the clause by reference to Article 3 Rome I Regulation, the reason being that there was a similarly dual choice-of-court clause, which resulted in the Cypriot court staying the proceedings before it for the dispute to be heard by the Bulgarian courts.

A fourth case mentioned Article 6(1) Rome I Regulation, rightly noting that it is restricted to business-to-consumer contracts and does not apply to consumer-to-consumer contracts according to CJEU case law. The case did not, however, involve an application of that provision.[13] A fifth case involved an application of Article 4 Rome I Regulation.[14] It concerned an interim application for injunctions in the context of a dispute over a contract of services between the parties. The court rightly found that, by operation of Article 4(1)(b) Rome I Regulation, the applicable law was the law of Ukraine, where the service provider had his habitual services. It also noted that even if the contract was not one of services, Article 4(2) Rome I Regulation would lead to the same result. Furthermore, in another case, the court considered Article 11 Rome I Regulation and concluded that the contract at issue, which was concluded in Cyprus, was formally valid because it was valid according to Cypriot law, i.e. the law of the place where the contract was concluded.[15] All of these cases only involved a quick – to some extent even hasty – application of the rules of Rome I Regulation. For example, in the last of the cases above,[16] the court chose to apply Article 11 Rome I Regulation (as opposed to Article 10, which governs the issue of substantive validity) without first explaining whether the issue at stake related to formal as opposed to substantive contract validity. Moreover, it cited both Article 11(1) and (2) Rome I Regulation and avoided making a choice in favour of the one that was actually applicable.

More recently, in the context of an interim application only involving a quick reference to the Regulation, the Court rightly acknowledged that because of Article 2 of the Regulation, the applicable law can very well be Russian law, i.e., a law of a country, which is not a Member State of the EU.[17] Finally, in another recent case, reference is made to Article 7 of the Regulation on insurance contracts, however this reference is contained in the affidavit supporting

---

13 *Alpha Bank Cyprus Limited v. Simon John Valder and others*, civil action no. 3704/2010, 02.05.2014.

14 *Igor Surkis and others v. Vadim Novinsky and others*, civil action no. 4958/15, 07.03.2017.

15 *Lanuria Limited v. Utterlan Limited and others*, civil action no. 2176/2016, 18.10.2016.

16 *Ibid.*

17 *Snapbox Holdings Limited v. Folsten Holdings Limited and Others*, civil action no. 5592/2016, 10.01.2020.

an interim application of the applicant and the relevant provision was not discussed or applied by the Court.[18]

It should be added that the Rome I Regulation makes no appearance in the case law of the Cyprus Supreme Court. The scarcity of case law on it is further confirmed by the fact that, in discussing the Regulation, a textbook on Cypriot private international law does not cite any Cypriot judicial decisions and only refers to relevant English and CJEU case law.[19] This lack of case law cannot be attributed to any substantive issue pertaining to the Regulation as such or an unwillingness on the part of the courts to make use of it. One possible reason is that given that by virtue of its Article 28, the Regulation applies to contracts concluded after 17 December 2009, most of the disputes arising out of such contracts are not likely to have reached the stage of a final court decision yet.

In the light of the above, there is no experience in Cyprus regarding the rest of the provisions of Rome I Regulation, such as Article 4 (which governs the applicable law in the absence of choice), Article 9 (regarding the application of overriding mandatory rules), or Article 21 (which allows courts to avoid the application of a rule of the applicable law that is clearly inconsistent with the public policy of the forum). However, some issues do merit discussion and are thus discussed immediately below.

3.2. *LOIS DE POLICE*

The concept of *lois de police* (or overriding mandatory provisions) is not mentioned at all in Cypriot case law and it is therefore uncertain whether Cypriot courts would, for example, consider 'employment law' provisions protecting certain basic rights of employees to be *lois de police*, as is the case in Greece.[20] It is worth noting that at least one rule would most likely be considered an overriding mandatory provision and thus applicable regardless of the applicable law, were the issue ever to arise. Given the status quo in Cyprus, a result of the Turkish invasion in 1974, the Turkish-Cypriot properties in the areas remaining under the control of the Republic of Cyprus have been placed under the guardianship of the Ministry of the Interior. According to section 3 of the Turkish Cypriot Properties (Administration and Other Matters) (Temporary Provisions) Law 139/1991, a contract for the sale of a property under guardianship is void unless it has been entered into with the prior written consent of the guardian, i.e. the Minister of the Interior. It must be assumed that

18 *Cyprus Electricity Authority v. HSB Engineering Insurance Limited and Others*, civil action no. 626/18, 30.01.2019.

19 Emilianides et al., supra n. 1, pp. 57–65.

20 V.S. Vrellis, *Private International Law*, 3rd Edition, Nomiki Vivliothiki: 2008, at p. 228.

a contract for the sale of such property governed by foreign law, i.e. by a law other than Cypriot law to which the aforementioned provision belongs, would still be affected by the said rule. In other words, section 3 would probably apply even if the law chosen by the parties – and hence the applicable law by virtue of Article 3 Rome I Regulation – were not Cypriot law. Of course, by virtue of Article 11(5) Rome I Regulation, the formal validity of 'immovable property' contracts is governed by the law of the place of the property, provided that the national rules on formal validity cannot be derogated from by agreement and are imposed irrespective of the applicable law. Therefore, in the context of this provision too, the relevant Cypriot rule must again be considered as applicable irrespective of the applicable law (and, thus, as an overriding mandatory provision) for it to be given precedence over the rules of the applicable law. The legislative restrictions on the acquiring of immovable property in Cyprus by foreigners[21] would most probably also be considered overriding mandatory provisions.

3.3. PUBLIC POLICY

The doctrine of public policy is discussed in Cypriot case law and also in the literature,[22] yet there is no case in which it has been applied by the court to disregard a provision of foreign law arising as the applicable law by operation of the Rome I Regulation or otherwise. There are several cases in which the court made reference to the *lex fori*; however, these relate to its application to procedural, as opposed to substantive, issues in accordance with the basic rule of private international law, according to which procedural matters are governed by the *lex fori*.[23] None of these cases involved applying the *lex fori* to fill in a gap arising as a result of a rule of the applicable law being disregarded on grounds of public policy.

---

21 The Acquisition of Immovable Property (Foreigners) Law Cap. 109.

22 *Glamor Development Ltd v. Christodoulos Christodoulou* (1984) 1 CLR 444; *Attorney-General v. Bank für Arbeit und Wirtschaft AG* (1999) 1 CLR 585 (in Greek); Emilianides et al., supra n. 1, p. 45.

23 *Hassanein Kamal v. 'Hellenic Island' and/or 'Island' and others (Number 2)* (1994) 1 CLR 578; *Fredericou Schools Co Ltd and others v. ACUAC Inc*, civil appeal 8266, 21 April 2000; *Hassanein v. Ship 'Hellenic Island'* (1989) 1 CLR 406; *Shehata v. Ellias and others* (1995) 1 CLR 621; *Nikolaou Panayiotis Psara v. Zois Tsakkiri* (2003) 1 CLR 1656; *'Archangelos Domain Adriatica' v. Adriatica* (1978) 1 CLR 439; *Joseph P Lasala and others v. Lykourgou Kyprianou and others*, civil action no. 5581/05, 28.02.2006; *Costas Stylianou v. 'The Fishing Trawler "Narkissos"' and two others* (1965) 1 CLR 291; *Preece v. 'Estias'* (1991) 1 CLR 568; *Saven Enterprises Ltd v. OAO Tomusinsky Open Pit Mine and others*, civil case no. 2680/2014, 30.04.2015; *Williams Glyn's Bank v. 'Ship Maria'* (1992) 1 CLR 309; *Ceska Konsolidanci Agentura v. Sampratrans Shipping Ltd* (2009) 1 CLR 615; *'Commercial Bank Ship Pegasos III' v. 'Ship Pegasos III'* (1978) 1 CLR 597; *Taito v. Ship 'Armar'* (1985) 1 CLR 142; *Economides v. M/V Cometa 23* (1986) 1 CLR 443; *Kayat Trading Limited v. Genzyme Corporation* (2011) 1 CLR 2330; *Amasa Hellas SA v. The Green Bird Ltd*, civil action no. 1129/07, 06.06.2011; *Synergatiki Pistotiki Etaireia*

3.4. *RENVOI*

Cypriot case law on renvoi is almost non-existent. Unlike Greek law and Article 32 of the Greek Civil Code, (national) Cypriot law does not explicitly exclude the application of *renvoi*. This means that common law would be adopted, leading to the application of *double renvoi*. This seems to have been confirmed by the Cyprus Supreme Court in *Christopoulou v. Christopoulou*,[24] which concerned a transfer of immovable property. However, this is the only case in Cyprus containing a reference to *renvoi* – something that seems to also be consistent with the rarity of the application of the doctrine in common law.[25] Given that Article 24 of the Regulation excludes *renvoi*, the number of cases on the particular principle is not expected to increase.

3.5. CHARACTERISATION OF ISSUES AS PROCEDURAL OR SUBSTANTIVE

According to Cypriot case law, the issue of time limits for bringing legal actions is, under Cypriot law, considered a procedural issue governed by the *lex fori*,[26] whereas Article 12(1)(d) Rome I Regulation characterises it as a substantive issue governed by the applicable law. The issue has not arisen in the context of the Rome I Regulation as yet. However, if it ever does so, the Cypriot courts will have to apply Article 12 Rome I Regulation, giving it precedence over the conflicting national case law, thereby treating the issue of limitations of actions as a substantive issue.

It should also be added that Article 12 Rome I Regulation makes no specific reference to the issue of interest on the amount that a court awards as damages, and it does not therefore explicitly state whether or not this is considered a matter to be governed by the applicable law (as opposed to the *lex fori*). Cypriot case law has expressed a preference for the view that the interest forms part of the measure of damages and is thus a procedural issue to be decided in accordance with the *lex fori*.[27] Article 12(c) Rome I Regulation, however, refers

Polemiou v. Georgios Ktoris and others, civil action no. 3084/13, 06.10.2014; *Ethimex SA v. Christ Haggipavlu Sons Limited*, civil case no. 1804/2013, 11.01.2016; *Keranis Panayiotis v. Ship 'Avantis II' (IMO 7432305)*, civil appeal 317/14, 17.11.2015. These decisions are available in Greek at <http://www.cylaw.org/cgi-bin/sinocgi.pl?&searchoption=1&query=lex%20fori&hitsnom=20&nexthit=1&view=relevance&masks=apofaseis/aad&masks=apofaseised>.

24 *Christopoulou v. Christopoulou* (1971) 1 CLR 437.

25 Emilianides et al., supra n. 1, p. 48.

26 *Shehata v. Ellias and others* (1995) 1 AAΔ 621; *Commercial Bank Ship 'Pegasos III' v. Ship 'Pegasos III'* (1978) 1 CLR 597.

27 *Williams Glyn's Bank v. Ship 'Maria'* (1992) 1 CLR 309.

to 'the assessment of damages in so far as it is governed by rules of law' as a matter to be decided by the applicable law. If, therefore, the interest is part of the measure of damages, as per the view endorsed in Cypriot case law, then this issue should be considered one of substance for the applicable law to determine, consistently with Article 12(c) Rome I Regulation, and not as a procedural issue as is the case under Cypriot (case) law.

There is also the view in Cypriot case law that the issue of whether a party is entitled to interest on the amount of damages awarded is substantive in nature to be decided by the applicable law, but that the question as to *how much* that interest should be is procedural to be resolved by an application of the *lex fori*. It seems, therefore, that there is a lack of clarity as to the law that should apply to the issue of interest. Most certainly, the fact that Article 12(c) Rome I Regulation is confined to a reference to the assessment of damages and remains silent as to the issue of interest on such damages does not help in achieving the necessary certainty.

3.6. PROVING FOREIGN LAW

In Cyprus, the content of foreign law is considered to be an issue of fact that must therefore be pleaded and proved with clarity before the court through expert evidence, in particular evidence from foreign legal experts that must be brought by the party seeking to invoke or rely on the provisions of the foreign law.[28] Cypriot courts cannot therefore freely seek to ascertain the content of foreign applicable law and must rely on the relevant evidence presented by the parties. When the evidence is conflicting, they will have to conduct their own research, but this must be confined to the information and sources put before them by the parties.[29] Thus, though Cyprus has ratified the European Convention on Information on Foreign Law, which enables judicial authorities of a contracting state to seek information about the content of the law of any of the other contracting states (if that law is relevant in the context of legal proceedings pending before the court), this option cannot be exercised in practice by Cypriot courts, as the latter are obliged to hear and confine themselves to relevant evidence. The ratification of said Convention seems to have been decided by the Cypriot legislature without due regard to the rules pertaining to the proof of foreign law, which definitely restrict its practical utility.

---

28 *Bank of Scotland v. Geodrill Ltd and others* (1993) 1 CLR 753; *China Wandao Engin Corporation v. Δημοκρατίας* (1997) 4 CLR 2084; *Federal Bank of Lebanon (SAL) v. Νίκου Κ. Shiakola*, civil appeal 10341, 19.01.1999.

29 *Williams Glyn's Bank v. Ship 'Maria'* (1992) 1 CLR 309.

Where the foreign law is not pleaded or proven, the Cypriot courts, as a rule derived from common law, apply the *lex fori*.[30] There are, however, examples of cases in which the court rejected an interim application for an injunction in the context of a contractual dispute, on the ground that the applicants failed to prove sufficiently the content of the applicable law.[31] This is the result of the equitable rule applicable in the context of applications for interim relief, that the applicant must make full and frank disclosure of all material facts, including the fact that a foreign law is the applicable one.

3.7. CASE LAW INVOLVING APPLICATION OF THE REGULATIONS IN THE YEARS TO COME

The fact that the Cypriot courts *must* rely on the parties to plead (or invoke) and prove the content of foreign law might be one of the culprits behind the relatively limited application of the Rome I (and II) Regulation and, more generally, foreign (applicable) law in Cypriot case law. More specifically, if none of the parties points to or raises the issue of the relevance of foreign applicable law, the court will probably simply proceed with deciding the case applying the Cypriot law.

The application in Cyprus of the doctrine of *forum non conveniens*, which derives from common law may also prevent a utilisation of the Regulations in some cases. More specifically, several cases involving a foreign applicable law may not get to be adjudicated by a Cypriot court due to that court deciding that it has no jurisdiction over the dispute (because a foreign court is a more suitable or proper forum).[32] However, of course not every case involving foreign applicable law is stayed by the Cypriot courts on the grounds of *forum non conveniens*.[33] Moreover, in the context of applying that doctrine, the court should look into the law applicable to the particular case, as the applicable law is considered to be a factor affecting the convenience of a forum.[34] The particular doctrine does not therefore exclude the application of the Regulations. Additionally, given

---

30 *Georgiades v. Kaminaras* (1958) 23 CLR 276; *Vlachos v. Dorothea* (1980) 1 CLR 113; *Standard Fruit Company v. Gold Seal Shipping* (1997) 1 CLR 489.

31 *Geniki Taxidromiki Ellados (Cyprus) Ltd v. Nan Global Ltd*, civil action no. 2650/2015, 22.12.2015; *Aimiliou Stylianou v. Andreas Karasiazis and others*, civil action no. 5928/15, 19.08.2016; *Igor Surkis and others v. Vadim Novinsky and others*, civil action no. 4958/15, 07.03.2017.

32 See for example *Saber Yacoup Shehata and others v. Assil Sabit Ellias* (1995) 1 CLR 621 and *Far Eastern Shipping Company Plc v. BN Marine Company Limited*, Admiralty court case no. 5/2013, 28.11.2014 (first instance decision).

33 *Oterom Ltd v. Kyriakou Z Christodoulidi* (2002) 1 CLR 1081.

34 *Konstantopoulou v. M/V Mediterranean* (1990) 1 CLR 782.

that the recast Brussels Regulation[35] does *not* allow for the application of the principle of *forum non conveniens* in cases involving a defendant domiciled in the EU, to which the Regulation applies,[36] any (limiting) effect that that principle could possibly have on the use or application of the Regulations is bound to be weakened. Though it is true that the principle of *forum non conveniens* had in fact been rendered inapplicable in those cases by the predecessor to the recast Brussels Regulation, which had bound Cypriot courts since 2004 when Cyprus joined the EU,[37] there was some misunderstanding about the relationship between the Regulation and the doctrine of *forum non conveniens*. The inapplicability of the doctrine was only explicitly recognised in Cypriot case law (by the Supreme Court) in 2012[38] and has since been taken up in more recent case law.[39]

More generally, it should be expected that the appearance of the Regulations in Cypriot case law is bound to increase as time goes on and as more and more cases fall within their temporal scope of application.

3.8. HAGUE CONVENTIONS AND BILATERAL AGREEMENTS

Cyprus does not apply any of the Hague Conventions containing rules on the law applicable to contractual disputes, and therefore no issue of overlap between the Rome I Regulation and any of the Hague Conventions has arisen in Cypriot case law. Cyprus is a signatory to the Convention of 1 July 1985 on the Law Applicable to Trusts and on their Recognition, yet trusts are exempted from the scope of the Regulation by virtue of Article 1(2)(h) Rome I. It is worth mentioning that Cyprus has also signed numerous bilateral agreements concerning merchant shipping with various non-EU Member States, which it has notified the European Commission in compliance with Article 26(1) Rome I Regulation.[40] These, however, contain rules providing, amongst other things, for freedom of establishment to the benefit of merchant shipping companies, the

---

35 Regulation (EU) 1215/2012 of the European Parliament and of the Council of 12 December 2012 on jurisdiction and the recognition and enforcement of judgments in civil and commercial matters.

36 Case C-281/02, *Owusu v. Jackson*, ECLI:EU:C:2005:120.

37 The decision of the CJEU which clarified the relevant point, namely *Owusu* (*ibid.*) was issued in 2005 under the previous Brussels I Regulation (Regulation 44/2001).

38 *Hampton Advisory Group SA v. Bost AD and others* (2012) 1 CLR 549.

39 See for example, *Gorsoan Limited and others v. Janna Bullock and others*, civil action no. 3573/2012, 05.11.2013; *Joint Stock Company Rodovid Bank v. Ledoyen Holdings Ltd and others*, civil action no. 1052/2015, 19.11.2015; *Bank of Cyprus Public company Ltd v. Lumley Craig and others*, civil action no. 3102/2013, 07.11.2016.

40 Notifications under Article 26(1) of Regulation (EC) No. 593/2008 of the European Parliament and of the Council on the law applicable to contractual obligations (Rome I) (2010/C 343/04), <http://www.ejtn.eu/PageFiles/12473/CELEX_52010XC1217(01)_EN_TXT.pdf>.

mutual recognition of ship documents, and jurisdictional rules on employment disputes over contracts between ship owners and crew members.[41] There is therefore no room for a conflict between any such bilateral agreement and the Rome I Regulation.

4. ROME II

4.1. THE NATIONAL LANDSCAPE

The national landscape for the Rome II Regulation is even poorer than that for the Rome I Regulation. Indeed, only very few first instance court decisions refer to the Rome II Regulation. One of them concerned a *contractual* dispute in which the court simply observed that the Rome II Regulation was totally irrelevant.[42] Another was an interim application for injunctions, in the context of which the court found that the applicable law was that of Russia; the court left a thorough examination of the matter for later (when the substance of the legal action were to heard), confining itself to referring to Article 3 Rome II Regulation and the universal application of the Regulation.[43] The only textbook on private international law in Cyprus does not refer to any relevant Cypriot case law either,[44] thereby confirming that the Cypriot courts have not been called upon to apply the Regulation as yet. By way of exception, more recently, the court, in the context of an application for stay of the proceedings in Cyprus on the ground that Cyprus was not a proper or convenient forum, applied Article 4(1) Rome II Regulation.[45] It concluded that the damage, i.e. the loss of money deposited in a bank account of the plaintiffs in Hong Kong, occurred in Hong Kong and, thus, the applicable law was that of Hong Kong. The court also noted that Hong Kong had the closest connection with the dispute and that the same result could be reached through an application of Article 4(3) Rome II Regulation. It is submitted that the reference to Article 4(3) was unnecessary; given that Article 4(1) clearly led to Hong Kong and there were no facts manifestly connecting the case with a country other than Hong Kong. Article 4(3), being an escape route from Article 4(1) (and Article 4(2) Rome II Regulation) when there is a manifest connection with a country other than the one to which the aforementioned provisions lead to, should not have been considered.

---

41 See for example, the Agreement between the Government of the Republic of Cyprus and the Government of the Syrian Arab Republic on cooperation in the field of merchant shipping, signed on 12 February 2004, entered into force on 11 February 2005, Articles 5, 8 and 14.

42 Civil action no. 2650/2015, supra n. 8.

43 *Reverta AS v. Bolmeno Commercial Ltd and others*, civil action no. 2989/16, 11.05.2017.

44 Emilianides et al., supra n. 1, pp. 66–71.

45 *Alterra International Holdings Limited v. Bank of Communications Co. Limited, Hong Kong Branch and others*, civil action no. 6078/15, 17.11.2017.

Cypriot courts most often have to resolve non-contractual disputes that arise out of actions or omissions that occurred in Cyprus, causing damage in Cyprus, in which no question regarding the application of the Rome II Regulation arises. This holds also true when the plaintiff (i.e. the party seeking compensation) is a foreigner, such as a tourist. As a result, most cases are dealt with as purely internal, with Cypriot tort law naturally being applied to the dispute, thus leaving no room for the invocation or consideration of the Rome II Regulation. It should be added that when the person seeking compensation is a foreigner, such as a tourist, the damages awarded are calculated in accordance with the standard rules and principles governing the measurement of damages that apply to purely internal cases, i.e. where the victim is a Cypriot national.[46] Thus, though the principle of *restitutio in integrum* is generally adopted in Cyprus,[47] the courts do not take into account the possibly higher standard of living of the victim when assessing non-pecuniary damages. Partly for this reason, Cyprus was in 2007 found to be one of the four Member States 'most concerned by the problem of cross-border road traffic accidents', which meant, amongst other things, that under Cypriot law there was a high likelihood of a low award of damages.[48] Of course, it has rightly been recognised[49] that there is a trend in Cyprus towards increasingly higher awards of damages and showing more sensitivity to human pain and suffering.[50]

Cap. 148, which largely codifies Cypriot tort law (in particular the relevant common law), provides in section 3 that, without prejudice to any other case in which Cypriot tort law applies by virtue of any rule of private international law, it applies to any tort committed in the territory of Cyprus or against any person or immovable property situated in the territory of Cyprus, irrespective of whether the act or omission constituting the tort is actionable under the law of the country in which the said act or omission has occurred.[51] Though, in cases falling within the scope of the Rome II Regulation, the latter will prevail over section 3 of Cap. 148,[52] it is worth mentioning that, while Article 4(1) Rome II Regulation adopts the rule of *lex loci damni* (i.e. the law of the place where the

46 *Lankuttis Anjia v. Andreas Nikola* (2002) 1 CLR 1128; *Christiansen Nicola Huxtable, through his father and lawful guardian T J Christiansen v. Blue Med. Hotels Ltd* (1998) 1 CLR 1542.

47 *Giallouros Takis v. Eugeniou Nikolaou* (2001) 1 CLR 558.

48 A. Renda and L. Schrefler, *Compensation of Victims of Cross-Border Road Traffic Accidents in the Eu: Assessment of Selected Options*, Centre for European Policy Studies, Brussels European Parliament, <http://www.europarl.europa.eu/RegData/etudes/etudes/join/2007/378292/IPOL-JURI_ET(2007)378292_EN.pdf> pp. 19–21.

49 *Ibid.*, p. 20.

50 *Charalampus Chrysi v. Christoforou Christoforou* (2012) 1 CLR 2812.

51 For the history of this provision and how it limited the 'double actionability' rule previously adopted in the Cypriot private international law, see Emilianides et al., supra n.1 at pp. 65–66.

52 On the supremacy of EU law over national provisions in Cypriot law, see supra at section 2 of this Chapter.

damage has occurred), section 3, Cap. 148 may be taken to render the Cypriot tort law applicable *both* when the damage has occurred in Cyprus *and* when the harmful event has occurred in Cyprus. Thus, if a negligent act is committed in Cyprus causing damage in Greece for example, Cypriot law may be applicable under Section 3, Cap. 148 but *not* under the Rome II Regulation; by operation of Article 4(1) of the latter, Greek law will be applicable.

4.2. QUASI-DELICTS

Some interesting issues may arise in Cyprus as a result of Chapter III Rome II Regulation, which contains rules on non-contractual obligations stemming from acts or omissions that do not constitute torts, namely unjust enrichment, *negotiorum gestio* and *culpa in contrahendo*. *Negotiorum gestio* is unknown in Cypriot law, both as a concept and as a cause of action, though the person whose affairs have been managed without that person's authority can recover any losses resulting from an omission to exercise reasonable care (on the part of the person undertaking the management of the affairs) under the law of the general tort of negligence.[53] With this in mind, in cases where Cypriot law is applicable, the plaintiff (or the person seeking damages) will not be able to derive everything (or anything) that may be encompassed by *negotiorum gestio* in jurisdictions that recognise the concept as a distinct cause of action. Indeed, the Rome II Regulation is limited to dictating the conflict-of-law rules for torts and other non-contractual obligations, and by no means introduces any torts or non-contractual obligations into the national substantive laws of the Member States. Under Article 15(a) Rome II Regulation, the 'basis of liability' is a matter to be decided by the applicable law and therefore, if no liability is attached to the breach of a non-contractual obligation under the applicable law, then no damages can successfully be sought.

The same holds true of *culpa in contrahendo*. It does not exist as a distinct tort or quasi-delict under Cypriot law, or even common law in general, but actions to recover loss as a result of bad faith during the negotiations for a contract can be recovered on the basis of other torts such as fraud and negligence.[54]

Similarly, unjust enrichment does not exist as an independent or distinct cause of action under common law or Cypriot law.[55] Of course, certain principles

---

53 Emilianides et al., supra n. 1, p. 70.

54 P. B. Quagliato, 'The Duty to Negotiate in Good Faith', (2008) 50(5) *International Journal of Law and Management* 213–225, <http://www.quagliatoadvogados.com.br/artigos/The-duty-to-negotiate-in-good-faith.pdf>.

55 *A I Karpasitis and sons (Industry) LTD and others v. Eugenias Karafoka and others* (1999) 1 CLR 1980.

of unjust enrichment are codified in Cyprus in the Cyprus Contract Law, Cap. 149, sections 70–72, which provide for *specific* and sufficiently delimited cases in which a person can recover damages from another. The interesting issue here is that in searching for the applicable law in the context of an action for unjust enrichment – which is considered quasi-contractual in Cyprus and indeed is governed by provisions within Cypriot contract law – a Cypriot court will have to apply the Rome II Regulation, which applies to non-contractual obligations, rather than the Rome I Regulation, which refers to contractual obligations. In other words, the Regulation concerning *non-contractual obligations* will decide whether Cypriot courts will apply (national) *contract* law.

Though this may initially strike one as odd, it should be recalled that concepts in EU legislative instruments are independent concepts of Community law, and should be interpreted by national courts by reference to those instruments and relevant CJEU case law and not by reference to national law.[56] Moreover, causes of action such as unjust enrichment or *culpa in contrahendo* stand between tort and contract law,[57] and hence both the Rome I and the Rome II Regulations could accommodate the relevant private international law rules.

4.3. *LOIS DE POLICE*, PUBLIC POLICY AND PROVING OF FOREIGN LAW

What was said above in the context of the Rome I Regulation about *lois de police*, public policy and proving foreign law also holds true in relation to the Rome II Regulation. As regards the latter, an interim application for an injunction, in which the applicants did not seek to prove the content of Russian law, which appeared to be the applicable law,[58] is noteworthy. The case concerned a non-contractual dispute, specifically fraud and other torts allegedly committed in various countries. This was a case in which the Rome II Regulation could have been utilised, *if* the harmful events occurred after 11 January 2009 (to which the Regulation is applicable by virtue of its Article 31). Yet the court opined that, given that the case was at an interim (preliminary) stage of the proceedings, it was too early for the applicable law to be established, and that it could decide the application by reference to Cypriot law relying on the presumption that it is identical to the foreign (applicable) law as per the general rule in cases where the foreign law is not proven.[59] It may appear that this approach does not sit easily

56 Case C-189/87, *Kalfelis v. Schröder and Others*, ECLI:EU:C:1988:459, paras. 15–18.

57 J. Dietrich, 'Classifying Precontractual Liability: a Comparative Analysis' (2001) 21 *Legal Studies* 153, 191.

58 *Gorsoan Limited κ.α. v. Janna Bullock and others*, civil action no. 3573/2012, 06.03.2013.

59 *Ibid.* On this general rule, see supra n. 31 and associated text.

with other case law in which relevant applications were rejected on the ground of the applicants' failure to disclose the applicable law.[60] Yet, it should be noted that in that case, the respondents too, omitted to provide any evidence as to the existence of a foreign applicable law, something that has affected the decision of the court. Moreover, as the case involved fraud committed in various countries, the applicable law could not readily or easily be established at that stage.

However, under Article 15(d) Rome II Regulation, 'the measures which a court may take to prevent or terminate injury or damage or to ensure the provision of compensation' are a matter for the applicable law. It would therefore appear that the Rome II Regulation also applies to interim (or interlocutory) applications, in which context it is not early for the applicable law to be established. In fact, the applicable law has to be established in order for the court to decide whether the interim injunction sought should be granted or not. As stated by Bach, 'whether a measure can be taken in general is a question to be answered by the *lex fori*, whereas whether the requirements of such measure are satisfied under the concrete circumstances is to be answered by Rome II-applicable law.'[61] Article 15(d) does *not* explicitly refer to interlocutory injunctions, unlike the corresponding Article 12(d) of the Proposal for the Regulation.[62] Article 2(3) Rome II Regulation states that the references in the Regulation to 'events' and 'damage' cover events and damage that are likely to occur, yet nowhere in the Regulation is it explicitly stated that the Regulation should apply to preliminary proceedings such as interlocutory applications for injunctions. An explicit relevant reference would certainly enhance certainty.

4.4. CHARACTERISATION OF ISSUES AS PROCEDURAL OR SUBSTANTIAL

In relation to the characterisation of issues as procedural or substantive, what has been stated in the context of the Rome I Regulation applies to the Rome II Regulation as well. Indeed, Article 15(h) Rome II Regulation includes the limitation of actions in the list of the issues of substance governed by the applicable law and therefore, when the issue arises, Cypriot courts must take care to follow the opposite course to the existing case law and thus comply with the Regulation. With regard to the issue of interest on the amount awarded as damages and the uncertainty surrounding the question as to whether it

---

60 See supra section 3.6 (in relation to the Rome I Regulation). A similar approach has also been adopted in a case involving the Rome II Regulation, see supra n. 45.

61 I. Bach (2011) 'Common Rules' in P. Huber (ed.) *Rome II Regulation, Pocket Commentary*, European Law Publishers, 342–409 at pp. 348–349.

62 Proposal for a Regulation of the European Parliament and the Council on the law applicable to non-contractual obligations ('ROME II') COM (2003) 0427 final.

is a procedural or a substantive issue,[63] the Rome II Regulation, just like the Rome I Regulation, does not offer clarification. Indeed, Article 15(c) Rome II Regulation states that 'the existence, the nature and the assessment of damage or the remedy claimed' is an issue governed by the applicable law, without obviously making any reference to the interest on any assessed and awarded damages. It is worth mentioning that in Cyprus the interest payable on the amount of damages for death or personal injury caused by a tort is dictated by rules of law, namely section 58A of the Cyprus Tort Law, Cap. 148. Accordingly, an EU court bound by the Rome II Regulation that arrives at the conclusion that Cypriot law is the applicable law must order the payment of interest on the amount of damages awarded in accordance with the aforementioned provision of Cap. 148 (if interest is taken to be part of the measure of damages and thus, subject to the applicable law).

4.5. HAGUE CONVENTIONS

Cyprus is not a party to and does not therefore apply any of the Hague Conventions containing rules on the law applicable to non-contractual disputes. Therefore, the issue has not arisen of overlap between the Rome II Regulation and any of the Hague Conventions, which would be given priority over the Regulation by virtue of Article 28 of the Regulation. Cyprus is a signatory to the Convention of 1 July 1985 on the Law Applicable to Trusts and on their Recognition and has notified the European Commission in compliance with Article 29(1) Rome II Regulation.[64] However, the non-contractual obligations of the parties to a trust – namely the settlor, the trustee and the beneficiary – are exempted from the scope of the Regulation by Article 1(2)(e) Rome II Regulation.

5. CONCLUSION

It has been seen that the Rome I and Rome II Regulations have not extensively been utilised by the Cypriot courts. Given that Cyprus is a commercial centre attracting business and investments from abroad, as well as a tourist destination visited by thousands of foreign nationals every year, the limited appearance of the Regulations in the case law could be explained by reference to the fact that both Regulations are only applicable to contracts or harmful events which

---

63 See supra at section 3.5 of this Chapter.

64 <http://eur-lex.europa.eu/legal-content/EN/TXT/?uri=CELEX%3A52010XC1217(02)>, notifications under Article 29(1) of Regulation (EC) No. 864/2007 on the law applicable to non-contractual obligations (Rome II).

have occurred from 2009 onwards However, the predecessor of the Rome I Regulation, namely the 1980 Rome Convention, is also not found in Cypriot case law and, more generally, the cases in which Cypriot courts have actually applied foreign law are fairly limited too.

More specifically, there is not in Cypriot case law a clear and/or detailed application of any of the provisions of the two Regulations, with the exception of Article 3 Rome I Regulation, which is perhaps the simplest to apply. When there is an explicit reference to foreign (applicable) law in a choice-of-law contract clause, it is impossible for the parties or the court to miss (or ignore) the relevance of that law to the dispute. It is probably for this reason that the scarce case law on the Regulations currently centres on Article 3 Rome I Regulation. What is certain, however, is that no substantial conclusions can be drawn from the limited Cypriot experience with the Regulations.

However, it can be seen that Cypriot law considers the issue of the limitation of actions to be a procedural issue for the *lex fori*, whereas under the Rome I and Rome II Regulations, specifically Article 12(1)(d) and Article 15(h) respectively, it is considered to be a substantive issue to be decided by the applicable law. This is not, however, a problem pertaining to the Regulations, as both of them leave no room for doubt as to how the issue of limitation of actions should be categorised. Rather, the Cypriot courts should take care to address the issue as a substantive one to be decided by the applicable law when dealing with cases falling within the ambit of the Regulations.

There seems also to be some uncertainty over whether the issue of interest on the amount of damages awarded is a procedural issue for the *lex fori* or a substantive one for the applicable law. Moreover, it may not be clear to the courts whether the Regulations should be applied also in the context of preliminary (or interlocutory) proceedings. In relation to these two issues, improvement may be needed at EU level; the Regulations could, as explained, be made more explicit, thereby preventing uncertainty and confusion.

The challenge ahead in the case of Cyprus is for lawyers and judges to familiarise themselves with the Rome I and Rome II Regulations, thereby ensuring they invoke and/or correctly apply the Regulations in appropriate cases. Of course, there are more complex issues relating to the Regulations, such as the rise of collective actions. Such actions definitely create issues, particularly in relation to Article 6 Rome I Regulation and Articles 4(2) and 5 Rome II Regulation. This is because while these provisions tie the applicable law to the habitual residence of the consumer or the party seeking compensation respectively, in a collective action there may be numerous claimants with different habitual residences. For the time being, Cyprus need not be concerned with such issues, as the Cypriot civil procedure law does not provide for the possibility of such collective actions. The focus can therefore be on the standard application of the Regulations in which Cyprus still lacks experience.

THE APPLICATION OF THE ROME I AND ROME II REGULATIONS IN THE CZECH REPUBLIC

Petr Bříza and Tomáš Hokr

1. THE NATIONAL LANDSCAPE

1.1. FACILITATIVE AND IMPLEMENTING MEASURES

In the Czech Republic, there are some provisions facilitating the application of the Rome I and Rome II Regulations, which can be found in the Act on Private International Law (No. 91/2012 Coll., effective as of 1 January 2014, hereinafter the 'APIL').[1] One of the prime examples of these provisions is

[1] The full English translation is available at <https://www.brizatrubac.cz/files/translation-czech-pil.pdf>.

section 84, which introduces a chapter entitled 'Law of Obligations', dealing with the determination of the applicable law and jurisdiction both for contractual and non-contractual obligations. The section declares the primacy of the directly applicable provisions of EU law and international treaties, referring explicitly to the Rome I Regulation and the Rome II Regulation in footnote 5, allowing the national (APIL) provisions to be applicable only insofar as the EU/international norms permit.[2] A more specific manifestation of this principle can be found in section 87 paragraph 3 of the APIL, implementing Article 7(3) of the Rome I Regulation, which empowers the Member States to grant greater freedom as regards the choice of the law applicable to insurance contracts that fall under Article 7(3)(a), (b) or (e). The Czech legislature has taken up that opportunity and section 87 paragraph 3 permits the parties in these cases to choose any applicable law they see fit, i.e. they are granted an unlimited freedom of choice of law.[3] In addition, the APIL fills the void regarding the general issues of private international law left by the Rome Regulations, like the question of ascertaining and applying foreign law.[4]

The rules of the Rome Regulations have not been extended beyond their normal scope of application by Czech law. Instead, the issues that are (felt) not (to be) covered by these Regulations are governed by specific APIL provisions. Thus, for example, defamation is dealt with by section 101 APIL, unilateral legal acts are governed by sections 90 and 91, and there are also – quite controversially – rules on employment relationships not established by an employment contract (section 89)[5] or on set-off (section 92).[6]

---

[2] Section 84 APIL reads as follows: 'The provisions of this Title shall apply in connection to the directly applicable provisions of the European Union law and international treaties. This Title shall be limited to the issues not falling into the scope of these laws and treaties, unless these laws and treaties allow the application of this Act.'

[3] 'Insurance contracts shall be governed by the law of the state where the policyholder is habitually resident. Contractual parties may choose the law applicable to the insurance contract; *should an insurance contract covered by a directly applicable provision of the European Union law be concerned, the parties may to an extent admitted by such a provision choose any applicable law*' (emphasis added).

[4] Cf., in particular, section 23 APIL and see more below in section 2.8 of this chapter.

[5] We believe that in the light of Giuliano–Lagarde Report on the Rome Convention (pp. 25–26) and the case law of the CJEU (cf. e.g. Case C-384/10, *Jan Voogsgeerd v. Navimer SA*, ECLI:EU:C:2011:842, para. 46), the notion 'employment contract' under Art. 8 of Rome I should be given a broad meaning that should effectively also cover other means of establishing an employment relationship, as the proper employment relationship should always be (in some form) based on a mutual agreement between the employer and employee, i.e. on a *contract* of some sort.

[6] The Czech legislature apparently did not share the view of some authors advocating that Art. 17 of the Rome I Regulation is also applicable (by analogy) to the set offs of non-contractual obligations (see e.g. M. Hellner, 'Set-off', in F. Ferrarri and S. Leible, *Rome I Regulation*, Munich: Sellier European Law Publishers, 2009, p. 264) – for more on this see also section 3 of this chapter. However, that does not matter much in practice before Czech courts, as section 92 APIL contains the same wording, as does Art. 17 of the Rome I Regulation.

1.2. NATIONAL DECISIONS APPLYING ROME I AND ROME II

There are only a handful of reported (publicly available)[7] court decisions that apply the Rome I or Rome II Regulations, or at least the Rome Convention. There are no reported arbitral awards issued in the Czech Republic that apply these laws.[8]

Given the limited number of reported decisions, it is difficult to specify the most commonly applied provisions of both Regulations. The available decisions deal with various provisions. However, based on our experience, probably the most frequently applied provision of the Rome I Regulation is Article 3, honouring freedom of choice of law. Nevertheless, courts usually apply this provision implicitly, by simply allowing parties to choose a law for their contract and respecting this choice. As to the Rome II Regulation, we believe that the most applied frequently provision is the general rule of Article 4, but again this is just our inference from practice, necessitated by the lack of representative case law.

Based on our practical experience, we are sure that there are quite a few decisions where the national conflict-of-laws provisions (the APIL or the 'old' Act on Private International Law, No. 97/1963 Coll., effective up to the end of 2013, hereinafter referred to as 'the old APIL') were wrongly applied instead of the Regulations. Most of them never reached the Supreme Court and thus are not published, as the application of the national rules led to the same result

7 There are roughly 20 decisions publicly available (some unpublished that the present authors are aware of from practice), most of them from the Czech Supreme Court (all decisions of which are publicly available); however, some of them concern primarily the Rome Convention, or the Rome I or Rome II Regulation is just mentioned by way of illustration without any deeper discussion thereof.

8 The fact that there are no reported Czech arbitral awards applying the Rome I or Rome II Regulations does not necessarily mean that the issues covered by the Regulations are not dealt with in the Czech Republic at all. First of all, most of the arbitration awards are confidential. Second, the Czech Republic is not that often a seat of international arbitration (compared to Vienna for example), which stems from many factors, including the relatively low significance of the Czech Republic in international trade, out-of-date arbitration laws and perhaps an ill-deserved reputation with regard to the efficiency of the judiciary. In our practice, however, we have encountered an LCIA award rendered between a Czech and a Russian party (seated in London) that touched upon the Rome I Regulation and its Article 1(2)(e). The parties to that arbitration had not made an express choice of law in their underlying agreement, thus it was discussed in the written submissions whether the arbitrators are under obligation to apply the Rome I Regulation as long as the Regulation itself mentions only the courts (and also excludes arbitration agreements from its scope). The arbitral tribunal has taken the side in favour of mandatory application of the Rome I Regulation. You can read more about this case on the Kluwer Arbitration Blog at <http://arbitrationblog.kluwerarbitration.com/2017/05/24/international-arbitration-in-london-from-the-perspective-of-a-civil-law-lawyer-rome-i-regulation-and-contractual-penalties/>. Petr Bříza has also applied Rome I Regulation in his practice as an arbitrator both in Prague and in Vienna (VIAC), but for the reasons of confidentiality cannot disclose the details of those cases.

(and thus nobody contested it)[9] or the parties (their lawyers) simply did not know that the Regulations should have been applicable.

2. THE OPERATION OF ROME I AND ROME II IN PRACTICE

2.1. SCOPE OF ROME I

In its decisions of 30 September 2015,[10] the Supreme Court of the Czech Republic touched upon a very important question, at least from a practical point of view. It dealt with a question whether so-called share-purchase agreements fall within the scope of the Rome I Regulation or whether they are outside the unified regime on the basis of the 'corporate law' exception contained in Article 1(2)(f) of the Rome I Regulation. Although the case at hand was decided on the basis on the Rome Convention (the contract was concluded in 2007), it should not matter, as the wording of Rome Convention exception in Article 1(2)(e) is exactly the same. The facts of the case were simple. A Czech entity (the seller) allegedly concluded agreements with two Austrian entities (the buyers) by which the seller sold to each of the buyers a 50 per cent share in a Czech limited liability company. A dispute arose over the payment of the purchase price and the seller brought an action against the buyers before a Czech court in České Budějovice (a city in the south of the Czech Republic), where the purchased company had its seat.[11] The seller invoked jurisdiction of this court under Article 5(1)(a) of the Brussels I Regulation, arguing that the place of the company's seat is the place where the obligation in question (payment of the purchase price) should have been performed. The buyers contested the jurisdiction of Czech courts, arguing that the Austrian courts, as the country where the defendants were domiciled, were competent to decide the case. The seminal question the Supreme Court thus faced was the interpretation of the Brussels I Regulation, namely whether share-purchase agreements fall under the scope of

9 See the decision of the Czech Supreme Court decision of 25 November 2014, docket no. 28 Cdo 3204/2014, where the court made a 'side note' that the lower court wrongly applied, in the context of an unjust enrichment case (which arose after 11 January 2009), the old APIL instead of the Rome II Regulation; however, it had no impact on the case, as both laws led to the determination of the same (in this case Czech) applicable law.

10 The English summary of the judgment is available on the Czech Supreme Court's website: <http://www.nsoud.cz/JudikaturaNS_new/ns_web.nsf/web/DecisionMaking~Decisions~2015_9_30___29_Cdo_2842_2013__summary_~?openDocument&lng=EN>, docket nos. 29 Cdo 1029/2014 and 29 Cdo 2842/2013.

11 In fact there were two separate actions, each against one of the buyers; therefore there are also two (although identical) decisions of the Supreme Court.

Article 5(1)(a) of the Regulation. The court undertook a fairly profound analysis[12] to conclude that they do. However, under the CJEU case law, the place of the performed obligation in question under Article 5(1)(a) is to be determined under the law applicable to the underlying contract[13] and thus the Supreme Court had also to determine the applicable law. This is where it came across the question whether share-purchase agreements fall under the scope of the Rome Convention (and thus also the Rome I Regulation). Quite surprisingly, the court rejected the Convention's application in one sentence, simply referring to Article 1(2)(e) of the Convention, unfortunately without giving a single reason why the exclusion should be applicable to these agreements. Having concluded that the Rome Convention was not applicable to the case at hand, it went on to apply the national conflict-of-laws rules, namely the old APIL. However, instead of applying its conflict provision covering corporate law matters (as one would guess given that the share-purchase agreements were found to be covered by the corporate law matters exception of the Rome Convention), it applied the old APIL's conflict provisions on ordinary contracts. This led the court to the conclusion that the choice of law was permissible for the share-purchase agreements,[14] which was the conclusion that would have been much more difficult to reach under the corporate law matters provision (where choice of law is essentially impermissible). Based on this case, we could conclude that the Czech Supreme Court permits choice of law in share-purchase agreements and treats them like ordinary contracts, yet excludes them from the scope of the Rome I Regulation on the basis of the corporate law matters exception.

We believe that the court wrongly applied the corporate law matters exception to the share-purchase agreement. Its decision is inconsistent with its own (correct) conclusion adopted in the very same case that these agreements do not fall into exclusive jurisdiction for corporate matters under Article 22(2) of the Brussels I Regulation. Moreover, the court's approach, in our view, reads too much into the corporate exception, given its legislative history and the simple fact that every exception should be interpreted restrictively. The text of the exclusion itself[15] speaks only of the matters closely related with the incorporation, dissolution and internal structure of a company or with liability

---

12 As the Brussels I Regulation is outside the scope of this book, we do not delve into the details of this analysis.

13 Case 12/76, *Industrie Tessili Italiana Como v. Dunlop AG*, ECLI:EU:C:1976:133.

14 There was no choice of law in the underlying contracts, however, and the court determined Czech law as the law applicable, based on section 10 of the old APIL (the law that reflects the best – from the conflict-of-laws perspective – the parties' relationship).

15 '[Q]uestions governed by the law of companies and other bodies, corporate or unincorporated, such as the creation, by registration or otherwise, legal capacity, internal organisation or winding-up of companies and other bodies, corporate or unincorporated, and the personal liability of officers and members as such for the obligations of the company or body'.

of its directors (executive body members). As the explanatory report to the Rome Convention (the so-called Giuliano–Lagarde Report)[16] explains, this exclusion 'affects all the complex acts (contractual, administrative, registration) which are necessary to the creation of a company or firm and to the regulation of its internal organization and winding-up, i.e. acts which fall within the scope of company law.'[17] The Report gives some examples of these acts, including 'the calling of meetings, the right to vote, the necessary quorum, the appointment of officers of the company or firm, etc.'[18]

Even though a share-purchase agreement has a direct influence on the internal structure of the company in the sense that it determines its ownership structure, it neither incorporates (establishes) the company nor lays down its internal rules like the articles of association or statutes of the company. The predominant character of the share-purchase agreement is contractual, as it is just a tool for transfer (change) of ownership, like other purchase (sales) contracts. Moreover, in public limited companies the shares are freely transferrable securities and the Giuliano–Lagarde Report states that contracts for the purchase and sale of negotiable instruments are not excluded from the scope of the Rome Convention; only the obligations arising out of their negotiable character are excluded.[19] In our opinion, it is possible to draw an analogy here and conclude that while the (contracts on) transfer of shares should not be excluded, the rights and liabilities attached to the shares are excluded. For these reasons, we do not agree with the Supreme Court's conclusion and consider it to be an example of an incorrect application of the Rome Convention (and indirectly also the Rome I Regulation). We believe that the court focused too much on the analysis of the Brussels I Regulation (which it conducted comprehensively and persuasively) and it paid much less (if any) attention to the similarly important question of the interpretation of the Rome Convention. This is regrettable, as share-purchase agreements are some of the most frequently concluded commercial contracts and yet the CJEU has not had an opportunity to speak on the subject and in addition the doctrinal debate is scarce.[20] From this perspective, the case was a missed

16 M. Giuliano and P. Lagarde, *Report on the Convention on the law applicable to contractual obligations* [1980] OJ C 282/1.

17 *Ibid.*, p. 12.

18 *Ibid.*, p. 12.

19 *Ibid.*, p. 11. The Report states this in connection with the exclusion on negotiable instruments contained in Art. 1(2)(d) of the Rome Convention (the same provision of the Rome I Regulation).

20 We are not aware of any English-language publication that would advocate exclusion of share-purchase agreements from the scope of the Rome I Regulation (Rome Convention). However, we also know of only one that would expressly advocate their inclusion in the scope of the law – see H. van Houtte, *The Law of Cross-border Securities Transaction*, London: Sweet & Maxwell, 1999, p. 8. In Czech, see on this point P. Bříza, *Volba práva a volba soudu v mezinárodním obchodě*. Prague: C.H. Beck, 2012, p. 22.

opportunity for the Czech Supreme Court, which could (and as the court of last resort should) have made a preliminary reference to the CJEU. Alternatively, it could at least have attempted a much deeper analysis of the issue, which could have been a more meaningful contribution and started a serious debate on the scope of the corporate matters exclusion.

2.2. *LOIS DE POLICE*

The Czech Supreme Court advocates a rather restrictive approach to applying overriding mandatory provisions (*lois de police*) and it does not essentially go beyond the definition adopted by the CJEU in *Arblade* case (C-369/96), which is also reflected in Article 9(1) of the Rome I Regulation. The approach of the Czech Supreme Court in this area is shown further below in section 2.9 dealing with public order (punitive damages case), but may be also demonstrated by several cross-border cases from the labour law area. There were a couple of cases decided in years 2008–2013[21] that concerned employment contracts that even predated the Rome Convention's application in the Czech Republic (which is, in the Czech Republic, applicable to contracts concluded on or after 1 July 2006[22]). The fact that the Rome Convention was not applicable to the cases at hand led the court to consider whether the employee-protective provisions of the Czech Labour Code are overriding mandatory rules applicable regardless of the law applicable to the employment contract (the old APIL did not contain any special provisions specifically protecting employees as a weaker party, as Article 8 of the Rome I Regulation does; thus the court had to look at the general category of overriding mandatory provisions). The employment contracts (in all cases) were governed by some of the law of District of Columbia. Under the scrutiny for (not) being overriding mandatory provisions were Czech Labour Code rules requiring employers to have (and state) a specific reason for dismissal of an employee and laying down a minimum length for the termination period (the period during which the contract continues after the employee is notified of its termination). The Czech Supreme Court refused to deem these provisions to be *lois de police*. The court said that not every mandatory provision that cannot be derogated from by agreement (contract) in domestic relations is an overriding mandatory provision in an international sense (which cannot be derogated from by a choice of law in a cross-border relationship). According to the court, the only truly overriding mandatory provisions are those the of which subject

21 See the Supreme Court decision of 8 December 2008, docket no. 21 Cdo 4196/2007 and decision of 19 March 2013, docket no. 21 Cdo 4534/2011.

22 See the Supreme Court decision of 28 November 2013, docket no. 33 Cdo 2377/2012, which provides a correct account of the temporal applicability of the old APIL, the Rome Convention and the Rome I Regulation.

matter has essential and irreplaceable importance for society. As the social protection from the undesirable social consequences of dismissal provided by the Labour Code provisions in question might be ensured otherwise (by other means), these provisions of themselves are not overriding (irreplaceable) mandatory provisions. The court noted that in the case at hand, the protection of the termination period was ensured by the fact that under the foreign law the employee was given a lump-sum payment for the whole termination period instead of having to continue to work during that period. The court then also ruled out that the application of the foreign law would be manifestly repugnant to the *ordre public* of the Czech Republic. The court gave an example of provisions that have to be deemed to be internationally overriding mandatory provisions even in the area of labour law, highlighting explicitly the provisions prohibiting any form of discrimination (both direct and indirect) in labour law relationships. A violation of such provisions was not, however, involved in these cases, and thus the Supreme Court found no violation of the Czech Republic's *lois de police*.

In these cases, the Czech Supreme Court provided a restrictive interpretation of the notion of overriding mandatory provisions, which is the correct approach, in our view, as far as the overriding mandatory provisions governed by Article 9(1) of the Rome I Regulation (and Article 16 of the Rome II Regulation) are concerned. However, it seems that the court slightly mixed up overriding mandatory provisions with the (simple) mandatory provisions protecting employees under Article 6(1) of the Rome Convention (Article 8(1) of the Rome I Regulation). The latter should, in our opinion, cover all the provisions from which it is not possible to derogate by agreement (contract), provided that they (overall) guarantee a higher protection of the employee than the foreign law. It is not entirely clear from the text of the judgments cited above whether the Supreme Court wanted to say that the Labour Code provisions in question are – apart from not being overriding mandatory provisions in international sense – not even mandatory provisions in the sense of Article 8(1) of the Rome I Regulation. While it is true that on the facts of these cases the conclusion that, in these particular circumstances, those provisions did not provide (clearly) greater protection for the employee than the foreign law was defensible (to some extent), in many other situations these rules will certainly be mandatory within Article 8(1) of the Rome I Regulation. The future will hopefully clarify the Supreme Court's exact position on employee-protective rules under Article 8(1) of the Rome I Regulation.

In any event, it seems that Czech courts (led by the guiding example of the Supreme Court) will be reluctant to find the rules protecting only private interests of parties (and balancing their inequality) to be *lois de police*. We think that it is the right approach, as the private interests of parties with less bargaining power are protected by Article 6 (consumers) and Article 8 (employees) of the

Rome I Regulation and by the choice-of-law restriction for all non-commercial tortious relations provided in Article 14 of the Rome II Regulation.[23]

As to the treatment of third states' *lois de police* (Article 9(3) of the Rome I Regulation and Article 16 of the Rome II Regulation), we have not witnessed any particular difficulties in practice; however, there is no publicly available decision dealing with this question. We consider the solution of Article 9(3) of the Rome I Regulation to strike the correct balance between legal certainty and the public interests of a third state whose laws make a particular contractual performance on its territory illegal. On the other hand, in the area of non-contractual obligations there is slightly less room (and it is also far less common) for parties to avoid mandatory rules by choice of law and, moreover, Article 17 of the Rome II Regulation gives some room for protection of the interests of the country where the event giving rise to the liability occurred. For these reasons, we believe that in the area of non-contractual relations there is no real need to introduce *lois de police* of third states, as this would only make the application of conflict rules in this area more complex and less predictable.

2.3. PARTY AUTONOMY

The rules on party autonomy, especially Article 3 of the Rome I Regulation, work very well in practice and the flexibility they give to parties can only be welcome. We have seen several contracts where the *dépeçage* was usefully employed by the parties to overcome some uncertainties in the law otherwise applicable, and it does not seem difficult to determine which part of the contract is severable from the rest and thus might be subject to a different law. On the other hand, we do not see it advisable or even necessary to introduce the possibility of choosing the *lex mercatoria*. There should always be some underlying 'full-scale' law and within its boundaries the parties should be (and are, under the Rome I Regulation – see Recital 13) free to choose and incorporate into their contract by reference a non-state body of law. Our opinion is not driven by a perceived need for a state-authored body of law, but by the fact that there is no *lex mercatoria* that could fully and exhaustively regulate all the questions that might arise in a contractual relationship and therefore the choice of *lex mercatoria* always brings

---

23 Even though it is not a case seated within the Czech Republic's jurisdiction, we deem it worth mentioning that in a recent LCIA arbitration with arbitral seat in London (referred to above in n. 8) we faced an arbitral tribunal considering whether a contractual penalty under Russian law is not of a penal nature and thus against the *ordre public* of England. The tribunal, taking into account the restrictive interpretation of overriding mandatory provisions and *ordre public* under the Rome I Regulation and reflecting the fact that the case's only connection with England was the seat of arbitration, finally decided to uphold the contractual penalty and awarded it in full. For more see article referred to in n. 8.

a great deal of uncertainty, which is not welcome, especially in commercial relations. Furthermore, in practice, there are not many contracts in which parties make a 'full-fledged' and transparent choice of a non-state body of law; rather it is often the arbitrators who somehow infer that there was such a choice, which gives them the ability to decide the case as they see fit, without the need to grapple with the peculiarities of a law that is either unfamiliar to them or seems to them to be unfair (or underdeveloped, etc.).

As to party autonomy under Article 14 of the Rome II Regulation, there is no relevant Czech case law available. In any event, it is a novelty in Czech law, as the previous national legislation (the old APIL) did not allow for choice of law in non-contractual matters. We think it is a useful tool and it is used in practice, in particular to extend the application of the law chosen by the parties for their contract to related non-contractual issues. We admit that the possibility of *ex post* choice of law in non-commercial relationships (permitted by Article 14(1) of the Rome II Regulation) might be abused against an uninformed weaker party, but we have not yet witnessed such a case in our practice.

2.4. ABSENCE OF CHOICE OF LAW

Czech courts are used to fixed rules; thus, we have not identified any opposition, either in the Czech doctrine or in the case law, to the fixed rules system of Article 4 of the Rome I Regulation. We believe that it is safe to say that Czech courts and practitioners have adhered to the approach introduced by that Regulation. There is also no evidence that Czech courts tend to overuse the so-called 'escape clauses' from the fixed rules (e.g. Article 4(4) of the Rome I Regulation). Probably the most significant judgment dealing with Article 4 issues so far was handed down by the Czech Supreme Court in January 2019.[24] The case dealt with a cross-border sales contract and a factoring contract (the parties involved were Czech and Slovak companies). The court applied the CISG[25] (which takes priority over the Rome I Regulation) to the sales contract and concluded that the factoring contract is a contract for the provision of services under Article 4(1)(b) of the Regulation. Thus, the applicable law is the law of the country where the service provider, i.e., the factor, has his or her habitual residence. However, the court added that if the assignment is not part of the factoring, but just a separate legal act (outside the factoring), then

---

24 See the decision of the Czech Supreme Court decision of 29 January 2019, docket no. 23 Cdo 427/2017. For a detailed case comment see P. Bříza, The CISG and the Law Applicable to International Factoring, Assignment, Set-off and Late Payment Interests, (2020) 1 *The European Legal Forum* 13.

25 *United Nations Convention on Contracts for the International Sale of Goods*, 11 April 1980, Vienna.

Article 4(2) of the Regulation steps in and the law applicable is the law of the country where the party required to effect the characteristic performance of the contract has his or her habitual residence. The assignor is such a party, being the one who 'effects' the transfer of the claim. It is submitted that both these conclusions are correct, despite some doctrinal views to the contrary.[26]

As to Article 4(1) of the Rome II Regulation, we are unfortunately again faced with an absolute lack of relevant Czech case law. We have been working on a case dealing with the concept of indirect damage, clarified by the CJEU's *Lazar* case (C-350/14), which confirmed that pure financial loss is not a direct damage under Article 4(1) of the Rome II Regulation. In our case the appellate court found that the violation in question amounts not to a damage, but to an unjust enrichment. Nevertheless, the court also applied the same principles regarding pure financial loss for the concept governed by Article 10 of the Rome II Regulation.[27] While the localisation of the place of direct damage might prove complex in some cases, it is in our opinion very difficult to come up with precise fixed rules that would improve the current system. We believe it is best to leave it to judicial practice to define more precisely the rules for various specific situations. Any attempt to change the current wording of Article 4 of the Rome II Regulation would be premature.

2.5. SPECIFIC RULES

In general, the specific rules that the Rome II Regulation sets forth for certain torts are seldom applied in the Czech Republic. This is either because the tort claims covered are hard to bring to court (in terms of the burden of proof or accessibility of evidence) or they arise only in purely domestic contexts (i.e. not involving cross-border issues).[28] As a result, from the perspective of the Czech

---

26 For more detail see P Bříza, above n. 24, pp. 15–16.

27 See the decision of the Municipal Court in Prague of 13 November 2019, docket no. 18 Co 304,305/2019-547 (not publicly available, on record with the authors). The case is now pending at the Czech Supreme Court.

28 As an example, hardship in enforcing claims can be illustrated in a claim covered by Article 6 of the Rome II Regulation. Indeed, private enforcement (unlike public enforcement) of obligations arising out of restrictions of competition (so-called 'private antitrust claims') is still virtually non-existent in the Czech Republic. Although such a claim could be enforced under sections 2990 and 2988 of the Civil Code (Act No. 89/2012 Coll.), no specific regulation in this respect is provided under the Act on Protection of Competition (Act No. 143/2001 Coll.). A plaintiff in the Czech Republic would usually be unable to prove the extent of damages and meet its burden of proof, mainly because of the discovery limitations. In addition, private antitrust claims are hindered by the issues relating to the limitation period or litigation costs. The new bill on collective claims (or at least its version adopted by the Czech government and currently discussed in Parliament) has also effectively excluded these claims from its scope as it applies to claims raised by consumers; in this

Republic, Articles 5–9 of the Rome II Regulation have so far had limited – if any – practical applicability.

That being said, of all the specific torts regulated, cross-border product liability claims covered by Article 5 of the Rome II Regulation have the greatest potential to occur.[29] An issue that may be of particular importance for this type of claim is connected to the *lex domicilii*, i.e. the law of the place of a natural person's habitual residence. Indeed, a product liability claim would typically occur in a setting where a private individual (a consumer) is confronted with a defective product. Unlike for a legal person or a natural person acting in the course of his or her business activity, no definition is provided under Article 23 of the habitual residence of a natural person. This is a well-known lacuna not only in the Rome II Regulation but also in the Rome I Regulation, which is essentially the same in this respect.[30] If we were to accept the solution proposed by the Brussels I *bis* Regulation,[31] the notion of 'habitual residence' is governed by national law and not the Regulations. Under Czech law, the habitual residence of a natural person is understood as the place (municipality) in which the person resides with the intent to reside permanently. This is not only an objective criterion – an actual economic or social connection of that person to a place – but also a subjective one: an intent is required.[32] This concept roughly corresponds to what is perceived as a habitual residence under the applicable case law of the CJEU, where habitual residence is a meeting of two elements – the place must be a centre of that person's interests and an element of permanency must be present.[33]

---

respect it mirrors the scope of applicability of the proposed Directive on representative actions for the protection of the collective interests of consumers (i.e., the document referenced as COM(2018) 184 final). As a matter of fact, the Czech legal framework has not been the only one to be largely inadequate in this sense; rather, it is a widespread issue among EU Member States and as such it was addressed by Directive 2014/104/EU on antitrust damages actions. The deadline to transpose the Directive passed on 27 December 2016. Although the Czech legislature failed to implement the Directive, a new bill on the compensation has been drafted and made into law No. 262/2017, effective as of 1 September 2017. It is fair to say that, unlike in many EU Member States, a plaintiff in the Czech Republic does not need to be concerned with proving violation of competition rules if so decided by the Czech competition authority; as far as the existence of the violation and a person responsible for it is concerned, such a decision of the competition authority would also bind the Czech courts (cf. section 135 of Act No. 99/1963 Coll., the Civil Procedure Code).

29 This is mainly due to the common EU framework provided by the Council Directive 85/374/EEC of 25 July 1985.

30 Cf. Art. 19 of the Rome I Regulation.

31 Art. 62 of the Brussels I bis Regulation.

32 Cf. the decisions of the Czech Supreme Court decision of 2 June 2005, docket no. 30 Cdo 444/2004 and decision of 20 November 2013, docket no. 28 Cdo 797/2013; and the decision of the Czech Constitutional Court, docket no. III. ÚS 3436/10 of 5 January 2011.

33 Cf. M. McParland, *The Rome I Regulation on the Law Applicable to Contractual Obligations*, Oxford: Oxford University Press, 2015, pp. 177–178.

2.6. RULES OF SAFETY AND CONDUCT

Czech courts have not yet expressed their opinion on Article 17 of the Rome II Regulation and thus we can only try to predict their approach. In our view, they should take proper account of the rules applicable on the territory where the event giving rise to the liability took place, provided that a party invokes such rules and proves their content. In particular, courts should not ignore the rules that make the conduct in question illegal in that territory (i.e. the rules that Article 9(3) of the Rome I Regulation counts among overriding mandatory norms); also in addition, the foreign rules requiring an administrative permit for any given conduct should not be overlooked. Undoubtedly, it will often be the case that the lack of an administrative permit will make the conduct illegal and therefore these rules should be taken into account under Article 17 of the Rome II Regulation, albeit only as a fact.

2.7 SCOPE OF APPLICABLE LAW

The Czech Supreme Court addressed Article 12 of the Rome I Regulation in its decision of 14 January 2016.[34] In this decision the court touched upon the question whether a claim for contractual penalty falls under the scope of the law applicable to the contract as set out in Article 12(1) of the Rome I Regulation. The court had no doubts in arriving in the conclusion that a contractual penalty claim belongs among 'the consequences of a total or partial breach of obligations' and thus is covered by the law applicable to the contract. The court used this analysis to buttress its conclusion that a contractual penalty claim falls under the matters related to contract within Article 5(1) of the Brussels I Regulation. Importantly, the court showed its willingness to characterise the issue in a European-wide, autonomous manner, looking at private international law regulations and doctrine, not at its national substantive definition (although, admittedly, the contractual penalty claim would also be a contractual issue under the Czech contract law). The Supreme Court's example might serve as a model (and arguably the right one) for lower Czech courts to try to characterise the issues referred to in the Rome Regulations in an autonomous,[35] EU-wide manner and to look at domestic law concepts only in the event of an apparent lack of any definition (or broader consensus).

---

34 Docket no. 30 Cdo 1941/2015. The English summary is available at the Supreme Court's webpage: <http://www.nsoud.cz/JudikaturaNS_new/ns_web.nsf/web/DecisionMaking~Decisions~2016_1_14___30_Cdo_1941_2015__summary_~?openDocument&lng=EN>.

35 See Recital 11 of the Rome II Regulation explicitly advocating this approach to the definition of 'non-contractual obligation'.

Also, in the 'factoring case' referred to above,[36] the Czech Supreme Court confirmed that the issue of the late payment interests falls under Article 12(1)(c) of the Rome I Regulation and the applicable law would be that of the contract at stake.

In the very same case, the Supreme Court also dealt with the scope of the respective laws determined under Article 14 (the Regulation's rules on assignments). The court clarified that the scope of the applicable law under Article 14(1) of the Regulation covers not only the validity of the (assignment) contract, but also its obligation (*inter partes*) effects, including the question, which party (assignor or assignee) is obliged to notify the debtor about the assignment. The court added that this applicable law also governs the contractual effects (*inter partes*) if the assignment is not effective (vis-a-vis third parties or the debtor). The court also commented on Article 14(2) of the Rome I Regulation, under which the law governing the relationship between the assignee and the debtor is the same as the law governing the assigned claim. This law determines the assignability of the claim, the relationship between the assignee and the debtor, the conditions under which the assignment can be invoked against the debtor and whether the debtor's obligations have been discharged. The court recalled the purpose of Article 14(2), which is the protection of the debtor, and emphasised the main aspects that are governed by the law determined under this provision, namely whether the assignment is at all permissible (the conditions of assignability) or invokable against the debtor.[37]

2.8. THE ASCERTAINMENT AND USE OF FOREIGN LAW

The questions of ascertainment and use of foreign law in the Czech Republic are governed by section 23 APIL. This provision contains a universal rule that applies irrespective of whether the conflict-of-law rule pointing to a foreign law stems from the Rome I or Rome II Regulations, the APIL itself or any other statute or treaty.

If a foreign law is to be used pursuant to a conflict-of-law rule, it should be ascertained as a matter of obligation (*ex officio*), i.e. even without the submission or a motion to do so. The court (public administration body) enjoys a wide discretion as to which means to use to ascertain the content of a given foreign law. Generally, it is acceptable for the court to rely on its own research, ask the

36 The decision of the Czech Supreme Court decision of 29 January 2019, docket no. 23 Cdo 427/2017, see n. 24, above.

37 For more detail on Article 14 discussion see the factoring case decision, n. 24, above, paras. 35–39.

parties for assistance or appoint a foreign law expert. In doing so the court is only limited by the requirements of reliability and credibility of the source. A court may even seek (and Czech courts often do) the assistance of the Ministry of Justice in this respect. However, a statement (opinion) on the content of a foreign law obtained from the Ministry of Justice is treated like any other evidence and thus does not formally bind the court,[38] even though in practice the courts consider it to be the most reliable and trustworthy source of evidence. In addition, depending on the particular foreign law to be applied, a court may decide to follow the channel prescribed in the European Convention on Information on Foreign Law, provided within the European Judicial Network[39] or any other mechanism provided for under a bilateral treaty. If information concerning the content of the foreign law cannot be obtained within a reasonable amount of time or is impossible to obtain, Czech law – as the *lex fori* – would be applied, as directed by section 23 paragraph 5 APIL.

The use of foreign law is governed by two basic principles. First, foreign law should be used even without the parties' submission or a motion to do so. This means that no formal step by either party is needed in the court proceeding: a court is obliged to use foreign law on its own initiative. Second, it must be applied in the way it is applied in the territory where it is used. This requires that the Czech judge address the question falling within the scope of the conflict-of-law rule and apply the foreign law that was determined in the same way as a foreign judge from that jurisdiction would. It follows that all facets (e.g. hierarchy) and sources of foreign law (including case law or the law of equity if applicable) should be taken into consideration in determining the issue that falls within the limits of the conflict-of-law rule. Due regard should be also had to the temporal application of the foreign law.[40]

Foreign law is treated as a *law* not as a *fact*, and in this respect it is treated by courts in the same way as Czech law. Any error made by a lower court in applying foreign law generates the same variety of appeals (reliefs) as an error in applying Czech law.[41] Notwithstanding any applicable foreign law, the *lex fori* would still be applied in matters involving public policy (Article 21 of the Rome I Regulation and Article 26 of the Rome I Regulation) and overriding mandatory provisions (Article 9 of the Rome I Regulation and Article 16 of the Rome II Regulation),[42] as well as to questions of procedure.

---

38 Cf. P. Bříza et al., *Act on Private International Law. Commentary* (in Czech: Zákon o mezinárodním právu soukromém. Komentář), Prague: C.H. Beck, 2014, p. 147.

39 See, the Council Decision of 28 May 2001, 2001/470/EC.

40 Cf. P. Bříza, above n. 38, p. 146.

41 *Ibid.*, pp. 146–147.

42 Cf. sections 3 and 4 APIL.

2.9. *ORDRE PUBLIC*

A definition of public policy (*ordre public*) in terms of conflict rules can be found in section 4 APIL, which states that the contents of any foreign law that is supposed to be used in accordance with the provisions of the APIL cannot be applied if the effects of such application would clearly contravene public order. The public order exception under the APIL covers not only the applicability of foreign law but extends to recognition and enforcement of foreign judgments, foreign court settlements and foreign arbitration awards.

The public order exception under the APIL is rather narrow in scope. For instance, the exception should not be triggered if the foreign law is simply less favourable than the Czech law for a Czech party dealing with a foreign party. In contrast, if the application of the contents of a foreign law conflicts with fundamental rights and freedoms, such effects would contravene Czech public order and the foreign law would thus have to be disregarded.[43]

Since Czech law attributes a compensatory function to damages, public policy is often raised in Czech courts as an objection to the application of a foreign law with regard to punitive or exemplary damages. Indeed, the Czech Supreme Court has thoroughly reviewed the issue (in the context of recognition and enforcement of foreign judgments) and maintains that the public order exception is available only so long as the amount of punitive damages is manifestly disproportionate to the amount of actual harm to be compensated.[44] Thus, punitive damages as such are not against Czech public order. Only excessive and disproportionate damages would amount to a violation of the right to own property under Article 11(1) of the Czech Charter of Fundamental Rights and Basic Freedoms; as such, this reasoning is in line with Recital 32 of the Rome II Regulation.[45] The determination as to whether damages that are awarded under the head of

---

43 Cf. the decisions of the Czech Constitutional Court, docket nos. II. ÚS 2455/09 and I. ÚS 709/05. It should be noted that the intensity of violation of a right is germane to its qualification as contravening Czech public policy. Only fundamental principles of the Czech legal system are protected. In our opinion, it would thus be against public order if a foreign law, for instance, were to strongly interfere with the freedom of contract, unjustifiably deny the opportunity to one party to exercise its rights under a contract (e.g., resulting in *de facto* expropriation), or manifestly over-extensively expand the liability of one party beyond the mere counterbalancing of the parties' private interests. See also section 2.2 above dealing with *lois de police*.

44 See the decision of the Czech Supreme Court decision of 22 August 2014, docket no. 30 Cdo 3157/2013 (for the non-existence of punitive or exemplary damages in Czech domestic law, cf. the Czech Supreme Court decision of 15 March 2012, docket no. 30 Cdo 1796/2011, or the decision of 28 February 2013, docket no. 30 Cdo 2778/2011).

45 This recital as well as the original Article 24 on punitive damages contained in the Commission's draft of the Rome II Regulation is discussed in the Supreme Court's judgment, docket no. 30 Cdo 3157/2013. The Supreme Court in this remarkable decision has also provided a broad comparison of approaches to punitive damages in various European countries.

punitive damages contravene public policy is therefore carried out on a case-by-case basis, taking the relevant circumstances of the case into account. As determining factors, the Supreme Court has put forward the following three criteria: the gravity of the harm sustained, whether the punitive damages are not out of all proportion to the harm sustained, and whether the punitive damages interfere with the right to property in an unacceptable manner (the so-called strangling effect).[46]

2.10. COMPENSATION

As the Czech Republic adheres to the compensatory concept of damages, any compensation awarded to cross-border victims of delicts reflects the harm sustained and proved. In this respect, Czech law treats cross-border victims in the same way as it treats domestic victims.

Under Czech law, victims can claim damages on the grounds of both harm to property and personal injury. With the Civil Code that came into effect on 1 January 2014, the Czech law on damages recovery underwent a dramatic shift, especially with respect to non-pecuniary damages for personal injury. Before the Civil Code, it was an implementation ordinance that provided the formula for the calculation of damages. Since the beginning of 2014, non-pecuniary damages for personal injury have been governed by section 2958 of the Civil Code, pursuant to which, as a principle, a victim is compensated for the pain and other non-pecuniary harm suffered (or for the victim's deteriorated social position, should the harm have resulted in an obstacle to a better future). If the amount of compensation cannot be determined in this manner, it must be determined according to the principles of decency. Since this concept is ill-designed for the determination of the amount of damages as far as out-of-court settlements are concerned, as well as for unification of case law, the Czech Supreme Court has recommended using guidelines (issued by the Supreme Court) setting forth the criteria for deteriorated social position and attributing a points evaluation to each category of pain.[47] The points total is then entered into a formula that takes into account the average gross income in the Czech Republic, which as such eliminates the need for further updates.

The guidelines, albeit not formally binding, are widely respected and adhered to by the lower courts. On the one hand, this practice contributes to legal certainty and predictability. On the other hand, however, this methodology, if relied too heavily on by the courts, may hamper the goal of section 2958 of

46 See the decision of the Czech Supreme Court decision of 22 August 2014, docket no. 30 Cdo 3157/2013.

47 See the Collection of Decisions and Standpoints of the Supreme Court, R 63/2014 civ. and R 1/2015.

the Civil Code, i.e. to provide fair compensation according to the principles of decency. Indeed, in our opinion, Czech courts tend to apply the formulas overly mechanically, without distinguishing cases that require individual approach. As such, this feature is to the detriment of section 2958 – which position has also been held by the Constitutional Court.[48] Another flaw worth mentioning relates to the methodology's points system, which for most categories is too low and thus inadequate.

3. GENERAL EVALUATION AND CONCLUSION

Overall, we are of the opinion that the Regulations have brought about a beneficial change into the Czech legal environment. The main benefit of a unified regime throughout the EU limiting the possibility of forum shopping is clear. However, also from the internal perspective of Czech private international law, we consider the Regulations to have had a positive impact. Even though the old APIL was a modern and progressive instrument back in the 1960s, it did not entirely cope with all the challenges of the 21st century. This was apparent especially in the field of delicts (torts), which were all covered by just one section of the old APIL, namely section 15, which stated that non-contractual claims for damages are governed either by the law of the country in which the damage occurs or, alternatively, by the law of the country in which the event giving rise to the damage occurs.[49] There were neither special rules for specific situations (different kinds of delicts and quasi-delicts), nor the possibility of choice of law by the parties. The system of the Rome II Regulation is thus more elaborate and brings more legal certainty than the too broad and discretionary rule of section 15 of the old APIL. In addition, the Rome Convention and the Rome I Regulation have also introduced some useful innovations into the Czech private international law, such as the special rules for weaker parties or regulation of third countries' overriding mandatory rules.[50] However, it is still too early for

---

48 See the decision of the Czech Constitutional Court of 16 February 2016, docket no. IV. ÚS 3122/15, in which the court stated that even limited guidelines determining points for categorised injuries can be problematic from the constitutionality perspective since any compensation for an injury must be based on evidence paying due regard to circumstances of each case.

49 It was up to the court to decide in each particular case, which of these laws (in case the place of damage and the place of the harmful event were in different countries) has a closer connection with the situation in question, given all the material facts. See Z. Kučera and L. Tichý, *Zákon o mezinárodním právu soukromém a procesním. Komentář* (Act on Private and Procedural International Law. Commentary), Prague: Panorama, 1989, p. 133.

50 The shift in the definition/role of the third countries' overriding mandatory norms introduced by the Rome I Regulation (Art. 9(3)) is to be welcomed, from the perspective

any reliable evaluations of the Regulations' benefits in terms of predictability and legal certainty, as the Czech case law on the Regulations is scarce. On the other hand, the lack of case law might also signify that the interpretation of these laws does not cause that many problems.[51]

Admittedly, the Regulations have both gaps and overlaps. Apart from the well-known and acknowledged gaps like the rules on defamation, there are other areas that might not be covered by the Regulations. In the area of contractual obligations, it would be useful if a clear rule on the (main) contract-related arrangements like (bank) guarantees were introduced. In the Czech Republic, there have been discussions about whether guarantees are unilateral or bilateral legal acts (arrangements) and given section 91 APIL, which deals with (among other things) unilaterally given security, it might still be felt that at least some of the unilateral legal acts related to contracts are left outside of the Rome I Regulation and that national regulation of the issue is thus necessary. Unilateral legal acts might also be left intact by the Rome II Regulation, as it is difficult to find a rule therein that would be suitable for acts like *public promises* (sections 2884 ff. of the Czech Civil Code) or *promises of indemnity* (sections 2890 ff. of the Czech Civil Code). As to the overlaps, it is not clear how broad the scope of set-off rule is (Article 17 of the Rome I Regulation). Does it cover all set-offs, including non-contractual ones, or is it limited only to the set-off of contractual obligations? What about the set-off of a non-contractual obligation against a contractual one?[52] These are the questions that should be considered in any future reform of the Regulations, together with new challenges like collective actions and private enforcement of competition law that give rise to complex problems of the multiplicity of claimants and/or defendants, the laws involved and related procedural aspects.

Looking at the Czech courts' take on the Regulations, there are judgments providing deep and interesting discussion of issues that are 'hot' across the EU, whether questions of punitive damages[53] or of the uniform characterisation of terms (institutes) used by the Regulations.[54] The Supreme Court judgment

of both party autonomy and legal certainty. It limits the situations in which these rules may be invoked to only those where the legitimate interest of the third country is clearly involved.

51 This may be true especially for choice of law under Art. 3 of the Rome I Regulation, which is in our experience used on a daily basis and yet is discussed only exceptionally in Czech courts.

52 For different views and solutions to this question see M Hellner, above n. 6, pp. 263–265 or McParland, above n. 33, p. 830.

53 See the decision of the Czech Supreme Court decision of 22 August 2014, docket no. 30 Cdo 3157/2013.

54 See the decision of the Czech Supreme Court decision of 14 January 2016, docket no. 30 Cdo 1941/2015.

clarifying the conflict-of-law regime of factoring contracts and assignments is also worth attention. On the other hand, the 'SPA case',[55] dealing with the question whether share-purchase agreements fall under the scope of the Rome I Regulation, was a big missed opportunity. Nevertheless, such a missed opportunity might be a push to clarify/remedy the issue in the future reform of the Regulations.

55 See the decision of the Czech Supreme Court decision of 30 September 2015, docket no. 29 Cdo 1029/2014.

THE APPLICATION OF THE ROME I AND ROME II REGULATIONS IN FRANCE

Marie-Elodie ANCEL*

* The author hereby wishes to express her sincere thanks to Mr Jean-Thomas Brière, for his linguistic revision of this contribution.

1. THE NATIONAL LANDSCAPE

1.1. APPLICATION OF ROME I AND ROME II IN GENERAL

The two Regulations, though eagerly anticipated and discussed by French legal scholars, have not stirred particular concern from the Ministry of Justice or from the Parliament. No particular measure aimed at facilitating the implementation of the two Regulations, which are directly applicable in the French legal order, has been enacted. Significantly, the French Ministry of Justice has not issued any circular on this topic. Under the aegis of the European Judicial Network in Civil and Commercial Matters, a national point of contact is instituted at the Department of Civil Affairs of the Ministry of Justice. There is also a local point of contact in each court of appeal and another one at the Cour de cassation level. However, no specific difficulty relating to the content of the two Regulations has been reported so far – but this does not mean there is none, as it will be shown hereafter. According to the judge designated as the national point of contact, references mostly come from abroad and relate to the French rules regarding road traffic accidents and compensation of personal and material damages.

To the author's knowledge, some French legislation mentions the Rome I Regulation (but none mentions the Rome II Regulation). Several provisions enacted in the field of prevention and resolution of banking crises are expressly characterised by the *Code monétaire et financier* as *lois de police* within the meaning of Article 9 of the Rome I Regulation (Article L. 613-50-4 and Article L. 613-45-1). A ministerial ruling regarding a national collective agreement also mentions the Rome I Regulation (along with the Rome Convention) in order to consider one paragraph as contrary to Article 8 (Article 1, arrêté du 21 août 2008 refusing to extend Article 3.11.3 of the national collective agreement on independent private education). Yet such a reference remains within the material limits of the Rome I Regulation because the contrary paragraph is included in a provision dedicated to the regime for employment contracts. Furthermore, a circular from the

Ministry of Justice recommends (subject to the assessment of the courts) that the measures taken in France to alleviate the legal consequences of the lockdown provoked by the COVID-19 crisis should be regarded as *lois de police* within the meaning of the Rome I Regulation.[1]

1.2. CASE LAW

French case law provides more insight into the implementation of the two Regulations. Not many cases have reached the Cour de cassation thus far (less than 20 by the end of July 2020[2] plus five more rendered in October 2018 but related to the same case),[3] though courts of appeal have issued more than a hundred decisions up to May 2017 (with some exceptions, decisions of the lower courts after this date are not examined in this contribution). In decreasing order of frequency, the most commonly applied provisions of the Rome I Regulation are Articles 8, 9, 3, 5 and 4. So far, the application of the Rome II Regulation has mostly focused on Articles 4 and 6.

Lower courts seem to be well aware of the existence of the Regulations. For instance, the temporal application of the Rome I Regulation is frequently examined in relation to employment contracts and usually correctly established.[4] Courts seldom refuse to apply the European instruments for incorrect reasons; however, some unjustified grounds for refusal can be found. For instance, a court

---

1 French Ministry of Justice, Circular, 17 April 2020, referring to the Ordinance No. 2020-427.

2 Cass. 1re civ., 30 April 2014, No. 13-11932 (Rome II); Cass. com., 1 March 2016, No. 14-22608 (Rome I); Cass. com., 2 November 2016, No. 15-10296 (Rome I); Cass. soc., 19 January 2017, No. 15-20095 (Rome I); Cass. soc., 1 February 2017, No. 15-23723 (Rome I); Cass. com., 4 May 2017, No. 15-22712 (Rome I); Cass. com., 8 November 2017, No. 16-10850 (Rome II); Cass. 1re civ., 24 January 2018, No. 17-10959 (Rome II); Cass. 1re civ., 5 September 2018, No. 16-24109 (Rome II); Cass. soc., 5 December 2018, No. 17-11224; Cass. 1re civ., 19 December 2018, No. 17-26663 (Rome I); Cass. soc., 20 February 2019, Nos. 17-20532, 17-20536 (Rome I); Cass. com., 7 May 2019, No. 17-15340 (Rome I and Rome II); Cass. com., 7 May 2019, No. 17-27229 (Rome II); Civ. 2e civ., 16 May 2019, No. 18-12005 (Rome I); Cass. 2e civ., 16 May 2019, No. 18-12006 (Rome I); Cass. com., 15 January 2020, No.17-22295 (Rome II); Cass. com., 8 July 2020, No. 17-31536 (Rome I and Rome II). Also worth mentioning, Conseil d'Etat, 15 June 2019, No. 417837 (Rome I).

3 Applying the Rome II Regulation, Cass. 1re civ., 5 October 2018, No. 17-14401; Cass. 1re civ., 5 October 2018, No. 16-19430; Cass. 1re civ., 5 October 2018, Nos. 15-26115, 15-26.388; Cass. 1re civ., 5 October 2018, No. 15-28531; Cass. 1re civ., 5 October 2018, No. 15-28891.

4 Colmar, 31 March 2016, No. 15/05844; Paris, 2 June 2015, No. 13/01874; Paris, 21 May 2015, No. 12/09680; Douai, 20 February 2015, No. 14/01536; Colmar, 7 February 2013, No. 11/04065; Colmar, 12 January 2012, No. 11/01146 (all explaining that the Rome I Regulation shall not be applied to an employment contract concluded before 17 December 2009). See also Grenoble, 21 May 2015, No. 14/03912. Following another line of reasoning, some courts applied the Rome I Regulation to cases regarding contracts concluded before 2009 because employer and employee agreed on its application (Aix-en-Provence, 27 April 2017, No. 16/06204; Chambéry, 29 September 2016, No. 16/0025) or because the employee did not challenge its application (Lyon, 26 January 2016, No. 14/06457).

of appeal refused to apply the Rome I Regulation to a contract entered into by parties who had their habitual residence in Switzerland because this state is not a member of the EU.[5] Even more surprisingly, another court ruled out the Rome I Regulation, holding that it is not applicable when the parties have chosen the law of their contract.[6]

French lower courts often struggle to decide which Regulation they should apply or whether they should give precedence to other sets of rules. Probably because the Rome I Regulation replaces the rather well-known Rome Convention, court practice seems to be more familiar with this Regulation than with the Rome II Regulation. For instance, in a May 2016 decision, the Aix-en-Provence Court of Appeal correctly applied the Rome I Regulation to validate the choice of the law applicable to an insurance contract, but appeared to be unaware of Article 18 of the Rome II Regulation. Regarding the admissibility of a direct action brought by the victim against the insurer of the liable person, the Court based its decision on prior French case law, which points solely to the law of the place of damage.[7] In another decision, the Nîmes Court of Appeal rightly held that the Rome I Regulation was not applicable *ratione temporis* (to an action brought by a French consumer against a German company which had manufactured the car that the consumer had bought in France from a reseller), whereas the issue should have been characterised as non-contractual, thus leading to the application of the Rome II Regulation.[8] However, in a dispute between two competitors, the Paris Court of Appeal was confronted with unfair competition activities initiated before 11 January 2009 but giving rise to ongoing alleged damages. The Rome II Regulation was held to be applicable to the dispute in its entirety.[9] Similarly, the Aix-en-Provence Court of Appeal applied exclusively the Rome II Regulation to a series of harmful events that took place between 1997 and 2010.[10] The Cour de cassation upheld its decision on the ground that previous French case law was identical to Article 4 of the Rome II Regulation (which is questionable) and that both rules were to be applied in that case.[11]

---

5 Chambéry, 8 December 2015, No. 15/01124.

6 Orléans, 9 April 2015, No. 13/03196.

7 Aix-en-Provence, 12 May 2016, No. 13/06987. To be compared with Versailles, 2 May 2017, No. 16/01166, correctly applying Article 18 of the Rome II Regulation.

8 Nîmes, 5 March 2015, No. 14/01736: the characterisation of the case as contractual comes from French case law.

9 Paris, 1 December 2015, No. 14/02708. This holding has not been challenged before the Cour de cassation (Cass. com., 8 November 2017, No. 16-10850).

10 Aix-en-Provence, 2 July 2015, No. 13/22482.

11 Cass. 1re civ., 5 October 2018, No. 17-14401 (Rome II); Cass. 1re civ., 5 October 2018, No. 16-19430 (Rome II); Cass. 1re civ., 5 October 2018, No. 15-26115-15-26.388 (Rome II); Cass. 1re civ., 5 October 2018, No. 15-28531 (Rome II); Cass. 1re civ., 5 October 2018, No. 15-28891 (Rome II).

In fact, the Regulations are more often invoked *outside* their scope of application rather than ignored. There are various reasons for this tropism. Firstly, many French courts base their decisions on the Rome I Regulation and simply overlook the fact that the cases under consideration fall outside its temporal scope.[12] Secondly, in at least two instances, the Rome I Regulation has been deliberately used as *ratio scripta*. In 2013, the Paris Court of Appeal used Article 4(1)(f) to identify the characteristic performance of a distribution agreement according to Article 4(2) of the Rome Convention.[13] A few days before, the Lyon Court of Appeal had based its construction of Article 6(1) of the Rome Convention (referring to 'mandatory rules') on the new wording of Article 8(1) of the Rome I Regulation (referring to 'provisions that cannot be derogated from by agreement').[14] Thirdly, in other cases, courts highlighted that the rules set out by the Rome Convention (held to be applicable to the pending cases) are confirmed, replicated or reinforced by the Rome I Regulation.[15] Finally, regarding the Rome II Regulation, it seems to have been wrongly applied (i) twice in lieu of the 1971 Hague Convention on the Law Applicable to Traffic

12 Paris (International Commercial Chamber), 5 March 2019, No. 18/04137, about a contract concluded in 2001, on the erroneous ground that it was terminated in 2011; Cass. soc., 20 February 2019, Nos. 17-20532, 17-20536 (having asked the lower court to apply the Rome I Regulation, a party cannot claim before the Cour de cassation the application of the Rome Convention); Metz, 17 May 2016, No. 14/00973, about a personal guarantee concluded in 1999 – Article 9 of the Rome I Regulation is mentioned together with Article 3 of the French Civil Code and Article 7 of the Rome Convention; Orléans, 3 March 2016, No. 15/01485, for an agency contract concluded 'in 2007 or 2008'; Lyon, 9 February 2016, No. 13/03208, for a contract concluded in 2008; Pau, 9 September 2015, No. 15/03304, about a publishing contract concluded in November 2008; Pau, 13 July 2015, No. 15/2847, about a framework contract concluded in 2007 with litigious operations concluded on 9 October 2009 and 9 December 2009; Versailles, 22 October 2014, No. 13/01771, on an employment contract concluded in 2003; Lyon, 22 April 2014, No. 12/00822, on a contract concluded in 2008; Poitiers, 28 September 2012, No. 10/03643; Douai, 29 June 2012, No. 12/00975, on a contract concluded in 1999, modified in 2008, with references to the Rome Convention too; Metz, 15 May 2012, No. 10/04280, on a contract concluded in 2008.
On the contrary some courts have rightly applied the Rome Convention: Nîmes, 2 October 2014, No. 13/00118; Versailles, 14 May 2013, No. 12/00913; Paris, 4 June 2013, No. 12/15944; Colmar, 30 March 2012, No. 11/04490; Aix-en-Provence, 14 September 2011, No. 09/22729; Colmar, 15 June 2011, No. 08/02971.

13 Paris, 4 June 2013, No. 12/15944.

14 Lyon, 28 May 2013, No. 12/05631.

15 Nîmes, 5 March 2015, No. 14/01736 (Article 4 of both texts); Montpellier, 11 May 2011, No. 10/06887 (Article 4(4) of the Rome Convention and Article 5 of the Rome I Regulation); Metz, 8 April 2014, No. 14/00294; Nancy, 26 October 2012, No. 12/00890 (Article 6 of the Rome Convention and Article 8 of the Rome I Regulation). More loosely, applying both the Rome Convention and the Rome I Regulation to an employment contract concluded in 2012, Aix-en-Provence, 21 May 2015, No. 13/22838.

Accidents;[16] (ii) once in lieu of national conflict-of-law rules and the Rome I Regulation;[17] (iii) once in lieu of national conflict-of-law rules.[18]

1.3. ARBITRATION

In France, arbitration appears to be a less fertile ground for the application of the two Regulations than litigation. No award referring to the Regulations has been recorded by the Association Française d'Arbitrage (AFA, also known as the Association for Arbitration). According to the International Arbitration Court of the ICC based in Paris, only two awards had applied the Rome Regulations by the end of 2013. One, rendered by an arbitral tribunal seated in Helsinki, is of very great interest because it thoroughly applied and discussed the two Regulations.[19] The dispute arose out of the sudden termination of a distribution contract, binding a Finnish manufacturer and its distributor for Greece. Finnish law expressly governed the contract. The distributor argued that its claims were non-contractual and should be adjudicated under Greek law, viewed as the law of the market affected and/or as the law of the place where the damages had occurred. Because the defendant was domiciled in the EU (as was the claimant), the arbitral tribunal found it appropriate to resort to the two Regulations.[20] The content of the award will be examined in further detail below.

2. THE OPERATION OF ROME I AND ROME II IN PRACTICE

2.1. *LOIS DE POLICE*

2.1.1. Identification of French lois de police

The interference of French overriding mandatory rules (*lois de police*) is often discussed before courts, since French case law traditionally tends to recognise such rules in contractual and non-contractual matters. For instance, in a 2006 decision, the Cour de cassation held that a provision of the French *Code de la*

---

16 See section 2.7.

17 Cass. 1re civ., 24 January 2018: lower court judges applied Article 18 of the Rome II Regulation whereas the insured obligations were contractual.

18 Cass. 1re civ., 24 September 2018, No. 16-24109: lower court judges applied the Rome II Regulation whereas the event giving rise to the damage occurred in 2006. See also, for a partial over-application, the above-mentioned decision of the Aix-en-Provence Court of Appeal, 2 July 2015, No. 13/22482.

19 ICC Award No. 16981 rendered in May 2012 and published in the ICC Dispute Resolution Bulletin 2016.

20 Even if the terminated agreement appears to have been entered into in 2000.

consommation was a *loi de police*. Further, in 2007, the Court held that the French provisions protecting sub-contractors (which give them a direct legal action against employers for payment) were also *lois de police*, to be applied whenever the building was located in France, although this reasoning was not obvious for all the judges.[21] Regarding non-contractual obligations, acts that create national funds for compensating victims of terrorism or of other specific torts are also considered *lois de police*.[22]

However, the enactment of the Rome I Regulation and the drafting of Article 9(1) seem to have reduced the judicial characterisation of *lois de police*. Under the Rome Convention, the Cour de cassation decided in 2010 that the French provision that gives carriers a direct claim for payment against recipients of the goods[23] is not a *loi de police*.[24] Consequently, for lower courts, such a direct action is admissible only if French law governs the contract for the carriage of goods.[25] The Cour de cassation also refused to label as *lois de police* the provisions of the *Code de la consommation* protecting individuals who act as personal guarantors for the benefit of a bank.[26] Under the Rome I Regulation, lower courts now follow this ruling.[27] More surprisingly, the Cour de cassation recently decided, again under the Rome Convention, that the French legislation transposing the Directive No. 86/653/EEC on commercial agents is not a *loi de police*.[28] Conversely, the *Conseil d'Etat* (the supreme administrative jurisdiction in France,) labelled as *loi de police* the French provision prohibiting the hiring

---

21 Cass. Ch. mixte, 30 November 2007, No. 06-14006.

22 For instance, Cass. 2e civ., 25 January 2007, No. 06-10514. However, they could also be considered to be public law matters.

23 *Code de commerce*, Article L. 132-8: 'The bill of lading shall form a contract between the consignor, the carrier and the recipient or between the consignor, the recipient, the agent on commission and the carrier. Carriers shall therefore have a direct claim for payment of their services against the consignor and the recipient, both of whom shall guarantee payment of the transport cost. Any clause to the contrary shall be deemed unwritten'.

24 Cass. com., 13 July 2010, No. 10-12154.

25 Angers, 8 September 2015, No. 13/01460; Versailles, 6 January 2015, No. 14/02383.

26 Cass. 1re civ., 16 September 2015, No. 14-10373.

27 About Articles L. 341-1, L. 341-2, L. 341-3 and L. 341-6 of the *Code de la consommation*: Metz, 17 May 2016, No. 14/00973; Douai, 28 January 2016, No. 15/00343. The position adopted by the Cour de cassation in September 2015 was anticipated earlier that year by the Metz Court of Appeal (16 April 2015, No. 12/03750).

28 Cass. com., 5 January 2016, No. 14-10628. Such a decision is at first sight hard to reconcile with the *Ingmar* and *Unamar* rulings (Case C-381/98, *Ingmar GB Ltd v. Eaton Leonard Technologies Inc.*, ECLI:EU:C:2000:605; Case C-184/12, *United Antwerp Maritime Agencies (Unamar) NV v. Navigation Maritime Bulgare*, ECLI:EU:C:2013:663). However its practical result is that the agent is only entitled to the compensation provided by the chosen law, i.e. German law, which happens to be the law of the country where the agent had to act on behalf of his French principal. The compensation due to the agent has therefore to be determined only by the German transposition of the Directive.

of a foreigner who is not authorised to carry out a salaried activity in France (Article L. 8251-1, *Code du travail*).[29]

French provisions regulating practices that restrict competition are more difficult to assess.[30] Article L. 442-6, I, 5° (now Article L. 442-1, II) of the *Code de commerce* allows a party to an 'established business relationship' to seek compensation from its counterpart if the latter abruptly breaks off the relationship. Since the CJEU's 2016 ruling in *Granarolo*,[31] a claim based on Article L. 442-6, I, 5° has to be considered as raising a contractual issue if an at least tacit long-standing contract has been terminated. Before this ruling, French courts tended to classify the issue as either a matter of tort or delict (this was the often-repeated position of the Commercial Court of the Cour de cassation)[32] or sometimes as a *loi de police*.[33] In fact, the two approaches often resulted in the application of Article L. 442-6, I, 5°. Indeed, the damage had often occurred in France[34] or the case was considered to fall within the spatial scope of the French *loi de police*. The *Granarolo* ruling now prohibits the 'non-contractual' approach in many cases.[35] This could theoretically give more strength to the approach in terms of overriding mandatory rules, meaning that French courts still could hold Article L. 442-6, I, 5° applicable. Nonetheless, given the restrictive conception of *loi de police* now adopted by the Cour de cassation in other fields, it seems more likely that the abrupt termination of a long-standing contract (whether tacit or express) will remain under the

---

29 Conseil d'Etat, 15 June 2019, No. 417837.

30 It is worth noting that the French Senate recently proposed to expressly indicate in Articles L. 441-7 and L. 442-6 of the *Code de commerce* are *lois de police* the meaning of Article 9 of the Rome I Regulation (Sénat, Article 10 *bis* A of the Draft Law for the balance of trade relations in the agricultural and food sector and for healthy, sustainable and accessible food for all, 2 July 2018). However, the Government opposed such a mention on various grounds. First, it held that *loi de police* is 'a notion defined by international conventions and applied by courts' and that it is not up to legislative characterisation. Secondly, and more convincingly, the Government insisted on the fact that French provisions had already been applied by courts in international situations and that a legislative characterisation of specific French provisions might impede a judicial characterisation of other provisions (Assemblée nationale, Report on the Draft Law for the balance of trade relations in the agricultural and food sector and for healthy, sustainable and accessible food for all, 18 July 2018).

31 Case C-196/15, *Granarolo SpA v. Ambrosi Emmi France SA*, ECLI:EU:C:2016:559.

32 For instance, Cass. com., 13 December 2011, No. 11-12024. See also Paris, 3 April 2014, No. 13/09590.

33 Grenoble, 28 May 2015, No. 12/02016 (applying Article 7 of the Rome Convention).

34 Or the escape clause enshrined in Article 4(3) of the Rome II Regulation could be used to revert to French law: Paris, 30 September 2016, No. 14/04908.

35 Paris, 10 May 2017, No. 14/15261 (French law is applicable to the breaking off of a tacit contract aiming at the distribution of products in France, on the ground of Article 4(1)(f) of the Rome I Regulation); Paris (International Commercial Chamber), 5 March 2019, No. 18/04137 (breaking off governed by French law, which applies by virtue of Article 4(4) of the Rome I Regulation).

lex contractus.[36] In May 2019, the Cour de cassation again avoided taking a position by approving the application of Article L. 442-6, I, 5° both on the basis of the Rome I Regulation and the Rome II Regulation, adding that to argue that the French provision was a *loi de police* was overabundant.[37]

Article L. 442-6, I, 2° and Article L. 442-6, II (d) of the *Code de commerce* were also confronted with Article 9(1) of the Rome I Regulation in the *Expedia* case lodged at the Paris lower courts. As permitted by Article L. 442-6, III, the Minister for Economic Affairs asked for the cancellation of parity clauses included in contracts governed by English law and entered into by an Internet platform and owners of hotels located in France. These clauses were challenged on the basis of Article L. 442-6, II (d), which prohibits most-favoured-customer clauses, and of Article L. 442-6, I, 2°, which requires protection against significant imbalance in the rights and obligations of the parties. According to the Minister for Economic Affairs, the case was non-contractual by nature and, in any event, the whole Article L. 442-6 was a *loi de police*. The Paris Commercial Court decided differently in May 2015.[38] First of all, it characterised the case as contractual and thus as falling under the Rome I Regulation: the choice of English law was therefore totally admissible. The Court added that Article 9 requires a cautious approach, each provision having to be examined closely and separately. On this basis, the *loi de police* label was denied to Article L. 442-6, II (d) because this provision is specific to sectors where several small suppliers face one large buyer. On the other hand, Article L. 442-6, I, 2° could be a *loi de police* because the need for rebalancing a contract is generic and systemic. Such an analysis, based on the economic facet of the provision (specific sectors versus systemic value) under examination, is not entirely convincing.[39] The Minister for Economic Affairs successfully appealed against the Paris Commercial Court's judgment. In June 2017 the Paris Court of Appeal decided that his claims were tortious by nature and that the Rome II Regulation had to be applied.[40] As a consequence, English law was disregarded, on the grounds of Article 14 of the Regulation, because the Minister was not bound by the choice-of-law clauses. Article 4 thus led to French law as the law of the country where the damage had occurred.

---

36 Paris (International Commercial Chamber), 3 June 2020, No. 19/03758. In the ICC Award No. 16981, the majority of the arbitral tribunal was not convinced that Article 18A of Greek Law 146/1914, also prohibiting the sudden and unjustified termination of long-term commercial relationships where one party is in a position of economic dependence on the other, is a *loi d'application immédiate* (in other words, an overriding mandatory rule). In particular, according to the arbitrators' views, 'the protection of a weaker party in contracts does not as such in all and every circumstance amount to an essential policy'.

37 Cass. com., 7 May 2019, No. 17-15340.

38 Trib. com. Paris, 7 May 2015, No. 2015000040, *Ministère de l'Economie et de l'Industrie et du Numérique v. Expedia, Inc. et al.; Ministère de l'Economie et de l'Industrie et du Numérique v. Hotels.com LP.*

39 Especially because it is not in line with the *Unamar* ruling.

40 Paris, 21 June 2017, No. 15/18784.

Resorting to *lois de police* was therefore unnecessary, but this did not prevent the Paris Court of Appeal from stating in an *obiter dictum* that both Articles L. 442-6, II (d) and L. 442-6, I, 2° are overriding mandatory provisions, within the meaning of Article 16 of the Rome II Regulation, because they promote 'equality of arms and faithfulness between economic partners'. This rationale was recently endorsed by the Cour de cassation.[41] Furthermore, in 2016, the French contract law reform introduced into the Civil Code the prohibition of significant imbalance,[42] broadening its range considerably. However, it is unlikely, of the provisions in the Civil Code, that this one in particular will ultimately be labelled as a *loi de police*. Were this to be the case, it would cause much uncertainty in international contractual relationships.

2.1.2. Effects to be Given to Foreign lois de police

To the present author's knowledge, only one case has been rendered by a French court regarding third states' *lois de police* in the context of the Rome I Regulation.[43] The treatment that was given to foreign overriding mandatory provisions does not appear completely satisfactory. In 2015, the Paris Court of Appeal had to adjudicate a claim brought by an Iranian agent against the French subsidiary of a US company.[44] Their contractual relationships were governed by French law but, because of US federal legislation prohibiting trade with Iran, the French subsidiary was prevented by its parent company from doing further business with its Iranian partner. The Court of Appeal refused 'to give effect' to the federal provisions, taking the view that the provisions did not originate from the state of the place of performance, as referred to in Article 9(3) of the Rome I Regulation. As a consequence, the French subsidiary was held to be contractually liable. Nevertheless, the Court of Appeal drew some legal consequences from the existence of the embargo in assessing the damages invoked by the Iranian party. The Court dismissed any loss of chance claimed by the agent, holding that 'because of the embargo on Iran decided by the U.S. government since 1995, the continuation of commercial relations [between the French subsidiary and the Iranian partner] was not serious' (under French law, any loss of chance has

---

41 Cass. com., 8 July 2020, No. 17-31536. It remains to be seen whether this judgment will reactivate a wider use of *lois de police* in business relationships.

42 Civil Code, Article 1171: any term of a standard form contract that creates a significant imbalance in the rights and obligations of the parties to the contract is deemed not written.

43 ICC Award No. 16981 needs to be treated separately because arbitral tribunals are not faced with *lois de police* of their own forum. In the case at hand, the arbitral tribunal felt to have only 'a duty' to enforce national overriding mandatory rules contained in the law chosen by the parties. Nevertheless, it hypothetically took the Greek provision invoked by the distributor as a *loi de police* and examined the consequences of its application or non-application. It concluded that the consequences of its non-application would be 'minimal, considering that Finnish law recognises and protects the same policy'.

44 Paris, 25 February 2015, No. 12/23757.

to be serious to be compensated). This shows that at least the existence of the US overriding mandatory rules was used as a fact that shaped the reasonable expectations of the Iranian partner. However, the Paris Court of Appeal's ruling could also have taken into consideration the threat to trade with Iran represented by the US embargo in assessing the validity of the contractual relationships on the ground of the French governing law.[45] The CJEU's 2016 *Nikiforidis* ruling will probably foster further analysis and examination of foreign *lois de police* in the light of the law of the contract.[46]

2.2. PARTY AUTONOMY

2.2.1. Party Autonomy under Rome I

Party autonomy has been acknowledged for more than a century in French conflict of laws on contracts. Contemporary case law shows that the express choice of law is unproblematic[47] and *dépeçage* almost non-existent.[48] When no express choice is made, tacit or implicit consensus is quite easily accepted[49] (except in employment contracts).[50] For instance, the Metz Court of Appeal has considered, on the ground of Article 3(1) of the Rome I Regulation, that where both parties base their written submissions on French law, it clearly demonstrates a choice of that law.[51] Such a characterisation could be discussed because reference to French law could have been limited to the issue at stake before that Court in relation to the differing temporal reach of each agreement. In instances where the parties can assign or waive the rights available in disputes (*droits disponibles*), the parties can choose the law that a French court will apply. However, they are relieved of this choice as soon as the dispute is solved (this is why this kind of agreement is called *accord procédural*). Party autonomy under the Rome I Regulation binds both parties without a time limit, unless they both decide to change their initial choice. Nonetheless, in the Metz Court of Appeal decision, such a distinction was not really material because the sales contract at issue was very simple and no other dispute was likely to arise.

---

45 Compare with Poitiers, 29 November 2011, No. 10/03500 (on the grounds of the Rome Convention and French law), where it was decided that a contract for carriage of goods violating a Ghanaian embargo was void because it had as its object an impossible thing.

46 Case C-135/15, *Republik Griechenland v. Grigorios Nikiforidis*, ECLI:EU:C:2016:774.

47 For instance, Paris, 11 October 2012, No. 11/20657 (express choice of English law) or, improperly grounded on French prior case law, Orléans, 25 April 2015, No. 13/03196. However, choice of non-state law provisions remains a blind spot before French courts.

48 Cass. soc., 4 December 2012, No. 11-22166 (on the ground of the Rome Convention, regarding an employment contract).

49 Paris (International Commercial Chamber), 3 June 2020, No. 19/03758.

50 See section 2.4.3.

51 Metz, 26 November 2015, No. 15/00561 (implicit choice of French law).

Tacit or implicit choice is also very often relied on for personal guarantees. In this context, various elements can serve as evidence. In one case, the Metz Court of Appeal held that the parties had made an implicit choice of Luxembourg law because of their choice of the Court of Luxembourg City, supported by the reference in the contract to two provisions of the Luxembourg Civil Code. Even though the French Civil Code once included the same provisions, the Court underlined that at the time of the conclusion of the contract these provisions had been relocated in the French Civil Code under a different number.[52] In another case, an Austrian company guaranteed the debt of another Austrian company that had bought wood from a French municipality.[53] Sales of wood by French public entities are strictly regulated under the French Forestry Code and, in this case, the sales contract was expressly submitted to French law. Moreover, the French Forestry Code requires that, when payment is deferred, an approved body must give a personal guarantee. The guarantee given by the Austrian company mentioned that specific provision and was written in French (although it was signed in Austria). Considering all these elements and given the ancillary nature of personal guarantees, the Metz Court of Appeal concluded that French law also implicitly governed the contract at issue. In yet another case, the Douai Court of Appeal decided, in a short reasoning, that because Belgian law expressly governed the guaranteed contract, it should also govern the guarantee. The Court may have felt the weakness of the argument and tried, not very convincingly, to conclude that Belgian law was applicable to the guarantee under Article 4 of the Rome I Regulation.[54]

2.2.2. *Party Autonomy under Rome II*

Party autonomy has not been completely ignored in tort matters, but until the Rome II Regulation the parties' choice could only stem from an *accord procédural* reached by the parties once they were litigating in a French court. Under the Rome II Regulation, party autonomy is theoretically wider; however, no such case has yet been brought in French court practice.

So far, Article 14 principally appears in the aforementioned ICC Award No. 16981.[55] The distribution contract at issue included a choice-of-law clause stating that the 'agreement shall be governed by and construed in accordance with Finnish law'. However, the distributor presented its claim for sudden

52 Metz, 16 April 2015, No. 12/03750.

53 Pau, 22 March 2016, No. 16/01183.

54 Douai, 28 January 2016, No. 15/00343. See section 2.3.2.

55 In the dispute between the Internet platform and owners of hotels in France (the *Expedia* case, see section 2.1.1), the Paris Court of Appeal noted that the Minister for Economic Affairs had not given its consent to the contractual clauses choosing English law. Therefore, his claims, characterised as tortious, were not governed by this law (Paris, 21 June 2017, No. 15/18784).

termination of the contract as tortious in nature, relying on elements of its counterpart's behaviour 'which made the relevant acts tort'. Because the arbitral tribunal had jurisdiction to adjudicate contractual and non-contractual claims, it had to decide whether the choice of Finnish law for the contract deserved to be extended to a claim that was allegedly tortious in nature. Firstly, the majority of the arbitral tribunal disagreed with the distributor, considering that its claims derived 'from the performance of the contract and [were] therefore contractual by nature'. Secondly, 'for the sake of completeness', the arbitrators addressed the issue of the law governing these claims, had the distributor's claims been characterised as tortious. The majority of the arbitral tribunal was satisfied that the conditions provided under Article 14 were fulfilled:

> 'the Parties, which both pursue a commercial activity, entered into a clear and written choice of law before the event giving rise to the alleged damage occurred; and the record does not evidence that the choice of law was not "freely negotiated" at the time it was made'.

However, readers are left with the impression that the arbitrators overlooked one point: was a choice of Finnish law for non-contractual claims related to the distribution contract really 'demonstrated with reasonable certainty by the circumstances of the case'? At an earlier stage of its reasoning, the majority of the arbitral tribunal had noted that:

> 'it is well established in international arbitration that, except where otherwise provided, it may generally be assumed that the parties agreed on an all-encompassing reference to the chosen substantive law, i.e. such reference includes not only contractual claims in the strict sense of the term but also e.g. tort claims arising out of and in connection with the contract containing the choice-of-law clause'.

Because this contention is grounded in a general assumption and not in the circumstances of the case, the award appears to be a little fragile when it comes to this aspect.[56]

2.3. ABSENCE OF CHOICE OF LAW

2.3.1. Fixed Rules under Rome I

Regarding contractual matters, French courts are comfortable with fixed rules. The method echoes national case law that was, under the influence of Batiffol, based on presumptions. In this favourable context, fixed rules enshrined in the

56 See also Paris (International Commercial Chamber), 3 June 2020, No. 19/03758.

Rome I Regulation have been used to determine the law applicable to a great variety of contracts: to an auction held in France,[57] to medical surgery performed in Belgium by a doctor established in France,[58] to the rental and setting up of tents for memorial ceremonies on the D-Day beaches in Normandy,[59] etc.

2.3.2. *Escape Clauses under Rome I*

So far, only a few decisions have addressed escape clauses under the Rome I Regulation and it is difficult to draw any consistent conclusion from them. However, it should be noted that escape clauses are not used in order to systematically revert to French law. Personal guarantees, carriage of goods and employment contracts offer the most relevant examples.

With regard to personal guarantees, absent a choice of law by the parties, French courts historically tended to presume that they were submitted to the law governing the secured obligation. Article 4(2) of the Rome Convention challenged this presumption and the Cour de cassation seemed to hesitate between a restrictive[60] and a looser[61] usage of the escape clause. The aforementioned decision rendered by the Douai Court of Appeal in 2016 seems to pick up the former presumption again.[62] The Court's reasoning is a bit confused: it appears only to rely on Article 4(2) of the Rome I Regulation, but in reality it ended up placing the guarantee concluded by two French nationals with their habitual residence in France under Belgian law, which expressly governed the main contract.[63] In any event, nowhere does the Court seem to realise that the escape clause under Article 4(3) of the Rome I Regulation should be used more sparingly than under the Rome Convention. Conversely, the Paris Court of Appeal ruled that a comfort letter granted by a Luxembourg parent company to the French Post Office to guarantee the debts of its French or other subsidiaries should remain under Luxembourg law. The Court insisted on the limited use to be made of Article 4(3) of the Regulation.[64]

---

57 Paris, 15 January 2013, No. 12/01720 (Article 4(1)(g)).

58 Paris, 15 May 2014, No. 13/02356.

59 Poitiers, 28 September 2012, No. 10/03643 (whether a pure provision of contract or a renting contract, the contract is to be governed by French law on the grounds of Article 4(1)(b) or (2)).

60 Cass. com., 8 March 2011, No. 09-11751.

61 Cass. 1re civ., 16 September 2015, No. 14-10373.

62 See section 2.2.1: Douai, 28 January 2016, No. 15/00343.

63 It is hard to tell whether the Court improperly applied Article 4(2) by confusing the 'characteristic performance' under the main contract and the one of the personal guarantee, or if it tried to align with the outcome of the decision rendered by the Cour de cassation on 16 September 2015.

64 Paris (International Commercial Chamber), 10 September 2019, No. 19/06981.

The escape clause spelled out in Article 5(3) of the Rome I Regulation for the carriage of goods was at play in a decision rendered by the Cour de cassation.[65] A French company was responsible for the operation of the carriage of goods within France as part of the goods' longer journey to their ultimate destination, Italy. Judges held that a single contract had been entered into with several carriers but parties did not choose the applicable law. Because the place of receipt (France) and the place of delivery (Italy) or the habitual residence of the consignor (France) were not situated in the country of the habitual residence of the main carrier (Switzerland), Article 5(1) led the judges towards the law of the country where the place of delivery was situated, as agreed by the parties (Italy). However, pursuant to Article 5(3), the French carrier argued that manifestly closer links existed with France. This position was sternly rebutted by the Court of Appeal and, afterwards, by the Cour de cassation. Furthermore, when the habitual residence of the carrier and the place of delivery are located in the same country, French judges are very reluctant to apply the escape clause.[66]

Finally, two decisions relate to Article 8(4). In the first case, a captain was hired to sail in the Western Mediterranean and it was impossible to identify one location where he habitually carried out his work.[67] The connection with the country of the place of business of his employer (a company incorporated in the Isle of Man) was weak, since the captain had never sailed in this region. The Aix-en-Provence Court of Appeal held that closest links, within the meaning of Article 8(4), existed with France, where the captain was domiciled during the contract and where from time to time he sailed the boat in performance of the contract. In a later case, the parties had expressly submitted an employment contract to Lebanese law, though the employee was to carry out his activities in Algeria.[68] The Aix-en-Provence Court of Appeal had to examine whether a closer link existed with France, because both parties were French, the salary was paid in euros and the employer had organised the employee's return to France. These circumstances were not considered sufficient to establish a closer link with France. As a principle, when an employee carries out his activities exclusively or almost exclusively in one country, French judges do not tend to depart from the law of this country.[69]

65 Cass. com., 1 March 2016, No. 14-22608 (it should be noted that judges mentioned Article 5(2) by mistake).

66 See section 2.4.1.

67 Aix-en-Provence, 22 January 2016, No. 15/02788.

68 Aix-en-Provence, 2 June 2016, No. 14/21676.

69 Sticking to the law of the place where the activities are carried out: Colmar, 29 April 2016, No. 14/02955; Colmar, 19 January 2016, No. 14/01854 and 14/01853; Douai, 19 December 2014, No. 14/01422.

2.3.3. *Fixed Rules under Rome II*

With respect to non-contractual issues, courts are keen to rely on Article 4 of the Rome II Regulation whenever the dispute is about non-material[70] or material[71] damages or personal injury.[72] Compared to contracts, the move towards fixed rules is more dramatic because, previously, the law applicable to non-contractual relationships whose elements are spread across different countries (*délits complexes*) was mostly determined on a case-by-case basis, which resulted in judicial uncertainty.[73] Against this background, the guidance provided by Article 4 of the Rome II Regulation seems to be appreciated.[74]

Still, factual constellations that occurred before and after 11 January 2009 can be problematic.[75] For instance, an important case involved thousands of victims of defective breast prostheses, who were domiciled in many countries, and various foreign distributors that operated on behalf of the French company producing the prostheses.[76] One action was specifically brought against an organisation incorporated in Germany and its French subsidiary, which were both in charge of assessing the medical devices between 1997 and 2010. The Aix-en-Provence Court of Appeal held that, pursuant to Article 4 of the Rome II Regulation, only one law was applicable to the claims:

> 'the tort/delict occurred in the French factories of [the producer] situated in [city X] where the audits took place, the responsibility of [the French subsidiary of the German organisation], a company governed by French law, was sought by the respondents and interveners. It follows, therefore, from [Article 4], from the facts and from the procedure described above, that French law is applicable to the present proceedings'.

It may be that the manifestly closest connection existed with France, but the Court of Appeal was not willing to go into further detail. Notably, it did not mention that decisions (related to the issue of compliance certificates, their

70 For the non-material injury caused to a French national who had married a woman in Tunisia but who suffered from the deliberate refusal of his wife to join him in France after the wedding: Douai, 8 January 2015, No. 13/07208; for the damage caused to a woman deserted by a husband, Paris, 30 June 2016, No. 14/09535.

71 Versailles, 2 May 2017, No. 16/01166.

72 Aix-en-Provence, 24 May 2017, No. 16/06254.

73 Cass. com., 25 March 2014, No. 12-29534; Cass. com., 4 November 2014, No. 12-27072.

74 See, using Article 4(1) of the Rome II Regulation as support for the case-by-case search for the law applicable to a situation falling outside the temporal scope of the Regulation, Montpellier, 21 June 2011, No. 10/03569.

75 See section 1.2.

76 Aix-en-Provence, 2 July 2015, No. 13/22482.

maintenance and renewal, for instance) had been taken in Germany.[77] Then the claimants, split into five groups, challenged the decision of the Court of Appeal on various procedural and substantive aspects. In turn, the German and French firms in charge of the monitoring of the products asked for the application of German law. This is how the Cour de cassation was led to hold that both the previous case-by-case approach and Article 4 of the Rome II Regulation were applicable and that, fortunately,[78] they conciliated in designating French law. However, the reading of the Aix-en-Provence Court of Appeal decision by the Cour de cassation required to reintroduce clearer references to paragraphs 1 and 3 of Article 4 of the Rome II Regulation:

> 'the judgment states, first, that [the German firm's] liability is sought on the basis of shortcomings both in the conduct of the certification procedure and in the implementation of the monitoring and recertification, provided for in Directive 93/42, in particular during surveillance inspections of the quality carried out in the premises of the [French company], located in France; (…) it then notes that the [German firm's] actions took place from 1997 to 2010; that in the current state of these statements and findings, the Court of Appeal was able to conclude that the damage had occurred in the [French company's] plants where the defective breast implants had been manufactured and inspections carried out, indicating that the fact that the tort/delict also had the closest links with France, within the meaning of Article 4(3) of the Rome II Regulation'.

Naturally, torts committed through the Internet make the localisation of direct damage difficult. In a September 2016 decision, the Rennes Court of Appeal made a considerable effort to justify that French law was applicable to a claim brought by a French company on the ground of denigration against a Japanese competitor, which had published a press release on its website alleging that the claimant was a patent infringer.[79] According to the Court, the Japanese defendant had deliberately caused damage in France to the French claimant. The Court highlighted that (i) the press release was published in English by the Japanese firm on its '.com' website, (ii) it clearly mentioned that the French company was involved in infringement proceedings initiated in Germany, and (iii) it had been shared many times in a highly competitive sector and relied on by customers

---

77 Under previous case law, such kind of decisions had been taken into account or even held decisive for the determination of the applicable law: Cass. 1re civ., 19 May 1999, No. 97-13972; Cass. 1re civ., 27 March 2007, No. 05-10480 (to be compared with Cass. 1re civ., 27 May 2010, No. 09-65906).

78 Luck favours the bold: very few French scholars would agree with the Cour de cassation on its assertion that 'Article 3 of the Civil Code' has been 'interpreted consistently' before the entry into force of the Rome II Regulation.

79 Rennes, 13 September 2016, No. 15/05875. However, Article 4 was improperly applied to this dispute that fell under Article 6(2).

of the French company. Clearly, in this case, the Court used 'targeting' as a criterion to localise damages allegedly caused through the Internet.

Financial disputes are another source of difficulty, as a Paris Court of Appeal decision illustrates.[80] In 2006, a French bank invested several million euros in hedge funds established under Cayman Islands law by a French investment firm. Two days after the collapse of Lehman Brothers, the bank started to secure its investments and, by 2009, it had taken over all the assets of the 'master' hedge fund. At the end of that year, the French firm and the master fund initiated proceedings in France. They blamed the bank for its abrupt withdrawal, which, according to the claimants, amounted to the French tort of abuse of right. The bank contended that Cayman Islands law should be applied. It argued that the Cayman Islands-incorporated hedge fund was the direct victim and that, because Cayman Islands law governed the contract between the bank and the hedge fund, the escape clause could not lead to any other law. However, the Court decided that French law was applicable to the case. First, it held that two of the parties (one of the claimants and the defendant) were French and that all the natural persons involved were also French. This may sound like a slightly distorted echo of Article 4(2) of the Rome II Regulation. Second, it analysed the damage claimed by the French investment firm as the loss of its fees combined with a forced standby, which had to be localised in France. The Court considered that the damages claimed by the master fund were indirect, because they were a consequence of the damage first suffered by the other fund (the so-called 'feed' fund), which was not a party to the proceedings. Thirdly, the Paris Court of Appeal rebutted any recourse to the escape clause, holding (a bit too quickly perhaps) that, because the claim had no contractual basis, the governing law of the contract did not matter. In another decision, the Paris Court of Appeal had to decide on the liability of a British bank for failure to fulfil its obligations of supervision and vigilance regarding an account opened in its books by a company, which had 'lost' the funds entrusted by a French investor. English law is held applicable on the ground of Article 4(1) of the Rome II Regulation. Again, the Paris Court of Appeal rebutted any recourse to the escape clause, holding that the sole circumstance that the funds had been invested through a transfer order made from an account opened in France did not suffice to justify the application of French law.[81]

2.3.4. Escape Clause under Rome II

Generally speaking, the escape clause included in Article 4(3) does not seem to be overused.[82] In the dispute between the French and Japanese competitors,

80 Paris, 26 March 2013, No. 12/02707.

81 Paris (International Commercial Court), 12 November 2019, No. 19/03149.

82 See section 2.3.3: Aix-en-Provence, 2 July 2015, No. 13/22482.

the Japanese defendant tried to argue that German law should apply to the case.[83] It argued that the denigration proceedings before the French court were related to the infringement claim first brought in Germany and that the parties' counsels had previously exchanged correspondence, so there was 'a pre-existing relationship between the parties' within the meaning of Article 4(3) of the Rome II Regulation. The Rennes Court of Appeal found that this was insufficient grounds to maintain that 'a manifestly closer connection' existed as required by Article 4(3).[84]

Of course, the Court's self-restraint in this case and in similar ones[85] might result from the fact that French courts considered that fixed rules led to French law and were not willing to move away from this analysis. However, the decision handed down in favour of British law by the Paris Court of Appeal about the liability of a British bank shows that the escape clause is not manipulated to designate French law.[86]

2.4. SPECIFIC RULES

2.4.1. Carriage of Goods under Rome I

When faced with a carrier that has its central administration in France and goods delivered in France, French courts readily follow Article 5(1) of the Rome I Regulation and are happy to apply French law.[87] In one decision, the Douai Court of Appeal even completely denied the existence of the escape clause in Article 5.[88] Nevertheless, when courts are confronted with the opposite situation (a carrier based in a foreign country and delivery – or receipt – in the same country), the foreign law is equally held applicable because of the convergence of some of the factors listed in Article 5(1).[89] Furthermore, under such circumstances, recourse to the escape clause does not appear to be an option. For instance, in a case relating to the delivery of goods in Chile by a Chilean carrier, even though French law governed the commission contract related to this carriage, French judges did not consider the possibility of submitting the contract for the carriage of goods to French law.[90]

---

83 See section 2.3.3: Rennes, 13 September 2016, No. 15/05875.

84 Nevertheless, it has to be reminded that Article 4 was improperly applied to this dispute that fell under Article 6(2).

85 See section 2.3.3: Paris, 26 March 2013, No. 12/02707.

86 Paris (International Commercial Court), 12 November 2019, No. 19/03149.

87 Versailles, 6 January 2015, No. 14/02383; Angers, 8 September 2015, No. 13/01460.

88 Douai, 2 July 2015, No. 14/04317.

89 Versailles, 19 May 2015, No. 14/04111.

90 Paris, 29 September 2016, No. 14/21772.

Moreover, commission contracts for the carriage of goods are still problematic despite the CJEU's *ICF* and *Haeger* rulings.[91] In a very unclear decision, the Versailles Court of Appeal tried to draw on the *Haeger & Schmidt* ruling, but it is impossible to understand whether the Court tried to apply Article 5(1) and (3) or Article 4(3) of the Rome I Regulation.[92]

2.4.2. *Carriage of Passengers under Rome I*

Article 5(2) only appears in the background of a case rendered by the Cour de cassation in 2018.[93] An Israeli resident had taken a flight, operated by an Israeli airline company, from France to Israel. However the flight landed more than three hours late. The French first instance court directly applied EU Regulation No. 261/2004 on compensation and assistance to passengers in the event of, among others, long delay of flights. Before the Cour de cassation, the airline company contended that Israeli law was applicable by virtue of Article 5(2) of the Rome I Regulation. However, the Cour de cassation rightfully upheld that the EU Regulation directly applies in such a case (i.e. in the case of a flight departure from a Member State), the determination of the law governing the contract being irrelevant. Curiously though, the Cour added that it had not been argued that Israeli compensation would have been 'at least equivalent' to the one resulting from the EU Regulation, as if it might have changed the outcome.

2.4.3. *Consumer Contracts under Rome I*

Only two cases are directly related to Article 6 of the Rome I Regulation. They both involve consumers with their habitual residence in France when the proceedings were initiated and professionals established abroad, in Belgium and in Germany respectively. The amounts at issue were rather high, around 15,000 euros. Quite surprisingly, no choice of law had been made and the main difficulty was to determine whether the consumers were entitled to the protection provided by Article 6(1). In the first case, the question was easily solved: a German firm had sold a fitted kitchen to a couple living in Alsace in the context of a commercial fair in Strasbourg;[94] as a consequence, French law was held to be applicable. The second case was more complicated. A consumer, allegedly living in Luxembourg at the time of the conclusion of the contract, hired a Belgian firm

---

91 Case C-133/08, *Intercontainer Interfrigo SC (ICF) v. Balkenende Oosthuizen BV and MIC Operations BV*, ECLI:EU:C:2009:617; Case C-305/13, *Haeger & Schmidt GmbH v. Mutuelles du Mans assurances IARD (MMA IARD) and Others*, ECLI:EU:C:2014:2320.

92 Versailles, 1 March 2016, No. 14/08465.

93 Cass. 1re civ., 19 December 2018, No. 17-26663.

94 Colmar, 19 October 2015, No. 14/02375.

to install frames, blinds and rolling shutters in his house in France.[95] The Metz Court of Appeal merely noted that the Belgian firm had agreed to perform its obligation in France, from which it inferred that it had 'directed its activities to France', where, meanwhile, the consumer had (apparently) transferred his habitual residence. One cannot help thinking that the application of the protective regime could have been more carefully thought through.

2.4.4. Individual Employment Contracts under Rome I

Article 8 is the most commonly applied provision of the Rome I Regulation. Case law essentially points to two findings.[96] First, French courts tend to be reluctant to characterise a tacit choice of law. Second, they still have to improve the comparison process of the chosen law (when there is one) with the objectively applicable law.

On the first topic, several decisions follow more or less the same pattern: when references to foreign provisions are included in employment contracts, a tacit choice of the foreign law has been considered not to be 'clearly demonstrated' pursuant to Article 3(1) (to which Article 8(1) refers) because of other connecting factors pointing to France. For instance, in a 2015 Orléans Court of Appeal decision, French law was applied to an employment contract drafted in Polish, entered into by Polish parties and including many references to Polish law provisions (notably on the duration of work, vacation, notice of departure) because these connections with Poland were outweighed by several other connections with France: the French residence of the employee, the performance of the work in France, the salary paid in euros, payslips worded in French, and the express reference to a French collective agreement.[97] The Orléans Court of Appeal was cautious enough to add that even if there were a choice of Polish law, French provisions on redundancy should apply by virtue of Article 8(2). In other cases, express reference to foreign labour provisions (from Belgium in one case, from Luxembourg in the others), only identified by their date (reference was made to 'the act dated …') and not by the state from which they emanated, was not considered to demonstrate the clear intention of the French employees to accept the application of foreign law. Because the contract had to be performed in France, French law was therefore held to be applicable on the grounds of Article 8(2).[98]

---

95 Metz, 8 March 2016, Nos. 15/00060, 16/00064.

96 Regarding the escape clause enshrined in Article 8(4), see section 2.3.2; on the scope of application of the governing law, see Cass. soc., 20 February 2019, Nos. 17-20532, 17-20536 (the status of co-employer is governed by the law applicable to the employment contract).

97 Orléans, 17 September 2015, No. 14/02920.

98 Douai, 29 May 2015, No. 14/0297; Metz, 13 October 2015, Nos. 15/00477 to 15/00485.

Regarding the comparison between the chosen law and the objectively applicable law (most of the time, the law of the country where the employee carries out his work),[99] the Cour de cassation had to provide some guidance to judges and parties on Article 6 of the Rome Convention. In a decision rendered in January 2017, the highest judges held that the employee at least had to allege that the objectively applicable law was more protective than the chosen law in relation to the legal basis of his claims.[100] It was not up to the judges hearing the case to make this point. In a second decision rendered in February 2017, the Cour de cassation underlined that judges have to demonstrate that French mandatory rules, and especially the provisions on fixed-term contracts and redundancy, give employees better protection than the chosen law (in this case, the law of St Vincent and the Grenadines).[101] It is true that the reasoning of French decisions is not always very clear on this aspect.[102] The comparison was better made in a decision, based on the Rome I Regulation, in which the judges relied on a legal study comparing French and English laws. The study, provided by the employee who was challenging his dismissal, pointed out that for some aspects of the redundancy procedure French law was more employee-protective. However, in a spill-over effect, all the employee's claims, and not merely the ones directly relating to the procedure of dismissal, were adjudicated on the basis of French law.[103]

2.4.5. *Unfair Competition and Acts Restricting Free Competition under Rome II*

Of the rules on specific torts and delicts, only Article 6 of the Rome II Regulation has been applied,[104] and it has rarely happened.[105] In a 2014 decision, the Paris

99 Cass. soc., 5 December 2018, No. 17-11224: the Cour de cassation denies any relevance to the E101 certificate issued on the basis of Regulation (EEC) No. 1408/71 to establish the place where the employee habitually carries out his work. It holds the same within the meaning of Article 19 of the Brussels I Regulation (Cass. soc., 29 September 2014, No. 13-15802; Cass. soc., 10 June 2015, No. 13-27799).

100 Cass. soc., 19 January 2017, No. 15-20095. Already on this line, Aix-en-Provence, 2 June 2016, No. 14/21676.

101 Cass. soc., 1 February 2017, No. 15-23723.

102 Chambéry, 7 April 2016, No. 15/01583: French provisions on redundancy protection prevail over the chosen law but no indication is given on the lesser protection provided by this law.

103 Aix-en-Provence, 27 April 2017, No. 16/06204, upheld by Cass. soc., 20 February 2019, Nos. 17-20532, 17-20536.

104 In case of copyright infringement, French courts do not have recourse to Article 8 of the Rome II Regulation because Article 5(2) of the 1886 Berne Convention for the Protection of Literary and Artistic Works is read as a choice-of-law rule and takes precedence over the Regulation pursuant to its Article 28 (see for instance Cass. com., 8 November 2017, No. 16-10850).

105 Rennes, 13 September 2016, No. 15/05875, for a missed opportunity (denigration); in the *Expedia* case, application of Article 6 of the Rome II Regulation to claims based on practices restricting competition was not seriously discussed (Paris, 21 June 2017, No. 15/18784).

Court of Appeal correctly refused to resort to Article 6(2) and, from there, to Article 4.[106] According to the Court, the alleged activities (unfair competition and passing off related to a likelihood of confusion on the part of the public) had a collective impact, which required them to be governed by the law of the place where the market was affected. Because the website at issue had an URL ending with '/fr' and offered a magazine written in French for download, French law was applied pursuant to Article 6(1). In another case, also based on unfair competition and passing off, the same court also relied on Article 6(1) and held that Singaporean law was applicable.[107] The Court noted that the defendant had no commercial activities in France and that the acts at issue could not have taken place outside of Singapore; as a consequence, Singapore was the country where competitive relations and the market had been affected.

However, the interface between Article 6(2) and Article 4 of the Rome II Regulation is not always so well handled. As an example, the Cour de cassation recently overturned a ruling (again rendered by the Paris Court of Appeal) applying, on the ground of Articles 6(2) and 4(2), French law between two French companies, which were competing in Japan. According to the Cour de cassation, in order to do so, the lower court should have ascertained that the disputed conduct was not likely to affect the Japanese market.[108]

2.5. SCOPE OF APPLICABLE LAW AND CHARACTERISATION ISSUES

For many years, the sudden termination of an established business relationship, which is regulated by a specific provision in the French *Code de commerce* (and also under Greek law),[109] has raised a characterisation issue when the dispute has an international dimension. One could contend that it recognises a tortious relationship on the grounds that, as the Advocate General Kokott put it in relation to the *Granarolo* case:

> 'the basis for the claim is not to be found in the agreements of the parties, but in a statutory provision which, for the purposes of ensuring order in economic life, reproves any abrupt termination of business relationships and provides in such cases for claims for damages by the former business partner'.[110]

---

106 Paris, 9 May 2014, No. 12/10744.

107 Paris, 1 December 2015, No. 14/02708.

108 Cass. com., 15 January 2020, No. 17-22295.

109 See section 2.1.1.

110 Case C-196/15, Opinion of Advocate General Kokott delivered on 23 December 2015.

Hence, regarding the applicable law, the Rome II Regulation would have been the relevant instrument. However, the CJEU expressed a different view in its 2016 ruling in *Granarolo*. Provided that a contract exists between the parties (and such a contract can be tacit, simply relying on a body of consistent evidence), the Court considered that its termination, whatever the circumstances and the alleged statutory basis for the claim, falls under contractual matters. If the *Granarolo* ruling is adequately taken into account by French judges, it should in general lead to the application of the Rome I Regulation.

A distinct characterisation issue is raised by the action that the Minister for Economic Affairs can take to request an injunction to cease practices restricting competition, a declaration of nullity of illegal clauses or contracts and the recovery of the mistaken payments on the basis of Article L. 442-6, III of the *Code de commerce*. As the above reported *Expedia* case shows,[111] in its 2015 judgment, the Paris First Instance Commercial Court characterised such an action as pertaining to contractual matters and discussed the possible existence of *lois de police* within the meaning of the Rome I Regulation. Two years later, the Paris Court of Appeal characterised the same claims as tortious and applied Article 4 of the Rome II Regulation.[112] According to the CJEU's 2016 *VKI v. Amazon* ruling, characterisation should probably be refined.[113] In the light of this ruling, the existence of the action brought by the Minister for Economic Affairs should be determined in accordance with Article 6(1) of the Rome II Regulation, whereas the law applicable to the assessment of a particular contractual term should continue to be determined pursuant to the Rome I Regulation.

Another issue concerns the law applicable to the prescription and limitation of actions. Although Article 12(1)(d) is now formally echoed in the French Civil Code (Article 2221), the Cour de cassation had to reaffirm that the prescription of a contractual obligation, along with the claim that the contract is void, is to be governed by the law applicable to this contract and not by the *lex fori*.[114]

2.6. FOREIGN LAW AND *ORDRE PUBLIC*

2.6.1. Foreign Law

The treatment of foreign law rests on a key distinction in French law: are the rights in dispute available (*disponibles*) or not? If they are and they usually are when contracts and torts are involved and proceedings have begun – parties

---

111 Trib. com. Paris, 7 May 2015, No. 2015000040. See section 2.1.1.

112 Paris, 21 June 2017, no. 15/18784. See section 2.1.1.

113 Case C-191/15, *Verein für Konsumenteninformation v. Amazon EU Sàrl*, ECLI:EU:C:2016:612.

114 Cass. 2e civ., 16 May 2019, No. 18-12005; Cass. 2e civ., 16 May 2019, No. 18-12006.

can ask, either expressly or even implicitly, French courts not to apply the relevant conflict-of-law rules. This is the aforementioned *accord procédural*.[115] Moreover, if the international dimension of the case is not taken into account during the proceedings before the lower court judges, the Cour de cassation will not overturn their decision. On the other hand, if one party specifically asks for the application of foreign law, lower court judges are legally required to determine the applicable law.[116] In addition, if the parties do not plead foreign law, lower court judges are free to raise the choice-of-law issue of their own motion, provided that the adversarial principle is observed (litigants being called to enter into a debate on the applicability and the content of foreign law).

Given the universal application of the two Regulations, French courts can be required, or can decide, to apply foreign law. However, numerous practical elements may restrict this outcome. Firstly, as stated above, litigants (or their counsel) might be interested in applying French law instead of the foreign law designated pursuant to the relevant Regulation.[117] This is understandable, since French provisions are obviously more familiar to counsel pleading in France, whichever side they are on. Courts are not hostile to this kind of agreement, because it also greatly simplifies the judges' task. Secondly, when faced with employment contracts, French courts, whose jurisdiction usually results from the performance of work in France, show a tendency to resort to French law. This trend, however, may be explained by the judicial aversion to party autonomy in this field.[118] Thirdly, one might expect parties and the court in proceedings related to torts committed through the Internet to try to apply a single law, even if it is foreign, because this is easier to manage than the application of multiple laws.[119]

In practice, when foreign law is declared to be applicable, French judges bear the final burden of proof regarding establishing its content. As a consequence, they cannot reject a claim governed by a foreign law because the claimant has not established its content or because the claimant based their claim on another foreign law.[120]

Most of the time, litigants will contribute to the ascertainment of the applicable foreign law by providing *certificats de coutume* supplied by a consular

---

115 See section 2.2.2.

116 Cass. com., 2 November 2016, No. 15-10296 (one party asked for the application of Spanish law).

117 See section 2.2.1.

118 See section 2.4.3.

119 See Paris, 1 December 2015, No. 14/02708 (it is plausible that other markets than the Singapore one were affected by the litigious activities of the competitor).

120 Cass. com., 4 May 2017, No. 15-22712 (Portuguese law applicable pursuant to Article 5 of the Rome I Regulation).

authority or a foreign lawyer. Judges can also rely on their personal knowledge, or commission an expert's report, or resort to international cooperation (notably thanks to the London Convention on Information on Foreign Law). The European Judicial Network can also play a role in the determination of the content of an EU Member State's law. However, these means of access to foreign law are clearly underused by French courts.

2.6.2. Ordre public

On several occasions, parties have tried to challenge, before French courts, the applicable law for the reason that its application to the case would have been inconsistent with international *ordre public* of the forum. So far, this attempt has never been successful. For instance, in a case related to the non-competition clause in an employment contract, the employee criticised the chosen law (Swiss law) as being contrary to 'essential values, such as the protection of the employee and the principles of free trade and industry'. However, this contention was considered too imprecise.[121] Besides, a law that does not offer carriers a direct action against recipients for payment (whereas the *Code de commerce* does) is not contrary to French international *ordre public*.[122] From another standpoint, in ICC Award No. 16981, the majority of the arbitral tribunal found no reason to consider the Greek provision prohibiting the sudden termination of a long-term commercial relationship to be international public policy. In particular, the arbitrators noted:

> 'that the Greek legislator enacted this provision in 1913, then repealed it and last re-established it in 2005. It is difficult to accept that the objective and effects of a law could be that fundamental for the Greek State if it seems hesitant about its adequacy in the first place'.

2.7. RELATIONS WITH INTERNATIONAL CONVENTIONS

Conflict with international conventions is addressed by the two Regulations. As far as matters covered by either of the Regulations are concerned, a pre-existing convention laying down choice-of-law rules and binding one or more Member States with third states will prevail over the Regulations. Otherwise, the relevant Regulation has to be applied by the court hearing the case. In France, several

---

121 Chambéry, 29 September 2016, No. 16/00025.

122 Douai, 2 July 2015, No. 14/04317.

conventions are relevant, most notably the Hague Conventions.[123] However, the effectiveness of Article 28 of the Rome II Regulation and Article 25 of the Rome I Regulation should be carefully set out.

On the one hand, the 1955 Hague Convention on the Law Applicable to International Sales of Goods seems to be frequently ignored by litigants and French courts in favour of Article 4(1)(a) of the Rome I Regulation.[124]

On the other hand, the Hague Conventions on torts are more important in French courts. For instance, one of the decisions that the Cour de cassation expressly rendered on the Regulations is related to the application of the 1971 Hague Convention.[125] In this case, the lower court judges had tried to solve the conflict between the Convention and the Rome II Regulation, and they did so in favour of the Regulation. As a result, because the claimant and defendant both had their habitual residence in France, the lower court judges declared French law to be applicable on the grounds of Article 4(2) of the Rome II Convention, instead of Article 3 of the 1971 Hague Convention, which designated the law of the state where the accident occurred (i.e. Spain). Their judgment was overturned only because they misunderstood and misapplied Article 28,[126] not because they had completely ignored the 1971 Hague Convention.[127] In another case, which came before the Chambéry Court of Appeal, the 1973 Hague Convention on the Law Applicable to Product Liability was given precedence over the Rome II Regulation.[128] French law was held to be applicable pursuant to Article 4(a) of the Convention (France was the place of injury and the place of the habitual residence of the person who directly suffered damage). A different outcome would have been reached under Article 5(1) of the Rome II Regulation because the defective product had apparently not been marketed in France. Case law clearly shows that the persistence of the 1971 and 1973 Hague Conventions in the French legal order is not devoid of consequences.

---

123 See Notifications under Article 26(1) of Regulation (EC) No. 593/2008 of the European Parliament and of the Council on the law applicable to contractual obligations (Rome I) [2010] OJ C 343/4; Notifications under Article 29(1) of Regulation (EC) No. 864/2007 on the law applicable to non-contractual obligations (Rome II) [2010] OJ C 343/5.

124 Paris, 26 June 2014, No. 12/15277; Paris, 3 June 2014, No. 13/23508; Lyon, 22 April 2014, No. 12/00822. See also Nancy, 4 April 2012, No. 11/00422, resorting to Article 19 of the Rome I Regulation to assess the domestic nature of the sale of goods in dispute.

125 Cass. 1re civ., 30 April 2014, No. 13-11932.

126 According to them, the Rome II Regulation should prevail because the dispute had contacts with two EU Member States.

127 For another mistake, Aix-en-Provence, 6 April 2017, No. 16/09190 (according to which the 1971 Hague Convention did not apply because Italy – the state where the accident occurred – is not bound by this Convention).

128 Chambéry, 13 March 2014, No. 13/01863.

3. GENERAL EVALUATION

3.1. THE COURTS' APPROACH AND COMPARISON WITH PREVIOUS REGIMES

French case law is still in the early years of the application of the two Regulations and, so far, the Cour de cassation has not had many opportunities to provide guidance. In such circumstances, it remains difficult to assess the innovations brought in by the Rome I and Rome II Regulations.

As far as the Rome I Regulation is concerned, French courts may feel a false sense of familiarity and not be sufficiently aware of the changes effected by the new instrument. For instance, the application of escape clauses – which are formulated more strictly under the Rome I Regulation than under the Rome Convention – is still uncertain, particularly when related contracts are at stake. As observed above, personal guarantees are often placed under the aegis of the law applicable to the secured obligation, whereas a commission for the carriage of goods tends to remain apart from the law governing the contract for the carriage of goods. By contrast, Article 9(1) of the Rome I Regulation seems to have had a huge influence on French judges, who are now less prone to labelling French law provisions as *lois de police*. This anti-*lois de police* trend has been reinforced by the refusal to give effect to Article 9(3) in the case pertaining to the US embargo against Iran. Because the *Unamar* and *Nikiforidis* rulings are more accommodating, French courts will have to improve the handling of (alleged) overriding mandatory rules, be they French or foreign.

The situation of the Rome II Regulation is different, as it directly replaces French case law. Courts appreciate the clarity and the legal certainty it brings to the field.[129] Nevertheless, many innovations (such as Articles 9–14) have not yet been 'tested' in French courts.

On the whole, French courts appear to be comfortable with private international law legislative instruments such as EU Regulations: written rules provide legal certainty, whereas, under the previous national private international law regime (an anomaly in the French legal order), lower court judges may have considered case law too subtle and too fragmentary. It is indicative of this trust in black-letter rules (sometimes based on a misunderstanding) that, so far, no French court, either high or low, has made a request to the CJEU for a

---

[129] Despite the Cour de cassation complimenting itself for the consistent interpretation of Article 3 of the Code civil in the field of torts/delicts: Cass. 1re civ., 5 October 2018, No. 17-14401; Cass. 1re civ., 5 October 2018, No. 16-19430; Cass. 1re civ., 5 October 2018, No. 15-26115-15-26.388; Cass. 1re civ., 5 October 2018, No. 15-28531; Cass. 1re civ., 5 October 2018, No. 15-28891. See section 2.3.3.

preliminary ruling on the Rome I or Rome II Regulations. However, judges often rely on CJEU rulings about the application of the Brussels I Regulation: it seems to satisfy their need for consistency.

An intermediate conclusion would be that uniformity is progressing. This optimistic view needs to be put into perspective, firstly because of the precedence that the Hague Conventions still have (at least in the field of non-contractual matters; by contrast, the 1955 Hague Convention seems to have fallen in disuse), and secondly because of the *accord procédural* that will quite often allow resort to be had to French law.

3.2. TAXONOMY AND GAPS IN ROME I AND ROME II

Under the Rome I Regulation, commission contracts for the carriage of goods appear to be difficult to handle. It is possible that the *ICF* and *Haeger & Schmidt* rulings have not explained with sufficient clarity how commission contracts for the carriage of goods are to be distinguished from the carriage of goods itself under the Rome Convention. The silence of the Rome I Regulation on this topic (apart from Recital 20) does not help. In terms of characterisation and coordination, other contracts, like framework and implementation contracts, could create difficulties; however, such cases have yet to be brought before French courts.

Given the limited application of the Rome II Regulation, French courts have been confronted most of all with the handling of the taxonomy used in Article 6 and its relationship with Article 4. Proceedings between members of a group of contracts can also be problematic because, under French rules, judges are used to reasoning on contractual grounds. The cases discussed above also show that localising financial and Internet-caused damages is not an easy task. However, the CJEU rulings on Article 5(3) of the Brussels I Regulation and Article 7(2) of the Brussels Ia Regulation may be of some use to judges.

4. CONCLUSION

4.1. SUMMARY OF FINDINGS

4.1.1. General Findings

French authorities are under the impression that the Regulations are not revolutionary and that they will bring clarity and simplification in their respective fields.

French courts are quite aware of the existence of the Regulations. Whether for good or bad reasons, these EU instruments are more often invoked *outside* their scope of application rather than ignored. However, the persistence of the 1971 and 1973 Hague Conventions in the French legal order has significant consequences.

Only one published ICC award on claims related to the sudden termination of a long-term contract appears worthy of interest because arbitrators thoroughly applied and discussed the two Regulations.

Characterisation issues exist but can generally be solved by reference to the rulings of the CJEU. Unfortunately, for issues that have not yet been addressed, French courts are not prone to making requests for preliminary rulings related to the Rome I and Rome II Regulations.

When foreign law is declared applicable, its procedural regime is rather favourable. Moreover, *ordre public* has not been a successful defence so far. Nevertheless, an accommodating vision of *accord procédural* allows resort, from time to time, to French law.

4.1.2. Rome I

The provisions of the Rome I Regulation most commonly applied by French courts are, in order, Articles 8, 9, 3, 5 and 4.

The enactment of the Rome I Regulation and the drafting of Article 9(1) seem to have reduced, at least during the first period, the judicial characterisation of *lois de police*. Besides, only one case was rendered by a French court regarding third states' *lois de police* and, in appearance only, the court denied any influence to overriding mandatory provisions emanating from a state not directly related to the performance of the contract.

French courts usually give effect to express choice of law and they rarely encounter *dépeçage*. When no express choice is made, they quite readily accept tacit or implicit choice, except in employment contracts.

French courts are comfortable with fixed rules; only a few decisions have addressed escape clauses under the Rome I Regulation and it is difficult to draw any consistent conclusion from these decisions.

While cases pertaining to Article 6 are infrequent, several decisions have been rendered on the grounds of Article 5. French courts seem to be at ease with Article 5(1) and reluctant to fall back on the escape clause, probably because the grouping of contracts that the former involves makes the latter less relevant.

Regarding employment contracts, as stated above, French courts tend to be reluctant to characterise a tacit choice of law. They also have to improve the process of comparing the chosen law (when there is one) with the objectively applicable law.

4.1.3. *Rome II*

At present, the application of the Rome II Regulation is mostly focused on Articles 4 and 6. Under the Rome II Regulation, only one significant occurrence of *loi de police* has been found.[130]

Compared to pre-Rome II case law, which was characterised by legal uncertainty, the guidance provided by Article 4 of the Regulation seems to be appreciated. Still, difficulties remain in terms of the localisation of the place of direct damage. Moreover, French courts seem to have difficulty identifying whether they should apply Article 4 or Article 6 and under what circumstances Article 6(2) enables them to apply Article 4 (i.e. when 'an act of unfair competition affects exclusively the interests of a specific competitor'). Generally speaking, the escape clause included in Article 4(3) does not seem to be overused.

4.2. MAIN RECOMMENDATIONS

So far, no specific changes to the two Regulations are recommended. More time should be allowed for the development and analysis of national case law. Room should also be left for preliminary rulings by the CJEU.

At the national level, some efforts could be made to improve the judicial application of the Regulations. For instance, the Ministry of Justice could issue a circular aiming to at least clarify the temporal, material and spatial scopes of the two Regulations. Furthermore, there have been exchanges between the Cour de cassation and the CJEU, which is highly valuable, but the benefits of this relationship should flow more systematically towards lower court judges.

Finally, the question arises whether, for the sake of uniformity, France should denounce the 1955 Hague Convention on the Law Applicable to International Sales of Goods and the 1973 Hague Convention on the Law Applicable to Product Liability.

---

130 Cass. com., 8 July 2020, No. 17-31536, based on both Article 9 of the Rome I Regulation and Article 16 of the Rome II Regulation.

THE APPLICATION OF THE ROME I AND ROME II REGULATIONS IN GREECE

Apostolos ANTHIMOS

1. THE NATIONAL LANDSCAPE

There are no national rules in Greece implementing the Rome I and Rome II Regulations, but it is worth noting that this is common behaviour for Greek governments, i.e. not to take any further action with respect to EU Regulations. The same was the case for the Rome Convention, i.e. no further action beyond ratification.[1] The rules of the Rome I and Rome II Regulations have not been

[1] See K.D. KERAMEUS / P.J. KOZYRIS (eds.), *Introduction to Greek Law*, 3rd edition, Kluwer Law International / Ant. N. Sakkoulas Publishers 2008, 381.

extended in Greece beyond their normal scope of application. In one reported decision, the court ruled out the application of the Rome II Regulation tacitly in defamation cases, applying Article 26 of the Greek Civil Code (CC).[2] Very recently, the Supreme Court applied the same domestic rule.[3]

There are nearly 80 decisions applying the Rome I Regulation in Greece, of which almost 80 per cent were rendered by first instance courts. For the Rome II Regulation, the figure is nearly 100 decisions, of which again almost 80 per cent were rendered by first instance courts. No arbitral awards have so far applied the Rome I or Rome II Regulations. The publication of domestic arbitral awards is virtually non-existent.

The most commonly applied provisions of the Rome I Regulation are: Articles 1 (scope), 3 (freedom of choice), 4 (applicable law in the absence of choice), 7 (insurance contracts), and 8 (individual employment contracts). For the Rome II Regulation: Articles 1 (scope), 2 (non-contractual obligations), 4(1) and (3) (general rule), 10(1) (unjust enrichment), and 14(1) (freedom of choice).

In terms of instances where courts should have applied the Rome I Regulation and failed to do so, Greek courts have not made any reference to the Rome I Regulation in international sales contracts,[4] employment contracts,[5] marine salvage contracts,[6] and sea labour accident cases,[7] founded on contractual agreements concluded after the entry into force of the Regulation. At the same time, courts have correctly applied the 1980 Rome Convention on the grounds of Article 28 Rome I.[8] On the other hand, Greek courts have focused correctly on domestic conflict-of-laws provisions in cases related to bills of lading (exclusion rule of Article 1(2)(d)),[9] arbitration agreements

---

2 Dodecanese CoA 220/2013, *Media and Communication Law* (= Δίκαιο Μέσων Ενημέρωσης και Επικοινωνίας) 2014, 198.

3 Supreme Court 848/2019, unreported. Unfortunately, the rationale behind the non-application of Rome II Regulation is false: The court underlined that the Regulation did not apply, because the tort was committed in 2007, hence it did not take into account the existence of Article 1 para. 2(g).

4 Thessaloniki 1st Instance Court (three-member panel) 1095/2016, *ISOCRATES*. The Greek plaintiff filed an action against his Canadian counterpart for damages. Not only did the court not make any reference to the Rome I Regulation; it went further, stating that the CISG is not a mandatory piece of legislation, and that therefore Art. 25 CC was to be applied.

5 Piraeus 1st Instance Court 334/2016, *Piraeus Court database*.

6 Piraeus 1st Instance Court 2932/2015, *Piraeus Court database*, and Piraeus 1st Instance Court 705/2016, *Piraeus Court database*.

7 Piraeus 1st Instance Court 4147/2015, *Piraeus Court database*. The court underlined that those accidents do not fall under the category of delicts; hence, Art. 25 CC (i.e. the applicable law provision for contractual obligations) applies.

8 Piraeus 1st Instance Court 1540/2014, *NOMOS*, Supreme Court 613/2017, *ISOCRATES*, Supreme Court 423/2018, *Chronicles of Private Law* (=Χρονικά Ιδιωτικού Δικαίου) 2019, 204.

9 Piraeus 1st Instance Court 721/2015, *Piraeus Court database*. See also Kavala 1st Instance Court 440/2011, *Armenopoulos* (=Αρμενόπουλος) 2012, 272.

(exclusion rule of Article 1(2)(e)),[10] questions governed by the law of companies (exclusion rule of Article 1(2)(f)),[11] and insurance contracts (exclusion rule of Article 1(2)(j)).[12]

There are several decisions to be found where the Rome I and/or Rome II Regulation(s) should have applied but, ultimately and wrongly, a different set of rules was applied instead. In the first case (trademark infringement of a very well-known German automobile giant by a Greek spare-parts seller), Greek law on trademarks and unfair competition was directly applied.[13] In the second case (traffic accident in Thessaloniki), the court directly invoked the provisions of the Greek Civil Code, even though the victim was a foreigner.[14] In the third case, involving an Albanian motorbike driver killed in June 2009, the Rhodes court applied Article 26 CC in examining the standing of his relatives to file an action for damages for pain and suffering.[15] Finally, in yet another traffic accident, involving citizens of North Macedonia as the victims of a car accident in Greece, the court ordered the production of additional evidence with respect to the standing of the plaintiffs to sue, because there was no information as to the law on subrogation in force in North Macedonia. Again the court founded its ruling directly on domestic conflict-of-laws rules, i.e. Article 26 CC.[16] A minority of recent Supreme Court rulings demonstrates similar problems of proper application.[17]

A significant number of judgments have applied Article 26 CC or the 1980 Rome Convention, because the harmful event occurred before the entry of

---

10 Piraeus 1st Instance Court (three-member panel) 4145/2015, *Piraeus Court database* (direct application of Greek law without reference to the Rome I Regulation exclusion), and Piraeus 1st Instance Court 4345/2015, *Piraeus Court database* (referring to the Rome Convention exclusion). Although examining exequatur applications, Art. 1(2)(e) Rome I Regulation was unnecessarily invoked by Trikala 1st Instance Court 43/2013, *Enterprises and Companies Law* (= Δίκαιο Επιχειρήσεων & Εταιριών) 2013, 363, and Thessaloniki 1st Instance Court 6458/2014, *Commercial Law Survey* (= Επισκόπηση Εμπορικού Δικαίου) 2014, 396.

11 Expressly Piraeus 1st Instance Court 3707/2015, *Piraeus Court database* (form and binding effect of a power of attorney for the conclusion of a contract on behalf of a Greek company). Similarly Piraeus 1st Instance Court 875/2016, *Piraeus Court database*.

12 Piraeus 1st Instance Court 2366, 2823 and 3108/2015, *Piraeus Court database* (policy issued for transportation by sea).

13 Thessaloniki 1st Instance Court (three-member panel) 559/2011, *ISOCRATES*.

14 Thessaloniki 1st Instance Court 101/2016, *ISOCRATES*.

15 Rhodes 1st Instance Court 65/2011, *Dodecanese Law Reports* (= Δωδεκανησιακή Νομολογία) 2013, 399.

16 Thessaloniki 1st Instance Court 7264/2015, unreported.

17 Supreme Court 249/2018, *ISOCRATES*: Wrongful application of the Rome II Regulation, instead of domestic law; Supreme Court 270/2018, *ISOCRATES*, erroneous application of domestic law, instead of Article 4 Rome II Regulation. However, if erroneous application leads to the same result, there is no ground for appeal, Supreme Court 755 and 756/2019, *ISOCRATES*.

the Regulation into force.[18] Finally, there are three more decisions in which the court mistakenly applied the Rome II Regulation in conjunction with Article 26 CC, even though the damage occurred before 11 January 2009.[19]

Finally, an issue emanating from maritime law deserves special attention. According to Article 106 of the Greek Code of Private Maritime Law, the ship owner is liable for any claims against the ship's operator. Greek courts have construed this provision as follows: notwithstanding that the ship owner's liability is *in rem*, Article 106 establishes an *ex lege* (non-contractual) obligation; however, it is not a conflict-of-laws rule. Moreover, there is no special provision regulating the matter from the private international law point of view. Therefore, the issue has to be solved by an analogous application of Article 4(3) and (4) of Rome I Regulation, because the Rome II Regulation refers to the main non-contractual obligations, hence the liability of the ship owner falls outside of its ambit.[20] This interpretation is premised on the misconceived assumption that the Regulation is confined to specific non-contractual obligations, and will be hopefully refuted soon.

2. THE OPERATION OF ROME I AND ROME II IN PRACTICE

2.1. *LOIS D'APPLICATION IMMÉDIATE*

As yet, there have been no reported decisions on the supremacy of overriding mandatory provisions over the provisions of the Rome I[21] or

18 Supreme Court 1166 and 1295/2019, unreported; Piraeus 1st Instance Court (three-member panel) 277/2014, *Hellenic Justice* (= Ελληνική Δικαιοσύνη) 2014, 879; Piraeus 1st Instance Court (three-member panel) 778/2016, *Piraeus Court database*; Athens CoA 683/2013, *ISOCRATES*; Thessaloniki 1st Instance Court 4719/2011, *ISOCRATES*; Piraeus 1st Instance Court (three-member panel) 464/2014, *ISOCRATES*; Athens 1st Instance Court (three-member panel) 1738/2012, *Armenopoulos* 2013, 1071 = *Civil Procedure Law Review* (= Επιθεώρηση Πολιτικής Δικονομίας) 2013, 523; Piraeus 1st Instance Court (three-member panel) 3839/2014, *Commercial Law Review* (= Επιθεώρηση Εμπορικού Δικαίου) 2014, 872; and Athens 1st Instance Court (three-member panel) 2528/2012, *ISOCRATES*.

19 Piraeus CoA 714/2012, *ISOCRATES;* Chania 1st Instance Court 123/2012, *Hellenic Justice* 2013, 858 (joint application of Article 19 Rome II Regulation with Art. 25 CC); Thessaloniki 1st Instance Court (three-member panel) 10369/2009, *ISOCRATES* (car producer's liability based on Art. 5(1) Rome II Regulation for damage that occurred during 2004).

20 Piraeus 1st Instance Court 210/2016, *Piraeus Court database*. Similarly Piraeus 1st Instance Court 860/2015, *Piraeus Court database*, although not expressly excluding the matter from the radius of the Rome II Regulation.

21 From a theoretical point of view, see C.H. TSOUKA, 'Overriding mandatory rules in the field of Regulation (EC) No 864/2007 of the European Parliament and of the Council of 11 July 2007 on the law applicable to non-contractual obligations (Rome II) and Regulation (EC) No 593/2008 of the European Parliament and of the Council of 17 June 2008 on the law

Rome II[22] Regulations. There is no commonly accepted definition of overriding mandatory provisions in Greece.[23] Pursuant to a definition adopted by Greek courts, *jus cogens* is the general term that covers both public policy and mandatory rules.[24] Public policy rules are regulated under Articles 3 and 33 CC.[25] They are activated in a negative fashion, i.e. they hinder the application of the foreign rule. Unlike the latter, mandatory rules protect core values of the country's political, social and economic foundations, and are imposed irrespective of the applicable rule pursuant to private international law provisions.[26] Hence, conflict-of-laws rules are set aside by mandatory rules.[27] It must be underlined that all mandatory rules fall under the ambit of *jus cogens*; however, not all *jus cogens* rules are automatically mandatory rules.[28]

Examples of mandatory rules in the Greek legal order are as follows: the provisions on the protection of professional tenement;[29] the law on consumer protection;[30] the law implementing Directive 96/71/EC on the posting of

---

applicable to contractual obligations (Rome I)' = 'Οι κανόνες αμέσου εφαρμογής στο πλαίσιο του Κανονισμού 864/2007 για το εφαρμοστέο δίκαιο στις εξωσυμβατικές ενοχές (Ρώμη II) και του Κανονισμού 593/2008 για το εφαρμοστέο δίκαιο στις συμβατικές ενοχές (Ρώμη I)' [2011] *Chronicles of Private Law* 393, 397 et seq.

22 See A. BOLOS / D. TZAKAS (E. LIASKOS), *Conflict of Laws in Torts – A Commentary of Regulation 864/2007 on the applicable law in non-contractual obligations = Το Ιδιωτικό Διεθνές Δίκαιο των Αδικοπραξιών – Κατ' άρθρον ερμηνεία του Κανονισμού 864/2007 για το εφαρμοστέο δίκαιο στις εξωσυμβατικές ενοχές ("Ρώμη II")*, Law & Economy = Δίκαιο & Οικονομία 2014, Art. 16, n. 55–60, n. 66–68. Compare C.H. TSOUKA, n. 21 above, 397.

23 A. KAISSIS, *Public policy aspects in the recognition and enforcement of foreign court judgments and arbitral awards* = Εκφάνσεις της δημόσιας τάξης στην αναγνώριση και εκτέλεση αλλοδαπών δικαστικών και διαιτητικών αποφάσεων, Sakkoulas Publications = Εκδόσεις Σάκκουλα 2003, 37. See C.H. TSOUKA, n. 21 above, 393, for a thorough analysis in light of the implementation of the Rome Regulations.

24 A terminological clarification is imperative, given the different terms used: the Greek term in use is *κανόνες άμεσης εφαρμογής*, a term coined by Francescakis in its French equivalent, i.e. *lois d'application immédiate*. The Greek versions of Art. 9 Rome I and Art. 16 Rome II differ in their title: the former refers to overriding mandatory provisions (υπερισχύουσες διατάξεις αναγκαστικού δικαίου), whereas the latter refers to mandatory rules, i.e. *lois d'application immédiate* (διατάξεις αμέσου εφαρμογής). This deviation is encountered in the French and Romanian versions, but not in the English, German, Spanish and Portuguese versions. Greek legal scholarship agrees that both terms are to be understood as meaning the same, i.e. mandatory rules. See also E. VASSILAKAKIS, 'Recent private international law codifications' [2010] 63 *RHDI (Revue hellénique de droit international)* 103, 106 (4c).

25 Ad hoc E. VASSILAKAKIS, n. 24 above, 107 (6).

26 Supreme Court (Full Bench) 561/2001, *Maritime Law Review* (= Επιθεώρηση Ναυτιλιακού Δικαίου) 2001, 283.

27 A. GRAMMATIKAKI-ALEXIOU / Z. PAPASSIOPI PASSIA / E. VASSILAKAKIS, *Private International Law = Ιδιωτικό Διεθνές Δίκαιο*, Sakkoulas Publications = Εκδόσεις Σάκκουλα 2012, 323.

28 C.H. TSOUKA, n. 21 above, 395.

29 Supreme Court 765/1985, *Legal Tribune* (= Νομικό Βήμα) 1986, 667 et seq.

30 S. VRELLIS, *Private International Law = Ιδιωτικό Διεθνές Δίκαιο*, 3rd edition, Nomiki Bibliothiki = Νομική Βιβλιοθήκη 2008, 24 et seq.

workers in the framework of the provision of services;[31] Article 46 of Law 3959/2011 on competition, providing that Greek law applies to all restrictions affecting Greece, even if they are related to agreements concluded between enterprises with no seat in the country.[32] Finally, Greek employees working in Asia or Africa are protected by special conflict-of-laws rules.[33]

In general terms, case law on the application of mandatory rules is scarce in Greece and does not take a systematic approach. Under the Rome Convention regime, Greek courts considered collective bargaining[34] and accidents relating to labour at sea[35] to be provisions of an overriding mandatory nature. No pertinent case law has been reported since the Rome I Regulation entered into force. As regards non-contractual obligations, it has been ruled that the notion of the *family* of the victim in a car accident is defined by domestic law. Finally, mandatory rules also include Law 551/1915 on compensation for maritime labour accidents, and Law 762/1978 on the liability of foreign employer's representatives in maritime labour disputes.[36] The issue of the treatment of third states' *lois d'application immediate* has not been considered in the Greek doctrine.[37]

2.2. PARTY AUTONOMY[38]

From the Greek perspective, there is no need to amend Article 3 of the Rome I Regulation because of the excessive use of *dépeçage* or the need to choose the *lex mercatoria*, with one sole exception of *dépeçage*,[39] which will be discussed shortly. On the whole, courts apply Article 3 of the Rome I Regulation in

---

31 A. GRAMMATIKAKI-ALEXIOU / Z. PAPASSIOPI PASSIA / E. VASSILAKAKIS, n. 27 above, 327–329.

32 A. BOLOS / D. TZAKAS (E. LIASKOS), n. 22 above, Art. 16, n. 57.

33 See E. VASSILAKAKIS, n. 24 above, 106.

34 Piraeus CoA 761/2013, *Maritime Law Review* 2013, 197, and Piraeus CoA 309/2013, *ISOCRATES*.

35 Piraeus CoA 407/2013, *ISOCRATES*.

36 A. BOLOS / D. TZAKAS (E. LIASKOS), n. 22 above, Art. 16, n. 67.

37 See A. BOLOS / D. TZAKAS (E. LIASKOS), n. 22 above, Art. 16, nn. 8–18, where the issue is presented on the basis of foreign legal scholarship.

38 A special monograph has been published on the matter by D. STAMATIADIS, *Private autonomy in the field of international contractual obligations = Η αυτονομία της ιδιωτικής βούλησης στο πεδίο των διεθνών συμβατικών ενοχών*, Nomiki Bibliothiki = Νομική Βιβλιοθήκη 2011, passim.

39 Piraeus 1st Instance Court 1420/2015, *ISOCRATES*: The court applied English law with respect to the formation and the validity of the warranty agreement, due to explicit stipulation made by the parties in the respective document. At the same time, it applied Greek law in regard to the defences available to the guarantor (Art. 853 et seq. CC).

two situations: either on the basis of a choice-of-law clause (a), or in the form of a post-contractual determination (b):

(a) The existing case law indicates that the parties usually opt for the application of English law in marine insurance (under Article 7(2) Rome I)[40] and guaranty[41] cases.
(b) A post-contractual determination of the applicable law is frequently accepted, either through tacit consent on the examination of the merits under domestic provisions,[42] or explicit reference of both parties to Greek law.[43]

Article 14 Rome II Regulation has been applied in Greece only in regard to its paragraph 1(a). In a number of cases, courts have invoked the provision when the parties relied solely on domestic law, as evidenced in the documents and pleadings submitted,[44] or when the defendant did not challenge the application of domestic law at the hearing[45] (so called post-contractual tacit agreement). In case an agreement exists, it must specifically refer to the inclusion of tortious liability.[46]

---

40 Piraeus CoA 768/2014, *NOMOS*.

41 Piraeus 1st Instance Court 1420/2015, *ISOCRATES*.

42 Patras 1st Instance Court (three-member panel) 244/2015, *NOMOS*; Piraeus 1st Instance Court (three-member panel) 3562/2015, *Piraeus Court database*; Piraeus 1st Instance Court 875/2016, *Piraeus Court database*; Piraeus 1st Instance Court 33/2016, *ISOCRATES*; Piraeus 1st Instance Court 3189/2015, *Piraeus Court database*; Piraeus 1st Instance Court 1671/2014, *ISOCRATES*; Piraeus 1st Instance Court 5261/2013, *Hellenic Justice* 2014, 889; Thessaloniki 1st Instance Court 840/2016, unreported. Default of appearance is considered equivalent to a tacit consent, see Piraeus 1st Instance Court 335, 337 and 4416/2015, *Piraeus Court database*.

43 Piraeus CoA 28/2017, *Enterprises & Companies Law Review* 2017, 944; Piraeus 1st Instance Court (three-member panel) 1326/2015, *NOMOS*, and Piraeus 1st Instance Court 7/2016, *Piraeus Court database*. See especially Piraeus CoA 149/2015, *ISOCRATES*: although the appellees challenged the application of Greek law in first instance proceedings, they invoked exclusively domestic provisions, leaving the supposedly applicable foreign law aside. See also Piraeus 1st Instance Court 860/2015, *Piraeus Court database*.

44 Piraeus CoA 149/2015, *ISOCRATES*: the defendants (a company registered in the Marshall Islands and a resident of Piraeus) challenged the application of domestic law, but founded their allegations solely on Greek law. Similarly Piraeus 1st Instance Court 1420/2015, *ISOCRATES*: following frictions in the course of a chartering contract, a Norwegian company requested a freezing order against three companies located in Panama and the Marshall Islands, and two persons residing in Greece, founding its application upon Greek maritime and tort law respectively. The defendants did not oppose the selection of Greek law, and countered in a similar fashion.

45 Piraeus 1st Instance Court 339/2015, *Piraeus Court database*; Piraeus 1st Instance Court 1286/2015, *Piraeus Court database*; Piraeus 1st Instance Court 875/2016, *Piraeus Court database*; Piraeus 1st Instance Court (three-member panel) 3562/2015, *Piraeus Court database*; Piraeus 1st Instance Court (three-member panel) 2447/2014, *NOMOS*; Piraeus 1st Instance Court 5261/2013, *Hellenic Justice* 2014, 889.

46 Athens 1st Instance Court 2993/2019, *NOMOS*.

2.3. ABSENCE OF CHOICE OF LAW

Of all the provisions of the Rome I Regulation, Article 4 has been the one most commonly applied by Greek courts. One has to distinguish between a clear-cut reference to a specific provision and a significant number of mixed models of inconsistent references.

As expected, Article 4(1) of the Rome I Regulation is the provision applied most frequently. Greek courts have referred frequently to Article 4(1)(a) (habitual residence of the seller)[47] and (b) (habitual residence of the service provider).[48] Article 4(2) has been invoked individually only once, but was misconstrued.[49] On the other hand, Article 4(3) has been engaged several times by courts under the following circumstances: in a sales contract, because of the removal of the seller to another country,[50] and in matters related to the sale and purchase of vessels,[51] because the foreign defendant company was administered

---

47 Patras 1st Instance Court 420/2018, *Commercial law Review* 2018, 694; Piraeus 1st Instance Court 2168/2014, *ISOCRATES*; Volos 1st Instance Court 599/2013, *Legal Tribune* 2014, 1139; Thessaloniki 1st Instance Court 17682/2015, *ISOCRATES* (here: application of Italian law, given that the seller was an Italian company); Thessaloniki 1st Instance Court 4535/2013, *ISOCRATES* (here: application of German law, the seller being a German legal entity), Thessaloniki 1st Instance Court 15289/2015, unreported (here: Austrian law, the seller being an Austrian legal entity; eventually, the CISG was applied). Similarly Thessaloniki 1st Instance Court 4715/2013, *Theory and Practice of Civil Law and Civil Procedure Law* (= Εφαρμογές Αστικού & Αστικού Δικονομικού Δικαίου) 2014, 848 (application of the CISG through selection of Cypriot law).

48 Piraeus 1st Instance Court 2442/2015, *Piraeus Court database* (dockage services); Thessaloniki 1st Instance Court 15289/2015, unreported (legal services of a Greek lawyer to a Cypriot company); Piraeus 1st Instance Court 3707/2015, *Piraeus Court database* (boat-cleaning services); Piraeus 1st Instance Court 294/2015, *ISOCRATES* (transport of provisions and ship crew within the Eleusis port, to the benefit of a foreign shipping company); Piraeus 1st Instance Court 2190/2014, *ISOCRATES* (shipping agency services, agent resident in Italy, hence Italian law applicable).

49 Piraeus 1st Instance Court 283/2015, *ISOCRATES*: the claimant was a Cypriot security company. In October 2013, it concluded a contract for security services with a shipping company in Athens, the latter having its registered seat in Monrovia, Liberia, and its actual administrative headquarters in Attica district. The agreed services were to be provided on board the defendant's ship during its passage from Fujairah port, UAE, to the Red Sea. The court applied Greek law, basing its position on Art. 25b CC and 4(2) Rome I. The court erred with regard to the latter provision: the *locus contractus* is not relevant for the purposes of applying Art. 4(2) Rome I, which refers to the law of the country where the party required to effect the characteristic performance of the contract has its habitual residence. Hence, in the case at hand, Cypriot law should have been applied.

50 Thessaloniki 1st Instance Court 1136/2015, *Armenopoulos* 2015, 420: the plaintiff was a resident of Greece when he concluded the sales contract. At the time he filed the action he was already living in Cyprus. The court stated that Cypriot law was not relevant, and instead of referring to Art. 4(1)(a) it invoked Art. 4(3) Rome I.

51 Ad hoc H. MEIDANIS, 'Sale and purchase of vessels before Greek courts – How safe is the choice of foreign law made by the parties? The controversial discussion on Article 479 of the Greek Civil Code' [2008] 61 *RHDI* 455.

by a person residing in Greece.[52] In one case, the court referred erroneously to Article 4(3) even though the conditions for applying Article 4(1) had been met, leading nonetheless to the application of the same applicable law (law of the same country).[53] In other cases, the court opted for Article 4(3) even though, judging from the facts, the application of Articles 4(4)[54] or 5(1)[55] would have been more appropriate.

Greek courts have repeatedly incorporated a variety of Article 4's paragraphs in their judgments as they appear to be uncertain as to the article's correct application, creating confusion as to their reasoning for doing so in the process. In particular, in genuine service contracts, Article 4(1)(a) has been referred to in conjunction with Article 4(1)(b).[56] Despite the unambiguous wording of Article 4(2), this paragraph has been cumulatively invoked in conjunction with Article 4(1)(a)[57] or (b).[58] Along the same lines, Article 4(3) and (4) were jointly

---

52 Piraeus 1st Instance Court 135/2016, *ISOCRATES.*

53 Piraeus 1st Instance Court 1028/2015, *ISOCRATES*: the claimant was a company situated in Piraeus. It concluded a contract with the defendant for the purchase of spare parts and the delivery of repair services to the ship of the defendant. Instead of invoking Art. 4(1)(a) and (b), the court preferred to resort to Art. 4(3) for no apparent reason. See however Thessaloniki 1st Instance Court (three-member panel) 4048/2014, *ISOCRATES*: a Dutch company filed proceedings against a Greek company arising from a sales contract. The Thessaloniki court chose to apply Greek law, by referring to Art. 4(3), thus unjustifiably defying Art. 4(1)(a).

54 Thessaloniki 1st Instance Court (three-member panel) 9059/2014, *ISOCRATES*: an Austrian transport company (plaintiff) concluded a contract with a Greek company (respondent), by virtue of which all trucks of the former would tank from specific petrol stations of a certain petrol company in Northern Greece, with which the respondent agreed to a special price. The latter was obliged to pay the respective amounts to the petrol stations, and to collect subsequently the amounts by the plaintiff, offering a discount of €5 per 1000 litres. Due to misappropriation of advance payments by the respondent, the Austrian company filed an action for damages. The court considered that Art. 4(3) Rome I should be directly applied, without elaborating on the reasoning of its conclusion. If the court tacitly considered that the law applicable cannot be determined pursuant to Art. 4(1) or (2), as was seemingly the case, it should have opted for Art. 4(4). On an equal footing, in a case concerning a debt acknowledge agreement, the court again invoked Art. 4(3), thus failing to take into account Art. 4(4), which would have been the appropriate rule for the circumstances of the dispute: see Piraeus 1st Instance Court 276/2016, *Piraeus Court database.* In a previous decision, the same court simply referred jointly to Art. 4(2)–(4): see Piraeus 1st Instance Court 2932/2015, *Piraeus Court database.*

55 Piraeus 1st Instance Court 909/2016, *Piraeus Court database*: the plaintiff, a Belgian carrier, sued a Greek company, which was supposed to receive merchandise shipped from Cape Town, to be delivered to Piraeus port. The court made a hasty reference to Art. 4(3), even though Art. 5(1) was applicable, which would have led to the same result, i.e. the application of Greek law, since the habitual residence of the carrier did not coincide with any of the locations mentioned therein. Hence, Greek law would have been applied as the law of the country where the place of delivery, as agreed by the parties, is situated.

56 Piraeus 1st Instance Court 209 and 210/2016, *Piraeus Court database.*

57 Piraeus 1st Instance Court 209 and 210/2016, *Piraeus Court database.*

58 Piraeus 1st Instance Court 335, 337, 355 and 4416/2015, *Piraeus Court database.*

invoked in a case concerning salvage at sea.[59] Finally, Article 4(4) has been additionally invoked in conjunction with Article 4(1)(a)[60] or (b).[61]

Turning to Article 4(1) of the Rome II Regulation, this provision has been repeatedly used by Greek courts to establish the applicable law in cross border disputes. Starting with the interdependence of this provision with Article 1(2), it has been ruled that the Regulation (i.e. Article 4) applies with respect to securities when the claimant founds his action on tort, i.e. not on the negotiable character of the financial instrument.[62] In addition, courts also refer to Article 4(3) Rome II Regulation whenever a manifestly closer connection has been demonstrated.[63] The rule has been implemented in a number of disputes arising out of carriage by road torts,[64] labour accidents,[65] ship collision incidents,[66] fraud in maritime matters,[67] negotiable instruments,[68] company[69] and stock market disputes,[70] intellectual property infringements,[71]

---

59 Piraeus 1st Instance Court 1230/2016, *Piraeus Court database*: The court stated that the above rules are applied by analogy, given the legal nature of salvage at sea as a contract of undertaking.

60 Piraeus 1st Instance Court 2191/2014, *ISOCRATES*.

61 Piraeus 1st Instance Court 335, 337, 355, 3189, 3823 and 4416/2015, *Piraeus Court database*.

62 Piraeus 1st Instance Court 339/2015, *Piraeus Court database* and Piraeus 1st Instance Court 601/2015, *Piraeus Court database* (cheques); Larissa 1st Instance Court (three-member panel) 35/2015, *NOMOS* (convertible bonds); and Athens 1st Instance Court (three-member panel) 606/2010, *ISOCRATES* (stock market transactions). See also A. BOLOS / D. TZAKAS (E. LIASKOS), n. 22 above, Art. 1, nn. 83–85.

63 Piraeus 1st Instance Court 601/2015, *Piraeus Court database*.

64 Euboea CoA 142/2018, *NOMOS*.

65 Piraeus 1st Instance Court (three-member panel) 3139/2015, *Piraeus Court database* (location of the accident: Piraeus port).

66 Piraeus 1st Instance Court (three-member panel) 3707/2013, *Hellenic Justice* 2014, 1502 (location of the collision: Salamina shipyard, Attica).

67 Piraeus 1st Instance Court (three-member panel) 2751/2015, *NOMOS* (place where the harmful event occurred: Piraeus, i.e. the residence of both parties).

68 Larissa 1st Instance Court (three-member panel) 35/2015, *NOMOS* (place where the harmful event occurred: Larissa, i.e. the residence of the consumer).

69 Piraeus 1st Instance Court 2166/2011, *Legal Tribune* 2012, 98: the applicant was a company with its statutory seat in the Marshall Islands. One of the applicant's associates illegally transferred part of the company's funds to the defendant. The incident was discovered later, i.e. following the associate's death. The court applied Greek law, as the law of the place where the harmful event occurred, which was Piraeus, i.e. the seat of the branch from which the money was transferred to the defendant.

70 Athens 1st Instance Court (three-member panel) 606/2010, *ISOCRATES* (tortious liability; the place of the harmful event was located in Greece, i.e. where the market manipulation occurred).

71 Athens 1st Instance Court 4658/2012, *Armenopoulos* 2013, 27: interim measures of the Greek Intellectual Property collective management body against Greek service providers, whose websites were offering unauthorised access to protected audiovisual material through connection to other web sites in Russia and the USA. The court applied Art. 4(1) Rome II,

theft,[72] piercing the corporate veil,[73] banking law,[74] and *culpa in contrahendo*[75] cases. There have not yet been any reported cases involving multiple tortfeasors or victims in which Article 4(2) of the Rome II Regulation has been applied.

2.4. ESCAPE CLAUSES

Article 4(4) of the Rome I Regulation is frequently applied in Greece, albeit sometimes analogously,[76] vaguely,[77] erroneously[78] or unnecessarily.[79]

stating that the infringement of intellectual property rights, i.e. the harmful event, occurred in Greece. It must be underlined that the applicant acted within its jurisdictional limits: it filed proceedings only in regard to audiovisual material related to Greek authors and artists. Strangely, no reference to Article 8 Rome II was made by the court.

72 Thessaloniki 1st Instance Court 20455/2014, *ISOCRATES* (place where the load bins of the foreign claimant were stolen: Thessaloniki).

73 Piraeus 1st Instance Court (three-member panel) 1743/2014, *ISOCRATES* (respondents: a Panamanian shipping company and their shareholders, residents of Greece; place of the harmful event: Piraeus). Similarly Thessaloniki 1st Instance Court (three-member panel), 9059/2014, *ISOCRATES*.

74 Piraeus 1st Instance Court (three-member panel) 4526/2014, *NOMOS*: garnishment order on a Greek account against a Piraeus branch of an English bank. The owner sued the bank for tortious liability, because it issued and handed over a cheque to the benefit of the person initiating execution. The court ruled that Greek law was to be applied, because the harmful event occurred in Greece, i.e. where the bank account was opened.

75 Larissa CoA 348/2015, *ISOCRATES* (in conjunction with Art. 12 Rome II Regulation).

76 Piraeus 1st Instance Court 210/2016, *Piraeus Court database*; Piraeus 1st Instance Court 860/2015, *Piraeus Court database*; Piraeus 1st Instance Court 4068/2013, *Maritime Law Review* 2013, 193; Thesprotia 1st Instance Court, *Legal Tribune* 2014, 4.

77 See for instance Piraeus 1st Instance Court 1812/2014, *Piraeus Court database*: a Greek company filed proceedings against a company registered in the Marshall Islands for shipbroker services offered in Greece. The court applied Greek law referring generally to Art. 4, i.e. with no further specification as to the exact paragraph it referred to; still, by the wording of the ruling, it becomes obvious that it meant Art. 4(4), in referring to the law of the country with which the case is most closely connected.

78 Piraeus 1st Instance Court 5261/2013, *Hellenic Justice* 2014, 889: the plaintiff was a Spanish company, providing goods and services to ships. Following talks with the second defendant, a resident of Piraeus, it concluded an agreement with the first defendant, a company registered in the Marshall Islands, with the aim of providing the above services to a ship under Moldovan flag, belonging to the first defendant, at the Las Palmas port. The first defendant presented himself as the legal representative of the second defendant. The court stated that the action for damages based on the breach of the contract should be examined under Greek law pursuant to Art. 4(4), since the parties did not agree on the applicable law, omitting any reference to Art. 4(1)(a) Rome I. The mistake was repeated at second instance: see Piraeus CoA 149/2015, *ISOCRATES*.

79 See Piraeus 1st Instance Court 339/2015, *Piraeus Court database*: the court characterised the legal relationship of the parties as a sales contract; still, instead of applying Art. 4(1)(a), it directly referred to Art. 4(4) Rome I, under the erroneous assumption that the lack of a choice-of -law agreement led unavoidably to the application of Art. 4(4) Rome I.

The provision has been used to determine the law applicable to the sale and purchase of vessels,[80] a relationship for which, as we saw earlier,[81] Article 4(3) has also been selected (by the same court, and within the same year, surprisingly).

Greek courts proceed to the application of Article 4(3) of the Rome II Regulation, sometimes in odd connection with Article 4(1),[82] mainly in two situations: when it is clear from all surrounding circumstances that the case is manifestly more closely connected with Greece (a), and when a pre-existing relationship between the parties is proven, that being a contractual one (b):

(a) The establishment of a manifestly closer connection to Greece has been accepted in the following cases: when it results from the facts that either both parties[83] or solely the respondent conduct(s) business and/or live(s) in Greece,[84] or in instances of an omission of a required action, that led to the harmful event, which was supposed to take place in Greece.[85]

---

80 Piraeus 1st Instance Court 875/2016, *Piraeus Court database*; Piraeus 1st Instance Court 860/2015, *Piraeus Court database*; and Piraeus 1st Instance Court 2190/2014, *ISOCRATES*.

81 Piraeus 1st Instance Court 135/2016, *ISOCRATES*.

82 See for instance Piraeus 1st Instance Court (three-member panel) 2447/2014, *NOMOS*.

83 Piraeus 1st Instance Court 1817/2014, *ISOCRATES*: request for an attachment order of a Belgian company, legally represented in Greece by a company registered in the Marshall Islands, legally represented in Piraeus, against three Greek shipping companies and one company registered in the Marshall Islands, legally represented in Piraeus. The court applied Greek law as being closely connected to the case at hand, given that the actual seat of all companies, and the place where the harmful event occurred (i.e. both the *situs* of action and the place of direct harm) was Piraeus.

84 Piraeus CoA 149/2015, *ISOCRATES*: the court stated that the action for damages should be examined under Greek law, since the second defendant was carrying out all activities related to the first defendant from his residence, i.e. Piraeus. See also Piraeus 1st Instance Court 5261/2013, *Hellenic Justice* 2014, 889 (same case in first instance). See more recently Piraeus CoA 28/2017, *Enterprises & Companies Law Review* 2017, 944: *Actio pauliana* of a Finnish company against two Greek companies, regarding transfer of property in Greece.

85 Thessaloniki 1st Instance Court 2508/2016, unreported. The facts of the case were as follows: the claimant was a Bulgarian carrier. He agreed with a shipper, located in Thessaloniki, to load merchandise from Chalkida (a city in Central Greece), and deliver it to Germany. At the Hungarian border the truck was refused entrance due to a violation of the provisions of Regulation 1013/2006 on shipments of waste. The truck remained there for nearly a year. As a consequence, the carrier sued the shipper, the Greek seller and the German buyer for damages. The German company did not appear in the proceedings. Both the carrier and the shipper resorted to Greek law. The court opted for the application of Art. 4(3), by virtue of which Greek law was applicable, because the harmful event of omitting to take the necessary measures of compliance with the above EU Regulation occurred in Greece.

Occasionally, the court simply reiterates the wording of the provision, in order to conclude that Greek law is to be applied.[86]

(b) The pre-existing contractual relationship between the parties was invoked mostly in maritime disputes, which usually concern an insurance contract,[87] a transport agreement,[88] or a vessel purchase deal,[89] the sole exception being a banking law case.[90]

---

86 Piraeus 1st Instance Court 601/2015, *Piraeus Court database*: the claimant was a Turkish company, whereas the respondents were two Greeks and one company registered in Monrovia, Liberia. In their capacity as legal representatives of the latter company, the Greek defendants issued two cheques in Piraeus, which were later not paid due to lack of funds. The court found that the above facts were sufficiently connected with Greece, as allowing it to examine the case under domestic law. Similarly Piraeus 1st Instance Court (three-member panel) 2447/2014, *NOMOS*: a company located in Guernsey, Channel Islands, filed proceedings for damages on tortious liability against two residents of Greece, acting as legal representatives of a company registered under the law of the Marshall Islands, and an English credit institution, legally represented in Greece. The claimant had already a writ of attachment against the English bank, which however became ineffective due to the machinations of the latter in the enforcement stage. The court concluded that domestic law was the proper law of the case, given the fact that the tort committed was evidently closely connected with Greece, i.e. the place where the harmful event occurred.

87 Piraeus 1st Instance Court 1286/2015, *Piraeus Court database*: a foreign company specialising in Mexican food concluded an insurance agreement with a Greek insurer for the transport of goods by sea to a UAE company. The freight was inspected at the port of Jebel Ali, where the container was found to be rusty and in bad condition, i.e. full of insects. The foreign company sued the Greek insurer for damages arising out of the contractual obligations. Ancillary relief was grounded on tortious liability. The court applied Greek law, because it was the law agreed on by the parties in the insurance contract, from which the tort of the respondent stemmed.

88 Piraeus 1st Instance Court 860/2015, *Piraeus Court database*: the claimant suffered an accident during the trip from Ancona (Italy) to Patras (Greece) on a ship owned by the first defendant, an Italian company. She filed an action for damages against the Italian company and a Greek company entrusted with the management of the ship (registered in Italy). With respect to the liability of the second defendant, the court applied Greek law, which was the proper law under Art. 4(3) Rome II, most importantly because of the contractual relationship (transportation contract) between the claimant and the Italian company, which was governed by Greek law.

89 Piraeus 1st Instance Court 602/2015, *Piraeus Court database*: following negotiations in Piraeus, the claimant, a Liberian company, proceeded to an advance payment for the purchase of a Turkish vessel, owned by two Liberian companies, legally represented by two Greeks, residents of Piraeus. In spite of the advance payment, the representatives transferred ownership of the vessel to a third company not involved in the proceedings. The claimant sued for damages. The court opted for the application of Greek law, by simply reiterating the wording of Art. 4(3) Rome II.

90 Patras 1st Instance Court (three-member panel) 244/2015, *NOMOS*: the claimant, a resident of Patras, filed an action for damages against a Cypriot bank, on the basis of an agreement for a time deposit he had ostensibly concluded in his hometown. Without specifically referring to Art. 4(3) Rome II, the court applied Greek law (*lex causa*) as the *lex delicti*, given that this joinder of action was closely connected with the credit contract, concluded in Greece.

In terms of typical situations in which the escape clauses have been applied, maritime disputes[91] are clearly the frontrunners.[92] Escape clauses also appear in traffic accidents[93] and banking law.[94]

2.5. SPECIFIC RULES

With respect to the carriage of goods (Article 5(1) and (3) Rome I Regulation), the rule of Article 5(1)(b) was applied, given that the requirements for applying Article 5(1)(a) were not met in the pertinent circumstances of the cases.[95] Article 5(1) was not applied in one case because of a post-contractual tacit agreement.[96] Finally, in another case, Article 5 was not considered by the court due to the supremacy accorded to the International Convention for the Unification of Certain Rules of Law relating to Bills of Lading (the Hague Rules).[97]

In relation to contracts for the carriage of passengers (Article 5(2) and (3) Rome I Regulation), Article 5(2) was examined in a case where the claimant

91 For the overall influence of the Rome II Regulation on maritime disputes, see K. KOROTZIS, 'EU Regulation 864/2007 on the applicable law in non-contractual disputes (Rome II) and its impact on Greek Maritime Law' = 'Ο Κανονισμός 864/2007 της Ευρωπαϊκής Ένωσης για το εφαρμοστέο δίκαιο στις εξωσυμβατικές ενοχές (Ρώμη II) και η επίδρασή του στο ελληνικό ναυτικό δίκαιο' [2009] *Legal Tribune* 278.

92 Piraeus CoA 149/2015, *ISOCRATES*; Piraeus 1st Instance Court 5261/2013, *Hellenic Justice* 2014, 889; Piraeus 1st Instance Court 602/2015, *Piraeus Court database*; Piraeus 1st Instance Court 860/2015, *Piraeus Court database*; Piraeus 1st Instance Court (three-member panel) 2447/2014, *NOMOS*; Piraeus 1st Instance Court 1286/2015, *Piraeus Court database*; and Piraeus 1st Instance Court 1817/2014, *ISOCRATES*.

93 Thessaloniki 1st Instance Court 126/2016, *ISOCRATES*.

94 Patras 1st Instance Court (three-member panel) 244/2015, *NOMOS*.

95 Piraeus 1st Instance Court 721/2015, *Piraeus Court database*: the carrier was a Danish company, the place of receipt was in Spain, the place of delivery in Greece, and the habitual residence of the consignor in France.

96 Thessaloniki 1st Instance Court 2508/2016, unreported: the carrier was a Bulgarian company, the place of receipt was in Greece, the place of delivery in Germany, and the habitual residence of the consignor in Greece. Pursuant to Art. 5(1)(a), Bulgarian law would be applicable; this was however not possible, because none of the other parties resided in this country. German law could have applied in accordance with Art. 5(1)(b), if the German company would have challenged the application of Greek law; however the German company was in default, which gave rise to the court invoking Art. 3(1) Rome I.

97 Kavala 1st Instance Court 440/2011, *Armenopoulos* 2012, 272: the applicant filed a writ of attachment regarding a ship docked in the port of Kariani, whose owner was the defendant. The latter asserted that Syrian law should apply, pursuant to Art. 5(1)(b), because the place of delivery was Tartus, Syria. Had the court accepted this assertion, it would have had to dismiss the application as time-barred. However, it gave prevalence to the international convention, which contains a provision concerning limitation of actions. Eventually the application was dismissed as time-barred pursuant to the Hague Rules.

suffered damage on board. The court applied Greek law because the habitual residence of the injured party and the place of destination coincided.[98]

In the sole reported case on consumer contracts (Article 6 of the Rome I Regulation),[99] the court applied Greek law on the basis of Article 6(4). The claimant initiated proceedings against a Cypriot bank for inaccurate and misleading information resulting in the loss of the sum he invested in a presumable time deposit. The court considered that the case fell under Article 6(4)(d).[100]

Disputes related to insurance contracts (Article 7 of the Rome I Regulation)[101] are beginning to appear more frequently, especially in the maritime sector. In this context, Greek,[102] but especially English,[103] law has been repeatedly applied by reference to Article 7(2), following a pertinent choice-of-law clause in the insurance policy by the parties involved. In the absence of a choice-of-law clause, courts resort to the law of the country where the insurer has his habitual residence.[104]

As in the case of insurance matters, individual employment contract disputes (Article 8 of the Rome I Regulation) have appeared often before Greek courts, mainly emanating from the maritime industry.[105] Practice shows the tendency of the courts to apply the law most favourable to the employee,[106]

---

98 Piraeus 1st Instance Court 860/2015, *Piraeus Court database*.

99 For a detailed analysis from the Greek point of view, see Z. PAPASSIOPI-PASSIA, 'Consumer protection in Greek private international law' [2010] 63 *RHDI* 79, 90–97.

100 Patras 1st Instance Court (three-member panel) 244/2015, *NOMOS*. Greek law was applied due to tacit post-contractual determination. In this respect, see also C.H. TSOUKA, 'Regulation (EC) No 593/2008 of the European Parliament and of the Council of 17 June 2008 on the law applicable to contractual obligations (Rome I) with regard to financial instruments and services' = 'Η ρύθμιση του Κανονισμού 593/2008 του Ευρωπαϊκού Κοινοβουλίου και του Συμβουλίου της 17ης Ιουνίου 2008 για το εφαρμοστέο δίκαιο στις συμβατικές ενοχές ("Ρώμη Ι") σχετικά με τις συμβάσεις που αφορούν χρηματοπιστωτικά μέσα και υπηρεσίες' [2010] *Chronicles of Private Law* 86.

101 The provision is thoroughly analysed by A. TSAVDARIDIS in I. ROKAS (ed.), *Commentary on Insurance Contract Act (UCA) = Ασφαλιστική Σύμβαση – Κατ' άρθρον ερμηνεία του Ν 2496/1997*, Nomiki Bibliothiki = Νομική Βιβλιοθήκη 2014, 23 et seq. See also A. TSAVDARIDIS, 'Conflict of laws rules on insurance contracts: From the Rome Convention and the EC directives on insurance to Regulation Rome I' = 'Το ιδ.δ.δ. της σύμβασης ασφάλισης: Από τη Σύμβαση της Ρώμης και τις κοινοτικές Οδηγίες για την ασφάλιση στον κανονισμό 'Ρώμη Ι' [2010] *Legal Tribune* 1952.

102 Piraeus 1st Instance Court 1286/2015, *Piraeus Court database*.

103 Piraeus CoA 768/2014, *NOMOS*; Piraeus 1st Instance Court (three-member panel) 4067/2015, *Piraeus Court database*; Piraeus 1st Instance Court 44/2016, *Piraeus Court database*; Piraeus 1st Instance Court 780/2016, *Piraeus Court database*.

104 Piraeus 1st Instance Court 1202/2015, *ISOCRATES* (here: German law).

105 Ad hoc N. MATHIOPOULOS, 'The applicable law in seamen's accidents' = 'Το εφαρμοστέο δίκαιο επί ναυτεργατικού ατυχήματος' [2015] *Piraeus Law Reports* (= Πειραϊκή Νομολογία) 292.

106 Piraeus 1st Instance Court 2950/2015, *Piraeus Court database*: an employment contract was concluded in the Philippines between the claimant, a Filipino national, and a company registered in the Philippines. The claimant worked as an oiler on board a ship under the

sporadically resorting to Article 9 of the Rome I Regulation (overriding mandatory provision),[107] sometimes with unconvincing or insufficient[108] reasoning.[109]

As for the Rome II Regulation, the existing case law does not allow generalisations regarding the proper implementation of the Regulation's rules on specific torts and delicts (αδικοπραξία). Overall, there are only a few decisions on the application of Articles 5–9.

---

flag of the Isle of Man, owned by the respondent. At a certain point he suffered a severe labour accident close to Port Elizabeth, South Africa. The court applied Greek law, as the law of the country where the place of business through which the employee was engaged was situated. It founded its decision on the fact that the respondent had its actual seat and administrative establishment in Piraeus. Hence, it referred (indirectly though) to Art. 8(3), given that no choice-of-law clause was present (Art. 8(1)) and no specific country from which the employee habitually carried out his work in performance of the contract (Art. 8(2)) could be determined. Similarly Piraeus 1st Instance Court 97/2015, *Piraeus Court database*: Ukrainian employees concluded an agreement in Greece to work on ship under the flag of Kiribati, owned by a company registered in the Marshall Islands, but with its administrative seat established in Greece. See further Piraeus 1st Instance Court 1844/2015, *Piraeus Court database*: a Greek employee concluded an oral agreement with a Greek resident, representing a foreign company, the latter being the owner of a ship under the Liberian flag. He started working in Luanda, Angola, as a first engineer, and terminated his work in Lagos, Nigeria. The court referred to Art. 8(2)–(4), and concluded that Greek law should apply as the law of the country where the respondent had its actual seat and administrative establishment in Piraeus; hence it applied tacitly Art. 8(3). Following the same direction: Piraeus 1st Instance Court 2783/2014, *ISOCRATES*, and Piraeus 1st Instance Court 3068/2011, *NOMOS*.

107 Piraeus 1st Instance Court 122/2016, *ISOCRATES*: an employment contract was concluded in Manila between a Filipino national (the claimant) and a company registered in Monrovia, Liberia (the defendant). The claimant worked as a sailor on a ship of the defendant under Liberian flag. The parties agreed that the contract would be governed by the Standard Terms and Conditions Governing the Employment of Filipino Seafarers on Board Ocean Going Vessels, which forms part of the law of the Philippines. The court refused to abide by the choice-of-law clause, stating that Filipino law diminishes the labour rights of the sailor compared to Greek legislation, which is to be applied in accordance with Art. 8, i.e. on the grounds of the actual seat and operative establishment of the defendant.

108 Piraeus 1st Instance Court 585/2015, *ISOCRATES*: a Greek national (the applicant) concluded an employment contract with a company registered in the Marshall Islands (the defendant), with the aim of working as a first captain on board a ship under the flag of the Saint Vincent and the Grenadines, owned by the defendant. His application for an attachment order was examined under Greek law on the basis of Art. 8(4). Nevertheless, the court underlined that the country which the employee habitually carried out his work in performance of the contract was the Hellenic Republic. Having said that, it failed to invoke Art. 8(2) in its ruling. The same mistake was committed by Piraeus 1st Instance Court 1351/2015, *ISOCRATES*: Georgian employees working on a ship under the Togolese flag, owned by a company registered in the Marshall Islands, but actually administered by an office in Piraeus. The close connection of Art. 8(4) was unnecessary, given that the court acknowledged that the applicants were habitually working in Greece; hence, Art. 8(2) was the appropriate provision to apply.

109 Example: Piraeus 1st Instance Court (acting as an appellate court for judgments of the Justice of the Peace) 4364/2015, *Piraeus Court database*: a company registered in the Marshall Islands (appellant) concluded an employment contract with a Greek person (appellee) in Piraeus.

In relation to product liability (Article 5 Rome II Regulation),[110] there is only one relevant case, which concerned the liability of a German automobile producer. Although the harmful events occurred before the entry into force of the Rome II Regulation, it is interesting to present the findings of the court in regard to the interpretation of the rule: The court referred to Article 5, without specifying which paragraph it was applying, concluding that Greek law on consumer protection was to be applied. *Mutatis mutandis* it applied Article 5(1)(a) Rome II Regulation, because it emphasised the habitual residence of the claimant, which was Thessaloniki, Greece. However, the court dismissed the action for damages, because the law on product liability does not give rise for compensation related to damages caused to the product itself.[111]

Similarly to Article 5, only a couple of decisions have been found in Greece on the interpretation of Article 6 Rome II Regulation on unfair competition and acts restricting free competition.[112] The first case concerned the violation of a Swiss pharmaceutical company's patent rights in Greece. The court referred to Article 6(1), stating that Greece was the location where competitive relations were likely to be affected by the actions of the defendant.[113] In the second case, the court applied the mosaic approach.[114]

The latter would work as a refrigerationist on board a ship under Maltese flag, travelling through many Mediterranean countries. The parties agreed that the law of Malta would govern the contract, as the law of the flag. For this reason, the company invoked Art. 3(1) in the hearing. The court applied Greek law in both instances, presenting four grounds on the basis of Art. 8: (a) the pre-contract was signed in Piraeus, which was the place of residence for the company representing the appellant and the legal representative of the appellant's representative in Greece; (b) the ship administration was operated solely from Greek soil; (c) the Maltese flag was a flag of convenience; and (d) the captain and most of the crew members on the ship were Greek nationals. It is hard to trace the precise provision supposedly put forward; presumably, the court's intention was to refer to Art. 8(4), but it failed to include it in the text of the decision.

110 For a detailed analysis of the topic before the entry into force of the Regulation, see V. KOURTIS, *The producer's liability for defective products in private international law* = *Η ευθύνη του παραγωγού ελαττωματικών προϊόντων στο ιδιωτικό διεθνές δίκαιο*, Sakkoulas Publications = Εκδόσεις Σάκκουλα 2006, passim.

111 Thessaloniki 1st Instance Court (three-member panel) 10369/2009, *ISOCRATES*.

112 See in detail D. STAMATIADIS, 'Private international law of unfair competition' = 'Το ιδιωτικό διεθνές δίκαιο του αθέμιτου ανταγωνισμού' [2008] *Chronicles of Private Law* 7.

113 Athens 1st Instance Court (three-member panel) 3955/2015, *ISOCRATES*. Similarly recently Athens CoA 2756/2018, *Enterprises & Companies Law Review* 2019, 80 (concerted action of the defendants (Swedish and Greek companies) with the aim to exclude the plaintiff from the fabrication and maintenance of dialysis machines (kidney treatment) in the Greek market).

114 Athens 1st Instance Court (three-member panel) 3008/2018, *Enterprises & Companies Law Review* 2019, 218: Unfair competition against a Greek olive oil producer and distributor by a Greek competitor in the Dutch and Belgian market; the court applied Art. 6.1 Rome II Regulation, and stayed proceedings, in order for the parties to furnish information on the applicable law in the countries aforementioned.

Article 8 of the Rome II Regulation on the infringement of intellectual property rights sets aside Article 67 of the Law on Intellectual Property.[115] The provision has appeared in three decisions: The first concerned a Greek architect who filed an action against three Greek companies and one Cypriot company for intellectual property infringement, resulting from the unauthorised reproduction of one of his pictures for commercial purposes at a fair, and in a promotional material which was broadcast both in television and on the Internet. He requested compensation for pain and suffering. The court referred to Article 8(1) of the Rome II Regulation because of the foreign element of the dispute, arising from the involvement of the Cypriot company.[116] The second ruling was in the patent rights[117] violation case mentioned above in relation to Article 6 of the Rome II Regulation.[118] Finally, Article 8(2) was applied in a Community Trade Mark violation.[119]

As for industrial damage, no reported case has been found dealing with the application of Article 9 Rome II Regulation.[120]

2.6. RULES APPLICABLE TO NON-CONTRACTUAL OBLIGATIONS OTHER THAN TORTS OR DELICTS

With the exception of unjust enrichment, the existing case law does not allow generalisations regarding the proper implementation of the Rome II Regulation's rules on *negotiorum gestio* (Article 11) and *culpa in contrahendo* (Article 12). Overall, there are approximately 15 decisions on the application of Articles 10–12 Rome II Regulation.

Courts apply the rule on unjust enrichment (Article 10 Rome II Regulation)[121] on the basis of three connecting factors: the existing relationship between the

115 For this rule, see E. VASSILAKAKIS, n. 24 above, 109.

116 Athens 1st Instance Court (three-member panel) 3141/2015, *Chronicles of Private Law* 2016, 59.

117 Specifically on the matter, see M. PERRAKI, 'Patent infringement and private international law issues in Greece' [2009] 62 *RHDI* 413, 415 et seq.

118 See n. 113 above.

119 Athens 1st Instance Court (three-member panel) 3008/2018, *Enterprises & Companies Law Review* 2019, 218 [act of infringement committed in Greece; hence, application of Greek law].

120 Ad hoc see C.H. TSOUKA, 'Regulation (EC) No 864/2007 of the European Parliament and of the Council of 11 July 2007 on the law applicable to non-contractual obligations (Rome II) and Greek shipping. Brief remarks on Article 9 on industrial action' = 'Ο κανονισμός (ΕΚ) αριθ. 864/2007 του Ευρωπαϊκού Κοινοβουλίου και του συμβουλίου της 11ης Ιουλίου 2007 για το εφαρμοστέο δίκαιο στις εξωσυμβατικές ενοχές ("Ρωμη ΙΙ") και η Ελληνική Ναυτιλία. Σύντομες σκέψεις για το άρθρο 9 περί συνδικαλιστικών κινητοποιήσεων' [2008] *Commercial Law Review* 253.

121 Ad hoc C.H. TSOUKA, *The applicable law in unjustified enrichment = Το εφαρμοστέο δίκαιο στον αδικαιολόγητο πλουτισμό*, Nomiki Bibliothiki = Νομική Βιβλιοθήκη 2013, passim.

parties (a), the post-contractual tacit agreement (b), and the close connection element (c):

(a) Article 10(1) was applied in three cases. In the first case, the court simply mentioned the provision, with no further analysis.[122] In the second case, the court directly connected the main contract (an insurance agreement) to the unjust enrichment obligation submitted by the claimant.[123] In the third case, Article 10(1) was connected to an existing non-contractual relationship (*culpa in contrahendo*).[124]
(b) On several occasions, courts have opted for an additional reference to Article 14(1) of the Rome II Regulation, in order to vest the application of domestic law with an additional legal ground.[125]
(c) Article 10(3) was applied in a single case: a Danish maritime transporter sued a Greek company for damages arising from the reluctance of the latter to receive goods transported from Spain to Piraeus in Greece. It added as an ancillary claim compensation due to unjustified enrichment. The court concluded that the contractual bond between the parties should be examined under Greek law. However, instead of referring to Article 10(1) of the Rome II Regulation, it opted for a direct reference to Article 10(3), which again resulted in the application of Greek law, i.e. the law of the country in which the unjustified enrichment took place.[126]

Negotiorum gestio (Article 11 of the Rome II Regulation) was applied in two cases. The first one has already been mentioned above in relation to Article 10 of the Rome II Regulation.[127] In a similar fashion, the court opted for a direct

---

122 Piraeus CoA 768/2014, *NOMOS*, Piraeus 1st Instance Court 875/2016, *Piraeus Court database*. Obviously the court suggested that the contract between the parties (vessel repair services in Greek shipyards and factories) was closely connected to Greece, irrespective of the ship's flag (registered in Saint Vincent and the Grenadines), and the registered seat of the defendants abroad, because the administration of the companies was operated from Piraeus. See also Piraeus 1st Instance Court 339/2015, *Piraeus Court database*: the court failed to underline the existence of successive sale contracts between the parties, which would have empowered the position taken in favour of the application of Art. 10(1) Rome II. Similarly Piraeus 1st Instance Court (three-member panel) 3562/2015, *Piraeus Court database*.

123 Piraeus 1st Instance Court 1286/2015, *Piraeus Court database*.

124 Piraeus 1st Instance Court 602/2015, *Piraeus Court database*. The court referred to a number of Rome II Regulation provisions, among them Art. 10(1).

125 Piraeus 1st Instance Court 875/2016, *Piraeus Court database*; Piraeus 1st Instance Court 339/2015, *Piraeus Court database*; Piraeus 1st Instance Court (three-member panel) 3562/2015, *Piraeus Court database*; and Piraeus 1st Instance Court 1286/2015, *Piraeus Court database*.

126 Piraeus 1st Instance Court 721/2015, *Piraeus Court database*.

127 See n. 126 above.

reference to Article 11(3) (emphasising the place where *negotiorum gestio* took place),[128] instead of referring to Article 11(1),[129] in spite of the existing relationship between the parties. The second case involved a genuine application of Article 11(3): the parties had no previous relationship and they were not habitually resident in the same country.[130]

Three decisions have been found related to *culpa in contrahendo* (Article 12 of the Rome II Regulation).[131] The first decision did not actually apply the provision, presumably because the claimant did not specifically refer to.[132] The second decision made direct reference to Article 12(1), pointing out the connection to the law that would have been applied to the contract (habitual residence of the seller).[133] Finally, the third decision proceeded in a similar fashion to the previous one, but without clearly stating that the law applicable to the contract would have been that of Greece. The latter was not indisputable, taking into account the parties' exchange of correspondence regarding a choice-of-law clause in favour of German law.[134]

2.7. SCOPE OF APPLICABLE LAW

No reported case law has been found on the question whether the courts have included issues not mentioned in the (non-exhaustive) list of issues in Article 12

---

128 i.e. Piraeus, where the claimant assumed the task of disposing of the rotten merchandise and cleaning the containers.

129 Art. 11(2) could not be applied, because of the place of residence in different countries (Denmark / Greece).

130 Piraeus 1st Instance Court 766/2015, *NOMOS*: the applicant, a Greek shipping company, requested an attachment order of a certain quantity of merchandise which was on board a ship anchored at the Salamina port, Greece. The goods were property of the defendant, an English company. The ship was auctioned in Piraeus and awarded to the applicant. The latter based its application on the grounds of outstanding sums arising from acts performed in relation to the merchandise without the defendant's due authority. Hence, no contractual or non-contractual obligation pre-existed between the parties, which gave rise to the court invoking directly Art. 11(3) Rome II.

131 For a primary presentation, see I. THOMA, 'Culpa in contrahendo in the Rome II Regulation' [2008] 61 *RHDI* 669. In detail, see A. BOLOS, 'Precontractual liability and applicable law after Regulation 864/2007 (Rome II)' = 'Προσυμβατική ευθύνη και εφαρμοστέο δίκαιο μετά τον Κανονισμό 864/2007 ("Ρώμη II")' [2009] *Chronicles of Private Law* 585.

132 Piraeus 1st Instance Court 602/2015, *Piraeus Court database*. Following negotiations in Piraeus, the claimant, a Liberian company, proceeded to an advance payment for the purchase of a Turkish vessel, owned by two Liberian companies, legally represented by two Greeks, residents of Piraeus. In spite of the advance payment, the representatives transferred ownership of the vessel to a third company, not involved in the proceedings. The claimant sued for damages. The court referred to a number of Rome II Regulation provisions in its reasoning; however, Art. 12 was not among them.

133 Volos 1st Instance Court (three-member panel) 199/2013, *Legal Tribune* 2014, 1139.

134 Larissa CoA 348/2015, *ISOCRATES*.

of the Rome I Regulation and Article 15 of the Rome II Regulation (scope of the law applicable). In fact, the courts rarely refer to those provisions, with a sole exception where the rule of Article 12(1)(d) of the Rome I Regulation was applied.[135]

There is also no reported case law on the issue of characterisation. Regarding Article 15 of the Rome II Regulation, its subsection (f) is one of the most significant features of the provision. It applies almost exclusively to traffic/labour accidents, and relates to the question of the legal standing of the victim's relatives.[136]

2.8. FOREIGN LAW

Cases in Greece involving foreign law are tried only rarely because of the insufficiency of information furnished by the parties. Courts order the production of a legal opinion by the Hellenic Institute of International and Foreign Law, which was established in 1939 and has since then been the main Greek research institution in the fields of international, foreign and comparative law. The Institute's main activity relates to the supply of legal information on foreign laws, EU law, international law and Greek law to certain categories of natural and legal persons. 'Legal information' is defined as information provided to the interested party in writing as regards a specific question of law, including – as the case may be – any relevant legislative provisions and case law. In providing legal information, the Institute does not in any way interpret the relevant rules of law. Similarly, it neither submits facts to such rules nor does it provide expert opinions or legal advice.

The courts usually make requests for the submission of legal information by either of the parties. This is triggered by the fact that the latter have not furnished the necessary material for the application of foreign law by the court.

---

135 Piraeus 1st Instance Court 875/2016, *Piraeus Court database*.

136 Piraeus 1st Instance Court (three-member panel) 3139/2015, *Piraeus Court database*: the wife and children of a deceased seafarer are entitled to compensation for emotional distress. See also Thessaloniki 1st Instance Court 101/2016, *ISOCRATES*: the parents, brothers and grandfather of the deceased in a traffic accident are entitled to compensation for emotional distress in accordance with domestic provisions (Art. 932 CC). The court mistakenly referred to Art. 26 CC, although the accident occurred in March 2015. Similarly, Rhodes 1st Instance Court 65/2011, *Dodecanese Reports* 2013, 399, again wrongly applying Art. 26 CC to a traffic accident that occurred in June 2009. For the application of Art. 4 in conjunction with Art. 15(f), see more recently Supreme Court 1863/2017, *Legal Tribune* 2018, 1041 (children, daughter in law, mother and sister); Supreme Court 1414/2019, unreported (parents and brothers of the deceased), and Dodecanese CoA 282/2017, *NOMOS* (grandparents and fiancé).

There are no lists as to the costs involving in pleading foreign law. The parties are burdened with all pertinent expenses; the court simply adjourns the hearing and orders the production of a legal report, specifying in the interim order what the exact content of that report must be.

In summary proceedings relating to the Rome I Regulation, courts unanimously apply Greek law, regardless of whether they have acknowledged that foreign law applies. This phenomenon is caused by the failure of the parties to furnish the court with information on the provisions of foreign law. The omission cannot be remedied by the court, because, unlike the powers with which courts are vested in ordinary proceedings, they are not entitled to order discontinuance for the production of foreign law in the course of expedited proceedings.[137] Hence, Greek law applies exceptionally, with the additional but somewhat unfounded assertion that the latter resembles the foreign law provisions that should have been applied.[138]

The universal application of Rome I Regulation has been repeatedly confirmed by Greek courts.[139] It was also confirmed in a case involving a Danish company: the court stated that the provisions of the Rome I Regulation applied in full, notwithstanding the fact that Denmark is not considered as a Member State for the purposes of the Regulation (Article 1(4)).[140]

In summary proceedings relating to the Rome II Regulation, courts sporadically apply Greek law, even if they have acknowledged that foreign law applies. Within the ambit of non-contractual obligations, there is one noteworthy decision that needs to be discussed in depth. The applicant was a Romanian citizen living in Craiova, Romania, and was a truck driver by profession, working in the field of transportation. The first defendant was also a citizen and resident of Romania – in fact, a colleague of the applicant. In the course of their professional duties, they were ordered to load a shipment of fruit from Greece and return to Romania. The defendant was at the wheel and the applicant was in the third (back) seat. On their way back and within the administrative region of Thessaloniki, an accident occurred. The defendant lost control of the vehicle and crashed the truck. As a result, a third person within the truck (sitting next to the driver) was killed, and the applicant was severely injured. The applicant initiated summary proceedings against the driver (the first defendant), the owner of the vehicle, and the Motor Insurers' Bureau, which is a legal private law entity based in Athens, supervised by the Bank of Greece. He claimed damages

137 Piraeus 1st Instance Court 1564/2014, *ISOCRATES*.

138 Piraeus 1st Instance Court 84/2016, *ISOCRATES*; Piraeus 1st Instance Court 2155/2014, *ISOCRATES*; and Kavala 1st Instance Court 440/2011, *Armenopoulos* 2012, 272.

139 See for instance Piraeus 1st Instance Court 4535 and 4715/2015, *Theory and Practice of Civil Law and Civil Procedure Law* 2014, 850 and 848.

140 Piraeus 1st Instance Court 721/2015, *Piraeus Court database*. Ad hoc S. VRELLIS, n. 30 above, 178.

for economic loss and additional expenses caused because of the accident. At the hearing, the applicant withdrew the proceedings with respect to the driver and the truck owner. The Thessaloniki court referred to the Rome II Regulation and concluded that, applying Article 4(3), the case was more closely connected with Romania: both the driver and the victim were Romanian citizens living in Romania, the vehicle was registered in Dolj County, Romania, and the green card (for insurance purposes) was issued by the Romanian authorities. Hence, Romanian law should be applied in the case at hand. However, due to the urgency of the matter, the court opted to apply Greek law, because it was not aware of the pertinent provisions under Romanian law, nor it was possible for the court to find them out on short notice, i.e. without ordering the production of relevant evidence, thus excessively delaying the pending proceedings. For the reasons stated above, the Thessaloniki court proceeded to the examination of the merits, applying fully and exclusively domestic law.[141]

What is probably most striking is that the court proceeded to the application of Greek law even though it had concluded that Romanian law should be applied. This is however a path followed almost religiously by Greek courts, which generally include an additional argument, namely that foreign law would presumably not deviate significantly from domestic legislation. Legal scholarship supports this position almost unanimously.[142] There are only a handful of suggestions that courts should use all the available means and exhaust all possible sources of information, especially by making use of technological tools, in order to find out the foreign law provisions applicable to the case at hand.[143]

A final remark on this point relates to Article 14 Rome II Regulation. The court omitted to make reference to Article 14(1) (freedom of choice by the parties). It is not clear from the text of the judgment whether the parties invoked Greek or Romanian law. Usually Greek lawyers tend to refer to the provisions of their own jurisdiction. Hence, if no issue of applicable law was raised by the parties, the court could have easily directly applied domestic law, without passing through the thorny corridors of Article 4 Rome II Regulation.

The universal application of the Rome II Regulation has been confirmed in many decisions,[144] including in a case involving a Danish company.

---

141 Thessaloniki 1st Instance Court 126/2016, *ISOCRATES*.

142 D. STAMATIADIS, 'Note to Thessaloniki 1st Instance Court 17171/2008' [2009] *Civil Procedure Law Review* 697 et seq.; P. YIANNOPOULOS, 'Note on Piraeus 1st Instance Court 56/2009' [2009] *Civil Procedure Law Review* 241.

143 K. GEORGIOU, 'The problem of application of Article 337 CCivP in summary proceedings: Note on Thessaloniki 1st Instance Court 467/2015' [2015] *Hellenic Justice* 1094.

144 See for instance Piraeus 1st Instance Court (three-member panel) 3707/2013, *Hellenic Justice* 2014, 1502; Piraeus 1st Instance Court (three-member panel) 3139/2015, *Piraeus Court database*; Thessaloniki 1st Instance Court (three-member panel), 9059/2014, *ISOCRATES*; and Piraeus 1st Instance Court (three-member panel) 1743/2014, *ISOCRATES*.

The court stated that the provisions of the Rome II Regulation applied in full, notwithstanding the fact that Denmark is not considered as a Member State for the purposes of the Regulation (Article 1(4)).[145]

2.9. RELATIONS WITH INTERNATIONAL CONVENTIONS

No pertinent Hague Convention has been ratified by the Hellenic Republic. Greek case law demonstrates a tendency to jointly invoke both international conventions (e.g. CISG) and conflict-of-laws rules. This stance has been criticised as lacking the proper methodological tools for the examination and determination of the proper applicable law.[146]

3. GENERAL EVALUATION

There have been no particular changes in the treatment of cases compared to the Rome Convention era, nor any obvious improvements or decline in standards following the introduction of the Rome I and Rome II Regulations. However, it should be noted that Greek courts are not yet sufficiently familiar with the developments brought in by the Regulations. They tend to apply the letter of the law, mostly influenced by the previous private international law regime, i.e. both the Rome Convention and domestic provisions (Articles 25–26 CC). Nevertheless, the situation is no worse than before the entry into force of the Regulations. Courts have not opted for different solutions; they simply follow the lines of previous case law, just changing the legal provisions they refer to.

4. CONCLUSION

4.1. SUMMARY OF FINDINGS

The major findings of the survey demonstrate an adherence by courts to the prioritisation of Greek law. To be sure, this is intertwined with immanent difficulties concerning the trying of a case on the basis of foreign law.

---

145 Piraeus 1st Instance Court 721/2015, *Piraeus Court database*. Ad hoc S. VRELLIS, n. 30 above, 178.

146 See S. LOISOU, 'Methodological aspects of treating contracts for the international sale of goods' = 'Μέθοδος προσέγγισης διαφορών από συμβάσεις διεθνούς πώλησης κινητών πραγμάτων' [2012] *Theory and Practice of Private Law* 990; I. THOMA, 'Relations between conflict of laws rules and uniform law' [2000] 53 *RHDI* 169.

No complaints may be expressed regarding unclear provisions. At the same time, it must be underlined that no case law has been ascertained on the interpretation of Articles 7, 9, 17, 18, 20, 21, 22, 23, 24, 25, 26, 27, 28 Rome II Regulation. Finally, no objections have been voiced regarding provisions that are out of line with recent policies changes.

4.2. MAIN RECOMMENDATIONS

From a national judicial perspective, initial and in-service training on cross-border disputes by the Training Institutes of the Judiciary could contribute to a better understanding of the Regulations. From a national legislative perspective, implementing legislation on the proper application of the Rome Regulations, as well as the development of a database encompassing reported and unreported domestic judgments, would undoubtedly lead to an improvement of the existing landscape. From an EU judicial perspective, the participation of Greek judges in initial and in-service training on cross-border disputes organised by the EJTN would promote awareness and facilitate access to the best practices of other Member State jurisdictions. From an EU legislative perspective, it is imperative to enhance the development of a database of reported and unreported judgments rendered by national courts.

THE APPLICATION OF THE ROME I AND ROME II REGULATIONS IN HUNGARY

Csongor István Nagy*

1. INTRODUCTION

Hungarian courts have produced a decent amount of case law on the application of the Rome I and Rome II Regulations. The Rome I Regulation has been applied in 26 published cases, and the Rome II Regulation in nine published cases.[1]

* The research for this article was supported by the project nr. EFOP-3.6.2-16-2017-00007, titled Aspects on the development of intelligent, sustainable and inclusive society: social, technological, innovation networks in employment and digital economy. The project has been supported by the European Union, co-financed by the European Social Fund and the budget of Hungary.

1 It has to be noted that while all Hungarian judgments are publicly available, court orders are not published, unless they are selected by one of the judicial collections. The court adopts an order when it does not decide on the merits of the case, for instance in the event that it terminates the proceedings on procedural grounds.

Before the entry into force of the Rome I Regulation, Hungarian courts applied the 1980 Rome Convention to contractual obligations. The Convention was promulgated in Hungary in 2006 by Act XXVIII of 2006 and entered into force on 1 June 2006. It remained applicable until 17 December 2009, when the Rome I Regulation replaced the Convention.

For long, Hungarian private international law[2] was included in Law-Decree[3] (Act) 13 of 1979 on Private International Law (the old Hungarian Act on Private International Law).[4] Recently, the Hungarian Parliament re-codified and adopted a new Act which came into effect on 1 January 2018 (the new Hungarian Act on Private International Law).[5]

2. STATUS AND TREATMENT OF FOREIGN LAW

According to Hungarian private international law, foreign law is to be applied in the form it is applied in the foreign country by foreign courts, i.e. not only the statutory language but also judicial practice and social context are to be taken into account.[6]

The forum is assumed to be *ex officio* familiar with its own law and to be its most authentic interpreter (*iura novit curia*). Nevertheless, in the case of foreign law, this may not be the case. Moreover, the application and identification of the foreign law might be burdensome. The question is who should bear the burden and risk of ascertaining the content of foreign law. In this regard, the starting point is the question whether foreign law is considered to be a factual or a legal issue. Facts are, in principle, to be proved by the parties and it is, normally, the plaintiff who bears the burden of proof. Legal questions do not have to be proved

2 For a general introduction into Hungarian private international law, see Csongor István Nagy, *Private International Law in Hungary* (Kluwer 2012).

3 Law-decrees are sources of law which have the same rank in the hierarchy of norms as the acts of the parliament; in fact, they can be regarded as statutes. Law-decrees cannot be issued anymore, however, as the power to adopt them was abolished in 1989. At the same time, several law-decrees adopted prior to this abolishment remain still in force. Law-decrees were adopted by the Presidential Council of the People's Republic in the period when the Parliament was adjourned, allowing the Presidential Council to regulate any matter with the exception of any amendment of the Constitution. This state of affairs ran counter to the principle of the separation of powers, hence its abolishment in 1989. Nevertheless, several important laws were adopted in this form and numerous international treaties were promulgated as law-decrees.

4 In Hungarian: *1979. évi 13. törvényerejű rendelet a nemzetközi magánjogról.*

5 Act XXVIII of 2018 on Private International Law (in Hungarian: *2017. évi XXVIII. törvény a nemzetközi magánjogról*).

6 Csongor István Nagy, *Nemzetközi magánjog* (HVG-Orac 2012), p. 37. Section 7(2) of the new Hungarian Act of Private International Law.

by the parties; though the latter may certainly make allegations, it is for the court to know and to interpret the law. Hungarian law is clear in this regard: foreign law is not a factual issue; Hungarian courts have to apply foreign law of their own motion (*ex officio*) and they bear the burden of ascertaining it.

Section 5 of the old Hungarian Act of Private International Law and Section 7 of the new Hungarian Act of Private International Law deals with the determination of foreign law and provide for different tools that were meant to help the court or administrative authority to determine the content of foreign law. The court may appoint an expert[7] familiar with the foreign law and take into account the allegations made and evidence submitted by the parties. The court may also contact the Minister of Justice, who can provide information about the foreign law. Although this is a tool of last resort, it is normally used in judicial practice automatically. The Minister of Justice contacts the state concerned for information. Hungary is party to the 1968 European Convention on Information on Foreign Law (London) and to its Strasbourg Protocol of 1978; hence, the Minister may seek information on the basis of the Convention.[8]

In Case *Pf.VI.26.608/2001/6*, the Supreme Court vacated the first instance judgment and remanded the case because the first instance court had failed to realise that there was an international element in the matter, and applied Hungarian law instead of German law, which was applicable in this case according to the Hungarian Act on Private International Law. In the judgment it was stressed that the court has to apply the foreign law of its own motion and hence the failure to apply the *lex causae* is a ground that necessitates the repetition of the entire evidentiary procedure.

In Case *Gf.4.30.112/2006/5*, the High Court of Appeal of Debrecen held that the court has to determine the content of foreign law of its own motion; hence, it cannot establish the content of the foreign law solely on the basis of the plaintiff's submission. The court is not relieved of the obligation to determine the content of foreign law *ex officio* even if there is no dispute between the parties as to the question of the applicable law. The Court stressed that the determination of the content of the foreign law is not the task of the parties but of the court.

Similarly to Section 5(3) of the old Hungarian Act on Private International Law, Section 7(3) of the new Hungarian Act on Private International Law provides that, if the content of the foreign law cannot be established within reasonable time, Hungarian law has to be applied. However, if the case cannot be adjudicated on the basis of the rules of Hungarian law, the law closest to the applicable law has to be applied.

---

7 Note that Hungarian civil procedural law follows the model of court-appointed experts, contrary to the common law notion of expert witness.

8 Promulgated by Government Decree 140 of 1992.

3. ROME I

The Rome I Regulation has been discussed in 42 published cases. The bulk of these matters raised no substantive issues of interpretation: in 14 cases the court established that the Rome I Regulation was not applicable *ratione temporis*,[9] while in 15 other cases the interpretation of the Regulation was clear.[10]

---

9 Case *Pf.20271/2014/3* (High Court of Appeal of Budapest), appealed from Case *P.20648/2011/40* (Budapest-Capital Regional Court); Case *G.40110/2013/45* (Zalaegerszeg Regional Court); Case *Pf.639898/2014/5* (Budapest-Capital Regional Court), appealed from Case *P.20986/2014/12* (Budapest District Court for the II and III Districts); Case *Gf.40100/2013/8* (High Court of Appeal of Budapest); Case *Pf.20267/2013/3* (High Court of Appeal of Győr); Case *B.12/2012/144* (Budapest Environs Regional Court); Case *G.20348/2013/83* (Győr Regional Court); Case *G.40138/2010/64* (Budapest Environs Regional Court); Case *Gf.30372/2012/7* (High Court of Appeal of Debrecen); Case *P.22877/2012/10* (Budapest-Capital Regional Court); Case *Pfv.20919/2015/6* (Supreme Court); Case *Pfv.22111/2015/12* (Supreme Court); Case *Pfv.V.20.366/2016/11* (Supreme Court), reported as BH 2017.5.155; Case *Pfv.20932/2017/12* (Supreme Court).

10 Case *Gf.40333/2015/5* (High Court of Appeal of Budapest), appealed from Case *G.42072/2014/17* (Budapest-Capital Regional Court) (The Court applied the law of the seller, which was Hungarian law.); Case *Pf.20074/2011/5* (High Court of Appeal of Győr), also reported as Case ÍH 2012.66 (An Austrian lawyer claimed an attorney's fee from his client; the Court applied Austrian law as the law of the service provider.); Case *Gf.20013/2015/4* (High Court of Appeal of Győr), appealed from Case *G.40031/2014/8* (Veszprém Court of Appeal) (As to a contract for the carriage of goods, the Court applied the law of the habitual residence of the person providing the service.); Case *Pf.20095/2015/5* (High Court of Appeal of Budapest) (The case contains references to the Rome I Regulation but the Court in fact applied the 1980 Rome Convention to a consumer contract and found that Hungarian law was applicable.); Case *Pf.20168/2013/5* (High Court of Appeal of Győr), appeal from Case *P.20197/2012/33* (Győr Regional Court) (Mere reference to the Rome I Regulation.); Case *Gf.30587/2013/4* (High Court of Appeal of Debrecen), appealed from Case *G.40186/2011/34* (Debrecen Regional Court) (The law applicable to the assignment was not to be established because the assigned claim was rejected.); Case *Gf.40117/2013/7* (High Court of Appeal of Budapest) (The cases concerned a contract of carriage and Hungarian law was applicable due to Article 5(1) of the Rome I Regulation; the Court also applied the COTIF-CÍM, promulgated in Hungary by Law-Decree 2 of 1986.); Case *G.40864/2008/169* (Budapest-Capital Regional Court); Case *G.40685/2012/38* (Budapest-Capital Regional Court) (The parties chose the applicable law.); Case *Pf.20234/2014/2* (Kaposvár Regional Court) (Absent party choice, the Court applied Hungarian law with reference to Article 4(1)(c) of the Rome I Regulation.); Case *Gf.40496/2012/5* (High Court of Appeal of Budapest), appealed from Case *G.40313/2011/27* (Budapest Environs Regional Court) (The Court applied the law of the seller's habitual residence, which was Slovak law.); Case *Gf.30147/2013/5* (High Court of Appeal of Szeged) (The law of the seller's habitual residence was applied, which was Hungarian law.); Case *G.40464/2015/16* (Budapest Environs Regional Court) (The parties chose Hungarian law at the trial.); Case *Mfv.10003/2017/5* (Supreme Court); Case *Gf.30475/2017/7* (High Court of Appeal of Debrecen) (The Court applied the seller's law, which was Hungarian law.); Case *Pf.20053/2018/13* (High Court of Appeal of Pécs) (The Court applied the law of the seller's habitual residence, which was Austrian law.); Case *G.40006/2017/35* (Szombathely Regional Court) (The Court wrongfully stated that since the case was governed by Hungarian law, Hungarian courts had jurisdiction.).

3.1. SCOPE OF APPLICATION

In Case *G.20348/2013/83*, the Rome I Regulation was not applicable *ratione temporis*. However, the Győr Regional Court, in *obiter dicta*, indicated that the Rome I Regulation would not apply anyway: one of the contracting parties was Austrian, but the other was from the Cayman Islands.

It seems that the court conceived the scope of the Rome I Regulation as applying only to EU matters. This stance appears to be flawed, since the Rome I Regulation has universal application and is applicable irrespective of whether the case has an EU element or not (Article 2 of the Rome I Regulation).

In Case *Gf.40063/2017/13*,[11] the dispute centred around the right of representation. The parties concluded a guarantee agreement, however, the signatory on the side of the guarantor had no right of representation. This question may be considered to fall out of the scope of the Rome I Regulation, as Article 1(2)(f) excludes, from the scope of the Regulation, 'questions governed by the law of companies', while Article 1(2)(g) excludes 'the question whether an agent is able to bind a principal, or an organ to bind a company or other body corporate or unincorporated, in relation to a third party.' Nonetheless, the High Court of Appeal of Budapest affirmed the Budapest-Capital Regional Court's judgment which extended the *lex contractus* established under the Rome I Regulation (Hungarian law) to the question of representation, presumably because the above issue qualifies as a contractual question[12] under Hungarian law.

3.2. DOMESTIC CONTRACTS

It is an interesting question of interpretation whether the branch of a foreign company qualifies as a foreign entity and, accordingly, whether as regards contracts between the branch and a domestic party the parties have the full right to choose the applicable law. Article 3(3)–(4) of the Rome I Regulation gives the parties the right to also choose the applicable law in domestic matters. However, if all the relevant elements of the case other than the choice itself are located in a country other than the one whose law was chosen, the parties' agreement will qualify as a 'choice in substantive sense' – unlike party choice in genuine international matters, where, as a principle, the chosen law has to be applied

---

11 Appealed from Case *G.42206/2012/102* (Budapest-Capital Regional Court).

12 Under Hungarian law, the actions of a person may bind the principal even if the former has no right of representation if the principal approves them either explicitly, or implicitly (that is, by indicative behavior). See Section 221(1) of the old Civil Code, which was applied in this case, and Section 6:14 of the Civil Code, the currently effective provision.

irrespective of the law applicable absent a party choice. Accordingly, as a matter of practice, it is crucial to establish whether the branch of a foreign company is a domestic or a foreign entity. Despite its considerable practical significance, this question has no judicial practice.

There are several rules in the Act on the Branch of Foreign Undertakings[13] that support the position that the branch of a foreign undertaking is not domestic. First, the branch is the foreign undertaking's organisational unit.[14] Second, the foreign undertaking pursues its entrepreneurial activities in Hungary through the branch;[15] consequently, at the end of the day, the actor is the foreign undertaking itself. Third, although the foreign undertaking, in principle, cannot dispose of the branch's property (assets, rights and obligations), it can do so in proceedings instituted abroad that are connected to the branch's property, rights and obligations.[16] Fourth, the foreign undertaking's liability for the branch's operation goes well beyond subsidiary liability; the foreign undertaking has to ensure steadily that the branch has the property necessary for its operation and it has joint and several liability with the branch for the latter's debts.[17] What is more, when effecting enforcement measures due to the debts of the branch, all assets of the foreign undertaking can be brought under enforcement.[18] Finally and interestingly, the fifth rule is that the branch's employees are legally employed by the foreign undertaking; accordingly, there is a substantial foreign element, at least as regards the employees' labour contract.[19]

Likewise, there are several arguments supporting the position that the branch is a domestic entity. First, the branch of the foreign undertaking is registered in the Hungarian company registry as a peculiar type of business organisation. Second, the branch is the subject of rights and obligations; although it has no legal personality, it has legal capacity. Its representatives act and sign in the name of the branch (and not in the name of the foreign undertaking). It is the branch that acts before the authorities and in legal relations with third parties.[20] Third, in principle, the foreign undertaking cannot dispose of the branch's property: the foreign undertaking can dispose of the property, rights and obligations acquired under the name of the branch only at the termination (winding-up)

---

13 Act CXXXII of 1997 on the Branch and Commercial Representation of Undertakings Seated Abroad (in Hungarian: *1997. évi CXXXII. törvény a külföldi székhelyű vállalkozások magyarországi fióktelepeiről és kereskedelmi képviseleteiről*).

14 Section 2(b) of Act CXXXII of 1997.

15 Section 3 of Act CXXXII of 1997.

16 Section 10(2) of Act CXXXII of 1997

17 Section 11(1) of Act CXXXII of 1997.

18 Section 11(3) of Act CXXXII of 1997.

19 Section 18(2) of Act CXXXII of 1997.

20 Section 3 of Act CXXXII of 1997.

of the branch and during insolvency proceedings.[21] Fourth, the branch cannot pursue representative activity on behalf of the foreign undertaking.[22]

The literature advocates the position that even though the status of the branch of a foreign undertaking is controversial, this business entity is deemed to be more domestic than not. Hence, in contracts between the branch of a foreign undertaking and a Hungarian company, the parties' stipulation of the applicable law will come under Article 3(3)–(4) of the Rome I Regulation.[23]

3.3. PARTY AUTONOMY

Hungarian private international law, in the field of contractual obligations, is traditionally based on party autonomy. The new Hungarian Act on Private International Law that came into effect on 1 January 2018 provides that the parties may choose the law applicable to the contract by the end of the procedure for the preparation of the case, within the deadline specified by the judge.[24] Arguably, this provision also governs cases that fall within the scope of the Rome I Regulation.

Hungarian courts have encountered various cases centring around the parties' implicit choice of law. In Case *Gf.40321/2014/9*,[25] the parties stipulated that the Hungarian Civil Code applied. The High Court of Appeal of Budapest considered this to be an implicit choice of Hungarian law. On the other hand, in Case *Gf.40051/2014/8*,[26] the High Court of Appeal of Pécs, when examining whether the parties had chosen German law, found the references to the German Civil Code (BGB) insufficient, because the contract also referred to the Hungarian Civil Code. The parties were Hungarian companies (seated and registered in Hungary) and entered into a construction contract, which used the *Vergabe- und Vertragsordnung für Bauleistungen* (VOB), a German standard contract worked out for construction projects. The VOB contains references to German law. The High Court of Appeal of Pécs held that that the references of the VOB to the provisions of the German Civil Code (BGB) were not sufficient to establish the choice of German law, as the contract also contained references

---

21 Section 10(2) of Act CXXXII of 1997.

22 Section 10(1) of Act CXXXII of 1997.

23 Csongor István Nagy, 'Külföldi-e a fióktelep: ki lehet-e kötni külföldi jogot a külföldi vállalkozás magyarországi fióktelepével kötött szerződésekben?', *Magyar Jog*, no. 5 (2011): 3–13 ('Is the branch a foreigner: can foreign law be stipulated in contracts concluded with the Hungarian branch of a foreign undertaking?').

24 Section 50(2) of the new Hungarian Act on Private International Law.

25 Appealed from Case *G.40368/2012/52* (Budapest-Capital Regional Court).

26 Appealed from Case *G.40161/2013/47* (Zalaegerszeg Regional Court).

to certain sources of Hungarian law. In Case *Pf.20370/2013/6*, the High Court of Appeal of Pécs apparently misconceived party autonomy and ignored the parties' choice of law without any detailed analysis. It also found that the contract was invalid because Austrian law was stipulated, which goes counter to the Rome I Regulation and the general principle that the law of the country to which the case is most closely connected has to be applied.

In Case *Pf.20024/2016/3*, the parties chose Austrian law in the contract but, during the civil procedure, jointly asked the court to apply Hungarian law concerning the question of validity. The High Court of Appeal of Pécs confirmed that the parties were free to choose different laws as to different parts of the contract or different issues of the contractual relationship.

In Case *Gf.40063/2017/13*,[27] the defendant, as the distributor's parent company, provided a guarantee (suretyship) to the supplier. In the distribution agreement the parties chose Austrian courts and Austrian law. The guarantee agreement, which was a separate contract, was not explicit as to the applicable law. While here the parties stipulated the exclusive jurisdiction of Hungarian courts, as to the applicable law, the guarantee agreement simply referred to the 'Act of the Civil Code'. The High Court of Appeal of Budapest found that, taking into account the circumstances of the case, the above clause embedded an implicit choice of Hungarian law. The parties chose Hungarian courts and one of them, the party seeking a security, was Hungarian. The Court found that it could be reasonably inferred that the term 'Act of the Civil Code' referred to the Hungarian Civil Code and, in turn, the parties implicitly chose Hungarian law.

In Case *P.25471/2015/47*, the Budapest-Capital Regional Court held that the law chosen by the parties does bind third parties. Contrary to choice-of-court agreements, which involve the derogation of jurisdiction, which, as a waiver of right, cannot bind non-parties, in choice of law, the parties' agreement cannot be conceived as a mutual waiver of a right and it qualifies as a connecting factor and, as such, determines the applicable law *erga omnes*.

In Case *Gfv.VII.30.130/2016*,[28] in relation to a claim that was submitted in the frame of an insolvency procedure, the Supreme Court established that it was the party's duty to refer to any choice-of-law agreement and submit the pertinent evidence; this implies that in case, according to the applicable rules of procedure, no new fact may be raised, the party is barred from referring to the choice-of-court agreement.[29]

27 Appealed from Case *G.42206/2012/102* (Budapest-Capital Regional Court).
28 Reported as BH 2017.3.97.
29 Para. 23.

3.4. OBJECTIVE CONNECTING FACTORS

In Case *Gf.20100/2017/5*, the defendant, a Hungarian company, was a contractor of a construction project in Romania and hired the plaintiff, a German company, as sub-contractor. The High Court of Appeal of Győr held that the works contract between the Hungarian contractor and the German sub-contractor was governed by German law, as this was the law of the party providing the characteristic performance (Article 4(2) of the Rome II Regulation). It found that the circumstances, that the contract was concluded in Hungary and that the construction was coordinated by the Hungarian company and it was related, in economic terms, to another construction contract, were irrelevant.

3.5. ESCAPE CLAUSE

In Case *Pfv.V.20.594/2017/6*,[30] the plaintiff, a German national, and a Hungarian company concluded a contract where the plaintiff promised to establish a company in Russia and to become the managing director of this company (as well as acquire a work permit). The plaintiff's place of living could not be ascertained on the basis of the fact of the case, it was either Germany or Russia. The parties did not choose the applicable law.

The Supreme Court held that Hungarian law was applicable. Article 4(1)(b) of the Rome I Regulation refers to the law of the service provider's habitual residence, hence, either Russian or German law should have been applied, as the plaintiff's place of business could not be clearly ascertained. Nonetheless, this question was jumped on by the Supreme Court, as it found that 'the contract is manifestly more closely connected with' Hungary and, hence, due to Article 4(3) of the Rome I Regulation, Hungarian law applied.

The Supreme Court reasoned that the contract had no connection to either German or Russian law. The parties envisaged entering into an employment contract under Russian law once the plaintiff acquired the necessary work permit and concluded the mandate contract for the interim period. When concluding the contract, the parties were aware of the possibility to choose the applicable law. For the employment contract to be concluded after the acquisition of the work permit, they wished to stipulate Russian law but did not choose the applicable law for the provisional service agreement. In fact, the purpose of the latter was to avoid breaching the Russian rules on employment (the contract was concluded between the plaintiff and the defendant and not the plaintiff and the Russian company that was supposed to be his later employer). The Court inferred that

30 Reported as BH 2018.9.250.

the reason why the parties did not choose the applicable law for the service contract was that they considered it to be truly provisional and considered the choice of the applicable law not to be relevant. The Supreme Court noted that this also underpinned the conclusion that the business relationship between the parties and the contractual construction was more closely connected to the defendant's personal law, that is, Hungarian law.[31]

3.6. IMPERATIVE NORMS

In Case *Gf.20062/2015/8*, the 1980 Rome Convention was applied, but the High Court of Appeal of Győr also referred to the Rome I Regulation when interpreting the Convention, specifically as to the concept of imperative norms.

Austrian law was applicable to the case. Contrary to the defendants' allegations, the court established that the Hungarian rules on the coming into existence, form, validity, substantive elements, rights and obligations, their performance and the termination of the legal relationship did not meet the requirements of Article 9(1) of the Rome I Regulation. Furthermore, the court also held that the application of the imperative rules is warranted chiefly in cases where the parties choose the law of a state to which the fact pattern has no connection. This condition was not met either, since the fact pattern, through the plaintiff and its business activity, was connected to Austria.

In Case *Gf.40608/2017/12*, the plaintiff sought a declaratory judgment establishing that due to the civil war in Libya and the embargo measures adopted by the European Union against Libya, it was freed from the duties emerging from the bank guarantee it issued. Although, in the declaration, the bank chose Libyan law, in its statement of claim, it relied exclusively on the European embargo measures without any reference to Libyan law and argued that the latter was irrelevant in relation to its request for a declaratory judgment. The High Court of Appeal of Budapest held that the provisions of the Libyan Embargo Regulation[32] qualify as imperative norms under Article 9 of the Rome I Regulation and, as such, replace the rules of the applicable law. However, the Court also noted that the impact of these rules on the plaintiff's contractual obligations can be established only on the basis of the joint interpretation of these imperative norms and the rules of *lex causae*, as the public policy exception enshrined in Article 21 of the Rome I Regulation does not rule out the application of the *lex causae* in its totality.

---

31 Para. 52.

32 Regulation 204/2011 of 2 March 2011 concerning restrictive measures in view of the situation in Libya. [2011] OJ L 58, pp. 1-13.

3.7. NATIONAL CHOICE-OF-LAW RULES

The old Hungarian Act on Private International Law was amended in 2009[33] in order to align it with the Rome I Regulation. Legally speaking, there cannot be a contradiction between the Hungarian Act and the Regulation, since the latter is directly applicable throughout the EU and has supremacy over Member State law. Nevertheless, the Hungarian legislator still considered it to be desirable to amend the Act on Private International Law. The new rules of the Act entered into force in step with the Rome I Regulation: they have been applicable as from 17 December 2009.

Section 24 of the old Act states the obvious: its rules on contractual relations are applicable to matters not covered by the Rome I Regulation. The general rule is party autonomy.[34] Sections 26–27 establish conflict rules concerning different types of contracts. Contracts concluded on stock exchange, tender or auction are governed by the law of the place where the exchange is located or the tender or auction is organised. Articles of association are governed by the law of the company's place of operation (however, the articles of association of a legal person are governed by the personal law of the legal person). The existence and extent of obligations based on negotiable instruments are governed by the law of the place of performance. Rights and obligations based on bonds issued on the basis of public loans come under the personal law of the issuer. *In rem* effects concerning negotiable instruments ensuring the right to dispose of goods (e.g. bills of lading, warehouse receipts) come under the Act's provisions on property law. Negotiable instruments embodying membership rights (e.g. shares) are governed by the legal person's personal law. Section 28 provides that all contracts not covered by the foregoing provisions are governed by the law to which the contract is most closely connected according to the substantial elements of the given contractual relationship. Sections 29(1) and (3) of the Act define the reach of the *lex contractus*.

Section 29(2) of the Act contains special connecting factors regarding formal validity; the determination of these subsidiary factors is led by the desire to save the contract. If the contract is invalid under the *lex contractus*, it is to be regarded as valid if it complies with the formal requirements of the *lex fori*, of the place where the contract was concluded or where the targeted legal effects are to emerge.

Unilateral declarations are governed by the same conflict rules as contracts, unless the Act on Private International Law provides otherwise.[35]

---

33 Act IX of 2009.

34 Section 25 of the Hungarian Act of Private International Law.

35 Section 30 of the Hungarian Act of Private International Law.

The new Act on Private International Law aligns itself with the regime of the Rome I Regulation. The general principle is party autonomy, which may be explicit or implicit (clearly ascertainable from the contract's provisions or the circumstances of the case) and may cover the whole contract or part of it. The parties may choose the law applicable to the contract by the end of the procedure for the preparation of the case, within the deadline specified by the judge. If the contract is connected only to a single country, the parties' choice of the applicable law may not impair the mandatory rules of that country.[36] Absent party choice, the contract is governed by the law of the country to which the contract, due to its substantial elements, is most closely connected.[37]

3.8. CONCLUSION

Hungarian courts have encountered the Rome I Regulation in numerous cases and applied it without substantive issues. In Case *G.20348/2013/83*, the Győr Regional Court erroneously suggested that the Rome I Regulation would not apply to cases with a significant non-EU element. A similar error can be perceived in Case *Pf.20370/2013/6*, where the High Court of Appeal of Pécs suggested that the parties may choose only the law that is connected to the matter.

4. ROME II

The survey of the publicly available judgments produced 12 Hungarian cases where a reference was made to the Rome II Regulation. In half of these cases, no substantive issues of interpretation emerged: in one of the cases the court established that the Rome II Regulation was not applicable *ratione temporis*,[38] while in five other cases the interpretation of the Regulation raised no substantive issues.[39]

4.1. SCOPE OF APPLICATION AND CHARACTERISATION

In Case *P.24487/2012/47*, the Hungarian plaintiff sued a Greek hospital for medical malpractice that occurred in Greece. The plaintiff was spending his

36 Section 50 of the new Hungarian Act of Private International Law.

37 Section 51 of the new Hungarian Act of Private International Law.

38 Case *Gf.40013/2015/15* (High Court of Appeal of Pécs).

39 Case *Pf.20095/2015/5* (High Court of Appeal of Budapest); Case *Gf.40117/2013/7* (High Court of Appeal of Budapest); Case *Pf.20174/2011/10* (High Court of Appeal of Győr); Case *G.40057/2012/118* (Debrecen Regional Court); Case *Pf.21326/2017/9* (High Court of Appeal of Budapest).

vacation in Greece and suffered serious injuries in a traffic accident. In the hospital, he was mistreated, which resulted in his permanent bodily injury. The case could have given rise to both contractual and delictual claims against the hospital. The Budapest-Capital Regional Court avoided deciding the issue whether the claim was contractual or delictual in nature (or both). It identified the applicable law both under the Rome II Regulation and the conflicts rules of contracts (the case occurred before the Rome I Regulation's entry into force) and concluded that both led to the same law (Greek law).

Issues of characterisation and scope emerged in cases involving traffic accidents. The courts have considered the law applicable to delictual liability to extend to the rules on compulsory motor vehicle liability insurance. While in the cases encountered by the courts this entailed no practical problems (because the *lex contractus* for the insurance contract and the law applicable to the tort were the same), this summary approach will have to be rectified in cases where the tortfeasor's insurance contract is governed by a law different from that of the tort.

In Case *Pfv.20852/2014/6*,[40] although both the tortfeasor and the victim were Hungarian citizens and the accident happened in Hungary, the Supreme Court examined the question of applicable law, as the car owned by the plaintiff was registered in Germany. The Supreme Court held that Hungarian law was applicable to the claim and, as part of that, also applied Act LXII of 2009 on Mandatory Motor Vehicle Liability Insurance. Interestingly, the Act addresses various issues related to the motor vehicle liability insurance contract: the duty to have insurance coverage, the conclusion and termination of the insurance contract, the insurance company's payment obligation and extent, the geographical and temporal scope of the insurance contract, the payment of the insurance fee, the insurance company's right of subrogation, etc.

Although in the case concerned this made no substantive difference, it has to be noted that the court's reference appears to have been excessive and treating the rules on mandatory motor vehicle insurance as delictual in nature may be regarded as an error of characterisation. Specifically, the Rome II Regulation determines the law applicable to non-contractual obligations (the relationship between the tortfeasor and the injured person) and does not apply to contractual obligations (the relationship between the tortfeasor and the insurance company it has a contract with). It may have made a difference (which could have made the Supreme Court engage in a more detailed characterisation) if the tortfeasor had been stationed in another Member State and he had had a contract with a foreign insurance company.

---

40 Appealed from Case *Pf.640701/2013/4* (Budapest-Capital Regional Court).

The same was established in Case *Pf.641647/2013/4*, where the Budapest-Capital Regional Court applied Hungarian law (as the place of the accident) and the Hungarian rules on mandatory motor vehicle liability insurance.

4.2. PARTY AUTONOMY

The new Hungarian Act on Private International Law that came into effect on 1 January 2018 provides that the parties may choose the law applicable to the non-contractual obligation by the end of the procedure for the preparation of the case, within the deadline specified by the judge.[41] Arguably, this provision also governs cases that fall within the scope of the Rome II Regulation.

The new Act establishes the same time limit in relation to Article 7 of the Rome II Regulation. In cases concerning environmental damages, the person seeking compensation may choose to base his claim on the law of the country in which the event giving rise to the damage occurred. This right may be exercised by the end of the procedure for the preparation of the case, within the deadline specified by the judge.[42]

Hungarian courts have been very permissive in relation to party autonomy in tort cases. In Case *P.21013/2011/49*, the parties requested the application of Hungarian law, which the Győr Regional Court treated as a choice-of-law agreement under Article 14(1) of the Rome II Regulation. In Case *Pf.631007/2014/3*,[43] the parties chose Hungarian law in the second instance procedure and the Budapest-Capital Regional Court considered this a valid choice. It should be noted that the court of first instance applied Hungarian law as the law applicable absent the parties' choice; the court of second instance disagreed with the first instance court on this, but accepted the parties' agreement on the application of Hungarian law.

This approach sanctioning a belated party choice goes against the scholarship's majority opinion on the old Hungarian Act on Private International Law that the law can be chosen the latest until the first instance judgment is entered[44] and, as from 1 January 2018, was superseded by the new Hungarian Act on Private International Law, which, as noted above, provides that such a choice may be made only by the end of the procedure for the preparation of the case, within the deadline specified by the judge.[45]

41 Section 63(2) of the new Hungarian Act on Private International Law.

42 Section 59 of the new Hungarian Act on Private International Law.

43 Appealed from Case *P.89765/2012/31* (Central District Court of Pest).

44 Csongor István Nagy, *Private International Law in Hungary* (Kluwer 2012), pp. 76–77, para. 158.

45 Section 63(2) of the new Hungarian Act on Private International Law.

4.3. OBJECTIVE CONNECTING FACTORS

In Case *P.24487/2012/47*, when it came to the application of the principle of *lex loci damni*, the Budapest-Capital Regional Court, in line with preamble (17) of the Rome II Regulation, took solely the direct damages into account (personal injury in Greece) and considered the indirect (consequential) damages occurring in Hungary to be irrelevant in the context of determining the applicable law.

In Case *Pfv.V.20.490/2018/10*,[46] the Supreme Court held, in the context of a traffic accident that occurred in Germany, that the existence and extent of delictual liability is governed by the Rome II Regulation and, hence, German law applied irrespective of whether the injured person sues the tortfeasor or the insurer directly. It also held that default interests come under Article 15(c) of the Rome II Regulation and, hence, in this case they were governed by German law.

4.4. NATIONAL CHOICE-OF-LAW RULES

The old Hungarian Act on Private International Law was amended in 2009[47] in order to align it with the Rome II Regulation. Legally speaking, there cannot be any contradiction between the Act and the Regulation, since the latter is directly applicable throughout the EU and has supremacy over Member State law. Nevertheless, the Hungarian legislator still considered it to be desirable to amend the Act. Unfortunately, the new rules of the Act did not enter into force in step with the Rome II Regulation: they have been applicable as from 4 April 2009, while the Regulation entered into force on 11 January 2009. Nonetheless, there is no doubt that the Rome II Regulation has supremacy over the national provisions and, hence, in its scope of application, it displaced them on 11 January 2009.

The amendment of 2009, in essence, preserved the traditional Hungarian approach to torts (*lex loci delicti commissi*) and did not extend the Rome II Regulation's approach (*lex loci damni*) beyond its scope of application. Currently, these two regimes operate in parallel. However, the new Hungarian Act on Private International Law that came into effect on 1 January 2018 aligns itself with the Rome II Regulation.

The old Hungarian Act on Private International Law provided for the following rules concerning the law applicable to torts. Section 32 of the Act states the obvious: its rules on non-contractual relations are applicable to matters not covered by the Rome II Regulation. Sections 33–34 essentially preserve the

---

46 Reported as BH 2019.10.270.

47 Act IX of 2009.

approach of the Act's old rules: the general rule is the *lex loci delicti commissi* (where *delictum* implies both conduct and omission), which is supplemented by the ubiquity principle (the law of the country where the damages occurred, i.e. the *lex loci damni*, is to be applied if it is more favourable to the injured person), the notion of common domicile (common place of living) and the application of the *lex bandi* in the case of registered watercrafts and aircrafts. Special connecting factors are applied to the question whether a person is capable of being liable for the loss and to traffic regulations. If under the law of the place where the damaging conduct or omission occurred liability is based on fault, tortious capacity can be established either on the basis of the tortfeasor's personal law or the law of the place of violation. Furthermore, the issue of whether the allegedly tortious conduct violated the traffic regulations or other security rules is governed by the law of the place of the delict/tort.

The provisions on unjust enrichment were completely repealed.

The new Act on Private International Law provides that non-contractual obligations are governed by the law of the country where the effect of the legal fact entailing the obligation occurred.[48] The law of common habitual residence has to be applied if the obligor and the obligee have their habitual residence or registered seat in the same country at the time of the occurrence of the legal fact entailing the obligation.[49] If the non-contractual obligation is closely linked to a legal relationship that existed at the time the legal fact entailing the obligation occurred, the non-contractual obligation will also be governed by that other legal relationship.[50]

The parties may choose the applicable law after the occurrence of the legal fact entailing the obligation. At this point, the new Hungarian Act on Private International Law departs from the rules of the Rome II Regulation, as the latter permit undertakings to stipulate the applicable law also before the occurrence of the damage.[51] The choice has to be made by the end of the procedure for the preparation of the case, within the deadline specified by the judge. If the legal relationship is connected only to a single country, the parties' choice may not violate the mandatory rules of that country.[52]

It should be noted that the law applicable to violations of personality rights (a subject excluded from the scope of the Rome II Regulation)[53] is not covered

48 Section 60 of the new Hungarian Act on Private International Law.

49 Section 61 of the new Hungarian Act on Private International Law.

50 Section 62 of the new Hungarian Act on Private International Law.

51 Article 14 of the Rome II Regulation.

52 Section 63 of the new Hungarian Act on Private International Law.

53 According to Article 1(2)(g) of the Rome II Regulation, 'non-contractual obligations arising out of violations of privacy and rights relating to personality, including defamation' shall be excluded from the Regulation's scope.

by the choice-of-law rules applicable to torts. The approach of the Hungarian Act on Private International Law in the field of personality rights is twofold. On the one hand, the existence of the individual personality rights comes under the purview of personal law.[54] On the other hand, the legal consequences of the violation of personality rights (as this is a question having delictual features) are governed by the law of the place where the violation was committed. If Hungarian law is more favourable to the injured person (in terms of damages or satisfaction), Hungarian law must be applied. According to Section 10(3) of the Act, claims emerging from the violation of personality rights are governed by the law of the place and time of the violation; nevertheless, if Hungarian law is more favourable to the injured party as regards damages or satisfaction, the claim is to be adjudicated according to this law.

The new Act on Private International Law aims to adopt an arrangement that complies with the principles set out in the judgment of the CJEU in *e-Date* and *Martinez*.[55] Although this ruling, as to choice of law, dealt solely with the E-Commerce Directive[56] and is, hence, applicable only to online violations of personality rights, it inspired the rules of the new Hungarian Act in general. According to these, violations of personality rights are governed by the law of the victim's place of habitual residence (in the case of legal persons, the law of the registered seat). This law governs the question whether a violation occurred and the legal consequences of this. The victim may, by the end of the procedure for the preparation of the case, within the deadline specified by the judge, choose the law of the country where the centre of his main interests is located, or the law of the country where the tortfeasor's habitual residence (the registered seat in the case of legal persons) is to be found, or Hungarian law. These rules apply also in case there is a danger that the personality rights will be violated.[57]

4.5. CONCLUSION

Issues of characterisation emerged in matters involving traffic accidents (distinction between the tort and the motor vehicle liability insurance). Hungarian courts have treated these issues in a rather summary manner, as the characterisation appeared to have no impact on the final outcome of the case.

---

54 Sections 10(1) and 18(1) of the Hungarian Act of Private International Law.

55 Joined Cases C-509/09 and C-161/10, *eDate Advertising GmbH v. X and Olivier Martinez and Robert Martinez v. MGN Limited.*

56 Directive 2000/31/EC of the European Parliament and of the Council of 8 June 2000 on certain legal aspects of information society services, in particular electronic commerce, in the Internal Market ('Directive on electronic commerce') [2000] OJ L 178/1.

57 Section 23 of the new Hungarian Act on Private International Law.

Hungarian courts have been very permissive in relation to party autonomy. The parties could choose the applicable law during the procedure, and in one case the court sanctioned a choice-of-law agreement concluded in the second instance proceeding. However, the new Hungarian Act on Private International Law that came into effect on 1 January 2018 has introduced a stricter time-bar (the law applicable may be chosen by the end of the procedure for the preparation of the case, within the deadline specified by the judge).

THE APPLICATION OF THE ROME I AND ROME II REGULATIONS IN IRELAND

Máire Ní Shúilleabháin

1. THE NATIONAL LANDSCAPE

While jurisdiction disputes have long been a regular feature of Irish litigation practice (and judges are very familiar with this aspect of private international law), the same cannot be said of choice of law. The reality is that choice-of-law disputes, particularly in tort matters, were, until recently, very rare indeed in the Irish legal context.[1]

The adoption of the Rome I and II Regulations (and the 1980 Rome Convention on the Law Applicable to Contractual Obligations) appears to have increased awareness of potential choice-of-law dimensions to contract and tort disputes. The volume of case law on choice-of-law questions has increased dramatically, albeit from an extremely low base. One would expect, therefore, that the Irish courts (and Irish legal practitioners) will soon develop a more in-depth understanding of choice-of-law principles (particularly as EU Court of Justice guidance becomes more readily available). However, as things stand, some of the Irish jurisprudence is rather rudimentary and exhibits signs of a preference for the application of the *lex fori*,[2] and a tendency to conceptualise foreign laws by reference to their similarities (or dissimilarities) to the *lex fori*.[3]

There are no national rules facilitating the application of Rome I and Rome II in Ireland.[4] There has been no extension of the rules laid down in Rome I and Rome II into areas beyond the scope of these instruments. There have been seven cases[5] before the Irish courts in which the Rome II Regulation has been considered, and five[6] where the Rome I Regulation has been considered. There are also some Irish decisions applying the 1980 Rome Convention that may be of use in interpreting the Rome I Regulation.[7]

---

1 See W. Binchy, *Irish Conflicts of Law*, Butterworths, Dublin 1988, pp. 517–582; L. Heffernan, 'Rome II: Implications for Irish Tort Litigation' in J. Ahern and W. Binchy (eds.), *The Rome II Regulation on the Law Applicable to Non-Contractual Obligations*, Martinus Nijhoff, Leiden 2009, pp. 257–276.

2 See e.g. *AIB v. Diamond* [2011] IEHC 505; [2012] 3 IR 549 and *Kelly v. Groupama* [2012] IEHC 177 discussed below. Commenting on *Kelly v. Groupama*, Danaher has observed that contrary to the expectation of an all-consuming *lex causae* under Rome II, 'there would still appear to be some fight left in the forum' (see G. Danaher, 'Accidents Abroad and the Assessment of Damages' (2012) 17(5) *Bar Review* 109, 113).

3 See e.g. *ICDL GCC Foundation FZ-LLC v. European Computer Driving Licence Foundation* [2011] IEHC 343, para. 10.3; *Kelly v. Groupama* [2012] IEHC 177, para. 16.

4 The 1980 Rome Convention was given force of law through the Contractual Obligations (Applicable Law) Act 1991.

5 *ICDL GCC Foundation FZ-LLC v. European Computer Driving Licence Foundation* [2011] IEHC 343; *AIB v. Diamond* [2011] IEHC 505; [2012] 3 IR 549; *Kelly v. Groupama* [2012] IEHC 177; *SPV Sam Dragon v. GE Transportation Finance (Ireland) Ltd* [2012] IEHC 240; *C&F Green Energy v. Bakker Magnetic* [2015] IEHC 773; *Unicredit Global Leasing Export GmbH v. Business Aviation Ltd* [2019] IEHC 139; *HKR Middle East Architects Engineering LC v. English* [2019] IEHC 306.

6 *AIB v. Diamond* [2011] IEHC 505; [2012] 3 IR 549; *C&F Green Energy v. Bakker Magnetic* [2015] IEHC 773; *Colclough v. The Association of Chartered Certified Accountants* [2018] IEHC 85; *Defender Ltd v. HSBC Institutional Trust Services (Ireland) Ltd* [2018] IEHC 706; *Unicredit Global Leasing Export GmbH v. Business Aviation Ltd* [2019] IEHC 139.

7 See e.g. *McDonald v. AZ Sint Elisabeth Hospital* [2015] IEHC 62; *Zimmerman v. Der Deutsche Schulverein* (1999) 10 ELR 211.

The author is not aware of any decisions of the Irish courts which should have applied Rome I or Rome II but which applied the former national rules in error. The existing Irish case law tends to focus with some care on the date of coming into force of each instrument[8] – although in one case it appeared to be assumed that the Rome I Regulation applied in circumstances where the contracts at issue were likely to have been concluded prior to 17 December 2009.[9]

The Irish cases on Rome II have focused mainly on Article 4,[10] but have also addressed Articles 6,[11] 10[12] and 15.[13] Articles 3, 4, 9 and 12 of Rome I have been considered.[14]

At this juncture it is useful to recall that Ireland, in line with its common law traditions, has an adversarial rather than an inquisitorial legal system. It follows that the onus is on the parties to the litigation to raise questions of foreign law and to adduce expert evidence of the content of the relevant foreign law.[15] The court cannot of its own motion investigate the foreign law. Therefore, in Ireland, the application of Rome I and Rome II depends on these instruments being invoked by legal practitioners (and on the willingness of clients to provide the extra funds necessary to the proof of foreign law). If there is no (or insufficient) evidence as to the content of a foreign law applicable pursuant to Rome I or Rome II, the Irish judge will apply the *lex fori*.[16]

---

8 See *McDonald v. AZ Sint Elisabeth Hospital* [2015] IEHC 62, para. 2; *Kelly v. Groupama* [2012] IEHC 177, para. 10.

9 *AIB v. Diamond* [2011] IEHC 505; [2012] 3 IR 549. This case concerned the employment contracts of some senior employees of the plaintiff bank. There was no suggestion that they were all recent recruits at the time of the litigation in 2011; yet it appeared to be assumed that the Rome I Regulation was potentially applicable.

10 *ICDL GCC Foundation FZ-LLC v. European Computer Driving Licence Foundation* [2011] IEHC 343; *AIB v. Diamond* [2011] IEHC 505; [2012] 3 IR 549; *SPV Sam Dragon v. GE Transportation Finance (Ireland) Ltd* [2012] IEHC 240; *C&F Green Energy v. Bakker Magnetic* [2015] IEHC 773.

11 *AIB v. Diamond* [2011] IEHC 505; [2012] 3 IR 549.

12 *Unicredit Global Leasing Export GmbH v. Business Aviation Ltd* [2019] IEHC 139; *HKR Middle East Architects Engineering LC v. English* [2019] IEHC 306.

13 *Kelly v. Groupama* [2012] IEHC 177 (Article 15 was not explicitly mentioned in this case but the case was concerned with the assessment of damages under the applicable law).

14 *C&F Green Energy v. Bakker Magnetic* [2015] IEHC 773; *AIB v. Diamond* [2011] IEHC 505; [2012] 3 IR 549; *Colclough v. The Association of Chartered Certified Accountants* [2018] IEHC 85; *Defender Ltd v. HSBC Institutional Trust Services (Ireland) Ltd* [2018] IEHC 706; *Unicredit Global Leasing Export GmbH v. Business Aviation Ltd* [2019] IEHC 139.

15 See W. Binchy, *Irish Conflicts of Law*, Butterworths, Dublin 1988, pp. 104–118; *Kutchera v. Buckingham International Holdings* [1988] IR 61, 68; *Nestorway v. Ambaflex* [2006] IEHC 235; M. Sychold, 'Ireland' in Swiss Institute of Comparative Law, *The Application of Foreign Law in Civil Matters in the EU Member States and its Perspectives for the Future*, JLS/2009/JCIV/PR/0005/E4, Lausanne 2011, pp. 247–262, available at <http://ec.europa.eu/justice/civil/files/foreign_law_en.pdf>.

16 See W. Binchy, *Irish Conflicts of Law*, Butterworths, Dublin 1988, p. 113; *Kutchera v. Buckingham International Holdings* [1988] IR 61, 68. But see also *HKR Middle East Architects Engineering LC v. English* [2019] IEHC 306, para. 382 et seq.

2. THE OPERATION OF ROME I AND ROME II IN PRACTICE

2.1. *LOIS DE POLICE* (OVERRIDING MANDATORY PROVISIONS)

Section 23 of the Sale of Goods and Supply of Services Act 1980 furnishes an example of an Irish 'overriding mandatory provision' which is expressed to be applicable even in the event of the governing law being a foreign law. Section 23 inserts a new section 55A into the Sale of Goods Act 1893, as follows:

> 'Where the proper law of a contract of sale of goods would, apart from a term that it should be the law of some other country or a term to the like effect, be the law of Ireland ... sections 12 to 15 and 55 ... of this Act ... shall, notwithstanding that term ... apply to the contract.'[17]

Sections 12–15 and 55 impose mandatory implied terms as to title, quality and description of goods in certain circumstances. Section 24 of the 1980 Act inserts a new section 61(6) into the 1893 Act allowing an exception to section 55A for certain international sales contracts between businesses located in different countries.

Statutory instruments giving effect to EU consumer protection measures also include clauses giving overriding mandatory effect to the domestic instrument: see for example Regulation 4 of the European Communities (Certain Aspects of the Sale of Consumer Goods and Associated Guarantees) Regulations 2003 (Statutory Instrument No. 11 of 2003) and Regulation 7 of the European Communities (Unfair Terms in Consumer Contracts) Regulations 1995 (Statutory Instrument No. 27 of 1995).

Zimmerman v. Der Deutsche Schulverein[18] furnishes an example of an Irish tribunal suggesting (by analogy with the Court of Justice judgment in *Ingmar v. Eaton Leonard*)[19] that legislative provisions having mandatory effect are to be elevated to the status of overriding mandatory provisions. This case was concerned with the interpretation of the 1980 Rome Convention and, as discussed below, Irish employment legislation was considered to be applicable pursuant to Article 6(1) notwithstanding an express choice of German law. However, the Irish Tribunal also suggested that the relevant legislation (which precluded any contracting out – but did not specify that it should apply even in the event of a choice of foreign law) should be applicable pursuant to Article 7(2) of the Rome Convention.

---

17 See also section 42 of the 1980 Act which gives overriding mandatory effect to sections 39 and 40 of the 1980 Act laying down implied terms for the benefit of recipients of services.

18 (1999) 10 ELR 211.

19 Case C-381/98, ECLI:EU:C:2000:605.

In *Colclough v. The Association of Chartered Certified Accountants*[20] it was determined that rights under the Constitution of Ireland (*Bunreacht na hÉireann*) could not operate as 'overriding mandatory provisions' under Article 9 Rome I. This is because constitutional rights may be waived.

Beyond the general pronouncements in the *Colclough* case, there is as yet no Irish case law on Article 9(3) Rome I. Ireland had entered a reservation on Article 7(1) of the Rome Convention, citing the 'vagueness and uncertainty that would result from its application'.[21] However, there is Irish common law authority which supports the non-enforcement of a contract which is valid under the proper law but illegal at the place of performance.[22]

2.2. PARTY AUTONOMY

2.2.1. Challenges to Choice-of-Law Clauses under Rome I

In the context of determining jurisdiction under the Brussels I Convention and Regulation, the Irish courts have often been faced with arguments that an alleged jurisdiction clause was not agreed at all,[23] or if it was agreed, is not applicable to the dispute at hand.[24] A recent case, *C&F Green Energy v. Bakker Magnetic*[25] suggests that similar arguments are likely to be made where one party seeks to rely on a choice-of-law clause. In *C&F Green Energy* the parties were in dispute respecting the supply of magnets to an Irish manufacturer of wind turbines. The Irish plaintiff claimed that the magnets were defective, a charge denied by the Dutch defendant who claimed that the Irish plaintiff had failed to comply with its payment obligations. Following the initiation of proceedings in Ireland, the Dutch defendant sought to rely on a choice of Dutch law included in the defendant's general conditions of sale. The defendant argued that these general conditions were incorporated into the contract because of their attachment to a series of quotations delivered by email and their inclusion in their order confirmation forms. The plaintiff sought to characterise the emails relied upon by the defendant as merely pre-contractual correspondence, and it argued that its orders for goods were not made subject to the condition importing Dutch law.

---

20 [2018] IEHC 85, para. 55.

21 See 407 *Dáil Debates* Col. 1938; G. Hogan, 'Contractual Obligations (Applicable Law) Act 1991' (annotation), *Irish Current Law Statutes Annotated* (edited by R. Clark), Round Hall, Dublin 1991; section 2(2) Contractual Obligations (Applicable Law) Act 1991.

22 See *Stanhope v. Hospitals Trust Ltd* [1936] Ir Jur Rep 25; *Apicella v. Scala* (1931) 66 ILTR 33 discussed by W. Binchy, *Irish Conflicts of Law*, Butterworths, Dublin 1988, pp. 546–547.

23 See e.g. *Unidare v. Scott* [1991] 2 IR 88; *Ryanair v. Billigfluege* [2010] IEHC 47; *Grosso v. Lamsouguer* [2012] IEHC 230; *Ryanair v. On the Beach* [2013] IEHC 124.

24 See e.g. *Bio-medical Research v. Delatex* [2000] 4 IR 307; *Bushell v. Leicht* [2015] IECA 211.

25 [2015] IEHC 773.

In the case at hand, the Court was only concerned with a pre-trial application for the separate determination of applicable law as a preliminary issue. This application was rejected (on the basis that the Irish law criteria for separate determination of a question of law were not satisfied) and the Court did not have to resolve the substantive question as to whether the alleged choice-of-law clause was in fact binding.

Of course, if, as predicted, choice-of-law clauses tend to be challenged in the same circumstances as choice-of-court clauses, the law governing the validity and interpretation of the clause will be the putative applicable law pursuant to Articles 3(5), 10 and 12 of the Rome I Regulation, and the existing Irish case law on the validity and scope of choice-of-court agreements under Brussels I will be of limited relevance.

2.2.2. *Implied Choices under Rome I*

Article 3 of the Rome I Regulation requires an implied choice-of-law to be 'clearly demonstrated' and this requirement is intended to be more onerous than the Rome Convention requirement that such a choice be 'demonstrated with reasonable certainty'.[26] In *AIB v. Diamond*,[27] however, the Irish High Court appeared to be quick to infer an implied choice in circumstances where no clear evidence of such a choice was presented.

This case (which is discussed in more detail below) concerned a contractual action by an employer against certain employees who were alleged to be making unlawful use of confidential information for the benefit of a prospective employer. (The prospective employers were also being sued by the plaintiff bank, by way of a tort action.) The plaintiff employer was seeking a short-term pre-trial 'springboard'[28] injunction to prevent the employees (and their new employers) obtaining an unfair advantage. The employees had been assigned to work for subsidiaries of the first plaintiff in Luxembourg, Hungary, Switzerland and the Netherlands, and upon being so assigned, each was issued with a contractual document, supplemental to the original contract of employment, providing as follows:

> 'While in [ ], you will be subject to the laws of that country, including those laws relating to personal taxation. Any provisions of the Laws of [ ] which relate to

---

26 M. McParland, *The Rome I Regulation on the Law Applicable to Contractual Obligations*, Oxford University Press, Oxford 2015, p. 301; O. Lando and P. Nielsen, 'The Rome I Regulation' (2008) 45 *Common Market Law Review* 1687, 1698.

27 [2011] IEHC 505; [2012] 3 IR 549.

28 As the judge described it, a springboard injunction 'may be granted to cancel out the head start gained from certain kinds of wrongdoing, in particular where such advantage necessarily lasts for a limited period of time': see *AIB v. Diamond* [2011] IEHC 505; [2012] 3 IR 549, 566.

employment there, which are not contained in this letter, shall be deemed to be contained and shall be binding on you and AIB now and into the future.'[29]

The Irish High Court took the view that there was 'at least' a strong arguable case that the defendants' contracts of employment remained governed by Irish law, notwithstanding their assignment to another jurisdiction, and notwithstanding the inclusion of the above clause in the supplemental contractual document.[30] The Court thought it was arguable that the above clause was simply an 'add-on' to the obligations which the relevant employee undertook, and that it was only intended to ensure compliance with the old maxim 'when in Rome, do as the Romans do'.[31] Thus, for the purposes of the interlocutory application, the Court accepted that the plaintiff had made out a strong arguable case that 'the employment contracts, by implied agreement, are governed by Irish law'.[32]

One would not, of course, expect an exhaustive analysis in an interlocutory hearing, but one would have hoped for a little more explanation as to why this 'strong arguable case' was made out (in particular when – as the Court acknowledged – the grant of the springboard injunction was likely to lead to a final resolution of the dispute in this case).[33] There was no reference to the factors set out in the Giuliano and Lagarde report on the Rome Convention[34] and no reference to the increased threshold for implied choices under the Rome I Regulation.

2.3. ABSENCE OF CHOICE OF LAW (AND THE USE OF ESCAPE CLAUSES)

The Irish courts experienced little difficulty in determining the location of the (direct) damage for the purposes of Article 4(1) Rome II and in distinguishing 'indirect consequences' in the personal injuries context in *Kelly v. Groupama*.[35] The plaintiff (an Irish resident) had been struck by a van in Cannes, France, and

29 *AIB v. Diamond* [2011] IEHC 505; [2012] 3 IR 549, 568.
30 *Ibid.*
31 *Ibid.*
32 *Ibid.*, 564.
33 *Ibid.*, 566.
34 M. Giuliano and P. Lagarde, Report on the Convention on the Law Applicable to Contractual Obligations [1980] OJ C 282/1, 17. The Giuliano and Lagarde Report has been instrumental in guiding the Irish courts in other cases: see e.g. *McDonald v. AZ Sint Elisabeth Hospital* [2015] IEHC 62 (a Rome Convention case).
35 *Kelly v. Groupama* [2012] IEHC 177. In *SPV Sam Dragon v. GE Transportation Finance (Ireland) Ltd* [2012] IEHC 240, para. 15 the Court appeared to accept that the Brussels I case law on the location of direct (and indirect) damage (under Article 5(3) of the Brussels Convention, now Article 7(2) of the Recast) should be utilised in interpreting Article 4(1) Rome II.

had suffered a fractured femur. Whilst the prognosis was initially very positive (and it was envisaged that the bone would heal without the need for surgery), the plaintiff's condition subsequently deteriorated with the result that he required a total hip replacement. While this deterioration in the plaintiff's condition occurred in Ireland, it was accepted that the applicable law was French law, 'the law of the place where the damage occurred.'[36]

In other contexts, however, the identification of 'the country in which the damage occurs' has proven more challenging, and the reasoning of the Irish courts in applying Article 4(1) – and in having recourse to Article 4(3) – has not been entirely clear.

In *ICDL GCC Foundation FZ-LLC v. European Computer Driving Licence Foundation*,[37] the Irish High Court was asked to determine the locus of damage suffered by a licensee and sub-licensee of an education programme, in circumstances where the defendant licensor was alleged to be liable in tort for wrongful interference in the plaintiffs' economic interests and for acts of negligence. The first plaintiff (licensee) was also suing for a breach of contract and the alleged wrongs (in tort and contract) flowed from the defendant licensor's purported termination of the licence. The licensor was an Irish company, the licensee was a Dubai-based corporation and the sub-licensee was a Saudi Arabian company. It was intended that the programme would be operated by the sub-licensee in Saudi Arabia in the first instance, but that the creation of the Dubai-based licensee (at the instigation of the sub-licensee) would allow for the subsequent expansion of operations in the Gulf Region at a later date. In these circumstances, the Irish High Court was satisfied that any damage suffered by the sub-licensee (second plaintiff) was sustained in Saudi Arabia and that the sub-licensee's claims in tort were governed by Saudi Arabian law pursuant to Article 4(1) of Rome II.[38] The Irish High Court encountered greater difficulty in determining the locus of the damage suffered by the Dubai-based licensee (first plaintiff) and in applying Article 4(1) to the licensee's claims in tort:

> '[T]he position regarding the Dubai Company is perhaps less clear cut. It is a UAE based company, whose connected company, TAM, operates in Saudi Arabia. There was no suggestion that the Dubai Company has any commercial interests, concerning the Licence and the operation of the Programme which were damaged, bar those which are conducted through TAM. Thus in view of the principles of separate legal personality which are common throughout many if not most jurisdictions, it is difficult to see how the Dubai Company suffered any damage in Saudi Arabia, save to the extent to which its return has been reduced by the damage caused to TAM. If the Dubai Company were, therefore, to have suffered any non-contractual damage as a

36 *Kelly v. Groupama* [2012] IEHC 177, para. 10.
37 [2011] IEHC 343.
38 *Ibid.*, para. 9.5.

result of the Foundation's termination then it would appear that, at least at the level of principle, such damage might be said to have occurred in the UAE.'[39]

Having indicated therefore that the licensee's (first plaintiff's) tort action should be governed by the laws of the United Arab Emirates (of which Dubai forms part) pursuant to Article 4(1) of Rome II, the Irish High Court went on to observe that this outcome would require 'the separate plaintiffs' claims to be decided under the laws of the UAE and Saudi Arabia respectively' and would involve the 'splitting of the applicable law'.[40] The Court proceeded then, somewhat confusingly, to observe that *depéçage* is not permitted under Article 4(2) and (3) of Rome II,[41] and concluded that both plaintiffs' tort claims should, in the end, be governed by the law of Saudi Arabia.[42] In an apparent reference to Recital 14 of Rome II, this position was said to be 'consistent with the requirements for legal certainty and the need to do justice in individual cases which the Regulation seeks to achieve'.[43] The Irish High Court also referred to the close connections between the two plaintiffs' claims in tort and the fact that they arose 'out of the same set of circumstances'.[44] One might infer that Article 4(3) Rome II was being applied, although this was not explicit. If Article 4(3) was being applied (as appeared to be the case), it is perhaps surprising that no account was taken of the law governing the licensing contract (Irish law)[45] or of the law governing the sub-licence (UAE law)[46] in determining the law governing the first plaintiff's tort claims pursuant to Article 4(3).[47] It would have been preferable if the Irish High Court, in considering the invocation of Article 4(3), had explored all relevant connections (as was done by the English High Court in *Winrow v. Hemphill*).[48]

The 2012 case of *SPV Sam Dragon v. GE Transportation Finance (Ireland) Ltd*[49] is also unclear in its application of Article 4(1) and (3) Rome II. This case concerned a vessel which had been owned by a South Korean company and had been registered on the South Korean Shipping Register. The defendant, an Irish

39 *Ibid.*, para. 9.6.
40 *Ibid.*, para. 9.7.
41 Referring to A. Dickinson, *The Rome II Regulation*, Oxford University Press, Oxford 2008, p. 335.
42 [2011] IEHC 343, paras. 9.7–9.9.
43 *Ibid.*, para. 9.8. The Court also emphasised that the first plaintiff's claims in tort were unlikely to be of consequence since the first plaintiff was in any event entitled to damages for breach of contract. The Court also noted that the defendant did not 'vigorously dispute' the application of Saudi Arabian law to both claims in tort (see para. 9.8).
44 [2011] IEHC 343, para. 9.8.
45 *ICDL GCC Foundation FZ-LLC v. European Computer Driving Licence Foundation* [2012] IESC 55, para. 75.
46 [2011] IEHC 343, para. 3.10.
47 The language of Article 4(3) gives specific emphasis to the law governing pre-existing relationships in determining a 'manifestly closer connection'.
48 [2014] EWHC 3164 (QB).
49 [2012] IEHC 240.

company, held a mortgage on the vessel and this mortgage was entered on the South Korean Register. Subsequently, the vessel was arrested by various creditors in Belgium and was sold by a Belgian bailiff to the plaintiff, a Panamanian company. The plaintiff wished to register the vessel on the Hong Kong Shipping Register but encountered difficulties in so doing. The plaintiff alleged that these difficulties were attributable to the defendant's initial failure to comply with the plaintiff's request for removal of the entry of the mortgage from the South Korean Register, and argued that this omission gave rise to liability in tort.

The Irish High Court found that the plaintiff's action was governed by South Korean law. The defendant had argued that South Korean law was applicable pursuant to Article 4(3) Rome II, insofar as the case concerned a vessel originally owned by a South Korean company and a mortgage governed by the law of South Korea, and insofar as the dispute centred on the deregistration of a ship from the Korean Shipping Register and the removal of a mortgage from that Register.[50] The Court appeared to agree with the defendant, reasoning as follows:

> 'Having considered the evidence, it seems to me that the country most connected with the alleged wrong arising out of the failure by the defendant to delete the entry of the mortgage from the Korean Register is Korea, and that the consequences in other jurisdictions were "indirect consequences" within the meaning of Article 4(1) of the Rome II Regulation. Accordingly, I hold that Korean law applies to this issue.'[51]

In so reasoning, the Court appears initially to be applying Article 4(3) Rome II: South Korean law is chosen as the law of the 'most connected' country. However, the Court goes on to emphasise that the consequences in other jurisdictions were 'indirect consequences', thereby suggesting that the direct damage was sustained in South Korea, and that the law of South Korea is applicable pursuant to Article 4(1).

The conclusion that South Korean law is the applicable law is a sound conclusion (and consistent with Rome II) and there is no reason to criticise the *result* of the Court's analysis. However, the reasoning itself is most unclear and it is impossible to determine whether South Korean law was applicable pursuant to Article 4(1) or (3). Of course, the identification of the location of the direct damage is far from straightforward in a case like this, and one would have some sympathy with a court which seeks to move directly to Article 4(3) where the application of Article 4(1) is fraught with difficulty. Nonetheless, Article 4 Rome II lays down a clear methodology for the determination of applicable law and national courts are bound to observe that methodology. The *SPV Sam Dragon*

---

50 *Ibid.*, paras. 16–17.

51 *Ibid.*, para. 18.

case is also concerning insofar as it fails to recognise the exceptionality of Article 4(3) and the primacy of Article 4(1).[52]

Similar methodological concerns arise in the context of the more recent case of *C&F Green Energy v. Bakker Magnetic*[53] discussed above. In this case, as already indicated, the Irish plaintiff disputed the existence of a choice-of-law agreement and the application of Dutch law pursuant to Article 3 of the Rome I Regulation, and it was contended that Irish law was applicable pursuant to Article 4 Rome I. This argument was summarised by the Irish Court as follows:

> 'The plaintiffs argue that it is not Article 3 but Article 4(3) of the Rome I Regulation that should apply. This Article provides that it is the law of the country most closely connected to the contract that shall apply ... They will argue that the choice of law should be determined pursuant to Article 4(3) by an examination of all of the numerous connections between the contract and Ireland.'[54]

Aside from the claim of breach of contract, the Irish plaintiff also alleged negligence on the part of the Dutch supplier, and the plaintiff's argument that Irish law also governed the claim in tort was summarised as follows:

> 'In relation to their claim in tort, they argue that the general rule under Rome II Article 4(1) should apply i.e. the law of the country where the damage occurred. They argue that Article 4(3) of Rome II further brings into play evidence as to manifest proximity.'[55]

As discussed above, in the case at hand, the Court was only seeking to resolve a preliminary question of whether applicable law should be determined separately or as part of a unitary trial – and the arguments outlined above were raised and considered only in that context. There was no question of the Court seeking to resolve the substantive question of applicable law based on these preliminary submissions. It is also important to note that the judge (in the text quoted above) was merely summarising the submissions of counsel. These extracts from the judgment are nonetheless concerning. Like the *ICDL* and *SPV Sam Dragon* cases, the *C&F Green Energy* case fails to recognise the exceptionality of the

---

52 See Recital 18 Rome II highlighting that Article 4(1) lays down the 'general rule' and that Article 4(3) should be understood as an 'escape clause'. That Article 4(3) should 'be reserved for the most exceptional of cases' is recognised in the literature: see L. Heffernan, 'Rome II: Implications for Irish Tort Litigation' in J. Ahern and W. Binchy (eds.), *The Rome II Regulation on the Law Applicable to Non-Contractual Obligations*, Martinus Nijhoff, Leiden 2009, p. 270.

53 [2015] IEHC 773.

54 *Ibid.*, para. 5.3.

55 *Ibid.*, para. 5.3. The text of the judgment reported on <https://beta.courts.ie/judgments> actually refers to 'Article 4(1)(i)' of Rome II (instead of 'Article 4(1)') but one must assume that this was a typographical error.

escape clause. Of course, Article 4(1)(a) Rome I did not serve the plaintiff's argument in *C&F Green Energy* and it is no surprise that the plaintiff should seek to rely on Article 4(3) Rome I. In that event, however, one would hope to see the plaintiff's argument framed in a manner that accepts the primacy of Article 4(1)(a)[56] and the need to establish that the contract 'is manifestly more closely connected with a country other than that indicated' in Article 4(1)(a).[57] Indeed, it is noteworthy that the Irish case law often omits the word 'manifestly' in its references to Article 4(3) Rome I and Article 4(3) Rome II.[58]

A final case in point is *AIB v. Diamond*.[59] As discussed above, this case was not concerned with a final determination of applicable law (but rather with a pre-trial 'springboard' injunction to restrict the use of confidential information) and this may explain the very rudimentary analysis of Article 4 Rome II. As already indicated, the High Court accepted that there was a strong arguable case that the employee defendants had impliedly agreed that their contracts would be governed by Irish law. Since the tort claim (against the prospective employers) was 'so closely connected with that contractual dispute',[60] it was contended that there was a strong arguable case that the law applicable to the tort claim was also Irish law. Having thus argued for the application of Irish law pursuant to Article 4(3) Rome II, the Court noted that the plaintiff was also asserting that 'independent of that close connection, the location of the damage suffered was sufficient to make Irish law applicable to the latter claim'.[61] Therefore – as in the *SPV Sam Dragon* judgment – counsel's argument in *AIB v. Diamond* appears to put the cart before the horse: the initial focus appeared to be on the escape clause, and the primary rule (of Article 4(1) Rome II) is mentioned almost as an afterthought.

This error is corrected to some extent in the judge's final determination on Article 4 Rome II: in concluding that AIB had established a strong arguable case of Irish law being applicable, he relies firstly on the likelihood of the damage having occurred in Ireland (Article 4(1)),[62] and only secondly (and subsequently) on the close connection to the contractual dispute apparently governed by Irish

---

56 For a relatively orthodox (and faithful) application of Article 4 of the Rome I Regulation (leading to the application of the law of the habitual residence of the characteristic performer), see *Unicredit Global Leasing Export GmbH v. Business Aviation Ltd* [2019] IEHC 139, paras. 69–73.

57 For a practitioner perspective, emphasising the need to restrict reliance on Article 4(3), see G. O'Connor, 'When in Rome: An Examination of Article 4 of the Rome Regime on the Governing Law of International Contracts' (2010) 9 *Hibernian Law Journal* 39.

58 See also *AIB v. Diamond* [2011] IEHC 505; [2012] 3 IR 549, 564.

59 *Ibid.*

60 *Ibid.*

61 *Ibid.*

62 While the primary focus on Article 4(1) is to be welcomed, one might question the view that the initial (direct) damage was incurred in Ireland (the seat of the parent company), in circumstances where confidential information was alleged to have been taken from foreign-based subsidiaries. It was argued by AIB that the damage was 'ultimately' suffered in Ireland (see [2012] 3 IR 549, 569) – but such damage might be characterised as 'indirect consequences' for the purposes of Article 4(1).

law (Article 4(3)).[63] Nonetheless, the judge also appears to overstate the role of the escape clause in apparently accepting that 'it would be incumbent on the court to hear the cases against the landscape of a single legal system' and thus to apply Irish law to the tortious claims, if Irish law were applicable to the associated contracts.[64] This particular emphasis of the need to apply a single law to all tort and contract claims stands in contrast to the approach taken in *ICDL* – where the law governing the associated contracts was not mentioned in applying Rome II and in determining the law applicable to the tort elements of the case.[65] Of course the Article 4(3) assessment is necessarily fact sensitive, but the Regulation's ambition of creating 'legal certainty'[66] will not be realised if the case law fails to provide reasoned guidance as to why a particular factor is of utmost importance in one case, but of very little moment in another.

Finally, it is also worth noting that Irish constitutional protection may have the potential to complicate the determination of the locus of the direct damage for the purposes of Article 4(1) Rome II. Under emerging Irish law, breaches of constitutional rights may be actionable in tort – and so, an Irish resident severely harmed in a road traffic accident abroad might be able to allege tortious liability for the breach of his or her right to bodily integrity and of association (assuming the accident severely curtailed the plaintiff's capacity to work and socialise).[67] While there is no difficulty in localising the immediate physical harm in such a case (and this would ordinarily be a straightforward case for the determination of the place of 'direct damage'), the violation of Irish constitutional rights is ongoing and by its nature localised in Ireland.[68]

2.4. SPECIFIC RULES

2.4.1. Article 6 Rome I

Whilst the fact situation in *McDonald v. AZ Sint Elisabeth Hospital* fell outside of the temporal scope of the Rome I Regulation (insofar as the contract was

---

63 *AIB v. Diamond* [2011] IEHC 505; [2012] 3 IR 549, 569.

64 *Ibid.*

65 Ironically in making the case for applying a single law, the Court in *AIB v. Diamond* refers to *ICDL* insofar as that case had emphasised the desirability of applying one single law to all tort aspects of the case.

66 See Recitals 6 and 14.

67 This example is derived from a discussion of Article 5(3) of the Brussels Convention in R. Byrne and W. Binchy, *Annual Review of Irish Law 1994*, Round Hall, Dublin 1994, pp. 100–102. It should be emphasised that this notion of private law liability for breaches of constitutional rights is still at the early stages of development – and tends to focus on breaches which are inadequately protected by existing torts.

68 See R. Byrne and W. Binchy, *Annual Review of Irish Law 1994*, Round Hall, Dublin 1994, pp. 101–102.

concluded in March 2007), the judgments of the Irish High Court are nonetheless instructive in interpreting Article 6 of the Rome I Regulation and in exploring its interaction with Article 17 Brussels I Recast. The plaintiff in this case was an Irish resident who travelled to Belgium for a gastric bypass procedure. The first defendant was the Belgian hospital with which the plaintiff had contracted, and the second defendant was the consultant doctor who performed the operation. Applying Article 15 of the Brussels I Regulation (the predecessor of Article 17 Brussels I Recast), the Irish High Court accepted that since the plaintiff had no contract with the second defendant, the Court could not exercise jurisdiction pursuant to Article 15 in the action against the second defendant.[69] The Irish Court was however satisfied that it had jurisdiction in the contractual action against the first defendant. Having discussed the Court of Justice's judgment in *Pammer v. Reederei Karl Schlüter*,[70] the Irish High Court determined that the Belgian hospital had 'directed' its activities to Ireland.[71] In concluding that the hospital 'clearly envisaged doing business with patients domiciled in Ireland', the Court laid emphasis on the fact that its website[72] had provided a telephone number especially for Irish patients, included a testimonial from an Irish patient and made specific reference to the possibility of pre-travel consultations in Dublin and Cork.[73] While the plaintiff was thus characterised as a protected consumer for the purposes of Article 15 of the Brussels I Regulation, he was subsequently denied such characterisation under the Rome Convention, and Belgian law (rather than Irish law) was found to be the law governing the contract.[74] In concluding that the plaintiff was not a 'consumer' for the purposes of Article 5 of the Rome Convention, the Court noted that he had not completed 'all the steps necessary ... for the conclusion of the contract' in Ireland (but

---

69 The plaintiff had telephoned the second defendant, prior to travelling for the procedure, and had paid the second defendant personally, but it was accepted that such payment was received on behalf of the hospital and that there was no contractual relationship with the second defendant: see [2014] IEHC 88; [2014] 1 IR 311, paras. 9 and 19. The Court accepted that the concept of 'contract' had to be determined autonomously and that it 'cannot be diluted or qualified by reference to purely national practices or understandings' (see para. 28).

70 Joined Cases C-585/08 and C-144/09, ECLI:EU:C:2010:740.

71 *McDonald v. AZ Sint Elisabeth Hospital* [2014] IEHC 88; [2014] 1 IR 311, 326.

72 While the contract had been entered into in 2007, neither party was in a position to produce the precise version of the website which was operational in 2007 – and the Court was required to proceed on the assumption that the 2011 version was broadly similar to the 2007 version: see [2014] IEHC 88; [2014] 1 IR 311, 315.

73 The Court distinguished the case at hand from *Harkin v. Towpik* [2013] IEHC 351; [2014] 1 ILRM 51 where an Irish-resident woman who had similarly availed of a surgical procedure abroad (in Poland), was found not to be a protected consumer under Article 15 Brussels I Regulation: the website in *Harkin v. Towpik* had been targeted towards the British market (with a UK domain name, an English telephone number, and indicating the acceptance of sterling) and there was no basis for inferring that the defendants were directing their activities to Ireland.

74 *McDonald v. AZ Sint Elisabeth Hospital* [2015] IEHC 62.

rather had completed some of them in Belgium – for example, he had signed the consent forms and had effected payment in Belgium).[75] More significantly (insofar as this requirement persists under the Rome I Regulation), the Court held that the plaintiff was debarred by Article 5(4)(b) of the Rome Convention (now Article 6(4)(a) Rome I) insofar as the services were 'to be supplied to the consumer exclusively in a country other than that in which he has his habitual residence'. Relying on the fact that he had had two telephone conversations with the hospital consultant in advance of his departure from Ireland, the plaintiff had argued that the relevant services had not been provided 'exclusively' in Belgium, but the Irish Court rejected this argument, characterising such consultations as 'at best pre-contractual in nature'.[76]

The *McDonald* judgments expose the technicality and precariousness of the consumer protection afforded under EU private international law. While one can readily appreciate the view that the service provider's law is much more closely connected in (what are now) cases affected by Article 6(4)(a),[77] the same might be said of the service provider's courts, yet the Brussels I Recast does not include an equivalent limitation on its consumer protection regime.[78] Also insofar as the consumer protection provisions of the Brussels I Recast and Rome I Regulations entail very similar criteria, this distinction is particularly liable to trip up the unwary practitioner.

2.4.2. *Article 11(4) Rome I*

As far as consumer protection is concerned, it is also noteworthy that, in its interaction with Irish domestic law on the sale of goods, the Rome I Regulation can have the opposite effect to that intended. Section 4 of the Sale of Goods Act 1893 renders unenforceable any contract for the sale of goods worth more than €12.70 in the absence of evidence in writing or certain specified acts of part performance. Section 4 can clearly work to the advantage of consumers (where it is the consumer who wishes to escape a contractual obligation); however, section 4 can equally work to the consumer's disadvantage – for example, where a seller no longer wishes to honour the consumer's order in a rising market. In the latter case, the consumer habitually resident in Ireland is exposed to the Irish formality rule pursuant to Article 11(4) Rome I, which exempts consumer contracts from

75 *Ibid.*, para. 34.
76 *Ibid.*, para. 42.
77 See *ibid.*, paras. 40–41 referring to the Giuliano and Lagarde Report and the underlying policy of Article 5(4) of the Rome Convention.
78 See M. McParland, *The Rome I Regulation on the Law Applicable to Contractual Obligations*, Oxford University Press, Oxford 2015, p. 554: Article 6(4)(a) Rome I has attracted significant criticism and it was at one point proposed to exclude this limitation on the application of the law of the consumer's habitual residence.

the general *favor validitatis* provisions of Article 11 Rome I. This illustrates that while Article 11(4) is intended as a consumer protection measure,[79] it may in fact undermine the interests of an Irish resident consumer (in circumstances where his or her interests would have been better served by the generality of the formality provisions of Article 11 Rome I).

2.4.3. *Article 8 Rome I*

In the absence of an agreed of choice of law, Article 8(2) Rome I provides for the application of the 'law of the country in which, or failing that, from which the employee habitually carries out his work in performance of the contract'. In *A Retail Company v. A Worker*,[80] the Irish Labour Court, in interpreting a similar provision under the Brussels Convention ('where the employee habitually carries out his work'), held that the employee of a company based in Northern Ireland habitually carried out his work there, despite the fact that he spent approximately 60 per cent of his working time in the Republic of Ireland. It was material in reaching this conclusion that his office and reporting managers were based in Northern Ireland.

In *Zimmerman v. Der Deutsche Schulverein*,[81] an employee working in Ireland had agreed that his employment contract would be governed by German law. The Irish Employment Appeals Tribunal found that he was nonetheless entitled to rely on the Irish Unfair Dismissals Act 1977, which provided in section 13 that any contractual provision seeking to exclude or limit the application of the Act was void. The Tribunal held that the terms of the 1977 Act were applicable pursuant to Article 6(1) of the Rome Convention (the predecessor of Article 8(1) Rome I Regulation) as 'mandatory rules' of Irish law.

2.4.4. *Article 12 Rome I*

Article 12(1)(d) Rome I arose for consideration in *Defender Ltd v. HSBC Institutional Trust Services (Ireland) Ltd*.[82] This action arose out of a custodian agreement, pursuant to which the plaintiff had invested substantial sums in a third-party company which was subsequently discovered to be 'the world's

---

79 See M. McParland, *The Rome I Regulation on the Law Applicable to Contractual Obligations*, Oxford University Press, Oxford 2015, p. 734.

80 (2002) 13 ELR 366, discussed by R. Byrne and W. Binchy, *Annual Review of Irish Law 2002*, Round Hall, Dublin 2002, pp. 73–77.

81 (1999) 10 ELR 211.

82 [2018] IEHC 706.

largest Ponzi scheme'.[83] Having settled its claim against the third party, the plaintiff pursued its custodian, the defendant, as an alleged concurrent wrongdoer, for the balance of its loss. The defendant sought to invoke a provision of Irish law (section 17(2) Civil Liability Act 1961) which could extinguish the claim against an alleged concurrent wrongdoer following a settlement or 'accord' with the other concurrent wrongdoer. Irish law was acknowledged to be the law governing the custodian agreement (pursuant to an express choice-of-law clause) and New York law to be the law governing the settlement agreement with the third party (again pursuant to an express choice-of-law clause).

The plaintiff contended that since the defendant was arguing that the settlement agreement extinguished the defendant's obligations to the plaintiff, New York law applied (pursuant to Article 12(1)(d) Rome I), as the law applicable to that contract, to 'the various ways of extinguishing obligations'.[84] Thus, it was argued that New York law should apply as respects the liability of alleged concurrent wrongdoers, and that the relevant defence under the Irish Civil Liability Act was inapplicable.

The Irish High Court held, however, that while New York law governed the question of whether there was a valid 'accord' for the purposes of the Irish Civil Liability Act, that was the extent of its relevance.[85] The substantive establishment of the liability of the custodian, and the effect of the settlement or 'accord' on that liability, was governed by the law applicable to the custodian agreement (Irish law), and the Irish Civil Liability Act could therefore be invoked by the defendant custodian in that context.[86]

2.4.5. Article 5 Rome II

Article 5 Rome II is singled out for particular criticism in the Irish literature. Article 5 is described as a 'convoluted', 'unsatisfactory' and 'ambiguous' provision which is likely to vex practitioners and courts.[87] Heffernan describes the 'cascade of connecting factors' as 'unnecessarily cumbersome and complex', and questions its capacity to provide a 'balanced solution' to the 'lofty objectives' set out in Recital 20.[88]

---

83 *Ibid.*, para. 2.
84 *Ibid.*, paras. 72–73.
85 *Ibid.*, paras. 61–64.
86 *Ibid.*, paras. 77–78.
87 L. Heffernan, 'Rome II: Implications for Irish Tort Litigation' in J. Ahern and W. Binchy (eds.), *The Rome II Regulation on the Law Applicable to Non-Contractual Obligations*, Martinus Nijhoff, Leiden 2009, pp. 272–273.
88 *Ibid.*, p. 272.

2.4.6. *Article 6 Rome II*

In *AIB v. Diamond*,[89] as indicated above, the corporate defendants were accused of benefitting from confidential information (including customer information) alleged to have been taken from the plaintiff bank by its employees (the personal defendants). The corporate defendants argued that the laws of the countries where the corporate defendants were established were applicable pursuant to Article 6 Rome II.[90] The plaintiff bank argued that 'the true nature of its case' was not one which sought 'to prevent unfair competition as such' but 'rather one where it seeks to protect its property rights (both intellectual property and goodwill) from being wrongfully used by a third party'.[91] It was argued that Article 6 was inapplicable where the corporate defendants had found themselves 'in a position to exploit those rights in circumstances where it is said that the ability of [those corporate defendants] to exploit those rights stems from illegality on the part of the personal defendants'.[92] The Court accepted that if AIB were correct in this argument, Article 6 would have no application. It concluded that there was a strong arguable case that Article 6 was inapplicable and that Article 4 Rome II applied.

The Court offered no further insights as to why Article 6 ought to be considered inapplicable on these facts – and indeed gave no explanation as to why Article 8 might not be applicable if (as alleged) the action were in truth concerned with intellectual property infringement. It may be that the Court believed (in accordance with Article 6(2)) that the corporate defendants' acts affected 'exclusively the interests of a specific competitor' and that Article 4 was applicable on that basis – but, if this was so, it was not explicitly stated. While an elaboration on the implications of Article 6 Rome II would have been helpful (and conducive to the appropriate development of the law), one also feels a degree of sympathy with a common law court faced with an argument based on Article 6 Rome II. 'Unfair competition' is alien to the common law conception of torts and civil wrongs, and Article 6 is widely acknowledged to be a troublesome, poorly drafted provision.[93]

2.4.7. *Article 10 Rome II*

Article 10(3) Rome II was applied to identify the law governing unjust enrichment claims in *Unicredit Global Leasing Export GmbH v. Business Aviation Ltd*[94] and in

---

89 [2011] IEHC 505; [2012] 3 IR 549.

90 *Ibid.*, 561–562 and 568–569.

91 *Ibid.*, 569.

92 *Ibid.*

93 See e.g. A. Dickinson, *The Rome II Regulation*, Oxford University Press, Oxford 2008, pp. 392–407; L. Collins et al., *Dicey, Morris and Collins: The Conflict of Laws*, 15th ed., Sweet & Maxwell, London 2012, pp. 2229–2233.

94 [2019] IEHC 139.

HKR Middle East Architects Engineering LC v. English.[95] In the former case, it was determined that the unjust enrichment took place in Austria, where the money was received by the company alleged to be obliged to make repayment.[96] In the latter case, the Irish High Court expressed some doubt. The monies had been received by a company with its registered office in the British Virgin Islands but with its bank account in Guernsey. In those circumstances, the Court thought that the unjust enrichment occurred either in the British Virgin Islands or in Guernsey.[97]

2.5. SCOPE OF APPLICABLE LAW

Existing Irish case law suggests an incomplete understanding of the division of substance and procedure under Rome I and Rome II. This distinction also existed in the pre-existing common law choice-of-law doctrine, but the common law gave 'procedure' a wider remit, with the result that remedies were considered to be a matter for the *lex fori*. While the Irish literature on the Rome Convention suggested a positive attitude towards the recalibration of the substance/procedure divide,[98] two recent Irish cases indicate an ongoing tendency to continue to cleave to the common law conception of procedure and a disinclination to apply foreign remedial law. This tendency was first apparent in *AIB v. Diamond* where (as indicated earlier) the plaintiff, an Irish bank, sought an interim 'springboard' injunction to prevent its employees and their prospective (new) employers from benefitting from information which the plaintiff alleged was illegally acquired. The defendant employees had been assigned to various subsidiaries of the plaintiff located in Luxembourg, Hungary, Switzerland and the Netherlands, and it was argued by the defendants that their employment contracts were governed by the laws of the countries where they had been working and not by Irish law.[99] As discussed above, it was also argued that insofar as the defendant employers were concerned, any liability in tort on their part was governed by foreign law pursuant to Article 6 Rome II.[100] The plaintiff bank had advanced its claims on the basis that Irish law was applicable,[101] and the defendants argued that the injunction application should be dismissed insofar as the various actions were

---

95 [2019] IEHC 306.

96 *Unicredit Global Leasing Export GmbH v. Business Aviation Ltd* [2019] IEHC 139, para. 64.

97 *HKR Middle East Architects Engineering LC v. English* [2019] IEHC 306, para. 393.

98 R. Byrne and W. Binchy, *Annual Review of Irish Law 1991,* Round Hall, Dublin 1991, p. 71; G. Hogan, 'Contractual Obligations (Applicable Law) Act 1991' (annotation), *Irish Current Law Statutes Annotated* (edited by R. Clark), Round Hall, Dublin 1991.

99 *AIB v. Diamond* [2011] IEHC 505; [2012] 3 IR 549, 561.

100 *Ibid.*, 568–569.

101 *Ibid.*, 562, 564.

governed by foreign law and the plaintiff had failed to adduce any evidence of wrongdoing under the relevant foreign laws.[102]

At common law there was a tendency to view interlocutory injunction applications as procedural matters governed by the law of the forum.[103] Citing some traditional common law jurisprudence on the characterisation of substance and procedure,[104] the Irish High Court concluded that AIB's injunction application was governed by Irish law and that the 'applicable law' issue should not be regarded as a threshold question.[105] The judge accepted that applicable law should be one of the many factors to be weighed in the balance of convenience (part of the Irish law test for the grant of an interlocutory injunction),[106] although he declared himself satisfied that the plaintiff had made out a strong arguable case that Irish law was the applicable law.

AIB v. Diamond is problematic in several respects (and the application of Article 3 Rome I and Articles 4 and 6 Rome II are criticised above). In terms of the division of substance and procedure, one would have expected a close analysis of Article 12 of Rome I[107] and Article 15 of Rome II, and of the extent to which remedies are governed by the applicable law pursuant to those provisions. In the *AIB v. Diamond* judgment, however, these rules were not mentioned and the division of substance and procedure was assessed purely from a common law perspective. It is now widely accepted that interlocutory relief is determined by reference to the applicable law under Rome I and Rome II[108] (and that the substance/procedure divide is to be determined by autonomous EU standards), but this orthodoxy is not reflected in the *AIB v. Diamond* judgment. It may however be unfair to criticise the judge for this shortcoming: defence counsel appeared only to contend that the alleged wrongdoing must be assessed according to foreign standards, and it did not appear to have been argued that the remedy itself must be determined in accordance with the foreign law.[109]

---

102 *Ibid.*, 561–562.

103 A. Briggs, *Private International Law in the English Courts*, Oxford University Press, Oxford 2014, pp. 147–148.

104 *AIB v. Diamond* [2011] IEHC 505; [2012] 3 IR 549, 564–565.

105 *Ibid.*, 566.

106 *Ibid.*, 566–567.

107 As pointed out at n. 9 above, it is likely that the contracts at issue pre-dated the coming into force of the Rome I Regulation; it appeared however to be assumed that the Rome I Regulation was applicable and, that being the case, Article 12 ought to have arisen for consideration.

108 See A. Dickinson, *The Rome II Regulation*, Oxford University Press, Oxford 2008, pp. 581–582; also *OJSC TNK-BP v. Lazurenko* [2012] EWHC 2781 (Ch), para. 20. In fact, there are also indications that even in common law choice-of-law systems, the availability of interlocutory relief is increasingly being seen as a matter for the *lex causae*: R. Garnett, *Substance and Procedure in Private International Law*, Oxford University Press, Oxford 2012, pp. 299–301.

109 See *AIB v. Diamond* [2011] IEHC 505; [2012] 3 IR 549, 561–562. It is reported that the defendants contended that foreign law was applicable 'in considering the obligations of the defendants' and that the plaintiff had failed to establish that 'any of the alleged actions of

In addition, insofar as Irish law, as a common law legal system, requires the party seeking to rely on foreign law to establish its applicability and to prove its content, it is arguable that the defendants were not entitled to expect that the plaintiff must establish its case under the relevant foreign law.[110] Rather it was for the defendants, relying on foreign law, to establish its applicability and to adduce evidence of its contents, and to the extent that the defendants failed to do that, the judge was justified in applying the law of the forum.[111]

As indicated above, in *Kelly v. Groupama*, it was accepted that French law was the applicable law for a personal injuries action arising from a road traffic accident taking place in France. Liability was not in issue in this case. Without referring to Article 15 Rome II, the Irish High Court appeared (initially) to accept without question that 'the substantive law applicable to the assessment of damages in this case is French law'.[112] The Court noted that the experts on French law were generally in agreement 'as to the way that French law requires an assessment of damages of this kind to be carried out'.[113] It was accepted that in France, a medical expert would be asked either by order of the court or by agreement of the parties, to conduct a medical examination 'in accordance with French law as laid down by the Cour de Cassation'.[114] The Irish judge also accepted that the injuries and consequences would be assessed under a number of headings by the medical expert, with the expert expressing his opinion of the degree of deficit or disability in percentage terms – and that the French judge would then determine the amount of the compensation under each of the relevant headings, taking account of the medical expert's assessment and having regard to the French 'book of quantum'.[115] The 'book of quantum' is 'a compilation of the awards made in the courts throughout France from which a judge can select a comparable case or comparable cases to ascertain the appropriate level of damages to ascribe to each category of loss or deficit'.[116] It was accepted by the Irish Court that while the French judge 'retains a full discretion in deciding on the amount of compensation to be awarded in each

---

the defendants were in breach of [that] law'. The report also indicates that the defendants contended that 'the question of the applicable law was … a threshold question' and that the plaintiff could only satisfy the (Irish) 'fair issue' requirement if it adduced evidence as to the relevant foreign law. It did not appear to have been argued that the Irish interlocutory relief requirements (e.g. of a fair issue to be tried) were in themselves irrelevant where the matter was governed by foreign law.

110 See S. Geeroms, *Foreign Law in Civil Litigation*, Oxford University Press, Oxford 2004, pp. 79–80; R. Fentiman, *Foreign Law in English Courts*, Oxford University Press, Oxford 1998, p. 100.

111 *Kutchera v. Buckingham International Holdings* [1988] IR 61, 68.

112 *Kelly v. Groupama* [2012] IEHC 177, para. 10.

113 *Ibid.*, para. 11.

114 *Ibid.*, para. 12.

115 *Ibid.*, paras. 13–14.

116 *Ibid.*, para. 14.

category so that the individual features of every case can sound in damages', it was nevertheless 'the invariable practice of judges throughout France to consult or have regard to this book in making awards of damages so that awards are consistent throughout France and thereby, ultimately, to maximise fairness and consistency in awarding of damages'.[117]

The procedure envisaged by French law was, to a large extent, followed by the Irish Court in *Kelly v. Groupama*. The defendant's expert witness on French law submitted the pleadings and the plaintiff's medical reports (from an Irish hospital) to a French medical expert.[118] The French medical expert's analysis (and percentages under each of the headings) were put before the Irish Court and the corresponding awards under the French book of quantum were identified. The Irish judge then made his assessment under each of the French headings, taking account of the French book of quantum.[119] In the end, however, the Irish judge awarded sums far in excess of the sums identified pursuant to the French book of quantum and his overall award of damages was €63,900 in contrast to the 'suggested' French award of €38,706.[120]

The Irish judge offered a number of (sometimes contradictory) explanations for his quantification of damages. He emphasised the residual discretion of the judge under French law and the non-binding nature of the book of quantum – and to that extent appeared to suggest that the quantification of damages was carried out in accordance with French law.[121] However, he also indicated that since 'matters of practice are governed by the *lex fori*', he was entitled to apply Irish law 'in choosing the amounts of compensation' and to 'have regard to levels of compensation awarded in the Irish courts in respect of similar losses'.[122] The Irish judgment also emphasised the similarity of French and Irish law on damages in tort,[123] suggesting that the outcome would have been the same under either of these two laws. In substituting the higher Irish awards for the lower French figures, the Irish judge tended to characterise the suggested French sums as unreasonable having regard to the particular suffering endured by this plaintiff.[124]

There was no explicit reference to Article 1(3), Article 15 or Recital 33 of Rome II in *Kelly v. Groupama*. It is true that these provisions do not provide any very clear guidance as to how a national judge should approach questions of quantification (and the inter-relationship of the *lex fori* and *lex cauase* in this

---

117 *Ibid.*, para. 15.
118 *Ibid.*, para. 12.
119 *Ibid.*, paras. 18–25.
120 The Irish judge increased the award under four of the six headings and accepted the suggested French quantum only under two headings.
121 *Kelly v. Groupama* [2012] IEHC 177, paras. 15, 17.
122 *Ibid.*, para. 17.
123 *Ibid.*, para. 16.
124 *Ibid.*, paras. 18, 21–23.

context has been the subject of much academic debate).[125] Nonetheless, it would have been preferable if the Irish judge had anchored his reasoning within the provisions of the Regulation and had clarified the precise extent to which he thought French and Irish rules were applicable. For example, the Irish judge might reasonably have asserted that he was applying French law (pursuant to Article 4(1)), but taking 'into account all the relevant actual circumstances of the specific victim' (in accordance with Recital 33) – and this would have provided a relatively satisfactory basis for the judgment. The Irish Court's suggestion that quantification remains a matter for the *lex fori* is probably untenable in view of the text of Article 15[126] (and the EU Court of Justice's emphasis of the desirability of unitary application of the *lex causae* designated under Article 4(1)).[127]

2.6. FOREIGN LAW

In Ireland, foreign law is a matter of fact, proven by way of expert evidence (usually from foreign lawyers with expertise and experience in the relevant area of practice in the foreign legal system in question).[128] For example, in *SPV Sam Dragon*, discussed above, evidence of South Korean law was given by Korean lawyers with extensive experience in maritime law.[129] While written sworn evidence may be sufficient (i.e. an affidavit sworn by a foreign lawyer), foreign law cannot be proven simply by exhibiting a letter from a foreign lawyer or by (Irish) counsel citing case law from the relevant foreign legal system.[130] Of course, the Irish court will rely on any available case law from the relevant foreign legal system in determining the content of the applicable foreign law, where such cases are cited by the expert foreign lawyer.[131]

If there is conflicting evidence as to what is the foreign law, or what is the correct interpretation of the foreign law, then it is a matter for the Irish court to decide between the conflicting expert testimonies.[132] In *SPV Sam Dragon*, where there was a conflict of evidence as to the nature of Korean maritime law, the evidence of experts on international maritime trade was used to resolve the conflicts in the evidence on Korean law.[133] In resolving conflicts of

125 See A. Dickinson, *The Rome II Regulation*, Oxford University Press, Oxford 2008, pp. 575–582, 591–597; A Briggs, *Private International Law in the English Courts*, Oxford University Press, Oxford 2014, pp. 676–680.

126 A. Dickinson, *The Rome II Regulation*, Oxford University Press, Oxford 2008, p. 575.

127 Case C-350/14, *Lazar v. Allianz*, ECLI:EU:C:2015:802, para. 29.

128 W. Binchy, *Irish Conflicts of Law*, Butterworths, Dublin 1988, pp. 105–110.

129 [2012] IEHC 240, para. 34.

130 *Walsh v. National Irish Bank* [2013] IESC 2, paras. 6.2–6.3, 8.2.

131 *SPV Sam Dragon v. GE Transportation Finance (Ireland) Ltd* [2012] IEHC 240, paras. 30, 34.

132 *Kutchera v. Buckingham International Holdings* [1988] IR 61, 68.

133 [2012] IEHC 240, paras. 19, 37 and 44.

expert evidence on particular points, the Irish judge will prefer the evidence that is more convincing and more consistent with the expert evidence as a whole.[134]

The Irish judge may still encounter difficulty in determining the content of the relevant foreign law, even in the absence of a conflict in the expert testimony. For instance, in *ICDL GCC Foundation FZ-LLC v. European Computer Driving Licence Foundation*, the expert witnesses were broadly in agreement on the applicable principles of Saudi law, but the Irish Court still struggled with the very general nature of the descriptions of Saudi law.[135] In this context, the Court noted that the Saudi principles on tortious liability were very similar to Irish principles but also cautioned against any over-reliance on Irish law in this context:

> '[O]nly the broad principles can be relied on and not the case law or interpretation which is available from Irish sources, i.e. textbooks and case law. Therefore, any similarity between Saudi and Irish law can only be seen as superficial at best and at worst there is a danger of conflating the two.'[136]

2.7. *ORDRE PUBLIC*

There are as yet no cases on Article 21 Rome I and Article 26 Rome II. Common law authorities and judgment recognition cases suggest that these provisions may be invoked against an aspect of the applicable foreign law which is penal or discriminatory[137] or otherwise at odds with the norms of the European Convention on Human Rights.[138] If there is an action on a gambling debt[139] or a champertous contract,[140] enforceable under the applicable law, the Irish courts may refuse enforcement under Article 21 Rome I. Irish constitutional law may also have some relevance here (for example, the rights to property under Articles 40(3)(2) and 43), although it is noteworthy that recent case law has tended to restrict the role of Irish constitutional norms in the international legal order.[141]

---

134 *Ibid.*, para. 40. See also *Unicredit Global Leasing Export GmbH v. Business Aviation Ltd* [2019] IEHC 139, paras. 81–89.

135 [2011] IEHC 343, paras. 10.3–10.4.

136 *Ibid.*, para. 10.3.

137 W. Binchy, *Irish Conflicts of Law*, Butterworths, Dublin 1988, pp. 192–197.

138 *Emo v. Mulligan* [2011] IEHC 552.

139 *Sporting Index v. O'Shea* [2015] IEHC 407.

140 *Fraser v. Buckle* [1996] 2 ILRM 24.

141 *Nottinghamshire County Council v. B* [2011] IESC 48, para. 64 (O'Donnell J).

2.8. RELATIONS WITH INTERNATIONAL CONVENTIONS

Ireland is not party to any of the international conventions that supersede Rome I and Rome II (i.e. the 1955 Hague Convention on the Law Applicable to International Sales of Goods, the 1971 Hague Traffic Accidents Convention, the 1973 Hague Products Liability Convention, the 1978 Hague Agency Convention and the 2001 Budapest Convention on the Contract for the Carriage of Goods by Inland Waterways).

3. GENERAL EVALUATION

In substantive terms, Rome II is likely to have had a more radical impact on Irish private international law than Rome I. Of course, Rome I was preceded by the Rome Convention, which was broadly similar in content, but even prior to the coming into force of the Rome Convention the principle of party autonomy was supported in Irish law – and it was accepted that contracting parties had full freedom to select an unconnected law.[142] In default of choice, the English 'proper law of the contract' doctrine was assumed to be applicable.[143]

Choice of law for torts was much more uncertain prior to the coming into force of Rome II – and Rome II is to be welcomed for providing much-needed clarity. Prior to 1986 it was assumed that the 'double actionability' doctrine laid down in *Phillips v. Eyre*[144] represented the law in Ireland[145] – but some obiter dicta in a jurisdiction case (*Grehan v. Medical Incorporated*)[146] were extremely critical of *Phillips v. Eyre* and a preference was expressed for some form of flexible interest analysis doctrine.[147] As Heffernan and Binchy have noted, this flirtation with interest analysis failed to develop into any kind of concrete legal doctrine[148] and the Irish approach to choice of law for tort remains a matter of speculation in those areas where Rome II does not apply. The *lex loci damni* rule laid down

142 See 407 *Dáil Debates* Col. 1935; *Kutchera v. Buckingham International Holdings* [1988] IR 61, 68.

143 W. Binchy, *Irish Conflicts of Law*, Butterworths, Dublin 1988, pp. 517–531.

144 (1879) LR 6 QB 1. Under the 'double actionability' doctrine, the plaintiff's case must be actionable under both the *lex fori* and the *lex loci delicti*.

145 W. Binchy, *Irish Conflicts of Law*, Butterworths, Dublin 1988, p. 572.

146 [1986] ILRM 627, 638.

147 A.V. Gill, 'The Locus Delicti and Choice of Law in Tort in Irish Private International Law' (1987) 5 *Irish Law Times* 3.

148 L. Heffernan, 'Rome II: Implications for Irish Tort Litigation' in J. Ahern and W. Binchy (eds.), *The Rome II Regulation on the Law Applicable to Non-Contractual Obligations*, Martinus Nijhoff, Leiden 2009, pp. 263–264; R. Byrne and W. Binchy, *Annual Review of Irish Law 1999*, Round Hall, Dublin 1999, p. 76; R. Byrne and W. Binchy, *Annual Review of Irish Law 2003*, Round Hall, Dublin 2003, p. 118.

in Rome II is generally welcomed as an improvement on 'double actionability' insofar as the latter doctrine sets the bar extremely high for victims of foreign torts.[149]

4. CONCLUSION

The Irish case law suggests that Rome I and Rome II are not yet fully embedded into Irish litigation practice. Existing decisions show some signs of a preference for the *lex fori* (even in cases where the applicable law is a foreign law) and of a tendency for rather frequent recourse to the escape clauses. Article 4(1) Rome II appears to have caused some difficulty insofar as it is premised on a clear location of 'direct damage', and Articles 5 and 6 Rome II are perceived to be problematic. The Irish case law also raises questions as to how parallel tort and contract actions are to be handled. One would expect that the Irish case law will become more authoritative and sure-footed as the EU Court of Justice jurisprudence develops clear guidelines on the application of Rome I and Rome II.

149 L. Heffernan, 'Rome II: Implications for Irish Tort Litigation' in J. Ahern and W. Binchy (eds.), *The Rome II Regulation on the Law Applicable to Non-Contractual Obligations*, Martinus Nijhoff, Leiden 2009, pp. 259–260, 275–276.

THE APPLICATION OF THE ROME I AND ROME II REGULATIONS IN ITALY

Pietro FRANZINA*

* The author is grateful to Irene Maccagnani for contributing to an early version of this chapter.

1. THE NATIONAL LANDSCAPE

1.1. CONTRACTS

1.1.1. From the Rome Convention to the Rome I Regulation

Italy has been a party to the Rome Convention of 19 June 1980 on the Law Applicable to Contractual Obligations[1] ever since the latter entered into force on the international plane, on 1 April 1991.

Consistent with the usual practice followed for uniform texts concerning private international law, the Rome Convention was implemented domestically through a mere 'implementation order',[2] that is a legislative measure which limited itself to prescribing the application of the Convention in Italy, without restating its provisions into a piece of internal legislation.

Regulation (EC) No. 593/2008 of 17 June 2008 on the Law Applicable to Contractual Obligations (Rome I)[3] entered into force on 24 July 2008 and became applicable in Italy, as in the other Member States of the European Union, on 17 December 2009 to contracts concluded after that date.

1.1.2. Quantitative Findings

The body of case law of Italian courts concerning the Rome Convention is rather significant.[4] The Supreme Court (Corte di Cassazione) alone has considered, or made reference to, the Convention in some 30 rulings.

The number of judgments regarding the Rome I Regulation remains, instead, rather limited. The Supreme Court referred to the Regulation in

---

1 [2005] OJ C 334/1 (consolidated version).

2 Law No. 975 of 18 December 1984. One of the advantages of this approach is that courts are immediately aware of the international character of the rules concerned and of the need to promote uniformity in their application. Italian courts have often voiced a concern for the uniform interpretation of harmonised rules of private (international) law: see e.g. Cass. (SU), 9 January 2008, No. 169, *RDIPP* 2008, 1081 on the Lugano Convention on Jurisdiction and the Recognition of Judgments in Civil and Commercial Matters. In addressing this concern, courts have occasionally stressed that international conventions of private international law ought to be construed in accordance with the rules on treaty interpretation laid down in the Vienna Convention on the Law of Treaties of 23 May 1969, rather than the canons used for domestic legislation. See, for instance, on matters other than the law applicable to contractual (and non-contractual) obligations: Cass., 21 July 1995, No. 7950, *RDI* 1996, 524; CA Firenze, 21 May 1999, *Famiglia e diritto* 2000, 270; and Cass., 14 July 2015, No. 14666, *DeJure*.

3 [2008] OJ L 177/6.

4 See, for an overview, J. Re, 'Rapporto sull'applicazione in Italia della Convenzione di Roma del 19 giugno 1980 e del Regolamento (CE) n. 593/2008 del 17 giugno 2008 sulla legge applicabile alle obbligazioni contrattuali («Roma I»)', in S. Bariatti, I. Viarengo and F.C. Villata (eds.), *La giurisprudenza italiana sui regolamenti europei in materia civile e commerciale e di famiglia* (Wolters Kluwer 2016), 83 ff.

five rulings. None of them, however, was concerned with contracts governed by the Regulation, or addressed issues within the purview of the Regulation.[5] Some 20 judgments rendered by first instance or appellate court could be found where the Regulation is considered, discussed or applied.

Very few references to the Rome Convention and the Rome I Regulation have been found in awards given by arbitral tribunals seated in Italy.

1.1.3. Other Rules on Contracts

Situations arise where Italian courts must resort to rules other than those in the Rome I Regulation or the Rome Convention for the purposes of determining the law applicable to a contract.

This basically occurs in two situations. The first situation arises with matters within the scope of an international convention in force for Italy that lays down conflict-of-law rules relating to contracts, such as the Hague Convention of 15 June 1955 on the Law Applicable to International Sales of Goods.[6] Neither the Rome Convention, pursuant to its Article 1(2)(d), nor the Rome I Regulation, according to its Article 1(2)(d), prejudice the application of such conventions. Thus, in principle, Italian courts are required to apply the relevant conventions instead of the two European texts. The second situation arises with matters that, in spite of their contractual nature (broadly understood), fall outside the scope of the Rome Convention and the Rome I Regulation, as well as of any other international instrument. These matters are governed by domestic rules of private international law.

The latter rules are peculiar in Italy, for they provide for the application of the European texts themselves. Article 57 of the Italian Statute on Private International Law (Law No. 218 of 31 May 1995)[7] provides that the law applicable to contracts must 'in any case' ('in ogni caso') be determined in accordance with the Rome Convention. This is understood to mean that, by virtue of Article 57, the Convention applies, in Italy, to *any* situation in the field of contracts, including situations that the Convention itself is unwilling to regulate.

Arbitration agreements provide an illustration of the function performed by Article 57. The Rome Convention, as stated in Article 1(2)(d), explicitly

---

5 See, for instance, Cass., 26 October 2018, No. 27311, *Pluris*, concerning a joint venture created between two Italian companies for works to be carried out in Spain. The Court conceded that the matter involved, in principle, the application of the Rome I Regulation, but noted that, at first instance and on appeal, the parties had failed to give evidence of the foreign element of the contract, and held, accordingly, that they were precluded, on procedural grounds, from raising the issue of the applicable law.

6 <http://hcch.net>. See further below, section 8.1.

7 For an English translation of the Statute, by A. Montanari and V.A. Narcisi, see J. Basedow, G. Rühl, F. Ferrari and P. De Miguel Asensio (eds.), *Encyclopedia of Private International Law* (Edward Elgar 2017), 3329 ff.

excludes arbitration and choice-of-court agreements from its scope (the same is true of the Rome I Regulation, pursuant to Article 1(2)(e)). According to Article 57 of the Italian Statute of Private International Law, Italian courts are nevertheless required to resort to the Convention whenever the issue arises of determining the law applicable to such an agreement, on the assumption that these are contractual in nature (or may be assimilated to a contract). The Corte di Cassazione, for example, followed this approach in a ruling of 2013 where the question raised concerned the validity of an arbitration agreement.[8]

With the adoption of the Rome I Regulation, the issue arose of whether Article 57 should be understood as providing for the extended operation of the Regulation, rather than the Rome Convention. The wording of the provision, with its explicit reference to the Rome Convention, has remained unchanged. The case law of Italian courts is inconclusive on the issue. Persuasive arguments have been advanced in legal literature to support the view that, as a result of the entry into application of the Regulation, Article 57 ought to be read as referring to the Regulation itself, and no longer to the Convention.[9]

It is worth noting, on a more general note, that Italian courts tend to use Article 57 of the Statute as a *general* gateway to the application of the Rome Convention and the Rome I Regulation. Courts, in fact, often rely on that provision also in matters indisputably within the scope of those texts.[10] This practice is unfortunate, if not mistaken outright. The Convention and the Regulation apply *by their own force*, not by virtue of Article 57, to situations within their scope. Things could hardly be otherwise in view of the implementation order mentioned above, as regards the Convention, and in view of Article 288 of the Treaty on the Functioning of the European Union, as concerns the Regulation.[11]

---

8 Cass. (SU), 25 October 2013, No. 24153, *RDIPP* 2014, 663.

9 F. Marongiu Buonaiuti, 'Note introduttive – II', in F. Salerno and P. Franzina (eds.), *Regolamento CE n. 593/2008 del Parlamento europeo e del Consiglio del 17 giugno 2008 sulla legge applicabile alle obbligazioni contrattuali (Roma I) – Commentario, Le nuove leggi civili commentate* 2009, 535 ff. See, for the opposite view, F. Salerno, 'Note introduttive I', *ibid.*, 533 ff.

10 See, for instance, Cass., 26 October 2015, No. 21712, *Pluris*, concerning a gambling contract concluded (prior to the date of application of the Rome I Regulation) between a French company running a casino in Nice and a player based in Italy. For the purposes of determining the law applicable to the contract, the Supreme Court considered, first, Article 57 of the Italian Statute of Private International Law. Only in view of the reference made in that provision to the Rome Convention did the Court rely on the Convention itself to conclude that the contract was governed by French law.

11 Recent rulings suggest that the trend described above is gradually being abandoned. See, for instance, Cass., 10 April 2019, No. 10045, *Pluris*, regarding an employment contract between RAI, the Italian national broadcasting corporation, and one of its employees working at the RAI's offices in Istanbul. The Supreme Court, while mentioning that the impugned judgment included a reference to Article 57, refrained from relying on the latter provision in its own reasoning and rather applied directly the Rome Convention (applicable in the circumstances *ratione temporis*).

When the Italian Statute of Private International Law was enacted, some authors submitted that Article 57 was meant to perform, inter alia, a 'pedagogic' function: this consisted of reminding courts of the existence of the Convention, thereby fostering its proper operation.[12] The argument is no longer convincing, provided it ever was. In fact, practice shows that Article 57 has become a source of disorientation for some courts.[13]

For instance, in a ruling of 2018, the Tribunal of Monza resorted to the Rome Convention to determine the law governing a demand guarantee concluded three years earlier between an Italian company and a person living in Switzerland, i.e. a contract that clearly fell as such within the scope of the Regulation.[14] In its reasoning, the Tribunal made in fact no reference to the Regulation, and rather mentioned Article 57 of the Italian Statute of Private International Law.

A judgment given in 2015 by the Tribunal of Livorno provides another example of the kind of difficulties that courts may run into when they rely on Article 57.[15] The case was about a charter party concluded in 2012. The issue arose of the law applicable to the contract. The Tribunal resorted for this to the Rome Convention, via Article 57, not to the Rome I Regulation. Ironically, the Tribunal, having reached the conclusion that the contract was governed by Italian law based on the choice made by the parties under Article 3 of the Rome Convention, observed, as a side note, that the principle of party autonomy is also enshrined in Article 3 of the Rome I Regulation, as if the latter had not been directly applicable to the case.

1.2. NON-CONTRACTUAL OBLIGATIONS

1.2.1. From Domestic Conflict-of-Law Rules to the Rome II Regulation

Prior to 11 July 2008, the date on which the Regulation No. 864/2007 of 11 July 2007 on the Law Applicable to Non-contractual Obligations (Rome II)[16] became applicable in its entirety, the law applicable to torts and

---

12 A. Giardina, 'Il rinvio alle convenzioni di diritto internazionale privato e processuale', in F. Salerno (ed.), *Convenzioni internazionali e legge di riforma del diritto internazionale privato* (Cedam 1997), 11 ff.

13 See further, on the reasons for a reform of Article 57, A. Malatesta, 'Riflessioni per una revisione della legge n. 218/1995 in materia di legge applicabile alle obbligazioni contrattuali ed extracontrattuali', in C. Campiglio (ed.), *Un nuovo diritto internazionale privato* (Wolters Kluwer 2019), 115 ff.

14 Trib. Monza, 23 October 2018, *DeJure*.

15 Trib. Livorno, 12 November 2015, *GiustUp*.

16 [2007] OJ L 199/40.

other non-contractual obligations was to be determined in Italy pursuant to Articles 61, 62 and 63 of the Italian Statute on Private International Law.[17]

The three provisions are still in force and have not been amended in light of the Regulation. Of course, they currently apply only to cases outside the scope of the Regulation itself.

The Tribunal of Trento dealt with one such case in a ruling of 2017.[18] At issue was the liability of the defendant, an Italian national, in his capacity as the sole director of an English company. The plaintiff, an Italian company, had obtained a payment order against the said English company, but had been unable to enforce it as a result of the insolvency of the latter and its voluntary winding-up. The claimant alleged that the insolvency was fraudulent in nature, and sought to recover the debt from the director, personally. The Tribunal held that the matter fell outside the scope of the Rome II Regulation, noting that, pursuant to Article 1(2)(d), the Regulation does not apply to non-contractual obligations arising out of the law of companies, as regards matters such as the creation or winding-up of a company, or the personal liability of officers as such for the company's obligations. In light of this finding, the Tribunal turned to Article 62 of the Italian Statute of Private International Law.

1.2.2. Quantitative Findings

The vast majority of the Italian judgments that refer to the Rome II Regulation are first instance or appellate court judgments.[19] More than 30 such judgments can be found in publicly available databases. The Corte di Cassazione, for its part, referred to the Regulation in no less than five decisions, none of which, however, raised issues governed by the Regulation itself.[20]

---

17 Article 61 applies to obligations that arise from the operation of law, as opposed to obligations based on consent and obligations resulting from a tort. Articles 62 and 63, instead, apply to torts. Pursuant to the former – the general rule on torts – torts are governed by the law of the country in which the damage occurred. The person who has sustained the damage, however, has the right to request that the tort be governed by the law of the country in which the event giving rise to the damage occurred. As an exception, if the tort involved only persons who are nationals of, and reside in, the same country, the law of that country applies. Article 63 lays down a special rule on product liability.

18 Trib. Trento, 17 February 2017, *GiustUp*.

19 See, F. Marchetti, 'Rapporto sull'applicazione in Italia del Regolamento (CE) n. 864/2007 dell'11 luglio 2008 sulla legge applicabile alle obbligazioni extracontrattuali («Roma II»)', in S. Bariatti, I. Viarengo and F.C. Villata (eds.), above n. 4, 119 ff.

20 See, for instance, Cass. (SU), 26 October 2018, No. 27164, *Pluris*. The Court had been asked to determine whether Italian courts possessed jurisdiction to entertain a case of unfair competition brought by an Italian radio broadcaster against a radio broadcaster based in Slovenia. Only for the purpose of interpreting Article 5(3) of Regulation (EC) No. 44/2001 on Jurisdiction and the Recognition and Enforcement of Judgments in Civil and Commercial Matters did the Court refer, as a reinforcing argument, to Article 6 of the Rome II Regulation.

1.2.3. *Other Rules Relevant on Non-Contractual Obligations*

As far as torts are concerned, Italian courts have only occasionally referred to international conventions enjoying primacy over the Rome II Regulation. Further information on those conventions are provided below in this chapter.[21]

2. THE SCOPE OF THE REGULATIONS

2.1. CONTRACTS

Pursuant to Article 1(1), the Rome I Regulation applies, 'in situations involving a conflict of laws, to contractual obligations in civil and commercial matters'. A list of excluded matters appears in Article 1(2). The two provisions only slightly depart from the corresponding provisions in the Rome Convention.

The material scope of the Regulation was discussed by the Corte di Cassazione in a ruling of 2012.[22] A woman sought to recover a debt from an Italian company that was the subject of insolvency proceedings. The claim related to the work carried out by the woman as a representative of the said company in France. The Court held that Regulation No. 1346/2000 on insolvency proceedings, then in force, rather than the Rome Regulation or the Rome Convention, applied to the matter. The Court acknowledged that, pursuant to Article 10 of Regulation No. 1346/2000, 'the effects of insolvency proceedings on employment contracts and relationships shall be governed by the law of the Member State applicable to the contract of employment', but observed that the scope of the latter provision is limited to civil law issues relating to the continuation of contractual relationships once insolvency proceedings have been opened. As stated in Article 4(2) of Regulation No. 1346/2000, it is for the law of the Member State where insolvency proceedings have been opened to regulate the impact of insolvency on current contracts to which the debtor is a party, the claims to be lodged against the debtor's estate, the treatment of claims arising after the opening of insolvency proceedings, or the distribution of proceeds from the realisation of the debtor's assets.

Both the Rome Convention (Article 1(2)(e)) and the Rome I Regulation (Article 1(2)(f)) clarify that they are not concerned with questions governed by the law of companies and other bodies, such as the creation, legal capacity, internal organisation or winding-up of those entities, and the personal liability

---

21 See further below, section 8.2.

22 Cass. (SU), 4 June 2012, No. 8931, *DeJure*.

of officers and members for the obligations thereof. In a judgment of 2012, the Tribunal of Monza held, on this basis, that the Rome Convention does not apply to the liability of the directors and other officers of a company in liquidation that allegedly results from the protracted activity of the company itself, despite the total loss of the share capital.[23]

In 2010, the Corte di Cassazione referred to the above exclusion to assert that the Rome Convention does not apply to the issues of the formal and substantive validity of a preliminary contract for the setting-up of a company.[24] By contrast, the Rome Convention has been deemed to apply to: a contract for the transfer of shares;[25] an option agreement contemplating the repurchase by a company of its own shares;[26] and the transactions whereby the shareholders of a company transferred the ownership of immoveable property to the company itself.[27]

2.2. NON-CONTRACTUAL OBLIGATIONS

Apart from the 2017 ruling of the Tribunal of Trento on the liability of a company's officer, illustrated above,[28] the material scope of the Rome II Regulation has apparently never been discussed at length by Italian courts.

Rather, various courts have addressed the issue of the temporal scope of application of the Regulation. Only a few cases, however, proved problematic. In a ruling of 2013, the Tribunal of Trieste resorted to the Regulation to determine the law governing liability resulting from a traffic accident which occurred after the entry into force of the Regulation (20 August 2007), but prior to its date of application, as specified in Article 32 (11 January 2009).[29] In fact, the Tribunal failed to consider the ruling of the CJEU in *Homawoo*, where it was clarified that Articles 31 and 32 of the Rome II Regulation, read in conjunction with Article 297 TFEU, 'must be interpreted as requiring a national court to apply the Regulation only to events giving rise to damage occurring after 11 January 2009'.[30]

23 Trib. Monza, 9 July 2012, *Pluris*.
24 Cass., 19 April 2010, No. 9276, *RDIPP* 2011, 194.
25 Trib. Roma, 8 May 2007, *Pluris*.
26 CA Milano, 15 July 2003, *RDIPP* 2004, 1367.
27 CA Milano, 27 October 2009, *RDIPP* 2010, 722.
28 See above n. 18.
29 Trib. Trieste, 11 July 2013, *RDIPP* 2013, 796.
30 Case C-412/10, *Homawoo v. GMF Assurances* ECLI:EU:C:2011:747. The ruling of the CJEU has instead been noted, and followed, by several other courts: see, among others, CA Genova, 12 May 2015, *GiustUp*, and Trib. Torino, 16 March 2017, *ibid*.

3. CHOICE OF LAW

3.1. CONTRACTS

Italian courts have addressed numerous cases concerning contracts featuring a choice-of-law clause. Several judgments involve a rather straightforward application of the relevant rules of the Rome Convention and the Rome I Regulation.[31] The majority of these judgments bring little added value to the understanding of the two instruments and will not be the object of detailed analysis in this report.

The focus will rather be on a selection of rulings dealing with controversial or less common issues, such as: the evidence needed to assert the existence and content of a tacit choice of law; the circumstances in which the parties to a contract should be considered to have resorted to *dépeçage*; and the legal treatment of clauses that materially incorporate foreign rules or non-State rules into the contract, or provide that the contract be governed as such by a body of non-State rules.

3.1.1. Tacit Choice

Article 3(1) of the Rome I Regulation requires that choice-of-law agreements be made expressly or be 'clearly demonstrated by the terms of the contract or the circumstances of the case'. Similarly, according to Article 3(1) of the Rome Convention, a tacit choice may be enforced so long as its existence and content are 'demonstrated with reasonable certainty by the terms of the contract or the circumstances of the case'. The Supreme Court noted in a ruling of 2019 that the provisions on tacit choice in the Rome Convention and in the Rome I Regulation, while not identical in their wording, must be understood to have, in substance, the same meaning.[32]

Italian courts have dealt with tacit choices on various occasions. The Tribunal of Rome, for example, considered the rules on tacit choice in a case of 2007 concerning the transfer of shares in an Italian company between an Italian company, on the one hand, and an Italian national and a Luxembourg company, on the other. The Tribunal found that the parties had tacitly agreed that the contract be governed by Italian law. According to the Tribunal, this was demonstrated, inter alia, by the fact that the contract was drafted in Italian and that its clauses made use of Italian legal terminology and included references to specific provisions of the Italian Civil Code.[33]

---

31 See, among others, Cass. (SU), 11 July 1997, No. 6328, *Giustizia civile - Massimario* 1997, 1184; Cass. (SU), 25 October 2013, No. 24153, *RDIPP* 2014, 663.

32 Cass., 10 April 2019, No. 10045, *Pluris*.

33 Trib. Roma, 8 May 2007, *Pluris*.

In a ruling of 2010, the Corte di Cassazione concluded that an employment contract between a German company and an Italian employee posted to a subsidiary in Italy had been tacitly submitted by the parties to German law.[34] The Court relied on several indicia, including the language of the agreement (the German language), the place of negotiation and conclusion (in Germany), and the fact that the salary ought to be paid in German marks. Additionally, the Court observed that, during the life of the contract, none of the parties had raised any objection to the alleged application of German law.

The same year, in another ruling concerning an employment contract between an Italian company and a worker posted to a foreign subsidiary, the Court found that the parties had tacitly chosen Italian law.[35] One decisive element was that the agreement included various references to Italian law and Italian legal concepts. The finding, the Court added, was confirmed by the fact that the parties had agreed to confer jurisdiction over disputes relating to the contract on the Tribunal of Milan.

In a ruling of 2018 concerning a demand guarantee, the Tribunal of Monza held that the parties, an Italian company and a resident of Switzerland, had tacitly agreed that the contract be submitted to Italian law pursuant to Article 3 of the Rome Convention.[36] According to the Tribunal, the choice resulted from an explicit reference made in the contract to a particular provision of the Italian Civil Code. Specifically, a clause provided that, by derogation to Article 1944, paragraph 2, of the Code, the beneficiary was not required to demand payment from the main debtor as a pre-condition for enforcing the guarantee. While acknowledging that the reference was meant to exclude the application of the said provision, the Tribunal observed that such an exclusion implied that the parties intended to have the contract governed by Italian law: the exclusion, the Tribunal noted, would have made little sense otherwise.

In 2019, the Court of Appeal of Florence, seised of a dispute concerning a commercial agency agreement concluded in 2003 between a company incorporated in the United States and an Italian company (as agent), concluded that the parties had tacitly agreed on the application of Italian law. The Court relied for that on the following indicia: the parties had conferred exclusive jurisdiction over their disputes to an Italian court; the agreement, which the parties had drafted both in Italian and in English, included a clause whereby the Italian version was to be considered the sole authentic version; the agreement included a reference to the opening provision of the section of the Italian Civil Code devoted to agency contracts.[37]

---

34 Cass., 25 November 2010, No. 23933, *RDIPP* 2011, 474.

35 Cass., 15 July 2010, No. 16579, *RDIPP* 2011, 1045.

36 Trib. Monza, 23 October 2018, *DeJure*.

37 CA Firenze, 1 October 2019, *GiustUp*.

3.1.2. Dépeçage

Article 3(1) of the Rome I Regulation, like Article 3(1) of the Rome Convention, stipulates that the parties may, by their choice, 'select the law applicable to the whole or to part only of the contract'. A partial choice results in the *dépeçage* of the contract, meaning that the contract is split into two or more parts, each governed by a different law.

The Italian Supreme Court referred to *dépeçage* in two rulings. The first, rendered in 2001, concerned an exclusive distribution agreement concluded between an Italian and an Austrian company.[38] The Supreme Court found that the parties had referred to Austrian law in their agreement, but held that that reference could not be construed as a choice of law for the whole contract. Austrian law was referred to in a single clause of the agreement, concerning the remedies available to the buyer in the event of delivery of defective goods. No references to Austrian law featured in other clauses, in particular those governing the commercial cooperation between the parties, which appeared to be the key element of the relationship. The Court concluded that Austrian law merely applied to the remedies referred to above, and turned to Article 4 of the Convention to determine the law applicable to the remaining aspects of the relationship.

The second decision dates from 2014 and regards a shipwreck insurance contract.[39] The contract included a 'classification clause', listing the requirements that the insured vessel had to comply with for the insurance to apply. The clause featured an express choice of English law, which was deemed by the Court to apply to the classification clause alone, based on its language and the circumstances. All other aspects of the contract, the Court held, were governed by Italian law.

3.1.3. Clauses Incorporating Foreign Rules or Designating Non-State Law

The view is generally accepted among scholars that a choice-of-law agreement substantially differs from an agreement to incorporate into the contract one or more provisions belonging to a law other than the *lex contractus*, or to a body of non-State rules.[40] The Rome I Regulation itself refers to the distinction. As stated in Recital 13, the Regulation 'does not preclude parties from incorporating by reference into their contract a non-State body of law or an international convention'. It is for the applicable (State) law to determine whether, to what

---

38 Cass. (SU), 11 June 2001, No. 7860, *RDIPP* 2002, 157.

39 Cass., 5 December 2014, No. 25735, *DeJure*.

40 See, among others, P. Mankowski, 'Article 3', in U. Magnus and P. Mankowski (eds.), *The Rome I Regulation – Commentary* (Otto Schmidt 2016), 189 f.

extent and subject to which conditions the incorporated terms are valid and enforceable.

The issue of incorporation has been considered in one Italian ruling, rendered by the Administrative Tribunal for the Region of Lazio in 2009.[41] The Tribunal was seised of a dispute concerning an employment contract concluded between the Italian Institute for Foreign Trade (a governmental agency) and an Italian national, hired to work in Germany. The parties had agreed to submit certain aspects of their relationship to specific German provisions relating to public employment contracts. The Tribunal held that the clause could not be construed as an agreement to submit the entire relationship to German law.[42] It noted that the parties' intention, as evidenced by the language of the clause and the circumstances in which the contract had been concluded, was simply to incorporate the above German provisions into their agreement.

As indicated in Recital 13 of the Rome I Regulation, incorporation is also at issue where the parties agree to have their contract governed by *lex mercatoria*, by a body of non-State rules, or by an international convention that would not apply to the contract by its own force. No judgment could be found concerning contracts featuring these kinds of clauses.[43] It is worth noting, however, that Italian courts have displayed, albeit occasionally, a rather open attitude towards non-State law. In an old case, rendered in 1982, the Corte di Cassazione referred to *lex mercatoria* as a body of regularly observed rules, which the *societas mercatorum*, that is, the actors of international trade considered as a community, perceive as binding despite the lack of formal recognition by States.[44] The Court's statement has been welcomed by some as the beginning of a promising development (and criticised by others), but has only rarely referred to in later case law.[45]

Rather, references to non-State rules have surfaced in decisions regarding specific non-State instruments. In 2005, for example, the Tribunal of Reggio Emilia ruled on a dispute concerning a documentary credit.[46] The Tribunal

41 Administrative Tribunal for the Region of Lazio, 30 November 2009, No. 12025, *Pluris*.

42 Since the contract predated the entry into force of the Rome Convention, the conflict-of-law issues raised by the case were settled by the Tribunal with reference to Article 25 of the introductory book of the Italian Civil Code, as it applied then. The provision enabled the parties to agree on a choice of law. Though not based on the European regime on contract conflicts, the reasoning of the Tribunal illustrates the way in which the issue of incorporation would plausibly be approached under the Rome I Regulation.

43 Things are different when reference is made to arbitral, as opposed to judicial, proceedings. See, for example, the award rendered in Rome on 4 December 1996 in a dispute between Morgan Stanley Capital Group and Enel, *Diritto del commercio internazionale* 1999, 474, where the arbitral tribunal applied the Unidroit Principles on International Commercial Contracts.

44 Cass., 8 February 1982, No. 722, *RDIPP* 1982, 829.

45 See further F. Marrella, *La nuova lex mercatoria – Principi Unidroit ed usi dei contratti del commercio internazionale* (Cedam 2003), 539 ff.

46 Trib. Reggio Emilia, 16 August 2005, *Pluris*.

observed that the obligations undertaken by the issuing bank were the object of detailed and well-settled rules developed through international commercial practice, whereas the Italian Civil Code only devoted to the topic few provisions of a general character. This led the Tribunal to decide the case in accordance with the practice evidenced in the Uniform Customs and Practice for Documentary Credits (UCP 600) prepared by the International Chamber of Commerce (ICC). The finding can hardly be assimilated to the enforcement, by the Tribunal, of a 'choice' of the UCP 600. Rather, the reference to the ICC rules UCP 600 seems to rest on the fact that, as a matter of Italian law (the law applicable to the matter), the parties to a contract, absent evidence of an intention to the contrary, are presumed to have incorporated such (trade) usages as are relevant to their relationship.

3.2. NON-CONTRACTUAL OBLIGATIONS

Article 14 of the Rome II Regulation enables the parties to a non-contractual obligation to choose the law applicable to their relationship. The choice can be made by an agreement entered into after the event giving rise to the damage occurred or, where all the parties are pursuing a commercial activity, by an agreement freely negotiated before the event. The provision clarifies that the choice can be made expressly or 'demonstrated with reasonable certainty by the circumstances of the case'.

The Tribunal of Varese considered Article 14 in a ruling rendered in 2012.[47] The case revolved around the compensation sought by an Italian woman for the harm she suffered as a result of a road accident in Spain. The governing law would have normally been Spanish law, pursuant to Article 4(1) of the Regulation. The Tribunal, however, considered that the parties, though not expressly, had agreed on the application of Italian law. In the course of the proceedings, the parties constantly referred to rules, institutions and concepts that are typical of the Italian legal system, as well as to the case law of Italian courts. According to the Tribunal, this amounted to an agreement by the parties to have the case decided, as to its substance, in conformity with Italian law.

The reasoning of the Tribunal of Varese does not differ from the reasoning that a court would normally use to assert the existence of a procedural agreement (or *accord procédural*, to use the expression by which these agreements are known in France, where they have been the subject of extensive scholarly consideration).[48] Procedural agreements, it is submitted, should be distinguished

---

47 Trib. Varese, 13 January 2012, *RDIPP* 2013, 798.

48 See, among others, B. Fauvarque-Cosson, 'L'accord procédural à l'épreuve du temps', in *Le droit international privé: esprit et méthodes – Mélanges en l'honneur de Paul Lagarde* (Dalloz 2005), 263.

from choice-of-law agreements. The latter represent the exercise of a freedom of choice the foundation of which lies in the applicable conflict-of-law rules. As such, choice-of-law agreements are only enforceable to the extent they meet the requirements provided for in those rules. Procedural agreements, by contrast, are legal devices whereby litigants are given the opportunity to 'deactivate' the conflict-of-law rule(s) that would otherwise apply in the circumstances. They are 'procedural' in the sense that they purport to affect the standards upon which the seised court will adjudicate the matter, whereas choice-of-law agreements ultimately aim at shaping the substance of the legal relationship concerned, with effects that are not limited to a given set of proceedings.

The Rome II Regulation enables the parties to agree on a choice of law. Arguably, however, it does not permit the parties to exclude, by agreement, the operation of the Regulation itself, if only by reference to specific court proceedings. Nothing in the wording or in the purpose of the Regulation indicates that its rules are optional in nature. Besides, the primacy of EU law and the general conditions that frame the procedural autonomy of Member States in matters governed by EU law prevent a procedural rule of the forum – one that would enable the litigants to instruct the court as to the adjudication of the case – from subverting, let alone ruling out, the operation of the Regulation.

In scenarios like the one considered by the Tribunal of Varese, the issue is, basically, whether the parties to the non-contractual relationship under consideration intended to agree on the law governing the substance of such relationship (rather than the conduct of the proceedings) and, if so, whether their agreement complied with the requirements in Article 14 of the Rome II Regulation. Various elements need to be considered when carrying out a similar inquiry, including whether the lawyers in fact had the power to bind the parties as to the substance of their relationship (as opposed to merely represent them for the purposes of the proceedings). One further question is whether the Regulation leaves the parties free to enter into a choice-of-law agreement as late as after proceedings are initiated on the non-contractual obligation in question. The Regulation does not take an explicit stance on the issue, and apparently leaves the matter with the *lex processus* (provided, of course, that the latter does not undermine the effectiveness of the Regulation). None of these questions were raised, let alone addressed, by the Tribunal of Varese in its decision. The reasoning of the Tribunal on this aspect is thus, at most, simplistic.

The Tribunal of Bologna displayed a more cautious attitude in a judgment issued in 2014.[49] The dispute concerned a road accident in Romania involving two Romanian nationals, one living in Italy, the other in Romania. The Tribunal rejected the view that, as in the previous case, the parties had agreed, by their

49 Trib. Bologna, 17 March 2014, *RDIPP* 2017, 126.

procedural conduct, on the application of Italian law. The victim had agreed to undergo a medical examination at the premises of the insurance company in Italy, and an out-of-court dispute settlement had been negotiated there between the parties. The Tribunal, however, found that these elements were not enough to substantiate a tacit choice of the applicable law and ultimately ruled on the substance of the case in accordance with Romanian law.

4. THE LAW APPLICABLE IN THE ABSENCE OF CHOICE

4.1. CONTRACTS

4.1.1. The Law Applicable Pursuant to Article 4 Rome I Regulation

In the absence of a choice by the parties, the law applicable to a contract must be determined, as a rule, in accordance with Article 4 of the Rome I Regulation. Article 4(1) sets forth eight special conflict-of-law rules, each referring to a type of contract. Pursuant to Article 4(2), where the contract is not covered by any of those special rules, or where the elements of the contract would be covered by more than one of them, the governing law shall be the law of the country where the party required to effect the characteristic performance habitually resides. Article 4(3) provides for an escape clause. This applies '[w]here it is clear from all the circumstances of the case that the contract is manifestly more closely connected with a country other than that indicated' in the previous rules, and results in the application of the law of that other country. Finally, Article 4(4) sets forth a residual rule according to which, where the applicable law cannot be determined pursuant to Article 4(1) and (2), the governing law shall be the law of the country with which the contract is most closely connected.

The number of published judgments that apply Article 4 of the Rome I Regulation is still relatively limited in Italy. So far, only one ruling – rendered by the Tribunal of Bologna in 2015 – features a rather detailed analysis of the provision.[50] The facts of the case are rather peculiar. A Panamanian company had transferred monies to an Italian national living in Italy. According to the company, the monies were meant to be used by the recipient to purchase an apartment in Italy on behalf of the company. The company sued the recipient before the Tribunal of Bologna seeking restitution of the funds. The defendant acknowledged that he had received an amount of money from the Panamanian company, but argued that he was entitled to keep it. He explained that he had been in an emotional relationship with the representative of the company for about ten years, and claimed that the funds in fact represented a donation

---

50 Trib. Bologna, 9 November 2015, *Pluris*.

made to him by her through the company, which she in fact controlled. The defendant produced a document, which the company unsuccessfully challenged as false, in which the woman had expressed the intention to make a gift to him. The Tribunal held that the law applicable to a donation must be determined in conformity with the Rome I Regulation.[51] It found that the document signed by the woman did not include a choice of law and accordingly turned to Article 4 of the Rome I Regulation. Donations, it observed, are not among the types of contracts listed in Article 4(1) of the Regulation. It thus turned to Article 4(2) and held that the law applicable to a gift is the law of the country where the party who is to perform the characteristic obligation – the donor – has his or her habitual residence or its central administration: Panama, in the circumstances.

4.1.2. The Law Applicable Pursuant to Article 4 Rome Convention

Italian courts have applied Article 4 of the Rome Convention in several cases. It is worth recalling that the approach followed by the Convention to identify the law applicable to a contract in the absence of a choice of law by the parties differs significantly from the approach of the Regulation.

Article 4(1) of the Convention submits the contract to 'the law of the country with which it is most closely connected', that is, based on the general presumption in Article 4(2): 'the country where the party who is to effect the performance which is characteristic of the contract has, at the time of conclusion of the contract, his habitual residence, or, in the case of a body corporate or unincorporate, its central administration'. The general presumption in Article 4(2), as well as the specific presumptions in Article 4(3) and (4) of the Convention for contracts having as their object a right *in rem* over immovable property (or the right to use immovable property) and contracts for the carriage of goods may be displaced under the escape clause in Article 4(5) whenever the contract appears to be more closely connected with another country, in which case the law of that other country applies. All in all, the Convention's approach is more flexible than the Regulation's. The main concern underlying the Regulation is abstract predictability. In the Convention, the balance between proximity and predictability was struck closer to proximity.

Most of the judgments rendered in Italy on the basis of Article 4 of the Convention are of limited or no practical interest today. This is due not only to the fact that, as mentioned, the approach of the Convention substantially differs from that of the Regulation. The limited relevance of those rulings is also due to the predominant interpretive posture taken by Italian courts towards Article 4 of the Convention.

---

51 On the applicability of the European regime on contract conflicts to 'contractual' donations, see the Giuliano–Lagarde report on the Rome Convention [1980] OJ C 282/1, under Article 1(30).

For a long time, the prevailing view in Italy has been that the Convention gives the authority seised of the case a very broad margin of appreciation. Most Italian courts, including the Corte di Cassazione, held the opinion that, in the absence of a choice by the parties, the seised court is not required, strictly speaking, to consider the general presumption in Article 4(2) or the special presumptions as may be relevant to the circumstances. In determining the country with which the contract is most closely connected, the seised court – according to the Italian case law – is free to decide on a case-by-case basis whether to rely on the above presumptions or to carry out a 'free' assessment of the case at issue and its connections.

A ruling of the Tribunal of Monza, concerning a contract for the sale of goods between an Italian buyer and a Moroccan seller, provides an illustration of this approach.[52] The contract in question was a rather ordinary sale of goods. Yet the Tribunal had no hesitation in disregarding the presumption in Article 4(2), which would have resulted in the application of Moroccan law. The Tribunal held that the most significant ties of the contract were with Italy, noting that the parties had agreed that the goods would be delivered in Italy and that the price would be paid under a letter of credit issued by an Italian bank. The Tribunal considered that this was enough to conclude that the case ought to be decided under Italian law.

Italian courts only reconsidered their overly flexible posture after the CJEU clarified in *Intercontainer Interfrigo* that the applicable law must always be determined on the basis of the presumptions set out in Article 4, as these 'satisfy the general requirement of foreseeability of the law and thus of legal certainty in contractual relationships'.[53] Only where the above presumptions appear to lack any genuine connecting value, the CJEU added, should the seised court be allowed to freely assess the circumstances of the case for the purposes of Article 4(5).

For instance, the Corte di Cassazione made a rather plain application of the presumptions set out in Article 4 in a ruling of 2019.[54] An independent asset management counsel, who had been instructed to manage the personal property of one of his clients, was not paid in full for his services. To determine the law governing the relationship between the counsel and his client, the Court limited itself to observing that the former had his habitual residence in Italy and concluded on this basis that the contract was governed by Italian law.

---

52 Trib. Monza, 15 February 2007, *Pluris*. This is one out of many rulings where Italian courts failed to apply the 1955 Hague Convention on Contracts for International Sales of Goods, and rather referred to either the Rome Convention or the Rome I Regulation in spite of the fact that, under the latter instruments, the Convention should prevail. See further below, section 8.1.

53 Case C-133/08, *Intercontainer Interfrigo SC (ICF) v. Balkenende Oosthuizen BV and MIC Operations BV*, ECLI:EU:C:2009:617, para. 62.

54 Cass. (SU), 12 June 2019, No. 15748, *Pluris*.

There are further reasons why a significant part of the case law of Italian courts relating to Article 4 of the Rome Convention is devoid, today, of practical interest.

Several Italian judgments have discussed the issue of whether the characteristic obligation of a distribution agreement is, in principle, the obligation of the grantor or of the distributor.[55] Now that the Rome I Regulation includes a special conflict-of-law rule for distribution contracts, the whole discussion is no longer relevant in practice: pursuant to Article 4(1)(f), a distribution contract, absent a choice by the parties, 'is governed by the law of the country where the distributor has his habitual residence'.

In the end, just a few judgments referring to Article 4 of the Rome Convention plausibly retain some practical relevance under the Regulation. These are basically cases that would need to be addressed today under Article 4(2) of the Rome I Regulation, under the escape clause in Article 4(3), or under the residual rule in Article 4(4).

One such judgment was rendered in 2005 by the Corte di Cassazione concerning a joint venture agreement between a German company and an Italian company in contemplation of a contract with a US company for the licence of a trademark owned by the latter.[56] The Court held that none of the parties to the joint venture could be regarded as the party required to perform the characteristic performance for the purposes of Article 4(2) of the Convention. Consequently, the Court moved on to identify, based on the circumstances of the case, the country with which the contract was most closely connected. The Court began by noting that, under the joint venture agreement, the parties had undertaken to cooperate in the negotiation of a licence agreement that would enable them to market shoes bearing the licensed trademark in several European countries. Those countries had been divided into two groups, and the parties had agreed that they would be, respectively, the sole distributor of the shoes in the countries of each group. The parties had also agreed that the goods would be manufactured in Italy by the Italian company. Based on the above circumstances, weighed one against each other, the Court concluded that the joint venture agreement was most closely connected to Italy.

It is submitted that, in a similar scenario, an analogous inquiry would need to be carried out today for the purposes of Article 4(4) of the Rome I Regulation. Doubts may instead be expressed as to the weight accorded, in the assessment, to the various ties considered. Where a contract is essentially aimed at *marketing* certain goods, the place where those goods ought to be *manufactured*, though certainly not irrelevant, can hardly be considered decisive. When the issue arises

---

55 See Cass. (SU), 11 June 2001, No. 7860, *RDIPP* 2002, 157; Cass. (SU), 4 May 2006, No. 10223, *RDIPP* 2007, 194; CA Roma, 18 December 2008, *Pluris*.

56 Cass. (SU), 3 May 2005, No. 9107, *Pluris*.

of a contract's closest connections, the focus should be on the circumstances that strictly relate to the (main) purpose of the contract, or the economic crux of the transaction. Only where the latter circumstances fail to provide a clear localisation of the contract should less pertinent indicia come to the fore.

The reasoning underlying a judgment given by the Corte di Cassazione in 2008 proves more persuasive in this respect.[57] An Italian company complained of the non-performance by a French company of the obligations undertaken under a joint venture agreement that also involved a third company based in Germany. Specifically, the French company had undertaken to submit a bid in its own name and on behalf of the two other parties in response to a tender issued by an Italian governmental agency, regarding services to be supplied in Italy. The French company lost interest in the tender and ultimately failed to submit the bid. The Corte di Cassazione referred to Article 4(5) of the Rome Convention and found that the contract's most significant ties were with Italy, where the services were to be provided and the bid was to be submitted.

4.2. NON-CONTRACTUAL OBLIGATIONS

4.2.1. Torts

Failing a choice of law under Article 14 of the Rome II Regulation, the law applicable to the non-contractual obligations arising out of a tort, is – according to the general rule set out in Article 4(1) of the Regulation – 'the law of the country in which the damage occurs irrespective of the country in which the event giving rise to the damage occurred and irrespective of the country or countries in which the indirect consequences of that event occur'. In accordance with Article 4(2), if both the person claimed to be liable and the victim of the tort have their habitual residence in the same country, the law of that country applies. An escape clause appears in Article 4(3) to cover cases where it is clear 'from all the circumstances' that the tort is 'manifestly more closely connected' with a country other than the country indicated in the Article 4(1) and (2).

Most of the cases decided by Italian courts on the grounds of Article 4 of the Rome II Regulation concern traffic accidents. In 2014, the Tribunal of Bologna held that Romanian law applied to the non-contractual obligations resulting from a car accident that occurred in Romania.[58] The fact that the accident had involved a car that was registered in Italy and insured by an Italian insurer was not enough to entail, the Tribunal observed, the application of Italian law under Article 4(3). In a ruling of 2015, the Tribunal of Modena, seised of an action for

57 Cass. (SU), 27 February 2008, No. 5091, *RDIPP* 2008, 1090.

58 Trib. Bologna, 17 March 2014, *RDIPP* 2017, 126.

damages brought by an Italian national living in Italy, similarly held that the liability arising out of an accident that occurred in Hungary was governed by Hungarian law.[59]

The Tribunal of Torino held in 2015 that Italian law applied to the liability arising out of a car accident which occurred in Morocco.[60] It did so on the basis of Article 4(2) of the Regulation, noting that both the driver and the victim (a pedestrian), had their habitual residence in Italy when the accident took place. The Tribunal of Monza followed a similar reasoning in a judgment of 2017, regarding the liability arising from an accident which occurred in Spain, given that the negligent driver and the injured passengers were all habitually resident in Italy at the time of the facts.[61] The Tribunal of Reggio Emilia, too, relied on Article 4(2) of the Rome II Regulation to state that Italian law applied to a case regarding an accident which occurred in Spain, which only involved persons whose habitual residence was in Italy.[62]

In a ruling of 2016, the Tribunal of Bolzano relied on Article 4(1) of the Rome II Regulation in a case regarding the liability arising from a ski accident caused by a child whose habitual residence was in Germany.[63] The Tribunal held that Italian law was applicable since the accident had occurred in Italy.

4.2.2. Other Non-Contractual Obligations

The author of this report is not aware of any Italian decisions referring to the rules set out in the Rome II Regulation for unjust enrichment (Article 10) and *negotiorum gestio* (Article 11).

One judgment, given by the Tribunal of Udine in 2018, involved, instead, the special conflict-of-laws rule on pre-contractual liability (Article 12).[64] The case may be summarised as follows. A Slovenian company wished to submit a tender for the realisation of a storing facility at the port of Koper, in Slovenia. To this end, the Slovenian company got in touch with an Italian company, with the understanding that, had the contract been awarded to the former, the two companies would have joined forces to perform the resulting obligations together. The contract was in fact awarded to the Slovenian company, but the two companies proved unable to agree on a framework of cooperation. The Italian company complained, among other things, that, in submitting the tender, the Slovenian company had indicated, for the work to be done by the Italian company, a significantly lower remuneration than the amount that the parties

59 Trib. Modena, 4 December 2015, *Pluris*.
60 Trib. Torino, 20 October 2015, *GiustUp*.
61 Trib. Monza, 6 April 2017, *GiustUp*.
62 Trib. Reggio Emilia, 1 April 2019, *GiustUp*.
63 Trib. Bolzano, 13 October 2016, *GiustUp*.
64 Trib. Udine, 10 August 2018, *GiustUp*.

had discussed in preparation of the tender. In view of the inability to reach an agreement, the Slovenian company ultimately entered into a cooperation agreement with another undertaking.

The Italian company sued the Slovenian company, claiming that the latter had acted in breach of its duties of good faith in pre-contractual dealings. The Tribunal noted that Article 12(1) was not applicable in the circumstances, since the law that would have been applicable to the cooperation contract had it been entered into could not be determined. It turned then to Article 12(2)(a), according to which the law applicable to *culpa in contrahendo* is the law of the country in which the damage occurred. The Tribunal held on this basis that the alleged liability of the Slovenian company was governed by Italian law, since the prejudice complained of by the plaintiff had allegedly occurred in Italy.

The Tribunal's reasoning is very short in this passage. Overall, its conclusions fall short of being persuasive. The Tribunal apparently relied very much on the allegations made by the Italian company, i.e. the latter's assertions as to the existence (and localisation) of the harm. This way, however, the Tribunal failed to distinguish between the localisation of the event giving rise to the damage and the localisation of the 'indirect consequences' thereof. Only the former, not the latter, is relevant under Article 12(2)(a) to determining the law applicable to *culpa in contrahendo*.

5. SPECIAL CONFLICT-OF-LAWS RULES

5.1. CONTRACTS

The case law of Italian courts regarding the special conflict-of-laws rules set out in the Rome I Regulation and the Rome Convention concerning contracts of carriage and insurance contracts appears to consist of a handful of rulings. By contrast, various decisions may be found in databases that involve the application of the special rules on consumer contracts and, more often, individual contracts of employment.

5.1.1. Contracts Concluded by Consumers

The Milan Chamber of the 'Arbitro Bancario Finanziario', an institution created under a law of 2005 to promote the settlement of disputes between banks, financial intermediaries and private investors, heard in 2014 a case relating to a financial contract concluded between a natural person residing in Italy, acting as a consumer, and a financial entity based in an unspecified country.[65]

65 Arbitro Bancario Finanziario, 15 October 2014, *Foro italiano* 2015, I, 1111.

The contract featured a choice-of-law clause indicating German law as the law applicable to the contract.

The consumer had undertaken to make periodical contributions to a fund in contemplation of the purchase of a house, with the understanding that he would, in due course, borrow from the fund the rest of the money needed for the purchase. The consumer, however, decided to quit the fund. The financial entity paid him back all the contributions made, but withheld – in accordance with the contract, and as permitted by German law – an amount equal to 1 per cent of the contemplated loan, as a non-reimbursable fee.

The Chamber, relying on Article 5(2) of the Rome Convention (corresponding to Article 6(2) of the Rome I Regulation), held that the choice of German law could not have the result of depriving the consumer of the protection afforded to him by the mandatory provisions of the Italian legislation on financial contracts, specifically, the provisions according to which no costs and fees may be claimed by the professional upon the consumer's withdrawal from a contract, unless it is established that those costs and fees have in fact been incurred by the professional for the purposes of providing the consumer with additional services, required by him.

5.1.2. Individual Contracts of Employment

Italian courts have heard various cases relating to employment contracts featuring a choice-of-law clause,[66] or involving a tacit choice.[67] However, only in a few judgments have Italian courts discussed the provision in Article 6(1) of the Rome Convention, now Article 8(1) of the Rome I Regulation. This is the provision according to which the parties' choice may not have the effect of depriving the employee of the protection afforded to him by the mandatory provisions of the law that would have been applicable to the contract in the absence of choice.

The Corte di Cassazione heard in 2019 a case which, apparently, fitted precisely in the above provision.[68] The case revolved around a series of fixed-term employment contracts concluded in the space of nine years between the British Council and one of its staff working in Rome. The contracts in the series all featured a choice of English law. After the last contract in the series expired, the employee claimed that, pursuant to Italian law, the employment relationship had turned into a relationship of indefinite duration by operation of law. He sued the Council seeking the payment of resulting unpaid wages. The Supreme Court

---

66 See e.g. Trib. Milano, 15 July 2016, *Pluris*, concerning an employment contract that the parties had agreed to submit to the law of the Emirate of Abu Dhabi. See also below, section 7.1.2, for further references.

67 See above, section 3.1.1.

68 Cass. (SU), 8 March 2019, No. 6884, *Pluris*.

noted that Italian labour legislation (as it stood at the material time) did not permit fixed-term contracts to be reiterated in the manner the parties had done in the circumstances. However, instead of disregarding the choice of English law made by the parties on the ground that it deprived the employee of the protection afforded to him by mandatory provisions of Italian law, the Court held that the application of English law, which in fact permitted such a reiteration, would be at odds with the public policy of Italy.

Where disputes have been brought before Italian courts regarding employment contracts lacking a choice-of-law clause, the applicable law has almost invariably been determined by reference to the country in which (or from which) the employee habitually carried out his or her work in performance of the contract,[69] rather than the country where the place of business through which the employee was engaged is situated. Only occasionally did the actual identification of the country of habitual work prove problematic.

In a ruling of 2018, the Corte di Cassazione dealt with a dispute concerning the dismissal of a manager of a German bank.[70] The Court acknowledged that the manager carried out his work in different countries, including Italy, but concluded that the country where the latter habitually carried out his work, for the purposes of Article 6 of the Rome Convention (which applied to the contract *ratione temporis*), was in fact the United Kingdom. Building on the indications provided by the CJEU in *Mulox*,[71] *Petrus Wilhelmus Rutten*[72] and *Herbert Weber*,[73] the Court observed that, in fact, the manager's activity was centred in London: he had an office there, where he was assisted by a secretary; the contacts with his superiors mostly occurred there; his own family lived in the United Kingdom; his domicile for tax purposes was there; and his stays in Italy had been discontinuous in nature and had not been, globally, particularly long.

5.2. NON-CONTRACTUAL OBLIGATIONS

The author of this report is aware of only a few cases concerning the conflict-of-law rules laid down in the Rome II Regulation as regards special torts and

---

69 See e.g. Cass., 11 November 2002, No. 15822, *RDIPP* 2003, 978, regarding an employment contract between a bank whose seat and central administration were in Italy and one of his employees, who had been hired to work at the New York branch of the bank. The contract, which did not include a choice-of-law clause, was found to be governed by the law of the State of New York. The Corte di Cassazione, as will be discussed below, held, however, that the rules of that law regarding the unilateral termination of labour contracts ought to be disregarded on public policy grounds.

70 Cass., 4 June 2018, No. 14199, *Pluris*.

71 Case C-125/92, *Mulox IBC Ltd v. Hendrick Geels*, ECLI:EU:C:1993:306.

72 Case C-383/95, *Petrus Wilhelmus Rutten v. Cross Medical Ltd*, ECLI:EU:C:1997:7.

73 Case C-37/00, *Herbert Weber v. Universal Ogden Services Ltd*, ECLI:EU:C:2002:122.

non-contractual obligations other than torts. Regard will be had here to competition cases and cases involving the infringement of intellectual property rights.

5.2.1. *Acts Restricting Free Competition*

The Italian Competition Authority (Autorità garante della concorrenza e del mercato) issued two decisions on the repression of unfair commercial practices and misleading and unlawful comparative advertising that involved conflict-of-law issues.

The Authority was asked in 2016 to assess the fairness of the standard terms that PayPal was using at that time.[74] The terms included a choice of English law and provided that English courts and the courts of Luxembourg were to have non-exclusive jurisdiction over disputes. The request came from two consumer associations and was made under Article 37 *bis* of the Italian Consumer Code, which provides for administrative protection (performed by the Authority through injunctions and pecuniary sanctions), against unfair terms. The Authority did not explicitly address the issue of the applicable law, but in fact referred to Italian law to assess whether the contractual terms used by PayPal should be regarded as fair. Specifically, the Authority referred to Article 33 of the Italian Consumer Code, enacted to implement Directive 93/13/EEC of 5 April 1993 on unfair terms in consumer contracts.

It is worth noting that the decision of the Authority came a few months earlier than the judgment of the CJEU in *Amazon EU*.[75] The Court held in that ruling that Article 6(1) of the Rome II Regulation 'covers the use of unfair terms inserted into general terms and conditions', and added that, in the case of an action for an injunction according to Directive 2009/22 on injunctions for the protection of consumers' interests, the country in which the collective interests of consumers are affected 'is the country of residence of the consumers to whom the undertaking directs its activities and whose interests are defended by the relevant consumer protection association by means of that action'. The Court further observed, however, that the law applicable to the examination of the unfairness of terms in consumer contracts that are the subject of an action for an injunction must be determined independently in accordance with the nature of those terms. Therefore, where the action aims to prevent such terms from being included in consumer contracts, 'the law applicable to the assessment of the terms must be determined in accordance with the Rome I Regulation', whether the action is individual or collective. The Court reiterated that, in assessing whether a term is unfair, Article 6(2) of the Rome I Regulation may need to

---

74 Decision No. 25881 of 24 February 2016, *PayPal-(EUROPE) & PayPal.it*, <http://agcm.it>.

75 Case C-191/15, *Verein für Konsumenteninformation v. Amazon EU Sàrl*, ECLI:EU:C:2016:612.

be considered. This provides that the parties to a consumer contract are free to choose the law applicable to their contract, but that the choice cannot have the result of depriving the consumer of the protection afforded to him by provisions that cannot be derogated from by agreement by virtue of the law which, in the absence of choice, would have been applicable on the basis of Article 6(1), that is, in principle, the law of the country where the consumers whose interests are being defended have their habitual residence. Such provisions, the Court noted, may include the provisions transposing Directive 93/13, provided that they ensure a higher level of protection for the consumer.

It is submitted that the Italian Competition Authority, though failing to provide a clear illustration of its reasoning on the issue, ultimately followed in the *PayPal* case the approach that the CJEU later endorsed in *Amazon EU*. For the tortious aspects, the Authority implicitly relied on Article 6(1) of the Rome II Regulation and considered that the use of allegedly unfair terms, as complained of by the two associations, was likely to affect, among other things, the collective interests of consumers residing in Italy. As to the contractual aspects, it found that, pursuant to Article 6(2) of the Rome I Regulation, the choice of English law could not deprive the consumers of the protection afforded by the mandatory provisions on unfair terms set forth by the Italian Consumer Code.

In another decision, the Authority was asked to assess whether the fact that a low-cost airline company provided consumers with allegedly misleading information on credit card charges amounted to an unfair commercial practice, and should accordingly be fined by the Authority in accordance with Article 27(9) of the Italian Consumer Code.[76] The company challenged the competence of the Authority to deal with the matter. It argued that it was no longer selling tickets through a website with an Italian domain name (.it), but rather through a generic top-level domain name (.com), addressing clients worldwide. The Authority dismissed the objection. It found it was entitled to examine the claim and to decide it in accordance with Italian law. It relied for this on the concept of 'directed' activity as understood by Article 6(1)(b) of the Rome I Regulation and Article 17(1)(c) of the Brussels I *bis* Regulation, in the interpretation provided by the CJEU in *Hotel Alpenhof*.[77] The activity to which the latter provisions refer is the commercial activity directed by a professional to several States including the State of the consumer's habitual residence. The author of this report contends that, as in the previous case, the Authority, though failing to mention the Rome II Regulation, was essentially concerned with determining whether the unlawful commercial practice at issue was governed by Italian law pursuant to Article 6 of the Rome II Regulation, and accordingly

76 Decision No. 26183 of 28 September 2016, *Norwegian Air Shuttle*, <http://agcm.it>.

77 Joined Cases C-585/08 and C-144/09, *Peter Pammer v. Reederei Karl Schlüter GmbH & Co. KG* and *Hotel Alpenhof GesmbH v. Oliver Heller*, ECLI:EU:C:2010:740, especially paras. 81 ff.

fell within the reach of the powers of the Authority itself.[78] It is plausible that the Authority inquired into whether the company's activities were directed to Italy to assess whether the practice complained of affected the interests of consumers in Italy.

5.2.2. *Infringement of Intellectual Property Rights*

In 2018, the Tribunal of Torino ruled on a matter involving the application of Article 8 of the Rome II Regulation.[79]

An Italian company, holder of the television rights of several series for Italy, complained that excerpts of those series had been unlawfully uploaded on an online platform, operated by a French company, by individual users of the platform itself, and had thus become available to other users without authorisation. After obtaining an injunction to have the infringing contents removed from the platform, the Italian company sought monetary reparation from the French operator, on the ground that the latter had failed to abide by the injunction and to take measures to prevent further infringements from happening.

The Tribunal held that the alleged liability of the platform operator was governed by Italian law. It relied for this finding both on Article 8 of the Rome II Regulation and on Article 4, noting that, in the circumstances, Italy was both the country for which protection of the rights in question was claimed and the country in which the damage occurred. Based on these premises, the Tribunal decided the merits of the case in accordance with the legislation enacted in Italy to implement Articles 14 and 15 of the Directive on electronic commerce,[80] regarding liability arising from hosting activities and the duties of service providers with respect to alleged illegal activities undertaken by the recipients of their services.

6. SCOPE OF THE APPLICABLE LAW

6.1. CONTRACTS

According to Article 12 of the Rome I Regulation, the law applicable to a contract, as designated under the conflict-of-laws rules of the Regulation itself,

---

[78] The reasoning seems to rest on the assumption that the task of national supervisory authorities is to ensure compliance, within the territory of their respective States, with the provisions of the State in question. For a similar remark, referring to the supervisory authorities established to ensure compliance with the rules on data protection, see Case C-230/14, *Weltimmo s.r.o. v. Nemzeti Adatvédelmi és Információszabadság Hatóság*, ECLI:EU:C:2015:639, para. 48.

[79] Trib. Torino, 24 January 2018, *GiustUp*.

[80] Directive 2000/31/EC of the European Parliament and of the Council of 8 June 2000 on certain legal aspects of information society services, in particular electronic commerce, in the Internal Market [2000] OJ L 178/1.

governs, inter alia, the interpretation of the contract, the performance of the obligations arising thereunder, the various ways of extinguishing those obligations and the consequences of the nullity of the contract. According to Article 10, the existence and validity of the contract must be assessed, as a rule, against the law that would govern the contract if it were valid. The formal validity of the parties' agreement must be assessed against the law that governs the contract in substance or against the different law specified for this purpose in Article 11. Further indications as to which issues must be deemed to be governed by the *lex contractus* are provided in Articles 13–18 with respect to incapacity, voluntary assignment and contractual subrogation, legal subrogation, multiple liability, set-off and the burden of proof.

6.1.1. Core Contractual Issues

The author of this report is aware of only few published judgments issued by Italian courts that are specifically concerned with whether a particular issue ought to be included in the scope of the *lex contractus*.

The issue of contract interpretation proved somewhat problematic in this respect. According to Article 10(1)(a) of the Rome Convention, now Article 12(1)(a) of the Rome I Regulation, the law applicable to a contract pursuant to the Convention, or the Regulation, governs, in particular, the interpretation of the contract.

The Corte di Cassazione apparently failed to consider this provision in a ruling of 2016, in a case concerning a 'buying agency agreement' concluded between an Italian agent and a US company.[81] Asked to clarify the interpretation of the contract, the Court disregarded the fact that the latter was governed by the law of the State of New York, which the parties had chosen, and rather applied the rules on contract interpretation of the Italian Civil Code.

In a later ruling, the Supreme Court, instead, seemed to take the above provision into account. A dispute had arisen between a company incorporated in Luxembourg and one of its directors. The latter complained that the company had dismissed him without just cause, and claimed an indemnity based on an agreement in force between the parties. The Corte di Cassazione, noting that the agreement was governed by the law of Luxembourg, ruled that the agreement itself ought to be construed in conformity with the rules of contract interpretation laid down in the Civil Code of Luxembourg.[82]

Apart from the above cases, the vast majority of the decisions that relate to either the Rome Convention or the Rome I Regulation concern issues that

81 Cass., 28 December 2016, No. 27072, *Pluris*.
82 Cass., 5 July 2019, No. 18182, *Pluris*.

fall indisputably within the scope of the law governing the contract, such as the performance of the obligations arising from the contract. Article 10(1)(b) of the Convention and Article 12(1)(b) of the Regulation list performance among the issues submitted to the *lex contractus*, as specified by the Convention and the Regulation themselves. As a matter of fact, determining the law applicable to the performance of a particular obligation is, in some cases, the main reason for resorting to the Convention or the Regulation. This occurs where the seised court must assess its jurisdiction based on the place where the obligation in question is to be performed, pursuant to the rule that is presently set forth in Article 7(1)(a) of the Brussels I *bis* Regulation, as interpreted by the CJEU in *Tessili*[83] and reiterated in *Falco Privatstiftung*.[84]

6.1.2. *Formal Validity and Capacity*

The Tribunal of Bologna discussed in 2015 the issue of which law applies to capacity and formal validity in connection with a case concerning a donation made by a Panamanian company.[85]

The Tribunal relied on Article 4(2) of the Rome I Regulation to state that the law of Panama applied to the donation of a sum of money made to an Italian national. The Tribunal referred to Panamanian law to assess, among other things, the formal validity of the donation. The donor, noting that the gift had been executed in Italy, had challenged the validity of the act. Under Italian law, donations must be made in the form of a notarial act, whereas the gift at issue merely resulted from a private agreement. The Tribunal dismissed the challenge. It implicitly relied for this on Article 11(1) of the Regulation. This stipulates that contracts concluded between persons (or their agents) who were in the same country when the agreement was made are formally valid if they satisfy either the requirements of the *lex contractus* or those of the *lex loci actus*, i.e. the law of the country where the agreement itself was concluded. The Tribunal found that Panamanian law does not prescribe that donations (other than donations of immoveable property) be drafted, authenticated or witnessed by a notary public in his or her official capacity, and accordingly concluded that the gift was valid.

The Tribunal found that two more questions had to be decided in conformity with Panamanian law. The first question was whether the donor, the Panamanian company, could lawfully grant a third party (i.e. the woman who had represented the company in relation to the gift) the power to make a donation on its behalf.

---

83 Case 12/76, *Industrie Tessili Italiana Como v. Dunlop AG*, ECLI:EU:C:1976:133.

84 Case C-533/07, *Falco Privatstiftung and Thomas Rabitsch v. Gisela Weller-Lindhorst*, ECLI:EU:2009:257.

85 Trib. Bologna, 9 November 2015, *Pluris*. Other aspects of the ruling were discussed above, in section 4.1.1.

The validity of the donation had been challenged on this ground, too. The Panamanian company submitted that, under Italian law, donations must be made personally by the donor and can in no case be made by an attorney, no matter how broad their powers. The Tribunal found that Panamanian law does not prevent donations from being made through a duly authorised representative, and accordingly dismissed the challenge.

Doubts may be expressed as to the inclusion of the above issue among those governed by the *lex contractus*. The question at stake, it is submitted, was whether the woman, acting as an agent, was able to bind the principal (the donor) in relation to a third party (the donee). This question is excluded altogether from the material scope of the Rome I Regulation pursuant to Article 1(2)(g). It is thus contended that it was not for the Regulation, but rather for the domestic conflict-of-law rules on agency and representation – Article 60 of the Italian Statute on Private International Law – to determine the law applicable to the issue under discussion. Had Article 60 of the Statute be considered, instead of the Regulation, Italian law would have applied. Under Article 60, outside of the cases where the attorney acts in the course of his or her business activity, the law applicable to representation is in fact the law of the country where the attorney performs (for the most part, as the case may be) his or her powers of representation.[86]

The second issue for which the Tribunal of Bologna relied on Panamanian law was whether the donor could be regarded as being capable of donating. The Tribunal observed that, under the law of some countries, companies lack capacity to donate, but found that this is not the case of Panamanian law, and accordingly also dismissed the challenge raised by the donor on this ground.

The Tribunal was correct in applying the law of Panama to the question of capacity, but erred, in the view of the author of this report, in drawing that conclusion from the Rome I Regulation. The Regulation, as stated in Article 1(2)(a), does not address 'questions involving the status or legal capacity of natural persons'. Questions involving the capacity of persons other than natural persons are likewise excluded, it is submitted, from the scope of application of the European regime. Those questions should rather be dealt with under the conflict-of-law rules of the forum. In the circumstances, the relevant provision would have been Article 25 of the Italian Statute on Private International Law,

---

86 Pursuant to Article 60(1), voluntary representation is governed by the law of the State in which the agent has his place of business, provided that he acts professionally and that the third party was, or ought to be, aware of that place. The provision goes on to state that, where the latter conditions are not met, the applicable law is the law of the country in which the agent primarily exercised his powers in the circumstances. Article 60(2) deals with the formal validity of powers of attorney. For a power of attorney to be formally valid, it must comply either with the law that governs representation in substance or with the law of the country where the agent exercised his powers.

according to which the law applicable to companies is the law of the country of incorporation (Panama, in the circumstances).

6.1.3. *Subrogation*

In a 2016 ruling, the Corte di Cassazione discussed the issue of the law applicable to subrogation.[87] Some naval engines had been supplied by an Italian manufacturer to an Italian company and then sold by the latter to a French company. The engines had subsequently been the object of further sales down the chain. It eventually turned out that the engines were defective. The final purchaser sought damages from the company it had bought the engines from, but the claim was settled by an insurance company. Relying on subrogation, the insurance company sought repayment, through a direct action, from the Italian company which had sold the engines to the first French buyer. The issue arose of whether the insurer was in fact entitled to exercise that right against the Italian seller. The Court took the view that the issue ought to be decided in accordance with the law applicable to the contract under which the Italian seller in question had sold the engines. The Court found that the contract was governed by Italian law pursuant to Article 4 of the Rome Convention. On this basis, it dismissed the claim, noting that Italian law, contrary to French law, does not make room for the kind of direct claim that the insurance company had relied upon in the circumstances.

The Court's reasoning is far from persuasive. The Court raised the issue of the characterisation of the claim for repayment, that is, as to whether the claim was contractual in nature, rather than non-contractual. The question was relevant, but the answer given is unconvincing. To characterise the claim, the Court saw fit to refer to the categories of Italian law, rather than to the notion of contract which is employed under the private international law rules of the EU, namely as results from the *Handte* case of the CJEU.[88] Had it used the *Handte* test, the Corte di Cassazione would have probably concluded that the claim was non-contractual. The Court would have then turned to (the domestic provision, applicable *ratione temporis*, corresponding to) Article 19 of the Rome II Regulation. Article 4 of the Rome Convention – the provision on which the Court in fact based its reasoning – did not have, it is contended, any role to play for the purposes of determining whether the insurance company was entitled to repayment from the Italian seller. Even if the Court had concluded that the claim was contractual, the relevant provision in the Convention would not have been Article 4, but rather Article 13, on subrogation.

---

87 Cass., 29 July 2016, No. 15895, *DeJure*.

88 Case C-26/91, *Jakob Handte & Co. GmbH v. Traitements Mécano-chimiques des Surfaces SA*, ECLI:EU:C:1992:268.

6.2. NON-CONTRACTUAL OBLIGATIONS

Article 15 of the Rome II Regulation features a non-exhaustive list of issues that must be decided in accordance with the law specified by the Regulation itself. These include issues relating to 'the basis and extent of liability' and 'the grounds for exemption from liability, any limitation of liability and any division of liability', as well as the question of 'whether a right to claim damages or a remedy may be transferred, including by inheritance', and the question of which persons are entitled to compensation for damage sustained personally. The *lex delicti* also governs the 'assessment' of the 'damage or the remedy claimed'.[89] Only the latter issue will be considered here.

In 2014, the Tribunal of Bologna ruled on the damage suffered by a Romanian child as a result of an accident that occurred in Romania, caused by a Romanian national who habitually resided in Italy.[90] Having stated that Romanian law applied to the case pursuant to Article 4(1) of the Rome II Regulation, the Tribunal, based on Romanian law, held that the driver was liable. It held, however, that the child had, through his own negligence, contributed to the harm he suffered, and estimated that the child's contribution amounted to 20 per cent of the whole damage. Regarding the amount of compensation, the Tribunal asserted that Romanian law, like Italian law, provides for non-pecuniary losses to be assessed by the seised court equitably. This approach, the Tribunal noted, does not rule out the possibility of referring to the tables drawn up by the Tribunal of Milan that generally guide Italian courts in assessing this kind of damages. Based on those tables, and having regard to the 20 per cent reduction corresponding to the child's contributory negligence, the compensation due to the victim ought to amount, in principle, to about 25,000 euros. That said, the Tribunal found that the amount thus calculated had to be reduced to take into account the fact that the socio-economic environment and the cost of living – which served as standards for the creation of the tables above – differed significantly between Romania and Italy. As a conclusion, the Tribunal awarded the child damages slightly in excess of 8,000 euros.

---

89 Italian courts have acknowledged on various occasions that it belongs to the *lex delicti*, as specified by the Regulation, to set out the legal standards for the assessment of the prejudice suffered. See, for instance, Trib. Bolzano, 13 October 2016, *GiustUp*, regarding a traffic accident occurred in Italy, caused by a car driven by a person whose habitual residence was in Germany and resulting in damages for a biker and his wife, whose habitual residence was also in Germany. The Tribunal, considering that the liability of the former was governed by German law pursuant to Article 4(2) of the Rome II Regulation, dismissed the claim of the plaintiff that the damage be assessed in accordance with the tables in force in Italy for these purposes.

90 Trib. Bologna, 17 March 2014, *RDIPP* 2017, 126.

By adopting this approach, the Tribunal of Bologna clearly departed from the currently prevailing view of the Corte di Cassazione.[91] The latter warned on several occasions of the risks of the described approach,[92] arguing that a person's right to compensation should be enforced irrespective of his or her economic conditions, as doing otherwise might result in discrimination.[93] In its judgment of 2014, the Tribunal of Bologna reversed the latter argument by observing that discrimination would rather arise if victims living in countries with very different socio-economic conditions were to be awarded the same level of compensation: the formally equal treatment that they had received would involve, in substance, a disparity.

No reference to support this conclusion was made by the Tribunal to the principle underlying Recital 33 of the Rome II Regulation. Recital 33 states that the court seised, 'when quantifying damages for personal injury in cases ... should take into account all the relevant actual circumstances of the specific victim, including in particular the actual losses and costs of after-care and medical attention'. By contrast, Recital 33 played an important role in the decision issued by the Tribunal of Modena in a case of 2015.[94] A dispute had arisen concerning an accident that occurred in Hungary. An ambulance had been hit by a lorry, and a woman, a paramedic living in Italy who was then on board the ambulance, had suffered serious injuries as a result. The Tribunal asserted that Hungarian law applied and held, on this basis, that damages were due to the woman. However, it relied on Recital 33 to refer to the Italian tables mentioned above – with no reductions or adaptations, in line with the approach of the Corte di Cassazione – for the purposes of quantifying compensation.

---

91 Other cases in which a similar reassessment was made are Cass., 14 February 2000, No. 1637, *Giustizia civile - Massimario* 2000, 332, that remained an isolated case in the case law of the Supreme Court, as further explained in the text; Trib. Torino, 20 July 2010, *RDIPP* 2012, 227; Trib. Monza, 2 November 2007, *Il civilista* 2010, 11, 68.

92 Cass., 18 May 2012, No. 7932, *Giustizia civile - Massimario* 2012, 5, 642; Cass. 13 November 2014, No. 24201, *Giustizia civile - Massimario* 2014; Cass. 12 June 2015, No. 12221, *DeJure;* Cass., 14 June 2016, No. 12146, *DeJure;* Cass. 7 October 2016, No. 20206, *RDIPP* 2017, 748. See also CA Milano, 11 February 2010, *Il civilista* 2010, 11, 67.

93 The clearest and most thorough illustration of the prevailing view is found in Cass., 15 February 2018, No. 3767, *DeJure*, a case concerning the damages claimed by the relatives of a traffic accident which occurred in Italy. The insurer had argued that, in quantifying the compensation due to the relatives for the suffering resulting from the loss of a loved one, the Court ought to take into account that the cost of living in Romania, the country where the claimants resided, is significantly lower than in Italy. The Court's reasoning rested on the premise that, as a matter of Italian law, non-pecuniary losses must be assessed in light of the consequences of the event, that is the detriment that the victim would be spared, had the event not occurred. The use that the victim may make of the amount awarded has no bearing on the assessment of the 'consequences' of the event. Actually, one cannot assume neither that the amount awarded will be spent (rather than invested, for example), nor that it will be spent in the country of residence (and not elsewhere).

94 Trib. Modena, 4 December 2015, *Pluris*.

7. MANDATORY PROVISIONS AND THE PUBLIC POLICY EXCEPTION

7.1. CONTRACTS

7.1.1. Overriding Mandatory Provisions

According to Article 9(1) of the Rome I Regulation, overriding mandatory provisions are 'provisions the respect for which is regarded as crucial by a country for safeguarding its public interests, such as its political, social or economic organisation, to such an extent that they are applicable to any situation falling within their scope, irrespective of the law otherwise applicable to the contract' pursuant to the Regulation.

As stated in Article 9(2), nothing in the Regulation prevents the courts of a Member State from applying an overriding mandatory provision, provided this belongs to the legal order of the forum. The same was true under Article 7(2) of the Rome Convention.

The overriding mandatory provisions of a law other than the law of the forum (and the *lex causae*) are subject to a different treatment. The Regulation provides in Article 9(3) that they may, at most, be 'given effect' in the forum. This may occur only for provisions that are part of the law of the country of performance of the contractual obligations in question, and only insofar as such provisions 'render the performance of the contract unlawful'. In considering whether to give effect to the overriding mandatory provisions of a third country, regard shall be had 'to their nature and purpose and to the consequences of their application or non-application'. Article 7(1) of the Rome Convention set forth a rather more liberal solution in this respect, as it allowed the overriding mandatory provisions of a third country to be given effect subject only to the condition that the situation had a 'close connection' with such third country.

So far, no decision has been published in Italy that specifically refers to Article 9 of the Rome I Regulation. Instead, case law reports record a few judgments in which Italian courts have considered Article 7 of the Rome Convention.

In 2007, the Tribunal of Rovereto ruled on a dispute concerning a licence and distribution agreement regarding a movie to be distributed in Italy, concluded between a Belgian company as the licensor and an Italian company as the licensee.[95] The agreement came with a choice-of-law clause which designated the law of England. The issue was raised in the proceedings of whether Article 1384 of the Italian Civil Code ought to be applied to the case as an overriding mandatory provision. Article 1384 deals with liquidated damages,

95 Trib. Rovereto, 15 March 2007, *RDIPP* 2008, 179.

that is, contract clauses that are intended to estimate damages in the event of non-performance. It provides that where the amount of damages due under the clause are manifestly disproportionate to the actual damages resulting from the breach, the failing party, provided its obligations have been performed at least in part, may seek a court order reducing the sum owed to the other party. The Tribunal acknowledged that Article 1384 of the Civil Code cannot, as a matter of Italian law, be derogated from by agreement. It held, however, that the provision did not qualify as an overriding mandatory provision for the purposes of Article 7(2) of the Rome Convention. Caution is needed in characterising a rule of the forum as an overriding mandatory provision, more so where, as in the circumstances, the interests protected under the domestic rule concerned are also considered under the *lex causae*. In the view of the Tribunal, the mere fact that the foreign law governing the contract accords less weight to the interests in question and protects them in a different manner is not enough to disregard the law chosen by the parties and apply the mandatory provisions of the forum instead.

Other Italian provisions are instead regarded, quite indisputably, to override the otherwise applicable foreign law. As stated by the Tribunal of Naples in a ruling of 2000, this applies, for example, to Article 4 of Law No. 154 of 17 February 1992 on the transparency of banking and financial transactions, under which banking contracts are invalid if they fail to state explicitly certain key terms, such as the applicable interest rate.[96]

The Italian legislator occasionally labelled certain of its legislative texts as overriding mandatory provisions. This occurred, for instance, with the Decree-Law No. 9 of 2 March 2020, part of the emergency measures adopted to tackle the COVID-19 crisis. Article 28 of the Decree-Law set forth provisions aimed to ensure the reimbursement of amounts paid in consideration of transport and accommodation services by persons affected either by the virus itself, or by confinement measures in connection therewith. Article 28(8) explicitly states that the above provisions are to be treated as overriding mandatory provisions for the purposes of Article 17 of the Italian Statute on Private International Law and Article 9 of the Rome I Regulation.[97]

Very few references exist in the Italian practice to the overriding mandatory provisions of third countries. In a ruling of 2016, the Tribunal of Modena considered the possibility of giving effect to the overriding mandatory provisions of a third country.[98] The case concerned a commercial agency contract between

---

96 Trib. Napoli, 13 July 2000, *Rivista del Notariato* 2001, 1198.

97 See further regarding this practice the blogposts by Ennio Piovesani on <http://conflictoflaws.net>, dated 19 March 2020, and by Giovanni Zarra on <http://www.sidiblog.org>, dated 30 March 2020.

98 Trib. Modena, 4 May 2016, *DeJure*.

an Italian company and a French agent. The parties had agreed that the contract be governed by Italian law. The Rome Convention applied to the matter *ratione temporis*. The issue arose of whether the Tribunal should have regard to the rules implementing the Commercial Agents Directive 86/653/EEC in the French legal order.[99] The Tribunal relied on the judgment of the CJEU in *Unamar*[100] to state that, in assessing the mandatory character of a piece of domestic legislation, one must take into account not only the wording of the legislation in question, but also its general structure and the circumstances in which it was adopted. It is against this standard, the Tribunal observed, that the question must be answered of whether a national provision – namely one providing the agent with a higher protection than required under the Directive – reflects an interest that the Member State concerned actually considers to be essential. The Tribunal reached the conclusion that the latter condition was not satisfied in the circumstances, and accordingly ruled out the possibility of giving effect to French law. Had the Rome I Regulation been applicable, instead of the Convention, the conclusion would have arguably been the same.

7.1.2. The Public Policy Exception

According to Article 21 of the Rome I Regulation, 'the application of a provision of the law of any country specified' by the Regulation itself may be refused 'if such application is manifestly incompatible with the public policy (*ordre public*) of the forum'. The Rome Convention featured in Article 16, an almost identical provision. The so-called public policy exception is meant to serve as a safeguard of the core values of the legal order of the forum. It is common ground that public policy can be used as a barrier to foreign law only in exceptional circumstances, where it is established that the application of one or more specific rules of the designated law would be irretrievably at odds with the fundamental principles of the *lex fori*. These principles may, depending on the circumstances, be enshrined in the constitution of the forum State or the international conventions to which the latter is a party, or may arise by way of interpretation from the legislation of that state. EU law, including the Charter of Fundamental Rights, may equally serve as a basis for the emergence of a Member State's public policy within the meaning of Article 21 of the Rome I Regulation.

Most of the Italian rulings that address the issue of public policy in the field of contracts relate to labour relations.

---

99 Council Directive 86/653/EEC of 18 December 1986 on the coordination of the laws of the Member States relating to self-employed commercial agents [1986] OJ L 382/17, as implemented in France under Law No. 523 of 1991.

100 Case C-184/12, *United Antwerp Maritime Agencies (Unamar) NV v. Navigation Maritime Bulgare*, ECLI:EU:C:2013:663.

The Corte di Cassazione ruled in 2002 on a dispute concerning an employment contract between an Italian national and a bank whose statutory seat and central administration were in Italy.[101] The employee had been hired to work at the bank's branch in New York. The bank later dismissed him without stating any reason for the dismissal. He then returned in Italy and sued the bank, seeking compensation for unlawful dismissal. The contract, which did not include a choice-of-law clause, appeared to be governed, pursuant to Article 6(2)(a) of the Rome Convention, corresponding to Article 8(2) of the Rome I Regulation, by the law of the State of New York. The Court considered the rules in force in the State of New York relating to the unilateral termination of employment contracts and concluded that the application of those rules in the circumstances would contradict the fundamental policies of the Italian legal system. Italian law, the Court stated, considers that employment contracts of indefinite duration deserve some degree of stability. Relying, in particular, on the Italian Constitution and on labour legislation, the Court added that absent a minimum protection of the right to stability, the dignity of employees is at risk. Against these premises, the Court found that the law of New York simply failed to provide workers with any protection against unjustified dismissals, and accordingly refused to apply that law on grounds of public policy.[102] As in other judgments relating to public policy,[103] the Court stressed that the applicable foreign law cannot be disregarded only because its rules provided a different kind of protection than the protection resulting from the corresponding Italian rules.[104] What triggers the public policy exception, the Court held, is rather the fact that, under the foreign law in question, taken as whole, the interests that Italian law considers to be fundamental are granted no protection at all, or that it fails to provide what Italian law regards as a minimum degree of protection. An illustration of this approach is provided by a judgment of the Corte di Cassazione in 2007.[105]

---

101 Cass., 11 November 2002, No. 15822, *RDIPP* 2003, 978.

102 See, for a similar finding, Cass., 9 May 2007, No. 10549, *RDIPP* 2008, 216, and Cass., 21 January 2013, No. 1302, *RDIPP* 2013, 472. See also CA Genova, 9 April 2013, *Pluris*.

103 Cass., 7 December 2005, No. 26976, *RDIPP* 2006, 1053; Cass., 26 May 2008, No. 13547, *RDIPP* 2009, 409.

104 See e.g. Cass., 19 July 2007, No. 16017, *RDIPP* 2008, 533, where the Court ruled out that the application of US law to the dismissal of all employees of the Alitalia airline branch in New York, which took place only after lengthy negotiations, with the mediation of public bodies and through meetings with trade unions could not be considered as being against public policy, since the minimum standards for the protection of the workers had been complied with. See also Cass., 26 November 2004, No. 22332, *RDIPP* 2005, 771, stating that public policy is not contravened where the foreign law applicable to an employment contract – Canadian law in the circumstances – does not provide for a thirteenth salary (Christmas bonus) or a severance indemnity, where it is established that the worker is granted a higher remunerative treatment than the one he would be entitled to under Italian law.

105 Cass., 4 May 2007, No. 10215, *RDIPP* 2008, 214. The case was decided in accordance with domestic conflict-of-law rules but is nevertheless believed to be of interest for the present survey.

Here, too, the case concerned a contract between an Italian bank and an Italian employee, whose work was to be carried out at one of the branches of the bank in the United States. Pursuant to the parties' agreement, the contract was governed by the law of the State where the branch was situated. The employee was dismissed, and the dispute turned on the lawfulness of his dismissal. The Corte di Cassazione acknowledged that the foreign applicable rules did not provide any specific guarantee against arbitrary dismissals, but observed that *in the circumstances* the application of those rules did not result in an infringement of Italian public policy. Indeed, the dismissal was based on a protracted failure by the employee to perform his duties under the contract – a scenario in which, under Italian standards, a dismissal appeared to be justified.

The Tribunal of Milan discussed rather extensively the issue of public policy in a case decided in 2016, concerning the dismissal of an employee of Italian nationality, who had been hired by a company of the United Arab Emirates to work there.[106] The man had been dismissed when his trial period had come to an end. He had not received any prior notice and he was left by the employer with no reasons for the dismissal. As agreed between the parties pursuant to Article 3 of the Rome I Regulation, the contract was governed by the law of the Emirate of Abu Dhabi. The dismissal had been made in conformity with the rules of the Emirate. The Tribunal, having examined the law of the Emirate and the federal rules of the United Arab Emirates, concluded that, in the circumstances, the application of the *lex contractus* did not conflict with Italian public policy. Italian law itself, the Tribunal noted, provides that the employer enjoys a broad discretion regarding dismissals made during the trial period or at the end of it, and does not require, in general, that reasons be given to justify the dismissal.

The public policy exception was relied upon by the Corte di Cassazione in 2013, in a case regarding two public employees.[107] The Italian Consulate in Buenos Aires had hired two women under a fixed-term contract. The contracts had been renewed twice, which was enough, under Argentinean law, to convert the relationship between the Consulate and the two employees into an employment contract of indefinite duration. The women then sued the Italian Ministry of Foreign Affairs to have the conversion judicially enforced. The Supreme Court dismissed the claim. It conceded that the contract was governed by the law of Argentina, pursuant to the 1980 Rome Convention (the Regulation was inapplicable *ratione temporis*), but found that, in the circumstances, the application of the Argentinean rules on conversion would have infringed Italian public policy. The Court relied for this on Article 97(3) of the Italian Constitution, according to which permanent posts in the public sector can only

106 Trib. Milano, 15 July 2016, *Pluris*.

107 Cass., 26 April 2013, No. 10070, *RDIPP* 2014, 178.

be accessed through competitive examinations, except in the cases established by law (none of which had occurred in the circumstances).

In another ruling, the issue was raised of whether the application of foreign law can be ruled out on grounds of public policy where the salary due to the employee in accordance with the law in question is grossly inadequate, that is, does not enable the employee and his or her family to live a free and dignified life. The Tribunal of Rome answered the question in the affirmative in a case regarding a former employee of the Embassy of Sri Lanka in Italy.[108] The man had worked for 12 years as a deliveryman and receptionist, five days a week, eight hours a day. He complained that his monthly salary was clearly not proportionate to the quantity and quality of the work provided, and that he had never received any of the bonuses that normally complement an employee's salary. He further noted that, upon dismissal, the Embassy had refused to pay any indemnity for lack of notice and any severance indemnity. The Tribunal relied on Article 36 of the Italian Constitution (according to which workers have the right to a remuneration commensurate to the quantity and quality of their work and in any case such as to ensure them and their families a free and dignified existence), and on other sources (including Article 23(3) of the Universal Declaration of Human Rights of 1948), to state that the law of Sri Lanka, which applied to the contract pursuant to a choice of law made by the parties, ought to be disregarded.

The opinions on the matter, however, remain divided, and the ruling of the Tribunal of Rome can hardly be regarded at this stage as a reliable and settled authority.

Public policy has only rarely been considered , in contractual disputes, outside the area of labour law. In 2015, the Tribunal of Rimini resorted to the public policy exception, as set out in Article 16 of the Rome Convention, in proceedings relating to a credit line agreement concluded by a bank in San Marino and some of its clients.[109] The bank had asked for the repayment of the monies that had been lent under the agreement. The clients, for their part, challenged the validity of the agreement and sought damages from the bank, arguing that the bank had failed to act with fairness and integrity, and had not complied with the Italian prescriptions on transparency in banking contracts. The Tribunal began by noting that the contract was governed by the law of San Marino pursuant to Article 4 of the Rome Convention. It acknowledged that the law of San Marino, as it stood then, did not require that banks supply the pre-contractual information that Italian law prescribed for the kind of contracts in question. The Tribunal, however, observed that the Italian rules on pre-contractual information in banking and

[108] Trib. Roma, 17 June 2010, *Pluris*.
[109] Trib. Rimini, 24 July 2015, *Pluris*.

financial transactions aim to ensure the proper functioning of the credit market and foster the protection of the weaker party. According to the Tribunal, this was enough to characterise those rules as an expression of Italian public policy. On these premises, the Tribunal disregarded the law of San Marino.

The Corte di Cassazione held that a foreign judgment enforcing a gambling debt cannot be refused recognition on grounds of public policy, since Italian law does not prohibit gambling as such, but instead regulates it.[110]

In a ruling in 2002, the Corte di Cassazione held that the public policy exception did not prevent the recognition of a foreign judgment that enforced a promise to pay particularly high interests on a certain amount of money.[111] The payment, it noted, was not due in the framework of a lending operation (a precondition for the application of Italian anti-usury legislation), but rather resulted from a judicially ascertained breach of contract.

7.2. NON-CONTRACTUAL OBLIGATIONS

7.2.1. *Overriding Mandatory Provisions*

The Rome II Regulation deals with overriding mandatory provisions in Article 16. Under this provision, nothing in the Regulation 'shall restrict the application of the provisions of the law of the forum in a situation where they are mandatory irrespective of the law otherwise applicable to the non-contractual obligation'. The Rome II Regulation, unlike Rome I, does not provide an explicit definition of the expression 'overriding mandatory provisions' and fails to clarify whether, and subject to which conditions, the courts of a Member State may give effect to the overriding mandatory provisions of a third country.

So far, Italian courts have never ruled on cases involving a reference to Article 16. Instead, prior to the adoption of the Regulation, the Corte di Cassazione relied on the Italian Statute on Private International Law (namely, Article 17 thereof, regarding overriding mandatory provisions)[112] to enforce certain mandatory provisions of the Italian legal order in a non-contractual dispute.[113] The case, decided in 2012, revolved around a traffic accident that occurred in Italy involving a car with a foreign licence plate. The Supreme

110 Cass., 15 June 2016, No. 12364, *DeJure*. Along the same lines, see also Cass., 27 September 2012, No. 16511, *Giustizia civile* 2012, 2263 and Cass., 17 January 2013, No. 1163, *Guida al diritto* 2013, 8, 50.

111 Cass., 6 December 2002, No. 17349, *Giustizia civile – Massimario* 2002, 2133.

112 Article 17 of Law No. 218 of 1995 specifies that the rules contained in this law do not prejudice those provisions of Italian law which, because of their object and purpose, are applicable irrespective of the reference made to a foreign law.

113 Cass., 18 May 2012, No. 7932, *DeJure*.

Court held that Articles 125 and 126 of the Italian Insurance Code, which make insurance compulsory for vehicles with foreign licence plates driving in Italy and impose obligations on the Italian Central Office in the event of accidents in Italy involving those vehicles, apply irrespective of the foreign law governing the liability arising from the accident. The same conclusion, it is submitted, would be reached today under Article 16 of the Rome II Regulation.

7.2.2. The Public Policy Exception

The Rome II Regulation refers to public policy in Article 26. Its wording does not differ from that of Article 21 of the Rome I Regulation. The general remarks made above as regards the latter provision also apply to the corresponding rule in the Rome II Regulation.

So far, Italian courts have only rarely addressed the issue of public policy in cases governed by the Rome II Regulation. Issues of this kind have instead been considered by Italian courts in cases regarding torts and other non-contractual obligations under Article 16 of the Italian Statute on Private International Law. This is the provision that enables Italian courts to disregard the applicable foreign law whenever its application would result in the infringement of the public policy of the forum. Article 16 of the Statute and Article 26 of the Rome II Regulation fundamentally refer, it is submitted, to the same notion of public policy. The rulings rendered by Italian courts pursuant to the former provision may thus be taken to provide a reliable indication of the way in which a public policy case would likely be addressed under the Regulation.

In 2013, the Corte di Cassazione ruled on an action for damages in connection with a traffic accident that occurred in Austria.[114] The accident involved an Austrian vehicle and an Italian camper van, parked on the hard shoulder of a motorway. Five of the occupants of the camper van died in the accident and one survived with serious injuries. Damages were sought by the surviving victim and the close relatives of the others. The Court held, based on Article 62 of the Italian Statute on Private International Law, that Austrian law was applicable. However, it refused to apply, on grounds of public policy, a particular Austrian provision pursuant to which the relatives of the victim of a tort are entitled to claim reparation solely in respect of the pecuniary damage they have suffered, and not in respect of the non-pecuniary damage consisting in the loss of a loved one.[115] To reach this conclusion, the Court asserted that the Italian Constitution protects family relationships. It observed that the legal value accorded to family ties further results from Article 8 of the European Convention

---

[114] Cass., 22 August 2013, No. 19405, *RDIPP* 2014, 698.

[115] In 2018, the Supreme Court came to a similar conclusion in a traffic accident case governed by Serbian law: Cass., 30 April 2018, No. 10321, *Pluris*.

on Human Rights and Article 7 of the Charter of Fundamental Rights of the European Union, on the right to respect for private and family life. According to the Supreme Court, the place occupied by family ties within the Italian legal system implies that family members have a fundamental right to civil redress in the event of infringement.[116]

The issue has also been raised of the applicability, on grounds of public policy, of foreign rules providing for punitive damages, and the recognition of foreign judgments that in fact awarded such damages. Punitive damages, as understood in the legal system of most common law countries, consist in compensation going beyond the amount which is necessary to compensate the injured party for the losses suffered by the latter. The aim of over-compensatory damages is basically to punish the tortfeasor for an act that is regarded as particularly reprehensible and/or to discourage the tortfeasor (or other potential wrongdoers) from repeating the act.

As a matter of Italian law, the victim of a tort is entitled, in principle, to receive full reparation for the harm suffered, but not more than that.

The traditional stance taken by Italian courts towards punitive damages is illustrated by a ruling given by the Corte di Cassazione in 2007.[117] At issue was whether a judgment rendered in the United States that awarded over-compensatory damages against an Italian manufacturer of protective helmets, which a US court had found to be defective, qualified for recognition and enforcement in Italy. The Supreme Court answered in the negative. It argued that the idea that compensation should punish, rather than restoring the status quo, is alien to the Italian rules on civil liability. When it comes to compensation, the Court observed, no regard should be had to elements such as the wealth of the wrongdoer or the fact that the victim is in need. The Court stressed that compensation, under Italian law, presupposes the assessment of the actual damage suffered by the victim. It is true that assessing the damage may, in appropriate circumstances, involve some discretion, but in no case can discretion go as far as enabling the seised court to award damages unrelated to real harm.

The latter finding was later called into question by the Supreme Court itself. In 2016, one of the chambers of the Court asked the United Chambers (Sezioni Unite) to reconsider the issue in a case regarding, once again, the recognition of a US judgment awarding punitive damages to the victim of an accident against the Italian manufacturer of a helmet.[118] In the request, the

---

116 See also, along these lines, Trib. Milano, 27 November 2019, *GiustUp*, where the Tribunal ruled that Dutch law ought to be disregarded on grounds of public policy insofar as it fails to recognise the right of close relatives to seek damages for the non-pecuniary prejudice consisting in the loss of a loved one.

117 Cass., 19 January 2007, No. 1183, *RDIPP* 2007, 777.

118 Cass., 16 May 2016, No. 9978, *DeJure*.

Chamber argued that the traditional position ought to be reconsidered in light of the evolution of the Italian law of civil liability and of the concept of public policy itself.

By the resulting ruling, given in 2017, the Corte di Cassazione actually inaugurated a new approach to punitive damages.[119] It noted that, under Italian law, civil liability is no longer concerned with compensation alone, but also serves other functions, such as the prevention of harmful conduct. The recognition of a foreign judgment awarding punitive damages (as well, arguably, the application of a foreign law contemplating the possibility of awarding those damages) does not infringe *as such* the public policy of Italy. Non-compensatory damages are permissible, in particular, in circumstances where the possibility of awarding such damages was provided for by the law, and where a fair balance is struck between the amount of the awarded damages and the seriousness of the violation complained of.[120]

8. RELATIONS WITH INTERNATIONAL CONVENTIONS

8.1. CONTRACTS

As stipulated in Article 25, the Rome I Regulation does not prejudice the international conventions to which one or more Member States were party at the time the Regulation was adopted and which lay down conflict-of-laws rules concerning contracts, provided that these conventions are in force internationally in the Member State concerned and one or more third countries. The Rome Convention features, in Article 21, a similar (albeit more broadly worded) provision.

Member States were required under Article 26 of the Regulation to inform the Commission of the international conventions to which they were a party with the characteristics described above. In its notification, as published in the Official Journal of the European Union, Italy declared that it was not a party to any such convention.[121]

This statement, it is submitted, is inaccurate. Italy is indeed a party to various international agreements that include conflict-of-laws rules applicable to contracts. One of these, the Hague Convention of 15 June 1955 on the Law

---

119 Cass. (SU), 5 July 2017, No. 16601, *RDIPP* 2017, 1049.

120 For an analysis in English of the ruling, see G. Ponzanelli, 'Punitive Damages and the Functions of Reparation: Some Preliminary Remarks After the Decision of the Italian Supreme Court, Joint Divisions, 5 July 20017, No. 16601', in S. Bariatti, L. Fumagalli and Z. Crespi Reghizzi (eds.), *Punitive Damages and Private International Law: State of the Art and Future Developments* (Wolters Kluwer 2019), 33 ff.

121 [2010] OJ C 343/3.

Applicable to International Sales of Goods, is particularly important in practice. No doubts seem to exist as to the fact that the Convention is fully in force in Italy. The Convention has never been denounced by Italy, and both the agreements database of the Italian Ministry of Foreign Affairs[122] and the website of the Hague Conference on Private International Law (populated by data from the Dutch Ministry of Foreign Affairs, the depositary of the Convention)[123] indicate that Italy is still among the contracting States. The failure by Italy to notify the existence of this and other international agreements is certainly unfortunate, but it does not render Article 25 inoperative.

8.1.1. 1955 Hague Convention on International Sale of Goods

The 1955 Hague Convention has been in force in Italy since 1 September 1964. It is currently in force also in Denmark, Finland, France, Niger, Norway, Sweden and Switzerland.

The Convention applies to contracts for the international sale of goods ('ventes à caractère international d'objets mobiliers corporels', according to the French authentic version). The Convention does not include an explicit definition of the expression 'sale of goods', and fails to specify what makes a contract international for the purposes of its rules. Article 1(3), however, clarifies that the Convention applies to contracts for the supply of goods to be manufactured or produced, unless the party who orders the goods undertakes to supply a substantial part of the materials necessary for such manufacture or production, and Article 1(4) states that the mere fact that the parties have entered into a choice-of-law or a choice-of-court agreement does not, as such, render the contract international. Some types of sales, such as the sale of registered ships and aircrafts, are excluded from the scope of the Convention altogether pursuant to Article 1(2). On a different note, the Convention does not explicitly distinguish between consumer sales and sales concluded between professionals or traders. The commonly accepted view is that the Convention is solely concerned with business-to-business contracts. An interpretative declaration adopted at the 14th session of the Hague Conference, in 1980,[124] endorses this reading.

The rules of the Convention are universal in nature, meaning that the law specified pursuant to the Convention applies whether or not it is the law of a contracting State. In practice, the Convention applies to all contracts within its scope, including those connected with a third State.

---

122 <http://itra.esteri.it>.

123 <http://hcch.net>. Regrettably, no corrigendum has ever appeared on the Official Journal of the European Union to amend the mistaken notification.

124 *RDIPP* 1981, 250.

Like the Rome I Regulation (and the Rome Convention), the Hague Convention provides in Article 2 that a sales contract is governed, in principle, by the law chosen by the parties. The parties can choose any law they wish, irrespective of whether the contract has a real and substantial connection with the country in question. The rules of the Hague Convention that deal with choice of law, however, differ in some respects from those of the Regulation (and, again, the Rome Convention). Unlike the European instruments, the Hague Convention does not expressly enable the parties to perform a *dépeçage* of the contract. In addition, the Convention requires that the choice of the parties, when made otherwise than expressly, result 'undoubtedly' ('indubitablement') from the provisions of the contract; under the European regime, on the other hand, a tacit choice is to be enforced whenever the existence and the content of the agreement of the parties is 'clearly demonstrated' either by the terms of the contract or by 'the circumstances of the case'.

In the absence of choice, sales of goods are governed, pursuant to Article 3(1) of the Convention, by the law of the country where the seller has its habitual residence. As a derogation to this rule, Article 3(2) provides for the application of the law of the country of the habitual residence of the buyer whenever the order was received in the latter country either by the seller or by his representative or commercial agent.[125] While the general rule in Article 3(1) is equivalent to the rule in Article 4(1)(a) of the Rome I Regulation, the exception in Article 3(2) has no corresponding provision in the European regime. Under appropriate circumstances, Article 3(2) is thus likely to lead in practice to outcomes that depart from those that would result from the Regulation.

The author of this report could not find any published judgments in Italian reports that specifically discuss choice of law under Article 2 of the Convention. Instead, several decisions are reported regarding Article 3 of the Convention. In 2000, for example, the Corte di Cassazione ruled on a case concerning a contract under which an Italian company undertook to deliver industrial equipment to a Malaysian company and to assemble it there. Absent a choice by the parties, the Court relied on Article 3(1) of the Hague Convention to hold that the contract was governed by Italian law, Italy being the country where the seller had its habitual residence.[126] In another ruling, rendered in 2004, the Tribunal of Padova referred to Article 3(1) of the Convention to determine the law applicable to a contract between an Austrian company and an Italian company. The Tribunal found that the contract was governed by the Vienna Convention of 11 April 1980

---

125 'Toutefois, la vente est régie par la loi interne du pays où l'acheteur a sa résidence habituelle, ou dans lequel il possède l'établissement qui a passé la commande, si c'est dans ce pays que la commande a été reçue, soit par le vendeur, soit par son représentant, agent ou commis-voyageur'.

126 Cass. (SU), 19 June 2000, No. 448, *RDIPP* 2001, 415.

on Contracts for the International Sale of Goods (CISG), but turned to the Hague Convention to address a question – the set-off of claims – that the CISG fails to settle expressly, and that should accordingly be decided, where the general principles of the CISG itself provide no guidance, in accordance with the law specified by the conflict-of-law rules of the forum.[127] In another judgment, again by the Tribunal of Padova, a similar reasoning was followed in a case concerning a contract between an Italian seller and a German buyer. The dispute revolved around another issue that the CISG fails to address, namely the determination of the interest rate due by the buyer in the event of late payment.[128]

Only a few judgments could be retrieved which refer to Article 3(2) of the Hague Convention. In an old case, decided in 1968, concerning a contract concluded between an Australian seller and an Italian buyer, the Court of Appeal of Rome, observing that the contract was concluded on the basis of the acceptance by the Italian agent of the Australian company of the counter-offer made by the Italian buyer and received by the seller in Italy (through his agent), stated that Italian law applied, this being the law of the country where the buyer had his habitual residence in accordance with Article 3(2) of the Hague Convention.[129]

In several judgments, the earliest of which were rendered towards the end of the 1990s, Italian courts, including the Corte di Cassazione, have failed to give precedence to the 1955 Hague Convention in cases relating to international sales of goods and have referred, instead, to the Rome Convention or the Rome I Regulation.[130] None of these judgments provides the reasons for the non-application of Article 25 of the Regulation or of Article 21 of the Rome Convention. In these instances, it is submitted, the latter provisions have simply been overlooked. There is something surprising in these repeated errors, since on other occasions the Corte di Cassazione itself has firmly asserted the primacy of the Hague Convention over the European regime, stressing that conflicts of laws involving contracts for the sale of goods should be dealt with, in Italy, under the former instrument.[131]

A ruling of the Tribunal of Monza of 2007 illustrates the trend of various Italian courts to disregard the Hague Convention.[132] The case concerned a sales contract between an Italian buyer and a Moroccan seller. The Tribunal sought to determine at the outset whether the CISG applied to the contract.

127 Trib. Padova, 25 February 2004, *RDIPP* 2004, 697.

128 Trib. Padova, 31 March 2004, *DeJure*. Further rulings along the same lines include CA Milano, 11 December 1998, *RDIPP* 1999, 112, and Trib. Roma, 14 July 2009, *Pluris*.

129 CA Roma, 7 May 1968, *RDIPP* 1969, 233.

130 See, among others, Trib. Reggio Emilia, 25 May 2005, *Pluris*; Trib. Modena, 9 December 2005, *RDIPP* 2007, 387; Trib. Gallarate, 13 January 2005; Trib. Nola, 11 December 2007; Trib. Bologna, 5 November 2008 and 13 May 2009; Trib. Bari, 15 May 2012, *Pluris*.

131 See, inter alia, Cass. (SU), 19 June 2000, No. 448, *RDIPP* 2001, 415.

132 Trib. Monza, 15 February 2007, *Pluris*.

Having found that Morocco is not a party to the CISG, the Tribunal turned to Article 1(1)(b) of the CISG itself. This provides that the CISG applies – regardless of the place of business of the parties – when the conflict-of-laws rules of the forum lead to the application of the law of a State that is bound by the CISG.[133] The Tribunal, instead of resorting to the Hague Convention, referred for this purpose to the Rome Convention. It found that the parties had not made a choice of law, and accordingly considered Article 4 of the Convention. In the view of the Tribunal, the general presumption in Article 4(2), which would have resulted in the application of Moroccan law (Morocco being the country where the seller had his habitual residence), ought to be discarded under the escape clause in Article 4(5). Italy, the Tribunal observed, was in fact the country with which the contract was most closely connected, since, according to the agreement of the parties, the goods were to be delivered at the buyer's premises in Italy and the price was to be paid in Italy via a letter of credit issued by an Italian bank. The reasoning of the Tribunal is hardly persuasive. For the purposes of this report it is worth noting that, had the Tribunal applied the 1955 Hague Convention, the outcome of the case would have been different. Since the Hague Convention does not include an escape clause, Article 3(1) would have led, in the circumstances, to the straightforward application of Moroccan law.

A judgment of the Corte di Cassazione rendered in 2016 provides a further example of the trend not to consider the Hague Convention in cases that, under the European regime, would in fact need to be decided in accordance with the Convention.[134] A dispute had arisen between a South African company and an Italian company over certain goods sold by the former to the latter. The contract between the parties did not feature a choice-of-law clause. The Court referred to the Rome Convention (the Rome I Regulation was not applicable *ratione temporis*), and more specifically to Article 4. It took the view that, under the general presumption in Article 4(2), the contract was governed by the law of South Africa. Based on this finding, the Corte di Cassazione held that the CISG did not apply to the contract either directly, under Article 1(1)(a), or indirectly, under Article 1(1)(b) of the CISG, since South Africa is not bound by the CISG. Ironically, had the 1955 Hague Convention been considered, the Court would have most probably concluded that the CISG was to govern the contract. As noted above, Article 3(2) of the Hague Convention provides that the law

133 According to Article 1(1), the CISG 'applies to contracts of sale of goods between parties whose places of business are in different States: (a) when the States are Contracting States; or (b) when the rules of private international law lead to the application of the law of a Contracting State.'

134 Cass., 29 December 2016, No. 27365, *RDIPP* 2017, 1031. For further illustrations of the disregard for the Hague Convention of 1955, see, among others, Trib. Rimini, 6 June 2013, *GiustUp*, and Trib. Prato, 4 March 2019, *GiustUp*.

applicable to a sales contract is the law of the country of the buyer's habitual residence, rather than the seller's, in the event that the order has been received in that country by the seller or his agent. Apparently, this is precisely what had occurred in the circumstances of that case: the Court in its judgment (albeit for reasons unrelated to the identification of the applicable law) mentioned that the South African company had acted in Italy through an agent.

8.1.2. Other Conventions Laying Down Conflict-of-Law Provisions

As noted above, the 1955 Hague Convention on the Law Applicable to Contracts for International Sales of Goods is not the only international convention to which Italy is a party that lays down conflict-of-laws rules in the field of contracts. Other conventions come with the purview of Article 25 of the Rome I Regulation, although none of these is concerned solely, or predominantly, with conflicts of laws. Of course, the primacy effect under Article 25 only refers to the specific provisions within these conventions that address conflict-of-laws issues.

One such provision may be found in an Agreement concluded on 14 January 1993 between Italy and the European Space Agency regarding the European Space Research Institute.[135] Article 14 of the Agreement provides that the Agency's activities in Italy are governed by Italian law, but further states that, if the conditions of employment of an employee of the Agency are not governed by the Agency's staff regulations, Italian law will apply.

Another treaty provision with the characteristics indicated in Article 25 of the Rome I Regulation, to name one more example, is Article 60 of the Munich Convention of 5 October 1973 on the Grant of European Patents (the European Patent Convention).[136] Article 60 sets forth the principle that the right to a European patent belongs to the inventor or his successor in title. It clarifies, however, that if the inventor is an employee, 'the right to a European patent shall be determined in accordance with the law of the State in which the employee is mainly employed', and adds that 'if the State in which the employee is mainly employed cannot be determined, the law to be applied shall be that of the State in which the employer has the place of business to which the employee is attached'.

---

135 The text of the Agreement is available through the treaty database of the Italian Ministry of Foreign Affairs at <http://itra.esteri.it>.

136 The Convention is in force in several EU Member States, including Austria, Belgium, Bulgaria, Croatia, Cyprus, the Czech Republic, Denmark, Estonia, Finland, France, Germany, Greece, Hungary, Ireland, Latvia, Lithuania, Luxembourg, Malta, the Netherlands, Poland, Portugal, Romania, Slovakia, Slovenia, Spain, Sweden and the United Kingdom. Of these, only Romania referred to Convention in its notification to the Commission under Articles 26(1) of the Rome I Regulation and 29(1) of the Rome II Regulation. For their part, Austria, Cyprus, the Czech Republic, Estonia, Finland, France, Germany, Ireland, Latvia, Lithuania, Luxembourg, Malta, Slovakia and the United Kingdom only mentioned the Convention in their notification under Article 29(1) of the Rome II Regulation.

The view has been convincingly advanced that the issues addressed in the last part of the provision would normally need to be decided, if the Munich Convention were inapplicable, in accordance with the law that governs the employment contract, as determined under Article 8 of the Rome I Regulation.[137]

8.1.3. Relations with Conventions Laying Down Uniform Substantive Rules

Article 25 of the Rome I Regulation is only concerned with the relationship with conventions that lay down conflict-of-laws rules, as opposed to conventions that provide for the international unification or harmonisation of substantive rules, such as the CISG. Article 21 of the Rome Convention featured a broader wording, and was considered by scholars to make the latter instrument subordinate to any international conventions in the field of contracts, whether specifically concerned with conflicts of laws or not.[138]

In spite of the different wording, the opinion is well settled among Italian courts that no regard should be had to conflict-of-laws rules, including the rules of the Rome Convention and the Rome I Regulation, so long as the matter is governed by a convention providing for the unification of substantive law.[139] In the words of the Corte di Cassazione, this is justified, as a matter of principle, by the 'special' character of uniform law.[140] As pointed out by the Tribunal of Padova in a case concerning a contract for the international sale of goods, one should not resort to a 'two-step' approach – i.e. the approach used by conflict-of-laws rules, which involves first identifying the applicable law, and second applying the law in question – whenever the conditions exist to adopt a 'single-step' approach, that is, the direct application of the relevant uniform substantive law.[141]

Various international conventions on the unification of substantive law have been found to prevail over the Rome Convention or the Rome I Regulation.

137 See M.-E. Ancel, 'France', in T. Kono, *Intellectual Property and Private International Law: Comparative Perspectives* (Hart Publishing 2012), 569.

138 G. Sacerdoti, 'Il coordinamento della Convenzione di Roma con altre convenzioni e con il diritto comunitario', in G. Sacerdoti and M. Frigo (eds.), *La Convenzione di Roma sul diritto applicabile ai contratti internazionali* (Giuffrè 1994), 78; and U. Villani, *La Convenzione di Roma sulla legge applicabile ai contratti* (Cacucci 2000), 15.

139 Cass. (SU), 18 October 2002, No. 14837, *RDIPP* 2003, 973; Cass. (SU), 20 April 2004, No. 7503, *RDIPP* 2005, 111; Cass. (SU), 15 February 2005, No. 2983, *RDIPP* 2005, 1077; Cass. (SU), 14 June 2007, No. 13891, *RDIPP* 2008, 505; Cass. (SU), 20 June 2007, No. 14299, *RDIPP* 2008, 511; Cass. (SU), 20 June 2007, No. 14300, *RDIPP* 2008, 511; Cass. (SU), 21 October 2009, No. 22239, *RDIPP* 2010, 481; Cass. (SU), 9 February 2009, No. 3059; Trib. Roma, 14 July 2009, *Pluris*.

140 Cass., 25 January 2018, No. 1867, *Pluris*. For earlier statements to the same effect see, inter alia: Trib. Pavia, 29 December 1999, *RDIPP* 2000, 770; Trib. Padova, 25 February 2004, *RDIPP* 2004, 697; Trib. Padova, 31 March 2004, *DeJure*.

141 Trib. Padova, 31 March 2004, *DeJure*.

Apart from the CISG, Italian courts have asserted, inter alia, the primacy of the Geneva Convention of 19 May 1956 on International Carriage of Goods by Road (CMR). In a case decided in 2005, the Corte di Cassazione acknowledged that, where litigation concerns a contract for the international carriage of goods by road, reference should be made directly to the CMR. Only where an issue falls outside the scope of the CMR, as occurred in the case at hand, which related to the payment of monies due upon the termination of the contract by agreement, the need arises to identify – via the applicable conflict-of-laws rules – the domestic law that governs the contract.[142]

8.2. NON-CONTRACTUAL OBLIGATIONS

Article 28 of the Rome II Regulation allows Member States, under the same terms as Article 25 of the Rome I Regulation, to apply the international conventions to which they became a party prior to the adoption of the Rome II Regulation and that include conflict-of-laws provisions in matters relating to non-contractual obligations. Italy is not a party to any international convention the main purpose of which is to provide for the unification of the conflict-of-law rules in a certain area, such as the Hague Convention of 4 May 1971 on the Law Applicable to Traffic Accidents, or the Hague Convention of 2 October 1973 on the Law Applicable to Product Liability. Italy is, however, party to various conventions that include conflict-of-law provisions concerning torts and/or other non-contractual obligations. As with the conventions relating to contractual obligations, Italy has failed to inform the Commission of the existence of these conventions. However, this does not affect the primacy of the latter instruments over the Rome II Regulation.

One treaty provision that prevails over the European regime on the ground of Article 28 of the Rome II Regulation is Article 9(2) of the above-mentioned European Patent Convention. Pursuant to Article 9(2) of the Convention, the non-contractual liability of the European Patent Organisation 'in respect of any damage caused by it or by the employees of the European Patent Office in the performance of their duties shall be governed by the law of the Federal Republic of Germany'. The provision goes on to state that, where the damage is caused by the branch of the Organisation at The Hague or by a sub-office or employees attached thereto, the applicable law shall be the law 'of the Contracting State in which such branch or sub-office is located'.

Other provisions that appear to fit in the description of Article 28 of the Regulation are Article 6(1) of the Convention of 29 May 1933 for the Unification

142 Cass. (SU), 3 May 2005, No. 9106, *RDIPP* 2006, 429.

of Certain Rules relating to the Precautionary Attachment of Aircraft[143] and Article 6(1) and (2) of the Convention of 10 May 1952 for the Unification of Certain Rules relating to the Arrest of Sea-Going Ships.[144]

The constituent instruments of international organisations and the seat agreements concluded by these organisations often include rules that determine the law applicable to the non-contractual liability of the organisation concerned. For example, Article 12 of the Agreement between Italy and the European Space Agency on the European Space Research Institute, mentioned above, provides that the Agency is responsible for any injury or damage arising from its activities in Italy, clarifying that, without prejudice to the relevant provisions of the constituent instrument of the Agency itself, such liability shall be governed by Italian law.

9. ISSUES NOT SETTLED BY ROME I AND ROME II

Issues may arise in the operation of the Rome I and Rome II Regulations that the two legislative measures fail to settle explicitly. As a rule, the task of filling these gaps lies with the law of the Member State of the forum.

There are various such issues. Most are procedural in nature. Both Regulations list 'evidence and procedure' among the matters excluded from their scope. Other excluded issues may arise in respect of any of the conflict-of-laws rules laid down in the Regulations, regardless of whether they are relied upon in the framework of court proceedings or elsewhere (e.g. before a notary public). Only two excluded issues (or groups of issues) will be considered here.

---

143 *League of Nations Treaty Series* 1938, vol. CXCII, Registration No. 4479, 291. The provision states that '[i]f an aircraft has been attached which is exempt from attachment according to the provisions of the present Convention, or if the debtor has had to furnish bond to prevent the attachment or to obtain the release thereof, the attaching claimant shall be liable in accordance with the law of the forum for the resulting damage to the operator or the owner'. Of the EU Member States which are bound by the Convention – Belgium, Germany, Hungary, Italy, the Netherlands, Poland, Romania and Spain – only three (Germany, Hungary and Romania) referred to the 1933 Convention in their notification to the Commission pursuant to Article 29(1) of the Rome II Regulation.

144 *United Nations Treaty Series* 1962, vol. 439, Registration No. 6330, 193. Pursuant to Article 6(1), '[a]ll questions whether in any case the claimant is liable in damages for the arrest of a ship or for the costs of the bail or other security furnished to release or prevent the arrest of a ship, shall be determined by the law of the Contracting State in whose jurisdiction the arrest was made or applied for'. Article 6(2) adds that '[t]he rules of procedure relating to the arrest of a ship, to the application for obtaining the authority referred to in Article 4, and to all matters of procedure which the arrest may entail, shall be governed by the law of the Contracting State in which the arrest was made or applied for'. The 1952 Convention was mentioned in the notification made under Article 29(1) of the Rome II Regulation by Germany, France, Ireland, Luxembourg, Portugal and the United Kingdom.

9.1. ASCERTAINING AND APPLYING FOREIGN LAW

Neither the Rome I nor the Rome II Regulation mention the legal status and the procedural treatment of foreign law. It is thus the task of the law of the forum to dictate, inter alia, the way in which the courts of a Member State should proceed to ascertain the content of the relevant provisions of the law specified under the Regulations, or the canons according to which those provisions should be interpreted.

The above questions must be answered, in Italy, pursuant to Articles 14 and 15 of the Italian Statute on Private International Law.

Article 14(1) stipulates that it is the task of the seised court to determine the content of the applicable foreign law. It must do so on its own motion.[145] To this end, the court can avail itself of the services offered by the Italian Ministry of Justice, rely on the applicable international conventions (such as the 1968 European Convention on Information on Foreign Law, to which Italy is a party along with some 40 other States), or ask for the assistance of experts or specialised institutions.[146] According to Article 14(2), if the content of the applicable foreign provisions cannot be determined,[147] then the seised court must turn to the law designated through another connecting factor as may be provided for under the conflict-of-law rule that applies in the circumstances. Only where the latter approach proves impossible or useless is the court allowed to apply the law of the forum. For example, in a Rome I scenario, if the parties to a contract for the provision of services have agreed on the applicable law, but the Italian court seised of the matter is unable to ascertain the content of the relevant provisions of the chosen law, then, according to Article 14(2), regard must be had to the law (which may be a foreign law) specified under Article 4(1)(b) of the Rome I Regulation. Italian law will only be resorted to if the latter provision results in the designation of a law that is equally unsuitable for application, as may occur, for instance, where the latter law happens to be the same law that the

145 This means, in practice, that the party seeking to enforce a right under a foreign law is not required to specify the foreign provisions on which his claims are based, or provide the court with evidence thereof. See recently in this respect Cass., 29 December 2016, No. 27365, *Pluris*.

146 As an alternative to the methods indicated in Article 14(1) of the Statute, Italian courts occasionally get in touch with the consular or diplomatic missions of the country whose law is applicable in Italy, and ask for assistance on their part. It is worth noting, however, that – absent specific provisions to the contrary – embassies and consulates are not, strictly speaking, under an obligation to provide this kind of assistance to the courts of the country where they operate.

147 This may occur where the study of the designated foreign legal system objectively raises special difficulties, or where the proceedings for the purposes of which the content of the foreign rules must be ascertained are urgent proceedings, incompatible with a thorough inquiry into the law in question. As to the latter occurrence, see, among other rulings, Trib. Savona, 14 November 2012, *RDIPP* 2015, 185.

parties had chosen, or where the court is unable to determine the content of that law either.

Pursuant to Article 15 of the Italian Statute on Private International Law, foreign law must be applied genuinely, that is, in accordance with the canons of interpretation of the designated foreign legal system and with the rules set out in that system to govern the temporal scope of local provisions and their succession over time.

The idea underlying Articles 14 and 15 of the Statute is, put shortly, that conflict-of-laws rules should be given full effect. Where they provide for the application of a foreign law, the court must make all reasonable efforts to determine the content of the pertinent foreign rules, and must apply foreign law in conformity with its original meaning. This approach is consistent with the bilateral nature of most conflict-of-law rules, including those in the Rome I and Rome II Regulations. Bilateral conflict-of-law rules are rules designed in such a way as to designate, depending on the circumstances, the *lex fori* or a foreign law. They build on the assumption that the *lex fori* and the applicable foreign law in principle enjoy the same status. Provisions such as Article 14(2) of the Italian Statute translate precisely this attitude, in that they confine the 'default' function of the *lex fori* to those cases where the applicable conflict-of-law rule has been exploited in full, but to no avail: that is, cases where the court seised has been unable to determine the content of the law designated under *any* pertinent connecting factor as may be provided for by the conflict-of-law rule that applies in the circumstances.

9.2. THE LAW APPLICABLE INSTEAD OF THE FOREIGN LAW CONFLICTING WITH PUBLIC POLICY

The second issue considered in this section has something in common with the problems regarding the treatment of foreign law. It, too, raises a concern for the effectiveness of the applicable conflict-of-law rule.

The Rome I and Rome II Regulations, as discussed above, provide that the application of the law specified under their rules may be refused if it would be at variance with the public policy of the forum. None of the two instruments explicitly address the issue of which law should apply once it is established that the designated foreign law must be disregarded.

Again, the answer lies in the law of the forum. In most Member States of the Union, courts are instructed to simply turn to the *lex fori*. The Italian Statute on Private International Law opts for a different and slightly more elaborate solution, which echoes the rule in Article 14(2), examined above. Pursuant to Article 16(2) of the Statute, when the application of the specified law must be ruled out on grounds of public policy, the case must be decided in accordance with the law designated under a different connecting factor that is applicable to the circumstances. This may well be the law of a foreign country. The law of the forum will only apply as a last resort, where no alternative connecting factors are available in the circumstances, or where such alternative connecting factors designate a law whose application is also objectionable in the circumstances.

Article 16(2) of the Italian Statute on Private International Law reflects the idea that the public policy exception should represent an exception to the normal operation of conflict-of-laws rules, and should not be interpreted as providing for an easy opportunity to fall back on the law of the forum. The fact that the law designated under a conflict-of-laws rule may be at odds with the fundamental principles of the forum is not a sufficient reason to conclude that the applicable conflict-of-law rule in question should become entirely inoperative. Rather, the potential of the latter rule should be exploited in full. Thus, if the rule in question sets out two or more connecting factors, the non-application of the law specified under one factor should result in the application of the law specified under another factor, rather than the immediate application of the *lex fori*.

10. GENERAL EVALUATION

It is probably too early to make a reliable assessment of the operation of the Rome I and Rome II Regulations in Italy. The rulings relating to the two instruments are growing in number, but they are not yet sufficiently numerous. It is true that the case law regarding the Rome Convention sheds light on some of the issues that Italian courts may be called upon to address today under the Rome I Regulation. Even so, the information collected for this report remains limited, and only covers a relatively narrow range of issues. All that being said, two general remarks can be made at this stage.

To begin with, the analysis of the decisions rendered in Italy suggest that Italian authorities are still insufficiently familiar with the rules regarding conflicts of laws in the fields of contracts and non-contractual obligations. Doubts tend to appear as soon as the issue arises of identifying the private international law rule(s) that apply to the situation at issue. Admittedly, the legal landscape is complex. However, it is a fact that Italian authorities have on various occasions simply failed to refer to the correct private international law text. For example, as shown in this report, the Rome Convention and the Rome I Regulation have frequently been resorted to in cases that should have instead been dealt with under the 1955 Hague Convention on the Law Applicable to Contracts for International Sales of Goods. Once the relevant legal instrument has been identified, the application of the relevant rules often leaves something to be desired. As illustrated in the report, serious objections can be raised regarding the way in which the Corte di Cassazione itself has in some cases approached the general issues it was seised of (for instance, the characterisation of a claim as contractual or non-contractual for the purposes of the conflict-of-law rules on subrogation). In addition, even where the final outcome of a judgment proves entirely convincing, the reasoning behind that judgment often proves unclear, as in the case of the two decisions of the Italian Competition Authority examined above. The blame, it is submitted, lies with the lack of specialised training. Private international law plays a very marginal role in the training of Italian jurists,[148] and is the subject of relatively few training events intended for practising lawyers and magistrates across the country.

Secondly, and somewhat in contrast to the previous remark, some aspects of the Italian practice on the Rome I and Rome II Regulations deserves to be considered either by the European institutions in the framework of a future review of the Regulations or by the legislators and the practitioners of other Member States. This is true, in particular of the way in which Italian courts deal with some of the issues that the Regulations fail to address, namely as regards the treatment of foreign law and the consequences of the non-application of the specified foreign law on grounds of public policy. The Italian approach, as discussed above, reflects a genuine concern for effectiveness. It is submitted that if uniform provisions were adopted, along the lines of Articles 14 and 15 of the Italian Statute on Private International Law, the operation of the Regulations would have a higher degree of consistency, and the objectives of the two measures would be served more efficiently.

148 See, in a comparative perspective, T. Kadner Graziano, 'Private International Law in Legal Education in Europe and Selected Other Countries', in J. von Hein, E.-M. Kieninger, G. Rühl (eds.), *How European is European Private International Law?* (Intersentia 2019), 339 ff.

THE APPLICATION OF THE ROME I AND ROME II REGULATIONS IN LATVIA

Inga KAČEVSKA and Aleksandrs FILLERS

1. THE NATIONAL LANDSCAPE

1.1. APPLICATION OF ROME I AND ROME II IN GENERAL

Latvia joined the European Union in 1 May 2004. With a separate law[1] Latvia adopted the Rome Convention, which became applicable from 1 May 2006.[2] In Latvia, the Rome I Regulation has been in force from 24 July 2008 but applies to

1 Likums par Konvenciju par Čehijas Republikas, Igaunijas Republikas, Kipras Republikas, Latvijas Republikas, Lietuvas Republikas, Ungārijas Republikas, Maltas Republikas, Polijas Republikas, Slovēnijas Republikas un Slovākijas Republikas pievienošanos Konvencijai par tiesību aktiem, kas piemērojami līgumsaistībām, kura atvērta parakstīšanai Romā 1980. gada 19.jūnijā, un Pirmajam un Otrajam protokolam par tās interpretāciju, ko veic Eiropas Kopienu Tiesa (Law on Convention on the Accession of the Czech Republic, the Republic of Estonia, the Republic of Cyprus, the Republic of Latvia, the Republic of Lithuania, the Republic of Hungary, the Republic of Malta, the Republic of Poland, the Republic of Slovenia and the Slovak Republic to the Convention on the law applicable to contractual obligations opened for signature in Rome on 19 June 1980, and to the First and Second Protocols on its interpretation by the Court of Justice of the European Communities) [2005] Latvijas Vēstnesis No. 209, 29.12.2005.

2 Ārlietu ministrijas dienesta informācija No. 41/326-2050 par Konvencijas spēkā stāšanos (Information No. 41/326-2050 of the Office of Ministry of Foreign Affairs on Force of Convention) [2006] Latvijas Vēstnesis No. 42, 14.03.2006.

contracts concluded after 17 December 2009, while the Rome II Regulation has been in force from 20 August 2007 and applies as of 11 January 2009.

There are no rules extending the scope of these instruments. Likewise, Latvian law does not have any special national rules facilitating the application of the Rome I and Rome II Regulations. In fact, even the Introduction to the Civil Law,[3] which contains the majority of the national conflict-of-laws rules, does not refer to these instruments. Similarly, Article 13 of the Labour Law,[4] which contains the national conflict-of-laws rule for employment contracts, does not indicate that it is superseded by the Rome I Regulation. This may partially explain why courts often apply national conflict-of-laws rules even though they have to apply the said EU instruments. They may simply not know about their existence and their applicability, because national laws make no references to EU conflict of laws.

1.2. CASE LAW APPLYING ROME I AND ROME II IN PRACTICE

There are no official statistics on how many cases both Regulations have been applied in; however, the authors have found a number of cases.[5] It should be noted that conflict-of-laws instruments are rarely applied by the Latvia courts. In some cases, courts have failed to refer to these instruments even when parties have referred to them in their submissions;[6] in other cases, courts have referred to the Rome Regulations without identifying the relevant provisions or evaluating the Regulation(s') applicability.[7] Overall, both party representatives and judges try to avoid applying conflict-of-laws rules as this may lead to the application of foreign law, the content of which is hard to determine, interpret and prove in the eyes of the Latvian lawyers. This is also the case because national rules do not facilitate the effective application of the foreign law and the determination of its content, as explained below.

It is difficult to identify the exact number of the most commonly applied provisions of the Rome Regulations or where they were applied wrongly. In many cases, authors have found that neither parties' representatives nor judges checked the scope of application of the Regulations. For example, in one case the counsel of the party in the statement of the claim suggested that the Rome I Regulation is applicable to a contract concluded on 3 June 2004, though the

---

3 Latvijas Republikas Civillikums (Civil Law of the Republic of Latvia) [1937] Valdības Vēstnesis No. 41, 20.02.1937.

4 Darba likums (Labour Law) [2002] Latvijas Vēstnesis No. 105, 06.07.2001.

5 The authors thank the Riga Regional Court for its help in collecting the cases.

6 See Riga Regional Court's judgment in the case No. C032265209, 26.11.2013; Valmiera District Court's decision in the case No. C39052915, 16.02.2016.

7 Kurzeme Regional Court's judgment in the case No. C02020713, 07.10.2013; Riga Regional Court's judgment in the case No. C2837210, 07.04.2014.

court did notice that the contract did not fall within the temporal scope of the Rome I Regulation.[8] However, the courts do not always check the applicability of the Regulations on their own initiative. For instance, in one case, the judge applied simultaneously both the Rome I Regulation and the Rome Convention, based on the submissions of the claimant's representative.[9] As we discuss below, in more complicated cases the misapplication is more obvious.

Arbitral awards are not reported in Latvia; thus there is no data on how many arbitral awards have applied the Rome I and Rome II Regulations.

2. THE OPERATION OF ROME I AND ROME II IN PRACTICE

2.1. *LOIS DE POLICE*

2.1.1. *Application of Overriding Mandatory Rules of the* lex fori

The authors have not identified any cases where the application of mandatory rules has been discussed by the courts. For that reason, we could not claim that the identification of mandatory rules is an issue in court practice.

However, overall, this absence may be caused by the rather limited number of cases where the Rome I and Rome II Regulations have been applied. Normally, mandatory rules are of importance only when a court applies laws other than the *lex fori*. Taking into account that the Latvian courts have preference for application of the *lex fori*, the number of such occasions is marginal. And even in cases where foreign law is applied, the issue comes into play only provided that some specific allegedly mandatory rules are in conflict with the *lex causae*. Given the small pool of cases available, it would have been unlikely that we would encounter the application of mandatory rules. Hence, we cannot identify any real-life difficulties related to the application of mandatory rules.

On a hypothetical level, the application of mandatory rules is problematic. It is well known that, as a rule, national legislators do not identify which rules are mandatory rules for the purposes of conflict-of-laws and what their territorial scope is.[10] Answering both questions requires extensive interpretation of the particular substantive rules. In particular, determination of the territorial scope is carried out via teleological interpretation.[11] While traditional conflict-of-laws

8 Riga Regional Court's decision in the case No. 3-10/0051, 29.10.2012.

9 Jurmala City Court's decision in the case No. C17119614, 01.08.2014.

10 F. FERRARI, *Rome I Regulation Pocket Commentary*, SELP, Munich, 2015, p. 326.

11 In principle, '[i]nterpretation of the forum's substantive rule as to its spatial applicability must … often be speculative.' A.A. EHRENZWEIG, 'Specific Principles of Private Transnational Law' [1968] *Collected Courses of The Hague Academy of International Law* 167, 187.

rules are bilateral – they determine the applicable law, the process of application of mandatory rules reflects unilateral methodology – the adjudicator does not need to determine the applicable law, but rather to determine whether a specific mandatory rule will apply to a given factual situation.

Taking into account the rather underdeveloped legal doctrine of conflict of laws in Latvia, there is hardly any doctrine on mandatory rules and their territorial scope. The lack of case law aggravates the situation. For example, for a long time Latvian legal environment suffered from excessive contractual penalties. To counter the problem, the legislator has set different limitations on the size of contractual penalties.[12] These recently enacted rules are important for the internal legal order and have resolved one of the most worrisome problems in Latvian civil law. It is, however, unclear whether these provisions, limiting the size of contractual penalties would trump provisions of otherwise applicable *lex causae*.

We have referred to this example because the problem of excessive contractual penalties was in the spotlight for years. However, even in respect of this question there are no indications either in doctrine or in practice as to how this problem would be resolved in the cross-border setting. There are numerous *lex fori* rules that could be mandatory, but their 'mandatory' nature and scope are not widely discussed even in the context of domestic law; hence, it is possible that nobody has even thought of how they were to be applied in a cross-border setting.

This means that, normally, parties and their lawyers can only try to make educated guesses about mandatory rules. Uncertainty is prevalent for each and every aspect of mandatory rules. It is utterly unknown what rules of Latvian law are mandatory in conflict-of-laws situations. Even if these rules were to be identified, it is entirely unclear whether a national court could establish any territorial limits for these provisions. Most likely, without any clear hints in the text of the provision, a judge would apply the mandatory rule, even if this were to be contrary to the teleology of the given rule.

The practical experience of the authors shows that, in some instances, the hypothetical presence of mandatory rules may reduce the planning of international transactions to an exercise in fortune-telling. A practitioner counselling a foreign party on a transaction in Latvia, if he/she is even aware of the problem, will not be able to say with any certainty what laws are mandatory. This is especially complicated in matters like labour law, where most substantive rules have a public law element. The only thing that counsel will be able to say with certainty is that 'it depends'. Of course, businesses do not find such

12 See Articles 1716, 1717 and 1724[1] of the Civil Law of the Republic of Latvia.

advice satisfactory. In fact – though this is a hypothetical assumption – such uncertainty could motivate foreign parties either to include a choice-of-court agreement combined with an agreement in favour of the law of the foreign forum, or to agree on the application of Latvian law in Latvian courts, making the problem of mandatory rules no longer relevant.

2.1.2. Giving Effect to Third States' Mandatory Rules

The treatment of third states' mandatory rules is an even more unlikely phenomenon than the application of mandatory rules of the *lex fori*. There are no examples of this known to the authors in Latvian practice. For this reason, it is impossible to draw any conclusions on whether giving effect to third states' mandatory rules should be extend to the Rome II Regulation or excluded from the Rome I Regulation. Taking into account the modest expertise of Latvian courts in conflict-of-laws issues, giving effect to third states' mandatory rules is not a topical issue.

However, it is necessary to make two theoretical remarks. Firstly, it could happen that a court of another Member State may consider giving effect to a Latvian mandatory rule. This exercise will be very complicated because, as stated before, the foreign court will most likely not be able to emulate the practice of Latvian courts in this respect as it will be lacking. That foreign court will have to decide on its own whether this Latvian rule is mandatory or not and what its territorial scope may be. This may not be a problem if courts are simply allowed to give effect to these rules, but it would be burdensome if this were a duty. Secondly, even a right to give effect to third states' mandatory rules generates additional uncertainty. In most cases, parties do not know *a priori* how the court (or courts) that could hear the case in the future is (are) to approach the issue and what the outcome may be. Giving effect to third states' mandatory rules must be approached with care. It should not be taken for granted that giving effect to a greater number of mandatory rules is always better. Most likely, such an extension would detract from the legal certainty and relative simplicity of the Rome I and Rome II Regulations.

2.2. PARTY AUTONOMY

2.2.1. Party Autonomy under Rome I

In most of the cases where parties have an agreement on the substantive law applicable to their contract, neither the parties nor the courts refer to Article 3 of the Rome I Regulation; thus, in the Latvian context it is very difficult to evaluate whether this article should be amended.

Moreover, excessive use of *dépeçage* was not identified in Latvia. However, there was one case that raised the interest of the authors.[13] In the context of an expedition and storage agreement, the Estonian claimant and the Latvian respondent agreed that their disputes would be resolved by the court where the claimant was situated, and the applicable law was the law of that state. Furthermore, in one of the clauses of the agreement, the parties agreed that the responsibility for the non-fulfilment of the contractual obligations would be assessed pursuant to the Latvian law. The claimant submitted that the claim had to be reviewed by the court of Latvia as the majority of the connecting factors were in Latvia – the goods, evidence and respondent were in Latvia. Moreover, in the claimant's view, the reference in the clause regarding responsibility, as well as parties' agreement on the respondent's duty to inform the claimant regarding the changes in Latvian law, referred to Latvian law as the applicable law.

The court decided that the claimant had violated the agreement on jurisdiction as, in accordance with the contract, the claimant was located in Estonia and thus the competent court was likewise in Estonia. Moreover, there was no evidence that the closest connection of the case was in Latvia; thus, the case was dismissed. The court made reference initially to Article 3(1) of the Rome I Regulation, and only then to Article 23(1) of the Brussels I Regulation.

This case illustrates rather typical practice of the Latvian courts, i.e. at the stage of determining jurisdiction, the courts apply the Brussels I Regulation and the Rome I Regulation 'interrelatedly' (quoted).[14] Still, the case above raises the question of what is the relation between a 'floating choice-of-law clause' and a tacit choice – the reference in the contract to a specific provision of the state's law.

There are no reported cases where parties had agreed on non-national rules. Parties most likely do not opt for the *lex mercatoria* because they are not aware of such an option. Some sets of non-state rules, for example, the UNIDROIT Principles of International Commercial Contracts,[15] harmonise contract law and are intended for international transactions. From the authors' point of view, it would be advisable to allow a greater choice of non-state laws to be used as the applicable law under the Rome I Regulation, because the choice of one parties' national law can put other party in a less favourable position. For example, Latvian contract law is to a large degree regulated by the Civil Law originating from 1937 and, as a result, the law does not always correspond to the modern need of traders, especially international ones.

13 Riga Regional Court's decision in the case No. 3-11-0177, 04.03.2013.

14 *Ibid.*

15 UNIDROIT Principles of International Commercial Contracts [2010] 45th CS A/67/17, 25.06–06.07.2012.

Moreover, the case law shows that if the parties have chosen the applicable law, one of the parties may nevertheless try to avoid application of this foreign law. For example, in one case, despite the fact that the parties had agreed to settle the disputes in Sweden and to apply Swedish law, the claimant tried to convince the Latvian court that the jurisdiction and applicable law clauses were not valid. The claimant argued that Article 4(1)(e) of the Rome I Regulation overrode Article 3, and that thus in the case at hand the applicable law was the law of the country where the franchisee had its habitual residence, i.e. Latvia. The court did not accept this reasoning, referring to Article 3(1) of the Rome I Regulation,[16] even though the Regulation was not applicable because the contract did not fall within the temporal scope of the Regulations (the contract was concluded in 2004).

2.2.2. Party Autonomy under Rome II

There are few cases where the courts have applied the Rome II Regulation, and the authors have found only one case where Article 14 was applied. This case between two Latvian companies concerned an insurance compensation claim arising from a traffic accident in Lithuania.

The second instance court, following the arguments of the claimant, acknowledged that, taking into consideration the fact that the respondent had not made any reference to Lithuanian law in its procedural documents and did not submit the translation of this law as required by Article 654 of the Civil Procedure Law, the respondent had thus, by its factual actions, in accordance with Article 14 of the Rome II Regulation, expressed its choice to apply Latvian substantive law. Before the court of cassation, the respondent denied the existence of an implied consensus of the choice of law and argued that the claimant had to prove its claim, including the applicable law.

The Supreme Court indicated, firstly, that a choice of forum did not automatically provide for choice of the applicable law. Then the Supreme Court briefly discussed the concept of 'an agreement freely negotiated' being a mandatory precondition for the consensus on the applicable law. In the case at hand, the respondent had objected to the application of Latvian law; thus there was no mutual agreement between the parties on the applicable law. The court annulled the judgment of the second instance court and sent the case back for re-consideration, noting that the regional court had to determine the relevant applicable law and also evaluate the interrelation between the Rome II Regulation and the Hague Convention of 4 May 1971 on the Law Applicable to Traffic Accidents (hereinafter: '1971 Hague Convention').[17]

---

16 Riga Regional Court's decision in the case No. 3-10-0150, 16.04.2012.

17 Supreme Court of Latvia's judgment in the case No. SKC-90/2015 01.07.2015.

The case clearly shows that the lower instance courts have limited expertise in EU conflict-of-laws instruments. The lack of legal analyses of the Regulation's text and available commentaries on this legal instrument lead to erroneous judgments. Moreover, the courts tend to follow the arguments of the party arguing for the application of the *lex fori* for reasons of judicial convenience.

2.2.3. *Law Applicable to Contracts in the Absence of Choice of Law*

Before Latvia joined the EU, its national conflict-of-laws rules determined the law applicable to a contract. Article 19 of the Latvian Civil Law made a contractual obligation subject to the law of its place of performance or, if that place could not be determined, to the *lex loci contractus*. This, of course, posed the question of the law applicable to synalagmatic contracts, which have two equal main obligations. Pursuant to the practice of the Supreme Court before World War II the place of performance of such contracts was the place where a non-monetary obligation was performed and not the place of payment.[18] Hence, the Supreme Court modified the wording of Article 19 and moved towards recognition of the characteristic performance rule. The authors are not aware of this type of reasoning having been re-adopted by the Supreme Court after Latvia regained independence in modern times.

However, even this problematic understanding of Article 19 is hardly an important part of Latvian legal culture. Conflict-of-laws rules found in the Latvian Civil Law were, in principle, rarely applied due to the scarcity of cross-border cases and hardly ever examined by the doctrine. Hence, there was probably hardly any historical resistance to Article 4 of the Rome I Regulation.

There seem to be two problems with the application of Article 4. Firstly, there is a more general problem related to the application of conflict-of-laws rules by Latvian courts. In some cases, where Article 4 could potentially be applied, it is simply ignored by the court, which instead applies the *lex fori* without any conflict-of-laws analysis.[19] Secondly, a more specific problem for courts is the understanding that the place of characteristic performance is interpreted autonomously. Courts tend to start their analyses of Article 4 by referring to one or other provision of the Latvian Civil Law that defines a particular contract. This seems to also be influenced by the fact that this mode of interpretation makes it possible to apply the *lex fori*. For example, in one case a court had to decide what law applies to a loan agreement under Article 4(2) of the Rome I Regulation.

---

18 B. BERENT, *Lettlands Zivilgesetzbuch vom 28. Januar 1937 in Einzeldarstellungen*, Verlag der A/G 'Ernst Platers', Riga, 1938, p. 132.

19 E.g. Valmiera District Court's judgment in the case No. C39056515, 12.08.2015 (in this case the claimant even referred to Article 4); City of Riga Northern District Court's judgment in the case No. C32296513/111014, 04.12.2014; Liepaja Court's judgment in the case No. C20248213, 17.10.2013.

The court reasoned that, under Latvian law, a loan is a real contract and the return of the money is the unique obligation arising from the contract. Since the debtor had its habitual residence in Latvia, this opened the door for the application of Latvian law.[20] In a very similar case, another court expressly stated that the characteristic performance of a loan agreement, even under Article 4(2) of the Rome I Regulation, must be determined pursuant to the construction of this contract found in the *lex fori*.[21] In another similar case, a court not only specified that the return of money was the characteristic performance of the loan agreement, but also emphasised that the claim before the court was about the return of the money.[22] In one more case, the court also found that the payment was a characteristic element of a sale of goods, in order to justify the application of Latvian law.[23] This latter case, however, was decided under Article 4 of the Rome Convention and probably even lower instance courts would have avoided such a solution, taking into account that Article 4(1)(a) of the Rome I Regulation contains an express rule on the law applicable to sale of goods contracts.

In this moment, this problem seems to have been resolved by the Supreme Court. The Supreme Court has indicated in respect of Article 4 of the Rome Convention that this practice is incorrect, and that payment does not normally constitute the characteristic performance.[24] The practice now being confirmed by the Supreme Court emphasises the importance of autonomous interpretation of European conflict-of-laws rules. Hopefully it will become dominant among all courts and will be extended to cases where the Rome I Regulation applies.

Overall, in the authors' view, Article 4 of the Rome I Regulation is an appropriate provision. In particular, the specific rules of Article 4(1) greatly simplify the determination of the law applicable to a number of frequently used

---

20 Jurmala Court's judgment in the case No. C17119614, 01.08.2014.

21 Riga Regional Court's judgment in the case No. C17132114, 09.10.2014.

22 Riga Regional Court's judgments in the case No. C17138713, 09.10.2014. All three cases mentioned in the report and dealing with the claim for return of the loan also raise much more important issues regarding the interplay of different conflict-of-laws rules. In these cases, the estate of a deceased Saudi Arabian national (also domiciled in Saudi Arabia) attempted to obtain recognition of its status of a creditor in insolvency proceedings against two Latvian companies. The estate claimed that the deceased person had given loans to these companies and had a right to be listed as one of the creditors in the insolvency proceedings. This raised a question of the law applicable in the insolvency proceedings *vis-à-vis* a creditor domiciled in a non-EU state, as well as the question of the relations between conflict-of-laws rules for insolvency proceedings and national conflict-of-laws rules on succession determining which person could represent an estate established abroad (these cases fell outside the temporal scope of Regulation 650/2012). Finally, these cases touched upon the question of the interplay between the Rome I Regulation and conflict-of-laws rules on insolvency and succession. Unfortunately, these questions were not discussed in detail by the national courts, which instead gave confusing reasoning driven by the preference for the *lex fori*.

23 This mode of reasoning was used by the court of appeals that was recited in the Supreme Court of Latvia's judgment in the case No. SKC-74/2016, 20.04.2016.

24 Supreme Court of Latvia's judgment in the case No. SKC-74/2016, 20.04.2016.

types of contracts. At the same time, even for contracts subject to Article 4(2), the determination of the place of characteristic performance in most cases is not especially difficult, making Article 4 comparatively simple in application.

Another advantage of Article 4 is that it provides a single connecting factor for the whole contract. It is superior in this sense to Article 19 of the Latvian Civil Law. On the one hand, if that provision is applied literally, it may make a single contract subject to multiple laws, depending upon the place where the obligations in question are performed. On the other hand, if Article 19 is understood to refer to the place of non-monetary performance as a single connecting factor, then that connection is often fortuitous. The disadvantages are absent from Article 4 of the Rome I Regulation.

However, the application of Article 4 of the Rome I Regulation, which is overall a superior rule, is complicated by the fact that courts tend to determine which party is to provide the characteristic performance by looking at the definitions of contracts found in Latvian legislation. Hopefully the intervention of the Supreme Court will be able to gradually change this trend.

2.2.4. *Law Applicable to Torts in the Absence of Choice of Law*

We have identified a few cases where a court has applied Article 4(1) of the Rome II Regulation.

In one case, where the owner of a bus brought a claim against Latvian and Lithuanian insurance companies, the court of first instance agreed with the defendant that Article 4(1) of the Rome II Regulation had to be applied as the traffic accident took place in Estonia, thus inviting the claimant to submit relevant Estonian law. The judge then referred to the Estonian law in order to determine whether damages, such as the loss of profit, were also compensated in traffic accident cases in general. However, despite the Estonian law applying, the court further analysed the concept 'damages' against the background of the Latvian legal tradition.[25]

In another similar insurance claim between two Latvian companies regarding a traffic accident in Germany, the court decided that the German law should be applied pursuant to Article 4 of the Rome II Regulation. The claimant

[25] Riga City Latgale Suburb Court's judgment in the case No. C29849910, 01.06.2016. Another problem with this case was that the claimant brought a claim for compensation of damages against the insurer, arguing that damages were caused by the insurer delaying payment payoff the compensation. However, it might be reasonably asked whether such a claim was even connected to the accident or whether it concerned an independent issue – the insurer's delay with the payment and as a consequence, its responsibility that required a separate applicable law analysis. Moreover, the court also ignored the possibility of applying the 1971 Hague Convention to determine the law applicable to the original traffic accident provided that determining that law was genuinely necessary to resolve the case.

only submitted the judgment of the German Supreme Court in which relevant German law had been referred to and interpreted. However, a judge decided that this judgment was not a legal act on which the claim could be based; the judge justified his decision by reference to Article 654 of the Civil Procedure Law which states that in cases where foreign laws shall be applied, the participant in the case who refers to the foreign law shall submit to the court a translation of the text in the official language as required by the specified procedures. As the claimant had not submitted German law and its translation, the court had no grounds to determine the applicable foreign law or its content and thus the claim was rejected.[26]

The second instance disagreed with such a 'formalistic approach' and decided that submission of the German law was not significant in the case at hand; firstly, because the judgment of the German Supreme Court was sufficient to determine the substance of the law; and secondly, because the defendant did not object on the application of this foreign court's judgment.[27]

Latvian courts have also considered a case dealing with law applicable to torts where however, the Rome II Regulation was not applied due to the priority of an international convention. The case dealt with a claim brought by the owner of a trailer against a branch of a Lithuanian insurance company in Latvia.[28] The trailer was destroyed during a traffic collision in Lithuania. The driver that caused the collision died, but he had liability insurance with a Lithuanian insurer. The Latvian company that owned the trailer brought a claim against the branch of the insurer in Latvia.

The Chamber of Civil Cases of the Supreme Court hearing the appeal decided that the respondent did not object to the application of Latvian law, and hence agreed to the choice of Latvian law under Article 14 of the Rome II Regulation. The Department of Civil Cases of the Supreme Court overturned the judgment of the Chamber of Civil Cases of the Supreme Court, finding that there was no tacit choice of law, because the respondent had invoked Lithuanian law during the proceedings and, in any case, the Rome II Regulation was not applicable. Rather, the applicable conflict-of-laws instrument was the 1971 Hague Convention. The case was returned to the Chamber of Civil Cases of the Supreme Court, which applied Article 3 of the Convention and found Lithuanian law to be applicable, since the collision took place in Lithuania.

While in this case the Rome II Regulation was not applicable, its Article 4 would have led to the same result – application of Lithuanian law – because the damage to the trailer occurred in Lithuania. Most likely, a national court would not have experienced any serious problems with the application of that

26 Riga City Ziemelu Suburb Court's judgment in the case No. C32288214, 14.11.2016.
27 Riga District Court's judgment in the case No. C32288214, 15.03.2017.
28 Supreme Court of Latvia's judgment in the case No. SKC-90/2015, 01.07.2015.

rule in such a simple case. More subtle fact patterns could easily cause problems, however. For example, in cases of thefts/fraud using electronic payment systems, the correct application of Article 4 does not seem to be self-evident at all. So far, Latvian courts have not faced such complex cases.

2.2.5. Application of Article 4(2) Rome II in Cases of Multiple Tortfeasors or Victims

The authors are not aware of any cases where a court has applied Article 4(2) of the Rome II Regulation in relation to multiple tortfeasors or victims. Hypothetically, its application would have been problematic. It seems that the provision would apply only to the most straightforward cases where there is only one tortfeasor and one victim.[29] The problem in practice would be that while such an interpretation may be based on some policy considerations (for example, the problem of applying different law to different victims or tortfeasors), this is not evident from the text of the provision. It is uncertain whether Latvian courts, mainly relying on the text of the Regulation and rarely (if ever) consulting legal doctrine (usually not available to judges at all or only available in a foreign language), would employ such an interpretation. It is more likely that they would prefer to apply Article 4(2) literally, even if this would amount to trying to fit a square peg in a round hole.

2.3. ESCAPE CLAUSES

The authors have identified one case where the escape clause was applied.[30] The case concerned an international carriage of goods. A Hungarian company hired a Latvian forwarding agent to organise a carriage of goods from Estonia to Hungary. The forwarding agent hired an Estonian carrier, who in turn employed an Estonian sub-carrier to perform the carriage. However, the latter could not perform the carriage as there were no goods for uploading at the agreed place of receipt. When the Estonian carrier informed the forwarding agent about the problem, the latter provided no further instructions, thus causing damages to the sub-carrier. The carrier compensated those damages to the sub-carrier and brought a claim for remuneration and compensation against the forwarding agent.

Hearing the case, the Latvian court came to a conclusion that the 1956 Convention on the Contract for the International Carriage of Goods by Road (CMR) was not applicable to the case as the sub-carrier did not begin the execution of the contract. Instead the court sought to determine the applicable

---

29 P. HUBER, *Rome II Regulation: Pocket Commentary*, Walter de Gruyter, Berlin, 2011, p. 95. *Contra*, G.-P. CALLIESS, *Rome Regulations: Commentary on the European Rules of the Conflict of Laws*, Wolters Kluwer, Alphen aan den Rijn, 2011, p. 417.

30 City of Riga Northern District Court's judgment in the case No. C33687116, 03.08.2017.

law under Article 5(1) of the Rome I Regulation. The court found that since the habitual residence of the carrier and the place of receipt of goods agreed by the parties were in Estonia, Estonian law applied. However, after reaching this solution, it continued its analysis by referring to the escape clause of Article 5(3) of the Rome I Regulation. The court underlined that the habitual residence of the consignor (the forwarding agent) was in Latvia and it was the consignor who determined the place of receipt. Moreover, both parties had referred to Latvian law in their submissions, indicating their will to be subjected to Latvian law. The sum of these circumstances showed that the contract was manifestly closer connected to Latvia than Estonia, hence Latvian law applied.

In its reasoning, the court made at least two mistakes. Firstly, the court combined the escape clause with an implicit choice of law. Secondly, the reasoning showed that the court used the escape clause for one purpose – to ensure the application of *lex fori*. In the given case, there was only one factor that connected the contract with Latvia – habitual residence of the consignor (forwarding agent). This was obviously not enough to evade application of Article 5(1) of the Rome I Regulation.

The case underlines two most obvious problems of the escape clauses. Firstly, it is not entirely clear what the underpinning policies of the escape clauses are. Is it legal certainty? In other words, are the escape clauses applied when the parties could not have foreseen the law applicable under the standard conflict-of-laws rule? Practice of other Member States does not confirm this approach. For example, an English court has taken into account the place where the victim of the tort suffered subsequent consequences (loss),[31] even though both the tortfeasor and victim would not have known about it before the tort took place. If the rule has an open-ended nature and even the policies behind it are not clear, then for Latvian courts, lacking the necessary experience, its application may be very complicated. It is probably better to have some teleological guidance in the text of the Regulations. In other words, courts must be aware what objective(s) should be attained via the use of the escape clauses. Secondly, the open-ended nature and the ambiguity of escape clauses make them a tempting tool to be used for the purpose of avoiding the application of foreign law.

2.4. SPECIFIC RULES

2.4.1. Contracts for Carriage, Consumer Contracts and Insurance Contracts

Rules regarding the special contracts covered by the Rome I Regulation are rarely applied in Latvia for the following reasons. Many aspects of carriage

31 *Winrow v. Hemphill & Anor* [2014] EWHC 3164 (QB) (06 October 2014).

of goods are covered in a number of international conventions, meaning that the courts usually apply those conventions. The authors have identified three relevant cases on carriage of goods. One of them we have discussed in the previous section on the escape clauses. In the second case, the court applied Article 5(1) of the Rome I Regulation and concluded that Latvian law applied to the claim of payment by the carrier.[32] The case was a simple one as Latvia was the place of habitual residence of both the consignor and the carrier and likewise the place of receipt of goods. In a third case, the court did not apply Article 5(1), instead determining the law applicable to a mis-delivery of goods by observing that the parties referred to Latvian law in their submissions, hence choosing Latvian law.[33] These three cases do not provide any genuinely valuable insights into Article 5(1) of the Rome I Regulation, but only underline the strong bias of Latvian courts in favour of *lex fori* and the prevalent perception of conflict-of-laws rules as tools to avoid application of foreign law.

Until recently, consumer disputes, including the disputes concerning the carriage of passengers, were reviewed in administrative proceedings. It was not uncommon for the parties to also refer to the Rome I Regulation in these proceedings, but the courts did not apply it in the reasoning for their judgments.[34]

The authors have not found any cases where Article 7 of the Rome I Regulation has been applied. However, as regards insurance contracts, it should be mentioned that the domestic Law on Insurance Contracts[35] also provides special conflict-of-laws rules. Article 2(5) of the Law states the specific rules that cover the situation where an insurance object related to insurance risk is located in a Member State of the EU or the European Economic Area. It firstly states that the insurance contract must comply with the provisions of private international law, but, secondly, the law also indicates the particular law that can be applied by the parties. These rules are unnecessary because the Rome I Regulation has to be applied directly; therefore, there is no need to duplicate Article 7 of the Regulation. Moreover, this encourages the application of the domestic conflict-of-laws rules instead of the Regulation.

2.4.2. Contracts for Individual Employment

The authors have identified only one case where the Latvian court could have potentially applied the Rome I Regulation to an individual employment contract. In the particular case, the court had to decide the law applicable to an employment contract of an employee working at sea.

---

32 Riga Regional Court's judgment in the case No. C-3651-17/1, 24.10.2017.

33 City of Riga Pardaugava Court's judgment in the case No. C-3747-17/6, 16.11.2017.

34 Administrative District Court's judgment in the case No. A42488806, 22.04.2008.

35 Par apdrošināšanas līgumu (On Insurance Contract) [1998] Latvijas Vēstnesis No. 188/189, 30.06.1998.

The application of Article 8(2) of the Rome I Regulation to employment contracts concerning work at sea has had some legislative debate, but as a consequence, for all workers in international transportation cases, the general rules in Article 8(2)–(4) apply to determine the applicable law in the absence of party choice.[36] However, the practice is not consistent, as demonstrated by the following case.

In the dispute between the sailor (presumably domiciled in Latvia, although it was not indicated in the judgment) and the ship flying under the flag of Saint Kitts and Nevis, owned by a Cypriot company, about the payment of the sailor's salary, the court did not even consider application of the Rome I Regulation, but directly applied the conflict-of-laws rules included in the Labour Law of the Republic of Latvia.

Article 13(4) of this Law provides that if the parties have not chosen the law applicable to their contract and the employee performs the contract in different states, the law applicable will be the law of the state where the which hired the employee is located.[37] Nevertheless, the judge applied the third part of this Article,[38] stating that if an employee and employer have not chosen the applicable law and the employee normally performs his or her work in another state in conformity with an employment contract, the law of that other state shall apply to the employment contract and employment-related legal relationships. The court decided that in the case at hand the employment contract was normally performed on the ship and as the ship flied under the flag of Saint Kitts and Nevis, the law of this federation should be applicable.[39] The judgment did not indicate what the route of the ship was or any other principal connecting factors with any particular state.

As with many other cases, the first problem is that the court applied the wrong conflict-of-laws instrument. It was not Article 13 of the Labour Law, but Article 8(2) of the Rome I Regulation that supplied the applicable conflict-of-laws rule. The second problem concerns the use of the flag as a connecting factor. Article 8 neither mentions the flag as a connecting factor, nor provides a specific conflict-of-laws rule for employees working at sea.[40] Moreover, often employees

---

36 M. MCPARLAND, *The Rome I Regulation on the Law Applicable to Contractual Obligations*, Oxford University Press, Oxford, 2015, p. 660.

37 Article 13(4): 'If an employee and employer have not chosen the applicable law and the employee in conformity with an employment contract does not perform his or her work in one and the same state, the law of the state in which is located the undertaking which hired the employee shall be applicable to the employment contract and employment legal relationships.'

38 Article 13(3): 'If an employee and employer have not chosen the applicable law and the employee in conformity with an employment contract normally performs his or her work in another state, the law of that other state shall apply to the employment contract and employment legal relationships.'

39 City of Riga Northern District Court's judgment in the case No. C32242113, 07.11.2013.

40 However, Article 13 of the Labour Law also did not mention the flag as a connecting factor, hence the correctness of the court's reasoning is doubtful even from the point of view of national conflict of laws.

bring their claims before the 'home courts'.[41] Application of the (foreign) law of the flag may put an administrative burden on these courts and at the same time diminish the territorial scope of their own labour law. Moreover, sometimes application of the law of the flag may also be unexpected for the employees. These considerations thus seem to speak against the use of the flag as a connecting factor. This conclusion also seems to follow from the *Voogsgeerd* case,[42] where the Court of Justice of the European Union (hereinafter: 'CJEU'), in determining the law applicable to a person employed on a vessel, made no mention of the state of the flag,[43] but rather used the habitual place of work as a connecting factor. Within the context of that judgment, the notion of the habitual place of work seems to be a very complex notion, and:

> 'the aspects characterising the employment relationship, as referred to in the order for reference, namely, the place of actual employment, the place where the employee receives instructions or where he must report before discharging his tasks, are relevant for the determination of the law applicable to that employment relationship in that, when those places are situated in the same country'.[44]

This is said to transform the habitual place of work from a foreseeable connecting factor into a proximity rule, similar to an escape clause[45] and difficult to apply. At the same time, some scholars still argue that the *Voogsgeerd* case dealt with specific factual circumstances (the employee was employed on two ships), hence the flag still survives as a connecting factor.[46] Others argue for immediate recourse to Article 8(3) of the Rome I Regulation with regard to employment relationships on the high seas where returning to the home harbour only plays a subordinate role,[47] while critics note that the place of engagement is equally at risk of manipulations by the employer.[48]

In our case, there are no doubts that the flag of Saint Kitts and Nevis was a flag of convenience. The court had to either attempt to pursue a factual test of habitual place of work proposed by the CJEU in the *Voogsgeerd* case or apply the law of the country where the place of business through which the employee

---

41 L.C. PIÑEIRO, *International Maritime Labour Law*, Springer, Heidelberg, 2015, p. 193.

42 Case C-384/10, *Jan Voogsgeerd v. Navimer SA*, ECLI:EU:C:2011:842.

43 L.C. PIÑEIRO, *International Maritime Labour Law*, Springer, Heidelberg, 2015, p. 195.

44 Case C-384/10, *Jan Voogsgeerd v. Navimer SA* [2011] ECR I-13275, para. 40.

45 L.C. PIÑEIRO, *International Maritime Labour Law*, Springer, Heidelberg, 2015, pp. 196–197.

46 *Ibid.*, p. 198.

47 F. FERRARI, *Rome I Regulation Pocket Commentary*, SELP, Munich, 2015, p. 309. See also, G.-P. CALLIESS, *Rome Regulations: Commentary on the European Rules of the Conflict of Laws*, Wolters Kluwer, Alphen aan den Rijn, 2011, p. 188 (arguing that Article 8(3) of the Rome I Regulation could be used for flag of convenience cases).

48 L.C. PIÑEIRO, *International Maritime Labour Law*, Springer, Heidelberg, 2015, p. 199.

was engaged was situated. The use of the latter connecting factor could have led to application of Cypriot law as the employer was formally registered in Cyprus. However, the application of Article 8(2) of the Rome Regulation itself seems to be very confusing and most likely the court would have to look beyond the formal place of registration of the employer, that is, at the place where the contract between the employee and the employer was genuinely concluded and the employee was engaged. As it currently stands, Article 8(2) is also a complicated fact-specific provision, one that is difficult to apply.

The case in question did not discuss these issues and did not even mention the factual circumstances necessary to apply these conflict-of-laws rules. Instead, the court ruled that the law of Saint Kitts and Nevis applied, because the employee carried out work on a ship flying under the flag of this state. Paradoxically, the court also mentioned that while the ship was located in the territorial waters of other states, their laws would likewise apply. This confusing statement should have opened the door for the application of Latvian law, since the ship was arrested in Latvia, but the court ignored its own statement, formally finding Saint Kitts and Nevis law to be applicable. Such a choice was illogical. Even from the scarce facts of the case reported in the judgment, it follows that the employee had nothing to do with Saint Kitts and Nevis, and at the same time, the court have had to apply a foreign and difficult-to-ascertain law. Here the court used another conflict-of-laws mechanism (or maybe a trick) in order to avoid the application of foreign law – it found that it was unaware of the content of the applicable substantive law. This was unsurprising. It seems that the defendant did not participate in the proceedings and the claimant was probably astonished to hear that the law of Saint Kitts and Nevis was to be applied. Saving itself from its own conflict-of-laws trap, the court then simply applied Latvian law, leaving all the conflict-of-laws mess behind, as if it had never happened.

This case illustrates a number of important issues. Firstly, it is indeed unclear what the current conflict-of-laws rule under Article 8 of the Rome I Regulation for employment at sea actually is. For less experienced courts, unaware of the sophisticated discussion about its interpretation or the scope of the *Voogsgeerd* case, this is an unpleasant situation. It may be possible for the legislator to address it, but an alternative route is to wait for another judgment by the CJEU on the application of Article 8 within the framework of more ordinary circumstances of employment at sea. A further point is that it seems that there has to be some answer provided by the EU law as to the *ex officio* application of EU conflict-of-laws rules. While it is not obvious from the text of the judgment, it is not impossible that the claimant (him/herself and/or counsel) did not understand the relevance of the conflict-of-laws rules and risks related to the application of different laws. The court was using non-mandatory application of conflict-of-laws rules to advance its preference for application of the *lex fori*.

2.4.3. *Specific Torts and Delicts in Rome II*

The application of the Rome II Regulation to specific torts is almost non-existent in Latvian practice. The authors have identified only one case where the court attempted to do this, yet the Rome II Regulation was not applicable in the first place.

In this particular case, the Chamber of Civil Cases of the Supreme Court had to decide whether a claim based on infringement of a trade secret fell within the scope of an arbitration agreement. Basically, the court had to rule on the interpretation of the arbitration agreement and then to consider whether the claim fell within the scope of the arbitration agreement.

The case contained an international element since the claimant was a foreign legal person. In its reasoning, the Chamber of Civil Cases of the Supreme Court referred simultaneously to national sources and the Rome II Regulation. In particular, it referred to Article 8, seemingly to justify its opinion that claims based on infringements of intellectual property were tort claims and hence fell outside the scope of the arbitration clause.

This reasoning has some flaws. Firstly, the interpretation of the arbitration agreement should have been the step in the reasoning and should have been done pursuant to international and national sources directly or indirectly dealing with the matter. Secondly, the distinction between contracts and torts in Latvian law is a matter of substantive law and must be based upon the understanding of these concepts in the national law. In principle, a conflict-of-laws instrument – the Rome II Regulation – meant to determine the applicable law is not a source that should be consulted, unless the national legislator has indicated otherwise. Thirdly, the reference to Article 8 was itself incorrect. Pursuant to the majority opinion, trade secrets do not fall within intellectual property rights under Article 8, but rather fall within the scope of Article 6, which deals with unfair competition.[49]

The problem, however, is that the Rome II Regulation does not provide any guidance as to the place of trade secrets within its structure. Analysis of scholarly works and legislative materials provides the answer, but Latvian courts seem to be quite reluctant to use such materials, particularly, when they are not brought up by litigants. One of the reasons for such reluctance may be fact, that usually these materials are available only in foreign languages and may not be among the books found in court libraries. Nevertheless, distinguishing between Articles 6 and 8 of the Rome II Regulation seems to be posing a problem for Latvian judges.

---

49 P. HUBER, *Rome II Regulation: Pocket Commentary*, Walter de Gruyter, Berlin, 2011, p. 233; C. WADLOW, 'Trade secrets and the Rome II Regulation on the law applicable to non-contractual obligations' [2008] *European Intellectual Property Review* 309, 311–312.

2.5. RULES APPLICABLE TO NON-CONTRACTUAL OBLIGATIONS OTHER THAN TORTS OR DELICTS

There is no known practice dealing specifically with the applicable law in cases of unjust enrichment, *negotiorum gestio* or *culpa in contrahendo*. For this reason, the authors cannot draw any conclusions from Latvian practice about the understanding of these concepts. However, the authors have identified a problem that does not deal specifically with the concept of unjust enrichment but is wider and deals with the scope of the Rome II Regulation.

There are at least three cases where a foreign insurer brought a claim before a Latvian court against a person domiciled in Latvia.[50] The fact pattern is always the same. A car is stolen from a person domiciled in another Member State. The insurer pays compensation and receives property rights. Then the insurer identifies a person in Latvia who has bought the stolen car.

In all three cases, we see the same basic structure of reasoning. In all cases, the claimants framed their claims as property claims for the return of possession of the vehicle. Overall, the reasoning on the application of conflict-of-laws rules in those cases was ambiguous. However, the courts mentioned Article 19 of the Rome II Regulation to verify whether the insurer was the owner of the vehicle. This was done even by the Supreme Court.[51] Other than that, these courts did not apply the Rome II Regulation. So, in reality, the courts did not use the Rome II Regulation to determine the law applicable to the claim, but only used Article 19 to justify the right of the insurer to bring a claim against the third party.

There are two problems arising from these cases. The first problem is that of the Rome II Regulation itself. The question is whether the Rome II Regulation applies to *rei vindicatio*, i.e. a claim for return of the property, at all. Some authors claim that the Rome II Regulation applies to such claims in all cases.[52] Theoretically, this is indirectly confirmed by the CJEU: in a case interpreting, the Brussels Convention, the CJEU stated that:

> 'actions for damages based on infringement of rights *in rem* or on damage to property in which rights *in rem* exist do not fall within the scope of Article 16(1)(a) since the existence and content of such rights *in rem*, usually rights of ownership, are of only marginal significance in that context.'[53]

---

50 Supreme Court of Latvia's judgment in the case No. SKC-79/2015, 17.12.2015; Riga Regional Court's decision in the case No. CA-2554-12/9, 20.11.2012; Kurzeme Regional Court's decision in the case No. C28381812, 14.07.2014.

51 Supreme Court of Latvia's judgment in the case No. SKC-79/2015, 17.12.2015.

52 P. HUBER, *Rome II Regulation: Pocket Commentary*, Walter de Gruyter, Berlin, 2011, p. 40.

53 Case C-343/04, *Land Oberösterreich v. ČEZ as*. ECLI:EU:C:2006:330, para. 33.

Others claim that the Rome II Regulation applies to *rei vindicatio*, 'insofar as the claim is premised on some behaviour or other responsibility of the defendant'.[54] Still others consider that claims based on property law are subject to the Regulation 'if the remedy sought is damages or a mandatory order other than one requiring that the defendant deliver up property to which the claimant has established a proprietary entitlement.'[55] Finally, some authors have expressed doubts about application of the Rome II Regulation to *rei vindicatio* in principle.[56] Obviously, such a split of opinion shows that the current text and structure of the Rome II Regulation do not make it possible to reach a uniform answer.

The second problem is with the courts' reasoning. The cases before the courts were complicated. The insurers brought claims against good faith acquirers. The claims were framed as property claims and requested return of the property. The reasoning of the courts was obviously inadequate, it did not attempt to determine the scope of the Rome II Regulation and strictly speaking did not apply the Regulation to determine the law applicable to the claims, rather making an incomprehensible reference to Article 19. Had the courts really applied the Rome II Regulation, the claims would most likely have been qualified as claims stemming from unjust enrichment, with the respective conflict-of-laws rules being applicable.

However, even if the courts were to answer the question about the applicability of the Rome II Regulation, it would have been difficult to provide a well-reasoned analysis. For courts that do not usually consult foreign academic contributions, answering the question about the applicability of the Rome II Regulation to *rei vindicatio* is not a simple task. Hence, the authors consider that the Rome II Regulation could be improved by clarifying what types of *rei vindicatio* claims fall within its scope, if at all. This would indirectly clarify the scope of the notion of unjust enrichment, as in most cases such claims would fall within the category of unjust enrichment.

2.6. RULES OF SAFETY AND CONDUCT

To the best of the authors' knowledge, the rules of safety and conduct have not been applied by Latvian courts. In particular, the authors have not found any cases where the Rome II Regulation would have been applied in the area of

54 G.-P. CALLIESS, *Rome Regulations: Commentary on the European Rules of the Conflict of Laws*, Wolters Kluwer, Alphen aan den Rijn, 2011, p. 382.

55 A. DICKINSON, *The Rome II Regulation: the law applicable to non-contractual obligations*, Oxford University Press, Oxford, 2008, para. 3.099.

56 A. CHONG, 'Choice of Law for Unjust Enrichment/Restitution and the Rome II Regulation' [2008] *International and Comparative Law Quarterly* 863, 893.

environmental torts – an area with greater potential for assessment of foreign administrative permits.

It is impossible to foresee how national courts would assess a foreign administrative permit allowing certain activity that is later claimed to be tortious. On the one hand, it is possible that courts would ignore such permits. Firstly, Article 17 of the Rome II Regulation does not mention such permits *expressis verbis*. Taking into account the somewhat positivistic inclinations of national courts (particularly in such unchartered territory as conflict of laws), a teleological interpretation of Article 17 may fail. Moreover, foreign administrative permits are deemed to be foreign public acts. Hence, it is possible that a national court would consider that such acts cannot have any impact on Latvian court, since the latter are not subject to foreign public acts. This is not impossible since the case law shows that courts lack confidence when dealing with conflict-of-laws rules. In such a state of affairs, reliance by courts on a formalistic and literal interpretation of conflict-of-laws rules would be of no surprise.

At the same time, in a number of cases where foreign insurers were trying to reclaim property stolen from their beneficiaries, courts did not analyse their property rights via the application of conflict-of-laws rules of the forum, simply recognising foreign documents confirming ownership.[57] This shows that recognition of foreign acts litigated before Latvian courts is not unknown. However, in these cases, the question of property was a preliminary question. Questions of liability are usually central to the case and courts may be less inclined to rely on foreign documents. For this reason, the authors can only note that no such case law exists and that, in the absence of clear language in the Rome II Regulation, the putative position of courts in relation to foreign administrative permits is uncertain.

2.7. SCOPE OF APPLICABLE LAW

The authors have not identified any cases posing the question of the interpretation of Article 12 of the Rome I Regulation or Article 15 of the Rome II Regulation. This is not surprising in the light of the limited case law.

2.8. *RENVOI*

Discussion of the problem of *renvoi* requires a preliminary distinction to be made between EU Member States and third states. The Member States do not have their own functioning conflict-of-laws rules, apart from the Rome I and Rome II

---

57 See section 2.5 of this chapter.

Regulations for matters falling within the scopes of these two Regulations. All the Member States, having adopted the Regulations in question, have agreed to avoid the application of their own conflict-of-laws rules. Hence, when the said Regulations indicate the law of a Member State, *renvoi* is technically impossible. When national legal systems have no functioning conflict-of-laws rules, one cannot speak of international harmony.

In theory, *renvoi* could be more relevant where the applicable law is that of a third state. Third states have their own conflict-of-laws systems, thus making *renvoi* possible. Would the re-introduction of *renvoi* in regard to third states be acceptable? In the authors' view, this would transform the conflict-of-laws Regulations from instruments identifying the applicable law into indicators of the competent legal order. This legal order then would have to decide what law applies. First of all, this would pose the question of what the policies behind international harmony are? Is international harmony intended to benefit parties' interests, via cementing legal certainty, or is it meant to achieve some other objectives, for example respect for sovereign legislators, etc.? It would seem to us that if the purpose for EU conflict-of-laws rules is to simplify individuals' lives[58] then the use of *renvoi* is an otiose or even counterproductive idea.

Secondly, it is doubtful that *renvoi* is even able to achieve international harmony, as it is mostly employed to support the application of the *lex fori* (at least in the case of remission), without truly advancing international harmony. Thirdly, it would endanger substantive policies behind the EU conflict-of-laws rules, empowering a third state legal order to decide what law applies.

Finally, prior identification of a competent legal order and then interpretation of its conflict-of-laws rules only to find the applicable law (or possibly just another competent legal order in case of transmission) would greatly complicate the functioning of conflict-of-laws. The case law analysed in this chapter shows that for some Member States even the current state of conflict of laws may be complicated. Adding any further levels of complexity will certainly make things worse, dispute settlement more expensive and lengthy, and courts even more inclined to avoid conflict of laws, falling back on the *lex fori*. For these reasons, the authors believe the re-introduction of *renvoi* to be counterproductive even when third state laws apply.

In the actual court practice of the majority of Latvian courts, the applicable law was that of Member States. Here *renvoi* is of no use. The application of the law of the third state is rare in Latvian court practice. For this reason and the reasons expressed above, there seems to be no need to re-introduce *renvoi* in the conflict of laws applicable to contractual and non-contractual obligations.

---

58 See Action Plan of the Council and the Commission on how best to implement the provisions of the Treaty of Amsterdam on an area of freedom, security and justice – Text adopted by the Justice and Home Affairs Council of 3 December 1998 [1999] OJ C 19/1–15, para. 39.

2.9. FOREIGN LAW

2.9.1. Application of Foreign Law in General

There are only a few formal provisions regarding the conflict-of-laws rules and foreign law in the national legal framework. The Civil Law of 1937 provides that where Latvian law allows the application of the law of a foreign state, the substance thereof shall be determined in accordance with the procedure prescribed by the law (first sentence of Article 22).[59] General rules on the application of foreign law are included in Part 80 ('Application of Foreign Law in Adjudicating Civil Cases') of the Civil Procedure Law, yet this Part consists only of two very short articles: Article 654 ('The Text of Foreign Law') and Article 655 ('Ascertaining Foreign Law'). Initially, it might seem that these articles provide a certain formula – the party submits the text of the foreign law, but the court then ascertains it. However, despite the titles of the articles, as explained below, those norms are understood differently.

Both Articles have not been changed since 2004, thus they are not up-to-date and do not facilitate the application of the Rome Regulations. Moreover, Part 80 of the Civil Procedure Law does not provide answers to many questions, including, but not limited to, whether the judge shall determine foreign law *ex officio* in the particular case, how to ascertain the law, what methods might be used to do so, and how foreign law is to be treated.[60] Even though it is not evident from the court practice, it is suggested that the foreign law is subject to the same treatment as the law of the forum, as Article 3 of the Civil Law provides that 'every civil legal relationship shall be adjudicated in accordance with the laws [*suggested: domestic and foreign*] which are in force at the time when such legal relations are created, varied or terminated.'[61] The authors consider that Article 3 governs the intertemporal application of the private laws and the suggested interpretation, extending its scope to the question of applicability of foreign law, is too broad.

As indicated, the relevant two articles of the Civil Procedure Law deal only with two questions on ascertaining foreign law: on the initiative of the party or the court. Accordingly, the authors discuss their application below.

---

59 Until 3 December 2015 it provided: 'Where Latvian law allows the application of the law of a foreign state, the substance thereof shall be determined in accordance with the procedure prescribed in the *Civil Procedure Law*.'

60 J. KOLOMIJCEVA, 'Ārvalsts likuma piemērošana civilprocesā' (Application of Foreign Law in Civil Procedure) [2010] *Jurista Vārds* 51.

61 'The Application of Foreign Law in Civil Matters in the EU Member States and Its Perspectives for the Future', Part I, Legal Analysis, Swiss Institute of Comparative Law, Lausanne, 11.07.2011, p. 290.

2.9.2. *Ascertaining of Foreign Law by the Party*

Article 654 of the Civil Procedure Law provides that in cases where foreign laws are to be applied, the party in the case who refers to the foreign law shall submit to the court a certified translation of the text into the court's official language according to specified procedures.

According to the commentaries to this article, the burden of proof of the applicability of foreign law is on the party and the court shall examine conflict-of-laws rules only when one of the parties refers to conflict of law or foreign law.[62] This is based on the notion that the Civil Procedure Law does not foresee a departure from the principles of adversarial proceedings.[63]

It is also suggested that 'once the applicable law is established, it is up to the parties to decide whether or not they choose to plead foreign law and subsequently to establish its contents. The only legal duty of the judge is to explain the legal consequences of their choice'.[64] This opinion is based on the notion that the foreign law is treated as a 'fact'. Nevertheless, if the foreign law is strictly treated as just a fact, then a misapplication of the foreign law cannot be argument at cassation, as the Supreme Court as the instance of cassation is not reviewing the substance of the dispute.[65] But this is not the case: even prior to World War II, the Supreme Court recognised that the erroneous application of foreign law was subject to appeal and cassation review,[66] the same is still true nowadays. Article 451 of the Civil Procedure Law states that a cassation complaint can be submitted inter alia if a court has applied a substantive law norm incorrectly, if it has been incorrectly applied to the facts of the case, or if a substantive law norm has been construed incorrectly. The case law also shows that cassation complaints can be based on an incorrect determination of the applicable foreign law.[67]

In the Latvian legal doctrine, it is implied that the parties shall prove that the foreign law is applicable and then prove its content, but that the court shall play a rather passive role. However, some authors have also proposed the 'active approach' to the treatment of foreign law should be introduced in Latvia,

---

62 K. TORGĀNS, *Civilprocesa likuma komentāri. III daļa. 61.–68. nodaļa* (Commentaries of Civil Procedure Law. Part III. Chapters 61–68), TNA, Riga, 2014, p. 836.

63 *Ibid.*, p. 837.

64 'The Application of Foreign Law in Civil Matters in the EU Member States and Its Perspectives for the Future', Part I, Legal Analysis, Swiss Institute of Comparative Law, Lausanne, 11.07.2011, p. 293.

65 K. TORGĀNS, *Civilprocesa likuma komentāri. II daļa. 29.–60.^{1} nodaļa* (Commentaries of Civil Procedure Law. Part II. Chapters 29–60^1), TNA, Riga, 2012, p. 756.

66 B. BERENT, *Lettlands Zivilgesetzbuch vom 28. Januar 1937 in Einzeldarstellungen*, Verlag der A/G 'Ernst Platers', Riga, 1938, p. 79.

67 Supreme Court's judgment in the case No. C27179312, 20.04.2016.

observing that it is necessary for the judiciary to establish a reliable approach to that application of foreign law *ex officio*, whereby any derogation is explained and justified by the court.[68]

Moreover, Article 654 of the Civil Procedure Law provides rather technical details regarding the submission of the text and translations of the foreign law. According to this provision, if a party refers to foreign law, it has to provide a translation of the particular law and prove the applicability of the foreign law and the consequences of its application to the claim.[69] Once again following one academic opinion, the party relying on foreign law, for the sake of its own interest, should also submit relevant additional information on the substance of the foreign law, its validity and examples of the case law and doctrine.[70] However, that makes the proceedings more expensive, complex, lengthy and unpredictable; as a result neither parties, nor judges are generally keen to apply foreign law.

2.9.3. Ascertaining of Foreign Law by the Court

Article 655(1) of the Civil Procedure Law states that in accordance with the specified procedures in international treaties binding the Republic of Latvia, a court shall ascertain the content of the foreign law to be applied. As indicated above, the parties themselves have to prove the application and the content of the foreign law and only in exceptional circumstances will the court itself determine the content of the foreign law.

Latvia is a party to the European Convention of 7 June 1968 on Information on Foreign Law (hereinafter: 'London Convention'). It is acknowledged that the assistance of the Ministry of Justice is very limited if the information on foreign law is required from a country other than an EU Member State, contracting state to the London Convention or state party to bilateral treaties on mutual judicial cooperation.[71] It is likely that the lack of information on foreign law leads to avoidance of the application of foreign law. There is also no official information how often the Convention is applied; there have been no reported cases where the Convention was applied. However, judges have admitted that the London Convention is not often used because there is the lack of awareness of it and that if the judge had used the Convention, he/she experienced a lengthy procedure

68 I. KAČEVSKA et al., *Recommendations and Guidelines: Effective adoption, transposition, implementation and application of European Union legislation in the area of civil justice*, Riga, 2015, p. 36.

69 K. TORGĀNS, *Civilprocesa likuma komentāri. III daļa. 61.–68. nodaļa* (Commentaries of Civil Procedure Law. Part III. Chapters 61–68), TNA, Riga, 2014, p. 840.

70 *Ibid.*

71 K. TORGĀNS, *Civilprocesa likuma komentāri. III daļa. 61.–68. nodaļa* (Commentaries of Civil Procedure Law. Part III. Chapters 61–68), TNA, Riga, 2014, p. 845.

and/or did not receive any information at all. Therefore, the Convention is not very effective.

The second part of Article 655 states that in other cases a court, through the intermediation of the Ministry of Justice and within the bounds of possibility, shall ascertain the contents of the foreign law to be applied. There are no practical examples of how this article is applied in the case law. In the commentaries, the court is advised to use also other means to discover the substance of the foreign law than those provided in the Civil Procedure Law – for example, using databases or Internet resources for research.[72] However, firstly, due to the overload of cases before the courts, the authors doubt whether the judges would take such an initiative. Secondly, the findings of such research, if it is carried out, may not be official, authoritative and valid sources of the particular foreign law.

In conclusion, it is recommended that the relevant part of the Civil Procedure Law should be updated and amended in order to facilitate the universal application of the Rome Regulations.

2.9.4. Failure to Determine Foreign Law

The second sentence of Article 22 of the Civil Law provides that if the court cannot determine the content of the foreign law, 'it shall be presumed that the legal system in the relevant foreign state, in the area of law to be adjudged, conforms to the Latvian legal system in the same area'.

Theoretically, this norm shall be applied if all possibilities of finding out the content of the foreign law have been exhausted, as provided by the law. Whether the content of the foreign law cannot be established shall be examined on a case-by-case basis, taking into consideration the facts of the case, including which state's law has to be ascertained, whether there is real judicial cooperation with that state, the practical possibility of accessing information on foreign law, and procedural economy, etc.[73] In the event of failure to determine the foreign law, the Latvian courts can apply Latvian law.

In practice, this norm is interpreted differently, and its interpretation allows courts to avoid the application of the foreign law. We have already discussed a case where the court was faced with a task of determining the law applicable to the cross-border maritime employment contract.[74] The case is also an example of failure to determine the content of foreign law. In the said case, a sailor (presumably domiciled in Latvia) brought a claim for unpaid salary against a foreign ship arrested and located in the harbour of Riga. The judge sitting in on the case conducted hearing with the participation of the representative of

---

72 *Ibid.*

73 *Ibid*, p. 847.

74 City of Riga Northern District Court's judgment in the case No. C32242113, 07.11.2013.

the claimant but without the participation of the respondent, even though, as indicated in the judgment, the summons was sent to the respondent at the place it was located (the harbour of Riga).[75]

Without referring to the Rome I Regulation, the court decided that the conflict-of-laws rules had to be determined by the Labour Law of Latvia.[76] Article 13(3) of this Law provides: 'if an employee and employer have not chosen the applicable law and the employee in conformity with an employment contract normally performs his or her work in another state, the law of that other state shall apply to the employment contract and employment legal relationships'. The judge established that the sailor had performed his work on a ship flying under the flag of Saint Kitts and Nevis; therefore, the law of Saint Kitts and Nevis had to be applied in the case at hand. Further, it was stated that as the law of Saint Kitts and Nevis was not known to the court and the parties had not submitted information on foreign law, in the consequence the foreign law could not be established. Therefore, the Latvian Labour Law was applied in accordance with the second sentence of Article 22 of the Civil Law. The claim was satisfied, the judgment was not appealed, and it entered into force.

As is evident, the court did not even consider looking at the Rome I Regulation, nevertheless, pursuant to the national conflict-of-laws rules foreign law was applicable. The judge disregarded the first part of Article 22 of the Civil Law stating that the content of foreign law must be determined in accordance with procedural laws. Instead, it decided to refer directly to the second part of this article as 'the court is unaware of such law'. Most likely, it seemed very exotic to request and apply the law of the Federation of Saint Kitts and Nevis (even though, in reality, it should not have been found to be the applicable law). Misapplication of the law cannot be excused; however, it is doubtful whether the court would have been able to review the case within a reasonable time if, indeed, the foreign law had been applicable and the information on the content of the law requested. This would notably be the case, since the Civil Procedure Law provides for expedited labour dispute resolution: such cases shall be decided no later than 15 days after receipt of the defendant's submissions, which in turn must be submitted 15–30 days after receipt of the statement of claim (Articles 148 and 149(8)).

2.10. *ORDRE PUBLIC*

The authors have not identified any cases where courts have refused to apply foreign law due to it being inconsistent with the *lex fori*. However, taking into account the fact that Latvian courts often simply ignore conflict-of-laws

---

75 This case is also discussed in section 2.4.2 of this chapter.

76 Darba likums (Labour Law) [2002] Latvijas Vēstnesis No. 105, 06.07.2001.

rules and instead apply the *lex fori*, it should not be taken for granted that the non-application of the public policy exception indicates a liberal approach on the part of Latvian courts to the application of foreign law.

Hypothetically, one of the problems is what the national court should do once it has applied the public policy exception under the Rome I and Rome II Regulations. For example, if the amount of the contractual penalty pursuant to foreign law is extremely large, it may be found to be contrary to Latvian public policy. However, when the foreign rule determining this amount is not applied, what should the judge should do? In Latvia, it is more than certain that the judge will apply the national law as it is applied in domestic cases, due to the strong homeward trend and lack of in-depth doctrine of private international law.

However, there are other possibilities. One possibility is to search for similar rules in different but related legal systems. Of course, due to practical problems, said possibility is unrealistic. Parties would not be able to predict the outcome of such an exercise. Firstly, since this method would be entirely in the hands of the court, the parties would not be able to know in advance which laws could be considered related to the *lex causae*. Secondly, in practice, the parties would not be able to know the content of these laws in advance. Thirdly, the parties would not be able to know in advance how a court would identify a common position among these different laws on the issue. Fourthly, it is likewise doubtful that the parties would be able to express their thoughts on the correct application of this method because neither the parties nor the judges are likely to know with certainty that the public policy exception will apply before the judgment is handed down. At that point, the parties can make no further submissions (except in the appeal proceedings). Finally, such course of action implies an overly active intervention on the part of the court, as well as being very expensive and time-consuming.

Another possible solution is to limit the effect of the public policy exception. If the foreign law provides for excessive contractual penalties, then the penalty may be decreased to a level acceptable for the Latvian legal system. This could be higher than that allowed by the *lex fori*, without being manifestly incompatible with it.

Unfortunately, neither case law nor doctrine currently provides any guidance in this respect. It is more likely that courts would simply rely on the *lex fori*, even if other more flexible solutions could ensure greater respect for the *lex causae*.

2.11. COMPENSATION

Currently, there is no case law where this question has been addressed. The authors can only offer some conjunctures. Firstly, if foreign law is applied, and it explicitly establishes how compensation must be calculated, then the application of foreign law implements the level of compensation provided. Secondly, it is possible that the foreign law may not specify the level of compensation, but that it can be derived from an in-depth analysis of foreign law in the light of scholarly discussion and case law. In that case, it is very unlikely that a national court would search for these sources *ex officio*. One can reasonably assume that the Latvian court would apply the written law, without deeper analysis, unless the parties were to argue for different interpretation. Thirdly, in a more complex situation – the amount of compensation is not always a question of interpreting a specific rule of the *lex causae*. Sometimes, it is a question of legal tradition. It is possible that foreign courts may simply award greater or more modest compensation than Latvian courts. The Rome II Regulation does not expressly require a national judge to take into account such traditions or foreign practices. In view of the positivistic approach of Latvian courts to conflict-of-laws rules, largely due to lack of doctrinal studies and extensive case law, it is very doubtful that a Latvian judge would attempt to educate him/herself on this foreign practice and mimic a foreign judge in respect of the level of compensation. Most likely, the level of compensation will be assessed pursuant to Latvian legal traditions.

2.12. RELATIONS WITH INTERNATIONAL CONVENTIONS

2.12.1. Relation with the 1971 Hague Convention

The 1971 Hague Convention entered into force in Latvia on 15 October 2000.[77] There are no official statistics regarding application of this Convention in Latvia; however, the authors found a few cases where it was relevant. One of the cases is exceptional, as the court of the second instance applied foreign law, which is very rare in the Latvian case law.[78] The court applied Lithuanian law, which was submitted by the claimant because the traffic accident occurred in Lithuania (Article 3 of the 1971 Hague Convention).[79] It did so because the Supreme Court returned this case for reconsideration to the second instance and instructed the court of appeal to consider the interrelation between the Rome II Regulation and the 1971 Hague Convention. Specifically, the Supreme Court noted that the 1971 Hague Convention did not allow the parties to implicitly choose the applicable law.[80]

In the case at hand, the 1971 Hague Convention played an important role as – atypically – the court applied the foreign law. However, since the practice is so

77 Par 1971. gada 4. maija Hāgas konvenciju par ceļu satiksmes negadījumiem piemērojamo likumu (Law on Convention on the Law Applicable to Traffic Accidents) [2000] Latvijas Vēstnesis No. 244/246, 30.06.2000.

78 See also discussion of this case in section 2.2.4 of the chapter.

79 Riga Regional Court's judgment in the case No. C30631610, 28.09.2015.

80 Supreme Court of Latvia's judgment in the case No. C30631610 SKC-90/2015, 01.07.2015.

limited, it is hard to elaborate on other aspects of the application of the Regulation and Convention. Nevertheless, as evident from this case, the claimant's claim was satisfied in all instances irrespective of the diverging conflict-of-laws solutions, while the Supreme Court showed its concern about the correct conflict-of-laws methodology.

2.12.2. Relations with Bilateral Treaties on Mutual Judicial Assistance

After 1990, Latvia concluded bilateral treaties on mutual legal assistance in civil and criminal matters with Russian, Ukraine, Belarus, Uzbekistan, Kyrgyzstan, Moldova, Poland and a trilateral treaty with Lithuania and Estonia. The treaties include also conflict-of-laws rules that may differ from the Rome I and Rome II Regulation rules. For example, the treaty between Latvia and Ukraine provides that unless the parties have agreed otherwise, the contractual relationship is governed by the law of the state where the contract was concluded.[81] Article 35 of the treaty between Latvia and Uzbekistan provides that obligations to compensate the damage shall be governed by the law of the state in which the event occurred or in which other circumstances giving rise to the claim in damages existed.[82]

In practice, the interaction between the Rome Regulations, bilateral treaties and the conflict-of-laws rules in the Civil Law raises a lot of questions. For example, in a dispute regarding a promissory note signed in Russia by the respondent (natural person domiciled in Russia), the respondent argued that in accordance with Article 19 of the Latvian Civil Law, the law applicable to promissory notes was the law of the Russian Federation. The court rejected the claimant's argument that the Rome I Regulation was applicable because, even if the promissory note was within the temporal and material scope of the Regulation, EU law should still not be applied in the case at hand.[83] In another case, the Supreme Court applied the Bilateral Treaty between Latvia and Moldova.[84] Whether the court should first make a reference to the Rome I Regulation and only then to bilateral treaties has not yet been discussed in the case law.

---

81 Līgums starp Latvijas Republiku un Ukrainu par tiesisko palīdzību un tiesiskajām attiecībām civilajās, ģimenes, darba un krimināllietās (Treaty between the Republic of Latvia and Ukraine on Judicial Assistance and Legal Relationship in Civil, Family, Labour and Criminal Cases) [1996] Latvijas Vēstnesis No. 169, 01.11.1995, Article 32.

82 Līgums starp Latvijas Republiku un Uzbekistānas Republiku par tiesisko palīdzību un tiesiskajām attiecībām civilajās, ģimenes, darba un krimināllietās (Treaty between the Republic of Latvia and Ukraine on Judicial Assistance and Legal Relationship in Civil, Family, Labour and Criminal Cases) [1997] Latvijas Vēstnesis No. 162/163, 27.09.1996.

83 Supreme Court of Latvia's judgment in the case No. C02058610, 07.09.2012.

84 Supreme Court of Latvia's judgment in the case No. SKC-131/2011, 27.04.2011.

It should be noted that the European Commission has required the 'Member States [to] renegotiate such agreement in order to eliminate any incompatibilities with the Community *acquis*, including on matters such as jurisdiction, recognition and enforcement in civil and commercial matters.'[85] While application of those international treaties is very topical and rare, re-negotiating is not an easy process, especially as they cover a number of areas that are simultaneously covered by different EU Regulations.

3. GENERAL EVALUATION

3.1. POTENTIALLY GREATER UNIFORMITY IN COMPARISON WITH THE PRE-ROME I AND ROME II REGIMES

The answer to the question of whether there is more uniformity in comparison with the pre-Rome I and Rome II regimes depends on what is meant by uniformity. If uniformity means uniformity of decisions between courts in different Member States, then there is an excellent legislative foundation for such uniformity. The fact that these instruments are often applied incorrectly by Latvian courts, or not applied when they should have been, diminishes this uniformity. Nevertheless, reverting to Latvian national conflict-of-laws rules would eliminate even theoretical grounds for international uniformity to begin with.

If uniformity means that Latvian courts decide similar cases similarly, then the same considerations apply here. Prior to the entry into force of the Rome Convention and later the Rome I and Rome II Regulations, most Latvian conflict-of-laws rules were archaic and underdeveloped. There was no unified practice on their application and the doctrine was underdeveloped. For this reason, uniformity was extremely limited, even non-existent.

Currently, we are still far from the optimal application of unified conflict-of-laws rules. Nevertheless, a few judgments of the Supreme Court clarifying the most basic issues relating to the application of the Rome I and Rome II Regulation are certainly strengthening uniformity. We may expect that as time goes by, the most basic issues will become undisputed for lower courts. Still, uniform understanding of more complex and often clandestine aspects of these instruments may require longer time to be settled in the light of the scarce case law. The practice of the CJEU may also be very important in giving guidance to Latvian courts.

---

85 Council Proposal for a Regulation of the European Parliament and of the Council establishing a procedure for the negotiation and conclusion of bilateral agreements between Member States and third countries concerning sectoral matters and covering applicable law in contractual and non-contractual obligations No. 11191/09 [2009] ADD 1 Rev 1.

3.2. THE PREVIOUS PRIVATE INTERNATIONAL LAW REGIME

It follows from everything said before that for non-contractual obligations we cannot even compare the obsolete and underdeveloped previous regime with the current one. Prior to the entry into force of the Rome II Regulation, the basic conflict-of-laws rule for non-contractual obligations was Article 20 of the Latvian Civil Law, which stated that:

> '[o]bligations not based on contract shall be adjudged, in respect of their substance and consequences, in accordance with the law of the place where the basis, from which the obligation arose, was created. Obligations arising from wrongful acts shall be adjudged in accordance with the law of the place where the wrongful acts took place.'

These laconic and simplistic rules were not developed by doctrine or case law.

As regards contractual obligations, the state of affairs is a bit more complex. Even before the entry into force of the Rome I Regulation, the domestic conflict-of-laws rules were replaced by the Rome Convention. The Rome Convention applied in Latvia only for a few years. Such a short period of application means that no definite conclusions can be drawn as to its efficiency. However, the Rome I Regulation is an improved version of the Rome Convention and is overall a more advanced legal document.

Let us mention just one example. Article 4 of the Rome Convention contained a complex conflict-of-laws rule presuming the closest relation between a country and a contract. This presumption diminished uniformity of conflict-of-laws rules, as different courts understood it differently. Such a provision would have been even more complex for Latvian courts, inexperienced in conflict-of-laws matters and facing a cumbersome and non-transparent rule. It would have likewise made it very difficult for parties to predict before and during litigation what law would eventually be applied by the court. Article 4 of the Rome I Regulation is a great step forward in terms of clarity and simplicity. In practice, it provides a fairly clear answer as to applicable law, preserving the option to apply another law but only in exceptional circumstances.

To summarise, it is beyond doubt that EU conflict-of-laws rules are much more evolved, and often less complicated than the previous national conflict-of-laws regime in Latvia.

3.3. PRACTICALITY OF THE TAXONOMY USED BY THE TWO REGULATIONS

In principle, the taxonomy used by the Regulations is practical. However, the case law indicates one specific problem. It seems that it is difficult to distinguish between 'non-contractual obligations' under the Rome II Regulation and *in rem* claims. In particular, the distinction between unjust enrichment claims and property claims is a difficult matter. The Rome II Regulation does not contain tools that help to draw the line between the two. Hence, courts may find it difficult to determine what types of claims related to the return of property are covered by the Regulation. Since it seems from the case law that vehicles stolen in other Member States are occasionally sold in Latvia, more clarity would be helpful for further, more consistent and thoughtful development of the case law.

3.4. GAPS IN THE REGULATIONS

The most important gaps are well known. The Rome II Regulation does not deal with obligations arising out of violations of privacy and personality rights, including defamation, while the Rome I Regulation does not deal with questions arising from agency. In cases dealing with several issues, some covered by EU conflict-of-laws instruments and others falling outside their scope, the parallel application of different conflict-of-laws regimes may be an excessive burden for both parties and courts. If the application of conflict-of-laws rules becomes too complicated, unsurprisingly, parties and courts will attempt to ignore conflict-of-laws rules whatsoever, moving directly towards the application of familiar *lex fori*.

Moreover, pursuant to Article 25 of the Brussels I *bis* Regime, the material validity of choice-of-court agreements is subject to the conflict-of-laws rules of the chosen court. The Rome I Regulation does not apply to such agreements. This exemption from its scope is an obvious gap in the Regulation.

3.5. APPLICATION OF THE REGULATIONS IN THE LIGHT OF THEIR SPIRIT

The case law shows that courts find it difficult to grasp the basic tenets of conflict-of-laws analysis and the correct application of EU conflict-of-laws rules. Even the most mundane issues – like the determination of the scope of the Rome I and Rome II Regulations, understanding that foreign law can be applied at all by Latvian courts, etc. – are often misunderstood by courts. Courts usually do not consult any doctrinal writings on EU conflict of laws and only on rare occasions are the CJEU cases consulted. In a situation where the level of expertise is not that high, it is not possible to speak of the application of EU conflict-of-laws using a sophisticated teleological methodology. On the contrary, even a literal application of these Regulations is rarely attempted by national courts.

3.6. NEGATIVE CONSEQUENCES ARISING FROM THE APPLICATION OF THE REGULATIONS

It seems to the authors that the main problem is the non-application of the Rome I and Rome II Regulations when they should apply. This creates an uncertain legal environment, where instead of using conflict-of-laws mechanisms to determine the applicable law, courts either ignore the question or use opportunistic interpretation, favouring the application of the *lex fori*. Such developments are certainly hindering the evolution of doctrine of conflict of laws and their reasonable in practice.

However, the authors have not identified any particular negative consequences arising from the application of the Regulations themselves. When they are applied correctly, nothing suggests that their application has any negative effect. Certainly, sometimes the application of foreign law may be a burden for parties and courts alike, but this is a normal side-effect of conflict of laws. In principle, however, the EU legislator should take into account the fact that conflict-of-laws rules that require very frequent application of foreign law may trigger greater opposition from national courts that lack the experience, resources and time to apply a body of foreign law that they do not really know or understand.

4. CONCLUSIONS

4.1. SUMMARY OF FINDINGS

In general, the authors can identify three main issues as regards the application of the Rome I and Rome II Regulations.

Firstly, the national legal environment does not facilitate the application of the Rome Regulations. Principal Latvian private law instruments made no reference to the Rome I and Rome II Regulations; therefore, lawyers are not aware of their existence. For this reason, the national conflict-of-laws rules or (directly) substantive national law is applied.

Secondly, even if the parties or the judge make reference to the Rome Regulations, still they lack the knowledge and methodology to apply them. Having insufficient knowledge about the correct application of the Rome I and Rome II Regulations, the courts tend to copy the reasoning from other national cases, without comparing fact patterns or the validity of the arguments, thus building incorrect case law.

In addition, the authors conclude that the first instance courts have little knowledge of EU conflict-of-laws rules and in most cases, they follow the misleading argumentation of the parties. The second instance courts and the Supreme Court try to correct the first instance's reasoning, but their efforts do not always succeed. Still, the judgments lack comprehensive and well-grounded reasoning, inter alia, possibly because there is a rather limited number of cases and commentaries.

Thirdly, even if the parties and the judge acknowledge that the Rome I and Rome II Regulations should be applied, they may escape doing so if it leads to application of foreign law and the determination of its substance. In the latter case, the national law does not give real guidance or help. Moreover, in practice it is difficult, time-consuming and expensive to determine the content of foreign law. The London Convention, unfortunately, is not helpful in this respect.

4.2. MAIN RECOMMENDATIONS

This chapter shows that Latvian courts often do not apply the Rome I and Rome II Regulations when they should, even if one of the parties refers to these instruments. Notably, courts do not proceed with a careful analysis of the scope of application of these instruments. Similarly, sometimes relatively simple issues, for example the autonomous interpretation of the place of characteristic performance of contracts, create difficulties for national courts due to their strong attachment to national legal concepts.

These problems cannot be fully resolved via amendments to the legal instruments. They must be approached from a different angle. Both national and EU measures are necessary to improve the quality of application of these instruments. At the national level, it is vital to have direct references to EU conflict-of-laws rules in the introduction to the Latvian Civil Law, so that national judges immediately see that national conflict-of-laws rules are subordinate to EU conflict-of-laws rules; currently, it seems that for some judges this is not common knowledge.

Other measures related to the further improvement of knowledge are necessary. At the national level there is training on this subject available to the judiciary, but as the application of conflict-of-laws rules and foreign law is today's reality, more attention should be paid to education, especially of the first instance judges. This is rather challenging because in Latvia judges do not specialise in particular areas of law.

Moreover, it may be appropriate either to commission the translation of foreign standard commentaries of these Regulations into Latvian or to commission an original commentary in Latvian that would take into account the specific problems faced by Latvian courts, as well as provide step-by-step guidance on the application of these Regulations. The existence of a significant number of commentaries in other European languages is not sufficient. National judges usually do not have access to the texts and sometimes may lack the necessary language skills.

The authors have also identified a number of problematic provisions in the Rome I and Rome II Regulations. They can be most easily solved by amending the Regulations or adding clarifying recitals.

The first problem is the conflict-of-laws regime for employees on the high seas. As the law stands today, it is not clear what the legal regime actually is. Do we still refer to the state of the flag? Do we employ a complex habitual place of work test that comes close to a closest connection test? The legislator should decide what policies are relevant in these types of employment relations and whether they justify a special conflict-of-laws rule. Even if no special rule is adopted, it may be useful to include a recital, allowing both parties and courts to know for sure whether the general conflict-of-laws rule applied to these relations and whether the state of the flag is relevant.

The second problem is relations between *in rem* claims and the scope of the Rome II Regulation. It is common knowledge that claims for recognition of property rights do not fall within the scope of the Rome II Regulation. However, claims are often not only for recognition of property rights, but also for the return of the property. These claims may be based on different grounds, including protection of the property or protection of possession (even without proving ownership). Latvian practice shows that this problem becomes particularly relevant in relation to the cross-border trade of stolen vehicles. The Rome II Regulation does not explain to what degree, if at all, it applies to claim for the return of the property, based on property claims or claims for the protection of possession. The views in the doctrine are very diverse, but the issue needs an answer, not only for theoretical clarity, but also for practical reasons. In particular, courts that are less exposed to EU conflict-of-laws rules hardly benefit from uncertainties that are embedded in the Regulations, making their job even more difficult. It would be useful for the EU legislator to clarify what the standing of the conflict-of-laws rules is on this issue.

The third problem is the uncertainty of the escape clauses. This may sound like an oxymoron since the escape clauses are meant to be vague. But it would seem to the authors that it would perhaps be better to specify what policies courts must achieve by using them. Are these clauses meant to advance legal certainty? In this case, courts cannot take into account *post factum* circumstances that would not have been foreseeable for the parties involved when the legal relation was formed. If they aim to achieve other policies, then there should be some indication of this in the text of the Regulations. Otherwise, an adjudicator may have the impression that the escapes clauses are technical provisions, applied mechanically without any true teleology. Such uncertainty may tempt some courts to substitute the non-identifiable policies of the escape clauses with their own favourite policy – the application of the *lex fori*.

The fourth problem is of lesser importance. It seems that there is a consensus among scholars that Article 8 of the Rome II Regulation does not cover infringement of trade secrets. The latter falls within the scope of Article 6.

Nevertheless, Latvian courts have failed to proceed with the correct analysis, instead classifying trade secrets under Article 8. While it may be questionable whether every little thing has to be spelled out in the text of the Regulations, it would possibly be useful to include a recital mentioning that Article 6 covers trade secrets.

In addition, there are certain gaps in the Regulations that have not been addressed by Latvian legal practice, most likely simply due to its scarcity. Such gaps complicate the existing conflict-of-laws regime. When this is the case, both counsel and courts may simply attempt to ignore conflict-of-laws rules entirely, because in most cases (particularly in smaller cases) the co-application of different conflict-of-laws regimes is too uncertain, expensive and tiresome for parties and the courts. At least for the purposes of simplification, it would be reasonable to extend the scope of the Rome II Regulation to obligations arising out of violations of privacy and personality rights, and that of the Rome I Regulation to those aspects of agency that are currently excluded from its scope pursuant to Article 1(2)(g). Likewise, the Rome I Regulation should be extended to choice-of-court agreements because, with the entry into force of the Brussels I *bis* Regulation, there are no unified conflict-of-laws rules on the validity of such agreements.

THE APPLICATION OF THE ROME I AND ROME II REGULATIONS IN LITHUANIA

Valentinas Mikelėnas

1. INTRODUCTION

To understand the specifics of the application of the Rome I and Rome II Regulations in Lithuania, it is necessary to describe, however briefly, the role of private international law in this country. Private international law was 'discovered' in Lithuania in 1990, after about 50 years of being ignored. It lost importance in the period between 1940 and 1990 due to the total economic, political and social isolation of Lithuania from the Western World during the Soviet era. The discipline of private international law was not included in university law curricula during this period. Because of this, private international law was *terra incognita* for lawyers and judges until 1990. The Civil Code of 1964 provided only a few rules on private international law. For example, Article 607 of the Civil Code established the principle of *lex loci delicti commisi* in respect of non-contractual obligations. Contractual obligations were governed by the *lex loci contractus* (Article 607). The Declaration of Independence of Lithuania on 11 March 1990 opened up new opportunities for the development of the national legal system and national law doctrine, including in private international law. On 18 July 2000, a new Civil Code was adopted (and entered into force on 1 July 2001). The rules on the conflict of laws were codified in Book One of the Civil Code (Articles 1.10–1.62). Thus, the real application and interpretation of the rules of private international law in Lithuania only started in 2001. Therefore, Lithuanian case law applying the rules of private international law is not plentiful and is rather controversial. The doctrine of private international law in Lithuania is also still being created. The first textbook on private international law was published only in 2001.[1]

As a result of these circumstances, it is quite difficult to discuss the application of EU rules of private international law in Lithuania.

2. THE NATIONAL LANDSCAPE

During the drafting of the Civil Code of 2000, the approach was to incorporate rules of modern private international law into its provisions instead of preparing a separate law on the subject. The Working Group used the latest examples of the codification of private international law inform around the world. The main foreign sources used by the Working Group were: Book Ten of the Civil Code of Quebec, the Italian Law on Private International Law of 1995, and the Swiss Law on Private International Law of 1987. Although Lithuania was not yet a member of the EU at the time the Civil Code was drafted, the political decision to join the EU had already been taken. For that reason, the 1980 Rome Convention was the main source for the choice-of-law rules for contractual relationships. Provisions of the 1980 Rome Convention were taken over into Article 1.37 of the Civil Code.

Lithuania became a member of the EU on 1 May 2004. Thus, before the entry into force of the Rome I Regulation, Lithuanian courts already had experience with conflict-of-laws rules like those established by the 1980 Rome Convention. On 30 March 2006 Lithuania ratified the 1980 Rome Convention and this Convention entered into force for the country on 1 December 2006. There is no

1 V. Mikelėnas, *An Introduction to Private International Law* (in Lithuanian), Justitia, Vilnius 2001. For more information about the development of private international law in Lithuania, see V. Mikelėnas, 'Reform of Private International Law in Lithuania' in P. Šarševič, P. Volken and A. Bonomi (eds.), *Yearbook of Private International Law*, vol. VII, Sellier European Law Publishers, Munich 2005, pp. 161–181; V. Mikelėnas, 'The present situation of private international law in Lithuania' (2005) 6 *European Legal Forum* 292–293; V. Mizaras, 'Roma II reglamentas ir Lietuvos tarptautinė privatinė teisė' in Privatinė teisė: praeitis, dabartis ir ateitis: Liber Amicorum Valentinas Mikelėnas, Justitia, Vilnius 2008, pp. 87–113.

Lithuanian case law on the application of the Rome Convention, except for one civil judgment by the Supreme Court. In that case, the Supreme Court indicated that the Rome Convention and Article 1.37 of the Civil Code provided similar rules. However, the Rome Convention was not applied in that case, because the contract was concluded before the entry into force of the Convention.[2]

No national legislation regarding the application of the Rome I and Rome II Regulations was adopted. The Civil Code (in Article 1.3) had established the principle of the supremacy of EU law over national law. Since EU Regulations have direct effect, there was no need to adopt any national legislation. From the moment of the entry into force of the Rome I and Rome II Regulations, the relevant conflict-of-laws rules of the Civil Code have no longer been applicable.

However, the Rome I and Rome II Regulations both provide an exception, i.e. cases for which these Regulations do not apply. In such cases, the conflict-of-laws rules of the Civil Code are to be applied. For instance, the Rome I Regulation excludes arbitration agreements, and the Rome II Regulation is not applicable in cases involving compensation for damage caused by defamation. Thus, Articles 1.37 and 1.45 of the Civil Code, respectively, are to be applied in such cases. Lithuanian case law does not provide any examples of the application of the Rome I or Rome II Regulations beyond their normal scope of application.

Lithuanian judicial statistics do not provide a number of judgments in which the Rome I and Rome II Regulations have been applied. The official data only indicate the number of civil cases in which rules of private international law were applied. For instance, in 2016 there was not a single case tried before courts of first instance where the rules of private international law were applied. However, surprisingly, the same source indicates that courts of first instance tried 564 civil cases in 2016 in which *renvoi* was applied. This shows that the courts either incorrectly provided statistical data, or failed to understand the meaning of private international law and *renvoi*.[3]

However, by entering the keywords *'Rome I'* and *'Rome II'* into the specialist judicial information database *Infolex*, it is possible to roughly determine the number of such decisions. This database includes 69 Supreme Court judgments in which the Rome I Regulation was applied and 72 judgments in which the Rome II Regulation was applied. The most commonly applied provisions are Articles 4 and 8 of the Rome I Regulation and Articles 4 and 28 of the Rome II Regulation.[4] However, these figures also need to be treated with caution, as a review of court rulings shows that, in fact, in many of these cases, none of the Regulations have been applied.

Due to the principle of confidentiality, arbitration awards or summaries thereof are not publicly available. Therefore, the number of arbitration awards

2 Supreme Court, judgment of 29 December 2011, civil case No. 3K-3-553/2011.

3 <http://www.teismai.lt/lt/visuomenei-ir-ziniasklaidai/statistika/106>.

4 <http://www.infolex.lt/tp/>. Data are as of 14 April 2020.

applying the Rome I or Rome II Regulations cannot be determined. Article 39 of the Law on Commercial Arbitration provides that the arbitral tribunal shall resolve disputes in accordance with the law selected by the parties as applicable to the dispute. The reference to the applicable foreign law means a reference to the national substantive law of the relevant state, rather than the international private law of that state. If the parties have failed to agree on the applicable law, the arbitral tribunal shall apply the law which, in the reasoned opinion of the arbitral tribunal, is applicable to the dispute, including trade customs (*lex mercatoria*). This rule means that arbitrators, unlike judges, are not strictly bound by conflict-of-laws rules, even if the place of arbitration is in Lithuania. Thus, the Rome I and Rome II Regulations will not necessarily apply in arbitral proceedings that take place in Lithuania.

Most courts have correctly applied the Rome I and Rome II rules. However, there also are some instances of incorrect application. In one such case, a court ignored Article 2 of the Rome I Regulation, which provides that any law specified by that Regulation shall be applied, whether it is the law of a Member State or of another state (principle of universal application).[5]

3. THE OPERATION OF ROME I AND ROME II IN PRACTICE

3.1. *LOIS DE POLICE*

The Civil Code also establishes some limitations on the application of foreign law. According to Part 1, Article 1.11 of the Civil Code, foreign law shall not be applied where the application thereof might be inconsistent with the public order established by the Constitution of the Republic of Lithuania and other laws. In such instances, the civil laws of the Republic of Lithuania shall apply. The concept of public policy is not defined in Lithuanian statutory law and is an object of interpretation. There are no examples in the Lithuanian case law of Lithuanian courts applying the case law of the CJEU or case law of foreign states when interpreting the concept of public policy. According to prevailing Lithuanian case law, the concept of public policy is understood quite widely and recognises that public policy includes all mandatory national rules. For instance, in its judgment of 7 December 2016, the Supreme Court refused to apply a Latvian law and resolved a labour dispute by applying the mandatory rules of the Lithuanian labour law. The Supreme Court applied not only Article 8 of the Rome I Regulation, but also Article 6 of the Lithuanian Labour Code, according

5 Supreme Court, judgment of 29 December 2011, civil case No. 3K-3-553/2011.

to which the mandatory Lithuanian labour law rules apply irrespective of the fact that the parties have chosen a foreign law.[6] Another example is the Law on Bankruptcy, most rules of which are also mandatory. For example, the Court of Appeal refused to apply Dutch law, which had been chosen by the parties for loan agreements, applying Lithuanian law instead, and reduced the interest rate from 15 and 23 per cent, as provided in the loan contracts, to 6 per cent as provided for by the Lithuanian Civil Code.[7]

Article 11 of the Civil Code provides two additional limitations on the application of foreign law. First, the mandatory legal rules of any other state more closely connected with a dispute shall apply even if another foreign law has been agreed upon by the parties. In deciding on these issues, the court shall take into consideration the nature of these provisions, their purpose, and the consequences of application or non-application thereof. Second, the applicable foreign law established in accordance with the conflict-of-laws rules may not be applied where, in light of all the attendant circumstances of the case, it becomes evident that the foreign law concerned is clearly not pertinent to the case or its separate claims, and that the case in question is more closely connected with the law of another state. However, this provision shall not apply where the applicable law is determined by the agreement of the parties. It is difficult to say whether these exceptions will apply when applying rules of the Rome I and Rome II Regulations. Keeping in mind the principle of supremacy of EU law, it is more likely that these exceptions will not apply, but, so far, such a conclusion has not been confirmed by case law.

3.2. PARTY AUTONOMY

The principle of freedom of contract is clearly established by Articles 1.2 and 6.156 of the Civil Code. The right of the parties to choose the applicable law is an integral part of the principle of the freedom of contract. According to Article 1.37 of the Civil Code, contractual obligations shall be governed by the law agreed by the parties. Such agreement of the parties may be expressed in the form of separate terms of the concluded contract or it may be determined in accordance with the factual circumstances of the case. The law of the state designated by the agreement of the contracting parties may be applied to the whole contract or only to a part or parts thereof. The freedom of parties to choose the applicable law is recognised and protected by case law.[8]

6 Supreme Court, judgment of 7 December 2016, civil case No. 3K-3-484-701/2016.
7 Court of Appeal, judgment of 12 March 2013, civil case No. 2-1003/2013.
8 Supreme Court, judgment of 29 December 2011, civil case No. 3K-3-553/2011.

However, the freedom of parties to choose the applicable law is restricted by both national and European Union law. The case law confirms that, in certain cases, the courts declare the choice of applicable law terms of a contract to be null and void by reason of their conflict with mandatory rules of law. For example, the Lithuanian Court of Appeal declared the term regarding the applicable law of an insurance contract concluded between an insurance company registered in Estonia and a policyholder company registered in Lithuania null and void. The court argued that the insurance contract provided for UK law as the applicable law. However, Article 7 of the Rome I Regulation, on the other hand, restricts the parties' choice of applicable law and, in that case, the law chosen by the parties did not comply with any of the exceptions provided for in Article 7(3) of the Rome I Regulation.[9]

Although the Civil Code use the wording 'foreign law' to refer to the national law of a foreign state, there are examples where courts apply the UNIDROIT Principles on International Commercial Contracts, the rules of the DCFR, etc.[10] Thus, the term 'foreign law' is understood more widely and includes the *lex mercatoria*. Therefore, from the perspective of Lithuanian case law, there is no need to modify Article 3 of the Rome I Regulation.

Limited party autonomy is also recognised in Lithuanian national conflict-of-laws rules regarding non-contractual relationships. According to Article 1.43 of the Civil Code, after damage has occurred, the parties may agree that the law applicable to the reparation for damage shall be the law of the state where the case concerned is being tried. Thus, Article 14 of the Rome II Regulation, which establishes the principle of limited party autonomy, was not a novelty for Lithuania. However, it is difficult to assess the efficacy of Article 14 of the Rome II Regulation, because in Lithuanian case law there is no example of the parties having used this possibility.

3.3. ABSENCE OF CHOICE OF LAW

Lithuanian case law recognises that the concepts and notions used in Article 4 of the Rome I Regulation are autonomous and Lithuanian courts try to interpret them in the same way in which they are being interpreted by the CJEU. So far, none of the Lithuanian courts have applied to the CJEU for a preliminary ruling regarding an interpretation of Article 4 of the Rome I Regulation.

---

9 Court of Appeal, judgment of 12 December 2019, civil case No. 2A-654-943/2019.

10 Supreme Court, judgment of 7 December 2016, civil case No. 3K-3-484-701/2016.

3.4. ESCAPE CLAUSES

The Lithuanian national conflict-of-laws rules provide an escape clause like the escape clauses contained in the Rome I and Rome II Regulations. Article 11 of the Civil Code gives Lithuanian courts a wide discretionary power to exclude foreign law which would apply in accordance with the rules of private international law. First, as mentioned previously in section 3.1, the court may refuse to apply foreign law on the basis of its contradiction with the public policy established by the Constitution and Lithuanian law. Second, the court may refuse to apply foreign law on the grounds that the law of another country is more closely related to the case in question. Both of these criteria are evaluative in nature, thereby permitting the courts to interpret them very broadly. It is therefore not surprising that Lithuanian courts apply the relevant Rome I and Rome II escape clauses. For example, in one civil case, it was established that two parties, both resident in Germany, had entered into a commission agreement, which was signed in Germany, and the goods were also located in Germany. The Supreme Court concluded that the contract was exclusively connected with Germany and that German law had to be applied.[11]

3.5. SPECIFIC RULES

Most of the problems in applying the Rome I rules are related to the classification of contracts and the application of Articles 4, 7, and 15 of the Rome I Regulation. For example, in one civil case, a court classified a contract between German and Lithuanian parties as a sales contract and applied the 1980 Vienna Convention on Contracts for the International Sale of Goods. However, the court did not consider the question of which law applies to matters not regulated by the Vienna Convention in this case since the seller's habitual residence was in Germany, therefore German law was applicable under Article 4(1)(a) of the Rome I Regulation.[12] In another case, the habitual residence of the seller also was in Switzerland, and in accordance with Article 4(1)(a) of the Rome I Regulation, Swiss law should have been applied; however, the court refused to apply Swiss law because Switzerland is not an EU Member State and EU law is not applicable in this case.[13] Accordingly, the court ignored Article 2 of the Rome I Regulation, which provides that any law specified by this Regulation shall be applied whether it is the law of a Member State or of another state (principle of universal application).

---

11 Supreme Court, judgment of 25 May 2015, civil case No. 3K-3-110-684/2015.
12 Supreme Court, judgment of 11 February 2014, civil case No. 3K-3-32/2014.
13 Supreme Court, judgment of 29 December 2011, civil case No. 3K-3-553/2011.

There also are problems regarding the delimitation of contractual and non-contractual liability, especially when the defendant is insured against civil liability. Some courts consider that the relationship between the victim and the defendant's insurer is governed by the rules of tort liability and apply the Rome II rules. However, another court classified the same situation as a contractual relationship and applied the Rome I rules.[14]

The difficulties experienced by Lithuanian courts in applying the Rome I and Rome II Regulations is confirmed by the fact that in 2014 the Supreme Court of Lithuania turned to the CJEU for a preliminary ruling regarding the relationship between the Rome I and Rome II Regulations and Directive 2009/103/EC.[15]

3.6. SCOPE OF APPLICABLE LAW

There are no examples of the application of Article 12 of the Rome I Regulation or Article 15 of the Rome II Regulation in Lithuanian case law. However, it is quite likely that the scope of applicable law will be interpreted more extensively than under these provisions. For example, it is likely that in applying Article 12 of the Rome I Regulation, courts will apply the rules regarding the grounds of nullity of a contract, remedies, interest, civil penalties, set-off, etc.

3.7. *RENVOI*

According to Article 1.10 of the Civil Code, an applicable foreign law means a reference to the national substantial law of the state concerned, but not a reference to the private international law of that state, except in situations provided for by the Civil Code. This means that Lithuanian law in general does not recognise *renvoi*. In this regard, Lithuanian national law is in line with the Rome I and Rome II Regulations, which also exclude *renvoi*.

3.8. FOREIGN LAW

The determination of the content of applicable foreign law is regulated by Article 1.12 of the Civil Code, which establishes two main rules. First, in the instances where the application of a foreign law is established by agreement between the parties, the content of the foreign law is a question of fact.

---

14 Court of Appeal, judgment of 10 February 2009, civil case No. 2A-241/2009.

15 Supreme Court, judgment of 8 October 2014, civil case No. 3K-3-415/2014. See also the CJEU's preliminary ruling in Joined Cases C-359/14 and C-475/14, *Ergo Insurance* <http://curia.europa.eu/juris/liste.jsf?num=C-359/14&language=en>.

This means that the burden of proof in relation to the content of the applicable foreign law – in accordance with its official interpretation, the practice of application and the legal doctrine in the relevant foreign state – rests on the party to the civil case that makes a reference to the foreign law. In such cases, the principle of *iura novit curia* does not apply. However, on request of a party, the court may assist in collecting information on the applicable foreign law. Case law shows that courts are reluctant to assist a party that relies on foreign law in such cases. Such reluctance can be explained by the substantive and procedural law rules that allow a court to apply Lithuanian law if the court believes that the information about the foreign law provided by the party is not sufficient. According to Article 1.12 of the Civil Code and Article 808 of the Code of Civil Procedure, if a party that refers to foreign law fails to fulfil the obligation to determine the content of the applicable foreign law, Lithuanian law shall apply. For example, in one case it was found that a contract between Danish and Lithuanian companies provided that the contract was governed by a Danish law. However, all courts, including the Supreme Court, refused to apply Danish law and the dispute was resolved by applying the law of Lithuania, as the information about Danish law supplied by the lawyers of the Danish company was considered to be insufficient. The courts stated that the Danish company had failed to prove the content of the Danish law, even though the Danish lawyers provided excerpts from the Danish Contract Law and excerpts from two textbooks.[16] Such a practice on the part of the courts is open to criticism because the autonomy of the parties is denied. On the other hand, if the court considers the material to be insufficient, it can always order a party to submit additional material and thus allow the party to fulfil its burden of proof. Alternatively, there are some positive examples of case law where the court, in order to create appropriate conditions for a party to prove the content of foreign law, suspended proceedings until the party submitted information to the court about the content of the foreign law.[17]

The second rule, established by Article 1.12 of the Civil Code, provides that, in cases established by international treaties of the Republic of Lithuania or by the laws of the Republic of Lithuania, the application, interpretation and determination of the content of a foreign law shall be performed by the court *ex officio*. The same rule also applies in respect of the Rome I and Rome II Regulations. It means that in such instances the content of foreign law is a question of law. In one civil case, the Supreme Court of Lithuania noted that the duty of the court to determine content of foreign law of its own motion did not affect the *lex fori* procedural rules, including the principle of cooperation between the court and the parties (Article 8 of the Code of Civil Procedure). This principle basically implies active

---

16 Supreme Court, judgment of 21 October 2015, civil case No. 3K-3-538-219/2015. See also Court of Appeal, judgment of 9 March 2017, civil case No. 2A-319-241/2017.

17 Court of Appeal, judgment of 29 December 2011, civil case No. 2-1895/2011.

action on the part of the court and parties, so that even in cases where the court has a duty *ex officio* to determine the content of a foreign law, the court may invite the parties to submit, in their view, any relevant evidence regarding the content of foreign law and its interpretation and application.[18]

Lithuania has ratified the European Convention on Information on Foreign Law; therefore, most information about the applicable foreign law is obtained in accordance with the procedure set out in this Convention. Another important source of information about the applicable foreign law is the materials submitted by the parties' lawyers, for example legal expert opinions, foreign statutory law official sources, case law and legal doctrine. In such cases, courts apply the *lex fori* procedural rules and require the information presented by the parties' lawyers to be appropriately approved by the public notary or other state official or institution e.g. the Ministry of Justice, otherwise the court may declare such information inadmissible.

3.9. *ORDRE PUBLIC*

So far, there have only been two cases in which Lithuanian courts relied on the public policy clause and refused to apply foreign law. The Supreme Court refused to apply a Latvian law and solved a labour dispute by applying the mandatory rules of Lithuanian labour law. The Supreme Court applied not only Article 8 of the Rome I Regulation, but also Article 6 of the Lithuanian Labour Code, according to which the mandatory Lithuanian labour law rules apply irrespective of the fact that the parties have chosen foreign law.[19]

Another example was a case heard by the Court of Appeal. This court refused to apply Dutch law, which had been chosen by the parties for loan agreements, applied Lithuanian law instead, and reduced the interest from 15 and 23 per cent, as provided in the loan contracts, to 6 per cent as provided by the Lithuanian Civil Code. The reasoning of the court was based on the Law on Bankruptcy, most of the rules of which are mandatory. The court ruled that protection of all creditors of an insolvent company is a matter of public policy; therefore the Lithuanian law, which is more favourable for all creditors, should apply.[20] In the majority of examined cases public policy is understood quite broadly and includes the mandatory rules of law as well as principles of law. For example, it is possible that Lithuanian courts may refuse to apply foreign law that provides for punitive damages, because Lithuanian tort law is based on the principle of full compensation and thus does not allow punitive damages.

---

18 Supreme Court, judgment of 1 February 2013, civil case No. 3K-3-78/2013.

19 Supreme Court, judgment of 7 December 2016, civil case No. 3K-3-484-701/2016.

20 Court of Appeal, judgment of 12 March 2013, civil case No. 2-1003/2013.

3.10. COMPENSATION

The law applicable to compensation for damage caused by traffic accidents is of special importance due to the substantial differences that sometimes exist between the national rules EU Member States. This fact can be illustrated by one Lithuanian civil case tried in 2009. A car of a Polish company caused a traffic accident in the territory of Lithuania in which two people were killed. Five victims – close relatives of the deceased – brought an action for compensation for pecuniary and non-pecuniary damage against the insurer of the Polish company. In 2009, the existing Lithuanian law provided that the defendant's insurer had a duty to compensate non-pecuniary damage not exceeding €500. Meanwhile, the Polish law provided that the maximum sum of compensation was €350,000. Therefore, the sum awarded as compensation for non-pecuniary damage differs significantly depending on whether Lithuanian law or Polish law were applied.[21] The problem of significant differences of compensation awards to cross-border victims of road traffic accidents was already discussed in a special study by the European Commission in 2008.[22]

3.11. RELATIONS WITH INTERNATIONAL INSTRUMENTS

Lithuania has informed the European Commission that the Rome I and Rome II Regulations shall not apply to its relations with Armenia, Azerbaijan, Belarus, Kazakhstan, Moldova, Ukraine and Uzbekistan.[23]

For non-contractual obligations, Lithuania applies the following international conventions instead of the Rome II Regulation:

- the 1971 Hague Convention on the Law Applicable to Traffic Accidents;
- the 1973 Convention on the Grant of European Patents, Munich;
- the 1989 London International Convention on Salvage, London; and
- the 2000 Convention on the Grant of European Patents, Munich.[24]

So far, there have been no court cases applying the above-mentioned Conventions, except for the 1971 Hague Convention.[25] We must admit that the Hague Convention's conflict-of-laws rules are clearer than those in the Rome II Regulation and courts apply them more easily. Furthermore, Article 8 of

---

21 Court of Appeal, judgment of 10 February 2009, civil case No. 2A-241/2009.
22 <http://ec.europa.eu/civiljustice/news/docs/study_compensation_road_victims_en.pdf>.
23 <http://www.ejtn.eu/PageFiles/12473/CELEX_52010XC1217(01)_EN_TXT.pdf>.
24 <http://eur-lex.europa.eu/legal-content/EN/TXT/?uri=CELEX%3A52010XC1217(02)>.
25 Supreme Court, judgment of 3 July 2015, civil case No. 3K-3-432-248/2015.

the Hague Convention clearly defines the scope of applicable law. Therefore, the Lithuanian choice not to apply the Rome II Regulations to those relationships involving the compensation of damage caused by traffic accidents seems reasonable.

4. GENERAL EVALUATION AND CONCLUSION

It is difficult, or even impossible, to draw a general conclusion about the efficacy of the Rome I and Rome II Regulations and their benefits or drawbacks from just a few court judgments. One thing is clear: it is always more difficult for national courts to apply EU law than national law. EU law often uses concepts and terms that are unknown to national law. Translations of EU legislation from the original language to a national language are not always precise. Even in cases where EU law uses the same concepts and terms as national law, the former is interpreted autonomously. Consequently, the content and meaning of certain EU notions can differ from the content and meaning of analogous concepts and terms of national law. National courts are not always inclined to apply to the CJEU for a preliminary ruling and seek to interpret EU law independently. Such independent interpretations often produce a different meaning and sense of EU law, or either narrow or expand its scope of application. The application of EU law is also complicated by the varying versatility of different instruments. For instance, the Rome I Regulation allow more discretion and flexibility for the courts, while the Rome II Regulation is less flexible and limits judicial discretion.

Another reason for the ineffective application of the Rome I and Rome II Regulations is inadequate training of judges and lawyers. Their training mainly focuses on national law rather than EU law. Little attention is paid to the interpretation and application of Rome I and Rome II by the Supreme Court of Lithuania. Although, according to Article 4 of the Lithuanian Code of Civil Procedure, one of the functions of the Supreme Court is to ensure a uniform interpretation and application of the law, including EU law, but the Supreme Court summarised the case law of lower courts when applying private international law for the one and only time in 2000. All this causes serious doubt as to whether the uniform and effective interpretation and application of the Rome I and Rome II Regulations will be achieved in the near future. However, despite judicial mistakes when applying the Rome I and Rome II Regulations, it remains to be hoped that legal doctrine will pay more attention to the theoretical analysis of Rome I and Rome II and criticism of case law. It is probable that the improvement in the training of judges, and the larger framework of supplementary measures, will help to ensure a more effective application of the Rome I and Rome II Regulations in future.

THE APPLICATION OF THE ROME I AND ROME II REGULATIONS IN LUXEMBOURG

Emilia FRONCZAK

1. THE NATIONAL LANDSCAPE

In Luxembourg, there are no national rules facilitating the application of the Rome I and Rome II Regulations, nor have the Regulations been extended beyond their normal scope of application. In terms of the number of national decisions applying the Regulations, it should be noted that, only recently (i.e. in the course of this project) a database (JUDOC) containing the 'most important' decisions has become publicly accessible. To obtain any other decision it has to be identified by date and case number so that it can be obtained upon individual request from Luxembourg's judicial documentation service. Therefore, case law research in Luxembourg is a difficult endeavour. The present author's own expertise, the skills of her firm's knowledge officer, and the kind help provided by Ms Céline Camara, a former researcher at the Max-Planck-Institute in Luxembourg, have made it possible to gather around 50 cases involving (pleas for) the application of the Rome I or Rome II Regulations. However, due to the difficulties highlighted above, it may well be that some decisions were simply not found. As regards arbitration, the Luxembourg Arbitration Centre also does not have a publicly accessible database, so no information concerning the number of arbitration awards applying the Rome I and Rome II Regulations could be obtained.

The most frequently applied provision of Rome I is Article 4(1)(a) and (b). For Rome II, the provisions are Articles 4 and 10(3).

No errors were found in the decisions that refer to the Rome I and Rome II Regulations but, in the end, apply a different set of rules. However, due to the limited research possibilities on the now publicly available database, it was impossible to establish the existence of cases with a cross-border element in which Rome I or Rome II should have been applied, but which were ultimately decided solely on the basis of Luxembourg law. It may therefore well be that such decisions exist, but were not found.

There are, however, judgments that in fact applied Rome II even though a different set of rules could have been applied, i.e. the 1971 Hague Convention on the Law Applicable to Traffic Accidents.[1] In three cases, the Luxembourg courts directly applied Rome II to find the applicable law, without considering the possibility of applying the 1971 Hague Convention.

One of these cases concerned a traffic accident that occurred in Luxembourg involving a Belgian and a Dutch car. The court applied the law of the place of the accident on the basis of the Rome II Regulation, although it seems that the 1971 Hague Convention should have been applied.[2] It should be noted, however, that this case was decided before the French *Cour de cassation* confirmed that, under Article 28 of the Rome II Regulation, the 1971 Hague Convention, as a convention non-exclusively concluded between the EU Member States, shall take precedence over the Regulation.[3] The Luxembourg literature at that point was of the opinion that after the entry into force of the Rome II Regulation, the

---

1 Convention on the Law Applicable to Traffic Accidents, of 04.05.1971, which entered into force on 03.06.1975.

2 TA Luxembourg, 15.11.2011, no. 156/2011, no. 138.290 du rôle.

3 Cass. fr., 30.04.2014, no. 13-11932. It should be noted that, due to limited national case law because of the size of the country, the case law of the French *Cour de cassation* is closely watched and very often followed by the Luxembourg courts.

1971 Hague Convention was to apply only to relations between Luxembourg and third countries.[4]

In another case, the accident occurred in Belgium but the parties were all (except one passenger) domiciled in Luxembourg. Although it is not specified in the judgment, it seems that the cars involved in the accident were also registered in Luxembourg. In this case, the accident took place in April 2013, the first instance decision was taken on 9 July 2014 – shortly after the abovementioned decision of the *Cour de cassation*. However, the appeal judgment was only delivered on 1 December 2015. In this case, an application of the 1971 Hague Convention would have allowed for a clear solution, as it provides for the application of the law of the state of the common registration of the vehicles involved in an accident. In fact, this Convention explicitly excludes in Article 4(a) the use of the habitual residence of a victim as a linking factor. On the contrary, for the Luxembourg court to designate, on the basis of the Rome II Regulation, *lex fori* as applicable law required 'ignoring' the fact that one of the defendants was domiciled in Belgium. This was achieved on the basis that his involvement in the accident, apart from being just another passenger, was not proven.[5] The implications for the applicability of the 1971 Hague Convention stemming from the subrogation of one of the insurance companies involved was not discussed in the judgment.

In addition, in a case where two motorbikes owned by persons domiciled in Belgium were involved in an accident in Luxembourg, Belgian law was identified as the applicable law on the basis of Article 4(2) Rome II.[6]

In all these cases, the application of the Rome II Regulation did not lead to the application of a different law than the one that would have been applied under the 1971 Hague Convention. One may therefore say that in these cases the solutions were different only in theory, but not in practice.

2. THE OPERATION OF ROME I AND ROME II IN PRACTICE

2.1. *LOIS DE POLICE*

In the analysed cases falling within the scope of Rome I and Rome II, *lois de police* (or overriding mandatory provisions) were not at stake.

4 J.-C. Wiwinius, *Le droit international privé au Grand-Duché de Luxembourg*, Paul Bauler, Luxembourg 2011, p. 203.

5 TA Luxembourg, 01.12.2015, no. 251/2015, no. 164.190 du rôle.

6 TP Luxembourg, 05.06.2014, Rép. fisc. no. 2389/14.

While the cases reviewed do not provide any examples, the Luxembourg legislature has insisted on the mandatory application of a number of provisions. In relation to contractual obligations, the following are considered to constitute *lois de police*:[7]

- employment law provisions regulating:
  - minimum required salary;
  - working hours and weekly rest;
  - amount of paid leave;
  - public holidays;
  - laws regulating interim work, part-time work and fixed-term contracts;
  - collective bargaining agreements; and
  - provisions regulating collective leave;
- legislation protecting the tenant;
- consumer protection legislation.

Due to the lack of pertinent case law, it is impossible to say for Luxembourg specifically whether the treatment of third states' *lois de police* needs to be reconsidered, taking into account the differences between Article 9 Rome I and Article 16 Rome II and their practice. It should be recalled, however, that under Article 7 of the Rome Convention, Luxembourg was one of the Member States that entered a reservation regarding the application of third states' *lois de police*, although its courts had previously been open to doing so.[8]

2.2. PARTY AUTONOMY

From the Luxembourg perspective, there is no need to amend Article 3 Rome I because of excessive use of *dépeçage* or the need to choose the *lex mercatoria*. The analysis of the available case law shows that the parties either do not choose the law that shall govern their contractual relationship or that they choose one particular law to govern all its aspects.

Regarding the introduction of party autonomy in Article 14 Rome II, its impact could not be assessed as there is no case law at all involving this provision.

2.3. ABSENCE OF CHOICE OF LAW

The fixed rules set out in Article 4 Rome I are used by the courts whenever the parties do not choose the applicable law. Most often used are the provisions

---

7 J.-C. Wiwinius, supra n. 4, p. 66 ff.

8 See J.-C. Wiwinius, supra n. 4, p. 69.

governing the law applicable to contracts for the sale of goods (Article 4(1)(a) Rome I)[9] and to contracts for the provision of services (Article 4(1)(b) Rome I).[10] However, there is no case law on the issue of the localisation of the place of direct damage (under Article 4 Rome II). In fact, in the available case law, this place was usually easily identifiable.

As to the application of Article 4(2) Rome II (law of the country of common residence of the parties), in instances of a multitude of tortfeasors or victims, the only available case concerned an insurance company and the passengers of a car involved in an accident with the insured vehicle.[11] In this case, there were multiple parties on both sides, all but one of them having their habitual residence in Luxembourg. The court applied Luxembourg law on the basis of the rule established in Article 4(2) Rome II, as the accident took place in Belgium. The fact that one of the passengers of the damaged car had his habitual residence in Belgium was left out on the basis that no facts were given to the court indicating any causal link between the actions of this passenger and the accident.

2.4. ESCAPE CLAUSES

Among the analysed cases only three involved the analysis of escape clauses (for example those in Article 4(4), 5(3) and 8(4) Rome I and Articles 4(3) and 5(2) Rome II). In none of them, did the courts come to the conclusion that the 'manifestly closer connection' had been established and should override the application of the law identified in accordance with the general rules. Luxembourg courts do not overuse these clauses.

Two of the above-mentioned cases concerned the analysis of the law applicable to contractual obligations.[12] The first case was still decided on the basis of the Rome Convention but is important to mention in order to understand the development of the approach that the Luxembourg courts take. The defendant, a construction company established in Germany, installed a heating system in a house in Luxembourg. The contract between the German company and the owner of the house had been signed in 2003. Probably in 2010 (the exact date is not mentioned in the judgment) a leakage in the heating pipes caused significant damage The plaintiff, i.e. an insurance company which indemnified the house owner for the reparation of these damages, was established in Belgium, with

9 TA Luxembourg, 18.11.2011, no. 1617/11; TP Luxembourg, 21.11.2013, no. 4366/2013; TP Luxembourg, 10.07.2015, no. 2932/2015.

10 TP Luxembourg, 11.11.2013, no. 2573/2013; TA Luxembourg, 31.01.2014 and 19.12.2014, no. 149.694 du rôle; TA Luxembourg, 04.12.2012, no. 154070 du rôle; CA Luxembourg, 02.02.2016, no. 41168 du rôle.

11 TA Luxembourg, 01.12.2015, no. 251/2015, no. 164.190 du rôle.

12 TA Diekirch, 15.09.2017, no. 17767 du rôle; CA Luxembourg, 02.02.2016, no. 41168 du rôle.

a branch in Luxembourg. The plaintiff sought to rely on Luxembourg law, whereas the defendant argued that German law should be applicable. The court established that because the contract between the construction company and the house owner had been signed in 2003, the Rome Convention had to be applied in order to determine the law applicable. In the absence of a choice of law in the underlying contract, the court had to identify the law of the country with which it was 'most closely connected'. This analysis was carried out in accordance with the guidance of Article 4(2) of the Rome Convention and German law was identified as applicable.

In the second case, a German company was contracted by a Luxembourg company to deliver and install a garage door for a building situated in Luxembourg. Since the invoice of the German company had not been paid, it started legal proceedings in Luxembourg. Having lost in the first instance, the Luxembourg company lodged an appeal and argued that the contract was 'manifestly more closely connected' with Luxembourg, since the services had been performed in Luxembourg and the debtor was domiciled in this country.

The court closely examined this argument and clearly stated that this Article introduces an exception allowing derogation from the law identified on the basis of Article 4(1)(b) Rome I where the contract's centre of gravity is situated in another country. In its analysis, the court looked at the case law of the French *Cour de cassation* and of the Court of Justice of the European Union (ECJ)[13] issued under the Rome Convention. Given the fact that Rome I allows derogation from the law applicable in accordance with Article 4(2) only in cases of identification of a country '*manifestly* more closely connected' with the contract, the court concluded that this exception should be used more restrictively than under the Rome Convention. Based on the assessment of all the factual elements, such as the language of the contract, the place of production, the place of delivery, etc., it concluded that the Luxembourg company had not established that the contract was 'manifestly more closely connected' with Luxembourg.

A case which analysed the law applicable to torts concerned a claim for compensation of an alleged prejudice consisting of legal fees incurred during multiple procedures linked to a divorce which was initiated by the other spouse.[14] Some of the procedures took place in Luxembourg and others in France. The defendant argued that the fact that some costs were linked to procedures that took place in France sufficed in order to establish that the underlying tort was

---

[13] Case C-133/08, *ICF*, ECLI:EU:C:2009:617 where the ECJ emphasised that the presumptions indicated in Article 4 of the Rome Convention provided for legal certainty.

[14] CA Luxembourg, 05.12.2018, no. 41168 du rôle. The Court of Appeal established that the prejudice linked to attorney fees paid in order to ensure representation in court proceedings are not excluded from the scope of Rome II.

'manifestly more closely connected' with France. The court dismissed this argument and decided on the basis of Article 4(2) Rome II that the law of the country where both parties had residence should apply.[15]

2.5. SPECIFIC RULES

Among the analysed case law, one judgment applied Article 5(1),[16] one applied Article 5(2)[17] and two applied Article 6 Rome I.[18] Article 5(1) Rome I was applied in a case where a Belgian transport and logistics company hired a Luxembourg company to perform transport services on its behalf for a client. The Luxembourg company was transporting goods from a warehouse located in France to different locations in Belgium. Once the client launched a procurement procedure in order to choose a transporter for the next period of time, both companies participated. Ultimately the client chose the Luxembourg company. Considering that the Luxembourg company committed an act of unfair competition, since it participated in the procurement procedure without informing the Belgian company, the latter refused to pay the latest invoices for transport services. The Luxembourg company thus started legal action. Given the clear factual situation, after establishing that the contract between the parties was a contract of carriage and not a distribution contract, it easily identified Belgian law as applicable to this contract.

The case in which Article 5(2) Rome I was applied dealt with a passenger living in Germany who, through a travel agent established in Germany, reserved tickets with Air France for a trip from Luxembourg to San Francisco via Paris. As the return flight from San Francisco was delayed, the passenger did not arrive on time in Luxembourg. The rights of the passengers are directly regulated by EU Regulation 261/2004.[19] However, Air France argued inter alia that the claim was time barred. Regulation 261/2004 does not specify the limitation periods for the claims it grants. Therefore, it was necessary to establish the law applicable to

15 It is clear form the merits of the judgment that the court of first instance took the same decision in this respect.

16 TA Diekirch, 27.11.2018, nos. 21057 and 21295 du rôle.

17 TP Luxembourg, 30.06.2015, Rép. fisc. no. 2690/2015. In another case, the *juge des référés* refused to decide on the applicability of either Art. 5(1) or Art. 4(1)(b), considering that the characterisation of a contract is not a matter to settle in interlocutory injunction proceedings: TA Luxembourg, 03.04.2014, réf. no. 212A/2014, no. 145580 du rôle.

18 TA Luxembourg, 08.06.2012, no. 123/2012, no. 139.898 du rôle; TP Luxembourg, 29.04.2015, Rép. fisc. no. 1747/2015.

19 Regulation (EC) No. 261/2004 of the European Parliament and of the Council of 11 February 2004 establishing common rules on compensation and assistance to passengers in the event of denied boarding and of cancellation or long delay of flights, and repealing Regulation (EEC) No. 295/91, OJ L 46, 17.2.2004, p. 1.

the contract at hand in order to determine whether the claim was indeed time barred. That is how Article 5(2) Rome I came into play. The court applied the provision of Article 5(2) Rome I literally and decided that, because the place of departure and the place of arrival were situated in Luxembourg and not in the country of residence of the passenger, French law was applicable as the law of the seat of the carrier.

As to the application of Article 6 Rome I, in a case decided by the district court of Luxembourg,[20] a consumer established in Luxembourg contracted a German company for garden works. In order to establish the law applicable to the case concerning the payment of VAT on the price for the work performed, the court applied the provision of Article 6 Rome I literally and decided that the law applicable to a dispute between a consumer and a professional who pursues his professional activities in the country in which the consumer has his/her habitual residence, i.e. Luxembourg, shall be governed by Luxembourg law.

In a case brought by a consumer residing in Germany against a professional established in Luxembourg, in which the consumer decided not to use the privilege to seise the courts of his/her place of residence, the German law was declared to be applicable.[21] In this case, the consumer had bought a product on eBay that turned out to be damaged. For the court seised, it was enough that the website of the professional used a top-level domain (.de) in order to judge that the professional was directing its activities to Germany which triggered the application of German law to the contract at hand.

Judging from this case law, the Luxembourg courts do not have a problem with the application of the specific rules established by the Rome I Regulation.

One case could be identified which applied the rules for specific torts or delicts in the Rome II Regulation, namely Article 6 concerning unfair competition.[22] In this case, as indicated above, a Belgian transport and logistics company took issue with the fact that the Luxembourg company it had hired to perform transport services on its behalf for a client did not inform it about its – eventually successful – participation in the following procurement procedure launched by that client. Considering that the Luxembourg company committed an act of unfair competition, the Belgian company refused to pay the latest invoices for transport services. In this case, the Luxembourg company started legal action. In response, the Belgian company requested compensation for an alleged damage resulting from the act of unfair competition allegedly committed by the Luxembourg company.

Given the facts of the case, the court applied Article 6(2) Rome II. It therefore had to establish the place where the alleged damage occurred in order to identify

20 TA Luxembourg, 08.06.2012, no. 123/2012, no. 139.898 du rôle.

21 TP Luxembourg, 29.04.2015, Rép. fisc. no. 1747/2015.

22 TA Diekirch, 27.11.2018, nos. 21057 and 21295 du rôle.

applicable law. This should have been the country where the specific competitor's interests, i.e. his competitive position vis-à-vis the acting competitor, had been affected.[23] From the judgment we know only that the transport services concerned goods from a warehouse located in France to the client's affiliates, authorised retailers and ateliers located in Belgium. Without any in-depth analysis the court stated that the alleged damage occurred in the place where the alleged victim was established, i.e. in Belgium. It therefore applied Belgian law.

In the case at hand, it seems that the competitor's interests in the Belgian market were affected and therefore the choice of law was correct, however the justification was not. Nevertheless, one case decided by a first instance court does not allow one to draw a general conclusion that the Luxembourg courts have difficulties with the application of the specific rules established by the Rome II Regulation.

2.6. RULES APPLICABLE TO NON-CONTRACTUAL OBLIGATIONS OTHER THAN TORTS OR DELICTS

2.6.1. Negotiorum gestio *and Unjust Enrichment*

Two examples can illustrate the understanding of these two concepts in Luxembourg. In the first case,[24] an aeroplane engine was shipped from Canada, where it had undergone a technical check, to Germany, from where it was to be shipped onwards to Luxembourg. The engine was supposed to undergo customs clearance in Luxembourg but, since this did not happen, the engine was sent to a depository in Germany where it stayed for over 20 days, which triggered its customs clearance in Germany. The VAT imposed on the company running the German depository was re-invoiced to the German company that was supposed to perform the customs clearance in Luxembourg. This company paid this sum and requested reimbursement from the Luxembourg company – i.e. the owner of the plane. Since that company refused to pay, the German company seised a Luxembourg court. Having found a document entitled 'Customs Clearance Instructions for Fiscal Representation' insufficient to prove a contractual relationship between the parties, the court analysed the possible existence of *negotiorum gestio*. Going through the plethora of rules indicated in Article 11 Rome II and in the absence of a contractual relationship or the habitual residence of the parties in the same Member State, the law of the place where the management of affairs was performed was found to apply. Payment of the invoice was identified as an action of management and therefore German

---

23 U. Magnus and P. Mankowski, *ECPIL: Rome II Regulation*, Otto Schmidt, Köln 2019, p. 264.

24 TA Luxembourg, 31.01.2014, no. 204/2014 and 19.12.2014, no. 2585/2014, no. 149.694 du rôle.

law was applicable. However, because the plaintiff did not prove the contents of German law in this respect, the plea was dismissed as unfounded.[25]

With regard to unjust enrichment, again, due to the absence of a contractual relationship or the habitual residence of the parties in the same Member State, this time in accordance with the plethora of rules established under Article 10 Rome I, the law of the Member State where the enrichment took place – in this case Luxembourg – was to be applied.

In both strands of the reasoning, it seems that the Luxembourg court did not consider the meaning of these terms as autonomous EU law concepts. Instead, when the plaintiff invoked *negotiorum gestio* or unjust enrichment as a basis for his claim, the court merely took the relevant provision of the Rome II Regulation and went through the cascade of norms to find the applicable law. It then evaluated the situation according to the law so determined. The court apparently considered that the concepts used in the Rome II Regulation were in line with their definition in civil law stemming from Roman law. As in the case at hand the court had no doubts about the acts being *negotiorum gestio*, or unjust enrichment, so that their qualification was not at stake and it could dispense with analysing the precise scope of these notions.

In two more parallel cases, a person residing in Luxembourg received invalidity and survivor's benefits granted to his mother for over four years after her death. In both cases, the law applicable to the action lodged by the social security institution and based on *répétition de l'indû* was determined on the basis of Article 10 of the Rome II Regulation.[26] In these cases, the applicability *ratione temporis* of the Rome II Regulation was not self-evident, since the pensions were received between 1 July 2006 and 31 October 2010, and the Regulation only applies to events occurring after 11 January 2009.[27] Consequently, the law applicable to the damage caused by the payments made before 11 January 2009 should have been ascertained on the basis of national private international law rules. Unfortunately, the court did not explain its choice to apply the Rome II Regulation to all events giving rise to the alleged damage.

2.6.2. Culpa in contrahendo

In a case decided before the entry into force of the Rome II Regulation and dealing with *culpa in contrahendo*, a party domiciled in Argentina and previously

---

25 It should be noted that it was a second decision in this case, as the court previously requested the parties in a separate decision to prove the German law as regards mandate and deposit contracts. It could therefore be argued that the party which subsidiarily relied on other civil law institutions to which foreign law could be found applicable should have proved it without further court's request. Further on the proof of foreign law see section 2.10 below.

26 TA Luxembourg, 09.01.2015, no. 8/2015, no. 166.013 du rôle, and 09.01.2015, no. 5/2015, no. 166.014 du rôle.

27 Case C-412/10, *Homawoo*, ECLI:EU:C:2011:747.

engaged as independent counsel for one member of a group of companies entered into negotiations to sign a framework agreement with another company in the same group concerning the restructuring of a daughter company to the company she worked for. This contract was to set out the conditions of participation of this party in this restructured company. However, the contract was to be signed only after a specific amount of money was transferred to the account of the company under restructuring. When this did not happen and the negotiations stalled, the counsel, *in spe*, set a deadline for her readiness to take the position in the company under restructuring. As the contract was not signed, she lodged an action in a Luxembourg court in order to obtain compensation for the parts of the company she was to own according to the framework contract after restructuring. The draft of this contract was subject to Luxembourg law. Although the Rome II Regulation was still not applicable *ratione temporis*, the court found Luxembourg law to apply to the dispute, considering this solution to be compatible inter alia with the conflict-of-law rules laid down in the future Rome II Regulation.[28]

The same approach was adopted in a case in which, by way of fraud, participation in a Luxembourg investment fund was sold on request not of the owners but of some unknown criminals. When the owners realised this, they lodged a claim against the investment fund. The fund itself lodged a claim against the German bank that had opened the account that allowed the fraud. The latter claim was based on tortious responsibility. In order to establish the law applicable to the fund's request, the court seised used the Rome II Regulation as a 'doctrinal source'[29] and decided that Luxembourg law should be applicable.

The available case law shows that the Luxembourg courts follow the path paved by the Court of Justice of the European Union in the *Henkel* case, which saw the ECJ interpret the Brussels Convention in the light of the upcoming Brussels I Regulation.[30]

2.7. RULES OF SAFETY AND CONDUCT

Examples of Luxembourg courts 'taking into account' foreign rules of safety and conduct notably concern traffic rules[31] and prudential rules for banks.[32]

The case concerning traffic rules was quite special due to the fact that two motorbikes owned by persons domiciled in Belgium were involved in an

---

28 TA Luxembourg, 18.11.2008, no. 202/2008, no. 108.103 du rôle.

29 TA Luxembourg, 04.05.2012, no. 706/2012, nos. 108.605, 111.262, 116.230 and 116.231 du rôle.

30 Case C-167/00, *Henkel*, ECLI:EU:C:2002:555.

31 TP Luxembourg, 05.06.2014, Rép. fisc. no. 2389/14.

32 TA Luxembourg, 04.05.2012, no. 706/2012, nos. 108.605, 111.262, 116.230 and 116.231 du rôle.

accident in Luxembourg, Belgian law was identified as the applicable law on the basis of Article 4(2) Rome II. However, because the accident took place in Luxembourg, the court applied domestic traffic rules before taking a decision concerning liability on the basis of foreign, i.e. Belgian, law.

The prudential rules for banks were taken into account in the investment fund case cited above (section 2.6.2) in order to determine the prudential responsibilities of the German bank. The court indicated that the German bank can only be liable under Luxembourg law if it violated its prudential obligations, but that the obligation it was subject to were the German prudential rules for banks. The court seems to actually apply these rules, rather than simply draw inspiration from them.

No available judgment has dealt with foreign administrative permits.

2.8. SCOPE OF APPLICABLE LAW

In Luxembourg, there is no issue of courts including elements not expressly included in the non-exhaustive lists in Article 12 Rome I or Article 15 Rome II framing the scope of applicable law. The few judgments regarding Rome I that have actually assessed the scope and content of the applicable law do not indicate any problems relating to characterisation (Article 12 Rome I). The only issue that comes to mind is the treatment of the legal presumption of *théorie de la facture acceptée* (theory of accepted invoice which consists in the presumption that the company which does not protest against an invoice within 30 days acknowledges the debt). In fact, some courts see it as a *lex fori* rule of proof and decide that even if foreign law applies to the contractual relation between the parties, the admissibility and the scope of an obligation proved by an accepted invoice is subject to Luxembourg law.[33] On the other hand, some courts decide that this '*théorie de la facture acceptée*' is subject to the *lex causae*.[34] Therefore the parties are invited to prove the scope of this theory in the applicable law in order to determine the scope of liability.

No characterisation issues have been identified with regard to Article 15 Rome II.

2.9. *RENVOI*

The case law reviewed has not provided any examples of where *renvoi* would have been helpful in order to reach international harmony of decisions.

---

33 CA Luxembourg, 21.05.2015, no. 399.08 du rôle.

34 TA Luxembourg, 18.03.2011, no. 48/2011, no. 131.450 du rôle; CA Luxembourg, 02.02.2016, no. 41168 du rôle.

2.10. FOREIGN LAW

Surprisingly – although Luxembourg has three official languages (French, German and Luxembourgish), the law is nowadays written exclusively in French,[35] French and Belgian case law is often cited, and most of the cases applying Rome I and Rome II Regulations concern Belgium, France or Germany – the courts often require that the parties prove foreign law. It is not uncommon for a court to decide on the applicability of a foreign law in a separate decision in which it requests the parties to prove this law before a subsequent hearing. What is more, if a party does not prove the law concerning, for example, a concept it relies on, the plea may be dismissed as unfounded.[36] Of course, in cases where the courts of first instance directly apply foreign law, it cannot be established beyond doubt that, knowing that the Luxembourg courts in principle require the parties to prove foreign applicable law, already in their submissions the attorneys proved the foreign law they relied on or considered applicable, so that an additional request from the court was not necessary. In fact, in some cases, a passage in the description of the requests indicates that the party invoked specific provisions of the foreign law.[37] The absence of such indications in other cases does not necessarily mean that the law was not proved in the submissions and therefore established in court.[38]

Nevertheless, in some first instance cases involving parties not represented by an attorney, the courts had to establish the law on their own motion.[39]

In situations where foreign law is applied, the burden of proof of its content is most often shifted to the parties, as the party seeking to rely on foreign law is required to prove it. This is not ideal as, firstly, the costs of litigation for the parties increase. Secondly, the courts do not have any certainty that the information provided is accurate and covers all the aspects of a certain concept. This may also compromise legal certainty. Especially in a small country such as Luxembourg, where cases with a cross-border element are quite common due to daily dealings with persons domiciled or companies established in neighbouring countries, but where the judges can without excessive difficulty have access to foreign law, such rule may be seen as unsatisfactory.

---

35 Previously, the statutes were in both French and German.

36 TA Luxembourg, 31.01.2014, no. 204/2014 and 19.12.2014, no. 2585/2014, no. 149.694 du rôle. In this case the plaintiff did not prove the German law concerning *negotiorum gestio*, and therefore the requests based on the plea that the relation between the parties amount to *negotiorum gestio* were dismissed as unfounded. In this case, the court requested the proof of German law in a separate judgment.

37 TP Luxembourg, 21.11.2013, Rép. fisc. no. 4366/2013; CA Luxembourg, 02.02.2016, no. 41168 du rôle.

38 TA Luxembourg, 09.10.2015, no. 201/2015, no. 171.604 du rôle; TA Luxembourg, 09.10.2015, no. 202/2015, no. 171.605 du rôle; CA Luxembourg, 08.01.2015, no. 40.561 du rôle; TA Diekirch, 27.11.2018, no. 21057 and 21295 du rôle.

39 See, for example, TP Luxembourg, 29.04.2015, Rép. fisc. no. 1747/2015.

On top of that, it should also be noted that the interpretation and application of foreign law by lower courts do not constitute grounds for appeal to the *Cour de cassation*.[40]

The judgments reviewed do not show any evidence of outside support in respect of foreign law. Previous judgments have occasionally[41] referred to assistance provided in the framework of the 1968 London Convention.[42]

Among the cases reviewed, only two[43] were decided on the basis of the *lex fori* applied by default. Considering that in Luxembourg a party bears the burden of proving the content of the foreign law relied on, this number is surprisingly low. One would have thought that the burden of proof would be harder to meet. On the other hand, almost all cases involved the laws of neighbouring countries with which the judges may feel sufficiently familiar as to easily accept the proof provided by the parties. Moreover, the sole case involving a non-EU Member State law concerned that of another European country, namely Liechtenstein.[44] Due to the lack of any further evidence, it is not possible to make claims as to the general impact of the Luxembourgish burden of proof principle on the universal application of Rome I and Rome II.

2.11. RELATIONS WITH INTERNATIONAL CONVENTIONS

Luxembourg is a party to the Hague Convention on Traffic Accidents.[45] Two cases come to mind in this respect. In the first one, the passenger of a car involved in an accident brought an action against the driver. The car was registered in Luxembourg and both parties were domiciled in Luxembourg. The accident, however, took place in Belgium and therefore Belgian law was applied on the basis of the 1971 Hague Convention.[46] If Rome II had been used, the applicable law would have been, according to Article 4(2), the law of the common domicile of the parties, which in this case was Luxembourg. While under Luxembourg law there is a presumption of liability of the guardian of the good where such

40 Cour Cass., 30.03.2006, no. 20/2006. See further J.-C. Wiwinius, supra n. 4, p. 57.

41 TA Luxembourg, 23.03.2010, no. 83/2010; TA Luxembourg, 07.10.2002, no. 292/2002.

42 European Convention on Information on Foreign Law, of 07.06.1968, which entered into force on 17.12.1969.

43 TA Luxembourg, 22.11.2011, no. 140635 – Rome II; TP Luxembourg, 12.07.2010, no. 2854/2010 – Rome I.

44 TA Luxembourg, 26.11.2014, no. 276/2014 – Rome I. There is, however, some evidence of the application of third state laws on the basis of the Rome Convention, see e.g. CA Luxembourg, 24.09.1998, Pas. 31, p. 58.

45 See above n. 1.

46 TA Luxembourg, 09.07.2014, no. 176/2014 and 19.10.2016, no. 369/2016, nos. 144.560 and 153.231 du rôle.

good causes damage, under Belgian law it is for the victim to prove the '*vice de la chose*', i.e. defect of the car, which caused the damage. Therefore, the plaintiff shall prove that the good causing damage was in an abnormal state, which puts it in a position to potentially cause damage. However, in this case it was clear that the damage was due to a collision with another car. The driver of the other car being responsible for the accident, no abnormality and therefore no 'vice' attributable to the good under the control of the defendant could have been proved. As a result, the plaintiff, meaning the victim passenger, lost. Under Luxembourg law, however, the result might have been the opposite, as the defendant would have had to rebut the presumption of his liability which requires one to establish the existence of one of the situations allowing his exoneration. Such exoneration of an alleged tortfeasor is only possible in the case of an event that is external, unforeseeable and irresistible, meaning in case of *force majeure*. The defendant could have been exonerated only if the court accepted the action of the driver of the other car constituted *force majeure*.

In another case, a traffic accident occurred in Luxembourg near the French border. French citizens domiciled in France and working in Luxembourg were hit by the drunk French driver of a car registered in France. One person died. The Luxembourg court dealing with the civil part of the claim applied the 1971 Hague Convention and, on the basis of Article 4(a), second indent, it decided that French law applied, as the victims were domiciled in the country of registration of the car that caused the accident.[47]

I do not think that the application of a specific set of private international law rules can be judged to be to the benefit of one of the parties. Such benefit will always depend on the content of the law that will be applied. Depending on the content of the applicable law designated by a certain set of private international law rules, one of the parties may indeed have an interest in the application of a different set of private international law rules designating a law more favourable to its claim.

Just like in the first case discussed above, it seems at first glance that the application of the Rome II Regulation would favour the victim. However, in order to assess the impact of the use of one or the other instrument, it is necessary to perform a thorough comparative analysis of the two competing sets of applicable rules. Civil liability is a complex issue and, even though the presumptions may give a better starting point to one of the parties, other elements, such as the standard of proof to be met or the application of the rules governing the impact of the victim's actions on the responsibility of the other party, etc., should be taken into account before it can be decided which instrument would be better for which party in a given case.

---

47 TA Luxembourg, 17.01.2014, no. 11/2014 and 07.03.2014, no. 60/2014, no. 148.665 du rôle.

3. GENERAL EVALUATION

The innovations brought in by the Rome I and Rome II Regulations can be judged to have been successful, as the application of the Regulations in about 50 cases in a small country like Luxembourg shows that the instruments have indeed been noticed by the courts.

In the absence of a database allowing advanced searches based on different criteria, it is unfortunately not possible to compare the uniformity we now have with the pre-Rome I and Rome II regimes, as this would require analysing not only the cases in which these instruments were applied but also those in which they were not applied, although the courts should have or could have applied them.

For the parties litigating in courts abroad, the new regime definitely provides for more clarity and judicial certainty as compared to the previous private international law regime.

In most cases the facts were quite straightforward allowing for the clear identification of a contract or tort/delict and, therefore, also the identification of an applicable corresponding rule defining applicable law. In addition, no overlaps were noticed between the concepts used by the Regulations. In the available judgments, the Luxembourg courts did not, however, deeply analyse the concepts used in the Rome I and Rome II Regulations.

The Luxembourg courts have applied these instruments literally, as the facts of the cases did not require their purposive interpretation. For example, as discussed in detail above, when notions such as *negotiorum gestio* or *culpa in contrahendo* were invoked, the court went straight to the relevant provision of the Rome II Regulation and applied it to determine the applicable law. Whether the relevant situation actually was a *negotiorum gestio* or *culpa in contrahendo* within the meaning of the Regulation was not discussed in the judgment.[48] However, there is no indication that Luxembourg courts would disregard the spirit of the Regulations.

4. CONCLUSION

4.1. SUMMARY OF FINDINGS

The Luxembourg courts seem to be comfortable with the Rome I and Rome II Regulations. They usually apply their rules literally, without discussing alternative interpretations or doctrinal doubts. On the other hand, in most of the cases

[48] TA Luxembourg, 31.01.2014, nos. 204/2014 and 19.12.2014, no. 2585/2014, no. 149.694 du rôle. TA Luxembourg, 18.11.2008, no. 202/2008, no. 108.103 du rôle.

reviewed for this chapter, the facts were quite straightforward. It thus may well be that some possible problems have simply not yet arisen before the Luxembourg courts.

So far, the Luxembourg courts have only got to apply the most common provisions of Rome I and Rome II. Therefore possible issues relating to other provisions could not be identified. Of the provisions actually applied, Article 28 of the Rome II Regulation proved problematic to some courts: its wording did not allow them to easily determine whether the Regulation supersedes only conventions signed between two or more Member States or any convention to which two or more Member States are parties. The former interpretation has now been accepted, quite rightly, in line with a judgment of the French *Cour de cassation*.[49] Finally, some judges found it – understandably[50] – difficult to determine the application *ratione temporis* of Rome II.[51]

4.2. MAIN RECOMMENDATIONS

More thought should be given to the interpretation of the notion of the 'place where the damage occurs'. In fact, for Luxembourg, where the financial markets play a significant economic role, it would be worth having clear guidelines on the localisation of financial damage. If the notions used in the Rome II Regulation are to be interpreted in coherence with those of the Brussels I *bis* Regulation, it would appear that, in accordance with *Kronhofer*[52] and *Kolassa*,[53] the damage does not necessarily occur in the place where the victim's assets are concentrated, if only financial damage was suffered there. Guidance on how to correctly localise the place where a purely financial damage occurs would thus be welcome.

One should also not forget the challenges that still lay ahead of us, one of them being the determination of the law applicable to the contracts and other business behaviour of retail giants such as Amazon Europe, established in Luxembourg, which has already become a challenge for some national courts. For the time being, however, a collective action concerning the general terms of that company, providing for the application of Luxembourg law, has only been brought in Austria.[54]

49 TA Luxembourg, 17.01.2014, no. 11/2014 and 07.03.2014, no. 60/2014, no. 148.665 du rôle.
50 See C-412/10, *Homawoo*, ECLI:EU:C:2011:747.
51 TA Luxembourg, 10.03.2011, no. 373/2011, no. 126.450 du rôle.
52 Case C-168/02, *Kronhofer*, ECLI:EU:C:2004:364.
53 Case C-375/13, *Kolassa*, ECLI:EU:C:2015:37.
54 Case before the Austrian Supreme Court: 2 Ob 204/14k. This case also already gave rise to a preliminary ruling from the CJEU (Case C-191/15, *VKI v. Amazon*, ECLI:EU:C:2016:612).

THE APPLICATION OF THE ROME I AND ROME II REGULATIONS IN THE NETHERLANDS

Laura Maria van Bochove

1. THE NATIONAL LANDSCAPE

1.1. THE REGULATIONS EMBEDDED IN NATIONAL LAW

Before the Rome I and Rome II Regulations entered into force, Dutch courts determined the law applicable to obligations arising out of contract and tort on the basis of the 1980 Rome Convention and the national Conflict of Laws (Torts) Act,[1] respectively. The Rome Convention remains relevant for contracts concluded before 17 December 2009, while the Conflict of Laws (Torts) Act still applies to harmful events that occurred before 11 January 2009.

Unlike the entry into force of other EU Regulations in the field of private international law, including the Brussels I *bis* Regulation, the entry into force of the Rome Regulations was not accompanied by separate Execution Acts (*Uitvoeringswetgeving*). However, Book 10 of the Dutch Civil Code (*Burgerlijk Wetboek*, DCC), which entered into force on 1 January 2012, contains several provisions relating to the application of Rome I and Rome II.

The Dutch legislator has extended the normal scope of application of the conflict rules of both Rome Regulations. Article 154 of Book 10 DCC states that the provisions of Rome I apply *mutatis mutandis* to obligations to be qualified as contractual but falling outside of the (substantive) scope of the Regulation or any other supranational source. Article 159 of Book 10 DCC contains a similar provision for non-contractual obligations outside of the scope of Rome II. Although it is not stated explicitly, the provisions of Rome I and Rome II do not apply if another European Regulation or a specific provision of national conflicts law regulates the applicable law in relation to the obligation in question. Case law now contains several examples of courts determining the applicable law using the extended application of the Regulations. In this way, courts have applied Rome I's provisions to determine the law applicable to the substantive validity of an arbitration clause,[2] and Rome II's conflict rules to cases of family law,[3] succession,[4] and infringements of personality rights.[5]

---

1 Wet van 11 april 2001, houdende regeling van het conflictenrecht met betrekking tot verbintenissen uit onrechtmatige daad, *Stb.* 2001, 190.

2 Rb. Amsterdam 11.11.2015, ECLI:NL:RBAMS:2015:8098; Rb. Overijssel 25.06.2014, ECLI:NL:RBOVE:2014:3551. On 01.01.2015 a new provision, Article 166 of Book 10 DCC, entered into force that specifically regulates the applicable law in relation to the substantive validity of an arbitration agreement. As a *lex specialis*, this provision takes precedence over Article 154 of Book 10 DCC.

3 Hof 's-Hertogenbosch 15.07.2014, ECLI:NL:GHSHE:2014:2181; Rb. Oost-Brabant 03.04.2013, ECLI:NL:RBOBR:2013:BZ7240.

4 Rb. Amsterdam 27.07.2016, ECLI:NL:RBAMS:2016:4704.

5 HR 03.06.2016, ECLI:NL:HR:2016:1054 (*Dahabshiil*); Rb. Amsterdam, 09.08.2017, ECLI:NL:RBAMS:2017:5415; Rb. Rotterdam 29.06.2017, ECLI:NL:RBROT:2017:4986; Rb. Amsterdam 21.05.2014, ECLI:NL:RBAMS:2014:3492; Hof 's-Hertogenbosch 17.09.2013, ECLI:NL:GHSHE:2013:4278; Rb. Amsterdam 15.06.2012, ECLI:NL:RBAMS:2012:BW9838.

Two provisions of Book 10 DCC concern the implementation of Article 7 Rome I: Article 155 extends the free choice of law for insurance contracts covered by Article 7(3) Rome I and in Article 156, the Dutch legislator determines that the insurance contract shall be governed by the law of the Member State that imposes the obligation to take out insurance.[6] Moreover, Article 158 of Book 10 DCC clarifies that the Hague Traffic Accident Convention and the Hague Product Liability Convention take precedence over Rome II. Remarkably, the DCC contains no similar provision to explicitly establish the hierarchy between the Rome I Regulation and the Hague Agency Convention.[7] However, the priority of the aforementioned conventions already follows from the Regulations themselves.[8]

1.2. CASE LAW ON ROME I AND ROME II

For the purposes of this report, the search engine 'Legal Intelligence' was used. It integrates the content of a large number of existing legal databases.[9] The search results show that as of January 2020, the Dutch courts had rendered approximately 350 different published decisions applying the Rome I Regulation, while in another 50 cases the Regulation was mentioned but found inapplicable *ratione temporis*. In about 250 decisions the courts had applied the Rome II Regulation, whereas the Regulation was mentioned in another 50 or so cases falling outside its temporal scope.

The five most-applied Rome I provisions are Article 3 (choice of law), Article 4 (applicable law in the absence of choice), Article 5 (transport contracts), Article 8 (employment contracts), and Article 10 (consent and material validity). The five Rome II provisions that are most often applied are Article 4 (general rule), Article 14 (choice of law), Article 6 (unfair competition and restricting

6 Compare Article 7(4)(b) Rome I.

7 However, Article 125 of Book 10 DCC states that the applicable law to agency is regulated by the Hague Agency Convention.

8 See Article 25(1) Rome I and Article 28(1) Rome II.

9 Although the vast majority of Dutch lower court decisions are not published, most lower and appellate court decisions by panels of three or more judges are made available on <www.rechtspraak.nl>, except for decisions that only consist of standard wording. In principle, all decisions of the Dutch Supreme Court are published. In addition, several legal journals publish case law, sometimes including cases that are not available on <www.rechtspraak.nl>. Dutch arbitration awards are not systematically published, due to their confidential and private nature. Out of the arbitration awards disclosed and included in the database of 'Legal Intelligence', the vast majority comes from the arbitration board for the building industry (Raad van Arbitrage voor de Bouw). In the rare cases that mention the Rome I Regulation or Rome II Regulation, the Regulation is mostly found inapplicable. For this reason, arbitration awards are further excluded from the present analysis.

free competition), Article 8 (infringement of intellectual property rights), and Article 10 (unjust enrichment).

In general, the Dutch courts apply the right set of conflict rules. However, there are some exceptions. In two cases, the courts disregarded the universal scope of the Rome I Regulation: they ruled that the Regulation was not applicable because one of the parties was domiciled in Denmark. One court held that the 1980 Rome Convention was applicable instead,[10] whereas the other applied the Rome I Regulation by analogy.[11] In another case, the court incorrectly held that the Rome II Regulation was not directly applicable since the case was connected to Serbia and Serbia is not an EU Member State and thus not a party to the Regulation.[12] In another case, the court assumed that Dutch law was applicable to an international loan agreement, without (explicit) consultation of the European conflict rules (in this case the Rome Convention was temporally applicable).[13]

In other cases, the Dutch courts have erroneously held Rome I/Rome II to be applicable instead of a special convention to which the Netherlands is a contracting state. In a case on agency, the court applied Article 4(1) Rome I, where it should have applied the 1978 Hague Agency Convention.[14] In a product liability case, the Dutch Court applied Article 5 Rome II, instead of the 1973 Hague Product Liability Convention.[15] In another case, which concerned a physical injury caused by a defective tea glass, the court overlooked not only the Hague Product Liability Convention, but also Article 5 Rome II; instead, the court applied the general rule of Article 4 Rome II.[16]

2. THE OPERATION OF ROME I AND ROME II IN PRACTICE

2.1. *LOIS DE POLICE*

In Dutch case law, the role of *lois de police* or overriding mandatory provisions is mainly limited to contracts (Article 9 Rome I). Case law on the Rome II Regulation contains no references to this concept.

One of the most well-known overriding mandatory provisions was Article 6 of the Extraordinary Decree on Labour Relations 1945 (*Buitengewoon Besluit Arbeidsverhoudingen 1945*, BBA). This provision required an employer to

10 Rb. Gelderland 09.12.2015, ECLI:NL:RBGEL:2015:8188.
11 Rb. Noord-Holland 18.04.2018, ECLI:NL:RBNHO:2018:3103.
12 Rb. Noord-Holland 28.06.2017, ECLI:NL:RBNNE:2017:2318.
13 Rb. Gelderland 27.07.2016, ECLI:NL:RBGEL:2016:4202.
14 Rb. Rotterdam 14.10.2015, ECLI:NL:RBROT:2015:7320.
15 Rb. Noord-Holland 08.12.2015, ECLI:NL:RBNHO:2015:10485.
16 Rb. Midden-Nederland 01.07.2016, ECLI:NL:RBMNE:2016:3598.

request permission from the authorities for a dismissal. Although the legislature remained silent about its application in international cases, in case law the provision has been recognised as an overriding mandatory rule. In the 1980s, the Dutch Supreme Court clarified its scope: employers should ask for permission when the dismissal has an impact on the Dutch labour market. This is especially the case when it is expected that the dismissed employee will seek a new job in the Netherlands or will make use of Dutch social welfare.[17] In 2012, the Dutch Supreme Court changed (or clarified) the scope of Article 6 BBA, by stating that this provision aims to protect employees against unfair dismissal and also applies when the employee's situation cannot be distinguished from that of a Dutch employee who is protected by this provision.[18] The court also confirmed that the application of Article 6 BBA does not depend on the law applicable to the employment contract. In the case in question, the employment contract contained a choice-of-law clause specifying Dutch law, and the employee worked in the Netherlands. The fact that Dutch labour law was applicable pursuant to Article 8 Rome I, however, did not automatically imply the application of Article 6 BBA.

Due to a major revision of Dutch labour law, Article 6 BBA was repealed on 1 July 2015. According to its legislative history, the scope of application of its successor – Article 671a of Book 7 DCC – aligns with Article 8 Rome I,[19] implying that the new provision is not an overriding mandatory provision. This does not mean, though, that the role of *lois de police* within the context of labour relations has been exhausted. Lower and appellate courts are divided on which rules of Dutch labour law are to be considered overriding mandatory rules, however. In 2013, the Court of Appeal of 's-Hertogenbosch held that the provisions of the European Posting of Workers Directive[20] should be regarded as *lois de police*. Moreover, the court held that its scope is extended by the Dutch Employment Conditions Cross-border Employment Act (*Wet Arbeidsvoorwaarden Grensoverschrijdende Arbeid*, WAGA) which transposes the Directive.[21] In a 2016 case, a first instance court qualified the Dutch Act on Compulsory Participation in an Industry-wide Pension Fund 2000 (*Wet verplichte deelneming in een bedrijfstakpensioenfonds 2000*) as an overriding mandatory rule within the meaning of Article 9 Rome I.[22] In 2015, however, a lower court did not find it necessary to clarify whether a provision of national law on the equal

[17] HR 23.10.1987, ECLI:NL:HR:1987:AD0017 (*Sorensen/Aramco*).
[18] HR 24.02.2012, ECLI:NL:HR:2012:BU8512 (*Nuon/Olbrych*).
[19] *Kamerstukken II* 2013/14, 33818, 3, p. 75.
[20] Directive 96/71/EC of the European Parliament and of the Council of 16 December 1996 concerning the posting of workers in the framework of the provision of services.
[21] Hof 's-Hertogenbosch 28.05.2013, ECLI:NL:GHSHE:2013:CA1457.
[22] Rb. Noord-Nederland 15.11.2016, ECLI:NL:RBNNE:2016:4935.

treatment of intermediaries should be considered an overriding mandatory rule, since this provision could be applied in any case via Article 8 Rome I.[23]

Outside the context of labour relations, the role of *lois de police* is much more limited. In one case, the court qualified Article 88 of Book 1 DCC as an overriding mandatory rule in the sense of Article 9 Rome I. This provision states that a spouse needs the permission of the other spouse to conclude a contract of guarantee (*borgtochtovereenkomst*). According to the court, the provision applies when the other spouse is domiciled in the Netherlands, irrespective of the law applicable to the contract.[24] However, the prevailing opinion in case law is that the permission of the other spouse falls outside of Rome I's substantive scope. Instead, it should be qualified as an issue of the personal legal relations between the spouses, for which Article 40 of Book 10 contains a specific conflicts rule.[25]

In 2015, the Amsterdam Court of Appeal had to decide whether a provision of Dutch rental law was to be considered an overriding mandatory rule.[26] The court answered the question in the negative. It held that in the case in question, public interests were not sufficiently involved. Yet, it can be inferred from the court's reasoning that another conclusion might have been reached in other circumstances, especially if the tenant was a weaker party protected under Dutch law.

Case law offers few examples of third country overriding mandatory rules. In one case, the court had to determine whether a Turkish rule requiring contracts to be drafted in the Turkish language qualified as an overriding mandatory rule. The court answered in the affirmative: since the rule aims at protecting Turkish citizens with insufficient knowledge of foreign languages, the provision serves a public interest. However, the court held that the case was insufficiently connected with the Turkish legal sphere to apply this provision.[27]

2.2. PARTY AUTONOMY

About 50 per cent of cases examined in which the courts applied the Rome I Regulation concern a choice of law. In the majority of these cases, the parties made an express choice of law, usually included in their contract. However, a choice of law made in the course of the proceedings is also accepted as a means to remedy an invalid choice of law.[28] In several cases, courts have accepted an implied or tacit choice for Dutch law, especially if the parties' pleadings were

[23] Rb. Midden-Nederland 18.03.2015, ECLI:NL:RBMNE:2015:1752.

[24] Rb. Midden-Nederland 02.08.2013, ECLI:NL:RBMNE:2013:3098.

[25] Rb. Noord-Nederland 01.06.2016, ECLI:NL:RBNNE:2016:2736; Hof's-Hertogenbosch 11.08.2015, ECLI:NL:GHSHE:2015:3191; Rb. Amsterdam 09.07.2014, ECLI:NL:RBAMS:2014:4641.

[26] Hof Amsterdam 24.02.2015, ECLI:NL:GHAMS:2015:523.

[27] Rb. Amsterdam 24.11.2014, ECLI:NL:RBAMS:2014:8502.

[28] e.g. Rb. Midden-Nederland 12.08.15, ECLI:NL:RBMNE:2015:5882.

based on Dutch legislation or case law.[29] However, an agreement to submit disputes to arbitration or court litigation in the Netherlands was regarded insufficient to accept a tacit choice for Dutch law.[30]

The validity of a choice of law can be an issue, especially when the choice of law is included in a party's general terms and conditions. In those cases the court will, pursuant to Article 10 Rome I, determine the validity on the basis of the chosen law.[31] Yet, in one case in which parties both referred to the choice-of-law clauses in their own general terms and conditions ('battle of the forms'), the court held that the question as to which party's terms and conditions were applicable had to be determined on the basis of the law applicable to the contract in the absence of choice.[32]

In comparison to Rome I, the role of choice of law is more limited under the Rome II Regulation. Case law shows, however, that courts are often willing to accept both express and implied choices of law in relation to cross-border torts. In practice this usually comes down to the application of Dutch law.[33] If parties make a choice of law, they usually do this in the course of proceedings.[34] This way, the choice of law is in keeping with Article 14(1)(a) Rome II, which states that parties may agree on the applicable law by an agreement entered into after the event giving rise to the damage occurred.

The courts' eagerness to respect party autonomy sometimes leads to dubious outcomes. Within the context of Rome I, courts have sometimes accepted a choice of law in disputes concerning a consumer or labour contract, disregarding the restrictions on party autonomy included in Article 6(2)[35] and Article 8(1) Rome I.[36] Under Rome II, courts have accepted a choice for Dutch law for copyright infringements that had taken place outside the Netherlands,[37] thereby violating Article 8(3) Rome II. Moreover, an implied choice in favour of Dutch

29 Rb. Rotterdam 21.03.2018, ECLI:NL:RBROT:2018:3237; Rb. Den Haag 26.10.2016, ECLI:NL:RBDHA:2016:13161; Rb. Rotterdam 23.10.2013, ECLI:NL:RBROT:2013:8186; Rb. Zutphen 15.08.2012, ECLI:NL:RBZUT:2012:BX4722.

30 Rb. Den Haag 28.05.2014, ECLI:NL:RBDHA:2014:7406; Hof Amsterdam 28.11.2017, ECLI:NL:GHAMS:2017:4959.

31 See e.g. Rb. Rotterdam 21.10.2015, ECLI:NL:RBROT:2015:8714; Rb. Oost-Brabant 16.04.2014, ECLI:NL:RBOBR:2014:1912; Rb. Rotterdam 29.08.2012, ECLI:NL:RBROT:2012:8663.

32 Rb. Gelderland 02.03.2016, ECLI:NL:RBGEL:2016:1328.

33 See e.g. Hof Amsterdam 25.10.2016, ECLI:NL:GHAMS:2016:4212; Rb. Amsterdam 21.09.2016, ECLI:NL:RBAMS:2016:5983; Rb. Rotterdam 30.03.2016, ECLI:NL:RBROT:2016:3638; Rb. Noord-Nederland 18.02.2015, ECLI:NL:RBNNE:2015:698.

34 Rb. Rotterdam 30.03.2016, ECLI:NL:RBROT:2016:3638; Rb. Amsterdam 18.12.2013, ECLI:NL:RBAMS:2013:9630; Rb. Oost-Brabant 02.12.2013, ECLI:NL:RBOBR:2013:6750.

35 Hof Arnhem-Leeuwarden 17.03.2015, ECLI:NL:GHARL:2015:1920.

36 See Hof 's-Hertogenbosch 12.12.2019, ECLI:NL:GHSHE:2019:4507; Rb. Limburg 25.08.2016, ECLI:NL:RBLIM:2016:7412; Rb. Zwolle 20.01.2010, ECLI:NL:RBZLY:2010:BO9945.

37 Rb. Amsterdam 21.09.2016, ECLI:NL:RBAMS:2016:5983; Rb. Zutphen 11.11.2009, ECLI:NL:RBZUT:2009:BN4069.

law was accepted in a case on unlawful comparative advertising, without making reference to Article 6(4) Rome II, which rules out choice of law for unfair competition.[38]

2.3. ABSENCE OF CHOICE OF LAW

2.3.1. Article 4 Rome I

Article 4(1) Rome I, which contains custom-made conflict rules for specific contracts, is new in comparison to the Rome Convention. Apparently, the change from Convention to Regulation has not given rise to many problems. In general, courts seem to be experiencing little difficulty in putting a contract into one of the categories of Article 4(1).

A large part of the Dutch case law on international contracts concerns the sale of movable goods. The Netherlands is party to the UN Convention on the International Sale of Goods (CISG). It contains uniform substantive rules that – as a general rule – take precedence over conflict-of-laws rules. However, the Rome I Regulation, in particular Article 4(1)(a), providing a conflict rule for sale of movable goods, remains relevant. Its role is twofold. Firstly, courts use the Rome I Regulation to determine the 'complementary' applicable national law[39] that governs issues not regulated by CISG.

Secondly, courts use the Regulation to establish whether CISG is applicable in geographical terms. Unless parties have opted out of CISG, the Convention is geographically applicable if the seller and the buyer have their places of business in a CISG contracting state (Article 1(1)(a) CISG). However, even if this is not the case, CISG is still applicable if – according to the conflict rules of the court seised – the law applicable to the contract is the law of a contracting state (Article 1(1)(b) CISG). This is where Rome I comes into view. In the absence of a choice of law, the court will determine the applicable law pursuant to Article 4 Rome I. Generally, the law of the country where the seller has his habitual residence will apply pursuant to Article 4(1)(a) Rome I, unless the contract is manifestly more closely connected with another country, in which case the law of that country applies (Article 4(3) Rome I). Consequently, if the provisions of Rome I refer to the law of a contracting state, the court will deem CISG applicable pursuant to Article 1(1)(b) CISG and apply the Convention's uniform rules.

---

38 Rb. Oost-Brabant 17.10.2014, ECLI:NL:RBOBR:2014:6281.

39 e.g. Rb. Gelderland 02.03.2016, ECLI:NL:RBGEL:2016:3134; Rb. Gelderland 14.10.2015, ECLI:NL:RBGEL:2015:7269; Hof Arnhem-Leeuwarden 15.09.2015, ECLI:NL:GHARL:2015:6805; Rb. Overijssel 07.01.2015, ECLI:NL:RBOVE:2015:380; Rb. Den Haag 12.03.2014, ECLI:NL:RBDHA:2014:3082.

If, on the other hand, Rome I refers to the law of a non-contracting state, CISG is not applicable and the court will apply this state's national sales law.

Some cases, however, take the following approach: the court first determines, on the basis of Rome I, which country's law is applicable to the contract and then checks whether this country is party to CISG.[40] In view of Article 1(1)(a) CISG, this approach should be considered incorrect: if both seller and buyer have their place of business in a (different) CISG contracting state, CISG is applicable even when the law applicable to the contract would be that of a non-contracting state.[41]

In a substantial part of the case law examined, the type of contract in question is not listed in Article 4(1) Rome I, and courts resort to Article 4(2) Rome I, which refers to the law of the country where the party required to effect the characteristic performance has his habitual residence. This provision has been applied to a wide variety of types of contracts.[42] In general, courts seem to face little difficulty in establishing which party has to effectuate the characteristic performance. For contracts of guarantee, this is the person who gives a guarantee for repayment.[43] For loan agreements, the person lending the money has been identified as the characteristic performer.[44] In a case concerning a sponsorship contract – in which a Uruguayan company sponsored the acquisition of a football player by Football Club Utrecht, the club was considered the characteristic performer as it had an obligation to let the football player play in the Dutch football league.[45] The company from Uruguay, on the other hand, only had to transfer the sponsorship fee.[46]

Only in rare instances have courts not been able to determine the applicable law pursuant to Article 4(1) and (2). In one case, concerning an agreement to cooperate, the court of The Hague could not identify the characteristic performer. Therefore, it applied Article 4(4) Rome I, which refers to the law of the country the contract was most closely connected with. It held that the contract was most closely connected with the Netherlands, since at the time

---

40 Rb. Arnhem 10.10.2012, ECLI:NL:RBARN:2012:BY2169; Rb. Rotterdam 08.07.2010, ECLI:NL:RBROT:2010:BN3275.

41 This could be the case if the law of a non-contracting state would be manifestly more closely connected within the meaning of Article 4(3) Rome II.

42 e.g. for a contract to reserve ambulances (see Rb. Overijssel 02.03.2016, ECLI:NL:RBOVE:2016:655), a consultancy agreement (see Rb. Leeuwarden 19.10.2012, ECLI:NL:RBLEE:2012:BY0812), combined sale of goods and provision services (see Rb. Rotterdam 29.06.2016, ECLI:NL:RBROT:2016:4913), and a sub-licence agreement (see Hof Arnhem-Leeuwarden 17.02.2015, ECLI:NL:GHARL:2015:1152).

43 Rb. Overijssel 27.06.2018, ECLI:NL:RBOVE:2018:2407; Rb. Den Haag 18.09.2013, ECLI:NL:RBDHA:2013:13451.

44 Rb. Rotterdam 24.06.2015, ECLI:NL:RBROT:2015:4512; Rb. Den Haag 23.04.2014, ECLI:NL:RBDHA:2014:6909.

45 Rb. Midden-Nederland 30.12.2015, ECLI:NL:RBMNE:2015:8754.

46 Rb. Overijssel 02.03.2016, ECLI:NL:RBOVE:2016:655.

of signing the agreement, the parties involved were habitually resident in the Netherlands and one other party had Dutch nationality.[47] In another case, the Amsterdam Court of First Instance applied Article 4(4) to determine the law applicable to a settlement agreement.[48]

2.3.2. *Article 4 Rome II*

Dutch courts have applied Article 4(1) Rome II, which refers to the law of the country where the damage was sustained (*lex loci damni*), in highly diverse cases. They include conspiracy,[49] endangerment,[50] and violation of ownership rights.[51] A relatively high proportion of cases, though, concern the collision of vessels, wrongful arrest/attachment, and director's liability.

The cases regarding the collision of vessels concern inland navigation.[52] The rules in this field of law – at least when the collision is *between* vessels – have been harmonised to a certain degree by the 1960 Geneva Convention,[53] to which the Netherlands is a contracting state. However, even when the Convention applies, the courts still need to determine the 'complementary' applicable law pursuant to Article 4 – which usually will refer to the law of the country where the collision took place.[54]

In cases concerning (alleged) wrongful arrest/attachment, courts generally locate the damage at the place where the arrest was made.[55] Yet, in 2011, in a case concerning the arrest of a ship, the court held that even though at the time of the arrest the ship was situated in Belgium, the damage was sustained in the Netherlands, where the victim resided and where the arrest was registered.[56]

---

47 Rb. Den Haag 28.05.2014, ECLI:NL:RBDHA:2014:7406. In Rb. Overijssel 22.10.2014, ECLI:NL:RBOVE:2014:5834, the court referred to Article 4(4), whereas it actually meant to apply Article 4(3) Rome I.

48 Rb. Amsterdam 31.05.2017, ECLI:NL:RBAMS:2017:3650.

49 Rb. Rotterdam 21.09.2016, ECLI:NL:RBROT:2016:7258.

50 e.g. Hof 's-Hertogenbosch 09.12.2014, ECLI:NL:GHSHE:2014:5184; Rb. Rotterdam 12.02.2014, ECLI:NL:RBROT:2014:1605.

51 e.g. Rb. Zeeland-West-Brabant 08.06.2016, ECLI:NL:RBZWB:2016:3515; Rb. Midden-Nederland 19.02.2014, ECLI:NL:RBMNE:2014:550; Rb. Limburg 15.07.2013, ECLI:NL:RBLIM:2013:4521.

52 e.g. Rb. Rotterdam 25.11.2015, ECLI:NL:RBROT:2015:8534; Rb. Rotterdam 03.07.2013, ECLI:NL:RBROT:2013:6173; Rb. Zwolle 02.05.2012, ECLI:NL:RBZLY:2012:1765.

53 Convention relating to the unification of certain rules concerning collisions in inland navigation, Geneva, 15.03.1960.

54 Rb. Rotterdam 17.07.2013, ECLI:NL:RBROT:2013:6174; Rb. Rotterdam 03.07.2013, ECLI:NL:RBROT:2013:6173.

55 e.g. Rb. Rotterdam 04.05.2016, ECLI:NL:RBROT:2016:3786; Rb. Amsterdam 06.04.2016, ECLI:NL:RBAMS:2016:1938; Rb. Zeeland-West-Brabant 12.03.2014, ECLI:NL:RBZWB:2014:1974; Rb. Arnhem 30.08.2012, ECLI:NL:RBARN:2012:BX8019.

56 Rb. Dordrecht 28.04.2011, ECLI:NL:RBDOR:2011:BQ4329. The Netherlands is also a contracting state to the 1952 Brussels Convention which contains uniform rules relating to the arrest of sea-going ships. In addition to uniform substantive law this Convention also contains a conflict-of-laws rule to determine the law applicable to a damages claim: Article 6

In cases concerning director's liability, the preliminary question arises whether this subject falls within the substantive scope of the Rome II Regulation. After all, Article 1(1)(d) Rome II determines that the Regulation is not applicable to non-contractual obligations arising out of the law of companies regarding matters such as the personal liability of officers. Although the Dutch legislator has 'extended' the substantive scope of the Regulation (see above, section 1.1), the extension will in principle not apply in this case, as Book 10 DCC contains specific conflict rules for issues of company law.[57] Moreover, courts have regularly held that the exception of Article 1(1)(d) Rome II and the specific rules of Book 10 DCC only apply in situations where the director's liability is based on company law, for example when the claims concern personal liability of the director for the company's debts.[58] If the claim against the director is based on general tort law (in the Netherlands: Article 162 of Book 6 DCC), the courts usually consider the claim as falling within the scope of the Rome II Regulation, and apply Article 4 Rome II to determine the applicable law.[59]

In general, the application of Article 4 Rome II does not appear to cause the courts many problems. In cases such as collision of vessels or endangerment, the place of damage is usually easy to establish.

However, sometimes the application of Article 4 Rome II may raise difficulties, for example in cases concerning medical liability or purely financial loss. In general, in medical cases the direct damage will occur at the place of treatment.[60] Sometimes the place of damage is more difficult establish, though. For the purpose of establishing jurisdiction, the Court of Appeal of The Hague had to establish where the damage resulting from a doctor incorrectly implanting birth control had occurred – at the place of the treatment, of the undesired conception, where the pregnancy was discovered, or where the child was born. The court held that the place of damage – which included costs for raising the child and loss of income – was the place where the baby was conceived.[61]

---

refers to the law of the contracting state in whose jurisdiction the arrest was made. In Rb. Rotterdam 27.05.2015, ECLI:NL:RBROT:2015:3919, the court held that the application of Article 6 of the 1952 Brussels Convention led to the same result as Article 4(1) Rome II.

57 See Article 117 ff. of Book 10 DCC.

58 See also the Conclusion of Advocate-General Vlas 18.03.2016, ECLI:NL:PHR:2016:139.

59 See e.g. Rb. Noord-Holland 17.05.2017, ECLI:NL:RBNHO:2017:4029; Rb. Amsterdam 10.02.2016, ECLI:NL:RBAMS:2016:356; Hof 's-Hertogenbosch 16.09.2014, ECLI:NL:GHSHE:2014:3665; Rb. Noord-Nederland 27.03.2013, ECLI:NL:RBNNE:2013:BZ6207; Rb. Utrecht 04.04.2012, ECLI:NL:RBUTR:2012:BW1752. In Rb. Overijssel 27.08.2014, ECLI:NL:RBOVE:2014:4875, the court held that the director's personal liability falls outside the scope of Rome II. However, the court still determined the applicable law pursuant to Article 4 Rome II, while referring to the extension of the substantive scope of Rome II in Article 159 of Book 10 DCC.

60 X.E. Kramer and H.L.E. Verhagen, *Mr. C. Assers handleiding tot de beoefening van het Nederlands burgerlijk recht. 10. Internationaal Privaatrecht. Deel III. Internationaal Vermogensrecht*, Kluwer, Deventer 2015, no. 1002.

61 Hof Den Haag 14.10.2004, ECLI:NL:GHSGR:2004:AR5850.

In cases of purely economic loss – often considered a potential pitfall[62] – courts have not been hesitant to locate the damage at the place where the victim has his bank account if he also resides there.[63]

Finally, the place of damage can be difficult to determine if the damage occurs in more than one country. The court can decide to apply the 'mosaic approach', which means that the damage occurring in country A will be governed by the law of country A, the damage occurring in country B by the law of country B, etc.[64] However, in the case of defamation and libel, the courts have adopted a different approach. As mentioned above, libel and defamation are excluded from Rome II's substantive scope, but pursuant to Article 159 of Book 10 DCC, the Dutch courts apply the Regulation's conflict rules to these types of cases.[65] In a case before the Dutch Supreme Court, the question arose as to where the damage should be located if defamatory statements are published on the Internet.[66] Based on the principle of coherent interpretation between EU private international law instruments, the Supreme Court deemed the CJEU case law on (now) Article 7(2) of the Brussels I *bis* Regulation to be guiding, in particular the *eDate Advertising and Martinez* case.[67] As a consequence, the Supreme Court held that the *locus damni* was situated at the place of the centre of the victim's interests.[68]

2.4. ESCAPE CLAUSES

2.4.1. Article 4(3) Rome I

In general, Dutch courts restrictively apply the escape clause of Article 4(3) Rome I in favour of the manifestly more closely connected law. However, in some cases, this provision has been used to avoid the application of Article 4(1) and (2) Rome I. In a case concerning a loan agreement and a deposit agreement,

---

62 See, inter alia, L.M. van Bochove, 'Purely economic loss in conflict of laws: the case of tortious interference with contract' [2016] *Nederlands Internationaal Privaatrecht* 456–465; X.E. Kramer and H.L.E. Verhagen, above n. 60, no. 998.

63 Rb. Amsterdam 29.07.2015, ECLI:NL:RBAMS:2015:4871; Rb. Rotterdam 19.08.2015, ECLI:NL:RBROT:2015:6045.

64 See Hof 's-Hertogenbosch 04.08.2015, ECLI:NL:GHSHE:2015:2992.

65 See e.g. Hof 's-Hertogenbosch 17.09.2013, ECLI:NL:GHSHE:2013:4278; Rb. Amsterdam 15.06.2012, ECLI:NL:RBAMS:2012:BW9838.

66 HR 03.06.2016, ECLI:NL:HR:2016:1054 (*Dahabshiil*).

67 Joined Cases C-509/09 and C-161/10, *eDate Advertising and Martinez*, ECLI:EU:C:2011:685.

68 HR 03.06.2016, ECLI:NL:HR:2016:1054 (*Dahabshiil*), para. 4.11.2. See in similar fashion Hof 's-Hertogenbosch 06.10.2015, ECLI:NL:GHSHE:2015:3904. See also L.M. van Bochove, 'Onlogisch analogisch. De overeenkomstige toepassing van Europese conflictregels in grensoverschrijdende smaadzaken ex artikel 10:159 BW', in F.Q. van der Pol et al. (eds.), *Vijftig weeffouten in het BW*, Ars Aequi Libri, Nijmegen 2017, pp. 377–383.

the court found it unnecessary to identify the characteristic performer since both agreements were clearly most closely connected to the Netherlands.[69]

Courts also restrictively interpret the other escape clauses of the Rome I Regulation, such as Article 8(4) for employment contracts.[70]

2.4.2. Article 4(3) Rome II

In general, the escape clause of Article 4(3) Rome II is not overused. Still, there are considerable differences in the way courts apply this provision. Sometimes the court only briefly states that the escape clause is not applicable.[71] In other instances, the court uses this provision as a 'safety net', by arguing that a certain law – for example Dutch law – applies pursuant to *either* Article 4(1) *or* (3) Rome II.[72] In addition to this, courts occasionally determine the applicable law solely on the basis of Article 4(3) Rome II.[73]

In some cases, courts adopt a more balanced approach to the escape clause. In general, courts draw specific attention to the fact that there is an agreement between the parties.[74] In a case concerning the non-payment of the earnings of a vessel sale, the court held that pursuant to Article 4(3) Rome II Dutch law was applicable. It took into account the parties' country of residence, the fact that there were pre-existing relationships between the parties governed by Dutch law, and that, at the time of the sale, the vessel was situated in the Netherlands.[75] In a case on the medical liability of a physician, pursuant to Article 4(3) Rome II the court applied Belgian law, which also governed the treatment agreement between the victim and the hospital. And this was despite the fact that both patient and physician were habitually resident in the Netherlands, which according to Article 4(2) Rome II would have led to the application of Dutch law. However, in a case concerning conspiracy, the court held that although the case was associated with loan agreements, the escape clause of Article 4(3) Rome II was not applicable since the agreements were not concluded between the two litigating parties.[76] However, even a pre-existing relationship *between the parties*

69 Rb. Amsterdam 12.11.2014, ECLI:NL:RBAMS:2014:7138.

70 e.g. Hof Amsterdam 28.11.2017, ECLI:NL:GHAMS:2017:4959; Rb. Midden-Nederland 22.07.2015, ECLI:NL:RBMNE:2015:5393.

71 Rb. Rotterdam 30.09.2015, ECLI:NL:RBROT:2015:6864; Rb. Rotterdam 19.08.2015, ECLI:NL:RBROT:2015:6045; Hof 's-Hertogenbosch 04.08.2015, ECLI:NL:GHSHE:2015:2992.

72 Rb. Rotterdam 09.12.2015, ECLI:NL:RBROT:2015:9110; Rb. Zeeland-West-Brabant 12.03.2014, ECLI:NL:RBZWB:2014:1974; Rb. Arnhem 30.08.2012, ECLI:NL:RBARN:2012:BX8019.

73 Rb. Gelderland 23.07.2014, ECLI:NL:RBGEL:2014:5618; Rb. Oost-Brabant 19.02.2014, ECLI:NL:RBOBR:2014:1584; Rb. Den Haag 23.04.2014, ECLI:NL:RBDHA:2014:6909.

74 e.g. Rb. Dordrecht 04.07.2012, ECLI:NL:RBDOR:2012:BX1353.

75 Rb. Noord-Nederland 13.03.2013, ECLI:NL:RBNNE:2013:BZ7200. The court, however, did not answer the question of which law would have been applicable pursuant to Article 4(1) Rome II, i.e. whether or not the escape clause was needed to apply Dutch law.

76 Rb. Rotterdam 21.09.2016, ECLI:NL:RBROT:2016:7258.

is in itself not necessarily sufficient to assume a manifestly closer connection; the court still has to take into account all the other circumstances of the case.[77]

2.5. SPECIFIC RULES

2.5.1. Specific Rules in Rome I

In the field of transport law, there are ample international instruments containing harmonised substantive law. Case law shows that Dutch courts usually first check whether or not such an instrument is applicable. However, the special conflict rules of Article 5 Rome I for transport contracts remain relevant for two reasons: (1) to establish the law applicable to transport contracts which fall outside the scope of the international instruments, such as multimodal carriage,[78] and (2) to determine the supplementary applicable law, i.e. the law applicable to specific issues not regulated by the relevant international instrument.[79]

The conflict rule for consumer contracts in Article 6 Rome I has been applied in only a limited number of cases. The question of whether or not a person is acting in the exercise of his trade or profession within the meaning of Article 6(1) Rome I was raised in a case concerning the renting of property. According to the court, the fact that the defendants rented out the property, in which they had previously lived themselves, at a profit, was not enough to consider them professional landlords.[80] One case, which was decided by the Amsterdam Court of Appeal, provides a good illustration of the courts' approach to a choice-of-law clause in contracts involving a consumer. First, the court checked whether or not the contract in question was a consumer contract within the meaning of Article 6(1) Rome I. After concluding that the requirements of Article 6(1) were fulfilled, the court held that the choice of law for Maltese law could not deprive the consumer of the protection he received on the basis of mandatory law of the country of his habitual residence, the Netherlands. The court did not make a comparison between Dutch and Maltese law to determine which law offers a higher degree of protection; instead it simply held the protective mandatory provisions of Dutch law to be applicable.[81] Not all courts, however, do things

77 Hof 's-Hertogenbosch 15.07.2014, ECLI:NL:GHSHE:2014:2181.

78 e.g. Rb. Rotterdam 29.06.2016, ECLI:NL:RBROT:2016:4923; Rb. Noord-Holland 03.04.2013, ECLI:NL:RBNHO:2013:CA0271.

79 Hof 's-Hertogenbosch 21.06.2016, ECLI:NL:GHSHE:2016:2474; Rb. Rotterdam 24.12.2014, ECLI:NL:RBROT:2014:10513.

80 Hof Amsterdam 24.02.2015, ECLI:NL:GHAMS:2015:523.

81 Hof Amsterdam 25.10.2016, ECLI:NL:GHAMS:2016:4212. For a different interpretation of Article 6(2) Rome I, see Rb. Limburg 01.08.2018, ECLI:NL:RBLIM:2018:7889. For a critical analysis of this case, see J.H.M. Spanjaard's case note in *Tijdschrift voor Consumentenrecht & handelspraktijken* 2018, pp. 255–259.

by the book. In one case, the Court of Appeal of Arnhem merely held that Article 6 does not stand in the way of a choice of law and applied the chosen (Dutch) law. The court did not consider it relevant to check whether or not the contract – concluded between a Dutch bank and a consumer habitually resident in Germany – fulfilled the requirements of Article 6(1).[82] In none of the cases did the court follow the CJEU's ruling in *VKI v. Amazon*. The CJEU ruled that a choice of law in the general terms and conditions is unfair within the meaning of Article 3(1) of Council Directive 93/13/EEC, in so far as it leads the consumer into error by giving him or her the impression that only the chosen law applies to the contract, without informing him or her that under Article 6(2) Rome I he or she also enjoys the protection of the mandatory provisions of his or her own law.[83]

In all cases found regarding insurance contracts, parties made a choice of law.[84] As said in the introduction, the Dutch legislature has extended the freedom to choose the applicable law to an insurance contract falling under the scope of Article 7(3) Rome I.

When determining the law applicable to an employment contract, the place where the employee habitually carries out his work is the primary connecting factor pursuant to Article 8 Rome I. Case law shows that locating the habitual place of work may raise difficulties, especially in relation to truck drivers.[85] In one decision, in order to establish this place, the Court of Appeal took into account the place from where the employee carried out his transport orders, received instructions and organised his work, in addition to the place where the trucks were located, the places where the transport was mainly carried out, where the goods were delivered and the place where the driver returned to after completing his orders.[86]

How should the habitual place of work of an employee who carries out a great deal of his work from home be determined? According to a (questionable) decision, remote work using an electronic connection with the employer's office in another country should be equated with working in that office.[87]

Article 8(2) Rome I states: 'The country where the work is habitually carried out shall not be deemed to have changed if he is temporarily employed in another country.' In a case concerning Portuguese and Polish temporary

82 Hof Arnhem-Leeuwarden 17.03.2015, ECLI:NL:GHARL:2015:1920.

83 Case C-191/15, *VKI/Amazon*, ECLI:EU:C:2016:612, para. 71.

84 Rb. Oost-Brabant 20.01.2016, ECLI:NL:RBOBR:2016:232; Rb. Rotterdam 23.12.2015, ECLI:NL:RBROT:2015:9586; Rb. Rotterdam 15.10.2014, ECLI:NL:RBROT:2014:8785.

85 e.g. Rb. Den Haag 09.06.2011, ECLI:NL:RBSGR:2011:BR1683; Rb. Maastricht 08.02.2011, ECLI:NL:RBMAA:2011:BP5801.

86 Hof Arnhem-Leeuwarden 17.05.2016, ECLI:NL:GHARL:2016:3792.

87 Rb. Den Haag 10.05.2016, ECLI:NL:RBDHA:2016:5102.

workers, employed by a Portuguese and an English temporary work agency, the court had to determine whether the work carried out by the employees on a Dutch road and tunnel, for which they had concluded a special agreement with their agency, was to be considered temporary in the sense of Article 8(2) Rome I. The court held that the fact that the workers had been employed by the agencies before in other countries was not relevant; the habitual place of work had to be determined solely for the employment contracts in question. It argued that a fixed-term contract does not necessarily imply temporary work. This decision has been criticised,[88] especially since Recital 36 Rome I states that the conclusion of a new employment contract with the employer 'should not preclude the employee from being regarded as carrying out his work in another country temporarily'.

The implications of Article 8(1) Rome I, which aims to protect the employee from a choice of law imposed on him by the employer, are sometimes overlooked. In several cases, courts have accepted a choice of law in the employment contract pursuant to Article 3 Rome I without further ado.[89] In another case, the court (wrongly) paraphrased Article 8(1) by stating that this provision merely makes explicit the fact that parties can choose the law applicable to their employment contract pursuant to Article 3 Rome I. Thus, the court ignored the second sentence of Article 8(1), which states that the choice of law may not deprive the employee of the protection offered by mandatory provisions of the objectively applicable law.[90]

2.5.2. Specific Rules in Rome II

Of the conflict rules for specific torts and delicts in Rome II, Dutch courts have almost exclusively applied Article 6 (unfair competition and restricting competition) and Article 8 (infringement of intellectual property rights). In only one case, which concerned the pollution of surface water as a result of a vessel collision, did the court hold that pursuant to Article 7 juncto 4(1) Rome II Dutch law was applicable as the *lex loci damni*.[91] Article 9 (industrial action) was applied in one case.[92] In addition, Article 5 Rome II was applied once, even

---

88 See E.J.A. Franssen's case note on ECLI:NL:RBDHA:2016:5102 in *Jurisprudentie Arbeidsrecht* 2015/203.

89 Rb. Limburg 25.08.2016, ECLI:NL:RBLIM:2016:7412; Rb. Zwolle 20.01.2010, ECLI:NL:RBZLY:2010:BO9945.

90 Rb. Limburg 29.09.2016, ECLI:NL:RBLIM:2016:8473.

91 Rb. Rotterdam 20.07.2016, ECLI:NL:RBROT:2016:6041. In Rb. Rotterdam 25.11.2015, ECLI:NL:RBROT:2015:8534 and Rb. Rotterdam 30.09.2015, ECLI:NL:RBROT:2015:6864 the court did not refer to Article 7 Rome II even though the cases concerned environmental damage.

92 Rb. Rotterdam 22.04.2015, ECLI:NL:RBROT:2015:3783.

though the court actually should have applied the 1973 Hague Product Liability Convention.[93]

Article 6 Rome II has been applied mostly in cases of unfair competition. In only one case, which concerned cartel damage, did the court make reference to the market rule of Article 6(3) Rome II, even though the Regulation was not temporally applicable to that case.[94] In all other cases, the courts have applied Article 6(1) and (2) Rome II. Two cases concern the taking advantage of a breach of contract, in which the courts (correctly) concluded that the act exclusively affects the interests of one specific competitor and applied Article 6(2) in conjunction with Article 4 Rome II.[95]

Misleading and unlawful comparative advertising is generally considered to affect more than just the interests of only one competitor and thus to fall within the scope of Article 6(1) Rome II.[96] However, in one case, the court failed to apply Article 6 to a claim based on unfair comparative advertising.[97] Instead, it found an implied choice for Dutch law on the basis of Article 14 Rome II. In a case concerning slavish product imitation, the court applied Article 4 instead of Article 6 Rome II.[98]

Article 8 Rome II is most frequently used in relation to copyright infringements.[99] Since intellectual property law is a field with a high degree of harmonisation of law at the international level, the question of concurrence of sources of law arises. An important question in this respect is whether or not the Berne Convention and Paris Convention contain a choice-of-law rule.[100] Both the Dutch Supreme Court and the Court of Appeal of The Hague have answered this question in the affirmative in respect to the Berne Convention.[101] In two cases, the Rotterdam Court of First Instance ruled accordingly, by giving preference to the Berne Convention on the basis of Article 28 Rome II.[102] Other courts have evaded the discussion by assuming that the conflict rule of the

---

93 Rb. Noord-Holland 08.12.2015, ECLI:NL:RBNHO:2015:10485. See above, section 1.2.

94 Rb. Gelderland 24.09.2014, ECLI:NL:RBGEL:2014:6118.

95 Rb. Midden-Nederland 15.07.2015, ECLI:NL:RBMNE:2015:5500; Rb. Almelo 07.03.2012, ECLI:NL:RBALM:2012:BV8702.

96 Rb. Rotterdam 10.06.2013, ECLI:NL:RBROT:2013:CA2928; Hof Den Haag 29.01.2013, ECLI:NL:GHDHA:2013:BZ0458.

97 Rb. Oost-Brabant 17.10.2014, ECLI:NL:RBOBR:2014:6281.

98 Rb. Arnhem 14.09.2012, ECLI:NL:RBARN:2012:BX9527.

99 e.g. Rb. Oost-Brabant 27.02.2015, ECLI:NL:RBOBR:2015:1328; Rb. Amsterdam 24.12.2014, ECLI:NL:RBAMS:2014:9087; Rb. Haarlem 07.12.2011, ECLI:NL:RBHAA:2011:BV6111; Hof Den Haag 12.07.2011, ECLI:NL:GHSGR:2011:BR1364.

100 See also S.J. Schaafsma, 'Rome II: intellectuele eigendom en oneerlijke concurrentie' [2008] *Weekblad voor Privaatrecht, Notariaat en Registratie* 998–1003.

101 HR 13.12.2013, ECLI:NL:HR:2013:1881; Hof Den Haag 22.09.2015, ECLI:NL:GHDHA:2015:2592.

102 Rb. Rotterdam 16.03.2016, ECLI:NL:RBROT:2016:2045; Rb. Rotterdam 20.01.2016, ECLI:NL:RBROT:2016:550.

Convention and Article 8(1) Rome II both lead to the application of the *lex loci protectionis*.[103] Finally, according to some courts, only Article 8(1) Rome II was relevant. Their approach implicitly rejects the view the Conventions contain a choice-of-law rule.[104]

The scope of Article 8 Rome II can give rise to difficulties, as is shown in a decision of 2009. In this case, the court wrongly qualified the law of database protection as *sui generis*, holding a choice by the parties for Dutch law valid pursuant to Article 14 Rome II.[105] In doing so, the court neglected Recital 26 Rome II, which states that the term 'intellectual property rights' of Article 8 Rome II also includes the right for the protection of databases. This means that the court should have determined the applicable law on the basis of this provision, which does not allow for a choice of law.

2.6. RULES APPLICABLE TO NON-CONTRACTUAL OBLIGATIONS OTHER THAN TORTS

The application of the conflict rules for non-contractual obligations other than torts does not appear to be problematic for the courts. In several cases, the courts have relied on the law applicable to the relationship (tort or contract) between the parties closely connected with the unjust enrichment (Article 10(1))[106] or *negotiorum gestio* (Article 11(1)).[107] In some instances, though, the courts have applied the law of the country where parties both have their habitual residence, on the basis of Article 10(2) Rome II.[108]

Only in a few cases has Article 12 Rome II on *culpa in contrahendo* been applied. In these cases, the courts connected the applicable law governing pre-contractual relations to the law which would have been applicable to the

---

103 e.g. Hof Den Haag 02.02.2016, ECLI:NL:GHDHA:2016:217; Hof Den Haag 12.07.2011, ECLI:NL:GHSGR:2011:BR1364. Compare also Rb. Den Haag 22.03.2011, ECLI:NL:RBSGR:2011:BS8763, in which the court argued that the national treatment principle of Article 2 of the Paris Convention for the Protection of Industrial Property can also be regarded as a conflict-of-laws rule for unfair competition. Yet the court held that Article 2 Paris Convention and Article 6(1) Rome II will lead to the same result: application of the law of the country where competitive relations are affected.

104 e.g. Rb. Midden-Nederland 25.03.2015, ECLI:NL:RBMNE:2015:1096; Rb. Haarlem 07.12.2011, ECLI:NL:RBHAA:2011:BV6111.

105 Rb. Amsterdam 01.10.2009, ECLI:NL:RBAMS:2009:BJ9179.

106 Rb. Zeeland-West-Brabant 08.06.2016, ECLI:NL:RBZWB:2016:3515; Rb. Rotterdam 23.05.2014, ECLI:NL:RBROT:2014:4707; Rb. Zwolle 17.09.2012, ECLI:NL:RBZLY:2012:BY1774.

107 Rb. Rotterdam 29.06.2016, ECLI:NL:RBROT:2016:4960; Rb. Rotterdam 07.08.2015, ECLI:NL:RBROT:2015:5907.

108 Rb. Noord-Holland 09.12.2015, ECLI:NL:RBNHO:2015:10691; Rb. Den Haag 22.02.2012, ECLI:NL:RBSGR:2012:BV7139.

contract had it been entered into.[109] Nevertheless, a different approach was adopted in a case in which the plaintiff argued that the defendant's behaviour during negotiations was contrary to the principles of reasonableness and fairness.[110] There can be little doubt that the claim concerned 'a non-contractual obligation arising out of dealings prior to the conclusion of a contract' within the meaning of Article 12 Rome II. The court, however, determined the applicable law on the basis of Article 4(1) Rome II, as the claim was based on tort/delict, thereby arguably overlooking the autonomous characterisation of *culpa in contrahendo* for the purposes of the Rome II Regulation.[111]

2.7. RULES OF SAFETY AND CONDUCT

Article 17 Rome II on rules of safety and conduct, was mentioned in two cases. One case concerned an observation balloon, to be used for surveillance at large events. The balloon, for which the British Civil Aviation Authority had issued an administrative permit, was released in England. The cable attached to the balloon broke, which caused the balloon to float away, all the way to the Netherlands. When it landed, the balloon damaged a high-tension cable. Although the court was concise in its reasoning, it appeared to accept that, pursuant to Article 17 Rome II, the British safety rules applied to the balloon's release.[112]

Another case concerned a person, domiciled in the Netherlands, who got injured in Turkey at a waterslide in a swimming pool. Although the incident took place in Turkey, the court held that the dispute was governed by Dutch law, since parties agreed on the application of Dutch law, including the Dutch rules of safety and conduct. The court explicitly stated that, along with the parties, it assumed the applicability in Turkey of the European safety standard for waterslides.[113] At first sight, it seems peculiar that the court did not determine whether or not Turkey was bound by this European safety standard. Yet, assuming the European safety standard is at least as high as the Turkish standards, it is difficult to argue that the court should have rejected the choice for this standard made by the parties.

---

109 Rb. Midden-Nederland 30.12.2013, ECLI:NL:RBMNE:2013:7419; Hof 's-Hertogenbosch 14.12.2010, ECLI:NL:GHSHE:2010:BO8197; Rb. Rotterdam 21.10.2009, ECLI:NL:RBROT:2009:BK3279.

110 Rb. Gelderland 14.10.2015, ECLI:NL:RBGEL:2015:6306.

111 See Recital 30 of Rome II's preamble.

112 Rb. Rotterdam 19.06.2015, ECLI:NL:RBROT:2015:4199.

113 Rb. Oost-Brabant 02.12.2013, ECLI:NL:RBOBR:2013:6750.

2.8. *RENVOI*

The exclusion of *renvoi* in the Rome I (Article 20) and Rome II Regulation (Article 24) is in line with Dutch national conflicts law (Article 5 of Book 10 DCC). This exclusion also corresponds with the Dutch courts' generally hostile attitude towards *renvoi*.[114] Only in exceptional cases – outside the scope of Rome I and Rome II and their predecessors – has *renvoi* been accepted to correct the result of the conflict rules.[115]

2.9. FOREIGN LAW

As a rule, a Dutch court has to apply the conflict rules as well as the substantive law applicable pursuant to these conflict rules *ex officio*. The application of foreign law on the court's own motion has been the prevailing opinion in case law for many years and has been confirmed in Article 2 of Book 10 DCC. There are, however, some restrictions to this rule. In the first place, the court of appeal is in principle bound by the decision of the lower court in relation to the applicable law, except when one of the parties files a complaint against this decision. The same is true for the court of final appeal: the Dutch Supreme Court cannot determine the applicable law *ex officio*. In addition to this, Article 79 of the Judicial Organisations Act (*Wet op de Rechterlijke Organisatie*) explicitly excludes violation of foreign law from the grounds of cassation. Furthermore, in interim proceedings, the courts may apply Dutch law, when (the contents of) the applicable law cannot be established with reasonable certainty, given the constraints of time.[116] Finally, in a judgment rendered in 2015, the Dutch Supreme Court seems to 'soften' the duty for courts to apply foreign law on their own motion.[117] One could infer from this case that it is up to the parties to inform the court on the contents of foreign law and – possibly – even substantiate this by submitting foreign legislation, case law or literature.

In order to establish the contents of foreign law, courts make use of several sources. They use legislation, case law and handbooks, available in specialised libraries such as the Peace Palace Library in the Hague, and/or Internet sources, including the information made available on the European e-Justice Portal.

---

114 A.P.M.J. Vonken, *Mr. C. Assers handleiding tot de beoefening van het Nederlands burgerlijk recht. 10. Internationaal Privaatrecht. Deel I. Algemeen deel IPR*, Kluwer, Deventer 2013, no. 437.

115 See the Conclusion of Advocate-General Strikwerda 01.10.2004, ECLI:NL:PHR:2004:AP2680, within the context of family law.

116 Rb. Noord-Nederland 01.06.2016, ECLI:NL:RBNNE:2016:2736.

117 HR 16.10.2015, ECLI:NL:HR:2015:3092. See for a critical analysis S.J. Schaafsma's case note, *Jurisprudentie Burgerlijk Procesrecht* 2017/44.

In addition to this, courts turn to one of the institutes specialising in the application of foreign law, such as the International Legal Institute (*Internationaal Juridisch Instituut*, IJI).[118] The more formal route provided for by the European Convention on Information on Foreign Law of the Council of Europe is rarely used, even though the Netherlands is one of the contracting parties.

The court has to determine the contents of foreign law on its own motion, but in practice parties and their lawyers have an important role in this regard. Parties often provide information on the contents of foreign law on their own initiative. The court also invite the parties to deliver this information, although this should not be seen as a court order to provide evidence. The parties' involvement in establishing the contents of foreign law has increased over the past few years. This may be explained by the fact that as of 2010 the Council for the Judiciary no longer bears the responsibility for the costs connected to the IJI providing advice on foreign law. Instead, the courts themselves have to finance 50 per cent of the hourly rate the IJI charges for its advisory service.

In general, Dutch courts do not compromise the universal scope of Rome I and Rome II. On the basis of these Regulations, Dutch courts have applied, inter alia, Singaporean law,[119] Saudi Arabian law,[120] Malaysian law,[121] Costa Rican law,[122] New York law,[123] Ukrainian law,[124] and the law of Greenland.[125] Still, as mentioned in section 2, courts regularly invite parties to make an explicit choice for Dutch law in the course of the proceedings, or derive an implied choice for the law of the Netherlands from the parties' behaviour.

2.10. *ORDRE PUBLIC*

In the cases examined, the public policy exception was rarely invoked. However, in one case involving a claim in tort the court held on the basis of national conflicts law – as Rome II was not applicable due to its temporal scope – that awarding punitive damages on the basis of Israeli law would be contrary to Dutch public policy. The court did not, however, apply the *lex fori*. Instead, it dismissed the claim.[126]

---

118 See e.g. Rb. Gelderland 05.02.2014, ECLI:NL:RBGEL:2014:586, in which the court referred to the Internationaal Juridisch Instituut's questions on the application/interpretation of Swedish contract law.

119 Rb. Rotterdam 01.08.2019, ECLI:NL:RBROT:2019:8191.

120 Hof Den Haag 24.07.2018, ECLI:NL:GHDHA:2018:1718.

121 Rb. Rotterdam 21.09.2016, ECLI:NL:RBROT:2016:7258.

122 Hof Arnhem-Leeuwarden 18.02.2014, ECLI:NL:GHARL:2014:1208.

123 Rb. Limburg 28.05.2014, ECLI:NL:RBLIM:2014:4725, confirmed in Hof 's-Hertogenbosch 06.06.2017, ECLI:NL:GHSHE:2017:2512.

124 Rb. Amsterdam 14.12.2016, ECLI:NL:RBAMS:2016:8264.

125 Rb. Amsterdam 09.06.2011, ECLI:NL:RBAMS:2011:BQ7690.

126 Rb. Utrecht 24.10.2012, ECLI:NL:RBUTR:2012: BY2102.

2.11. COMPENSATION

For a long time, the level of compensation for pecuniary and non-pecuniary damage in the Netherlands was on or even below the average of the other European countries.[127] However, based on more recent case law, an upward trend can be identified, in any event in the compensation of immaterial damage.[128] No conclusions on the sufficiency of compensation for victims in cross-border cases can be drawn from the available information.

2.12. RELATIONS WITH INTERNATIONAL CONVENTIONS

Being the host country of the Hague Conference on Private International Law, the Netherlands is party to many Hague Conventions. In view of the aim of this report, attention will be paid to the problem of concurrence between Rome I and the 1978 Hague Agency Convention, and between Rome II on the one hand and the 1971 Hague Traffic Accidents Convention and the 1973 Hague Product Liability Convention on the other hand.

The problem of concurrence between the Hague Agency Convention and Rome I does not arise in relation to the question whether an agent is able to bind a principal in relation to a third party, as this issue is excluded from Rome I's substantive scope (Article 1(2)(g) Rome I).[129] By contrast, both the relationship between the agent and the principal and the relationship between the agent and the third party fall within the scope of Rome I. Yet in these cases, the Hague Agency Convention should be given precedence pursuant to Article 28 Rome I.[130] The practical implications of this are limited, however. Both Article 6 Hague Agency Convention and Article 4 Rome I will generally refer to the law of the country of the agent's habitual residence. Moreover, both instruments accept party autonomy.

Both the Hague Traffic Accident Convention and the Hague Product Liability Convention take precedence over Rome II. This follows from Article 25 Rome II, and is confirmed in Article 158 of Book 10 DCC.

---

127 See in relation to non-pecuniary loss, inter alia, S.D. Lindenbergh, 'Smartengeld: ontwikkeling en stilstand', *Smartengeld*, ANWB, The Hague 2006, p. 6, 11; L.T. Visscher, 'QALY in de vaststelling van smartengeld bij letsel' [2013] *Tijdschrift voor Vergoeding Personenschade* 94.

128 S.D. Lindenbergh, 'Smartengeld anno 2017' <https://www.smartengeld.nl/pagina/smartengeld-anno-2017>. See also the Bill on Affectionate Damage (*Wetsvoorstel Affectieschade*), *Kamerstukken II* 2014/15, 34257, no. 2, which aims to introduce a legal basis for the compensation for bereavement.

129 Dutch courts determine the applicable law on the basis of Article 11 ff. of the Hague Agency Convention, See e.g. HR 16.09.2016, ECLI:NL:HR:2016:2118; Hof Amsterdam 02.02.2016, ECLI:NL:GHAMS:2016:362; Rb. Overijssel 17.06.2015, ECLI:NL:RBOVE:2015:3123.

130 e.g. Hof Den Haag 23.06.2015, ECLI:NL:GHDHA:2015:3304; Rb. Amsterdam 16.04.2013, ECLI:NL:RBAMS:2013:BZ9386; Rb. Utrecht 25.04.2012, ECLI:NL:RBUTR:2012:BW5342.

In the vast majority of cases,[131] the Hague Traffic Accident Convention and Rome II will refer to the law of the same country, namely the country where the traffic accident took place.[132] Usually, the place of the accident (*locus delicti*, the connecting factor of Article 3 Hague Convention) will also be the place of damage (*locus damni*, the connecting factor of Article 4(1) Rome II).[133] However, divergence between the results is more likely to occur when Article 4 of the Hague Traffic Accident Convention applies, which refers to the internal law of the country where the vehicle is registered.[134] This connecting factor is absent in Rome II. Conversely, the Hague Convention contains no equivalent of Article 4(2) Rome II, referring to the law of the country where both parties have their habitual residence. The question of which party would benefit from the application of Rome II instead of the Convention is not easy to answer. Case law offers two examples in which the conflict rules of the Hague Convention referred to foreign law, whereas, if Article 4(2) Rome II had been applied, Dutch law would have governed the claim.[135] However, in order to establish whether Dutch law actually offers the victim better protection than foreign legal systems, thorough comparative research would be required.

---

131 A search, conducted on 01.05.2018, on the Hague Traffic Accident Convention in 'Legal Intelligence' resulted in 30 cases in which the Convention was applied. In the vast majority of these cases, the application of Rome II would (most probably) have led to the same outcome.

132 e.g. Rb. Midden-Nederland 14.09.2016, ECLI:NL:RBMNE:2016:5346; Rb. Gelderland 23.03.2016, ECLI:NL:RBGEL:2016:1907; Rb. Amsterdam 26.07.2012, ECLI:NL:RBAMS:2012:BX4272.

133 However, in exceptional cases these places can be situated in different countries. In Rb. Zeeland-West-Brabant 17.12.2014, ECLI:NL:RBZWB:2014:8827, a car driver chased a horse and cart. He forced them into the kerb, thereby frightening the horse, which escaped and eventually ran through a glass shop window. Due to this, the horse was severely injured. Although both the accident and the damage occurred in the same country – the Netherlands – this could have been different, especially in view of the fact that the series of events took place in the town of Baarle-Nassau, which is closely linked to the Belgian exclaves of Baarle-Hertog.

134 In Hof Arnhem-Leeuwarden 19.08.2014, ECLI:NL:GHARL:2014:6502, concerning an accident in Scotland between motorbikes, the court held that Dutch law was applicable as the internal law of the country of registration (Article 4(a) and (b) Hague Traffic Accident Convention). However, as both parties where domiciled in the Netherlands, the application of Rome II, more specifically Article 4(2), would probably have led to the same result.

135 See Hof 's-Hertogenbosch 15.04.2003, ECLI:NL:GHSHE:2003:AF7941 and Hof Arnhem 18.05.2004, ECLI:NL:GHARN:2004:AP0037. The first case concerned a traffic accident in Indonesia with a rented car (registered in Indonesia). Pursuant to the Hague Traffic Accident Convention, Indonesian law, being the law of the country of the accident, applied. The result under Rome II would (probably) have been different, as both the person claimed to be liable and the victim were domiciled in the Netherlands. Pursuant to Article 4(2) Rome II, Dutch law would have been applicable, assuming that the court would not find Indonesia manifestly more closely connected with the tort (Article 4(3) Rome II). The second case concerned an accident in Turkey that involved a car registered in the Netherlands and a motorbike registered in Turkey. Pursuant to Article 3 Hague Traffic Accident Convention, Turkish law was applicable. Again, the result would have been different under Rome II as both the person whose liability was claimed (the insurance company) and the victim were habitually resident in the Netherlands.

Case law in which the Hague Product Liability Convention has been applied is scarce. Hence, it is difficult to draw general conclusions as to whether the solutions are truly different from the possible results of applying Rome II.[136] One case, however, shows that the fact that the connecting factors of Articles 4 and 5 of the Hague Convention, on the one hand, and Article 5 Rome II, on the other hand, diverge raises questions as to the scope of the latter provision.[137] The case concerned an employee (domiciled in the Netherlands) of a Dutch company who was posted to work for a Belgian company. One day, the employee was injured after the heavy door of the cabin in which the employee carried out his work fell down and hit his foot. The Dutch employer filed a damages claim against the Belgian company, submitting that the Belgian company produced and installed the cabin, and therefore was liable on the basis of product liability. On appeal, the court held that, pursuant to Article 4(b) of the Hague Product Liability Convention, Belgian law was applicable since the accident occurred in Belgium, which was also the principal place of business of the company claimed to be liable. However, the court made a reservation by adding that this was true 'insofar as the claim falls within the Convention's substantive scope'.[138] Judging by the wording of the Hague Convention, it is not unlikely that the claim indeed falls within the Convention's scope. Conversely, it is highly doubtful that the claim also falls within the substantive scope of Article 5 Rome II. After all, this provision attaches importance to the question of where the product was marketed, and the product in question (the cabin) was not marketed in any country. Presuming Article 5 Rome II would not apply, the applicable law has to be determined on the basis of Article 4 Rome I, which in this case would probably refer to Belgian law since the (initial) damage occurred in Belgium. Hence, the application of Rome II in this case would probably have led to the same outcome as the application of the Hague Product Liability Convention.

3. GENERAL EVALUATION AND CONCLUSION

It appears from the Dutch case law that the transition from the Rome Convention to the Rome I Regulation has caused few problems. Courts generally understand the functioning of the new Article 4 Rome I, including the list of the eight specific contracts in Article 4(1). The substitution of the Dutch Conflict

136 In Rb. Noord-Holland 08.12.2015, ECLI:NL:RBNHO:2015:10485, the court erroneously applied Article 5 Rome II, instead of Article 5 of the Hague Product Liability Convention. The application of the Hague Convention would nonetheless have led to the same result.

137 Hof 's-Hertogenbosch 02.12.2014, ECLI:NL:GHSHE:2014:5073.

138 *Ibid.*, para. 3.7.

of Laws (Torts) Act with Rome II was not problematic either. This can be attributed to the fact that the provisions of the Act are very similar to the Rome II provisions.[139]

In the majority of cases, Dutch courts do not encounter major difficulties when applying the Rome I and Rome II Regulations. Often, the courts accept a choice of law by the parties – made either in advance or during the proceedings, and either explicit or implicit. Although in most cases examined the courts ultimately applied Dutch law, the courts generally respect both their duty to apply the conflict rules of the Regulations *ex officio* and the universal scope of the Regulation. When the conflict rules of Rome I or Rome II refer to a foreign legal system, the court will apply this law on its own motion, although in practice parties often take the initiative to inform the court of the content of foreign law. Moreover, the exact scope of this duty has been called into question following a decision of the Dutch Supreme Court.[140]

The case law examined shows that courts sometimes make mistakes, however. In some instances, courts have ignored the precedence of a specific convention over the Rome II Regulation. A more common mistake is applying a general provision instead of the conflict rule that specifically regulates the law applicable to the contract, delict or quasi-delict in question. This can have significant implications, for example where the court accepts a choice of law in cases where the European legislator actually ruled out or limited party autonomy.

The abovementioned errors do not seem to point to structural problems in the application of the Regulations. They do, however, show that judges are occasionally not fully aware of the basics of European conflicts law. A possible explanation is that, in recent decades, most Dutch law schools have decreased the role of private international law in their educational programmes, despite the expansion of national, European and international legislation in this area of law. Continuing training of the judiciary, as well as the reinstatement of the position of private international law in the university curriculums, is therefore recommended.

Questions of a more fundamental nature relate to the application of Article 4(1) Rome II, which refers to the law of the country where the damage occurred. The first issue concerns the way in which courts apply this provision in purely economic loss cases, such as cases regarding investment losses. Case law shows the courts' current readiness to locate the place of damage at the place where the victim holds a bank account and is domiciled. However, the European case law casts certain doubts with regard to the correctness of this approach, since the CJEU – within the context of (now) Article 7(2) Brussels I *bis*

---

139 See also J.A. van der Weide, 'Het verwijzingsrecht voor niet-contractuele verbintenissen Europees geregeld. Een analyse van de Verordening Rome II' [2008] *Nederlands Tijdschrift voor Europees Recht* 214, 225.

140 See above, section 2.9.

Regulation – has held that purely financial damage which occurs directly in the applicant's bank account is not, in itself, a 'relevant connecting factor' for establishing jurisdiction, even when the victim is domiciled in the country where the bank account is held.[141] Nevertheless, the CJEU does not offer a ready-made alternative solution. In this context, reference can be made to a recent case concerning investment losses, where the Court of Rotterdam held that the place where the damage occurred was located at the place of the market on which the financial instruments were purchased.[142]

The second issue concerns the application of Article 4(1) Rome II in defamation cases. In order to establish the place of damage within the meaning of this provision, in 2016 the Dutch Supreme Court imported the 'centre-of-the-victim's-interests' criterion from CJEU case law. The 2016 case raises the question whether this criterion, developed within the context of the EU jurisdiction rules, is also appropriate for determining the applicable law in a defamation case, especially in view of the universal scope of the Rome II Regulation. There is a risk that a Dutch court will have to apply strict foreign defamation laws to claims against journalists, bloggers, etc., domiciled in the Netherlands.[143] This could result in a decision by a Dutch court stating that a publication is wrongful, whereas pursuant to Dutch law the publication is permitted. Evidently, the issue touches on fundamental principles underlying the Dutch legal order, in particular the freedom of expression. The public policy exception could possibly be used to correct an undesirable result, but given the narrow scope of this exception it is doubtful whether it is sufficient to avert the danger.

It should be noted that, at first glance, the European legislature is not to blame in this matter. After all, by excluding defamation from Rome II's the substantive scope it has made clear the Regulation's provisions do not apply to this field of law. The aforementioned risk is first and foremost a consequence of the fact that the Dutch legislature has extended the scope of Rome II, in combination with the way in which the Dutch Supreme Court interpreted the 'place of damage' within the context of Article 4(1) Rome II. Still, the problem would presumably not have occurred if either the Rome II Regulation had been applicable in defamation cases, particularly if it had contained a specific conflict rule on defamation. This is something to consider in preparation for the reform of Rome II. Alternatively, a provision explicitly dealing with the question of the law applicable in defamation cases could be introduced at the national level.

---

141 Case C-12/15, *Universal Music International Holding BV v. Michael Tétreault Schilling and Others*, ECLI:EU:C:2016:449, para. 38. See also Case C-168/02, *Rudolf Kronhofer v. Marianne Maier et al.*, ECLI:EU:C:2004:364, para. 21.

142 Rb. Rotterdam 29.01.2020, ECLI:NL:RBROT:2020:614. See also L.M. van Bochove's case note in *Ondernemingsrecht* 2020/49.

143 See M. Teekens's case note on ECLI:NL:HR:2016:1054 in *Jurisprudentie in Nederland* 2016/155.

Finally, attention should be paid to two new challenges for the European and/or national legislature, namely the rise of collective actions and the increasing importance attached to the concept of international corporate social responsibility.

Dutch law contains several provisions that provide for a remedy in mass damages cases. The Dutch Collective Settlements Act (*Wet Collectieve Afwikkelingen Massaschade*, WCAM), which entered into force on 27 July 2005, arranges for collective redress in mass damages on the basis of a settlement agreement binding all persons covered by its terms, except for those who choose to opt out. Over the past years, the private international law aspects of the Dutch provisions on collective redress have received considerable attention in scholarship.[144] The research focuses, however, mainly on international jurisdiction and recognition and enforcement. The role of the question of the applicable law is considered a matter of much less importance. This is especially true for WCAM settlements, which usually contain a choice-of-law clause.[145] In addition to the WCAM, Article 305a of Book 3 DCC contains a legal basis for representative collective action. This provision raises profound questions from a private international law perspective. In a recent case, the Court of Rotterdam held that the fact that the proceedings are instituted on the basis of Article 305a of Book 3 DCC, does not affect the determination of the applicable law on the basis of Article 4(1) Rome II.[146] Yet, this decision appears to be a bit premature, considering that, in the context of the question of jurisdiction, the Dutch Supreme Court deemed it necessary to request a preliminary ruling from the CJEU to clarify the relation between Article 305a of Book 3 DCC and Article 7(2) Brussels I *bis* Regulation.[147] In view of the recently extended scope of Article 305a of Book 3 DCC to pecuniary damages claims,[148] it is likely that in future the courts will increasingly encounter problems in relation to the applicable law in mass damages cases. Related to the topic of collective actions is the consolidation of claims for damages assigned to and brought before a

---

144 See, inter alia, T.M.C. Arons and W.H. van Boom, 'Beyond Tulips and Cheese: Exporting Mass Securities Claim Settlements from the Netherlands' [2010] *European Business Law Review* 857–883; H. van Lith, *The Dutch Collective Settlements Act and Private International Law*, Maklu, Apeldoorn 2011; A. Halfmeier, 'Recognition of a WCAM settlement in Germany' [2012] *Nederlands Internationaal Privaatrecht* 176–184; N. Peters and M.H. ten Wolde, 'De Wet collectieve afwikkeling massaschade: wat is zij waard in het buitenland?' [2013] *Nederlands Tijdschrift voor Burgerlijk Recht* 3–14; M.W.F. Bosters, *Collective redress and private international law in the European Union. Issues regarding jurisdiction and the recognition and enforcement of judgments in cross-border mass disputes relating to financial services*, T.M.C. Asser Press/Springer, The Hague 2016.

145 See Van Lith, above n. 144, pp. 137–139.

146 Rb. Rotterdam 29.01.2020, ECLI:NL:RBROT:2020:614.

147 See request for a preliminary ruling from the Hoge Raad der Nederlanden, lodged on 25 September 2019, Case C-709/19, *Vereniging voor Effectenbezitters*.

148 Wet afwikkeling massaschade in collectieve actie, *Stb.* 2019, 130.

court by a 'litigation vehicle'. A recent judgment concerning consolidated cartel damages claims[149] illustrates the complexities of determining the applicable law in such a case. As Rome II was inapplicable *ratio temporis*, the Court of Amsterdam had to apply the national conflict rules which referred to the law of the country of the affected market – just as per Article 6(3)(a) Rome II. However, the court held that, in this case, the application of the market criterion would lead to an undesirable dispersion of the applicable law and opted for a more practical solution: to apply the *lex fori* instead. While it is unlikely that the CJEU would approve such a solution under Rome II, the case does cast doubt on the suitability of the current connecting factors, such as the place of damage and the affected market, to determine the law applicable to consolidated claims.[150] Consequently, it is recommended that these issues be addressed during the preparations for the reform of Rome II.

A second issue that deserves further consideration is that of the legal duties in relation to human rights of EU-based companies who pursue business activities in developing countries (international corporate social responsibility). Under certain conditions, the general provisions of Dutch tort law provide for a legal basis to hold companies responsible for human rights violations committed in the course of their business activities or those of their subsidiaries or supply chain partners. However, it raises the question of the extent to which Dutch courts can apply Dutch legislation, especially in view of the fact that in the vast majority of cases the *locus damni* will be situated in the developing country, which may not provide possibilities for legal redress.[151] Therefore, it is recommended that the European legislature examines the possibilities of introducing a provision that specifically deals with the applicable law question in relation to non-contractual liability arising out of extra-territorial human rights violations committed within the context of business activities.[152]

---

149 Rb. Amsterdam 01.05.2019, ECLI:NL:RBAMS:2019:3393.

150 See L.M. van Bochove, 'Het toepasselijk recht op gebundelde kartelschadeclaims. Van mozaïek tot Rubik's Cube' [2020] *Maandblad voor Ondernemingsrecht* 9–15.

151 In three much-debated judgments of 18.01.2015, The Hague Court of Appeal accepted jurisdiction in cases brought by Nigerian residents and a Dutch environmental association against Shell for environmental damage caused in Nigeria by Shell's subsidiaries, see ECLI:NL:GHDHA:2015:3586, ECLI:NL:GHDHA:2015:3587 and ECLI:NL:GHDHA:2015:3588. The court held that pursuant to the Dutch Conflict of Laws (Torts) Act (Rome II was inapplicable *ratione temporis*) Nigerian law applied to the claims. Yet it should not be ruled out that the claims would succeed under Nigerian common law; see C. de Groot, 'The "Shell Nigeria Issue": Judgments by the Court of Appeal of The Hague, The Netherlands' [2016] *European Company Law* 98–104.

152 See also L. Enneking et al., 'Zorgplichten van Nederlandse ondernemingen inzake internationaal maatschappelijk verantwoord ondernemen. Een rechtsvergelijkend en empirisch onderzoek naar de stand van het Nederlandse recht in het licht van de UN Guiding Principles' <https://www.wodc.nl/binaries/2531-volledige-rapport_tcm28-73868.pdf>, p. 453.

THE APPLICATION OF THE ROME I AND ROME II REGULATIONS IN POLAND

Marcin CZEPELAK*

1. THE NATIONAL LANDSCAPE

Poland began to codify private international law just after regaining its independence after World War I (1914–1918).[1] Having been divided between the three occupying forces – Russia, Germany and Austria – in 1918 Poland

* Dr hab. Marcin Czepelak is a member of the Chair of Private International Law at the Faculty of Law and Administration of the Jagiellonian University in Kraków. The views and opinions expressed in this chapter are those of the author and shall not be understood as reflecting the official policy or position of institution the author has the honour of representing.

1 For further reading see: Adam Zamoyski, *Poland: A history*, Harper Collins Publishers, London 2015; Norman Davies, *God's Playground: A History of Poland, vol. II: 1975 to the Present*, revised ed., Oxford University Press, Oxford 2005.

had, roughly speaking,[2] three systems of civil law based on the French Civil Code,[3] the German Civil Code (BGB) and the Austrian Civil Code (ABGB). As the unification of these systems seemed to be a rather lengthy process, on 2 August 1926 two parallel laws were simultaneously enacted: the Act on Private International Law and the Act on Private Interlocal Law. The former was directed at the conflict of laws in the international dimension; the latter, the internal. They were complex modern codifications, highly appreciated in Poland and abroad, which shaped the Polish approach to the conflict of laws.

After World War II, Poland under Soviet occupation found herself behind the 'Iron Curtain'. In spite of that, the Act on Private International Law of 12 November 1965 was indeed anything but socialist law based on the Marxist ideology. On the contrary, it in fact resembled the codifications enacted in Western Europe in the 1970s and 1980s.[4]

The Polish Act on Private International Law of 4 February 2011 (Polish PIL Act of 2011) currently in force thus constitutes the third generation of Polish acts on conflict of laws.[5] It was, however, enacted after the EU had already shaped contemporary private international law. The centre of gravity for private international law in Poland had clearly already shifted from Warsaw to Brussels, which made it doubtful whether the attempt at national codification was the appropriate response to the process of 'creeping codification' that had been commenced and advanced by the EU.[6] In any case, there is the urgent problem of coordination between various sources of private international law.

The Polish private international law is composed of three different kinds of sources: firstly, EU Regulations, among them Rome I and Rome II; secondly, international conventions; and thirdly, the Polish PIL Act of 2011 and some other national laws. The key issue is how to coordinate these various sources.

What makes this problem more difficult in the case of Poland is the significant number of international conventions in the field of private international law to which Poland is a party. These include not only multilateral conventions concluded in the framework of the Hague Conference on Private International

2 On some parts of the Polish territory, the Hungarian law and the Russian X volume of 'Collection of Laws' had briefly been in force.

3 The French *Code Civil* – in Poland called the Code of Napoleon – had been in force in the Duchy of Warsaw, established by Napoleon in 1807, and after the Congress of Vienna in 1815 it remained in force in Polish lands occupied by Russia. For further reading see: Adam Zamoyski, *Rites of Peace: The Fall of Napoleon and the Congress of Vienna*, Harper Collins Publishers, London 2008.

4 Andrzej Mączyński, 'Polish Private International Law' (2005) VI *Yearbook of Private International Law* 203–220.

5 Tomasz Pajor, 'Introduction to the New Polish Act on Private International of 4 February 2011' (2011) XIII *Yearbook of Private International Law* 381–388.

6 Marcin Czepelak, 'Would We Like to Have a European Code of Private International Law?' (2010) 18(4) *European Review of Private Law* 705–728.

Law, but also numerous bilateral conventions. In the main, those concluded by Poland with other EU Member States have been superseded by the EU law. Those concluded with non-Member States (Ukraine, Belarus, Russia, Vietnam, Mongolia) need to be carefully interpreted, as it often remains unclear to which instrument priority should be given.

Article 93 of the Polish Constitution of 2 April 1997 enables the law of the EU to be applied directly in Poland. Accordingly, the Rome I and Rome II Regulations have binding force resulting directly from the Polish Constitution and from the Treaty Establishing the European Union. Nevertheless, in the Polish PIL Act of 2011, there are some provisions 'reminding' courts about EU Regulations and the international conventions. Two such provisions aim at the application of the Rome I and Rome II Regulations. Firstly, Article 28(1) of the Polish PIL Act of 2011 reads as follows: 'The law applicable to the contractual obligations shall be determined by the Regulation (EC) No. 593/2008 of the European Parliament and of the Council of 17 June 2008 on the law applicable to contractual obligations (Rome I)'. Secondly, Article 33 of the Polish PIL Act of 2011 states that 'the law applicable to the obligation arising from the event other than a legal act shall be determined by the Regulation (EC) Regulation (EC) No. 864/2007 of the European Parliament and of the Council of 11 July 2007 on the law applicable to non-contractual obligations (Rome II)'. A couple of similar provisions refer to other EU Regulations and international conventions concluded in the framework of the Hague Conference on Private International Law.

Although such provisions do not have binding force (i.e. the role of international conventions and the EU law has already been decided by the Polish Constitution), the Polish courts tend to invoke these provisions as if they provided the legal basis for the application of the Rome I and Rome II Regulations. However, as the Supreme Court aptly put it in a judgment on 23 May 2013,[7] the Rome I and Rome II Regulations would be applicable even if Article 28(1) and Article 33 of the Polish PIL Act had not been enacted at all.

The Polish PIL Act of 2011 interacts in several circumstances with the Rome I and Rome II Regulations. Firstly, Article 28(2) of the Polish PIL Act of 2011 refer to the matters excluded from the scope of application of the Rome I Regulation under Article 1(2)(j), stating that Rome I shall be nevertheless applied to these matters.

Secondly, there are two additional rules concerning insurance contracts that need to be taken into account together with Article 7 Rome I. According to Article 29(1) of the Polish PIL Act of 2011, insurance contracts shall be governed by Polish law if the law relating to a particular field requires compulsory insurance. The same rule applies under Article 29(2) of the Polish PIL Act of 2011 in cases where the law of a Member State of the European Economic Area requires compulsory insurance.

---

7 Case II CSK 250/12.

Thirdly, Article 30(1) of the Polish PIL Act of 2011 establishes some limitations of the choice of law for consumer contracts in cases not covered by the Rome I Regulation. Accordingly, a choice of law of a country that is not a Member State of the European Economic Area for a contract that has a close connection with the territory of at least one Member State shall not deprive the consumer of the protection granted by Polish law implementing the following Directives:

1. Council Directive 93/13/EEC of 5 April 1993 on unfair terms in consumer contracts;
2. Directive 97/7/EC of the European Parliament and of the Council of 20 May 1997 on the protection of consumers in respect of distance contracts;
3. Directive 1999/44/EC of the European Parliament and of the Council of 25 May 1999 on certain aspects of the sale of consumer goods and associated guarantees;
4. Directive 2002/65/EC of the European Parliament and of the Council of 23 September 2002 concerning the distance marketing of consumer financial services and amending Council Directive 90/619/EEC and Directives 97/7/EC and 98/27/EC;
5. Council Directive 87/102/EEC of 22 December 1986 for the approximation of the laws, regulations and administrative provisions of the Member States concerning consumer credit; Polish Special Edition: Ch. 15, Vol. 1, p. 326.

Fourthly, Article 30(2) of the Polish PIL Act of 2011 concerns contracts within the scope of Directive 2008/122/EC of 14 January 2009 on the protection of consumers in respect of certain aspects of timeshare, long-term holiday product, resale and exchange contracts.[8] In cases where the law applicable to such a contract is the law of a non-Member State of the European Economic Area, the consumer shall not be deprived of the protection granted by the Polish law implementing the Directive, provided that:

1. any such immovables are situated within the territory of one of the Member States, or
2. if the contract not directly related to the immovable, the professional carries on his business or profession in a Member State, or by any means directs such activities to a Member State, and the contract falls within the scope of this activity.

The Polish legislator did not decide to broaden the scope of the Rome I and Rome II Regulations extensively. For example Article 32 of the Polish PIL Act of 2011

[8] [2009] OJ L 33/10.

establishes an autonomous rule on the law applicable to unilateral judicial acts and does not refer to the solutions adopted in the Rome I Regulation.

There are two important conflict-of-laws rules that come into operation in the areas excluded from the scope of application of the Rome II Regulation. The first concerns defamation, the other responsibility of public authorities.

Article 16 of the Polish PIL Act of 2011 reads as follows:

> '1. The rights of personality of a natural person shall be governed by the law of his nationality.
>
> 2. The natural person whose rights of personality are threatened by the violation or have been adversely affected may claim protection under the law of the country in whose territory the event giving rise to the risk of infringement or to the violation took place, or under the law of the country in whose territory the effects of the infringement occurred.
>
> 3. If the breach of rights of personality of a natural person took place in the mass media, the right to reply, correction, or other similar safeguard measures shall be subject to the law of the country in which the broadcaster or publisher is established or has his habitual residence.'[9]

Finally, according to Article 35 of the Polish PIL Act of 2011, civil liability for the acts and omissions of state organs with public authority shall be governed by the law of that state.

In the various legal databases there are altogether around 300 decisions of Polish courts mentioning either the Rome I or Rome II Regulations, or both.[10] This is the number of judgments published in the official as well as commercial sources, yet the real number must be considered to be higher, as not all cases are published. It is important to note that this statistic encompasses all levels of so-called 'common courts' (i.e. district courts, regional courts, courts of appeal and the Supreme Court), as well as the administrative courts (i.e. regional administrative courts and the Supreme Administrative Court). The number of arbitral awards applying the Rome I and Rome II Regulations remains unknown, as arbitral awards are not published.

In the published cases, in which the Rome I and Rome II Regulations are mentioned, Polish courts did not apply these Regulations in every case. On many occasions, courts only noted that the Regulations are in force, but that the case had to be decided on the basis of the provision which were no longer binding (for example the Polish PIL Act of 1965, or the Rome Convention if the contract was concluded before 17 December 2009).

---

9 Translation: Mateusz Pilich and Andrzej W. Wiśniewski, 2012.

10 The case law of the courts is published by the Polish Ministry of Justice at the website: <www.orzeczenia.ms.gov.pl>; the Supreme Court publishes its case law at the website: <www.sn.pl/orzecznictwo/>. All cases quoted in this article are accessible there.

The first most commonly applied provision is Article 3 Rome I, as the courts start the conflict-of-laws analysis by checking whether there was a choice-of-court agreement. This is often the case if one party relies on the general terms and conditions of the contract. Separately from the question whether the choice-of-law agreement has or has not been effectively concluded, the courts decide on the issue of the scope of such clauses.

The second most commonly applied provision is Article 4 Rome II. First and foremost, Article 4(1) is invoked to designate the law of the place of damage as concerns the determination of the law applicable to responsibility in tort. However, the Polish courts have also considered whether to apply the escape clause from Article 4(3). In some cases they did it, in other cases not. Article 4(2) was also invoked in one case (an accident in a coal-mine in the Czech Republic where the claimant was a worker with habitual residence in Poland and the defendant was his employer, a company with its seat in Poland).

The third most commonly applied provision is probably Article 17 Rome I. It is quite common in cases where the plaintiff claims that the defendant failed to pay, for the latter to invoke its application.

The fourth most commonly applied provision is Article 18 Rome II, as quite often in cases of road accidents the claim is brought directly against the insurer.[11] Conversely, in several cases it was the insurer who sued the person responsible for the accident, which meant, in turn, that Article 19 came into operation.

The fifth most commonly applied provision is probably Article 4 Rome I (taken together with Article 4 Rome Convention), designating the law applicable to the contract in the absence of a choice made by the parties.

The number of cases in which Polish courts should have applied either Rome I or Rome II (but did not do) cannot be precisely identified, because some courts might have ignored the foreign element and adjudicated by simply applying Polish law. If there is no appeal against such a judgment, in which a party claims that the foreign law should have been applied, it is quite possible for this problem to go unnoticed. On the other hand, an important part of the published case law is that these are judgments rendered by the courts in cases in which the appeal was based on the reproach of the court's non-application of foreign law. Accordingly, it is impossible to determine all the cases, in which parties were satisfied with the application of the Polish law, although Polish courts should have applied foreign law on the basis of either Rome I or Rome II.

There are however a few cases where it is clear that the court had a problem with the scope of application of the Rome I or Rome II Regulations. In terms of the scope of application *ratione temporis*, Polish courts have been able to deal

11 The application of Article 18 of the Rome II Regulation can be also triggered by Articles 13(2) and 11(1)(b) of the Brussels I bis Regulation: Judgment of the Supreme Court of 22 March 2019, case IV CSK 417/17.

with the somewhat obscure wording of Article 31 and 32 Rome II. As far as the scope *ratione loci* is concerned, in at least one case the Court of Appeal in Białystok[12] applied Danish law, invoking the Rome Convention instead of the Rome I Regulation. The court was clearly confused by the fact that it had to apply the law of a state in which the Rome I Regulation was not in force. This is why the Rome Convention, which was in force in Denmark, came into operation. Surely, the Danish law would be applicable under the Rome I Regulation as well. Nevertheless, it is rather unusual for the Polish courts to misunderstand the concept of the universal application of the Rome I and Rome II Regulations.[13]

2. THE OPERATION OF ROME I AND ROME II IN PRACTICE

2.1. *LOIS DE POLICE*

Despite the fact that the so-called *lois de police*, or *lois d'application necessaire*, have become a highly disputed object of doctrinal debate, it seems that the Polish courts could have lived without the explicit provision on that issue. The concept as such was certainly known before the Rome I Regulation and the Rome Convention came into operation in Poland, but there is a clear discrepancy between how much attention is paid to this problem in legal writing and how often it is the question at issue in court proceedings.

In fact, the only example of this problem where the internationally mandatory rules were at issue concerned the posted workers and Directive 96/71/EC. In a series of more than ten similar reported cases, Polish courts considered that:

> 'This directive obliged the EU Member States to enact in their national legal systems the unilateral conflict-of-laws rules designating the law of the Member State to which the worker was delegated by a service provider as applicable to each condition of employment outlined in Article 3.1. of the said directive. The directive 96/71/EC did not leave any margin of appreciation to the Member States in that context. In all Member States of the European Union the national provision of the labour law regulating the condition of the employment mention in Article 3.1. of the directive 96/71/EC constitute *lois de police*'.[14]

---

12 Judgment of 4 April 2017, joint cases: I ACa 442/16 and IACz 587/16.

13 For example, it clearly follows from the Judgment of the Supreme Court of 25 June 2019, case I CZ 48/19, that the conflict-of-laws rules established by Rome I are universal, so that they can determine the law of the state where it is not in force (in this case – the law of the State of New York) as applicable.

14 See for example the judgment of the Court of Appeal in Wrocław of 27 March 2012, joint cases: III APa 32/10 and III Apz 20/10.

The Polish courts misuse neither Article 9 Rome I nor Article 16 Rome II. Despite what may have been feared, the concept of the *loi de police* has not served as 'a shortcut' to the *lex fori*. In any case, it is not the definition, as such, that could be problematic. Nor does the lack of such a definition in Rome II constitute a problem in legal practice, as there is no doubt that the Rome I and Rome II Regulations, together with the amended Brussels I *bis* Regulation, must be interpreted as 'three complementary instruments'.[15] Accordingly, it is clear in Polish legal doctrine that the definition set out in Article 9(1) of Rome I applies equally to Rome II.

Even before Rome I, or indeed the Rome Convention, entered into force, Polish courts had in several cases declared some provisions of financial law to be *lois d'application necessaire*. This was the case for some limitations on the currency exchange, namely the requirement to obtain special permission for specific transactions, without which such contracts should be declared void.

Also undisputable is the international mandatory character of provisions regulating transactions concerning military equipment, explosives, etc., or provisions aiming at the protection of national cultural heritage. Some authors also argue that the special provision establishing the highest interest rate is a *loi de police* as well.

Finally, there is no reported case law in which Polish courts have applied the *lois de police* on the basis of Article 16 Rome II.

The above-mentioned case law concerning the national labour law provisions implementing Directive 96/71/EC brought some problems to light. If a Polish worker is employed in Poland (i.e. he performs his work in Poland), then his contract is governed by Polish law. When such a worker is sent to work in another Member State, its provisions implementing Directive 96/71/EC must be applied as *lois de police*. Accordingly, a Polish court must consider them to be *lois de police* of the third state. According to the wording of Article 9(3) Rome I, such rules must be taken into consideration if they make the contract void. This is, however, not the case for the provisions implementing Directive 96/71/EC, as they do not make the contract void but change its terms instead, meaning that the standard foreseen by the Directive applies in its place. Accordingly, if the courts had followed the literal interpretation, they could have not applied such rules. They did so, however, in those cases where the Rome Convention was applicable and not Rome I, so that the court was not faced with the somewhat rigid wording of Article 9(3) Rome I. This example clearly demonstrates that the said provision might be in need of some improvement.

---

15 Green Paper on the conversion of the Rome Convention of 1980 on the law applicable to contractual obligations into a Community instrument and its modernisation, COM/2002/0654 final, at 1.3.

2.2. PARTY AUTONOMY

It has already been mentioned that Article 3 of Rome I (as its predecessor – Article 3 of the Rome Convention), which is the pillar of party autonomy in EU private international law, is the most commonly applied provision. Polish courts took note of the construction guideline established in point 12 of the Preamble to Rome I.[16] The Supreme Court pointed out that a court can imply the choice of law from a choice of agreement fulfilling the requirements set out in the Article 25 of the Brussels I *bis* Regulation, but it cannot be implied the other way around.[17] Whilst deciding this case, the Polish Supreme Court referred to the case *Sherdley v. Nordea.*[18]

As expected, choice-of-law clauses are often a matter of construction as to what the clause effectively means. The most common scenario is when the court applies Polish law because the parties have agreed that 'in matters not covered by the contract the Polish Civil Code applies'.[19]

Whether a choice-of-law clause can be interpreted as ruling out the application of the New York Convention on the Limitation Period in the International Sale of Goods of 1974 is equally a matter of construction. It is possible only if intention clearly results from the clause, because this Convention forms part of the Polish legal system. In other words, if parties chose the Polish law as applicable, they have chosen the Polish legal system and not merely the Polish Civil Code.[20]

Overall, there is no evidence in Polish case law suggesting that Article 3(1) of Rome I needs to be amended. On the one hand, *dépeçage* is very seldom (if at all) inserted into the choice-of-law clauses. On the other hand, it is very unlikely that parties would decide to choose the *lex mercatoria*, unless they also conclude an arbitration agreement.

Choice-of-law agreements are unlikely as far as the extra-contractual obligations are at stake. If parties are willing to settle the case, they negotiate the amount of compensation rather than the choice-of-law agreement. Moreover, in

---

16 'An agreement between the parties to confer on one or more courts or tribunals of a Member State exclusive jurisdiction to determine disputes under the contract should be one of the factors to be taken into account in determining whether a choice of law has been clearly demonstrated'.

17 Judgment of the Supreme Court of 23 March 2018, case I CSK 363/17, (OSNC 2019/2/20).

18 *Sherdley & Anor v. Nordea Life and Pension SA (Societe Anonyme)* [2012] EWCA Civ 88.

19 For example, Judgment of the Supreme Court of 31 January 2019, case III PK 64/19. However, in this case one can see a problem of autonomous qualification. The issue at dispute was whether the parties to a contract labelled as the 'contract for performance of the specific task' had actually entered into the employment contract. Accordingly, it was necessary to apply either Article 3 or Article 8 of the Rome I Regulation, depending on the qualification of this contract. The Supreme Court found that the parties had implicitly chosen the Polish law, only after having the Polish law applied to determine that under the Polish law it would have been the contract of employment.

20 Judgment of the Supreme Court of 24 November 2017, case III CZP 73/17.

order to conclude such an agreement one must assume that there is a risk of the event giving rise to the damage. Therefore, it is realistic only in connection with the choice-of-law agreement for the contract.[21] For the time being, the above-mentioned issues are discussed by the legal doctrine rather than by the courts.

2.3. ABSENCE OF CHOICE OF LAW

The Polish PIL Act of 1965, in force before the Rome Convention came into operation in Poland, established a set of fixed conflict-of-law rules similar to the rules set forth by Rome I. Moreover, Polish courts tended to interpret Article 4 of the Convention not in the same way the English courts did. Accordingly, Polish courts, underlying the need to ensure predictability, adhered to the rules established by Article 4 of Rome I.

In relation to Article 4(1) Rome II, only the localisation of the place of direct damage becomes the question at issue. What the Polish courts would do in case of financial fraud remains to be seen in the future.

There is no reported Polish case law directly concerning a situation of multiple tortfeasors (Article 4(2) Rome II). Were this to arise, the response would be probably that Article 4(2) comes into operation only in situations where all tortfeasors and the victim have habitual residence in the same state.

2.4. ESCAPE CLAUSES

It suffices to say that Polish courts have been able to strike a fair balance between the fixed conflict-of-law rules and the escape clauses. There is no evidence of excessive use of such provisions, which by their very nature must be applied exceptionally. Although Polish courts apply the escape clauses on a case-by-case basis, and so it is not possible to categorise typical situations where this happens, there have been some cases in which the escape clauses came into operation.

For example, in its judgment on 5 February 2015,[22] the Supreme Court applied Article 4(3) Rome II in legal proceedings brought by the insurer against the insured. The latter, a company established in Poland, had entered into a contract with a German enterprise. The Polish company was to perform construction work on a site in Germany. Part of this commitment was carried out by a subcontractor, a Polish entrepreneur, who caused an accident that damaged some of the German company's technical equipment. The insurer brought a claim against the Polish

---

21 Marcin Czepelak, 'Concurrent Causes of Action in the Rome I and II Regulations' (2011) 7(2) *Journal of Private International Law* 393–410.

22 Case V CSK 164/14.

company after compensating the owner of the damaged property. The court stated that although Article 4(1) and (2) Rome II would have led to the application of German law, Polish law was instead to govern the case; thus it invoked the 'escape clause' of Article 4(3) Rome II. The court noted that there were four parties involved altogether, of which three had either their seat or their place of habitual residence in Poland (the service provider, its subcontractor and the insurer). Moreover, these parties were bound by contracts governed by the Polish law (the insurance contract and the contract between the contractor and subcontractor). Accordingly, the Supreme Court found an application of Article 4(3) Rome II to be fully justified by the circumstances of the case.

Although the question of how the Polish courts would apply Article 4(3) Rome II in the case of a collision of a ship in international waters has not been dealt with directly, it may be possible to deduce the likely response from the *obiter dictum* in the Supreme Court's judgment of 23 May 2013.[23] This case concerned an accident in which a Polish sailor was injured. However, this happened not on the high seas, but in Nigerian territorial waters; thus the Supreme Court explained the difference between the coastal area and the high seas from the perspective of the conflict of laws. If the event giving rise to the damage had occurred on the high seas, then, according to the former version of Article 356 of the Polish Maritime Code, it would have been governed the law of the flag (*lex banderae*). Having been amended by the Polish PIL Act of 2011, this provision now reads as follows: 'if the place of event designates the applicable law, it shall be presumed, that, in case of the ship sailing outside the territory of the coastal state, the event occurred on the territory of the State of flag'. One could derive two following conclusions from that fact.

Firstly, the Polish courts do not follow the principle of the *lex fori* as applicable to the high seas, as used to be the case under English law.[24] Instead, they try to look for the genuine connecting factor. That is why Article 356 of the Polish Maritime Code does not establish a conflict-of-law rule, i.e. it does not designate the applicable law, but merely defines how the courts should consider the notion of the 'place of event' in relation to a ship sailing on the high seas. This rule of interpretation is limited to events on the ship; accordingly, it does not refer to torts outside the ship (for example, damage caused by a ship to another ship or to a submarine pipeline).

Secondly, Article 356 of the Polish Maritime Code cannot be directly applicable, because it uses the notion of the 'place of event' and not the 'place of damage', which is the point of attachment (or connecting factor) under the general rule established by Article 4(1) Rome II. Moreover, Rome II requires a uniform

23 Case II CSK 250/12.

24 Sarah Fiona Gahlen, *Civil Liability for Accidents at Sea*, Springer, Berlin/Heidelberg 2015, pp. 350–351.

and autonomous interpretation, so one cannot use national law definitions to interpret the uniform conflict-of-law rule established by the European legislator. Nevertheless, the law of the flag as applicable to extra-contractual liability for damage that occurs on a ship might be considered to be in line with Rome II. This way, the principle resulting from Article 356 of the Polish Maritime Code could nevertheless be applicable – *non ratione imperii, sed imperio rationis.*

2.5. SPECIFIC RULES

The overall evaluation of the Polish case law concerning Articles 5, 6, 7 and 8 Rome I shows that these provisions have not been applied often enough to prove whether they work well in practice.

The Polish courts have applied Article 5 Rome I in several cases, but simply to state that the law designated by this provision is overridden by the international conventions establishing uniform rules in the field of transport law (the Convention on the Contract for the International Carriage of Goods by Road, the Convention concerning International Carriage by Rail, etc.). However, in some cases it was nonetheless necessary for the court to designate the applicable law; then, Article 5 Rome I led to the law of (the seat of) the carrier.[25]

Secondly, in a case where consumer contracts were at stake, the question at issue was the choice-of-law agreement inserted into the general terms and conditions of the ticket provider for the UEFA Euro 2012. The Polish Supreme Court held[26] that the choice of Swiss law could not deprive the consumer of the protection of Polish law granted by Article 6 Rome I. Instead of invalidating such a clause, as the lower court had done, the Supreme Court explained the mechanism established by Article 6(2) Rome I, which entails the incorporation of the chosen foreign law in the manner of general terms and conditions of contract, which need to conform with the law of the state where a consumer has his habitual residence.

Thirdly, in the case of Article 7 (insurance contracts), as might be expected, it usually leads to the application of the law of the insurer.[27]

Fourthly, individual employment contracts have been at issue in some case not because of problems with the application of Article 8 Rome I, but because of the application of the international mandatory rules of the third state (see section 2.1 above).

---

25 For example judgment of the Regional Court in Warszawa of 1 December 2016, case XXVII Ca 3352/16.

26 Judgment 17 September 2013, case I CSK 555/13.

27 For example the judgment of the Court of Appeal in Szczecin of 13 December 2016, case I ACa 1036/15.

2.6. SCOPE OF THE APPLICABLE LAW

It can be seen from the reported case law of the Polish courts that the problems with characterisation are more likely to appear at the first stage of characterisation, rather than at the second. The former boils down to the question of which conflict-of-laws rule to apply; the latter, which rules of the applicable law apply to decide the case. For example, the Court of Appeal of Szczecin had to decide how to qualify a claim for unduly enforced money.[28]

The problem is when an issue of qualification goes unnoticed – like in the case in which the Supreme Court decided that the restrictions imposed on the contracts between a company and its shareholders form part of the law applicable to the contract (*lex contractus*).[29] However, it seems that they are matters which are explicitly excluded from the scope of the law of contract by Article 1.2. of Rome I as 'questions governed by the law of companies and other bodies, corporate or unincorporated'.

An interesting question concerning Article 12 Rome I and Article 15 Rome II is the relation between the characterisation for the purpose of the designation of the applicable law and the scope of the applicable law. In a case decided by the Polish Supreme Court on 13 March 2014,[30] the respondent was supposed to offer the plaintiff in Dubai the job of director coordinating the activity of a company in the United Arab Emirates. The respondent, however, ultimately appeared not to be the entitled to act on behalf of the company, as he had only pretended to be one of the partners. His offer of employment could be characterised at the same as a contractual issue and as fraud. In explaining this problem from a conflict-of-laws perspective, the Polish Supreme Court reasoned as follows.

The determination of the applicable law by a court cannot depend on how the plaintiff phrased his claim, i.e. whether he invokes contract, tort or any other legal cause of action. Neither does it matter whether the claimant maintains that the contract was legally binding or void and seeks remedy for unjust enrichment. In other words, when the existence of consent or validity of a contract are in dispute and the plaintiff phrases his claim in contract, it is not enough for the court to designate the applicable law by means of the 'contractual' connecting factor, i.e. to characterise the claim as a 'contract' for the purpose of the conflict-of-law rules. Nor, if a plaintiff phrases his claim in tort and seeks compensation for the damage resulting therefrom, it means that the applicable law is to be designated by the 'delictual' (or 'tortious') connecting factor. When the event

---

28 Judgment of 29 May 2014, case I ACa 212/14.

29 Judgment of 16 May 2019, case III CSK 322/18. Perhaps the reason why this issue went unnoticed was the fact that, in any case, the law of Czech Republic would have been applicable, and actually was applied.

30 Case I CSK 274/13.

giving rise to the damage is more closely connected to the contract than to the place of damage, then the law applicable to the contract nevertheless governs the liability in tort.

This approach to characterisation also has a bearing on the application of the law designated by the conflict-of-laws rule. One shall apply all the rules of the law governing the case which are applicable under the circumstances. Accordingly, it does not matter whether the claim has been characterised as a 'contract' or 'tort' for the purposes of the designation of the applicable law. Indeed, regardless of whether Polish or English law is applicable to the 'contract' under Rome I, the court shall apply those Polish or English provisions that cover the case with their scope of application, notwithstanding whether they concern liability in contract, in tort or restitution. The conflict-of-laws rules themselves do not provide guidance on the character of liability in a case. Accordingly, the application of a given conflict-of-law rule means only that the applicable law is to be designated by a particular connecting factor (a point of attachment suitable for situations labelled as 'contracts', 'torts' or 'unjust enrichment'). In other words, the choice between the conflict-of-law rules applicable to a contract or a tort does not mean choosing between two kinds of liability, but rather a choice between two different connecting factors. One might say a choice-of-law rule does not determine the law applicable to a contract, since one does not know whether it has actually been concluded, but to a 'contractual situation'. Accordingly, once the law applicable to the contract is determined, it also covers the effects of the nullity of this contract, therefore Article 12(1)(e) of Rome I precludes the application of Article 10(1) of Rome II.[31]

2.7. *RENVOI*

There is no evidence that *renvoi* would have been helpful in the field of law of obligations in Poland. If the overall goals of the Rome I and Rome II Regulations are to determine the law that has the closest connection to the case and to improve predictability, then these goals would be undermined by *renvoi*. Certainly, there is no room for this institution in cases where a choice-of-law agreement has been concluded.

2.8. FOREIGN LAW

According to Article 1143 §1 of the Polish Code of Civil Procedure as amended from 1 July 2009, the court is obliged to determine the applicable law and its content.

---

31 Judgment of the Supreme Court of 9 February 2017, case III CSK 60/16.

Accordingly, the court applies foreign law *ex officio* and the parties need neither request it nor provide the court with the evidence of foreign law.[32] For that purpose, the court may[33] apply to the Ministry of Justice for a translation of the text of the foreign law, as well as for an explanation of foreign judicial practice. In other words, Polish courts are to apply foreign law as it is applied by foreign courts.[34] Moreover, according to Article 1143 §1 of the Polish Code of Civil Procedure, the court can appoint an expert, ask for expert evidence, or use any other necessary measures in order to ascertain the foreign law to be applied.

This approach dates as far as the first Polish Act on Private International Law of 2 August 1926, which established the principle of equal treatment of Polish and foreign law. Thus, Polish conflict-of-law rules have always had a universal scope of application, as is now the case of the uniform rules established by the Rome I and Rome II Regulations.

The application of Article 1143 §1 of the Polish Code of Civil Procedure and placing the *lex fori* and foreign law on the same footing has had considerable impact on the civil procedure. The case law concerning the Rome I and Rome II Regulations shows that an appeal from a judgment of the court of first instance or cassation to the Supreme Court is often based on the alleged misapplication of foreign law. The appellate courts and the Supreme Court often carefully scrutinise how the content of foreign law and foreign case law has been ascertained. If the court has wrongly determined the applicable law, the Supreme Court considers this to be a reason to reverse the judgment and thus to return the case to the lower court with instructions on which law is to be applied (see, for example, the judgment of the Supreme Court of 23 May 2013).[35]

The Polish Supreme Court pays special attention to ascertaining not merely the text of the foreign law but also the way it is interpreted and applied by the foreign courts. In case concerning a loan agreement governed by German law,[36] the Regional Court and the Court of Appeal, as well as the Supreme Court, applied German law; however, the question at issue was how to apply it. The Court of Appeal found the judgment of the lower court to be insufficiently justified, as no text of the German Civil Code was quoted. The Supreme Court, in turn, insisted on interpreting the foreign law at least in the light of academic commentaries.

---

32 Judgment of the Supreme Court of 17 October 2008, case I CSK 105/08; judgment of the Supreme Court of 3 March 2011, case II PK 208/10.

33 It is a possibility, not an obligation, as was underlined in the judgment of the Supreme Court of 9 April 2015, case II CSK 550/14.

34 Judgment of the Supreme Court of 11 August 2004, case II CK 489/03; judgment of the Supreme Court of 9 May 2007, case II CSK 60/07; judgment of the Supreme Court of 11 January 2008, case V CSK 372/07.

35 Case II CSK 250/12.

36 Judgment of the Supreme Court of 23 June 2016, case V CSK 536/15.

Generally speaking, in cases in which the Rome I and Rome II Regulations have been at stake, there has been no problem of proving foreign law. This may be, however, because the foreign applicable law was the law of a European state or the law of one of the United States of America. Only in one case, in which Liberian law was supposed to be applicable, was there a problem of ascertaining the content of the Liberian law on responsibility for an accident that happened to person employed on a ship. In the first instance proceedings, the court applied Polish law, because it had not received a reply from the Ministry of Justice to its enquiry about Liberian law. Only after did the Court of Appeal point out that a lack of response did not equate to the impossibility of establishing the content of the foreign law; if that is the case, then expert evidence was required. Eventually, the Supreme Court, in its judgment of 23 May 2013,[37] decided that instead of Liberian law, Nigerian law should apply.

Sometimes lower courts try to make their life easier. They admit that the foreign law is indeed applicable, but that its provisions are 'convergent' with Polish law. They then abandon their analysis of the foreign law (which should cover the text of the relevant legal provisions as well as the foreign case law) and swiftly proceed to decide the case by applying Polish law. Even if such the court's decision would truly be the same had the applicable foreign law been applied, this practice is against Polish law.

2.9. *ORDRE PUBLIC*

It follows from the reported case law that the Polish courts are likely to invoke *ordre public* in two cases from the field of the law of obligations: punitive damages and money compensation for immaterial damage. Accordingly, two principles are considered to be part of Polish public policy (or 'the fundamental principles of the Polish legal system', as it is phrased in Article 7 of the Polish PIL Act of 2011). Firstly, the Polish Supreme Court has held that compensation should be proportionate to the damage and cannot play a punitive role.[38] Secondly, the Court of Appeal in Szczecin, in its judgment of 7 February 2014,[39] stated that some form of judicial protection must be available in all cases that concern immaterial damage (see section 2.10 below). However, the fact that German law does not allow the acquisition of movable property *bona fide* from a person not entitled to transfer the ownership has not been considered as contrary to the Polish *ordre public*, even if the latter legal system differs in this case.[40] This issue is, however, not covered by the scope of Rome I.

---

37 Case II CSK 250/12.

38 Judgment of 11 October 2013, case I CSK 697/12.

39 Case I ACa 660/12.

40 Judgment of the Supreme Court of 28 February 2018, case IV CSK 433/17.

2.10. COMPENSATION

The case law shows that Polish courts are reluctant to award high compensation in domestic as well as in international cases. At the same time, the courts consider some aspects of compensation to be of crucial importance. For example, in its judgment of 7 February 2014,[41] the Court of Appeal in Szczecin stated that some form of judicial protection must be available in cases where plaintiff has lost a close family member of in a road accident. After noting that under German law – unlike in other European legal systems – a child cannot claim compensation for the suffering caused by the death of his or her mother, the Court of Appeal considered German law to be manifestly contrary to the Polish public policy.

2.11. RELATIONS WITH INTERNATIONAL CONVENTIONS

Much has been written about the relation between Rome I and Rome II and the international conventions. Both Regulations are equipped with provisions that deal with this problem (Articles 25 and 26 of Rome I and Articles 28 and 29 of Rome II). However, the international conventions often have similar clauses, so the method of establishing priority among two prima facie 'competing' instruments always remains a matter of construction. In practice one can distinguish two situations.

Firstly, Rome I and Rome II give priority to various international conventions establishing the uniform material rules – such as the Convention providing a uniform law for bills of exchange and promissory notes, signed in Geneva on 7 June 1930, or *Convention relative au contrat de transport international de marchandises par route* (CMR), or other international convention from the field of transport law.[42] However, Rome I and Rome II designate the applicable law outside the scope of such conventions.

Secondly, the relation between Rome I and Rome II and the international conventions establishing conflict-of-law rules is much more complicated. One can see it in the example of the relation between the Rome II Regulation and the 1971 Hague Convention on the law Applicable to Road Accidents. Not only are the Polish courts clearly confused, but even some scholars are too. Generally speaking, Poland is a party to the Hague Convention, which takes priority over Article 4 Rome II. Accordingly, the Court of Appeal in Szczecin was obviously wrong when, in dealing with a road accident in Germany, it applied Rome II

41 Case I ACa 660/12.

42 For example, the Judgments of the Supreme Court of 6 April 2017, case III CSK 174/16; 14 March 2019, case IV CSK 6/18.

instead of the 1971 Hague Convention, pointing out that Germany is not a party to this Convention.[43]

The priority of the Hague Convention over it notwithstanding, the Rome II Regulation applies outside the scope of application of this Convention, namely to designate the law applicable to subrogation. Finally, the Hague Convention in turn gives priority to bilateral conventions, to which Poland is a party, meaning that this problem becomes an even more complicated issue.

3. GENERAL EVALUATION

The overall evaluation of the application of Rome I and Rome II Regulations by the Polish courts is definitively positive. It is, however, hard to say what could be considered to be 'the innovation', as the main solutions adopted by these Regulations are quite similar to those which were previously in force under the domestic Polish law.

Uniformity is achieved only when the courts of different states apply the same rules in the same way, i.e. they render the same reasoned judgments as concerns the same factual circumstances in cases. The Rome I and Rome II Regulations provide a means through which this harmonisation may be achieved, in which the uniform choice-of-law rules are in force.

In terms of party autonomy, the Rome I Regulation has brought about necessary improvements in comparison to the Polish PIL Act of 1965. In terms of the absence of choice, the Polish PIL Act of 1965 was in general terms not very different from the Rome I and Rome II Regulations.

Generally speaking, the Rome I and Rome II Regulations must be considered to be useful tools for resolving conflicts of laws. They respect party autonomy and increase the predictability of the law applicable to contractual and extra-contractual obligations.

The only true lacuna, which makes international transactions less secure, is the question of the effects of the assignment against third parties.[44] It is also very important to find a uniform solution in relation to the law applicable to defamation, as many Polish citizens live abroad. If there is a problem in terms of the comprehension of conflict-of-law rules, then this would probably also be the case for rules originating from the national legislator. Certainly, there have been several cases where Polish courts have had problems with the interpretation and application of the Rome I and Rome II Regulations; however, in many other cases they shown deep insight into and knowledge of private international law.

---

43 Judgment of 7 February 2014, case I ACa 660/12.

44 The Commission submitted the proposal of the Regulation on the law applicable to the third-party effects of the assignments of claims, COM(2018) 96 final, 2018/0044 (COD).

As already noted, the overall evaluation of the application of the Rome I and Rome II Regulation by the Polish courts is definitively positive.

4. CONCLUSION

4.1. SUMMARY OF FINDINGS

The conflict-of-law rules as they are established in the Rome I and Rome II Regulations are very useful tools for courts. These rules, however, need to be simple, i.e. phrased in a way that enables comprehension and interpretation. Moreover, the courts need time to learn how to apply them. That is why changes should be introduced only where case law has proved it to be necessary.

4.2. MAIN RECOMMENDATIONS

It is highly disputable what the law applicable to the effects of the assignment of claims towards third parties other than the debtor actually is. Some authors maintained that this issue should be governed by the law of the assignment, as established under Article 14(1) Rome I. Others, however, considered this matter to be excluded from the scope of application of the said provision. The report prepared by the British Institute for Comparative Law suggests that the European Commission leaned towards the former opinion and was looking for possible solutions. After the report was published, the Commission submitted the proposal of the Regulation on the law applicable to the third-party effects of the assignments of claims.[45] Perhaps, one of the important new challenges would be to unify conflict-of-laws aspects of factoring transactions. Referring to this proposal, the CJEU has recently confirmed that 'under EU law as it currently stands, the absence of rules of conflict expressly governing the third-party effects of assignments of claims is a choice of the EU legislature.'[46]

The Polish legislator has already sought a solution. That is why Article 36 of the Polish PIL Act 2011 makes the effects of the assignment against third parties subject to the law that governs the obligation relating to the assignment.

It would be necessary and at the same time easy to correct some discrepancies between the Rome I and Rome II Regulations in terms of choice-of-law agreements. Simultaneously, a quite misleading provision, i.e. Article 3(5) Rome I should be deleted as far as the formal validity of such agreements is concerned.

---

45 12.03.2018; COM(2018) 96 final, 2018/0044 (COD).

46 ECJ Judgment of 9 October 2019, case 548/18, at 37.

One cannot reasonably maintain that 'the choice shall be … clearly demonstrated by the terms of the contract or the circumstances of the case' and at the same apply Article 11, which may potentially lead to the application of a rule requiring that this agreement be concluded in writing or in notarial deed. This is at the same time irreconcilable with the very concept of uniform EU private international law, which aims to establish uniform criteria of validity for the choice-of-law clauses.[47] It is also misleading because it may suggest that the formal requirements for the choice-of-law agreement are the same as those established by Article 11 Rome I for the main contract.

[47] See for example the judgment of the Court of Appeal in Katowice of 21 July 2016, case V ACa 938/15, V ACz 1269/15.

THE APPLICATION OF THE ROME I AND ROME II REGULATIONS IN PORTUGAL

Afonso Patrão

1. INTRODUCTION

This chapter analyses how Portuguese courts are applying two European Regulations on the conflict of laws – the Rome I Regulation on the law applicable to contractual obligations; and the Rome II Regulation on the law applicable to non-contractual obligations.

Some preliminary clarifications are required.

Firstly, this study does not consider all rulings of Portuguese courts. In fact, decisions of lower courts are not available to academics in a digital format nor organised by subject matter; therefore, the lower court rulings analysed were obtained by directly contacting the courts, which means not all the case law of lower courts could be considered. Furthermore, regarding superior courts (Courts of Appeal and the Portuguese Supreme Court of Justice),[1] not all verdicts are available on the Internet or in Court reports published by the Ministry of Justice, only the most significant and consequential judgments are selected.[2] As for arbitration awards, no are data publicly available, making it impossible to find out how the Rome I and Rome II Regulations are applied.

This means that there are no accurate public data on the application of these Regulations by the clear majority of Portuguese courts, which may weaken the conclusions drawn in this chapter.

Secondly, Portuguese law does not provide any national rules facilitating the application of the Rome I and Rome II Regulations; in fact, since the direct application of European Regulations is established in the Portuguese Constitution,[3] the courts have simply replaced the use of previous national conflict-of-laws rules with the European rules.

Thirdly, some national rules on the general problems of private international law must be stressed, since they influence the way Portuguese courts apply European conflict-of-laws rules.[4] The most decisive are the rules on characterisation and application of foreign law.

On characterisation, the Portuguese Civil Code includes a rule establishing the autonomous interpretation of conflict-of-laws norms and prescribing

1 In Portuguese: Courts of Appeal – Tribunais da Relação; and Supreme Court of Justice – Supremo Tribunal de Justiça.

2 The Portuguese Ministry of Justice publish Court Reports – *Boletim do Ministério da Justiça* – available via <http://www.gddc.pt/actividade-editorial/actividade-editorial.html>. However, the online reports consist of only a selection of court decisions depending on their significance.
Additionally, superior courts release their decisions via <www.dgsi.pt>. Nevertheless, the rapporteur for each case decides if the judgment is sufficiently important to be available online, which means only some rulings are available via the Internet.

3 Cf. Article 8(3) of the Portuguese Constitution: 'The norms issued by the competent organs of international organisations to which Portugal belongs come directly into force in Portuguese internal law, on condition that this is laid down in the respective constituent treaties'.

4 Cf. Luís de Lima Pinheiro, *Direito Internacional Privado*, Vol. I, Introdução e Direito de Conflitos – Parte Geral, 3rd edition, Almedina, Coimbra, 2014, p. 237; Geraldo Ribeiro, 'A Europeização do Direito Internacional Privado e Direito Processual Internacional: Algumas Notas sobre o problema da interpretação do âmbito objectivo dos regulamentos comunitários', *Julgar*, no. 23, 2014, pp. 263–293, p. 271; Jan von Hein and Giesela Rühl, 'Towards a European Code on Private International Law', *Cross-border activities in the EU – Making life easier for citizens*, Directorate General for Internal Policies, European Parliament, Brussels, 2015, pp. 8–53, pp. 14 and 21 ff.; Hans Jürgen Sonnenberger, 'Eingriffsnormen', *Brauchen wir eine Rom 0-Verordnung?*, Stefan Leible and Hannes Unberath, Jenaer Wissenschaftliche Verlagsgesellschaft, Jena, 2013, pp. 429–444, pp. 429 ff.; Wolfgang Wurmnest, 'Ordre public', *Brauchen wir eine Rom 0-Verordnung?*, Stefan Leible and Hannes Unberath, Jenaer Wissenschaftliche Verlagsgesellschaft, Jena, 2013, pp. 445–478, pp. 445 ff.

lege causae characterisation,[5] in harmony with the guidelines of the Court of Justice of the European Union.[6]

Regarding the application of foreign law, within the Portuguese system it must be acknowledged *ex officio* by the courts – *iura novit curiae.*[7] This means there is no risk of endangering the objective of international uniformity of decisions, since the applicable law is *ex officio* sought and employed by national judges, even if the parties do not plead it and do not prove its content.[8]

---

5 Article 15 of the Portuguese Civil Code: 'The reference made by a conflict-of-laws rule to a certain legislation relates only to the norms which report to the subject of that rule, considering their content and purpose within the legal system they belong to'.

6 In fact, it is now clear that the CJEU discourages characterisation *lege fori* and instructs that concepts should be interpreted autonomously. Therefore, the characterisation method contained in Article 15 of the Portuguese Civil Code matches the one prescribed by European case law, even in the absence of a 'Rome 0 Regulation'. Cf. Luís de Lima Pinheiro, 'The methodology and the general part of the Portuguese Private International Law Codification: a possible source of inspiration for the European Legislator?', *Yearbook of Private International Law*, Vol. XIV, 2012–2013, pp. 153–172, p. 155 ff.; Benedetta Ubertazzi, 'La legge applicabile alle obbligazioni contrattuali nel Regolamento "Roma I"', *Diritto Internazionale Privato e Cooperazione Giudiziaria in Materia Civile – Trattato di Diritto Privato dell'Unione Europea, Vol. XIV*, Andrea Bonomi, Giappichelli Editore, Turin, 2009, pp. 345–408, p. 351; Christian Heinze, 'Bausteine eines Allgemeinen Teils des europäischen Internationalen Privatrechts', *Die richtige Ordnung – Festschrift für Jan Kropholler zum 70. Geburtstag*, Dietmar Baetge, Jan von Hein and Michael von Hinden, Mohr Siebeck, Tübingen, 2008, pp. 105–127, p. 108 ff.; Helmut Heiss and Emese Kaufmann-Mohi, '"Qualifikation" – Ein Regelungsgegenstand für eine Rom 0-Verordnung?', *Brauchen wir eine Rom 0-Verordnung?*, Stefan Leible and Hannes Unberath, Jenaer Wissenschaftliche Verlagsgesellschaft, Jena, 2013, pp. 181–199, p. 197; Andrea Bonomi, 'Il diritto internazionale privato dell'Unione europea: considerazioni generali', *Diritto Internazionale Privato e Cooperazione Giudiziaria in Materia Civile – Trattato di Diritto Privato dell'Unione Europea, Vol. XIV*, Andrea Bonomi, Giappichelli Editore, Turin, 2009, pp. 1–54, p. 35 ff.; Rafael Arenas García, 'La distinción entre obligaciones contractuales y obligaciones extracontractuales en los instrumentos comunitarios de derecho internacional privado', *Anuario Español de Derecho Internacional Privado*, Vol. VI, 2006, pp. 393–415, p. 414; Hélène Gaudemet-Tallon, 'Le nouveau droit international privé européen des contrats (Commentaire de la convention C.E.E. no. 80/934 sur la loi applicable aux obligations contractuelles, ouverte à la signature à Rome le 19 juin 1980)', *Revue Trimestrielle de Droit Européen*, Vol. 17, 1981, pp. 215–285, p. 258; Geraldo Ribeiro, n. 4 above, p. 271.

7 Article 348 of the Portuguese Civil Code. Cf. António Ferrer Correia, *Lições de Direito Internacional Privado*, Almedina, Coimbra, 2000, p. 427; Luís de Lima Pinheiro, n. 4 above, p. 648; António Marques dos Santos, 'A Aplicação do Direito Estrangeiro', *Estudos de Direito Internacional Privado e de Direito Público*, Almedina, Coimbra, 2004, pp. 33–53, p. 45; Trevor C. Hartley, 'Pleading and Proof of Foreign Law: the Major European Systems Compared', *International and Comparative Law Quarterly*, Vol. 45, 1996, pp. 271–292, p. 275; Afonso Patrão, 'Poderes e deveres de Notário e Conservador na Cognição de direito estrangeiro', *Cadernos do CENoR – Centro de Estudos Notariais e Registais*, no. 2, 2014, pp. 9–38, pp. 13 ff.

8 In fact, the *iura novit curiae* maxim is the only system that prevents the undermining of the purposes of European unification of the conflict-of-laws rules. Cf. Luís de Lima Pinheiro, n. 6 above, p. 171; Stefan Leible and Michael Müller, 'A General Part for European Private International Law?', *Yearbook of Private International Law*, Vol. XIV, 2012–2013,

In addition, it must be underlined that the position on *renvoi* in the Rome I and Rome II Regulations is different from the system of private international law. In fact, internal rules establish a pragmatic system on *renvoi*, accepting it only when it ensures international uniformity of decisions.[9]

2. APPLICATION OF ROME II

2.1. THE NATIONAL LANDSCAPE

To my knowledge, there are very few judicial rulings by Portuguese courts directly concerning the application of the Rome II Regulation – I identified only seven verdicts.[10] Additionally, there are other rulings discussing whether

pp. 137–152, p. 149; Urs Peter Gruber and Ivo Bach, 'The Application of Foreign Law – A progress report on a new European project', *Yearbook of Private International Law*, Vol. 11, 2009, pp. 157–169, p. 167; José Luis Iglesias Buhigues, 'Luces y sombras de la cooperación judicial en materia civil en la UE', *Entre Bruselas y la Haya: Estudios sobre la unificación internacional y regional del Derecho internacional privado – Liber Amicorum Alegría Borrás*, Joaquin Forner Delaygua, Cristina González Beilfuss and Ramón Viñas Farré, Marcial Pons, Madrid, 2013, pp. 535–552, p. 551; Rainer Hausmann, 'Pleading and Proof of Foreign Law – a Comparative Analysis', *The European Legal Forum*, Vol. 8, no. 1, 2008, pp. 1–13, p. 13; Aurelio López-Tarruella Martínez, '¿Constituye la aplicación de la lex fori en defecto de prueba del Derecho extranjero designado por una norma de conflicto unionista un incumplimiento del Derecho de la Unión Europea?', *Nuevas Fronteras del Derecho de la Unión Europea – Liber amicorum José Luis Iglesias Buhigues*, Carlos Esplugues Mota and Guillermo Palao Moreno, Tirant lo Blanch, Valencia, 2012, pp. 537–554, p. 552.

9 Articles 16–18 of the 1966 Portuguese Civil Code. The Portuguese system, as a principle, excludes *renvoi* (Article 16). However, *renvoi* is accepted in cases in which harmony of decisions can be achieved: if the foreign law makes a *renvoi* to a third state that would apply its own law (Article 17(1)), and if the foreign law makes a *renvoi* to Portuguese internal law (Article 18(1)).
The system is more complex regarding the law applicable to personal status, in which the system accepts *renvoi* only when the most relevant legislation (nationality and habitual residence) agree on the law applicable – Articles 17(2) and 18(2) of the Portuguese Civil Code. For further explanations, João Baptista Machado, *Lições de Direito Internacional Privado*, Almedina, Coimbra, 1999, pp. 178 ff.; António Ferrer Correia, n. 7 above, p. 256 ff.; Luís de Lima Pinheiro, n. 4 above, pp. 542 ff.; Helena Mota, 'A autonomia conflitual e o reenvio no âmbito do Regulamento (UE) no. 650/2012, do Parlamento Europeu e do Conselho, de 4 de Julho de 2012', *Revista Electrónica de Direito*, no. 1, 2014, available via <www.cije.up.pt/revistared>, p. 17 (comparing the Portuguese *renvoi* rules with Article 34 of Regulation 650/2012).

10 Judgment of the Lisbon Court of Appeal of 10 July 2013, case 3774/12.2TJLSB-A.L1-7 (available via <http://www.dgsi.pt/jtrl.nsf/33182fc732316039802565fa00497eec/d0306eb0c5b0994980257bc200692f35?OpenDocument&Highlight=0,3774%2F12.2TJLSB-A.L1-7>); Judgment of the Guimarães Court of Appeal of 29 October 2013, case 225/12.6TBAMR.G1 (available via <http://www.dgsi.pt/jtrg.nsf/86c25a698e4e7cb7802579ec004d3832/296884764e6120cb80257c28003d756b?OpenDocument&Highlight=0,225%2F12.6TBAMR.G1>); Judgment of the Supreme Court of Justice of 1 April 2014, case 1061/12.5TVLSB.L1.S1 (available

the Rome II Regulation should be applicable, in terms of when it entered into force.[11] However, it is not certain that these are the only decisions applying the Rome II Regulation: on the one hand, there is no central place of publication of lower courts' decisions; on the other hand, there may exist more rulings of the superior courts on the Rome II Regulation that were not selected for publication.

Surprisingly, the decisions where the Rome II Regulation (specifically its rule that the Regulation applies to events that occurred after 11 January 2009) has been applied wrongly in Portugal are not judgments that apply national rules on the law applicable to torts in cases that should be subject to the Rome II Regulation: I found none of these. Rather, I found judgments where the Rome II Regulation was wrongly applied to events that occurred *before* its entry into force. These decisions were made by lower courts and then amended by the Supreme Court of Justice.[12]

The European rules on torts are not very different from the national set of norms, which may explain the fact that not many discussions have arisen on the application of the Rome II Regulation. In fact, Portuguese internal conflict-of-laws norms already contained an exception clause allowing for the setting aside

via <http://www.dgsi.pt/jstj.nsf/954f0ce6ad9dd8b980256b5f003fa814/e29fb62bf946e5d980257cad004f7726?OpenDocument&Highlight=0,1061%2F12.5TVLSB.L1.S1>); Judgment of the Court of Póvoa do Varzim (Lower Court) of 7 June 2016, case 406/14.8TBMAI; Judgment of the Court of Póvoa do Varzim (Lower Court) of 15 June 2016, case 21/14.6TBSTS; Judgment of the Court of Póvoa do Varzim (Lower Court) of 30 August 2016, case 461/13.8TBPVZ.

11 Cf. Judgment of the Supreme Court of Justice of 1 March 2012, case 186/10.6TBCBT.S1 (available via <http://www.dgsi.pt/jstj.nsf/954f0ce6ad9dd8b980256b5f003fa814/a26b538186b9c0df802579bc004147a2?OpenDocument&Highlight=0,186%2F10.6TBCBT.S1>) and Judgment of the Supreme Court of Justice of 11 April 2013, case 186/10.6TBCBT.S2 (available via <http://www.dgsi.pt/jstj.nsf/954f0ce6ad9dd8b980256b5f003fa814/d04217db6aaf52b980257b5000354078?OpenDocument&Highlight=0,186%2F10.6TBCBT.S2>). In these cases, the event giving rise to damage occurred *before* the entry into force of the Rome II Regulation, even though the claim was only filed after that date. The Supreme Court of Justice declared that the Rome II Regulation was not applicable, amending the lower court decisions and determining that the national set of rules on tort law was applicable (Article 45 of the Portuguese Civil Code).
The application in time rules are also discussed in Judgment of the Lisbon Court of Appeal of 29 October 2015, case 2691/13.3TCLRS.L1-2 (available via <http://www.dgsi.pt/jtrl.nsf/33182fc732316039802565fa00497eec/794ce7c47b07215b80257f0a00439624?OpenDocument&Highlight=0,2691%2F13.3TCLRS.L1-2>) and in Judgment of the Coimbra Court of Appeal of 9 January 2012, case 1473/10.9T2AVR.C1 (available via <http://www.dgsi.pt/jtrc.nsf/c3fb530030ea1c61802568d9005cd5bb/43eafe5d809eb893802579950059b777?OpenDocument&Highlight=0,1473%2F10.9T2AVR.C1>): they both concerned a road accident that occurred in Spain (the first one on 28 March 2008; the second one on 27 August 2007) in which one of the parties set aside the application of the Rome II Regulation, but the arguments were not accepted by the courts.

12 Cf. n. 11 above.

of the general rule if there was a common habitual residence of both the person claimed to be liable and the person sustaining the damage.[13] Additionally, the national set of rules on the law applicable to tort had already established an escape clause in favour of *lex loci damni* in cases in which the general rule (*lex loci delicti commissi*) did not provide for compensation.[14]

Therefore, just like in most Member States, the main distinction between the Rome II Regulation (*lex loci damni*) and national private international law rules (*lex delicti commissi*) is the general criterion: previously, the law applicable to torts was *lex loci delicti commissi*, whereas now the European conflict-of-laws rule elects *lex loci damni*. Hence, the aspect of the Rome II Regulation that has been most often considered by the national courts is the determination of the place where the damage occurred. In fact, Article 4(1) and Recital 17, which deal with the determination of the place of the *direct consequences* of the tort, are the most commonly applied rules of the Rome II Regulation.

The other main difference is the existence in the Rome II Regulation of party autonomy. However, no case has come before the Portuguese courts in which the parties had chosen the law applicable to tort.

2.2. RELEVANT CASES

Most of the cases decided by Portuguese courts that apply the Rome II Regulation have concerned traffic accidents that occurred in Spain, causing damage to persons with habitual residence (or central administration) in Portugal. In these cases, it has been discussed *what damages* were relevant to establish the *country in which the damage occurred*. These rulings have used two different solutions, one of them clearly undermining the purpose of the Rome II Regulation via the erroneous application of Article 4.

To show the tendencies of Portuguese courts as regards the interpretation of Article 4(1) of the Rome II Regulation, I highlight three cases on traffic

13 Cf. Article 45(3) of the Portuguese Civil Code. Internal rules on the conflict of laws also admitted the overlook of the general rule if both parties had the same nationality: 'If, however, the person claimed to be liable and the person sustaining damage both have the nationality of the same country or their habitual residence in the same country, and were occasionally abroad, the law of that country shall be applicable, without prejudice of the mandatory provisions of the law of the country where the event occurred'.

14 Unlike the one in Article 4(3) of the Rome II Regulation, this escape clause has a substantive purpose, overriding the general rule not because of the existence of a closer connection but to fulfil a goal (compensation of damages) when the *lex loci delicti commissi* did not hold the person liable. Emphasising the contrast, cf. Rui Moura Ramos, *Estudos de Direito Internacional Privado da União Europeia*, Imprensa da Universidade de Coimbra, Coimbra, 2016, p. 117.

collisions: two correct decisions and the one in which, in my understanding, the court wrongly applied the European rules.

The first case came before the Lisbon Court of Appeal and concerned a traffic accident in Spanish territory, in which a car driven by a Spanish citizen (with habitual residence in Spain) caused damage to a truck owned by a Portuguese company governed from Portugal.[15] In court, the Portuguese company (the legal person sustaining the damage) claimed compensation for the *time the truck was stopped for repairs* and not being used in the company's activity. Thus, it was argued that the 'country where the damage occurred' was Portugal (Article 4(1)) and, therefore, there was no ground for exemption from liability, since Portuguese law establishes a limitation period of three years (which had not been exhausted). On the other hand, the Spanish driver argued that there were grounds for exemption: he claimed the damage was *the harm done to the truck in Spain* and, therefore, Spanish law would be applicable, with its one-year limitation period (which had already been exhausted).

Similarly, in the second case,[16] a Portuguese driver with habitual residence in Portugal sustained damage as a result of a road accident that occurred in Spain and claimed liability of a Spanish driver with habitual residence in Spain. The Portuguese driver asked for compensation for the costs of repairing the car, a service which had taken place in a garage in Portugal. Thus, the person sustaining the damage argued that Portuguese law was applicable (with its three-year limitation period), since the costs were incurred in Portugal. The person claimed to be liable, however, argued that the only relevant damage was the *direct harm to the car*, thus contending that Spanish law and its limitation period of one year applied.

In both cases, the court was required to interpret the concept of the relevant 'damage', in order to determine the *place where the damage occurred*: the victims argued for the relevance of 'the location from which reparation was demanded in court'; while the persons claimed to be liable held that what was relevant was the *first consequence of the event*. On this matter, both the Lisbon Court of Appeal as the Supreme Court of Justice decided, referring to Recitals 16 and 17, that the relevant damage is the first consequence of the event – the place where people were injured or the property was damaged – notwithstanding its indirect

15 Judgment of the Lisbon Court of Appeal of 11 January 2013, case 3774/12.2TJLSB-A.L1-7 (available via <http://www.dgsi.pt/jtrl.nsf/33182fc732316039802565fa00497eec/d0306eb0c5b0994980257bc200692f35?OpenDocument>).

16 Judgment of the Supreme Court of Justice of 1 April 2014, case 1061/12.5TVLSB.L1.S1 (available via <http://www.dgsi.pt/jstj.nsf/954f0ce6ad9dd8b980256b5f003fa814/e29fb62bf946e5d980257cad004f7726?OpenDocument&Highlight=0,1061%2F12.5TVLSB.L1.S1>).

consequences. Therefore, Spanish law was established as being applicable to the tort.[17] In my understanding, these rulings show a correct application of the Rome II Regulation.[18]

A very different solution – and, in my view, an incorrect decision – was given by the Guimarães Court of Appeal in a similar case concerning a road accident that occurred in Spain between a person with habitual residence in Portugal (the person sustaining the damage) and a Spanish citizen living in Spain.[19] In this case, the court established that the relevant damage was the cost of repairing the car, which had been carried out in a garage in Portugal. Therefore, the court established that Portuguese law was applicable and, in my opinion, contradicted Recitals 16 and 17.[20]

---

17 In these cases, even though the parties had different interpretations of Article 4 of the Rome II Regulation, no preliminary ruling was requested from the CJEU. Regarding the first case (the one from the Lisbon Court of Appeal), perhaps the national court decided not to refer the case because there was a judicial remedy under national law (according to Article 672 of the Portuguese Civil Procedure Code). However, in the case decided by the Supreme Court of Justice, no judicial remedy existed. Therefore, it was possibly assumed that 'the correct application of Community law may be so obvious as to leave no scope for any reasonable doubt as to the manner in which the question raised is to be resolved' and that, consequently, 'the national court or tribunal [may] refrain from submitting the question to the court of justice and take upon itself the responsibility for resolving it' – Case 283/81, *CILFIT* [1982] ECR 3415, Recital 16.
In fact, the absence of preliminary ruling cannot be explained by the existence of a previous decision of the CJEU on the interpretation of Article 4(1) of the Rome II Regulation, since the only verdict was given in Case C-350/14, *Florin Lazar*.

18 Other good examples must be stressed. Firstly, the Judgment of the Coimbra Court of Appeal of 9 January 2012, case 1473/10.9T2AVR.C1 (available via <http://www.dgsi.pt/jtrc.nsf/c3fb530030ea1c61802568d9005cd5bb/43eafe5d809eb893802579950059b777?OpenDocument>). In this case, although the court decided that the Rome II Regulation was not applicable (since the road accident occurred on 27 August 2007), the judges highlighted the concept of *direct damage* as the place where persons were injured or property was harmed. Secondly, a decision from a lower court (Judgment of the Court of Póvoa do Varzim of 30 August 2016, case 461/13.8TBPVZ), between a Spanish citizen living in Spain and a Portuguese citizen living in Portugal, concerning a road accident which took place in Portugal. The court decided in favour of the application the law of the country where the road accident occurred (Portugal), thus holding that the *direct damage* was the relevant fact to be ascertained.

19 Judgment of the Guimarães Court of Appeal of 29 October 2013, case 225/12.6TBAMR.G1 (available via <http://www.dgsi.pt/jtrg.nsf/86c25a698e4e7cb7802579ec004d3832/296884764e6120cb80257c28003d756b?OpenDocument>).

20 Again, just like in the judgment referred to in n. 17 above), although the parties had different interpretations of Article 4 of the Rome II Regulation, no preliminary ruling was requested from the CJEU. It is not clear whether the court decided not to make such a reference because it thought there was a judicial remedy under national law (according to Article 672 of the Portuguese Civil Procedure Code). However, because this interpretation contradicts the opinion of the CJEU in Case C-350/14, *Florin Lazar*, the Portuguese court should have referred the case for a preliminary ruling if it was not intending on following the CJEU's interpretation.

Beyond the interpretation of Article 4(1), I identified a judgment where Article 4(2) was used – applying the law of common habitual residence of both the person claimed to be liable and the person sustaining damage. The case concerned a traffic collision that occurred in Portugal between two Ukrainian citizens living in Portugal; the court applied Portuguese law because it was the law of the country of the habitual residence of both the parties.[21] Although this rule did not lead to a different solution (since the general rule of *lex loci damni* already indicated Portuguese law), this is an example of the use of this special norm.

Beyond traffic accidents, I identified only one decision on tort given by a lower court. It concerned the professional liability of a Portuguese notary in not having informed the buyer of a property located in Portugal (a Spanish citizen living in Spain) of the existence of a real security right over the property bought in the notary's office (in Portugal). In this case, the court submitted the case to Portuguese law, without giving much of an explanation. It seems that the court believed the *direct damage* was the harm to the assets of the person sustaining the damage at the moment he purchased the building bearing a real security right.[22]

2.3. ISSUES NOT COVERED IN CASE LAW

As can be seen, most aspects of the Rome II Regulation have not been dealt with by Portuguese courts. In fact, there is no case in which the parties chose the law applicable to torts (Article 14) and no judgment concerning *lois de police* (whether of the *lex fori* or of third countries). The application of overriding mandatory provisions of third countries is, however, broadly debated by legal doctrine when there is no rule on its treatment (like in Article 16 Rome II Regulation).[23]

---

21 Cf. Judgment of the Court of Póvoa do Varzim (Lower Court) of 15 June 2016, case 21/14.6TBSTS.

22 Cf. Judgment of the Court of Póvoa do Varzim (Lower Court) of 7 June 2016, case 406/14.8TBMAI.

23 Rui Moura Ramos, *Da Lei Aplicável ao Contrato de Trabalho Internacional*, Almedina, Coimbra, 1990, p. 719, argues the equal treatment of *lois de police* of the *lex fori* and of third countries prompts uniformity of decisions. However, António Marques dos Santos, *As Normas de Aplicação Imediata no Direito Internacional Privado – Esboço de uma Teoria Geral*, Vol. II, Almedina, Coimbra, 1991, pp. 1046 and 1047, and *Direito Internacional Privado*, Vol. I, Introdução, Associação Académica da Faculdade de Direito de Lisboa, Lisbon, 2001, p. 300; Nuno Andrade Pissarra, 'Normas de Aplicação Imediata e Direito Comunitário', *Normas de Aplicação Imediata, Ordem Pública Internacional e Direito Comunitário*, Almedina, Coimbra, 2004, pp. 9–140, p. 46; Dário Moura Vicente, *Da Responsabilidade Pré-Contratual em Direito Internacional Privado*, Almedina, Coimbra, 2001, p. 637, and 'Método Jurídico e Direito Internacional Privado', *Direito Internacional Privado – Ensaios*, Vol. II, Almedina, Coimbra, 2005, pp. 7–37, p. 30, all hold that the *lois de police* of third countries can only be applied if there is a special rule on that matter.

I found no case using Rome II's special rules on product liability, unfair competition, environmental damage, intellectual property rights or industrial action, no judicial decisions on either unjust enrichment or *negotiorum gestio;* no case in which overriding mandatory provisions were applied or even considered; no ruling referencing rules of safety and conduct (Article 17); no ruling applying the escape clauses; and no case invoking *ordre public.*

3. APPLICATION OF ROME I

3.1. THE NATIONAL LANDSCAPE

Compared to the Rome II Regulation, the application of the Rome I Regulation is noticeably more frequent. In fact, within the selection of publicly available court rulings, dozens of decisions can be found. Some of these decisions discuss only the Regulations rule on application in time (Article 28), declaring that contracts concluded before 17 December 2009 are subject to the 1980 Rome Convention on the Law Applicable to Contractual Obligations.[24]

According to Luís de Lima Pinheiro, 'Apontamento sobre as normas de aplicação necessária perante o direito internacional privado português e o artigo 21.º do Código Civil de Macau', *Revista da Ordem dos Advogados*, Year 60, Vol. I (January), 2000, pp. 23–48, p. 41, there must be a rule of *lex fori* indicating a certain category of norms of some foreign legislation which could be considered if they are *lois de police* i.e. you can only give preference to foreign *lois de police* if national law provides a rule explicitly allowing it (Luís de Lima Pinheiro, n. 6 above, p. 162, and n. 4 above, pp. 296 and 308 ff.).

24 Cf. Judgment of the Évora Court of Appeal of 4 November 2013, case 202/11.4TBLLE.E1 (available via <http://www.dgsi.pt/jtre.nsf/134973db04f39bf2802579bf005f080b/54d2598ebd97112980257de10056fc2a?OpenDocument&Highlight=0,202%2F11.4TBLLE.E1>), concerning a contract concluded in London on 17 June 2009 between two British citizens; Judgment of the Porto Court of Appeal of 29 May 2015, case 529/13.0TTOAZ.P1 (available via <http://www.dgsi.pt/jtrp.nsf/56a6e7121657f91e80257cda00381fdf/4c304f5b3a31e5fd80257e7c00481136?OpenDocument&Highlight=0,529%2F13.0TTOAZ.P1>), concerning an individual employment contract concluded on 9 February 2009; Judgment of the Porto Court of Appeal of 29 May 2014, case 254/05.6TBVLP.P1, (available via <http://www.dgsi.pt/jtrp.nsf/56a6e7121657f91e80257cda00381fdf/de1d31c36619152480257cf2004e6fda?OpenDocument&Highlight=0,254%2F05.6TBVLP.P1>), concerning a sales contract concluded on 18 November 2004; Judgment of the Porto Court of Appeal of 5 May 2014, case 525/09.2TTPRT.P1 (available via <http://www.dgsi.pt/jtrp.nsf/56a6e7121657f91e80257cda00381fdf/4eb265e1211558b280257cd9003eb679?OpenDocument&Highlight=0,525%2F09.2TTPRT.P1>), concerning an individual employment contract concluded on 17 March 2003; Judgment of the Lisbon Court of Appeal of 11 April 2015, case 2998.14.2TTLSB.L1-4 (available via <http://www.dgsi.pt/jtrl.nsf/33182fc732316039802565fa00497eec/55018aca6d94e18c80257efa003ac208?OpenDocument&Highlight=0,2998.14.2TTLSB.L1-4%20>) concerning an individual employment contract concluded on 1 December 2005; Judgment of the Lisbon Court of Appeal of 18 April 2012, case 914/09.2TTLSB.L1-4 (available via <http://www.dgsi.pt/jtrl.nsf/33182fc732316039802565fa00497eec/cbdd4c5052a0ecaf802579ec00450e55?OpenDocument&Highlight=0,914%2F09.2TTLSB.L1-4>), concerning an individual employment contract

I have not found any case where the Rome I Regulation was overlooked by the national courts: in all cases concerning contracts involving a conflict of laws concluded after its entry into force, the Rome I Regulation was applied.[25]

The European rules on contractual obligations have two important differences from the national set of norms (Articles 41 and 42 of the Portuguese Civil Code), although the national conflict-of-laws rules already establish party autonomy (allowing express or tacit choice of the law applicable to contracts).[26]

The first difference is the generosity of party autonomy under the Rome I Regulation. The national rules only allowed the choice of the laws of countries that had a connection to the contract or of laws the application of which served a rightful interest of the parties.[27] In addition, the possibility of choosing a law applicable to only part of the contract and of having interchangeable laws governing the contract was not explicitly legally authorised.

---

concluded in July 2007 between a Portuguese employee and a Dutch company; Judgment of the Lisbon Court of Appeal of 16 June 2011, case 6422/06.6TVLSB.L1-2 (available via <http://www.dgsi.pt/jtrl.nsf/33182fc732316039802565fa00497eec/084161208851801a802578cc003d497f?OpenDocument&Highlight=0,6422%2F06.6TVLSB.L1-2>) concerning a contract on the sale of goods concluded in 2005 between a company with central administration in Portugal and a company with central administration in Spain; Judgment of the Supreme Court of Justice of 12 May 2016, case 2998/14.2TTLSB.L1.S1 (available <http://www.dgsi.pt/jstj.nsf/954f0ce6ad9dd8b980256b5f003fa814/b89a5ec177e3159e80257fb2003d31e2?OpenDocument&Highlight=0,2998%2F14.2TTLSB.L1.S1>), concerning an individual employment contract concluded on 1 December 2005; Judgment of the Supreme Court of Justice of 12 May 2016, case 2998/14.2TTLSB.L1.S1 (available via <http://www.dgsi.pt/jstj.nsf/954f0ce6ad9dd8b980256b5f003fa814/b89a5ec177e3159e80257fb2003d31e2?OpenDocument&Highlight=0,2998%2F14.2TTLSB.L1.S1>), concerning an individual employment contract concluded on 9 February 2009; Judgment of the Porto Court of Appeal of 2 June 2014, case 930/08.1TTPRT.P2 (available via <http://www.dgsi.pt/jtrp.nsf/56a6e7121657f91e80257cda00381fdf/bdb6210bbadf9a9780257cfb0045f055?OpenDocument&Highlight=0,930%2F08.1TTPRT.P2%20>), concerning an individual employment contract concluded on 20 October 2005; Judgment of the Coimbra Court of Appeal of 20 April 2016, case 234/10.0TTCTB.C1 (available via <http://www.dgsi.pt/jtrc.nsf/c3fb530030ea1c61802568d9005cd5bb/0d990c317ee7dbb380257fa20049854d?OpenDocument&Highlight=0,234%2F10.0TTCTB.C1>), concerning an individual employment contract concluded on 5 March 2008.

25 However, with regard to contracts concluded before 11 December 2009, I identified one ruling where a lower court determined the applicable law by using national rules on the conflict of laws, instead of following, as it should have, the 1980 Rome Convention (which has been in force in Portugal since 1 January 1994, since Portugal acceded via the 1992 Funchal Convention on the Accession of the Kingdom of Spain and the Portuguese Republic to the Rome Convention on the Law Applicable to Contractual Obligations). Cf. Judgment of the Penela Lower Court of 17 March 2014, case 51/11.0TBPNL. In this decision, the court debated the validity of a contract between two British citizens with habitual residence in Portugal concluded on 17 March 2008. The court established that the Rome I Regulation was not applicable (Article 28 Rome I) and used the national set of rules on the conflict of laws, instead of following, as it should have, the 1980 Rome Convention.

26 In fact, Article 41 of the Portuguese Civil Code establishes that contracts shall be governed by the law chosen by the parties, explicitly or tacitly.

27 Article 41(2) of the Portuguese Civil Code. For a comparison of both systems, cf. Rui Moura Ramos, n. 14 above, p. 81.

The second main difference is the determination of the law applicable in the absence of choice. The national rules did not provide different criteria depending on the type of contract: in the absence of choice, *all contracts* were to be submitted to the law of the country of habitual residence of both parties. If the parties had habitual residence in different countries, contracts in which only one of the individuals could be deemed a beneficiary were submitted to the law of the country where the sponsor had habitual residence; in all other cases, the *lex loci celebrationis* rule applied. In addition, it must be emphasised that no escape clause was provided, making these rules mandatory.

However, with the 1980 Rome Convention having come into force in Portugal on 1 January 1994,[28] the national rules on the conflict of laws had already been relegated to contracts concluded before that date.

3.2. RELEVANT CASES

Although most cases dealt with by the Portuguese courts have concerned the law applicable to individual employment contracts, there are decisions on most of the Rome I Regulation's rules. Therefore, I have decided to select just a few, in order to show how these rules are being interpreted by Portuguese judges.

3.2.1. Implicit Choice of Law

When the parties expressly choose the law applicable to the contract, determining it is unproblematic.[29] More interesting are the judgments in which one of the parties argued for the existence of an *implicit* choice of law with the opposition of the other (who claimed that there had been no choice of law and, therefore, asked for the application of Article 4 of Rome I Regulation).

The courts' criteria for the determination of an implicit choice of law were not developed from the Rome I Regulation, since both the national set of rules and the 1980 Rome Convention already granted the possibility of tacit *professio iuris* – case law which it seems will still be used within the scope of the Rome I Regulation. Within previous conflict-of-laws rules, Portuguese courts decided that a tacit choice of law could be determined by the existence of allusions to

---

28 Portugal acceded to the 1980 Rome Convention via the 1992 Funchal Convention on the Accession of the Kingdom of Spain and the Portuguese Republic to the Rome Convention on the Law Applicable to Contractual Obligations.

29 It must be stressed that the Rome I Regulation's solution to the impossibility of choosing rules that are not in force in any country (like the *lex mercatoria*) as the *lex contractus* is strongly criticised, among Portuguese authors, by Luís de Lima Pinheiro, 'Rome I Regulation: Some Controversial Issues', *Grenzen überwinden – Prinzipien bewahren: Festschrift für Bernd von Hoffmann*, Herbert Kronke and Karsten Thorn, Ernst und Werner Gieseking, Bielefeld, 2011, pp. 242–257.

collective labour agreements, by the existence of a choice of court, and by the legal style in which the contract was written. On the other hand, the nationality of the parties and the currency established in the contract were seen as irrelevant for determining an implicit *professio iuris.*[30]

Within the scope of the Rome I Regulation, I identified only one ruling that added new criteria for determining an implicit choice of law: Portuguese courts decided the *language in which the contract was written* could not be used as a relevant circumstance for declaring a tacit choice of law.[31]

3.2.2. *General Rules on the Applicable Law in the Absence of Choice*

There are some cases determining the law applicable to contracts by using the Rome I Regulation's general rules in the absence of choice. Most of them are

30 Cf. Judgment of the Porto Court of Appeal of 29 May 2015, case 529/13.0TTOAZ.P1 (available via <http://www.dgsi.pt/jtrp.nsf/56a6e7121657f91e80257cda00381fdf/4c304f5b3a31e5fd80257e7c00481136?OpenDocument&Highlight=0,529%2F13.0TTOAZ.P1>). In this ruling, the court decided – in relation to an individual employment contract submitted to the 1980 Rome Convention on the Law Applicable to Contractual Obligations – that there had been an implicit choice of Portuguese law because the contract mentioned specific rules of a Portuguese collective labour agreement and because the parties made an agreement giving Portuguese courts exclusive jurisdiction.
In the same direction, in the Judgment of the Supreme Court of Justice of 12 May 2016, case 2998/14.2TTLSB.L1.S1 (available via <http://www.dgsi.pt/jstj.nsf/954f0ce6ad9dd8b980256b5f003fa814/b89a5ec177e3159e80257fb2003d31e2?OpenDocument&Highlight=0,2998%2F14.2TTLSB.L1.S1>), the court decided – in relation to an individual employment contract submitted to the 1980 Rome Convention – that there had been an implicit choice of Portuguese law was made because the contract mentioned specific rules of a Portuguese collective labour agreement, because the parties gave Portuguese courts exclusive jurisdiction, and because the contract explicitly established the employee should take the national holidays of the place in which the employee carried out his work (and not Portuguese national holidays), a clause interpreted by the court within a tacit assumption that, in its absence, Portuguese law would define the holidays and was therefore applicable to the contract.
It is not clear whether the courts used these criteria cumulatively or not. It seems the conclusion on the existence of an implicit choice of law was a result of the cumulative verification of all facts, which implies that the presence of just one of the criteria would not be enough.
Additionally, Judgment of the Coimbra Court of Appeal of 20 April 2016, case 234/10.0TTCTB.C1 (available via <http://www.dgsi.pt/jtrc.nsf/c3fb530030ea1c61802568d9005cd5bb/0d990c317ee7dbb380257fa20049854d?OpenDocument&Highlight=0,234%2F10.0TTCTB.C1>) determined that the nationality of the parties and the currency used in the contract were not relevant circumstances to justify an implicit choice of law. In this ruling, the court seemed to find that the legal style in which contract was written could be a relevant indicator for an implicit choice of law; however, because the contract related to Portuguese law and to Santomean law (which are very similar), that criterion could not be used.

31 In fact, in the Judgment of the Lisbon Court of Appeal of 19 November 2015, case 604/12.9TCFUN.L1-6 (available via <http://www.dgsi.pt/jtrl.nsf/33182fc732316039802565fa00497eec/720e4cdff38aafca80257f10003ea1d6?OpenDocument&Highlight=0,604%2F12.9TCFUN.L1-6>), the court held that the fact the contract was written in Italian did not imply an implicit choice of law.

simple, applying the law of the country where the central administration of the seller was located.[32] In other cases, it was discussed whether the relevant connecting factor was the central administration of the company or the place of its branch, agency or establishment (Article 19(2)).[33] I identified only one case concerning the law applicable to a contract relating to a right *in rem* in immovable property situated in Portugal, for which the parties did not choose the applicable law.[34]

An interesting verdict, discussing which criterion of Article 4 was appropriate, concerned a contract concluded in France between an Italian citizen with habitual residence in Italy and a company with central administration in Portugal, through which the Italian citizen engaged the Portuguese company to rent his flat in Monaco. The contract was written in Italian, but the court decided that the language of the contract did not imply an implicit choice of law; consequently, it discussed whether the law applicable to that kind of contract was the law of the country where the immovable property was situated (Article 4(1)(c)), or the law of the country of the landlord's habitual residence (Article 4(1)(d)), or the law of the country where the service provider had its habitual residence (Article 4(1)(b)). The applicable law depended on the characterisation of the contract: it mattered whether the contract was considered a *contract relating a right in rem in immovable property*, or a *tenancy of immovable property for temporary use for a period of no more than six consecutive months*, or a *contract for the provision of services.*

The court decided, against the argument of the Italian citizen, that it was a *contract for the provision of services*, since none of the parties used the flat and because the Portuguese company could rent the flat to any tenant and decide the

32 Cf. Judgment of the Porto Court of Appeal of 3 October 2014, case 693/10.0TVPRT.C1.P1 (available via <http://www.dgsi.pt/jtrp.nsf/56a6e7121657f91e80257cda00381fdf/a8cb2fdd8bde561480257ca2004cb3b5?OpenDocument&Highlight=0,693%2F10.0TVPRT.C1.P1>); Judgment of the Supreme Court of Justice of 26 February 2015, case 693/10.0TVPRT.C1.P1.S1 (available via <http://www.dgsi.pt/jstj.nsf/954f0ce6ad9dd8b980256b5f003fa814/3b5d7150f7a5535480257df8005e3e87?OpenDocument&Highlight=0,693%2F10.0TVPRT.C1.P1.S1>).

33 Judgment of the Guimarães Court of Appeal of 9 June 2016, case 4085/15.7T8GMR-A.G1 (available via <http://www.dgsi.pt/jtrg.nsf/86c25a698e4e7cb7802579ec004d3832/165b5a6cfe92c24f80258014004a4039?OpenDocument&Highlight=0,4085%2F15.7T8GMR-A.G1>).

34 Cf. Decision of Technical Council of the Institute of Notariats and Registries of 26 May 2011 (available via <http://www.irn.mj.pt/sections/irn/doutrina/pareceres/predial/2010/p-r-p-223-2010-sjc-ct/downloadFile/file/RP223-2010.pdf?nocache=1318328677.59>). The decision was not given by a court *stricto sensu*, but by the Legal Advisory Board of the National Institute on Land Registry, which settles appeals from land registrars' decisions. Within the Portuguese legal system, one can challenge decisions of registrars in court or by appealing to the President of the Institute of Notariats and Registries; in the latter case, the President's decision will be made, taking into account an opinion of the Legal Advisory Board of the Institute of Notariats and Registries. An analysis of the case law shows that in every single case the President's decision acknowledged the opinion of this council, which grants it almost the same authority as a court decision.

duration of each rental; therefore, Portuguese law was applicable, since it was the law of the country of habitual residence of the service provider.[35]

3.2.3. *Specific Rules on the Law Applicable to Individual Employment Contracts and to Contracts of Carriage*

Although many rulings of Portuguese courts have used specific European rules on the law applicable to individual employment contracts, all decisions concerned contracts submitted to the 1980 Rome Convention: in these cases, Portuguese courts compared the rules of the chosen law and the law applicable in the absence of choice, affording the employee the protection of the last.[36] This case law will probably be taken as a reference in cases concerning employment contracts submitted to the Rome I Regulation; however, I found no decisions on disputes arising from contracts concluded after 17 December 2009.

Beyond rulings on individual employment contracts, I found a single decision concerning a contract for the carriage of goods, in which the court submitted the contract to the law of the country of the habitual residence of the carrier.[37]

3.2.4. *Overriding Mandatory Provisions*

Portuguese courts apply often a mandatory provision of the *lex fori* concerning the law applicable to individual employment contracts, namely a rule of the Portuguese Constitution prohibiting dismissal without fair cause,[38] which is

---

35 Cf. Judgment of the Lisbon Court of Appeal of 19 November 2015, case 604/12.9TCFUN.L1-6 (available via <http://www.dgsi.pt/jtrl.nsf/33182fc732316039802565fa00497eec/720e4cdff38aafca80257f10003ea1d6?OpenDocument&Highlight=0,604%2F12.9TCFUN.L1-6>).

36 Cf. Judgment of the Supreme Court of Justice of 12 May 2016, case 2998/14.2TTLSB.L1.S1 (available <http://www.dgsi.pt/jstj.nsf/954f0ce6ad9dd8b980256b5f003fa814/b89a5ec177e3159e80257fb2003d31e2?OpenDocument&Highlight=0,2998%2F14.2TTLSB.L1.S1>), concerning an individual employment contract concluded on 1 December 2005 between a Portuguese employee with habitual residence in Portugal and a Spanish company, in which Spanish law had been explicitly chosen. The court compared the provisions of the chosen law and of the law applicable in the absence of choice and gave the employee the protection afforded by Portuguese law (applicable in the absence of choice).
The same solution was provided in Judgment of the Porto Court of Appeal of 2 June 2014, case 930/08.1TTPRT.P2 (available via <http://www.dgsi.pt/jtrp.nsf/56a6e7121657f91e80257cda00381fdf/bdb6210bbadf9a9780257cfb0045f055?OpenDocument&Highlight=0,930%2F08.1TTPRT.P2%20>): even though the parties had expressly chosen French law, the court compared the provisions on dismissal of French law with Portuguese law (applicable in the absence of choice) and gave the employee the protection afforded by Portuguese law.

37 Cf. Judgment of the Torres Vedras Lower Court of 11 March 2013, case 293447/11.1YIPRT.

38 Cf. Article 53 of the Constitution of Portuguese Republic: 'Workers are guaranteed job security, and dismissal without fair cause or for political or ideological reasons is prohibited'.

deemed to be an implicit *loi d'application immédiate* of Portuguese law.[39] The concept of *overriding mandatory provisions* traditionally used by the courts is similar to the definition provided by Francescakis, since it is used by Portuguese legal authors. The courts define such provisions as those 'which, by the essentiality of their commands, transcend the spatial competence of the system in which they are integrated, applying directly to international situations, taking precedence over the law of the country designated by the conflict-of-laws rule'.[40] However, none of these cases concerned contracts within the temporal scope of the Rome I Regulation. Additionally, I found no case dealing with the application of *lois de police* of third countries.

3.2.5. *Formal Validity of Contracts and Characterisation Issues*

There is a very interesting decision regarding the characterisation of provisions on the formal validity of contracts when those norms are established to ensure the contract's *substantive validity*. The decision was not addressed by a court but

---

39 Cf. Judgment of the Porto Court of Appeal of 5 May 2014, case 525/09.2TTPRT.P1 (available via <http://www.dgsi.pt/jtrp.nsf/56a6e7121657f91e80257cda00381fdf/4eb265e1211558b280257cd9003eb679?OpenDocument&Highlight=0,525%2F09.2TTPRT.P1>); Judgment of the Lisbon Court of Appeal of 11 April 2015, case 2998.14.2TTLSB.L1-4 (available via <http://www.dgsi.pt/jtrl.nsf/33182fc732316039802565fa00497eec/55018aca6d94e18c80257efa003ac208?OpenDocument&Highlight=0,2998.14.2TTLSB.L1-4%20>); Judgment of the Supreme Court of Justice of 30 September 1998, case 98S131 (available via <http://www.dgsi.pt/jstj.nsf/954f0ce6ad9dd8b980256b5f003fa814/782a5a05901e6e7b802568fc003bb047?OpenDocument&Highlight=0,98S131>); Judgment of the Supreme Court of Justice of 7 November 2012, case 377/07.7TTFUN.L1.S1 (available via <http://www.dgsi.pt/jstj.nsf/954f0ce6ad9dd8b980256b5f003fa814/43918af5a031701080257a3d002d3a73?OpenDocument&Highlight=0,98S131>); Judgment of the Lisbon Court of Appeal of 20 February 2013, case 3319/07.6TTLSB.L3-4 (available via <http://www.dgsi.pt/jtrl.nsf/33182fc732316039802565fa00497eec/4fcfba3d6a3f79d680257bc2004d67cf?OpenDocument&Highlight=0,3319%2F07.6TTLSB.L3-4>).

40 Judgment of the Porto Court of Appeal of 5 May 2014, case 525/09.2TTPRT.P1 (available via <http://www.dgsi.pt/jtrp.nsf/56a6e7121657f91e80257cda00381fdf/4eb265e1211558b280257cd9003eb679?OpenDocument&Highlight=0,525%2F09.2TTPRT.P1>). The concept is developed by Rui Moura Ramos, n. 23 above, p. 672; António Marques dos Santos, 'Alguns Princípios de Direito Internacional Privado e de Direito Internacional Público do Trabalho', *Estudos de Direito Internacional Privado e de Direito Público*, Almedina, Coimbra, 2004, pp. 93–130, p. 105; António Marques dos Santos, n. 23 above, p. 940; António Ferrer Correia, n. 7 above, p. 161; António Ferrer Correia, 'Considerações sobre o método do Direito Internacional Privado', *Estudos em Homenagem ao Prof. Doutor J. J. Teixeira Ribeiro*, Vol. III, Coimbra, 1983, pp. 1–92, p. 85; António Ferrer Correia, *Direito Internacional Privado - Alguns Problemas*, Almedina, Coimbra, 1997, p. 60; João Baptista Machado, *Âmbito de Eficácia e Âmbito de Competência das Leis* (reimpressão), Almedina, Coimbra, 1998, p. 279; Maria Helena Brito, 'Os Contratos Bancários e a Convenção de Roma de 19 de Junho de 1980 sobre a lei aplicável às obrigações contratuais', *Revista da Banca*, no. 28, 1993, pp. 75–124, p. 118.

by the Legal Advisory Board of the National Institute on Land Registry, which settles appeals from land registrars' decisions.[41]

In a contract relating to a right *in rem* in immovable property situated in Portugal (for which the parties did not choose the applicable law), concluded in California, Portuguese law was established as the *lex contractus* (Article 4(1)(c) of the Rome I Regulation) but the formal validity was debated. The contract satisfied the formal requirements of the *lex loci celebrationis* (California), since it was concluded in a private document before a witness (a common-law notary). However, if Portuguese law were applicable, the contract would be found invalid; in fact, Portuguese law establishes that contracts concerning rights *in rem* in immovable property are formally valid only if concluded by an authentic instrument or by authenticated private documents (where a civil law notary or other official certifies the substantive legality of the contract); if not, the contracts are declared *substantively invalid*, since those are requirements *ad substantiam* and not only *ad probationem*.[42]

The problem dealt with was the characterisation of those requirements of Portuguese law: if they were taken to be *formal requirements*, the contract would be valid, since Article 11(1) of the Rome I Regulation established the sufficiency of the form prescribed in Californian law; however, if the *ad substantiam* requirement of an authentic instrument – since it is meant to ensure the fulfilment of *lex contractus* – was characterised as a requirement for the substantive validity of the contract, Portuguese law would be applicable (because the contract was submitted to Portuguese law) and the nullity of contract should be declared.

It was decided that the *ad substantiam* requirement of Portuguese law for an authentic instrument was intended to prevent the substantive invalidity of the contract and, therefore, was a validity requisite of *substance* and not of *form*. Accordingly, because Portuguese law was the *lex contractus*, the nullity of the contract was declared. This ruling followed the opinion of most Portuguese legal authors on the characterisation of those provisions.[43]

---

41 Cf. Decision of Technical Council of the Institute of Notariats and Registries of 26 May 2011 (available via <http://www.irn.mj.pt/sections/irn/doutrina/pareceres/predial/2010/p-r-p-223-2010-sjc-ct/downloadFile/file/RP223-2010.pdf>). Cf., on the authority of this council, n. 34 above.

42 This means that overlooking those requirements of form give rise to the *substantive invalidity* of the contract – Article 220 of the Portuguese Civil Code.

43 Cf. João Baptista Machado, n. 9 above, p. 357; Luís de Lima Pinheiro, *Direito Internacional Privado*, Vol. II, Direito de Conflitos – Parte Especial, 3rd edition, Almedina, Coimbra, 2009, p. 159; Afonso Patrão, 'A aplicação internacionalmente ampliada das regras de notariado latino nos negócios imobiliários', *Estudos em Homenagem ao Conselheiro Presidente Rui Moura Ramos*, Vol. II, Tribunal Constitucional, Lisbon, 2016, pp. 551–609, p. 557.

3.2.6. *Escape Clause*

There are no cases I know of the effectively use the escape clauses of the Rome I Regulation. There are, however, rulings in which the court searched for relevant elements to determine a country more closely connected with the contract other than the national law indicated in Article 4.[44] Additionally, there are court decisions that apply the escape clause of the 1980 Rome Convention, using criteria which will probably be employed within the scope of the Rome I Regulation: the court used it when the parties had the same nationality, belonged to the same family, and spoke the language of the country of both parties' nationality.[45]

4. CONCLUSION

As has been seen, the case law of Portuguese courts does not cover all the issues relating to the Rome I and Rome II Regulations. As regards the Rome I Regulation, there is no case on overriding mandatory provisions of third states, no judgment applying specific rules on consumer contracts or insurance contracts, and no verdict applying the *lex fori* because of the inconsistency of foreign law with international *ordre public.*

Regarding the Rome II Regulation, the situation is even worse. The publicly available judgments applying the Rome II Regulation are scarce; as a result, I found no case in which the parties chose the law applicable to torts; no verdict applying specific conflict-of-laws rules to product liability, unfair competition, environmental damage, intellectual property rights or industrial action; no judicial decisions on either unjust enrichment or *negotiorum gestio;* no case in which overriding mandatory provisions were applied or even considered; and no ruling referencing rules of safety and conduct (Article 17).

Although this collection of judicial rulings is not enough to draw any conclusions, the lack of cases in which the parties had designated the law

---

44 Cf. Judgment of the Porto Court of Appeal of 10 January 2015, case 588/13.6TVPRT.P1 (available via <http://www.dgsi.pt/jtrp.nsf/56a6e7121657f91e80257cda00381fdf/03469e2b51f3065480257edc004a3748?OpenDocument&Highlight=0,588%2F13.6TVPRT.P1>).

45 Judgment of the Lisbon Court of Appeal of 18 April 2012, case 914/09.2TTLSB.L1-4 (available via <http://www.dgsi.pt/jtrl.nsf/33182fc732316039802565fa00497eec/cbdd4c5052a0ecaf802579ec00450e55?OpenDocument&Highlight=0,914%2F09.2TTLSB.L1-4>) concerning an individual employment contract concluded in July 2007 between a Portuguese employee and a Dutch company. In this contract, the court used the exception clause of Article 6 (2) of the 1980 Rome Convention on the Law Applicable to Contractual Obligations, considering the fact that both the employee and the administrator of the Dutch company were Portuguese citizens and from the same (Portuguese) family, the labour orders were given in Portuguese, and the employee was in the Netherlands only during the execution of the contract.

applicable to torts could perhaps be expected: if the parties could agree on the applicable law, the dispute may have been solved out of court.

Considering exclusively the existing case law, I must address some interesting issues on the application of these Regulations, which could identify both difficulties and virtues of the European rules on the conflict of laws.

The first issue concerns the characterisation of rules on the formal validity of a contract. Despite not being addressed in Article 12 of the Rome I Regulation, I believe that the Portuguese authorities decided correctly in assuming that the rules of the *lex contractus* on form, which are intended to ensure the substantive validity of the contract (by having a notary or other public official oversee it), are to be employed if their infringement would cause the *substantive invalidity* of the contract. In fact, in notarial systems where the conveyancer assumes a *preventive role*, ensuring a superior degree of legal certainty, these rules on form concern the substantive validity of the contract.

The second conclusion concerns Article 4(1) of the Rome II Regulation, which was wrongly interpreted once in Portugal, which could suggest a certain lack of clarity. In fact, even though most decisions of Portuguese courts are correct in this respect (applying the law of the country where the first damage arose), it must be emphasised that in most cases there was a discussion between the parties on the analysis of Article 4(1). As aforementioned, I found one incorrect decision where it was held that the law of indirect consequences of the event was applicable. Therefore, for the sake of clarity, the inclusion of the criteria of Recitals 16 and 17 into the text of Article 4 could be considered.

The third conclusion concerns the disappearance of *renvoi* in the Rome I and Rome II Regulations, *vis-à-vis* the internal rules of Portuguese law (in which *renvoi* was pragmatically oriented, having only been accepted as it achieved international consistency of decisions).[46] In contrast to what might have been expected, no judgment was found that applied the Regulations gave rise to inconsistency of decisions; in fact, all cases exclusively concerned Member States, which means international consistency was achieved in the fields of contractual and non-contractual obligations, even without a *renvoi* system. This proves that the unification of conflict-of-laws rules at the European level is a successful way of promoting international stability.

[46] Cf. Articles 16–18 of the Portuguese Civil Code.

THE APPLICATION OF THE ROME I AND ROME II REGULATIONS IN SLOVAKIA

Elena JUDOVA and Miloš LEVRINC

1. INTRODUCTION

Sixteen years after joining the European Union,[1] it can be stated that the knowledge of European law in the legal practice of the Slovak Republic is good. The courts, as well as attorneys and members of other legal professions, are, in

1 The Slovak Republic has been a Member State of the European Union since 1 May 2004.

dealing with some legal questions, accustomed to check whether there is also any European legislation available, to refer to European rules (the Regulations as well as the Directives) in their decisions or submissions, and to refer to the case law of the European Court of Justice. Judges are regularly trained through the Judicial Academy of the Slovak Republic, and professional literature also plays supporting role here, in particular regularly published and widely respected professional journals, such as the *Judicial Review* (*Justičná revue*), published by the Ministry of Justice, and journals published by professional chambers, such as *Advocacy Bulletin* (*Bulletin advokácie*), *Ars notaria* and others.

Despite that, the range of issues addressed in the case law of the courts of the Slovak Republic in relation to the application of the Rome I and Rome II Regulations is not large. The majority of cases deal with the issue of determining the applicable law, i.e. the application of Articles 3–8 of the Rome I Regulation and Article 4 of the Rome II Regulation. Only rarely are issues such as the scope of the applicable law dealt with in the case law.

There are several reasons for this. First of all, it has to do with the position of case law as a source of law, or with the slow adoption of the idea that courts can shape the law through the formulation of rigorous argumentation in handing down the decisions of the courts of the Slovak Republic.

Another reason is that the courts have a large overload of cases. According to the data of the Ministry of Justice of the Slovak Republic, the average number of new submissions to the courts of first instance is 393 per judge per year totalled (approximately 33 per month); however, in some district courts this figure exceeded 500 or even more new submissions per judge per year.[2] Generally, the courts of first and second instances are not specialised, however. The same courts decide civil, commercial, labour, family and criminal matters.[3] Thus, the courts are expected to have a detailed overview of all areas of law. We should also not fail to mention the frequent legislative changes in Slovak law. As a result, it is very difficult for courts to follow in detail the development of European law, including its interpretation in the case law of the EU courts, and there is great uncertainty about the requirements for the application of standards of European law.

Given the above, it is not surprising that the decisions of the courts of the Slovak Republic deal in much more detail with European standards of consumer

2 <https://www.justice.gov.sk/Stranky/Sudy/Statistika-OS-2012-2016.aspx>.

3 In the Slovak Republic, there is a unitary court system, consisting of district courts, regional courts and the Supreme Court of the Slovak Republic (Sec. 5, Act no. 757/2004 Coll. of laws on courts). The only specialised court is a specialised criminal court with jurisdiction over the entire Slovak Republic, which decides on the most serious offences. On the basis of the internal work plan of the court, an individual judge can be assigned mainly to agenda civil, family, commercial, or other specific matters. However, this assignment of a judge need not be exclusive and is not unchangeable. There is no separate agenda of matters with a foreign element.

law or company law than European standards relating to the determination of the applicable law and court jurisdiction. The reason for this is that the courts focus on flawless decisions on the merits, and the determination of jurisdiction and the applicable law is for the court basically only an intermediate step on the way to deciding on the merits of the case.

This basic level of argumentation regarding the determination of applicable law and jurisdiction is also caused by courts' limited experience in dealing with cases with a foreign element, i.e. cross-border legal relations. The Slovak Republic is a small country, and was until 1989 part of the socialist bloc. It became an open market economy only after the change in the system of government in 1989. The increased mobility of the population, through the establishment of cross-border commercial and non-commercial relations, has only really come about in the last 25 years, in particular since Slovakia's accession to the EU in 2004. So far, cases with a foreign element have only come before Slovak courts relatively infrequently. A particular judge may face the need to apply the rules of private international law only once or twice a year. This is also the reason why a larger space is not given to the questions of determining the applicable law in the judgments of the court of the Slovak Republic.

2. THE POSITION OF COURT DECISIONS IN SLOVAK LAW

The Slovak legal system belongs to the civil law family. A court decision – a judgment – is not considered a source of law, but only an act of law enforcement. In the first civil codes adopted in continental Europe in the early nineteenth century, any possibility of creating legal rules by the courts was completely rejected.[4] Gradually, however, judicial practice has become an accepted tool of interpretation of generally formulated rules of law and their operation in a particular cause. Today, in countries belonging to the continental civil law family, the established case law of the courts is recognised to have a certain degree of normative binding force.[5]

In the Slovak Republic, the idea of the binding force of established judicial practice does not have such a tradition as in the countries of continental Western Europe. During the totalitarian regime in the years 1948–1989, in accordance with promoted statutory positivism, it was inconceivable that the courts would in any way create or complement socialist law. The legal monopoly belonged

4 See Bogdan, M.: *Concise Introduction to Comparative Law*, Groningen: Europa Law Publishing, 2013, p. 140.

5 Bobek, M. – Kühn, Z. et al.: *Judikatura a právní argumentace*, 2nd ed, Prague: Auditorium, 2013, p. 26 et seq.

to the ruling Communist Party and was exercised through the parliament composed solely of its candidates. The judge was required to mechanically follow the law; any creative interpretation of the law would carry a risk of uncontrolled departure from socialist ideas.

Whole generations of lawyers were trained in this spirit, and to some extent this continues in the teaching of law and judicial practice today. Gradually, however, numerous voices from the academic and judicial community have started to appear, pointing to the need for constant decision-making of the courts in accordance with established practice of supreme courts in order to assure predictability of court decisions and the outcome of the lawsuit, without which the existence of one of basic principles of the rule of law – the principle of legal certainty – is not possible.[6]

The obligation to follow the established case law of higher courts was legislatively enshrined in the new legislation on civil procedural law effective from 1 July 2016. The Civil Contentious Procedure Code (*Civilný sporový poriadok*), Act no. 160/2015 Coll. of Laws (CCPC), as the only one of the three procedural codes that is general and not specialised,[7] enshrines in its initial part, dedicated to the basic principles, the rules in accordance with which these procedural codes are to be applied and interpreted. In this part, Article 2 sets out the obligation to follow the established decision-making practice of the highest judicial authorities and the obligation to justify possible departure from this practice.[8] The explanatory memorandum to this provision expressly mentions

---

6 See e.g. Ľalík, M.: 'Menej pozitivisticky a viac prirodzenoprávne. Editoriál', in: *Zo súdnej praxe*, vol. 11, 2006, no. 4; or Demčák, S.: 'O záväznosti judikatúry v podmienkach Slovenskej republiky', in: *Bulletin slovenskej advokácie*, vol. XV, 2009, no. 6, pp. 8–13. Similarly even the Constitutional Court, in its order of 22 November 2011, case no. IV. ÚS 499/2011-25: 'Diametrically opposed decision-making activity of the General Court on the same question of law for the same or an analogous factual situation, unless it may be objectively and reasonably justified, is constitutionally unsustainable. Although legal conclusions of general courts contained in their decisions do not have in the legal system of the Slovak Republic a character of a precedent, that would bind other judges deciding on similar matters to rule identically, despite that conflicting legal conclusions expressed in analogous cases do not contribute to the fulfilment of the main purpose of the principle of legal certainty nor confidence in fair trial.'

7 The Civil Procedure Code 1963 was replaced with effect from 1 July 2016 by three new procedural codes: Act no. 160/2015 Coll. – the Civil Contentious Procedure Code; Act no. 161/2015 Coll. – the Civil Non-Contentious Procedure Code; and Act no. 162/2015 Coll. – the Administrative Procedure Code, which are in a mutual relationship of subsidiarity. The Civil Contentious Procedure Code acts as a general rule, the Civil Non-Contentious Procedure Code and Administrative Procedure Code as *lex specialis*, and in issues not regulated in the latter two, the Civil Contentious Procedure Code is followed.

8 Article 2(2) CCPC: 'Legal certainty is a condition in which anyone can legitimately expect that the dispute will be resolved in line with the established practice of the highest judicial authorities; if there is no such established practice, it is a condition in which anyone can legitimately expect that the dispute will be resolved fairly.' Article 2(3) CCPC: 'If the dispute, under consideration of the relevant facts and legal specificities of the case, is decided otherwise, everyone has the right to a thorough and convincing justification for this departure.'

the established case law line of the highest judicial authorities of the Slovak Republic, i.e. the Supreme Court and the Constitutional Court,[9] as well as the European Court of Human Rights and the European Court of Justice.

The case law of these judicial authorities, including the European courts, has been regularly analysed by law journals and debated in professional training for judges, but the courts have rarely relied on the case law in issue in their decisions. However, the situation is slowly changing, especially with regard to higher court judgments and especially from recent years.

As a novelty, the courts have an obligation (section 220(3) CCPC) to give detailed justification for any departure from established judicial practice, either their own or that of the highest judicial authorities, if they decide to depart from such an established practice in their decision, in accordance with Article 2 of the Basic principles of the CCPC. The court is required to comment on the arguments of the parties, including on the case law and jurisprudence raised by the parties in the dispute. This in turn is likely to place higher demands on the court to acquire a greater working knowledge, in the case law of the European Court of Justice (ECJ) for example, as it is not unusual for the parties' lawyers to choose certain judgments from the body of the ECJ's case law, where it is interpreting a certain provision of a Regulation in the context of certain factual circumstances, potentially favourable to their case.

It can therefore be expected that this new legislation will lead to the development of the case law of the Slovak courts and strengthen the line of argumentation of judicial decisions.[10] The courts, in their decisions, are supposed to be more motivated than they have been so far to take into account the case law, whether of domestic or of European courts, in their decisions. They are obliged to consider case law if the parties raise it in their submissions, which may also give an incentive to lawyers representing the parties to search

---

9 The system of general courts in the Slovak Republic consists of district courts, regional courts and the Supreme Court. Civil cases are decided in the first instance by district courts, except in matters where the law provides that regional courts decide in the first instance. Regional courts decide as the courts of second instance on appeals from decisions of the district courts. The Supreme Court decides on extraordinary legal remedies against decisions of district and regional courts. The Constitutional Court decides in matters of protection of constitutional values.

10 For example, the Regional Court in Bratislava, in the reasoning of its judgment concerning the determination of the law applicable to an individual employment contract, referred to earlier decisions of different chambers of the same regional court in similar cases and stated that: 'if, in the same legal question, in the same or analogous factual situation, the current decision-making practice of the courts is the same and the Supreme Court of the Slovak Republic has not yet expressed a different legal opinion, then the Court, in order to comply with the principle of legal certainty and in the interest of trust in a fair trial (Article 2 para 2 CCPC), has no reason to deviate from the established legal opinion expressed in previous cases.' – Judgment of the Regional Court Bratislava of 25 September 2018, file ref. 3Co/162/2017.

for relevant case law and submit it to support their claims. On the other hand, it is uncertain whether this will be equally reflected in the interpretation and application of the Regulations on the law applicable to contractual and non-contractual obligations, particularly for the reasons referred to in section 1.

Greater quality and coherence in decision-making on cross-border contractual obligations would be achieved if the Supreme Court were to deal more often with these issues in its case law. Only its repeatedly confirmed legal opinions (together with the opinions of the Constitutional Court in matters relating to the review of constitutionality) can be considered established decision-making practice under Article 2 of the Basic principles of the CCPC.[11] However, for the Supreme Court to be able to deal with these issues repeatedly, it is essential that they are regularly submitted to the court for a decision, which is currently only possible by filing an extraordinary remedy (appellate review), which requires action on the part of the parties and for the grounds for appellate review under section 421 CCPC to be met.[12]

So far, district and regional courts have approached the interpretation of Regulations differently, according to their personal understanding and working knowledge of the Regulation, ultimately influenced by the arguments of the parties' lawyers. They are sometimes also inspired by the decisions of their colleagues from other courts, but nothing binds them to follow the case law of other Slovak courts, or to deal with it.[13] Therefore, the application of certain provisions of the Rome I and Rome II Regulations is in the Slovak judicial practice very heterogeneous, and that is why, despite the majority taking a certain approach to the application of a specific provision of the Regulation, we dare not say that it is an established approach that will persist in Slovakia.

---

11 As to the criteria that the case law of the Supreme Court must meet in order to be considered 'established case law' that should be followed by Slovak courts, see closer Moravčíková, A.: 'Postavenie a povaha judikatúry v novej procesnej právnej úprave', in: *Právny obzor*, vol. 99, 2016, no. 4, pp. 259–273.

12 Tóth-Vaňo, P.: 'O precedenčnej záväznosti súdneho rozhodnutia (aj podľa Civilného sporového poriadku)', in: *Justičná revue*, vol. 68, 2016, no. 5, p. 609 et seq. It should be noted that during the analysed period of 2006–2019, there were minimal such decisions by the Supreme Court of the Slovak Republic. Only two decision of the Supreme Court of the Slovak Republic concerned the question of the law applicable to contractual obligations (and none to non-contractual obligations). The first decision, Resolution of the Supreme Court of 27 August 2015, file ref. 2MCdo 16/2014, could affect the application of Article 3 of the Rome I Regulation, namely the validity of the choice of law for consumer contracts enshrined in the general terms of the entrepreneur. The core of the subject was, however, related to the method of application of substantive Czech law as the law applicable in the matter. The second decision, Resolution of the Supreme Court of 25 October 2017, file ref. 7Cdo 19/2017, concerning the interpretation of the 'place where the work is habitually carried out' was even challenged by one of the parties before the Constitutional Court of the Slovak Republic, and is described in section 4.4.4.

13 The opinion of a higher court on appeal from the decision of the lower court is individually binding. It is, however, binding only for the specific case in which the appeal was lodged.

3. PREVIOUS PRIVATE INTERNATIONAL LAW REGIME: THE PIL ACT

The legal order of the Slovak Republic has a long tradition of codified private international law. Private international law was first codified in 1948 by Act no. 41/1948 Coll. on international and interregional private law and the legal status of foreigners in the field of private law of 10 April 1948. That statute was replaced in 1963 by the currently valid Act no. 97/1963 Coll. on Private International Law and the Rules of Procedure of 4 December 1963, effective from 1 April 1964. The new law built on the existing provisions of the Act of 10 April 1948 in many ways the continuity in handling situations with a foreign element was thus preserved.

The currently effective Act on Private International Law and the Rules of Procedure of 4 December 1963 (the PIL Act) has therefore been applied for over fifty years. Generations of judges and lawyers have been educated on the basis of the PIL Act and still tend to look for solutions in this statute that comprehensively address the entire area of legal relations with foreign elements.

After 1990, and especially in connection with the entry of Slovakia into the EU, there have been several changes to the PIL Act, but they more substantially affected several issues of family relationships or the recognition and enforcement of foreign judgments, and only to a minor extent the regulation of obligations. It is interesting that the regulation of contractual and non-contractual obligations in the PIL Act is based on similar principles as the European regulation.

The law applicable to contractual relations is set forth in sections 9 and 10; labour law relations are governed separately by section 16. Section 14 sets forth the law applicable to unilateral legal acts and section 15 sets forth the law applicable to claims for damages incurred other than by a breach of obligations under contract and other legal actions. Specifically governed are ancillary issues such as modifications, security or consequences of a breach of contractual obligations in section 11, or limitation and set-off in section 13. The public policy exception (section 36) and the use of *renvoi* (section 35) are governed separately, within the common provisions.

Legal regulation of contractual obligations is based, similarly to the Rome Convention and the Rome I Regulation, on the principles of the choice of law and the law of the party that provides the characteristic performance for the contract. Choice of law is unlimited and may be made expressly or tacitly, if there are no doubts about the will expressed, given the circumstances. Regulation of the choice of law was amended in 2003[14] due to the transposition

[14] Act no. 589/20003 Coll. of laws.

of the consumer directives[15] with the provision that says that if the parties to a consumer contract choose a law that provides the consumer with less protection of his rights than Slovak law, their relations shall be governed unilaterally by Slovak law (section 9(3) of the PIL Act).

If there is no choice of law, contractual relationships between the contracting parties, in accordance with section 10 of the PIL Act, shall be governed by the law corresponding to the reasonable arrangement of such relationship. This provision also contains precisely formulated conflict-of-laws rules for the selected contracts – sales contracts, contracts for the provision of services, real estate-related contracts, contracts of carriage, insurance contracts, mandate contracts, agency contracts, and contracts of multilateral barter.

These precisely formulated conflict-of-laws rules are present in the first two paragraphs of section 10 of the PIL Act, with the first paragraph establishing the general principle and the second setting out the specificities of conflict-of-laws rules. They are introduced with the words: 'With respect to it [the principle of reasonable arrangement of the relationship], unless special legislation provides otherwise, the following principles shall in general apply: a) a sales contract …'. Specifically formulated conflict-of-laws rules are thus the norm that should typically be followed; the principle of reasonable arrangement of the relationship functions as an escape clause. The criteria used to determine the applicable law are also closely related to those enshrined by the Rome I Regulation – for instance, sales contracts shall be governed by the law of the place of seat (domicile) of the seller, contracts for the provision of services by the law of the place of seat (domicile) of the service provider, and real estate-related contracts by the law of the place where the property is situated.[16]

---

15 Article 6 of Council Directive 93/13/EEC on unfair terms in consumer contracts; Article 7 of Directive 1999/44/EC on certain aspects of the sale of consumer goods and associated guarantees; and Article 9 of the Directive 94/47/EC on the protection of purchasers in respect of certain aspects of contracts relating to the purchase of the right to use immovable properties on a timeshare basis. The provision of section 9(3) of the PIL Act persisted in an unchanged form even after the adoption of Directive 2011/83/EU on consumer rights, amending Directive 93/13/EEC and Directive 1999/44/EC and repealing of the Directive 94/47/EC by the Directive 2008/122/EC on the protection of consumers in respect of certain aspects of timeshare, long-term holiday product, resale and exchange contracts.

16 The only deviation from the principle of the law of domicile of the party that provides the characteristic performance is a provision on agency contracts in section 10(2)(f), under which the law of the person for whom a representative carries out activities (the principal) is to be used. This regulation was the product of the period during which it originated and the monopoly on foreign trade that was carried out by state-owned foreign trade enterprises. It has not been modified since 1990, it was merely pointed out that it has been overcome through practice and that the law that corresponds to the reasonable arrangement of the given relationship is to prevail, as enshrined in the introduction of section 10.

With the exception of the above, contracts are to be governed, within the meaning of section 10 of the PIL Act (unless a specific law provides otherwise), by the law of the country in which both parties have their seat (domicile) or, if their seat (domicile) is not in the same country, by the law of the place where the contract was concluded – except for distance contracts, for which the law of the seat (domicile) of the recipient of an offer to conclude a contract prevails. Reference to the law of the seat (domicile) of the recipient of an offer to conclude a contract will also in most cases lead to the application of the law of the party that provides characteristic performance; however, this may not be so in the case of contracts like distribution contracts or franchise contracts. Moreover, section 10 of PIL Act was amended in 2014,[17] with the provision ensuring consumer protection, this time following the transposition of the Directive 2011/83/EU on consumer rights. For more detail on the effect of this provision on judicial practice, see section 4.5.1.

The PIL Act also specifically deals with issues related to modification, security or consequences of a breach of contractual obligations (section 11). If a choice of law was not made by the parties, or in the absence of a law the use of which corresponds to a reasonable arrangement of the relationship, these issues are governed by the same law as the contractual obligation itself, similarly to the Rome I Regulation. Within the meaning of the PIL Act, the limitation period (section 13(1)) is governed by the same law as the law of obligations. Set-off shall be governed by the same law as the claim against which it is pursued, unless anything else results from the requirement of a reasonable arrangement of the legal relationship (section 13(2)).

Similarly, the validity of the contract and the consequences of its invalidity are governed by the law that would be applicable were the contract to be valid. However, in terms of formal validity, the applicable law is either the law by which the contract would be governed, or the law of the place where the will to act was expressed (section 4).

As regards non-contractual obligations, the PIL Act states that the applicable law is either the law of the place where the damage occurred, or the law of the place where the event occurred that gave rise to damages (section 15). However, it was not the choice of the parties but that of the court hearing the case and taking into account the facts as to which legal system the situation should have a closer relationship. Legal doctrine on this provision has stated that the conflict-of-law criteria laid down in section 15 are not suitable for certain types of damage (namely if the damage is caused by unfair competition, defective products or the infringement of intellectual property rights, or where the parties are domiciled in the same country and their presence in the place where the damage occurred

[17] Act no. 102/2014 Coll. of laws.

is strictly a coincidence).[18] Choice of law for non-contractual obligations was not possible under Slovak private international law.

The provisions of the Slovak PIL Act are clear, understandable, formulated simply and are generally known to the Slovak legal community. The basic principles are comparable to those of the Rome I and Rome II Regulations, and in many cases the use of PIL Act may lead to the same results as the application of EU Regulations.[19] Therefore, the use of the PIL Act is nowadays still attractive. In several judgments, we encountered the fact that court cited the PIL Act alongside the provisions of the Rome I Regulation (it is interesting though that this was rarely the case in relation to the Rome II Regulation) and in the event that both instruments referred to the same applicable law, they did not consider any further the question which one was applicable in the situation in question. On the other hand, courts also cite the PIL Act alongside the Rome I and Rome II Regulations to illustrate the existing sources regulating both contractual and non-contractual obligations with foreign elements, then subsequently deduce which of these sets of rules is applicable to the case (and why).

The proportion of cases where the PIL Act was wrongly used in situations to which the Rome Convention or the Rome I Regulation should have been applied is no higher than 26 per cent. However, in a number of decisions in which the court correctly applied the Rome I Regulation, it was clear that the court interpreted its provisions through the PIL Act.

On the other hand, this may be a useful way to bring the EU legislation on the law applicable to contractual and non-contractual obligations closer to the courts, and to legal practice in general. This could be done by pointing out the existing similarities and highlighting the differences between the EU and Slovak law, including different rules governing their interpretation. The fact is that the national legislation does not cease to operate alongside the provisions of the EU Regulations at least until aspects of contractual and non-contractual relationships are excluded from the scope of the Rome I and Rome II Regulations. Legal practice then often perceives such a duplicate system as highly complex and takes recourse to what it knows already.

---

18 Kučera, Z. – Tichý, L.: Zákon o mezinárodním právu soukromém a procesním, Prague: Panorama, 1989, pp. 133–134.

19 This is very well illustrated by the decision of the Regional Court Žilina, of 29 May 2014, file ref. 6Co/502/2013, issued on appeal from the decision of the District Court Žilina. The Regional Court in its judgment also commented on the determination of the applicable law made by the District Court, in relation to its decision to proceed pursuant to sections 9 and 10 of the Slovak PIL Act. The Regional Court pointed out that since the contractual relationship of the parties in question arose on 23 December 2006, the applicable law should have been determined under the 1980 Rome Convention on the Law Applicable to Contractual Obligations. At the same time, however, the Regional Court concluded that the applicable law under the Convention was also Slovak law and therefore the District Court was correct in applying Slovak law in the case, even though the court used the provisions of Slovak private international law as the basis for its consideration.

4. THE EU RULES ON THE LAW APPLICABLE TO OBLIGATIONS IN PRACTICE

4.1. THE ROME CONVENTION AND ROME I AND ROME II REGULATIONS IN PRACTICE

4.1.1. General Information

The Slovak Republic, as a Member State of the EU since 2004, has been bound by the Rome I and Rome II Regulations from the date of their entry into force. The rules for the application in time of these Regulations (Article 28 Rome I, Article 31 Rome II) also apply in their unchanged form to the Slovak Republic and its judicial authorities. The Slovak Republic acceded to the Rome Convention on the Law Applicable to Contractual Obligations, along with nine other new Member States, via the Luxembourg Convention of 2005.[20] In accordance with Article 5 of the Luxembourg Convention, and following the ratification of this Convention by the Slovak Republic, the Rome Convention came into force for the Slovak Republic on 1 August 2006, and pursuant to the provision of Article 17 should be applied by the Slovak courts to contracts concluded after 1 August 2006.

The first court decisions based on the EU regulation of the law applicable to contractual obligations in the Rome Convention occurred very soon after these rules became applicable for the Slovak Republic. Nevertheless, cases still occur in which courts completely ignore European legislation on the law applicable to contractual relationships with cross-border elements. What is even more surprising is that in many such decisions of the Slovak district courts, the jurisdiction is correctly based on the Brussels I Regulation 44/2001 (most of the proceedings in which the judgments studied were delivered started before 10 January 2015). As noted above, this was the case for about 26 per cent of judgments that we have had the opportunity to study.[21]

In the course of preparing this chapter, judgments delivered between 2006 and 2019 have been examined. Judgments were sought from courts of all instances; however, the core of the collected decisions is composed of decisions of the first instance courts. To select judgments, we used the official, freely accessible Slov-lex database, operated by the Ministry of Justice of the Slovak Republic,[22] and several private databases, especially ASPI, EPI, etc.

---

20 [2005] OJ C 169/1–9.

21 This number is really only approximate, due to the fact that the courts often cited the PIL Act in addition to the Rome I Regulation and the Rome Convention, and those judgments also appeared in the group of judgments applying the PIL Act as well as a group of judgments applying the Regulation or the Convention.

22 <https://www.slov-lex.sk/vseobecne-sudy-sr>.

From these databases, we obtained in total 63 decisions on the Rome II Regulation, 728 decisions on the Rome I Regulation and 39 decisions on the Rome Convention. However, these numbers should only be regarded as indicative, as some decisions could be classified into several categories if the court referred to more than one of these instruments in order to choose between them. Since we are dealing with the issue of whether the courts of the Slovak Republic neglected to apply the European rules on the law applicable to contractual and non-contractual obligations, we also made a control selection of decisions referring to the previous Slovak regulation in this area, in particular sections 9, 10 and 15 of the PIL Act.

Most of the decisions referred to Czech–Slovak cases, i.e. situations in which litigants had their seat or habitual residence in the Czech or Slovak Republic, and there was a choice to be made between these two legal orders. Linguistic differences between the two countries are not large; they do not lead to serious complications in the identification and study of applicable law. Czech law is relatively easily accessible, and along with the case law of the Czech courts, it is systematically monitored in Slovakia and regularly analysed and compared in the academic literature. The absence of a language barrier and the proximity of the two legal systems are a positive factor in these situations. There is no secondary motivation of the courts to seek ways to interpret conflict-of-laws rules to make Slovak law applicable, and they are not burdened with the problems of the identification and application of foreign law.

The nature of the cases was often very similar. Most concerned transport contracts, credit agreements, sales contracts and contracts for the provision of services, while a smaller number dealt with insurance contracts and employment contracts. As for non-contractual obligations, the cases mainly involved claims for damages and, less frequently, unjust enrichment, product liability, or infringement of intellectual property rights. The most frequently applied provisions of the Rome I Regulation were Articles 3, 4 and 6 (under the Rome Convention, Articles 3, 4 and 5), but the courts also applied Articles 7, 8, 9 and 14. Article 12 was also repeatedly cited by the courts, mostly in connection with Articles 3 and 4, often without further explanation of its impact on the case at hand. In the case of the Rome II Regulation, by far the most commonly applied provision was Article 4, followed by Articles 5, 8, 10 and 12 respectively.

4.1.2. Arbitration Awards

The legal framework regulating the performance of the Slovak arbitration judiciary is Act no. 244/2002 Coll. of laws on Arbitration, which has recently been radically altered, in particular as regards the possibility of establishing permanent arbitration courts. Amendments no. 336/2014 Coll. of laws and 125/2016 Coll. of laws responded to a significant increase in the number of arbitration courts: under previous legislation it was possible for any legal person to set up an arbitration court, which had an impact on the quantity and the quality of arbitration awards, with the quality not always meeting the appropriate standard. In some cases, there was even a suspicion of deliberate links between certain permanent arbitral tribunals and entrepreneurs that had their disputes repeatedly heard by a given court of arbitration. In conjunction with the (perceived and real) defects in consumer arbitration, this situation evoked mistrust of arbitration as such. The Slovak legislator considered the regulation of permanent arbitration courts to be an important instrument of public policy.[23]

As clear is from current practice, almost all arbitration proceedings conducted in the Slovak Republic are held within institutionalised permanent arbitration courts, which are legally obliged to publish the statutes and rules of procedure and keep a list of arbitrators acting for the Permanent Court of Arbitration, open for inspection by anyone. Towards the end of 2016, the number of permanent arbitration courts registered with the Ministry of Justice of the Slovak Republic came to 197 permanent arbitration courts and eight permanent arbitration courts competent to decide consumer disputes whose founder held a licence granted by the Ministry under Act no. 335/2014 Coll. Amendment 125/2016 Coll. to the Arbitration Act, in effect from 1 January 2017, significantly affected the number of permanent arbitration courts. Not even 10 per cent of the founders of permanent arbitration courts registered in the list of permanent arbitration courts, maintained by the Ministry of Justice of the Slovak Republic, met the new conditions for the establishment of permanent arbitration courts within the statutory deadlines.

From the previous activities and practice of arbitration courts, no publicly available information exists on the awards, their content and the number of cases to which the provisions of the Rome I and Rome II Regulations were applied. Arbitration proceedings come under the framework Act no. 244/2002 Coll. of laws non-public proceedings, and therefore there is no database of decisions relating to matters decided by arbitration courts. Certain limited information may be obtained only indirectly from the decisions of the ordinary courts, based on section 40 of the Arbitration Act. Ordinary courts may, under the conditions exhaustively defined by law, annul the arbitration decisions if one of the parties to arbitration proceedings files an action for the annulment of the arbitration award.

A review pursuant to section 40 of the Arbitration Act is not an ordinary review, but considers whether or not a private entity (the arbitration court) infringed legal provisions in the course of private relations; it is thus something like an assessment of the validity of a contract under substantive law. The fact

---

23 Gyárfáš, J. – Števček, M., et al.: *Zákon o rozhodcovskom konaní. Komentár*, Prague: C.H. Beck, 2016, p. 225.

that the Arbitration Act allows for a gentle review of arbitral decisions is simply a case of the legislator striking a balance between private autonomy and the fundamental right to a fair trial.

From the published judgments of ordinary courts relating to these kinds of actions for annulment of arbitration awards pursuant to section 40 of the Arbitration Act, it can be concluded that for the most part such proceedings concern arbitration awards relating to consumer matters and where the arbitration clause (the arbitration agreement) was assessed as an unfair contract term. In these cases, the arbitration award was consequently annulled or, if the execution proceedings already begin, the execution proceedings was cancelled due to the absence of the material enforceability of the arbitration clause.

On the websites of permanent arbitration courts in the territory of the Slovak Republic, there can be found proposals for arbitration clauses on the agreement on the jurisdiction of the given arbitration court. As regards the applicable law in disputes with a foreign element (cross-border disputes), the websites recommend that the parties to arbitration proceedings choose the applicable law. Even from the rules of procedure and the arbitration rules of a given arbitration court, it largely follows that in disputes arising from private law relations with a foreign element, on which the arbitration court is entitled to decide, this court will *a priori* decide on the basis of the law on which the parties to the arbitration have agreed. If the parties to the arbitration have not agreed on the applicable law, the arbitration court shall decide according to the law determined by domestic conflict-of-laws rules. The arbitration court is also entitled by law to decide commercial disputes following the principles of justice (*ex aequo et bono*), but only if the parties to the arbitration agreed to that or, more precisely, if the parties to the arbitration expressly authorised it to.

4.2. TEMPORAL APPLICATION OF THE ROME REGULATIONS AND CONVENTION

As mentioned above, except for a certain percentage of cases where the courts routinely applied Slovak national conflict-of-laws rules, Slovak courts began to apply either the Rome Convention or the Rome I and Rome II Regulations relatively flexibly, that is since the date these instruments became applicable for the Slovak Republic.

Perhaps not so surprising is that the courts often apply the Regulations and the Convention retroactively, i.e. also to situations to which, due to their rules on temporal application, the Regulations or the Convention should not be applied, but the court decided to do so after the new legislation was adopted and published. The courts have treated these instruments simply as a valid law that is binding on them. The courts have dealt with the transitional provisions of the Regulations and Convention only in a small percentage of cases.

This approach to the application of the Regulations was probably helped by the fact that private international law in the Slovak Republic has remained unchanged for a long time – the current PIL Act has been in force since 1 April 1964, and although there have been several amendments to it, they have never been associated with the transitional provisions (the PIL Act only includes one transitional provision relating to the procedural rules on the recognition and enforcement of foreign decisions).[24] Another factor that could have contributed to the courts' approach may have been, as already mentioned, the similarity of the provisions of the PIL Act and the European legislation, in particular in the field of conflict of laws applicable to contractual obligations. At first sight, there was no significant change in the criteria used to determine the applicable law, thus no significant differences in determining the applicable law arose.

In the majority of decisions, however, a routine approach will be used in dealing with the issues of private international law, which are perceived, as already mentioned in the introduction, as only a precursor to addressing much more fundamental and complex problems connected with the merits of the case.

4.3. MATERIAL SCOPE OF APPLICATION OF THE REGULATIONS AND CONVENTION

In identifying the material scope of the Regulations, Slovak courts rely heavily on Article 1 of both Regulations; in relation to the application of the Rome II Regulation, they normally also cite Article 2(1), which contains a definition of what is meant by 'damage' for the purposes of the Regulation. Disputes most frequently concerned claims from either failure to fulfil obligations under the contract, or claims for damages occasioned by an accident or by damaging the claimant's property.

The situations in which the application of the Rome I Regulation was rejected, with reference to its material scope of application, mainly included bills of exchange disputes. In all those cases, the creditor claimed payment of debts from the debtor. The courts, referring to Article 1(2)(d), excluded the application of the Rome I Regulation and determined the applicable law under the Slovak PIL Act.

Another such case was pending before District Court in Trenčín.[25] The subject of the dispute was the determination of the right of ownership to a motor vehicle (the motor vehicle was purchased in good faith, but from the non-owner, rather than the owner). The court pointed out that the law applicable cannot

---

24 The temporal application of private international law as it has been addressed previously in the doctrine, that is by the doctrine of 'intertemporal collisions'.

25 Judgment of the District Court Trenčín of 6 November 2018, file ref. 16C/154/2016.

be determined under the Rome II Regulation, since that regulation does not contain criteria for determining the law applicable to the question of ownership, nor under the Rome I Regulation, since there is no relationship of obligation between the plaintiff and the defendant. The applicable law was therefore determined by the court pursuant to Section 6 of the Slovak PIL Act.

Also sometimes problematic was the actual distribution of the issue between the Rome I and Rome II Regulations, that is, determining whether the claim qualified as contractual or non-contractual. It was generally evident that the majority of the courts did not know how to qualify ancillary questions, such as damages caused by breach of contractual obligations of the parties to the contract or the assignment of the claim to the insurer. The courts often went against how these issues were categorised by the Slovak substantive law.

This situation arose in a case decided by the Regional Court in Prešov.[26] The key issue in the dispute was the existence of a claim for damages of a consignor against the carrier. The consignor (a company with its seat in Slovakia) ordered from the carrier (a company with its seat in the Czech Republic) the carriage of goods from Prešov (in the Slovak Republic) to Cartagena in Colombia. The goods were intended for the consignor's business partner in Colombia. As a result of the carrier's misconduct, the wrong consignment was delivered to Colombia. The carrier then delivered the correct consignment to Colombia, but extra costs were incurred by the consignor's business partner associated with paying twice for customs clearance and nationalisation for both the incorrect and correct consignments. The additional amount paid was claimed by the consignor's Colombian business partner against the Slovak consignor. The Slovak consignor then subsequently claimed the damage against the carrier in the form of set-off. The carrier challenged the validity of the set-off in court.

The court found that the claimant and the defendant had entered into contractual relationship – a contract for the carriage of goods by sea. The contract, as agreed by the parties, had to be governed by the UN Convention on the Carriage of Goods by Sea. However, since the Convention does not allow for redress for damage other than that occurring to goods or causally linked to the delayed delivery of the goods, it was necessary to establish the applicable law under the applicable conflict-of-laws rules in order to arrange on compensation for other damage. Although the court from the beginning considered the relationship between the claimant and the defendant to be a contractual one, in determining the law applicable to compensation it referred to section 10(2)(c) of the PIL Act and simultaneously to Article 4(1) of the Rome II Regulation. Subsequently, without any detailed analysis of the provisions in question, the court held that the applicable law should be determined on the basis of the place where the damage occurred. This procedure was all the more interesting given

26 Judgment of the Regional Court Prešov, of 12 November 2014, file ref. 1Cob93/2013.

that the existing section 10(2)(c) of the PIL Act governed the law applicable to contracts of transport, thus to the contractual obligation, but in the identification of the European rule governing this question the court referred to the Regulation governing non-contractual obligations.

However, even according to the Slovak national rules on private international law the question whether the carrier is liable for damage to the consignor, or in other words whether the resulting damage can be attributed to non-fulfilment of duties of the carrier, should not be resolved according to section 10(2)(c) of the PIL Act. The law applicable to claims for damages arising from a breach of contractual obligations is to be determined pursuant to section 11, dealing with general ancillary questions on contractual obligations, i.e. modifications, security and the consequences of breaches of contractual obligations. According to this provision the law applicable is the law governing the contract itself (*lex causae*), unless the parties have chosen another law for this purpose, different from the law applicable to contract.

The District Court in Bratislava[27] took a different approach in a case of compensation for damage suffered by a carrier as a result of the consignor's delay with payments made for transport. After the consignor did not pay duly and on time for the service provided, the carrier hired a lawyer. Only after the carrier filed a petition for a European order for payment through a lawyer did the consignor gradually, in several instalments, pay the amount due. The carrier, however, in separate proceedings, claimed compensation for costs incurred for the lawyer's services. The court considered that there was a causal link between the defendant's delay and the damage (i.e. costs incurred by the hiring of the lawyer) and that these were deliberately incurred costs, as the plaintiff (the carrier) had no legal training and the defendant (the consignor) only fulfilled its obligation following the lawyer's involvement. The court therefore upheld the plaintiff's claim, considering that party entitled to compensation as a consequence of the other party's failure to fulfil its obligations. The law applied was, with reference to Article 12(1)(c) of the Rome I Regulation, the law that governed the contract for the carriage of goods.

Another such example is the subrogation of the claim from the purchase contract to the insurer in the decisions of the District Court in Trenčín of 24 February 2011[28] and the District Court in Bardejov of 6 May 2015.[29]

---

27 Judgment of the District Court Bratislava I, of 14 August 2015, file ref. 25Cb/64/2013.

28 Judgment of the District Court Trenčín, of 24 February 2011, file ref. 39Cb/146/2010.

29 Judgment for the acknowledgment District Court Bardejov, of 6 May 2015, file ref. 7C/56/2014. A 'judgment for acknowledgement' is a specificity of Slovak civil procedure law and is issued in instances where a defendant acknowledges the claim made against them; the reasoning in such a judgment is shorter as there need only be an identification of the claim and a description of the reasons for issuing the judgment.

In the case decided by the District Court in Trenčín, the insurer (the plaintiff) sought a recovery of a claim which had passed on to him under the insurance contract concluded; the buyer had not honoured the sales contract with the supplier by not paying the purchase price and this situation was covered under the insurance contract between the supplier and the insurance company. The insured, a company engaged in the manufacturing and sales of food products, delivered to the debtor (the defendant) goods for which the debtor, also a company, failed to pay. Unfortunately, we have not been able to identify the precise location of the seats of all the parties concerned, because of anonymisation,[30] but the description of the circumstances of the case implied that the insured was established in the Slovak Republic and the insurance company was a foreign entity. Since the contract of insurance also covered the situation of the insured not receiving payments for goods or services as a result of legally confirmed or factual insolvency of the customer, the insurance company paid the insured the price of the goods supplied on the basis of which the right to compensation for the consideration provided passed to an insurance company. The court concluded that the applicable law was determined under Article 10(3), in conjunction with Articles 2(2) and 3, of the Rome II Regulation. On the basis of the law it considered applicable to unjust enrichment, the court held that the defendant had an obligation to pay the payments due for the goods.

In this case, the situation was clearly one that should have been dealt with under the rules of the law applicable to contractual obligations. Since both the insurance and purchase contracts, from the latter of which the claim arose, were concluded in 2008, the Rome Convention and the PIL Act were applicable. The authorisation of the insurer to recover the claim in question could be resolved by a court in accordance with the law determined under Article 13 of the Rome Convention. However, the Convention excluded from its scope insurance contracts covering risks situated in the territories of the Member States. In this situation, the national law was applicable, specifically section 11 of the PIL Act, according to which the law applicable to the subrogation of the claim is *lex causae*. The content of the claim should be assessed according the law applicable to the purchase contract, specified under Article 4 of the Rome Convention.

Somewhat more accurate was the procedure used by the District Court in Bardejov in dealing with an insurer's claim for compensation for damage. This case thus concerned a non-contractual claim. However, in determining the applicable law, the court referred to Article 4(1) of the Rome II Regulation,

[30] Pursuant to the Slovak legislation, information the disclosure of which could endanger or undermine rights and interests protected by law, in particular personal data of natural persons (not businessmen), including the residence of a natural person, are subject to anonymisation. Anonymisation is carried out so that the words are replaced by initials and figures are replaced with X. This often makes an academic analysis of the court decision difficult. Some courts also go beyond legal obligation and anonymise the data of all litigants.

without reference to Article 19 of the Regulation, which governs the transfer of the claim. It is uncertain whether or not the court considered Article 19. As the defendant recognised the applicant's claim and since it was a dispute that the parties can end by a court settlement, the court did not address the circumstances of the case in detail.

The Regional Court in Žilina, in its decision of 19 September 2019,[31] referred to the case law of the Court of Justice of the European Union (CJEU) in assessing the nature of the claim. The court ruled on the right to reimbursement of costs incurred by the participant in the accident, not directly as a result of the accident, but in connection with it. The injured party was forced to borrow a spare car during the repair of his car which was damaged in the accident, and he claimed these costs from the perpetrator of the accident. The Regional Court referred to the CJEU judgment C-27/02 *Engler* and stated that the claim should be considered as non-contractual, as there is no obligation freely assumed by any of the parties.

Sometimes it can be difficult to determine whether the obligation at issue is contractual or non-contractual, despite the due diligence on the part of the court dealing with the issue. This is the case for example when a passenger gets onto public transport without purchasing a ticket, and is therefore a 'deadhead'. If the passenger is a Slovak citizen with his or her permanent domicile in the territory of the Slovak Republic[32] and he got on a vehicle in the Czech Republic, and the vehicle is operated by a Czech transport company, this is a situation with cross-border implications and it is necessary to determine the applicable law. Between 2010 and 2016, Slovak courts dealt with a whole series of such cases where transport companies with their seat in the Czech Republic assigned their claims against Slovak debtors to companies with their seat either in the Slovak Republic or the Czech Republic, which subsequently brought actions in the Slovak courts.

In these cases, the Slovak courts mainly applied Article 5(2) of the Rome I Regulation, which governs contracts for the carriage of passengers. The contract of carriage should have been made in an implied way, i.e. by a passenger boarding a vehicle.[33] In contrast, the District Court in Revúca, in its judgment of 11 September 2014, stated that the contract of carriage between the legal predecessor of the applicant (the carrier) and the defendant (the passenger) had

---

31 Judgment of the Regional Court Žilina of 19 September 2019, file ref. 14Cob/45/2019.

32 The courts in these situations invariably fail to address the habitual residence of the 'deadhead'; however, from the fact that actions against such persons have been filed in the Slovak Republic and the courts, having considered the provisions of the Brussels I Regulation, established that they had jurisdiction with regard to the existence of the defendant's domicile in the territory of the Slovak Republic, it can be estimated that they were Slovak nationals habitually resident in the Slovak Republic.

33 For example, the judgment of the District Court Ružomberok, of 30 November 2011, file ref. 2C/134/2011, p. 3.

not been concluded, as the condition and the method of proof of the creation of the carriage contract and the rights and obligations resulting from it is the obligation of the passenger to present a valid travel document, a condition which in this case was not fulfilled. This, however, did not, according to the court, preclude the creation of the non-contractual liability of the defendant. The District Court therefore determined the applicable law under Article 4(1) of the Rome II Regulation and applied the law of the Czech Republic, as the damage occurred on its territory.[34] The District Court in Revúca, however, remained alone in this view; only two other district courts decided identically.

Nevertheless, it is difficult to say whether claims of 'travelling as a deadhead' have been established to be contractual in the Slovak Republic. The decisions in question were issued during the short period when it was usually the one and the same applicant who filed actions with different courts of the Slovak Republic with very similar content, and courts could either identify with a qualification by the applicant or be inspired by earlier judgments of their colleagues in similar cases (as mentioned already, Slovak courts do not like to venture into a long analysis of private international law and prefer to focus more on the substance of the case). Until the Supreme Court of the Slovak Republic or the CJEU shall decide on the application of the Rome I or Rome II Regulations, any other court of the Slovak Republic may choose to apply either the Rome I Regulation or the Rome II Regulation.

The situation is similar to that in *Pula Parking v. Tedeheran*.[35] The question is thus not so much whether the claim is of a public or private nature, but whether the situation may actually be qualified as a contractual relationship, as Advocate General Bobek did in his conclusions of 27 October 2016.[36] In his commentary on the conclusions of AG Bobek, Professor Hess critically pointed out that such a qualification of the situation is in conflict with the foundational principle of private autonomy and runs counter to the express will of the parties. Professor Hess further stated that in contemporary modern German doctrine, if someone uses the services or goods of common interest without paying the price, such a situation is qualified as unjust enrichment.[37]

---

34 Judgment of the District Court Revúca, of 11 September 2014, file ref. 7C/368/2013, p. 3.

35 In Case C-551/15, *Pula Parking*, ECLI:EU:C:2017:193, the issue was parking in a public parking space belonging to the city of Pula (Croatia) and the use of a parking space without paying a parking fee.

36 The CJEU in its decision of 9 March 2017, without specific justification, accepted the contractual classification of the situation (p. 35). The CJEU concentrated rather on responding to the question of whether the situation as such fell within the concept of the 'civil and commercial matters' and thus within the scope of the Brussels I *bis* Regulation (its answer was positive) and whether the notaries acting in enforcement proceedings based on an 'authentic document' fall within the concept of 'court' within the meaning of the Regulation (its answer was negative).

37 Hess, B. 'Factual Contracts in European Law? Critical Reflections on the Conclusions of AG Bobek of October 27, 2016 in Case C-551/15 Pula Parking ./. Tederahan', *Conflict of Laws.net. News and Views in Private International Law*, 22 November 2016.

Such a classification of the claim would also seem to be logical in the case of travelling as a deadhead on public transport or intercity trains. Fundamentally, the situation concerns the use of these means of transport with no intention to pay for the services used; thus, the deadhead is enriched at the expense of the carrier. Interestingly, however, the District Court in Revúca did not consider this alternative but, after qualifying the claim as non-contractual, the court relied upon one of the introductory provisions of the Rome II Regulation, the general rule on the law applicable to torts (Article 4), in order to decide that there was no instance of unjust enrichment. The outcome of determining the applicable law, however, would in this case be the same: regardless of whether the court were to apply Article 4 or Article 10 of the Regulation, the applicable law was that of the Czech Republic, where the alleged damage occurred – or where the unjust enrichment occurred.

On the edge of public or private nature was a claim asserted by a hospital in Olomouc in the Czech Republic against the defendant domiciled in the Slovak Republic. The subject of the claim was the payment of treatment and hospital stay costs of the defendant, who was in a state of intoxication, in special areas of the hospital designated for such cases (detention centre). The hospital's claim was based on a law according to which a person who, under the influence of alcohol or other addictive substances, endangers himself or others or violates a public order is obliged to undergo a stay in such a special area and is obliged to pay the costs. In this case, too, the District Court applied Article 4 of the Rome II Regulation. The court stated that a specific legal relationship had been established between the parties to the proceedings, which did not arise on a contractual basis, but was closest to the relationship between the wrongdoer and the harmed. The court determined the Czech law as the applicable law, pointing out that the damage occurred in the territory of the Czech Republic.[38]

Of a similar nature was a series of claims for unpaid tolls for the use of sections of toll roads in the Czech Republic, lodged before the Slovak courts. The decisions in these disputes were very similar in two respects: the law applicable to the claims lodged by the Road and Motorway Directorate of the Czech Republic was determined by the courts under Article 4(1) of the Rome II Regulation, and the Regulation was applied retroactively. However, since the entitled entity was a public organisation – Road and Motorway Directorate of the Czech Republic, which exercises ownership rights over real property constituting state motorways and first-class roads and is responsible for the administration and maintenance of these roads – in this case it is appropriate to ask whether these claims are of a public or private nature.

---

38 Judgment of the District Court Prešov, of 25 October 2019, file ref. 8C/19/2019.

4.4. APPLICATION OF ROME I AND ROME II RULES

4.4.1. *Party Autonomy*

The regulation of the choice of law in the Rome I Regulation is very similarly formulated as in the PIL Act, which has been applied in Slovak territory since 1 April 1964. Under section 9 of the PIL Act, parties to the contract can choose the law to govern their contractual relations. They can choose any law and this choice is considered to be unrestricted in accordance with the explanatory note to the PIL Act. However, the chosen law has to be in force, i.e. it must be the law actually applicable in the territory of a state. The choice of law can be made by explicit demonstration of the parties' will, either in writing in the contract's provisions or verbally, or even tacitly (implicitly); however, the court must have no doubt about the will expressed.[39]

Professional Czechoslovak literature has cited as an indicator of the tacit choice of law that the parties referred to the provisions of a particular legal order or to a particular legal institution typical of some legal order in the text of the treaty. However, it was admitted that the participants could have intended to use certain provisions of a particular legal order in isolation, for which it was recommended to admit the application of those provisions, but only to the extent that is allowed by the rules of the law applicable to contractual obligations. It meant that the mandatory rules of the law applicable to the contractual obligation as a whole couldn't been overturned.[40] It was not recommended to see a choice of forum as an indicator of the choice of law. References to a specific provision of a particular legal order are generally accepted by the Slovak courts as indicators of tacit choice.[41]

---

[39] Section 9 PIL Act: '(1) The parties to the contract may choose the law which shall govern their mutual property relations, unless specific legislation provides otherwise; they can do so tacitly, if, with regard to the circumstances, there is no doubt as to their expressed will. (2) Unless the expressed will of the contracting parties indicates otherwise, the conflict of law provisions of the chosen law shall be disregarded.' This provision remains unchanged; only section 9(3) was added, by an amendment from 2003, to respond to the commitments made by the Slovak Republic to join the EU: '(3) If the parties to the consumer contract have chosen a law which gives the consumer smaller protection of his rights than the Slovak legal order, their relations are governed by the Slovak law.' The chosen law governs only the contractual relations of the parties; property rights are governed by the law determined on the basis of sections 5–7 PIL Act.

[40] Kučera, Z. – Tichý, L.: *Zákon o mezinárodním právu soukromém a procesním*, Prague: Panorama, 1989, p. 99.

[41] For example, the judgment of the District Court Košice II, of 28 March 2012, file ref. 15C/101/2010 states that the parties did not expressly choose the applicable law, but the loan agreement was concluded in accordance with section 497 et seq. of the Commercial Code of the Czech Republic, so it was necessary to apply Czech law to the contractual obligation of the participants. For the sake of completeness, it is necessary to add that the opposite conclusions are rare – the judgment of the District Court Vranov nad Topľou, of 30 September 2014,

In the majority of cases that the Slovak courts have dealt with, the choice of law was made in writing, as one of the contractual provisions. It was also regularly included in the general business terms of the service provider – banks, insurance companies or travel agents, for example.[42] In addition to the choice of national law, the contracting parties also chose INCOTERMS (International Commercial Terms of the International Chamber of Commerce). These clauses have already been used in the practice of Czechoslovakian foreign trade enterprises, state-owned enterprises who were the only entities permitted to carry out foreign trade operations in the socialist era. We did not find any reported cases where there was a choice of another uniform law instrument, such as the UNIDROIT Principles or PECL, even translated into the Slovak language and published with the commentary.[43] However, it is reasonable to assume that parties that choose such instruments are more likely to resolve their disputes in arbitration tribunals, and indeed often in arbitration tribunals abroad.

One of the most interesting cases on the silent choice of law was the situation decided by the Prešov Regional Court.[44] The dispute arose from a shipping contract from Prešov (Slovak Republic) to Cartagena (Colombia), in which a Czech company acted as the carrier and the consignor was a Slovak company. The contract was made orally; no explicit choice of law was made. The claimant pleaded for the application of the UN Convention on the Carriage of Goods by Sea[45] as a commercial usage. The Slovak Republic is considered to be a signatory state to the Convention, based on its succession to the Czechoslovak Federal Republic, but the Slovak Republic never ratified the Convention and is therefore not bound by it. The court rejected the application of the Convention as a commercial usage. On the other hand, it accepted that the Convention was chosen by the parties to the contract as the set of rules governing their contractual relations, based on the fact that the bill of lading issued by the carrier contained a statement that the contract of carriage would be governed by the Convention. Ultimately, the claim was assessed under the Slovak legal order, as the court

---

file ref. 13Cb/37/2014 came to the conclusion that the provision of Article IV of the contract, under which the rights and obligations of this contract were not expressly governed by the Civil Code of the Czech Republic, could not be considered as a choice of law.

42 Judgment of the District Court Banská Bystrica, of 6 July 2016, file ref. 8C/366/2015. However, in this case, the court dealt with the choice of law very strangely. It cited Article 3(1) Rome I Regulation, and subsequently Article 6(2), compared the specific provisions of Czech law as the chosen law and Slovak law as the law of the consumer's habitual residence, and stated that both legal orders provide the consumer with the same legal protection – and then with reference to Article 6(1) used Slovak law.

43 *Zásady medzinárodných obchodných zmlúv*, Bratislava: Iura Edition, 1996; *Princípy Európskeho zmluvného práva*, Bratislava: Iura Edition, 2009.

44 Judgment of the Regional Court Prešov, of 12 November 2014, file ref. 1Cob/93/2013.

45 It is likely a reference to the UN Convention on the Carriage of Goods by Sea from 1978, the so-called 'Hamburg Rules', but no official Slovak translation was made of its name nor a specific designation in the judgment.

considered that the unconfirmed issues in the Convention were governed by the law that is applicable under the provisions of the relevant conflict-of-law rule.

In another case, the choice of law made by the parties after the commencement of legal proceedings was accepted by the District Court in Námestovo[46] for a contract concerning the supply and installation of windows at the client's family home. The contract could be qualified as a consumer contract, but the consumer travelled to the seller to the country of his habitual residence and concluded a contract there, so the specific rule on consumer contracts was not applicable.[47] The contract was concluded verbally, at the beginning of 2009 (the parties did not specify the exact date); therefore, the court decided the case on the basis of the provisions of the 1980 Rome Convention. At the hearing, the legal representative of the claimant (the seller) proposed the use of the Slovak legal order, and the defendant (the consumer) agreed with such a choice in his written statement. The court then considered the question of whether or not to accept such a choice of law. It referred to Article 3(2) of the Rome Convention, which says that 'the parties may, at any time, agree to subject the contract to a law other than that previously governed by it, whether by virtue of a previous choice of law or of other provisions of the Convention'. From this the court concluded that the parties may choose the applicable law even after the contract has been concluded, since the Rome Convention allows the choice of the law 'at any time', and so accepted the choice of Slovak law.

In the case of non-contractual obligations, no choice of law seems to have been made in the reported cases. It is worth mentioning that until the arrival of the Rome II Regulation, under Slovak private international law (and similarly Czech law, which was based until 2014 on the same Act no. 97/1963 Coll. adopted during the existence of the common Czechoslovak Republic), choice of law for non-contractual obligations was not possible. It is debatable whether the parties from the Czech and Slovak Republics are aware that they can make a choice of law for these kinds of obligations.

4.4.2. *Absence of Choice of Law*

In the absence of a choice of law, the Slovak courts have automatically applied the fixed conflict-of-laws rules as laid down in Article 4(1) of the Rome I Regulation. After all, such a system is very close to what the courts have been accustomed to under Slovak national law. For the purposes of Article 4, the law

46 Judgment of the District Court Námestovo, of 23 November 2011, file ref. 8C/209/2010.

47 The court never considered the potential application of Article 5 of the Rome Convention in the judgment, so it is difficult to judge whether it was omitted or simply considered inapplicable in this matter.

applicable to contracts of sale, service contracts, credit agreements or consumer contracts was determined in cases where the court found that they were not covered by Article 6 of the Rome I Regulation, in particular for failing to meet the criteria laid down in Article 6(1) or because they were situations referred to in Article 6(4)(a).

In principle, the courts had not had the problem of determining what performance is characteristic of the contract, although, in particular, when implementing the Rome Convention, they simplified the procedure by estimating which law has a closer relationship to the legal relationship without considering the characteristic performance.[48] The applicable law on the basis of Article 4(2) was determined by the District Court in Revúca,[49] for a contract for assignment of a claim. With reference to the first sentence of Article 14 of the Rome I Regulation, the court came to the conclusion that the contract for the assignment of claims had to be reassessed under the conflict rules in the Regulation, namely Article 4. It stated that the contract of assignment of the claim does not fall under any of the contracts referred to in Article 4(1) and moved on to Article 4(2). In assessing what performance is characteristic of the contract, the court referred to the provisions of the Slovak Commercial Code, according to which the arrangement of remuneration is not an essential part (*essentialia negotii*) of the contract for the assignment of a claim and, therefore, as a characteristic performance the court assessed the activity of an assignor.

Article 4(4) of the Rome I Regulation was used to determine the applicable law in the case of a guarantor's obligation. The court found that a guarantor's obligation is an autonomous contractual obligation that establishes the legal relationship between the creditor and the guarantor, but that liability is ancillary to the obligation between the debtor and the creditor whose security has been secured. On that basis, the court, referring to Article 4(4) of the Rome I Regulation, held that the guarantor's obligation was closely linked to the purchase contract concluded between the creditor and the debtor and was therefore governed by the same law as the purchase contract in question.[50]

---

48 For example, the judgment of the District Court Malacky, of 16 July 2014, file ref. 4Ccud/3/2009 applied Austrian law in the matter, because, according to the court, the situation has the closest connection to the substantive law of Austria, as that was where the performance – namely the providing of services – was carried out. In the present case, the court would have drawn the same conclusion even if the applicable law was determined on the basis of the habitual residence of the party, providing the characteristic performance for the contract, since the service provider had a habitual residence in Austria. But this does not always have to be the case. For example, the use of an escape clause could have been considered.

49 Judgment of the District Court Revúca, of 11 February 2016, file ref. 7C/192/2015.

50 Judgment of the District Court Galanta, of 10 September 2015, file ref. 17Cb/45/2014.

4.4.3. *Escape Clauses*

Slovak courts use the escape clauses only in rare cases. For example, there were complex cases in which transport operators claimed payment of transport costs arising from several transport contracts in the same proceedings. The services of a lawyer were required. Only after the lawyer's call did the customer pay the transport costs. If the court were to determine the law applicable to each of the transport contracts in question, some would be governed by different applicable law from others. It was not possible or useful to separate the claims and decide them separately. In this situation, the court used the escape clause in Article 5(3) of the Rome I Regulation and, referring to the fact that the carrier was based in the Czech Republic and the place of destination of the goods was in several cases in the Czech Republic, used Czech law as the law with the closest connection to the contract of carriage.[51]

In another case, the court departed from the law applicable within the meaning of Article 4(1) of the Rome I Regulation. The subject of the dispute was the right to pay the cost of providing services. The court found that a contract such as this should be governed by the law of the country of the habitual residence of the service provider, but in the circumstances it was clear that the contract has a manifestly closer connection with another country – the work was done in the territory of the Slovak Republic for a client established in the Slovak Republic, based on an order placed in the territory of the Slovak Republic. The court therefore applied the law of the Slovak Republic.[52]

The escape clause, enshrined in Article 4(3) of the Rome I Regulation, was also used by the District Court in Liptovsky Mikulas.[53] The District Court ruled on a commission claim made by an agent against a professional hockey player, for whom he was to conclude a professional player's contract. The professional player's contract was indeed concluded, but the player questioned whether the agent contributed. According to the player, the club with which he concluded contract contacted him directly and negotiated and signed the contract without the involvement of the agent. The court dealt with the determination of the law applicable to the contract concluded between the player and the agent. The agent, a company based in Germany, was under a contract to offer the player, a Slovak citizen, the opportunity to conclude a professional contract in Germany and Europe. The professional player's contract was ultimately concluded with a Slovak legal entity, with sporting activities being carried out on the territory of Slovakia.

---

51 Judgment of the District Court Bratislava I, of 14 August 2015, file ref. 25Cb/64/2013.

52 Judgment of the District Court Martin, of 27 March 2015, file ref. 17Cb/32/2015.

53 Judgment of the District Court Liptovský Mikuláš, of 22 March 2012, file ref. 8C/101/2011.

It is apparent from the reasoning of the judgment in question that the court excluded the application of Article 4(1) of the Rome I Regulation and, in determining the applicable law, assessed Article 4(2) and (3). It found that within the meaning of Article 4(2) it is possible to consider the settlement of the dispute under German substantive law – apparently taking into account the habitual residence of the agent (the claimant), whom the court seemed to consider to be the party providing the characteristic performance of the contract. The court, however, considered that the contract had a closer relationship with the Slovak Republic and, therefore, within the meaning of Article 4(3), the substantive law of the Slovak Republic was applicable. In support of its conclusion that the contract had a closer relationship with the Slovak Republic, the court stated that the agent's activities were to be carried out for a Slovak citizen, and the professional player's contract from which the commission was claimed was negotiated in the Slovak Republic, with a Slovak legal entity, under Slovak law.

4.4.4. Specific Rules

Among the specific rules, Article 6 of the Rome I Regulation, formerly Article 5 of the Rome Convention, has a special status. Consumer contracts are probably the most numerous group of disputes with a foreign element before the Slovak courts in which the application of the Rome I Regulation may be considered. The interpretation and application of Article 6 have a number of specific features, which makes it hard to compare with the other specific rules of this Regulation. The application of Article 6 is based on the concept of the so-called 'passive consumer'. In order for this provision to be applicable, it is not sufficient for the contract to qualify as a consumer contract; rather, it is necessary to examine whether the stronger party (the entrepreneur) has directed his activity to the country of the consumer's habitual residence and whether the contract falls within the scope of such activities. There is also a complex system of choice of law. The choice of law may not have the result of depriving the consumer of the protection afforded to him by provisions that cannot be derogated from by agreement by virtue of the law which, in the absence of choice, would have been applicable.

In general, the Slovak courts have not avoided Article 6 in consumer cases, but only a small number of them have dealt with the question whether a foreign businessman really directed his business activity to the country where the consumer was habitually resident, or whether a consumer who, at the time of commencement of the proceedings, was habitually resident in the Slovak Republic had no habitual residence at the time of the conclusion of the contract in the country in which the entrepreneur was established and also operates. Mostly, they have only cited Article 6 and decided on the basis of the chosen law or the law of consumer's habitual residence. Where they have done so, they have not always been fully aware of the functioning of the relationship between Article 6 and Articles 3 and 4.

The District Court in Humenné[54] resolved a dispute between a bank established in the Czech Republic (the claimant) and a consumer (the defendant, a natural person with Slovak nationality and a permanent residence in the Slovak Republic), in which in the claimant's general terms and conditions contained the choice-of-law clause where Czech law was chosen. The court found that it could not be identified from the case file that the applicant would be engaged in business or business activity in Slovakia, where the defendant had his residence. Similarly, it had not been established that this creditor would direct his activity to Slovakia and that the contract under review would be within the scope of such activity. On the basis of these findings, the court should have concluded that Article 6 was not applicable and should have considered the choice of law under Article 3 of the Rome I Regulation. However, the court continued its argument in line with Article 6. The court concluded that the law applicable to the case was the law in force in the Czech Republic, on the basis of the choice of law made by the parties. In the event that Czech substantive law would deprive the sued consumer of the protection afforded to him by the provisions of Slovak substantive law, it would be possible to derogate from Czech law, as provided for in Article 6(2) of the Rome I Regulation.

In another case, the District Court in Michalovce[55] applied the law of the Slovak Republic on the basis of Article 6(1). Its conclusions were based on the fact that the consumer had his habitual residence in the territory of the Slovak Republic and the business entity also carried out its business activities in the territory of the Slovak Republic through its organisational unit registered in the Commercial Register of the Slovak Republic. However, the claimant was not an organisational unit of a business entity (a bank), but a parent company established in the Czech Republic. The loan that was the subject of the dispute was provided in Czech crowns. Was it sufficient for the court that the defendant also carried out, through its organisational unit, business activity in the country of the consumer's habitual residence, as is stated in the text of Article 6(1)(a), without examining whether the contract was concluded through the local branch of the entrepreneur and without examining whether or not the contract was concluded during the Slovak consumer's stay in the Czech Republic? It is possible. However, to evaluate with certainty the procedure of the District Court in Michalovce is not possible, as the court did not deal with this key information in the judgment. The situation is similar for other judgments by district courts, since the key data are anonymised in the judgment or the court failed to ascertain them at all.

On the other hand, there are also cases of the correct application of Article 6 of the Rome I Regulation. We can mention the judgment of the District Court in Revúca,[56] in a dispute concerning non-payment for a gas supply. The claimant

54 Judgment of the District Court Humenné, of 25 May 2015, file ref. 5C/282/2014.

55 Judgment of the District Court Michalovce, of 27 July 2012, file ref. 8C/57/2012.

56 Judgment of the District Court Revúca, of 14 December 2016, file ref. 5C/152/2015.

(the gas supplier) was domiciled in the Czech Republic, while the defendant (the receiver) was domiciled in the Slovak Republic at the time of the dispute. The court applied the law of the Czech Republic, on the grounds that the contractual relationship between the claimant and the defendant was based on an explicit agreement on the choice of law made by the parties in Article 10.6. of the supplier's terms and conditions, namely that the contractual relationship would be governed by the law of the Czech Republic. The court further considered that Czech law would also be applicable to a given contractual relationship even in the absence of a choice-of-law agreement under Article 6(1) of Rome I Regulation, since it was clear from the circumstances of the case that at the time of the conclusion and performance of the contract, the defendant had stayed and lived at the place of supply for which he had concluded a gas supply contract, i.e. he resided in the territory of the Czech Republic.

In the present case, a question may arise as to whether the court should not have excluded the use of Article 6 within the meaning of paragraph 4, since services (the supply of gas) were supplied to the consumer exclusively in a country that was not the country of his habitual residence. In the present case, however, the country of the consumer's habitual residence at the time the service was provided was the Czech Republic. Thus, at the time of the establishment and implementation of the contractual relationship, the trader actually pursued his activity in the country of the consumer's habitual residence; the conditions in Article 6(1)(a) were satisfied, but their application led to the use of the law of the Czech Republic. A less vigilant judge could, in the austere, formalistic interpretation of Article 6, be confused by this fact.

The application of Article 6, on the grounds that the service was provided in the Czech Republic, was rejected by the District Court in Senica.[57] In the present case, the service (supply of natural gas to the defendant's place of delivery) was provided in the Czech Republic by a distribution company based in Brno in the Czech Republic. The customer was a Slovak national, and at the time of the opening of proceedings the place of his habitual residence was unknown. The place of the customer's habitual residence at the time of the conclusion of the combined services contract and at the time the service was performed is not mentioned in the judgment. The court stated that it had determined the applicable law within the meaning of Article 4(1)(b) and Article 6(3), holding that the country of the habitual residence of the service provider was the Czech Republic, but that this was not the country of the habitual residence of the consumer.

The District Court in Spišská Nová Ves decided a case under the provisions of the Rome Convention.[58] The court first rightly held that the Rome I Regulation should not be applied to the contractual relationship in question, as

[57] Judgment of the District Court Senica, of 29 June 2016, file ref. 3C/94/2015.
[58] Judgment of the District Court Spišská Nová Ves, of 30 January 2012, file ref. 1C/210/2009.

the Regulation, according to its Article 28, applies to contracts entered into after 17 December 2009, and the conclusion of the contract giving rise to the dispute took place in July 2008. In relation to Article 5(1) of the Rome Convention, the court found that the service contract in question was a consumer contract since the services were to be provided for a purpose which may not be regarded as part of the business or occupation of the customer. However, the court also found that the services (the building of the weekend house) were to be provided in Switzerland, i.e. in a country other than the country of the habitual residence of the consumer, which was Germany. Therefore, within the meaning of Article 5(4), this article should not apply in the matter. The court then determined the applicable law under Article 4(1).

In recent years there have also been cases involving invalidating the choice of law in consumer contracts, especially where the choice of law was made in the general terms and conditions of a stronger party, and was therefore not individually negotiated, as required by Directive 93/13/EEC on unfair terms in consumer contracts and its Slovak transposition into section 53 of the Civil Code. In other words, the court considered such a choice of law to be an unfair term. Such a conclusion by the District Court in Bardejov[59] was confirmed in the appeal proceedings by the Regional Court in Prešov.[60] However, the Regional Court in Prešov wrongly assessed the applicable legislation. It pointed out that the Rome I Regulation did not apply to the contract in respect of the date of its conclusion before 17 December 2009, but completely failed to mention the Rome Convention and proceeded according to Slovak law, namely the provision of section 10(4) of the PIL Act.

Also of interest is another statement made by the Regional Court in Prešov, where it notes that, even if the choice of law was valid, the procedure under section 9(3) of the PIL Act should have been applied. Section 9(3) says that, if the parties to a consumer contract have chosen a law which confers less protection to the consumer than that received under the Slovak legal order, their relations will be governed by the Slovak legal order. The key question in the case at hand was the length of the limitation period. If Czech law applied, the limitation period would be four years, whereas under Slovak law the limitation period in such cases is three years. As a result, the otherwise substantiated and undisputed claim against the consumer was declared to be subject to limitation. The court obviously considered the different length of the limitation period between the chosen law and the law of the consumer's habitual residence to lead to a lower level of protection for the consumer. Such an approach to consumer protection in the application of Article 6(2) could lead to a broad rejection of the law chosen by the parties to consumer contracts.

---

59 Judgment of the District Court Bardejov, of 14 March 2014, file ref. 1C/121/2013.

60 Judgment of the Regional Court Prešov, of 31 March 2016, file ref. 20Co/289/2014.

It should be noted that the Regional Court in Prešov, which is generally known in the Slovak Republic for its pro-consumer line of decision-making, continues in this practice,[61] even after the decision of the Supreme Court of the Slovak Republic of 27 August 2015 mentioned in section 4.5.2. Sometimes it has followers in other courts.[62] The common feature of these decisions is the statement that Slovak law provides the consumer with greater protection than Czech law, inter alia, a more favourable length of limitation period. The parties in these proceedings were unsuccessful in their attempts to argue the case law of the courts of the Czech Republic and the above-mentioned judgment of the Supreme Court of the Slovak Republic. At the same time, this practice of the Regional Court in Prešov confirms that it is still not possible to talk about a uniform line of decision-making in matters of application of the Rome I and Rome II Regulations in the Slovak Republic.

A serious problem from the point of view of applying Article 6(2) of the Rome I Regulation may be the above-mentioned paragraph 4 of section 10 of the PIL Act. This new paragraph was added to section 10 of the PIL Act by an amendment in 2014 with effect from 1 May 2014[63] for the purpose of transposing Directive 2011/83/EU on consumer rights. Its wording does not seem to be problematic at first glance: 'Contractual relations related to a consumer contract shall be governed by Slovakian law, unless the law that would otherwise be applicable, provides the consumer with better protection of their rights.' The apparent serious deficiency of this provision is that it does not take into account whether the consumer has or does not have habitual residence in the territory of the Slovak Republic when it confirms the application of Slovak law (but this situation has already been repeated under section 9(3) of the PIL Act). However, this provision was unduly described as an *imperatívna norma* – an overriding mandatory rule (*loi de police*)[64] by the explanatory note.

Some courts have understood this to mean that the provisions of the Slovak legislation on consumer rights should be applied as an overriding mandatory

---

61 See Judgment of the Regional Court Prešov, of 10 January 2019, file ref. 5Co/18/2018 and Judgment of the Regional Court Prešov, of 29 April 2019, file ref. 2Co/169/2018.

62 Judgment of the Regional Court Banská Bystrica, of 19 September 2018, file ref. 17Co/265/2017.

63 Act no. 102/2014 Coll. of 25 March 2014, on the protection of the consumer in the sale of goods or the provision of services on the basis of a distance contract or a contract concluded outside the seller's business premises and on the amendment of certain laws, effective from 1 May 2014.

64 The explanatory report to the amendment states: 'In line with the logic of the PIL Act, Section 10 is supplemented by an overriding mandatory rule applicable to obligations that originate or relate to a consumer contract. It does not appear to be appropriate to define overriding mandatory rules in individual consumer protection laws, but it would be better to incorporate them in the provisions on obligations with the international element in Act no. 97/1963 Coll. In accordance with the philosophy of the Rome I Regulation, the preference for the consumer of a more favourable legal regime is also incorporated'.

rule, so always in the case of a consumer contract with a foreign element. The District Court in Košice I in its judgment of 24 April 2015[65] stated that the contract in that case had been concluded under the provisions of the Commercial Code in force in the Czech Republic, from which it could be inferred that the legal relationship between the parties should be governed by the law in force in the Czech Republic. However, the court could not omit Article 7 of the Rome Convention (the contract in question was concluded on 13 April 2007) and also had to take into account the mandatory standards in force in the Slovak Republic. The District Court further referred to section 10(4) of the PIL Act and noted that with this provision the Slovak Republic has made it clear that consumer protection standards are considered mandatory. Subsequently, the court referred to the provisions of the Slovak Consumer Protection Act[66] prohibiting aggressive (unfair) trade practices and dismissed the action on the grounds of their use by the applicant.

In contrast, the Regional Court in Trenčín[67] did not accept the reasoning of the District Court in Partizánske[68] which, with reference to section 10(4) of the PIL Act, applied the provisions of the Slovak Consumer Protection Act. According to the Slovak Consumer Act, the authority deciding on the claims of a consumer contract takes into account, even without a motion, the grounds of weakening the claim of the seller against the consumer, including the limitation period. Subsequently the District Court applied the limitation period as it is provided by the Slovak law. The Regional Court in Trenčín was of the opinion that for the contract concluded in accordance with the legislation of the Czech Republic this law had been validly chosen and the legal relations between the parties should be assessed according to this law. However, it is necessary to take into account the provisions of the relevant legislation on consumer protection in force in the Czech Republic, since the contract in question was a consumer contract.

On the contrary, a reference to overriding mandatory rules could probably be used by the Regional Court in Košice in a judgment of 9 October 2019.[69] The court ruled on the claim arising out of an unjust enrichment originating from the performance of an invalid contract. The loan agreement was concluded in the Slovak Republic, according to Czech law, between the Czech company as the loan provider and a consumer with a habitual residence in the Slovak Republic. The invalidity of the contract resulted from Slovak Act no. 129/2010 Coll. of laws, according to which loans may be provided to consumers in the territory of the Slovak Republic only by entities that have the authorisation of the National

65 Judgment of the District Court Košice I, of 24 April 2015, file ref. 12C/406/2011.
66 Act no. 250/2007 Coll. of 9 May 2007 on consumer protection.
67 Judgment of the Regional Court Trenčín, of 31 March 2016, file ref. 4Co/147/2015.
68 Judgment of the District Court Partizánske, of 17 December 2014, file ref. 1C/43/2014.
69 Judgment of the Regional Court Košice, of 9 October 2019, file ref. 2Co/243/2019.

Bank of Slovakia for such activities. As the Czech company did not have such an authorisation, the contract was considered invalid. The relevant provision of Act no. 129/2010 Coll. of laws seems to be an overriding mandatory rule (*loi de police*). But the Regional Court referred to it as a provision of the law of the country of the consumer's habitual residence, from which it is not possible to deviate by agreement, within the meaning of Article 6(2) Rome I Regulation and thus applied Slovak law.

Regarding other specific rules, it seems that, from the point of view of their systematic classification or interpretation, the application of Articles 5, 7 and 8 of the Rome I Regulation does not led to any more serious problems. However, it should be noted that Articles 7 and 8 have been applied in only a very small number of cases.[70] However, Article 5 on transport contracts has been frequently applied (some of these judgments have already been discussed in the previous sections).

In connection with the application of Article 8 of the Rome I Regulation, it may sometimes be difficult to determine the place where the work is habitually carried out, as was the situation, for example, in a case decided by the District Court Bratislava I.[71] The subject of the dispute was a claims arising from an employment contract concluded on 30 April 2009, with an amendment on 20 February 2012, under which the place of work changed from the Slovak Republic to Sweden. The employee actually performed work in Sweden from February to June 2012 for the employer's branch in Sweden. He was paid in Swedish crowns, according to Swedish regulations. On this basis, the employer argued that the place of work had changed and that the employment relationship was governed by Swedish law after the employee had been recruited to work in Sweden. The District Court rejected the arguments of the employer and assessed the performance of work in Sweden as a temporary posting, during which the 'hard core' of the employee's working conditions were governed by the law of the host state, but the remainder were governed by Slovak law, which was, according to the provisions of the employment contract, chosen as the law applicable to the employment relationship.

This decision of the District Court was challenged before the Regional Court by an appeal,[72] next before the Supreme Court by an extraordinary remedy[73]

---

70 For example, judgment of the District Court Ružomberok, of 25 April 2012, file ref. 2C/35/2012. The court ruled on the unpaid instalments of an insurance premium from an insurance contract for liability for damage caused by the operation of a motor vehicle. The court, referring to Article 7(1) and (3) last sentence applied Czech law. Although this is not stated in the judgment, given the mandatory nature of the insurance involved in the registration of a motor vehicle in that country, it can be assumed that the insured risk was situated in the Czech Republic.

71 Judgment of the District Court Bratislava I, of 27 October 2014, file ref. 4Cpr/6/2013.

72 Judgment of the Regional Court Bratislava, of 16 June 2016, file ref. 3CoPr 6/2015.

73 Resolution of the Supreme Court of the Slovak Republic, of 25 October 2017, file ref. 7Cdo 19/2017.

and finally, before the Constitutional Court of the Slovak Republic.[74] All courts upheld the judgment of the District Court. Crucial for the court's decision was the interpretation of the 'place where the work was habitually carried out', as the determination of this place was the basis for assessing whether the employee was posted within the meaning of Directive no. 96/71/EC or not. In this argument, the employer also referred to the judgments of the CJEU in cases C-65/85 *Lawrie-Blum* and C-125/92 *Mulox*, but the higher courts rejected that argument, pointing out that none of those judgments applied to the present case. For example, in relation to the *Mulox* judgment, it has been pointed out that that judgment was given for the purpose of determining jurisdiction (Article 5 paragraph 1 of the Brussels Convention) and was therefore not applicable in the present case. However, none of the courts used later judgments of the CJEU for interpreting the concept of the place where the work is habitually carried out, in support of their conclusions.[75]

On the other hand, when applying the Rome II Regulation, courts have only minimally used the specific rules. Overall, the Rome II Regulation has been used very little; however, in our opinion, this is also due to a misqualification of the claims, which could in fact have been qualified, for example, as unjust enrichment.[76] A reference to one of the specific rules, Article 5 on product liability, was found only in one judgment;[77] however, the court did not discuss the use the Article in any way and applied the law chosen by the parties to the distribution contract with which the claim for damages was linked.

Article 8 of the Rome II Regulation was referred in to in Judgments of the District Court Bratislava I of 22 March 2019[78] and of 17 October 2019.[79] In the first dispute, a Czech television company asserted claims from the unauthorised retransmission of its programmes in the Slovak Republic. The second dispute concerned a claimant's copyright infringement by the unauthorised publication of photographs taken by him. In both cases, the courts designated the Slovak law

---

74 Resolution of the Constitutional Court of the Slovak Republic, of 10 May 2018, file ref. II. ÚS 233/2018. By a complaint (Article 127 of the Constitution of the SR, Act no. 460/1992 Coll.) filed with the Constitutional Court the employer objected that his right to a fair trial within the meaning of Article 46(1) of the Constitution of the SR, as well as in accordance with Article 6(1) of the European Convention for the Protection of Human Rights and Fundamental Freedoms of 1950, had been violated by the fact that neither the Regional Court nor the Supreme Court had dealt with the arguments presented by him and also by the fact that the decisions of both courts were not duly and convincingly reasoned, as required by the above-mentioned human rights standards and their interpretation.

75 For example Case C-29/10 *Koezelsch*, or Case C-384/10 *Bogsgeerd*. Discussed, for example, in Júdová, E.: *Pracovnoprávne vzťahy s cudzím prvkom*, in: Aktuálne problémy pracovného práva a sociálnej legislatívy po novele Zákonníka práce. Sládkovičovo: Fakulta práva J.Jesenského, 2012, pp. 101–118.

76 See section 4.3.

77 Judgment of the District Court Trenčín, of 17 December 2012, file ref. 39Cb/182/2010.

78 Judgment of the District Court Bratislava I, of 22 March 2019, file ref. 10Ca/9/2019.

79 Judgment of the District Court Bratislava I, of 17 October 2019, file ref. 19Ca/50/2019.

as the applicable law, on the basis of Article 8(1) of the Rome II Regulation, on the grounds that the protection of intellectual property rights is required in the territory of the Slovak Republic.

4.5. RELATED QUESTIONS

4.5.1. Lois de police

The use of mandatory rules (*lois de police*) did not exist in Slovak and previously in Czechoslovak private international law enshrined legislatively, but it was addressed in the doctrine[80] and in the textbooks of private international law.[81] Such rules mainly included foreign exchange regulations, currency and customs regulations, regulations imposing permissions for the import or export of goods, and the like. The importance of types of provisions is weakening with the transition of the Slovak Republic to a market economy and its membership of the EU and the eurozone. The vast majority of disputes from contractual or non-contractual obligations heard by the Slovak courts in the last decade concerned 'intra-Union' relations, i.e. they were disputes not going beyond the borders of the EU. Most of them also had a non-commercial nature.

A relatively new feature in Slovak private international law is the inclusion among the mandatory rules of standards protecting private interests, i.e. standards balancing the unequal position of the weaker parties to contractual obligations, such as consumers, employees, commercial agents, etc.[82] Protection of the weaker party was brought into Slovak law by European law, and following the European approach it has also established itself in private international law. So far, the Rome I Regulation and its interpretation has had a greater impact

80 See Pauknerová, M.: 'Přímo použitelné administrativněprávní normy a mezinárodní právo soukromé', in: *Právník*, vol. CXXII, no. 5, 1983, pp. 477–489, or Kopáč, L.: 'Druhy právních norem upravujících mezinárodní obchod a jejich vzájemný vztah', in: *Právník*, vol. CXXIV, no. 12, 1985, pp. 1099–1114. These articles referred to the well-known article by Phocion Francescakis from 1966: Francescakis, P., 'Quelques precisions sur les "lois d'application immediate" et leurs rapports avec les règles sur les conflicts de lois' in *Revue critique de droit international privé*, 1966, pp. 1–18. The Francescakis definition of the overriding mandatory rules (*lois d'application immediate*) formulated in the article, influenced via the Belgian law and judgment of the CJEU C-369/96 *Arblade*, the formulation of Article 9 of the Rome I Regulation. See Bonomi, A., Overriding mandatory provisions in the Rome I Regulation on the law applicable to contracts, *Yearbook of Private International Law*, vol. 10, 2008, p. 287 et seq. See also Proposal for a Regulation of the European Parliament and the Council on the law applicable to contractual obligations (Rome I), COM (2005) 650 final, commentary on Article 8. In Slovakia, except for the private international law experts, this theory is unknown to the legal public.

81 Kučera, Z.: *Mezinárodní právo soukromé*, 2nd ed., Prague: Panorama, 1980, p. 175 et seq.

82 Lysina, P. – Ďuriš, M. – Haťapka, M. et al.: *Medzinárodné právo súkromné*, 2nd ed., Bratislava: C.H. Beck, 2016, p. 280.

on the interpretation and application of the mandatory rules in Slovak private international law than the previous domestic doctrine.

In particular, consumer protection is a topic that resonates strongly in Slovak judicial practice. Slovak courts are aware of the emphasis that the EU accords to the protection of the consumer as the weaker party. Consumer disputes are numerous already at national level. There is some nervousness among the courts for fear of neglecting or ignoring the application of any rule of consumer law. Therefore, when the legislator in the explanatory note referred to the provision of section 10(4) of the PIL Act as an overriding mandatory rule, the courts, such as the District Court in Košice I[83] (judgment of 24 April 2015, cited in section 4.4.4) immediately reacted and automatically identified the rules of Slovak law governing consumer rights as rules that cannot be derogated from, even where foreign law is applicable.

As already mentioned in section 4.4.4, a new paragraph 4 was inserted into section 10 of the PIL Act by an amendment made by the law adopted in 2014 for the purpose of transposing Directive 2011/83/EU on consumer rights (it is probably the transposition of Article 25 of the Directive). Paragraph 4 is, however, formulated as a conflict-of-law rule. Denoting a conflict-of-law rule as an overriding mandatory rule is very unusual.[84] We dare say that this does not imply a good understanding by the legislator of the concept of the *loi de police*. For the courts, the designation of the conflict-of-laws rule as an overriding mandatory rule, may even be misleading. However, as the case law cited in section 4.4.4 demonstrates, the courts have interpreted the provision in question in such a way as to give preference to the provisions of Slovak consumer law qualifying them as an overriding mandatory rule. This, on the other hand, may result in the systematic invalidation of a foreign law applicable to a consumer contract, whether by choice of law or on the basis of choice-of-law rules. The provision in question can thus act counter-productively against Article 6. However, as it can be seen from the example of the Regional Court in Trenčín of 31 March 2016[85] (see section 4.4.4), it also depends on the judge's personal experience and knowledge.

---

83 Judgment of the District Court Košice I, of 24 April 2015, file ref. 12C/406/2011.

84 The suitability of this rule as a transposition of Directive 2011/83/EU on consumer rights should be given a separate section. The provision in question is part of section 10 of the PIL Act on the law applicable in the absence of a choice of law, and therefore does not cover situations where a law has been chosen for a consumer contract. The provision unilaterally applies the Slovak legal order if a law which would otherwise be decisive for a consumer contract does not guarantee the consumer greater protection of his rights, no matter where the consumer has his habitual residence. In addition, the transposition of any protection standard in consumer directives by way of a conflict-of-law rule is not the most appropriate means, as without knowledge of its origin, a judge may logically give precedence to the Rome Regulation I. We are not even certain that the provision fulfils the objective set in the Directive.

85 Judgment of the Regional Court Trenčín, of 31 March 2016, file ref. 4Co/147/2015.

4.5.2. *Treatment of Foreign Law*

Czechoslovak private international law, and after that also Slovak private international law, is based on the idea that the foreign law referred to by the conflict rule is treated as a 'law', not a factual circumstance.[86] Accordingly, in line with the principle of *iura novit curia*, it is the court which is required to determine the content of a foreign law. This obligation is imposed by the PIL Act in section 53(1), with the words 'For the determination of a foreign law, the judicial authority will take all necessary measures'. Both the older and more recent doctrine on this subject emphasises that the court is obliged to apply foreign law ex officio because of the binding legal norm – a conflict-of-law rule (even a conflict-of-law rule in an international treaty, or an EU regulation such as Rome I or Rome II), which binds the court.[87]

The judge is therefore required not only to make use of all the means available to find foreign law, but also to ascertain how the foreign regulation in his country of origin is interpreted and applied so that the foreign law can be used in the way it is used in his country of origin. Even in the cases of the application of foreign law on the basis of a reference to the conflict-of-law rules in the Rome I Regulation, it was therefore common in the cases to be decided under Czech law, for the parties to the dispute, or even the court itself, to base their arguments on the case law of the highest judicial authorities of the Czech Republic.

Similarly, the Supreme Court of the Slovak Republic, when interpreting the disputed provision of Czech law (section 262(4) of the Commercial Code), proceeded according to its interpretation in the case law of the Supreme Court of the Czech Republic.[88] Both the District and Regional Courts[89] dismissed the defendant's claim because the limitation period had elapsed. The defendant's claim arising from the loan agreement was governed, under the choice of law, by Czech law. As a loan agreement, this contract was governed by the Czech Commercial Code, Act no. 513/1991 Coll., which provided for a general limitation period of four years. However, the loan agreement was also a consumer contract, so the Slovak courts applied the limitation period under the Civil Code

[86] From the older literature, e.g. Kučera, Z.: *Mezinárodní právo soukromé*, 2nd ed., Prague: Panorama, 1980, p. 129 et seq.; from more current literature, e.g. Lysina, P. – Ďuriš, M. – Haťapka, M. et al.: *Medzinárodné právo súkromné*, 2nd ed., Bratislava: C.H. Beck, 2016, p. 148 et seq.

[87] Pekár, B. – Slašťan, M.: 'Zisťovanie a používanie cudzieho práva v Slovenskej republike', in: *Dny práva 2015. Část IV. Kodifikace obecné části kolizního práva – cesta či omyl. Acta Universitatis Brunensis Iuridica*, vol. 548, Brno: Masarykova univerzita, 2016, p. 184.

[88] Resolution of the Supreme Court of the Slovak Republic, of 27 August 2015, file ref. 2 MCdo 16/2014.

[89] Judgment of the District Court Stará Ľubovňa, of 9 May 2013, file ref. 1 C 58/2012; Judgment of the Regional Court Prešov, of 10 April 2014, file ref. 5 Co 122/2013.

of the Czech Republic, i.e. three years, with reference to section 262(4) of the Commercial Code of the Czech Republic, which states that contracts covered by the Commercial Code are governed by the provisions of the Civil Code or special regulations on consumer contracts, adhesion contracts, unfair terms and other provisions aimed at consumer protection, if this is in favour of the contracting party (so long as they are not an entrepreneur).

The General Prosecutor of the Slovak Republic filed an extraordinary appeal against the decision of the first and second instance courts for an incorrect legal assessment of the case. The Slovak Supreme Court joined the opinion of the Prosecutor General. According to the Slovak Supreme Court, it was necessary to apply the limitation period in accordance with the Commercial Code of the Czech Republic and not the Civil Code of the Czech Republic. The Slovak Supreme Court based its argument on the case law of the Czech Supreme Court, according to which the provision of section 262(4) should not be interpreted as justifying the application of any provision which may be more advantageous to the consumer. According to the Czech Supreme Court, the regulation on the limitation period is not one aimed at protecting the consumer; rather the different lengths of the limitation periods in the Civil and Commercial Codes of the Czech Republic are only a result of various legislative processes. The limitation affects both parties equally. The Slovak Supreme Court, in its interpretation of the Czech Commercial Code, also referred to the explanatory memorandum to the relevant section and to Czech literature.

The requirement to apply the foreign law to which the conflict-of-law rule referred as it is interpreted and applied in its country of origin also places high demands on the court. While the continuing education of judges also involves courses on the world's legal systems, it is only possible to give the judges a basic guidance as to what legal system they have to take into account and to what extent, for example, to take into account relevant case law or doctrine and so on. However, if the court adjudicates in a specific case this is not sufficient; in order to properly understand the foreign law and to apply it correctly the court needs to select the relevant legal standard in a foreign legal system applicable in the matter, it needs to find the relevant case law, commentaries or other academic literature.

If the Slovak court enforces Czech law – which is currently the case in the majority of cases – this does not have to be complicated. The court has an advantage given the absence of a language barrier, the wide availability of Czech literature in the Slovak Republic, and the fact that Czech and Slovak law are based on the same historical foundations and that legal thinking is very close in these countries. Where another foreign law is applied, in particular the law of another 'legal family', the courts are more motivated to seek elements connecting the situation with Slovak law so that they can apply this law.

As regards the choice of permissible means of proving foreign law, the court may use any means it considers reliable. Section 53 of the PIL Act gives the examples of ascertaining the content of foreign law by the court's own means[90] or from publicly available sources, by imposing an obligation on the parties, or by requesting information from the Ministry of Justice. If the court imposes an obligation on the parties to present a document proving the foreign law and the parties do not submit that document within the prescribed time limit, this, according to the prevailing opinions, does not exempt the court from the obligation to determine the content of the foreign law.[91] Only if 'the content of a foreign law will not be determined or the determination of the content of a foreign law is connected with difficulties to overcome obstacles or impossible, the Slovak law shall apply' (section 53(1) last sentence of the PIL Act).

In practice, the courts usually turn to the Ministry of Justice for information. The Ministry of Justice of the Slovak Republic identifies such information on the basis of cooperation through bilateral[92] or multilateral treaties,[93] or through the diplomatic representations of the Slovak Republic abroad. Information from the Ministry of Justice is not formally binding on the court – it is for the court to judge whether it considers the information relevant. In another way in which Slovak courts are informed of the content of foreign law and the relevant case law is the information submitted by the parties, in the context of the arguments put forward in support of their claims; it is again the court that decides whether it considers this information relevant.[94]

4.5.3. *Relations with International Conventions*

The most frequently applied international treaties in contractual matters heard by Slovak courts were the UN Convention on Contracts for the International Sale of Goods from 1980 (CISG)[95] and the Convention on the Contract for the

---

90 For example, the judge's own knowledge of foreign law acquired during an internship abroad, or information provided by personal contact with a judicial colleague from a foreign state, see Lysina, P. – Ďuriš, M. – Haťapka, M. et al.: *Medzinárodné právo súkromné*, 2nd ed., Bratislava: C.H. Beck, 2016, p. 149.

91 Kučera, Z. – Tichý, L.: *Zákon o mezinárodním právu soukromém a procesním*, Prague: Panorama, 1989, p. 282.

92 In particular, bilateral agreements on legal aid – a complete list of agreements is available at the Ministry of Justice of the Slovak Republic website: <https://www.justice.gov.sk/Stranky/Nase-sluzby/Medzinarodne-pravo/Justicna%20spolupraca%20v%20obcianskych%20a%20obchodnych%20veciach/Pramene%20prava/Dvojstranne-zmluvy.aspx>.

93 The Slovak Republic is bound by the European Convention on Information on Foreign Law of 1968, together with the Additional Protocol to the European Convention on Information on Foreign Law of 1978.

94 However, if the parties submit a certificate on a foreign law in the prescribed form, accompanied by a legalisation clause, it has a probative value of the public instrument.

95 The Slovak Republic is bound by the Convention on the basis of succession to the Czech and Slovak Federal Republic from 1.1.1993. The Convention was published in the Collection of Laws no. 160/1991 Coll.

International Carriage of Goods by Road from 1956 (CMR).[96] In general, the assessment of the relationship between the above conventions and the Rome I Regulation does not pose a problem in the practice of Slovak courts. The courts primarily apply the conventions as a unified substantive law and only to matters not governed by the conventions; applicable national law is determined on the basis of the Rome I Regulation.[97]

In extra-contractual matters, the most frequently applied is the Hague Convention on the law applicable to traffic accidents from 1971,[98] which, in accordance with Article 28 of the Rome II Regulation, takes precedence over the provisions of the Rome II Regulation. It turns out that the interpretation of the Hague Convention can be problematic in cases where the right to compensation for damage caused by a traffic accident that occurred in another state and with a foreign vehicle, is asserted by a Slovak co-driver against another Slovak driver (who is also the perpetrator of the accident) of the car which is registered in the Slovak Republic. Under the Convention, the law of the State where the accident occurred is applied in principle (Article 3 of the Convention) and exceptions to this rule apply only in situations involving a vehicle, or vehicles, registered in a State other than that in which the accident occurred (Article 4 of the Convention). The Convention does not contain a provision similar to Article 4 paragraph 2 of the Rome II Regulation, which gives priority to the law of the State of the common habitual residence of the parties.

In a similar situation, the Regional Court in Bratislava distinguished claims for damages caused by a vehicle registered in the Slovak Republic on a vehicle registered in the country where the accident occurred – for this the applicable law is to be determined in accordance with Article 3 of the Hague Convention – from a claim for damage caused to a Slovak passenger in a vehicle registered in the Slovak Republic (claim asserted in proceedings before this court) and for which the applicable law is to be determined in accordance with Article 4(b) of the Hague Convention. In this way, the Regional Court came to apply Slovak law.[99]

On the contrary, the District Court in Nové Mesto nad Váhom proceeded differently in a similar situation.[100] Due to the fact that two vehicles registered in different countries (Slovakia and Hungary) were involved in the accident that

---

96 The Slovak Republic is bound by the Convention on the basis of succession to the Czech and Slovak Federal Republic from 1.1.1993. The Convention was published in the Collection of Laws no. 11/1975 Coll.

97 For example, Judgment of the Regional Court Bratislava of 21 November 2018, file ref. 3Cob/61/2018.

98 The Slovak Republic is bound by the Convention on the basis of succession to the Czech and Slovak Federal Republic from 1.1.1993. The Convention was published in the Collection of Laws no. 130/1976 Coll.

99 Judgment of the Regional Court Bratislava, of 29 January 2019, file ref. 5 Co/314/2017.

100 Judgment of the District Court Nové Mesto nad Váhom, of 25 October 2012, file ref. 4C/144/2008.

took place in Hungary, the application of the exceptions to the Hague Convention enshrined in Article 4 was not possible according to the court. However, since the claim was asserted by a co-driver against the driver of a vehicle registered in the Slovak Republic, both of them being Slovak citizens residing in the Slovak Republic, the court held that it was not a legal relationship with a foreign element and therefore is governed by Slovak law. The law of the place where the accident took place should have been decisive for assessing whether liability has arisen.

5. GENERAL EVALUATION

The judicial practice of the Slovak Courts in the application of the Rome I and Rome II Regulations is rather incoherent. This is despite the fact that the Rome I Regulation did not bring about a fundamental turning point in the determination of the applicable law for contractual obligations – in many cases the system established by the Regulation is similar to the previous regime based on the PIL Act, which might have been expected to have had a positive impact on the correct application of the Regulation. The courts try to interpret the Regulations in particular with regard to their wording, and the CJEU case law is only exceptionally cited interpreting the provisions of the Regulations. However, this approach is partly due to the surviving formalistic method of interpretation and application of law by the courts, which is currently being criticised by the judiciary itself in the Slovak Republic.

The errors in the application of the Rome I and Rome II Regulations are also caused by judges' inexperience in deciding on cross-border legal relations. These cases form only a small percentage of the courts' caseload, and so the courts do not regularly have to deal with decisions in these matters. The determination of the applicable law is considered to be only a precursor to the decision on the key factual issues of the dispute. The attention paid to private international law issues is very small overall: for example, only single-semester courses on private international law are currently being taught in law schools in the Slovak Republic. Students and lawyers in practice perceive this area to be very complicated, and they are moreover discouraged by the large number of competing sources; as a result, they rarely go any deeper into the subject. In addition, there are no complete or thematic CJEU case law collections in the field of European private international law or specialised monographs devoted to the individual Regulations.

One of the basic problems faced by the Slovak courts is the qualification of an obligation as a contractual or non-contractual, or the solution to the question of when to proceed according to the Rome I Regulation and when according to the Rome II Regulation. Judicial practice also points to their weak working knowledge of the provisions of the Regulations: sometimes we feel like the courts have not read the Regulations to the end.

The problem also arises from the provision of Article 6 of the Rome I Regulation and the overall decision on consumer disputes. These disputes make up a large percentage of disputes with cross-border implications. The very application of Article 6 is based on the fulfilment of the specified conditions plus the assessment whether or not the situations are excluded, which is not always mastered by the courts. There are also concerns about consumer law, which is why the court does not neglect any important consumer protection clause, and therefore often goes beyond what is mandated in reviewing the Regulations. Thus, it is easy to confuse the mechanism of Article 6(3) with overriding mandatory rules.

6. CONCLUSION

Experience with the practical application of the Rome I and Rome II Regulations in the conditions of the Slovak Republic shows, in the first place, the need to deepen the education of judges in this area. At the national level, it will be necessary to provide the courts, as well as the legal public and obviously the parties, with tools to help them make quick reference to the provisions of the Regulations, such as different casebooks containing case law on individual regulations, practical manuals (experience shows that these being available online is not enough) and books.

A great deal of reluctance in connection with European private international law and private international law generally is also caused by the multitude of sources and the problem of getting familiar with them. As the practice of the Slovak courts shows, the division of the subject of contractual and non-contractual obligations into two separate regulations can cause serious problems. The Slovak courts have sometimes gone against how they would naturally have qualified the situations in question in order to comply with the letter of the Rome I and Rome II Regulations. Combining the conflict of law between contractual and non-contractual obligations into a single legal act would eliminate the problem of determining whether the situation falls within the scope of one or the other Regulation and would enable the court to focus on the correct application of the provisions of this instrument.

Even though a lot of the problems could be eliminated by improving the training of judges and access to reference material, this study also shows that the ideal rule should be formulated as simply as possible, supplemented by a more extensive interpretation.

THE APPLICATION OF THE ROME I AND ROME II REGULATIONS IN SLOVENIA

Jerca KRAMBERGER ŠKERL and Aleš GALIČ

1. THE NATIONAL LANDSCAPE

In small countries like Slovenia case law develops slowly. It takes more time before a sufficient number of relevant issues reach the courts. In addition, a smaller population means fewer academics and therefore less discussion and critical confrontation of ideas on an academic level. As case law and doctrine cannot sufficiently play their role in ensuring the development of law, the result is often a lack of legal certainty and predictability. In the case of a broad international harmonisation of law, however, the case law of foreign courts and positions of foreign legal writing can be used as a valuable persuasive authority. For small EU Member States, this is a very positive, yet often overlooked, effect of EU-wide harmonisation of law.

Since Slovenia's accession to the EU – or more precisely since the accession negotiations started in the late 1990s – EU law has received much scholarly attention. However, in relation to the resolution of cross-border disputes, much more attention has been paid to procedural issues than to the conflict of laws. The first systematic textbook regarding all existing EU private international law, including the conflict of laws, was published in 2018.[1] There have been very few legislative changes influenced by the development of EU private international law in general; the Slovenian legislature often remains passive even in areas of law where intervention would be necessary in order to ensure the effective transposition of EU directives and the smooth application of EU Regulations.

In Slovenia, the Rome I and II Regulations are applicable within their 'original' scope of application, since the Slovenian legislature has not adopted any act which would broaden such scope. For matters falling outside the scope of application of the EU Regulations, the ratified international treaties or the national legislation are applicable (i.e. the Slovenian Private International Law and Procedure Act of 1999, hereinafter: the PILPA).[2]

All judgments of the Supreme Court of Slovenia (*Vrhovno sodišče*) and the four appellate courts (*višja sodišča*) are available online free of charge, but with a certain delay.[3] However, the judgments of the first instance courts (i.e. the local (*okrajna*) and the district courts (*okrožna sodišča*)) are only available physically at the courts and therefore *de facto* are not available for systematic scholarly research. Thus, we can only provide information on the case law of the appellate courts and the Supreme Court published to date (April 2020).

---

1 M. Repas and V. Rijavec (eds), 'Mednarodno zasebno pravo Evropske unije' *[Private International Law of the European Union]*, Uradni list, Ljubljana 2018.

2 *Zakon o mednarodnem zasebnem pravu in postopku*, Official Gazette of the Republic of Slovenia No. 56/1999 and 45/2008.

3 These judgments are available on the website <http://www.sodnapraksa.si/>.

The judgments analysed in this contribution are those in which the Rome I and Rome II Regulations were actually applied to determine the applicable substantive law; contrary to the judgments where these Regulations were only mentioned for comparison or for the determination that the dispute falls outside of their scope of application. Since the 1980 Rome Convention was applicable in Slovenia from June 2006 to December 2009, it seemed important to also mention the judgments where this convention was applied.

In the judgments published as of April 2020, the *Rome Convention* was applied in seven judgments of the Appellate Court in Maribor,[4] the *Rome I Regulation* was applied in 13 judgments of the Appellate Court in Ljubljana,[5] in three judgments of the Appellate Court in Koper,[6] in two judgments of the Appellate Court in Celje,[7] in two judgments of the Appellate Court in Maribor,[8] and in two judgments of the Supreme Court of Slovenia.[9] The *Rome II Regulation* was applied in 13 judgments of the Appellate Court in Ljubljana,[10] two judgments of the Supreme Court of Slovenia,[11] 13 judgments of the Appellate Court in Maribor,[12] and one judgment of the Appellate Labour and Social Court.[13]

As to arbitration, the overall number of proceedings, where the seat of arbitration is in Slovenia (in practice: proceedings administered by the Ljubljana Arbitration Centre, previously known as the Permanent Court of Arbitration Attached to the Slovenian Chamber of Commerce) is low. None of the publicly available arbitral awards make any reference to the Rome I and II Regulations.

4 Nos. I Ip 387/2012 of 31 May 2012, I Ip 567/2012 of 14 June 2012, I Ip 513/2013 of 4 July 2013, I Ip 196/2015 of 29 May 2015, I Ip 1081/2015-1 of 3 February 2016, I Cp 338/2016 of 5 April 2016, and I Ip 544/2016 of 23 September 2016.

5 Nos. I Cp 1951/2014 of 3 December 2014, I Cpg 1709/2014 of 11 February 2015, I Cp 836/2015 of 29 June 2015, I Cpg 23/2016 of 5 April 2016, I Cpg 412/2016 of 31 January 2017, I Cp 171/2017 of 31 May 2017, I Cp 2164/2016 of 25 January 2017, II Cp 2213/2017 of 16 May 2018, and II Cp 2226/2017 of 21 March 2018. I Cpg 664/2017 of 20 July 2017, II Cp 3249/2016 of 29 March 2017, V Cpg 164/2018 of 5 April 2018, I Cp 2219/2017 of 18 April 2018, I Cpg 1084/2016 of 25 October 2017, I Cpg 73/2018 of 8 November 2018, I Cpg 581/2017 of 21 February 2019, I Cpg 259/2019 of 28 August 2019 and I Cp 994/2019 of 16 October 2019.

6 Nos. I Cp 246/2017 of 4 July 2017, Cpg 172/2016 of 14 September 2016 and 21 February 2019.

7 No. Cpg 41/2018 of 13 June 2018 and Cpg 18/2019 of 17 April 2019.

8 No. I Ip 100/2017 of 22 February 2017 and I Cp 87/2019 of 12 March 2019.

9 Nos. VIII Ips 39/2017 and VIII Ips 311/2016, both of 6 June 2017.

10 II Cp 2009/2009 of 30 September 2015, II Cp 1356/2012 of 24 October 2012, II Cp 2926/2012 of 29 May 2013, II Cp 1909/2014 of 1 October 2014, I Cp 1591/2015 of 23 September 2015, III Cp 942/2016 of 15 June 2016, I Cpg 1084/2016 of 25 October 2017, II Cp 3249/2016 of 20 March 2017, I Cpg 664/2017 of 20 July 2017, V Cpg 164/2018 of 5 April 2018, I Cp 2219/2017 of 18 April 2018, I Cp 522/2019 of 3 April 2019 and II Cp 2314/2018 of 12 June 2019.

11 Nos. III Ips 32/2015 of 20 September 2016, Cpg 3/2019 of 15 July 2019.

12 Nos. I Cp 615/2016 of 13 April 2016, I Cp 8/2017 of 7 February 2017 and ten more judgments, all relating to the same factual and legal matrix (individual claims concerning the same mass-harm event). On a different subject matter: No. I Cp 295/2019 of 11 June 2019.

13 No. Pdp 599/2012 of 16 August 2012.

In any case pursuant to the Slovenian Arbitration Act[14] (which is the *lex arbitri* for arbitration with a seat in Slovenia), an arbitral tribunal is not obliged to apply any conflict-of-laws norms. Article 32(2) of the Arbitration Act provides that an arbitral tribunal shall (in the absence of a choice-of-law agreement of the parties) apply the legal rules – thus directly rules of substantive law and not conflict-of-laws rules – that it considers appropriate.[15] Hence, unlike in Article 28 of the UNCITRAL Model Law, a reference is made directly to the substantive law and not merely to the legal system's conflict-of-law norms that the tribunal finds appropriate to apply. Thus an arbitral tribunal applying the Slovenian Arbitration Act as *lex arbitri* can *stricto sensu* never fail to apply the Rome I or Rome II Regulations.

In relation to the most commonly applied provisions, in the seven judgments applying the Rome Convention, Articles 3[16] and 7[17] were applied three times, Article 4[18] was applied twice, and Articles 1[19] and 5[20] were applied once. In judgments applying the Rome I Regulation, Article 3 was applied seven times,[21] Article 6 four times,[22] Article 4 eight times,[23] Article 8 twice,[24] and Articles 1,[25] 5,[26] 7,[27] 12[28] and 14[29] were applied once.

14 *Zakon o arbitraži*, Official Gazette of the Republic of Slovenia No. 45/2008.

15 See e.g. Š. Mežnar, 'Uporaba materialnega prava v postopkih pred mednarodnimi trgovinskimi arbitražami' *[Applicable Substantive Law in International Arbitration]* (2004) 64 *Zbornik znanstvenih razprav Pravne fakultete Ljubljana* 281 et seq.

16 Appellate Court in Maribor, Nos. I Ip 567/2012 of 14 June 2012, I Ip 544/2016 of 23 September 2016 and I Ip 1081/2015-1 of 3 February 2016.

17 Appellate Court in Maribor, Nos. I Ip 567/2012 of 14 June 2012, I Ip 196/2015 of 29 May 2015 and I Ip 513/2013 of 4 July 2013.

18 Appellate Court in Maribor, Nos. I Ip 196/2015 of 29 May 2015 and I Ip 513/2013 of 4 July 2013.

19 Appellate Court in Maribor, No. I Ip 387/2012 of 31 May 2012.

20 Appellate Court in Maribor, No. I Cp 338/2016 of 5 April 2016.

21 Appellate Court in Ljubljana, Nos. I Cpg 1709/2014 of 11 February 2015, I Cpg 23/2016 of 5 April 2016, I Cp 171/2017 of 31 May 2017, I Cpg 412/2016 of 31 January 2017, I Cpg 259/2019 of 28 August 2019, Appellate Court in Maribor, No. I Ip 100/2017 of 22 February 2017 and Appellate Court in Celje, No. Cpg 18/2019 of 17 April 2019.

22 Appellate Court in Ljubljana, Nos. I Cp 1951/2014 of 3 December 2014, I Cp 2164/2016 of 25 January 2017, II Cp 2226/2017 of 21 March 2018, and II Cp 2213/2017 of 16 May 2018.

23 Appellate Court in Koper, Nos. I Cp 246/2017 of 4 July 2017, Cpg 172/2016 of 14 September 2016 and I Cpg 266/2018 of 21 February 2019, Appellate Court in Celje, Nos. Cpg 41/2018 of 13 June 2018 and Cpg 18/2019 of 17 April 2019, Appellate Court in Maribor, No. I Cp 87/2019 of 12 March 2019, Appellate Court in Ljubljana, Nos. I Cpg 581/2017 of 21 February 2019 and I Cpg 73/2018 of 8 November 2018.

24 Supreme Court of Slovenia, Nos. VIII Ips 39/2017 and VIII Ips 311/2016, both of 6 June 2017.

25 Appellate Court in Ljubljana, No. I Cp 836/2015 of 29 June 2015.

26 Appellate Court in Ljubljana, No. I Cpg 581/2017 of 21 February 2019.

27 Appellate Court in Ljubljana, No. I Cpg 23/2016 of 5 April 2016.

28 Appellate Court in Ljubljana, No. I Cp 994/2019 of 16 October 2019.

29 Appellate Court in Ljubljana, No. I Cpg 73/2018 of 8 November 2018.

For the Rome II Regulation, the concept of the place of the damage (Article 4) in a cross-border delict (environmental damage) has been most often applied, in particular in the context of distinguishing between a direct and a consequential damage.[30] While some of these cases relate to personal injuries (skiing and traffic accidents), most of them concern individual claims relating to the same mass harm – flooding of the river Drava in Slovenia, whereas the event giving rise to the damage (alleged mishandling of the hydro-power dam) occurred in Austria. These cases were assessed under the general regime of Article 4, and it has not been discussed whether they could also be assessed under Article 7 (environmental damage). Article 8(1) (infringement of intellectual property rights) has also been an often-applied provision with four cases.[31] All these cases are, however, practically identical insofar as the determination of applicable law is concerned (Slovenian law, which is the law of the country for which the protection was sought). They all refer to collective management of copyright (actions brought by a Slovenian collective management organisation for collection of rights revenue). The courts have also applied the rule concerning product liability (Article 5),[32] the rule determining the law applicable to a non-contractual obligation arising out of an act of unfair competition (Article 6),[33] the general rule of Article 4, specifically relating to the question of indirect damage,[34] and have attempted to resolve the question whether a determination of whether the case indeed relates to tort should be based on either the *lex fori* or the *lex causae*.[35] Relationship between the Rome II Regulation and the Hague Convention of 4 May 1971 on the Law Applicable to Traffic Accidents has also been scrutinised, along with the issue of quantification of damages (the relevance of the non-binding scale system of damages for personal injury issued by the Supreme Court in the country which law is applicable).[36]

Given the limited ability to search for them, it is not possible to give the exact number of decisions that should have applied the Rome I or Rome II Regulations but ultimately – and wrongly – applied a different set of rules. Examples of such decisions can, however, be found, and include not only decisions where

30 By way of example: Appellate Court in Maribor, No. I Cp 8/2017 of 7 February 2017.

31 By way of example: Appellate Court in Ljubljana, No. II Cp 2009/2009 of 30 September 2015.

32 Supreme Court of Slovenia, No. III Ips 32/2015 of 20 September 2016.

33 Appellate Court in Ljubljana, No. V Cpg 164/2018 of 5 April 2018.

34 Appellate Court in Maribor, No. I Cp 615/2016 of 13 April 2016 and I Cp 8/2017 of 7 February 2017, Appellate Labour and Social Court, No. Pdp 599/2012 of 16 August 2012. I Cp 8/2017 of 7 February 2017.

35 Appellate Court in Ljubljana, No. III Cp 942/2016 of 15 June 2016.

36 Appellate Court in Ljubljana, No. II Cp 3249/2016 of 29 March 2017.

courts applied the formerly applicable national conflict-of-laws rule,[37] but also decisions where courts did not establish a foreign element at all.[38]

It can be seen that Slovenian judges' knowledge of the conflict-of-laws rules for contractual and non-contractual obligations varies considerably. There are judgments where the reasons for the application of EU Regulations (or previously the Rome Convention) are explained in an absolutely correct and almost scholarly manner, yet there are also those where it seems the judge has not even heard of these Regulations. Examples of the latter are two 2016 judgments of the Appellate Labour and Social Court, where one of the parties contended that the Rome I Regulation applied (which is mentioned in the judgment, where the court summarises the contentions of the parties), but the court completely ignored this and founded its decision on the applicable law under the formerly applicable national legislation (PILPA).[39] This error was later corrected by the Supreme Court.[40]

2. THE OPERATION OF ROME I AND ROME II IN PRACTICE

2.1. *LOIS DE POLICE*

The Slovenian national legislation (PILPA) does not provide for overriding mandatory provisions, so there is no case law on the subject on the basis of the national rules. Nevertheless, the concept was already recognised and referred to in the doctrine before the entry into force of the EU legislation.

Concerning the Rome I Regulation, there are no published judgments as of April 2020 in which the courts would apply *lois de police*. Two judgments could,

---

37 Typically, Appellate Labour and Social Court, No. Pdp 599/2012 of 16 August 2012 (relating to the law applicable to a dispute over an accident at work). In one judgment, the Appellate Court in Ljubljana wrongly rejected the application of the Rome I Regulation, stating that the legal relationship was connected to the United Kingdom where the Regulation does not apply, therefore the Slovenian national conflict-of-laws rules must be applied: No. I Cp 1900/2017 of 10 January 2018.

38 See e.g. Appellate Court in Ljubljana, No. I Cp 836/2015 of 29 June 2015, where the appellate court quashed the first instance judgment, where the court simply applied the Slovenian law to a dispute between an Austrian attorney and his Slovenian client (for due payment of services), failing to realise that the question of applicable law should be addressed first.

39 Appellate Labour and Social Court, Nos. Pdp 1088/2015 of 15 September 2016, and Pdp 596/2015 of 28 January 2016. In a more recent case, the same court, again after the parties had invoked the Rome I Regulation and Directive No. 96/71/EC, even resolved the case solely on the basis of the Slovenian national labour law legislation, with no regard to the EU legal sources: Appellate Labour and Social Court, No. Pdp 62/2019 of 20 June 2019.

40 Judgment Nos. VIII Ips 39/2017 and VIII Ips 311/2016, both of 6 June 2017.

however, be found where the courts applied Article 7(2) of the Rome Convention, stating that the limitation of the interest rate for consumer loans represented an example of Slovenian overriding mandatory rules. In the judgment of the Appellate Court in Maribor,[41] the court stated:

> 'The limitation of the interest rate in consumer loans is an overriding mandatory rule, which is confirmed by the public interest of the prevention of an unjustified enrichment of the commercially strong suppliers of the means of financing, on behalf of the weaker parties who do not hold the role of a commercial subject on the market. This interest is surely even more emphasised in the current global crisis situation. The background of the public interest in the protection of the consumer in the field of financing by loans is the protection of values of constitutional level. In this regard, the principle of welfare state and the protection of the human right to social security are emphasised (Articles 2 and 50 of the Constitution), where the obligations arising out of a loan influence importantly the individual's social situation and consequently their possibilities of personal development also from the point of view of the human right to personal dignity (Article 34 of the Constitution).'

These judgments are interesting, as they provide an example of what kind of provision the Slovenian courts could deem to be of an overriding mandatory nature. However, Article 5 of the Rome Convention already ensures the protection of the consumers in a way that makes the application of Article 7(2) of the Rome Convention redundant. Namely, Article 5 provides that the mandatory rules (the national *ius cogens*, i.e. the nationally mandatory rules, which is a much wider category than the *lois de police*) of the consumer's home state shall apply even if the contract is in general governed by the law of another state. In these cases, the defendants were consumers domiciled in Slovenia, so there was no need to apply Article 7(2) of the Convention. Furthermore, the authors deem that the public policy defence would have been a more appropriate means of protecting the consumers from too-high interest rates. The application of the domestic law would thus replace those foreign laws that provided for unacceptably high interest rates.

As regards the *lois de police* of third states, we believe that a unique solution should be found for the Rome I and Rome II Regulations. *Lois de police* are general instruments that should not be regulated differently regarding different areas of conflict-of-laws rules (if, in the future, there is European code of private international law, *lois de police* should be regulated in the general part).

---

41 No. I Ip 567/2012 of 14 June 2012.

2.2. PARTY AUTONOMY

2.2.1. Express and Implicit Choice of Law by the Parties

No case law is reported on the choice of applicable law by the parties in non-contractual obligations, whereas numerous decisions can be found in the field of contractual obligations, under the Rome I Regulation and formerly under the PILPA. Interestingly, in most reported cases, the parties had not chosen the applicable law before the dispute and the courts construed an implicit choice of law from the circumstances of the case and/or from the allegations of the parties during the court proceedings. In one of the cases, the court recognised an implicit choice-of-law agreement in that the parties referred to a Slovenian act in their contract.[42]

Quite frequently, if the parties argue their case on the grounds of Slovenian law, the courts tend to construe an implicit choice-of-law agreement and deem that the parties thereby wished to exclude the application of a foreign law.[43] Realistically, however, this situation is probably often merely a consequence of the fact that the parties (or their lawyers) failed to realise that there is a cross-border case and that the question of applicable law should be resolved in the first place.

In one case, such references to the Slovenian Code of Obligations were interpreted by the court, first, as a choice of the Slovenian law and second, as a revocation of the application of the CISG.[44] In another, more recent case, however, the court deemed that the referring of both parties to the Slovenian Code of Obligations (and not to Slovenian law in general) indeed amounted to the choice of Slovenian law under Rome I, but did not exclude the application of the CISG.[45] In yet another case, one party invoked an implicit choice-of-law agreement in favour of Slovenian national law and the other party the applicability of Hungarian national law. The first instance court, applying the law on its own motion, decided the case pursuant to the CISG and to the Convention on the Limitation Period in the International Sale of Goods. The appellate court considered that, first, the first instance court should have examined whether the parties concluded an implicit choice-of-court agreement, and second, if they did, had they excluded the application of the CISG which otherwise constitutes a part of Slovenian (as well as Hungarian) law. If the application of the UN instruments showed to be justified, the first instance court should have, on the basis of the applicable Slovenian procedural

---

42 Appellate Court in Maribor, No. I Ip 100/2017 of 22 February 2017.

43 See e.g. Appellate Court in Ljubljana, Nos. I Cp 2137/2015 of 23 December 2015, I Cp 1951/2014 of 3 December 2014, I Cp 171/2017 of 31 May 2017, I Cpg 1084/2016.

44 Appellate Court in Ljubljana, No. I Cpg 1709/2014 of 11 February 2015.

45 Appellate Court in Ljubljana, No. I Cpg 259/2019 of 28 August 2019.

law, informed the parties of its intention to apply those instruments, so as to prevent a so-called surprise judgment.[46] These cases show that construing an implicit choice-of-law agreement can be a sensible issue, particularly when combined with the question of the applicability of the CISG (or another supranational legal source). The lack of coherent case law can be the source of important legal uncertainty for the parties.

Another case is worth mentioning, concerning an explicit choice-of-law agreement and its effects on third parties. In this case, the court (wrongly, in our opinion) deemed that the explicit choice-of-law agreement, contained in the contract of loan, also stretched to the obligation of the surety, as the connection between the contracts was such that it would have been impossible that they were ruled by different laws.[47]

2.2.2. Choice of a Non-State Body of Law

The lack of option, under the Rome I Regulation, to choose a non-state body of law seems rigid, especially in the light of the growing alignment between court and arbitration proceedings. In business-to-business relations it is difficult to find a good reason to preclude parties from choosing one of the established sets of rules, such as the UNIDROIT Principles or PECL, or even the *lex mercatoria*.[48] It should however be agreed which state law applies to fill the lacunae in such sets of rules. The current wording of Recital 13 of the Rome I Regulation makes the choice of a non-state body of law or an international convention subordinate to the conditions under the otherwise applicable state law, which is stricter than allowing the parties to choose one of these sets of rules and determine the subsidiarily applicable state law.

The application of an international convention is, however, only potentially problematic when the otherwise applicable law is that of a non-contracting state to that convention. Otherwise, the conventions themselves set out when they are applicable – the most prominent example is the CISG, which provides for the possibility of opting out, but is otherwise automatically applicable if the dispute falls within its scope of application.

Recital 14 of the Rome I also enables future EU instruments to provide whether the parties can choose them as the applicable law or not. Although the CESL project seems to have failed, new relevant EU instruments will surely emerge, thus such possibility is welcome.

---

46 Appellate Court in Celje, No. Cpg 18/2019 of 17 April 2019.

47 Appellate Court in Ljubljana, No. I Cpg 412/2016 of 31 January 2017.

48 This should be contrasted to Article 32(1) of the Slovenian Arbitration Act, which explicitly refers to 'legal rules' (which is a broader concept than the 'law' of the state) and thus allows for the applicability of e.g. *lex mercatoria* or inter-, supra- or transnational rules and principles on contract law, such as the UNIDROIT Principles or PECL, and not only of the legal system of a certain state.

2.2.3. Depeçage

Dépeçage is a problem and hinders the conclusion of cross-border contracts especially in contracts with weaker parties that are protected by the mandatory rules of their state of domicile. Smaller Member States are particularly affected: since the market is small, sellers could prefer not to conclude contracts with consumers in those countries, rather than studying the mandatory rules of that state and adapting the contract. In light of the efforts to harmonise certain areas of law in the EU, it would be good to give the parties the option to choose a common set of rules (an optional instrument) that meets the minimum standards of the EU.[49]

2.3. ABSENCE OF CHOICE OF LAW

2.3.1. *Absence of Choice of Law in Contractual Obligations*

In Slovenian case law, Article 4 of the Rome I Regulation was applied seven times to date. In one case, the Slovenian plaintiff filed a lawsuit seeking compensation from an Italian defendant who supposedly did not respect professional standards in performing a dental surgery.[50] The court applied Italian law, being that the service provider had their habitual residence in Italy. Regarding the circumstances of the case as described in the appellate judgment, it remains unclear why the court did not at least consider applying Article 6 of the Regulation.

In another case, the court applied Article 4(3), i.e. the escape clause.[51] In a dispute between the contractor and the subcontractor regarding the construction of a building, the court deemed that Slovenian law was applicable, despite the fact that the service provider had their habitual residence in Italy. Considering all circumstances, the case was manifestly more closely connected to Slovenia.

The third case considered the international sale of goods, governed by the CISG.[52] However, as the latter does not regulate the statute of limitations regarding warranty claims, the court applied the law of the country in which the service provider had their company headquarters. The court cited two possible bases for such decision, namely Article 4 of the Rome I Regulation, and a similar provision in the PILPA, without clearly stating which of these acts applied.[53]

---

49 Such as, for example, the Principles of European Insurance Contract Law (PEICL).
50 Appellate Court in Koper, No. I Cp 246/2017 of 4 July 2017.
51 Appellate Court in Koper, No. Cpg 172/2016 of 14 September 2016.
52 Appellate Court in Celje, No. Cpg 41/2018 of 13 June 2018.
53 Since the contract was concluded in 2013, the applicable act was the Rome I Regulation.

In the most recent case, a contract of factoring was concluded between two Austrian commercial companies regarding claims which arose in Austria, *in casu* regarding a claim for payment of the helicopter transfer of the defendant who was injured in a skiing accident. The Appellate Court in Maribor applied Article 4(4) of the Rome I Regulation, i.e. the rule of the closest connection, and applied Austrian law when deciding on the assignment of a claim and thus on the plaintiff's status of creditor regarding the litigious claim.[54] As the dispute centred around the question of whether the claim against the defendant was included in the contract of factoring (i.e. whether this claim was indeed transferred to the plaintiff), it is unclear why the court did not apply Article 14 of Rome I.

In another reported case, the dispute arose between a Slovenian and a German company first as to the contract of carriage and, in the absence of choice by the parties, the court applied Slovenian law pursuant to Article 5(1) of the Rome I Regulation.[55] Since the dispute also concerned the contract for forwarding, the court further applied Article 4(1)(b) of the Rome I Regulation and applied the law of the State of the habitual residence of the service provider.

In a 2019 case, the court had to resolve a dispute regarding a distribution contract. In the absence of choice by the parties, the court applied Slovenian law on the basis of Article 4(1)(f) of the Rome I Regulation, as Slovenia was the country where the distributor had his habitual residence.[56]

In a 2018 case, the Slovenian defendant was the assignee of a claim from a German assignor. Article 14(2) of the Rome I Regulation provides that the law governing the assigned claim shall determine, inter alia, the relationship between the assignee and the debtor. Therefore, the court examined which law was applicable to the claim arising from what seemed to be an orally concluded contract of agency, by applying Article 4(1)(b) of the Rome I Regulation. It then applied German law.[57]

2.3.2. Absence of Choice of Law in Non-Contractual Obligations

Under the previously applicable national legislation (Article 30 of PILPA) and in contrast to the Rome II regime, the law applicable to tort/delict was (unless the court established that the case was manifestly more closely connected with

54 No. I Cp 87/2019 of 12 March 2019.

55 Appellate Court in Ljubljana, No. I Cpg 581/2017 of 21 February 2019. The court applied Slovenian law to the questions not regulated by the UN Convention on the Contract for the International Carriage of Goods by Road (CMR), which was applicable to the case at hand.

56 Appellate Court in Koper, No. I Cpg 266/2018 of 21 February 2019. It must, however, be noted that the court uses the formulation that it 'has jurisdiction under the Rome I Regulation' and it is not entirely clear from the reasoning that the court indeed separately examined the issues of jurisdiction and applicable law.

57 Appellate Court in Ljubljana, No. I Cpg 73/2018 of 8 November 2018.

the law of another country) the law of the country where the tortfeasor acted. Nevertheless, the law of the country where the damage occurred was applicable provided that the tortfeasor could and should have foreseen that the damage could occur in that country.

In principle, the courts acknowledge (both with regard to jurisdiction as well as with regard to the applicable law) that in cases of personal injury or damage to property, the country in which the damage occurred is only the country where the injury was sustained or the property was damaged respectively, and that it is irrelevant where the injured person thereafter suffered pain and suffering, deterioration of health, emotional distress, loss of enjoyment or incurred financial losses (e.g. loss of income or the costs of medical treatment).[58] No complex cases (e.g. involving multiple tortfeasors) have been reported yet.

2.4. ESCAPE CLAUSES

The escape clauses have been overused by Slovenian courts. This is probably related to the fact that under national private international law (at least concerning contractual obligations) the flexible criterion of the closest connection has been perceived as the main principle and the modern and the preferred approach, whereas the list for certain categories of contracts (typically characteristic performance) amounted to a mere presumption, i.e. the rule which applies if the closest connection cannot be established.

This concept, which has often been repeated both in case law and in legal writing, has spilled over to the application of the Rome I and II Regulations. Quite frequently, the courts refer to the doctrines established under the national PILPA and state that the same approach also prevails in relation to the Rome I and II Regulations (failing to realise that the escape clauses in these Regulations were only supposed to be applied in exceptional circumstances).[59] One court even explicitly stated that the 'escape clauses' are not meant to be an exception but rather an expression of the main principle that the law most closely connected

---

58 E.g. Appellate Court in Ljubljana, No. I Cp 2219/2017 of 18 April 2018 (skiing accident abroad, medical treatment, costs and further pain and suffering and loss of enjoyment in Slovenia), Appellate Court in Maribor, No. I Cp 295/2019 of 11 June 2019 (traffic accident abroad, indirect/consequential damage in Slovenia), Appellate Labour and Social Court, No. Pdp 599/2012 of 16 August 2012 (concerning an accident at work), Appellate Court in Maribor, No. I Cp 615/2016 of 13 April 2016 (jurisdictional issue, concerning environmental damage; alleged reckless flood management by a hydro-power plant operator in Austria, which allegedly aggravated floods in Slovenia). The court rejected the defence that Slovenia was merely a place of indirect consequences and ruled that the flooding of land in Slovenia amounted to a direct damage.

59 See e.g. Supreme Court of Slovenia, No. II Ips 1001/2007 of 16 December 2010; Appellate Labour and Social Court, No. Pdp 767/2011 of 13 July 2012; Appellate Labour and Social Court, No. Pdp 599/2012 of 16 August 2012.

with a dispute should always be applied.[60] Perhaps, however, the courts are eager to apply 'escape clauses' because in all cases where they were applied it resulted in the application of the court's own national – thus Slovenian – law.

In a case already mentioned above, the court applied the escape clause of Article 4(3) correctly, at least in our opinion.[61] The court argued that even though the service provider (*in casu* the contractor) had their habitual residence in Italy, the court applied Slovenian law, because the client and the subcontractor had their residence in Slovenia, the building was to be constructed and the materials delivered in Slovenia, and the subcontractor was established with the aim of performing market activities together with the contractor.

2.5. SPECIFIC RULES

2.5.1. Insurance

In a 2016 judgment concerning the determination of applicable law relating to an insurance contract (and a direct claim against the insurer), the court did not seem to apply the Rome regime correctly. Faced with the question whether it had jurisdiction over a direct claim, filed by the victim against the insurer of the person liable to pay compensation (Article 11 of the Brussels I Regulation), the court correctly stated that it first needed to determine whether this kind of direct claim was admissible.[62] However, it then went on to state that the issue of admissibility of a direct claim should be resolved pursuant to the law applicable to the liability insurance contract, thus pursuant to the Rome I Regulation (and concluded that under the chosen law applicable to the insurance contract, a direct claim was not admissible). The court overlooked Article 18 of the Rome II Regulation, under which a direct action would nevertheless be admissible if it were available under the law applicable to the non-contractual obligation (*in casu*, the law of the place where the damage occurred).

Another recent case concerned the claim of an (Austrian) social security institution, acting as the statutory assignee of the rights of the directly injured party in a motor accident which occurred in Slovenia.[63] The injured party

60 Appellate Labour and Social Court, No. Pdp 767/2011 of 13 July 2012. In another case (No. Pdp 599/2012 of 16 August 2012) the same court reasoned that 'there are no circumstances, which would support the conclusion that the Italian law (law which would be applicable under Article 4(1) Rome II) is more closely connected to the dispute than Slovenian law.' The court therefore applied Slovenian law.

61 Appellate Court in Koper, No. Cpg 172/2016 of 14 September 2016.

62 Appellate Court in Ljubljana, No. I Cpg 23/2016 of 5 April 2016.

63 Appellate Court in Ljubljana, No. II Cp 2314/2018 of 12 June 2019.

received compensation from her social security institution and the latter then brought proceedings against the person responsible for the accident claiming the subrogation of the rights that passed to it from the directly injured party. The court (correctly) determined, applying Article 19 of the Rome II Regulation, that the question of subrogation is governed by Austrian law (as this was the law that governs the social security institution's duty to satisfy the creditor[64]). The court then went on to say that the Austrian law also governs the statute of limitations, which was invoked by the defendant. In view of the court, the statute of limitations is inseparably linked to the claim, therefore it would not be possible to apply Austrian law as to the issue of subrogation, but Slovenian law as to the issue of statute of limitations. Yet, this reasoning of the court is wrong. It is true that the statute of limitations is inseparably linked to the claim – but in this case, the statute of limitations was not invoked regarding any separate issue of subrogation, but regarding the main obligation in tort. As the damage occurred in Slovenia, the law applicable to the non-contractual obligation arising out of a tort/delict is Slovenian law. It should be clear that the law applicable to such obligation does not change only because the rights of the injured person passed to a third party by way of subrogation. Thereby, the law governing the non-contractual obligation (*in casu*: Slovenian law) also governs the issue of prescription/limitation (Article 15(h) Rome II).

2.5.2. *Consumers*

In a judgment applying provisions of the Rome I Regulation concerning the law applicable to consumer contracts, the court had to assess the validity of a choice-of-law clause in a consumer credit contract. The court correctly invoked Article 6(2) and ruled that the chosen law (*in casu*, Slovak law) could not deprive a Slovenian consumer of the protection afforded to him by mandatory provisions of Slovenian law (which would have been applicable on the basis of Article 6(1) of the Rome I Regulation).[65] Applying mandatory rules of Slovenian law, the court concluded that the consumer credit contract was null and void (since the trader was not properly licensed to offer consumer credit). It then, however, went on to state that because the consumer credit contract was null and void, the choice-of-law agreement in this contract was null and void as well (and concluded that therefore Slovenian law was exclusively applicable). The court thus failed to respect the principle of the separability of the choice-of-law agreement from the main contract.

---

64 A reference was also made to Art. 85 of the Regulation (EC) No. 883/2004 of the European Parliament and of the Council of 29 April 2004 on the coordination of social security systems.

65 Appellate Court in Ljubljana, No. I Cp 1951/2014 of 3 December 2014.

In three cases involving Czech lenders of money and Slovenian borrowers, the court equally applied Article 6(2) of the Rome I Regulation and applied Slovenian law, despite the contractual agreement on the choice of Czech law.[66] It deemed that the Slovenian rule regarding the obligatory licence for offering consumer credits was of a mandatory nature and protected the consumer, and therefore, the parties could not depart from it via choice-of-law agreement.

In our opinion, it would be better to apply Article 9 of the Rome I Regulation in these cases. In applying Article 6(2), the court should probably have performed a broader examination of the provisions of both laws, so as to see which law and which specific provisions were in fact more protective of the consumer.

2.5.3. *Employees*

In two judgments, the Supreme Court applied Article 8 of the Rome I Regulation.[67] The cases concerned Bulgarian citizens who worked for the Bulgarian embassy in Slovenia on the basis of contracts containing a choice-of-law clause in favour of the Bulgarian law. The defendant (the embassy) argued, among other things, that there was no employment relationship and that Bulgarian law should be applied. The court applied the autonomous interpretation of 'labour contracts' given by the Court of Justice of the EU in *Holterman*[68] and established that Article 8 of the Rome I Regulation was indeed applicable. It disregarded the choice-of-law clause, since it deprived the employee of the benefits of the Slovenian law, which was the law of the country where he habitually carried out his work.

2.5.4. *Product Liability*

There is only one published judgment of the Slovenian Supreme Court relating to a determination of the applicable law in a cross-border case of product liability. This case is of interest in relation to the Rome II Regulation, but it must be noted that the application of Rome II was incorrect, since the court should have applied the 1973 Hague Convention on the Law Applicable to Products Liability.

The court had to assess a situation where the product was not marketed in any of the countries referred to in Article 5(1)(a)–(c) Rome II Regulation. The court ruled that in the event that Article 5 as the *lex specialis* cannot be applied at all, recourse must be had to the general rule of Article 4 – thus the place where the damage occurred (*in casu*, Slovenia).[69] In our opinion, however, this result

66 Appellate Court in Ljubljana, Nos. I Cp 2164/2016 of 25 January 2017, II Cp 2226/2017 of 21 March 2018, and II Cp 2213/2017 of 16 May 2018.

67 Nos. VIII Ips 39/2017 and VIII Ips 311/2016, both of 6 June 2017.

68 No. C-47/14 of 10 September 2015, ECLI:EU:C:2015:574.

69 Supreme Court of Slovenia, No. III Ips 32/2015 of 20 September 2016.

is not convincing. Pursuant to Article 5(1)(c) Rome II Regulation, the law of the country where the damage occurred is applicable, but only if the product was marketed in that country. It is thus clear that if the product was not marketed in the country where the damage occurred, the law of this country cannot apply. This condition would, however, become obsolete if the law of the country where the damage occurred could apply anyway – if not pursuant to Article 5(1)(c), then pursuant to the general rule of Article 4. It would thus be more convincing in cases where the product was not marketed in any of the countries referred to in Article 5(1)(a)–(c) to apply the law of the country of the producer pursuant to Article 5(1) second paragraph by way of analogy. Article 5(1) second paragraph explicitly makes the law of the country of the producer applicable in the event that he could not have foreseen that the product would be marketed in the relevant states. The *ratio legis* of this rule supports the conclusion that this should all the more be the case when the product was not marketed in the relevant states at all.

In any case, the difficulty that the Supreme Court had in interpreting Article 5 of the Rome II Regulation shows that it would be advisable to have a solution to the lacuna in Article 5 (no explicit rule for a situation where the product was marketed neither in the country where the person who sustained damage was habitually resident, nor in the country where the product was purchased, nor in the country where the damage occurred).

2.6. RULES APPLICABLE TO NON-CONTRACTUAL OBLIGATIONS OTHER THAN TORTS OR DELICTS

2.6.1. Unjust Enrichment

There is one reported case on unjust enrichment, which was resolved on the basis of the Rome II Regulation. The Appellate Court in Ljubljana stated:

> 'Since during the procedure both parties referred to the provisions of the Slovenian law, the appellate court will verify if the first instance decision was correct on the basis of the domestic law … The applicable law regarding the contractual relationship will, pursuant to Article 20 of PILPA, or, in case of an unjust enrichment which came to existence after 11 July 2007,[70] pursuant to Article 10/1 of the Rome II Regulation, be decisive also for the resolution of the dispute regarding the unjust enrichment'.

The case concerned unpaid invoices issued by the plaintiff, who was an intermediary between the defendant as the buyer and a third person as the

[70] The court seems not to be familiar with the CJEU judgment in Case C-412/10, *Deo Antoine Homawoo v. GMF Assurances SA* of 17 November 2011, ECLI:EU:C:2011:747, concerning the application *ratione temporis* of the Rome II Regulation.

provider of ordered equipment. The plaintiff alleged that she paid the provider for this equipment and thus replaced them in the legal relationship with the defendant, which the latter denied.[71]

In the absence of further case law issued in application of the Rome II Regulation, it might be useful to look at the interpretation of the unjust enrichment by Slovenian courts when they have applied the national conflict of laws rules. For example, in 2011, the Supreme Court dealt with a case of unjust enrichment under the PILPA, where the Slovenian defendants withdrew money from their bank accounts in Slovenia and Austria. This money was given to them by the French plaintiffs, allegedly without the intention of being a donation. The court concluded that the defendants were unjustly enriched and applied Article 29 PILPA which refers to the law which would be applicable to the presumed legal relationship that gave rise to the enrichment. In this case, the presumed legal relationship was a contract, which means that in the absence of choice, the most closely connected law applies (Articles 19 and 20 PILPA). The court deemed that the closest connection existed with Slovenian law because:

> 'the money was delivered also in Slovenia, one of the bank accounts was in Slovenia, the defendants bought a house in Slovenia for the disputed money, the defendants have their domicile in Slovenia, the plaintiffs are of Slovenian origin, despite the French citizenship, since they are children of two Slovenian brothers etc.'[72]

In a judgment by the Supreme Court of 2009, the plaintiff invoked unjust enrichment, because the defendant had unjustly received payment for costs related to a loan.[73] The court applied the PILPA, which referred to the law of the contract of loan, which was Italian law. Since the PILPA provides for *renvoi*, the court then verified the Italian choice-of-law provision on unjust enrichment and found that Italian law referred back to Slovenian law. On that basis, the Supreme Court then applied Slovenian law.

2.6.2. Negotiorum gestio, culpa in contrahendo

There is no reported case law on cross-border *negotiorum gestio* or *culpa in contrahendo* based on the Rome II Regulation, or even based on the PILPA. There are, however, several judgments decided on the basis of the national legislation that can shed some light onto the comprehension of the latter notion in Slovenian private international law.

---

[71] Appellate Court in Ljubljana, No. I Cp 338/2016 of 5 April 2016.
[72] Supreme Court of Slovenia, No. II Ips 648/2008 of 27 October 2011.
[73] Supreme Court of Slovenia, No. III Ips 18/2007 of 18 February 2009.

In a judgment of the Appellate Court in Ljubljana, *culpa in contrahendo* was defined as follows: '"*Culpa in contrahendo*" is a notion broader than the substance of the liability for negotiations, it encompasses all rights and obligations related to the conclusion of a contract, and not only those related to dishonest negotiations.'[74] In another judgment of the same court, it is stated that: 'liability based on *culpa in contrahendo* … gives the right to the honest party to demand compensation only for the damage resulting from the negative contractual interest'.[75]

2.7. SCOPE OF APPLICABLE LAW

Regarding the scope of applicable law, in a 2019 judgment, the Appellate Court in Ljubljana decided on a question of the remainder of a debt which has partly been repaid in enforcement proceedings in Croatia.[76] In the proceedings in Slovenia, the debtor invoked that the amount of the repaid debt should be calculated according to Slovenian law, which is applicable to the contract of loan under the Rome I Regulation. The court, however, decided that Croatian enforcement law determines the consequences of the Croatian enforcement proceedings (i.e. the answer to the question up to which amount the creditor was repaid within those proceedings) and that Slovenian law can only be applicable to the contract of loan itself. The court, however, unfortunately overlooked Article 28 of the Rome I Regulation, under which the Regulation is only applicable to contracts concluded after 17 December 2009, whereas the contract at stake was concluded in April 2009.

The issue of characterisation has so far been discussed in only one reported case. The Appellate Court in Ljubljana ruled that characterisation (the question of whether the case relates to tort and thus whether the Rome II Regulation should apply) should be achieved by reference to the *lex causae* (the law to be applied to determine the case).[77] The appellate court criticised the first instance court, which characterised the relevant legal question by reference to the *lex fori*. In the view of the appellate court, that approach amounted to a logical fallacy. In our view, however, at least in the context of the application of *national* private international law, it is the other way around: at least in the first stage of the characterisation process, the *lex fori* has to be applied.[78] Nevertheless, the

[74] Appellate Court in Ljubljana, No. I Cpg 837/2006 of 24 January 2008.

[75] Appellate Court in Ljubljana, No. II Cp 3712/2008 of 22 April 2009.

[76] Appellate Court in Ljubljana, No. I Cp 994/2019 of 16 October 2019.

[77] Appellate Court in Ljubljana, No. III Cp 942/2016 of 15 June 2016.

[78] The majority view in Slovenian legal writing supports the 'two-stage process of characterisation' doctrine. Ilešič, Polajnar Pavčnik, Wedam Lukić, *Mednarodno zasebno pravo – komentar zakona*, Ljubljana, 1992, p. 32 (with further references to other authors).

crucial aspect remained overlooked by both (first and second instance) courts; namely that by interpreting concepts in the EU Rome I and Rome II Regulations the euroautonomous approach should apply. Hence, the questions whether the case concerns e.g. 'tort' or 'contractual obligation' should not be solved pursuant to any national law, thus neither by *lex causae* nor by *lex fori*, but by way of euroautonomous interpretation. In case of doubt, the CJEU should be addressed to clarify the issue.

2.8. *RENVOI*

It is very difficult to assess the possible utility of *renvoi* in concrete cases. Even though the PILPA provides for *renvoi*, Slovenian courts have never expressed any concerns about applying the substantive law directly on the basis of the Regulations. In general, we believe that *renvoi* greatly limits the effectiveness of the international harmonisation of private international law rules and should continue to be excluded from the Rome I and Rome II Regulations.

2.9. FOREIGN LAW

If a dispute has a cross-border character, the Slovenian court of its own motion has to apply choice-of-law rules to determine the applicable substantive law. If the applicable law is a foreign law, the court has to determine its content *ex officio*, since foreign law has the same status as domestic law and the *iura novit curia* rule applies. There is thus no requirement for the parties to request the application of foreign law or an obligation to adduce evidence regarding the content of such law.

According to Article 12(3) PILPA, however, the parties may contribute to establishing the content of the applicable foreign law in that they may submit to the court a public document or other document issued by a competent foreign authority providing this content. If the court has any difficulty in determining the content of the applicable foreign law, it can request relevant information from the Ministry of Justice or, as provided by Article 12(2) PILPA, 'establish its content in another suitable manner'. If the court deems it necessary, the Ministry will carry out the procedure under the 1968 European Convention on Information on Foreign Law. Thus, the Ministry, as the transmitting authority under the Convention, will contact the receiving authority of the state the law of which is applicable to the case before the Slovenian court in order to receive information on the content of that law.

The Yugoslav Act on Private International Law of 1982, the predecessor of the PILPA, provided that foreign law had to be applied according to its sense and its terms. This provision was omitted in the PILPA, since it is self-evident – albeit difficult in practice – that foreign law must be applied as in its country of origin, including its interpretation in the case law and theory. The non-application or erroneous application of foreign law may be corrected by the appellate court via an appeal or the Supreme Court through a legal remedy called revision.[79]

When applying foreign law, the court will only apply the substantive provisions and will normally apply Slovenian domestic procedural rules (*lex fori regit processum*). Regarding the distinction between procedural and substantive issues, it has been ruled (under the PILPA) that the standard of proof constitutes a procedural issue, meaning that, according to the Civil Procedure Act, the court has to be 'convinced' of the veracity of the fact that is being proven. Thus the Slovenian Civil Procedure Act must be applied.[80] On the other hand, it is a generally accepted view that the rules governing the burden of proof are based in substantive and not in procedural law.[81] Equally, under Slovenian law, prescription (statute of limitations) is a substantive issue, meaning that the *lex causae* applies (Article 8 PILPA).

Currently, foreign law cannot be ascertained by experts as a means of evidence. The doctrinal explanation for this is that the expert evidence as means of evidence can only be provided on matters of fact, whereas foreign law is considered a question of law, like for domestic law. We believe that this should change, following the examples of Austria and Germany, for instance. Without questioning the status of foreign law as the law and not as a fact, there are strong practical reasons for allowing the court to appoint experts for the applicable foreign law. When establishing the contents of a foreign law, the *iura novit curia* principle can only mean that the court must ascertain the foreign law *ex officio*, it does not impose restrictions on how it is ascertained. It is extremely difficult to apply foreign law correctly without knowing the foreign system – as well as the foreign language – very well, which cannot be expected from judges. The option to appoint a lawyer practising in the foreign legal system would be of great help in terms of saving time and improving the accuracy of the final decision.

In practice, the courts' approach to determining the foreign law has been quite flexible. Information provided online has been deemed sufficient, as have (official) translations of foreign judgments (*in casu*, an Austrian judgment applying Greek law, which was the applicable law in a case before a Slovenian court).[82] In another case, the appellate court even accepted (although describing it as 'awkward') the approach of a first instance court, which determined the

79 It must, however, be noted that the application of a wrong conflict-of-law rule leading to the application of the same substantial law as the correct conflict-of-law rule does not constitute an erroneous application of law as one of the reasons for appeal or revision. See e.g. Appellate Court in Koper, No. Cpg 172/2016 of 14 September 2016.

80 See e.g. Supreme Court of the Republic of Slovenia, No. III Ips 125/2007 of 22 September 2009.

81 Supreme Court of Slovenia, No. II Ips 405/2000 of 29 March 2001.

82 Appellate Court in Ljubljana, No. I Cpg 23/2016 of 5 April 2016.

content of the applicable German law by relying on its (assumed) similarity with Slovenian law. The first instance court reasoned that the relevant Slovenian legislation had been adopted following the German model, and that it could thus be concluded with a sufficient degree of probability that the German law was identical.[83] In any case, the Slovenian courts reject the view that the content of foreign law can only be established via the Ministry of Justice.[84] If the content of the applicable foreign law cannot be established, the court applies Slovenian law.

2.10. *ORDRE PUBLIC*

There are no reported cases of the application of the public policy defence pursuant to the Rome I or Rome II Regulations.

Even pursuant to the national legislation, in force as of 1999, the public policy defence was never successfully adduced regarding the choice of law (unlike in the field of the recognition and enforcement of judgments). In a case from 2016, the Appellate Court in Maribor explained:

> 'Each mandatory (imperative) rule is not a part of the public policy, but only those, of which a violation would endanger the legal and moral integrity of the domestic legal order. That said, it is completely clear that rules on the statute of limitations regarding civil claims do not fall into the scope of public policy.'[85]

One issue that could be problematic from the point of view of public policy is punitive damages, rejected by the Slovenian law of obligations, which defines damages as the satisfaction for the victim and leaves the possible sanctioning of the tortfeasor to the criminal law.

2.11. COMPENSATION

One case where the claimant argued that the amount of compensation pursuant to Croatian law (the law applicable pursuant to the 1971 Hague Convention) for the damage suffered in a traffic accident was disproportionately low came before the Slovenian Constitutional Court. The court upheld the judgment and stated that the application of a foreign law pursuant to the Convention had been based on reasonable grounds and that, although it could lead to awarding lower damages, did not amount to discrimination.[86]

---

83 Appellate Court in Ljubljana, No. I Cpg 563/2010 of 20 May 2010.

84 *Ibid.*

85 Appellate Court in Maribor, No. I Cpg 10/2016 of 12 April 2016.

86 Constitutional Court of Slovenia, No. Up-1802/08 of 16 December 2009.

2.12. RELATIONS WITH INTERNATIONAL CONVENTIONS

Slovenia is a party to the 1971 Hague Convention on the Law Applicable to Traffic Accidents and to the 1973 Hague Convention on the Law Applicable to Products Liability. These conventions supersede the Rome II Regulation, as Slovenia has notified on the basis of Article 29(1) of the Rome II Regulation.

In reported cases where the Convention on Traffic Accidents has been applied, the result regarding the applicable law would have been the same if the Rome II Regulation had been applied.[87] This is not surprising. If the notion of place of the damage (Rome II) is construed restrictively so as to relate only to the place of injury or damage of the property, the place of the damage in the case of a traffic accident can rarely be different from the place where the accident occurred (the Hague Convention). Likewise, in cases where the place of the car's registration is relevant pursuant to the Hague Convention (Articles 4 and 5), this would rarely be different from the place of the (common) habitual residence of the injured persons.

It must, however, be noted that Slovenian courts' knowledge of both the Hague Conventions and the fact that they supersede the Rome II Regulation, and, formerly, the national legislation, is inadequate. Judgments can be found where a court misapplied the Rome II Regulation instead of the Hague Convention on Traffic Accidents,[88] as well as instead of the Hague Product Liability Convention.[89]

3. GENERAL EVALUATION

Slovenia has had a private international law code since the 1980s, and the current act (PILPA) has been in force since 1999. This act comprises conflict-of-law rules, rules on international jurisdiction and rules on recognition and enforcement of foreign judgments. Slovenian judges are thus used to have at their disposal a coherent legal text on all the main private international law questions. With the 'explosion' of the European private international law texts in the last two decades, arguably the biggest problem for the judges currently seems to be finding the applicable legislation. Many examples can be found where national legislation

---

87 Appellate Court in Ljubljana, No. I Cp 1591/2015 of 23 September 2015; Constitutional Court of Slovenia, No. Up-1802/08 of 16 December 2009.

88 See e.g. Appellate Court in Ljubljana, No. I Cpg 23/2016 of 5 April 2016, where the court even applied the Rome I Regulation instead of the Hague Convention (if the Hague Convention had not been applicable, it would have been correct to apply the Rome II Regulation, since the dispute was about a direct lawsuit of the victim against the insurance company).

89 Supreme Court of Slovenia, No. III Ips 32/2015 of 20 September 2016.

was applied instead of the EU Regulations, as well as EU Regulations instead of a Hague Convention, etc.

It was wise and without any doubt a step forward to enact common conflict-of-law rules on the EU level – this has never been disputed in Slovenia. They are not ideal, but the CJEU is helping to fill the lacunae and imprecisions, and, above all, resolve the characterisation issues that inevitably arise. It is also important that national judges interpret and qualify different notions according not only to the judgments of the CJEU concerning Rome I and Rome II Regulations, but also to the interpretations already provided on the basis of other texts, for example the Brussels I *bis* Regulation.

However, we believe that further steps should be taken towards a European private international law code or at least towards a Regulation on the 'general part' of the conflict of laws, as is comprised in national private international law legislation (where they exist). It is confusing for practitioners and from a theoretical point of view that certain general notions like overriding mandatory rules or *renvoi* are regulated differently in different European conflict-of-laws Regulations.

4. CONCLUSION

In Slovenia, no real controversies regarding the Rome I and II Regulations have developed in legal writing or in the case law. In general, the Regulations' framework is considered to work well. The main problem in Slovenia is that the Regulations are still insufficiently known by judges and lawyers alike. The case law analysis shows that the courts sometimes still struggle to identify the applicable conflict-of-law act and hesitate between the Rome II Regulation, the national rules and the Hague Conventions in relation to torts, and between the Rome I Regulation, the Rome Convention (which was applicable in Slovenia from 2006 to 2009) and the national law on the contractual side. In the motivation for their judgments, the courts thus sometimes explain that the same substantive law is applicable under all or some of these acts, without clearly stating which of them is actually applicable.[90] Likewise, the applicability of the CISG is sometimes overlooked. Lawyers often argue cross-border cases on the basis of Slovenian substantive law, without mentioning the conflict-of-law rules, which could also mean that they did not realise that there is a conflict-of-law issue at all. The court must apply the conflict-of-laws rules *ex officio*, but they tend to characterise such contentions of the parties as a silent choice-of-law agreement and accordingly apply the Slovenian law.

90 See e.g. Appellate Court in Celje, No. Cpg 41/2018 of 13 June 2018.

What is thus needed is intensified judicial training and continuous training of lawyers. In addition, a creation of EU-wide databases of national case law applying the Regulations and a publication of (multilingual) European commentaries would be most valuable, in order to achieve both correct and uniform application EU-wide of the Regulations. An approach promoting better knowledge and more uniform use of existing instruments would, from the perspective of Slovenia at least, be preferred over a large-scale reform of the Rome I regime.

THE APPLICATION OF THE ROME I AND ROME II REGULATIONS IN SPAIN

Diana SANCHO-VILLA

1. INTRODUCTION

This chapter evaluates the judicial practice on the Rome I and Rome II Regulations in Spain, which are concerned with the determination of the law applicable to contractual and non-contractual obligations.[1] It analyses more than 70 judgments

[1] Regulation 593/2008 [2008] OJ L177/6 and Regulation 864/2007 [2007] OJ L199/40.

delivered by national courts, which involve cases that decide international commercial disputes by reference to either Rome I or Rome II provisions.[2]

The study seeks to identify common threads in international commercial litigation in order to ascertain the extent to which the advent of Rome I and Rome II has contributed to transforming the practice in Spain.[3] To this end, the chapter examines the following key aspects: the interplay between universal law and national law (section 2), the interaction between Rome I, Rome II and other international conventions (section 3), party autonomy and the determination of the applicable law in the absence of choice (section 4), the tension between the *lex fori* and the *lex causae* (section 5) and the practice on the scope of the *lex contractus* (section 6). Concluding remarks follow in section 7.

2. THE INTERPLAY BETWEEN UNIVERSAL LAW AND NATIONAL LAW

2.1. PERCEPTIONS OF UNIVERSAL LAW

The Rome I Regulation on the law applicable to contractual obligations applies universally, i.e. it applies regardless of whether or not the law identified by its provisions is the law of a Member State.[4] Therefore, within its material and temporal scope of application, Rome I displaces domestic choice-of-law rules for contracts.

The universal nature of the Rome Convention on the Law Applicable to Contractual Obligations of 1980 (the predecessor to Rome I), and its ability to displace internal choice-of-law norms, was acknowledged early on by the Spanish Supreme Court (Tribunal Supremo), the highest judicial authority in

2 The judgments have been selected following a search on CENDOJ, the General Council of the Judiciary's legal database. CENDOJ is available at: <http://www.poderjudicial.es/search/indexAN.jsp>. Key words used included: 'Regulation 593/2008', 'Regulation 864/2007', 'Rome I' and 'Rome II'. A list of the judgments is provided at the start of the book.

3 Other works on the judicial application of Rome I and Rome II in Spain include: L. Carballo, 'La aplicación jurisprudencial del Convenio de Roma y el Reglamento Roma I: un viaje de ida y vuelta al Derecho español', and also, E. Torralba, 'Retos en la práctica española en materia de ley aplicable a las obligaciones extracontractuales', in C. Otero (ed.), *Justicia Civil en la Unión Europea. Evaluación de la experiencia española y perspectivas de futuro*, Dykinson, Madrid 2017, pp. 175–193 and pp. 159–173, respectively. Previous studies on the application of the Rome Convention include: P. Paradela, 'Quince años de aplicación en España del Convenio de Roma sobre ley aplicable a las obligaciones contractuales' (2008) 8 *Anuario Español de Derecho Internacional Privado* 469–480; also, E. Castellanos, 'El Convenio de Roma de 1980 ante los tribunales españoles: balance de 15 años de vigencia', in A. Calvo and E. Castellanos (eds.), *La Unión Europea ante el Derecho de la Globalización*, Colex, Madrid 2008, pp. 121–188.

4 Article 2 Rome I.

Spain.[5] Further litigation over contracts provided the Tribunal Supremo with additional opportunities to confirm the universal application of this Convention.[6] As a result, the universal reach of the Rome Convention was fully endorsed by Spanish courts, though not without occasional inconsistencies in decisions.[7]

At present, there is no doubt that the universal nature of the Rome I Regulation is unequivocally upheld in Spain: neither the application of the law of a third country to the contract (chosen by the parties,[8] or objectively determined)[9] nor the parties not having EU nationality (or not being domiciled in the EU)[10] prevents Spanish courts from applying Rome I, provided that the dispute falls within the material and temporal scope of the Regulation.

With regard to litigation over non-contractual obligations, the Rome II Regulation also applies universally and thus displaces, within its material and temporal scope, domestic choice-of-law rules for non-contractual obligations.[11]

The universal application of Rome II is also consistently upheld in Spain. The judgment delivered by the Tribunal Supremo in 2017 provides an example.[12] In this case, the Court proceeded to determine the applicable law to an unfair competition dispute by reference to Article 6 Rome II (before the adoption of Rome II, such disputes were decided under the choice-of-law rule in Article 4 of the Unfair Competition Act). Another example is the judgment given by the Audiencia Provincial de Córdoba in 2017 (also deciding an unfair competition dispute).[13] Further, in a judgment handed down by the Commercial Court of Madrid (Juzgado de lo Mercantil de Madrid) in 2014,[14] the Court explicitly acknowledged the 'multilateral' and 'universal' nature of Article 3 Rome II, in

---

5 Tribunal Supremo, Judgment (recourse no.) 4796/1997, 29/09/1998, ECLI:ES:TS:1998:5453.

6 For example, Tribunal Supremo, Judgment 76/2006, 20/07/2007, ECLI:ES:TS:2007:5913.

7 For example, the judgment given in 2006 by the Audiencia Provincial de Bizcaia, in which the Court refused to apply the Rome Convention because the seller was established in Costa Rica, a non-contracting country to the Convention (Judgment 170/2006, 11/10/2006, ECLI:ES:APBI:2006:1838).

8 For example, Tribunal Superior de Justicia de Madrid, Judgment 272/2019, 08/03/2019, on an employment contract submitted to the law of Turkey (ECLI:ES:TSJM:2017:2160); and Tribunal Superior de Justicia de Madrid, Judgment 427/2016, 06/06/2016, on an employment contract under the law of Hong Kong (ECLI:ES:TSJM:2016:6581).

9 For example, Judgment 1723/2015 of the Tribunal Superior de Justicia de Castilla-Leon, delivered on 21/11/2015, in which the Court confirmed the application of the law of Chile under Article 8(2) Rome I (ECLI:ES:TSJCL:2015:5597); also, Judgment 88/2013 of the Audiencia Provincial de Avila, given on 12/06/2013, in which the Court confirmed the application of the law of Lebanon under Article 4(1)(a) Rome I (ECLI:ES:APAV:2013:195).

10 For example, parties from Lebanon and Spain (Judgment 88/2013, Audiencia Provincial de Avila, 12/06/2013, ECLI:ES:APAV:2013:195); and parties from Spain and Chile (Judgment 1723/2015, Tribunal Superior de Justicia de Castilla-León, 21/11/2015, ECLI:ES:TSJCL:2015:5597).

11 Article 3 Rome II.

12 Tribunal Supremo, Judgment 306/2017, 17/05/2017, ECLI:ES:TS:2017:1910.

13 Audiencia Provincial de Córdoba, Judgment 453/2017, 14/07/2017, ECLI:ES:APCO:2017:666.

14 Juzgado de lo Mercantil de Madrid, Judgment 2/2014, 09/01/2014, ECLI:ES:JMM:2014:5.

the context of a dispute concerning an infringement of intellectual property rights.[15] However, despite generally consistent practice on the universal reach of Rome II, some inconsistencies can also be found. The judgment delivered by the Audiencia Provincial de Lleida provides an example.[16]

In short, domestic choice-of-law rules are no longer applied to disputes falling within the scope of Rome I and Rome II. Focusing, in particular, on Articles 10(5) and 10(9) of the Civil Code, the internal choice-of-law norms for general contracts and torts, the sections below explore the role that these two provisions play in practice.

2.2. INTERNATIONAL CONTRACTUAL DISPUTES

To determine the law applicable to contracts concluded before 1 September 1993, the courts rely on domestic choice-of-law rules. This is because these contracts fall outside the temporal scope of application of the 1980 Rome Convention,[17] which precedes the Rome I Regulation. The application of Article 10(5) of the Civil Code to contracts concluded before 1 September 1993 has never been problematic, as the case decided by the Tribunal Supremo in 2011 illustrates.[18]

However, the subsequent application of the Rome Convention and the Rome I Regulation, and the interplay of both of these instruments with Article 10(5), have caused difficulties in practice. According to Article 28 Rome I, contracts entered into after 1 September 1993 fall under the 1980 Rome Convention, whereas those concluded after 17 December 2009 fall under the Rome I Regulation. For example, in order to establish its competence, the Audiencia Provincial de Valencia had to determine the law governing the

---

15 The Court, however, did not decide the case under Article 8 Rome II because the alleged infringement had occurred before the entry into force of this Regulation.

16 In this case, the Court refused to apply Rome II to a dispute concerning the injuries sustained by the victim, who was skiing in Andorra. The Court considered that Rome II was not applicable because Andorra was not a Member State of the EU. Instead, it applied Article 10(9) of the Civil Code, the domestic choice-of-law rule for torts, and concluded that the law of Andorra was the governing law; (Audiencia Provincial de Lleida, Judgment 487/2015, 27/11/2015, ECLI:ES:APL:2015:955). It has to be noted that, had the Court applied Article 4(1) Rome II, the outcome would likely have been the same.

17 Article 29 Rome Convention (this Convention was adopted in Spain in 1993; *Boletín Oficial del Estado* 171, 19.07.1993 and 189, 09.08.1993).

18 Tribunal Supremo, Judgment 238/2011, 01/04/2011, which confirmed the application of Article 10(5) of the Civil Code to a contract concluded on 15 March 1985 (ECLI:ES:TS:2011:1805). Other examples include: Audiencia Provincial de Valencia, Judgment 31/2014, 05/02/2014, ECLI:ES:APV:2014:1188 (deciding a dispute over a contract for the sale of goods); also, Judgment 1087/2003 by the Tribunal Superior de Justicia de Madrid, delivered on 11/12/2003, which applied Article 1(4) of the Spanish Workers' Rights Statute (*Estatuto de los Trabajadores*) to an employment contract concluded before 1 September 1993 (ECLI:ES:TSJM:2003:16699).

contract under the *Tessili* doctrine.[19] Although the contract was concluded before 1 September 1993, the Court applied Article 4(2) of the Rome Convention (instead of Article 10(5) of the Civil Code) and concluded that German law governed the contract.[20]

The aforementioned judgment by the Audiencia Provincial de Bizcaia decided in 2006 was controversial.[21] In this case, the Court relied upon Article 10(5) Civil Code to justify the application of Spanish law to the contract in dispute, which had been concluded in Spain. Article 10(5) states that the law governing the contract is the law of the country where the contract has been celebrated (in the absence of express choice of law by the parties or the parties' common nationality/habitual residence).[22] As already discussed, the problem with this case was that the law governing the contract should have been determined by reference to the Rome Convention.[23]

This judgment was an isolated case. In Spain, the advent of Rome I has relegated Article 10(5) Civil Code to a purely residual role in international litigation (such as determining the applicable law to contracts celebrated before 1 September 1993). As discussed before, national courts do not rely upon Article 10(5) to solve disputes falling within the scope of application of the Rome I Regulation (or Rome Convention).

Notwithstanding this, redundant references to Article 10(5) in disputes involving contracts entered into in Spain can occasionally be found. The case decided by the Audiencia Provincial de A Coruña in 2015 is an example.[24] As the appellant failed to prove Portuguese law (applicable via Article 4(1)(a) Rome I), the Court proceeded to solve the dispute under Spanish law, in line with consistent case law of the Tribunal Supremo.[25] In this case, the application of Spanish law was entirely justified by long-established principles of procedural law, explicitly endorsed by the Court. Therefore, additional references to the choice-of-law rule in Article 10(5) Civil Code (and to Spain as the place where the contract had been celebrated) were unnecessary.

---

19 Audiencia Provincial de Valencia, Judgment 502/2013, 11/11/2013, ECLI:ES:APV:2013:5749.

20 It has to be noted, however, that under Article 10(5) of the Civil Code, the outcome would likely have been equivalent: Article 10(5) provides for the application of the parties' common nationality or habitual residence (in the absence of choice of law); in this case, the contract concerned a sale of shares between German companies.

21 Judgment 170/2006, 11/10/2006 (ECLI:ES:APBI:2006:1838); see *supra* n. 7.

22 Article 10(5) Civil Code reads: 'The law to which the parties have expressly submitted shall apply to contractual obligations, provided that it has some connection with the transaction in question; in the absence thereof, the national law common to the parties shall apply; in the absence thereof, that of their common habitual residence and, lastly, the law of the place where the contract has been entered into'. This translation is available at the WIPO website (No. WIPO Lex ES122), edited by the Spanish Ministry of Justice (Secretaría General Técnica): <http://www.wipo.int/wipolex/es/text.jsp?file_id=221319#LinkTarget_6329>.

23 Which was applicable to the dispute and which pointed to the law of Costa Rica (under Article 4(2) Rome Convention).

24 Audiencia Provincial de A Coruña, Judgment 168/2015, 15/06/2016, ECLI:ES:APC:2015:1556.

25 See *infra* n. 130.

2.3. INTERNATIONAL NON-CONTRACTUAL DISPUTES

There have been certain difficulties in interpreting the temporal scope of application of the Rome II Regulation. These have provided the Court of Justice of the European Union (CJEU) with an opportunity to clarify that the Regulation applies 'only to events giving rise to damage occurring after 11 January 2009.'[26] This aspect of Rome II has not been particularly controversial in Spain. Instead, difficulties that national courts appear to have encountered relate to the existence of several choice-of-law regimes *ratione materiae*.

In Spain, the Hague Convention of 4 May 1971 on the Law Applicable to Traffic Accidents and the Hague Convention of 2 October 1973 on the Law Applicable to Products Liability are in force.[27] These Conventions take prevalence over the Rome II Regulation.[28] Also, they apply even if the law applicable is not that of a contracting State,[29] which implies that they discard the application of Article 10(9) of the Civil Code, the internal choice-of-law rule for torts.

The application of these Conventions to traffic accidents and product liability disputes reduces the judicial practice on Rome II (otherwise applicable to such disputes). As things stand, in the absence of applicable international conventions, non-contractual disputes excluded from Rome II fall under Article 10(9) of the Civil Code.[30]

For example, Article 10(9) applies to non-contractual obligations arising out of violations of privacy and rights relating to personality. In 2013, the Tribunal Supremo resolved a dispute in which an individual sought compensation from Google Inc. for the damage sustained to their privacy as a result of information that the company had made available through its search engine.[31] In this case, the Court confirmed the application of the limited liability regime for intermediaries under the Spanish Electronic Commerce Act.[32]

Article 10(9) Civil Code states that non-contractual obligations shall be governed by the law of the place where the harmful event has occurred

---

26 CJEU, Case C-412/10, *Deo Antoine Homawoo v. GMF Assurances SA*, ECLI:EU:C:2011:747.

27 Convention on the Law Applicable to Traffic Accidents of 1971 (*Boletín Oficial del Estado* 264, 04.11.1987 and 307, 24.12.1987) and Convention on the Law Applicable to Products Liability of 1973 (*Boletín Oficial del Estado* 21, 25.01.1989).

28 Article 28 Rome II.

29 Article 11 of the 1971 Convention and Article 11 of the 1973 Convention.

30 Article 1(2) Rome II, on the matters excluded from this Regulation.

31 Tribunal Supremo, Judgment 144/2013, 04/03/2013, ECLI:ES:TS:2013:2245.

32 The Court solved the dispute under Spanish law without expressly referring to Article 10(9) to determine the law applicable. In any case, this provision pointed to Spanish law (as the harmful event had most likely occurred in Spain). On this decision, see P. De Miguel, 'Sentencia del Tribunal Supremo num. 144/2013, de 4 de marzo de 2013' (2013) LXV *Revista Española de Derecho Internacional* 333–336, 336.

(*lex loci delicti commissi*).[33] It has traditionally been disputed whether this provision refers to the place of the event giving rise to the damage or to the place of the damage itself.[34] References to the uncertainties surrounding the interpretation of Article 10(9) can be found in recent case law. This is illustrated in the judgment delivered by the Audiencia Provincial de Zaragoza in 2010, in which Article 10(9)'s ability to ensure the application of a law sufficiently connected to the dispute was questioned.[35] This contrasts with the case decided in 2018 by the Audiencia Provincial de Oviedo, in which the suitability of the *lex loci damni* rule under Article 4(1) Rome II to ensure the application of a law closely connected to the non-contractual dispute, was explicitly acknowledged.[36]

Spanish scholars have suggested that the advent of Rome II justifies the aligning of the rule in Article 10(9) Civil Code with that of Article 4(1) of the Regulation.[37] They advocate that the phrase 'place where the harmful event has occurred' of Article 10(9) be interpreted as referring to the place where the damage has occurred. In the context of defamation claims (which are excluded from Rome II and solved under Article 10(9) Civil Code), this has led to proposals that recommend the application of the law of the country of the victim's habitual residence (which is likely to coincide with the place of the damage, in most cases).[38]

Such developments demonstrate the ability of Rome II to positively influence the interpretation of Article 10(9) Civil Code. They also demonstrate that the relationship between these two instruments is not solely of mutual exclusion.

---

33 Article 10(9) Civil Code: '*Las obligaciones no contractuales se regirán por la ley del lugar donde hubiere ocurrido el hecho de que deriven*'.

34 M. Amores, 'Artículo 10, apartado 9', in M. Albaladejo and S. Díaz Alabart (eds.), *Comentarios al Código Civil y a las Compilaciones forales*, Edersa, Madrid 1995, pp. 729–769, 755; also, F. Rozas and S. Sanchez, *Derecho Internacional Privado*, Civitas, Pamplona 2016, p. 521.

35 Judgment 524/2010, decided on 22/11/2010, in which the Court stated: 'La doctrina criticó no sin razón [Article 10(9)] que puede llevar a aplicación de ordenamientos jurídicos carentes de cualquier conexión con las partes implicadas, como responsables o perjudicados con el daño. Este reproche a la norma de conflicto es particularmente intenso en relación [...]. Problema que se ha querido solucionar con el Reglamento de Roma II', at Fundamento de Derecho Decimonoveno, 25 (ECLI:ES:APZ:2010:2760). This case decided the civil liability of an air carrier for death, in the context of an accident that occurred in Turkey involving members of the Army (the so-called, Yak-42 Case).

36 Audiencia Provincial de Oviedo, Judgment 54/2018, 07/02/2018, ECLI:ES:APO:2018:293.

37 For example: F. Garcimartín, *Derecho Internacional Privado*, Civitas Thomson Reuters, Pamplona 2016, p. 419; also, A. Calvo and E. Carrascosa, *Derecho Internacional Privado*, Comares, Granada 2016, p. 1346.

38 See, E. Torralba, 'La difamación en la era de las comunicaciones: ¿Nuevas? Perspectivas de Derecho Internacional Privado' (2012) *Indret* 1–37, 21: <https://indret.com/la-difamacion-en-la-era-de-las-comunicaciones-nuevas-perspectivas-de-derecho-internacional-privado-europeo/>; also, L. García, 'Reglamento "Roma II" y derecho de la personalidad: reflexiones para formular una norma de conflicto que preserve adecuadamente el ejercicio del derecho a la información y de la libertad de expresión' (2012) *Revista de Derecho Comunitario Europeo* 851–874, 864–869.

2.4. INTERNAL DISPUTES

The Spanish Constitution acknowledges the existence of different legislative regimes on contractual and non-contractual obligations within the Spanish territory. These regimes include the Spanish Civil Code, which constitutes the 'common' regime, and the regimes of the *Comunidades Autonomas*, referred to as 'foral' regimes. Examples of the latter include the law of Catalonia, the law of Navarra and the law of the Basque Country.

This area of litigation develops outside of Rome I and Rome II, as internal disputes (as opposed to international disputes) are excluded from these Regulations.[39] Generally, the interpretative difficulties that these cases present arise from the lack of clarity of the constitutional mandate, and also the suitability of domestic choice-of-law rules to deal with such conflicts consistently.[40]

For the purpose of this chapter, it suffices to refer here to the important role that Article 10(5) Civil Code plays in resolving internal contractual disputes. Recent examples include: a judgment by the Audiencia Provincial de Navarra, which concerned a conflict between the law of the Basque Country and the foral law of Navarra;[41] also, a judgment by the Tribunal Superior de Justicia de Cataluña, which related to a conflict between the 'common' regime and the law of Catalonia.[42] Article 10(9) plays an equivalent role in determining the law applicable to non-contractual obligations in internal disputes, as illustrated in the 2011 judgment of the Audiencia Provincial de Barcelona.[43]

3. ROME I, ROME II AND INTERNATIONAL CONVENTIONS

3.1. CONTRACTUAL OBLIGATIONS

This section considers the interplay between Rome I, which provides a set of uniform choice-of-law rules to determine the law governing the contract (*lex contractus*), and substantive law conventions. The following remarks concern the Convention on Contracts for the International Sale of Goods (CISG) and the Convention on the Contract for the International Carriage of Goods by Road (CMR).

---

39 See Article 22(2) Rome I and Article 25(2) Rome II.

40 For example, see A. Font, 'Sentencia Audiencia Provincial Navarra núm. 297/2001 (Section 3ª), de 16 de noviembre' (2002) LIV *Revista Española de Derecho Internacional* 449–458, 451, 456.

41 Audiencia Provincial de Navarra, Judgment 297/2001, 16/11/2001, ECLI:ES:APNA:2001:1246.

42 Tribunal Superior de Justicia de Cataluña, Judgment 22/2011, 26/05/2011, ECLI:ES:TSJCAT:2011.

43 Audiencia Provincial de Barcelona, Judgment 65/2011, 16/02/2011, ECLI:ES:APB:2011:1797, in which the Court discussed the application of the law of Catalonia (applicable under Article 10(9) Civil Code) and its prevalence over the national regime.

CISG plays an important role in resolving international disputes over sale of goods contracts. This Convention, which entered into force in Spain in 1991,[44] applies if either party to the contract is established in the territory of contracting states, or if the law which governs the contract (according to the relevant private international rules) is that of a contracting state.[45]

The following recent cases illustrate how the courts implement the mandate in Article 7(2) CISG – which states that aspects to the dispute not regulated by the CISG are to be decided under the *lex contractus*. The case decided by the Audiencia Provincial de Valencia in 2014 provides a good example of balanced practice.[46] In the context of a dispute for breach of contract, the Court had to decide if the action was time-barred. As the CISG does not regulate limitation periods, the Court was right in applying German law as the *lex contractus*.[47] Similarly, in the case decided by the Audiencia Provincial de Zamora in 2017, the Court also had to determine if the action for breach of contract was time-barred.[48] The Court refused to apply the Unidroit Principles of International Commercial Contracts (as the appellant sought)[49] because there was no evidence that the parties had incorporated them into their contract. Instead, the Court decided the dispute under Italian law, the *lex contractus* determined via Article 4(1)(a) Rome I.[50]

Another example illustrating balanced practice on the CISG is the judgment delivered by the Audiencia Provincial de Lleida in 2019.[51] In this case, the Court considered whether the Spanish buyer was entitled to rely on the right to a lack of conformity under Article 39(2) CISG.[52] As to the relevant interests, the Court referred to Swiss law, the *lex contractus* under Article 4(1)(a) Rome I.[53]

44 See *Boletín Oficial del Estado* 26, 30.01.1991 and 282, 22.11.1996.

45 Article 1(1) CISG. Importantly, the parties can exclude the CISG or derogate from its provisions, as provided for under Article 6 CISG: an example of a case interpreting this provision is the dispute decided by the Audiencia Provincial de Avila on 12/06/2013 (Judgment 88/2013, ECLI:ES:APAV:2013:195).

46 Audiencia Provincial de Valencia, Judgment 31/2014, 05/02/2014, ECLI:ES:APV:2014:1188.

47 Determined under Article 4(2) Rome Convention, which was applicable to the dispute (the contract had been concluded before the 17 December 2019); under German law, the action was time-barred.

48 Audiencia Provincial de Zamora, Judgment 107/2017, 07/04/2017, ECLI:ES:APZA:2017:173.

49 Under Article 10(2) Unidroit Principles, the action brought by the claimant would have been time-barred.

50 However, the case ended up being decided under Spanish law as the parties failed to prove Italian law.

51 Audiencia Provincial de Lleida, Judgment 154/2019, 26/03/2019, ECLI:ES:APL:2019:169.

52 The Court refused to grant the Spanish buyer this right because, under the circumstances of the case, the legal requirements under Article 39(2) CISG had not been met.

53 It has to be noted, however, that the immediate reliance on the *lex contractus* to decide matters only partially regulated in CISG has been criticised in the literature for departing from the principle of interpretation in Article 7(2) CISG: see R. Arenas, 'Sentencia 114/2012, Juzgado de Instancia, Madrid, JUR/2012/211398' (2012) 12 *Anuario Español de Derecho Internacional Privado* 798–804.

With regard to the CMR, examples illustrating the equivalent interplay between Article 5(1) Rome I, the choice-of-law rule for contracts for the carriage of goods, and CMR also exist.[54] In the case decided by the Audiencia Provincial de Zaragoza in 2018, the Court unambiguously acknowledged the important regulatory role that the *lex contractus* determined under Rome I plays in this area.[55] After stating that the CMR did not intend to regulate all possible aspects concerning a relationship of carriage (as opposed to a contract of carriage), the Court conceded that the non-express regulation of the matter in dispute in the Convention represented an indirect remission to the national law applicable via Article 5(1) Rome I.[56]

Additional examples demonstrating balanced practice on the CMR include: a judgment by the Audiencia Provincial de Murcia, delivered in 2017, in which the Court decided the dispute under Article 13(1) CMR on the rights of the consignee against the carrier (instead of referring to the law of Austria determined via Article 5(1) of Rome I as the appellant sought);[57] also, a judgment by the Juzgado de lo Mercantil de Donostia, handed down in 2015, in which the Court decided whether a contract for the carriage of goods by road between parties established in France and Spain had been entered into, by reference to Spanish law (as the *lex contractus* under Article 5(1) Rome I).[58]

To sum up, the examples discussed in this section show the existence of a substantial body of cases that ensure a balanced interplay between choice-of-law rules under Rome I and substantive law conventions, such as the CISG and the CMR. These cases further confirm the important contribution to litigation that the *lex contractus*, determined by reference to Rome I, plays in this area.[59]

3.2. NON-CONTRACTUAL OBLIGATIONS

Different regimes apply to the determination of the applicable law to non-contractual obligations in Spain. As discussed before, the 1971 Hague

54 The CMR was adopted in Spain in 1974: *Boletín Oficial del Estado* 109, 07.05.1974.

55 Audiencia Provincial de Zaragoza, Judgment 716/2018, 06/11/2018, ECLI:ES:APZ:218:2474.

56 'El CMR dista de ser una realidad juridica acabada y ommicomprensiva de todas las relaciones jurídicas ue una relacion de transporte más amplia que un contrato de transporte puede originar. […] Estima la Sala que no puede hablarse de una laguna del derecho cuando lo que el convenio CMR ha pretendido regular es estrictamente el contrato, no aquellas cautelas o garantías legales de naturaleza extracontractual para el cumplimiento del mismo que cada Derecho quiere establecer', at Fundamento de Derecho Tercero (Audiencia Provincial de Zaragoza, Judgment 716/2018, 06/11/2018, ECLI:ES:APZ:218:2474).

57 Audiencia Provincial de Murcia, Judgment 250/2017, 27/04/2017, ECLI:ES:APMU:2017:993.

58 Juzgado de lo Mercantil de Donostia, Judgment 303/2015, 23/09/2015, ECLI:ES:JMSS:2015:3590.

59 See, L. Carballo, *supra* n. 3.

Convention on Traffic Accidents and the 1973 Hague Convention on Products Liability are in force, and take prevalence over Rome II.

Litigation on traffic accidents is not uncommon. An overall assessment of available cases shows that the prevalence of the Hague Convention 1971 (HCTA) over Rome II is consistently upheld. The following cases illustrate this: for example, the judgment delivered by the Tribunal Supremo in 2009, which decided upon a traffic accident that occurred in Switzerland (under Spanish law applicable via Article 4(a) HCTA);[60] the judgment of the Audiencia Provincial de Madrid of 2019, in which the Court applied Spanish law to an accident that occurred in France (involving two Spanish-registered vehicles, as provided for in Article 4(b) HCTA);[61] the judgment of the Audiencia Provincial de Barcelona of 2018 on a traffic accident that also occurred in France (decided under French law in accordance with Article 3 HCTA);[62] the judgment of the Audiencia Provincial de Barcelona of 2012, which considered a traffic accident that occurred in Morocco (solved under Spanish law as mandated by Article 4(a) HCTA);[63] the judgment of the Audiencia Provincial de Gijón of 2012 on a traffic accident that also occurred in Morocco (under the law of Morocco applicable via Article 3 HCTA);[64] and the judgment of the Audiencia Provincial de Pontevedra of 2012 on an accident that occurred in Portugal (decided under Portuguese law as provided for in Articles 3 and 4(c) HCTA).[65]

With regard to product liability, the landmark 2014 judgment of the Tribunal Supremo illustrates the application of this Convention in Spain. A failure of the collision-avoidance equipment of two aeroplanes caused a mid-air collision over Germany and proceedings were brought in Spain against the American manufacturers. In this case, Article 6 of the Convention was used to determine the liability of the manufacturers, who were based in Arizona and New Jersey.[66]

Inconsistencies in the determination of the law governing disputes arising out of traffic accidents can also be found. For example, the following cases were decided by reference to Article 4 Rome II: the judgment by the Audiencia Provincial de Barcelona of 2020 (on a traffic accident that occurred in England),[67] the judgment by the Audiencia Provincial de Madrid of 2019 (on a traffic accident

---

60 Tribunal Supremo, Judgment 722/2009, 23/03/2010, ECLI:ES:TS:2010:3313.

61 Audiencia Provincial de Madrid, Judgment 421/2019, 30/09/2019, ECLI:ES:APM:2019:11054.

62 Audiencia Provincial de Barcelona, Judgment 215/2018, 13/07/2018, ECLI:ES:APB:2018: 6940.

63 Audiencia Provincial de Barcelona, Judgment 13/2012, 13/01/2012, ECLI:ES:APB:2012:334.

64 Audiencia Provincial de Gijón, Judgment 56/2012, 10/02/2012, ECLI:ES:APO:2012:283.

65 Audiencia Provincial de Pontevedra, Judgment 521/2012, 13/12/2012, ECLI:ES:APPO:2012:3057.

66 Tribunal Supremo, Judgment 649/2014, 13/01/2015, ECLI:ES:TS:2015:181; on this case, see, A. Hernández, 'Accidentes aereos y *forum non conveniens*' (2012) 4 *Cuadernos de Derecho Transnacional* 307–321, 317: <https://e-revistas.uc3m.es/index.php/CDT/article/view/1624>.

67 Audiencia Provincial de Barcelona, Judgment 49/2020, 31/01/2020, ECLI:ES:APB:2020:491.

that occurred in Portugal);[68] and the judgment by the Audiencia Provincial de Pontevedra of 2012 (also on a traffic accident that occurred in Portugal).[69] Other cases have applied both Article 4 Rome II and the 1971 Hague Convention to solve the relevant traffic accident dispute,[70] or have relied upon the domestic choice-of-law rule, Article 10(9) of the Civil Code.[71]

Efforts have been made to ensure the smooth application of the Hague Conventions and the Rome II Regulation in Spain.[72] Although there is a well-established tradition of applying the Hague Conventions to traffic accidents and product liability disputes, non-contractual litigation under Rome II is generally preferred for the uniform interpretation of its norms, the flexibility of its rules and the possibility of party autonomy under Article 14.[73] This has contributed to a group of leading scholars suggesting the Spanish withdrawal from the 1971 and 1973 Hague Conventions.[74] This is not an unreasonable proposal. Should it be implemented, it would contribute towards the altering of the status quo of non-contractual litigation and further enhancement of Rome II's visibility in Spain.

4. PARTY AUTONOMY AND APPLICABLE LAW IN THE ABSENCE OF CHOICE

4.1. THE INTERPLAY BETWEEN PARTY AUTONOMY AND THE *LEX FORI*

The parties can freely choose the law applicable to their contractual obligation (Article 3 Rome I), and also to their non-contractual obligation (Article 14 Rome II). It has to be noted that litigation under Article 14 Rome II is rare compared to that occurring under Article 3 Rome I, and also that the courts clearly distinguish choice-of-law clauses from choice of court agreements.[75]

---

68 Audiencia Provincial de Madrid, Judgment 12/2019, 17/01/2019, ECLI:ES:APM:2019:773.

69 Audiencia Provincial de Pontevedra, Judgment 439/2012, 06/11/2012, ECLI:ES:APPO:2012:2888.

70 Audiencia Provincial de Cáceres, Judgment 93/2013, 10/04/2013, ECLI:ES:APCC:2013:264.

71 Audiencia Provincial de Pontevedra, Judgment 293/2014, 16/05/2014, ECLI:ES:APPO:2014:1255.

72 On the Hague Convention of 1971, in particular, see A. Espiniella, 'Accidentes de circulación por carretera: del Convenio de la Haya de 4 de mayo de 1971 al Reglamento (CE) no 864/2007 ("Roma II")' (2007) 7 *Anuario Español de Derecho Internacional Privado* 505–532.

73 For example, in the academic literature, see E. Torralba, *supra* n. 3; A. Espiniella, *supra* n. 72; and also J. Maseda, 'Sentencia de 10 diciembre de 2015, asunto C-350/14, Florin Lazar v Allianz SpA' (2016) LXVIII *Revista Española de Derecho Internacional* 187–190, 190.

74 See, for example, E. Torralba, *supra* n. 3; A. Espiniella, *supra* n. 72; J. Maseda, *supra* n. 73; and A. Calvo and E. Carrascosa, *supra* n. 37, p. 1369.

75 For example: for contractual disputes (Tribunal Superior de Justicia de Madrid, Judgment 10351/2004, 16/11/2004, ECLI:ES:TSJM:2004:14142); and for non-contractual disputes (Audiencia Provincial de Barcelona, Judgment 242/2016, 01/09/2016, ECLI:ES:APB:2016:9245).

Party autonomy is widely accepted in international contractual litigation in Spain. Consistent with the mandate in Article 3(1) Rome I, the reviewed cases show the courts' reliance on the parties' subjective intentions as the main justification for party autonomy. This is illustrated in the judgment by the Audiencia Provincial de Barcelona of 2017, in which the court made this point explicit.[76] Most cases in Spain are straightforward as to the enforcement of express choice-of-law clauses. Recent examples include the aforementioned case by the Audiencia Provincial de Barcelona and also the judgment by the Audiencia Provincial de Logroño of 2014, which considers the validity of an express choice of Italian law.[77] Nothing in case law suggests that the requirement of an objective connection under the old Article 10(5) Civil Code (between the law chosen by the parties and the transaction in question) has ever interfered with the interpretation of Article 3(1) Rome I in Spain.

The Tribunal Supremo has taken a restrictive view on choice-of-law agreements included in financial instruments, as the judgment decided in 2017 illustrates.[78] A Spanish investor acquired a structured note, issued by Morgan Stanley, through a financial intermediary commercialising the note in Spain. The investor brought proceedings in Spain for frustration by impossibility against Morgan Stanley and the intermediary. The prospectus produced by the issuer contained a choice-of-law clause in favour of English law, and was available on the Luxembourg Stock Exchange website and also on the National Securities Market Commission (CNMV) website. Notwithstanding this, the Court refused to recognise the choice of law. It argued that the order of purchase did not contain a choice of law, nor was it included in the pre-contractual documents provided to the investor.[79] This interpretation restrains party autonomy in choice of law

---

76 In the context of a dispute over a distribution contract, the Court stated that the express choice of Belgian law had to be enforced to honour what the parties had clearly and unambiguously decided. As the Court stated, 'de manera clara y rotunda' and also, 'que las partes decidieron someter su relación jurídica al derecho belga, como así se confirma, correctamente [...]' (Audiencia Provincial de Barcelona, Judgment 514/2017, 19/12/2017, ECLI:ES:APB:2017:12794).

77 Audiencia Provincial de Logroño, Judgment 252/2014, 26/11/2013, ECLI:ES:APLO:2014:483; in this case, however, the Court did not explicitly evaluate the validity of the clause under Article 3(5) Rome I.

78 Tribunal Supremo, Judgment 342/2015, 20/07/2017, ECLI:ES:TS:2017:3027; the case was decided under the Rome Convention, applicable to the contract in dispute.

79 The Court also interpreted that the pre-contractual documentation failed to include a clear and sufficiently visible reference which could be interpreted as supporting an implied choice of law: 'No puede entenderse que haya existido una elección expresa de la ley inglesa por parte del demandante al adquirir la Nota estructurada, ni que tal elección resulte de manera segura de los términos del contrato suscrito por el demandante ni de las circunstancias concurrentes, por el hecho de que los documentos en los que se recoge la sumisión a la ley inglesa se encontraran disponibles en la página web de la Bolsa de Luxemburgo o en la página web de la Comisión Nacional del Mercado de Valores.
En la orden de compra firmada por el demandante no aparecía esa elección del Derecho inglés. En los documentos informativos que se suministró al demandante antes de la firma

regarding financial instruments. It also contrasts with the more permissive approach of the CJEU regarding choice-of-court agreements included in financial instruments.[80]

According to the mandate in Article 3(1) Rome I, which is worded restrictively,[81] Spanish courts will only imply choice of law in the context of a specific dispute if they are left in no doubt that the parties intended to choose the governing law. For example, it is an established practice to interpret the parties' conduct in the context of court proceedings, which consists of relying upon Spanish law to justify their claims and legal rights as to the substance, as a clear indication that they intend to solve their dispute by reference to the *lex fori*. This is illustrated in the case decided by the Audiencia Provincial de Avila in 2013.[82]

The judgment of the Audiencia Provincial de Barcelona of 2019 confirmed the existence of an implied choice of Spanish law, in the context of a dispute over the termination of an agency contract.[83] In this case, proceedings were brought by the German-based agent against the defendant, a company established in Spain, to recover a payment of commissions. The Court implied the existence of a choice of Spanish law using a number of factors, such as the absence of references to any other law, the language used and common practices that the parties knew or should have known.[84]

The Audiencia Provincial de Palma Mallorca handed down a less straightforward case in 2017, interpreting Article 3(1) Rome Convention.[85]

---

de la orden de compra tampoco aparecía esa elección del Derecho inglés, por lo que tampoco puede considerarse que, pese a no constar expresamente esa elección en el contrato puesto a la firma del cliente, existiera una mención clara y suficientemente visible en la documentación precontractual que pudiera ser interpretada como indicativa del conocimiento y aceptación por el comprador de esa elección de un Derecho extranjero para que rigiera la relación contractual'.

80 As in CJEU, Case C-366/13, *Profit Investment Sim Spa*, ECLI:EU:C:2016:282, see F. Garcimartin, 'A propósito de la Sentencia del Tribunal Supremo de 20 de Julio de 2017': <https://almacendederecho.org/clausulas-ley-aplicable-instrumentos-financieros/>.

81 Under Article 3(1) Rome I, the choice must be 'clearly demonstrated by the terms of the contract or the circumstances of the case'.

82 Judgment 88/2013, in which the Court interpreted that Spanish law was applicable on this ground. The Court stated '[...] en el presente supuesto no existió expresa elección -aunque sí actos propios posteriores que sugieren la aplicación del Código Civil y el Código de Comercio' (ECLI:ES:APAV:2013:195).

83 Audiencia Provincial de Barcelona, Judgment 448/2019, 03/07/2019, ECLI:ES:APB:2019:8380.

84 Such as the principal's conduct of including an express choice-of-law clause in the contract with the new agent (who substituted the claimant) to ensure that the same law governed the net of agency contracts under the principal's control: see H. Aguilar, 'Problemas de ley aplicable en el marco de un contrato internacional de agencia comercial: comentario a la Sentencia de la Audiencia Provincial de Barcelona (Sección 11ª) de 3 de Julio de 2019' (2020) 12 *Cuadernos de Derecho Transnacional* 435–443, 440: <https://e-revistas.uc3m.es/index.php/CDT/article/view/5196>.

85 Audiencia Provincial de Palma de Mallorca, Judgment 341/2017, 31/10/2017, ECLI:ES:APIB:2017:1916; decided under the Rome Convention, which applied to the contract in dispute.

In this case, the Court had to determine whether a lease contract of immovable property located in Spain and celebrated in 2007, between two Spanish-registered companies with German-based headquarters, included an implied choice of German law. The Court took into account the circumstances of the case, in particular, the fact that the parties had celebrated a second contract in 2015, which substituted the 2007 contract. Importantly, both contracts included equivalent references to provisions of German law. However, the 2015 contract contained an express choice-of-law clause nominating German law that the contract in dispute, the 2007 contract, did not include.

Under the 'previous course of dealing' ground, the Guiliano-Lagarde Report suggests that it may be possible to imply that the parties have submitted the relevant contract to the same law they had chosen in a previous contract, where 'the choice of law has been omitted in circumstances which do not indicate a deliberate change of policy by the parties'.[86] The application of this ground to the present dispute is not self-evident: the case in dispute refers to the reverse situation (only the second contract included an express choice-of-law clause); also, the interpretation of this ground is completely dependent on the circumstances of the case, i.e. the absence of a choice-of-law clause in a contract may simply be evidence that the parties did not reach an agreement.[87] There is another ground in the Guiliano-Lagarde Report that could be relevant to the case decided by the Audiencia Provincial. References to provisions of domestic law may be interpreted as indicating the existence of a choice-of-law agreement that has not been explicitly stated. However, this is not conclusive and requires an analysis under the circumstances of the case. References to substantive provisions of domestic law do not automatically imply a choice of law.[88]

In the case in dispute, the Audiencia Provincial concluded that the absence of an express choice of German law in the first contract (the 2007 contract) demonstrated that the parties did not intend German law to govern this contract.[89] Under the Court's construct, the absence of express choice of German law in the first contract (which only included references to German law) was to be interpreted by reference to the second contract (the 2015 contract, which

86 [1980] OJ C287/17.

87 J. Hill and A. Chong, *Commercial Conflict of Laws in English Courts*, Hart Publishing, Oxford 2010, p. 512.

88 J. Hill and A. Chong, *supra* n. 87, p. 515.

89 'El hecho de que el contrato suscrito por la actora y la nueva arrendataria el 18 de febrero de 2015 contengauna cláusula expresa de sujeción a la ley alemana demuestra que si el arrendamiento de 2007 no contenía una estipulación semejante, a pesar de tener ambos las mismas remisiones concretas al derecho alemán, es porque la voluntad de las partes al suscribir el contrato anual de 2007 no fue la de someter todo lo pactado, incluso cuando no hubiese remisión expresa, a la ley alemana', Fundamento de Derecho Segundo, Audiencia Provincial de Palma de Mallorca, Judgment 341/2017, 31/10/2017, ECLI:ES:APIB:2017:1916.

included equivalent references to German law and an express choice of German law) to completely exclude implied party autonomy in the former.

It could be argued whether it was possible for the Court to interpret the facts of the case more permissively, i.e. as demonstrating with 'reasonable certainty' that an implied agreement between the parties existed.[90] However, the strict approach that the Audiencia Provincial took in this case was fully justified under the applicable legislative framework. Although worded more permissively than the equivalent provision in Rome I, the mandate in Article 3(1) Rome Convention is still strict and based on the real intentions of the parties;[91] and in this case, as interpreted by the Court, what prevented party autonomy was not that an alleged agreement could not be demonstrated with reasonable certainty, but that an agreement did not exist.

4.2. LAW APPLICABLE IN THE ABSENCE OF CHOICE

4.2.1. Contractual Disputes

Article 4 Rome I represents a compromise between legal certainty and flexibility. Whereas the list of choice-of-law rules (rather than presumptions) in Article 4(1) Rome I effectively contributes to legal certainty by narrowing down judicial discretion, the escape clause in Article 4(3) allows for some degree of flexibility.

The higher level of certainty secured by Article 4(1) may explain why there is little litigation in Spain regarding this provision. The following examples involving Article 4(1) Rome I are straightforward: a contract for the sale of goods governed by the law of Portugal as the law of the seller under Article 4(1)(a);[92] a contract for the provision of consulting services regulated by German law as the law of the provider of services under Article 4(1)(b);[93] and a tenancy of immovable property in Spain decided under Spanish law according to Article 4(1)(c).[94] With regard to the new rule for franchise and distribution contracts under Article 4(1)(f) and (g) Rome I (based on the habitual residence

---

90 According to the wording in Article 3(1) Rome Convention, which applied to the contract in dispute, the choice has to be 'demonstrated with reasonable certainty' (rather than 'clearly demonstrated' as in Article 3(1) Rome I).

91 See A. Mills, *Party Autonomy in Private International Law*, Cambridge University Press, Cambridge 2018, pp. 327–328; see also J. Hill and A. Chong, *supra* n. 87, p. 510.

92 Audiencia Provincial de A Coruña, Judgment 168/2015, 15/06/2016, ECLI:ES:APC:2015:1556.

93 Audiencia Provincial de Barcelona, Judgment 206/2016, 26/05/2016, ECLI:ES:APB:2016:9018 (though German law was eventually discarded under the escape clause in Article 4(3) Rome I).

94 Between two parties from Pakistan, Audiencia Provincial de Barcelona, Judgment 464/2014, 11/11/2014, ECLI:ES:APB:2014:12300.

of the franchisee and distributor), it has to be noted that this was already the practice in Spain under the Rome Convention.[95]

As to the judicial interpretation of the concept of characteristic performance in Article 4(2) Rome I, which only applies if the contract does not fit within one of the categories in Article 4(1), it is important to consider how this notion was interpreted under the Rome Convention's legislative framework. For example, the Audiencia Provincial de Valencia clearly stated in its 2014 judgment that the concept of characteristic performance referred to the non-monetary obligation under the contract.[96] The Court, however, elaborated further on this concept and stated that additional elements, such as the place where the contract was concluded and the place of the offer, could also qualify for consideration. This broad approach was controversial since such elements do not play a role in defining the concept of characteristic performance. Nothing in case law suggests, however, that this broad interpretation has been further upheld in practice.

In review, the practice in relation to the presumptions in Article 4(2)–(4) of the Rome Convention, and Article 4(1) and (2) Rome I, has never been particularly problematic in Spain. The courts have generally endorsed a rigid approach to them and only under exceptional circumstances have they had recourse to the escape clause in Article 4(3) Rome I (Article 4(5) Rome Convention).[97] Overall, there is evidence that the practice regarding Article 4 Rome I is generally consistent and that this provision has helped enhance legal certainty in Spain.

4.2.2. Non-Contractual Disputes

With regard to litigation under Article 4 Rome II, the Audiencia Provincial de Oviedo provides a good illustration on the application of the *lex loci damni* rule under paragraph (1), in a judgment it delivered in 2018.[98] In this case, the

95 See H. Aguilar, 'Los contratos internacionales de distribucion commercial en el Reglamento Roma I' (2009) 1 *Cuadernos de Derecho Transnacional* 19–35 (quoting at n. 51 the Judgment by Audiencia Provincia de Barcelona of 08.04.2000): <https://e-revistas.uc3m.es/index.php/CDT/article/view/67>.

96 Audiencia Provincial de Valencia, Judgment 31/2014, 05/02/2014, ECLI:ES:APV:2014:1188: 'la mayoría de la doctrina se inclina por considerar como prestación característica la prestación no dineraria, en la medida en que el pago de un precio, renta, honorarios … es común a la mayor parte de contratos, y no específicamente identificativo de un contrato'.

97 An example of a case applying Article 4(3) Rome I is Judgment 206/2016 by the Audiencia Provincial de Barcelona. In this case, the Court relied on the escape clause in Article 4(3) to take into account additional elements to which the contract related. In particular, the Court justified the application of Spanish law to a contract for the provision of services between a Spanish company and a German provider on Article 4(3) Rome I grounds, arguing that the services were to be provided in Spain (ECLI:ES:APB:2016:9018). On the application of Article 4(3) Rome I, see, W. Martinez, 'El artículo 4.3 del Reglamento Roma I. Una verdadera cláusula de excepción' (2012) *Revista Electrónica de Estudios Internacionales* 17: <www.reei.org>.

98 Audiencia Provincial de Oviedo, Judgment 54/2018, 07/02/2018, ECLI:ES:APO:2018:293.

Court confirmed the application of French law to the personal injuries sustained by a Spanish-based individual at a hotel in France. Notably, the Court stressed the ability of this rule to contribute to the sound administration of justice and to ensure the application of a law sufficiently connected to the dispute.[99] As discussed before, the clarity of this rule contrasts with the uncertainties that have traditionally surrounded the interpretation of Article 10(9) of the Civil Code. From this point of view, there is no doubt that Article 4 Rome II has contributed to the enhancement of legal certainty in Spain.

Another example shows how the court excluded the application of Article 4(1) Rome II to indirect damages suffered by the victim, as the case decided by the Audiencia Provincial de Barcelona in 2020 illustrates.[100]

Further, the judgment delivered by the Audiencia Provincial de Zaragoza in 2019 provides another example of the application of Article 4(1).[101] In this case, the claimant argued that a Polish-based bank was at fault for not conducting additional checks as to the beneficiary's identity, in the context of a transfer of money ordered by the former from Spain. The Court confirmed the application of Spanish law, where the damage had occurred, rather than the law of Poland, where a hacker had fraudulently accessed the monies.[102]

With regard to the special rules under Rome II, recent examples of unfair competition claims decided under Article 6 exist. This is a complex provision. For the purpose of this chapter, it is sufficient to refer here to the dispute decided in 2017 by the Tribunal Supremo, in which the Court clarified that a claim in Spain under Spanish law, was not to cover acts conducted in a different country and having effects in the territory of that country.[103] Another recent example is the claim decided by the Audiencia Provincial de Cordoba, brought by a global bagel and coffee chain against a Spanish company which had set up shops imitating the commercial trade dress used by the former.[104]

---

99 The Court stated, 'adoptando como criterio general el del lugar del daño (lex loci damni), de cuya bondad se parte por ser el más equitativo, mejor para administrar justicia y más conforme con la premisa del vínculo más estrecho [...]', at Fundamento de Derecho Tercero (ECLI:ES:APO:2018:293).

100 Though the problem with this case was that the Court decided the dispute, which concerned a traffic accident, by reference to Article 4(1) Rome II instead of relying upon the 1971 Hague Convention (Judgment 49/2020, 31/01/2020,ECLI:ES:APB:2020:491).

101 Audiencia Provincial de Zaragoza, Judgment 332/2019, 17/04/2019, ECLI:ES:APZ:2019:680.

102 The Court established that the damage had materialised in Spain, where the money had left the claimant's account, although the reasoning could have been clearer (regarding the determination of the jurisdiction of the court, in particular). Eventually, the Court conceded that the bank was not at fault under Article 59 of the Payment Services Act of 2018 (*Real Decreto 19/2018 de Servicios de Pago*).

103 Tribunal Supremo, Judgment 306/2017, 17/05/2017, ECLI:ES:TS:2017:1910.

104 The Court decided the case under Articles 6(2) and 4 Rome II, which pointed to Spanish law: see, Audiencia Provincial de Cordoba, Judgment 453/2017, 14/07/2017, ECLI:ES:APCO:2017:666.

5. THE INTERPLAY BETWEEN THE *LEX FORI* AND THE *LEX CAUSAE*

Under certain circumstances, the *lex causae* under Rome I and Rome II, chosen by the parties or objectively determined, can be displaced by the *lex fori*. The purpose of this section is to look at the interplay between the *lex causae* and the *lex fori* using a sample of recently decided cases in the following three areas: mandatory rules, public policy norms and failure to prove foreign law.

It should be noted that cases discussing the application of mandatory rules and public policy norms mostly deal with contractual disputes decided under Rome I. There appears to be sparse litigation on the application of both of these categories of provisions under Rome II.[105] By contrast, there are multiple examples illustrating the parties failing to prove foreign law.

5.1. MANDATORY RULES

5.1.1. Employment Contracts

Litigation over individual employment contracts is not uncommon in Spain. Consistent with the policy informing Article 8(1) Rome I, Spanish courts apply the chosen law only if it is more beneficial to the employee as the weaker party to the contract. Under the preferential law approach in Article 8(1), the parties are free to choose the applicable law to their contract, though this choice cannot deprive employees of the protection afforded to them by mandatory provisions of the *lex loci laboris*. Article 8(2) Rome I defines *lex loci laboris* as the 'law of the country in which [...] or from which the employee carries out his work in performance of the contract'.

The following cases illustrate the application of Article 8(1)–(2) Rome I. For example, the case decided by the Tribunal Superior de Justicia de Palma de Mallorca in 2017, on a claim for unfair dismissal, in which the Court confirmed that German law, as the chosen law, could not prevent the application of mandatory provisions of Spanish law where the employee performed their work.[106] Further, the judgment from the Tribunal Superior de Justicia de Bilbao

---

105 For a study on these norms under Rome II, see J. Maseda, 'El Juego de las normas imperativas en el Reglamento Roma II sobre ley aplicable a las obligaciones no contractuales: límites a la aplicación de la *lex causae*' (2013) *Revista Española de Estudios Internacionales* 2–45: <http://www.reei.org>.

106 Tribunal de Justicia de Palma de Mallorca, Judgment 199/2017, 01/06/2017, ECLI:ES: TSJBAL:2017:470.

delivered in 2017, also in the context of an unfair dismissal claim,[107] in which the Court confirmed that the application of the law chosen by the parties, the law of Cyprus, could not displace the mandatory provisions of Spanish law applicable as *lex loci laboris*. Finally, the same was upheld in a dispute decided by the Tribunal Superior de Justicia de Valladolid in 2015, in which the contract had been submitted to the law of Spain but the employee performed their work in Chile.[108]

The preferential law approach requires the courts to engage in a comparative analysis between the chosen law and the *lex loci laboris*, which in turn requires the parties to prove the relevant foreign law. This is an important point. According to long-established principles of procedural law, failing to prove foreign law will bring the dispute back to Spanish law.[109] For example, it has to be noted that, in the three cases just mentioned, the disputes were eventually decided under Spanish law because the relevant party failed to prove foreign law.

The judgment delivered by the Tribunal Superior de Justicia de Valladolid in 2018 provides a good illustration of how the Court compared relevant provisions of German law (the chosen law) and Spanish law (the *lex loci laboris*). This occurred in the context of an unfair dismissal action.[110] Eventually, the Court concluded that the protections under German law, which had been satisfactorily proven, were more favourable to the employee, and solved the dispute under this law.

With regard to the determination of the *lex loci laboris*, the Tribunal Supremo has recently interpreted the phrase 'the law of the country in which [...] the employee carries out his work in performance of the contract' in Article 8(2) Rome I.[111] In this case, the Court confirmed the application of Spanish law as *lex loci laboris* to the contract of employment between a senior executive and a group of companies for which he had continuously worked. The Court conceded that the employee had performed his work in the Spanish subsidiary, in accordance with Article 8(2), regardless of temporary transfers elsewhere. It also clarified that there had been one employment relationship only, despite the parties having celebrated different contracts.

---

107 Tribunal Superior de Jusitica de Bilbao, Judgment 1666/2017, 05/09/2017, ECLI:ES:TSJPV:2017:2852.

108 Tribunal Superior de Justicia de Castilla-León, Judgment 1723/2015, 21/11/2015, ECLI:ES:TSJCL:2015:5597.

109 On the failure to prove foreign law, see *infra* section 5.3.

110 The Court compared Articles 53–55 of the Workers' Rights Statute (*Estatuto de los Trabajadores*) with the relevant provisions of the Protection Against Dismissal Act (the applicable German Act): Tribunal Superior de Justicia de Valladolid, Judgment 489/2018, 15/03/2018 (ECLI:ES:TSJCL:2018:1001).

111 Tribunal Supremo, Decree (Auto) recourse no. 2112/2019, 17/05/2017, ECLI:ES:TS:2020:2180A.

Finally, the Tribunal Superior de Justicia de Cataluña decided in 2015 a claim for unfair dismissal brought by a flight attendant against Ryanair.[112] The contract included a choice-of-law clause in favour of Irish law. The Court decided that the employee had provided his services from Spain under Article 8(2) Rome I, as he always departed from and returned to Girona, from where he operated.[113] The Court confirmed that the choice-of-law clause in the contract was valid and effective, but only to the extent that the chosen law was more beneficial to the employee as mandated in Article 8(1) Rome I. Given that the Court found that Spanish norms for dismissal were more favourable than those of Ireland, it resolved the dispute under Spanish law.[114]

5.1.2. Contracts for the Carriage of Passengers

The case decided by the Juzgado de lo Mercantil de Madrid in 2013, which concerned the validity of a choice-of-law clause in the general terms of sale of an air carrier, was notable.[115] A consumer organisation brought a representative action on behalf of individuals residing in Spain who had entered into a contract with Ryanair; the contract was celebrated under the carrier's standard terms, which included a choice-of-law clause in favour of the law of Ireland. The clause satisfied the conditions in Article 5(2) second paragraph Rome I, yet the Court examined its validity under European mandatory principles of consumer protection. Relying on Article 90(3) of the 2007 Spanish Consumer Act, which transposes Directive 93/13/EEC on unfair terms, the Court decided that the choice of Irish law was void. This was based on the reasoning that the express clause, which designated the law of a country different from where the consumer had accepted the contract (i.e. Spain), had not been negotiated individually.

The Audiencia Provincial de Madrid, however, reversed this decision and considered that the choice-of-law clause included in the carrier's standard terms of sale was lawful, in a judgment delivered on 26 June 2017.[116] In this case, the Court validated the choice of Irish law under Article 5(2) Rome I, which allowed party autonomy under certain conditions (that had been met under the facts of the case as the carrier had its habitual residence in Ireland).

---

112 Tribunal Superior de Justicia de Cataluña, Barcelona, Judgment 4166/2015, 25/06/2015, ECLI:ES:TSJCAT:2015:6221.

113 On the interpretative difficulties of the concept of 'base' in Spanish case law, see P. Juarez, 'El conflicto de Ryanair: Una lectura desde el Derecho Internacional Privado' (2019) 11 *Cuadernos de Derecho Transnacional* 372–407, 384–389: <https://e-revistas.uc3m.es/index.php/CDT/article/view/4625>.

114 It has been reported that most cases deciding individual employment disputes against Ryanair in Spain end up being solved under Spanish law, which tends to be interpreted as being more beneficial to the employee (see, P. Juarez *supra* n. 113).

115 Juzgado de lo Mercantil of Madrid, Judgment 113/2013, 30/09/2013, ECLI:ES:JMM:2013:380.

116 Audiencia Provincial de Madrid, Judgment 392/2017, 26/07/2017, ECLI:ES:APM:2017:10881.

Then, the Court refused to strike down the choice-of-law clause by reference to Directive 93/13: it took the view that the clause was not at odds with the transparency requirements in Article 5 of Directive 93/13 as interpreted by the CJEU in the *Amazon* ruling, and refused to apply Spanish law to evaluate the fairness of the clause under Article 3 of the Directive.[117] That Article 5(2) Rome I validates party autonomy in contracts for the carriage of passengers, is beyond dispute. However, in building its argument, the Court could have elaborated further on the application of the fairness test in the context of this provision.[118]

5.2. PUBLIC POLICY RULES

The category of overriding mandatory provisions refers to the more limited group of norms referred to in Article 9(1) Rome I, in line with the definitions in the CJEU *Arblade* and *Leloup* rulings.[119] This category of norms, which apply regardless of the *lex contractus*, only includes rules that a country regards as crucial for safeguarding its public interests. There is evidence that the courts in Spain endorse this narrow approach and do not rely on Article 9(2) to implement norms designed to protect consumers' rights. The aforementioned judgment by the Audiencia Provincial de Madrid of 26 June 2017 made this point explicit. In this case, the Court unambiguously affirmed that using Article 9(2) Rome I to justify the application of mandatory provisions that protect consumers would be contrary to Rome I and to the principle of supremacy of European law.[120]

Employment courts also reserve the category of rules in Article 9(2) Rome I to those protecting public interests. This is shown, for example, in the

117 The Court stated, '[...] No solo la cláusula en examen resulta plenamente autorizada por el derecho de la Unión, sino que, además, no identificamos en el caso circunstancias que, conforme a los dictados de la Directiva 93/13, según el esquema de análisis que presenta el TJ en los apartados 66 y siguientes de la sentencia Vereinfür Konsumenteninformation [...]generen un desequilibrio importante entre los derechos y obligaciones de las partes', Fundamento de Derecho, paragraph 21.8 (ECLI:ES:APM:2017:10881).

118 In this case, the Court relied upon the CJEU *Amazon* ruling to support its interpretation (Case C-191/15, ECLI:EU:C:2016:612), but did not elaborate on how a substantial assessment of the fairness of the clause could be conducted for contracts falling outside Article 6 Rome I (i.e. not subjected to the preferential law approach). On the CJEU *Amazon* ruling, see, G. Rühl, 'The unfairness of choice-of-law clauses or: The (unclear) relationship between Article 6 Rome I Regulation and the Unfair Terms in Consumer Contracts Directive: VKI v. Amazon', (2018) 55 *Common Market Law Review* 201–224.

119 CJEU, Case C-369/96 and C-376/96, *Arblade and Leloup*, ECLI:EU:C:1999:575.

120 As the Court stated: 'debe descartarse que el artículo 9.2 del Reglamento Roma I pueda servir de fundamento a la entrada en juego del artículo 90.2 TRLGDCU, como norma de policía del foro. Tal enfoque supondría dejar sin efecto las reglas de conflicto del Reglamento [...] y, en tal sentido, una vulneración del principio de primacía del derecho de la Unión', paragraph 21.4 (Audiencia Provincial de Madrid, Judgment 392/2017, 26/07/2017, ECLI:ES:APM:2017:10881).

case decided by the Tribunal Superior de Justicia de Asturias in 2013.[121] In this case, the court considered that specific voluntary benefits sought by the employee were not to be classified as overriding mandatory rules of forum, in accordance with Article 3(1)(c) Directive concerning the Posting of Workers. Another example is provided by the Tribunal Superior de Justicia de Madrid, in a case it decided in 2019, in which the Court discussed the application of Spanish social security rules as overriding mandatory provisions.[122] Further, an additional illustration is provided in the case decided by the Tribunal Superior de Justicia de Madrid in 2016.[123] Acting in a private capacity, the Ministry for Foreign Affairs employed personnel to work in the Spanish Embassy in Uruguay. The contracts had been submitted to Spanish law and the annual salary increases were to be determined in accordance with the Spanish National Budget Act. As a result of austerity measures, no further pay rises applied to the contracts. The employees brought proceedings in Spain claiming the application of the law of Uruguay to the calculation of annual pay rises. The Court held that Spanish law governed the contracts under Article 8(1) Rome I and, even if a different outcome could be justified under Article 8(2), it confirmed that the rule fixing the pay rise was to be applied to the contract as a matter of public policy of the forum under Article 9(2) Rome I, on the grounds of budgetary sustainability.

More ambiguous statements concerning the scope of Article 9(2) Rome I can also be found in recent case law. The case decided by the Audiencia Provincial de Barcelona in 2019, on a dispute over the termination of an agency contract between a German-based agent and a Spanish company, provides an example.[124] In this case, the Court stated that the agent should not be deprived of their rights under Articles 28 and 29 of the Spanish Agency Contract Act and, in support of this, it referred to Article 9(2) Rome I and to the CJEU *Ingmar* case.[125] This is a complex area that the CJEU *Unamar* ruling has further developed.[126]

---

121 Tribunal Superior de Justicia de Asturias, Judgment 230/2013, 01/02/2013, ECLI:ES:TSJAS:2013:402.

122 Tribunal Superior de Justicia de Madrid, Judgment 529/2019, 28/06/2019, ECLI:ES:TSJM:2019:5382.

123 Tribunal Superior de Justicia de Madrid, Judgment 335/2016, 09/05/2016, ECLI:ES:TSJM:2016:5287.

124 Audiencia Provincial de Barcelona, Judgment 448/2019, 03/07/2019, ECLI:ES:APB:2019:8380; see, *supra* n. 83.

125 The Court stated, 'no cabría privar al agente de los derechos reconocidos en los arts. 28 y 29 LCA (Article 9.2 Reglamento y STJUE de 9/11/2000, Caso Ingmar)'; ECLI:ES:APB:2019:8380.

126 In the *Unamar* decision, the CJEU permitted the courts of a Member State to disregard the application of the law that the parties had freely chosen (which protected the agent as it transposed Directive 86/653/EEC) and to apply, instead, the law of the forum transposing the Directive, if the national courts found that it was essential, in the legal order concerned, to grant the commercial agent protection going beyond that provided for by the Directive (Case C-184/12, *Unamar*, ECLI:EU:C:2013:663).

With regard to the Audiencia Provincial's judgment, however, it has to be noted that the Court's remarks were made *obiter dicta* – as discussed before, the Court solved the case under Article 3(1) Rome I, interpreting that the contract contained an implied choice of Spanish law.[127]

5.3. FAILURE TO PROVE FOREIGN LAW

According to the mandate in Article 12(6) of the Spanish Civil Code, the courts apply choice-of-law rules *ex officio*. This, however, does not prevent international disputes from eventually being decided under the *lex fori* (Spanish law), when the parties fail to prove foreign law.[128]

In Spain, the litigating parties must prove the applicable foreign law to the court, which may cooperate in establishing it in accordance with Article 281(2) of the Spanish Civil Justice Act.[129] This has been the paradigm in Spain under the Tribunal Supremo's doctrine,[130] which Article 33(3) of the newly adopted International Civil Cooperation Act now codifies.[131] Articles 34 and 35 of the new Act provide for a mechanism enabling Spanish authorities to request information on foreign law. However, as the onus remains on the party claiming the application of foreign law, it has been suggested that these provisions do not substantially alter the status quo.[132]

In review, an important number of the cases discussed in this chapter ended up being decided under Spanish law because of the failure to prove foreign law. These include: the 2019 judgment of the Audiencia Provincial de Madrid on a traffic accident that occurred in Portugal;[133] the 2018 judgment by the Audiencia Provincial de Barcelona on a contract for the sale of goods by auction submitted to German law (in accordance with Article 3(1) Rome I);[134] the 2018 judgment by the Audiencia Provincial de Barcelona on a dispute over a non-contractual obligation to be decided under French law (as provided for under Article 4(1)

127 In this case, as the *lex contractus* coincided with the *lex fori*, it is not apparent that the Court intended to apply those protective norms via Article 9(2) Rome I.

128 See J. Iglesias, C. Esplugues, G. Palao, R. Espinosa and C. Azcárraga, 'Spain', in C. Esplugues, J. Iglesias and G. Palao (eds.), *Application of Foreign Law*, Sellier, Munich 2011, pp. 355–375.

129 *Ley 1/2000 de enjuiciamiento civil* (*Boletín Oficial del Estado* 7, 08.01.2000).

130 See Tribunal Supremo: Judgment 436/2005, 10/06/2005, ECLI:ES:TS:2005:3760; Judgment (recourse no.) 2421/1999, 04/07/2006, ECLI:ES:TS:2006:4079; Judgment 797/2007, 04/07/2007, ECLI:ES:TS:2007:4484; Judgment 338/2008, 30/04/2008, ECLI:ES:TS:2008:1632; Judgment 528/2014, 14/10/2014, ECLI:ES:TS:2014:5567; and Judgment 198/2015, 17/04/2015, ECLI:ES:TS:2015:1868.

131 *Ley 29/2015 de cooperación jurídica internacional en materia civil* (*Boletín Oficial del Estado* 182, 31.07.2015).

132 See E. Torralba, *supra* n. 3; see also A. Calvo, 'Aplicación judicial del derecho extranjero: consideraciones críticas' (2016) LXVIII *Revista Española de Derecho Internacional* 133–156.

133 Audiencia Provincial de Madrid, Judgment 12/2019, 17/01/2019, ECLI:ES:APM:2019:773.

134 Audiencia Provincial de Barcelona, Judgment 337/2018, 12/04/2018, ECLI:ES:APB:2018:2837.

Rome II);[135] the 2018 judgment by the Audiencia Provincial de Barcelona on a traffic accident to be decided under French law (under Article 3 of the 1971 Hague Convention);[136] the 2017 judgment by the Audiencia Provincial de Zamora on a contract for the sale of goods under Italian law;[137] the judgment of the Tribunal Supremo of 2015, in which the parties failed to prove the law of the Netherlands (applicable to the assignment of credits);[138] the 2014 judgment of the Tribunal Supremo on an employment contract under Italian law;[139] the 2015 judgment of the Audiencia Provincial de A Coruña on a contract for the sale of goods under the law of Portugal;[140] the 2013 judgment of the Audiencia Provincial de León on a contract submitted to German law;[141] and finally, the 2009 judgment of the Audiencia Provincial de Alicante on an agency contract governed by the law of Georgia.[142]

Clearly, despite the mandatory nature of choice-of-law norms, the courts will decide the dispute under the *lex fori* unless the interested party proves the content of foreign law. This may be burdensome for the party in terms of cost and delays and an incentive may also exist for a party to fail to plead foreign law if the substantive outcome under foreign law is less beneficial than it would be under the *lex fori*.[143] Therefore, it is apparent that the difficulties surrounding the proof of foreign law may compromise the mandatory nature of choice-of-law norms in Rome I and Rome II.

6. SCOPE OF THE *LEX CONTRACTUS*

A few recent cases concern litigation over the scope of the *lex contractus* under Article 12 Rome I. The 2010 judgment of the Audiencia Provincial de Murcia provides a good illustration. In this case, the Court held the view that the determination of the relevant interests could not be claimed under Spanish law, where the reimbursement of the principal payment was to be determined under Irish law. The Court made it clear that it was for the interested party to establish all the relevant concepts under the law applicable to the contract.[144]

Issues of capacity are excluded from the Rome I Regulation, as the 2015 judgment of the Audiencia Provincial de las Palmas de Gran Canarias illustrates.

---

135 Audiencia Provincial de Oviedo, Judgment 54/2018, 07/02/2018, ECLI:ES:APO:2018:293.

136 Audiencia Provincial de Barcelona, Judgment 215/2018, 13/07/2018, ECLI:ES:APB:2018:6940.

137 Audiencia Provincial de Zamora, Judgment 107/2017, 07/04/2017, ECLI:ES:APZA:2017:173.

138 Tribunal Supremo, Judgment 198/2015, 17/04/2015, ECLI:ES:TS:2015:1868.

139 Tribunal Supremo, Judgment (recourse no.) 257/2012, 22/12/2014, ECLI:ES:TS:2014:5639.

140 Audiencia Provincial de A Coruña, Judgment 168/2015, 15/06/2016, ECLI:ES:APC:2015:1556.

141 Audiencia Provincial de León, Judgment 373/2013, 25/09/2013, ECLI:ES:APLE:2013:1308.

142 Audiencia Provincial de Alicante, Judgment 446/2009, 21/07/2009, ECLI:ES:APA:2009:2489.

143 As pointed out in the academic literature, see *supra* n. 132.

144 Audiencia Provincial de Madrid, Judgment 25/2010, 27/12/2012, ECLI:ES:APM:2012:22783.

In this case, the Court was of the view that Article 13 Rome I could not be applied to confirm the validity of a contract concluded by an individual who lacked capacity under their personal law (i.e. the law of Austria) because the requirement in Article 13 – that such a person had capacity under Spanish law – was not satisfied.[145]

The practice on formal validity under Article 11 Rome I is notable. Under Spanish law, contracts for the sale of immovable property must be authorised by notaries, so that they can be registered in the Property Registry of Spain. In 2012, the Tribunal Supremo decided a case on whether the parties to a contract for the sale of immovable property (located in Spain), which had already been authorised by German notaries, could access the property registry in Spain.[146] The Court held that the contract could be registered in Spain, provided that German notaries were functionally equivalent to Spanish notaries (which was the case). As discussed in the literature, this decision put an end to Spanish notaries' monopoly over Spanish forms.[147]

7. CONCLUSION

The judgments examined in this chapter show how the application of the Rome I and Rome II Regulations has contributed to modernising the judicial practice on international commercial disputes in Spain.

On the one hand, Rome I has definitely relegated the domestic choice-of-law rule for contracts, Article 10(5) of the Civil Code, to a purely residual role in international litigation (such as deciding the applicable law to international contracts concluded before 1 September 1993). On the other hand, Rome II has positively influenced the interpretation of the domestic choice-of-law rule for non-contractual obligations, Article 10(9) of the Civil Code, which remains the relevant rule for disputes arising out of non-contractual obligations that are excluded from this Regulation (in the absence of applicable international conventions).

The cases reviewed in this chapter reveal consistent practice on express choice of law, which is generally upheld in Spain, especially in contractual disputes. The practice concerning implied choice of law has proven to be strict, according to the mandate in Article 3(1) Rome I. Moreover, although the practice in relation to the presumptions in Article 4(2) – (4) of the Rome Convention has never been

145 Audiencia Provincial de las Palmas de Gran Canaria, Judgment 385/2015, 15/10/2015, ECLI:ES:APGC:2015:2181.

146 Tribunal Supremo, Judgment 998/2011, 19/06/2012, ECLI:ES:TS:2012:5354.

147 See S. Sanchez, 'Eficacia registral de los documentos notariales extranjeros: STS (Sala 1ª) de 19 de junio de 2012' (2013) LXV *Revista Española de Derecho Internacional* 244–246.

particularly problematic in Spain (for the courts have generally endorsed a rigid approach to them), there is evidence that the application of Article 4 Rome I has helped achieve a higher degree of certainty in the determination of the law applicable to the contract in the absence of choice.

The cases examined show generally consistent practice regarding the classification of mandatory rules in Spain, both simple and overriding, and also concerning the implementation of the preferential law approach under Article 8 Rome I. In review, the importance of the role that higher instances and specialised courts (such as commercial courts and employment courts) have played in promoting a coherent application of these categories of norms, must be acknowledged.

However, the chapter has also identified more controversial aspects of the practice on Rome I and Rome II in Spain. Interpretative difficulties that the courts appear to have encountered relate, for example, to the complex interplay between Rome I and other European instruments (such as Directive 93/13 on unfair terms). With regard to non-contractual disputes, in particular, it needs to be considered whether the practice in Spain would benefit from the country withdrawing from the old 1971 and 1973 Hague Conventions.

Finally, there persists an unresolved problem, of a procedural law nature, concerning the parties' failure to prove foreign law. As discussed, failing to prove foreign law is likely to bring the dispute back to Spanish law, which may compromise the mandatory nature of the choice-of-law norms in Rome I and Rome II. The courts are not to be blamed for this though. Under the current paradigm, although the courts can help the parties establish foreign law, the courts cannot replace them as the onus remains on the parties to plead and prove foreign law.

THE APPLICATION OF THE ROME I AND ROME II REGULATIONS IN THE UNITED KINGDOM

Uglješa Grušić

1. INTRODUCTION

'All roads lead to Rome!' For a while, this saying could have been invoked by private international lawyers in the United Kingdom, as well as in the Member States of the European Union (apart from Denmark), to succinctly capture the evolution and reality of the part of this discipline dealing with choice of law for contractual and non-contractual obligations. But the voters of the UK have spoken – EU law and the writ of the Court of Justice of the EU are no longer welcome. This is why any presentation and assessment of the application of the Rome I and Rome II Regulations[1] in this country has to start with a brief note of what Brexit – the withdrawal of the UK from the EU – brings for private international law in general and the two Regulations in particular.

The UK left the European Union on 31 January 2020.[2] However, the EU-UK Withdrawal Agreement[3] provides for a Brexit implementation period, which is currently set to end on 31 December 2020. Until that time, the EU Treaties will continue to apply to the UK and the European Communities Act 1972, by virtue of which EU law is incorporated into UK law, will continue to have effect. This means that the Rome I and Rome II Regulations will continue to be directly effective in the UK until the expiry of the Brexit implementation period. The UK Government has decided to retain the provisions of the two Regulations as part of UK law and the retained provisions will be applicable after the expiry of the Brexit implementation period as part of domestic law.[4] The main consequence of this is that UK courts will not be bound by any principle laid down, or any decision made, by the CJEU and will not be able to refer any matter to the CJEU. Even though they will be able to 'have regard to anything done … by the European Court, another EU entity or the EU',[5] it is possible that the UK courts' interpretation of the retained provisions of the two Regulations will depart from that of the CJEU.

The Rome I and Rome II Regulations have been frequently applied by English courts, not so much in other parts of the UK. As of 1 April 2020, which has been chosen as the cut-off date for the purposes of this chapter, there had been 26 cases in which Rome I was applied[6] and 48 cases applying Rome II.[7] There have also

---

1 Regulation (EC) No. 593/2008 of the European Parliament and of the Council on the law applicable to contractual obligations (Rome I) [2008] OJ L177/6; Regulation (EC) No. 864/2007 of the European Parliament and of the Council on the law applicable to non-contractual obligations (Rome II) [2007] OJ L199/40.

2 European Union (Withdrawal) Act 2018; European Union (Withdrawal) Act 2018 (Exit Day) (Amendment) (No 3) Regulations (SI 2019/1423), regulation 2(2).

3 Agreement on the withdrawal of the United Kingdom of Great Britain and Northern Ireland from the European Union and the European Atomic Energy Community [2019] OJ C384I/1, implemented into UK law by the European Union (Withdrawal Agreement) Act 2020.

4 Law Applicable to Contractual Obligations and Non-Contractual Obligations (Amendment etc) (EU Exit) Regulations (SI 2019/834).

5 European Union (Withdrawal) Act 2018, section 6(2).

6 There are more cases applying the Rome Convention on the law applicable to contractual obligations [1980] OJ L266/1, as amended by later accession conventions. This chapter, however, deals only with cases applying Rome I or Rome II.

7 Two notes are in order here. First, I looked for UK cases on Rome I and Rome II in the Westlaw and LexisNexis databases. I searched for all judgments which contain either the term '864/2007' or the term '593/2008', which are the numbers of the two Regulations. My assumption was that any case applying, discussing or mentioning one of the Regulations would also include a complete reference to the Regulation, including its number. I then cross-checked my list of cases against the cases referred to in L. Collins (gen. ed.), *Dicey, Morris and Collins on the*

been other cases in which the provisions of Rome I or Rome II have been either mentioned or discussed, but not applied. In light of the large number of cases applying, mentioning or discussing the two Regulations, the aim of this chapter is not to offer an in-depth analysis of the issues that have arisen or could arise in the future. This is not necessary given the excellent commentaries on these two instruments, including by UK scholars and in UK journals.[8] What this chapter aims to do is, firstly, to describe the legal and commercial contexts in which disputes concerning choice of law for contractual and non-contractual obligations have arisen before UK courts. Next, this chapter will outline the treatment by UK courts of some of the key general issues that are common to the two Regulations and of certain specific issues that are idiosyncratic to either Rome I or Rome II.

Conflict of Laws (London: Sweet & Maxwell, 15th ed., 2012) and the fifth supplement of this book (2018). Second, 'the application of' Rome I and Rome II has been understood widely as covering not only the cases where the provisions of the Regulations were applied to determine the applicable law, regardless of whether that part of the judgment forms part of the ratio decidendi or is obiter, but also the cases where the provisions of the Regulations were applied for other purposes (e.g. in *Impala Warehousing and Logistics (Shanghai) Co. Ltd v. Wanxiang Resources (Singapore) PTE Ltd* [2015] EWHC 811 (Comm), [2015] 2 All ER (Comm) 234, the court applied the provisions on the subject-matter scope of the Regulations to determine whether a claim brought in China was contractual for the purposes of determining whether an exclusive English jurisdiction agreement had been breached and an anti-suit injunction should be granted). There are also cases where the courts applied an exclusion from the subject-matter scope of the Regulations, which cases have not been counted as 'applying' the Regulations: see *Enka Insaat ve Sanayi AS v. OOO 'Insurance Co. Chubb'* [2019] EWHC 3568 (Comm) (arbitration exclusion in Article 1(2)(e) of Rome I); *European Film Bonds A/S v. Lotus Holdings LLC* [2019] EWHC 2116 (Ch) (arbitration exclusion in Article 1(2)(e) of Rome I); *PJSC Tatneft v. Bogolyubov* [2017] EWCA Civ 1581, [2018] 4 WLR 14 (evidence and procedure exclusion in Article 1(3) of Rome II); *Actavis UK Ltd v. Eli Lilly & Co.* [2015] EWCA Civ 555, [2016] 4 All ER 666 (evidence and procedure exclusion in Article 1(3) of Rome II), reversed in part in [2017] UKSC 48, [2018] 1 All ER 171 without discussing this point; *Integral Petroleum SA v. SCU-Finanz AG* [2015] EWCA Civ 144, [2016] 1 All ER (Comm) 217 (company law exclusions in Article 1(2)(f) and (g) of Rome I); *Subotic v. Knezevic* [2013] EWHC 3011 (QB) (defamation exclusion in Article 1(2)(g) of Rome II); *Mauritius Commercial Bank Ltd v. Hestia Holdings Ltd* [2013] EWHC 1328 (Comm), [2013] 2 All ER (Comm) 898 (choice-of-court agreement exclusion in Article 1(2)(e) of Rome I); *Arsanovia Ltd v. Cruz City 1 Mauritius Holdings* [2012] EWHC 3702 (Comm), [2013] 2 All ER (Comm) 1 (arbitration exclusion in Article 1(2)(e) of Rome I). I have also not counted as 'applying' the Regulations the cases which discussed the temporal scope of Rome II and concluded that the matter fell outside its temporal scope: see *Docherty v. Secretary of State for Business, Innovation and Skills* [2018] CSOH 25, 2018 SLT 349, reversed on a different point in [2018] CSIH 57, 2019 SC 50; *Allen v. Depuy International Ltd* [2014] EWHC 753 (QB), [2015] 2 WLR 442; *Homawoo v. GMF Assurance SA* [2010] EWHC 1941 (QB), [2011] ILPr 12.

8 See, among others, A. Dickinson, *The Rome II Regulation* (Oxford: Oxford University Press, 2008); M. McParland, *The Rome I Regulation on the Law Applicable to Contractual Obligations* (Oxford: Oxford University Press, 2015); M. Wilderspin and R. Plender, *The European Private International Law of Obligations* (London: Sweet & Maxwell, 4th ed., 2015). The *International and Comparative Law Quarterly*, *Journal of Private International Law* and *Lloyd's Maritime and Commercial Law Quarterly* are among the UK academic journals that frequently feature articles on Rome I and Rome II. Excellent case notes can also be found in the *Cambridge Law Journal* and the *Law Quarterly Review*.

2. THE NATIONAL LANDSCAPE

Prior to the entry into force of the Rome I and Rome II Regulations, the law applicable to contracts and torts in the UK was largely determined pursuant to the choice-of-law rules of the Contracts (Applicable Law) Act 1990, which implemented the Rome Convention into UK law, and Part III of the Private International Law (Miscellaneous Provisions) Act 1995, which reformed choice-of-law rules in tort. Choice of law for matters and obligations not covered by the two instruments was determined by the common law choice-of-law rules. Initially, the UK did not participate in the adoption of Rome I,[9] but eventually decided to opt into it.[10] The UK participated in the adoption and application of Rome II.[11] The UK also decided to extend the application of the two Regulations (with the exception of insurance contracts) in the case of conflicts between the laws of different parts of the UK and between the laws of one or more parts of the UK and Gibraltar.[12]

In order to describe the context in which disputes concerning choice of law for contractual and non-contractual obligations have arisen before UK courts, the kinds of cases in which such disputes have arisen and their legal context will be presented first.

Rome I has been applied in the following circumstances:

- to determine the law applicable to the existence and validity of a contract for the sale of sugar to decide on a claim for a declaration that an arbitral tribunal had substantive jurisdiction over a dispute between the parties;[13]
- to a claim for injunctive relief and damages under a contract for the supply of condoms;[14]

9 Recital 45 of Rome I.

10 See Commission Decision 2009/26/EC of 22 December 2008 on the request from the United Kingdom to accept Regulation (EC) No. 593/2008 of the European Parliament and the Council on the law applicable to contractual obligations (Rome I) [2009] OJ L10/22.

11 Recital 39 of Rome II.

12 Law Applicable to Non-Contractual Obligations (England and Wales and Northern Ireland) Regulations (SI 2008/2986); Law Applicable to Non-Contractual Obligations (Scotland) Regulations (SSI 2008/404); Law Applicable to Contractual Obligations (England and Wales and Northern Ireland) Regulations (SI 2009/3064); Law Applicable to Contractual Obligations (Scotland) Regulations (SSI 2009/410). See also *Docherty v. Secretary of State for Business, Innovation and Skills* [2018] CSOH 25, 2018 SLT 349, reversed on a different point in [2018] CSIH 57, 2019 SC 50.

13 *Toyota Tsusho Sugar Trading Ltd v. Prolat Srl* [2014] EWHC 3649 (Comm), [2015] 1 Lloyd's Rep 344.

14 *SSL International Plc v. TTK LIG Ltd* [2011] EWCA Civ 1170, [2012] 1 WLR 1842.

- to a claim for a declaration of invalidity and unenforceability of an undertaking by deed to purchase certain assets upon the occurrence of certain events;[15]
- to a claim for damages under a contract for the sale of junk bonds;[16]
- to claims for payment under a contract for the sale of private placement notes;[17]
- to a claim for fraudulent misrepresentation and breach of contract in respect of a contract for the purchase of shares;[18]
- to a claim for recovery of sums paid to a third party under a contract of guarantee;[19]
- to determine the law applicable to a claim for a declaration of non-liability under a comfort letter concerning the financing of an airline;[20]
- to claims for breach of alleged contracts for the provision of services to refinance a company;[21]
- to a claim for damages for personal injuries suffered abroad during a travel package;[22]
- to a claim under a contract for organising an excursion for damages and other remedies for personal injuries suffered in a road accident abroad;[23]
- to a claim for the payment of sums due under a betting account contract;[24]
- to determine whether a claim under a warehouse receipt brought abroad was contractual in nature for the purposes of determining whether an exclusive English jurisdiction agreement had been breached and an anti-suit injunction should be granted;[25]
- to determine whether a party was the sole beneficiary or a joint promisee under a letter a credit for the purposes of deciding on the setting aside of an interim third party debt order;[26]

---

15 *Dana Gas PJSC v. Dana Gas Sukuk Ltd* [2017] EWHC 2928 (Comm), [2018] 1 Lloyd's Rep 177.

16 *Molton Street Capital LLP v. Shooters Hill Capital Partners LLP* [2015] EWHC 3419 (Comm).

17 *BNP Paribas SA v. Anchorage Capital Europe LLP* [2013] EWHC 3073 (Comm).

18 *Scott v. West* [2012] EWHC 1890 (Ch).

19 *European Union v. Syria* [2018] EWHC 1712 (Comm).

20 *Etihad Airways PJSC v. Flöther* [2019] EWHC 3107 (Comm), [2020] 2 WLR 333.

21 *Bazhanov v. Fosman* [2017] EWHC 3404 (Comm).

22 *Committeri v. Club Mediterranee SA* [2018] EWCA Civ 1889, [2019] ILPr 19.

23 *Brownlie v. Four Seasons Holdings Inc.* [2015] EWCA Civ 665, [2016] 1 WLR 1814, reversed in *Four Seasons Holdings Inc. v. Brownlie* [2017] UKSC 80, [2018] 1 WLR 192 without discussing choice of law under Rome I; *Brownlie v. Four Seasons Holdings Inc. (No 2)* [2019] EWHC 2533 (QB).

24 *Eurasia Sports Ltd v. Tsai* [2016] EWHC 2207 (QB), affirmed in [2018] EWCA Civ 1742, [2018] 1 WLR 6089 without discussing choice of law.

25 *Impala Warehousing and Logistics (Shanghai) Co. Ltd v. Wanxiang Resources (Singapore) PTE Ltd* [2015] EWHC 811 (Comm), [2015] 2 All ER (Comm) 234.

26 *Taurus Petroleum Ltd v. State Oil Marketing Co. of the Ministry of Oil, Iraq* [2015] EWCA Civ 835, [2016] 2 All ER (Comm) 1037, reversed in [2017] UKSC 64, [2018] AC 690 without discussing choice of law.

- to determine the situs of a debt for the purposes of deciding on the setting aside of an interim third party debt order;[27]
- to a claim on a guarantee ancillary to a contract of affreightment;[28]
- to determine whether a choice-of-law clause from a charterparty had been incorporated into bills of lading;[29]
- to determine the effect of incorporation into a bill of lading of the 'law and arbitration clause' of a charterparty, which clause provided, not for English law and arbitration, but for English law and court jurisdiction;[30]
- to a claim for damages related to a contract for the provision of brokerage services;[31]
- to a claim for the payment of commission for the provision of the service of introducing a purchaser to a broker which resulted in the sale of a luxury yacht;[32]
- to a claim for the payment of sums due under a settlement agreement concerning the provision of entertainment services;[33]
- to a claim for failure to pay the minimum wage and provide paid leave under an employment contract;[34]
- to a claim for unfair dismissal and a bonus payment under an employment contract;[35] and
- to determine the validity of the change of applicable law in the context of schemes of arrangement.[36]

There are also cases in which the provisions of Rome I have been either mentioned or discussed but not applied.

---

27 *Hardy Exploration and Production (India) Inc. v. India* [2018] EWHC 1916 (Comm), [2019] QB 544.

28 *Aquavita International SA v. Ashapura Minecham Ltd* [2014] EWHC 2806 (Comm); [2015] EWHC 2807 (QB).

29 *Seniority Shipping Corp SA v. City Seed Crushing Industries Ltd* [2019] EWHC 3541 (Comm).

30 *Caresse Navigation Ltd v. Office National de l'Electricité (Channel Ranger)* [2013] EWHC 3081 (Comm), [2014] 1 Lloyd's Rep 337, affirmed in [2014] EWCA Civ 1366, [2015] QB 366 without discussing choice of law.

31 *Pan Oceanic Chartering Inc. v. UNIPEC UK Co. Ltd* [2016] EWHC 2774 (Comm), [2017] 2 All ER (Comm) 196.

32 *Wrigley v. Wood* [2014] EWHC 3684 (Comm).

33 *Bill Kenwright Ltd v. Flash Entertainment FZ LLC* [2016] EWHC 1951 (QB).

34 *Aslam v. Uber BV* [2017] IRLR 4, ET, affirmed in [2018] ICR 453, EAT and [2018] EWCA Civ 2748, [2019] 3 All ER 489 without discussing choice of law.

35 *Olsen v. Gearbulk Services Ltd* [2015] IRLR 818, EAT.

36 *Re Syncreon Group BV* [2019] EWHC 2068 (Ch); *Re Far East Capital Ltd SA* [2017] EWHC 2878 (Ch); *In re APCOA Parking Holdings GmbH and others (No 2)* [2014] EWHC 3849 (Ch), [2015] 4 All ER 572.

Rome II has mostly been applied in road accident cases,[37] but has also been applied in the following circumstances:

- to other claims for damages for personal injuries suffered abroad;[38]
- to a claim for restitution in unjust enrichment arising from the end of a romantic relationship;[39]
- to a claim for damages and restitution following a fraud;[40]
- to a claim for damages for harassment;[41]
- to a claim for damages for diminishing the assets of a company with the purpose of preventing the claimant from satisfying an arbitration award;[42]
- to a claim against a co-worker for whistleblowing detriment;[43]
- to claims for damages for conspiracy, dishonest assistance, knowing receipt and bribery;[44]
- to claims concerning the infringement of unitary Community intellectual property rights;[45]

---

37 *Pandya v. Intersalonika General Insurance Co. SA* [2020] EWHC 273 (QB); *Brownlie v. Four Seasons Holdings Inc. (No 2)* [2019] EWHC 2533 (QB); *Folkes v. Generali Assurances* [2019] EWHC 801 (QB); *Gilmour v. Linea Directa Aseguradora Sa Compania De Seguros Y Reaseguros* 2017 GWD 39-603, Sheriff Court (Lothian and Borders) (Edinburgh); *Gunn v. Diaz* [2017] EWHC 157 (QB), [2017] 2 All ER (Comm) 129; *Moreno v. Motor Insurers' Bureau* [2016] UKSC 52, [2016] 1 WLR 3194; *Le Guevel-Mouly v. AIG Europe Ltd* [2016] EWHC 1794 (QB); *Syred v. Powszechny Zaklad Ubezpreczen (PZU) SA* [2016] EWHC 254 (QB), [2016] 1 WLR 3211; *XP v. Compensa Towarzystwo SA* [2016] EWHC 1728 (QB), [2016] Med LR 570; *Bianco v. Bennett* [2015] EWHC 626 (QB), [2015] ILPr 24; *Marshall v. Motor Insurers' Bureau* [2015] EWHC 3421 (QB), [2016] Lloyd's Rep IR 400, affirmed in *Pickard v. Marshall* [2017] EWCA Civ 17, [2017] RTR 20; *Vann v. Ocidental-Companhia De Seguros SA* [2015] EWCA Civ 572; *Wall v. Mutuelle de Poitiers Assurances* [2014] EWCA Civ 138, [2014] 1 WLR 4263; *Winrow v. Hemphill* [2014] EWHC 3164 (QB), [2015] ILPr 12; *Stylianou v. Toyoshima* [2013] EWHC 2188 (QB); *Wink v. Croatia Osiguranje DD* [2013] EWHC 1118 (QB); *Bacon v. Nacional Suiza Cia Seguros y Reseguros SA* [2010] EWHC 2017 (QB), [2010] ILPr 46; *Bonsall v. Cattolica Assicurazioni* [2010] ILPr 45, County Court (Winchester).

38 *Vilca v. Xstrata Ltd* [2018] EWHC 27 (QB); *His Royal Highness Okpabi v. Royal Dutch Shell Plc* [2017] EWHC 89 (TCC), [2017] Bus LR 1335, affirmed in [2018] EWCA Civ 191, [2018] Bus LR 1022 without discussing choice of law under Rome II; *Committeri v. Club Mediterranee SA* [2016] EWHC 1510 (QB), affirmed in [2018] EWCA Civ 1889, [2019] ILPr 19 without discussing choice of law under Rome II; *Rai v. Ministry of Defence*, Queen's Bench Division, 9 May 2016.

39 *Gray v. Hurley* [2019] EWHC 1636 (QB).

40 *ED&F Man Capital Markets Ltd v. Come Harvest Holdings Ltd* [2019] EWHC 1661 (Comm), [2019] ILPr 40.

41 *BVC v. EWF* [2019] EWHC 2506 (QB).

42 *KMG International NV v. Chen* [2019] EWHC 2389 (Comm), [2020] Bus LR 133.

43 *Foreign and Commonwealth Office v. Bamieh* [2019] EWCA Civ 803, [2019] IRLR 736.

44 *FM Capital Partners Ltd v. Marino* [2018] EWHC 1768 (Comm), affirmed in [2020] EWCA Civ 245 without discussing choice of law.

45 *W3 Ltd v. Easygroup Ltd* [2018] EWHC 7 (Ch), [2018] FSR 16; *Eli Lilly and Co. v. Genentech Inc.* [2017] EWHC 3104 (Pat), [2018] 1 WLR 1755; *Parainen Pearl Shipping Ltd v. Kristian Gerhard Jebsen Skipsrederi AS* [2017] EWHC 2570 (Pat).

- to a claim for conspiracy to injure by using a Twitter account to make allegations of bribery and corruption against the claimant and to disclose confidential information;[46]
- to claims for damages for breach of competition law brought by retailers for overpaying merchant service charges under the MasterCard payment scheme;[47]
- to a claim for damages for a conspiracy to defraud;[48]
- to a claim for restitution in unjust enrichment concerning non-existent contracts for the provision of services to refinance a company;[49]
- to a claim for damages for tortious interference with contractual relations;[50]
- to a claim for damages for the torts of fraudulent misrepresentation and conspiracy to injure by opening and debiting betting accounts;[51]
- to a claim for damages and interest founded on non-contractual liability of the defendant majority beneficial owner of the claimant who acted dishonestly and in breach of duties owed to the claimant;[52]
- to claims for damages in the tort of deceit and restitution in unjust enrichment arising out of a fraud;[53]
- to a claim for damages for unlawful means conspiracy and unlawful interference with economic interests and contractual relations;[54]
- to determine whether a claim under a warehouse receipt brought abroad was contractual in nature for the purposes of determining whether an exclusive English jurisdiction agreement had been breached and an anti-suit injunction should be granted;[55]
- to issues concerning public policy in a claim for contribution at the behest of the fraudster against the victim;[56]
- to an application for an interim injunction to restrain the publication of a book pending trial;[57]

---

46 *MX1 Ltd v. Farahzad* [2018] EWHC 1041 (Ch), [2018] 1 WLR 5553.

47 *Deutsche Bahn AG v. Mastercard Inc.* [2018] EWHC 412 (Ch), [2018] 4 CMLR 31.

48 *Angola v. Perfectbit Ltd* [2018] EWHC 965 (Comm), [2018] Lloyd's Rep FC 363.

49 *Bazhanov v. Fosman* [2017] EWHC 3404 (Comm).

50 *Pan Oceanic Chartering Inc. v. UNIPEC UK Co. Ltd* [2016] EWHC 2774 (Comm), [2017] 2 All ER (Comm) 196.

51 *Eurasia Sports Ltd v. Tsai* [2016] EWHC 2207 (QB), affirmed in [2018] EWCA Civ 1742, [2018] 1 WLR 6089 without discussing choice of law.

52 *AS Latvijas Krajbanka (In Liquidation) v. Antonov* [2016] EWHC 1679 (Comm).

53 *Banque Cantonale de Geneve v. Polevent Ltd* [2015] EWHC 1968 (Comm), [2016] QB 394.

54 *Erste Group Bank AG (London) v. JSC (VMZ Red October)* [2015] EWCA Civ 379, [2015] 1 CLC 706.

55 *Impala Warehousing and Logistics (Shanghai) Co. Ltd v. Wanxiang Resources (Singapore) PTE Ltd* [2015] EWHC 811 (Comm), [2015] 2 All ER (Comm) 234.

56 *Group Seven Ltd v. Allied Investment Corp Ltd* [2014] EWHC 2046 (Ch), affirmed in [2015] EWCA Civ 631 without discussing choice of law.

57 *OPO v. MLA* [2014] EWCA Civ 1277, [2015] EMLR 4, reversed in [2015] UKSC 32, [2016] AC 219 without discussing choice of law.

- to a claim for damages for the torts of conspiracy, unlawful interference, procuring breach of contract and dishonest assistance in relation to a complex investment;[58]
- to a claim for an interim injunction restraining a former employee from disclosing confidential information;[59]
- to a claim for injunctions restraining a party from breaching confidence in a patent dispute;[60]
- to a claim for a declaration of non-liability concerning the claimant's alleged negligence for the defendant's online betting losses;[61] and
- to a claim for damages for fraudulent misrepresentation inducing the claimant to enter a contract (ISDA master agreement).[62]

There are also cases in which the provisions of Rome II have been either mentioned or discussed but not applied.

UK judgments on the application of the Rome I and Rome II Regulations offer a wealth of empirical evidence on the operation of these two instruments. This evidence can be used to test two hypotheses that have been advanced in academic literature, which should help us to better understand the practical operation of the two Regulations before UK courts.

The first hypothesis is succinctly explained by McLachlan:

> 'Intuitively, one might have expected that the process of globalisation would have led to a welter of cases on that central concern of the conflict of laws, namely choice of law. In fact, the reverse has been true. There has been only a trickle of cases reported over the last 25 years in the English law reports on choice of law issues. By contrast, there have been a myriad of reported decisions on every aspect of the *process* of litigation, and in particular on jurisdiction. ...
>
> The internationalisation of the litigation process itself has wrought a revolution – or at least a major re-orientation – in the preoccupations of private international law of far greater significance in practice than anything achieved by the work of scholars in the so-called American Revolution in the conflict of laws.'[63]

While it is beyond the scope of this chapter to compare in detail the cases on choice of law and on the process of litigation, it is nevertheless possible to test

58 *Fortress Value Recovery Fund I LLC v. Blue Skye Special Opportunities Fund LP* [2013] EWHC 14 (Comm), [2013] 1 All ER (Comm) 973.

59 *OJSC TNK-BP Holding v. Lazurenko* [2012] EWHC 2781 (Ch).

60 *Innovia Films Ltd v. Frito-Lay North America Inc.* [2012] EWHC 790 (Pat), [2012] RPC 24.

61 *Hillside (New Media) Ltd v. Baasland* [2010] EWHC 3336 (Comm), [2010] 2 CLC 986.

62 *Morgan Stanley & Co. International Plc v. China Haisheng Juice Holdings Co. Ltd* [2009] EWHC 2409 (Comm), [2010] 2 All ER (Comm) 514.

63 C. McLachlan, 'International Litigation and the Reworking of the Conflict of Laws' (2004) 120 LQR 580, 581, with reference to P. North, 'Private International Law: Change or Decay?' (2001) 50 ICLQ 477, 500. See also McLachlan, ibid, 600–607.

this hypothesis by looking at the legal context in which choice-of-law disputes arise under the Rome I and Rome II Regulations. Out of the 26 cases in which Rome I was applied, choice of law was relevant for the process of litigation, not for deciding the case on the substance, in 17 cases or 65 per cent. Most of these 'procedural' choice-of-law cases concerned service out of the jurisdiction and/or the *forum (non) conveniens* doctrine.[64] Other cases concerned the application of Article 25 of the Brussels I Regulation,[65] an application for an anti-suit injunction,[66] an application for summary judgment,[67] an application under section 32 of the Arbitration Act 1996 seeking the court's determination of questions relating to the jurisdiction of an arbitral tribunal,[68] and an interim third-party debt order.[69] Out of the 48 cases applying Rome II, choice of law was relevant for the process of litigation in 25 cases or 52 per cent. Procedural contexts included: service out and/or *forum (non) conveniens*,[70] an application for

---

64 *Bazhanov v. Fosman* [2017] EWHC 3404 (Comm); *Bill Kenwright Ltd v. Flash Entertainment FZ LLC* [2016] EWHC 1951 (QB); *Eurasia Sports Ltd v. Tsai* [2016] EWHC 2207 (QB), affirmed in [2018] EWCA Civ 1742, [2018] 1 WLR 6089 without discussing choice of law; *Brownlie v. Four Seasons Holdings Inc.* [2015] EWCA Civ 665, [2016] 1 WLR 1814, reversed in *Four Seasons Holdings Inc. v. Brownlie* [2017] UKSC 80, [2018] 1 WLR 192 without discussing choice of law under Rome I; *Aquavita International SA v. Ashapura Minecham Ltd* [2014] EWHC 2806 (Comm) (this judgment was affirmed at trial in which the defendant did not participate [2015] EWHC 2807 (QB)); *Wrigley v. Wood* [2014] EWHC 3684 (Comm); *BNP Paribas SA v. Anchorage Capital Europe LLP* [2013] EWHC 3073 (Comm); *Caresse Navigation Ltd v. Office National de l'Electricité (Channel Ranger)* [2013] EWHC 3081 (Comm), [2014] 1 Lloyd's Rep 337, affirmed in [2014] EWCA Civ 1366, [2015] QB 366 without discussing choice of law; *Scott v. West* [2012] EWHC 1890 (Ch); *SSL International Plc v. TTK LIG Ltd* [2011] EWCA Civ 1170, [2012] 1 WLR 1842.

65 Regulation (EC) No. 1215/2012 of the European Parliament and of the Council on jurisdiction and the recognition and enforcement of judgments in civil and commercial matters (recast) [2012] OJ L351/1, superseding Council Regulation (EC) No. 44/2001 of 22 December 2000 on jurisdiction and the recognition and enforcement of judgments in civil and commercial matters [2001] OJ L12/1; *Etihad Airways PJSC v. Flöther* [2019] EWHC 3107 (Comm), [2020] 2 WLR 333.

66 *Seniority Shipping Corp SA v. City Seed Crushing Industries Ltd* [2019] EWHC 3541 (Comm); *Impala Warehousing and Logistics (Shanghai) Co. Ltd v. Wanxiang Resources (Singapore) PTE Ltd* [2015] EWHC 811 (Comm), [2015] 2 All ER (Comm) 234.

67 *European Union v. Syria* [2018] EWHC 1712 (Comm).

68 *Toyota Tsusho Sugar Trading Ltd v. Prolat Srl* [2014] EWHC 3649 (Comm), [2015] 1 Lloyd's Rep 344.

69 *Hardy Exploration and Production (India) Inc. v. India* [2018] EWHC 1916 (Comm), [2019] QB 544; *Taurus Petroleum Ltd v. State Oil Marketing Co. of the Ministry of Oil, Iraq* [2015] EWCA Civ 835, [2016] 2 All ER (Comm) 1037, reversed in [2017] UKSC 64, [2018] AC 690 without discussing choice of law.

70 *Brownlie v. Four Seasons Holdings Inc. (No 2)* [2019] EWHC 2533 (QB); *ED&F Man Capital Markets Ltd v. Come Harvest Holdings Ltd* [2019] EWHC 1661 (Comm), [2019] ILPr 40; *Gray v. Hurley* [2019] EWHC 1636 (QB); *Angola v. Perfectbit Ltd* [2018] EWHC 965 (Comm), [2018] Lloyd's Rep FC 363; *Bazhanov v. Fosman* [2017] EWHC 3404 (Comm); *Eli Lilly and Co. v. Genentech Inc.* [2017] EWHC 3104 (Pat), [2018] 1 WLR 1755; *Gunn v. Diaz* [2017] EWHC 157 (QB), [2017] 2 All ER (Comm) 129; *His Royal Highness Okpabi v. Royal Dutch Shell Plc* [2017] EWHC 89 (TCC), [2017] Bus LR 1335, affirmed in [2018] EWCA Civ 191,

an anti-suit injunction,[71] the way in which expert evidence was to be adduced,[72] an application to strike out a statement of case/for summary judgment,[73] and an application for an interim injunction.[74] There are two possible explanations for the fact that cases applying Rome II concern the process of litigation less frequently than cases applying Rome I. The first is that many cases falling into the former category involve road accidents, which usually raise issues of liability and quantum, typically between insurers. The second lies in the fact that one of the most popular jurisdictional 'gateways' under traditional English law is that the contract is governed by English law.[75] Overall, out of the 69 cases applying the two Regulations, choice of law was relevant for the process of litigation, not for deciding the case on the substance, in 39 cases, or 57 per cent.[76] This indicates not only that the number of cases on choice of law under the two Regulations is more than a 'trickle', but also that the majority of choice-of-law cases in fact concern procedure in which choice-of-law issues often arise in an incidental or accidental manner.

The legal context in which a choice-of-law dispute arises is important because it can affect the choice-of-law process. For example: in service out cases the claimant must show a reasonable prospect of success on the merits, which

[2018] Bus LR 1022 without discussing choice of law under Rome II; *Eurasia Sports Ltd v. Tsai* [2016] EWHC 2207 (QB), affirmed in [2018] EWCA Civ 1742, [2018] 1 WLR 6089 without discussing choice of law; *Le Guevel-Mouly v. AIG Europe Ltd* [2016] EWHC 1794 (QB); *Erste Group Bank AG (London) v. JSC (VMZ Red October)* [2015] EWCA Civ 379, [2015] 1 CLC 706; *Stylianou v. Toyoshima* [2013] EWHC 2188 (QB); *Wink v. Croatia Osiguranje DD* [2013] EWHC 1118 (QB); *Innovia Films Ltd v. Frito-Lay North America Inc.* [2012] EWHC 790 (Pat), [2012] RPC 24. Similarly, *Parainen Pearl Shipping Ltd v. Kristian Gerhard Jebsen Skipsrederi AS* [2017] EWHC 2570 (Pat) (jurisdiction under the Lugano Convention).

71 *Impala Warehousing and Logistics (Shanghai) Co. Ltd v. Wanxiang Resources (Singapore) PTE Ltd* [2015] EWHC 811 (Comm), [2015] 2 All ER (Comm) 234; *Morgan Stanley & Co. International Plc v. China Haisheng Juice Holdings Co. Ltd* [2009] EWHC 2409 (Comm), [2010] 2 All ER (Comm) 514.

72 *Wall v. Mutuelle de Poitiers Assurances* [2014] EWCA Civ 138, [2014] 1 WLR 4263.

73 *BVC v. EWF* [2019] EWHC 2506 (QB); *KMG International NV v. Chen* [2019] EWHC 2389 (Comm), [2020] Bus LR 133; *MX1 Ltd v. Farahzad* [2018] EWHC 1041 (Ch), [2018] 1 WLR 5553; *Fortress Value Recovery Fund I LLC v. Blue Skye Special Opportunities Fund LP* [2013] EWHC 14 (Comm), [2013] 1 All ER (Comm) 973; *Hillside (New Media) Ltd v. Baasland* [2010] EWHC 3336 (Comm), [2010] 2 CLC 986.

74 *OPO v. MLA* [2014] EWCA Civ 1277, [2015] EMLR 4, reversed [2015] UKSC 32, [2016] AC 219; *OJSC TNK-BP Holding v. Lazurenko* [2012] EWHC 2781 (Ch).

75 Civil Procedure Rules Practice Direction 6B, paragraph 3.1(6)(c).

76 This chapter lists 26 cases as applying Rome I and 48 cases as applying Rome II, but 'only' 69 cases as applying the two Regulations. This is because some cases applied both Rome I and Rome II and are therefore counted within both the 26 cases applying Rome I and the 48 cases applying Rome II. Similarly, this chapter lists 17 cases applying Rome I and 25 cases applying Rome II where choice of law was relevant for the process of litigation, not for deciding the case on the substance. But because some cases applied both Rome I and Rome II, the total number of cases applying either Regulation or both of them and where choice of law was relevant for the process of litigation is 39.

may include showing a reasonable prospect of success on a legal issue under the applicable law; the applicable standard of proof in service out cases and under the *forum (non) conveniens* doctrine is not the balance of probabilities, but the standard of a good arguable case; in an application to strike out a statement of case, one of the relevant issues is whether the statement of case discloses reasonable grounds for bringing or defending the claim under the governing law; in an application for summary judgment, one of the relevant issues is whether the claim or defence has a real prospect of success under the governing law; one of the requirements for obtaining an interim injunction is that there is a serious issue to be tried under the governing law. This is why the issue of applicable law in 'procedural' choice-of-law cases does not necessarily receive the same amount of scrutiny as at trial, where the applicable standard of proof is the balance of probabilities and the reasonable prospect of success test or its variant is not used, and why such cases should be read and used cautiously.[77]

The second hypothesis that can be tested is that the application of the Regulations is influenced not only by the legal context but also by the need to balance multiple policy issues generated by international commercial litigation. This hypothesis has been advanced by Penadés Fons,[78] who has demonstrated, in a study on implied choice and the application of the escape clauses of the Rome Convention and the Rome I Regulation by UK courts, that the judges support the national policy to promote England as a centre for commercial dispute resolution and to export English law in certain 'strategic industries', namely the shipping, banking and finance, and insurance sectors. It is justified to use this chapter to test this hypothesis for two reasons. Firstly, because the present chapter deals with both the Rome I and Rome II Regulations, whereas the mentioned study focused only on choice of law for contractual obligations. This is potentially important because disputes concerning 'strategic industries' give rise to choice-of-law issues concerning both contractual and non-contractual obligations. Secondly, because, with respect to choice of law for contractual obligations, the present chapter focuses on the 26 cases applying Rome I, whereas the mentioned study covered cases up to and including 1 April 2014 and was therefore able to include only three cases applying Rome I.[79] This is potentially important because the provisions of Rome I, at least in theory, should leave less room than the provisions of the Rome Convention for judicial discretion and,

77 See McLachlan (n. 63) 601; M. Penadés Fons, 'Commercial Choice of Law in Context: Looking Beyond Rome' (2015) 78 MLR 241; P. Rogerson, 'Problems of the Applicable Law of the Contract in the English Common Law Jurisdiction Rules: The Good Arguable Case' (2013) 9 JPIL 387.

78 Penadés Fons (n. 77).

79 These are the High Court judgment in *Brownlie v. Four Seasons Holdings Inc.* [2014] EWHC 273 (QB) (this case eventually went to the Supreme Court); *BNP Paribas SA v. Anchorage Capital Europe LLP* [2013] EWHC 3073 (Comm); *Scott v. West* [2012] EWHC 1890 (Ch). Importantly, Penadés Fons predicted the continuation of the English practice under Rome I.

therefore, for policy-influenced judgments. This second hypothesis will be tested in the following section after the examination of the way UK courts have dealt with party autonomy, including implied choice of law, and the determination of the applicable law in the absence of party autonomy.

3. ISSUES COMMON TO BOTH REGULATIONS

There are certain issues that are common to both Regulations, including: interpretation; temporal and subject-matter scope; party autonomy; application of escape clauses; legal certainty versus flexibility dilemma; overriding mandatory provisions; public policy; scope of applicable law, including the substance versus procedure dichotomy; pleading and proof of foreign law; habitual residence; and *renvoi*.

3.1. INTERPRETATION

A fundamental principle of interpretation of the two Regulations is that of autonomous European interpretation. This principle has been applied faithfully by UK courts.

For example, in *Committeri v. Club Mediterranee SA*[80] the question was whether a claim for damages for personal injuries suffered abroad during a package travel was based on the breach of a contractual or non-contractual obligation. The claimant's employer had made a contract with the defendant for the provision of travel and accommodation services for the claimant in France. The claimant injured his leg during a team-building exercise. The contract contained a clause providing that the booking conditions were governed by English law. The claimant, as a beneficiary under the contract, brought a claim against the defendant under French law, namely the *Code de tourisme*, which implemented Directive 90/314[81] into French law. The defendant disputed the application of French law on the basis that the obligation on which the claim was based was contractual in nature and that English law applied pursuant to the choice-of-law clause contained in the contract. The choice-of-law issue was crucial because liability under French law was strict, whereas English law required a breach of reasonable skill and care and the parties were in agreement that the defendant's conduct was not careless. The court found that under both European case law and the domestic laws of England and France the obligation that formed the basis of the claim was to be regarded as contractual.

80 [2018] EWCA Civ 1889, [2019] ILPr 19.

81 Council Directive 90/314/EEC on package travel, package holidays and package tours [1990] OJ L158/59.

One notable exception where the courts initially failed to give an autonomous interpretation to the Rome II Regulation was cases for compensation under the Motor Vehicles (Compulsory Insurance) (Information Centre and Compensation Body) Regulations 2003.[82] The Supreme Court has recently overturned these cases and given a correct interpretation, in line with the principle of autonomous European interpretation, to the relevant provisions of Rome II, as well as to Directive 2009/103/EC and the Directives which it superseded.[83] It is also worth mentioning in this respect that not all the judges have adopted the terminology of the two Regulations. One can thus still find references in judgments to the old common law term 'proper law' of the contract, issue or tort.[84]

UK courts have also frequently referred to cases decided under other European private international law instruments, such as the Rome Convention and the Brussels I Regulation, thus interpreting the provisions of the Rome I and Rome II Regulations in a systemic manner. There are some cases, however, in which the principle of systematic interpretation has been cautiously applied.[85]

---

82 SI 2003/37, implementing a series of Council Directives, which were subsequently superseded by the codifying Directive 2009/103/EC of the European Parliament and of the Council relating to insurance against civil liability in respect of the use of motor vehicles, and the enforcement of the obligation to insure against such liability [2009] OJ L263/11.

83 *Moreno v. Motor Insurers' Bureau* [2016] UKSC 52, [2016] 1 WLR 3194. Discussed below in sub-section 3.8.

84 See *KMG International NV v. Chen* [2019] EWHC 2389 (Comm), [2020] Bus LR 133 at [41], [50]; *Four Seasons Holdings Inc. v. Brownlie* [2017] UKSC 80, [2018] 1 WLR 192 at [18], [22]; *The Law Debenture Trust Corp Plc v. Ukraine* [2017] EWHC 655 (Comm), [2017] QB 1249 at [71], [75], [170], [175]; *Eurasia Sports Ltd v. Tsai* [2016] EWHC 2207 (QB) at [59], [60], affirmed in [2018] EWCA Civ 1742, [2018] 1 WLR 6089 without discussing choice of law; *Brownlie v. Four Seasons Holdings Inc.* [2015] EWCA Civ 665, [2016] 1 WLR 1814 at [38]; *Molton Street Capital LLP v. Shooters Hill Capital Partners LLP* [2015] EWHC 3419 (Comm) at [11], [81], [83], [91] et seq.; *Taurus Petroleum Ltd v. State Oil Marketing Co. of the Ministry of Oil, Iraq* [2015] EWCA Civ 835, [2016] 2 All ER (Comm) 1037 at [35]; *Integral Petroleum SA v. SCU-Finanz AG* [2014] EWHC 702 (Comm) at [61]; *OPO v. MLA* [2014] EWCA Civ 1277, [2015] EMLR 4 at [95], [97], [110]; *Toyota Tsusho Sugar Trading Ltd v. Prolat Srl* [2014] EWHC 3649 (Comm), [2015] 1 Lloyd's Rep 344 at [14]; *Winrow v. Hemphill* [2014] EWHC 3164 (QB), [2015] ILPr 12 at [43]; *Caresse Navigation Ltd v. Office National de l'Electricité (Channel Ranger)* [2013] EWHC 3081 (Comm), [2014] 1 Lloyd's Rep 337 at [34]; *SSL International Plc v. TTK LIG Ltd* [2011] EWCA Civ 1170, [2012] 1 WLR 1842 at [82]; *Hillside (New Media) Ltd v. Baasland* [2010] EWHC 3336 (Comm), [2010] 2 CLC 986 at [46].

85 *FM Capital Partners Ltd v. Marino* [2018] EWHC 1768 (Comm) at [485], [486], affirmed in [2020] EWCA Civ 245 without discussing choice of law (the case law under Article 7(2) of the Brussels I Regulation is 'likely to be useful' under the Rome II Regulation, referring to *Erste Group Bank AG (London) v. JSC (VMZ Red October)* [2015] EWCA Civ 379, [2015] 1 CLC 706 at [90], [91] and *Fortress Value Recovery Fund I LLC v. Blue Skye Special Opportunities Fund LP* [2013] EWHC 14 (Comm), [2013] 1 All ER (Comm) 973 at [44]). See also *Kennedy v. National Trust for Scotland* [2019] EWCA Civ 648, [2020] 2 WLR 275 at [55] (the meaning of 'elements' in 'international elements' for the purposes of determining the international scope of the Brussels I Regulation does not have the same meaning as 'elements' for the purposes of Article 3(3) of Rome I).

3.2. TEMPORAL AND SUBJECT-MATTER SCOPE

The two Regulations are of universal application,[86] in the sense that any law specified as applicable by the Regulations is applied regardless of whether it is the law of a Member State of the EU or of a non-EU state. However, in order for the choice-of-law rules of the two Regulations to apply, the matter must fall within their temporal and subject-matter scope.

The temporal scope of Rome I has not caused problems in practice. This is because Rome I uses a relatively simple criterion for determining its application in time that is based on the date of conclusion of the contract – it applies to contracts concluded after 17 December 2009.[87]

The same cannot be said about the temporal scope of Rome II. That Regulation provides in Article 31 ('Application in time') that it shall apply to events giving rise to damage which occur after its entry into force (which was on 20 August 2007) and in Article 32 ('Date of application') that it shall apply from 11 January 2009, except for Article 29 concerning certain notification duties of the Member States, which shall apply from 11 July 2008. These articles initially caused a considerable degree of legal uncertainty.[88] But the CJEU judgment in *Homawoo*,[89] which was given on a reference for a preliminary ruling from the High Court of England and Wales,[90] put the matter to rest. The CJEU held that Rome II applies 'to events giving rise to damage occurring after 11 January 2009 and that the date on which the proceedings seeking compensation for damage were brought or the date on which the applicable law was determined by the court seised have no bearing on determining the scope *ratione temporis*'. The *Homawoo* rule was interpreted in three subsequent cases. In *Docherty v. Secretary of State for Business, Innovation and Skills*,[91] the court dealt with an industrial illness case where the relatives of a deceased person brought a claim for damages against that person's previous employers who allegedly negligently exposed him to asbestos which caused the development of plural plaques and death. One feature of asbestos cases is that the causal event (the inhalation of asbestos fibres) typically takes place many years, even decades, before the development of symptoms of illness. The court held that the reference to 'events giving rise to damage' is linked to the distinction drawn in Article 4(1) of Rome II between

---

86 Article 2 of Rome I; Article 3 of Rome II.

87 Articles 28 and 29(2) of Rome I.

88 See in particular *Bacon v. Nacional Suiza Cia Seguros y Reseguros SA* [2010] EWHC 2017 (QB), [2010] ILPr 46 at [37]–[66]; *Bonsall v. Cattolica Assicurazioni* [2010] ILPr 45, County Court (Winchester); *Hillside (New Media) Ltd v. Baasland* [2010] EWHC 3336 (Comm), [2010] 2 CLC 986 at [23]–[25].

89 Case C-412/10 *Deo Antoine Homawoo v. GMF Assurances SA*, ECLI:EU:C:2011:747, [2012] ILPr 2.

90 *Homawoo v. GMF Assurance SA* [2010] EWHC 1941 (QB), [2011] ILPr 12.

91 [2018] CSOH 25, 2018 SLT 349, reversed on a different point in [2018] CSIH 57, 2019 SC 50.

three separate concepts: (i) the event giving rise to the damage; (ii) the damage; and (iii) the indirect consequences of the event. It held that the relevant event in the present case was the allegedly negligent exposure to asbestos which occurred long before 11 January 2009.[92] In *Allen v. Depuy International Ltd*,[93] a product (hip implants) liability case, the court held that the date of the 'events giving rise to damage' was the date of manufacture or distribution of the defective product or, if that was wrong, the date of implantation.[94] In *Alliance Bank JSC v. Aquanta Corp*,[95] the court pointed out that the wording 'events giving rise to damage occurring after 11 January 2009', as interpreted by the CJEU in *Homawoo*, was ambiguous as it could refer both to 'the date when the damage is caused' and 'the date of the event which subsequently, possibly years later, caused the damage'.[96] The court, nevertheless, expressed its preference for the former interpretation on the basis that Article 4(1) and (2) of Rome II refers to the law of the country in which and the time when the damage occurs,[97] but proceeded with the analysis of both the choice-of-law rules of Rome II and Part III of the Private International Law (Miscellaneous Provisions) Act 1995.[98]

With regard to the subject-matter scope of the two Regulations, they apply to 'civil and commercial matters',[99] although there are some undoubtedly civil and commercial matters which are excluded from the scope of the two instruments.[100] Furthermore, Rome I applies to contractual obligations,[101] whereas Rome II applies to non-contractual obligations.[102] Both Regulations apply if there is a situation involving a conflict of laws.[103]

The interpretation of the term 'civil and commercial matters' was one of the main issues in *Rai v. Ministry of Defence*.[104] The claimant was a soldier in the British Army. While stationed in Canada, he was undergoing a training exercise in horse management provided by a private company. A horse kicked him, causing him personal injuries. The court held that the claim did not relate to the 'liability of the State for acts and omissions in the exercise of State authority',

---

92 Ibid at [14], [15].

93 [2014] EWHC 753 (QB), [2015] 2 WLR 442.

94 Ibid at [14].

95 [2011] EWHC 3281 (Comm), [2012] 1 Lloyd's Rep 181, affirmed in [2012] EWCA Civ 1588, [2013] 1 All ER (Comm) 819 without discussing this point.

96 [2011] EWHC 3281 (Comm), [2012] 1 Lloyd's Rep 181 at [37].

97 Ibid at [38].

98 It is also worth noting that both the High Court and the Court of Appeal held that not even a provisional view could be reached on the law governing the tort without a full understanding of the facts.

99 Article 1(1) of Rome I; Article 1(1) of Rome II.

100 Article 1(2) of Rome I; Article 1(2) of Rome II.

101 Article 1(1) of Rome I.

102 Articles 1(1) and 2 of Rome II.

103 Articles 1(1) of Rome I; Article 1(1) of Rome II.

104 Queen's Bench Division, 9 May 2016 at [43]–[89].

since the basis of the claim did not arise out of some positive exercise or projection of a power that was peculiar to the state. Importantly, such type of training could have been undertaken within the private sector.

The application of the exclusions,[105] with the exception of the exclusion for evidence and procedure,[106] has not been problematic. Evidence and procedure will be addressed below in sub-section 3.8 concerning the scope of applicable law.

The fault line between contractual and non-contractual obligations was considered in *Committeri v. Club Mediterranee SA*,[107] presented in the preceding sub-section. The courts were faced with the problem of classification in two other cases. *Impala Warehousing and Logistics (Shanghai) Co. Ltd v. Wanxiang Resources (Singapore) PTE Ltd*[108] concerned an application for an anti-suit injunction. The relevant question was whether a claim under a warehouse receipt brought in the Shanghai courts was contractual in nature for the purposes of determining whether an exclusive English jurisdiction clause contained in the receipt had been breached. If so, there would be a basis for granting an anti-suit injunction. To answer this question, the court applied the provisions on the subject-matter scope of the Rome I and Rome II Regulations. It gave an autonomous interpretation to those provisions and held that the claim, which was based on an obligation under a warehouse receipt, was contractual and therefore covered by the jurisdiction clause. In *Pan Oceanic Chartering Inc. v. UNIPEC UK Co. Ltd*[109] the court dealt with the issue of relevance of the domestic law under which the claim is pleaded for the classification of the defendant's obligation. A ship chartering broker brought a claim for damages against the charterers of a vessel for breach of an 'implied in law' promise under the law of

---

105 See *Enka Insaat ve Sanayi AS v. OOO 'Insurance Co. Chubb'* [2019] EWHC 3568 (Comm) at [9] (arbitration exclusion in Article 1(2)(e) of Rome I); *European Film Bonds A/S v. Lotus Holdings LLC* [2019] EWHC 2116 (Ch) at [142] (arbitration exclusion in Article 1(2)(e) of Rome I); *AS Latvijas Krajbanka (In Liquidation) v. Antonov* [2016] EWHC 1679 (Comm) at [8] (company law exclusion in Article 1(2)(d) of Rome II); *Integral Petroleum SA v. SCU-Finanz AG* [2015] EWCA Civ 144, [2016] 1 All ER (Comm) 217 at [39]–[47] (company law exclusions in Article 1(2)(f) and (g) of Rome I); *Mauritius Commercial Bank Ltd v. Hestia Holdings Ltd* [2013] EWHC 1328 (Comm), [2013] 2 All ER (Comm) 898 at [15] (choice-of-court agreement exclusion in Article 1(2)(e) of Rome I); *Subotic v. Knezevic* [2013] EWHC 3011 (QB) at [51] (defamation exclusion in Article 1(2)(g) of Rome II); *Arsanovia Ltd v. Cruz City 1 Mauritius Holdings* [2012] EWHC 3702 (Comm), [2013] 2 All ER (Comm) 1 at [8] (arbitration exclusion in Article 1(2)(e) of Rome I). See also *BVC v. EWF* [2019] EWHC 2506 (QB) at [189] (the exclusion for claims arising from violations of privacy and rights relating to personality, including defamation in Article 1(2)(g) of Rome II does not apply to a claim for harassment); *Re Far East Capital Ltd SA* [2017] EWHC 2878 (Ch) at [39], [40] (company law exclusion in Article 1(2)(f) of Rome I does not apply to schemes of arrangement).

106 Article 1(3) of Rome I; Article 1(3) of Rome II.

107 [2018] EWCA Civ 1889, [2019] ILPr 19.

108 [2015] EWHC 811 (Comm), [2015] 2 All ER (Comm) 234 at [62], [74]–[75], [81].

109 [2016] EWHC 2774 (Comm), [2017] 2 All ER (Comm) 196 at [150]–[161], [173]–[181].

New Jersey not to do anything improper or unjustified that would deprive the broker of their commission. At the stage of determining whether the defendant's obligation is contractual or non-contractual for the purposes of determining the scope of the Rome I and Rome II Regulations, the law governing the relationship between the parties is unknown. It may be the law under which the claim is pleaded (e.g. New Jersey law), but it may well be another law (e.g. English law). The law governing the relationship between the parties will only be discovered after the defendant's obligation is classified and the relevant choice-of-law rules are applied. The court confirmed that determining the nature of an obligation was an autonomous exercise, to be conducted without regard to the *lex fori* or the *lex causae*. Nevertheless, the court had to look at the facts which, if made out, would give rise to an implied in law promise, and those facts could not be identified without an understanding of what the law under which the claim was pleaded (i.e. New Jersey law) required. The relevant facts were the provision of services by the broker, the buyer's knowledge of the mechanism by which the broker would be paid commission by the seller, and the entry into a contract for sale. Since the parties directly accepted the broker's services and negotiated and entered the contract in the knowledge of the brokerage commission arrangement, the implied in law promise was a contractual obligation for the purpose of Rome I. In other words, the court took into account the domestic law under which the claim was pleaded (i.e. New Jersey law) to ascertain the relevant facts. The relevant facts clearly indicated that the alleged obligation of the defendant was contractual and Rome I was applied. Under Rome I, the applicable law was English. Because the implied in law claim arose under the domestic law under which the claim was pleaded (i.e. New Jersey law), but not under the applicable English law, it fell away and the claim was dismissed.

3.3. PARTY AUTONOMY

Party autonomy is a cornerstone of the Rome I Regulation[110] and an important principle under Rome II.[111] Article 3 of Rome I, as well as Article 3 of its predecessor, the Rome Convention, have been frequently invoked by UK courts. The same cannot be said of Article 14 of Rome II, which has been considered in only three cases and applied in none.[112]

---

110 Recital 11 of Rome I.

111 Recital 31 of Rome II.

112 *Bazhanov v. Fosman* [2017] EWHC 3404 (Comm) at [71]–[73] (no choice of law for non-contractual obligations was expressed and no circumstances were relied on to support an implied choice beyond the mere fact of an alleged express agreement as to the contractual governing law and jurisdiction); *Pan Oceanic Chartering Inc. v. UNIPEC UK Co. Ltd* [2016] EWHC 2774 (Comm), [2017] 2 All ER (Comm) 196 at [185]–[192] (no choice of law to govern a tort because of choice-of-law or jurisdiction agreements in related contracts);

Party autonomy under Article 3 of Rome I can be exercised expressly or impliedly. An express choice of law can be made by means of incorporation of a choice-of-law clause contained in another document (e.g. incorporation into a bill of lading of the choice-of-law clause contained in a charterparty).[113] An implied choice of law was found to have been made in three cases. In *Etihad Airways PJSC v. Flöther*,[114] the court found an implied choice of English law on the basis that the parties had expressly agreed on the applicable law in related and previous contracts. In *Hardy Exploration and Production (India) Inc. v. India*,[115] the parties entered a contract which did not contain an express choice of law, but did contain an Indian jurisdiction clause and an Indian arbitration clause. Furthermore, the jurisdiction clause disapplied the Indian Arbitration and Conciliation Act 1996, the contract was related to other contracts which were expressly governed by Indian law and contained Indian jurisdiction clauses, and the payment under the contract was made to the Government of India in India. The party who commenced the English proceedings for the setting aside of an interim third party debt order argued that the parties to the contract had impliedly chosen Indian law, which was not contested. The court also found that the contract was governed by Indian law. *Aquavita International SA v. Ashapura Minecham Ltd*[116] concerned a guarantee ancillary to a contract of affreightment, which was expressly governed by English law. The court held that where a contract contained an express or implied choice of law and a guarantee was given in respect of obligations under the contract, the court would often infer that the parties had chosen that the guarantee should be governed by the same system of law as the contract to which it related in the absence of some contrary indication. If the rights and obligations under the main contract were governed by a chosen

---

Stylianou v. Toyoshima [2013] EWHC 2188 (QB) at [82] (no agreement arising by inference or implication from the 'choice' of commencing proceedings in Western Australia; nevertheless, the continued and active pursuit of the proceedings in Western Australia was an important factor under the escape clause).

113 *Caresse Navigation Ltd v. Office National de l'Electricité (Channel Ranger)* [2013] EWHC 3081 (Comm), [2014] 1 Lloyd's Rep 337 at [30]–[37], affirmed in [2014] EWCA Civ 1366, [2015] QB 366 without discussing choice of law. The court added that the choice of law was irrefutable, at any rate provided that the law so chosen was usual and proper for the trade in question. Since the Amwelsh (Americanised Welsh Coal Charter) form was a commonly used charter form for the carriage of coal, there was nothing surprising or unusual about the choice of English law, which was what the printed form provided. Similarly, *Seniority Shipping Corp SA v. City Seed Crushing Industries Ltd* [2019] EWHC 3541 (Comm) at [12]–[14], [16]; *Toyota Tsusho Sugar Trading Ltd v. Prolat Srl* [2014] EWHC 3649 (Comm), [2015] 1 Lloyd's Rep 344 at [18]; *Aquavita International SA v. Ashapura Minecham Ltd* [2014] EWHC 2806 (Comm) at [13]–[15], affirmed at trial in which the defendant did not participate [2015] EWHC 2807 (QB) at [97].

114 [2019] EWHC 3107 (Comm), [2020] 2 WLR 333 at [85].

115 [2018] EWHC 1916 (Comm), [2019] QB 544 at [84].

116 [2014] EWHC 2806 (Comm) at [16]–[31], affirmed at trial in which the defendant did not participate [2015] EWHC 2807 (QB) at [94]–[105].

system of law, it would be incongruous for the guarantee to be governed by a different system. Differences between the two systems might potentially result in a mismatch between the obligations of the party to the main contract which were the subject matter of the guarantee, and the obligations of the guarantor to fulfil those obligations. The rationale of the general principle was not merely that the guarantee had a close connection with the main contract, but also that businessmen would not normally choose to have their rights and obligations under the guarantee governed by a different system of law. The courts have also confirmed that the parties are free to change the applicable law.[117]

The courts have interpreted widely the scope of choice-of-law agreements. In *Committeri v. Club Mediterranee SA*,[118] for example, the High Court held that a choice-of-law clause in a contract for the provision of travel and accommodation services covered matters relating to payment, modification, cancellation, responsibility and performance. That left nothing to be governed by a separate or implied choice of law.

3.4. APPLICATION OF ESCAPE CLAUSES

One of the major problems with the Rome Convention, the resolution of which was an important impetus behind its conversion into a Regulation, was a perceived lack of legal certainty and foreseeability in the application of Article 4 of the Convention concerning the determination of the applicable law in the absence of party autonomy.[119] The two Regulations aim to infuse legal certainty and foreseeability into choice of law by laying down a number of fixed choice-of-law rules for contractual and non-contractual obligations[120]

---

117 *Re Syncreon Group BV* [2019] EWHC 2068 (Ch) at [31]; *In re APCOA Parking Holdings GmbH and others (No 2)* [2014] EWHC 3849 (Ch), [2015] 4 All ER 572 at [230], [231], [245]–[248].

118 [2016] EWHC 1510 (QB) at [54]–[56], affirmed in [2018] EWCA Civ 1889, [2019] ILPr 19. See also *BNP Paribas SA v. Anchorage Capital Europe LLP* [2013] EWHC 3073 (Comm) at [62], [63]. But see *Aslam v. Uber BV* [2017] IRLR 4, ET at [104]–[105], affirmed in [2018] ICR 453, EAT and [2018] EWCA Civ 2748, [2019] 3 All ER 489 without discussing choice of law.

119 See European Commission, Green Paper on the conversion of the Rome Convention of 1980 on the law applicable to contractual obligations into a Community instrument and its modernisation, COM(2002) 654 final; S. Atrill, 'Choice of Law in Contract: The Missing Pieces of the Article 4 Jigsaw' (2004) 53 ICLQ 549; J.J. Fawcett, 'A United Kingdom Perspective on the Rome I Regulation' in N. Boschiero (ed.), *La nuova disciplina comunitaria della legge applicabile ai contratti (Roma I)* (Rome: Giappichelli, 2009) 191; R. Fentiman, 'Choice of Law in Europe: Uniformity and Integration' (2008) 82 *Tulane Law Review* 2021; J. Hill, 'Choice of Law in Contract under the Rome Convention: The Approach of the UK Courts' (2004) 53 ICLQ 325; C.S.A. Okoli and G.O. Arishe, 'The Operation of the Escape Clause in the Rome Convention, Rome I Regulation and Rome II Regulation' (2012) 8 JPIL 513; Z. Tang, 'Law Applicable in the Absence of Choice: The New Article 4 of the Rome I Regulation' (2008) 71 MLR 785; cf. Penadés Fons (n. 77).

120 The fixed choice-of-law rules of Rome I and Rome II are dealt with in section 4 below.

and providing that the vast majority of these rules can be departed from where it is *clear* from all the circumstances of the case that the contract or non-contractual obligation (and not an individual issue) is *manifestly* more closely connected with another country.[121] The question arises whether UK courts have applied the fixed choice-of-law rules and the escape clauses with the intended strictness.

Judging from the reported cases, UK courts have generally followed a strict interpretation. Although they have been willing to take into account all factors as they stood at the date of the decision,[122] the escape clauses have not often led to the displacement of the law designated by the fixed choice-of-law rules.

The following two cases illustrate the strict approach adopted by UK courts. In *Molton Street Capital LLP v. Shooters Hill Capital Partners LLP*,[123] which concerned a claim for damages under a contract for the sale of junk bonds to an English buyer negotiated by an English broker, the court held that the contract was subject to New York law as the seller was habitually resident in New York and the contract was not manifestly more closely connected with England. The court stressed that the language and structure of Rome I suggested a higher threshold than in the Rome Convention and required that the cumulative weight of the factors connecting the contract to another country had to clearly and decisively outweigh the *desideratum* of certainty in applying the fixed choice-of-law rules. Decisive factors were that the bonds were essentially New York instruments, the issuing entity was a New York entity set up by a bank headquartered in New York, performance would take place in New York, the price was in US dollars, and the substantive rights attaching to the bonds were represented by a book

---

121 Cf. Article 8(4) of Rome I on individual employment contracts which is worded in slightly different terms.

122 *Winrow v. Hemphill* [2014] EWHC 3164 (QB), [2015] ILPr 12 at [42]–[63]: factors to be taken into account under Article 4(3) of Rome II include the country in which the accident and the damage occurred and the common habitual residence of the parties at the time of the accident, as well as all facts as they stood at the date of the decision, not limited to the date of the tort, regardless of whether connected with the tort or with the consequences of the tort. See also *Stylianou v. Toyoshima* [2013] EWHC 2188 (QB) at [62]; *FM Capital Partners Ltd v. Marino* [2018] EWHC 1768 (Comm) at [517], affirmed in [2020] EWCA Civ 245 without discussing choice of law. That a tort is part of a multi-party accident may be a highly relevant factor: *Pickard v. Marshall* [2017] EWCA Civ 17, [2017] RTR 20 at [14].

123 [2015] EWHC 3419 (Comm) at [91]–[106]. Similarly, *BNP Paribas SA v. Anchorage Capital Europe LLP* [2013] EWHC 3073 (Comm) (English law applicable under Article 4(1) of Rome I; the court spoke, at [64], of 'a high hurdle' which Article 4(3) deliberately places in the way of a party seeking to displace the primary rule). The courts also refused to apply the escape clause in Article 4(3) of Rome I in *Toyota Tsusho Sugar Trading Ltd v. Prolat Srl* [2014] EWHC 3649 (Comm), [2015] 1 Lloyd's Rep 344 at [18] (English law applicable under Article 4(1) of Rome I) and *Brownlie v. Four Seasons Holdings Inc.* [2015] EWCA Civ 665, [2016] 1 WLR 1814 at [32], [41], reversed in *Four Seasons Holdings Inc. v. Brownlie* [2017] UKSC 80, [2018] 1 WLR 192 without discussing choice of law under Rome I (Egyptian law applicable under Article 4(1) of Rome I) and the escape clause in Article 8(4) of Rome I concerning individual employment contracts in *Olsen v. Gearbulk Services Ltd* [2015] IRLR 818, EAT at [60] (Swiss law applicable under Article 8(2) of Rome I).

entry in New York. In *Committeri v. Club Mediterranee SA*,[124] a case concerning personal injuries suffered abroad, the High Court refused to apply the escape clause in Article 4(3) of Rome II. It held that there was a high hurdle in order to displace the law designated by the fixed choice-of-law rules in Article 4 and that there was nothing in this case which came close to overcoming that high hurdle. The law of the place of the damage, namely French law, governed under Rome II.

The adoption of the strict approach does not mean that the escape clauses have never been applied. The escape clause in Article 4 of Rome I was applied in one case and the escape clause in Article 4 of Rome II was applied in five cases. In *Bill Kenwright Ltd v. Flash Entertainment FZ LLC*,[125] after holding that in a settlement agreement the 'characteristic performance' for the purposes of Article 4(2) of Rome I was the payment of money, which in that case pointed to the law of Abu Dhabi, the court applied the escape clause in favour of English law. The court stated, seemingly without appreciating the difference between the escape clause in the Rome I Regulation and that in the Rome Convention, that 'in the present case, the presumption [was] weak and displaced by the fact that the Settlement Agreement [was] more closely connected with England than Abu Dhabi, in particular because the key meetings and negotiations took place in England … and the invoices provided for payment in England.'[126]

124 [2016] EWHC 1510 (QB) at [57], affirmed in [2018] EWCA Civ 1889, [2019] ILPr 19 without discussing choice of law under Rome II. Similarly, *Microsoft Mobile Oy (Ltd) v. Sony Europe Ltd* [2017] EWHC 374 (Ch), [2018] 1 All ER (Comm) 419 at [173]–[176] (the court said, at [176], that Article 4(3) of Rome II is a provision that will only rarely be triggered; it was not possible to identify the applicable law at the time); *Pan Oceanic Chartering Inc. v. UNIPEC UK Co. Ltd* [2016] EWHC 2774 (Comm), [2017] 2 All ER (Comm) 196 at [205]–[210] (New York law applicable under Article 4(1) of Rome II; the court spoke, at [206], of 'exceptional circumstances' and overcoming a 'high hurdle' that are needed to engage Article 4(3)); *Rai v. Ministry of Defence*, Queen's Bench Division, 9 May 2016 at [90]–[118] (English law applicable under Article 4(2) of Rome II; the court spoke, at [117], of 'the high hurdle contained in Article 4(3)'); *Winrow v. Hemphill* [2014] EWHC 3164 (QB), [2015] ILPr 12 at [38]–[63] (German law applicable under Article 4(1) of Rome II; the court clarified, at [42], that the standard required to satisfy Article 4(3) was 'high'); *Stylianou v. Toyoshima* [2013] EWHC 2188 (QB) at [55]–[83] (Western Australian law applicable under Article 4(1) of Rome II; the court spoke, at [83] of the need for an 'exceptional case' before the escape clause in Article 4(3) can apply). See also *Bazhanov v. Fosman* [2017] EWHC 3404 (Comm) at [76] and *Banque Cantonale de Geneve v. Polevent Ltd* [2015] EWHC 1968 (Comm), [2016] QB 394 at [19], where the courts refused to apply the escape clause in Article 10(4) of Rome II.

125 [2016] EWHC 1951 (QB) at [34]–[38].

126 Ibid at [38]. See also *Wrigley v. Wood* [2014] EWHC 3684 (Comm), where the court had to determine the applicable law of two contracts, one made before the entry into force of the Rome I Regulation, the other after that date. The court applied Article 4 of the Rome Convention, including the escape clause in Article 4(5), to determine the law applicable to the first contract. The court did not conduct a separate choice-of-law analysis under the Rome I Regulation and did not ask the question whether the fact that the escape clause under Article 4(3) of Rome I was meant to operate in exceptional circumstances where the contract was *manifestly* more closely connected with another country made a difference to the choice-of-law analysis. The court mentioned, at [19], that the second contract would be affected by Article 19(1) of the Rome I Regulation which deals with habitual residence of natural persons.

In *Marshall v. Motor Insurers' Bureau*,[127] after finding that the rule of the common habitual residence would point to English law, the court departed from this law in favour of the law of the place of the damage, namely French law. This was done by reliance on the following factors: (i) both parties were hit by another, French, car driven by a French driver in France and any claims brought against the French driver and her insurers were governed by French law; (ii) the collision was the cause of the accident and the injuries suffered by the claimants; and (iii) any claims against the insurer of the French vehicle recovery truck were also governed by French law. In *Hillside (New Media) Ltd v. Baasland*,[128] which concerned economic loss (nearly £3 million) suffered by a Norwegian who placed bets through the bet365 website, the court held that English law was applicable as the law of the country where the damage occurred because the *situs* of one of the claimant's online betting accounts was in England where the betting company was domiciled. The court also said obiter that the same result would have been reached under the escape clause of Article 4(3) of Rome II because the mentioned factors pointed to England and because the parties were bound by a contract governed by English law. A similar reasoning was applied in two other cases.[129] In *Innovia Films Ltd v. Frito-Lay North America Inc*[130] the court noted that neither party relied on Article 4(1) of Rome II and that the claim was more closely connected with England. There are three more cases where the courts said that there was an argument that Article 4(3) of Rome II applied and pointed to the application of English law,[131] that it was likely that English law applied by virtue of Article 4(3) of Rome II[132] and that the claimant had a real prospect of establishing at trial that English law governed because the tortious acts and conduct were manifestly more closely connected with England for the purposes of Article 4(3) of Rome II.[133]

---

127 [2015] EWHC 3421 (QB), [2016] Lloyd's Rep IR 400 at [9]–[23], affirmed in *Pickard v. Marshall* [2017] EWCA Civ 17, [2017] RTR 20 at [14]–[21].

128 [2010] EWHC 3336 (Comm), [2010] 2 CLC 986 at [28]–[37], [46].

129 *FM Capital Partners Ltd v. Marino* [2018] EWHC 1768 (Comm) at [511]–[519], affirmed in [2020] EWCA Civ 245 without discussing choice of law (English law governed under either Article 4(1) or Article 4(3)); *Erste Group Bank AG (London) v. JSC (VMZ Red October)* [2015] EWCA Civ 379, [2015] 1 CLC 706 at [84]–[100] (Article 4(1) did not point to England and, in any event, for the purposes of Article 4(3) the alleged tort was manifestly more closely connected with Russia than with any other place).

130 [2012] EWHC 790 (Pat), [2012] RPC 24 at [111].

131 *Angola v. Perfectbit Ltd* [2018] EWHC 965 (Comm), [2018] Lloyd's Rep FC 363 at [198], [200].

132 *OPO v. MLA* [2014] EWCA Civ 1277, [2015] EMLR 4 at [112], reversed in [2015] UKSC 32, [2016] AC 219 without discussing choice of law (the court could not make any final decision for the purposes of Article 4(3) because it was not making any findings of fact).

133 *Fortress Value Recovery Fund I LLC v. Blue Skye Special Opportunities Fund LP* [2013] EWHC 14 (Comm), [2013] 1 All ER (Comm) 973 at [42]–[75] (it was neither necessary nor appropriate to determine on a summary basis before trial whether the applicable law of any claim in tort was the law of England or Luxembourg).

3.5. LEGAL CERTAINTY VERSUS FLEXIBILITY DILEMMA

A good framework for analysing the exercise of judicial discretion in choice of law has been developed by Penadés Fons.[134] The starting point is that implied choice and the escape clauses are functional equivalents in that they represent the two means offered by the Regulations to the courts of the Member States to reach appropriate choice-of-law decisions. The exercise of discretion depends on a number of factors, most importantly the legal and commercial contexts of the claim.

With regard to the legal context, it has been mentioned that out of the 26 cases in which Rome I was applied, choice of law was relevant for the process of litigation, not for deciding the case on the substance, in 17 cases or 65 per cent. This is in line with the conclusions of the study by Penadés Fons, who found that approximately two thirds of choice-of-law disputes are dealt with in interlocutory proceedings.[135] Out of the 48 cases applying Rome II, choice of law was relevant for the process of litigation in 25 cases or 52 per cent.

A further question that can be asked is how frequently judicial discretion was exercised at the interlocutory stage or on an application to strike out a statement of case/for summary judgment as opposed to the trial stage. Implied choice under Rome I was demonstrated in three cases.[136] The escape clause of Article 4(3) of Rome I was applied in one case.[137] Article 4(4) of Rome I, under which the applicable law is decided through direct application of the principle of closest connection, was applied in two cases.[138] It was unclear in one case whether the applicable law was determined by the application of the escape clause in Article 4(3) or by the application of Article 4(4) of Rome I.[139] All of these cases, except one,[140] were decided at the interlocutory stage. This contrasts with ten cases applying the fixed choice-of-law rules of Rome I, five of which were at the interlocutory stage or decided on an application to strike out a statement

---

134 Penadés Fons (n. 77).

135 Ibid, 254.

136 *Etihad Airways PJSC v. Flöther* [2019] EWHC 3107 (Comm), [2020] 2 WLR 333 (application of Article 25 of the Brussels I Regulation; English law applicable); *Hardy Exploration and Production (India) Inc. v. India* [2018] EWHC 1916 (Comm), [2019] QB 544 (application for setting aside a third party debt order; Indian law applicable); *Aquavita International SA v. Ashapura Minecham Ltd* [2014] EWHC 2806 (Comm) (service out; English law applicable), affirmed at trial in which the defendant did not participate [2015] EWHC 2807 (QB).

137 *Bill Kenwright Ltd v. Flash Entertainment FZ LLC* [2016] EWHC 1951 (QB) (service out; English law applicable).

138 *Bazhanov v. Fosman* [2017] EWHC 3404 (Comm) (service out; Russian law applicable); *Scott v. West* [2012] EWHC 1890 (Ch) (service out; English law applicable).

139 *Wrigley v. Wood* [2014] EWHC 3684 (Comm) (service out; the law of Florida applicable).

140 *Hardy Exploration and Production (India) Inc. v. India* [2018] EWHC 1916 (Comm), [2019] QB 544.

of case/for summary judgment.[141] These results depart from the conclusions of the study by Penadés Fons, who found that, under the Rome Convention and Rome I, the gateways for discretion were applied in nearly 60 per cent of all choice-of-law decisions rendered before jurisdiction has been established and in 32 per cent of all choice-of-law decisions rendered at trial under a higher standard of proof.[142] One possible explanation for this is that the courts are now resorting to judicial discretion in choice of law more sparingly, in line with the tightening of the rules of Rome I. This appears to be consistent with the fact that the escape clauses of Rome II were applied in only five cases, twice at trial,[143] twice on an application for permission to serve out[144] and once on an application for summary judgment,[145] although there are three more cases where the courts said before trial that there was an argument that Article 4(3) of Rome II applied and pointed to the application of English law,[146] that it was

---

141 *European Union v. Syria* [2018] EWHC 1712 (Comm) (application for summary judgment; Belgian or Luxembourg law applicable); *Eurasia Sports Ltd v. Tsai* [2016] EWHC 2207 (QB), affirmed in [2018] EWCA Civ 1742, [2018] 1 WLR 6089 without discussing choice of law (service out; English law likely applicable); *Brownlie v. Four Seasons Holdings Inc.* [2015] EWCA Civ 665, [2016] 1 WLR 1814, reversed in *Four Seasons Holdings Inc. v. Brownlie* [2017] UKSC 80, [2018] 1 WLR 192 without discussing choice of law under Rome I (service out; Egyptian law applicable); *BNP Paribas SA v. Anchorage Capital Europe LLP* [2013] EWHC 3073 (Comm) (service out; English law applicable); *SSL International Plc v. TTK LIG Ltd* [2011] EWCA Civ 1170, [2012] 1 WLR 1842 (service out; Indian law applicable). Cf. *Aslam v. Uber BV* [2017] IRLR 4, ET, affirmed in [2018] ICR 453, EAT and [2018] EWCA Civ 2748, [2019] 3 All ER 489 without discussing choice of law (trial of a claim for failure to pay the minimum wage and provide paid leave; Dutch law applicable; English law also relevant under Articles 8 and 9); *Molton Street Capital LLP v. Shooters Hill Capital Partners LLP* [2015] EWHC 3419 (Comm) (trial of a claim for damages under a contract for the sale of junk bonds; New York law applicable); *Olsen v. Gearbulk Services Ltd* [2015] IRLR 818, EAT (trial of a claim for unfair dismissal and a bonus payment under an employment contract; Bermuda law applicable; Swiss law also relevant under Article 8); *Toyota Tsusho Sugar Trading Ltd v. Prolat Srl* [2014] EWHC 3649 (Comm), [2015] 1 Lloyd's Rep 344 (application under section 32 of the Arbitration Act 1996; English law applicable); *Taurus Petroleum Ltd v. State Oil Marketing Co. of the Ministry of Oil, Iraq* [2015] EWCA Civ 835, [2016] 2 All ER (Comm) 1037, reversed in [2017] UKSC 64, [2018] AC 690 without discussing choice of law (application for setting aside an interim third party debt order; English law applicable).

142 Penadés Fons (n. 77) 253.

143 *FM Capital Partners Ltd v. Marino* [2018] EWHC 1768 (Comm), affirmed in [2020] EWCA Civ 245 without discussing choice of law (conspiracy, dishonest assistance, knowing receipt and bribery; English law applicable); *Marshall v. Motor Insurers' Bureau* [2015] EWHC 3421 (QB), [2016] Lloyd's Rep IR 400, affirmed in *Pickard v. Marshall* [2017] EWCA Civ 17, [2017] RTR 20 (trial of a claim for damages for personal injury suffered in a road accident abroad; French law applicable).

144 *Erste Group Bank AG (London) v. JSC (VMZ Red October)* [2015] EWCA Civ 379, [2015] 1 CLC 706 (service out; Russian law applicable); *Innovia Films Ltd v. Frito-Lay North America Inc.* [2012] EWHC 790 (Pat), [2012] RPC 24 (service out; English law applicable).

145 *Hillside (New Media) Ltd v. Baasland* [2010] EWHC 3336 (Comm), [2010] 2 CLC 986 (English law applicable).

146 *Angola v. Perfectbit Ltd* [2018] EWHC 965 (Comm), [2018] Lloyd's Rep FC 363 (service out).

likely that English law applied[147] and that the claimant had a real prospect of establishing at trial that English law governed by virtue of Article 4(3) of Rome II.[148] The fixed choice-of-law rules of Rome II were applied in many more cases, both before and at trial.[149] Neither express nor implied choice has yet been demonstrated under Rome II.

The discussion in the preceding paragraph has not taken into account the commercial context of the claim, which according to Penadés Fons is the crucial factor for the outcome of the application of the gateways for discretion. Penadés Fons has found that in cases concerning 'strategic industries', namely shipping, banking and finance, and insurance, the courts resort to the discretional gateways and apply English law much more often than in cases concerning other sectors.[150] Looking at the cases under Rome I which actually or potentially concerned the exercise of judicial discretion at the interlocutory stage or on an application to strike out a statement of case/for summary judgment, English law was found to be applicable in six out of ten cases.[151] In the six cases under Rome I which

---

147 *OPO v. MLA* [2014] EWCA Civ 1277, [2015] EMLR 4, reversed in [2015] UKSC 32, [2016] AC 219 without discussing choice of law (application for an interim injunction; the court could not make any final decision for the purposes of Article 4(3) because it was not making any findings of fact).

148 *Fortress Value Recovery Fund I LLC v. Blue Skye Special Opportunities Fund LP* [2013] EWHC 14 (Comm), [2013] 1 All ER (Comm) 973 (application to strike out a statement of case/for summary judgment; it was neither necessary nor appropriate to determine on a summary basis before trial whether the applicable law of any claim in tort was the law of England or Luxembourg).

149 See sub-section 4.3 below.

150 Penadés Fons (n. 77) 257 et seq.

151 *Etihad Airways PJSC v. Flöther* [2019] EWHC 3107 (Comm), [2020] 2 WLR 333 (application of Article 25 of the Brussels I Regulation; comfort letter concerning the financing of an airline); *Bill Kenwright Ltd v. Flash Entertainment FZ LLC* [2016] EWHC 1951 (QB) (service out; settlement agreement concerning the provision of entertainment services); *Eurasia Sports Ltd v. Tsai* [2016] EWHC 2207 (QB), affirmed in [2018] EWCA Civ 1742, [2018] 1 WLR 6089 without discussing choice of law (service out; betting account contract); *Aquavita International SA v. Ashapura Minecham Ltd* [2014] EWHC 2806 (Comm) (service out; guarantee ancillary to a contract of affreightment), affirmed at trial in which the defendant did not participate [2015] EWHC 2807 (QB); *BNP Paribas SA v. Anchorage Capital Europe LLP* [2013] EWHC 3073 (Comm) (service out; contract for the sale of private placement notes); *Scott v. West* [2012] EWHC 1890 (Ch) (service out; sale of shares). Cf. *European Union v. Syria* [2018] EWHC 1712 (Comm) (application for summary judgment; contract of guarantee; Belgian or Luxembourg law applicable); *Bazhanov v. Fosman* [2017] EWHC 3404 (Comm) (service out; alleged contracts for the provision of services to refinance a company; Russian law applicable); *Brownlie v. Four Seasons Holdings Inc.* [2015] EWCA Civ 665, [2016] 1 WLR 1814, reversed in *Four Seasons Holdings Inc. v. Brownlie* [2017] UKSC 80, [2018] 1 WLR 192 without discussing choice of law under Rome I (service out; contract for organising an excursion; Egyptian law applicable); *Wrigley v. Wood* [2014] EWHC 3684 (Comm) (service out; provision of service of introducing a purchaser to a broker; the law of Florida applicable); *SSL International Plc v. TTK LIG Ltd* [2011] EWCA Civ 1170, [2012] 1 WLR 1842 (service out; supply of condoms; Indian law applicable).

actually or potentially concerned the exercise of judicial discretion and were not decided at the interlocutory stage or on an application for summary judgment, English law was applicable in two cases.[152] Only three of these cases in which foreign law was found to be applicable (as opposed to many cases in which English law was applicable) concerned a 'strategic industry', namely banking and finance. It should be noted, however, that the first case[153] concerned New York instruments which were found to be governed by New York law. The second case[154] concerned alleged contracts between Russian businessmen to refinance a Russian company. The third case concerned European Union's guarantee of Syria's repayment obligations under loan agreements entered between Syria and the European Investment Bank.[155] Looking at the cases which actually or potentially concerned the exercise of judicial discretion under Rome II at the interlocutory stage or on an application to strike out a statement of case/for summary judgment, English law was found to be applicable in nine out of 19 cases.[156] In the cases which actually or potentially concerned the exercise

152 *Toyota Tsusho Sugar Trading Ltd v. Prolat Srl* [2014] EWHC 3649 (Comm), [2015] 1 Lloyd's Rep 344 (sale of sugar); *Taurus Petroleum Ltd v. State Oil Marketing Co. of the Ministry of Oil, Iraq* [2015] EWCA Civ 835, [2016] 2 All ER (Comm) 1037, reversed in [2017] UKSC 64, [2018] AC 690 without discussing choice of law (letter of credit). Cf. *Hardy Exploration and Production (India) Inc. v. India* [2018] EWHC 1916 (Comm), [2019] QB 544 (fee guarantee contract; Indian law applicable); *Aslam v. Uber BV* [2017] IRLR 4, ET, affirmed in [2018] ICR 453, EAT and [2018] EWCA Civ 2748, [2019] 3 All ER 489 without discussing choice of law (employment contract; Dutch law applicable; English law also relevant under Articles 8 and 9); *Molton Street Capital LLP v. Shooters Hill Capital Partners LLP* [2015] EWHC 3419 (Comm) (sale of junk bonds; New York law applicable); *Olsen v. Gearbulk Services Ltd* [2015] IRLR 818, EAT (employment contract; Bermuda law applicable; Swiss law also relevant under Article 8).

153 *Molton Street Capital LLP v. Shooters Hill Capital Partners LLP* [2015] EWHC 3419 (Comm).

154 *Bazhanov v. Fosman* [2017] EWHC 3404 (Comm).

155 *European Union v. Syria* [2018] EWHC 1712 (Comm).

156 *ED&F Man Capital Markets Ltd v. Come Harvest Holdings Ltd* [2019] EWHC 1661 (Comm), [2019] ILPr 40 (service out; fraud; sale of goods); *Gray v. Hurley* [2019] EWHC 1636 (QB) (service out; claim for restitution in unjust enrichment arising from the end of a romantic relationship); *Angola v. Perfectbit Ltd* [2018] EWHC 965 (Comm), [2018] Lloyd's Rep FC 363 (service out; conspiracy to defraud; investment); *MX1 Ltd v. Farahzad* [2018] EWHC 1041 (Ch), [2018] 1 WLR 5553 (application to strike out a statement of case/for summary judgment; conspiracy to injure by using a Twitter account); *Eurasia Sports Ltd v. Tsai* [2016] EWHC 2207 (QB), affirmed in [2018] EWCA Civ 1742, [2018] 1 WLR 6089 without discussing choice of law (service out; fraud; online betting); *OPO v. MLA* [2014] EWCA Civ 1277, [2015] EMLR 4 at [112], reversed in [2015] UKSC 32, [2016] AC 219 without discussing choice of law (application for an interim injunction to restrain the publication of a book pending trial; intentional infliction of emotional harm); *Fortress Value Recovery Fund I LLC v. Blue Skye Special Opportunities Fund LP* [2013] EWHC 14 (Comm), [2013] 1 All ER (Comm) 973 (application for summary judgment; fraud; investment); *Innovia Films Ltd v. Frito-Lay North America Inc.* [2012] EWHC 790 (Pat), [2012] RPC 24 (service out; patent dispute); *Hillside (New Media) Ltd v. Baasland* [2010] EWHC 3336 (Comm), [2010] 2 CLC 986 (application for summary judgment; negligence and online betting losses). Cf. *Brownlie v. Four Seasons Holdings Inc. (No 2)* [2019] EWHC 2533 (QB) (road accident

of judicial discretion under Rome II at trial, English law was applied in four out of 23 cases (in one further case, both English and a foreign law were applied to different claims).[157]

These findings support the conclusion that the commercial context is very important for the exercise of discretion under Rome I. These findings also

abroad; Egyptian law applicable); *BVC v. EWF* [2019] EWHC 2506 (QB) (application for summary judgment; harassment; foreign law applicable); *Bazhanov v. Fosman* [2017] EWHC 3404 (Comm) (service out; unjust enrichment concerning non-existent contracts for the provision of services to refinance of a Russian company; Russian law applicable); *His Royal Highness Okpabi v. Royal Dutch Shell Plc* [2017] EWHC 89 (TCC), [2017] Bus LR 1335, affirmed in [2018] EWCA Civ 191, [2018] Bus LR 1022 without discussing choice of law under Rome II (service out; environmental damage; mining and extraction; Nigerian law applicable); *Gunn v. Diaz* [2017] EWHC 157 (QB), [2017] 2 All ER (Comm) 129 (service out; road accident abroad; Costa Rican law applicable); *Le Guevel-Mouly v. AIG Europe Ltd* [2016] EWHC 1794 (QB) (*forum non conveniens*; road accident in Scotland; French law applicable); *Erste Group Bank AG (London) v. JSC (VMZ Red October)* [2015] EWCA Civ 379, [2015] 1 CLC 706 (service out; unlawful means conspiracy; banking and finance; Russian law applicable); *Stylianou v. Toyoshima* [2013] EWHC 2188 (QB) (service out; road accident abroad; West Australian law applicable); *Wink v. Croatia Osiguranje DD* [2013] EWHC 1118 (QB) (service out; road accident abroad; Croatian law applicable); *OJSC TNK-BP Holding v. Lazurenko* [2012] EWHC 2781 (Ch) (application for an interim injunction; employment relationship; Russian law applicable).

157 *FM Capital Partners Ltd v. Marino* [2018] EWHC 1768 (Comm), affirmed in [2020] EWCA Civ 245 without discussing choice of law (conspiracy, dishonest assistance, knowing receipt and bribery; investment); *Rai v. Ministry of Defence*, Queen's Bench Division, 9 May 2016 (personal injury abroad; military training); *Bianco v. Bennett* [2015] EWHC 626 (QB), [2015] ILPr 24 (road accident in England); *Morgan Stanley & Co. International Plc v. China Haisheng Juice Holdings Co. Ltd* [2009] EWHC 2409 (Comm), [2010] 2 All ER (Comm) 514 (application for an ASI; *culpa in contrahendo*; ISDA master agreement). Cf. *Pandya v. Intersalonika General Insurance Co. SA* [2020] EWHC 273 (QB) (road accident abroad; Greek law applicable) *Foreign and Commonwealth Office v. Bamieh* [2019] EWCA Civ 803, [2019] IRLR 736 (whistleblowing detriment; Kosovan law applicable); *Folkes v. Generali Assurances* [2019] EWHC 801 (QB) (road accident abroad; French law applicable); *Vilca v. Xstrata Ltd* [2018] EWHC 27 (QB) (personal injury abroad; mining and extraction; Peruvian law applicable); *Gilmour v. Linea Directa Aseguradora Sa Compania De Seguros Y Reaseguros* 2017 GWD 39-603, Sheriff Court (Lothian and Borders) (Edinburgh) (road accident abroad; Spanish law applicable); *Pan Oceanic Chartering Inc. v. UNIPEC UK Co. Ltd* [2016] EWHC 2774 (Comm), [2017] 2 All ER (Comm) 196 (tortious interference with contractual relations; shipping; New York law applicable); *AS Latvijas Krajbanka (In Liquidation) v. Antonov* [2016] EWHC 1679 (Comm) (non-contractual liability of the defendant majority beneficial owner of the claimant who acted dishonestly and in breach of duties owed to the claimant; Latvian law applicable); *Committeri v. Club Mediterranee SA* [2016] EWHC 1510 (QB), affirmed in [2018] EWCA Civ 1889, [2019] ILPr 19 without discussing choice of law under Rome II (personal injury abroad; French law applicable); *Moreno v. Motor Insurers' Bureau* [2016] UKSC 52, [2016] 1 WLR 3194 (road accident abroad; Greek law applicable); *Syred v. Powszechny Zaklad Ubezpreczen (PZU) SA* [2016] EWHC 254 (QB), [2016] 1 WLR 3211 (road accident abroad; Polish law applicable); *XP v. Compensa Towarzystwo SA* [2016] EWHC 1728 (QB), [2016] Med LR 570 (road accident abroad; Polish law applicable); *Marshall v. Motor Insurers' Bureau* [2015] EWHC 3421 (QB), [2016] Lloyd's Rep IR 400, affirmed in *Pickard v. Marshall* [2017] EWCA Civ 17, [2017] RTR 20 (road accident abroad; French law applicable); *Vann v. Ocidental-Companhia De Seguros SA* [2015] EWCA Civ 572 (road accident abroad; Portuguese law

indicate that this framework for analysing the exercise of judicial discretion in choice of law is unsuitable for cases concerning the application of Rome II. This is because the functions of choice of law for contractual and non-contractual obligations are different. In particular, the function and operation of choice of law in cases concerning international torts, which comprise the bulk of cases concerning the application of Rome II, are different depending on whether the tort in question raises a conflict between laws that primarily regulate conduct ('conduct-regulating rules') or between laws that primarily allocate the loss resulting from the injury ('loss-allocating' or 'loss-distributing rules').[158] Any further analysis of the exercise of judicial discretion in choice of law under Rome II would have to take into account this alternative framework.[159]

3.6. OVERRIDING MANDATORY PROVISIONS

Both Rome I and Rome II allow the courts to apply the overriding mandatory provisions of the law of the forum.[160] Rome I also allows the courts to give effect, under certain conditions, to the overriding mandatory provisions of the law of the country of performance even if that law is not the governing law.[161] This is a major novelty in the Regulation as far as the UK is concerned because the UK exercised its right not to apply Article 7(1) of the Rome Convention on the effect of mandatory rules of third countries.

The identification and application of overriding mandatory provisions have not caused many problems in practice. In *KMG International NV v. Chen*,[162] the court found that the English rule against reflective loss was not an overriding mandatory provision for the purposes of Article 16 of Rome II. In *Syred v. Powszechny Zaklad Ubezpreczen (PZU) SA*,[163] the court was asked to find that

applicable); *Winrow v. Hemphill* [2014] EWHC 3164 (QB), [2015] ILPr 12 (road accident abroad; German law applicable); *Bacon v. Nacional Suiza Cia Seguros y Reseguros SA* [2010] EWHC 2017 (QB), [2010] ILPr 46 (road accident abroad; Spanish law applicable); *Bonsall v. Cattolica Assicurazioni* [2010] ILPr 45, County Court (Winchester) (road accident abroad; Italian law applicable). See also *Jacobs v. Motor Insurers' Bureau* [2010] EWCA Civ 1208, [2011] 1 WLR 2609 (road accident abroad; Spanish law applicable). In *Banque Cantonale de Geneve v. Polevent Ltd* [2015] EWHC 1968 (Comm), [2016] QB 394, which concerned the tort of deceit and restitution in unjust enrichment arising out of a fraud in the banking and finance sector, the claim in tort was governed by Swiss law, while the claim in restitution was governed by English law.

158 See further S.C. Symeonides, 'Rome II and Tort Conflicts: A Missed Opportunity' (2008) 56 AJCL 173.

159 See ibid, 188 et seq., for an analysis of the rules of Rome II along these lines.

160 Article 9(2) of Rome I; Article 16 of Rome II.

161 Article 9(3) of Rome I.

162 [2019] EWHC 2389 (Comm), [2020] Bus LR 133 at [50].

163 [2016] EWHC 254 (QB), [2016] 1 WLR 3211 at [144]–[152].

section 17 of the Social Security (Recovery of Benefits) Act 1997, which governs the assessment of damages in a claim by an injured person against the tortfeasor, was an overriding mandatory provision for the purposes of Article 16 of Rome II. The court held that this provision was not so crucial for the protection of the political, social or economic order of the UK as to override a rule of the applicable Polish law, which follows the general common law principle that damages should be compensatory. In *Eurobank Ergasias SA v. Kalliroi Navigation Co. Ltd*,[164] the court was asked to apply to a contract governed by English law the old common law rule on the effect of supervening illegality at the place of performance laid down in the famous case of *Ralli Bros v. Compania Naviera Sota y Aznar*.[165] The court was invited to find that this case was overridden by Article 9(3) of Rome I. The court refused to do this on the basis that the contract in question was governed by English law and applied the *Ralli Bros* case as part of the applicable English law. The court further held, obiter, in respect of another contract that Chapter F of Act No 2501 of the Governor of the Bank of Greece of 31 October 2002 prohibiting commission fees on lending was not an overriding mandatory provision because it was not exclusively or even mainly concerned with advancing consumer protection or some other interest serving what might be referred to as weaker contractual parties or the types of interest set out in Article 9(1) of Rome I. However, even if it was wrong, the court held that it would have exercised its discretion in favour of permitting the enforcement of the contract in question.

There is one case that arguably should have been dealt with under the framework of Article 9(3) of Rome I, but was instead treated as engaging the doctrine of public policy. In *Dana Gas PJSC v. Dana Gas Sukuk Ltd*,[166] the court considered whether an undertaking by deed governed by English law to purchase certain assets upon the occurrence of certain events was invalid and unenforceable, on the basis that it formed part of an Islamic financial transaction that was governed by the law of United Arab Emirates and was unlawful and unenforceable under that law. The claimant, who sought a declaration of invalidity and unenforceability, relied on a principle that, as a matter of public policy, the English courts will not enforce a contract entered for a purpose which is unlawful under the law of a friendly foreign state. This principle derives from the famous cases of *Foster v. Driscoll*[167] and *Regazzoni v. Sethia*,[168] which concern initial illegality at the place of performance and were decided long before the Rome I Regulation became part of UK law. The court in *Dana* held that in the

164 [2015] EWHC 2377 (Comm) at [31]–[37], [39], [40].
165 [1920] 2 KB 287 (CA).
166 [2017] EWHC 2928 (Comm), [2018] 1 Lloyd's Rep 177 at [81]–[83].
167 [1929] 1 KB 470 (CA).
168 [1958] AC 301 (HL).

present case there was nothing to indicate that the undertaking had as its object and intention the doing of anything in the UAE which was unlawful under the laws of the UAE and therefore was not contrary to English public policy. But as the UK Ministry of Justice observed in its consultation paper 'Rome I – Should the UK Opt In?',[169] Article 9(3) of Rome I is formulated in terms that are sufficiently broad to cover situations of unlawful contractual performance where the applicable law is foreign and removes the uncertainty that existed under the Rome Convention as to whether *Foster v. Driscoll* properly fell within the scope of the public policy rule.[170] In order not to reignite these old uncertainties, it is better to treat cases like *Dana Gas PJSC v. Dana Gas Sukuk Ltd* as engaging Article 9(3) of Rome I and not the old common law authorities.

Another problem concerning overriding mandatory provisions and Rome I is the choice-of-law treatment of so-called statutory claims. In certain areas, most importantly employment and consumer law, claimants often base their claims on the provisions of domestic statutes. UK courts approach these claims as raising not choice-of-law issues, but issues of statutory construction, which approach results in an over-application of domestic law. The questions that the courts ask are not whether the employment and consumer contracts in question are governed by domestic law or, if not, whether the domestic statutes should be applied as overriding mandatory provisions. The courts are only asking whether the claim falls within the territorial scope of the statute in question. It has been argued that this way of reasoning is contrary to the scheme and logic of Rome I.[171] Nevertheless, UK courts have not questioned this approach even after the coming into force of Rome I and have continued to approach statutory claims as raising only issues of statutory construction.[172]

3.7. PUBLIC POLICY

Both Rome I and Rome II allow the courts to refuse to apply a provision of the foreign applicable law if such application is manifestly incompatible with domestic public policy.[173]

---

169 Consultation Paper CP05/08, 2 April 2008.

170 Ibid, 33.

171 See C. Bisping, 'Avoid the Statutist Trap: The International Scope of the Consumer Credit Act' (2012) 8 JPIL 35; U. Grušić, *The European Private International Law of Employment* (Cambridge: Cambridge University Press, 2015) Ch. 3.

172 *Olsen v. Gearbulk Services Ltd* [2015] IRLR 818, EAT; *Aslam v. Uber BV* [2017] IRLR 4, ET at [115]–[118], [120] (see also [111]–[114] on the concept of 'individual employment contract'), affirmed in [2018] ICR 453, EAT and [2018] EWCA Civ 2748, [2019] 3 All ER 489 without discussing choice of law.

173 Article 21 of Rome I; Article 26 of Rome II.

Public policy has so far been raised in three cases. It has been argued in the preceding sub-section that *Dana Gas PJSC v. Dana Gas Sukuk Ltd*[174] was wrongly treated as engaging the doctrine of public policy, not Article 9(3) of Rome I. In *KMG International NV v. Chen*,[175] the court found that the English rule against reflective loss is not a rule of English public policy. In *Group Seven Ltd v. Allied Investment Corp Ltd*,[176] the court considered whether the rules on contributory negligence of the applicable Maltese law allowing a plea of contribution at the behest of a fraudster against the victim were contrary to domestic public policy. The court rejected this argument by holding that it is overwhelmingly the case that the normal position is that the courts in this jurisdiction recognise laws of foreign jurisdictions even when they are different. The court did not consider that the rule of Maltese law could lead to a result so wholly alien to the fundamental requirements of justice as administered by an English court.

3.8. SCOPE OF APPLICABLE LAW AND SUBSTANCE/PROCEDURE DICHOTOMY

The two Regulations contain non-exclusive lists of issues that fall within the scope of the law governing contractual and non-contractual obligations.[177] This is to be contrasted with issues of evidence and procedure, which are always governed by the law of the forum.[178]

In English private international law, the issue of assessment of damages was traditionally regarded as a procedural issue and therefore governed by the *lex fori*.[179] But the Rome I and Rome II Regulations now provide that this issue falls within the scope of the applicable law.[180] Nevertheless, it took a while for UK courts to completely give up the old reasoning. In the EU, the compensation scheme for victims of road accidents caused by uninsured drivers has been set up by Directive 2009/103/EC and the Directives which it superseded. These Directives are implemented into UK law by means of the Motor Vehicles (Compulsory Insurance) (Information Centre and Compensation Body) Regulations 2003, which enable UK residents to obtain compensation for injuries suffered

---

174 [2017] EWHC 2928 (Comm), [2018] 1 Lloyd's Rep 177.

175 [2019] EWHC 2389 (Comm), [2020] Bus LR 133 at [56], [57].

176 [2014] EWHC 2046 (Ch) at [405]–[410], affirmed in [2015] EWCA Civ 631 without discussing choice of law.

177 Article 12 of Rome I; Article 15 of Rome II. See also Article 18 of Rome I and Article 22 of Rome II on burden of proof.

178 Article 1(3) of Rome I; Article 1(3) of Rome II.

179 *Harding v. Wealands* [2006] UKHL 32, [2007] 2 AC 1.

180 Article 12(1)(c) of Rome I; Article 15(1)(c) of Rome II. This includes the discount rate and the multipliers which follow from them for the assessment of future loss: *Stylianou v. Toyoshima* [2013] EWHC 2188 (QB) at [84]–[93].

in a Member State of the EU in road accidents caused by uninsured drivers. The Directives do not state whether questions of liability and assessment of damages are to be determined by reference to the law governing the tort or the *lex fori*. The 2003 Regulations are also silent on this point. UK courts had accepted that the issue of liability is governed by the law governing the tort, but had initially held that the issue of assessment of damages was a matter for the *lex fori*.[181] But this case law was overturned by the Supreme Court in *Moreno v. Motor Insurers' Bureau*,[182] in which the court held that compensation under the 2003 Regulations should be assessed by reference to the law governing the tort.[183] In other cases, the Court of Appeal held that the law governing the tort was broad and included lawful[184] 'practices, conventions and guidelines regularly used by foreign judges in assessing damages under their law',[185] while the High Court held that evidence and procedure are restricted to 'the constitution, powers of courts and mode of trial'[186] and rules that are 'an indispensable feature of the forum's legal framework for resolving disputes'.[187]

Other decisions confirm that the following issues fall within the scope of the law governing contractual and non-contractual obligations: whether the English rule against reflective loss applies,[188] limitation,[189] remedies and interest,[190]

---

181 *Jacobs v. Motor Insurers' Bureau* [2010] EWCA Civ 1208, [2011] 1 WLR 2609; *Bloy v. Motor Insurers' Bureau* [2013] EWCA Civ 1543, [2014] Lloyd's Rep IR 75; *Marshall v. Motor Insurers' Bureau* [2015] EWHC 3421 (QB), [2016] Lloyd's Rep IR 400 at [64], [65], affirmed on other grounds [2017] EWCA Civ 17, [2017] RTR 20.

182 [2016] UKSC 52, [2016] 1 WLR 3194.

183 For the interpretation of controversial Recital 33 to Rome II, see *Stylianou v. Toyoshima* [2013] EWHC 2188 (QB) at [74]–[78], where the court concluded, at [78], that: 'The solution to the problem lies … in the court looking at the actual costs, for example, of aftercare in the victim's place of residence, and taking those into account when assessing damages, but only insofar as the applicable law permits it to do so.' See also *Gunn v. Diaz* [2017] EWHC 157 (QB), [2017] 2 All ER (Comm) 129 at [10]; *Wall v. Mutuelle de Poitiers Assurances* [2014] EWCA Civ 138, [2014] 1 WLR 4263 at [11] (Longmore LJ), [37] (Jackson LJ).

184 Unlawful practice will not be taken into account: *Syred v. Powszechny Zaklad Ubezpreczen (PZU) SA* [2016] EWHC 254 (QB), [2016] 1 WLR 3211 at [45]–[47].

185 *Wall v. Mutuelle de Poitiers Assurances* [2014] EWCA Civ 138, [2014] 1 WLR 4263 at [21]–[24] (Longmore LJ), [32]–[34] (Jackson LJ), [49]–[51] (Christopher Clarke LJ). See also *Gilmour v. Linea Directa Aseguradora Sa Compania De Seguros Y Reaseguros* 2017 GWD 39-603, Sheriff Court (Lothian and Borders) (Edinburgh) at [17].

186 *Stylianou v. Toyoshima* [2013] EWHC 2188 (QB) at [92], referring to *Dicey, Morris and Collins* and Tugendhat J in *Wall v. Mutuelle De Poitiers Assurances* [2013] EWHC 53 (QB), [2013] 1 WLR 3890.

187 *KMG International NV v. Chen* [2019] EWHC 2389 (Comm), [2020] Bus LR 133 at [36](6).

188 Ibid at [36], [42], [43].

189 *Pandya v. Intersalonika General Insurance Co. SA* [2020] EWHC 273 (QB); *Brownlie v. Four Seasons Holdings Inc. (No 2)* [2019] EWHC 2533 (QB) at [6], [38], [47]; *W3 Ltd v. Easygroup Ltd* [2018] EWHC 7 (Ch), [2018] FSR 16 at [360]; *Vilca v. Xstrata Ltd* [2018] EWHC 27 (QB) at [51]; *PJSC Tatneft v. Bogolyubov* [2017] EWCA Civ 1581, [2018] 4 WLR 14 at [72]; *Deutsche Bahn AG v. Mastercard Inc.* [2016] CAT 14, [2017] Bus LR 63 at [48]–[50], [69].

190 *AS Latvijas Krajbanka (In Liquidation) v. Antonov* [2016] EWHC 1679 (Comm) at [9], [10]; *OJSC TNK-BP Holding v. Lazurenko* [2012] EWHC 2781 (Ch) at [20].

and burden of proof.[191] By contrast, the following issues are to be treated as procedural and thus outside the scope of the applicable law: whether a change of parties is allowed,[192] standard of proof,[193] the power to order an interim payment,[194] whether amendments to particulars of claim raise a new cause of action,[195] rules or conditions for obtaining a declaration of non-liability,[196] the way in which evidence of fact or opinion is to be given to the court,[197] and what evidence is admissible.[198]

3.9. TREATMENT OF FOREIGN LAW

Pleading and proof of foreign law are considered to be matters of evidence and procedure and are thus outside the scope of the law governing contractual and non-contractual obligations.[199] In England, a party wishing to rely on foreign law needs to plead that foreign law and prove its content. This is done by means of expert evidence.[200]

The reason why the treatment of foreign law is singled out in this chapter, even though it is a procedural and evidentiary issue (which was dealt with in the preceding sub-section), is that the parties' decisions on whether to plead and prove foreign law can have substantive effects. In some cases, the courts have recorded that the parties were in agreement with respect to how a particular

191 *Gilmour v. Linea Directa Aseguradora Sa Compania De Seguros Y Reaseguros* 2017 GWD 39-603, Sheriff Court (Lothian and Borders) (Edinburgh) at [15]–[17]; *Marshall v. Motor Insurers' Bureau* [2015] EWHC 3421 (QB), [2016] Lloyd's Rep IR 400 at [25], affirmed in *Pickard v. Marshall* [2017] EWCA Civ 17, [2017] RTR 20.

192 *Brownlie v. Four Seasons Holdings Inc. (No 2)* [2019] EWHC 2533 (QB) at [53].

193 *Folkes v. Generali Assurances* [2019] EWHC 801 (QB) at [12]; *Marshall v. Motor Insurers' Bureau* [2015] EWHC 3421 (QB), [2016] Lloyd's Rep IR 400 at [25], affirmed in *Pickard v. Marshall* [2017] EWCA Civ 17, [2017] RTR 20; cf. *Gilmour v. Linea Directa Aseguradora Sa Compania De Seguros Y Reaseguros* 2017 GWD 39-603, Sheriff Court (Lothian and Borders) (Edinburgh) at [15]–[17].

194 *Folkes v. Generali Assurances* [2019] EWHC 801 (QB) at [16].

195 *PJSC Tatneft v. Bogolyubov* [2017] EWCA Civ 1581, [2018] 4 WLR 14 at [29]–[33].

196 *Parainen Pearl Shipping Ltd v. Kristian Gerhard Jebsen Skipsrederi AS* [2017] EWHC 2570 (Pat) at [19]; *Actavis UK Ltd v. Eli Lilly & Co.* [2015] EWCA Civ 555, [2016] 4 All ER 666 at [100]–[145], reversed in part in [2017] UKSC 48, [2018] 1 All ER 171 without discussing this point.

197 *Wall v. Mutuelle de Poitiers Assurances* [2014] EWCA Civ 138, [2014] 1 WLR 4263 at [11]–[20] (Longmore LJ), [39]–[46] (Jackson LJ), [48] (Christopher Clarke LJ).

198 *Gilmour v. Linea Directa Aseguradora Sa Compania De Seguros Y Reaseguros* 2017 GWD 39-603, Sheriff Court (Lothian and Borders) (Edinburgh) at [17].

199 Article 1(3) of Rome I; Article 1(3) of Rome II.

200 On pleading and proof of foreign law in a case concerning Rome II, see *OPO v. MLA* [2014] EWCA Civ 1277, [2015] EMLR 4 at [108]–[111], reversed in [2015] UKSC 32, [2016] AC 219 without discussing choice of law; *Brownlie v. Four Seasons Holdings Inc.* [2015] EWCA Civ 665, [2016] 1 WLR 1814 at [88], [89], [92], reversed in *Four Seasons Holdings Inc. v. Brownlie* [2017] UKSC 80, [2018] 1 WLR 192 without discussing pleading and proof of foreign law.

choice-of-law rule of the Regulations should be applied.[201] In such cases, the courts accept the agreement between the parties and do not conduct a separate choice-of-law analysis. In other cases, the parties refrain from mentioning foreign law altogether. In such cases, English courts are entitled to proceed on the basis of the presumption that the foreign law is the same as English law. In both types of case, the exclusion of evidence and procedure from the scope of the Regulations, coupled with the English rules on pleading and proof of foreign law, represent an instrument of party autonomy.

3.10. HABITUAL RESIDENCE

The concept of habitual residence of companies and natural persons acting in the course of a business activity is a legal concept. The habitual residence of a company is the place of its central administration.[202] There is also a special rule for determining the habitual residence of companies acting in the course of operations of a branch, agency or other establishment.[203] UK courts have not yet had an opportunity to address the concept of habitual residence of companies for the purposes of the Rome I and Rome II Regulations. The habitual residence of a natural person acting in the course of a business activity is his or her principal place of business.[204] In *Wrigley v. Wood*,[205] the court had to determine the applicable law of two contracts for the payment of commission for the provision of service of introducing a purchaser to a broker which resulted in the sale of a luxury yacht. One contract was made before the entry into force of the Rome I Regulation, the other after that date. The contracts were between the captain of the yacht and the broker. The court found that the captain had entered this contract in the course of his trade or profession as a yacht captain. The question arose as to whether or not the captain had a principal place of business or indeed any place of business. The evidence established that the captain effectively spent 47 weeks of his year on the yacht. The court felt that there was something wholly artificial in suggesting that the yacht was a place of business or indeed in seeking to ascribe a place, a location, in relation to it, because of its itinerant nature. The submission of the defendants was that Monaco was the place in question because that was where the yacht's managing agents were established. The court

201 See, for example, *PJSC Tatneft v. Bogolyubov* [2017] EWCA Civ 1581, [2018] 4 WLR 14 at [29] and *Lebara Mobile Ltd v. Lycamobile UK Ltd* [2015] EWHC 3318 (Ch) at [31].

202 Article 19(1) of Rome I; Article 23(1) of Rome II.

203 Article 19(2) of Rome I, on which see *Eurasia Sports Ltd v. Tsai* [2016] EWHC 2207 (QB), affirmed in [2018] EWCA Civ 1742, [2018] 1 WLR 6089 without discussing choice of law; Article 23(1) of Rome II.

204 Article 19(1) of Rome I; Article 23(2) of Rome II.

205 [2014] EWHC 3684 (Comm) at [19], [20].

concluded this part of the judgment by noting that 'There appear few, if any, other true candidates.'[206] The captain's habitual residence for the purposes of Rome I was therefore unclear.

The concept of habitual residence of natural persons not acting in the course of a business activity is a question of fact. This notion was interpreted in two cases. In *Gray v. Hurley*,[207] the defendant was found to have been habitually resident in England because he spent more time in London than anywhere else (763 days over the course of five years) and had a home in London. *Winrow v. Hemphill*[208] concerned a personal injury suffered abroad in a road accident. The claimant, a UK national, had been living and working in Germany for eight-and-a-half-years by the time of the accident. She was living there with her husband. Three of their children were at school in Germany. The claimant had moved to Germany because her husband was in the army and had been posted there. The claimant and her family returned to the UK approximately 18 months after the accident, which was earlier than they had originally planned. The court held that, although Germany had not been her husband's first choice, the residence of the claimant in Germany was voluntary and established for a considerable period of time. In light of the length of stay in this country, its purpose and the establishment of a life there, the habitual residence of the claimant at the time of the accident was held to be in Germany.

3.11. *RENVOI*

Renvoi is excluded in matters that fall within the scope of the Rome I and Rome II Regulations.[209] This exclusion has been mentioned by the courts on several occasions[210] and has not led to any problems in practice.

4. ISSUES SPECIFIC TO EITHER ROME I OR ROME II

This part of the chapter will examine certain issues that have come up in practice that are specific to either the Rome I or the Rome II Regulation, including: fixed choice-of-law rules in contract; choice-of-law rules for formal validity of contracts; choice-of-law rules in tort; choice-of-law rules for unjust enrichment; and choice-of-law rules for *culpa in contrahendo*.

---

206 Ibid at [20].

207 [2019] EWHC 1636 (QB) at [190].

208 [2014] EWHC 3164 (QB), [2015] ILPr 12 at [39]–[41].

209 Article 20 of Rome I; Article 24 of Rome II.

210 See *Integral Petroleum SA v. SCU-Finanz AG* [2015] EWCA Civ 144, [2016] 1 All ER (Comm) 217 at [23], [48]; *Jacobs v. Motor Insurers' Bureau* [2010] EWCA Civ 1208, [2011] 1 WLR 2609 at [27].

4.1. ROME I: CHOICE-OF-LAW RULES IN CONTRACT

Article 4 of Rome I lays down fixed choice-of-law rules for the vast majority of contracts (other than contracts of carriage, consumer, insurance and employment contracts). Article 4(1) sets out fixed choice-of-law rules for a number of nominate contracts. Article 4(2) covers innominate contracts that have a characteristic performance. Article 4(4) is a catch-all provisions that applies to innominate contracts without a characteristic performance.

Article 4(1) was applied in four cases.[211] The courts applied Article 4(2) in four cases.[212] In *European Union v. Syria*,[213] the court held that the characteristic performance under a contract of guarantee was that of payment of money by the guarantor. In *Bill Kenwright Ltd v. Flash Entertainment FZ LLC*,[214] the court held that in a settlement agreement the 'characteristic performance' was the payment of money. In *Eurasia Sports Ltd v. Tsai*,[215] the court considered (while leaving the point open) that a betting account contract was governed by the law of the place where the relevant branch of the betting company, as the provider of the characteristic obligation, was located, which was English law. In *Taurus Petroleum Ltd v. State Oil Marketing Co. of the Ministry of Oil, Iraq*,[216] the High Court held that a letter of credit fell within Article 4(2) and that the characteristic performance was effected by the bank making payment by taking steps to credit the payee's account, which pointed to English law. In the Court of Appeal, Moore-Bick VP[217] seems to have confused the Rome Convention and the Rome I Regulation,[218] but did express his disagreement with the judge that

211 *Brownlie v. Four Seasons Holdings Inc. (No 2)* [2019] EWHC 2533 (QB) at [6]; *Brownlie v. Four Seasons Holdings Inc.* [2015] EWCA Civ 665, [2016] 1 WLR 1814 at [32], [41] (provision of services under a contract for organising an excursion), reversed in *Four Seasons Holdings Inc. v. Brownlie* [2017] UKSC 80, [2018] 1 WLR 192 without discussing choice of law under Rome I; *Toyota Tsusho Sugar Trading Ltd v. Prolat Srl* [2014] EWHC 3649 (Comm), [2015] 1 Lloyd's Rep 344 at [18] (sale of sugar); *BNP Paribas SA v. Anchorage Capital Europe LLP* [2013] EWHC 3073 (Comm) at [62], [64] (sale of private placement notes regarded as a sale of goods); *SSL International Plc v. TTK LIG Ltd* [2011] EWCA Civ 1170, [2012] 1 WLR 1842 at [82] (supply of condoms).

212 See also *Molton Street Capital LLP v. Shooters Hill Capital Partners LLP* [2015] EWHC 3419 (Comm) at [92]–[94] (sale of junk bonds).

213 [2018] EWHC 1712 (Comm) at [74].

214 [2016] EWHC 1951 (QB) at [37].

215 [2016] EWHC 2207 (QB) at [37], [60], affirmed in [2018] EWCA Civ 1742, [2018] 1 WLR 6089 without discussing choice of law.

216 [2013] EWHC 3494 (Comm), [2014] 1 All ER (Comm) 942 at [18].

217 [2015] EWCA Civ 835, [2016] 2 All ER (Comm) 1037 at [35], reversed in [2017] UKSC 64, [2018] AC 690 without discussing this point.

218 See ibid: 'The letters of credit contain no express choice of proper law and in those circumstances, by virtue of art 4(1) of the Rome Convention ("Rome")'. The letter of credit in *Taurus* was issued after 17 December 2009, so Rome I applied.

the performance which was characteristic of the contract was taking steps to effect payment rather than actually making payment. Nevertheless, the result was the same – English law governed.

Article 4(4) was applied in two cases. In *Bazhanov v. Fosman*,[219] the court dealt with the law applicable to alleged contracts for the provision of services to refinance a Russian company. Since the alleged contracts contemplated that services would be provided by both parties, Article 4(1) and (2) did not apply. Had the judge been persuaded that there was a good arguable case that enforceable contracts had been made, he would have concluded that Russian law governed under Article 4(4). In *Scott v. West*,[220] which concerned a contract for the purchase of shares. The court held that the contract in question was most closely connected with England.

There is one case where the court had to apply Article 4 of Rome I, but where it is unclear which particular paragraph of Article 4 was relied upon. In *Wrigley v. Wood*,[221] the court had to determine the applicable law of two contracts for the payment of commission for the provision of service of introducing a purchaser to a broker which resulted in the sale of a luxury yacht. One contract was made before the entry into force of the Rome I Regulation, the other after that date. The contracts were between the captain of the yacht and the broker. It has already been mentioned[222] that the judgment is unclear with respect to the captain's habitual residence. It is also unclear which of the four paragraphs of Article 4 the court relied upon to determine that the applicable law was the law of Florida. This is because the court applied the Rome Convention to determine the law governing the contract entered before 17 December 2009, but failed to conduct a separate choice-of-law analysis under the Rome I Regulation for the contract entered after this date. The contract in question was for the provision of the service of introducing a purchaser to a broker, so it falls under Article 4(1)(b) of Rome I which points to the law of the country of the service provider's habitual residence. But given that the court struggled to determine the habitual residence of the claimant, it is unclear whether it applied the escape clause in Article 4(3) or the closest connection test in Article 4(4) to determine the applicable law. Ultimately, the outcome would have been the same, but the case demonstrates a lack of rigour in the application of Rome I.

---

219 [2017] EWHC 3404 (Comm) at [62]–[64].

220 [2012] EWHC 1890 (Ch) at [10], [11].

221 [2014] EWHC 3684 (Comm).

222 See n. 205 above.

4.2. ROME I: CHOICE-OF-LAW RULES FOR FORMAL VALIDITY OF CONTRACTS

The only case considering Article 11 of Rome I on formal validity of contracts is *Integral Petroleum SA v. SCU-Finanz AG*.[223] This case concerned an oil supply contract between two Swiss oil trading companies. Although the Swiss Register of Commerce listed two joint authorised signatories (*prokurists*) of the seller, only one had signed the supply contract. The buyer, alleging that no oil had been supplied under the contract, obtained judgment in default of defence in an action for damages for breach of contract. The judge held that the defence that the sole signatory could not bind it was bound to succeed. The buyer appealed. The main issue on appeal was which system of law should apply, namely Swiss law or the law applicable to the formal validity of contracts pursuant to Article 11 of Rome I. The court held that the issue was not one of formal validity, but one of the authority of a sole signatory to bind the company. Since that was a matter for the company's constitution, it was governed by common law principles of agent and principal. The court further held that even if the ability of the sole signatory to bind the company could be brought within Article 11, it would still be excluded from the scope of Rome I by Article 1(2)(f) and/or (g).

4.3. ROME II: CHOICE-OF-LAW RULES IN TORT

With regard to choice-of-law rules in tort, Article 4 has been by far the most frequently applied provision. In personal injury cases, the courts have usually applied the law designated by either the fixed choice-of-law rule in Article 4(1) (*lex loci damni*)[224] or Article 4(2) (the law of the common habitual residence

---

223 [2015] EWCA Civ 144, [2016] 1 All ER (Comm) 217 at [17]–[23], [39]–[48].

224 *Pandya v. Intersalonika General Insurance Co. SA* [2020] EWHC 273 (QB) at [9], [12]; *Brownlie v. Four Seasons Holdings Inc. (No 2)* [2019] EWHC 2533 (QB) at [6]; *Folkes v. Generali Assurances* [2019] EWHC 801 (QB) at [7]; *Vilca v. Xstrata Ltd* [2018] EWHC 27 (QB) at [3], [51]; *Gilmour v. Linea Directa Aseguradora Sa Compania De Seguros Y Reaseguros* 2017 GWD 39-603, Sheriff Court (Lothian and Borders) (Edinburgh) at [2], [15]; *Gunn v. Diaz* [2017] EWHC 157 (QB), [2017] 2 All ER (Comm) 129 at [9]; *Committeri v. Club Mediterranee SA* [2016] EWHC 1510 (QB) at [57], affirmed in [2018] EWCA Civ 1889, [2019] ILPr 19 without discussing choice of law under Rome II; *XP v. Compensa Towarzystwo SA* [2016] EWHC 1728 (QB), [2016] Med LR 570 at [55]; *Bianco v. Bennett* [2015] EWHC 626 (QB), [2015] ILPr 24 at [28]; *Vann v. Ocidental-Companhia De Seguros SA* [2015] EWCA Civ 572 at [17]; *Winrow v. Hemphill* [2014] EWHC 3164 (QB), [2015] ILPr 12 at [38]–[63]; *Stylianou v. Toyoshima* [2013] EWHC 2188 (QB) at [55]–[83]; *Wink v. Croatia Osiguranje DD* [2013] EWHC 1118 (QB) at [49]. See also *Jacobs v. Motor Insurers' Bureau* [2010] EWCA Civ 1208, [2011] 1 WLR 2609; *Bacon v. Nacional Suiza Cia Seguros y Reseguros SA* [2010] EWHC 2017 (QB), [2010] ILPr 46 at [25]; *Bonsall v. Cattolica Assicurazioni* [2010] ILPr 45, County Court (Winchester).

of the parties).[225] Cases concerning economic loss have caused particular difficulties for the application of Article 4(1). In such cases, the courts have been applying the law of the country where the losses were irreversibly suffered as the *lex loci damni*.[226] If economic loss is suffered in more than one country,

---

225 *Le Guevel-Mouly v. AIG Europe Ltd* [2016] EWHC 1794 (QB) at [19]; *Rai v. Ministry of Defence*, Queen's Bench Division, 9 May 2016 at [90]–[118]. See also *Winrow v. Hemphill* [2014] EWHC 3164 (QB), [2015] ILPr 12 at [39] (the court clarified that 'the person claimed to be liable' for the purposes of Article 4(2) was the first defendant driver, not the second defendant insurer); *Marshall v. Motor Insurers' Bureau* [2015] EWHC 3421 (QB), [2016] Lloyd's Rep IR 400 at [17], [18], affirmed in *Pickard v. Marshall* [2017] EWCA Civ 17, [2017] RTR 20 (Article 4(2) is not to be construed strictly to confine it to apply to proceedings where one person is bringing proceedings against another person and also applies to multi-party cases).

226 *ED&F Man Capital Markets Ltd v. Come Harvest Holdings Ltd* [2019] EWHC 1661 (Comm), [2019] ILPr 40 at [59]–[69] (unlawful means conspiracy; the damage occurred in the place in England where the claimant paid out funds to purchase goods and received allegedly forged warehouse receipts); *FM Capital Partners Ltd v. Marino* [2018] EWHC 1768 (Comm) at [484]–[510], in particular [493], affirmed in [2020] EWCA Civ 245 without discussing choice of law (conspiracy, dishonest assistance, knowing receipt and bribery; if economic loss consists in the non-receipt of money, the *lex loci damni* is the place where 'the claimant complains that he has not received a sum which he should have received'); *MX1 Ltd v. Farahzad* [2018] EWHC 1041 (Ch), [2018] 1 WLR 5553 at [31]–[40] (conspiracy to injure; according to the court, at [39](8), the 'touchstone' in cases of economic loss for identifying the applicable law appears to be reversibility; the losses in this case, which consisted in the costs incurred in uncovering the defendant's tracks as the person behind a Twitter account used to make allegations of bribery and corruption against the claimant and to disclose confidential information, were irreversibly suffered in England); *Pan Oceanic Chartering Inc. v. UNIPEC UK Co. Ltd* [2016] EWHC 2774 (Comm), [2017] 2 All ER (Comm) 196 at [193]–[204] (tortious interference with contractual relations; the damage was the loss of commission, which should have been paid in New York); *AS Latvijas Krajbanka (In Liquidation) v. Antonov* [2016] EWHC 1679 (Comm) at [8] (the bank argued that the defendant had caused the bank to enter transactions which were not in its interests and which were arranged to benefit the defendant; the bank's losses were incurred in Latvia); *Eurasia Sports Ltd v. Tsai* [2016] EWHC 2207 (QB) at [59], affirmed in [2018] EWCA Civ 1742, [2018] 1 WLR 6089 without discussing choice of law (the claimant argued that the defendants set up 11 betting accounts which went rapidly into debt; damage held to have been sustained in England); *Banque Cantonale de Geneve v. Polevent Ltd* [2015] EWHC 1968 (Comm), [2016] QB 394 (claim in deceit; an employee of the claimant Geneva bank had been defrauded to transfer the claimant's moneys to an account in London held by the defendant; bank's losses accepted to have occurred in Geneva); *Hillside (New Media) Ltd v. Baasland* [2010] EWHC 3336 (Comm), [2010] 2 CLC 986 at [28]–[37] (losses (nearly £3 million) suffered by a Norwegian who placed bets on the bet365 website were suffered in England because the *situs* of one of the claimant's online betting accounts was in England where the betting company was domiciled; the losses were suffered when the claimant used the funds to place bets). See also *PJSC Tatneft v. Bogolyubov* [2017] EWCA Civ 1581, [2018] 4 WLR 14 at [29] (dishonest scheme to misappropriate sums in Russia owed to a Russian assignor; common ground that Russian law applicable); *Fortress Value Recovery Fund I LLC v. Blue Skye Special Opportunities Fund LP* [2013] EWHC 14 (Comm), [2013] 1 All ER (Comm) 973 at [42]–[75] (the claimant was an investor in certain Italian assets; the investment structure was based around a fund, in the form of an English limited partnership, which held shares in a Luxembourg company which held the Italian assets; the principal limited partner in the fund was a Luxembourg company that was the joint venture vehicle

the applicable law pursuant to Article 4(1) is not the place where the damage predominantly occurs – where damage occurs across several jurisdictions there will be several applicable laws.[227]

UK courts have also considered the special choice-of-laws rules contained in Articles 6 (Unfair competition and acts restricting free competition), 7 (Environmental damage) and 8 (Infringement of intellectual property rights).

In *Innovia Films Ltd v. Frito-Lay North America Inc*,[228] the claimant commenced two actions concerning various patent applications made by the defendant. The claimant argued that it had devised the inventions for food packaging film described and claimed in those applications, and that they had been disclosed to the defendant in confidence. The claimant thus claimed to be the rightful owner of those applications and any patents resulting therefrom, and that the defendant had acted in breach of confidence. One of the issues was the law applicable to the claim for breach of confidence. The court indicated that claims for breach of an equitable obligation of confidence fell within Article 6. The court then specified that Article 6(2) was the applicable rule on the ground that the alleged acts of unfair competition affected the interests of a specific competitor, namely the claimant. It followed that Article 4 applied. The claim was held to be manifestly more closely connected with England, so English law applied. In *Deutsche Bahn AG v. Mastercard Inc*,[229] the court dealt with connected claims brought by 1,300 retailers operating in 18 EU countries that, in breach of EU/EEA and domestic competition rules, the merchant service charges which they had paid in respect of MasterCard credit card and Maestro debit card transactions under the MasterCard payment scheme were higher than they should have been. It was common ground that Article 6(3) was the relevant choice-of-law rule for the claims that fell within the temporal scope of Rome II. The parties also agreed that the country 'where the market is, or is likely to

by which the claimant and other investors invested in the fund; the claimant argued that it was the victim of a dishonest scheme to reorganise the fund and its assets, diminishing or eliminating its rights and interests in the assets and taking the control and benefit of the assets; it was neither necessary nor appropriate to determine on a summary basis before trial whether the applicable law of any claim in tort was the law of England or Luxembourg; the claimant had a real prospect of establishing at trial that English law governed on the basis that the direct damage occurred in England for the purposes of Article 4(1)); *Erste Group Bank AG (London) v. JSC (VMZ Red October)* [2015] EWCA Civ 379, [2015] 1 CLC 706 at [94]–[96] (if the loss suffered by the claimant as the result of a conspiracy was the damage to its right to repayment under a loan agreement and a guarantee, that loss was suffered in New York, as the place of payment under the two contracts).

227 *MX1 Ltd v. Farahzad* [2018] EWHC 1041 (Ch), [2018] 1 WLR 5553 at [41]–[44].

228 [2012] EWHC 790 (Pat), [2012] RPC 24 at [109]–[111]. See also *Conductive Inkjet Technology Ltd v. Uni-Pixel Displays Inc.* [2013] EWHC 2968 (Ch), [2014] 1 All ER (Comm) 654 at [125]; *Force India Formula One Team Ltd v. 1 Malaysia Racing Team SDN BHD* [2012] EWHC 616 (Ch), [2012] RPC 29 at [388].

229 [2018] EWHC 412 (Ch), [2018] 4 CMLR 31 at [21]–[23].

be, affected', within the meaning of Article 6(3), was the country in which the merchant was based at the time of the transaction upon which a merchant service charge was paid by the merchant to the acquiring bank. The parties also agreed that for practical reasons all UK transactions in respect of which a claim was made should be treated as having occurred in England, so that the applicable law was English law.

Article 7 was discussed in *His Royal Highness Okpabi v. Royal Dutch Shell Plc*.[230] The claim for damages was brought by Nigerian claimants against Royal Dutch Shell Plc, an Anglo-Dutch oil company incorporated in England, and its Nigerian subsidiary for environmental damage in Nigeria caused by oil leaks from pipelines and associated infrastructure operated by the subsidiary. The judge held that Article 7 applied and that the claimants were entitled to elect to pursue an environmental claim under the law where negligent supervisory acts and omissions occurred, rather than the place where the damage occurred. The claimants maintained that this entitled them to proceed against Royal Dutch Shell Plc under English law as the acts and omissions occurred (or were said to have occurred) in England. The defendants contended that the claim against Royal Dutch Shell Plc was governed by Nigerian law. The judge did not decide this issue because he found that, given the substantial similarity between English and Nigerian common law, the difference was immaterial.

Article 8 was applied in three cases, all of which concerned the infringement of unitary Community intellectual property rights. The courts applied the rule that the applicable law, for any question that is not governed by the relevant Community instrument, is the law of the country in which the act of infringement was committed.[231]

4.4. ROME II: CHOICE-OF-LAW RULES FOR UNJUST ENRICHMENT

Article 10 of Rome II was applied in four cases. It has already been mentioned that in *Bazhanov v. Fosman*[232] the court dealt with the law applicable to alleged contracts for the provision of services to refinance a Russian company. The claim in unjust enrichment was advanced as an alternative to a contract claim to cover the situation where, contrary to the claimant's primary case, no contract had

230 [2017] EWHC 89 (TCC), [2017] Bus LR 1335 at [55], affirmed in [2018] EWCA Civ 191, [2018] Bus LR 1022 without discussing choice of law under Rome II.

231 *W3 Ltd v. Easygroup Ltd* [2018] EWHC 7 (Ch), [2018] FSR 16 at [357]–[360] (EU trade marks); *Eli Lilly and Co. v. Genentech Inc.* [2017] EWHC 3104 (Pat), [2018] 1 WLR 1755 at [35] (European patent); *Parainen Pearl Shipping Ltd v. Kristian Gerhard Jebsen Skipsrederi AS* [2017] EWHC 2570 (Pat) at [18] (European patent).

232 [2017] EWHC 3404 (Comm).

been in fact entered. After having found that the parties had not agreed on the governing law, the judge held[233] that Article 10(1) did not apply because on the hypothesis that there was no contract, there was no governing law that could be derived from it for the purposes of Article 10(1). Article 10(2) did not apply because one party was habitually resident in England, the other in Russia. It was common ground that for the purposes of Article 10(3) the unjust enrichment took place in Russia and that Article 10(4) would not point to any other law. Because Russian law does not recognise claims based on unjust enrichment, the unjust enrichment claim did not raise a serious issue to be tried.

In *Gray v. Hurley*,[234] the court dealt with a claim for restitution in unjust enrichment arising from the end of a romantic relationship. The court held that Article 10(1) did not apply. Since both parties were habitually resident in England, English law applied by virtue of Article 10(2).

In *ED&F Man Capital Markets Ltd v. Come Harvest Holdings Ltd*,[235] the court held that the unjust enrichment concerned a closely connected relationship existing between the parties that arose out of the alleged unlawful means conspiracy to defraud. Since the law governing the tort was English law, the unjust enrichment was governed by the same law. But the court also held that, if Article 10(1) did not apply, Article 10(3) would lead to the application of Singaporean law since Singapore was the place where the unjust enrichment took place. The defendant was from Singapore and the allegedly forged warehouse receipts concerned goods which were located in warehouses in several countries, including Singapore.

In *Banque Cantonale de Geneve v. Polevent Ltd*,[236] the claimant was a bank in Geneva. One of its employees was defrauded by the defendant into believing that she was acting on instructions from the claimant's deputy chief executive officer and transferred moneys to an account in London held by the defendant. The claimant brought two claims against the defendant: a claim in the tort of deceit and a claim for restitution in unjust enrichment based on the mistaken transfer induced by fraud. The question was whether the restitution claim was governed by English law, as the law of the place where the unjust enrichment had taken place, or by Swiss law, either because it arose out of the tort of deceit and therefore Article 4 of Rome II was applicable or because it was a claim for unjust enrichment arising out of a 'relationship existing' between the parties and therefore, by virtue of Article 10(1), was governed by the law applicable to the relationship. The court held that Article 4 was not applicable because, while the deceit explained why the transfer had been made, it was not a necessary

233 Ibid at [70]–[77].
234 [2019] EWHC 1636 (QB) at [188]–[191].
235 [2019] EWHC 1661 (Comm), [2019] ILPr 40 at [70]–[73].
236 [2015] EWHC 1968 (Comm), [2016] QB 394.

ingredient of a claim for restitution. 'Relationship' for the purposes of Article 10(1) was not intended to refer to the mere 'relationship' of wrongdoer and victim created by the commission of the tort. It referred to a relationship in existence before the facts which had given rise to the claim had occurred. Accordingly, since there had been no relationship between the claimant and the defendant before the events which had led to money being mistakenly paid into the latter's account in London, Article 10(3) applied with the result that the law governing the restitution claim was English, as the law of the country where the unjust enrichment had occurred.

It has further been accepted by the parties in one case[237] that Article 10 is not applicable to claims in knowing receipt because these are not 'pure unjust enrichment' claims but claims relating to a wrong.

4.5. ROME II: CHOICE-OF-LAW RULES FOR *CULPA IN CONTRAHENDO*

The only case that applied Article 12 of Rome II is *Morgan Stanley & Co. International Plc v. China Haisheng Juice Holdings Co. Ltd.*[238] After noting that it was common ground that English law applied to a contract, the court held that the law applicable to a party's claim for damages for fraudulent misrepresentation inducing that party to enter the contract was likely to be English law.

5. CONCLUSION

The aim of this chapter was, firstly, to describe the legal and commercial contexts in which disputes concerning choice of law for contractual and non-contractual obligations have arisen before UK courts and, secondly, to outline the treatment by UK courts of some of the key general issues that are common to the Rome I and Rome II Regulations and of certain specific issues that are idiosyncratic to either Rome I or Rome II.

The two Regulations have been frequently applied by UK courts. On 1 April 2020, there had been 69 cases in which the courts applied the Regulations, 26 applying Rome I and 48 applying Rome II (as explained at fn. 76). There are many other cases where the courts mentioned or discussed the Regulations, without applying them. An interesting feature of the application of the

---

237 *FM Capital Partners Ltd v. Marino* [2018] EWHC 1768 (Comm) at [482], affirmed in [2020] EWCA Civ 245 without discussing choice of law; cf. *ED&F Man Capital Markets Ltd v. Come Harvest Holdings Ltd* [2019] EWHC 1661 (Comm), [2019] ILPr 40 at [70], [71].

238 [2009] EWHC 2409 (Comm), [2010] 2 All ER (Comm) 514 at [36].

Regulations in the UK is that choice of law was often (in 65 per cent of cases applying Rome I and in 52 per cent of cases applying Rome II) relevant for the process of litigation, not for deciding the case on the substance. Many cases thus concerned service out of the jurisdiction and/or the *forum (non) conveniens* doctrine, applications for an anti-suit injunction, to strike out a statement of case, for summary judgment or interim injunction and interim third party debt orders. The legal context is crucial for understanding the practical operation of the two Regulations because in many 'procedural' choice-of-law cases, choice-of-law issues arose in an incidental or accidental manner and were dealt with under a lower standard of proof or on a summary basis. Because choice-of-law issues do not necessarily receive the same amount of scrutiny in 'procedural' choice-of-law cases as at trial, such cases should be read and used cautiously. With regard to the commercial context, the cases concerned various types of disputes and kinds of contracts and non-contractual obligations. Of particular note is the fact that the majority of cases under Rome II concerned claims for damages for personal injuries suffered abroad. Most of the remaining cases under Rome II concerned economic loss.

The chapter reveals that UK courts are well versed in the application of the two Regulations. They have been applying faithfully the principle of autonomous European interpretation, even when this meant a departure from the traditional common law approach (e.g. with respect to the choice-of-law treatment of the issue of assessment of damages), and have often referred to other EU private international law instruments, most importantly the Rome Convention and the Brussels I Regulation. UK courts have had the opportunity to apply many different provisions of the two Regulations and, generally speaking, have been doing that correctly. In particular, implied choice of law and the escape clauses have been resorted to sparingly, although the courts have been more willing to exercise judicial discretion when dealing with choice-of-law issues at the interlocutory stage or on an application to strike out a statement of case/for summary judgment.

This is not to say that the two Regulations have been applied perfectly. An issue of particular concern is the choice-of-law treatment of so-called statutory claims under Rome I. In the areas of employment and consumer law, claimants often base their claims on the provisions of domestic statutes. UK courts approach these claims as raising not choice-of-law issues, but issues of statutory construction, which approach results in the over-application of domestic law. Another peculiarity of the application of the two Regulations in UK courts in the treatment of foreign law. Although this is a procedural and evidentiary issue, the parties' decisions on whether to plead and prove foreign law can have substantive effects. Whenever the parties are in agreement with respect to how a particular choice-of-law rule of the Regulations should be applied or the parties choose not to plead and prove foreign law, the courts have been willing to follow the parties' wishes. The rules on pleading and proof of foreign law have therefore been used as tools of party autonomy.

Overall, it can be concluded that the innovations introduced by the Rome I and Rome II Regulations have proved to be both satisfactory and successful. The Regulations have achieved greater legal certainty, foreseeability and uniformity in the area of choice of law for contractual and non-contractual obligations. The Rome I and Rome II Regulations have been applied on many occasions in the UK. UK courts have thus contributed significantly to the understanding of the provisions of two instruments. They will continue to do so even after the expiry of the Brexit implementation period because their provisions will continue to be applied indirectly in the UK, as UK domestic law by virtue of the European Union (Withdrawal) Act and the Law Applicable to Contractual Obligations and Non-Contractual Obligations (Amendment etc) (EU Exit) Regulations.

CONCLUSION

Emmanuel GUINCHARD*

* In the following footnotes, national reports are referred to by the name of the country (or countries) reported on. Where a footnote is provided, it may be a reference either to the footnote itself or (for the reader's convenience) to the text relating to the footnote or to both.

As in 2019 we celebrated the 10th anniversary of the entry into application of both the Rome I and the Rome II Regulations, it appeared useful to take stock and assess in particular whether these Regulations have been applied consistently and adequately by courts within the European Union – both at EU level (CJEU) and at national level – and identify any difficulties that may have arisen in their interpretation and application. This study appears relevant to those both within and outside the EU, especially since some states extended the application of Rome I and Rome II beyond their original scope of application (section 1). For the purpose of this study, the experts commendably looked at legislative measures, judicial practice and even non-judicial practice (section 2). Overall, the assessment is positive, but weaknesses remain, in particular in respect of the treatment and proof of foreign law (section 3). A look at the future will conclude the study (section 4).

1. THE RELEVANCY OF THE STUDY

1.1. THE RELEVANCY FOR EU AND NON-EU STAKEHOLDERS

A study of Rome I and Rome II in practice is of clear relevance to any EU legal professional, institution, business, or other interested party.[1] However, the study of the judicial application of the Rome I and Rome II Regulations is also of relevance to third-state stakeholders.

Firstly, it could provide them with a possible source of inspiration for the drafting and/or interpretation of their own set of rules, especially where the latter is already inspired at least in part by the European regime.[2] In relation to Rome I, one may think for example of the 2007 Turkish Private International Law and International Civil Procedure Act, which contains many similar provisions to Rome I, despite some differences on matters such as *culpa in contrahendo*, escape clauses and the *lois d'application immédiate* – a concept (roughly) translated as overriding mandatory provisions in the English version

---

1 See the Introduction to this volume above.

2 Or even in full for the very specific third state that is now technically the United Kingdom (considered elsewhere in this report as a Member State, as it had been so until recently, 1 February 2020, i.e. for the period covered by the national report, and is still subject to a transition regime, which will mean applying Rome I and Rome II long after the end of the transition period currently scheduled for 31 December 2020: see the Introduction to this volume). The United Kingdom currently intends to unilaterally apply Rome I and Rome II even afterwards, making this study extremely relevant not only for its past and present but also its future. The adoption is *mutatis mutandis*, including by revocation of associated Regulation 662/2009: see the adopted The Law Applicable to Contractual Obligations and Non-Contractual Obligations (Amendment etc.) (EU Exit) Regulations 2019, UK S.I. 2019/834, <https://www.legislation.gov.uk/uksi/2019/834/made>.

of Article 9 Rome I[3] – of a third state.[4] In relation to Rome II, one may think of the 2014 Argentinean Civil and Commercial Code, with its Article 2657 purely and simply mirroring Article 4(1) and (2)[5] Rome II, and the role of Article 4(3) being assumed by the general escape clause of Article 2597. The Draft OHADAC[6] Model Law relating to Private International Law also comes to mind, as the influence of Rome II appears exceptionally strong here, particularly through the often faithful replication of both the general rule (Article 4 Rome II) in Article 52(2) and (3) OHADAC, and almost all specific rules (Articles 5–8 Rome II) in Articles 53–56 OHADAC (liability for damage caused by defective products, unfair competition and acts restricting free competition, environmental damage and infringement of intellectual property rights).[7]

---

3 One wonders if the translation may not explain in part the confusion sometimes observed with *ordre public* in the sense of Article 21 Rome I and Article 26 Rome II, or mandatory rules referred to by paraphrase in Article 8 Rome I (e.g. Czech Republic, section 2.2). The expression 'rules of immediate application', already used in several countries (e.g. Croatia) and much closer to the original concept of *Francescakis* ('*lois d'application immédiate*'), could perhaps be preferred. The expression used in the French version of Article 9 ('*lois de police*') is widespread, including outside France, albeit not the most enlightening either.

4 See B. Yüksel, 'Choice of Law in Civil and Commercial Matters under Turkish Private International Law in Comparison with Their Equivalents under the Rome I and Rome II Regulations', in P. Beaumont and B. Yüksel (eds.), *Turkish and EU Private International Law. A comparison*, XII Lehva, Istanbul, 2014, p. 153, at p. 223. The author notes that, although the characterisation of *culpa in contrahendo* differs in EU and Turkish private international law, the main conflict-of-laws rule appears similar (p. 194). The difference on the question of the *lois d'application immédiate* of a third state stems from the source of inspiration of the Turkish Private International Law Act on this point, namely the Rome Convention (see pp. 189–191). For a finding of similarity regarding the law applicable to contracts on intellectual property rights, see, in the same book, B. Bahadir Erdem, 'Intellectual Property Rights in Turkish Private International Law and a Comparative Analysis on Applicable Law to Contractual Obligations', p. 225, at p. 241, who compares Article 28(1) of the Turkish Private International Law Act and Article 3 Rome I. In the absence of a choice-of-law clause in a licensing agreement, the consistency between the EU and Turkish regimes lies more in the interpretation of Article 4(2) Rome I, as Article 28(2) Turkish Private International Law Act offers a clear rule on the topic, in contrast with the EU Regulation, if the licensing agreement is not characterised as a contract for the provisions of services in the sense of Article 4(1)(b), should the CJEU's case law on Brussels I be transposed to Rome I (see p. 233 ff.). Here, the potential for inspiration could work in the opposite direction.

5 With the specification that common domicile is preferred in Article 2657, second paragraph, to common habitual residence in Article 4(2). See E. Guinchard, 'Du rayonnement extérieur de l'espace judiciaire civil européen. Un aperçu de deux législations récentes (Nouveau code civil et commercial argentin de 2014 et Projet de loi modèle OHADAC de droit international privé de 2014)', RTDE 2014, 919.

6 Organization for the Harmonization of Business Law in the Caribbean.

7 Although this does not exclude differences such as the even greater role accorded to party autonomy: compare Articles 6(4), 8(3) and 14 Rome II with Articles 52(1), 54(4) and 56(2) OHADAC. For a presentation of the Draft Model Law, see E. Guinchard, supra n. 5. For a commentary, see J.C. Fernández Rozas (ed.), *Armonización del Derecho Internacional Privado en el Caribe / L'harmonisation du Droit International Privé dans le Caraïbe / Harmonization of Private International Law in the Caribbean. Estudios y Materiales Preparatorios y Proyecto de Ley Modelo Ohadac de Derecho Internacional Privado de 2014*, Iprolex, Madrid, 2015.

Secondly, Rome I and Rome II regulate contractual and non-contractual relationships with third states following Article 2 Rome I/Article 3 Rome II and their principle of universal application: 'Any law specified by this Regulation shall be applied whether or not it is the law of a Member State'. The two Regulations therefore have a direct impact on (among others) non-EU-based individuals and companies who enter into relations with EU-based persons, or even on non-EU-based individuals and legal entities exclusively, for example if they have concluded an exclusive jurisdiction clause in favour of a national court in the EU, which will apply the Regulations.

1.2. ENRICHING THE SIGNIFICANCE OF THE STUDY: THE EXTENSION OF ROME I AND ROME II

Rome I and Rome II have not generally been applied beyond their original scope of application. Where this has been the case, three types of extension can be distinguished: deliberate, unplanned and erroneous.

1.2.1. Deliberate Extension

While most Member States have not deliberately extended the application of Rome I and/or Rome II beyond its/their original scope of application (e.g. Austria[8]), some states have indeed done so.

Firstly, this may have been done as a matter of principle. Thus, in Croatia, '[a]ccording to Article 25(2) of the 2017 Croatian Private International Law Act [which entered into force on 29 January 2019], the law applicable to contractual obligations that fall outside of the scope of application of the Rome I Regulation, and are not governed by another provision of national or international law in force in Croatia, is determined according to the provisions of the Rome I Regulation applicable to such contractual obligations'.[9] A similar extension of its scope of application benefits Rome II, according to Article 26(2) of the same Act.[10] In both cases, this extension is subject to conditions (a private law matter, a foreign element, a contractual or non-contractual obligation in the meaning of Croatian (not European) law and the absence of any other

8 Austria and Germany, section 2.2.2 (for Rome I), with none mentioned for Rome II either. See also Bulgaria, sections 1.1 (for Rome I) and 1.2 (for Rome II); Czech Republic, section 1.1; Greece, section 1; Ireland, section 1; Latvia, section 1.1; Lithuania, section 2; Luxembourg, section 1 *in limine*; Slovenia, section 1. The Cypriot, French, Portuguese, Slovak and Spanish reports do not mention any extension of Rome I or Rome II. Consideration is here given to an extension decided at national level.

9 Croatia, section 2.

10 Croatia, section 2.

provision of national or international law governing the same issue in Croatia). A wholesale extension of Rome I and Rome II may equally be found in the Netherlands.[11] An extension of Rome I (only) may also be found in Belgium, and probably in Italy, in both cases by a convincing interpretation of references to the Rome Convention in national private international law acts as references today to Rome I.[12]

Interestingly, as a result of its extension beyond its scope, a Regulation may have been applied to a particularly controversial issue whose exclusion from it was the outcome of an intense debate. An illustration would be the application of Rome II to defamation in the Netherlands. In a case involving defamatory statements on the Internet, the Dutch Supreme Court located the damage in the sense of Article 4(1) Rome II at the place of the centre of the victim's interests.[13] Whilst seemingly not raising a technical issue, this interpretation has been criticised from a values perspective as the application of the general rule of Rome II thus understood may endanger freedom of expression: '[t]here is a risk that a Dutch court will have to apply strict foreign defamation laws to claims against journalists, bloggers, etc., domiciled in the Netherlands'.[14] The suggested response was not to continue to exclude defamation from Rome II and to derogate to the national extension of Rome II on this point, but on the contrary to include defamation within the scope of application of Rome II, albeit with a dedicated rule of conflict of laws.[15] Its contents will – no doubt – be as debated, as in the years leading to the adoption of Rome II. Should it still prove difficult to insert such a provision despite the numerous proposals made,[16] even less a set of provisions on the applicable law covering all matters currently excluded by Article 1(2)(g) Rome II (that is all non-contractual obligations arising out of violations of privacy and rights relating to personality), a solution could be

11 The Netherlands, section 1.1.

12 Belgium, section 1 (Article 98 of the Belgian Private International Law Act); Italy, section 1.1.3 (Article 57 of the Italian Private International Law Act), with our expert however noting that case law is inconclusive on this point. These Acts referred to the Rome Convention, as Rome I was not in existence at the time of their enactment. For the same reason, Rome II is not mentioned in these Acts and no extension of Rome II to cases falling outside its scope of application is therefore foreseen in the absence of legislative intervention.

13 The Netherlands, section 2.3.2 *in fine*.

14 The Netherlands, section 3, where the expert adds that *ordre public* is unlikely to provide full relief.

15 The Netherlands, section 3, where our expert advocates, subsidiarily, for a dedicated conflict-of-laws rule at national level.

16 E.g. F.M. Meier, 'Unification of choice-of-law rules for defamation claims', Journal of Private International Law 2016, 492, 520 ('law of the country where the victim has his centre of interests at the time of the tort', subject to the law of the habitual residence of the broadcaster or publisher where the latter 'did not intend to distribute the publication or broadcast to the country where the victim has his centre of interests').

an exceptionally lower threshold for *ordre public* on this particular point,[17] for example without the adverb 'manifestly' of current Article 26 Rome II.[18]

Secondly, and by contrast with the first type of deliberate extension, the extension may be limited in scope, as illustrated by Poland, where the 2011 Private International Law Act states that Rome I shall apply to the specific insurances contracts excluded from its scope in Article 1(2)(j).[19]

Thirdly, a different and weaker form of deliberate extension may be found in Hungary, where Rome I and Rome II do not apply directly to matters outside their scope of application[20] but have strongly influenced the national rules on private international law which do apply in these circumstances, in particular the new Hungarian Act on Private International Law which came into force in 2018.[21] This alignment is however subject to limitations, such as the unavailability of party autonomy before the event giving rise to the damage, i.e. the most notable aspect of Article 14 Rome II.[22]

Finally, an extension *ratione loci* of Rome I and Rome II may be found in the United Kingdom, which decided to apply the Regulations to settle conflicts between the laws of its different countries – for example, between England and Scotland.[23]

---

17 In the application of *ordre public*, consideration could be given to the case law of the ECtHR (within the framework of the doctrine of *ordre public* in private international law as opposed to domestic law), for instance (Grand Chamber), *Springer v. Germany*, no. 39954/08, 7 February 2012, esp. paras. 89–95, where the following criteria are put forward in order to balance the right to freedom of expression against the right to respect for private life: 'contribution to a debate of general interest … How well known is the person concerned and what is the subject of the report? … Prior conduct of the person concerned … Method of obtaining the information and its veracity … Content, form and consequences of the publication … Severity of the sanction imposed'.

18 Subsidiarily, should the current exclusion of Article 1(2)(g) Rome II be maintained, clarification should be provided on its scope, as issues have been raised before national courts, in particular Austria and Germany, for instance whether claims by legal persons outside Article 6 Rome II are covered: see Austria and Germany, section 3.2.

19 Poland, section 1.

20 See however Hungary, section 3.1 where, by exception, the applicable law under Rome I (Hungarian law) was extended in a case to a matter normally excluded from Rome I, 'presumably because the [issue at stake] qualifies as a contractual question under Hungarian law'.

21 Hungary, sections 3.7 (for Rome I) and 4.4 (for Rome II). Similarly, the Rome Convention and the Rome II proposal inspired the drafting of the Bulgarian Code of Private International Law on, respectively, contractual and non-contractual obligations (Bulgaria, sections 1.1 and 1.2). One also notes that, in Spain, some leading authors have called for the national rule on the law applicable to non-contractual obligations (Article 10(9) Civil Code) to be interpreted in line with Article 4(1) Rome II due to its ambiguity (Spain, section 2.3 (n. 37)). Consideration is here given to an inspiration at national level. It therefore does not exclude the ad hoc inspiration in a specific case, e.g. France, section 1.2; Luxembourg, section 2.6.2.

22 Hungary, section 4.4.

23 For Rome II: The Law Applicable to Non-Contractual Obligations (England and Wales and Northern Ireland) Regulations 2008 (UK S.I. 2008/2986), regulation 6; and The

1.2.2. *Unplanned Extension*

Exceptionally, the extension may be the result less of a clear will to extend the Regulation(s) than of hastiness to repeal the relevant national private international law regime and the corresponding necessity to fill in the gap thus created. This is the case for Germany in the field of contractual obligations, where courts have, in the absence of national private international law provisions, applied Rome I to the material validity of choice-of-court agreements despite their exclusion from Rome I.[24] That said, the extension is not systematic, as courts have not always applied Rome I to fill in the gap, as illustrated by arbitration agreements.[25]

1.2.3. *Erroneous Extension*

Erroneous extensions of the scope of application of Rome I and Rome II took place when courts, in various Member States, mistakenly applied Rome I and/or Rome II to situations pre-dating their entry into force[26] or falling within the scope of Hague Conventions by virtue of the politeness clauses in Article 25 Rome I and Article 28 Rome II.[27] In other words, in these cases, the non-application of Rome I/Rome II led to the application of Rome I/Rome II. Interestingly, it seems that overall most of the mistakes made in respect of the scope of application of Rome I and Rome II resulted precisely in an extension of their scope rather than their non-application in cases where they should have been applied.[28]

Law Applicable to Non-Contractual Obligations (Scotland) Regulations 2008 (Scottish S.I. 2008/404), regulation 4. For Rome I: The Law Applicable to Contractual Obligations (England and Wales and Northern Ireland) Regulations 2009 (UK S.I. 2009/3064), regulation 5; and The Law Applicable to Contractual Obligations (Scotland) Regulations 2009 (Scottish S.I. 2009/410), regulation 4, both including Gibraltar and excluding insurance contracts (covered by the Financial Services and Markets Act 2000 (Law Applicable to Contracts of Insurance) Regulations 2009 (UK S.I. 2009/3075), regulation 3).

24 Austria and Germany, section 2.2.2 (n. 17).

25 Austria and Germany, section 2.2.2 (n. 18).

26 E.g. France, section 1.2 (the phenomenon does not exclude mistakes in the opposite direction; however it remains that 'the Regulations are more often invoked *outside* their scope of application rather than ignored' (italics in the original)); Greece, section 1 (nn. 17 (first decision) and 19, with, however, several reverse errors); Ireland, section 1; Luxembourg, section 2.6.1 *in fine* (see also section 2.6.2); Portugal, section 2.1 (n. 12), with the understanding that these mistakes by lower courts were later corrected by the Supreme Court.

27 E.g. France, sections 1.2 and 2.7; Italy, sections 4.1.2 (n. 51) and 8.1.1; Latvia, section 2.2.4 (n. 25 *in fine*); Luxembourg, section 1; the Netherlands, sections 1.2 and 2.5.2; Poland, section 2.11 (n. 43); Slovenia, sections 2.5.4 and 2.12; Spain, section 3.2 (nn. 67–69). In most countries, the primacy of the Hague Conventions is generally upheld (save perhaps that of the Hague Convention of 15 June 1955 on The Law Applicable to International Sales of Goods), albeit there are precisely mistakes 'benefiting' Rome I and Rome II.

28 For an example where Rome I and Rome II should have been applied instead of national rules: Slovenia, section 1 (n. 37).

2. THE METHODOLOGY OF THE STUDY

2.1. SEARCHING FOR NATIONAL MEASURES FACILITATING THE APPLICATION OF ROME I AND ROME II

A Regulation, by its very nature, does not require national measures of application (by contrast with the implementation measures required for a Directive). At times, however, the specific contents of a Regulation may require a national measure of application, for example in order for a state to avail itself of an option offered by the Regulation. Such is the case for Article 7(3) Rome I, which allows Member States to grant greater freedom of choice of the law applicable to insurance contracts (in specific circumstances); a few states used that opportunity.[29]

Moreover, both Rome I and Rome II require national measures preparing for their entry into application and facilitating the latter (without amending the legal order). Thus, according to Article 26(1) Rome I, Member States had – six months before the Regulation became applicable – to notify the European Commission of any binding international convention that they are party to laying down conflict-of-law rules relating to contractual obligations. This seems to have been done correctly by Member States, with the exception of Italy, which declared that it was not a party to any such convention despite being bound by the 1955 Hague Convention on International Sale of Goods, among others.[30] This inaccurate notification on the part of Italy may cause confusion in practice, especially outside the country, even if it is clear from a legal perspective that Italy remains bound by the convention as long as it has not been properly denounced and that correspondingly Article 25(1) Rome I

---

29 E.g. Czech Republic, section 1.1 (n. 3); the Netherlands, section 1.1. For Europe's largest insurance market, see the Financial Services and Markets Act 2000 (Law Applicable to Contracts of Insurance) Regulations 2009 (UK S.I. 2009/3075), regulation 4. It is interesting to note the specificity of insurance contracts in respect of Member States' wider discretion. For a critic of Article 7(3) Rome I, see H. Heiss, in U. Magnus and P. Mankowski (eds.), *European Commentaries on Private International Law Vol. II – Rome I Regulation*, Otto Schmidt, Köln, 2017, Article 7, especially para. 30 ff pp. 508-509 on the discrepancy between the purpose of Article 7(3) and its scope of application. The purpose of this provision is to have 'special conflict of law provisions for policyholder protection in the internal insurance market. However, this internal market also naturally includes Denmark and the EEA Contracting States'. Whilst Denmark is ultimately included through the exception of Article 1(4) Rome I *in fine*, the EFTA States who are parties to the EEA are not. The author therefore concludes that, in his opinion, the meaning of Member State in Article 7(3) Rome I should also cover 'the EEA Contracting States' (para. 31 p. 509). From the same author, see previously H. Heiss, 'Insurance Contracts in Rome I: Another Recent Failure of The European Legislature', YBPIL 2008 261.

30 Italy, section 8.1 (with n. 121 on the regrettable fact that no corrigendum has ever appeared in the Official Journal of the EU in this respect).

applies, i.e. that this international convention supersedes Rome I. Similarly, according to Article 29(1) Rome II, Member States had – six months before the Regulation became applicable – to notify the European Commission of any binding international convention laying down conflict-of-law rules relating to non-contractual obligations. Unfortunately, Italy also declared that it was not a party to any such convention despite being bound by several.[31] The inaccurate notification does not affect the legal validity and binding character of these conventions nor the application of Article 28(1) Rome II, i.e. that these international conventions supersede Rome II. However, it may again lead to confusion in practice. Interestingly, our expert notes, in relation to a particular convention (the 1933 Convention on the Precautionary Attachment of Aircraft), that other states (Belgium, the Netherlands, Poland and Spain) equally failed to acknowledge its existence in their notification to the European Union.[32] There may therefore be scope for Member States to revisit their notifications to the European Commission and ascertain their accuracy.[33]

Other national measures facilitating the application of Rome I and Rome II remain at the discretion of the Member States. In practice, they may prove extremely useful to help court staff and court users (including those from abroad) get acquainted with the practical operation of the new instruments in the country. Such measures do not necessarily have to be binding, with a typical example being guidelines for judges from the Ministry of Justice. However, no such national measures facilitating the application of Rome I and Rome II appear to have been adopted in many countries.[34]

---

31 Italy, section 8.2.

32 Italy, section 8.2 (n. 141), where the expert notes that on the contrary Germany, Hungary and Romania rightly referred to the Convention of 29 May 1933 for the Unification of Certain Rules relating to the Precautionary Attachment of Aircraft in their notifications.

33 Even where a Member State is not bound by any relevant international convention, a notification could still prove useful for clarification purposes. In this respect, we note that Belgium and Spain, in contrast with other states in a similar situation, did not notify the European Commission in relation to Rome I: see the list of 'Notifications under Article 26(1) of Regulation (EC) No 593/2008 of the European Parliament and of the Council on the law applicable to contractual obligations (Rome I)', OJ C343/3, 17 December 2010. Belgium also did not notify the European Commission in relation to Rome II (see the list of 'Notifications under Article 29(1) of Regulation (EC) No 864/2007 on the law applicable to non-contractual obligations (Rome II)', OJ C343/7, 17 December 2010). The latter, at least, appears to be inaccurate since Belgium should have declared that it is bound by conventions such as the 1933 Convention on the Precautionary Attachment of Aircraft and the Hague Convention of 4 May 1971 on the Law Applicable to Traffic Accidents.

34 Bulgaria, sections 1.1 (for Rome I) and 1.2 (for Rome II); Cyprus, section 3.1 (for Rome I), with none mentioned for Rome II either; France, section 1.1; Greece, section 1; Ireland, section 1; Latvia, section 1.1; Lithuania, section 2; Luxembourg, section 1 *in limine*; Portugal, section 1. By contrast, the United Kingdom's Ministry of Justice issued some 'Guidance on the law applicable to contractual obligations (Rome I). Outline of the main provisions' in February 2010.

2.2. COLLECTING CASE LAW

The authors of the report on the CJEU collected case law from the publicly available and comprehensive European database of this Court. The authors of the national reports collected judgments primarily through publicly available national databases,[35] which vary in their comprehensiveness. For example, in Portugal, only selected decisions of the Courts of Appeal and the Supreme Court of Justice are published in such a format,[36] whilst in Slovenia all judgments from the Courts of Appeal and the Supreme Court are available.[37] Unfortunately, in many – albeit not all – countries,[38] the decisions of first instance courts are not included in these databases, which hinders systematic research.[39] However, several authors alleviated this issue by complementing publicly available national databases with private national databases[40] or local databases or court reports (e.g. case law of the Piraeus Port, Athens or Dodecanese Law Reports, for Greece).[41] Specialist journals[42] were also considered, as one of their primary tasks is precisely to publish judgments,[43] including those unpublished elsewhere.[44] This proved particularly useful in Belgium, where decisions below the three Supreme Courts are normally unpublished, to the point that our expert wondered whether the aim was not in fact to hide case law.[45] A few authors

---

35 E.g. Spain, section 1 (n. 2).

36 Portugal, section 1.

37 Slovenia, section 1, where it is noted that it may be with a certain delay.

38 See for example Hungary, section 1 (n. 1), where it is noted that all Hungarian judgments are publicly available (by contrast with court orders).

39 It could also contribute to the overall paucity of collected case law in a few countries. However, one should be cautious in inferring from the lack of inclusion in databases that there are numerous first instance judgments to report on as several other factors may come into play, such as the attitude towards conflict-of-laws rules or the time needed for contractual disputes to arise or the slowness of proceedings (time to deliver a judgment), with further consequences for decisions of higher courts (time to consider recourses).

40 E.g. Poland, section 1, with reference to judgments published in databases from 'official as well as commercial sources'; or Slovakia, section 4.1.1 where the team accessed several private databases.

41 Greece, n. 5 (Piraeus Court database) and n. 15 (Dodecanese Law Reports), among many examples.

42 Specialist books have also been used for checking purposes in Cyprus (section 3.1 (n. 19)) and the United Kingdom (section 1 (n. 5)).

43 E.g. Italy, with multiple references to several journals, such as the world-leading *Rivista di diritto internazionale privato e processuale* (RDIPP).

44 E.g. Netherlands, section 1.2 (n. 9).

45 Belgium, section 1 *in limine*: 'Belgium has an abysmal method of publishing – more appropriately hiding – case law' (save for the Supreme Courts' decisions). Until recently, the situation in Luxembourg hardly appeared to be better as judgments had 'to be identified by date and case number so that [they] can be obtained upon individual request from Luxembourg's judicial documentation service' (Luxembourg, section 1). The situation has improved, even if only slightly, since a publicly accessible database containing the 'most important' decisions is now also available (Luxembourg, section 1).

even approached individual courts directly to collect case law (Latvia[46] and Portugal[47]). First instance court decisions are therefore analysed in this book,[48] alongside case law from Supreme Courts and Courts of Appeal (including a newly created International Commercial Chamber[49]), as well as of course case law from the CJEU. Whilst the vast majority of national decisions originate in courts with jurisdiction for private matters, administrative[50] and constitutional courts[51] have also been considered where relevant.

2.3. GOING BEYOND CASE LAW

Moreover, this book does not simply offer a 'snapshot' of (European and national) judicial practice. Several contributors went further. Consequently, the book at times provides information on practice before other bodies, whether public (e.g. decisions from the Italian Competition and Markets Authority[52]) or private (e.g. arbitral awards from the International Chamber of Commerce[53]). Moreover, practice has at times also been considered. For instance, the Czech team had access from their practice to undisclosed contracts employing *dépeçage* under Article 3 Rome I, unpublished arbitral awards and undisclosed contracts making use of Article 14 Rome II.[54]

3. THE OUTCOMES OF THE STUDY

3.1. QUANTITATIVE RESULTS

The evidence thus collected appears considerable – even if it cannot be exhaustive and does not pretend to be, given the methodological limitations noted above. It is submitted that it provides a good picture of Rome I and Rome II in practice.

46 Latvia, section 1.2 (n. 5: Riga Regional Court).
47 Portugal, section 1 (selected first instance courts).
48 E.g. Italy, at (among others) sections 3.2, 4.1.1 and 4.2.1.
49 France, e.g. sections 1.2 (n. 12) and 2.3.2 (n. 64).
50 Austria and Germany, sections 1 (n. 4), 2.3 (nn. 29 and 40) and 2.5.1 (n. 95); France, section 2.1.1 (n. 29); Italy, section 3.1.3 (n. 40); Latvia, section 2.4.1 (n. 34); Poland, section 1.
51 E.g. Czech Republic, section 2.9 (n. 43) and Slovenia, section 2.11. In both cases, the decisions of the Constitutional Courts seem to relate to the law prior to Rome I and Rome II, given their docket number and date, but are likely to be influential on their application. Moreover, the Slovenian decision is about the Hague Convention of 4 May 1971 on the Law Applicable to Traffic Accidents, which is still of relevance today through Article 28 Rome II.
52 Italy, section 5.2.1.
53 France, section 1.3.
54 Czech Republic, respectively: section 2.3 *in limine* on *dépeçage*; n. 8 (with n. 23) on a LCIA award in particular; and section 2.3 *in fine* on the use of Article 14 Rome II for non-contractual issues related to the contract.

The key results of the study – necessarily based only on the data collected[55] – are as follows. From a quantitative perspective, for judgments, as opposed to arbitral awards,[56] there is wide diversity between EU Member States. On one end of the spectrum, one finds Slovakia, the Netherlands and Germany, with respectively (up to) 791,[57] 600[58] and 460[59] judgments on Rome I and Rome II. These countries probably benefit from a highly (at least comparatively) effective case reporting system, whilst also having a specific historical background, in Slovakia's case (where most decisions relate to previously internal situations[60]), or being economically important, with the first port in Europe in the Netherlands' case and the first European economy in Germany's case (which is also the most populous country in the EU). On the other end of the spectrum, one finds Croatia, Cyprus and Ireland, with respectively 2,[61] 8[62] and 12[63] judgments on Rome I and Rome II. The situation in Croatia may be due in part to the specific scope of application *ratione temporis* of the Regulations in this country: by contrast with all other Member States, Croatia only joined the EU on 1 July 2013, i.e. after the entry

---

55 Exceptionally, the reliability of official statistics may be questioned: Lithuania, section 2, where no first instance case involving private international law (in the absence of specific data on Rome I and Rome II) is reported, whilst for the same year more than 550 are said to have applied *renvoi*. Our expert therefore turned to a legal database, unfortunately with inconclusive results here too: see infra n. 71.

56 Where arbitral awards could be accessed, experts very often noted that either there were no or very few references to Rome I or Rome II (e.g. Italy, section 1.1.2 *in fine*) or that these Regulations were mentioned only to be declared inapplicable (e.g. Netherlands, section 1.2 (n. 9)). Contra: the personal experience of one of the Czech experts (Czech Republic, n. 8, *in fine*).

57 Slovakia, section 4.1.1 (the actual numbers may be smaller 'as some decisions could be classified into several categories if the court referred to more than one of these instruments in order to choose between them'; however, the decrease cannot be too significant as the number of cases on Rome II is only 63 out of the total).

58 The Netherlands, section 1.2 (with around 100 other judgments mentioning Rome I/Rome II but ultimately not applying them as the matter was outside their scope of application *ratione temporis*).

59 Germany, in Austria and Germany, sections 2.1 (for Rome I) and 3.1 (for Rome II).

60 Slovakia, section 4.1.1: 'Most of the decisions referred to Czech–Slovak cases, i.e. situations in which litigants had their seat or habitual residence in the Czech or Slovak Republic, and there was a choice to be made between these two legal orders'.

61 Croatia, section 1: two appellate court decisions on Rome I and none on Rome II. Given the appellate nature of the decisions on Rome I, one may think that there are in reality four decisions in total. However, in both cases, the appellate court referred the case back to the lower court on the ground precisely that it had not applied Rome I despite the cross-border nature of the dispute (Croatia, section 1).

62 Cyprus, sections 3.1 (six decisions on Rome I, with a further one merely mentioning Rome I and the latter being referred to by the parties in another case) and 4.1 (two decisions on Rome II, with a further one merely mentioning Rome II).

63 Ireland, section 1. A small number of countries may potentially replace Ireland in the trio of countries having the fewest judgments on Rome I and Rome II. However, the exact number of judgments on Rome I and Rome II in these countries would need to be clarified (e.g. Czech Republic, section 1.2 (n. 7)).

into force of the Regulations, and consequently Rome I only applies to contracts concluded after 1 July 2013 and Rome II to events giving rise to damage occurring after the same date.[64] The size of the country may also play a role. However, it is difficult to establish a precise correlation between size and number of cases, as significant business investments are made for example in Cyprus, which is also a popular tourism destination: it may therefore be that the reason for the low number of cases after 10 years of application of Rome I and Rome II is, at times, to be found elsewhere. In this respect, it is worth noting that in the case of Cyprus lawyers are not yet familiar with Rome I and Rome II,[65] a lack of knowledge which proves decisive since 'Cypriot courts *must* rely on the parties to plead (or invoke) and prove the content of foreign law'.[66] It should be specified that a low number of cases in absolute terms may still represent substantial progress, as illustrated by Ireland, where by contrast with jurisdiction disputes 'choice-of-law disputes, particularly in tort matters, were, until recently, very rare indeed [so that if] case law on choice-of-law questions has increased dramatically [it is] from an extremely low base'.[67]

In between the two extremes, one finds countries such as Greece (around 180 cases), France (at least 125 cases), Bulgaria (around 100 cases), the United Kingdom (69 cases) or Slovenia (51 cases),[68] knowing that it may be difficult in some countries to ascertain the exact number of cases where Rome I and Rome II were effectively applied as opposed to merely pleaded by the parties or mentioned by the court.[69]

One notes, firstly, that in about half of the countries for which this information is available, the number of cases on Rome I is higher than the number of cases on Rome II. For example, in Slovakia, while there are (up to) 728 decisions on the Rome I Regulation, one finds at most only 63 decisions on

64 Croatia, section 1.

65 Cyprus, section 5: 'The challenge ahead in the case of Cyprus is for lawyers ... to familiarise themselves with [Rome I and Rome II], thereby ensuring they invoke ... the Regulations in appropriate cases'.

66 Cyprus, section 3.7 (italics in the original), where the expert adds: 'if none of the parties points to or raises the issue of the relevance of foreign applicable law, the court will probably simply proceed with deciding the case applying the Cypriot law'.

67 Ireland, section 1, where the expert adds that the adoption of Rome I and Rome II (and previously the Rome Convention) has increased awareness of choice-of-law dimensions.

68 Greece, section 1; France, section 1.2; Bulgaria, sections 1.1 (for Rome I) and 1.2 (for Rome II); United Kingdom, sections 2 (n. 76) and 5; Slovenia, section 1.

69 For example, in Poland, one finds around 300 decisions mentioning Rome I and/or Rome II. However, 'on many occasions, courts only noted that the Regulations are in force, but that the case had to be decided' according to the national private international law regime or the Rome Convention (Poland, section 1). On the other hand, the number of cases applying Rome I and/or Rome II is probably higher as not all cases are published. See also Luxembourg, section 1 ('around 50 cases involving (pleas for) the application' of Rome I or Rome II).

the Rome II Regulation.[70] The situation is the reverse in the other half of the countries studied.[71]

Secondly, the number of cases where Rome I and Rome II should have been applied may at times be much higher than the number of judgments on Rome I and Rome II (even those unpublished). One of the main reasons would be the failure to realise the existence of an international element or, worse, plain disregard for it. Thus, it has been noticed in Bulgaria that '[t]here are naturally court cases in which the foreign element in the relationships and the proceedings go unnoticed by the courts because the parties remain silent about it and, as a result, there is no reference to Rome I'.[72] In one country, moreover, the non-application of the Rome I and Rome II Regulations even seems to be actively pursued: in Latvia, '[o]verall, both party representatives and judges try to avoid applying conflict-of-laws rules'.[73] However, in a few countries, higher courts are taking steps to address the disregard by lower courts of the applicability of rules of conflict of laws. Thus, the only two decisions on Rome I in Croatia are decisions referring the case back to the lower court for lack of

---

70 Slovakia, section 4.1.1 (the actual numbers may be smaller 'as some decisions could be classified into several categories if the court referred to more than one of these instruments in order to choose between them'). Similarly, Bulgaria, sections 1.1 (for Rome I: 70 decisions) and 1.2 (for Rome II: 30 decisions); Croatia, section 1 (two decisions on Rome I and none on Rome II); Cyprus, sections 3.1 (for Rome I: six decisions) and 4.1 (for Rome II: two decisions); Germany, in Austria and Germany, sections 2.1 (for Rome I: 260 decisions) and 3.1 (for Rome II: 200 decisions); Hungary, sections 3 (for Rome I: 42 decisions, including 14 cases where the court merely established that the Regulation was not applicable *ratione temporis*) and 4 (for Rome II: 12 decisions, with one where the Regulation was not applicable *ratione temporis*); the Netherlands, section 1.2 (350 decisions on Rome I and 250 on Rome II); Portugal, sections 2.1 (for Rome II: seven decisions) and 3.1 (for Rome I: 'dozens of decisions').

71 Austria, in Austria and Germany, sections 2.1 and 3.1 (50 decisions on Rome II and 30 on Rome I); Greece, section 1 (100 decisions on Rome II and 80 on Rome I); Italy, sections 1.1.2 (for Rome I: 20 judgments considering, discussing or applying it, with five more merely mentioning it) and 1.2.2 (for Rome II: more than 30 decisions referring to it, and potentially applying it, with five more merely mentioning it); Ireland, section 1 (seven decisions on Rome II and five on Rome I); Slovenia, section 1 (29 decisions on Rome II and 22 on Rome I); United Kingdom, sections 1 (nn. 6 and 7), 2 (n. 76) and 5 (48 cases applying Rome II and 26 Rome I). Another example could be Lithuania, with 72 judgments on Rome II and 69 judgments on Rome I according to a database. However, the figures may not be relied upon 'as a review of court rulings shows that, in fact, in many of these cases, none of the Regulations have been applied' (Lithuania, section 2).

72 Bulgaria, section 1.1 (see also section 3). For an example, see also Italy, section 1.1.2 (n. 5), where at both first and second instances the parties neglected to provide evidence of the foreign element of the contract, the Supreme Court then holding that they were therefore precluded, on procedural grounds, from raising the issue of the applicable law before it despite Rome I being applicable.

73 Latvia, section 1.2, with examples in n. 6 of cases where courts failed to apply Rome I and Rome II despite the parties referring to them in their submissions. Several judgments have nonetheless been delivered on Rome I and Rome II in Latvia, as demonstrated in the national report. On the similar disregard of the applicable Regulations by some judges, see Slovenia, section 1 (n. 39; see also n. 38 where the court of first instance seemed to have ignored the rather obvious cross-border element).

application of the Regulation.[74] Another main reason for which the number of cases Rome I and Rome II should have been applied is higher than the number of judgments on Rome I and Rome II (even those unpublished) is the existence of basic mistakes on the scope of application of the Regulations, notably *ratione loci* and *ratione temporis*. In terms of scope of application *ratione loci*, in France, for example, the application of Rome I was ruled out in one case because the parties had their habitual residence in a third State.[75] In Germany, a small number of courts required one or both parties to reside in a Member State.[76] In Hungary, one court indicated (obiter dicta) that Rome I would not apply to cases involving a contracting party from outside the EU.[77] In the Netherlands, some courts declared the Regulations non applicable to cases connected to a State which did not apply them, in particular, where one of the parties was domiciled in such a State.[78] However, mistakes prejudicing the applicability of Rome I and Rome II tend, overall, to be relatively limited (despite some variations between countries and with the exception of Slovakia),[79] especially basic mistakes which are very infrequent, and should be balanced against those already mentioned in respect of the erroneous extension of Rome I and Rome II. It is hoped that these mistakes will fade away in time.

3.2. QUALITATIVE RESULTS

From a qualitative perspective, it appears that there is a wide discrepancy in the use of Rome I and Rome II rules of conflict of laws as several of them are hardly ever applied by courts in the EU. Fortunately, for those rules of conflict of laws

---

74 Croatia, section 1. See also Hungary, section 2 (in relation to the Hungarian Act on Private International Law rather than Rome I and Rome II, although it is hoped that this attitude will benefit the two Regulations); Poland, section 1 (where the expert notes, in a paragraph on the difficulty of identifying all cases in which courts should have applied Rome I and/or Rome II but ignored the foreign element, that 'an important part of the published case law is [composed of] judgments rendered by the courts in cases in which the appeal was based on the reproach of the court's non-application of foreign law'); Slovenia, section 1 (n. 40). In all these situations, the case must obviously reach the higher court(s), whatever the ground may be.

75 France, section 1.2.

76 Austria and Germany, section 1, with references in n. 4.

77 Hungary, section 3.1.

78 The Netherlands, section 1.2, with the understanding that the Regulations may ultimately have been applied by analogy because of their extension beyond their original scope of application in this country.

79 In Slovakia, the proportion of cases where Rome I (or the Rome Convention) should have been applied instead of the national private international law Act currently stands at about 25% (section 3, where our experts add that, where Rome I was rightly applied, the courts, at times, interpreted it through the lenses of the national private international law Act). The number of judgments on Rome I and Rome II should therefore be higher than it is, despite being already the highest in Europe: see this conclusion, section 3.1.

which are effectively applied, their judicial application is in many (albeit not all) respects satisfactory.

3.2.1. *The Existence of Unused or Near-Unused Conflict-of-Laws Rules*

It is quite striking to note that some provisions are hardly ever applied by courts in the EU. An excellent illustration would be Article 7 Rome II, with only two cases reported in the whole EU,[80] including none in countries where one would have expected an interested audience, such as in Germany where environmental considerations are traditionally taken seriously.[81] It could of course be argued that due to this consideration the environment is well protected and no litigation is foreseen. However, apart from the fact that environmental law is not always that respected in other countries (some having even made themselves famous before the CJEU for their repeated non-implementation of relevant Directives) and that there are no cases on Article 7 Rome II in those countries either, one should remember that it is cross-border cases that are under consideration here and therefore the event giving rise to the damage may be found in an entirely different state, including outside the EU. A question may therefore arise: is there no real need for a provision such as Article 7 Rome II, the difficulties highlighted by academics being exaggerated and in any case purely doctrinal, or are the difficulties so significant that these provisions cannot be applied? It is unfortunately very difficult to respond to this question, which may also be linked to a lack of in-depth knowledge of the Regulations by practitioners as Article 7 Rome II is rather innovative. This could notably explain why several Slovenian cases involving the flooding of a river in Slovenia with the event giving rise to the damage in Austria were exclusively dealt with under the general rule (Article 4 Rome II), with no discussion of Article 7 Rome II.[82] National rules governing questions not addressed in the Regulation, for instance the timeframe within which the choice offered by Article 7 Rome II must be made,[83] may also come into play here. However, it is likely that judicial

---

80 Cases on Article 7 Rome II have only been reported in the Netherlands, section 2.5.2 (one case) and the United Kingdom, section 4.3 (one case, with the proviso that whilst the judge declared Article 7 Rome II applicable he ultimately did not seem to fully draw the consequences, considering the difference between English and Nigerian law to be 'immaterial').

81 There is no application of Article 7 Rome II in both Austria and Germany: Austria and Germany, section 3.5.2.1.

82 Slovenia, section 1. See also the Netherlands, section 2.5.2, n. 91 *in fine*: twice, 'the court did not refer to Article 7 Rome II even though the cases concerned environmental damage' (the composition of the court probably differed from when it did apply Article 7 Rome II).

83 Recital 25 *in fine* Rome II. On the topic, see for example the rule introduced by the new Hungarian Act on Private International Law, which provides that the right of the person

application of Article 7 Rome II will increase in the future, as cross-border environmental litigation is slowly but surely rising.

It remains to be seen whether such a rise is also on the agenda for all the other rules of conflict of laws that are currently hardly ever applied by courts in the EU. Among them, one finds one of the most innovative provisions of Rome II:[84] Article 14. It has in fact been applied – more than Article 7 of the same Regulation – albeit still to a very limited extent, save in the Netherlands, where it is the second most applied provision of Rome II (including in circumstances where it should not be available).[85] In all the countries where

seeking compensation to choose the law of the country in which the event giving rise to the damage occurred 'may be exercised by the end of the procedure for the preparation of the case, within the deadline specified by the judge' (Hungary, section 4.2). It is submitted here that an harmonisation at EU level of the rule on this issue (resulting in the abolition of the last sentence of recital 25 Rome II) would be useful, either in Rome II itself, or in a Rome 0 Regulation or Code of EU Private International Law.

84 Even for a country such as Germany, which is one of the few countries that was not unfamiliar with party autonomy in torts before Rome II, albeit on a more restricted scale (ex post choice only): see E. Guinchard and S. Lamont-Black, 'Environmental Law – The Black Sheep in Rome II's Drive for Legal Certainty? Article 7 of Regulation (EC) No. 864/2007 on the Law Applicable to Non-Contractual Obligations in Context', Environmental Law Review 2009, 161, 167. For another country which allows party autonomy in torts, again ex post, albeit only in favour of the *lex fori*, see Lithuania, section 3.2.

85 The use of Article 14 Rome II was reported in the following countries: Austria and Germany, section 3.4; France, with no case (save to state that Article 14 Rome II could not be applied because of a lack of consent from one of the parties to the procedure, but not to the contract containing a choice-of-law clause, and Article 4 Rome II was subsequently applied: see sections 2.1.1 and 2.2.2 (n. 55)) until a very recent decision from the International Commercial Chamber of the Paris Court of Appeal on 3 June 2020 (section 2.2.2, n. 56), which applies Article 14 Rome II considering that 'it is clear from the circumstances of the case that the parties intended that French law applies', with the understanding that this choice complements the finding that French law equally applies on other grounds (no. 19/03758, spec. paragraphs 67 and 68); Greece, section 2.2 (with the understanding that at times the use of Article 14 Rome II was supplemental: see section 2.6); Hungary, section 4.2, where our expert provides two examples of the application of Article 14(1) Rome II, but notes that the choice took place before second instance courts and that this may now be inconsistent with the new Hungarian Act on Private International Law, which provides that 'such a choice may be made only by the end of the procedure for the preparation of the case, within the deadline specified by the judge' (it is submitted here that an harmonisation at EU level of the rule on this issue would be useful, either in Rome II itself, or in a Rome 0 Regulation or Code of EU Private International Law, as positions diverge: see for example the Austrian one in Austria and Germany, section 3.4, where our experts note that 'an implied choice of law by the parties' conduct in court proceedings is not possible at all'); Italy, section 3.2; the Netherlands, sections 1.2 (Article 14 Rome II is the second most applied provision of Rome II), 2.2 (on party autonomy in general, including examples of the correct application of Article 14 Rome II as well as three cases where courts disregarded the explicit prohibitions on party autonomy found in Articles 6(4) and 8(3) Rome II (nn. 37 and 38)) and 2.5.2 (with another example of incorrect application of Article 14 Rome II in n. 105); Spain, section 4.1. On the other hand, no judicial application of Article 14 Rome II was reported in the following countries: Bulgaria, section 2.2.2 *in limine* (by contrast, Article 14 has been used in complex commercial contracts); Czech Republic, section 2.3 (no case; however, the

the use of Article 14 Rome II in courts was reported, it is of clear interest to note that, save in one extremely recent case, the choice of law was always made only after the event giving rise to the damage occurred, i.e. no use was made of the most innovative aspect of Article 14 Rome II (one has to go out of court to exceptionally find such use).[86] Moreover, in the vast majority of decisions, albeit not all, the choice was in favour of the *lex fori*. It was also often an implied choice, which may at times cast some shadows on the reality of the agreement of the parties as the convenience of the court may have prevailed. In this respect, courts have been urged to be more cautious, and in particular consider 'whether the lawyers in fact had the power to bind the parties as to the substance of their relationship (as opposed to merely represent them for the purposes of the proceedings)'.[87]

It is worth observing that some rules of conflict of laws of Rome I and/or Rome II seem to be unused or near-unused by courts in certain countries, rather than the EU in general, and very much used in others. Party autonomy under Article 3 Rome I is a prime example of this, with 'numerous decisions' in Austria and Germany and hardly any in the Czech Republic.[88] However, a lack of judicial practice does not necessarily equate to a lack of practice,[89] as it is quite standard for international commercial contracts to include a choice-of-law clause. The latter will never have to be interpreted by a court in the absence of a dispute between the parties or where alternative dispute resolution (in the Anglo-American meaning of the expression) is preferred. The lack of case law here merely reflects a lack of issues.

Czech team had access from their practice to undisclosed contracts making use of Article 14 Rome II to extend the application of the chosen *lex contractus* to related non-contractual issues, presumably before the event giving rise to the damage occurred); Latvia, section 2.2.2 (no case, with the understanding that a second instance court applied Article 14 Rome II before seeing its judgment annulled on this point by the Supreme Court for lack of consent by one of the parties; see also a similar case at section 2.2.4: no tacit choice of law for lack of mutual agreement and in reality Rome II was not applicable); Lithuania, section 3.2 *in fine*; Luxembourg, section 2.2 *in fine*; Poland, section 2.2 *in fine*; Portugal, sections 2.1 *in fine* and 2.3; Slovakia, section 4.4.1; Slovenia, section 2.2.1 *in limine*; United Kingdom, section 3.3. The Belgian, Croatian, Cypriot and Irish reports do not mention any use of Article 14 Rome II either.

86 The sole judgment where Article 14(1)(b) was applied is the very recent decision from the International Commercial Chamber of the Paris Court of Appeal on 3 June 2020 (no. 19/03758). For other uses of the same provision, see Bulgaria, section 2.2.2 *in fine* (Article 14(1)(b) is used in complex commercial contracts); Czech Republic, section 2.3 (the Czech team had access from their practice to undisclosed contracts making use of Article 14 Rome II to extend the application of the chosen *lex contractus* to related non-contractual issues, presumably before the event giving rise to the damage occurred). See also an ICC award where the arbitrators considered that the conditions of Article 14(1)(b) Rome II were fulfilled (France, section 2.2.2).

87 Italy, section 3.2, where our expert also notes a difference of attitude between courts.

88 Austria and Germany, section 2.4 *in limine*; Czech Republic, section 3 (n. 51).

89 Czech Republic, section 3 (n. 51).

3.2.2. *The Rather Positive Assessment of Effectively Applied Conflict-of-Laws Rules*

By contrast with (among others) Articles 7 and 14 Rome II, some rules of conflict of laws are often, or relatively often, applied in courts. The 'General rule' of Rome II (Article 4) is thus effectively the most applied, or one of the most applied, provision(s) of this Regulation.[90] Other provisions are applied to varying degree. In respect of the effectively applied provisions, the overall assessment of their judicial application appears positive. In particular, one should not confuse numbers and issues. Many cases raise no particular issue of interpretation.[91] Moreover, fears expressed in relation to debated aspects of party autonomy such as the possibility for parties to select the law applicable to only part of their contract and consequently to choose different laws for different parts of their contract, i.e. *dépeçage*, have proven unfounded. The Czech experts thus noted that they came across several examples of *dépeçage* in their practice. None of the contracts raised any difficulty in respect of the severability of the different contractual parts and corresponding applicable laws; and parties put *dépeçage* to good use, in order to overcome the uncertainties of the law otherwise applicable[92] rather than to try to avoid being subject to state laws altogether.

Nevertheless, mistakes in the application of Rome I and Rome II conflict-of-laws rules do occur. At times, they may even be basic ones. For example, in Germany, a few courts ignored the exclusion of *renvoi* in Rome I and Rome II.[93] In Hungary, one court restricted party autonomy to 'the law that is connected to the matter'.[94] In the Netherlands, a few courts have forgotten the restrictions on party autonomy in consumer and employment contracts pursuant to Articles 6(2) and 8(1) Rome I.[95] However, overall these mistakes tend to be relatively limited.

---

90 E.g. Austria and Germany, section 3.1 (for both countries); Bulgaria, section 1.2; France, section 1.2; Ireland, section 1; Luxembourg, section 1; The Netherlands, section 1.2; Poland, section 1; Portugal, section 2.1; Slovenia, section 1.

91 Example: Hungary, sections 3 (15 out of 28 cases where Rome I was effectively applied) and 4 (five out of 11 cases where Rome II was effectively applied). Similarly, and among others, see Austria and Germany, section 2.5.2.1, where the experts note the 'very large number of decisions on Articles 5–8 Rome I Regulation' and add that 'the application of Articles 5 and 7 has not caused any major problems' with only one noteworthy decision.

92 Czech Republic, section 2.3. For a similar conclusion on *dépeçage*, see Austria and Germany, section 2.4 (no particular issue); Bulgaria, section 2.2.1 (no excessive use); Italy, section 3.1.2 (seemingly no difficulty); Latvia, section 2.2.1 (no excessive use). Contra: Slovenia, section 2.2.3. An example of *dépeçage* under Article 3 Rome I also came to light in a Cypriot case, albeit that the court did not decide on the clause as the case was ultimately heard by a Bulgarian court (Cyprus, section 3.1, which notes that *dépeçage* is a novelty in Cypriot private international law and that there is no case law on the matter, as opposed to case law on a clause where one law supplements another one).

93 Austria and Germany, section 1 (with references in n. 5).

94 Hungary, section 3.8.

95 The Netherlands, section 2.2.

Furthermore, and importantly, without disregarding the existence of issues in relation to specific conflict-of-laws rules (at least in some countries),[96] if one is to judge the application of conflict-of-laws rules in Rome I and Rome II by one of the oldest temptations in private international law – reverting to the *lex fori* – the picture is globally satisfactory until perhaps the stage of the proof of foreign law. The collected cases do not demonstrate a widespread use of three key derogatory private international law mechanisms (in particular with a view to reverting to the *lex fori*): the reverse may even said to be the norm in respect of *lois d'application immédiate*, escape clauses and *ordre public*.

3.2.2.1. *Lois d'application immédiate*

Lois d'application immédiate are, overall, seldom used under Rome I and Rome II (with the exception perhaps of Slovakia[97]). A good illustration of this stance would be Hungary, where only one example of application of a *loi d'application immédiate* was found.[98] It has even been said that 'there is a clear discrepancy

---

96 For an example on Rome I: Austria and Germany, section 2.5.2.1, where the experts note the 'critical issues' affecting the application of Articles 6 and 8 Rome I (in the absence of choice of law) before elaborating on them in sections 2.5.2.2 (Article 6 Rome I) and 2.5.2.3 (Article 8 Rome I). For an example on Rome II: Ireland, section 2.4.6, where the expert points out that not only is Article 6 Rome II poorly drafted but one of its key concepts (unfair competition) 'is alien to the common law conception of torts and civil wrongs'. Article 6 Rome II has also demonstrated its limitations in Austria and Germany, as Article 8 Rome II (section 3.5.2). See also this conclusion, section 4.2.

97 The exception derives from a confusion made by the legislator and relates solely to consumer contracts. The Slovak legislator characterised, in an explanatory note, a conflict-of-laws rule on consumer protection as a *loi d'application immediate*, a statement which led some courts (not all as highlighted in particular by a 2019 decision) to consider the entire Slovak consumer law as *loi d'application immediate* (Slovakia, sections 4.4.4 and 4.5.1). The point matters in practice as consumer contracts are the most important category of contracts appearing before Slovak courts under Rome I (and Rome I is by far the most used Regulation among Rome I and Rome II: see section 3.1 of this conclusion): Slovakia, section 4.4.4 *in limine*. It seems that, overall, Slovak courts are keen on consumer protection, with several having interpreted (too) liberally the conditions of applicability of Article 6 Rome I (section 4.4.4).

98 Hungary, section 3.6. In favour of a strict position, see also Belgium, section 3.4 (one decision, on Article 16 Rome II, with our expert interestingly pointing out at section 2.4.1 *in fine* the unlikely application of Article 9 Rome I to gold-plating in the field of commercial agents protection); Bulgaria, section 2.1 (one example); Croatia, section 3.1 (no case, by contrast with the situation pre-Rome I and Rome II where remarkably courts have not always identified *lois d'application immédiate* as such whilst still applying them); Cyprus, section 3.2 (no case, with the concept of *lois d'application immédiate* even unknown in case law, our expert mentioning nonetheless two examples of likely application, both in the field of immovable property); Czech Republic, section 2.2 (no example, and with a strict position from the Supreme Court even before Rome I and Rome II); Greece, section 2.1 *in limine* (no decision); Ireland, section 2.1 (no decision, whether under Rome I or Rome II); Italy, sections 7.1.1 (for Rome I: no decision) and 7.2.1 (for Rome II: no decision); Latvia, sections 2.1.1 and 2.1.2 (no decision, with our experts noting at section 2.1.1 the difficulty of

between how much attention is paid to this problem in legal writing and how often it is the question at issue in court proceedings'.[99] Several reasons may account for this restraint in the use of Article 9 Rome I and Article 16 Rome II.

Firstly, the provision may not be identified as a *loi d'application immédiate* by courts (on which the characterisation task generally falls[100]).[101] In France, it has thus been pointed out that 'the enactment of the Rome I Regulation and the drafting of Article 9(1) seem to have reduced the judicial characterisation of [*lois d'application immédiate*]', even for cases falling under the Rome

drawing conclusions from this fact given the relative paucity of decisions applying Rome I and Rome II due to the predilection of judges for the *lex fori*); Lithuania, section 3.1 (two examples, knowing that both the Supreme Court and the Court of Appeal seem to have used several grounds to apply the *lex fori* as the same cases are mentioned as applying *ordre public*: see Lithuania, section 3.9). Luxembourg, section 2.1 *in limine* (no case); the Netherlands, section 2.1 (three decisions on Article 9 Rome I and no decision on Article 16 Rome II, with the understanding that, prior to a major reform of employment law in 2015, cases on Article 9 Rome I were probably more numerous as two judgments from the Supreme Court characterised a 1945 provision requiring an employer to ask the permission of the authorities before a dismissal as a *loi d'application immediate* (applicable subject to conditions), even if no specific example of such cases is provided and the latest decision from the Supreme Court in 2012 seems to relate to an employment contract of 2005); Portugal, sections 2.3 (for Rome II: no case) and 3.2.4 (for Rome I: no case); Slovenia, section 2.1 (for Rome I: no decision; with none mentioned either on Rome II in the report); Spain, section 5.2 (two cases and one remark *obiter dicta*). For Austria and Germany, there is hardly any application of *lois d'application immédiate* under Rome II (Austria and Germany, section 3.3 *in limine*, with the sole case of effective application mentioned however being interesting, less perhaps for its result than for its methodology in the sense that the Austrian Supreme Court relied expressly on *Arblade*, and thus indirectly on the *Francescakis* definition, to identify *lois d'application immédiate* even though there is no equivalent of Article 9(1) Rome I in Rome II). Case law appears prima facie important in relation to Rome I, but often did not lead to the positive identification of *lois d'application immediate*, even less in these being applied or given effect on the ground of Article 9 Rome I (Austria and Germany, section 2.3).

99 Poland, section 2.1, with the only exception under Rome I (albeit importantly in line with its Recital 34) being employment law (more than ten similar cases on the posting of workers: 'the national provision[s] of the labour law regulating the condition[s] of the employment mention[ned] in Article 3(1) of Directive 96/71/EC constitute *lois de police*') and no reported case under Rome II.

100 The fact that courts are responsible in practice for the identification of most *lois d'application immédiate*, whilst deciding on an ad hoc and ex post basis in the absence of established case law, led our Latvian experts to declare that, in some instances, 'the planning of international transactions [is reduced] to an exercise in fortune-telling' (Latvia, section 2.1.1).

101 By exception, the legislator may identify specific provisions as *lois d'application immédiate*. Examples may be found notably in France, section 1.1 (prevention and resolution of banking crises); Ireland, section 2.1 (sale of goods and consumer protection); Luxembourg, section 2.1 (employment, housing and consumer laws). This is without prejudice to the extraordinary measures taken by governments throughout Europe to tackle the health crisis provoked by COVID-19 (e.g. Italy, section 7.1.1). Atypically, the intervention of the legislator may be anything but helpful, in the sense that it confuses two key mechanisms of private international law (*lois d'application immédiate* and rules of conflict of laws): see supra n. 97 on Slovakia.

Convention, with the Supreme Court refusing, among others, to characterise as *lois d'application immédiate* consumer law provisions 'protecting individuals who act as personal guarantors for the benefit of a bank' and even the national implementing legislation of Directive No. 86/653/EEC on commercial agents.[102]

When *lois d'application immédiate* are identified, it is mostly for good reasons, for example arms control[103] or embargos.[104]

Secondly, a provision may be identified as a *loi d'application immédiate* but its application (Article 9(2) Rome I) or effect (Article 9(3) Rome I) denied, for instance on the ground that the case is insufficiently connected with the country of the *loi d'application immédiate*. An example of the latter is provided by a Dutch case, in which the court characterised a Turkish rule requiring contracts to be drafted in the Turkish language as a *loi d'application immédiate* (on the ground that the rule serves a public interest since it 'aims at protecting Turkish citizens with insufficient knowledge of foreign languages'), before however holding that 'the case was insufficiently connected with the Turkish legal sphere to apply this provision'.[105] The requirement for such connection may not be found as such in Article 9(3) Rome I,[106] but the court was probably referring to the need for the *loi d'application immédiate* to be that of the country of performance of the contract (in any case, it will not come as a surprise to Turkish lawyers in the light of Article 31 of the Turkish Private International Law Act). By contrast, no similar connection restriction may be found in Article 9(2) Rome I. It has nevertheless been implied as common sense by the German Supreme Court in employment matters, leaving however the question of the required threshold unresolved.[107]

Overall, national judges have demonstrated clear restraint in the use of *lois d'application immédiate*. This is in line with the case law of the Court of Justice itself. In the judgment considered to be the most important one it delivered on Rome I,[108] the Court of Justice asserted that 'Article 9 of the Rome I Regulation must be interpreted strictly', before stating that its list of 'overriding mandatory provisions to which the court of the forum may give effect is exhaustive' and subsequently that a court is precluded from applying, as legal rules, *lois d'application immédiate* other than those of the forum state

---

102 France, section 2.1.1. For Rome II, 'only one significant occurrence' of *loi d'application immediate* has been found following a very recent judgment from the Supreme Court on 8 July 2020 (France, sections 4.1.3 (n. 130) and 2.1.1 (n. 41)).

103 Austria and Germany, section 2.3 (n. 37, with the reasoning criticised by the experts: see n. 29 and text).

104 Hungary, section 3.6 (EU Libyan Embargo Regulation).

105 The Netherlands, section 2.1.

106 Compare Article 7(1) of the 1980 Rome Convention: 'effect may be given to the mandatory rules of the law of another country with which the situation has a close connection'.

107 Austria and Germany, section 2.3 (n. 47).

108 CJEU, section 3.1.

or of the state where the obligations arising out of the contract have to be or have been performed, such as the Greek austerity laws at stake in the case.[109] The existence of specific conflict-of-law rules for several contracts, such as consumer contracts, may also explain in part why *lois d'application immédiate* are not really used by national courts.[110] One can here contrast the position in Europe with that in South America.[111] Nevertheless, this explanation faces limitations for employment contracts,[112] where specific rules on conflict of laws have been enacted, but courts do not demonstrate the same restraint. The main type of contracts for which courts have been lenient in the identification and

109 CJEU, 18 October 2016, Case C-135/15, *Republik Griechenland v. Grigorios Nikiforidis*, ECLI:EU:C:2016:774, paras. 44, 49 and 50. Note the important caveat of the Court of Justice: Article 9 does not preclude the national court 'from taking such other overriding mandatory provisions into account as matters of fact in so far as this is provided for by the national law that is applicable to the contract pursuant to the regulation' (operative part). For a comment, see CJEU, section 3.1 and E. Fohrer-Dedeurwaerder, Journal du droit international (Clunet) 2017, no. 1, Jurisprudence, comm. 5, spec. 2, A. A similar restraint in the use of *lois d'application immédiate* was demonstrated by the CJEU in relation to Rome II: 'Article 16 of [Rome II] must be interpreted as meaning that a national provision ... which provides that the limitation period for actions seeking compensation for damage resulting from an accident is three years, cannot be considered to be an overriding mandatory provision, within the meaning of that article, unless the court hearing the case finds, on the basis of a detailed analysis of the wording, general scheme, objectives and the context in which that provision was adopted, that it is of such importance in the national legal order that it justifies a departure from the law applicable, designated pursuant to Article 4 of that regulation' (CJEU, 31 January 2019, Case C-149/18, *Agostinho da Silva Martins v. Dekra Claims Services Portugal SA*, ECLI:EU:C:2019:84, reported at <https://europeanciviljustice.wordpress.com/2019/02/01/cjeu-on-articles-16-and-27-rome-ii-and-article-28-directive-2009-103/>). However, our experts rightly point out (CJEU, section 4.2) that, whilst sound *de lege lata*, the decision is too harsh in practice as, at best (see n. 30), '[s]hort one-year limitation periods are made, and may be fit, for domestic situations, and for such situations only'. They therefore suggest, *de lege ferenda*, an amendment to Rome II consisting in the cumulative application of the applicable law and the law of the country of the victim's habitual residence (at the time of the accident) to limitation periods.

110 Very exceptionally, a provision intended to protect the consumer may, in certain circumstances, have the opposite effect: see the interesting observation of the Irish expert in relation to Article 11(4) Rome I when it interacts with domestic law (Ireland, section 2.4.2).

111 C. Lima Marques, 'Brésil', in D.P. Fernández Arroyo (ed.), *Consumer Protection in International Private Relationships / La protection des consommateurs dans les relations privées internationales*, CEDEP, Paraguay, 2010, p. 47 at p. 48 *in fine* and p. 76 (the author notes that in the absence of specific consumer conflict of laws rules in Brazil the courts apply the Consumer Code as *loi d'application immédiate*); in the same book, D.P. Fernández Arroyo, 'Protection des consommateurs dans les relations privées internationales', p. 659 at p. 730. Note the rather recent Mercosur Agreement on the Law Applicable to International Consumer Contracts (*Acuerdo del Mercosur sobre derecho aplicable en materia de contratos internacionales de consumo*, adopted in Brasilia (Brazil) on 20 December 2017 (MERCOSUR/CMC/DEC No. 36/17)), available on the dedicated website of the depository (Paraguay): <https://www.mre.gov.py/tratados/public_web/ConsultaMercosur.aspx>.

112 It also faces limitations, in respect of consumer contracts themselves, in two specific countries: Slovakia (see supra n. 97) and the United Kingdom (see the next footnote). In both countries, it seems the cause lies in a lack of understanding in the way in which private international law operates.

application of *lois d'application immédiate* is indeed employment contracts[113] (even if this approach is not systematic[114]). However, this is not to say that this case law is necessarily out of line with Rome I, at least for the posting of workers as demonstrated by its Recital 34,[115] merely that it contributes to their specificity in practice, which also appears in the use of escape clauses.

---

113 The Netherlands, section 2.1: 'Outside the context of labour relations, the role of *lois de police* is much more limited'; Poland, section 2.1 where employment law appears to be the only exception to the non-use of *lois d'application immédiate* under Rome I. See also Austria and Germany, section 2.3: 'The identification of overriding mandatory provisions (*lois de police*) has played a major role in German and Austrian case law, mostly in labour law disputes', with our experts adding that in 'most cases, however, the courts have denied the existence of an overriding mandatory provision' (with nonetheless several examples of effective identification given, in particular in employment law); France, section 2.1.1 (n. 29) with one out of only two case-law examples of a clear-cut characterisation as a French *loi d'application immediate* since the enactment of Rome I relating to employment law (and the only one until the very recent characterisation of some non-employment law provisions as *lois d'application immediate* by the Supreme Court on 8 July 2020 (n. 41; ECLI:FR:CCASS:2020:CO00314)). Adde the case law prior to Rome I, although in all likelihood transposable to contracts concluded after 17 December 2009, in Ireland and Portugal: Ireland, section 2.1 where the only example given of a tribunal suggesting the application of a *loi d'application immediate* (by virtue of Article 7(2) Rome Convention) relates to employment law (with the understanding that the tribunal considered the legislation at stake already applicable under Article 6(1) Rome Convention); Portugal, section 3.2.4 where the only contracts for which the use of *lois d'application immédiate* is mentioned (moreover as frequent) are individual employment contracts (in their respect, 'Portuguese courts apply often … a rule of the Portuguese Constitution prohibiting dismissal without fair cause, which is deemed to be an implicit *loi d'application immédiate*'). The situation of the United Kingdom appears similar (especially in respect of the end result in most cases), although not identical, with no decision mentioned as applying *lois d'application immédiate* as such (despite attempts by the parties), albeit with cases in employment (and consumer law) where courts 'are only asking whether the claim falls within the territorial scope of the statute in question' (so-called statutory claims), an approach which results in the over-application of the *lex fori* (United Kingdom, section 3.6) and which seems to us reminiscent of the unilateralist approach underlying *lois d'application immédiate*, though without the surrounding conflict-of-laws reasoning. The expert also notes one case which, he believes, 'should have been dealt with under' Article 9(3) Rome I rather than *ordre public*.

114 See for example cases from the Czech Supreme Court likely to be transposed to Rome I and holding that Czech employment rules requiring employers to state a specific ground for dismissal and abiding by a minimum termination period are neither *lois d'application immédiate* nor part of *ordre public*, subject to conditions (Czech Republic, section 2.2).

115 Recital 34 Rome I: 'The rule on individual employment contracts should not prejudice the application of the overriding mandatory provisions of the country to which a worker is posted in accordance with Directive 96/71/EC of the European Parliament and of the Council of 16 December 1996 concerning the posting of workers in the framework of the provision of services' (with the understanding that the latter has been quite significantly amended by Directive (EU) 2018/957 of the European Parliament and of the Council of 28 June 2018 amending Directive 96/71/EC concerning the posting of workers in the framework of the provision of services, reported at <https://europeanciviljustice.wordpress.com/2018/07/09/amendment-to-the-directive-on-the-posting-of-workers/> (with further amendment reported at <https://europeanciviljustice.wordpress.com/2019/04/01/corrigendum-to-directive-eu-2018-957-concerning-the-posting-of-workers/>)). For a characterisation of Articles 3(1) and 3(1)(a) of amended Directive 96/71 as '*special rules* on conflict of laws' (italics in the original) rather

3.2.2.2. Escape Clauses

The use of escape clauses under Rome I and Rome II appears either non-existent or limited in most countries, albeit not all.

No application of escape clauses has for example been reported in Bulgaria, despite attempts from the parties.[116] The situation is identical in several other countries.[117] A sole application of an escape clause was accounted for in Cyprus, Hungary, Latvia and Spain.[118] In other countries, courts have had resort to escape clauses, albeit only sporadically. For example, Austrian and German courts have used escape clauses restrictively, whether in relation to Rome I or Rome II.[119] This appears to be particularly true for Rome I, where only two decisions have applied Article 4(3) and none Article 5(3) or Article 7(2) *in fine*.[120] Similarly, in France, the Netherlands, Poland, Slovakia and the United Kingdom, overall, courts do not overuse escape clauses. However, they do use them on an occasional basis.[121]

than *lois d'application immediate*, see the 28 May 2020 opinions of Advocate-General Manuel Campos Sánchez-Bordona in case C-620/18 (*Hungary v European Parliament and Council of the European Union*) and case C-626/18 (*Poland v European Parliament and Council of the European Union*), respectively at 191 ff. (notably 194) and at 83 ff. (notably 84). The Court of Justice has yet to deliver its judgments in the two cases.

116 Bulgaria, sections 2.4.1 (for Rome I) and 2.4.2 (for Rome II).

117 Luxembourg, section 2.4 (for both Rome I and Rome II); Portugal, sections 2.3 *in fine* (for Rome II) and 3.2.6 *in limine* (for Rome I). The Belgian (sections 2.2 for Rome I and 3.2 for Rome II), Croatian and Italian reports mention no application of escape clauses under either Rome I or Rome II (with the proviso that there is simply no reported decision on Rome II in Croatia). The Czech report (section 2.4) states that there is no evidence that the courts overuse the escape clauses of Rome I, at least in respect of its Article 4, and no example of use in relation to other relevant Articles of Rome I or Rome II is mentioned either. This non-application of escape clauses under Rome I and Rome II is without prejudice of the use of escape clauses under national private international law or the Rome Convention (for examples of the latter, see Belgium, section 2.2, with one example in favour of a foreign law and one in favour of the *lex fori*).

118 Cyprus, section 4.1 (Article 4(3) Rome II); Hungary, section 3.5 (Article 4(3) Rome I); Latvia, section 2.3 *in limine* (Article 5(3) Rome I); Spain, section 4.2.1 (nn. 93 and 97: Article 4(3) Rome I).

119 Austria and Germany, sections 2.6 (for Rome I), and 3.7 (for Rome II).

120 Austria and Germany, section 2.6, with the only exception to this restrictive attitude appearing to be employment disputes (Article 8(4) Rome I), at least in Germany more than Austria.

121 France, sections 2.3.2 (for Rome I in general, with details of successful and unsuccessful attempts by the parties to resort to the escape clauses, leading to ultimately few effective applications), 2.4.1 (for Article 5(3) Rome I, with no example of effective application as there is no departure from the normally applicable law, whether of the forum or foreign) and 2.3.4 (for Article 4(3) Rome II, with no example of effective application and no mention of the use of any other escape clause of Rome II); Netherlands, sections 2.4.1 *in limine* and *in fine* (for Rome I) and 2.4.2 *in limine* (for Rome II); Poland, sections 1 (on Article 4(3) Rome II) and 2.4 (for both Rome I and Rome II, and with an example of application of Article 4(3) Rome II); Slovakia, section 4.4.3 *in limine* ('rare cases'); United Kingdom, section 3.4 (one application of Article 4(3) Rome I and five of Article 4(3) Rome II), with another application of Article 4(3) Rome II in the extremely recently delivered judgment in *Avonwick*

Such restraint is particularly welcomed in relation to Article 4(3) Rome I when it comes from countries which had at times adopted a very loose interpretation of the presumptions of Article 4(2)–(4) Rome Convention and demonstrated an unfortunate tendency to have resort primarily to the escape clause of Article 4(5) Rome Convention. It is quite remarkable in this respect that, whilst Italy was one of these countries,[122] no use of Article 4(3) Rome I has been reported so far[123] and that, whilst 'English courts have been regarded as those most ready to apply the escape clause of Article 4(5) [Rome Convention]',[124] they have shown clear restraint in relation to Article 4(3) Rome I, which demonstrates that the strengthening of Article 4 Rome Convention has proven successful.[125] A good example of the restraint shown by English judges in the use of escape clauses under Rome I would be the judgment of the High Court of England and Wales (Commercial Court) delivered on 26 November 2015 in *Molton Street Capital LLP v. Shooters Hill*

Holdings Ltd v. Azitio Holdings Ltd & Ors [2020] EWHC 1844 (Comm) (14 July 2020), paragraph 176 (with the understanding that the displacement of the normally applicable law related only to the issue of limitation).

122 Italy, section 4.1.2, where our expert notes that this behaviour was endorsed by the Supreme Court and only changed following the *Intercontainer Interfrigo* decision of the CJEU in 2009, i.e. the same year Rome I came into force (CJEU, 6 October 2009, Case C-133/08, *Intercontainer Interfrigo SC (ICF) v. Balkenende Oosthuizen BV and MIC Operations BV*, ECLI:EU:C:2009:617).

123 Italy, section 4.1.1. In section 4.1.2, the expert refers to a 2008 Supreme Court decision under Article 4(5) of the Rome Convention which may still be relevant today for the purposes of Article 4(3) Rome I.

124 C. Heinze, in P. Torremans (ed., with consultant editor J.J. Fawcett), *Cheshire, North & Fawcett: Private International Law*, 15th ed., Oxford University Press, Oxford, 2017, p. 736.

125 Serious fears to the contrary had been expressed in some quarters, for instance by R. Morse ('Franchise Contracts and the Conflicts of Laws', in *Essays in Honour of Michael Bogdan*, Juristförlaget i Lund, Sweden, 2013, p. 363), who concluded his contribution by stating: 'Having specific rules for particular contracts, as in Art. 4(1) at least, of Rome I may be thought by some to be more conducive to certainty and predictability than the rather general approach taken in the Rome Convention. But it does not come without its own, perhaps considerable, uncertainty and unpredictability' (p. 371). The author previously criticised in rather strong words several alleged uncertainties, considering for example that the escape clause of Article 4(3) Rome I 'will cause misery to lawyers and their clients' beyond its accepted non-application in the case where the franchisor is based in another country from which he performs his obligations. Collected judicial practice on Article 4(3) Rome I points to a very different picture. Moreover, it is submitted that the uncertainties singled out may be overstated in the sense that any uncertainty in the application of a prima facie clear provision ('a franchise contract shall be governed by the law of the country where the franchisee has his habitual residence', Article 4(1)(e) Rome I) cannot be compared with the uncertainty arising from the absence of such provision, as the latter takes place at an entirely different level from the former. It is precisely because the previous regime consisting in a mere presumption in favour of the law of the habitual residence of the party who is to effect the characteristic performance along with the absence of provisions on specific contracts (save two: see Article 4(3) and (4) Rome Convention) in the absence of choice of law by the parties (see Article 4(2) Rome Convention) demonstrated its severe limits in terms of predictability that Article 4(1) Rome I was introduced.

Capital Partners LLP and Odeon Capital Group LLC.[126] The case concerned damages for breach of an alleged contract of sale of junk bonds. The claimant and buyer was based in London, the (first) defendant was a broker based in London with whom the contract was negotiated, and the (second) defendant and seller was based in New York. The judge (Popplewell J) applied Article 4 Rome I, a point uncontested by both parties. He highlighted the difference between Rome I and the Rome Convention:

> 'The text and architecture of Article 4 of the Rome I Regulation is very different from that of the Rome Convention. In particular, the test is no longer expressed as one of closest connection; the test is that contained in the rules set out in Articles 4.1 and 4.2, which are no longer expressed as presumptions or as being subject to the closest connection test; and the closest connection test has become an "escape clause" to be applied only where it is clear that the connection is manifestly closer to a country other than that dictated by the tests in Articles 4.1 and 4.2 so that they are to be disregarded. The word "clear" reflects what the ECJ had already said was the effect of Article 4.5 of the Rome Convention in the *Interfrigo* case, but the word "manifestly" suggests a more stringent standard than before, as does the elevation of the criteria in Articles 4.1 and 4.2 to tests from mere presumptions of closest connection. The new language and structure suggests a higher threshold, which requires that the cumulative weight of the factors connecting the contract to another country must clearly and decisively outweigh the desideratum of certainty in applying the relevant test in Article 4.1 or 4.2' (paragraph 94).

Article 4 pointed to New York law unless the escape clause could apply, an argument put forward by the claimant. However, the judge was of a different opinion. He started with the fact that:

> 'there are considerable connecting factors with New York, quite apart from that being Odeon's place of business. The Bonds themselves are closely connected with New York, and not with England. … [T]he Bonds are essentially New York instruments in which the primary rights they confer are against … a New York common law trust, and/or … a New York chartered limited purpose trust company, acting on its behalf. BS Trust is the issuing entity, which was a special purpose vehicle set up by … a bank headquartered in New York. … On analysis it is also the case that performance of the contract between Molton Street and Odeon was to take place in New York. As to payment, the price was in US$ and was to be paid by Molton Street to Odeon through their respective settlement agents in New York for clearing purposes' (paragraphs 98–99).

After considering some more contentious points, the judge specifically addressed the factors put forward by the claimant in favour of English law.

---

126 [2015] EWHC 3419 (Comm), reported at <https://europeancivil justice.wordpress.com/2015/12/02/high-court-on-rome-i/>. See United Kingdom, section 3.4.

He stated that those factors in reality either pointed to New York law (i.e. the place of delivery of the bonds) or were neutral (regulatory argument). For example, 'the fact that negotiations took place between exclusively English parties carries little weight when they were conducted on the understanding that the contract would be with a US party, and against the background that it ought to have been contemplated that the US party would itself have to decide whether to give its independent assent by adopting the outcome of those negotiations' (paragraph 105). The judge subsequently refused to apply Article 4(3) (i.e. the escape clause) because he found himself unable to accept that the contract was manifestly more closely connected with England than New York. The law of the contract was deemed to be the law of New York. The judgment is important in itself, but also because it comes from a country where flexibility in the court's determination of the applicable law has traditionally been cherished, perhaps overly. This should not be understood as meaning that that the escape clause of Article 4(3) Rome I has never been applied in England. However, practice rightly demonstrates a clear restraint in doing so and only one case has applied it so far.[127] This strict position on the use of escape clauses is reflected in the practice of most EU Member States.

From this (overall) limited practice, one may tentatively identify four interesting features. Firstly, courts may refer to an escape clause in order to better support their determination of the applicable law pursuant to the normal rules,[128] an approach which appears unnecessary and perhaps reveals a certain lack of confidence. Secondly, courts at times go directly to the escape clause, thus giving priority to efficiency over the robustness of their conflict-of-laws reasoning (with the inherent dangers of such approach).[129] Thirdly, the escape clause is not always just seen as a means to revert to the *lex fori*.[130] For instance, the sole example of the use of an escape clause provided for in Lithuania involves

---

[127] United Kingdom, sections 3.4 (displacement of the applicable law of Abu Dhabi in favour of English law) and 3.5.

[128] Cyprus, section 4.1 and the Netherlands, section 2.4.2. In both cases, the escape clause of Article 4(3) Rome II was used in order to better support the determination of the applicable law pursuant to the general rule of Article 4(1) Rome II.

[129] Austria and Germany, section 3.7 (n. 263, on German courts resorting directly to Article 4(3) Rome II without applying Article 4(1) and (2)); the Netherlands, sections 2.4.1 (for Article 4(3) Rome I) and 2.4.2 (for Article 4(3) Rome II).

[130] France, sections 2.3.2 (noting that the escape clauses of Rome I are not used to systematically revert to the *lex fori*), 2.4.1 (for Article 5(3) Rome I, whose use is not an option even when it could lead to French law) and 2.3.4 *in fine* (with a recent decision alleviating fears that the use of the escape clauses of Rome II would have led to a departure from French law in previous cases where they were considered and that this might have come into play in the decision of judges); the Netherlands, section 2.4.2 (the escape clause of Article 4(3) Rome II has been applied to set aside the *lex fori* applicable pursuant to Article 4(2) Rome II). Adde the most recent application of an escape clause in the United Kingdom, where Article 4(3) Rome II is applied to displace Cypriot law in favour of Ukrainian law on the issue of limitation (*Avonwick Holdings Ltd v. Azitio Holdings Ltd & Ors* [2020] EWHC 1844 (Comm), para. 176).

the application of German law by the Supreme Court.[131] However, some may succumb to the temptation.[132] Last but not least, where an escape clause has effectively been applied, its use often appears reasonable. For example, following damage to the equipment of a German company in Germany by a Polish subcontractor acting for a Polish company, the Polish insurer of the latter compensated the German company before bringing proceedings against the insured in Poland. The Polish Supreme Court displaced German law in favour of Polish law pursuant to Article 4(3) Rome II, taking into account in particular the fact that out of four parties involved, three had either their seat or place of habitual residence in Poland (the service provider, the subcontractor and the insurer), and that these parties were bound by contracts governed by Polish law (the insurance contract and the subcontracting contract).[133] Cases of refusal of application of an escape clause equally seem reasonable. For example, an Italian tribunal declined to apply the *lex fori* pursuant to Article 4(3) Rome II, and thus to displace the Romanian law of the place of the car accident, on the sole ground that the car was registered in Italy and insured by an Italian insurer.[134] Caution has nevertheless been expressed at times in relation to particular judgments.[135]

Moreover, one may identify two main types of exceptions to the overall restraint demonstrated by courts in the use of escape clauses, one *ratione materiae* and one *ratione loci*. *Ratione materiae*, courts do not always seem to demonstrate the same level of restraint in the use of escape clauses in relation to employment disputes. This specificity can nevertheless objectively be justified by the difference of wording in the escape clauses, with a lower threshold in Article 8(4) Rome I due to the absence of the adverb 'manifestly' in comparison to Article 4(3) Rome I. In other words, case law is here in line with Rome I itself (subject to a closer analysis on a case-by-case basis). Furthermore, this practice may only be observed in a handful of countries (within the already limited number of those who actually use escape clauses under Rome I and/or Rome II).[136] However, it may be necessary to go beyond this explanation as, looking at the overall picture, one cannot escape from the impression that many

---

131 Lithuania, section 3.4.

132 Latvia, section 2.3 (where our experts note that, in the sole application of an escape clause in the country, 'the reasoning showed that the court used the escape clause for one purpose – to ensure the application of *lex fori*').

133 Poland, section 2.4.

134 Italy, section 4.2.1.

135 Netherlands, section 2.4.2 (where the expert notes that in their application of the escape clause of Article 4(3) Rome II courts tend to give particular importance to the existence of a pre-existing relationship between the parties, perhaps at times excessively, as such a pre-existing relationship is not sufficient in itself); Latvia, section 2.3 (where the experts note that, in the sole application of an escape clause in the country, the court 'made at least two mistakes', namely combining the escape clause with an implicit choice of law and reverting to the *lex fori* despite a weak connection of the contract with Latvia).

136 Mainly Germany: 'With respect to labour contracts, the courts tend to be more liberal', at least in Germany more than Austria (Austria and Germany, section 2.6).

courts in the European Union tend to approach employment disputes differently, in the sense that this area is characterised by a higher (even if not systematic) use of a variety of mechanisms to revert to the *lex fori* (deemed more favourable to the employee). It has thus already been highlighted that courts in some Member States have – as an exception – been lenient in the identification and application of *lois d'application immédiate* in the field of employment contracts.[137] It will be seen that courts in other Member States have for their part been (relatively) lenient on the use of *ordre public* in the context of employment disputes.[138] A more liberal use of escape clauses could appear to be a further means to reach the same end, thus highlighting the specificity of employment disputes in many countries,[139] albeit expressed through the use of different derogatory mechanisms (or an atypical use of a classical conflict-of-laws rule such as party autonomy[140]). By contrast with *lois d'application immédiate* of the forum and *ordre public* (in the practice of most states), escape clauses do not however per se lead to the *lex fori*. It would therefore be useful to carry out a further analysis of whether, in employment contracts, the effective use of Article 8(4) Rome I led in the vast majority of cases to the *lex fori* (this could be complemented by an analysis of cases of refusal to apply the escape clause, including those which could have led to foreign law). The sample here at our disposal is far too limited to draw definitive conclusions, even if the sole (detailed) example of effective use of Article 8(4) Rome I provided for France and Germany[141] did lead to

137 See supra n. 113.

138 See infra n. 157 and text.

139 An added specificity of employment disputes appears in Germany, where the relevant Supreme Court (Bundesarbeitsgericht) reviews the application of foreign law. This stands in contrast with other civil and commercial disputes where the relevant Supreme Court (Bundesgerichtshof) has repeatedly declined to do so (Austria and Germany, section 4). The experts note that the position of the BGH differs from that of its Austrian equivalent (the Oberste Gerichtshof). At times, it does not however exclude a de facto review of foreign law by the BGH through the review of the procedural provision on how to establish the contents of foreign law.

140 Such is the case in France: 'When no express choice is made, tacit or implicit consensus is quite easily accepted (except in employment contracts)' (France, section 2.2.1; adde section 2.4.4 where the expert explains that courts consider that a tacit choice of foreign law is not clearly demonstrated by references to foreign provisions in individual employment contracts where there are other connecting factors with France). The point matters in practice as Article 8 is the most applied provision of Rome I in this country (section 2.4.4 *in limine*). The final result is that, 'when faced with employment contracts, French courts, whose jurisdiction usually results from the performance of work in France, show a tendency to resort to French law' (section 2.6.1). Note that the above is merely intended to highlight the specificity of employment contracts in France and does not express any opinion on whether the approach of courts in this country, in respect of implied choice in contracts other than employment contracts, should be commended.

141 France, section 2.3.2 (albeit the same French court also rejected the application of the escape clause in favour of the *lex fori* in another case and our expert notes that '[a]s a principle, when an employee carries out his activities exclusively or almost exclusively in one country, French judges do not tend to depart from the law of this country'; beyond the specific provision of Article 8(4) Rome I, see nevertheless the previous footnote on the whole of Article 8 Rome I as applied in this country); Austria and Germany, section 2.6.

the application of the *lex fori*, like the two decisions on Article 8(4) Rome I mentioned for Greece.[142]

Ratione loci, in terms of Member States, the only two exceptions to the restraint demonstrated by courts in the use of escape clauses appear to be Greece and Slovenia (with perhaps Ireland on the way[143]). In Greece, judges seem to generously use escape clauses,[144] including in non-warranted circumstances,[145] seemingly always in favour of the *lex fori*.[146] In Slovenia, a misunderstanding on the nature and function of escape clauses under Rome I and Rome II was expressed in particular by one court, which 'explicitly stated that the "escape clauses" are not meant to be an exception but rather an expression of the main principle that the law most closely connected with a dispute should always be applied'.[147] Such reversal of the hierarchy, where the exception becomes the rule, is due to a spill-over effect from the Slovenian Private International Law and Procedure Act endorsed by the Supreme Court itself.[148] It has unfortunately led

142 Greece, section 2.5, n. 108 (where our expert notes that in reality the use of Article 8(4) was unnecessary, Article 8(2) being sufficient), with a further presumed application of Article 8(4) Rome I in favour of Greek law in n. 109. Overall, 'Practice shows the tendency of the [Greek] courts to apply the law most favourable to the employee' (Greece, section 2.5), with this law apparently being understood to be the *lex fori* (see n. 106). Adde the existence of specific conflict-of-laws rules for Greek employees working in Africa and Asia (Greece, section 2.1 (n. 33)).

143 Ireland, sections 2.3 (where the expert interestingly points out 'that the Irish case law often omits the word "manifestly" in its references to Article 4(3) Rome I and Article 4(3) Rome II') and 4. The paucity of cases overall in Ireland means that the use of escape clauses may be high in relative, albeit not absolute, numbers. One also notes that the Lithuanian report states that courts apply the escape clauses of Rome I and Rome II, seemingly quite liberally; however, only one example is provided (Lithuania, section 3.4).

144 Greece, sections 2.3 and 2.4.

145 E.g. Greece, section 2.3, nn. 53 to 55 (in relation to Article 4(3) Rome I).

146 See for instance the outcome in the cases applying Article 4(3) Rome II mentioned in section 2.4, nn. 83 to 90. Overall, the expert observes that '[c]ases in Greece involving foreign law are tried only rarely' (section 2.8 *in limine*).

147 Slovenia, section 2.4 (n. 60). For a similar statement, see the Brussels Court of Appeal which, in 2011, identified Article 4(3) Rome II 'as the general rule: applicable law should be the law with the closest connection' (Belgium, section 3.2 (n. 25)). However, our expert notes that Rome II was not in reality applicable in this case and reference to it was made in support of other findings; moreover, the court rejected the application of Article 4(3) Rome II after contemplating it, and the Belgian report overall mentions no case of application of the escape clauses of Rome I or Rome II. It is nonetheless hoped that such statement remains isolated.

148 Slovenia, section 2.4 (n. 59). One may also wonder if the excessive use of escape clauses in the country is not related to the fact that *lois d'application immédiate* is a concept unknown in the Slovenian Private International Law and Procedure Act, thus depriving the courts of a traditional means to revert to the *lex fori* (there is no case law on *lois d'application immédiate* under the national rules: Slovenia, section 2.1). In support of this balancing act, one notes that in all cases where the escape clauses were (by spill-over effect from the national Private International Law Act) applied under Rome I and Rome II they led to the *lex fori*; and our experts suggest this may have been the intention in the first place (Slovenia, section 2.4). Interestingly, the concept of *lois d'application immédiate* was equally ignored in Slovak legislation, and whilst this country does not overuse escape clauses today, it tends to liberally apply *lois d'application immédiate* in relation to consumer contracts (Slovakia, sections 4.4.3, 4.4.4 and 4.5.1). However, Rome I and Rome II now provide for both *lois d'application immédiate* (currently unused in Slovenia since

to an overuse of the escape clauses in the country,[149] always in favour of the *lex fori*.[150] A reminder of the clear differences between national and European legislation in their approach to escape clauses would appear to be extremely useful here.

3.2.2.3. *Ordre public*

Ordre public under Rome I or Rome II appears to be hardly ever used. In the vast majority of countries, there are simply no reported cases where *ordre public* under these Regulations was effectively applied, as illustrated by Austria and Germany.[151] However, the fact that no use of *ordre public* was recorded does not mean that parties did not try, simply that the courts did not give way, as exemplified by the British, French, or German cases where *ordre public* was raised.[152] This appears all the more remarkable given that Rome I and Rome II

---

there is no decision on Rome I, with none mentioned either on Rome II; by contrast with two on the Rome Convention: Slovenia, section 2.1) and escape clauses (currently overused in the same country) in conditions which must be abided by. The Czech Republic proves this is possible as it also ignored the concept of *lois d'application immédiate* in legislation (Slovakia, 4.5.1 *in limine*), albeit overuses neither *lois d'application immédiate* nor escape clauses (Czech Republic, sections 2.2 and 2.4).

149 Slovenia, section 2.4, *in limine*.

150 Slovenia, section 2.4.

151 Austria and Germany, sections 2.8 *in limine* (for Rome I) and 3.10 (for Rome II). See also Bulgaria, sections 2.8.1 (for Rome I, with the understanding that a court applied *ordre public* before its decision was overturned on this point by a higher court) and 2.8.2 (for Rome II); Croatia, section 3.7 (for both Rome I and Rome II, since the only decision mentioned as applying *ordre public* was delivered prior to the entry in force of these Regulations, and that overall Rome II has not yet been applied in this country, whilst the two decisions on Rome I do not seem to involve *ordre public* according to their presentation in sections 1 and 3.2); Cyprus, sections 3.1 and 3.3 (for Rome I) and 4.3 (for Rome II); France, section 2.6.2 (for both Rome I and Rome II); Greece, section 4.1 (for Rome II), with no application of Article 21 Rome I mentioned in the report either; Ireland, section 2.7 (for both Rome I and Rome II); Latvia, section 2.10 *in limine* (for both Rome I and Rome II); Portugal, sections 2.3 *in fine* (for Rome II) and 4 (for Rome I); Slovenia, section 2.10 *in limine* (for both Rome I and Rome II); United Kingdom, section 3.7 (and section 3.6 for the first case). No effective application of *ordre public* under Rome I and Rome II is mentioned in the Belgian, Czech, Luxembourgian, Slovak and Spanish reports. The Dutch report (section 2.10) mentions one case where the court declared foreign law (Israeli law on punitive damages) inconsistent with *ordre public*, however it was not decided on the basis of Rome I or Rome II but national conflict of laws (interestingly, the *lex fori* was subsequently not applied, as the claim was instead dismissed). The Hungarian report mentions in section 3.6 a court referring to Article 21 Rome I, albeit after having (rightly) characterised the EU Libyan Embargo Regulation as a *loi d'application immédiate* under Article 9 Rome I and held that it thus replaces the rules of the applicable law; it seems that the court did not so much apply Article 21 Rome I as made a (confusing and unnecessary) analogy between Articles 9 and 21 Rome I in order to state that the application of the *lex causae* is not necessarily ruled out in its totality by the application of the *loi d'application immédiate*.

152 United Kingdom, section 3.7 (and section 3.6 for the first case); France, section 2.6.2; Austria and Germany, sections 2.8 (for Rome I) and 3.10 (for Rome II). See also, albeit under the

have universal application and that courts may therefore be confronted with very different legal systems, for instance Kuwaiti law in Germany.[153] The absence of cases where *ordre public* was applied may be understood as demonstrating a liberal approach to the application of foreign law, save where (by exception) courts tend to simply ignore Rome I and Rome II in the first place and directly apply the *lex fori*, making the question of *ordre public* meaningless.[154]

By exception, *ordre public* was applied in Italy, Lithuania and Poland, albeit only sporadically, and interestingly each time in respect of the law of another Member State. In Italy in 2019, a first instance court thus set aside Dutch law on the ground that it did not recognise the right of close relatives to seek damages for the non-pecuniary prejudice resulting from the death of a loved one.[155] Similarly, in Poland, a court of appeal deemed German law inconsistent with Polish *ordre public* on the ground that it does not allow a child to claim compensation for the suffering caused by the death of his mother (immaterial damage).[156] In Lithuania, the Supreme Court set aside Latvian law in the context of an employment dispute – contributing to the specificity of such disputes[157] – whilst the Court of Appeal declined to apply the Dutch law chosen by the parties and reduced the contractually agreed interest rates (15% and 23%) to the rate

---

1971 Hague Convention (even if the applicable law would have been the same under Rome II: Slovenia, section 2.12 (n. 87)), Slovenia, section 2.11, on the Constitutional Court rejecting a claim of discrimination made against Croatian law, in all likelihood under the *ordre public* exception, on the ground that the amount of compensation was disproportionately low.

153 Austria and Germany, section 2.8.

154 Latvia, section 2.10.

155 Italy, section 7.2.2 (n. 114, with the decision very likely to have been delivered under Rome II given its date). No other example of effective application of *ordre public* under the Regulations is provided for Italy, neither under Rome I (section 7.1.2, where all cases mentioned where *ordre public* was effectively applied relate to the Rome Convention; see also section 5.1.2 on the 2019 Supreme Court decision considering English employment law inconsistent with *ordre public* under the Rome Convention, a Supreme Court which has not yet delivered any ruling under Rome I (Italy, section 1.1.2)) nor Rome II (section 7.2.2, where all other cases mentioned where *ordre public* was effectively applied relate to the Italian Private International Law Act or the recognition and enforcement of foreign judgments, in particular all the decisions from the Supreme Court which has not yet delivered any ruling on Rome II (see section 1.2.2)). On the law applicable to damage claims brought by secondary victims, see CJEU, section 4.1.

156 Poland, sections 2.9 and 2.10. The judgment seemed to have been delivered under Rome II. The Polish report (section 2.9) also mentions a decision from the Supreme Court holding that compensation should be proportionate to the damage and not punitive in nature, although it is unclear if *ordre public* was effectively applied in the case at hand (and against which foreign law) and if this was done under Rome II.

157 See also Italy, section 7.1.2: 'Most of the Italian rulings that address the issue of public policy in the field of contracts relate to labour relations', albeit under the Rome Convention for those cases where *ordre public* was effectively applied, with one case under Rome I where it was merely discussed (see also section 5.1.2 on the 2019 Supreme Court decision considering English employment law inconsistent with *ordre public* under the Rome Convention).

foreseen by the *lex fori* (6%) in a loan agreements dispute in an insolvency context.[158]

In Lithuanian cases where *ordre public* was applied, the application of the *lex fori* was indeed the next step.[159] However, courts could consider solutions more respectful of the *lex causae*. For example, it has been rightly pointed out that where foreign law provides for excessive contractual penalties, the latter could be decreased to an acceptable level whilst still being higher than the one foreseen by the *lex fori*.[160] This principle of proportionality in the application of *ordre public* could perhaps have been applied by the Lithuanian Court of Appeal in the above case. It could certainly be one of the topics on the agenda when Rome I and Rome II are revised, or in the event a Rome 0 Regulation or Code of Private International Law/Code of European Civil Justice is drafted, along with any other solution which avoids an automatic and immediate fall-back on the *lex fori* in cases of application of *ordre public*. Inspiration could here be drawn from Bulgaria, where the Code of Private International Law provides that another appropriate provision of the same foreign law should be applied in such a situation,[161] or Italy, where the Statute on Private International Law states that in that case the applicable law shall be determined on the basis of other connecting factors possibly provided for with respect to the same matter.[162] In both countries, the *lex fori* applies only as a last resort. Such refined alternatives may contribute to deterring judges from an excessive application of *ordre public*, as the possibility of falling back on the *lex fori* is no longer guaranteed. Nevertheless, it is likely that the *lex fori* will appear to many countries to be the easiest and most suitable fall-back solution in cases of application of *ordre public*, especially since overall there is clearly no overuse of *ordre public* under Rome I or Rome II for the time being.

In the future, there is near certainty that the application of *ordre public* will increase in absolute numbers, although there is no reason at this stage

---

158 Lithuania, section 3.9. One notes that both the Supreme Court and the Court of Appeal seem to have used several grounds to apply the *lex fori* as the same cases are mentioned as applying *ordre public* but also Lithuanian law as a *loi d'application immédiate* (see Lithuania, section 3.1).

159 Lithuania, section 3.9 (with the same remark as in the preceding footnote). In the absence of an indication to the contrary, in all likelihood, this was also the case for Poland. On Italian law, see infra this conclusion (text relating to n. 162) on the interesting provision of the Italian Private International Law Act which avoids an immediate fall-back on the *lex fori*.

160 Latvia, section 2.10. The authors also discuss the possibility of searching for similar rules to the *lex causae* in different but related legal systems before setting aside this solution notably for lack of predictability, fear of excessive judicial discretion and additional delay to the decision on the merits. Overall, they believe that in practice, in Latvia, courts will apply the *lex fori* where *ordre public* is used.

161 Bulgaria, section 2.8.1.

162 Italy, section 9.2.

to predict overuse.[163] This view may find support in the fact that judgments applying *ordre public* outside Rome I and Rome II,[164] and which seem likely to be transposed to Rome I and Rome II, do not overall appear to be unjustified. It could even be argued that, at times, a very fair balance has been reached. A good illustration would be the recent trend to consider that punitive damages do not per se infringe *ordre public*, and only do so where they are disproportionate, a position endorsed in the decisions of the Czech and Italian Supreme Courts in 2014 and 2017 respectively.[165] By contrast, and rather exceptionally, one may perhaps have wished for a more robust reasoning, if not a different outcome, in a Croatian decision which considered the Czech law chosen by the parties to be inconsistent with *ordre public* because the contract resulted in a severe imbalance of rights and obligations in favour of the Czech party, albeit without explaining which particular principle of the *lex fori* had been breached and why it was so important as to be part of *ordre public*.[166]

3.2.2.4. Treatment and Proof of Foreign Law

The application of foreign law is important for all conflict-of-laws provisions; it is at times even crucial for their operation. A comparison of the substance of the chosen law and the law applicable in the absence of choice is thus built into Article 8 Rome I on employment contracts:[167] how may such a comparison be done if it is nearly impossible to know the contents of foreign law?

Unfortunately, the main weakness of Rome I and Rome II is probably the lack of appropriate rules and support in respect of the treatment and proof of

---

163 A monitoring of the use of *ordre public* in employment disputes may however prove necessary given their specificity, in the sense that this area seems characterised by a greater use of a variety of mechanisms to revert to the *lex fori* in many countries. Greater does not per se mean unjustified (see Italy, section 7.1.2 where a 2002 Supreme Court decision held inconsistent with *ordre public* the law of New York as it failed to provide workers with permanent contracts (contracts of indefinite duration) any protection against unjustified dismissals). It also does not mean systematic: see for example cases from the Czech Supreme Court likely to be transposed to Rome I and Rome II and holding that Czech employment rules requiring employers to state a specific ground for dismissal and abiding by a minimum termination period are neither *lois d'application immédiate* nor part of *ordre public*, subject to conditions (Czech Republic, section 2.2).

164 This would be either under the legal regime which preceded Rome I or Rome II or in the field of recognition and enforcement of foreign judgments.

165 Czech Republic, section 2.9; Italy, section 7.2.2. It remains to be seen whether such case law will inspire courts in countries likely to consider punitive damages as per se contrary to *ordre public* under Rome I and Rome II, such as Lithuania (section 3.9), the Netherlands (section 2.10), Poland (section 2.9) and Slovenia (section 2.10 *in fine*).

166 Croatia, section 3.7.

167 On the difficulty of the comparison, see in particular M.-E. Ancel, P. Deumier and M. Laazouzi, *Droit des contrats internationaux*, 2nd ed., Sirey, Paris, 2020, para. 1020.

foreign law. This is not an issue which is specific to Rome I and Rome II, but it does have a major impact on their application in too many countries. In extreme cases, it may be the main reason for the paucity of case law. In Latvia, it has thus been said that lawyers and judges try to avoid applying conflict-of-laws rules 'as this may lead to the application of foreign law, the content of which is hard to determine, interpret and prove in the eyes of the Latvian lawyers. This is also the case because national rules do not facilitate the effective application of the foreign law and the determination of its content'.[168] Another country where the (lack of) success of the Regulations seems to be directly related to the rules on the treatment and proof of foreign law is Cyprus, where lawyers are not yet familiar with Rome I and Rome II,[169] a lack of knowledge which proves decisive since 'Cypriot courts *must* rely on the parties to plead (or invoke) and prove the content of foreign law'.[170] Elsewhere, in Lithuania, issues relating to the treatment and proof of foreign law may, at times, undermine basic principles of Rome I and Rome II such as party autonomy. This is illustrated by a case where parties had chosen Danish law to govern their contract, but courts, including the Supreme Court, reverted to Lithuanian law on the ground that Danish law had not been proven to their satisfaction, interestingly despite the Danish party providing excerpts from Danish contract law as well as from textbooks.[171] For similar reasons, in Greece, the application of foreign law appears to be exceptional.[172] This is especially true in summary proceedings, where Greek courts, after having declared foreign law applicable under Rome I or Rome II, revert 'almost religiously' to the *lex fori* on the ground that the foreign law cannot be proved within a reasonable amount of time and resembles Greek law.[173] States with a wider practice of private international law are not unfamiliar with this last type of assertion, as one learns for instance with some surprise

168 Latvia, section 1.2.

169 Cyprus, section 5: 'The challenge ahead in the case of Cyprus is for lawyers … to familiarise themselves with [Rome I and Rome II], thereby ensuring they invoke … the Regulations in appropriate cases'.

170 Cyprus, section 3.7 (italics in the original), where the expert adds: 'if none of the parties points to or raises the issue of the relevance of foreign applicable law, the court will probably simply proceed with deciding the case applying the Cypriot law'.

171 Lithuania, section 3.8. Assuming the information provided was not enough, indeed, a point which seems debated, the courts do not appear to have granted lawyers additional time (as was done in other cases), or sought alternative ways to provide the required information. Our expert rightly points out that party autonomy seems to have been denied in this case.

172 Greece, section 2.8 *in limine*.

173 Greece, section 2.8, where, in respect of summary proceedings, the expert observes, in relation to Rome I, that 'courts unanimously apply Greek law' and, in relation to Rome II, after providing an example where the court acknowledged the application of foreign law on the basis of the Regulation before applying the *lex fori*, that this is 'a path followed almost religiously by Greek courts' (on the assumed resemblance of foreign law with Greek law, see nn. 138 and 142).

that Egyptian law is the same as English law.[174] The non-application of foreign law is however not limited to third states with a fundamentally different legal culture from the forum. It does seem odd that, for example, the law of another Member State of the EU – moreover a close one from both a geographical and legal family perspective – might not be ultimately applied in some cases, such as in a Spanish decision where in the end Portuguese law was not applied.[175] Interestingly, even in countries that are on the opposite ends of the spectrum in terms of application of foreign law, calls have been made to harmonise the proof and treatment of foreign law,[176] the relevant legal regime for which varies immensely from one country to another.[177]

Rome I and Rome II (and similar instruments) could therefore be usefully complemented by a Rome 0 Regulation or a Code of Private International Law/Code of European Civil Justice,[178] or a part thereof, dealing with the

[174] Court of Appeal of England and Wales, *Lady Christine Brownlie v. Four Seasons Holdings Inc.* [2015] EWCA Civ 665, reported at <https://europeanciviljustice.wordpress.com/2015/07/14/egyptian-law-is-the-same-as-english-law/>. To the question 'whether this court can, under Rome II, in the absence of proof as to Egyptian law, apply the presumption that Egyptian law is the same as English law' (para. 88), Lady Justice Arden replied without hesitation: 'I reject Mr Palmer's submissions that the presumption as to foreign law being the same as English law does not apply' (para. 89 *in fine*).

[175] Spain, sections 2.2 (n. 25) and 5.3 (with other examples involving in particular Dutch, French, German, Italian and Portuguese laws).

[176] Austria and Germany, sections 4 ('Due to the good legal infrastructure in Austria and Germany, adequate access to foreign law is provided, at least generally') and 5 (Rome 0 to 'address issues like the application of foreign law by domestic courts'). For other countries where the application of foreign law did not – overall – raise any specific difficulty, see Luxembourg, section 2.10 (with our expert nonetheless advocating for some changes); Poland, section 2.8 (with our expert noting, however, the practice *contra legem* of some first instance courts who apply the *lex fori* on the ground that foreign law seems 'convergent' with Polish law). The main reason seems to be that the laws applied were, for the most, those of fellow European States or other Western States (USA). The multilingual capacity of Luxembourg judges seems to be a key factor in the smooth application of foreign law as these languages are also those of the neighbouring countries whose laws are being applied (with Luxembourg judges already spontaneously taking into consideration the case law of some of these countries in the domestic context).

[177] As demonstrated in this study. Several experts have advocated for changes at country level in relation to the treatment and proof of foreign law, e.g. Slovenia, section 2.9 on the need to allow foreign law to be ascertained by experts.

[178] On a Rome 0 Regulation, see notably S. Leible and H. Unberath, *Brauchen wir eine Rom 0-Verordnung?*, JWV (Jenaer Wissenschaftliche Verlagsgesellschaft), 2013. On a Code of Private International Law, see notably P. Lagarde, 'Embryon de règlement portant Code européen de droit international privé', RabelsZ 2011; C. Nourissat, 'La codification de l'espace judiciaire civil européen', in M. Douchy-Oudot and E. Guinchard (eds.), *La justice civile européenne en marche*, Dalloz, Paris, 2012, p. 175. An alternative would be to complement the existing suggestion of a Directive on European Civil Procedure, notably its Article 9(2). On the suggestion, see the draft report of MEP Emil Radev of 10 February 2017 on 'Common minimum standards of civil procedure', PE593.974v01-00. The report of MEP Radev was adopted by the JURI Committee in June 2017 and by the Parliament in July 2017. For an interview with E. Radev, see <https://europeanciviljustice.wordpress.com/2016/02/26/

treatment and proof of the foreign law.[179] Regarding the contents of such a provision, most commentators focus on what the respective duties of the judge and parties should be or the status of foreign law, notably for judicial recourses purposes. It is indeed necessary to do so, and a good starting point in this respect could be the relevant provisions of the recent GEDIP proposal on a general part of private international law.[180] However, whilst being crucial, it is submitted that this part should be complemented by practical measures, perhaps through action grants from the European Commission. Practical resources may even be in greater demand here than legal principles. Should the EU budget remain constant, which is understandable given the over-indebtedness of most EU Member States even before the coronavirus-related economic crisis, some of the money very generously distributed abroad could be redirected to support the correct implementation of EU law (for example, the €10 million given annually to support intra-African academic mobility,[181] not European or inter-African–European mobility, which is merely a drop in the ocean of European aid to third states when considering how EU taxpayers' money is spent in various categories). Practical resources could be put and remain in place even if a proposal for a Rome 0 Regulation or Code of Private International Law is rejected as the EU does not seem inclined to take this path.

---

interview-with-mep-emil-radev-on-civil-procedure-in-the-eu/>. For a study on the topic, see J. Fitchen, 'Unharmonised Procedural Rules: Is there a Case for Further Harmonisation at EU Level?', in P. Beaumont, M. Danov, K. Trimmings and B. Yüksel (eds.), *Cross-Border Litigation in Europe*, Hart Publishing, Oxford, 2017, p. 55.

179 The European legislator is aware of the importance of the topic, as demonstrated by Article 30(1)(i) Rome II, which makes it compulsory for the European Commission to submit a study on the application of foreign law: 'a study on the effects of the way in which foreign law is treated in the different jurisdictions and on the extent to which courts in the Member States apply foreign law in practice pursuant to this Regulation' (there does not unfortunately seem to be an equivalent provision in Rome I whilst the issue is equally pressing). Sadly, no legislative proposal seems to have been published so far.

180 Groupe européen de droit international privé (GEDIP)/European Group for Private International Law (EGPIL), minutes of the 29th working session held in Katowice on 13–15 September 2019, III, p. 39 ff., and Annex 3 on a 'Proposition d'un document de travail pour une Partie générale d'un code de DIP européen' (H. Gaudemet-Tallon, F. Jault-Seseke, C. Kessedjian, P. Lagarde and E. Pataut), p. 86, specifically Article 18, p. 90, available at <https://www.gedip-egpil.eu/reunionstravail/2019_Katowice/PVTrav-Final-2.12.19.pdf>. Article 18 reads: 'Établissement du droit étranger. 1. Le contenu du droit étranger applicable en vertu du présent règlement est établi d'office par le juge, qui peut requérir la collaboration des parties. 2. Le droit du for est applicable lorsqu'il est manifestement impossible d'établir le contenu du droit étranger'. See also the interesting suggestion of the Italian expert, drawing on provisions currently in force in Italy, to avoid an immediate fall-back on the *lex fori* where the normally applicable foreign law cannot be proven (Italy, sections 9.1 and 10).

181 Call for proposals – EACEA/03/2019 – Intra-Africa Academic Mobility Scheme, OJ C91/2, 11 March 2019. On the Intra-Africa Academic Mobility Scheme 2020 (EACEA/07/2020), see <https://eacea.ec.europa.eu/intra-africa/funding/intra-africa-academic-mobility-scheme-2020_en> (with guidelines, including on the budget available).

4. CONCLUSION

4.1. PROPOSAL ON THE LAW APPLICABLE TO THE THIRD-PARTY EFFECTS OF ASSIGNMENTS OF CLAIMS

The striking feature of the proposal on the law applicable to the third-party effects of assignments of claims[182] is indeed that it does not aim to amend Rome I but to complement it[183] by enacting a fully autonomous instrument. However, this does not appear to be consistent with the intention of the European legislator as expressed in Article 27(2) Rome I, which refers to a proposal amending 'this' Regulation (i.e. Rome I itself). The (undisputable) economic importance of the proposal may not reasonably constitute a valid justification for such specific treatment. If it were to be a question of scope of application of Rome I, the argument may not be fully convincing either, as appropriate amendments could be drafted. The fact that numerous provisions of the proposal are identical *mutatis mutandis* to those of Rome I (universal application, *lois d'application immédiate*,[184] *ordre public*, exclusion of *renvoi*, states with more than one legal system, etc.) or drafted along similar lines (e.g. scope of application) may be seen as an incentive to find a solution leading to the inclusion of the proposal in Rome I, if necessary (and inter alia) with a specific paragraph tailored to

182 Proposal for a Regulation of the European Parliament and of the Council on the law applicable to the third-party effects of assignments of claims (12 March 2018, COM/2018/096 final – 2018/044 (COD)), reported at <https://europeancivilјustice.wordpress.com/2018/03/13/proposal-for-a-regulation-on-the-law-applicable-to-the-third-party-effects-of-assignments-of-claims/>. The key provision is Article 4 on the applicable law, with the main rule being in favour of 'the law of the country in which the assignor has its habitual residence at the material time' (Article 4(1), subject to some exceptions and limited party autonomy). On the current state of the procedure, see <https://oeil.secure.europarl.europa.eu/oeil/popups/ficheprocedure.do?reference=2018%2F0044(COD)&l=en> (the latest key event being the position of the European Parliament adopted at first reading on 13 February 2019 with a view to the adoption of Regulation (EU) … / … of the European Parliament and of the Council on the law applicable to the third-party effects of assignments of claims, available at <https://www.europarl.europa.eu/doceo/document/TA-8-2019-0086_EN.html>).

183 On the gap left by existing Article 14 Rome I, see CJEU, 9 October 2019, Case C-548/18, *BGL BNP Paribas SA v. TeamBank AG Nürnberg*: 'Article 14 of the Rome I Regulation must be interpreted as not designating, directly or by analogy, the applicable law concerning the third-party effects of the assignment of a claim in the event of multiple assignments of the claim by the same creditor to successive assignees'. In favour of the law that governs the obligation relating to the assignment, see Article 36 of the Polish Private International Law Act 2011 (Poland, section 4.2). For a recent case on existing Article 14 Rome I (including the scope of the applicable law under Article 14(1)), see the Czech Supreme Court in 2019 (Czech Republic, section 2.7).

184 In respect of the first two paragraphs of Article 9 Rome I. The third paragraph is not included in Article 6 of the proposal. However, see the amendment suggested by the European Parliament in this respect in its position of 13 February 2019 referred to supra n. 182 (addition of paragraph 2(a), which replicates *mutatis mutandis* the main part of paragraph 3 of Article 9 Rome I).

the needs of the new Article 14 *bis* in Article 1 Rome I. At the very least, if the proposal is not included in Rome I, both instruments should be included in a codification of European private international law[185] in order to avoid adding to the existing confusion perceptible in several countries arising from the multitude of sources of private international law and their delimitation and coordination.[186]

4.2. TOWARDS ROME I *BIS* AND ROME II *BIS*?

The current legislative priority in relation to Rome I and Rome II undoubtedly appears to be the proposal on the law applicable to the third-party effects of assignments of claims. It is true that delay has characterised this topic, since the report on it, to be accompanied (if appropriate) by a legislative proposal, which was initially scheduled for 17 June 2010 at the latest,[187] only saw the light in 2016 (for the report)[188] and 2018 (for the proposal). One of the next steps initially scheduled in Rome II and Rome I themselves is the reports on their application, to be accompanied (if appropriate) by legislative proposals, initially planned for (respectively) no later than 20 August 2011 and 17 June 2013.[189] Once the proposal on the law applicable to the third-party effects of assignments of claims is adopted, such reports and proposals could well be the next legislative priority.

---

185 '[H]aving a comprehensive PIL codification has numerous advantages when compared with having the PIL rules distributed over a large number of separate acts or regulations: a comprehensive codification makes all PIL rules readily accessible in one place, helps to avoid friction between the rules on jurisdiction on the one hand and applicable law on the other, promotes a uniform view of the whole matter, favours clarity and coherence between the different sets of rules, reduces complexity, increases legal certainty, and considerably adds to the user-friendliness of the rules on PIL' (T. Kadner Graziano, 'Codifying European Union private international law: The Swiss Private International Law Act – a model for a comprehensive EU private international law regulation?', Journal of Private International Law 2015, 11(3), 585, 606). Regarding the Rome I and Rome II Regulations in particular, a codification has the obvious advantage of avoiding a tough (and necessarily unsatisfactory) choice to make for any private international lawyer entitled to take only one Regulation onto a desert island. For this single reason, a codification appears necessary.

186 Several national courts tend to cumulatively apply provisions of various sources, for instance in Bulgaria (section 1.1), or just be confused (Slovenia, section 3, where the experts consider that 'arguably the biggest problem for the judges currently seems to be finding the applicable legislation', and section 4). See also Poland, section 1 ('urgent problem of coordination between various sources of private international law'); Slovakia, sections 5 and 6.

187 Article 27(2) Rome I.

188 Report from the Commission to the European Parliament, the Council and the European Economic and Social Committee on the question of the effectiveness of an assignment or subrogation of a claim against third parties and the priority of the assigned or subrogated claim over the right of another person, COM/2016/0626 final.

189 Respectively Article 30 Rome II and Article 27(1) Rome I.

The overall satisfactory application of Rome I and Rome II in respect of those key mechanisms of conflict of laws that are *lois d'application immédiate*, escape clauses and *ordre public* should not indeed be understood as meaning that Rome I and Rome II are without flaws. In addition to the issue of the treatment and proof of foreign law previously mentioned, several weaknesses have been identified in this study. Some are structural, such as the dichotomy created in the EU by the primacy of the 1971 and 1973 Hague Conventions over Rome II,[190] or the lack of legal education and training on the Regulations.[191] Others are analytical, such as the need (in selected countries) for guidance on what should be understood as an implied choice of law in (notably) Article 3 Rome I and Article 14 Rome II,[192] or on how to localise financial damage,[193] or on how to

190 See the concern expressed by national experts for, notably, France, section 4.2; Germany, section 3.13; Spain, sections 3.2 and 7 (contra: Lithuania, section 3.11, where the 1971 Hague Convention is deemed to be clearer than Rome II and its application over the latter correspondingly valued). Denunciation of the relevant Hague Conventions has been advocated. For a compromise, see T. Kadner Graziano, 'Cross-border traffic accidents in the EU – the potential impact of driverless cars', Study for the JURI Committee of the European Parliament, PE571.362, 2016, specifically 3.2.6, where the author suggests adding a new paragraph to Article 28 Rome II: 'Where the person claimed to be liable and the injured person have their habitual residence in EU Member States at the time the damage occurred, this Regulation will take precedence over other conventions to which the Member States are or become party'. However, as he observed, this amendment implies a renegotiation 'between the EU and the Hague Conference' (or current third states parties to the Hague Conventions), which may take some time. For a discussion of possible solutions, see also E. Guinchard, 'Unfinished Business: Rome II in Practice and the Need for a Hague Convention on Non-Contractual Obligations', European Law Review 2015, 100, 106 ff.

191 See Greece, section 4.2; Italy, section 10; Latvia, section 4.2; Lithuania, section 4; the Netherlands, section 3; Slovakia, sections 5 and 6; Slovenia, section 4. In many other countries, the level of judges varies greatly at times, with several courts struggling with the interpretation and application of Rome I and Rome II, even in countries where, overall, the evaluation is very positive in this respect, e.g. Poland, section 3. See also section 3.1 of this conclusion on some basic mistakes made by national courts, even if they tend to be limited in number. Very odd errors such as the following ones are absolutely exceptional: in France, the application of Rome I was ruled out in one case because the parties had chosen the law of their contract (France, section 1.2), and in Germany a few courts determined international jurisdiction on the basis of Rome I and Rome II (Austria and Germany, section 1, with references in n. 6). The solution lies in enhanced support to national judges, in particular through the European Judicial Training Institute, and a change of approach in academic and professional curricula where necessary.

192 Austria and Germany, sections 2.4.3 for Rome I ('Subsequent choice of law', interestingly with more issues observed than in the context of an original implied choice of law where courts approach was deemed overall satisfactory: see section 2.4.2) and 3.4 for Rome II; Ireland, section 2.2.2. See also Slovenia, section 4, where courts tend to construe pleadings on the *lex fori* as implied choice-of-law agreements, perhaps too easily. Contra: Bulgaria, section 2.2.1; Spain, 7; United Kingdom, sections 3.5 (for both Rome I (three cases only where implied choice was demonstrated) and Rome II (no case), by contrast perhaps with the previous situation under the Rome Convention) and 5.

193 France, section 2.3.3. (also Internet-related torts); Luxembourg, section 4.2; Poland, section 2.3. For guidance on the localisation of the damage to be provided by courts rather than the legislator, see Czech Republic, section 2.4.

identify the law applicable to employees on the high seas.[194] Several national reports have indeed identified one or more particular issue(s) with a specific provision, or lack thereof, thus demonstrating the need for a reform of Rome I and/or Rome II at times. Moreover, the fact that the judicial practice collected has not demonstrated any major problem in relation to a specific provision does not mean that a reform of that specific provision (or its interaction with other provisions) – or the creation of one where it is lacking – should not be considered,[195] simply that one should distinguish the provisions that have already caused difficulties in judicial practice and could therefore usefully be improved with some sense of urgency from the provisions that could be amended even though they have not yet raised any difficulty in judicial practice, including because they are not really applied in judicial practice. Should Rome I *bis* and Rome II *bis* Regulations be drafted, a preference should be expressed for a comprehensive reform.

4.3. FINAL WORD

The weaknesses in the drafting, interpretation and application of Rome I and Rome II highlighted in this study should not detract from the overall positive assessment of the Regulations in their first ten years of judicial practice.[196] It may

194 Latvia, section 4.2. For other issues, see for instance supra n. 96.

195 For an example of an issue stemming from an existing provision, see M.-E. Ancel, 'The Rome I Regulation and Distribution Contracts', Yearbook of Private International Law 2008, vol. 10, p. 221, specifically III.B.1 (lack of definition of distribution contracts in Article 4(1) Rome I; on distribution contracts in general, see in particular Á. Espiniella Menéndez, *El contrato de distribución comercial internacional*, Aranzadi, Navarra, 2018) or S. Zheng Tang, 'Law Applicable in the Absence of Choice – The New Article 4 of the Rome I Regulation', Modern Law Review 2008, 71(5), p. 785 (classification issues between the different types of contracts foreseen in Article 4(1) Rome I). For an example of an issue stemming from the interaction between an existing provision and other relevant/surrounding norms, see J. Van Hein, 'Protecting Victims Of Cross-Border Torts Under Article 7 No. 2 Brussels Ibis: Towards A More Differentiated And Balanced Approach', Yearbook of Private International Law 2014/2015, vol. 16, p. 241, specifically p. 255 ff. ('2. Frictions between Brussels Ibis and Rome II'). For an example of a gap: S. Corneloup, 'Vers une réforme du Règlement Rome II: la réparation des dommages causés par une violation du droit des marchés financiers nécessite-t-elle une règle de conflit spéciale ?', in M. Douchy-Oudot and E. Guinchard (eds.), *La justice civile européenne en marche*, Dalloz, Paris, 2012, p. 63 (with suggestions for several other reforms of Rome II in the introduction).

196 E.g. Bulgaria, section 3 *in limine*; Czech Republic, section 3 *in limine*; Luxembourg, section 3 *in limine*; Poland, section 3 *in limine*. See also CJEU, section 7 *in limine*. Contra: Slovakia, section 5 *in limine* (in relation to the application of Rome I and Rome II by courts, judged to be 'rather incoherent', despite the similarity with national provisions). For an interesting observation that Rome I and Rome II had no real impact in practice, see Greece, section 3 *in fine*: 'the situation is no worse than before the entry into force of the Regulations. Courts have not opted for different solutions; they simply follow the lines of previous case law, just changing the legal provisions they refer to'. In Croatia, Rome I and Rome II have been applied for less than ten years.

be necessary at this stage to remind ourselves that their very existence is to be commended. In particular, it has ensured a much greater degree of uniformity and predictability across the EU, starting with the countries whose national rules were not fully adequate, markedly in the field of non-contractual obligations.[197] Harmonisation at European level also represents a huge advantage for small countries, as it offers the possibility of using the case law and academic literature of other Member States to balance out the objective/quantitative paucity of case law and small number of specialist academics and lawyers at national level; this point was raised by the Slovenian team and could equally apply to the many other EU Member States of comparable size.[198] This should not be lost sight of. Therefore, overall, subject to the reform needs already pointed out, one can only wish Rome I and Rome II a very happy birthday!

[197] Czech Republic, section 3 (n. 49); France, section 3.1 (n. 129); Ireland, section 3; Latvia, section 3.2. It is submitted that an extension of Rome II to all non-contractual obligations by the European legislator would, for the same reason, be of much benefit to these countries (subject to the appropriateness of the new conflict-of-laws rules).

[198] Slovenia, section 1, *in limine*. As an exception, one notes the high number of cases in Slovakia: see this conclusion, section 3.1.

ABOUT THE EDITOR

Emmanuel Guinchard is Senior Lecturer in Law and the Full-Time LLM Framework Programme Leader (cyber law, international commercial law and space law) at Northumbria Law School, United Kingdom. His teaching and research focuses on private international law, European Union law, World Trade Organization law and competition law. He has published widely in the field of European Civil Justice and blogs at https://europeanciviljustice.wordpress.com/.

www.ingramcontent.com/pod-product-compliance
Ingram Content Group UK Ltd.
Pitfield, Milton Keynes, MK11 3LW, UK
UKHW051846100926
8556IPUK00005B/468

9 781780 686714